Magruder's
American Government

Magruder's American Government

1981

Revised by **William A. McClenaghan**
Department of Political Science
Oregon State University

Allyn and Bacon, Inc.
Boston   Rockleigh, NJ   Atlanta   Dallas   San Jose

AMERICAN GOVERNMENT, first published in 1917, and revised annually, is an enduring symbol of the author's faith in American ideals and American institutions. The life of Frank Abbott Magruder (1882–1949) was an outstanding example of Americanism at its very best. His career as a teacher, author, and tireless worker in civic and religious undertakings remains an inspiring memory to all who knew him.

Graphic material and maps prepared by: Lee Ames & Zak, Ltd., and Visual Services

ISBN: 0-205-07285-2

Library of Congress Catalog Card Number: 17–13472

Printed in the United States of America

56789   85 84 83

The first edition of *American Government* was published more than six decades ago, in 1917. This edition of *American Government* is the latest in a long line of succesors to that original text. It is, in fact, the 61st edition of the book. That first edition and each of the succeeding volumes, up to and including this one, have had one basic purpose: to describe, analyze, and explain the American system of government.

American Government, 1981, is a carefully and a very comprehensively revised book. Altogether, the many changes which have been made in it appear on more than 400 of its pages.

As with each of its predecessors, this edition has been so very extensively revised for a quite important reason:

The American system of government is extraordinarily dynamic. Change—growth, adaptation, innovation—is a basic element of its character. While it is true that its fundamental principles and its basic structure have remained constant over time, many of its other characteristics have changed. And they continue to do so—from year to year and, frequently, from one day to the next, and sometimes remarkably.

To underscore the critical importance of this fact of continuing change, dwell for a moment on the phrase "the American system of government." You will encounter it again and again, for it is an apt description of government in the United States. And, as you will soon discover, that system of government is a very complex one.

It is complex because it is composed of many different parts, performing many different functions. And it is a system because all of those many different parts are interrelated. The whole cannot be understood without a knowledge of its various interacting parts; and those parts cannot be understood without a knowledge of the whole. Given all of this, the vital effects of ongoing change in the system should be fairly obvious.

Ronald Reagan's victory in the presidential election, and the other Republican successes of 1980, produced a number of the changes in this 1981 edition, of course. The results of the 1980 elections and the inauguration of the Reagan administration are reflected in many places—in written comments, in graphic materials, and in several other ways.

Here are but a few of the many other changes to be found in this edition:

—A fresh consideration of the policy of affirmative action in the light of the Supreme Court's decisions in the *Bakke, Weber,* and *Fullilove* cases.

—A revised treatment of campaign finance and its regulation, including the recent changes in federal law and their impact on the 1980 elections.

—A new look at the voter registration process, with a pro-con discussion of its impact on voter turnout.

—Revised treatments of several topics relating to Congress: bicameralism; the reapportionment of seats in the House; the disciplining of its members; the filibuster in the Senate; and the characteristics of its present membership and the shape of their various roles.

—A description of the Executive Office of the President at the beginning of the Reagan administration and a revamped consideration of the Cabinet and its role.

And there is much else, too—dozens upon hundreds of changes, including new comment and data upon such varied topics as the federal budget, the public debt, the energy problem, social security, aid to parochial schools and the 1st Amendment, the most recent FBI crime reports, and the new federal judicial circuit. And still more: diplomatic immunity and the hostage crisis in Iran, renewed registration for the draft, the new shape of the SALT process, the new relationship between the United States and Taiwan, and immigration policies. And the several chapters on State and local government reflect new developments at those levels, too: constitutional revision, changes in legislative organization and procedures, the use of the initiative and referendum, current data on State and local finance, and, once again, much else.

Again, all of the many changes incorporated in this volume reflect the complex and the dynamic character of American government. Every effort has been made to make it as accurate, as up-to-date, and as relevant as possible. The wealth of factual material it contains has been drawn from the most current and reliable of sources. This is not a book on current events, however. Much of its content is topical; it contains much data and draws many examples from the contemporary scene. But they are purposefully woven into the context of the book's main purpose: the description, analysis, and explanation of the American system of government.

American Government, 1981, is intended to serve as a basic tool in the learning process. It is built to encourage inquiry and discovery by students—to prompt them to engage in that most difficult, and rewarding, of all human activities: thinking. To that end, it includes 35 case studies, extensively revised for this edition. Each of them raises a problem in some area of public policy and then poses a series of questions designed to provoke reasoned responses. Each chapter is preceded by a series of open-ended questions relating to basic aspects of that chapter. And at the end of each chapter there are several review questions, questions for further inquiry, a number of suggestions for both individual and group activities, and a listing of recently published books for further reading. Then, too, the book contains a large

number of visual materials—maps, photographs, cartoons, graphs, tables, charts, and diagrams—to complement the text and to illustrate trends, concepts, principles, problems, and facts in a striking way. Finally, the supplementary pieces, *Workbook for Magruder's American Government* and *Tests for American Government,* round out a planned set of instructional resources.

Some criticize textbooks because, they claim, they are "too large" and "too factual," and they sometimes argue that they should be "more interpretive." *This* textbook includes that material which, in the author's judgment, is necessary to a basic knowledge and understanding of the American governmental system. If it is a "large" one, it is because its subject is a *large* and an *important* one.

Every book, no matter its subject, reflects in at least some degree the biases of its author. And this book is no exception. A very conscious effort has been made to minimize their appearance, and to present a fair and balanced view of government in the United States. But, inevitably, those biases are present. Whenever they appear they should be subjected to critical examination by the reader, of course. One of them is outstandingly obvious: the conviction that the American system of government, although it contains many and sometimes glaring imperfections, is and should be government of the people, by the people, and for the people.

One final comment here: Both the original author, the late Frank Abbott Magruder, and the present one have sought to make each new edition of *American Government* as accurate, as up-to-date, as readable, and as useable as possible. Over the years we have received much valuable help from the many teachers and students actually using the book in classrooms across the nation. A special word of thanks is gratefully given to all of those teachers gratefully given to all of those persons throughout the country who have so generously contributed their suggestions and ideas to this new edition.

WILLIAM A. McCLENAGHAN,
Department of Political Science
Oregon State University,
Corvallis, Oregon

CONTENTS

Case Studies

CANADA

CEDED BY GREAT BRITAIN – 1818

LOUISIANA PURCHASE – 1803

OREGON TREATY – 1846

MEXICAN CESSION – 1848

GADSDEN PURCHASE 1853

TEXAS ANNEXATION – 1845

WASHINGTON

Seattle
Olympia
Spokane

OREGON
Portland
Salem
Mt. Hood 11,245

Mt. Rainier 14,410

Grand Coulee Dam

Bonneville Dam

MONTANA
Helena
Billings

NORTH DAKOTA
Bismarck

SOUTH DAKOTA
Pierre

IDAHO
Boise
Lewiston

GLACIER NATL PARK

INTERNATIONAL PEACE PARK

YELLOWSTONE NATL PARK

Grand Teton 13,766

WYOMING

Cheyenne

NEBRASKA

CALIFORNIA

NEVADA
Reno
Carson City
Ely

GREAT BASIN

Great Salt Lake
Salt Lake City

UTAH

UINTA MTS.

COLORADO
Denver

KANSAS
Salina
Dodge City
Wichita

San Francisco
Oakland
San Jose
Monterey
Sacramento

SIERRA NEVADA
CENTRAL VALLEY

Mt. Whitney 14,495

DEATH VALLEY –282

Lake Mead

Hoover Dam

ZION NATL PARK

GRAND CANYON NATL PARK

COLORADO PLATEAU

CONTINENTAL DIVIDE

Santa Fe
Albuquerque

Santa Barbara
LOS ANGELES

San Diego

ARIZONA
Phoenix
Tucson

NEW MEXICO

OKLAHOMA
Oklahoma City

El Paso

TEXAS
Fort Worth
Austin
San Antonio

EDWARDS PLATEAU

PACIFIC OCEAN

COAST RANGES
CASCADE RANGES
ROCKY MTS.
CONTINENTAL DIVIDE
COLUMBIA PLATEAU
SNAKE RIVER PLAIN

Columbia R.
Snake River
Green River
Colorado River
Gila River
Rio Grande
Pecos River
Red River
Arkansas River
Platte River
North Platte River
Missouri River
Little Missouri River
Yellowstone River
Bighorn
Black Hills
GREAT PLAINS
Red River of the North

0   600 mi.
1 inch to 600 miles

0   420 km
1 centimeter to 420 kilometers

0   200 mi.
1 inch to 200 miles

0   125 km
1 centimeter to 125 kilometers

POINT BARROW • Barrow

BROOKS RANGE

ARCTIC CIRCLE

Nome

Fort Yukon

ALASKA

Mt. McKinley 20,320

ALASKA RANGE

Yukon R.
Tanana R.

Anchorage

Seward

Juneau

CANADA

Bering Sea

ALEUTIAN ISLANDS

ALASKA PURCHASE – 1867

NIIHAU
KAUAI
OAHU
Pearl Harbor
Honolulu
MOLOKAI
LANAI
MAUI
KAHOOLAWE
Mauna Kea 13,796
Hilo
HAWAII

HAWAII ANNEXATION –1898

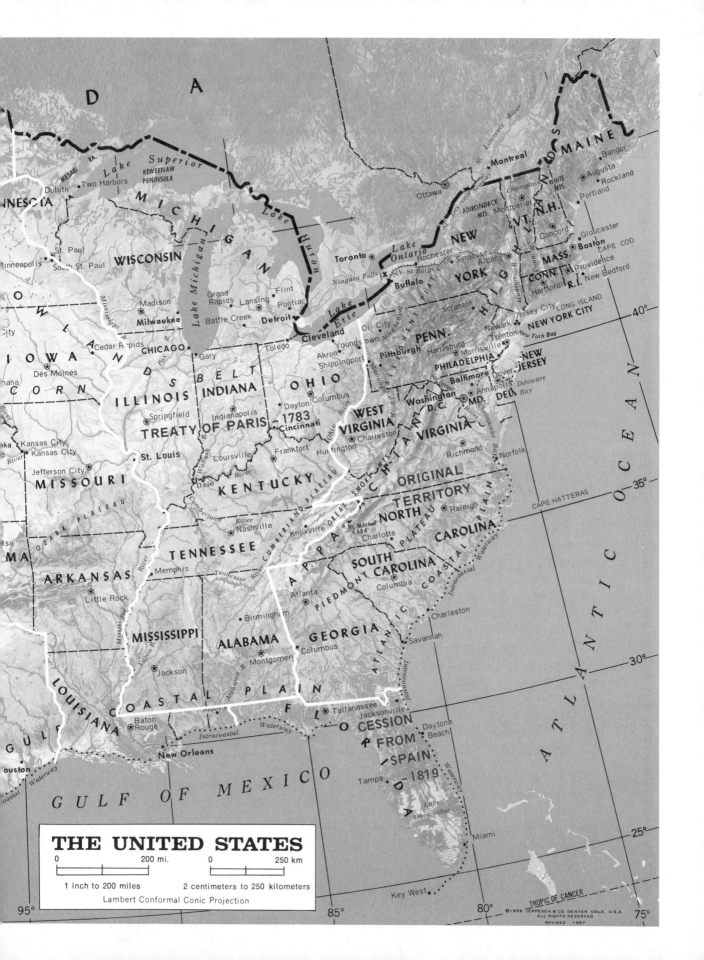

THE UNITED STATES

| 0 | | 200 mi. | 0 | | 250 km |

1 inch to 200 miles   2 centimeters to 250 kilometers

Lambert Conformal Conic Projection

CANADA

MINNESOTA
Duluth • Two Harbors
MESABI
Lake Superior
KEWEENAW PENINSULA
St. Paul
Minneapolis • South St. Paul
WISCONSIN
Madison
Milwaukee
MICHIGAN
Lake Michigan
Lake Huron
Grand Rapids • Lansing • Flint • Pontiac
Battle Creek
Detroit

IOWA
Des Moines
Cedar Rapids
CHICAGO
Gary
Toledo
Cleveland
Lake Erie

CORN BELT
ILLINOIS   INDIANA   OHIO
Springfield   Indianapolis   Dayton • Columbus
Cincinnati
1783
TREATY OF PARIS

Kansas City
Kansas City
Jefferson City
MISSOURI
St. Louis
Louisville   Frankfort
Nashville
KENTUCKY
Huntington

OZARK PLATEAU
ARKANSAS
Little Rock
TENNESSEE
Memphis
Cumberland River
CUMBERLAND PLATEAU
GREAT SMOKY MTS.
Mt. Mitchell 6,684'
Knoxville
Charlotte

MISSISSIPPI   ALABAMA
Jackson
Birmingham
Montgomery
Columbus
GEORGIA
Atlanta
PIEDMONT
SOUTH CAROLINA
Columbia
Charleston

LOUISIANA
Baton Rouge
New Orleans
COASTAL PLAIN
GULF
Mobile
Intracoastal Waterway
Tallahassee
Jacksonville
FLORIDA
CESSION FROM SPAIN 1819
Daytona Beach
Tampa
Lake Okeechobee
Miami
Key West

GULF OF MEXICO
Houston
Intracoastal Waterway

Montreal
St. Lawrence Seaway
Ottawa
Lake Ontario
Toronto
Niagara Falls
Buffalo
Rochester
Syracuse
Albany
NEW YORK
Scranton
ADIRONDACK MTS.
Lake Champlain
Montpelier
MAINE
Bangor
Augusta
Rockland
Portland
WHITE MTS.
VT. N.H.
Concord
Gloucester
Boston
MASS.
CAPE COD
CONN.
Hartford
Providence
R.I.
New Bedford
LONG ISLAND
Jersey City
NEW YORK CITY
Newark
Trenton
New York Bay
NEW JERSEY
Harrisburg
Morrisville
PENN.
Pittsburgh
Youngstown
Akron
Oil City
Shippingport
ALLEGHENY PLATEAU
PHILADELPHIA
Baltimore
Dover
Delaware Bay
DEL.
MD.
Washington D.C.
Annapolis
Chesapeake Bay
WEST VIRGINIA
Charleston
VIRGINIA
Richmond
Norfolk
ORIGINAL TERRITORY
NORTH CAROLINA
Raleigh
ATLANTIC COASTAL PLAIN
CAPE HATTERAS
Intracoastal Waterway

ATLANTIC OCEAN

40°
35°
30°
25°
TROPIC OF CANCER

95°   85°   80°   75°

©1958, JEPPESEN & CO. DENVER, COLO., U.S.A.
ALL RIGHTS RESERVED
REVISED 1967

Part ONE

THE FOUNDATIONS OF THE AMERICAN GOVERNMENTAL SYSTEM

This is a book about government. More particularly, it is a book about government in the United States. Over the course of its pages, we shall consider the ways in which it is organized, the ways it is controlled by the people, and the ways it functions.

You will soon see that the American governmental system is almost certainly the most complicated of the more than 150 such systems which now exist in the world. You will soon see, too, that our governmental system is a democratic one—one in which government may be conducted *only* on the basis of the consent of the governed. And you will also see that in this country government is an all-pervading social force; there is not a single moment in our daily lives when government does not play a meaningful part in our existence.

Before we become involved in the details of our subject, however, a few preliminary words are in order.

The American Heritage. Our governmental system rests upon two mighty pillars: the Declaration of Independence and the Constitution of the United States of America. This nation was born with the bold words of the Declaration. Its very heart is in these hallowed lines:

We hold these truths to be self-evident: that all men are created equal; that they are endowed by their Creator with certain unalienable Rights; that among these are Life, Liberty, and the pursuit of Happiness.

The Union was created by the lofty phrases of the Constitution. Its very first words are among the most important of all:

We the People of the United States, in Order to form a more perfect Union, establish Justice, insure domestic Tranquillity, provide for the common defence, promote the general Welfare, and secure the Blessings of Liberty to ourselves and our Posterity, do ordain and establish this Constitution for the United States of America.

These two passages are brief, yes; and their words are simple. Yet they are of deep and lasting significance. In them is to be found the fundamental expression of the American heritage—a deep and abiding faith in individualism, in freedom, and in equality. It is the task of all of us to carry that great heritage forward, so that together we may sustain and strengthen the values of a free and open society.

You will find that many things are indispensable as you prepare yourself to meet that high purpose—and, certainly, not the least of them is the thing that this book hopes to further: a knowledge and understanding of the nature and workings of the American system of government.

The Basic Tasks of Government. The nature of our governmental system can be better understood if we look at the basic tasks it performs. They are—as they have been from our beginnings—the great purposes set forth in the Preamble to the Constitution: to "form a more perfect union," "establish justice," "insure domestic tranquillity," "provide for the common defence," "promote the general welfare," and "secure the blessings of liberty."

12

An 18th-century engraving depicts delegates to the Second Continental Congress during the signing of the Declaration of Independence in 1776.

FORM A MORE PERFECT UNION. We the People of the United States are a highly diverse and, at the same time, a strikingly similar lot—a heterogeneous, yet homogeneous people. We are composed of many stocks and ethnic groups—English, Irish, Scots, Spanish, French, German, Italian, Polish, Jewish, Russian, Scandinavian, Indian, African, Oriental, and a great many others. The now more than 50 million immigrants who followed in the wake of our earliest settlers came from widely varied places and backgrounds. They brought with them several different languages, customs, and religious, political, economic, and social ideas.

Yet, regardless of ancestry, place of birth, religious and political views, and other differences among us, we share the same basic ideals, a common language, similar customs, and a single nationality. We are *all* Americans.

ESTABLISH JUSTICE. We have said that the American heritage is a faith in individualism, in freedom, and in equality. It is a belief in the fundamental worth and dignity of each and every human being. Those who framed the Constitution recognized that an ordered system of justice is essential to the maintenance of this belief. They agreed with Thomas Jefferson that the establishing and maintaining of justice is "the most sacred of the duties of government."

INSURE DOMESTIC TRANQUILLITY. Order is essential to the well-being of any society, and keeping the peace at home has always been one of the major functions of government. In fact, it is quite likely the oldest of all governmental functions.

Government maintains order in several different ways. Essentially, however, it does so through the making of rules (laws) for the regulation of human behavior and by providing the machinery through which those rules can be enforced. Thus government makes it possible for disputes between or among its citizens to be settled by peaceful means, without recourse to violence.

PROVIDE FOR THE COMMON DEFENSE. Just as government must keep the peace at home, it must also defend the homeland and its people against foreign attack. Today the task of providing for the common defense is one of the most pressing and most expensive of all governmental functions. We know that wars and national defense are extremely costly in terms of dollars and natural resources—and terribly and incalculably more so in terms of human lives. But we know, too, that in a world as unsettled as this one, we must be prepared for any eventuality. We hope, pray, and work for peace—but we keep our powder dry.

PROMOTE THE GENERAL WELFARE. Over the centuries, government—especially in democratic countries such as the United States—has become the *servant*, as well as the protector, of the people. Few Americans fully realize the many and varied ways in which government in this country—at all levels, National, State, and local—provides us with services we could hardly live without. From the instant a person is born (usually in a government-regulated hospital under the care of a government-licensed doctor) until one dies and is buried (after proper legal certification of death and in a government-regulated cemetery), each American citizen is in constant contact, and in myriad ways, with the agencies and services of government—that is, with government serving the people to "promote the general welfare."

SECURE THE BLESSINGS OF LIBERTY. One need not look far—into history or in the contemporary world—to discover that government can be and often has been the mortal enemy of human freedom. For us, however, this has not been so. The United States was founded by people who loved liberty and prized it above all earthly possessions. For it they pledged their lives, their fortunes, and their sacred honor. They declared "life, liberty, and the pursuit of happiness" to be the unalienable rights of all people. They *also* declared "that to *secure* these rights *governments* are instituted among men." For us, then, one of government's prime tasks today is, as it has always been, that of protecting and promoting freedom for the individual— that of securing "the blessings of liberty" to each and to all Americans.

At the beginning of this introductory comment, we noted that in this book we shall consider the ways in which our governmental system is organized, the ways in which it is controlled, and the ways in which it functions. We shall, in fact, be concerned with those matters throughout *all* of the book. In this first part of it, however—over its first four chapters—we shall be concerned with them in a basic sense. That is, we shall consider what may be called the foundations of the American system of government. We shall look at its origins and development, the fundamental principles upon which it is laid, and the structure of the American federal system. In Part Two, we turn to American citizenship and civil rights, and we explore the politics of the American democracy in Part Three. Parts Four, Five, and Six deal respectively with the legislative, executive, and judicial branches of government and with the shaping of national policy in many areas. Finally, we turn to the many facets of State and local government in Part Seven.

Modern Political and Economic Systems

He who considers things in their first growth, whether a state or anything else, will obtain the best view of them.

ARISTOTLE

■ Was John Adams correct when he observed: "If men were angels no government would be necessary"?

■ Why do people regularly accept the authority and abide by the decisions of government? Should government always be obeyed?

■ Is the will of the majority always obeyed in a democracy? Should it be?

"We the People of the United States . . ." With these words the Constitution of the United States begins, and no other words in all of that remarkable document are more meaningful or more important. For here, in this short phrase, is to be found the very essence of the American system of government.

As Americans, we take great and justifiable pride in that system of government. We are proud that it is a system of self-government under law. And we are proud that it is a system in which "We the People" rule and in which government exists only to do our bidding.

We take pride, too, in the fact that the Government of the United States is, and for generations has been, the envy of peoples the world over. Several other nations have experimented with governmental systems not unlike our own; but none of them has lasted for so long nor been developed on so large a scale.

As we take pride, however, it seems wise to remember that we have learned much from—and that we owe much to—some of those other peoples and nations. Our debts to the ancient Greeks and to the not-so-ancient English are especially large.

It seems wise to recall another fact, too: Systems of self-government have been exceedingly rare over the course of human history. Our own, now in its third century, has existed for a longer time than has any other. Authoritarian systems, on the other hand—whether known as tyrannies, despotisms, or dictatorships—have been much more durable and far more numerous.

Viewed against this backdrop, and against the backdrop of the conflict-ridden world in which we live, this also seems wise: That we begin our study of the American system of government with a brief examination of the various governmental systems to be found in the world today. Much of what exists and many of the things that occur in even the most remote corners of the globe may have an immediate and a vital effect upon our daily lives. They may even affect the very future of our existence as a nation.

Governments in the World Today

Government is among the oldest of all human inventions. Its origins are lost in the mists of pre-historic time. More than 2300 years ago, Aristotle wrote that "man is by nature a political animal." When he did so, he was but recording what had, even then, been obvious for thousands of years.

Government first appeared when human beings realized that they could not live without it. That is, it appeared when humans first realized that they could not survive without some form of authority, some power, which could regulate both their own and their neighbors' conduct.

The State. Over the long course of human history the *state* has emerged as the dominant political institution in the world. It may be defined as a body of people, occupying a defined territory, organized politically, and having the power to make and enforce law without the consent of any higher authority.

There are more than 150 states in the world today. They vary greatly in terms of size, economic importance, military power, and many other factors. But each state possesses the four characteristics set out in the preceding definition—that is, population, territory, sovereignty, and government.[1]

POPULATION.   Obviously, there must be people. The size of the population is not essential to the existence of a state, however. The smallest of them all, in terms of population, is San Marino.[2] Nestled high in the Apennines and bounded on all sides by Italy, it contains only some 21,000 people. The People's Republic of China is the largest. Its population is now well over 900 million—so many that if they were all to line up in single file the Chinese people could encircle the globe nearly 18 times.

TERRITORY.   Just as there must be people, so must there be land, territory with known and recognized boundaries. In terms of territory as well as population, San Marino ranks as the smallest of the states in the world today. It has an area of only some 63 square kilometers (24 square miles). The largest state, on the other hand, is the Soviet Union. It encompasses 22,490,000 square kilometers (8,650,000 square miles) and covers about one-sixth of all of the land surface of the earth. The total area of the United States is 9,365,600 square kilometers (3,615,122 square miles).

SOVEREIGNTY.   Every state is *sovereign*. That is, every state possesses supreme and absolute power within its own territory. And it may wield that power as it chooses.

---

[1] Note that what we have defined here—the *state*—is a *legal* entity. In popular usage, a state is often called a "nation" or a "country." In a strict sense, however, *nation* is an *ethnic* term, referring to races or other large groups of people. The term *country* is a *geographic* term, referring to a particular place, region, or area of land.

[2] The Vatican is not cited here primarily because the United States does not recognize its existence as a sovereign state; however, it is recognized by some 80 other states today. Vatican City, with a population of about 1000, occupies a roughly triangular area of approximately 44 hectares (109 acres) and is wholly surrounded by the City of Rome. Nor is the principality of Monaco cited; its several legal ties to France deny its sovereignty. Monaco, with a population of about 30,000, is bounded on three sides by France and by the Mediterranean on the south; it contains some 243 hectares (600 acres, less than one square mile).

In Great Britain, all of the power held by government is lodged in Parliament—and, more precisely, in its lower chamber, the House of Commons. Most other democratic governments in the world today are patterned on the British parliamentary system.

It may determine its own policies, chart its own courses of action, both foreign and domestic. It is neither subordinate nor responsible to any external authority.

Thus, as a sovereign state, the United States may determine its own form of government, may form its own economic system, may shape its own foreign policies, and may decide as it will on all other matters—and so, too, may all other states.[3]

---

[3] Note that sovereignty is *the* distinctive characteristic of a state—the factor that distinguishes it from all other (lesser) political units in the world. The States within the United States are not sovereign and thus are not states in the international legal sense. A superior force, the Constitution of the United States, stands above each of them. Neither do the various dependent areas of the world (*e.g.* Puerto Rico, Guam, Hong Kong) qualify as states. In this book, *state* printed with a small "s" denotes a state in the family of nations, such as France, the United States, and the Soviet Union. *State* printed with a capital "S" refers to a State in the American Union, such as California, Illinois, and North Carolina.

The *location* of sovereignty within a state—that is, who holds and exercises the sovereign power—is of supreme importance. Its location determines whether the government of the state is democratic or dictatorial in form. If the people are sovereign, then the governmental system is a democratic one. If, on the other hand, the power is held by a single person or a small group, a dictatorship exists.

GOVERNMENT. Every state is politically organized. That is, every state has a *government*. Government is the institution through which the public policies of a state are made and enforced and all of its other affairs are conducted. To put the definition another way, government is the agency through which the state exerts its will and attempts to accomplish its ends. It consists of the machinery and the personnel by which the state is ruled (governed). In effect, government may be likened to the

Reproduced by permission of Johnny Hart and Field Enterprises, Inc.

engine which makes an automobile (the state) move.

Origins of the State. For centuries historians, political scientists, philosophers, and others have pondered the question of the origin of the state. How did it arise? What factor or set of circumstances first brought it into being? Over time, several different answers have been offered; but history provides no conclusive evidence to support any of them. Among them, the four which have been most widely accepted, and had the greatest impact, are:

THE FORCE THEORY. Many scholars have long argued that the state was born of force. They hold that it developed because one man—or perhaps a small group of men—claimed control over an area and forced all within it to submit to his—or their—rule. When that rule was established, they argue, all of the basic elements of the state—population, territory, sovereignty, and government—were present.

THE EVOLUTIONARY THEORY. Others claim that the state developed naturally and gradually out of the early family. They maintain that the primitive family, of which the father was the head and thus the "government," was the first stage in human political development. Over countless years the original family became a network of closely related families; that is, it became a clan. Eventually the clan became a tribe. When the tribe first turned to settled agriculture—when it abandoned its nomadic ways and first tied itself to the land —the state was born.

THE DIVINE RIGHT THEORY. Some theorists have argued that the state arose as the result of the "divine right of kings." According to this view, God granted to those of royal birth the right to rule other men. Of course, the theory seems to most of us today to be a patently ridiculous one. But it was widely accepted in the seventeenth and eighteenth centuries. And much of the thought upon which present-day democratic government was built was first developed as an argument or protest against the "divine-right" theory.

THE SOCIAL CONTRACT THEORY. In terms of our political system, the most significant of the various theories concerning the origin of the state is that of the social contract. It was developed in the seventeenth and eighteenth centuries by such philosophers as John Locke, James Harrington, and Thomas Hobbes in England and Jean Jacques Rousseau in France.

Hobbes wrote that in his earliest history man lived in unbridled freedom, in a "state of nature." No government existed; no man was subject to any power superior to that of his own will. Each man could do as he pleased and in whatever manner he chose, at least to the extent that he was physically capable of so doing. That which he could take by force was his, and for as long as he could hold it. But all men were similarly free. Thus, each man was only as secure as his own physical prowess and watchfulness could make him. His life in the state of nature, wrote Hobbes, was "nasty, brutish, and short."

Men overcame their unpleasant condition, says the theory, by agreeing with one another to create a state. By *contract,* men within a given area joined together, each surrendering to the state as much power to control his own behavior as was necessary to promote the safety and well-being of all. In the contract (that is, through a constitution), the members of the state created a government to exercise the powers they had voluntarily granted to the state.

In short, the social contract theory argues that the state arose as the result of a voluntary act of free men. It holds that the state exists only to serve the will of the people, that the people are the sole source of political power, and that the people are free to grant or withhold that power as they choose. The theory seems farfetched to many of us today. But the great concepts it fostered—popular sovereignty, limited government, and individual rights—were, as we shall see, immensely important to the shaping of our own governmental system.[4]

Forms of Government.   No two governments are, or ever have been, exactly alike. Obviously this must be so, for governments are the products of human needs and human experiences. And all of them have been shaped by many other factors— geography, climate, history, customs, resources, the capacities of the people, and several others.

While no two governments are identical, each may be classified according to one or more of its basic features. Political scientists have developed a number of different bases upon which to classify—and so to describe and to analyze—governments. Three of those classifications are especially important and useful for our purposes— classifications according to: (1) the geographical distribution of governmental power within the state, (2) the nature of the relationship between the legislative (law-making) and the executive (law-executing) branches of the government, and (3) the number of persons who may participate in the governing process.

(1) Geographic Distribution of Power. In every governmental system the power to govern is located in one or more places, geographically. Viewing governments from this standpoint, three basic forms exist: *unitary* governments, *federal* governments, and *confederate* governments.

Unitary Government.   A *unitary* government is often described as a centralized government. It is one in which all of the powers possessed by the government are held by a single central agency. Local units of government do exist in the typical unitary system. But these units are created by and for the convenience of the central government, and they derive whatever powers they have only from that source.

Most governments in the world today are unitary in form. Great Britain affords a classic illustration of the type. All of the power that the British government possesses is held by one central organ, the Parliament. Local governments exist only to relieve Parliament of burdens it could perform only with much difficulty and inconvenience. Although it isn't likely, Parliament could abolish all agencies of local government in Great Britain at any time.

Be careful *not* to confuse the unitary form of government with a dictatorship. In the unitary form *all of the powers the government possesses* are concentrated in the central government. But that government might not possess *all* power. In Great Britain, for

---

[4] The Declaration of Independence (see text, pages 783–785) laid its justification for revolution on the social contract theory, arguing that the king and his ministers had violated the contract. Indeed, the principal author of the Declaration, Thomas Jefferson, described the document as "pure Locke."

example, the powers held by the government are strictly limited. British government is unitary and is also, at the same time, democratic.

Federal Government. A *federal* government is one in which the powers of government are divided between a central government and several regional (local) governments. This *division of powers* is made on a geographic basis by an authority superior to both the central and the local governments and cannot be changed by either level acting alone.

In the United States, for example, certain powers are possessed by the National Government and others by the 50 States. This division of powers is set out in the Constitution of the United States. The Constitution stands above both levels of government and cannot be altered unless the people, acting through both the National Government and the States, approve such a change. Australia, Canada, Mexico, New Zealand, Switzerland, West Germany, Yugoslavia, and some 20 other states also utilize the federal form today. (Note that the government of each of the 50 States in the American Union is *unitary,* not federal, in form.)

Confederate Government. A *confederation* is an alliance of independent states. A central organ (the confederate government) possesses the power to handle only those matters of common concern which the member states have delegated to it. Typically, confederate governments have possessed limited powers and only in such fields as defense and foreign commerce. There are no confederations in the world today. But, in our own history, the United States under the Articles of Confederation (1781-1789) and the Confederate States (1861-1865) afford examples of the form.

(2) RELATIONSHIP BETWEEN LEGISLATIVE AND EXECUTIVE BRANCHES. Viewing governments from the standpoint of the relationship that exists between their legislative (law-making) and their executive (law-executing) agencies yields two basic forms: *presidential* and *parliamentary.*

Presidential Government. The *presidential* form features a *separation of powers* between the executive and legislative branches of the government. The two branches are independent of and co-equal with one another. The chief executive (president) is chosen independently of the legislature, holds office for a fixed term, and has broad powers not subject to the direct control of the legislature.

Usually, as in the United States (and each of the 50 States) a written constitution provides for the separation of powers between the branches of government. Thus, the Constitution of the United States provides for the selection of the President, independently of the Congress, for a fixed four-year term. It also assigns to the President and to the Congress their respective fields of power.

Parliamentary Government. In the *parliamentary* form, the executive is composed of the prime minister (or premier) and that official's cabinet. They themselves are members of the legislative branch (the parliament). The prime minister is the leader of the majority party—or of a coalition of two or more parties—in parliament, and is chosen to office by that body. With its approval, he or she selects the members of the cabinet from among the members of parliament. The executive is thus chosen by the legislature, is a part of it, and is subject to its direct control.

The prime minister and the cabinet— referred to as "the government"—remain in office only as long as their policies and administration retain the confidence and support of a majority in parliament. If they are defeated on an important matter (if they do not receive a "vote of confidence"), they must resign from office. Then a new "government" must be formed. Either parliament chooses a new prime minister or, as often happens, a general election is held in which all of the seats in parliament go

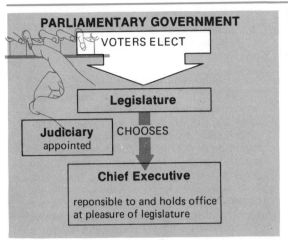

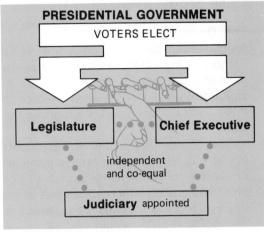

before the voters. The British, most European, and a majority of all other governments in the world today are parliamentary in form.

(3) THE NUMBER WHO MAY PARTICIPATE. What is probably the most meaningful of classifications of government is that based upon the number of individuals who may participate in the governmental process. Formal legal institutions are important to the mechanical operation of government, but the degree of popular participation is the vital heart of the matter. Here we have two basic forms to consider: *dictatorships* and *democracies*.

Dictatorship.   Where the power to govern is held by one person or a small group, a *dictatorship* exists. It is probably the oldest, and certainly the most common, form of government known to history.

All dictatorships are *authoritarian* in nature. That is, they are governmental systems in which the ruling power exercises absolute and unchallengeable authority over the people. Modern dictatorships have tended to be *totalitarian,* as well. That is, they exercise dictatorial (authoritarian) power with regard to virtually *every* aspect of human affairs; their power embraces all (the *totality of*) matters of human concern.

The prime examples of dictatorship in the 20th century are those which existed in

Fascist Italy (from 1922 to 1943) and Nazi Germany (from 1933 to 1945), and those which continue to exist in the Soviet Union (where the present dictatorial regime was established in 1917) and the People's Republic of China (where the dictatorship came to power in 1949). But notice that dictatorships outnumber democracies by a wide margin—historically *and* presently.

One-man dictatorships have been and are relatively uncommon. They are not unknown, however. The recently-deposed regime in Uganda provides a classic example of the point. Idi Amin Dada seized control of the government of that East African state in 1971. Immediately, Amin proclaimed himself the nation's "President-for-Life"; and for eight years he ruled with a harsh and *autocratic* (absolute, unlimited) hand. His government was finally toppled by the armies of Tanzania in 1979.

Dictatorships are much more often dominated by the will of a small, tight-knit group. For example, the premier of the Soviet Union may be properly described as a dictator. But he is, in fact, powerless to act without the support and approval of the potent *politburo* (executive council) of the Communist Party of the USSR.

The primary characteristic of any dictatorship is that *it is not responsible to the people and cannot be limited by them.* It is not ac-

Case Study

The Declaration of Independence was proclaimed to the world on July 4, 1776. For more than 200 years now that remarkable document has stood as an inspiration to millions of persons—both in this country and, indeed, throughout the world.

One of the Declaration's basic purposes was, of course, to proclaim the independence of the United States. Another and equally vital purpose was to set out the basic principles upon which a new political order would be built in the new and independent United States.

These principles were so much a part of American thought at that time that the Declaration described them as "self-evident":

> We hold these truths to be self-evident, that all men are created equal, that they are endowed by their Creator with certain unalienable Rights, that among these are Life, Liberty, and the pursuit of Happiness. That to secure these rights, Governments are instituted among Men, deriving their just powers from the consent of the governed; That whenever any Form of Government becomes destructive of these ends it is the Right of the People to alter or abolish it, and to institute new Government, laying its foundation on such principles and organizing its powers in such form, as to them shall seem most likely to effect their Safety and Happiness.

- What basic principles of government are set out here?
- Did the promulgation of the Declaration amount to an American commitment to democratic government?

- Why, according to the Declaration, do governments exist?
- Does the Declaration proclaim a right to revolution? If so, when, and to what end, may that right be exercised?

countable to any higher authority for its actions or for the manner in which they are taken.

Dictatorships often present the outward appearance of control by the people. Thus, popular elections are usually held. But elections are rigidly controlled and, typically, the voter is offered the candidates of only one political party. An elected legislative body often exists; but it functions only to rubber-stamp the policies and programs of the dictatorship.

Public support for the regime is mobilized through massive propaganda programs and absolute control of the educational system. Opposition is suppressed, often ruthlessly by a secret police. Only one political party, highly organized and rigidly disciplined, is permitted. Freedom of speech, thought, and association—so vital in democracy—are not tolerated.

Typically, dictatorial regimes are quite militaristic in character. They usually gain power by force; many of the major posts in the government are held by militarists. Moreover, after crushing all effective opposition at home, they may turn to foreign aggression and other adventures to enhance the nation's military power and prestige.

Benito Mussolini stated the basic philosophy of the modern-day totalitarian dictatorship when he proclaimed:

> All is in the state and for the state, nothing outside the state, nothing against the state.

Democracy. In the *democratic* form of government, supreme political authority rests with the people. The people hold the sovereign power and government is conducted only by and with their consent.[5]

---

[5] The word *democracy* is derived from the Greek words *demos*, meaning "the people," and *kratos*, meaning "rule" or "authority." The Greek word *demokratia* means, literally, "rule by the people."

Abraham Lincoln gave immortality to this definition of democracy in the Gettysburg Address in 1863: "government of the people, by the people, for the people." Nowhere is there a better, more concise statement of the American appreciation of the term. But notice that it is the *second* of Lincoln's three phrases which distinguishes a democracy from any other form of government. All governments are *of* the people—at least in the sense that they operate "over" the people. Even a dictatorship may function *for* the people. But only a democracy is of, for, *and by* the people.

A democracy may be either *direct* or *indirect* in form. A *direct* (or *pure*) democracy exists where the will of the people is translated into public policy (law) directly by the people themselves in mass meetings. Obviously, such a system is practicable only in very small communities where it is possible for the citizens to assemble in a given place and where the problems of government are few and simple. Direct democracy does not exist at the national level anywhere in the world today. But the old New England town meeting and the *Landsgemeinde* in a few of the smaller Swiss cantons are excellent examples of direct democracy in action.[6]

In the United States we are more familiar with the *indirect* form—that is, with *representative* democracy. In a representative democracy the popular will is formulated and expressed through a relatively small group of persons chosen by the people to act as their representatives. These representatives act as the people's agents. They are responsible for the ongoing, day-to-day conduct of government. And they are held accountable to the people for the manner in which they meet that responsibility, especially through periodic elections.

To put it another way, representative democracy is government by popular consent—government with the consent of the governed.

There are some who insist that the United States is a *republic* rather than a democracy. They hold that, in a republic, the sovereign power is held by the electorate and is exercised by representatives chosen by and held responsible to the electorate. For them, a democracy may be defined only in terms of direct democracy. Of course, they are entitled to their view. To most Americans, however, the terms democracy, republic, representative democracy, and republican form of government generally mean the same thing.

Regardless of the terms used, remember that above all else in a democracy the people are sovereign—that is, the people are the only source for any and all governmental power. In short, the people rule. Today, most of the states of the Western World are representative democracies—although, certainly, some are more democratic than others.

Basic Concepts of Democracy. There is nothing inevitable about democracy. It does not exist in the United States simply because we regard it as the best of all possible political systems.[7] Nor will it continue to exist for that reason. Rather, democracy exists in this country because, as a people, we believe in the concepts upon which it is based. It will continue to exist, and be improved in practice, only for so long as we continue to subscribe to—and *seriously attempt to practice*—those concepts.

The basic concepts of democracy—es-

---

6 The *Landsgemeinde*, like the original New England town meeting, is an assembly open to all local citizens qualified to vote. In a more limited sense, lawmaking by initiative petition is also an example of direct democracy (see page 705).

7 The late Sir Winston Churchill once argued for democracy in these terms: "Many forms of government have been tried in this world of sin and woe. No one pretends that democracy is perfect or all-wise. Indeed, it has been said that democracy is the worst form of government except all of those other forms which have been tried from time to time . . ."

pecially as we understand and apply the term in the United States—are:

(1) A recognition of the fundamental worth and dignity of each and every person.

(2) A respect for the equality of all persons.

(3) A faith in majority rule and an insistence upon minority rights.

(4) An acceptance of the necessity of compromise.

(5) An insistence upon the widest possible area of individual freedom.

Of course, these ideas may be, and often are, phrased in other ways. No matter what the phrasing, however, any formulation of the basic concepts of democracy must include the five presented here. They form the very *minimum* that must be subscribed to by anyone who professes to believe in democracy. Some will argue that other concepts belong in such a listing; for example, the right of each person to at least a certain minimum level of economic security. But the point here is that, no matter what else *might* be included, at least those cited *must* be.

FUNDAMENTAL WORTH OF THE INDIVIDUAL. Democracy is firmly based upon a belief in the fundamental importance of the individual. Each and every individual, no matter what his or her station in life may be, is a separate and distinct being. Democracy

insists that *each person's worth and dignity must be recognized and respected by all other individuals, and by all of society, at all times.*

This concept of the sanctity of the individual is of overriding importance in democratic thought. It is the *central concept* from which all else in democracy flows. Anything and everything a democratic society does must and should be done within the limits of this great concept.

It is true that the welfare of one or a few individuals is sometimes subordinated to the interests of the many in a democracy. For example, an individual may be forced to pay taxes to support the functions of government, whether he or she wants to or not. One may be required to serve in the armed forces, be prohibited from constructing a building in a certain location, or even be forced to give up his or her home for some public purpose, such as a new highway. When these or similar things are done, a democratic society is serving the interests of the many. But it is *not* serving them simply as the interests of a mass of people who happen to outnumber the few. Rather, it is serving the many who, *as individuals*, altogether, make up the society.

The distinction we are trying to make here—between *an* individual and *all* individuals—may be a very fine one. It is, however, a most important one to a true understanding of the meaning of democracy.

EQUALITY OF ALL PERSONS. Hand-in-

the small society　　　　　　　　**by Brickman**

HOO-BOY! IT'S SURE NICE TO LIVE IN A COUNTRY WHERE HEADS ARE COUNTED ON ELECTION DAY...

NOT BROKEN—

Washington Star Syndicate, Inc.

BRICKMAN

11-7

hand with the belief in the sanctity of the individual, democracy stresses the equality of all individuals. It holds, with Jefferson, that "all men are created equal."

Certainly, democracy does *not* insist upon an equality of *condition* for all persons. Thus, it does not claim that all are born with the same mental or physical abilities. Nor does it argue that all persons are entitled to an equal share of worldly goods.

Rather, the democratic concept of equality insists that all are entitled to: (1) *equality of opportunity* and (2) *equality before the law.* That is, the democratic concept of equality holds that no person should be held back for any such artificial or arbitrary reasons as those based upon race, color, religion, or economic or social status. It holds that each person must be free to develop himself or herself as fully as he or she can (or cares to) and that each person should be treated as the equal of all others by the law.

We have come a great distance toward realizing the goal of equality for all in this country. But only the willfully blind will not see that we are yet a considerable distance from a genuine, universally recognized, and universally respected equality for all of our people.

MAJORITY RULE AND MINORITY RIGHTS. In a democracy public policy is to be made *not* by the dictate of a ruling few but in accord with the will of the people.

But what is the "popular will," and how is it to be determined? How, that is, are public policy questions to be decided and public policies made? Clearly, there must be some standard, some device, by which these crucial questions can be answered. The only satisfactory device that democracy knows is that of *majority rule.*

An ancient Arab proverb tells us that it is better to knock heads together than it is to count them. It suggests that one is more likely to find out what is inside those heads by breaking them open than by simply counting them. But, again, and most emphatically, democracy *does* believe in counting heads.

Democracy is firmly committed to the proposition that a majority of the people will be right more often than they will be wrong. And it is also committed to the belief that the majority will be right more often than will one person or small group.

Democracy may be quite usefully described as an experiment—and as a "trial-and-error" process—designed to find satisfactory ways of ordering human relations. Notice that it does *not* argue that the majority will *always* be "right," that it will always arrive at the best of all possible decisions on public matters. In fact, the democratic process (the process of majority rule) does not intend to provide "right" or "best" answers. Rather, it searches for *satisfactory* solutions to public problems.

Of course, democracy insists that the decisions that are made will more often be *more* rather than *less* satisfactory. But it does admit of the possibility of mistakes, of the finding of "wrong" or less satisfactory answers. And it also recognizes that seldom is any solution to a public problem so satisfactory that there is no room for improvement. So, the process of experimentation, of seeking answers to public questions, is a continuous one.

Certainly, a democracy cannot function without the principle of majority rule. Unchecked, however, a majority could readily become a tyranny. Unchecked, it could easily destroy its opposition and, in the process, destroy democracy, as well. Thus, democracy insists upon majority rule *restrained by minority rights.* The majority must always recognize the right of any minority to become, if it can, by fair and lawful means, itself the majority. The majority must always be willing to listen to a minority argument, to hear its objections, to bear its criticisms, and to welcome its suggestions. Anything less contradicts the very meaning of democracy.

NECESSITY OF COMPROMISE.   In a democracy public decision-making is (must be) very largely a process of give-and-take, of accommodating competing views and interests with one another. That is, it is very largely a matter of *compromise.* Compromise is the process of blending and adjusting, of reconciling, in order to find the position most acceptable to the largest number of people.

Compromise is an essential part of the democratic concept for two major reasons. *First,* recall that democracy exalts the *individual* and, at the same time, it insists that each individual is the *equal* of all others. How—in a society composed of many individuals (and groups) with widely varying opinions and interests—can public decisions be made except by compromise? *Secondly,* few public questions have only "two sides." Most have many different sides and can be answered in several ways. As an illustration, take the apparently simple question of how a city should finance the paving of a public street. Should it charge the costs to those who own property along the street? Or should all of the city's residents pay the costs from the city's general treasury? Or should the city and the adjacent property owners share the costs? What of those who will use the street but do not live within the city? Should they be required to pay a toll or buy a license for that use?

Again, the point here is that *most* public policy questions can be answered in several different ways. But the fact remains that *some* answer must be found.

It would be impossible for the people in a democratic society to decide most public questions without the element of compromise. Remember, however, that compromise is a *process,* a way of achieving majority agreement. It is never an end in itself. Not all compromises are good, and not all are necessary. There are some things—the equality of all persons, for example—that can never be and should

never be the subject of any kind of compromise if democracy is to survive.

INDIVIDUAL FREEDOM.   From all that has been said to this point, it should be clear that democracy can thrive only in an atmosphere of individual freedom. But democracy *does not* and *cannot* insist upon complete freedom for the individual. No person can be absolutely free to do as he or she pleases, for this would ultimately mean that no one would be free. Absolute freedom can exist only in a state of *anarchy*—in the total absence of government. Moreover, anarchy can only lead, inevitably and quickly, to rule by the strong and ruthless.

Democracy does insist, however, that each individual must be as free to do as he or she pleases as the freedom of all will permit. In other words, each individual's liberty is relative to and dependent upon the liberties of all other persons. Justice Oliver Wendell Holmes once emphasized the relative nature of each individual's rights this way: "The right to swing my fist ends where the other man's nose begins."

Drawing the line between the rights of one individual and those of another is a far-from-easy task. But the drawing of that line is a continuingly necessary and vitally important function of democratic government. It is because, as John F. Kennedy once observed: "The rights of every man are diminished when the rights of one man are threatened."

And striking the proper balance between freedom for the individual and the rights of society as a whole is similarly difficult—and is, too, a similarly vital function of democratic government. Abraham Lincoln once posed democracy's problem here in these words:

> Must a government of necessity be too *strong* for the liberties of its own people, or too *weak* to maintain its own existence?

The problem goes to the very heart of democracy. Human beings desire both liberty and authority. Democratic government must strike the balance between the two. The authority of government must be adequate to the needs of society. But this authority must never be so great as to restrict the individual beyond the point of necessity.

Democracy regards all civil rights as vital, but it places its highest value on those guarantees necessary to the free exchange of ideas: on *freedom of expression* and *freedom of thought*. Several years ago, the President's Committee on Civil Rights made the point this way:

> In a free society there is faith in the ability of the people to make sound, rational judgments. But such judgments are possible only when the people have access to all relevant facts and to all prevailing interpretations of the facts. How can such judgments be formed on a sound basis if arguments, viewpoints, or opinions are arbitrarily suppressed? How can the concept of the marketplace of thought in which truth ultimately prevails retain its validity if the thought of certain individuals is denied the right of circulation?

We shall return to the whole subject of individual rights later—especially in Chapters 6 and 7. And we shall return to each of the other basic democratic concepts, again and again, throughout the pages of this book.

Capitalism, Socialism, Communism

What are the functions which, whatever its form, a government ought to undertake? What should it have the power to do? What should it not be permitted to do? Certainly these questions may be, and often are, posed with reference to virtually all areas of human activity. But these questions are raised most often, and most significantly, in the realm of economic affairs.

Questions of politics and of economics are, in fact, inseparable. Many of the most important and most difficult questions governments face are economic ones. What, for example, should be the nature of the relationship between management and labor in a nation's economy? What role should government play in that relationship? On what basis should goods and services be distributed and exchanged within the nation? Should such basic industries as transportation, steel, and oil be privately or publicly owned and operated? And what of banking? What provisions, if any, ought to be made for the welfare of the nation's elderly? And what of the poor, the physically or mentally handicapped, and those who are otherwise disadvantaged? Obviously, a large number of other important questions can be posed.

Clearly, these are critical *economic* questions—and, just as clearly, they are critical *political* questions, as well.

Three major economic systems predominate in the world today: capitalism, socialism, and communism.

Capitalism. The American economic system—and that found in several other nations today—is known as *capitalism*. It is based upon private ownership, individual initiative, profit, and competition. Capitalism is often described, as well, as the *free enterprise* or *private enterprise* system.

BASIC NATURE OF THE CAPITALISTIC SYSTEM. In the capitalistic system the means by which goods and services are produced are held, very largely, as private property—as the property of individuals and companies (formed, owned, and controlled by one or a few or many individuals). That is, the instruments of production, of distribution, and of exchange (as factories, mines, stores, farms, railroads, airlines, banks) are privately owned and managed.

Those who own these means hire labor and *compete* with one another to produce goods and services at a *profit*. Competition is the lifeblood of the system, and in its purest form involves the providing of the best possible product at the lowest possible price. Profit is the motive power of the system. The profits of an enterprise are its earnings, the excess of income over expenditures; that is, the returns realized by the owners over and above the costs of doing business. In short, profits represent the rewards received for the risks taken and the initiative shown.

Generally speaking, any person or group may start an enterprise—attempt to produce or sell goods or offer services—and the risks and rewards are theirs. Most of the larger and many of the smaller businesses in the United States today are actually owned by large numbers of persons—by stockholders who own shares in them.

The American Telephone and Telegraph Company, the world's largest private utility, for example, is now owned by nearly three million stockholders. Altogether, more than 25 million persons in the United States own shares in some 11,000 business firms today.

Typically, a portion of the profits earned by an enterprise is paid out as *dividends* and a portion is reinvested in the business. Thus, the investor receives a return on his or her investment, the business expands, more jobs are created, individual purchasing power increases, and a still higher standard of living results.

LAISSEZ-FAIRE THEORY. American capitalism as we know it today bears only a distant resemblance to classical capitalistic economics. The origins of capitalism are laid in the concepts of *laissez-faire*, a doctrine developed in the late eighteenth and early nineteenth centuries.[8]

According to *laissez-faire* theory, government should play only a very limited—virtually a "hands-off"—role in society. Its activities should be confined to three areas: (1) the conduct of foreign relations and national defense, (2) the maintenance of police and courts to protect private property and the health, safety, and morals of the people, and (3) the performance of certain necessary functions which cannot be provided by private enterprise at a profit.

The theory was given its classic expression by Adam Smith in *The Wealth of Nations*, first published in London in 1776. Its basic assumption was well summarized in Thomas Jefferson's often quoted remark: "That government is best which governs least." Its supporters opposed any governmental activity which tended to hamper free enterprise. They insisted that government's place in economic affairs ought to be limited to those functions designed to protect and promote the unhampered, free play of competition and the operation of the law of supply and demand.

The theory of *laissez-faire* economics never operated in fact in this country, even in the earliest days of the Republic. Government at both the National and the State levels has played a meaningful role in economic affairs throughout our history. Even so, it is obvious that the concepts of *laissez-faire* had, and continue to have, a profound effect upon the nature of our economic system. Most business enterprises in the United States are private in character. They are owned by private persons, not by government. They are financed with private capital, not with public funds. And, they are managed by private citizens, not by public officials.

A "MIXED ECONOMY." While the American economic system is essentially private in character, government has always played a considerable, and an increasing, role in it. Indeed, our system may be properly described as a "mixed economy." That is, it is one in which private enterprise is combined with and supported by considerable governmental regulation and promotion.

---

[8] The term *laissez-faire* comes from a French idiom meaning "to let alone." Translated literally, it means "allow to act."

It is one in which there is a substantial amount of governmental activity and control designed to protect the public interest and to preserve private enterprise. To put the point another way, we have recognized that unregulated capitalism would result in a system of injustice and selfishness, a system in which the cruel philosophy of "dog-eat-dog" would prevail.

A vast amount of economic regulation and promotion occurs at all levels of government in the United States—National, State, and local. To cite only a very few of an almost unlimited number of examples, economic activities are regulated by government in this country through: antitrust laws, labor-management relations statutes, pure food and drug laws, the regulation of environmental pollution, the policing of investment practices, and city and county zoning ordinances and building codes.

Similarly, the nation's economic life is promoted in a myriad of public ways; for example: by direct subsidies, public roads and highways, such services as the postal system and weather reports, public housing programs, research at State universities, a variety of loan programs for a multitude of purposes, and planting and marketing advice to farmers.

Our economy is also "mixed" in the sense that some enterprises and functions which might be carried on privately are, in fact, operated by government. Public education, the postal system, the monetary system, some forms of public transportation, and roadbuilding are familiar examples of long standing.

To what extent should government participate, regulate and promote, police and serve? Many of our most heated political debates revolve about the question. In the constant search for answers, we tend to follow the general rule expressed by Abraham Lincoln:

The legitimate object of government is to do for the community of people whatever they need to have done, but cannot

The brokers here, engaged in the buying and selling of a commodity (as eggs, potatoes, lumber), are subject to government regulations designed to prevent fraudulent trading practices.

do so well for themselves, in their separate and individual capacities.

One needs only to look at the great achievements and the standard of living of the American people to see the advantages of our economic system. Most of the people of the United States believe that a well-regulated capitalistic system—one of free choice, individual incentive, private enterprise—is the best guarantee of the better life for everyone.

Socialism. Socialism is a philosophy of *economic collectivism*. It advocates the *collective*—that is, the social, public—ownership of the instruments of production, distribution, and exchange. It insists that the means by which goods and services are produced should be *publicly* owned and managed.

Socialism argues that the economic order should be designed and operated in behalf of all, for the use and benefit of all. It

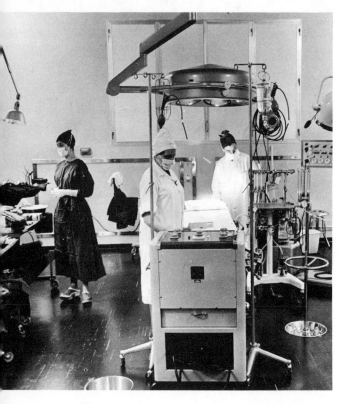

An operating room in a hospital in Sweden, where medical care is provided by the government.

alone. They came to believe that the power of the state must be used to bring about a collective economy.

The most extreme form of socialism today is *communism,* to which we shall turn in a moment. Most socialists outside the Soviet and Chinese orbits are *evolutionary socialists,* or, as they are often called, *social democrats.* They believe that socialism can best be achieved gradually and peaceably, by lawful means, and by working within the established framework of government. They believe that, even after they have won control of government, the new order should be introduced only in stages. The first stage, they believe, should be the *nationalization* (socialization) of a few key enterprises, such as banking, transportation, and the steel industry.

Evolutionary socialists argue that political democracy, with its emphasis upon popular participation in government, is incomplete. True democracy can exist, they claim, only when the people share in the management of their economic destinies as well. The British Labor Party and the major socialist parties of Western Europe and the Scandinavian countries are prime examples of evolutionary socialism in action today.[9]

To the socialist, the philosophy of socialism is based on justice because it aims at a more equitable distribution of wealth and opportunity among people. Economic affairs should be organized and managed, says the socialist, for the good of the entire community.

Opponents of socialism condemn it because they believe that it stifles individual initiative and denies to the capable and the

thus rejects the concepts of private ownership, competition, and profit which lie at the heart of capitalist thought and practice.

The roots of socialism lie deep in history. Almost from the beginning there have been those who have dreamed and planned for a society built upon socialist doctrine. Most of the earlier socialists foresaw a collective economy arising out of and managed by voluntary private action. With few exceptions, they considered governmental action unnecessary to the realization of their goals. Thus, early socialist doctrine is often referred to as "private socialism."

Socialism in its modern form—that is, *state socialism*—has emerged only over the course of the past 100 years or so. Only since the middle of the last century have most socialists argued that the reaching of their goal is too big a task for private action

---

[9] Although socialism and communism are often identified with each other, the socialists of the non-communist world (the evolutionary socialists) are usually bitter foes of the communists. They share many of the ideas supported by the Russian, Chinese, and other Marxists. But most evolutionary socialists reject the theory of the class struggle, the necessity of violent revolution, and the dictatorship of the proletariat—all fundamental to Marxian communism.

industrious the justifiable rewards of their efforts. Many also argue that the increased governmental regulation necessary to socialism must inevitably lead to dictatorship.

The complexities of modern society have led to vast expansion of governmental functions in most countries, including the United States. Many of the activities undertaken by government in this country in the past four decades or so have been attacked by opponents who insist that they are "socialistic" and thus ill-advised and a threat to the nation and its future.

Communism. As we know it today, communism was born in 1848 with the publication of *The Communist Manifesto*. A brief, inflammatory pamphlet, it was written by Karl Marx with the aid of his close colleague, Friedrich Engels. In *The Communist Manifesto* and his later and very extensive writings, Marx laid down the cardinal premises of *scientific socialism*, or communism.[10]

From the death of Marx in 1883, and that of Engels in 1895, communism has been interpreted and expanded by his followers. The most important of the latter-day "high priests of communism" have been Vladimir Ilyich Lenin, Josef Stalin, Nikita Khrushchev and Leonid Brezhnev in the Soviet Union, and Mao Tse-tung in the People's Republic of China. The doctrine they have developed is distinctly both political and economic in nature.[11]

COMMUNIST THEORY. In its essence, the communist ideology rests upon four basic, and closely related, propositions: (1) its theory of history, (2) the labor theory of value, (3) its theory of the nature of the state, and (4) its concept of the dictatorship of the proletariat.

(1) The Communist Theory of History. According to Marx, all of human history has been a story of the "class struggle." The communists say that there have always been two opposing classes in society—one an oppressor (dominating) class and the other an oppressed (dominated) class. In feudal times the two classes were the nobility and the serfs. Today, say the communists, the capitalists (the *bourgeoisie*) keep the workers (the *proletariat*) in bondage. Workers in capitalistic countries are described as "wage slaves." These workers, say the communists, are paid barely enough to permit them to eke out a starvation living as they continue to toil for their masters.

The communists contend that the class struggle has become so bitter and the divisions between the classes so sharp that the situation cannot continue. They claim that a revolt of the masses and the destruction of the bourgeoisie are inevitable. They see their function as that of speeding up the "natural" course of history, by violence if necessary.

(2) The Labor Theory of Value. The communist ideology also holds that the value of any commodity is determined by the amount of labor necessary to produce it. In other words, a suit of clothes is worth so much because it takes so much labor to produce it. Because the laborer produced the suit and thus created its value, the communists claim that the laborer should receive that value in full. They maintain that all income should come from work. They are fiercely opposed to the free enterprise profit system and condemn profits as "surplus value" which should go to the worker.

(3) The Nature of the State. To the communists, the state is the instrument or "tool" of the dominating class—a tool with

[10] The term *scientific socialism* was used to distinguish Marxian thought from the older and less extreme forms of socialism. In later years, Marx and his followers came to prefer the term *communism*.

[11] Capitalism is also a political and an economic doctrine, but in a much more limited sense. To the capitalist, the proper role of government is that of stimulator, servant, and regulator or referee. Socialism is much more a political as well as an economic theory than is capitalism, but it is not nearly so distinctly political as is communism.

In the Soviet Union, ballots may be cast only for those candidates approved by the Communist Party. Below are deputies of the Soviet of the Union and the Soviet of Nationalities as they vote on a resolution. Although "representatives of the people," they are never entrusted with independent choices and decisions.

which the bourgeoisie keeps the proletariat in bondage. Because the bourgeoisie is so firmly entrenched in its control of the state and its power, said Lenin, it is only through a "violent and bloody revolution" that the situation can be altered. (The communists also claim that other institutions are used as "tools" as well. Thus, Marx described religion as "the opiate of the people." Religion, he claimed, was a drug fed to the people as a hoax through which they are led to tolerate their supposed harsh lot in this life in order to gain a "fictional afterlife.")

(4) *The Dictatorship of the Proletariat.* The communists do not foresee a proletariat able to govern themselves after a revolution. Rather, the proletariat would need "guidance and education"—from the Communist Party, of course. Hence, the dogma calls for a *dictatorship of the proletariat.* That is, a totalitarian regime is to be estab-

lished to lead the people to the theoretical goal of communism: a "free classless society." As that goal is realized, it is claimed, the state would "wither away." The cardinal principle of the new society would be: "From each according to his ability, to each according to his need."

EVALUATION OF COMMUNISM. The Soviet Union presents the outstanding example of communism in action. Strictly speaking, the Russians do not practice pure communism today, but an extreme form of socialism.[12] Their present system stems from the

---

[12] According to Marx, the guiding principle in a communist society should be "From each according to his ability, to each according to his need." But compare this with this provision (Article 13) of the Soviet Constitution of 1977: "The State shall control the measure of labor and consumption in accordance with the principle: 'From each according to his ability, to each according to his work.' . . . Socially useful work and its results shall determine a citizen's status in society."

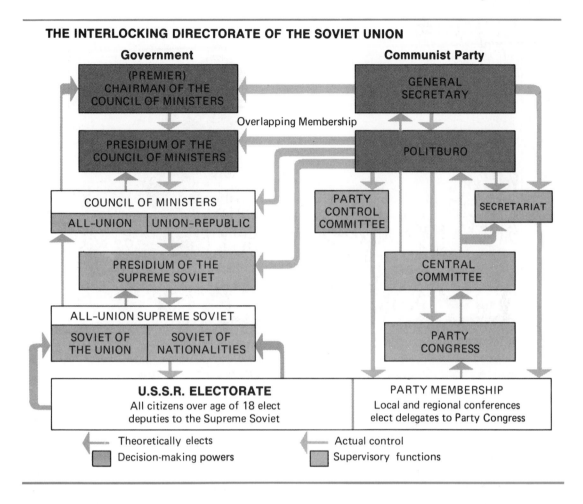

THE INTERLOCKING DIRECTORATE OF THE SOVIET UNION

October Revolution of 1917 when Lenin and his followers came to power.[13] Immediately, Lenin attempted to establish a communist system. But the attempt compounded the chaos of Russia's defeat and withdrawal from World War I, and it failed. The inefficient and the lazy received as much as the efficient and the industrious. Workers and peasants rebelled. The new government imposed severe reprisals; many thousands were executed. Finally, the Soviet leaders modified their approach, turning to their version of socialism. The Soviets now claim to be working *toward* the eventual goal of pure communism.

More than a century of Marxist theory and more than a half-century of Soviet communism have exposed many of the fallacies of communist doctrine. We note the major ones here.

Marx argued that the divisions between the bourgeoisie and the proletariat would continue to deepen. Ultimately, they would reach a point where capitalism would collapse under its own weight. The rich, said Marx, would become richer and the poor would become poorer. The struggle between the bourgeoisie and the prole-

[13] The revolution occurred on October 25, 1917, by the calendar then in use in Russia. By the Western calendar, now also used in the Soviet Union, the date was November 7. The communists did not, as is often supposed, revolt against the czarist regime. Rather, they overthrew the fledgling democratic government headed by Alexander Kerensky. The Kerensky government had been created as a consequence of a revolution in March of 1917. It was this earlier, noncommunist revolt that deposed the czarist tyranny.

© 8/20/80. THE PHILADELPHIA INQUIRER. THE WASHINGTON POST WRITERS GROUP. AUTH

'WORKERS OF THE WORLD, UNITE!' —MARX

POLISH WORKERS ON STRIKE! FREE SPEECH! STRIKE FREE TRADE UNIONS POLISH POLISH WORKERS STRIKE STRIKE

Through the years, the confidence of Marxists that communism would appeal to workers throughout the world, regardless of nationality, has proven to be ill-founded.

tariat would grind the middle class down into the ranks of the proletariat.

In fact, the contrary has happened. The economic gap between workers and owners has narrowed almost to the point of extinction, especially in the United States. Marx and his followers failed to foresee the tremendous growth of the middle class. The poor have not become poorer; they have, in fact, become much, much richer.

Communist theory has little room for individual initiative and incentive, so vital in our own economic system. One of the basic differences between our system and the communists' should be noted here. It is that: Where we strive to promote *equality of opportunity,* the communists argue for *equality of condition.* Experience has forced the communists to recognize the importance of incentive, however. The labor theory of value has been very largely ignored in communist practice. Income in the Soviet Union today is based largely on the amount or the importance of the work one does. Thus, scientists, managers, administrators, teachers, and others in the professions receive larger incomes and many more privileges than do the masses in the working class.

The state has not been the tool of the dominant class in the non-communist world. Rather, the state—acting through government controlled by, and responsive to, the will of the people—has become one of the major agents through which the welfare of the people has advanced.

Marx predicted that the emergence of communism would promote peace among the nations of the world. Obviously, quite the opposite has occurred. Further, he and his followers confidently expected communism to appeal to workers throughout the world, regardless of nationality. *The Communist Manifesto* closed with the cry: "Workingmen of all countries, unite!" But, in fact, communism has failed to eliminate nationalistic sentiments. And that point is aptly demonstrated by the conflict-ridden relationships between the Soviet Union and the People's Republic of China.

The state in the Soviet Union, the People's Republic of China, and other communist countries shows no sign of "withering away." Indeed, under communism the power of the state has been drastically *increased*. The dictatorships established in these countries have become the most totalitarian the world has ever seen. All forms of opposition are ruthlessly suppressed. Basic freedoms are not permitted, lest the people examine and question the policies of the state. Fear is a weapon in the hands of the ruling group. The dictatorship easily perpetuates itself.

SUMMARY

A knowledge of the governmental and economic systems which exist today is essential in our conflict-ridden world.

The *state,* the dominant political unit in the world today, is a body of people occupying a defined territory and organized politically with the power to make and enforce law without the consent of any higher authority. Every state possesses four essential characteristics: (1) population; (2) territory; (3) sovereignty; and (4) government.

While no two governments are identical, each may be classified in various ways on the basis of certain factors. A *unitary* government is one in which all the powers possessed by the government are lodged in a single central organ, as in Great Britain. A *federal* government is one in which governmental powers are distributed on a geographic basis between a central and several local governments, as in the United States. A *confederate* government is an alliance of independent states with a weak central government which has limited powers over such matters of common concern as defense and foreign affairs.

A *presidential* government is one in which the executive (president) is independent of and co-equal with the legislature, as in the United States. In a *parliamentary* form of government the executive (prime minister and cabinet) is a part of—and subordinate to—the legislature, as in Great Britain.

A *dictatorship* exists where the power to govern is held by one person or, as is typically the case, a small group. All dictatorships are authoritarian in character, and modern dictatorships have tended to be totalitarian, as well. The primary characteristic of a dictatorship is that it is not responsible to, and cannot be limited by, the people.

A *democracy* exists where the power to govern is held by the people themselves, where government is conducted by, and with the consent of, the people. Modern democracies are indirect—that is, representative democracies—rather than direct (or pure) in form. Democratic thought insists upon belief in: (1) the fundamental worth of every individual; (2) the equality of all persons; (3) majority rule and minority rights; (4) the necessity of compromise; and (5) individual freedom.

Capitalism is an economic doctrine based upon private ownership of the means by which goods and services are produced and upon individual initiative, profit, and competition.

Socialism is a philosophy of economic collectivism, advocating public ownership of the major instruments of production, distribution, and exchange. *Evolutionary* socialists are to be distinguished from *revolutionary* socialists; most of the latter are communists.

Communism is an extreme form of socialism. In its present-day form it dates from the teachings of Karl Marx as interpreted and applied especially by Lenin, Stalin, Khrushchev, and Mao. It is built around four central concepts: (1) its theory of history, (2) the labor theory of value, (3) its theory of the nature of the state, and (4) the dictatorship of the proletariat.

Concept Development

Questions for Review

1. What is a *state?* What are its four essential characteristics? Which of these distinguishes it from any other political entity?

2. What is the difference between state and government?

3. Why is the location of sovereignty within a state of such vital importance?

4. Why is the social contract theory so significant in terms of the development of our own political system?

5. On what particular basis can a unitary government be distinguished from a federal one? Presidential from parliamentary? Dictatorial from democratic?

6. What characteristic determines whether a dictatorship is totalitarian or not?

7. How useful is Abraham Lincoln's definition of democracy?

8. What does the text suggest are the five basic concepts of democracy?

9. Upon what key factors is capitalism based?

10. According to *laissez-faire* theory, what is the proper role of government in a society?

11. Why may the American economic system properly be described as a "mixed economy"?

12. What is the general rule we have followed in determining the proper role of government in the nation's economy?

13. What is the main distinction to be drawn between capitalism and socialism?

14. Why is modern socialism often referred to as "state socialism"?

15. Why are the terms "social democrat" and "evolutionary socialist" regularly applied to the major socialist parties of Western Europe?

16. Who founded present-day communism? When?

17. What are the four central tenets of communist theory?

18. What fallacies in communist thought and practice are cited in the text?

For Further Inquiry

1. In 1733, the English author Alexander Pope penned these lines in his "Essay on Man":

For forms of government let fools
   contest;
Whate'er is best administer'd is best.

Do you agree or disagree with Pope's view?

2. Of the various forms of government, why has democracy been practiced in only a comparatively few places and for only relatively brief periods of time?

3. Do you agree with James Bryce's observation that: "No government demands so much from the citizens as democracy and none gives back so much." Why?

4. Democracy has been described as "a never-ending search for truth." How apt is this description? Why must the search be a never-ending one?

5. Karl Marx predicted that successful communist revolutions would occur first in the more highly industrialized nations, particularly in Germany and England and then in the United States. But history has shown this to be another of his false prophecies. Communist revolutions have occurred, instead, in underdeveloped and predominantly agrarian countries. Why?

Suggested Activities

1. Examine the governmental systems of selected foreign states and present a class report based upon your research.

2. Construct a glossary of key words and phrases in American politics. Each term could be defined or described on a separate card or sheet, filed alphabetically, and improved throughout the year.

3. Prepare a series of posters or other displays to illustrate the basic concepts of democracy cited in the text.

4. Make a list of: (a) examples of the ways in which economic activities are regulated by the National, State, and local governments in your area; (b) examples of the ways in which the three levels of government aid the economy of your locale; or (c) the publicly conducted enterprises in your community.

5. Invite the owner of a local business to discuss with the class the various ways in which government regulates and aids that particular business.

6. Stage a debate or class forum on the following: (a) *Resolved,* That the United States may be described properly as both a democracy and a republic; (b) *Resolved,* That it is more desirable that government strive to promote equality of opportunity for all than that it strive to promote an equality of condition for all.

Suggested Reading

Almond, Gabriel A. and Powell, G. B., *Comparative Politics Today: A World View.* Little, Brown, 1980.

Beloff, Max and Peels, Gillian, *The Government of the United Kingdom.* Norton, 1980.

Coulter, Edwin M., *Principles of Politics and Government.* Allyn and Bacon, 1981.

Glassner, Martin and DeBlij, Ham, *Systematic Political Geography.* Wiley, 3rd ed., 1980.

Gross, Bertram, *Friendly Fascism: The New Face of Power in America.* Evans, 1980.

Lefever, Ernest (ed.), *Will Capitalism Survive? Ethics and Public Policy Center,* 1980.

Hough, Jerry F., *Soviet Leadership in Transition.* The Brookings Institution, 1980.

Lipson, Leslie, *The Great Issues of Politics: An Introduction to Political Science.* Prentice-Hall, 6th ed., 1981.

Paxton, John (ed.), *The Statesman's Yearbook, 1980-1981.* St. Martin's Press, 1980.

Plano, Jack C. and Greenberg, Milton, *The American Political Dictionary.* Holt, Rinehart and Winston, 5th ed., 1979.

Rose, Richard, *Politics in England.* Little, Brown, 3rd ed., 1980.

Sargent, Lyman T., *Contemporary Political Ideologies.* Dorsey, 5th ed., 1981.

Solzhenitsyn, Aleksandr, *The Mortal Danger: How Misconceptions About Russia Imperil America.* Harper & Row, 1980.

Townsend, James R., *Politics in China.* Little, Brown, 2nd ed., 1980.

2

To Form a More Perfect Union

We hold these truths to be self-evident, that all men are created equal, that they are endowed by their Creator with certain unalienable Rights, that among these are Life, Liberty and the pursuit of Happiness.

THE DECLARATION OF INDEPENDENCE

■ Out of what historical setting did the government of the United States emerge?

■ How and why did the Constitution, written in 1787, differ so markedly from the Declaration of Independence, written only 11 years earlier?

■ Why may it be argued that the words "We the People" are the most important of all in the Constitution?

The American system of government did not suddenly spring into being at the wave of some political magician's wand on the 4th of July in 1776. Nor was it pulled out of thin air by the Founding Fathers at Philadelphia in the summer of 1787. Rather, its roots reach deep into the past. Indeed, its origins may be traced back to the very beginnings of Western civilization.

Those who built the Constitution worked with what they knew. They worked with a knowledge of ideas and institutions gained in their own lives and with a knowledge that had come to them as the product of centuries of experience, tradition, thought, and deed.

We review here the major aspects of the background of the American governmental system, carrying our treatment through the creating of the Constitution. But as we do so, recall that the job of constitution-making was *not* finished in 1787. Nor, indeed, has it been completed since, for it is a continuing and never-ending process, as we shall see.

The Colonial Period

Our English Heritage. Peoples of many different nationalities came to explore and to settle in various parts of what was to become the United States. They included the French, the Dutch, the Spanish, the Swedes, the Norwegians, and others. But it was the English who came in the largest

Even in the 16th century, England had a long tradition of parliamentary checks on royal power. At left is a 16th-century print showing Queen Elizabeth meeting with Parliament. The woodcut above shows the meeting of the first legislative assembly in America in 1619.

numbers. And it was the English who came to control the 13 colonies that stretched for some 1300 miles along the Atlantic seaboard of North America.

The earliest English settlers were pioneers. They had to clear the wilderness, establish their homes and farms, deal with the Indians, and quite literally hack out their own economic future in the New World. But they came here in search of greater freedom and brought much of their political future with them, ready-made. They brought with them knowledge of and experience with a political system that had been developing in England for centuries. Especially, they brought with them three political ideas that were to loom large in the shaping of government in the United States: the concepts of *ordered government,* of *limited government,* and of *representative government.*

ORDERED GOVERNMENT. The early colonists recognized the necessity of an orderly

regulation of their relationships with one another—that is, for government. They promptly established local governments based on those they had known in England. Many of the offices and units they established are still to be found in American government today, especially at the local level: the sheriff, coroner, justice of the peace, county, township, borough, and grand jury, for example.

LIMITED GOVERNMENT. The first colonists brought with them, too, the idea that government is *not* all-powerful. That is, that government is *limited* in what it may do. And, especially, the idea that government is limited in the sense that each person has certain rights that government cannot injure or take away. The concept of limited government was deeply embedded in English practice by the time the first colonists reached the New World. It had been enshrined there in such historic documents as the Magna Carta of 1215, the

Petition of Right of 1628, and the Bill of Rights and the Act of Toleration of 1689.

REPRESENTATIVE GOVERNMENT. A third and profoundly important concept brought to America by English settlers was that of representative government. For centuries there had been developing in England the idea that government exists to serve the people and that the people should have a voice in the shaping of the policies of government. As with the concept of limited government, representative government found fertile soil in America and flourished quickly.

We have changed, developed, and added to the institutions and ideas which came to us from England. Even so, there is much in the American governmental system that bears the stamp of our English heritage. Certainly, this is not so strange when we recall that the Colonial Period of American history lasted for 168 years (1607–1775) and that the United States has existed as a nation for only a slightly longer period of time.

Government in the Colonies. The colonies have been aptly described as "thirteen schools of government"—schools in which Americans first began to learn the difficult art of government.

The first of the colonies, Virginia, was established with the first permanent English settlement in the New World, at Jamestown in 1607. The other 12 were established over the next century and a quarter, the last being Georgia in 1732.

The Virginia colony was founded by a group of settlers sent out by a commercial corporation, the London Company. Acting under a royal charter granted by King James I, the company established the colony as a money-making venture.

Scant provision was made for local government in the colony's earliest years. A governor and council were created, but tight control was held by the Company in London. In 1619 the Company did permit the creation of a legislature of burgesses[1] elected from each settlement in the colony. That assembly, the first representative legislature to meet in America, convened on July 30, 1619, in the church at Jamestown. In its first session it passed laws to aid the farmers of the colony and to curb idleness, gambling, improper dress, and drunkenness.

Because the London Company had failed to create a prosperous colony, King James I withdrew its charter in 1624. From then until it became an independent State, Virginia was a *royal colony.*

Types of Colonies. According to the form of government in each—particularly the way in which the governor was chosen—there were three types of colonies: *royal, proprietary,* and *charter.*

Royal Colonies. The royal colonies were the most numerous. By the beginning of the American Revolution, they included: New Hampshire, New York, New Jersey, Virginia, North Carolina, South Carolina, Georgia, and Massachusetts. For each of these colonies a royal governor and a council (or "upper house") was appointed by the king, and a popular assembly (or "lower house") was elected in the colony. The governor, together with the governor's council and the assembly, ruled the colony according to written instructions issued from time to time by the Crown. The royal governors most often ruled with a stern hand, and much of the resentment that ultimately flared into revolution was fanned by their actions.

Proprietary Colonies. The proprietary colonies were Pennsylvania, Delaware, and Maryland. The name "proprietary" came from the term "proprietor." The *proprietor*

---

[1] The term "burgesses" was used because it was expected that the settlements would develop into *boroughs* (towns). After 1634 the burgesses represented counties, and in 1776 their title was changed to "assemblymen." Virginia called the lower house of its colonial legislature the House of Burgesses; South Carolina, the House of Commons; Massachusetts, the House of Representatives.

was an individual to whom the king had made a grant of land. That land could be settled and governed as the proprietor (owner) saw fit, subject only to the general supervision of the Crown. The proprietor appointed the governor and established a legislature, court system, and local governments. The proprietor was, in effect, a "little king." The *Frame of Government* (a constitution) that William Penn first drew for Pennsylvania in 1682 was, for that day and age, exceedingly democratic.

Charter Colonies. The charter colonies were Connecticut and Rhode Island. In each of these colonies the king granted a charter to the colonists themselves, as a group. The charter was a written document outlining certain rights of self-government which could be withdrawn by the king if he chose to do so. The governor was elected annually by the freemen of the colony; and although the king's approval was required, it was seldom asked. The council and assembly were elected annually, and the governor had no veto over the assembly's acts.

The Connecticut and Rhode Island charters were so liberal that, after independence, they continued to serve as State constitutions until 1818 and 1842, respectively.

The Colonies and England. The colonists were British subjects, and as such they owed allegiance to the Crown. In the minds of the king and his ministers, the colonies existed as handmaids to serve the parent country. They were regarded as sources of raw materials and as markets for finished products. They were far-off lands to be ruled for England's benefit.

In *theory*, the colonies were controlled in all important matters from London. But London was 4800 kilometers (3000 miles) away. It took almost two months to sail from England to America. So, in *practice*, the colonists became quite accustomed to doing much as they pleased. They made their own laws, and the few regulations imposed by Parliament, concerned largely with trade, were generally ignored.

This relatively loose supervision of the colonies was tightened, dramatically, in the early 1760's, however. George III ascended the throne in 1760, and shortly the British began to deal much more firmly with their American possessions. Restrictive trading laws were expanded and enforced, and new taxes were imposed, mostly for the support of British troops stationed in North America.

Many colonists took strong exception to these moves. They saw no need for the troops—the power of the French had been broken in the French and Indian Wars (1754–1763). They objected to taxes they had no part in levying—it was "taxation without representation." They recognized the sovereignty of the king, but they flatly

The British began rigorous enforcement of the restrictive trade acts in the 1760's; the major colonial shipping centers, especially Boston and Philadelphia, were quickly affected.

refused to recognize the right of Parliament to control affairs within the colonies. In short, the colonists maintained that they possessed the same rights as the English people at home and that they had the right to manage their own local affairs as they saw fit.

The king's ministers were poorly informed and stubborn. They pushed ahead with their plans despite the resentments their policies stirred in America. Within a few years the colonists were to find themselves faced with a fateful choice—to submit or to revolt.

The Colonies Unite. Long before the fateful 1770's attempts had been made to bring the separate colonies together for collective action.

EARLY ATTEMPTS. In 1643 the Massachusetts Bay, Plymouth, Connecticut, and New Haven settlements had joined in the New England Confederation, a "league of friendship" for defense against the Indians. But as the Indian danger passed and frictions between the settlements developed, the confederation lost importance and finally died in 1684. William Penn, in 1697, offered an elaborate plan for intercolonial cooperation, especially in trade, defense, and criminal matters; but it was largely ignored and soon forgotten.

THE ALBANY PLAN, 1754. In 1754 the Lords of Trade called a conference of seven of the northern colonies[2] at Albany to consider the problems of colonial trade and the threat of French and Indian attacks. Here Benjamin Franklin proposed what came to be known as his "Albany Plan of Union."

Franklin would have created an annual *congress* (conference) consisting of one delegate from each of the 13 colonies. This body would have power to raise military and naval forces, to make war and peace with the Indians, to regulate trade with the Indians, and to collect customs and levy taxes.

Franklin's plan was ahead of its time, but it was to be remembered later when independence came. Although it was adopted by the Albany meeting, it was rejected by each of the colonies as a *surrender of too much* local power.

THE STAMP ACT CONGRESS, 1765. The harsh tax and trade policies of the 1760's fanned colonial resentment. A series of new laws had been passed by Parliament, among them the Stamp Act of 1765. This law required the use of tax stamps on all legal documents, on various commercial agreements, and on all newspapers circulating in the colonies.

The new taxes were widely denounced—in part because the rates were severe, but largely because their imposition amounted to "taxation without representation." In October of 1765 delegates from nine of the colonies[3] met in the Stamp Act Congress in New York. They drafted a Declaration of Rights and Grievances, a stern protest against the taxes and other policies of the King's ministers. Their meeting marked the first occasion on which a significant number of the colonies joined together to oppose England.

Parliament repealed the Stamp Act, but events were moving rapidly toward the final break. Resentment and anger were expressed in wholesale evasion of the laws; mob violence took place at the ports; English goods were boycotted; and such outbreaks as the Boston Tea Party of December 16, 1773, occurred. Organized resistance was carried on through Committees of Correspondence, which had grown out of a group formed in 1772 by Samuel Adams in Boston. By 1773 committees were to be found throughout the colonies, providing a network for cooperation and the exchange of information among the

---

[2] Connecticut, Maryland, Massachusetts, New Hampshire, New York, Pennsylvania, and Rhode Island.

[3] All except Georgia, New Hampshire, North Carolina, and Virginia.

patriots. In many places the committees even took over the management of local public affairs.

THE FIRST CONTINENTAL CONGRESS, 1774. In the spring of 1774 Parliament passed another set of laws, this time intended to punish the colonists for the disturbances in Boston and elsewhere. The "Intolerable Acts," as they were called, prompted the Massachusetts and Virginia assemblies to call a general meeting of the colonies.

Fifty-six delegates, from every colony except Georgia, assembled in Philadelphia on September 5, 1774. Many of the leaders of the day were there—men such as Patrick Henry, Samuel Adams, Richard Henry Lee, and George Washington. For nearly two months the members of this First Continental Congress debated the strained and critical situation with England.

A Declaration of Rights, protesting British colonial policies, was addressed to George III. The delegates urged each of the colonies to refuse all trade with England and called for the creation of local committees to enforce the boycott. Before they adjourned on October 26, the delegates also called for a second congress to meet the following May. Later, the assemblies in each of the colonies, including Georgia, approved the actions of the First Continental Congress.

Independence

Events moved swiftly in the months following the adjournment of the First Continental Congress. The British, instead of compromising to pacify the colonists, applied even stricter measures. Then it happened. On April 19, 1775, at Lexington and Concord, open and armed conflict occurred. The "shot heard 'round the world" was fired just three weeks before the Second Continental Congress assembled.

The Second Continental Congress, 1775. All 13 colonies sent delegates to the Second Continental Congress. It convened

A British cartoonist comments on the kind of treatment which Boston's Sons of Liberty gave customs officials who collected a tax on tea.

on May 10, 1775, in Independence Hall in Philadelphia. Most of the delegates who had attended the First Continental Congress a year earlier were again present. Especially notable among the new members were Benjamin Franklin and John Hancock.

Hancock was chosen president of the Second Continental Congress.[4] Almost immediately a "continental army" was organized, and George Washington was appointed its commander in chief. Washington took formal command of the army at Cambridge, Massachusetts, on July 3, 1775. Thomas Jefferson then replaced Washington as one of the delegates from Virginia.

The Second Continental Congress became, by force of circumstance, our first

---

[4] Peyton Randolph, who had also served as President of the First Continental Congress, was originally chosen to the office. He resigned on May 24, however, because the Virginia Assembly, of which he was the Speaker, had been called into session. Hancock was then chosen to succeed him.

Philadelphians hear that the Declaration of Independence has just been signed.

national government. Although it rested upon no constitutional basis, it served as the first government of the United States for five fateful years—from the signing of the Declaration of Independence in July of 1776 until the Articles of Confederation went into effect on March 1, 1781. It prosecuted a war, raised armies and a navy, borrowed, purchased supplies, created a monetary system, negotiated treaties with foreign powers, and performed the other functions any government would have had to under the circumstances.

The Second Continental Congress exercised both legislative and executive functions. In legislative matters each colonial (later State) delegation had one vote. Executive functions were performed by the delegates through committees.

The Declaration of Independence. On June 7, 1776, over a year after open rebellion had broken out in the colonies,

Richard Henry Lee of Virginia proposed to the Second Continental Congress:

Resolved, That these United Colonies are, and of right ought to be, free and independent States, that they are absolved from all allegiance to the British Crown, and that all political connection between them and the state of Great Britain is, and ought to be, totally dissolved.

A committee of five of the ablest men in the Congress—Benjamin Franklin, John Adams, Roger Sherman, Robert Livingston, and Thomas Jefferson—was appointed to draft a statement to proclaim independence. Their momentous product, the Declaration of Independence,[5] was almost wholly the work of the young and brilliant Jefferson.

On July 2 the final break came. By unanimous vote the delegates adopted Lee's resolution. Two days later, on July 4, the Declaration of Independence itself was adopted and announced to the world.

WHAT THE DECLARATION SAYS. Most of the great document deals with the grievances the colonists felt toward England and George III. Its real heart, the lines which have made it our most precious charter, are found in the second paragraph of the Declaration.

Its second paragraph proclaims:

We hold these truths to be self-evident, that all men are created equal, that they are endowed by their Creator with certain unalienable Rights, that among these are Life, Liberty and the pursuit of Happiness. That to secure these rights, Governments are instituted among Men, deriving their just powers from the consent of the governed; That whenever any Form of Government becomes destructive of these ends, it is the Right of the People to alter or to abolish it, and to institute new Government, laying its foundations on such

---

[5] The full text of the Declaration appears at pages 783-785.

Case Study

With the first State constitutions, the Articles of Confederation, and then the Constitution of 1787, the United States inaugurated what has been called "the era of the written constitution." This nation set a pattern which has been followed by most new nations ever since: that of establishing a government on the basis of a written fundamental law.

The American practice marked a sharp break with the past. Writing in 1793, Lord Bolingbrooke penned this still-accurate description of the British Constitution:

By constitution we mean, whenever we speak with propriety and exactness, that assemblage of laws, institutions and customs, derived from certain fixed principles of reason, directed to certain fixed objects of public good, that compose the general system, according to which the community hath agreed to be governed.

■ Why did Americans of the 1770's and 1780's insist upon writing constitutions? What advantages might there be in having an unwritten constitution? What dangers might be involved?

---

principles and organizing its power in such form, as to them shall seem most likely to effect their Safety and Happiness.

With these brave words the United States of America was born. The 13 former colonies were now free and independent States. The 56 men who gave birth to the new nation sealed the Declaration with this final sentence:

And for the support of this Declaration, with a firm reliance in the protection of Divine Providence, we mutually pledge to each other our Lives, our Fortunes and our sacred Honor.

The First State Constitutions

In January of 1776 New Hampshire adopted a constitution to replace royal control. Within three months South Carolina had done the same. Then, on May 10, 1776, nearly two months before the Declaration of Independence, the Second Continental Congress urged each of the colonies to adopt:

. . . such governments as shall, in the opinion of the representatives of the people, best conduce to the happiness and safety of their constituents.

Most of the States adopted written constitutions in 1776 and 1777. With minor changes, Connecticut and Rhode Island transformed their colonial charters into State constitutions. Assemblies or conventions were commonly used to draft and approve the new documents. Massachusetts set a lasting precedent when it submitted its new fundamental law to the voters for approval. The Massachusetts constitution of 1780, still in force, is the oldest of the present-day State constitutions.[6] In fact, it is the oldest written constitution in force in the world today.

The First State Constitutions. Although the new State constitutions differed widely in detail, they had many features in common. Four of these features should be noted here—for, within a few years, these documents were to have a marked effect on the drafting of the Constitution of the United States.

POPULAR SOVEREIGNTY. The people were recognized as the *sole* source of governmental authority. All power held by government could come from one, and *only* one, fountain: the people themselves.

---

[6] From independence until the adoption of its constitution in 1780, Massachusetts relied on the charter in force prior to 1691 as its fundamental law.

The Fugio cent of 1787, the first coin to be struck by authority of the United States, symbolized the unification of 13 colonies into a single nation of 13 States.

LIMITED GOVERNMENT. Government could exercise *only* those powers granted to it by the people. Because of the oppression experienced by the people in the colonies under British rule, the new State constitutions granted powers very sparingly.

CIVIL LIBERTIES. Seven of the first State constitutions[7] began with a bill of rights setting out the "unalienable rights" of the people. In every State it was made clear that the sovereign people had rights that government must at all times respect.

SEPARATION OF POWERS AND CHECKS AND BALANCES. The powers that were given to the new State governments were purposely divided among three distinct branches— legislative, executive, and judicial.

Each branch of the government was given powers with which to "check" the other branches of the government.

The first State constitutions were very short compared to those of today. Since the memory of royal governors was fresh in

---

[7] Those of Delaware, Maryland, Massachusetts, New Hampshire, North Carolina, Pennsylvania, and Virginia.

the minds of the people, the new State governors were given little real power. Most of the authority granted to each State was vested in its legislature. The right to vote was limited to those adult males who could meet property ownership and other rigid suffrage qualifications.

The Confederation and the Critical Period

Our First National Constitution. The First and Second Continental Congresses rested on no legal base. They were called in haste to meet an emergency, and they were intended to be temporary. Something more regular and permanent was clearly needed.

When Richard Henry Lee introduced his resolution which led to the Declaration of Independence, he also called for a "plan of confederation." Off and on—for 17 months—the Second Continental Congress debated and considered a scheme to unite the former colonies. Then on November 15, 1777, the Articles of Confederation were approved.

The Articles did not go into effect immediately, however. The ratifications (formal approval) of all 13 States were required. Eleven States approved the document within the year following their proposal. Delaware added its approval in mid-1779. But Maryland did not ratify until February 27, 1781. The Second Continental Congress then set March 1, 1781, as the date upon which the Articles finally were to become effective.

The Articles of Confederation established "a firm league of friendship" among the States. Each State retained "its sovereignty, freedom, and independence, and every power, jurisdiction, and right . . . not . . . expressly delegated to the United States, in Congress assembled." The States came together "for their common defense, the security of their liberties, and their mutual and general welfare."

The government established by the Articles was exceedingly simple. A Congress, composed of delegates appointed annually by the States in whatever manner their legislatures might direct, was the single organ created. Each State had one vote in the Congress, regardless of its population or wealth. Neither an executive nor a judicial branch was provided. These functions were to be handled by committees of the Congress, and civil officers (postmasters, for example) were to be appointed by the Congress.

The powers of the Congress appear, at first glance, to have been considerable. Its more important powers included those to make war and peace, send and receive ambassadors, enter into treaties, borrow money, raise and equip a navy, maintain an army by requesting troops from the States, request funds from the States to meet the costs of government, regulate Indian affairs, fix standards of weights and measures, and establish post offices.

Several important powers were *not* granted to the Congress, however. The lack of them, together with other weaknesses in the Articles, soon proved the document inadequate to the pressing needs of the times.

The Congress was not given the power to tax. It could raise needed funds in only two ways: by borrowing and by requesting money from the States. Heavy borrowing had been necessary to finance the American Revolution, and many of those debts had not been repaid. At best, then, this source for funds was none too good. And, throughout the period the Articles of Confederation were in force, not one of the States came close to meeting the financial requests made by the Congress.

Nor was Congress granted the power to regulate trade between the States. It could not even levy duties on imports or exports.

Still worse, the Congress had no power to force either the States or the people to obey the Articles of Confederation or its

WEAKNESSES IN THE ARTICLES OF CONFEDERATION

1. One vote for each State, regardless of size.

2. Congress had no power to lay and collect taxes or duties.

3. Congress had no power to regulate foreign and interstate commerce.

4. No executive to enforce acts of Congress.

5. No national court system.

6. Amendment only with consent of all of the States.

7. A 9/13 majority required to pass laws.

8. Articles only a "firm league of friendship."

own laws. All that the Congress could do was to *advise* and *request* the States to do this or to do that. In effect, all it could do was to say "please" and wait with hat in hand—often in vain.

Finally, most of the important powers that the Congress did have could be exercised only with the consent of the delegates from *nine* of the thirteen States. No changes could be made in the Articles unless *all* of the States agreed.[8]

In sum, these weaknesses in the Articles made an effective *national* government a virtual impossibility, as we shall see.

---

[8] To get all 13 jealous and increasingly unfriendly States to agree on anything seemed hopeless. In 1785 Congress made a final attempt to solve its financial problems by proposing an amendment to the Articles to provide for import duties. Only New York, reaping a handsome return from its own tax on imports, refused to approve the proposal.

The Critical Period, 1781–1787. On October 19, 1781, a British band played the old tune, "The World Turned Upside Down," as Lord Cornwallis formally surrendered his army to General Washington at Yorktown. Victory had come at last to the United States. It was confirmed by the Treaty of Paris in 1783.

The coming of peace brought the political, social, and economic difficulties of the new nation into sharp focus. With a central government powerless to act, the States bickered among themselves and became increasingly jealous of one another. They levied tariffs on one another's goods and even banned some trade. They negotiated directly with foreign governments, even though this was forbidden in the Articles of Confederation. They often refused to obey laws and treaties made by the Congress. Most States even raised their own armies and navies. They printed their own money, often supporting it with little backing. Prices soared. Debts, public and private, went unpaid. Sound credit vanished. National respect began to disintegrate, since the States refused to support the central government, financially and in almost every other way.

George Washington was moved to complain:

We are one nation today and thirteen tomorrow. Who will treat with us on such terms?

The historian John Fiske thus described existing commercial conditions:

The city of New York, with its population of 30,000 souls, had long been supplied with firewood from Connecticut, and with butter and cheese, chickens and garden vegetables from the thrifty farms of New Jersey. This trade, it was observed, carried thousands of dollars out of the city and into the pockets of the detested Yankees and despised Jerseymen. "It was ruinous to domestic industry," said the men of New York. "It must be stopped by . . . a navigation act and a protective tariff." Acts were accordingly passed, obliging every Yankee sloop which came down through Hell Gate, and every Jersey market boat which was rowed across from Paulus Hook to Cortlandt Street, to pay entrance fees and obtain clearances at the custom house, just as was done by ships from London and Hamburg; and not a cartload of Connecticut firewood could be delivered at the back door of a country house in Beekman Street until it should have paid a heavy duty. Great and just was the wrath of the farmers and lumbermen. The New Jersey legislature made up its mind to retaliate. The city of New York had lately bought a small patch of ground on Sandy Hook, and had built a lighthouse there. This lighthouse was the one weak spot in the heel of Achilles where a hostile arrow could strike, and New Jersey gave vent to her indignation by laying a tax of $1800 a

"IT IS UNTHINKABLE THAT THE CITIZENS OF RHODE ISLAND SHOULD EVER SURRENDER THEIR SOVEREIGNTY TO SOME CENTRAL AUTHORITY WAY OFF IN PHILADELPHIA."

By Burr Shafer, © 1960

year on it. Connecticut was equally prompt. At a great meeting of businessmen, held at New London, it was unanimously agreed to suspend all commercial intercourse with New York. Every merchant signed an agreement, under a penalty of $250 for the first offence, not to send any goods whatever into the hated State for a period of twelve months.[9]

Such distressing conditions led many to yearn for a stronger central government better able to cope with the problems besetting the new nation. Rather naturally, the groups most menaced by instability—the large property owners, the merchants, and other creditors—became the driving force behind efforts to accomplish that end.

The Conventions at Mount Vernon and Annapolis. Several disputes between Maryland and Virginia, most of them centering on trade and navigation of the Potomac River and Chesapeake Bay, led to a meeting of representatives of the two States. They met at Alexandria, in Virginia, in March of 1785. At George Washington's invitation their sessions were moved to his home at Mount Vernon. Their deliberations proved so successful that, on January 21, 1786, the Virginia Assembly called for "a joint meeting of . . . [all of] the States to recommend a federal plan for regulating commerce."

When that convention opened at Annapolis, in Maryland, in September of 1786, however, only five of the 13 States were represented. Disappointed, but not discouraged, the delegates to the Annapolis Convention issued a call for yet another meeting of the States:

. . . at Philadelphia on the second Monday in May next . . . to devise such further provisions as shall appear to them necessary to render the constitution of

the Federal Government adequate to the exigencies of the Union . . .

By mid-February of 1787, seven of the States[10] had named delegates to the Philadelphia meeting. Then, on February 21, the Congress, which had been hesitating, also called upon the States to send delegates to Philadelphia:

. . . for the sole and express purpose of revising the Articles of Confederation and reporting to Congress and the several legislatures such alterations and provisions therein as shall when agreed to in Congress and confirmed by the States render the [Articles of Confederation] adequate to the exigencies of Government and the preservation of the Union.

The Constitutional Convention

The Constitutional Convention began its work on Friday, May 25, 1787.[11] In all, 12 of the 13 States were represented: Rhode Island did not participate.[12]

The Founding Fathers. All told, 74 delegates were chosen by the various State legislatures. But, in fact, only 55 of them actually attended any of the sessions of the Philadelphia Convention.

Of those who did attend, surely this can be said: Never before, or since, has so remarkable a group been gathered under one roof. Among the most outstanding of them were George Washington, James Madison, and Edmund Randolph from Virginia; Benjamin Franklin, Gouverneur

---

9 John Fiske, *The Critical Period of American History.* Boston: Houghton Mifflin, 1888, p. 146.

10 Delaware, Georgia, New Hampshire, New Jersey, North Carolina, Pennsylvania, Virginia.

11 Not enough of the States were represented on the date originally set, Monday, May 14. Those delegates who were present met and adjourned each day until May 25, when a quorum (majority) of the States was on hand.

12 The Rhode Island legislature was controlled by the "soft-money" group—mainly debtors and farmers who were benefited by inflation and thus against the creation of a stronger central government. New Hampshire's delegation, delayed especially by a lack of funds, did not reach Philadelphia until late July.

Morris, Robert Morris, and James Wilson from Pennsylvania; Alexander Hamilton from New York; William Livingston and William Paterson from New Jersey; Elbridge Gerry and Rufus King from Massachusetts; Luther Martin from Maryland; Oliver Ellsworth and Roger Sherman from Connecticut; John Dickinson from Delaware; and John Rutledge and the two Pinckneys from South Carolina.

These were men of wide knowledge and public experience, and of wealth and prestige. Many of them had served in the American Revolution. Thirty-nine had served in the Continental Congresses or the Congress of the Confederation or both, eight in constitutional conventions in their own States, and seven had been State governors. Thirty-one of the delegates had college educations, and their number included two college presidents and three professors. Eight had signed the Declaration of Independence. Two were to become President of the United States, and one a Vice President. Seventeen were later to serve in the Senate and 11 in the House of Representatives.

Is it any wonder that the product of such a gathering was described by the English statesman, William E. Gladstone, nearly a century later as "the most wonderful work ever struck off at a given time by the brain and purpose of man"?

Remarkably, the average age of the Founding Fathers was only 42, and half of them were only in their 30's. Indeed, most of the real leaders were all in that age bracket—Madison was 36, Gouverneur Morris 35, Randolph 34, and Hamilton 32. Franklin, at 81 the oldest member, was failing and unable to attend many of the sessions. Washington, at 55, was one of the few older members who played a key part in the making of the Constitution.

By and large, the Framers of the Constitution represented a new generation in

Case Study

Much praise has been heaped upon the men who drafted the Constitution of the United States. Thus, Thomas Jefferson, writing from Paris, described the Framers as "an assembly of demi-gods." A French diplomat, reporting to his government, wrote: ". . . if all the delegates named for this Philadelphia Convention are present, one will never have seen, even in Europe, an assembly more respectable for talents, knowledge, disinterestedness and patriotism than those who will compose it."

Well over a century later the historian Charles Beard was to write that ". . . never in the history of assemblies has there been a convention of men richer in political experience and in practical knowledge, or endowed with a profounder insight into the springs of human action and in intimate essence of government." (*The Supreme Court and the Constitution*, 1912, pages 86–87.)

But another noted constitutional scholar, Max Farrand, has concluded that: "Great men here and there, it is true, but the convention as a whole was comprised of such as would be appointed to a similar gathering at the present time: professional men, businessmen, and gentlemen of leisure; patriotic statesmen and clever, scheming politicians; some trained by experience and study for the task before them, and others utterly unfit. It was essentially a representative body, taking possibly a somewhat higher tone from the social conditions of the time, the seriousness of the crisis, and the character of the leaders." (*The Framing of the Constitution of the United States*, 1940, pages 40–41.)

■ Which of these views of the Founding Fathers do you think is the more likely or accurate? Do you think that a "similar gathering at the present time" could, in fact, be had? Explain.

American politics. Several of the more prominent leaders of the Revolutionary period were notable by their absence. Patrick Henry said that he "smelt a rat" and refused to attend. Samuel Adams, John Hancock, and Richard Henry Lee were not selected as delegates by their respective States. Thomas Jefferson was our minister to France, and John Adams was serving in a similar capacity to England and Holland at the time.

Organization and Procedure. The convention met in Independence Hall, probably in the same room in which 11 years earlier the Declaration of Independence had been signed. Of the 55 delegates who reached Philadelphia, some attended only a part of the time. About 30 attended most daily sessions.

When the convention organized itself on May 25, George Washington was the unanimous choice to preside. It was de-cided that each State should have one vote on all questions and that a simple majority of the votes cast would carry any proposal.

The meeting naturally attracted much public attention. Thus, to ensure free and unrestrained debate, and to protect themselves as much as possible from outside pressures, the delegates pledged themselves to the strictest secrecy concerning their proceedings. The pledge was kept in remarkable fashion.

A secretary (William Jackson) was appointed, and a *Journal* was kept. The official record, however, was little more than a bare listing of formal motions and votes, and it was not always accurate, at that. Fortunately, some of the delegates—most notably James Madison—kept private accounts of the proceedings. Most of what we know today of the work of the Constitutional Convention comes from Madison's careful and voluminous *Notes.* His

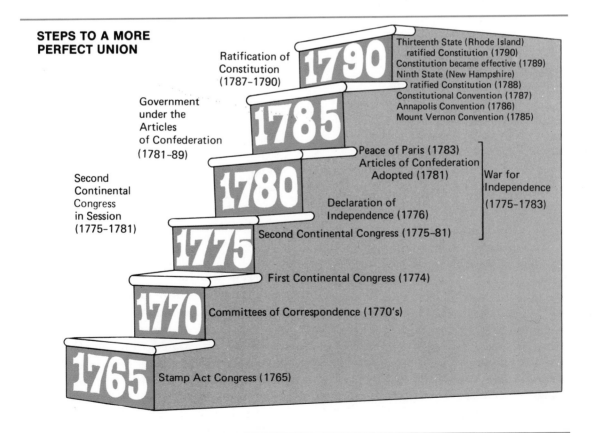

STEPS TO A MORE PERFECT UNION

Ratification of Constitution (1787–1790)

Thirteenth State (Rhode Island) ratified Constitution (1790)
Constitution became effective (1789)
Ninth State (New Hampshire) ratified Constitution (1788)

Constitutional Convention (1787)
Annapolis Convention (1786)
Mount Vernon Convention (1785)

Government under the Articles of Confederation (1781–89)

Peace of Paris (1783)
Articles of Confederation Adopted (1781)

War for Independence (1775–1783)

Second Continental Congress in Session (1775–1781)

Declaration of Independence (1776)

Second Continental Congress (1775–81)

First Continental Congress (1774)

Committees of Correspondence (1770's)

Stamp Act Congress (1765)

brilliance and vast knowledge led his colleagues to hold him in profound respect. He was, in effect, the floor leader at the convention. Madison contributed more to the Constitution than did any of the others—and, still, he was able to keep such a close record. Certainly, he deserves his title: "Father of the Constitution."

The relatively small number of delegates made it possible for them to do most of their work on the convention floor. Some matters were dealt with by committees, but all questions were ultimately settled by the full body. Daily sessions usually began at 10:00 in the morning and adjourned by mid-afternoon.

The Great Agreement. Almost at once the delegates agreed that they were meeting to create a *new* government for the United States. On May 30 they adopted this proposal, put by Edmund Randolph:

> *Resolved, . . .* that a *national* Government ought to be established consisting of a *supreme* Legislative, Executive, and Judiciary.

An 18th century engraving shows Philadelphia's Independence Hall in 1776.

They had been appointed to "recommend revisions" in the Articles of Confederation. But, with this decision, the Framers set about writing a whole new constitution. This meant the creation of a vastly expanded government with extensive new powers—a national government with powers supreme over the powers of the States.

The debates were often bitter, and at times the convention even seemed on the verge of collapse. Once the Great Agreement was reached, however, the determination of the majority of the delegates never wavered.

The Virginia Plan. No State had been more responsible for the calling of the Constitutional Convention than Virginia. It was natural, then, that its delegates should present the first plan for a new constitution. On May 29 the Virginia Plan, 15 separate resolutions drafted largely by Madison, was presented by Edmund Randolph.

The Virginia Plan called for a new government to be composed of three branches—legislative, executive, and judicial. The legislature (Congress) would be *bicameral*—that is, consist of two houses. Representation in each house was to be based upon either each State's population or the amount of money it contributed to the support of the central government. The members of the lower house (the House of Representatives) were to be elected popularly and those of the upper house (the Senate) were to be chosen by the lower house from candidates nominated by the State Legislatures. Congress was to be given all the powers it held under the Articles of Confederation. In addition, it was to have the power to legislate "in all cases in which the States are incompetent" to act, the power to veto any State law in conflict with national law, and the power to use the armed forces to compel a State to obey national law.

The Virginia Plan also called for a "national executive" and a "national judiciary" to be chosen by Congress. Together, these two branches would compose a "council of revision." They would have the power to veto acts of Congress, but such an action could be overridden by a vote of the two houses. It also provided that all State officers should take an oath to support the Union and that each State should be guaranteed a republican form of government. It further provided that new States might be admitted to the Union by a majority vote of Congress.

The Virginia Plan, then, proposed a *thorough* revision of the Articles of Confederation. It proposed the creation of a *national* government with vastly expanded powers and, importantly, with the power to enforce its decisions.

The Virginia Plan served as a model for discussion through the remainder of the convention. But some of the delegates—especially those from the smaller States of Delaware, Maryland, and New Jersey and from New York[13]—considered its proposals too radical and far-reaching. In the course of discussions of the Virginia Plan, they developed their counterproposals. On June 15, William Paterson of New Jersey presented the position of the small States to the convention.

The New Jersey Plan. Paterson and his colleagues proposed amendments to the Articles of Confederation, but not nearly so thorough a revision as that offered by the Virginia Plan. The New Jersey Plan would have retained the unicameral (one-house) Congress of the Confederation, with each of the States equally represented. To the existing powers of the

Congress would be added a limited power to tax and the power to regulate interstate commerce. It also called for a "federal executive" and a "federal judiciary" to be elected by the Congress.

The major point of difference between the rival plans concerned representation in Congress. Should the States be represented on the basis of their populations (or financial contributions) or should they each be represented equally? For weeks the delegates returned to this conflict, debating it again and again. The lines were sharply drawn. Several delegates on both sides threatened to withdraw. But, finally and fortunately, a compromise was reached. It proved to be one of the truly great compromises of the Constitutional Convention.

The Great Compromises. The Constitution, as it was drafted at Philadelphia, has often been described as a "bundle of compromises." The description is an apt one—*if* it is properly understood.

By no means all, or even most, of what went into the document resulted from compromises among the delegates. The Founding Fathers were, in fact, in close agreement on many of the basic issues they faced. Virtually all of them were convinced that a *new* central government was essential. Virtually all felt that the government had to have the powers necessary to cope with the nation's economic and social problems. They were dedicated, too, to the concepts of popular sovereignty and of limited government. None of them questioned for a moment the wisdom of representative government. The principles of separation of powers and checks and balances were accepted by the delegates almost as a matter of course.

There were differences of opinion among them, of course, and often very important ones. Matters could hardly have been otherwise. After all, the delegates came from 12 different States which were, in 1787, widely separated in both geographic and economic terms. And, quite

---

[13] The Virginia Plan's major support came from the delegations of the three largest States: Virginia, Pennsylvania, and Massachusetts. New York was then only the fifth largest. Alexander Hamilton, the convention's most outspoken champion of a stronger central government, was regularly out-voted by his fellow delegates from New York.

naturally, the delegates tended to reflect the interests of their respective States.

Many disputes did occur, and the compromises by which they were resolved often were reached only after hours and days or even weeks of intense debate. But the point here is that the differences were *not* over the *most fundamental* of questions. Rather, the differences were over such vital but lesser questions as the details of the composition of Congress, the manner by which the President should be chosen, and the specific limitations that should be placed upon such grants as the taxing power and the commerce power.

THE CONNECTICUT COMPROMISE. The most famous of the disputes was that between the large and the small States over representation in Congress. The former expected to dominate the new government, and the latter feared that they would be unable to protect their interests. The conflict between the rival Virginia and New Jersey Plans was finally settled by a compromise first suggested by Roger Sherman of Connecticut. It was agreed that Congress should be composed of two houses, a Senate and a House of Representatives. In the smaller Senate the States would be represented equally. In the House representation would be in accordance with population. Thus, by combining basic features of both the Virginia and New Jersey Plans, the convention's most serious conflict was resolved.

THE THREE-FIFTHS COMPROMISE. Once it had been agreed that representation in the lower house would be based on population, another question arose. Should the Southern States be permitted to count their slaves in determining their populations? Again, the arguments were fierce. Some delegates contended that *all* slaves should be counted in a State's population while others argued that *none* should be. But, finally, the delegates agreed that all "free persons" would be counted and so, too, would "three-fifths of all other per-

sons." The "three-fifths" won by the Southern States was balanced by the fact that it was to be used *not only* for setting each State's quota of seats in the House of Representatives *but also* its quota of money to be raised under any direct tax levied by Congress. Of course, this curious compromise was nullified by the adoption of the 13th Amendment (which abolished slavery) in 1865.

THE COMMERCE AND SLAVE TRADE COMPROMISE. Much of the agitation that had led to the calling of the Philadelphia Convention came from those who were most interested in bringing order to the economic chaos of the times. Most urgent was the need for national regulation of interstate and foreign trade. But if the National Government controlled commerce, Southerners were afraid that Northerners, in control of Congress, might tax their flourishing agricultural trade with England. They were particularly fearful that their cotton trade might be forced to the less profitable markets in the North.

Again, compromise was reached. Congress was given the power to regulate interstate and foreign commerce. But it was expressly forbidden the power to tax exports or to favor one port over another in the regulation of trade. Congress was also prohibited from interfering with the slave trade. It could not interfere "with the migration or importation of such persons as any of the States now existing shall think proper to admit"—except for a small head tax, at least until the year 1808.[14]

OTHER COMPROMISES. Several other compromises went into the making of the Constitution. For example, several methods for selecting the President were proposed, including election by the people, by Congress, and by the State legislatures. Twice the delegates approved election by Congress. Opponents of that scheme argued that it would inevitably lead to legis-

14 Article I, Section 9, Clause 1.

An 18th century engraving depicts George Washington (standing) presiding over the Constitutional Convention.

lative domination of the executive branch and would thus destroy the concept of separation of powers. They finally won their point in the closing weeks. The Electoral College system was devised as a compromise among the various alternatives.

The President's four-year term and eligibility for re-election came from a compromise between those who favored a longer term and those who feared that long tenure in office was a threat to liberty. The question of who could vote in national as well as State elections was left to each of the States. This was the result of a compromise between those who favored a small, aristocratic electorate and those who wanted to broaden the suffrage.

The method of choosing Senators, the manner of selecting judges, the admission of new States, the amendment process— these and many other topics provoked debate and painstaking consideration. As Benjamin Franklin put it, the convention spent much time "sawing boards to make them fit."

Sources of the Constitution. As we noted, the Framers were, by and large, well-educated men. In drafting the Constitution they drew upon their knowledge of history of the governments of antiquity and of contemporary England and Europe. They were familiar with the political writings of their time—especially with Blackstone's *Commentaries on the Laws of England,* Montesquieu's *Spirit of the Laws,* Rousseau's *Social Contract,* and John Locke's *Two Treatises on Government.* As one writer has put it, they were "saturated with the revolutionary literature that some of their contemporaries, including some of those at the Convention, helped write and disseminate."

More immediately, they drew upon their experience with and the records of the Second Continental Congress, the Articles of Confederation, and their respective State governments. Thus, much that went

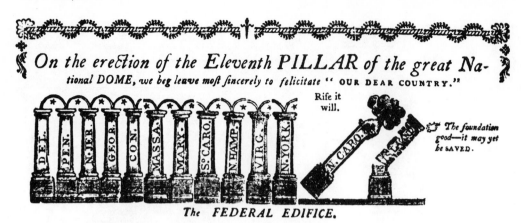

On the erection of the Eleventh PILLAR of the great National DOME, we beg leave most sincerely to felicitate " OUR DEAR COUNTRY."

Rise it will.

The foundation good—it may yet be SAVED.

The FEDERAL EDIFICE.

Newspapers figured prominently in the campaign for ratification of the Constitution. This drawing appeared in a Massachusetts paper in 1788.

into the Constitution came directly—sometimes word for word—from the Articles of Confederation and from various of the State constitutions.

The Convention Completes Its Work. By the end of July the delegates had tailored a series of resolutions into an organized text. The next several weeks were spent in analyzing, debating, and perfecting their handiwork. On September 8, a Committee on Style was named to "revise the style and arrange the articles which had been agreed to by the house." This group, headed by Gouverneur Morris, put the Constitution in its final, clear, concise form. At last, on the 17th of September, the convention approved its handiwork and 39 names were affixed to the finished document.[15]

Perhaps none of the Framers was *completely* satisfied with their work, but Benjamin Franklin spoke for most of them when he said:

I agree to this Constitution, with all its faults, if they are such; . . . I doubt whether any other Convention we can obtain may be able to make a better Constitution. For when you assemble a number of men to have the advantage of their joint wisdom, you inevitably assemble with those men all their prejudices, their passions, their errors of opinion, their local interests, and their selfish views. From such an assembly can a perfect production be expected? It therefore astonishes me, Sir, to find this system approaching so near to perfection as it does; and I think it will astonish our enemies. . . .

While the Constitution was being signed, Madison tells us that:

Doctr Franklin looking toward the President's chair, at the back of which a rising sun happened to be painted, observed to a few members near him, that Painters had found it difficult to distinguish in their art a rising from a setting sun. I have, said he, often and often in the course of the Session . . . looked at that behind the President without being able to tell whether it was rising or setting. But now at length I have the happiness to know that it is a rising and not a setting sun.

Ratification. The new Constitution was intended to replace the Articles of Confederation—which provided that

---

[15] Three of the 41 delegates present refused to sign: Edmund Randolph of Virginia, who later did support ratification and then served as Attorney General and then Secretary of State in the Washington administration; Elbridge Gerry of Massachusetts, who later became Vice President under Madison, and George Mason of Virginia, who maintained his opposition to the Constitution through the remainder of his life. George Read of Delaware signed both for himself and for his absent colleague, John Dickinson.

changes in them could be made *only* with the approval of *all* of the States. But the Framers had seen how crippling the unanimity requirement could be. So, the new Constitution provided (in Article VII) that the ratifications "of nine States shall be sufficient for the establishment of this Constitution between the States so ratifying the same." The Congress of the Confederation agreed to this irregular procedure when it sent the new document on to the States for their action on September 28, 1787.

FEDERALISTS AND ANTI-FEDERALISTS. The proposed Constitution was printed, circulated, and debated throughout the country. Two factions quickly emerged in each of the States: the *Federalists*, who supported ratification, and the *Anti-Federalists*, who opposed it.

The Federalists were led in the main by many of those who had attended the Philadelphia Convention. Among them, the most active and the most effective were James Madison and Alexander Hamilton. Their opposition was headed by such respected Revolutionary War figures as Patrick Henry, Richard Henry Lee, John Hancock, and Samuel Adams.

Hamilton's arguments supporting the Constitution figured prominently in its final ratification.

In arguing their case the Federalists emphasized the weaknesses of the Articles of Confederation. They insisted that the many difficulties facing the Republic could be overcome only by replacing the existing governmental system with a new one founded upon the proposed Constitution.

The Anti-Federalists attacked nearly every feature of the new document. Many objected to the fact that they had either to accept or to reject it as it stood, without an opportunity to amend it before a final decision was made. Some complained that nowhere did it specifically recognize the existence of God. Others criticized the Framers for providing a method of ratification contrary to that required by the Articles of Confederation. Still others, especially debtors, were vehemently opposed to the denial to the States of the power to print money.

The largest amount of criticism focused upon two aspects of the Constitution, however: (1) the vast increases it provided in the powers of the central government and (2) its lack of a bill of rights. There was no general listing of such fundamental liberties as freedom of speech, press, and religion and guarantees of fair trial. Patrick

RATIFICATION OF THE CONSTITUTION

State	Date	Vote
Delaware	Dec. 7, 1787	30–0
Pennsylvania	Dec. 12, 1787	46–23
New Jersey	Dec. 19, 1787	38–0
Georgia	Jan. 2, 1788	26–0
Connecticut	Jan. 9, 1788	128–40
Massachusetts	Feb. 6, 1788	187–168
Maryland	Apr. 28, 1788	63–11
South Carolina	May 23, 1788	149–73
New Hampshire	June 21, 1788	57–46
Virginia	June 25, 1788	89–79
New York	July 26, 1788	30–27
North Carolina	Nov. 21, 1789*	184–77
Rhode Island	May 29, 1790	34–32

* Second vote; ratification was originally defeated on August 4, 1788, by a vote of 184–84.

George Washington makes a triumphant entry into New York Harbor on his way to taking the oath of office as the first President of the United States.

Henry expressed the view of many when he said of the proposed Constitution:

> I look upon that paper as the most fatal plan that could possibly be conceived to enslave a free people.

SUCCESS. Although the struggle for ratification was a bitter one in many States, the Federalists ultimately prevailed in all of them. The Constitution was ratified by the convention called in each State on the date and by the vote shown in the table on page 57.

On June 21, 1788, New Hampshire brought the number of ratifying States to nine. According to Article VII, its action should have brought the Constitution into effect. But, in fact, it did not. Neither Virginia nor New York had yet ratified, and without either of them the new government could not hope to succeed.

Virginia. Virginia's ratification fol-lowed New Hampshire's by a scant four days. The debates in its convention were intense and brilliant, and they were followed closely throughout the State. The Federalist cause was led by Madison, the young John Marshall, and Governor Edmund Randolph (even though, recall, he had refused to sign the Constitution at Philadelphia). Patrick Henry led the opposition and was joined by such outstanding Virginians as James Monroe, Richard Henry Lee, and George Mason (another of the non-signers).

Although George Washington was not a delegate, his strong support for ratification proved vital in persuading the convention. Together with Madison, he was able to convince a reluctant Jefferson to agree. Had Jefferson fought as did other Anti-Federalists, Virginia might never have ratified the Constitution.

New York. A narrow vote in the New

York convention brought the number of States to 11 on July 26, 1788. New York's approval was in no small part the result of the appearance of *The Federalist*—a remarkable series of 85 essays. These essays discussed the Constitution virtually line by line and defended it against its critics. These "papers" were written by Madison, Hamilton, and John Jay. They were first published in various newspapers of the State and shortly thereafter in book form. They remain today an excellent commentary on the Constitution and continue to rank among the very best of political writings in the English language.

Inauguration of the New Government. On September 13, 1788, with 11 of the 13 States "under the federal roof," the Congress of the Confederation paved the way for its successor. It chose New York City as the temporary capitol. It provided for the selection of presidential electors in the States, and set the first Wednesday in February as the day on which they would vote. And it decided that the new government should be inaugurated on March 4, 1789.

The new Congress did convene on March 4th, in Federal Hall on Wall Street. But, because a quorum was lacking, the First Session of the First Congress did not count the electoral vote until the 6th of April. Then on April 30th, after a memorable trip from Mount Vernon to New York, George Washington, the unanimous choice of the electors, took the oath of office as the first President of the United States.

SUMMARY

Government in the United States is the product of centuries of development.

The English, who settled the 13 colonies, contributed much to the shaping of the American governmental system: especially, the pattern of early government in America and the concepts of limited government and representative government.

Beginning with the founding of Jamestown, Virginia, in 1607, all 13 of the colonies were established by 1732. Three types of colonies existed: royal, proprietary, and charter. The eight royal colonies were ruled by a royal governor under the king. The three proprietary colonies were governed under a proprietor who was, in turn, responsible to the king. The two charter colonies, the most democratic, governed themselves much as they saw fit.

England's control over its colonies was tightened in the 1760's, and the resentment this created led to the American Revolution. England looked on the colonies as handmaids to serve the mother country; the colonists demanded the right to manage their own affairs. The colonists did attempt to head off the break, especially in the First Continental Congress in 1774.

By the meeting of the Second Continental Congress in 1775, the American Revolution had actually begun. This body functioned as our first national government. It proclaimed the Declaration of Independence on July 4, 1776, and drew up our first national constitution, the Articles of Confederation, which went into effect in March of 1781.

The government set up under the Articles of Confederation proved too weak for the times. The chaos of the Critical Period led to the meeting of the Constitutional Convention.

From May 25 to September 17, 1787, the Founding Fathers worked to produce the Constitution. It replaced the Articles of Confederation in 1789 when George Washington was inaugurated as the first President of the United States of America.

Concept Development

Questions for Review

1. What were the major political concepts the early English settlers brought to America?

2. What distinguished the three major types of colonies from each other?

3. What was the English attitude toward the colonies? What was the colonial attitude toward the relationship with England after 1763?

4. What body became our first national government? How?

5. The Declaration of Independence was drafted by whom?

6. Which portion of the Declaration of Independence is the most important? Why?

7. What, in brief, was the nature of the first State governments?

8. What were the Articles of Confederation? When and by whom were they framed? When did they become effective?

9. What was the structure of the government created by the Articles?

10. What were the major powers of the Congress under the Articles? What were the document's major weaknesses?

11. When and where was the Constitution framed?

12. Who were the outstanding members of the Constitutional Convention?

13. What momentous decision did the Founding Fathers make at the outset of the convention?

14. Who is called the "Father of the Constitution"? Why?

15. What were the similarities and the differences between the Virginia Plan and the New Jersey Plan?

16. What were the three major compromises made at the Convention?

17. In what sense was the Constitution a "bundle of compromises"?

18. From what sources did the Founding Fathers draw in drafting the Constitution?

19. What were the major objections raised against the proposed new Constitution?

20. When did the new government begin functioning?

For Further Inquiry

1. On the first day, May 25, 1787, the delegates to the Constitutional Convention unanimously elected George Washington the presiding officer. Why was this action so significant? What was Washington's status with the people of the day? Could the fact that he presided at the Convention have had any effect in the ratification controversy?

2. Why has it been said that the fact that such men as Patrick Henry, Samuel Adams, and John Hancock were not delegates to the Constitutional Convention was

probably a fortunate thing? How might their absence be considered unfortunate?

3. In what ways did the Constitution provide for "a more perfect Union" than the Articles of Confederation?

4. The Preamble of the Constitution declares that the document was ordained and established by "We the People of the United States." Yet, in fact, it was drafted by 55 men at Philadelphia and ratified by conventions in the 13 States. How can one reconcile the apparent contradiction here?

5. It has been said that the Declaration of Independence was a radical and revolutionary document but that the Constitution was not. Do you agree? Explain.

6. What do you think James Madison meant when he remarked on the floor of the Philadelphia Convention: "In truth, all men with power ought to be distrusted to a certain degree"?

Suggested Activities

1. Prepare short biographical sketches of such outstanding Revolutionary War leaders and of the Founding Fathers as George Washington, Benjamin Franklin, Thomas Jefferson, Alexander Hamilton, Samuel Adams, Patrick Henry, James Madison, John Hancock, Richard Henry Lee, Gouverneur Morris.

2. Stage a debate or class forum on the following: (a) *Resolved,* That the Framers of the Constitution should have provided for a unicameral Congress in which each State would have been equally represented; (b) *Resolved,* That the States should have rejected the Constitution proposed by the Philadelphia Convention and that the governmental arrangements provided by the Articles of Confederation should have been continued; (c) *Resolved,* That the 13

colonies should have remained within the British Empire.

3. Prepare a wall chart or bulletin board display depicting the major steps and events leading finally to the Constitution and its ratification.

4. Compare the organization, length, and contents of the Constitution of the United States and the constitution of your State. (If a copy of the latter is not available in the school or other library, one can be obtained from the office of the Secretary of State in the State capital.)

5. Prepare a wall chart or bulletin board display depicting the major weaknesses of the Articles of Confederation and the manner in which they were corrected in the Constitution.

Suggested Reading

Boyd, Steven R., *The Politics of Opposition: Anti-Federalists and the Acceptance of the Constitution.* KTO Press, 1979.

Garraty, John, *The American Nation.* Harper & Row, 4th ed., 1979.

Jensen, Merrill, *The Making of the American Constitution.* Krieger, 1979.

McCaughey, Elizabeth P., *From Loyalist to Founding Father: The Political Odyssey of William Samuel Johnson.* Columbia University Press, 1980.

Moynihan, Daniel P., *Counting Our Blessings.* Little, Brown, 1980.

Pritchett, C. Herman, *The American Constitutional System.* McGraw-Hill, 5th ed., 1980.

Urdang, Laurence, *The Timetable of American History.* Simon & Schuster, 1981.

Wood, Gordon S., *The Confederation and the Constitution: The Critical Issues.* University Press of America, 1979.

The Living Constitution

. . . a Constitution intended to endure for ages to come, and, consequently, to be adapted to the various crises of human affairs.

CHIEF JUSTICE JOHN MARSHALL
McCulloch v. *Maryland* (1819)

■ Why are brevity and flexibility profoundly important characteristics of the Constitution?

■ Why may it be said that the Constitution today *is*, and at the same time, *is not* the document that was written in 1787?

■ Is the Constitution too easily amended—either formally or informally?

The Constitution of the United States is the nation's fundamental law. It sets forth the basic principles upon which government in the United States was established and upon which it is maintained. And it sets forth the basic framework and procedures by which, and the limits within which, the governmental system must operate.

Even with its 26 amendments, the Constitution is brief. It contains only a few more than 7000 words and can be read in a leisurely half hour. You will find the text of the Constitution on pages 788–800—preceded by a two-page outline of its contents. As you read the document, note that it deals very largely with matters of basic principle rather than with the specific details of governmental structure, organization, and procedure.

In this chapter we consider the basic principles of the American constitutional system: the concepts of popular sovereignty, limited government, separation of powers, checks and balances, judicial review, and federalism. Then we turn to the various ways the Constitution has changed and developed over the past 19 decades.

The Basic Principles

Popular Sovereignty. In the United States the people are sovereign. All political power resides in them. From them must flow any and all authority for any governmental action. Government may act only with the consent of the governed.

The principle of popular sovereignty is most clearly stated in the Preamble to the Constitution:

> We the People of the United States . . . do ordain and establish this Constitution for the United States of America.

Acting through the medium of the Constitution, the sovereign people created the National Government and have given to it certain powers. And, too, through the Constitution of the United States and its own fundamental law, each of the 50 States has received its life and its powers from the people.

Limited Government. The principle of limited government is equally basic to the American constitutional system. It holds that government is *not* all-powerful, that government may do only *certain* things—*only* those things that the people have seen fit to give it the power to do.

In effect, the principle of limited government is the other side of the coin of popular sovereignty: The people are the only source for any and all of government's authority, and government has only that authority the people have given to it.

The concept of limited government may be put another way: Government must obey the law. This fundamentally vital notion is often described as *constitutionalism*—that is, that government must be conducted according to constitutional principles. And it is also frequently identified as the *rule of law*—that is, that government and its officers, in all that they do, are under, never above the law.

In very large part, the Constitution is a statement of the principle of limited government. Many of its provisions are written as explicit prohibitions of power to government.[1] As but one of many examples of the point, notice the great guaran-

LePelly in *The Christian Science Monitor* © 1970 TCSPS

'I'M NOT GOING TO MARRY EITHER ONE OF YOU'

tees of freedom of expression. Those guarantees—of freedom of religion, speech, press, assembly, and petition—are altogether indispensible to democratic government. And they are enshrined in the 1st Amendment, which begins with the words "Congress shall make no law . . ."

Separation of Powers. Recall our brief discussion of the parliamentary and presidential forms of government on page 20. In a parliamentary system the basic powers of a government—its legislative, executive, and judicial powers—are all gathered in the hands of a single agency. British government affords an excellent illustration of the type. In a presidential system, on the other hand, these basic powers are distributed (separated) among three distinct and independent branches.

The Constitution distributes the powers of the National Government among the Congress (the legislative branch), the President (the executive branch), and the

---

[1] See, especially, Article I, Sections 9 and 10; Article IV; the 1st through the 10th Amendments; and the 13th, 14th, 15th, 19th, 24th, and 26th Amendments.

courts (the judicial branch). This separation of powers is expressly provided for in three constitutional provisions. Article I, Section 1 provides: "All legislative powers herein granted shall be vested in a Congress of the United States . . ." Article II, Section 1 provides: "The executive power shall be vested in a President of the United States of America." Article III, Section 1 provides: "The judicial power of the United States shall be vested in one Supreme Court, and in such inferior courts as the Congress may from time to time ordain and establish."

In defense of this arrangement James Madison wrote in *The Federalist* No. 47:

> The accumulation of all powers, legislative, executive, and judiciary, in the same hands, whether of one, a few, or many, and whether hereditary, self-appointed, or elective, may justly be pronounced the very definition of tyranny.

The Congress exercises *legislative* (law-making) powers. It cannot authorize any other agency or person to make laws in its stead. But it can, and often does, pass acts which outline general policies and set certain standards while leaving the actual details of day-to-day administration to some agency under the President. For instance, Congress has provided for the regulation of air transportation and has set out the standards to be followed in this respect. The details of that regulation—involving such complex matters as navigational aids, air traffic control, and pilot licensing—are handled by executive agencies. (In this case, by the Federal Aviation Administration and the Civil Aeronautics Board.)

The President possesses *executive* (law-executing, law-enforcing, law-administering) powers. Of course, the President is assisted by all of the several departments, agencies, officers, and employees in the vast executive branch. But the President alone is personally and finally responsible for the exercise of the executive power of the United States.

The courts, and most importantly the Supreme Court, exercise the *judicial* (law-interpreting, law-applying) powers. The courts exercise their powers in actual disputes as those disputes are presented to them—in the form of cases brought either by government or by private parties.

The earliest of the State constitutions had provided for a separation of powers among legislative, executive, and judicial agencies (as they all still do today). The fact that they did was a reflection of the mistrust and suspicion of *any* government common to the people of the United States of the late 1700's. Thus, separation of powers was both natural and inevitable in the writing of the Constitution.

Checks and Balances. While the Constitution establishes three *separate* and *distinct* branches of the National Government, it does not make these branches *completely* independent of one another. Rather, each branch has its own field of powers, but it is also subject to a series of constitutional *checks* (restraints) which either of the other two branches may exercise against it.

The Constitution interlaces the three branches with several of these checks. For example, Congress has the power to make laws, but the President may veto an act of Congress. And, in turn, Congress may pass legislation over a President's veto by a two-thirds vote in each house. Congress may refuse to appropriate funds requested by the President, or the Senate may refuse to approve appointments or treaties the President has made. The President has the power to appoint all federal judges, but the Senate must give its approval. The courts have the power to determine the constitutionality of acts of Congress or the executive actions of the President.

Head-on clashes between the branches seldom occur. The check and balance system, however, operates constantly, and in almost routine fashion. The very *existence* of the system shapes much that happens in the National Government. Consider two

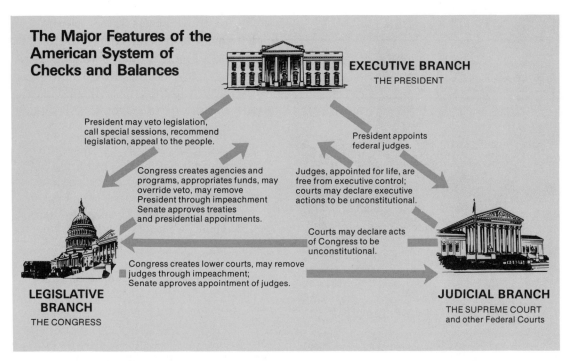

The Major Features of the American System of Checks and Balances

EXECUTIVE BRANCH
THE PRESIDENT

President may veto legislation, call special sessions, recommend legislation, appeal to the people.

President appoints federal judges.

Congress creates agencies and programs, appropriates funds, may override veto, may remove President through impeachment Senate approves treaties and presidential appointments.

Judges, appointed for life, are free from executive control; courts may declare executive actions to be unconstitutional.

Courts may declare acts of Congress to be unconstitutional.

Congress creates lower courts, may remove judges through impeachment; Senate approves appointment of judges.

LEGISLATIVE BRANCH
THE CONGRESS

JUDICIAL BRANCH
THE SUPREME COURT
and other Federal Courts

The balance of power among the three branches of government is maintained through the system of constitutional checks which help keep the National Government on an even keel.

common examples of the point: In selecting someone to an important post in the administration, the President must always bear in mind that the person appointed *must* be acceptable to a majority of the Senate. Similarly, as it frames legislation, Congress must keep in mind both the President's veto power and the power of the courts to declare a statute unconstitutional.

Of course, spectacular clashes, dramatic applications of the check and balance system, do sometimes occur. And no more pithy illustration of this fact can be cited than the several chapters of the Watergate Affair. That eventful, many-faceted topic dominated the nation's politics for a year and a half and tremors from it will be felt for years to come. It involved a series of clashes between the President and Congress and the courts. And the whole matter climaxed on August 9, 1974—the day Richard Nixon—facing almost certain impeachment by the House and conviction and re-

moval from office by the Senate—resigned the Presidency.

But, again, stark confrontations are rare. The check and balance system makes compromises necessary, and compromise is indispensable to democratic government.

Over time, the check and balance system has worked quite well. It has done what the Framers designed it to do. It has prevented "an unjust combination of the majority."

At the same time, it has not worked to prevent a fairly close relationship between the executive and legislative branches. The President and Congress usually do work in rather close cooperation with one another.

But, notice, this has been especially true when the President and a majority of both houses of Congress have been of the same political party. When the other major party controls one or both houses, partisan frictions tend to play a larger-than-usual role in that relationship. The point can be

A series of clashes took place between the President, Congress, and the courts during the Watergate Affair. Here, the Senate Watergate Investigating Committee is shown during a hearing.

seen in that link today—with a Republican President and a Republican majority in the Senate, but a Democratic majority in the House of Representatives.

Judicial Review. *Judicial review* may be defined as the power of a court to determine the constitutionality of a governmental action. It involves the power to declare *unconstitutional* (null and void, of no force and effect) a governmental action found to be in violation of some provision in the Constitution. The power is held by all of the courts in the federal judiciary and by most State courts, as well.[2]

The Constitution does not provide for the power of judicial review *in so many words*. But the Framers rather clearly intended that the federal courts, and especially the Supreme Court, should possess the power. They felt that its existence was clearly implied in the words of the Constitution.[3] In *The Federalist* No. 78, Alexander Hamilton wrote:

> The interpretation of the laws is the proper and peculiar province of the courts. A constitution is, in fact, and must be regarded by the judges as a fundamental law. It therefore belongs to them to ascertain its meaning, as well as the meaning of any particular act proceeding from the legislative body. If there should happen to be an irreconcilable conflict between the two, that which has the superior obligation and validity ought, of course, to be preferred; or, in other words, the Constitution ought to be preferred to the Statute, the intention of the people to the intention of their agents.

The Supreme Court first exercised the power of judicial review in *Marbury* v. *Madison*, 1803.[4] By 1981 it had declared some 120 acts or portions of acts of Congress unconstitutional. It has also voided many presidential and other executive branch actions. And it has held hundreds of actions of the States and their local governments unconstitutional, including nearly 900 State laws and more than 100 local ordinances.

Federalism. When we discussed various forms of government in Chapter 1, we learned that governments may be classified in a number of different ways. Among the several possible classifications is that based on the geographic distribution of the powers of government. From this standpoint, recall, governments may be *unitary, confederate,* or *federal* in form.

As we know, the Government of the

---

[2] Generally, the power is held by all State courts which are *courts of record.* These are courts which keep a record of their proceedings and have the power to punish for contempt of court. Only the lowest State courts (for example, justice of the peace and municipal courts) are not usually courts of record.

[3] See Article III, Section 2 and Article IV, Section 2.

[4] See pages 73, 86–87. We shall return, often, to the Court's exercise of the power of judicial review—and also examine it at greater length in Chapter 26, "The Federal Court System."

United States is a federal government. That is, the powers of government are distributed between the National Government on the one hand and the 50 States on the other.

None of the basic principles of the American constitutional system was a more natural result of the birth of the United States than federalism. The colonists had rebelled against the harsh rule of a powerful central government. They had rebelled because, they insisted, they had the right to handle their own local affairs without meddling and dictation from the King and his ministers. Surely, they would not now consent to the creation of another strongly centralized government.

Even so, it was obvious that a National Government much stronger than the weak Congress under the Articles of Confederation was necessary. The economic and political chaos of the 1780's had more than proved that need. The Framers resolved the problem by constructing a *federal government*—a compromise between the system of nearly-independent States loosely joined to one another in the Confederation and a much-dreaded, too-powerful central government.

We shall explore the nature of the American federal system at length in the next chapter, Chapter 4, "The Nation and the States: Federalism."

Our Changing Constitution

The Constitution of the United States has now been in force for more than 190 years—for longer, by far, than has the written constitution of any other nation in the world.[5]

In the more than 19 decades since the Constitution was drafted great changes have taken place. In 1787 the young Republic was a small agricultural nation of less than four million people scattered for some 2090 kilometers (1300 miles) along the eastern edge of the continent. The original 13 States, joined to one another only by horses and sailing ships, struggled to stay alive in an essentially hostile world.

Today, however, the United States has grown to a population of more than 226 million. The now 50 States span the continent and beyond, and the nation has many far-flung dependencies and commitments. This nation is the most powerful one on earth, and our modern, highly industrialized and technological society has produced the highest standard of living any nation has ever known.

How has the Constitution, written in 1787, managed to endure, to keep pace with this astounding change and growth? The answer to that question is to be found in the fact that the Constitution today, at one and the same time, *is* and *is not* the document of 1787. Many of the words are the same, and much of their meaning remains the same, too. But some words have been changed, some have been eliminated, and some have been added. And meanings have been modified through 19 decades, too.

This process of constitutional change, modification, and growth has come about in two basic ways: by *formal amendment* and by *informal amendment*.

Formal Amendment. The Framers were well aware that even the wisest of constitution-makers cannot hope to build for all time—and, so, the Constitution includes provisions for its own amendment.

Article V sets out two methods for the *proposal* and two methods for the *ratification* of constitutional amendments. So, as the diagram on page 68 indicates, it provides for four different methods of amendment.

First: An amendment may be proposed by a two-thirds vote in each house of Congress and be ratified by three-fourths of

---

[5] The British constitution dates from well before the Norman Conquest of 1066; but it is not a single, written document, as is the Constitution of the United States. Rather, it is an "unwritten constitution," a collection of principles, customs, traditions, and significant parliamentary acts which guide British government and practice.

AMENDING THE UNITED STATES CONSTITUTION

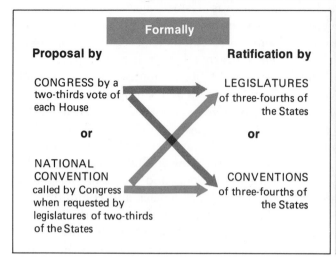

Formally

Proposal by

CONGRESS by a
two-thirds vote of
each House

or

NATIONAL
CONVENTION
called by Congress
when requested by
legislatures of two-thirds
of the States

Ratification by

LEGISLATURES
of three-fourths of
the States

or

CONVENTIONS
of three-fourths of
the States

Informally

Through:

1. Basic Legislation: creation of lower
   federal courts, enactment of labor
   laws by Congress.
2. Executive Action: war-making, use
   of executive agreements by President.
3. Court Decisions: Judicial Review
   (*Marbury v. Madison*).
4. Party Practices: national conventions
   to nominate presidential, vice-presidential candidates.
5. Custom: Cabinet, senatorial courtesy.

the State legislatures. Today, then, 38 State legislatures must approve an amendment to make it a part of the Constitution. Twenty-five of the Constitution's now 26 amendments were adopted in this manner.

Second: An amendment may be proposed by Congress and ratified by conventions called for that purpose in three-fourths of the States. Only the 21st Amendment, added in 1933, was adopted in this way.[6]

Third: An amendment may be proposed by a national convention, called by Congress at the request of two-thirds of the State legislatures (today, 34) and ratified by the legislatures of three-fourths of the States. To date, Congress has not had occasion to call such a convention.[7]

Fourth: An amendment may be proposed by a national convention and ratified by conventions in three-fourths of the States. Recall that the Constitution itself was originally adopted in a closely similar process.

The Constitution places only one restriction on the subjects with which a proposed amendment may deal. Article V declares that "no State, without its consent, shall be deprived of its equal suffrage in the Senate."

Note that the formal amendment process emphasizes the federal character of our governmental system. Proposal occurs at the *national* level and ratification is a *State-by-State* matter. And note, too, that our political theory holds that the adoption of an amendment represents an expression of the people's sovereign will.

When Congress passes a joint resolution proposing an amendment, the measure is not sent to the President to be signed or vetoed—despite the fact that the Constitution would seem to require it.[8] When Congress proposes an amendment it is not making law (not legislating). And, note, the vote necessary to propose an amendment (two-thirds of each house) is

---

[6] The 21st Amendment repealed the 18th (which had established national prohibition). Conventions were used here largely because Congress felt that their popularly elected delegates would be more inclined to favor the repeal of prohibition than would State legislators.

[7] Congress was very nearly required to call one a decade ago. Between 1963 and 1969, 33 State legislatures—one short of the necessary two-thirds—sought an amendment to erase several of the Supreme Court's "one-man, one-vote" decisions. They supported a proposal to allow one house of a bicameral State legislature to be apportioned on some basis other than population; see pages 692-695. Currently (1981), some 30 States have asked for a convention for an amendment that would require that the federal budget be balanced each year, except in time of war or other national emergency.

---

[8] Article I, Section 7, Clause 3.

Case Study

In 1972 Congress proposed the Equal Rights Amendment to the States. The proposed amendment reads:

SECTION 1. Equality of rights under the law shall not be denied or abridged by the United States or by an State on account of sex.
SECTION 2. The Congress shall have the power to enforce, by appropriate legislation, the provisions of this article.
SECTION 3. This amendment shall take effect two years after the date of ratification.

In the joint resolution submitting ERA to the States, Congress fixed a seven-year time limit on the ratification process. It declared that the amendment:

. . . shall be valid to all intents and purposes as part of the Constitution when ratified by the legislatures of three-fourths of the several States within seven years from the date of its submission by the Congress.

As the deadline for ratification (March 22, 1979) approached, it became increasingly clear that ERA would not be approved in timely fashion. Only 35 of the

necessary 38 State legislatures had voted to do so.

After heated debate, in both houses and throughout the country. Congress voted to extend the time limit—to June 30, 1982.

By 1981, ERA remained three States shy of ratification. And five of the State legislatures which had approved it (Idaho, Kentucky, Nebraska, South Dakota, and Tennessee) had later acted to withdraw their ratifications.

■ Has your State's legislature ratified or rejected ERA? When? By what margin in each chamber? Do you favor or oppose the action it took? Why?
■ Do you agree with the congressional decision to extend the ERA deadline?
■ Should three more States ratify ERA by June 30, 1982, this question will then have to be answered: Can a State rescind its approval of a proposed constitutional amendment? Presumably, Congress will have to provide that answer. If you were a member of Congress, how would you vote on the matter? Why?

the same as the vote necessary to override a presidential veto.

The practice of sending proposed amendments to the State legislatures rather than to ratifying conventions is sometimes criticized—especially because it permits a constitutional change without a clear-cut expression by the people. The critics lay their argument on these points: The State legislators, who do the ratifying, are chosen to office for a mix of reasons—party membership, incumbency, personal popularity, their stands on such matters as taxes, schools, welfare programs, and many others. But they are almost never chosen because of their stand on a proposed amendment to the Federal Constitution; in fact, many of them may have been elected even before the proposal was submitted to the States. On the other hand,

the delegates to a ratifying convention would be selected by the people on the basis of one overriding factor: a yes-or-no stand on the proposed amendment.

In *Hawke* v. *Smith*, 1920, the Supreme Court held that Ohio (or any other States) could not require that an amendment proposed by Congress be approved by a vote of the people of the State before it could be ratified by the legislature. But a State legislature can call for an *advisory* vote by the people before it acts—as the Court most recently indicated in a case from Nevada, *Kimble* v. *Swackhamer*, 1978.

If a State rejects a proposed amendment it may later reconsider that action—and ratify the proposal if it chooses to do so. But both historical precedent and most constitutional scholars hold that the reverse is not true. That is, once a State has ratified an amendment it may not later reverse itself.[9]

Some 6000 joint resolutions proposing amendments have been presented to Congress since the Constitution became effective in 1789. To 1981, Congress has sent but 33 of them on to the States. And, of those, only 26 have been finally ratified.[10]

The 26 Amendments. The first 10 amendments were all added to the Constitution in a body in 1791. They had been proposed by the First Congress in 1789. Their proposal was a direct response to the fact that many, including Thomas Jefferson, had agreed to support the original Constitution only on condition that a listing of the basic rights held by the people against the new National Government be added to the document immediately. Collectively, these amendments are known as the Bill of Rights. Their provisions include the great constitutional guarantees of freedom of expression and belief, of personal rights, and of fair treatment before the law. We shall turn to them in detail in Chapters 6 and 7. The 10th Amendment does not deal with civil rights. Rather, it expressly provides for the concept of *reserved powers* in the federal system—a matter we shall consider in the next chapter.

The 11th Amendment, added in 1795, provides that a State may not be sued in a federal court by a citizen of another State or of a foreign state. The 12th Amendment (1804) made some revision in the presidential election system.

The 13th Amendment (1865) abolished slavery and prohibited most other forms of "involuntary servitude." The 14th (1868) defined American citizenship and thus extended it to former slaves. This amendment also contains the Due Process and Equal Protection Clauses which guarantee basic civil rights against infringements by the States. The 15th (1870) forbids any restrictions on the suffrage based upon "race, color, or previous condition of servitude."

The 16th Amendment, authorizing a federal income tax, and the 17th, providing for the direct popular election of United States Senators, were ratified in the same year, 1913. The 18th Amendment (1919) established nationwide prohibition. The 19th (1920) provided for woman suffrage. The 20th provided a new date for the convening of each regular session of Congress and for the inauguration of the President. The 21st repealed the 18th Amendment. Both the 20th and 21st were adopted in the same year—1933.

The 22nd Amendment, ratified in 1951, limits a President to two full terms or not more than 10 years in office. The 23rd (1961) provides for three presidential electors from the District of Columbia. The 24th (1964) bans the payment of any tax as a prerequisite to voting in any federal election. And the 25th (1967) provides for presidential succession, the filling of a vacancy in the Vice Presidency, and procedures for determining presidential disability.

The most recently adopted Amendment, the 26th, was added to the Constitution in record time in 1971. It sets age 18 as

---

[9] The Supreme Court has never ruled on the point directly. However, its decisions in related cases strongly suggest that it would find that a State's attempt to *rescind*, or cancel, a ratification (a *recision*) presents a "political question"—that is, a nonjusticiable matter, one to be resolved by Congress rather than the courts. Of the 35 States which have thus far (to 1981), ratified the proposed Equal Rights Amendment (ERA), five (Idaho, Kentucky, Nebraska, Tennessee, and South Dakota) subsequently reversed their decisions; what effect, if any, those recisions will have remains to be seen; see note 10 and page 800.

[10] To date, seven amendments have been offered but not ratified. Two of them were proposed in 1789 together with the 10 which became the Bill of Rights; one dealt with the apportionment of the House of Representatives, the other with the compensation of members of Congress. A third, proposed in 1810, would have voided the citizenship of any person accepting a foreign title or other honor. A fourth, in 1861, would have prohibited adoption of any amendment relating to slavery. A fifth, in 1924, would have given Congress the power to regulate child labor. A sixth, the Equal Rights Amendment, proposed in 1972, is now before the States. So, too, is the seventh one, proposed in 1978, to grant full congressional representation to the District of Columbia; see page 800.

Suffragettes march to the Capitol in Washington, D.C., in 1913. Seven years later their efforts to win the right to vote became the law of the land when the 19th Amendment was ratified.

AMENDMENTS TO THE CONSTITUTION

Amendments	Subject	Year Adopted	Time Required For Ratification
1st–10th	The Bill of Rights	1791	2 years, 2 months, 20 days
11th	Immunity of States from certain suits	1795	11 months, 3 days
12th	Changes in Electoral College procedure	1804	6 months, 3 days
13th	Prohibition of slavery	1865	10 months, 3 days
14th	Citizenship, due process, and equal protection	1868	2 years, 26 days
15th	No denial of vote because of race, color, or previous condition of servitude	1870	11 months, 8 days
16th	Power of Congress to tax incomes	1913	3 years, 6 months, 22 days
17th	Direct election of U.S. Senators	1913	10 months, 26 days
18th	National (liquor) prohibition	1919	1 year, 29 days
19th	Woman suffrage	1920	1 year, 2 months, 14 days
20th	Change of dates for congressional and presidential terms	1933	10 months, 21 days
21st	Repeal of the 18th Amendment	1933	9 months, 15 days
22nd	Limit on presidential tenure	1951	3 years, 11 months, 3 days
23rd	District of Columbia electoral vote	1961	9 months, 13 days
24th	Prohibition of tax payment as a qualification to vote in federal elections	1964	1 year, 4 months, 9 days
25th	Procedures for determining presidential disability, presidential succession, and for filling a vice presidential vacancy	1967	1 year, 7 months, 4 days
26th	Sets the minimum age for voting in all elections at 18	1971	3 months, 7 days

the minimum age for voting in *all* elections—federal, State, or local—held in this country.

The 26 amendments, the year in which each of them was adopted, and the period of time required for the ratification of each is shown in the table on page 71.

Informal Amendment. Important as they are, the formal amendments have *not* been especially responsible for the Constitution's amazing vitality. Rather, the *informal* amendments have been and are most responsible. That is, as the United States has changed and grown through the years, the Constitution has kept pace through changes (informal amendments) which have *not* involved additions or deletions in its actual wording. These changes have come through the day-to-day, year-to-year experiences of government under the Constitution.

Certainly, the Framers did not intend to place future generations in a constitutional straitjacket. Rather, they recognized that, inevitably, the future would call for changes in what they had done.

In order to gain a true understanding of the nature of our constitutional system as it exists today, we must consider five means by which informal amendment has occurred: by *basic legislation, executive action, court decisions, party practices,* and *custom.*

BASIC LEGISLATION. The Constitution deals very largely with matters of basic principle. So, much of its language is general and, often, skeletal. The Framers purposely left it to Congress to fill in the details as circumstances required. In doing so, Congress has spelled out—and, in effect, added to—many of the Constitution's provisions. For example, starting with the Judiciary Act of 1789, the entire federal court system, except for the Supreme Court itself, has been created by acts of Congress. So, too, have all of the numerous departments, agencies, and offices in the executive branch, except for the offices of President and Vice President.

Then, too, Congress has added to the Constitution by the manner in which it has exercised its various powers. For example, the Constitution gives Congress the expressed power to regulate interstate and foreign commerce.[11] But what *is* interstate commerce? And what is foreign commerce? The Constitution does not say. In passing literally thousands of statutes under the Commerce Clause, Congress has done much to define its meaning. And, in the process, it has informally amended—in fact, added a great deal to the words of—the document.

EXECUTIVE ACTION. The manner in which the various Presidents have exercised their power has contributed significantly to the informal amendment process. This has been especially true of the stronger Presidents: George Washington, Thomas Jefferson, Andrew Jackson, Abraham Lincoln, Grover Cleveland, Theodore Roosevelt, Woodrow Wilson, Franklin Roosevelt, and Harry S Truman.

For example, only Congress may declare war.[12] But the President is made Commander in Chief of the Armed Forces.[13] And, acting as Commander in Chief, various Presidents have used the Armed Forces for military action abroad—*without a declaration of war*—on no fewer than 150 occasions in our history thus far.

Among the many other examples, the device of "executive agreements" is illustrative. Recent Presidents have made many such agreements instead of using the treaty-making process outlined in the Constitution.[14] *Executive agreements* are agreements made between the President and the head of a foreign state (or between their subordinates). Though they do not require Senate approval, the courts consider them to be as legally binding as are formal treaties.

---

[11] Article I, Section 8, Clause 3.
[12] Article I, Section 8, Clause 11.
[13] Article II, Section 2, Clause 1.
[14] Article II, Section 2, Clause 2.

In meetings with heads of state or their representatives, a President may make executive agreements which are binding on the nation. President Carter is shown with Teng Hsiao-ping, Vice Premier of China, during his visit to the White House.

COURT DECISIONS. The courts—and most importantly the Supreme Court—interpret and apply pertinent provisions of the Constitution to cases that come before them. We have already made reference to some instances of constitutional interpretation (that is, informal amendment) by the Supreme Court—most notably, *Marbury* v. *Madison,* 1803. We shall refer to many more elsewhere in the text. But, in short, the Court may be viewed, as Woodrow Wilson once put it, as a "constitutional convention in continuous session." Or, as the late Chief Justice Charles Evans Hughes said: "The Constitution means what the judges say it means."

In expanding the Constitution through judicial interpretation, the Supreme Court has leaned most heavily on the Necessary and Proper Clause, the Commerce Power, and the Taxing Power.

PARTY PRACTICES. Political parties have also contributed to the informal amendment process. Parties themselves have developed *extra-constitutionally.* Not only does the Constitution not even mention parties, but most of the Framers were opposed to their growth. In his Farewell Address in 1796 George Washington warned the people against "the baneful effects of the spirit of party."

Yet, in many ways today, government in the United States is government through party. For example, the Electoral College system for electing Presidents has become a "rubber stamp" for party action. The national convention system for selecting party candidates for the Presidency is not provided for in the Constitution; the device was originated by the parties. Both houses of Congress are organized and conduct much of their business on the basis of party. The President makes appointments to major federal offices with an eye to party politics.

CUSTOM. Unwritten custom may be as strong as written law. For example, on each of the eight occasions when Presidents have died in office, the Vice President then became President. Yet, the Constitution did not provide for this *until* the adoption of the 25th Amendment *in 1967.* Until then, the Constitution in fact provided only that *the powers and duties of the office* of President—but *not the office* itself—should be transferred to the Vice President.

The "no-third-term tradition" was broken twice by Franklin D. Roosevelt, who served as President for 12 years—from 1933 until his death in 1945.

It is a well-established custom for the Senate to reject a presidential appointment if it is opposed by a Senator of the majority party from the State where the appointee is to serve. This practice, known as *senatorial courtesy*, shifts a large share of the real power to appoint many federal officers from the President to individual members of the Senate.

The strength and importance of unwritten customs is well illustrated by the rare instance in which one of them was nullified. From the time George Washington refused a third term as President in 1796, there had existed the so-called "no-third-term tradition." In 1940, and again in 1944, Franklin D. Roosevelt broke with tradition, however, by seeking and winning a third, and then a fourth, term. As a result, the 22nd Amendment was added to the Constitution in 1951—and so what had been an unwritten custom became a part of the written law of the land.

SUMMARY

The Constitution of the United States is the nation's fundamental law. It contains the basic principles of our governmental system and sets forth the basic organization and procedures by which, and the limits within which, government in the United States must operate. The six basic principles are:

(1) Popular Sovereignty—that the people are the only source for *any* and *all* governmental authority.

(2) Limited Government—that government is not all-powerful, that it may do *only* what the *sovereign* (the people) permit it to do.

(3) Separation of Powers—that the legislative, executive, and judicial powers are separated among three independent and co-equal branches of government.

(4) Checks and Balances—that the three branches of government are tied together through a series of *checks* (restraints) that each may exercise against the others.

(5) Judicial Review—that the courts possess the power to review executive and legislative actions in the light of their constitutionality.

(6) Federalism—that the powers of government are distributed on a territorial basis between the National Government on the one hand and the States on the other.

The amendment process clearly demonstrates the federal nature of our governmental system—proposal being a *national* function and ratification a *State* matter. With two methods of proposal and two of ratification, there are four ways in which the Constitution may be formally amended. To date, however, only two of them have been used. Twenty-six formal amendments have been added to the Constitution since it was drawn up in 1787.

In addition to the formal amendments, the Constitution has been changed and has kept pace with the changing times by "informal amendment." The change and development has come about in five ways—by: (1) basic acts of Congress; (2) precedent-setting actions of various Presidents; (3) significant decisions of the Supreme Court; (4) political party practices; and (5) custom.

Concept Development

Questions for Review

1. What, in general terms, is the Constitution?

2. What are the six basic principles of the American constitutional system?

3. Why is the wording of the Preamble so important?

4. How do people delegate to governments in the United States the powers those governments possess?

5. What are the three great branches of the National Government, and what basic powers does each possess?

6. Why does each branch have powers with which it can restrain the others?

7. What is the power of judicial review? How does the Constitution make provision for it?

8. Why was a federal system a natural outgrowth of our earlier experiences?

9. Why did the Framers of the Constitution make specific provisions for constitutional amendment?

10. In what particular ways may the Constitution be amended formally? Which of these have actually been used?

11. How many formal amendments have been added to the Constitution?

12. How has the Constitution been changed and developed otherwise?

13. What are the five methods by which this change and development has been accomplished?

For Further Inquiry

1. Select a particular provision of the Constitution which illustrates one of the basic principles of our constitutional system (for example, the President's veto power which illustrates the principle of checks and balances). Why was the particular provision included in the Constitution? What arguments for and against its inclusion would you have made as a member of the Constitutional Convention?

2. Many view the Constitution as a sacred document that should not be changed. Thomas Jefferson, however, expressed the contrary view in these words:

Some men ascribe to the men of the preceding age a wisdom more than human, and suppose what they did to be beyond amendment. I knew that age [of the late 1700's] well. I belonged to it and labored with it. It deserved well of its country. It was very like the present, but without the experience of the present; and forty years of experience is worth a century of book reading; and this they would say themselves were they to arise from the dead.

Do you agree or disagree with Jefferson's viewpoint? Are these words more or less valid today than when they were written?

3. On several occasions Congress has refused to approve proposals which would permit constitutional amendments to be proposed by a simple majority in each house and ratified by a majority vote of the people at a national election. Do you think that Congress has acted wisely in this matter?

4. What prompted the proposal and ratification of each of the Constitution's 26 amendments?

5. In what particular terms, if any, do you feel the Constitution should be further amended?

6. What restrictions, if any, are there on the lengths to which the process of informal amendment may be carried?

7. The Constitution is often described as a "living document." What do you think is meant by that phrase?

Suggested Activities

1. Ask a prominent local attorney or judge to speak to the class on the place of the judiciary in the American system of government.

2. Prepare a large poster display illustrating: (a) the principles of separation of powers and checks and balances; and (b) the constitutional amendment process.

3. Write a report on the historical background of one of the 26 formal amendments.

4. From current newspapers and peri-

odicals make a bulletin board display of several examples of the informal amendment process in action.

5. Stage a debate or class forum on the following: (a) *Resolved,* That in today's world a unitary system of government is more practical than a federal system; (b) *Resolved,* That in today's world it is more practical for the basic powers of government to be concentrated in one supreme agency than to be divided among three distinct branches.

6. Compare the methods by which the Constitution of the United States may be amended with the amendment procedures prescribed in the constitution of your State.

Suggested Reading

Chase, Harold W., Holt, Robert T., and Turner, John E., *American Government in Comparative Perspective.* Franklin Watts, 1979.

Chistenson, Reo M., *American Politics: Understanding What Counts.* Harper & Row, 1980.

Corwin, Edward S. and Peltason, J. W., *Understanding the Constitution.* Holt, Rinehart and Winston, 8th ed., 1979.

Cushman, Robert F., *Cases in Constitutional Law.* Prentice-Hall, 5th ed., 1979.

Grimes, Alan P., *Democracy and the Amendments to the Constitution.* Heath, 1979.

Hillan, Ray C., *The Hands of Wise Men: Essays on the U.S. Constitution.* Brigham Young University Press, 1979.

King, Anthony (ed.), *The New American Political System.* American Enterprise Institute, 1979.

Lundberg, Ferdinand, *Cracks in the Constitution,* Lyle Stuart, 1980.

Pritchett, C. Herman, *The American Constitutional System.* McGraw-Hill, 5th ed., 1980.

Rembar, Charles, *The Law of the Land: The Evolution of Our Legal System.* Simon & Schuster, 1980.

The Nation
and the States:
Federalism

The Constitution, in all its provisions, looks to an indestructible Union, composed of indestructible States.

CHIEF JUSTICE SALMON P. CHASE
Texas v. White (1868)

■ Why does the United States have a federal rather than a unitary form of government?

■ Why can the concept of division of powers be termed, as well, a concept of shared powers?

■ What factors account for the marked growth in the scope of the powers and functions of the National Government?

■ Has there been a corresponding decline in the role of the States in the federal system?

The authors of the Constitution built their proposals for a new governmental system for the United States upon the concept of *federalism.* That is, they invented a governmental arrangement in which the powers of government were to be divided on a geographic basis—some of them to be held, on the one hand, by the new National Government and others by the already existing States.

The creation of a federal union under the Constitution was the result of both experience and logic. The Framers had to deal with a number of difficult and profoundly important problems at Philadelphia in the summer of 1787. Among the most significant, and complex, of them, was this: How were they to provide for a *strong, national* government, with power sufficient to meet the nation's needs and, at *the same time,* preserve the existing States?

Few, if any, of the Founding Fathers favored the creation of a strong centralized (*unitary*) government in the British pattern. They knew how stoutly the people had fought for the right of local self-government. Still, they knew that the governmental system provided by the Articles (a *confederation*) was largely impotent, too weak to manage the nation's difficulties.

Recall, too, that the authors of the Constitution were absolutely dedicated to the concept of limited government. They were convinced that: (1) the existence of *any* governmental power poses a threat to indi-

POPULATION OF THE UNITED STATES

Rank 1970	Rank 1980	State	Capital	Population 1970	Population 1980	Percent of Change
21	22	Alabama	Montgomery	3,444,354	3,890,061	+12.9%
50	50	Alaska	Juneau	302,583	400,481	+32.4
33	29	Arizona	Phoenix	1,775,399	2,717,866	+53.1
32	33	Arkansas	Little Rock	1,923,322	2,285,513	+18.8
1	1	California	Sacramento	19,975,069	23,668,562	+18.5
30	28	Colorado	Denver	2,209,596	2,888,834	+30.7
24	24	Connecticut	Hartford	3,032,217	3,107,576	+ 2.5
46	47	Delaware	Dover	548,104	595,225	+ 8.6
–	–	Dist. of Columbia		756,668	637,651	–15.7
9	7	Florida	Tallahassee	6,791,418	9,739,992	+43.3
15	13	Georgia	Atlanta	4,587,930	5,464,265	+19.1
40	39	Hawaii	Honolulu	769,913	965,000	+25.3
42	41	Idaho	Boise	713,015	943,935	+32.4
5	5	Illinois	Springfield	11,110,258	11,418,461	+ 2.8
11	12	Indiana	Indianapolis	5,195,392	5,490,179	+ 5.7
25	27	Iowa	Des Moines	2,825,368	2,913,387	+ 3.1
28	32	Kansas	Topeka	2,249,071	2,363,208	+ 5.1
23	23	Kentucky	Frankfort	3,220,711	3,661,433	+13.7
20	18	Louisiana	Baton Rouge	3,644,637	4,203,972	+15.3
38	38	Maine	Augusta	993,722	1,124,660	+13.2
18	19	Maryland	Annapolis	3,923,897	4,216,446	+ 7.5
10	11	Massachusetts	Boston	5,689,170	5,737,037	+ 0.8
7	8	Michigan	Lansing	8,881,826	9,258,344	+ 4.2
19	21	Minnesota	St. Paul	3,806,103	4,077,148	+ 7.1
29	31	Mississippi	Jackson	2,216,994	2,520,638	+13.7
13	15	Missouri	Jefferson City	4,677,623	4,917,444	+ 5.1
43	44	Montana	Helena	694,409	786,690	+13.3
35	35	Nebraska	Lincoln	1,485,333	1,570,006	+ 5.7
47	43	Nevada	Carson City	488,738	799,184	+63.5
41	42	New Hampshire	Concord	737,681	920,610	+24.8
8	9	New Jersey	Trenton	7,171,112	7,364,158	+ 2.7
37	37	New Mexico	Santa Fe	1,017,055	1,299,968	+27.8
2	2	New York	Albany	18,241,391	17,557,288	– 3.8
12	10	North Carolina	Raleigh	5,084,411	5,874,429	+15.5
45	46	North Dakota	Bismarck	617,792	652,695	+ 5.6
6	6	Ohio	Columbus	10,657,423	10,797,419	+ 1.3
27	26	Oklahoma	Oklahoma City	2,559,463	3,025,266	+18.2
31	30	Oregon	Salem	2,091,533	2,632,663	+25.9
3	4	Pennsylvania	Harrisburg	11,800,766	11,866,728	+ 0.6
39	40	Rhode Island	Providence	949,723	947,154	– 0.3
26	25	South Carolina	Columbia	2,590,713	3,119,208	+20.4
44	45	South Dakota	Pierre	662,257	690,178	+ 4.2
17	17	Tennessee	Nashville	3,926,018	4,590,750	+16.9
4	3	Texas	Austin	11,198,655	14,228,383	+27.1
36	36	Utah	Salt Lake City	1,059,273	1,461,037	+37.9
48	48	Vermont	Montpelier	444,732	511,456	+15.0
14	14	Virginia	Richmond	4,651,448	5,346,279	+14.9
22	20	Washington	Olympia	3,413,244	4,130,163	+21.0
34	34	West Virginia	Charleston	1,744,237	1,949,644	+11.8
16	16	Wisconsin	Madison	4,417,821	4,705,335	+ 6.5
49	49	Wyoming	Cheyenne	332,416	470,816	+41.6
		United States		203,302,031	226,504,825	+11.4%

Source: Census Bureau

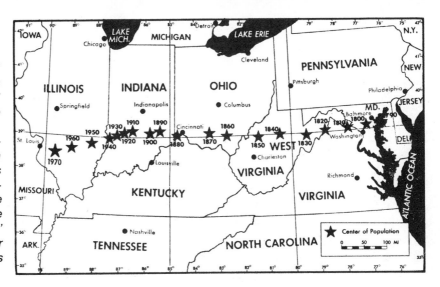

Using the symbol of a "star," this map shows the steady westward shift of the nation's "center of population" since 1790, when the first census was taken. The center of population is that point which may be considered as the center of population gravity in the United States. Where do you think the "star" will be located after the 1980 census has been tabulated?

vidual liberty, (2) the exercise of power must therefore be limited, and (3) to divide governmental power is to restrict it and thus prevent tyranny.

Federalism provided them with a solution to both the problem of establishing a strong *national* government and, at the same time, maintaining a *limited* government.

Federalism Defined. A federal system of government is one in which a constitution divides governmental powers on a territorial basis, between a central (or national) government and several regional (local) governments. Each level possesses and exercises its own distinct field of powers. Neither level of government, acting alone, can alter the basic division of powers the constitution makes between them. Each of the levels of government operates through its own agencies and exercises power directly upon individuals. In the United States, of course, the central government is the National Government and the regional governments are those of the 50 States.

In effect, federalism produces a dual system of government—two basic levels of government, each with its own separate sphere of authority.

Federalism's major strength lies in the fact that it permits *local* action in matters of primarily local concern and, at the same time, allows *national* action in matters of

wider concern. Local needs and desires may vary from one State to another, and federalism allows for this. Illustrations of the point are nearly limitless. Thus: Many forms of gambling are legal in Nevada but are outlawed in most of the other States. New Jersey provides free bus transportation for private as well as public school students but most other States do not. Nebraska has the only unicameral (one house) legislature among the 50 States. A third of the States regulate and operate the liquor business as a public monopoly, but in the others private enterprise holds sway.

While federalism permits and encourages local preferences in many matters, it also provides for the strength that comes from union.

National defense and foreign affairs furnish ready illustrations of the point, of course. But so, too, do domestic affairs. Take, for example, a natural disaster—such as severe flooding or prolonged drought—that occurs in a particular State. When a disaster strikes, the resources of the National Government and all of the States can be mobilized to aid the stricken area. Similarly, when a serious problem blankets the country—for example, high unemployment or some other serious economic difficulty—the resources of all of the Union are available to meet it.

The terms *federalism* and *democracy* are not synonymous. Remember, federalism

Federal Aviation Administration (FAA) personnel are on duty here at an air traffic control tower. This agency is one of many created by Congress to regulate interstate and foreign commerce.

involves a territorial division of the powers of government, while democracy involves the role of the people in the governing process. Still, it is virtually impossible to imagine a democratic system operating over any large area in which there is not also present a large degree of local self-government.

The Division of Powers

The Constitution sets out the basic design of the American federal system. At base, it provides for a *division of powers* between the National Government on the one hand and the States on the other. The division was intended (implied) in the provisions of the original Constitution and explicitly stated in the 10th Amendment:

> The powers not delegated to the United States by the Constitution nor prohibited by it to the States, are reserved to the States respectively, or to the people.

The table and chart on pages 81 and 85 present the division of powers in graphic form.

The National Government, One of Delegated Powers. The National Government is a government of *delegated powers.* That is, it possesses only those powers delegated (granted) to it in the Constitution. Constitutionally, there are three distinct types of delegated powers: the *expressed,* the *implied,* and the *inherent* powers.

THE EXPRESSED POWERS. The expressed powers are those delegated to the National Government in so many words—literally, expressly—in the Constitution. Most of them are to be found in Article I, Section 8. There, in 18 separate clauses, 27 different powers are expressly vested in Congress. They include, for example, the power to lay and collect taxes, to coin money, to regulate foreign and interstate commerce, to raise and maintain armed forces, to declare war, fix standards of weights and measures, grant patents and copyrights, and several others.

But notice that many of the expressed powers are to be found elsewhere in the Constitution. For example, Article II, Section 2 gives the President several powers, including the power to act as commander-in-chief of the armed forces, to grant reprieves and pardons, to make treaties, and to appoint major federal officeholders. Article III grants "the judicial power of the United States" to the Supreme Court and to the other courts in the federal judiciary. And, several expressed powers are to be found in various of the amendments to the Constitution—for example, the 16th Amendment gives to Congress the power to levy an income tax.

THE IMPLIED POWERS. The implied powers are those which are not expressly stated in the Constitution but which may be *reasonably* implied from those which are.

The constitutional basis for the existence of the implied powers is to be found among the expressed powers. Article I, Section 8, Clause 18 gives to Congress the "necessary and proper" power. The provision reads:

THE DIVISION OF POWERS IN THE AMERICAN FEDERAL SYSTEM

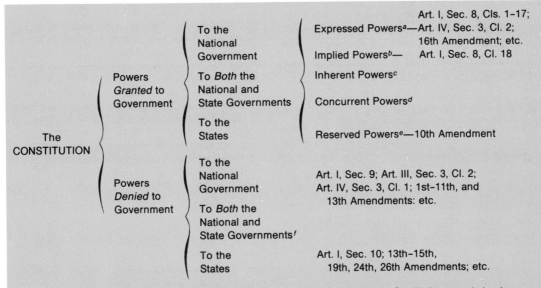

a Those powers *expressly* (explicitly) granted to the National Government in the Constitution—*e.g.*, to tax, to regulate foreign and interstate commerce.

b Those powers which may be reasonably implied from the expressed powers—*e.g.*, to aid States in highway construction, declare certain defined actions to be federal crimes, regulate labor-management relations.

c Those powers, although not explicitly granted, which are possessed by virtue of the fact that the National Government is the *national* government of a sovereign state—*e.g.*, the power to regulate immigration.

d Those powers which may be exercised by *both* National and State Governments. Some powers of the National Government are of such nature as to be "exclusive powers"—*e.g.*, to declare war.

e Those powers not granted to the National Government and not denied to the States by the Constitution—*e.g.*, to create local government and to provide public schools.

f E.g., to pass *ex post facto* laws or bills of attainder (Art. I, Secs. 9 and 10) or deprive any persons of life, liberty, or property without due process (5th and 14th Amendments). The National Government is denied power by: (1) several expressed prohibitions in the Constitution; (2) the Constitution's silence on many subjects; (3) the fact that the exercise of certain powers (*e.g.*, taxing governmental functions of the States) could endanger the federal system itself. The States are denied powers by: (1) several expressed prohibitions in the Constitution; (2) many provisions in their own constitutions; (3) the fact that the exercise of certain powers (*e.g.*, taxing the National Government) could endanger the federal system itself.

Congress shall have power . . . to make all laws which shall be necessary and proper for carrying into execution the foregoing powers, and all other powers vested by this Constitution in the Government of the United States, or in any department or officer thereof.

Through congressional and court interpretation, the words "necessary and proper" have come to mean, in effect, "convenient and expedient." Indeed, the Necessary and Proper Clause is sometimes called the "Elastic Clause."

To cite but a few of the literally thousands of illustrations of the exercise of the doctrine of implied powers, note the following examples: Congress has provided for the regulation of labor-management relations, the building of hydro-electric power dams, and the making of river and harbor improvements. It has provided for the punishment as a federal crime the transportation of stolen goods, gambling information, or kidnapped persons across State lines. And, Congress has prohibited racial discrimination in access to such public accommodations as restaurants, theaters, and hotels. All of these actions, and a great many more, have been reasonably implied from but *one* of the expressed pow-

Case Study

The constitutional validity of the concept of implied powers was first tested in the Supreme Court in the landmark case *McCulloch* v. *Maryland*, 1819. The State of Maryland, defending its view of the federal division of powers, had challenged the constitutionality of the creation by Congress of the Bank of the United States. The Court unanimously upheld the establishment of the Bank as a necessary and proper means for carrying into execution such expressed powers as those to tax, to borrow, and to coin money and regulate its value. Declared Chief Justice John Marshall:

> We admit, as all must admit, that the powers of the government are limited, and that its limits are not to be transcended. But we think the sound construction of the Constitution must allow to the national legislature that discretion, with respect to the means by which the powers it confers are to be carried into execution, which will enable that body to perform the high duties assigned to it, in the manner most beneficial to the people. Let the end be legitimate, let it be within the scope of the Constitution, and all means which are appropriate, which are plainly adapted to the end, which are not prohibited, but consist with the letter and spirit of the Constitution, are constitutional.

■ Why do you think the Supreme Court provided so broad and sweeping a definition to the powers of Congress? Should the Court have done so?

---

ers—the power to regulate interstate commerce.[1]

THE INHERENT POWERS. The inherent powers are those which belong to the National Government by *virtue of its existence* as the national government of a sovereign state in the world community. Although they are not expressly set out in the Constitution, they are powers which national governments have historically possessed. It is only logical to assume that the Framers intended that these powers would belong to and be exercised by the National Government. The inherent powers are few in number. The chief ones include: the powers to regulate immigration, deport aliens, acquire territory, extend diplomatic recognition, and protect the nation against rebellion or internal subversion.

It is possible to *imply* the existence of most of the inherent powers from one or more of the expressed powers. Thus, for example, the power to regulate immigra-

tion can be rather readily implied from the expressed power to regulate foreign commerce. Or, the power to acquire territory may be implied from the treaty-making and war powers. But the doctrine of inherent powers holds that it is not necessary to go to those lengths to establish these powers. In short, they exist because the United States exists.

Powers Denied to the National Government. While the Constitution *delegates* certain powers to the National Government, it also *denies* certain powers to it. It does so in three ways.

First, some powers are denied to the National Government *in so many words* in the Constitution.[2] Among them are the power to levy duties on exports, to deny freedom of religion, speech, press, or assembly, to conduct illegal searches or seizures, to deny one accused of crime a speedy and public trial, and to inflict cruel and unusual punishments.

---

[1] Article I, Section 8, Clause 3. We shall return to the doctrine of implied powers in greater detail in Chapter 14, "The Powers of Congress."

[2] *Most* of these expressed denials of power are found in Article I, Section 9 and in the 1st through the 8th Amendments.

When a national disaster strikes, the Government stands ready to aid the stricken area. Here U.S. Army equipment and personnel help to clear a snow-clogged highway after a huge winter storm had crippled much of the Northeast.

Secondly, some powers are denied to the National Government because of the Constitution's *silence* concerning them. Remember, the National Government is *a government of delegated powers;* it has *only* those powers delegated to it by the Constitution. Many powers are *not* granted to the National Government. Among them are such powers as those to create a public school system for the nation, to enact a uniform marriage and divorce law, or to establish units of local government. The Constitution says nothing about these matters. It does not give to the National Government power to do any of these things—expressly, implicitly, or inherently. And that silence effectively denies them to the National Government.

Thirdly, some powers are denied to the National Government because of the nature of the federal system. That is, the National Government cannot be permitted to do those things which would threaten the existence of the federal system. For example, in the exercise of its power to tax it cannot tax any of the States (or their local units) in the performance of their governmental functions. If it could, it could conceivably destroy (tax out of existence) one or more, or all, of the States.[3]

The States, Governments of Reserved Powers. The Constitution *reserves* certain powers to the States. The *reserved powers* are the powers held by the States in the federal system. They are those powers which are not granted to the National Government and which are not at the same time denied to the States. Read again the words of the 10th Amendment.

Thus, Alabama (or any other State) may forbid persons under 18 to marry without parental consent or those under 19 to buy liquor. It may restrict, or even prohibit, the carrying of handguns. It may re-

---

[3] But note that when a State (or one of its local units) is engaged in the performance of a so-called *nongovernmental* function—*e.g.,* operating liquor stores, a bus system, a farmer's market, and so forth—it is liable to taxation by the National Government; see pages 446, 770.

Case Study

The 26th Amendment to the Constitution, ratified in 1971, declares:

> The right of citizens of the United States, who are 18 years of age or older, to vote shall not be denied or abridged by the United States or by any State on account of age.

In enacting the Voting Rights Act Amendments of 1970 Congress had provided for 18 as the minimum age for voting in all elections held in the United States—national, State, and local. In *Oregon* v. *Mitchell*, 1970, however, the Supreme Court held that although Congress could set a minimum age for voting in *national* elections, it lacked the constitutional power to do so for State and local elections.

In response to the Court's decision, Congress promptly proposed, and the States speedily ratified, the 18-year-old Vote Amendment.

■ Do you think that the adoption of the 26th Amendment was a wise move? Why? Do you think it would have been better to leave the determination of the minimum voting age to the individual States? Why?

quire that doctors, lawyers, plumbers, and hairdressers be licensed in order to practice in the State. It may charter and regulate corporations doing business in the State. It may establish public school systems and units of local government. It may set the conditions under which divorces may be granted, and permit certain forms of gambling and prohibit others.

The sphere of State powers is vast, indeed. Alabama can do all of those things we have just suggested, and much more, because there is nothing in the Constitution to prohibit it from doing so. The National Government cannot do these things because the Constitution does not delegate to it the power to do so. The power to do these things has been *reserved* to the States.

Powers Denied to the States. Just as the Constitution denies certain powers to the National Government it also prohibits the States from doing certain things. Some powers are denied to the States in *so many words* in the Constitution.[4] For example, no State may enter into any treaty, alliance, or confederation. No state may coin or print money, make any law impairing the obli-

gations of a contract, or grant titles of nobility. Nor may a State deprive any person of life, liberty, or property without due process of law.

Some powers are also denied to the States because of the existence of the federal system. Thus, no State (or local government) may tax any of the agencies or functions of the National Government. Note, too, that each of the States has its own constitution and that document contains many denials of power to the State.[5]

The Exclusive Powers. The exclusive powers are those which, in the federal system, may be exercised *only* by the National Government. They include most, but not all, of the delegated (expressed, implied, and inherent) powers of the National Government.

Some of the powers delegated to the National Government are expressly denied to the States. For example, the powers to coin money, make treaties, and levy import duties are expressly granted to the Na-

---

[4] Most of these expressed prohibitions of power to the States are found in Article I, Section 10, and in the 13th, 14th, 15th, 19th, 24th, and 26th Amendments.

[5] Examine your own State's constitution on this point—and note, then, the significance of the words "or to the people" in the 10th Amendment. If a copy of the State constitution is not available locally, one can be obtained from the office of the Secretary of State in the State capital. We treat State constitutions in some detail in Chapter 28.

THE DIVISION OF POWERS BETWEEN THE NATIONAL GOVERNMENT AND THE STATES

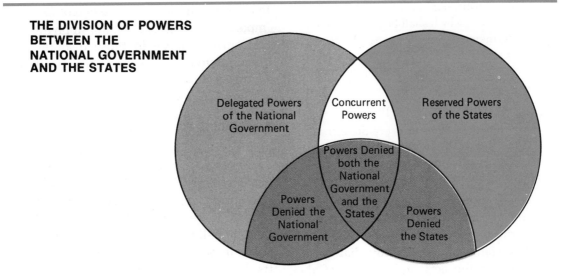

tional Government, and they are expressly denied to the States. Thus, these powers belong exclusively to—are *exclusive powers* of—the National Government.

Some of the powers which are delegated to the National Government but which are *not expressly* denied to the States are also among the exclusive powers of the National Government. This is so because of the nature of the particular powers involved. For example, the States are not expressly denied the power to regulate interstate commerce; but, if they were to be permitted to do so, chaos would result.[6]

The Concurrent Powers. The concurrent powers are those which belong to and are exercised by both the National Government *and* the States. They include, for example, the power to lay and collect taxes, to define crimes and provide for their punishment, and to condemn private property for public use. The concurrent powers are

not held and exercised *jointly* by the two basic levels of government in the federal system, but, rather, *separately* and *simultaneously.*

To put the description of concurrent powers another way: The States may exercise concurrently with the National Government any power which is not exclusively granted to the latter by the Constitution and not, at the same time, denied by it to the States.

The Supreme Law of the Land

The division of powers between the National Government and the States is a quite complicated matter, as we have seen. It produces what has been described as a "dual system of government." That is, it produces a system in which two basic levels of government operate over the same territory and the same people at one and the same time.

In such an arrangement there are bound to be conflicts between the two levels, conflicts between national law on the one hand and State law on the other. Anticipating this, the Framers wrote the Supremacy Clause into the Constitution. Article VI, Section 2 provides:

---

[6] The States may not regulate interstate commerce as such. But in the exercise of their various powers they inevitably *affect* it. For example, in regulating highway speeds, the States regulate vehicles operating not only within the State (that is, in *intrastate* commerce) but also those operating from State to State, as well. Generally, States may *affect* interstate commerce, but may not impose an unreasonable burden upon it.

This Constitution, and the laws of the United States which shall be made in pursuance thereof, and all treaties made or which shall be made under the authority of the United States, shall be the supreme law of the land; . . .

And, significantly, the provision adds:

. . . and the judges in every State shall be bound thereby, anything in the constitution or laws of any State to the contrary notwithstanding.

This section, then, makes the Constitution and the acts and treaties of the United States the highest forms of law. The Constitution stands above all; immediately beneath it are the acts and treaties of the United States.[7]

No form of State law may conflict with *any* form of national law. As an illustration, when Oregon entered the Union in 1859, its constitution prohibited voting by any person of Chinese descent. In 1870, the 15th Amendment was added to the United States Constitution, prohibiting any of the States the power to deny to any person the right to vote on account of either race or color. Thus, the provision in the Oregon constitution ceased to be effective in 1870.

In effect, the Supremacy Clause creates a "ladder of laws" in the United States. The Constitution occupies the topmost rung. Immediately beneath it stand acts of Congress and treaties of the United States. Each State's constitution—supreme over all other forms of *a State's law*—stands beneath *all* forms of federal law. At the base of the ladder are those other forms of State law, such as statutes, city and county charters and ordinances, and so forth.

The Supreme Court as the Umpire in the Federal System. The Supreme Court has often been called the "umpire" in the

federal system. It is because one of its most important functions is that of applying the Supremacy Clause to those disputes our "dual system of government" inevitably produces.

The Court was first called upon to play its role as umpire—to settle a clash between a national law and a State law—in a landmark case in 1819. The case, *McCulloch v. Maryland,* involved the controversial Second Bank of the United States.[8] The Bank had been established (chartered) by act of Congress in 1816. In 1818 the Maryland legislature, hoping to cripple the Bank, imposed a tax on all notes issued by its Baltimore branch. McCulloch, the branch cashier, refused to pay the tax and was convicted in the State courts for his refusal.

The Supreme Court unanimously reversed the Maryland courts, however. Speaking for the Court, Chief Justice John Marshall based his opinion squarely on the Supremacy Clause: "If any one proposition could command the universal assent of mankind," he wrote, "we might expect that it would be this—that the government of the Union, though limited in its powers, is supreme within its sphere of action." Hence, no State possesses any power "to retard, impede, burden, or in any manner control, the operations of the constitutional laws enacted by Congress."

It is impossible to overstate the historical, and the continuing, significance of the Court's function as the umpire of the federal system. Had the Court not assumed the role it is altogether likely that the federal system—and probably the United States itself—could not have survived its early years. Justice Oliver Wendell Holmes once made this point in these words:

---

[7] Acts of Congress and treaties stand on an equal plane with one another and beneath the Constitution. Neither may conflict with any provision in the Constitution. In case of conflict between the provisions of an act and those of a treaty, the more recently adopted takes precedence—as the latest expression of the popular will.

[8] The case is also critically important in the development of our constitutional system because, in deciding it, the Court for the first time upheld the doctrine of implied powers (see pages 80–82, 343–345). It also held the National Government immune from any form of State taxation (see pages 345, 770). We shall return to the case at some length in Chapter 14, "The Powers of Congress."

I do not think the United States would come to an end if we [the Court] lost our power to declare an Act of Congress void. I do think the Union would be imperiled if we could not make that declaration as to the laws of the several States.[9]

The National Government's Obligations to the States

The Constitution imposes several obligations upon the National Government for the benefit of the States. Most of them are to be found in Article IV.

Guarantee of a Republican Form of Government. The National Government is required to "guarantee to every State in this Union a republican form of government."[10] The Constitution does not define the phrase "a republican form of government," and the Supreme Court has regularly refused to do so. It is, nevertheless, generally understood to mean a "representative democracy."

The Supreme Court has held that the question of whether or not a State has a republican form of government is a *political question*. That is, it is a question to be decided not by the courts but by the political branches of the government—the President and Congress.

The leading case here is *Luther* v. *Borden,* 1849. It grew out of an incident known to history as Dorr's Rebellion—a revolt led by Thomas W. Dorr against the State of Rhode Island in 1841–1842. Dorr and his

Under the strong leadership of John Marshall, Chief Justice of the United States from 1801 to 1835, the Supreme Court established itself as a potent institution in the American governmental system.

followers proclaimed a new constitution for the State and named Dorr the governor. When he attempted to put his new government into operation, however, the governor in office under the original constitution declared martial law and promptly appealed to President John Tyler for assistance. When the President took steps to put down the revolt, it collapsed.

The question of which of the two competing governments was the legitimate one at the time was a central issue in *Luther* v. *Borden.* Again, the Supreme Court refused to decide the matter—holding it to be a political question.

The only extensive use ever made of the guarantee of a republican form of government came in the period immediately following the Civil War. During the Reconstruction Period, Congress declared that several of the Southern States did not have governments of a republican form. It

9 *Collected Legal Papers.* Harcourt, 1920, pages 295–96. The Supreme Court first found a State law to be unconstitutional in a case from Georgia, *Fletcher* v. *Peck,* 1810. The case involved the Contract Clause. The Court held that an act of the Georgia legislature in which a grant of land had been made was a valid contract between Georgia and the grantee. It held that the legislature's later attempt to rescind the contract was an unconstitutional violation of Article I, Section 10, Clause 1's command that "No State shall . . . pass any . . . law impairing the obligation of contracts." Since then the Court has found more than 900 State statutes unconstitutional—while upholding the constitutionality of thousands of others.

10 Article IV, Section 4.

refused to admit Senators and Representatives chosen in those States until they had ratified the 13th, 14th, and 15th Amendments and had broadened their laws to recognize the voting and other rights of blacks.

Protection Against Invasion and Domestic Violence. The National Government also is required to ". . . protect each of them against invasion; and on application of the legislature, or of the executive (when the legislature cannot be convened), against domestic violence."[11]

FOREIGN INVASION. It is clear beyond any question today that an invasion of any one of the 50 States would be met as an attack upon the United States itself. But, recall, that was *not* the case in 1787. Then it was far from certain that all 13 States would stand together if one of them were attacked by a foreign power. So, before the original States agreed to relinquish their war-making powers, each of them insisted upon an iron-clad pledge that an attack upon any one of them would be met as an attack upon all.

DOMESTIC VIOLENCE. The federal system assumes that each of the 50 States will maintain the peace within its own borders. Thus, the primary responsibility for curbing insurrection, riot, and other internal disorder rests upon the individual States. However, the Constitution does recognize the possibility that, on occasion, a State may find itself unable to control a particular situation. Hence, the Constitution's guarantee of protection against domestic violence in each of them.

Historically, the use of federal force to restore order within a State has been a rare event. The most recent uses occurred more than a decade ago. When racial unrest exploded into violence in Detroit in the midst of the "long, hot summer" of 1967, President Johnson ordered units of the Regular Army into the city. He acted at the request of Michigan's Governor George Romney, and only after Detroit's police and firefighters, supported by State Police and National Guard units, found themselves unable to cope with widespread rioting, arson, looting, and other pillage in the city's ghetto areas. In 1968, again at the request of the governors involved, President Johnson sent federal troops into Chicago and Baltimore. They were sent to help State and local forces quell the violence that erupted in those cities following the assassination of Dr. Martin Luther King, Jr.

Normally, a President has sent troops into a State only in response to a request from its governor (or legislature). But when national laws are being violated, or national functions interfered with, or national property endangered, a President need not wait for such a request.[12]

The ravages of nature, such as hurricanes, tornadoes, and floods, can be far more destructive than the violence of humans. Here, too, acting to protect the States against "domestic violence," the Government stands ready to, and regularly does, come to the aid of stricken areas.

Respect for Territorial Integrity. The National Government is constitutionally bound to respect the territorial integrity— the legal existence and physical boundaries—of each of the States. Several provisions of the Constitution impose this obligation. Thus, Congress, must include, in both of its houses, members chosen in

---

[11] Article IV, Section 4.

[12] President Cleveland sent federal troops to restore order in the Chicago railyards during the Pullman Strike of 1894, *acting over the express objections* of Governor Altgeld of Illinois. The Supreme Court upheld his action (*In re Debs*, 1896) because rioters had threatened federal property and impeded the mails and interstate commerce. Several Presidents since have acted without a request. Most recently, Mr. Eisenhower did so at Little Rock in 1957, and Mr. Kennedy at the University of Mississippi in 1962 and again at the University of Alabama in 1963, to halt the unlawful obstruction of school integration orders issued by federal courts.

each one of the States.[13] And Congress, acting alone, cannot create a new State from territory belonging to one of the existing States. To do so, it first must have the consent of the legislature of the State involved.[14] And, recall, Article V provides that no State may be deprived of its equal representation in the Senate without its own consent.

Federal-State Cooperation

The concept of a division of powers on a territorial basis is the primary and distinctive characteristic of any government which is federal in form. And we have just examined the basic features of the division of powers between the National Government and the States in the American federal system.

Again, the division of powers in the American federal system is a very complicated matter. As we noted a moment ago, it involves a *dual* system of government. Two basic levels of government operate over the same territory and the same people at one and the same time. Given this complex arrangement, it should come as no surprise that competition, tensions, and even conflicts have been, and are, an ongoing feature of American federalism.

The federal system also produces what is often described as "a checkerboard of governments" in this country. An almost bewildering variety of governmental units, many of them with overlapping and sometimes conflicting powers and functions, blankets the nation. According to the most recent Census Bureau count, there are now nearly 80,000 units of government in the United States. That total includes the one National Government and the 50 State governments, of course. Beyond those basic units, it also includes 3042 counties,

over 18,800 municipalities (cities, towns, villages, and boroughs), and nearly 17,000 townships. An then, too, there are more than 15,000 school districts and some 26,000 special districts (which provide fire protection, water supply, sewage treatment, and a host of other public services, usually in suburban and rural areas).

Each of these local units of government is located *within* one of the 50 States; none of them has an existence apart from its parent State. That is, each of them is a creature—a sub-part—of its State. To put the point another way, the two basic levels in the federal system are the nation and the 50 States; all of the local units exist as subordinate parts of their respective States.

We shall consider the very important and necessary place of these thousands of local governments later, and in considerable detail, in Chapter 32. But, for now, notice this vital point: The concept of a *division* of powers in the federal arrangement can also be described, quite accurately, as one of *shared* powers, as well. That is, in addition to the two *separate* spheres of power held and exercised by the two basic levels of government in this country, there are large, and constantly growing, areas of *cooperation* between them.

Federal Grants-In-Aid. Perhaps the best known example of this cooperation is the system of federal grants-in-aid to the States (and to their cities and other local units, as well).

Federal aid to the States dates back to the Northwest Ordinance of 1785. In that statute, the Congress under the Articles directed that certain lands in the Northwest Territory be set aside for the support of public schools.

Currently, Congress appropriates some $88 billion a year for grants to States and locales, to support dozens of different programs. Most of this funding goes to the States or their local units on a *categorical* basis—that is, for particular purposes. These monies are targeted for such pur-

---

[13] In the House: Article I, Section 2, Clause 1; in the Senate: Article I, Section 3, Clause 1.
[14] Article IV, Section 3, Clause 1.

poses as highway construction and maintenance, aid to dependent children, aid to education, school lunch programs, law enforcement, mass transit facilities, urban renewal and slum clearance, unemployment insurance, on-the-job training programs, and for many, many other things.

The constitutional basis for the grant-in-aid approach is found in the taxing power. Article I, Section 8, Clause 1 gives to Congress the power to tax in order

> . . . to pay the debts, and provide for the common defense and general welfare, of the United States.

In providing for the grants, Congress normally attaches conditions which the States must meet in accepting them. These usually require a State to: (1) use the grant only for the purpose specified; (2) make a matching appropriation (ordinarily an amount equal to that provided in federal funds, but occasionally much less); (3) create a suitable agency to administer the program; and (4) meet certain standards set for the project for which the aid is furnished.

GRANTS-IN-AID: PRO AND CON. Some people object to the grants-in-aid system because, they insist, it forces States to undertake programs for which many of them have neither the desire nor money. In theory, each State is free to accept or reject the federal funds; in practice, however, and even with the "strings" attached, they prove politically irresistible.

Another ground for criticism is that the arrangement enables the National Government to participate in activities in which it would otherwise have no constitutional authority—for example, public education, urban renewal, and mental health programs. Critics also contend that, because the funds come from those who pay federal taxes, the residents of the wealthier States bear an unjust burden.

Supporters of the system insist that grants-in-aid have encouraged the States to undertake worthwhile activities they would not have otherwise performed. They argue that minimum standards are necessary to insure proper use of funds and success for programs. They also add that what benefits one State or section of the nation, in effect, benefits all.

Whatever the merit of the arguments, it is clear that the grants-in-aid device *does* extend federal authority into areas from which the Constitution otherwise excludes it. But notice in this connection that the grants-in-aid arrangement is in fact simply an aspect of the doctrine of implied powers. (See page 80.)

Revenue Sharing. The federal revenue sharing program is a newer and entirely separate feature of cooperative federalism. It is an arrangement through which Congress gives to the States, and especially to their local governments, an annual share of the national government's huge tax-take.

Congress first provided for the revenue sharing program in the State and Local Fiscal Assistance Act of 1972. That law has now been revised and extended—twice in 1976 and most recently in 1980.

Thus far, from 1972 through 1980, the revenue sharing program has funneled more than $20 billion to the States. And, over that same period, it has produced nearly $42 billion for their local governments.

In the current (1980) law, Congress provided no revenue sharing funds for the States for 1981. However, they will get some $2.3 billion in 1982 and a like amount in 1983. Their local units are scheduled to receive approximately $4.6 billion in each of those three fiscal years.

The specific amount given to each State each year is determined by a rather complex formula; at base, it is pegged to the total amount of federal income taxes collected in that State during the previous year.

The revenue sharing and the grants-in-aid programs are strikingly different. Most importantly: (1) no State or local matching funds are involved in the revenue sharing program. And (2) the revenue sharing monies are provided with virtually no strings attached. Congress has placed only one major restriction on the use of revenue sharing funds. That it cannot be spent for any function in which discrimination on any of these bases is practiced: race, color, sex, age, national origin, religious belief, or physical disabilities.

Revenue sharing serves three broad purposes: *First,* It attempts to relieve the chronic, steadily worsening fiscal woes of the States and their local governments. *Second,* it seeks to shift power—in the form of control over spending decisions—from the national level to the State and local arena. And *third,* it works to lessen the burden borne by those least able to pay for the support of State and local activities. It does this by reducing the need to rely on generally more regressive State and local tax sources, notably the property tax (thus shifting a greater portion of the tax load to the more progressive federal income tax).

Revenue sharing has proved to be both a fairly successful and a popular device. Quite understandably, it is strongly supported by most governors, mayors, and other State and local officials. It does have its critics, however. Many opponents argue that it is a "Trojan horse." That is, they claim that while it appears to return power to the local level, it actually *increases* local dependence on Washington for federal assistance. Some critics also argue that, as the Federal Government is putting up the monies involved, it should retain a larger measure of control over their spending. They insist that Congress should target specific State and local problems—as in the grant-in-aid programs—and so insure more effective use of the funds.

Other Forms of Federal Aid. The National Government furnishes aid to the States in a number of other ways. Thus, it shares with them the revenues it receives from certain activities. For example, it shares revenue from the sale of timber from national forest lands, mineral leases on public lands, migratory bird hunting licenses, and leases of power sites on federal lands. It also makes some direct payments to local governments in areas where there are large federal land-holdings. The payments are made *in lieu of* (in place of) the property taxes the local governments cannot collect. (These allocations are often referred to as "lulu payments.")

There are many other ways in which the National Government renders aid to the States. For example, the FBI assists State and local police in criminal law enforcement. The Census Bureau makes its studies available to State and local school systems to help them plan for the future. The Army and Air Force equip and train each State's National Guard units. Congress has prohibited, as federal crimes, the

Alaska's oil-rich North Slope is public land, and large sums are paid for mineral leases there. This revenue is shared with the State.

movement of certain persons (such as escaped prisoners) and goods (such as those stolen) across State lines. A listing of this sort may be carried on and on; numerous other illustrations appear throughout the remainder of this book.

State Aid to the National Government. Federal-State cooperation is distinctly a two-way street. The States and their local units also aid the National Government in a variety of ways. For example, national elections are conducted in each State by State and local election officials. They are financed by State and local funds, and are regulated to a very great extent by State laws.

Among many other illustrations of the point: The legal process by which aliens become citizens of the United States (naturalization) is conducted in large part through the State courts, rather than in the federal courts. Fugitives from federal justice are often apprehended by State and local police. Federal prisoners are regularly lodged in local jails while awaiting trial in federal courts and, if convicted, while awaiting transportation to federal penitentiaries.

Again, we shall encounter many other instances of intergovernmental cooperation as we continue our examination of the American governmental system.

Interstate Relations

The rivalries, jealousies, and disputes among the States under the Articles of Confederation furnished a major reason for the drafting of the Constitution in 1787. The fact that the new Constitution strengthened the hand of the National Government—especially in the field of commerce—eliminated many of those interstate frictions. The States were restrained even more closely by several constitutional provisions dealing directly with the matter of interstate relationships.

States Legally Separate. Each State is legally separate from every other State in the Union. When the States are acting within the sphere of their reserved powers, they stand toward one another as independent and wholly separate. Put the other way around, each State has no jurisdiction outside the limits of its own boundaries.[15]

Obviously, however, the States must have dealings with one another. These interstate relationships are covered by the Constitution in several important respects.

Interstate Compacts. As we have seen, no State may enter into any treaty, alliance, or confederation. The States may, with the consent of Congress, enter into *compacts* or agreements among themselves and with foreign states, however.[16]

Little use was made of interstate compacts until relatively recently. In fact, to 1900 Congress had approved only 19 of them, and they were very largely directed to common boundary problems. In this century, however, and particularly since the mid-1930's, their use has increased considerably. New Jersey and New York led the way in 1921 when, by compact, they created the Port of New York Authority to manage and develop the harbor facilities of that great metropolis.

---

[15] This statement must be qualified slightly. Various States now cooperate with one another in some common programs, usually through interstate compacts. For example, several States now have "hot-pursuit agreements" with neighboring States. These States permit police officers from an adjoining State to pursue a lawbreaker across the State line. When a fugitive is captured in such circumstances, however, that person must be turned over to local authorities. In effect, the "hot-pursuit agreements" make a police officer of one State temporarily an officer of another State.

[16] Article I, Section 10, Clause 3. The Supreme Court has held that congressional consent need not be obtained for compacts which do not "tend to increase the political power of the States," *Virginia* v. *Tennessee*, 1893. But it is often difficult to determine whether a particular agreement is "political" or "nonpolitical" in nature. Hence, most interstate agreements are submitted to Congress as a matter of course. Increasingly in recent years, Congress has given consent to the making of compacts in certain areas *in advance* of the actual concluding of the agreements—among them, compacts providing for cooperation in such fields as forest fire prevention, nuclear research, and higher education.

The huge New York Port Authority Bus Terminal serves tens of thousands of commuters who travel between New York and New Jersey each day.

Nearly 200 compacts are in force today, and many of them involve several States. In fact, all 50 States have now joined in two of these agreements: the Interstate Compact for the Supervision of Parollees and Probationers and the Interstate Compact on Juveniles. Other pacts, many with multi-State membership, cover a widening range of topics. Several deal with the development and conservation of such natural resources as fish, wildlife, water, coal, or oil and with regional cooperation in higher education or forest fire protection. Still others involve motor vehicle safety, the licensing of drivers, stream and harbor pollution, and the coordination of civil defense programs.

Most compacts deal with the common use of natural resources. The Colorado River (Hoover Dam) Compact of 1928 involved the States of the Colorado River Basin. It was the first great attempt to bring several of the States together for the development, control, and management of a regional river.

Full Faith and Credit. The Constitution requires each State to give "full faith and credit . . . to the public acts, records, and judicial proceedings of every other State."[17] The phrase "public acts" refers to the laws of a State; "records" to such documentary materials as birth certificates, marriage licenses, car registrations, and the like; and "judicial proceedings" to the outcome of court actions: judgments for debt, criminal convictions, divorce decrees, and the like.

Suppose that a person dies in Baltimore and leaves a will disposing of property in Chicago. With regard to that property Illinois must give *full faith and credit* (respect the validity of) the *probating* (proving) of that will as a judicial proceeding of the State of Maryland. One may prove age, marital status, title to property, or similar facts by securing the necessary document or documents from the State where the record was made.

EXCEPTIONS. The Full Faith and Credit Clause is regularly observed and usually operates in a routine manner between and among the States. Two exceptions to the rule must be noted, however. *First,* it applies only to *civil* matters; that is, one State will not (cannot) enforce another State's criminal law. *Second,* full faith and credit need not be given to certain divorces granted by one State to residents of another State.

On the second exception, the key question is always this: Was the person who obtained the divorce in fact a resident of the State which granted it? If so, the divorce will be accorded full faith and credit in other States. If not, then the State granting the divorce did not have the authority to do so and another State may refuse to recognize its validity.

This whole matter of interstate (or

---

[17] Article IV, Section 1.

"quickie") divorces has been a most troublesome one for years. It has been especially so since the Supreme Court's decision in *Williams* v. *North Carolina,* 1945. In that case, a couple had traveled from North Carolina to Nevada, each to obtain a divorce in order to marry one another. After residing in Las Vegas for 6 weeks (the minimum period Nevada required in its divorce law), they obtained their divorces. They immediately married and then returned to North Carolina as husband and wife.

North Carolina authorities refused to recognize the validity of the Nevada divorces and the Williamses were each tried and convicted of the crime of bigamous cohabitation.

On appeal, the Supreme Court upheld North Carolina's denial of full faith and credit to the Nevada divorces. It held that the couple had not established *bona fide* (good faith, valid) residence in Nevada. It held that they were, in fact and throughout the incident, legal residents of North Carolina. In short, the Court found that Nevada lacked the authority to grant the divorces involved here.

A divorce granted by a State court to a *bona fide* resident of that State must be given full faith and credit in all other States. But to become a legal resident of a State a person must intend to reside there permanently, or at least indefinitely. Clearly, the Williamses had not intended to do so.

The *Williams* case, and several since, cast dark and continuing clouds of doubt over the validity of thousands of interstate divorces. The later marriages of persons involved in such divorces and/or the frequently tangled estate problems produced by their deaths suggest the confused and serious nature of this matter.

Extradition. The Constitution provides:

A person charged in any State with treason, felony, or other crime, who shall flee from justice, and be found in another State, shall, on demand of the executive authority of the State from which he fled, be delivered up, to be removed to the State having jurisdiction of the crime.[18]

The return of a fugitive is usually quite a routine matter. But, on occasion, a governor does refuse to surrender someone. And that practice, supported by Supreme Court decisions dating from 1861, has made the word "shall" actually read "may" in the Extradition Clause. There is no way in which a governor may be forced to act; the matter lies within the governor's discretion. When one governor refuses the request of another governor, whether the reasons be good, bad, or indifferent, there the matter ends.

Instances of a governor's refusal are not common, but they are not rare, either. In a fairly typical case, in 1978, Governor William G. Milliken of Michigan refused to return a woman to Alabama. She had been convicted of bank robbery there in 1942. Her part in the crime had been a largely unknowing one; nonetheless, she was sentenced to 30 years in prison. She escaped in 1952, made her way to Detroit, and had lived there ever since. The governor refused to extradite her because, in his view, her 1942 punishment had been overly severe and, too, because he felt that she had long since paid for her crime in her conscience.

Privileges and Immunities. The Constitution provides:

The citizens of each State shall be entitled to all privileges and immunities of citizens in the several States.[19]

---

[18] Article IV, Section 2, Clause 2. Extradition has been carried on between sovereign states from early times. The word *extradition* is the popular term used in the United States for what is technically known in the law as *interstate rendition.*

[19] Article IV, Section 2, Clause 1; the provision is reinforced in the 14th Amendment.

Essentially, this provision means that a resident of one State will not be discriminated against *unreasonably* by another State.

The courts have never given a complete list of the privileges and immunities of "interstate citizenship." But these are some of them: The right to pass through or reside in any other State for the purpose of trade, agriculture, professional pursuits, or otherwise. The right to demand the writ of *habeas corpus* and to sue in court. The right to make contracts, to buy, sell, and hold property, and to marry.

Of course, the provision does not mean that a resident of one State need not obey the laws of another State while in that State. Nor does it mean that a State may not make *reasonable* discrimination against residents of other States. For example, a State is not required to grant *public* or *political* privileges to nonresidents. It may require (and all States do) that one live in the State for a certain period before being eli-gible to vote or to hold public office. It may require a period of residence within the State before it grants one a license to practice medicine or dentistry. And it may restrict the practice of law to residents of the State.

Wild fish and game are the common property of the people of a State. Therefore, a nonresident may be compelled to pay a higher fee for a hunting or fishing license than a resident who pays taxes to maintain game, provide fish hatcheries, and the like. By the same token, State colleges and universities usually charge higher tuition to students from other States than to its own residents.

The Admission of New States

Only Congress has the power to admit new States to the Union. The Constitution places only one restriction on the power. A new State may not be created by taking territory from one or more of the existing

TERRITORIAL EXPANSION OF THE UNITED STATES AND ACQUISITIONS OF OTHER PRINCIPAL AREAS

Source: U.S. Bureau of the Census

ORIGIN AND ADMISSION OF THE 50 STATES

Order Of Admission	Source Of State Lands	Organized As Territory		Admitted As State	
Delaware	Swedish Charter, 1638; English Charter, 1683	. . .		7 Dec.	1787*
Pennsylvania	English Grant, 1680	. . .		12 Dec.	1787*
New Jersey	Dutch Settlement, 1623; English Charter, 1664	. . .		18 Dec.	1787*
Georgia	English Charter, 1732	. . .		2 Jan.	1788*
Connecticut	English Charter, 1662	. . .		9 Jan.	1788*
Massachusetts	English Charter, 1629	. . .		6 Feb.	1788*
Maryland	English Charter, 1632	. . .		28 Apr.	1788*
South Carolina	English Charter, 1663	. . .		23 May	1788*
New Hampshire	English Charter, 1622 and 1629	. . .		21 June	1788*
Virginia	English Charter, 1609	. . .		25 June	1788*
New York	Dutch Settlement, 1623; English Control, 1664	. . .		26 July	1788*
North Carolina	English Charter, 1663	. . .		21 Nov.	1789*
Rhode Island	English Charter, 1663	. . .		29 May	1790*
Vermont	Lands of New York and New Hampshire	**		4 Mar.	1791
Kentucky	Lands of Virginia	**		1 June	1792
Tennessee	Lands of North Carolina	**		1 June	1796
Ohio	Lands of Virginia; Northwest Territory, 1787	13 July	1787	1 Mar.	1803
Louisiana	Louisiana Purchase, 1803	24 Mar.	1804	30 Apr.	1812
Indiana	Lands of Virginia; Northwest Territory, 1787	7 May	1800	11 Dec.	1816
Mississippi	Lands of Georgia and South Carolina	17 Apr.	1798	10 Dec.	1817
Illinois	Lands of Virginia; Northwest Territory, 1787	3 Feb.	1809	3 Dec.	1818
Alabama	Lands of Georgia and South Carolina	3 Mar.	1817	14 Dec.	1819
Maine	Lands of Massachusetts	**		15 Mar.	1820
Missouri	Louisiana Purchase, 1803	4 June	1812	10 Aug.	1821
Arkansas	Louisiana Purchase, 1803	2 Mar.	1819	15 June	1836
Michigan	Lands from Virginia; Northwest Territory, 1787	11 Jan.	1805	26 Jan.	1837
Florida	Ceded by Spain, 1819	30 Mar.	1822	3 Mar.	1845
Texas	Republic of Texas, 1845	**		29 Dec.	1845
Iowa	Louisiana Purchase, 1803	12 June	1838	28 Dec.	1846
Wisconsin	Lands of Michigan; Northwest Territory, 1787	20 Apr.	1836	29 May	1848
California	Ceded by Mexico, 1848	**		9 Sept.	1850
Minnesota	Northwest Territory, 1787; and Louisiana Purchase, 1803	3 Mar.	1849	11 May	1858
Oregon	Louisiana Purchase, 1803; Treaty with Spain, 1819 and Treaty with Great Britain, 1846	14 Aug.	1848	14 Feb.	1859
Kansas	Louisiana Purchase, 1803; and lands from Texas	30 May	1854	29 Jan.	1861
West Virginia	Part of Virginia to 1863	**		20 June	1863
Nevada	Ceded by Mexico, 1848	2 Mar.	1861	31 Oct.	1864
Nebraska	Louisiana Purchase, 1803	30 May	1854	1 Mar.	1867
Colorado	Louisiana Purchase, 1803	28 Feb.	1861	1 Aug.	1876
South Dakota	Louisiana Purchase, 1803	2 Mar.	1861	2 Nov.	1889
North Dakota	Louisiana Purchase, 1803	2 Mar.	1861	2 Nov.	1889
Montana	Louisiana Purchase, 1803	26 May	1864	8 Nov.	1889
Washington	Louisiana Purchase, 1803; and Treaty with Great Britain, 1846	2 Mar.	1853	11 Nov.	1889
Idaho	Louisiana Purchase, 1803; and Oregon Territory	3 Mar.	1863	3 July	1890
Wyoming	Louisiana Purchase, 1803	25 July	1868	10 July	1890
Utah	Ceded by Mexico, 1848	9 Sept.	1850	4 Jan.	1896
Oklahoma	Louisiana Purchase, 1803	2 May	1890	16 Nov.	1907
New Mexico	Ceded by Mexico, 1848	9 Sept.	1850	6 Jan.	1912
Arizona	Ceded by Mexico, 1848; Gadsden Purchase, 1853	24 Feb.	1863	14 Feb.	1912
Alaska	Territory, Purchase from Russia, 1867	24 Aug.	1912	3 Jan.	1959
Hawaii	Territory, Annexed 1898	14 June	1900	21 Aug.	1959

*Date of ratification of U.S. Constitution   ** No territorial status before admission to the Union.

States without the consent of the State legislatures involved.[20]

Congress has admitted 37 States since the original 13 formed the Union. Five States—Vermont, Kentucky, Tennessee, Maine, and West Virginia—were created from parts of already existing States. Texas was an independent republic before admission. California was admitted after being ceded to the United States by Mexico. Each of the other 30 States entered the Union only after a period as an organized territory.

The table on page 96 indicates the sources of the lands comprising each of the 50 States, the dates upon which 30 of them were organized as territories, and the date each of them entered the Union.

Admission Procedure. The usual process of admission is relatively simple. The area desiring Statehood first *petitions* (applies to) Congress for admission. If and when it is favorably disposed, Congress passes an *enabling act* which directs the framing of a proposed State constitution. After that document has been drafted by a convention and approved by a popular vote, it is submitted to Congress. If Congress is still agreeable to Statehood, it then passes an *act of admission*.

The two newest States, Alaska and Hawaii, abbreviated the usual process. Each adopted a proposed constitution without waiting for an enabling act: Alaska in 1956 and Hawaii in 1950.

Conditions for Admission. Before finally admitting a new State, Congress has often imposed certain conditions. When

---

[20] Article IV, Section 3, Clause 1. It is sometimes argued that this restriction was violated in the admission of West Virginia in 1863. That State was formed out of the 40 western counties which broke away from Virginia over the issue of secession from the Union. The consent required by the Constitution was given by a minority of the members of the Virginia legislature—those representing the 40 western counties. Congress accepted their action on the ground that they were the only group legally capable of acting as the Virginia legislature at the time.

A Hawaiian student leads a parade in Honolulu after word of statehood reached Hawaii in 1959. He is wearing a hula skirt made of ti leaves.

Ohio entered the Union in 1803, it was forbidden to tax for five years any public lands sold within its borders by the United States. In 1896 Utah was admitted on condition that its constitution outlaw polygamy. In the act admitting Alaska in 1959, the State was forever prohibited from claiming title to any lands legally held by an Indian, Eskimo, or Aleut.

EACH STATE ENTERS THE UNION ON AN EQUAL FOOTING WITH EACH OF THE OTHER STATES. Thus, although it is possible for Congress to impose conditions like those just mentioned, it *cannot* impose conditions of a political nature. For example, when Oklahoma was admitted in 1907, Congress forbade the State to remove its capitol from Guthrie to any other place prior to 1913. In 1910, however, the legislature moved the capitol to Oklahoma City. When this step was challenged, the Supreme Court (*Coyle* v. *Smith*, 1911) held that Congress may impose conditions for admission as it pleases. *But,* held the Court, the conditions cannot be *enforced* when they compromise the independence of a State to manage its own internal affairs.

Arizona provides another example of the kind of condition that may be imposed but not enforced. President William Howard Taft vetoed a resolution admitting Arizona in 1911. He objected because Arizona's proposed constitution provided that judges might be recalled from office by a vote of the people. To President Taft this

meant that a judge would have to keep one eye on the law and the other on public opinion. The offending section was then removed from the proposed constitution. The next year Congress passed and the President signed a new act of admission, and Arizona then became the 48th State. Almost immediately thereafter the voters in Arizona amended the State constitution by adding a provision for the recall of judges. That provision remains a valid part of Arizona's constitution today.

SUMMARY

A *federal system* is one in which the powers of government are divided on a territorial basis between a central and several local governments, with each level exercising its own distinct field of powers. The Framers of the Constitution created the federal system to meet the need for a stronger national government and, at the same time, to preserve the rights of local self-government.

Our federal system's chief advantage is that it permits local problems to be dealt with in accord with local needs and desires while matters of wider concern may be handled on a national basis. It also provides for the strength of union. *Federalism* and *democracy* are not synonymous terms, but it is extremely difficult to conceive of a democracy involving a large area in which federalism is not also present.

The Constitution establishes a *division of powers* between the National Government and the States. The National Government possesses *only* those powers *delegated* to it in the Constitution. The *delegated powers* are of three kinds: (1) the *expressed powers*—those delegated in so many words in the Constitution, (2) the *implied powers*—those that may be reasonably implied from the expressed powers, and (3) the *inherent powers*—those that belong to (inhere in) the National Government because it *is a national* government. The Constitution also *denies* certain powers to the National Government—in so many words, through the silence of the Constitution, and as a result of the existence of a federal system.

The States possess the *reserved powers*—those powers which are not delegated to the National Government and not denied to the States by the Constitution. The States are also *denied* certain powers—in so many words in the Constitution, as a result of the existence of the federal system, and by their own constitutions.

The *exclusive powers* are those that belong *only* to the National Government. The *concurrent powers* are those that may be exercised by *both* the National Government and the States.

The Constitution is the "supreme law of the land." Immediately under it stands acts of Congress and treaties of the United States. No provision in a State constitution or in any State or local law may conflict with the "supreme law." The Supreme Court of the United States is the final interpreter of the Constitution and functions as the "umpire" in the federal system.

The National Government has certain obligations toward the States under the Constitution. It must guarantee to each State a republican form of government, protect each State against foreign invasion and domestic violence, and respect the territorial integrity of every State in the Union.

The States and the National Government cooperate with one another in many ways, from grant-in-aid programs and revenue sharing to election administration and law enforcement.

Each of the States is legally separate from all of the others. The Constitution does require the States to cooperate with one another through the Full Faith and Credit Clause, the Extradition Clause, and the Privileges and Immunities Clause. The States may, with the consent of Congress, enter into compacts among themselves.

New States may be admitted *only* by Congress. Since 1790, Congress has admitted 37 States into the Union.

Concept Development

Questions for Review

1. Why did the authors of the Constitution create a federal system?

2. What is *federalism?*

3. What is the chief advantage of a federal system?

4. What is meant by the term *division of powers?*

5. Why is the National Government properly described as a government of *delegated powers?*

6. What are the *expressed powers?* The *implied powers?* The *inherent powers?*

7. Why are the States properly described as governments of *reserved powers?*

8. What are the *exclusive powers?* The *concurrent powers?*

9. If the provisions of a State law conflict with those of a national law, which must yield? Why?

10. Why is the Court's decision in *McCulloch* v. *Maryland* of such importance?

11. What are the three obligations the Constitution imposes upon the National Government with regard to the States?

12. What is the phrase "a republican form of government" generally understood to mean?

13. What is probably the best known example of federal aid to the States? On what grounds is the arrangement sometimes criticized? On what grounds is it sometimes defended?

14. What are the three broad purposes of the revenue sharing program?

15. In what ways do the States aid the National Government?

16. What agreements are the States constitutionally forbidden to make? What agreements are the States permitted to make?

17. What, in brief, does the Full Faith and Credit Clause provide? The Extradition Clause? The Privileges and Immunities Clause?

18. Who has the exclusive power to admit new States?

For Further Inquiry

1. What do you think conditions might be like in what is now the United States if no federal system had been created and the 13 States had attempted to continue under the Articles of Confederation?

2. Why are the powers to declare war, to conduct foreign relations, and to regulate foreign and interstate commerce exclusive powers of the National Government?

3. The Constitution (Article I, Section 10, Clause 3) forbids the States to "engage in war." But there is a qualification to this prohibition. Why?

4. In 1954 the Supreme Court held (in *Brown* v. *Topeka Board of Education*) that segregation by race in the public schools was unconstitutional as a violation of the 14th Amendment's Equal Protection Clause. Why has it been said that the aftermath of that decision posed the most serious problem to face American federalism since 1865?

5. If you were a delegate to a convention called to "modernize" the Constitution, what changes in the federal system, if any, would you support?

6. What factors have been most responsible for the growth of the powers of the National Government in recent decades?

Suggested Activities

1. Using current newspapers and periodicals, find examples of each of the types of power and denials of power shown in the chart on page 81.

2. Invite your local chief of police or other local law enforcement official to speak to the class on the ways in which agencies of the National Government cooperate with local peace officers.

3. Construct a wall map illustrating the historical growth of the Union based on the data presented in the table on page 96.

4. Stage a debate or class forum on the question: *Resolved,* That the grants-in-aid system undermines the federal system and reduces the power and importance of the States.

5. Prepare a class report on the history of the admission of your State to the Union.

Suggested Reading

American Regionalism: Our Economic, Cultural and Political Makeup. Editorial Research Reports. 1980.

Berman, David R., *State and Local Politics.* Allyn and Bacon, 3rd ed., 1981.

Corwin, Edward S. and Peltason, J.W., *Understanding the Constitution.* Holt, Rinehart and Winston, 8th ed., 1979.

Dye, Thomas R., *Politics in States and Communities.* Prentice-Hall, 4th ed., 1981.

Hale, George E. and Palley, Marian L., *Politics and Federal Grants.* Congressional Quarterly Press, 1981.

Henry, Nicholas, *Governing at the Grassroots: State and Local Politics.* Prentice-Hall, 1980.

Pritchett, C. Herman, *The Federal System in Constitutional Law.* Prentice-Hall, 1978.

Reagan, Michael D. and Sanzone, John G., *The New Federalism.* Oxford, 2nd ed., 1981.

CITIZENSHIP AND CIVIL RIGHTS

Recall that the Preamble to the Constitution declares: "We the People of the United States, . . . do ordain and establish this Constitution for the United States of America." Thus, the Constitution declares that this nation was called into being by its people. The United States exists solely because its people chose to create it, and it has no existence apart from the people.

Who are "the People of the United States"? Who are the people who created this nation, who belong to this political community, for whom this nation exists and without whom it could not exist? The answer is, of course: the *citizens* of the United States.

Recall, too, that the Preamble identifies the cardinal reasons for the creation of the Constitution, including among them: to "establish justice . . . and secure the Blessings of Liberty to ourselves and our Posterity." Thus, with these words and in many other provisions, the Constitution stresses the unparalleled importance of freedom for the individual in this country.

In a moment we shall turn to a consideration of the subjects of citizenship and of individual rights in the American democracy. But, first, a few related thoughts.

In Chapter 1 we suggested that democracy exists in this country because, as a people, we subscribe to its basic concepts. That is, we, the people, believe in the *fundamental worth and dignity* and in the *equality* of each

and of all persons. We have faith in the principle of *majority rule* and, at the same time, assert a *respect for minority rights.* We recognize the indispensable *necessity of compromise* in the making of public policy decisions. And we insist upon the *widest possible area of freedom for the individual.*

The critics of American democracy are fond of telling us of our shortcomings, of reminding us that we do not always practice what we preach. And—certainly and unfortunately, and to a point—they are right. Only the completely bemused and the ignorant can pretend that we have achieved perfection in the building of a democratic society in this country.

But they are right *only* to a point. For only the willfully blind can pretend that we have not made great strides or that we are not constantly striving to translate the theory of democracy into the reality of its practice. We, the People of the United States, have come closer to the realization of democracy in practice than have the people of any other nation on earth.

In each of the next chapters we shall treat topics that illustrate our point abundantly. With respect to citizenship, for example, we have developed and we honor in practice a definition of citizenship that comes remarkably close to the democratic ideal. And our steadily improving record with respect to human dignity, equality, and freedom shines with the same light.

The Golden Door: Immigration and Citizenship

"Keep ancient lands, your storied
pomp," cries she
With silent lips. "Give me your
tired, your poor,
Your huddled masses, yearning to
breathe free,
The wretched refuse of your teeming
shore.
Send these, the homeless, tempest-tost
to me,
I lift my lamp beside the golden
door!"

EMMA LAZARUS, from the poem
The New Colossus (inscribed on tablet
at base of the Statue of Liberty)

■ Why might the United States be described as "a nation of nations"?

■ Is it either fair or reasonable for the law to draw distinctions between citizens and aliens?

■ What responsibilities should accompany the possession of United States citizenship?

Citizenship is the badge of membership in the political society.[1] Today every state in the world has rules by which citizenship is determined. And, much can be learned about the basic nature of a government from an examination of those rules. Who are and who may become citizens? Who are excluded from citizenship, and why? What rights do citizens possess? Are all citizens of equal rank, or are there different classes of citizenship? To what extent may and do citizens participate in the political process?

In this chapter we are concerned with the first two of the questions just posed—that is, with the American law of citizenship. In succeeding chapters we shall examine the other questions asked above.

Immigration

We are a nation of immigrants. Except for the American Indians—and even they are the descendants of earlier immigrants—all of us have come here from abroad or are descended from those who did.

Power to Regulate Immigration. In international law every sovereign state possesses the power to regulate the crossing of its borders, inward (immigration)

---

[1] The concept of citizenship—of the free inhabitants of a city—was developed by the ancient Greeks and Romans. It replaced the earlier concept of kinship—of the blood relationships of the family and the tribe—as the basis for community.

Some 600,000 Vietnamese refugees have been admitted to the United States since the end of the war in Vietnam in 1975.

and outward (emigration). In our law this power belongs inherently and exclusively to the National Government.

In a long line of cases, from 1849 on, the Supreme Court has held that—beyond its rank among the inherent powers—the power to regulate immigration is implied from the powers to regulate foreign commerce and to conduct foreign relations.[2]

The Nation's Population Growth. There were only some 2.5 million persons living in the United States when independence was declared in 1776. In the more than 200 years since, the nation's population has grown nearly ninety-fold and is now more than 226 million.

This tremendous population growth has come from two principal sources: (1) natural increase and (2) immigration.

A population of only 3,929,214 persons was reported by the First Census in 1790. The unsettled and seemingly unlimited expanse of the country, with its vast and untapped natural wealth begged for people.[3] By 1820 the population had more than doubled, to 9,638,453; and by 1830 it had nearly tripled, to 12,866,020.

As you can see from the table on page 104, the nation's population grew at the rate of about one-third from decade to dec-

---

[2] In *The Passenger Cases,* 1849, the Court voided New York and Massachusetts laws which had imposed taxes upon immigrants and those transporting immigrants to the United States. The Court held these laws to be regulations of foreign commerce and thus unconstitutional State exercises of power exclusively granted to the National Government.

[3] Recall, too, that the United States was founded in part as a haven for the oppressed. One of the complaints of the Declaration of Independence had been that George III "has endeavored to prevent the population of these States, for that purpose obstructing the Laws for the Naturalization of Foreigners, refusing to pass others to encourage their migration hither . . ."

IMMIGRATION AND OUR NATIONAL POPULATION, 1790–1980

Census Year	National Population	Since Preceding Census		
		Immigration	Population Increase	Percentage of Increase
1790	3,929,214	....	....	....
1800	5,308,483	....	1,379,269	35.1
1810	7,239,881	....	1,931,398	36.4
1820	9,638,453	(8,385)[a]	2,398,572	33.1
1830	12,866,020	143,439	3,227,567	33.5
1840	17,069,453	599,125	4,203,433	32.7
1850	23,191,876	1,713,251	6,122,423	35.3
1860	31,443,321	2,598,214	8,251,445	35.5
1870	38,558,371	2,314,824	7,115,050	22.2
1880	50,155,783	2,812,191	11,597,412	30.1
1890	62,947,714	5,246,613	12,791,931	25.5
1900	75,994,575	3,687,564	13,046,861	20.7
1910	91,972,266	8,795,386	15,977,691	21.0
1920	105,710,620	5,735,811	13,738,354	14.9
1930	122,775,046	4,107,209	17,064,426	16.1
1940	131,669,275	528,431	8,894,229	7.2
1950	150,697,361	1,035,039	19,028,086	14.5
1960	179,323,175	2,515,479	28,625,814	18.5
1970	203,235,298	3,321,677	23,912,123	13.3
1980	226,000,000[b]	4,100,000[c]	22,764,702[c]	11.2

[a] Immigration figures were not recorded until 1820; this figure is for that year.
[b] Preliminary. [c] Estimated.

ade until the 1860's. From then until the 1940's, the *rate of growth* dropped steadily. That is, although the total number of persons in the United States continued to increase from census to census, the total did not increase as rapidly after 1860 as it had before. The rate of growth fell to an all-time low of one-fourteenth during the depression years of the 1930's, but it climbed sharply in the 1940's and 1950's. The rate steadied at about the one-fifth level into the early 1960's, but has dropped sharply since then.[4]

Since 1820, when such figures were first recorded, some 50 million immigrants have entered the United States. Our population today is largely the result of that immigration.

[4] The decline is a direct result of a steady drop in the nation's birth rate in the last several years. In 1960 the rate was 23.7 live births per 1000 persons in the population. With but minor variations, it has dropped steadily since then—to an all-time low of 14.7 in 1976. It rallied slightly in 1977, to 15.4. The rate for both 1978 and 1979 was 15.3; early data put the 1980 data at the same figure.

Early Immigration Restrictions. The United States made no serious attempt to regulate immigration for more than a century after independence. Indeed, Congress did not enact its first statute in the field until 1819. That statute provided only for the collection of immigration statistics and for the regulation of the carrying of steerage passengers. As long as land was plentiful and rapidly expanding industry demanded more and still more laborers, immigration was actively encouraged.

By 1890, however, the open frontier had become a thing of the past, and labor was no longer in critically short supply. Then, too, the major source of immigration had shifted. Until the 1880's most immigrants had come from the countries of Northern and Western Europe. The "new immigration" from the 1880's onward consisted chiefly of immigrants from Southern and Central Europe.

Each of these factors—the closing of the frontier, a more abundant labor sup-

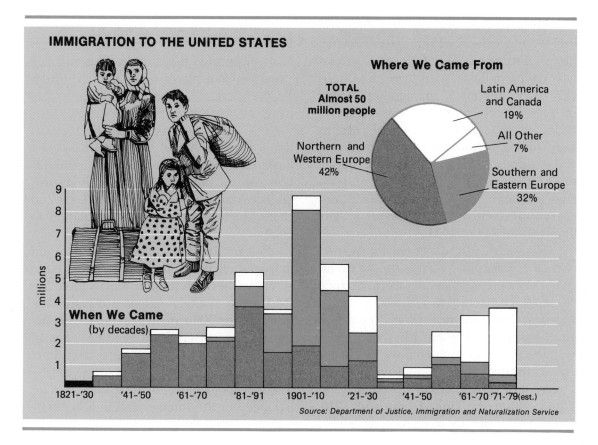

IMMIGRATION TO THE UNITED STATES

Where We Came From

TOTAL Almost 50 million people

Northern and Western Europe 42%

Latin America and Canada 19%

All Other 7%

Southern and Eastern Europe 32%

When We Came (by decades)

millions

1821–'30 '41–'50 '61–'70 '81–'91 1901–'10 '21–'30 '41–'50 '61–'70 '71–'79(est.)

Source: Department of Justice, Immigration and Naturalization Service

ply, and the shift in the major source of newcomers—combined to bring changes in our traditional policy of encouraging immigration. Ultimately, the policy was reversed.

Oriental and Personal Exclusion Policies. Congress placed the first major restrictions on immigration with the passage of the Chinese Exclusion Act of 1882.[5] At the same time it barred the entry of convicts, lunatics, paupers, and others likely to become public charges. Over the next sev-

eral years a long list of "undesirables" was composed. For example, contract laborers were excluded in 1885, immoral persons and anarchists in 1903, and illiterates in 1917.[6] By 1920 more than 30 groups were listed as ineligible on grounds of personal characteristics.

But, despite the growing restrictions, the tide of immigration mounted. In the 10 years from 1905 through 1914, an average of more than one million persons came to the United States annually. World War I slowed the tide to a mere trickle; but with the end of the war, it rose rapidly again.

---

[5] The law was intended to stem the flow of "coolie labor" to the Pacific Coast; the Chinese could and did work for far less than white laborers, especially in the mines and on the railroads. By 1924 *all* Orientals had been excluded except for temporary visits. The policy was relaxed somewhat during World War II when provision was made for the admission of limited numbers of Chinese, Filipinos, and natives of India. Since 1952, immigration from each independent country in the Far East has been regulated by the quota system.

[6] Congress had originally provided for the barring of those who could neither read nor write in 1897, but President Cleveland vetoed the bill. He held that literacy was much more a gauge of one's opportunities than of intelligence or other worthy qualifications. President Taft vetoed a similar bill in 1913 on the same basis, and the 1917 law was passed only over a veto by President Wilson.

NATIONAL ORIGINS. By 1921 Congress had become convinced that greater restrictions were necessary. Immigration was nearing the million-a-year level once more. Ellis Island, the major immigration facility in New York Harbor, was literally swamped; thousands of potential entrants were forced to remain there for months while administrative machinery determined their admissibility. Patriotic societies and labor unions were alarmed. Congress met the situation with the Immigration Act of 1921.

That statute placed a *quantitative* restriction on immigration. That is, to the exclusion policies based upon race and upon personal characteristics, Congress now added a numerical restriction. The maximum number of persons (the "quota") to be admitted from each country in Europe was established. The number was fixed at 3 percent of the natives of the country residing within the United States in 1910. That translated to a ceiling of about 355,000 European immigrants that could be admitted per year.

The 1921 law was intended as a stopgap measure. It was replaced by a more comprehensive and restrictive law, the Immigration (Johnson) Act of 1924. Under the 1924 statute, the quota admissible from each European country was reduced to 2 percent of those residing within the United States in 1890 (a total of approximately 165,000). By pushing the base back to the 1890 census, immigration from Northern and Western Europe was purposefully favored over that from Southern and Central Europe.[7]

Turning the clock back to 1890 reflected a view widely held at the time. Many suspected that the people coming to America from places other than Northern Europe, England, and Ireland might not have the attributes of an "American."

The 1924 law was refined by the National Origins Act of 1929 which set the basic pattern for our system of immigration control until 1965. The 1929 law established an overall figure of 150,000 and changed the base for quota calculation to 1920.

Present Immigration Policy. Present immigration policy is set out in two basic statutes: the Immigration and Nationality (McCarran-Walter) Act of 1952 and the Immigration Reform Act of 1965. The latter act made significant modifications in the 1952 law, but both statutes are direct descendants of the legislation of the 1920's. Major responsibility for their enforcement is lodged in the Immigration and Naturalization Service in the Department of Justice.

The now historic policy of strict control of immigration is continued under these two statutes—and in both *qualitative* and *quantitative* terms. That is, only a *limited number* of persons who possess *certain personal characteristics* (but do *not* possess others) can be admitted to the United States as immigrants.

PERSONAL QUALIFICATIONS. The list of "undesirable aliens" barred today takes up six pages in the *United States Code.* It includes, among many others: insane or mentally retarded persons, chronic alcoholics, drug addicts, vagrants, beggars, stowaways, paupers, those with any dangerous contagious disease, those who are criminals, polygamists, adults unable to read and understand any language or dialect, advocates of forcible overthrow of our government, present or former members of communist or other totalitarian groups, and those who advocate in any way world communism or other forms of totalitarian

---

[7] Recall that the largest proportion of immigration prior to 1890 had come from Northern and Western Europe. The Johnson Act also broadened the Oriental exclusion policy. It expressly prohibited immigration from Japan (which, in fact, had been virtually eliminated by the Gentleman's Agreement of 1907 which President Theodore Roosevelt had made with the Japanese government). The Oriental exclusion policy was finally abandoned in 1952; see note 5.

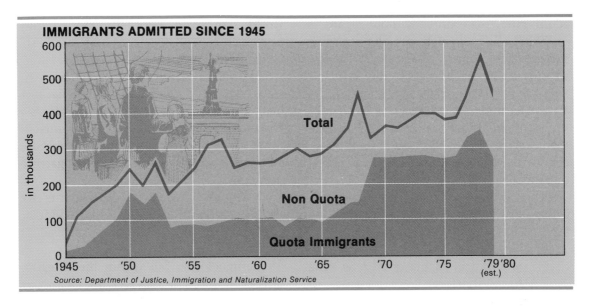

IMMIGRANTS ADMITTED SINCE 1945

Total

Non Quota

Quota Immigrants

in thousands

Source: Department of Justice, Immigration and Naturalization Service

dictatorship.[8] No person ineligible to become a citizen can enter the United States as an immigrant.

THE QUOTA SYSTEM. The Immigration Reform Act of 1965 made extensive changes in the *numerical* limits which are placed upon immigration to this country. The McCarran-Walter Act had continued the national origins quota system begun in the 1920's. And, in only slightly modified form, it continued to favor immigrants from Northern and Western Europe.

Under the 1952 law each nation outside the Western Hemisphere was assigned an annual quota. Each nation's quota was equal to one-sixth of one percent of the number of persons in the United States in 1920 who had been born in or were descended from those who had been born in that country.

Altogether, by 1965 a total of 158,561 *quota immigrants* could be admitted to this country each year. Of that total, by far the largest share was that assigned to Great

Britain (including Northern Ireland), 65,361. The second largest quota was that of Germany, 25,814, followed by Ireland (Eire), 17,756. Then came Poland, 6,488; Italy, 5,666; Sweden, 3,295; the Netherlands, 3,136; France, 3,069; Czechoslovakia, 2,859; and the USSR, 2,697. In all, Europe accounted for 149,697 slots in the total allowed. The number from *all* of the rest of the world—from all countries other than those in Europe and this hemisphere—amounted to a tiny share of the total allowed, only 8,864 persons.

The 1965 law abolished the national origins (country-by-country) quotas. Instead, it placed an annual ceiling on the number of quota immigrants who may be admitted each year. That overall limit is now 320,000 persons.[9]

Until 1968, anyone who was born in an independent country in this hemisphere

---

[8] Aliens who can prove that their membership in or support of a communist or other totalitarian group was unknowing, involuntary, or based on economic necessity or that they have honestly reformed may be admitted. The Attorney General may allow the admission of or deny entry to any alien whenever such action is found to be in the best interests of the United States.

[9] The 1965 law placed the annual ceiling at 290,000 persons, but Congress raised that figure to its present level in 1980. But, as we shall see in a moment, the current ceiling does not include the several classes of *special immigrants* who may be admitted to this country. From 1968 to 1978, the ceiling was imposed in two parts: 120,000 persons from countries in the Western Hemisphere and 170,000 persons from all other countries in the world. Since 1978, however, the ceiling has been imposed as a single, worldwide limit.

could enter this country without regard to numbers. But all such persons are now subject to the numerical as well as the personal characteristics limits of the law.

Each alien who applies for admission as a quota immigrant is assigned to one of several "preference classes." He or she then receives a *visa* (an entry permit) in accord with that ranking—and on a "first-qualified, first-served" basis.

The preference classes, in order of priority, and the percentage allocated to each are:

1. Unmarried adult sons and daughters of United States citizens—the first 20 percent of the total of 170,000.
2. Spouses and unmarried sons and daughters of resident aliens—20 percent of the total plus any unused portion of Class 1.
3. Members of the professions, such as doctors, lawyers, and teachers, and others with special talents or education—10 percent of the total.
4. Married sons and daughters of United States citizens—10 percent of the total plus any unused portion of the first three classes.
5. Brothers and sisters of United States citizens—24 percent of the total plus any unused portion of the first four classes.
6. Skilled and unskilled persons to fill specified labor needs in the country—10 percent.
7. Refugees from communist, or communist-dominated areas, and from the Middle East, and persons made homeless by natural calamity—6 percent.

If all the higher preference classes were filled, no places would be available in the seventh class and only a few in the sixth. Following allocation of these preferences, all of the unused places—if any, and up to the outside limit of 120,000 for this hemisphere and 170,000 for the rest of the world—are given to other qualified (but non-preference) applicants on a "first-come, first-served" basis.[10]

SPECIAL IMMIGRANTS. As we have just seen, not more than 320,000 immigrants may enter this country each year under the present quota system. But thousands of others—*special immigrants*—may be and are admitted each year, and without regard to numbers.

Many of these special immigrants are the alien wives, husbands, minor children, or parents of American citizens, or resident aliens returning from trips abroad.

Refugees also fall within the category of special immigrants. Over the past three decades or so, Congress has passed a number of laws to admit certain groups of them to this country. Thus, 415,744 refugees from war-torn Europe were admitted under the terms of the Displaced Persons Acts of 1948 and 1950; and another 214,000, mostly from Iron Curtain countries, were allowed to enter between 1953 and 1956. More recently, some 600,000 Vietnamese and Cambodians, who fled their homes after the end of the war in Southeast Asia, have been admitted.

At present, the law provides for the admission of up to 50,000 refugees as special immigrants each year. However, Congress has also given the President the power to admit a larger number whenever that action is prompted by an emergency "of great humanitarian concern." Thus, some 125,000 persons who fled Castro's Cuba entered the United States in 1980.

Each year Congress also enacts a number of "private laws" to permit the entry of certain persons without regard to the quota system. These laws usually allow the entry of "hardship" or "humanitarian" cases—for example, an alien child an American family plans to adopt.

---

[10] Except that a limit is imposed upon the number of immigrants who may be admitted from any one country in any one year. The limit is 20,000, not counting the parents, spouses, and unmarried minor children of U.S. citizens.

NONIMMIGRANTS. Many thousands of persons come to the United States each year as *nonimmigrants;* that is, for *temporary* purposes—including such visitors as students, newspaper reporters, tourists, people on business, touring entertainers, and athletes.

Aliens in the United States. More than five million aliens are legal residents of the United States today. Some 400,000 immigrants and more than four million nonimmigrants arrive each year.

In many respects aliens enjoy the same privileges and benefits held by citizens. Most of the great constitutional guarantees of freedom are written in terms of "persons" rather than "citizens"; thus, they apply to aliens. Generally, aliens may attend public schools, make contracts, use the courts, own property, and engage in most businesses. In short, aliens may do most of the things any citizen may do.

There are several disadvantages to the status, however. Contrary to a widespread impression, aliens must shoulder most of the responsibilities imposed upon citizens. They must obey the law and pay taxes, of course. They cannot vote in any election, and citizenship is regularly a qualification for elective office in this country. Many jobs in defense-related work are denied to them. In many States they cannot enter certain professions such as law, medicine, or dentistry. In a few States their right to own property is severely restricted. In some States they cannot own firearms. Several States also deny them unemployment compensation and various other welfare benefits available to citizens. When and if an alien does become a citizen, these disadvantages evaporate, and he or she assumes all of the rights and privileges of that cherished status.

How Immigrants Enter the United States. Every immigrant seeking to enter the United States must go before an American consul to obtain a *visa* (permit to enter). This visa establishes his or her ap-

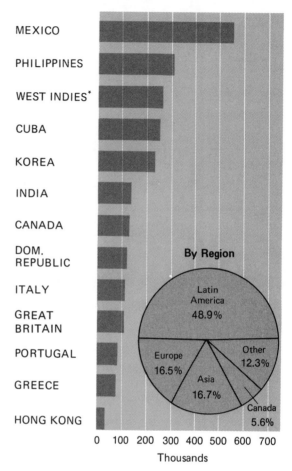

**IMMIGRANTS 1971-1979
By Selected Country of Birth**

(excluding Cuba and Dominican Republic)
Source: Immigration and Naturalization Service

parent right to enter the United States, subject to a further examination at the port of entry. Consuls deny visas to aliens who are legally inadmissible. Some immigrants are turned back on arrival at our ports of entry by immigration officials.

A steamship or airline which knowingly or carelessly brings an alien who is not admissible is required to return the alien to the port where the alien boarded. Once, a number of years ago, an alien from Brazil was rejected for insanity. Since he was not a Brazilian, Brazil refused to take him back and the steamship line was

Between 1901 and 1910, some 10 million immigrants arrived in America. Here, European immigrants await inspection at Ellis Island, New York, in 1907.

forced to carry him back and forth for years until his condition improved.

Deportation. A citizen cannot be deported. However, an alien may be forced to leave the country for a variety of reasons. Illegal entry is the most common cause. Aliens who enter with falsified passports, attempt to sneak in by plane or ship, or attempt to slip across the border at night are sometimes caught—and most often by the Border Patrol, the police arm of the Immigration and Naturalization Service.

Any alien who commits a crime involving moral turpitude, violates the narcotics laws, or commits practically any other felony may be deported. In recent years, a number of aliens with gambling, narcotics, and similar records have been deported.

Finally, any alien may be deported who teaches or advocates the forcible overthrow of the Government of the United States, or who belongs to an organization which does (the Communist Party, for example). We have no use for those who would come here to enjoy our liberties while working at the same time to destroy them.

THE ALIEN RECORD A GOOD ONE. Through the years, the record of the alien population has been quite good. According to FBI records, for example, the crime rate for aliens is well below that for citizens. Because those who are admitted must meet the high standards set by law, many times they become the very best of citizens.

American Citizenship

Every person living in the United States or in any of its territorial possessions falls into one of three classes: Most are citizens of the United States, a few are nationals of the United States, and the others are aliens.

Citizens are full-fledged members of the political community. They are entitled to all of the privileges of citizenship, including the protection of the United States while traveling or residing abroad. They owe full allegiance to this country and, with their fellow citizens, must bear the responsibilities of government.

Nationals are not full-fledged citizens. They do owe full allegiance to the United States, and they are entitled to its protection.[11] They enjoy many, but not all, of the rights of citizenship. For example, they do not possess political rights (the right to vote and to hold elective office). The few nationals of the United States come principally from smaller outlying possessions today.

Aliens are those persons within the United States or any of its possessions, either temporarily or permanently, who are neither citizens nor nationals.

The Constitution and Citizenship. As it was originally written, the Constitution contained no definition of citizenship. It mentioned both "citizens of the United States" and "citizens of the States."[12] Until the 1860's, it was generally agreed that national citizenship followed that of the States. That is, any person who was recognized as a citizen of one of the States was recognized as a citizen of the United States, as well.

Actually, the question was of little importance before the 1860's. Much of the population was the product of recent immigration, and little distinction was made between citizens and aliens. The Civil War and the subsequent adoption of the 13th Amendment forbidding slavery raised the need for a constitutional definition, however.[13]

Section 1 of the 14th Amendment, adopted in 1868, laid down the basic statement of national citizenship. The provision reads:

> All persons born or naturalized in the United States, and subject to the jurisdiction thereof, are citizens of the United States and of the State wherein they reside.

As the chart presented on page 113 shows, the 14th Amendment thus provides for two ways in which one may acquire citizenship: (1) by birth, and (2) by naturalization.

Citizenship by Birth. Approximately 200 million Americans—well over 90 percent of all of us—acquired American citizenship by having been born in the United States. It is quite possible, however, for one to gain American citizenship at birth even though he or she is born abroad. Two basic rules are applied to determine citizenship by birth: (1) *jus soli*—the law of the soil, *where* born, and (2) *jus sanguinus*—the law of the blood, *to whom* born.

Jus Soli. According to the 14th Amendment, any person born in the United States (and who is born subject to its jurisdiction) automatically becomes an American citizen at birth. That is, one becomes a native-born citizen because of the *location* of his or her birth. Thus, any person who is born in any one of the 50 States, in the District of Columbia, or in Guam, Puerto Rico, or the Virgin Islands acquires citizenship at birth. So, too, is any

---

[11] The term *national* is also used in international law to identify any persons, citizen or not, who owes allegiance to and is entitled to the protection of a particular state.

[12] Article I, Clause 8, Section 4 gives to Congress the power "to establish a uniform rule of naturalization."

---

[13] In the famous *Dred Scott Case* (*Dred Scott* v. *Sanford*) in 1857, the Supreme Court had ruled that neither the States nor the National Government had the power to confer national citizenship on Negroes, slave or free.

Case Study

There are literally millions of illegal aliens in the United States today—millions who have entered the country and remained here in violation of the immigration laws. Their number is unknown, even approximately. The Immigration and Naturalization Service places the figure at "somewhere between six and 12 million."

However many there are, their number is increasing. The INS estimates that at least half a million more arrive each year. Most do so by slipping across the Mexican or Canadian borders, usually at night, by using forged documents, or by entering with temporary visitor or student visas and then simply remaining.

Some 900,000 illegal entrants have been apprehended by the INS in each of the past several years. Nearly all have been sent home, either voluntarily or through formal deportation proceedings. But a sizable portion of that number includes repeats—aliens who have entered illegally and been deported two or three or even more times in the same year.

Most illegal aliens come from 15 countries. Well over half are from Mexico. The bulk of the rest come from seven other Latin-American countries and from Korea, the Philippines, Thailand, India, Iran, Greece, and Nigeria. The majority of those from Mexico remain here for only four to six months in a year, to do seasonal work. Most from other countries live here permanently, with many settling in the larger cities.

It is not unlawful to hire illegal aliens, and at least 3.5 million of them now hold jobs in this country.

■ What serious problems do these facts pose?
■ Why do many farm and business groups balk at effective solutions?
■ What position does organized labor take here?

---

person born in an American embassy in a foreign country, or any person born aboard an American public vessel anywhere in the world.[14]

Just how broad the 14th Amendment's statement of *jus soli* is can be seen from one of the leading cases in the law of citizenship, *United States* v. *Wong Kim Ark* (1898). Wong Kim Ark was born in San Francisco in 1873 to parents who were citizens of China. He made a brief trip to China in 1895. Upon his return, he was refused entry to the United States by immigration officials at San Francisco. They insisted that the 14th Amendment should not be applied so literally as to mean that he was a citizen. They declared that as an alien he was prohibited entry by the Chinese Exclusion Act of 1882. The Supreme Court, however, held that, under the clear words of the 14th Amendment, Wong Kim Ark was, indeed, a native-born citizen. Thus, said the Court, the Chinese Exclusion Act could not be applied to him.

A very small number of persons who are born *physically* in the United States do not become citizens at birth. They are those few who are born not "subject to the jurisdiction of the United States." They include children born to foreign diplomatic officials and children born on foreign public vessels in American waters.[15]

JUS SANGUINIS. It is altogether possible for one to become a citizen at birth even

---

[14] Under the international law doctrine of *extraterritoriality*, United States embassies abroad are, in effect, parts of the United States. A public vessel is any vessel, such as a warship, cutter, or lightship, operated by an agency of the United States Government.

[15] Until 1924 Indians born to tribal members living on reservations were not considered citizens, but *wards* (persons legally held to be under the guardianship of the government). In that year Congress conferred citizenship on all Indians not already possessing it.

HOW CITIZENSHIP IS ACQUIRED

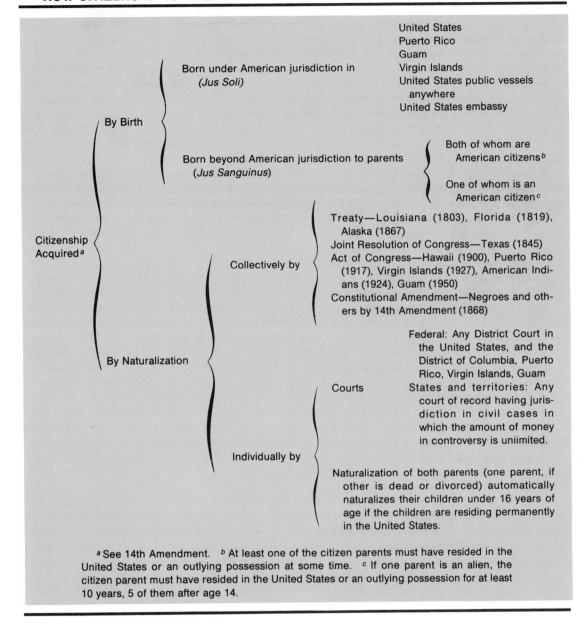

Born under American jurisdiction in *(Jus Soli)*
- United States
- Puerto Rico
- Guam
- Virgin Islands
- United States public vessels anywhere
- United States embassy

Born beyond American jurisdiction to parents *(Jus Sanguinus)*
- Both of whom are American citizens[b]
- One of whom is an American citizen[c]

By Birth

Citizenship Acquired[a]

By Naturalization

Collectively by
- Treaty—Louisiana (1803), Florida (1819), Alaska (1867)
- Joint Resolution of Congress—Texas (1845)
- Act of Congress—Hawaii (1900), Puerto Rico (1917), Virgin Islands (1927), American Indians (1924), Guam (1950)
- Constitutional Amendment—Negroes and others by 14th Amendment (1868)

Individually by

Courts
- Federal: Any District Court in the United States, and the District of Columbia, Puerto Rico, Virgin Islands, Guam
- States and territories: Any court of record having jurisdiction in civil cases in which the amount of money in controversy is unlimited.

Naturalization of both parents (one parent, if other is dead or divorced) automatically naturalizes their children under 16 years of age if the children are residing permanently in the United States.

[a] See 14th Amendment. [b] At least one of the citizen parents must have resided in the United States or an outlying possession at some time. [c] If one parent is an alien, the citizen parent must have resided in the United States or an outlying possession for at least 10 years, 5 of them after age 14.

though that person was born *outside* the United States. A child born abroad to parents, at least one of whom is an American citizen who has at some time resided in the United States, automatically acquires American citizenship at birth. That is, the child becomes a native-born citizen on the basis of the *parents to whom* he or she is born.

Although the 14th Amendment does not specifically provide for *jus sanguinis*, Congress has recognized it by law since 1790. The constitutionality of the arrangement has never been challenged. If it were to be challenged today, it would almost certainly be upheld—if for no other reason than the longstanding nature of the practice.

NATURALIZATION PROCESS

DECLARATION OF INTENTION (Optional)
Filed with clerk of court; petitioner must be at least 18 years of age; states intention to renounce allegiance to former country.

PETITION
Filed with clerk of court after 5 years of residence (3 if married to an American citizen); renounces allegiance to former country and declares not opposed to organized government nor a polygamist.

PETITION ATTESTED
2 American citizens (witnesses) verify petitioner's 5 years of continuous residence, good moral character, and belief in principles of the Constitution in sworn statement to clerk of court.

EXAMINATION
By judge, or appointee who reports findings and makes recommendations to judge.

CITIZENSHIP GRANTED
Not less than 30 days after filing of petition; judge administers oath of allegiance and signs certificate of citizenship.

When a child is born abroad to an American citizen parent or parents, the birth is usually recorded at the nearest American consulate. If both parents are citizens, only one of them must have resided within the United States (or one of its outlying possessions) at some time in order for the child to become an American citizen at birth. If one parent is a citizen and the other a *national,* the citizen parent must have lived in this country (or one of the possessions) for at least one year to establish the child's citizenship at birth. If one of the parents is a citizen and the other an *alien,* then the residence requirement is somewhat longer. The citizen parent must have lived in the United States (or one of the possessions) for at least 10 years, five of them after age 14, in order for the child to acquire his or her citizenship under the principle of *jus sanguinus.*

Citizenship by Naturalization. *Naturalization* is the legal process by which a person acquires a new citizenship at some time after birth. Congress has the *exclusive* power to provide for naturalization; no State may do so.[16] The naturalization process usually involves individual persons. On occasion, however, the process has involved particular groups. Thus, naturalization may be accomplished *individually* or *collectively.*

COLLECTIVE NATURALIZATION. At various times in our history it has seemed desirable for Congress to provide for the naturalization *en masse* of a number of persons at one time. This has usually happened when the United States has acquired new territory. The residents of the areas involved were naturalized by the

------

16 Article I, Section 8, Clause 4.

terms of treaties, by acts, or by joint resolutions—as the chart on page 113 indicates. All American Indians who had not by then become citizens were collectively naturalized by act of Congress in 1924.

INDIVIDUAL NATURALIZATION. Naturalization is much more commonly an individual process. Generally, any person eligible to enter the United States as an immigrant is eligible to become a naturalized citizen. The naturalization of both parents automatically naturalizes any of their children under the age of 16.[17] The naturalization of a husband or a wife, however, does not automatically naturalize the other. Congress has provided that one may be naturalized by any United States District Court or in any State or territorial court of record.

According to the McCarran-Walter Act, applicants for naturalization must satisfy the following requirements:[18]

(1) They must have entered the United States legally, have resided here continuously for at least five years (including six months in the State in which they file their petition for naturalization), and be at least 18 years old.

(2) They must be of "good moral character," be "attached to the principles of the Constitution of the United States," and be "well disposed to the good order and happiness of the United States."

(3) They must be able to read, write, speak, and understand words in ordinary usage in the English language (unless he or she is over 50 years of age and has lived in

Occasionally, several hundred newly naturalized Americans take the oath of citizenship en masse. More than 140,000 persons have been naturalized in each of the past few years.

this country for 20 years). And they must demonstrate "a knowledge and understanding of the fundamentals of the history, and the principles and form of government, of the United States."

(4) They must not, within 10 years prior to filing their petition, have advocated opposition to organized government *(anarchism)* or the overthrow of government by force or violence, or belonged to an organization advocating either of these ends. (This stipulation is lifted if one can show that membership was unknowing, invol-

---

[17] Such children must be living in the United States at the time of the parents' naturalization. The naturalization of one parent is sufficient if the other has died or in the case of divorce.

[18] Except that some of these requirements are eased for the alien spouses or children of citizens and for those serving or who have served in the Armed Forces. For example, a citizen's alien wife need reside in the United States for only three years (from date of marriage) rather than the five years normally required before the filing of a naturalization petition.

ALIEN ADDRESS REPORT | COMPLETE ALL ITEMS—PRINT IN BLOCK LETTERS WITH BALL-POINT PEN OR USE TYPEWRITER. THIS CARD MUST BE MAILED. PLACE A TEN CENT U.S. POSTAGE STAMP ON REVERSE AND DROP IN MAIL BOX. THIS CARD IS REVISED ANNUALLY. ONLY SUBMIT A CURRENT YEAR CARD.

1. (LAST NAME)   (FIRST)   (MIDDLE)

2. ADDRESS IN THE U.S. (EXCEPT COMMUTERS—SHOW ADDRESS IN MEXICO OR CANADA. SEE ITEM 15)

CITY OR TOWN | STATE | ZIP CODE | CHECK HERE IF ADDRESS IS CURRENT □

3. ALIEN NO. FROM ALIEN CARD A- | 4. PLACE ENTERED THE U.S. | 5. WHEN ENTERED U.S. (MO/DAY/YR) | 6. SEX □ MALE □ FEMALE

7. COUNTRY OF BIRTH | 8. DATE OF BIRTH (MO/DAY/YR) | 9. COUNTRY OF CITIZENSHIP | 10. ARE YOU NOW WORKING IN THE U.S.? □ YES □ NO

11. SOCIAL SECURITY NO. (IF ANY) | 12. FOR GOVERNMENT USE ONLY

13. PRESENT OR MOST RECENT OCCUPATION IN U.S. (MAIN JOB) | 14. TYPE OF FIRM OR BUSINESS OF PRESENT OR MOST RECENT EMPLOYMENT (MAIN JOB)

15. STATUS (CHECK APPROPRIATE BOX) WHEN DID YOU RECEIVE YOUR PRESENT IMMIGRATION STATUS? (MO/DAY/YR)
1 □ IMMIGRANT (PERMANENT RESIDENT) 3 □ VISITOR 4 □ CREWMAN 5 □ STUDENT
2 □ IMMIGRANT (COMMUTER WORKER-CHECK THIS BLOCK 6 □ EXCHANGE ALIEN 7 □ REFUGEE-PAROLEE
IF YOU ENTER THE U.S. DAILY OR AT LEAST TWICE A WEEK) 8 □ OTHER (SPECIFY)

16. I CERTIFY THAT THE STATEMENTS ON THIS CARD ARE TRUE TO THE BEST OF MY KNOWLEDGE
SIGNATURE (IF UNDER 14 YEARS OLD, SIGNATURE OF PARENT OR GUARDIAN) | DATE

Form I-53 (Rev.1-1-80)N U.S. DEPARTMENT OF JUSTICE—IMMIGRATION AND NATURALIZATION SERVICE
FORM APPROVED OMB NO. 43—R0306

All aliens, including those who apply for citizenship, must register with the Immigration and Naturalization Service during January of each year.

untary, or based upon economic necessity.) Of course, these stipulations are aimed at communists.

(5) They must take an oath (or affirmation) in which allegiance is renounced to any foreign state or ruler and pledge that they will support and defend the Constitution and laws of the United States against all enemies foreign and domestic. They must agree to take up arms in defense of this country or to perform noncombat service if called upon to do so by law.

Examiners from the Immigration and Naturalization Service usually play a very significant role in the process. They examine applicants, often very closely, to ensure that citizens-to-be meet the conditions that have just been outlined. The final decision to grant or to deny citizenship is made by the federal or State judge in whose court the petition has been filed.

In 1963 Congress enacted a statute directing the President to proclaim Sir Winston Churchill an "honorary citizen" of the United States. Lafayette was made an honorary citizen of two States during the American Revolution. But the honor accorded Great Britain's late wartime Prime Minister is unique in our history.

Loss of Citizenship. Under present law, one may lose one's citizenship in one of three ways: (1) as punishment for certain federal crimes, (2) by expatriation, or (3) by denaturalization.

PUNISHMENT FOR CRIME. Despite the popular impression, a person cannot lose his or her citizenship upon being convicted of *most* federal or *any* State crimes. Some of the *privileges* of citizenship, especially the right to vote, are often denied to felons in various States. But under *no* circumstances may a State deprive *anyone* of citizenship.

Citizens, naturalized or native-born, may be stripped of citizenship upon conviction of certain federal offenses. The only crimes to which this penalty may be attached are treason, inciting or engaging in rebellion, or attempting to overthrow the government by force or violence.[19]

---

[19] For many years, desertion from the armed forces in wartime and flight from the country to avoid wartime service also were punished with the loss of citizenship. However, the Supreme Court in *Trop* v. *Dulles,* 1958, held the desertion provision to be unconstitutional as a violation of the 8th Amendment's ban of cruel and unusual punishment. And, in *Kennedy* v. *Mendoza-Martinez,* 1963, it struck down the draft-evasion provision because the law did not allow to those persons charged with the offense any of the fair trial guarantees set out in the 5th and 6th Amendments. See pages 162–168.

EXPATRIATION. One may *expatriate* one-self (renounce one's citizenship) in a variety of ways; and one may do so either voluntarily or involuntarily, according to the statutes. For example, expatriation may occur if one takes an oath of allegiance to or is naturalized by a foreign state.[20] A child may be expatriated if the parents become naturalized citizens of another country.

Any American citizen may renounce his or her citizenship by making a formal declaration to that effect to a representative of the Attorney General or to an American diplomatic or consular officer abroad.[21]

DENATURALIZATION. The process by which naturalized citizens may be stripped of their citizenship is that of denaturaliza-tion. It is far easier for naturalized citizens to lose their citizenship than it is for native-born citizens. They can lose it on any of the grounds upon which native-born citizens can, of course.

In addition, one may be denaturalized if one joins a communist organization or other group, membership in which would have barred one's naturalization, within five years after becoming a citizen. One may be denaturalized if, at any time within 10 years after becoming a citizen, one refuses to testify before a congressional committee concerning alleged subversive activities. And, if it is shown that citizenship was obtained by fraud or that one took the oath of allegiance with mental reservations, a person may be denaturalized.[22]

[20] For many years the law also provided for the automatic loss of citizenship by a person who voted in a foreign election. The Supreme Court held that provision unconstitutional in 1967, however. In *Afroyim* v. *Rusk* it declared that the fact that the 14th Amendment defines citizenship has the effect of denying to Congress the power to provide for the loss of citizenship except on a voluntary basis. Said the Court, one has "a constitutional right to remain a citizen unless he voluntarily relinquishes that right." Although *Afroyim* involved only the matter of voting in a foreign election, the Court's opinion appears to say that Congress does not have the authority to provide for the involuntary loss of citizenship under any circumstances.

The Court narrowed its holding in *Afroyim* in some later cases, but only slightly. And, most recently, it has reaffirmed the essential thrust of that 1967 decision. In *Vance* v. *Terrazas*, 1980, it upheld the power of Congress to set the standards the Government uses when it claims that a person has voluntarily relinquished citizenship. But, in doing so, it also ruled that in such cases the Government must prove more than the mere fact that the person involved acted voluntarily. It must also show that that person specifically intended to renounce his or her citizenship.

[21] American citizenship is neither lost nor acquired by marriage today. The only significant effect marriage has on the subject now is to shorten the time required for naturalization in the case of the person who marries an American citizen.

[22] Until recently the law also provided that if naturalized citizens returned to their former country and resided there for a period of three years they would thereby be denaturalized. However, the Supreme Court held the provision unconstitutional in *Schneider* v. *Rusk*, 1964. It held that, as the Constitution draws no distinctions between naturalized and native-born citizens (except in eligibility to the Presidency), Congress has no authority to do so.

SUMMARY

We are a nation of immigrants. Some 50 million have come to this country since 1820. While immigration was encouraged for more than a century, the closing of the frontier by 1890, a lessening demand for new labor, and a shift in the main source of immigration prompted change.

The power to regulate immigration is an exclusive power of the National Government. The first major restrictions on admission came when Congress enacted the Chinese Exclusion Act of 1882. This was followed by the exclusion of several classes of undesirables. A continuing flood of immigration brought restrictions in the form of national quotas in the 1920's.

Today, under the Immigration and Nationality (McCarran-Walter) Act of 1952 and the Immigration Reform Act of 1965, immigration is rigidly controlled in terms of *both* quality and quantity. Immigrants must meet high personal qualifications. Under the quota system, only 170,000 quota immigrants may be admitted from countries outside the Western Hemisphere and only 120,000 from within this hemisphere each year. Many special immigrants are admitted, however, as are many nonimmigrants.

All persons living in the United States or its possessions are *citizens, nationals,* or *aliens.* The original Constitution contained no definition of citizenship; the 14th Amendment added one in 1868. Citizenship may be acquired either by birth or by naturalization. A person may become a native-born citizen by being born in the United States (*jus soli*) or by being born abroad to parents at least one of whom is an American citizen (*jus sanguinis*). Naturalization may be either individual or collective.

Citizenship imposes some duties and accords some privileges not extended to aliens. Over all, the alien record in the United States is quite good. One may be stripped of one's citizenship *only* by the National Government, *never* by a State. Citizenship is lost as a result of punishment for a few specific federal crimes, by expatriation, or by denaturalization.

Concept Development

Questions for Review

1. On what grounds does the Congress possess the power to regulate immigration?

2. What two factors have been especially responsible for our tremendous population growth?

3. How many immigrants have come to the United States since such records were first kept?

4. What factors were responsible for our early policy of encouraging immigration?

5. What factors brought a change in that policy?

6. What and when was the first major attempt made to restrict immigration?

7. What act of Congress set the basic pattern for our present system of immigration control?

8. What are the two major statutes under which immigration is regulated today?

9. May a person ineligible to become a citizen nonetheless enter as an immigrant?

10. Immigration is rigidly controlled today on the basis of what two factors?

11. What area of the world was favored by the former quota system?

12. What are special immigrants? Nonimmigrants?

13. Approximately how many aliens now live in the United States? Approximately how many immigrants come here each year?

14. On what two broad bases may one acquire citizenship?

15. What is the difference between *jus soli* and *jus sanguinis*?

16. Who may become a naturalized citizen?

17. May a State grant citizenship? May it deprive citizenship?

18. On what grounds may one be expatriated? Denaturalized?

For Further Inquiry

1. In *Ambach* v. *Norwick*, 1979, the Supreme Court upheld a New York State law which forbids aliens to become public school teachers if they are eligible for citizenship but have not applied for it. Said the Court: "Some State functions are so bound up with the operation of the State as a governmental entity as to permit the exclusion from those functions of all persons who have not become a part of the process of self-government." It found that education falls into that category of State functions—especially because the schools and teachers play a critical role in the shaping of students' attitudes toward the society, government, and the political process. Do you agree with the Court's ruling? Why, or why not? If so, what other public jobs (if any) do you think ought to be denied to such aliens?

2. Many argue that because the personal qualifications an alien must meet are so high we could well afford to raise the number of quota immigrants admissible in any one year. Do you agree? Why?

3. Do you think that aliens should be permitted to vote in your State? Do you think they should be permitted to practice law or medicine? If not, why not? If so, under what conditions?

4. In what particular ways can a nation's immigration history and its present policies have important consequences for its foreign relations?

5. For the alien about to be naturalized, the court ceremony involved is a unique, solemn, and significant occasion. Most judges regard it in this light and, despite the pressure of their other judicial duties, arrange proceedings in a fitting manner. A few judges do not, however; they seem to view the matter as an unwelcome interruption, a boring chore to be accomplished as quickly as possible. If you were a judge, what steps would you take to insure that the dignity of your courtroom ceremony matched the importance of the occasion?

Suggested Activities

1. Invite a naturalized citizen to speak to the class on his or her experiences in obtaining citizenship.

2. Arrange a class trip to attend a naturalization ceremony.

3. Prepare an essay on the subject: "What It Means to Be an American."

4. Stage a debate or class forum on the question: *Resolved,* That the present immigration policies of the United States are, in many particulars, much too restrictive.

5. Prepare a wall chart or bulletin board display presenting the material contained in the graph on page 105 or in the chart on page 113.

Suggested Reading

Brownstone, David M., *et. al., Island of Hope, Island of Tears.* Rawson, Wade, 1979.

Bryce-Laporte, Roy S. (ed.), *Source Book on the New Immigration.* Transaction Books. 1979.

Kraus, Michael and Snider, Louis, *Immigration: The American Mosaic from Pilgrims to Modern Refugees.* Krieger, 1979.

Lieberson, Stanley, *A Piece of the Pie: Black and White Immigrants Since 1880.* University of California Press, 1980.

"Making It in America: Story of the Vietnamese," *U.S. News,* Nov. 27, 1978.

Also: Office of Information, Immigration and Naturalization Service, Department of Justice, Washington, D.C. 20536.

6

Civil Rights: Fundamental Freedoms

The God who gave us life gave us liberty at the same time.

THOMAS JEFFERSON

■ Why is the relationship between liberty and authority so critical in a free society?

■ Where is the line to be drawn between the right of individuals to express themselves and the right of society to protect itself?

■ Why must it be that all civil rights are *relative* rights, that no person can possess the absolute right to do as he or she pleases?

The United States was born out of a struggle for freedom. Those who founded this nation loved liberty and prized it above all earthly possessions. For them, freedom for their country and freedom for the individual were the greatest of blessings that Providence could bestow. In proclaiming the independence of the United States, they declared:

> We hold these truths to be self-evident: that all men are created equal; that they are endowed by their Creator with certain unalienable Rights; that among these are Life, Liberty, and the pursuit of Happiness.

And, significantly, in the very next line of the Declaration of Independence they added:

> That to secure these rights, Governments are instituted among Men. . . .

The Founding Fathers repeated this justification for the existence of government in the Preamble to the Constitution:

> We the People of the United States, in Order to . . . secure the Blessings of Liberty to ourselves and our Posterity, do ordain and establish this Constitution for the United States of America.

Civil Rights and Limited Government. Government in the United States is firmly based upon the concept of *limited government.* That is, it is based on the principle that government is not all-powerful, that it

The right of individuals or groups to take steps to correct grievances or unfair practices is central to the preservation of a free society.

has *only* those powers the sovereign people have given to it. This fact is well illustrated in the field of civil rights. The Constitution is studded with guarantees of personal freedom—that is, with prohibitions of governmental action.

All governments exercise authority over individuals. The crucial difference between democracies and dictatorships lies in the *extent* of that authority. In a dictatorship that authority is practically unlimited. In the Soviet Union, for example, opposition to the dictatorship is ruthlessly suppressed. Even such forms of expression as art, music, and literature must glorify the state. In the United States, on the other hand, governmental authority is severely limited. Peaceable opposition to the government is not only permitted, it is actively encouraged. The late Justice Robert H. Jackson put it well:

If there is any fixed star in our constitutional constellation, it is that no official, high or petty, can prescribe what shall be orthodox in politics, nationalism, religion, or other matters of opinion or force citizens to confess by word or act their faith therein.[1]

Our System of Civil Rights

Historical Background. As we noted in Chapter 2, our system of civil rights is one of those valuable legacies which came to us from England and played a vitally important role in the shaping of government in the United States. Over a period of centuries, the English people had waged a continuing struggle to establish individual liberties. The early colonists brought a dedication to that cause with them to the New World.

The concept of civil rights took root and flourished in the fertile soil of America. The Revolutionary War was fought to

---

[1] *West Virginia Board of Education* v. *Barnette,* 1943; see page 134.

maintain and expand the rights of the individual against government. The very first State constitutions contained long lists of rights held by the people.

The National Constitution, as it was drafted at Philadelphia in 1787, contained a number of important civil rights guarantees—especially in Article I, Sections 9 and 10 and in Article III. But it did not contain—as several of the first State constitutions had—a bill of rights, a general listing of the rights held by the people.

The outcry this omission raised was so marked that several of the States ratified the original Constitution only on condition that a Bill of Rights be immediately added. The very first session of Congress in 1789 proposed a series of amendments to meet this demand. Ten of them, the Bill of Rights, were ratified by the States and became a part of the Constitution on December 15, 1791. Later Amendments, especially the 13th and 14th, have added to the freedoms guaranteed by the Constitution.

The Courts and Civil Rights. In the United States the courts, especially the Supreme Court of the United States, stand as the principal guardian of individual liberties. The executive and legislative branches of the National and State Governments are also responsible for safeguarding the people's rights, of course. But it is the courts which must *interpret* and *apply* the constitutional guarantees whenever an individual claims that government has infringed upon his or her liberty.

The fact that the courts do stand as guardians does *not* mean that the citizen can sit back in assured safety, however. Nor does the fact that the National Constitution and the State constitutions contain lists of basic rights mean that our founders bought and paid for them and that they are ours forever. To preserve and protect those liberties, each generation must learn and understand them anew, and be willing to fight for their preservation. The late

Learned Hand, one of the nation's great jurists, put it this way:

> I often wonder whether we do not rest our hopes too much upon constitutions, upon laws and upon courts. These are false hopes; believe me, these are false hopes. Liberty lies in the hearts of men and women; when it dies there, no constitution, no law, no court can ever do much to help it. While it lies there it needs no constitution, no law, no court to save it.[2]

Civil Rights Are Relative, Not Absolute. Even though basic civil rights are guaranteed to *everyone* in the United States, *no one* has the right to do whatever he or she pleases. Individuals have a right to do as they please *as long as* they do not interfere with the rights of others. That is, each person's rights are *relative* to the rights of all others. For example, each person in the United States enjoys the right of free speech. But no person has *absolute* freedom of speech. Thus, one who uses obscene language may be punished by a court for committing a crime. Or, one who damages another by what he or she says may be sued for slander. The great Justice Oliver Wendell Holmes once made the point in this oft-quoted passage:

> The most stringent protection of free speech would not protect a man in falsely shouting fire in a theatre and causing a panic.[3]

Persons to Whom Rights are Guaranteed. Most of the civil rights guaranteed in the Constitution are extended to *all persons.* The Supreme Court has often held that the word "persons" includes aliens in the United States as well as citizens.

Not *all* rights are extended to aliens,

---

[2] Quoted in Irving Dillard (ed.), *The Spirit of Liberty: Papers and Addresses of Learned Hand.* Knopf, 2nd edition, 1953, pages 189–190.
[3] *Schenck v. United States,* 1919; see page 138.

The right of free speech is protected by the 1st and 14th Amendments to the Constitution. But slander, libel, and inciting to riot are not protected.

however. For example, the right to travel freely throughout the United States is one of the rights guaranteed to all *citizens* by the Constitution's two Privileges and Immunities Clauses.[4] But aliens may be, and especially in wartime are, restricted in this regard.

Early in World War II all persons of Japanese descent living on the Pacific Coast were evacuated inland. Some 120,000 persons, two-thirds of whom were *native-born American citizens,* were involved. They were interned in "war relocation camps" operated by the Government. The relocation program caused severe economic and personal hardship for many. In 1944 the Supreme Court reluctantly upheld the forced evacuation as a reasonable wartime emergency measure.[5] The action has been severely criticized ever since. Japanese-Americans fought heroically in World War II, and not a single instance of *Nisei*

(American-born Japanese) disloyalty has ever been found.

Federalism Complicates Our System of Civil Rights. The existence of a federal system in the United States complicates our system of civil rights in these several ways:

(1) There are some civil rights which are enjoyed against the National Government only.

(2) There are some civil rights which are enjoyed against the States (and their local governments) only.

(3) There are some—a great many—which are enjoyed against both the National Government and the States.

(4) Some of the civil rights enjoyed against a State arise from the National Constitution whereas others arise from the particular State constitution.

As we shall see in a moment, the Supreme Court has lessened the complicated effects of federalism on our system of civil rights—especially through its broadening interpretation and application of the Due Process Clause in the 14th Amendment.

The Bill of Rights Restricts the National Government Only. The several guarantees contained in the Bill of Rights were originally intended as restrictions upon the National Government, *not the*

---

[4] Article IV, Section 2, Clause 1 and the 14th Amendment. Of course, the guarantee does not extend to those citizens under some form of legal restraint—in jail, on bail, committed to mental institutions, etc.

[5] *Korematsu* v. *United States,* 1944; however, on the very same day the Court held (in *Ex parte Endo*) that once the loyalty of any citizen internee was established, no restriction could be placed on that person's freedom to travel that was not legally imposed upon all other citizens.

HIGHLIGHTS OF THE BILL OF RIGHTS

Freedom of religion

Freedom of speech

Freedom of press

Protection against illegal searches

Freedom of assembly and petition

Right to trial by jury

Right to due process of law

Right to counsel

No cruel and unusual punishments

Just compensation for property

Congress OF THE *United States*
begun and held at the City of New-York on
Wednesday the fourth of March, one thousand seven hundred and eighty nine.

States.[6] To illustrate the point, take the 2nd Amendment. It reads:

> A well-regulated militia being necessary to the security of a free state, the right of the people to keep and bear arms shall not be infringed.

This restriction applies *only* to the National Government. The States may, and very often do, restrict the right to keep and bear arms. They may require licenses for guns, prohibit the carrying of concealed weapons, and so on. (As a matter of fact, the Amendment does not impose a very significant limit on the National Government, either—as we shall note shortly.)

MODIFYING EFFECT OF THE 14TH AMENDMENT. The provisions of the Bill of Rights apply *only* against the National Government. *But* notice that the Due Process Clause of the 14th Amendment provides:

> . . . nor shall any State deprive any person of life, liberty, or property, without due process of law, . . .

---

[6] Recall that Amendments 1–10 were added (in 1791) to meet one of the major objections raised during the struggle for ratification of the Constitution; see page 57. The Supreme Court held the amendments to apply only against the National Government in the first case in which the point was raised, *Barron* v. *Baltimore,* decided in 1833; it has followed that holding ever since.

In performing its task of interpreting and applying the Constitution, the Supreme Court has often held that the 14th Amendment's Due Process Clause guarantees to all persons *all* of those rights which are "basic or essential to the American concept of ordered liberty."

In a long series of cases the Court has held that most of the specific guarantees in the Bill of Rights are also contained in the 14th Amendment's Due Process Clause. That is, it has "read into the meaning" of the 14th Amendment most of the protections set out in the Bill of Rights—and thus made them applicable against the States.

The Court began this historic process in *Gitlow* v. *New York* in 1925. In that landmark case, it found that freedom of speech—which the 1st Amendment says cannot be denied by the National Government—is also "among the fundamental personal rights and liberties protected by the Due Process Clause of the 14th Amendment from impairment by the States."

Soon after *Gitlow,* the other 1st Amendment guarantees were held to be within the meaning of the 14th Amendment's Due Process Clause, as well. The Court did so with regard to: freedom of the press, in *Near* v. *Minnesota,* 1931; freedom of assembly and petition, in *De Jonge* v. *Oregon,* 1937; and freedom of religion, in *Cantwell* v. *Connecticut,* 1940. We shall return to each of these landmark cases, considering them more closely and in greater detail, later in this chapter.

The Supreme Court enlarged the scope of the 14th Amendment's Due Process Clause much further in several cases decided in the 1960's. Thus, in *Mapp* v. *Ohio,* 1961, it held that the Clause prohibits un-

reasonable searches and seizures by State and local authorities and forbids them the use of any evidence gained by those actions—just as the 4th Amendment prohibits such actions by federal officers. In *Robinson* v. *California,* 1962, it added the 8th Amendment's ban on cruel and unusual punishments to the list of essential rights covered by the 14th Amendment. The Court has since given the same 14th-Amendment coverage to:

—the 6th Amendment's guarantee of the right to counsel in *Gideon* v. *Wainwright,* 1963.
—the 5th Amendment's ban on self-incrimination in *Malloy* v. *Hogan,* 1964.
—the 6th Amendment's right of persons accused of crime to confront witnesses against them in *Pointer* v. *Texas,* 1965.
—the 6th Amendment's guarantee of a speedy trial in *Klopfer* v. *North Carolina,* 1967.
—the 6th Amendment's guarantee that those accused may compel witnesses in their behalf in *Washington* v. *Texas,* 1967.
—the 6th Amendment's guarantee of trial by jury (at least in cases involving serious crime) in *Duncan* v. *Louisiana,* 1968.
—the 5th Amendment's prohibition of double jeopardy in *Benton* v. *Maryland,* 1969.

We shall return to each of these latter guarantees. But for now, note the essential point here: In effect, the Supreme Court has "nationalized" these basic guarantees. That is, by holding that they exist *against the States* through the 14th Amendment, *as well as* against the National Government through the Bill of Rights, the Supreme Court has made their basic content and meaning uniform throughout the nation. In the process, much of the effect that federalism has upon our civil rights system

---

7 The case involved a communist who had been convicted of criminal anarchy in New York. He had published a pamphlet advocating the violent overthrow of government. In upholding his conviction the Court also sustained the constitutionality of the State law under which he had been tried.

Case Study

The history of the United States, from its earliest days to the present time, can be written around the continuing theme of individual liberty. Indeed, as a people, we have always proclaimed the primary importance of the concept. The nation was founded and settled chiefly by those in search of greater personal freedom. The Revolutionary War, the settlement of the West, the coming of tens of millions of the "huddled masses yearning to breathe free," our role in two great world wars, our struggles for economic and social justice and for equality for all—these and the other chapters in our history have all been dominated by the great theme of liberty.

As a matter of fact, our attitude toward the dignity, the sanctity, the inviolability of the individual finds such ready acceptance today—at least in theory if not always in practice, that most Americans seem almost to take it for granted.

At the same time, however, and in seeming paradox, we Americans have always placed an extremely high value on the concept of authority, on the need for "law and order." Recall that the earliest of the colonists lost no time in establishing authority, in such forms as town governments, organized churches, and in other ways. While the revolutionists of 1776 were proclaiming "Life, Liberty, and the pursuit of Happiness" to be "unalienable Rights," they were also quick to insist upon government "to secure these rights." And a century later, the western pioneers, storied for their rugged individualism, depended upon government to open the West, to guarantee their land claims, to protect them against Indians and outlaws, and to provide them with such public services as roads and schools.

■ Are liberty and authority opposing concepts? Why can it be said that the classic problem for a democracy is that of achieving a proper balance between these two forces? What did James Madison mean when he wrote, in *The Federalist No. 51:* "In framing a government which is to be administered by men over men, the great difficulty lies in this: you must first enable the government to control the governed; and in the next place, to control itself"? Even if the delicate balance between individual liberty and governmental authority can be satisfactorily struck, it must be continually maintained. Even then, still another crucial problem remains: How can the conflicts that arise be resolved when certain rights as exercised by some impinge on the rights of others? In what ways can you illustrate this problem?

has been very sharply reduced. But, notice, the 14th Amendment's Due Process Clause *does not* cover all of the rights provided in the Bill of Rights. Rather, it covers only those the Supreme Court has found to be "basic or essential to the American concept of ordered liberty."

No Complete Listing of Rights Possible. The Constitution contains a number of civil rights guarantees: in Article I, Sections 9 and 10; in Article III, Sections 2 and 3; in the 1st through the 8th Amendments; and in the 13th and 14th Amendments. But nowhere in the Constitution—and, indeed, nowhere else—can one find a complete and exhaustive listing of *all* of the rights held by the American people.

The too-seldom noted 9th Amendment declares that there are other rights, in addition to those in the Constitution:

> The enumeration in the Constitution of certain rights shall not be construed to deny or disparage others retained by the people.

Over the years, many additional rights have been found to be "retained by the people." As but one quick illustration, the

Supreme Court has often held that evidence gained as the result of an unlawful search or seizure cannot be used against any person accused of crime in any court in the land. See page 157.

Freedom of Expression

The right to freedom of expression is absolutely indispensable to the notion of democracy. Without it, a free society cannot exist.

The right is enshrined in the 1st Amendment, where freedom of religion, speech, press, assembly, and petition are protected against the National Government. It declares:

Congress shall make no law respecting an establishment of religion, or prohibiting the free exercise thereof; or abridging the freedom of speech, or of the press; or the right of the people peaceably to assemble, and to petition the Government for a redress of grievances.

As we have already noted, the 14th Amendment's Due Process Clause extends these fundamental freedoms against the States and their local governments.

Freedom of Religion. The 1st and 14th Amendments guarantee that: (1) there shall be no "establishment of religion" in the United States, and (2) there shall be no

The 1st Amendment guarantees freedom of worship to people of all faiths. Here, a Jewish worshipper is at morning prayers in a synagogue.

arbitrary governmental restriction of the personal exercise of religious belief.[8]

SEPARATION OF CHURCH AND STATE. The Establishment Clause creates, in Thomas Jefferson's phrase, a "wall of separation between church and state." But the wall is not infinitely high, nor is it impenetrable. That is, church and state, while constitutionally separated in the United States, are not enemies. Nor are they even strangers to one another. In fact, their relationship is a friendly one.

Government has done much to encourage churches and religion in this country. For example, nearly all church-owned property and contributions to churches and religious sects are exempted from federal, State, and local taxation. Chaplains serve with each branch of the armed forces. Most public officials take an oath of office in the name of God. Sessions of Congress and of most State legislatures and city councils are opened with prayer. Even the nation's anthem and its coins and currency contain references to God.

The content of the Establishment Clause cannot be described in precise terms. And the nature of the "wall of separation" remains a matter of continuing and often heated controversy.

Only a few cases involving the Clause have thus far been decided by the Supreme Court. In fact, the Court did not rule upon the meaning of the provision until as recently as 1947. A few earlier cases did bear on the problem, but each of them was decided without a direct consideration of the nature of the "wall of separation."

In 1925, in *Pierce* v. *Society of Sisters,* the Court voided an Oregon compulsory school attendance law. It had required that all persons between the ages of eight and sixteen attend *public* schools. The statute was purposely designed to eliminate the private—and especially the parochial (*i.e.,* church-related)—schools in the State. The Court held the law to be a deprivation of liberty and of property in violation of the 14th Amendment; see page 150.

In 1930, in *Cochran* v. *Louisiana,* the Court upheld a Louisiana law authorizing the use of public funds to supply "schoolbooks to the school children of the State." Under that law, textbooks were furnished to pupils in both public and private schools, including those attending parochial schools. Said the Court: "The school children and the State alone are the beneficiaries" of the law, not the schools they attend.

In 1934, in *Hamilton* v. *Board of Regents,* the Court also upheld a suspension by the University of California of two students who refused to take part in a compulsory ROTC program. The students had refused to do so on religious grounds. They argued that the University's requirement deprived them of their liberty as guaranteed by the 14th Amendment. The Court held that although the Constitution undoubtedly protects the right to object to such training on religious grounds, "California has not drafted or called them to attend the University."

The first direct ruling on the meaning of the Constitution's phrase "an establishment of religion" came in *Everson* v. *Board of Education,* 1947—a case often known as the *New Jersey School Bus Case.* In it, the Court upheld a State law that provided for the public (tax-supported) busing of students who attend parochial schools. It ruled, 5–4, that the statute was not an aid to religion but, rather, a safety measure intended to benefit school children no matter what school they might attend. Said the Court:

---

[8] Also, Article VI, Section 6 provides that: ". . . no religious test shall ever be required as a qualification to any office of trust or profit under the United States." In *Torcaso* v. *Watkins,* 1961, the Supreme Court held that the 14th Amendment applies the same ban upon the States when it unanimously invalidated a provision in the Maryland constitution requiring all public officeholders to declare a belief in the existence of God.

The "establishment of religion" clause of the 1st Amendment means at least this: Neither a State nor the Federal Government can set up a church. Neither can pass laws which aid one religion, aid all religions, or prefer one religion over another. . . . No tax in any amount, large or small, can be levied to support any religious activities or institutions, whatever they may be called, or whatever form they may adopt to teach or practice religion. Neither the State nor the Federal Government can, openly or secretly, participate in the affairs of any religious organizations or groups and *vice versa*.

Since that decision—over the past three decades, then—the Court has decided only a comparative handful of Establishment Clause cases. Most have involved, in one way or another, religion and education.

RELEASED TIME. Two of these cases have dealt with "released time" programs in public schools. Such programs, now found in most of the States, allow those students who wish to do so to be "released" from school time in order to attend classes in religious instruction.

In *McCollum* v. *Board of Education,* 1948, the Court struck down the program then in use in Champaign, Illinois. It did so because school classrooms and other public facilities were used for religious purposes.

In *Zorach* v. *Clauson,* 1952, however, New York City's program, similar in nearly all respects to that in Illinois, was upheld. The Court did so because New York's program requires that the religious classes be held *away* from the schools, in *private* places.

PRAYERS AND THE BIBLE. Two other decisions have involved the widespread practice of the recitation of prayers and the reading of the Bible in public schools. In *Engel* v. *Vitale,* 1962, the Court outlawed the use, even on a voluntary basis, of a nondenominational prayer written by the New York State Board of Regents. The "Regents' prayer" read:

Almighty God, we acknowledge our dependence upon Thee, and we beg Thy blessings upon us, our parents, our teachers, and our country.

The Supreme Court held that:

. . . the constitutional prohibition against laws respecting an establishment of religion must at least mean that in this country it is no part of the business of government to compose official prayers for any group of the American people to recite as part of a religious program carried on by government.

To those who insisted that the Regents' prayer posed no actual threat of religious establishment, the Court quoted the author of the 1st Amendment, James Madison:

. . . It is proper to take alarm at the first experiment on our liberties. . . . Who does not see that the same authority which can establish Christianity, in exclusion of all other Religions, may establish with the same ease any particular sect of Christians, in exclusion of all other Sects? That the same authority which can force a citizen to contribute three pence only of his property for the support of any one establishment, may force him to conform to any other establishment in all cases whatsoever?

In 1963 two cases, one from Pennsylvania and the other from Maryland, were combined for decision. In *Abington School District* v. *Schempp,* reading from the Bible—as required by State law—and reciting the Lord's Prayer at the beginning of each school day was challenged. In *Murray* v. *Baltimore School Board,* a board rule that required each day to open with "reading, without comment, a chapter in the Holy Bible and/or the use of the Lord's Prayer" was also challenged.

By an 8-1 majority, the Supreme Court held that both cases involved violation of "the command of the 1st Amendment that the government maintain strict neutrality, neither aiding nor opposing religion." And it added:

> . . . The place of religion in our society is an exalted one, achieved through a long tradition of reliance on the home, the church, and the inviolable citadel of the individual heart and mind. We have come to recognize through bitter experience that it is not within the power of government to invade that citadel, whether its purpose or effect be to aid or oppose, to advance or retard.

Most recently, the Court struck down a Kentucky law requiring that copies of the Ten Commandments be posted in all public school classrooms, *Stone* v. *Graham,* 1980.

To sum up these rulings, the Supreme Court has held that the public schools—which are agencies of government—cannot sponsor religious exercises. Specifically, it has held that the Establishment Clause forbids the organized reciting of prayers and the devotional reading of the Bible in public schools. But it has *not* held that individuals cannot pray, when and as they choose, in the schools—or in any other place. Nor has it held that the Bible cannot be studied in a literary or historic frame.

Despite these rulings, both organized prayers and Bible readings can be found in many public schools around the country.

EVOLUTION. In *Epperson* v. *Arkansas,* 1968, the Court held that State's law forbidding the teaching of evolution in the public schools invalid because the Establishment Clause:

> . . . forbids alike the preference of a religious doctrine or the prohibition of theory which is deemed antagonistic to a particular dogma. . . . The State has no legitimate interest in protecting any or all religions from views distasteful to them.

TAX EXEMPTION. Every State exempts houses of worship, and other church-owned property used for religious purposes, from both State and local taxation. The Court upheld this practice—found that it does not violate the wall of separa-tion—in *Walz* v. *Tax Commission,* 1970.

Walz, a New York City property owner, had challenged the exemption of churches from local property levies. He argued that these exemptions made his and others' property taxes higher than they would otherwise be, and that they amounted to a public support of religion.

The Court denied his plea. It found that such exemptions are only evidence of a State's "benevolent neutrality" toward religion. Said the Court, these exemptions "create only a minimal and remote"—and therefore permissible—"involvement between church and state."

STATE AID TO PAROCHIAL SCHOOLS. Most recent Establishment Clause cases center around this highly controversial question: What forms of State aid to parochial schools are constitutional?

Several States provide various forms of support to church-related schools—*e.g.,* transportation, textbooks, and standardized testing. And the pressures to expand both the amounts and the kinds of this aid have increased as school operating costs have soared in recent years.

Those who argue for such aid regularly note that parochial schools enroll large numbers of students who would otherwise have to be educated at public expense. They also point out that the Supreme Court has held that parents have a legal right to send their children to those schools (*Pierce* v. *Society of Sisters*). They insist that, to give that right real meaning, some aid must be given to those schools in order to relieve parents of some of the double burden imposed upon them because they must pay taxes to support public schools their children do not attend. Many of them insist, too, that church-run schools do not pose serious church-state problems. They take that position because, in their view, those schools devote most of their efforts to the teaching of *secular* (*i.e.,* nonreligious) subjects rather than to *sectarian* (*i.e.,* religious) ones.

Those who oppose such aid base their arguments on a number of grounds, too. They regularly note that the public schools play an important democratizing role by bringing together students from various religious backgrounds. They regard the separation of children in schools on the basis of religion as at least undesirable—and particularly so because religious differences are often related to ethnic, social, and economic distinctions among people. Many of them also insist that those parents who want to send their children to parochial schools should accept the financial consequences of that choice and should not expect the rest of society to bear that load. And many of them maintain that it is not possible to draw clear lines between secular and sectarian subjects; that is, they insist that religious points of view do have an effect upon the teaching of nonreligious subjects in the church-run schools.

For the past decade the Supreme Court has been picking its way through cases generated by various State aid programs. In the first of them, *Board of Education* v. *Allen,* 1968, it upheld a New York law providing secular textbooks for students in parochial schools. It thus followed the position set out in the *Cochran* and *Everson* cases. That is, it applied what has come to be known as the "child-benefit theory"— that the aid is directed to the student, not to the school.

In deciding *Allen,* the Court emphasized that a State may aid *only* secular education in church-related schools. But drawing the line between that aid which supports only the nonreligious activities of a parochial school and that which also promotes its religious purposes has proved to be a quite troublesome task.

Excessive Entanglement. Since 1971, the Court has added to the child-benefit theory another test: the *excessive entanglement standard.* This gauge of its constitutionality holds that a State's law must meet these requirements: (1) the purpose of the aid

must be clearly secular, not religious; (2) its primary effect must neither advance nor inhibit religion; and (3) it must avoid an "excessive entanglement of government with religion."

In other words, as the Court put it in the first case in which it applied the new test, the Establishment Clause is designed to prevent three main evils: "sponsorship, financial support, and active involvement of the sovereign in religious activity," *Lemon* v. *Kurtzman,* 1971.

In *Lemon,* the Court struck down a Pennsylvania law providing for the reimbursement of private schools for their expenditures for teachers' salaries, textbooks, and other instructional materials used in nonreligious courses. At the same time, it also voided a Rhode Island law providing salary supplements for teachers of secular courses in private elementary schools (*Earley* v. *DiCenso,* 1971).

In both of these cases the Court held that the State programs were of direct benefit to parochial schools—and, so, to the churches which sponsor them. And it held, too, that these programs required such strict State supervision that they produced an excessive entanglement of government with religion. (The Court found, for example, that both programs required close surveillance of parochial schools to determine what courses were being taught—and, beyond that, what was in fact being taught in those courses.)

The Court has been using the excessive entanglement standard in "parochaid" cases for a decade now. Over that span, it has upheld some State aid programs and has rejected others. Thus, it has ruled that public grants may not be made to parochial schools for maintenance and repair work, nor for tuition reimbursements to parents whose children attend those schools—in a New York case, *Committee for Public Education* v. *Nyquist,* 1973.

It allowed the use of public funds to loan textbooks to students in parochial schools—in a Pennsylvania case, *Meek* v. *Pittinger*, 1975. But, in that same case, it rejected the loan of such things as films, projectors, and recorders, and grants for counselling and speech therapy work. And it banned public payments for field trips by parochial school students—in an Ohio case, *Wolman* v. *Walter*, 1977.

Two recent New York cases may help lay out the shape of the Court's standard here. In *Levitt* v. *Committee for Public Education*, 1973, it struck down a program in which the State reimbursed church-related schools for their costs in certain testing and reporting functions. That ruling focused on the point that many of those tests had been prepared by teachers in those schools—and so could be considered a part of their program of religious instruction.

But in *Committee for Public Education* v. *Regan*, 1980, the Court allowed the State to pay church-related schools to administer, grade, and report the results of standardized tests prepared by the State Department of Education. And, in the same case, it upheld the use of public funds to defray those school's costs for reporting pupil attendance figures and other educational data required by the State.

The Court has taken a different view in cases involving public aid to church-related colleges and universities, however. Thus, in *Tilton* v. *Richardson*, 1971, it upheld federal grants to such institutions for the construction of academic buildings used for nonreligious purposes. It could find no excessive entanglement in these "one-shot" grants.[9] And it has sanctioned two somewhat similar State programs—one conducted by South Carolina (*Hunt* v. *McNair*, 1973) and the other by Maryland (*Roemer* v. *Maryland Board of Public Works*, 1976).

---

[9] But in *Tilton* the Court did hold one section of the Higher Education Facilities Act of 1963 unconstitutional. That section limited to 20 years a college's obligation not to use a federally-financed building for religious instruction or worship. In effect, the Court ruled that such buildings may never be used for those purposes.

Given the money problems facing the parochial schools, it seems obvious that the Court has many more such cases to hear.

THE FREE EXERCISE OF RELIGION. The Free Exercise Clause guarantees to each person the right to *believe* whatever that person chooses to believe in matters of religion. But no person has a right to *act* in whatever way he or she may choose on the basis or those beliefs. Freedom of religion is not a defense for those actions which violate criminal laws, offend the public morals, or threaten the health, welfare, or safety of the community.

The Supreme Court laid down the basic shape of the right in the first case it heard on the point, *Reynolds* v. *United States*, 1878. Reynolds, a Mormon living in Utah, had two wives—a circumstance allowed by the doctrine of his church but prohibited by a federal law banning polygamy in the territories of the United States.

Reynolds was tried and convicted under the law and, on appeal, argued that it violated his constitutional right to the free exercise of his religious beliefs. But the Court held that the 1st Amendment does not forbid Congress to punish actions which are "violations of social duties or subversive of good order." To hold otherwise, said the Court:

. . . would be to make the professed doctrines of religious belief superior to the law of the land, and in effect to permit every citizen to become a law unto himself. Government could exist only in name under such circumstances.

The Court has held to this position through the years, upholding many regulations in the face of free-exercise challenges. Thus, it has upheld laws requiring the compulsory vaccination of school children (*Jacobson* v. *Massachusetts*, 1905); forbidding the use of poisonous snakes in religious rites (*Bunn* v. *North Carolina*, 1949); and requiring businesses to close on Sundays—"blue laws" (*McGowan* v. *Maryland*, 1961). It has held that religious groups may

The Amish are often called the "plain people." A life apart from the modern world and its values is central to their faith. The Supreme Court has held that Amish children cannot be compelled to attend public schools beyond the eighth grade.

be required to obtain a permit before holding a parade on public streets (*Cox* v. *New Hampshire*, 1941). It has held that child labor laws may be applied to those who permit children under their care to sell religious literature in the streets (*Prince* v. *Massachusetts*, 1944). And it has held that one with religious objections to military service can nonetheless be drafted.[10]

But, of course, the Court has also found a number of governmental actions contrary to the free-exercise guarantee. Thus, it has found that the right is abridged if a city ordinance makes it illegal to distribute religious tracts within the city (*Marsh* v. *Alabama*, 1946) or if a State law requires the approval of a public official before one may solicit funds for a religious purpose (*Cantwell* v. *Connecticut*, 1940). It has found that right to be abridged if a local ordinance prohibits the door-to-door distribution of religious handbills (*Martin* v. *Struthers*, 1943). It has held that a State may not compel Amish children to attend school beyond the eighth grade—because the sect's centuries-old "self-sufficient agrarian lifestyle essential to their religious faith is threatened by . . . modern education" (*Wis-*

consin v. *Yoder*, 1972). And, most recently, it has ruled that a State may not bar ministers from holding public office (*McDaniel* v. *Paty*, 1978).

Many important religious freedom cases have been carried to the Supreme Court over the years by Jehovah's Witnesses, a fundamentalist group which very actively promotes its beliefs. Perhaps the stormiest controversy the sect stirred came from its defiance of compulsory flag salute requirements. That controversy and the two major Supreme Court decisions it produced tell us much about the guarantee of religious freedom. And, too, it reveals much about how difficult 1st Amendment questions can be for the courts.

The Witnesses refuse to salute the flag or to permit their children to do so. They regard such conduct as a violation of the commandment against idolatry. In *Minersville School District* v. *Gobitis*, 1940, the Court upheld a Pennsylvania school board regulation requiring students to salute the flag at the beginning of each school day. Gobitis had been convicted for forbidding his children to do so. He appealed, basing his argument on the constitutional guarantee. But the Court held, 8–1, that freedom of religion is not an absolute right. It held that the flag is a symbol of national unity upon which the nation's security depends, and that requiring the salute was not an infringement on religious liberty.

Less than three years later, in a remarkable turnabout, the Court reversed the

---

[10] In the leading case on the point during the Vietnam War, the Court held that those persons entitled to exemption from the draft as conscientious objectors were those "whose consciences, spurred by deeply held moral, ethical, or religious beliefs, would give them no rest if they allowed themselves to become part of an instrument of war." *Welsh* v. *United States*, 1970.

Gobitis decision. In *West Virginia Board of Education* v. *Barnette,* 1943, 6–3, it held that legislation requiring a flag salute *is* an unconstitutional interference with religious freedom. Mr. Justice Jackson's words quoted on page 121 are from the Court's powerful opinion in the case. To them the Court added:

> The case is made difficult not because the principles of its decision are obscure but because the flag involved is our own. Nevertheless, we apply the limitations of the Constitution without fear. . . . To believe that patriotism will not flourish if patriotic ceremonies are voluntary is to make an unflattering estimate of the appeal of our institutions to free minds.

Freedom of Speech and Press. The 1st and the 14th Amendments' protection of free speech and a free press serve two basic purposes. They (1) guarantee to *each person* the right of free expression, in the spoken and the written word and by all other means of communication, and (2) ensure to *all persons* an adequate and wide-ranging discussion of public affairs.

Freedom of speech and press are most often thought of in terms of the first purpose—that is, in terms of the right of each person to express his or her views. But the second purpose is just as vital. It is because our system of government rests on a faith in the ability of the people to make sound, reasoned judgments.

Clearly, such judgments can be made only where the people have the greatest possible access to all of the facts in a given matter *and,* as well, to any and all *interpretations* of those facts. Justice Oliver Wendell Holmes once put the point in these words:

> Persecution for the expression of opinions seems to me perfectly logical. If you have no doubt of your premises or your power and want a certain result with all your heart, you naturally express your wishes in law and sweep away all opposition. . . . But when men have realized that time has upset many fighting faiths, they

may come to believe even more than they believe the very foundations of their own conduct that the ultimate good desired is better reached by free trade in ideas— that the best test of truth is the power of the thought to get itself accepted in the competition of the market, and that truth is the only ground upon which their wishes safely can be carried out.[11]

Notice that the guarantees of free speech and press are especially intended to protect the expression of *unpopular* views. The opinions and ideas held by the majority need, after all, little or no constitutional protection. Again, in Justice Holmes' words:

> . . . if there is any principle of the Constitution that more imperatively calls for attachment than any other it is the principle of free thought—not free thought for those who agree with us but freedom for the thought that we hate.[12]

RIGHTS RELATIVE, NOT ABSOLUTE. The 1st and 14th Amendments do *not* provide for unbridled freedom of speech and press, however. Many reasonable restrictions may be and are imposed. For example, no one has a right to *libel* or *slander* another.[13] Similarly, such actions as the uttering of obscene words, the printing and distribution of obscene materials, or the sending of such materials through the mails may be and are prohibited by law.

---

[11] Dissenting in *Abrams* v. *United States,* 1919.

[12] Dissenting in *Schwimmer* v. *United States,* 1928.

[13] *Libel* (the printed word) and *slander* (the spoken word) involve the use of words *maliciously* (with vicious purpose) to injure one's character or reputation or expose one to public contempt, ridicule, or hatred. Truth is usually an absolute defense. The law is less restrictive concerning criticism of public officials, however. In *New York Times* v. *Sullivan,* 1964, the Supreme Court held that a public official may not recover damages for criticism, even if it is exaggerated or false, unless "the statement was made with actual malice—that is, with knowledge that it was false or with reckless disregard of whether it was false or not." Several later decisions have extended that ruling to cover "public figures" and even private individuals who become involved in newsworthy events.

Obscenity. Obscenity is not protected by the 1st and 14th Amendments. It is beyond the pale of constitutionally-protected speech and press. Even so, no civil rights issue has given the Supreme Court more difficulty in recent years.

Finding an adequate definition of the term has proved an elusive and troublesome thing. The Court has wrestled several times with these questions: What language, what printed matter, what films and other materials are, in fact, obscene? And what restrictions can properly be placed on the distribution and use of such materials?[14]

The leading case on the point today is *Miller* v. *California,* 1973. There the Court affirmed the position that obscenity is not constitutionally protected. And it laid down three standards by which to determine whether material is obscene or not: *First,* whether "the average person, applying contemporary [local] community standards," would find that the material, taken as a whole, "appeals to the prurient interest"—*i.e.,* tends to excite lust, produce lewd emotions. *Second,* "whether the work depicts or describes, in a patently offensive way," a form of sexual conduct specifically dealt with in the State's obscenity law. And *third,* "whether the work, taken as a whole, lacks serious literary, artistic, political, or scientific value." The very fact that the Court has developed so complex a set of standards is itself an indication of how difficult the obscenity problem is.

That obscenity is a knotty problem can also be seen from these cases: In *Stanley* v. *Georgia,* 1969, the Court held that a State

cannot make it a crime for a person to possess obscene materials for his or her own private use in his or her own home.[15] Yet, in two 1971 cases, *United States* v. *Thirty-Seven Photographs* and *United States* v. *Reidel,* the Court again held that Congress may bar such materials from the mails. And it also held that Congress may prohibit the importation of such materials from abroad, even for one's own private use. In short, the Court has sanctioned the right of an individual to read or view obscene materials in his or her own home; but it has also denied to any person the principal means of obtaining them.[16]

Prior Censorship Forbidden. The 1st and 14th Amendments permit government to punish *some* utterances, once made. But the Constitution does *not* permit government to establish a system of prior censorship—that is, to impose "previous restraints." Government may not curb ideas *before* they are expressed. Thus, the publishers of a newspaper or magazine may be punished for the printing of a libelous comment or an obscene photograph, *after* they have done so. But, except in the most extreme situations, publishers cannot be forbidden to publish.

The leading case here is *Near* v. *Minnesota,* 1931. In that case the Supreme Court struck down a State law prohibiting the publication of any "malicious, scandalous, and defamatory" periodical. Acting under the statute, a local court had issued an in-

---

[14] Congress enacted the first of a series of laws to exclude obscene matter from the mails in 1872. The Court upheld the current statute, which excludes "every obscene, lewd, lascivious, or filthy" piece of material in *Roth* v. *United States,* 1957. It held the statute a valid exercise of the postal power (Article I, Section 8, Clause 7) and not repugnant to the 1st Amendment. The decision in *Roth* also marked the Court's first attempt to devise an adequate definition of obscenity.

[15] Films were involved in this case. Said the Court: "If the 1st Amendment means anything, it means that the State has no business telling a man sitting alone in his own home, what books he may read or what films he may watch." But in *United States* v. *Orito,* 1973, it held that the "zone of privacy" protected in *Stanley* v. *Georgia* does not extend beyond one's own home.

[16] Another principal source for obscene materials is, of course, so-called "adult book stores." Although such matter can neither be mailed nor imported legally, these "porno shops" are usually well-supplied. In *Young* v. *American Mini Theatre,* 1976, the Court ruled that a city can regulate the location of "adult entertainment establishments" (presumably including the book stores) through its zoning ordinances—and many cities now do so.

Case Study

A free press is indispensable to a free society. Indeed, Thomas Jefferson once declared that "were it left to me to decide whether we should have a government without newspapers or newspapers without a government, I should not hesitate a moment to prefer the latter."

The Supreme Court has often said that the fundamental purpose of the guarantee of freedom of the press is to insure "such a free and general discussion of public matters" as "to prepare the people for an intelligent exercise of their rights as citizens"—as it did in an early leading case, *Grosjean* v. *American Press Company,* 1936.

But the free press guarantee is not absolute—*e.g.,* in matters involving libel or obscenity, as we have seen. And, too, the Supreme Court has often held that what the Constitution protects is the right to *communicate* information, not the right to *acquire* it. That is, the Court has drawn a distinction between the right to *gather* the news and the right to *publish* or *broadcast* it. In short, it has said that the 1st Amendment does not give to the news media any greater right of access to information than that it gives to the public generally.

The Court reiterated this acquire-communicate distinction most recently in deciding *Houchins* v. *KQED* in 1978. There, it refused to order the sheriff of Alameda County, California, to permit television reporters and cameras access to some portions of the county's jail facilities.

KQED had sought to visit and photograph the jail as part of its coverage of several stories—including a prisoner's suicide, several escapes, and allegations of gang rapes and poor physical conditions. The sheriff refused several such requests. Instead, he scheduled a series of closely supervised monthly tours. Although open to the public, each tour was limited to not more than 25 persons, including the press; and cameras, recording equipment, and inmate interviews were prohibited.

■ How would you make the choice that Jefferson posed? Why do most reporters oppose the Court's acquire-communicate distinction? Do you agree with the decision in *Houchins* v. *KQED?*

junction forbidding *continued* publication of *The Saturday Press,* a weekly published in Minneapolis. The paper had printed several articles charging public corruption and attacking "grafters" and "Jewish gangsters" in that city. Finding the law unconstitutional, the Court held the press to be immune to "prior restraint," except in such extreme cases as wartime or when a publication is obscene or incites its readers to violence. The Court reaffirmed that view in *New York Times* v. *United States,* 1971—the famous *Pentagon Papers Case.* The *Times* and several other newspapers had obtained copies of a set of classified documents and began to publish them. The documents, officially titled *History of U.S. Decision-Making Process on Viet Nam Policy* but popularly dubbed "The Pentagon Papers," had been stolen from the Defense Department. The Government, arguing that publication of the documents would endanger national security, sought court orders to forbid their printing. The Court rejected the Government's pleas, however. It held that there is a strong presumption that prior censorship is unconstitutional and that the Government had not satisfactorily overcome that presumption.

CONFIDENTIALITY. Do news reporters have a constitutional right to withhold certain information from government? Or, may they be compelled to testify before a grand jury, in court, or before a legislative committee—and there be required to identify their sources and furnish other confidential information?

While these questions are of immediate concern to those who gather and disseminate the news, they have a direct impact upon the free flow of information—and, therefore, on the public's right to know.

Many reporters and most news organizations insist that they must have the right to refuse to testify. They argue that without it they cannot assure confidentiality to their sources—cannot assure them that they will remain anonymous. And they contend that without that assurance many of their sources will not provide them the information they must have in order to keep the public informed.

Both State and federal courts have generally rejected the news media argument. In recent years several reporters have refused to obey court orders directing them to divulge information—and, as a consequence, a number of them have gone to jail. Their willingness to pay the penalty for contempt of court testifies to the importance of the issues involved here.

In the leading case, *Branzburg* v. *Hayes,* 1972, the Supreme Court held that the 1st Amendment does not grant a special privilege to reporters. They, "like other citizens, [must] respond to relevant questions put to them in the course of a valid grand jury investigation or criminal trial." If any special exemptions are to be given to the news media, said the Court, they must come from Congress and the States.

To date, Congress has not responded to the Court's suggestion. However, some 20 State legislatures have enacted so-called "shield laws"—statutes which do grant to reporters some degree of protection against the disclosure of their sources or the divulgence of other confidential information.

MOTION PICTURES. The question of whether motion pictures are protected by constitutional guarantees of freedom of expression reached the Supreme Court early in the history of the movie industry. In *Mutual Film Corporation* v. *Ohio,* 1915, the Court upheld a State law prohibiting the showing of films not of "moral, educational, or amusing and harmless character." The Court viewed the showing of motion pictures as "a business pure and simple, originated and conducted for profit like other spectacles, not to be regarded . . . as part of the press of the country or as organs of public opinion." Nearly all of the States and thousands of local communities then proceeded to establish strong movie censorship programs.

In 1952 the Supreme Court expressly overruled its 1915 decision, however. In *Burstyn* v. *Wilson,* involving movie censorship in New York, it held that "liberty of expression by means of motion pictures is guaranteed by the 1st and 14th Amendments." Movie censorship as such is *not* unconstitutional, however. The Court has struck down State and local censorship of films in many recent cases. But it has done so only when that censorship has conflicted with the basic principle of free expression.

RADIO AND TELEVISION. Congress has provided for very extensive control over radio and television broadcasting through the Federal Communications Commission; see pages 566–567. Although there has been no systematic effort to censor the content of radio or television programs, the FCC licenses on the basis of "the public interest, convenience, or necessity." And, the licenses are subject to renewal every three years and to cancellation. The FCC has on some occasions inquired into the content of programs. In some cases it has refused applications for the renewal of licenses on the basis of objectionable programs or practices. In upholding such regulation, in *National Broadcasting Company* v. *United States,* 1943, the Supreme Court said:

> The right of free speech does not include . . . the right to use the facilities of radio and television without a license. The licensing system established by Congress in the Communications Act of 1934 was a proper exercise of its power over

commerce. The standard it provided for the licensing of stations was "the public interest, convenience, or necessity." Denial of a station license on that ground, if valid under the Act, is not a denial of free speech.

THE CLEAR AND PRESENT DANGER RULE. Drawing the line between those expressions which are protected by the Constitution and those which are not is an extremely difficult task. Where is the line between the right of individuals to express themselves and the right of the society to protect itself?

When a conflict between free expression and the demands of public safety occur, judges frequently rely upon the "clear and present danger" rule. The test, formulated by Justice Holmes, was first laid down by the Supreme Court in *Schenck* v. *United States,* 1919.

Schenck, the general secretary of the Socialist Party, and another party member, had been convicted of attempting to obstruct the war effort in violation of the Espionage Act of 1917. They had sent some 15,000 strongly worded leaflets to men who had been called to military service, urging them to resist the draft. In upholding both the law and the conviction, the Court said:

> We admit that in many places and in ordinary times the defendants in saying

all that was said in the circular would have been within their constitutional rights. But the character of every act depends upon the circumstances in which it is done. . . .

And, the Court then said:

> Words can be weapons . . . The question in every case is whether the words used are used in such circumstances and are of such a nature as to create a clear and present danger that they will bring about the substantive evils [*i.e.,* actions] that Congress has a right to prevent.

Words themselves can be outlawed, and those who utter them can be punished when their use creates an immediate danger that criminal acts will follow.

But—and this is the vital nub of the matter—*what* words used in *what* circumstances constitute a clear and present danger? The question can be answered only on the basis of the facts in each particular case.

INTERNAL SECURITY. Government has an undoubted right to protect itself and the nation against internal subversion—against domestic threats to the nation's security. But how far can it go in its attempts to do so?

Clearly, government may punish espionage, sabotage, and treason. Sedition presents a much more delicate problem, however, because it inevitably involves the use

the small society   by Brickman

Washington Star Syndicate, Inc.

of spoken or written words.[17]

Congress first acted to curb opposition to government in the Alien and Sedition Acts of 1798. These statutes authorized the President to deport undesirable aliens and made "malicious writing" against the government a crime. They were intended to stifle the opponents of President John Adams and the Federalist Party. The acts were undoubtedly unconstitutional, but they were never tested in the courts. Even so, some 25 persons were fined or jailed for violating them.

The Alien and Sedition Acts were a major issue in the elections of 1800 and a major reason for the defeat of the Federalists that year. In 1801 President Thomas Jefferson pardoned all who had been convicted under the acts and Congress soon repealed them.

Another sedition law was enacted during the First World War, as a part of the Espionage Act of 1917. That statute made it a crime to encourage disloyalty, interfere with the draft, obstruct recruiting, incite insubordination in the armed forces, or hinder the sale of government bonds. It also made it a crime to "willfully utter, print, write, or publish any disloyal, profane, scurrilous, or abusive language about the form of government of the United States or the Constitution. . . ."

Recall that it was in interpreting this act that the Supreme Court, speaking through Justice Oliver Wendell Holmes, first formulated the "clear and present danger" rule. Despite that test, some 2000 persons were convicted under the law.

Congress had made the Espionage Act of 1917 effective only in wartime. How-

ever, in 1940 it passed a new sedition law applicable in peacetime, as well. And it later enacted two additional sedition statutes. These three laws are: the Alien Registration (Smith) Act of 1940, the Internal Security (McCarran) Act of 1950, and the Communist Control Act of 1954. In their most pertinent provisions:

The Smith Act makes it unlawful for any person to teach or advocate the violent overthrow of government in the United States or to organize or knowingly be a member of any group with such an aim. It also forbids *conspiring* (joining, plotting) with others to commit any of these acts.

The McCarran Act requires all "communist-action" and "communist-front" organizations to register with the Attorney General of the United States. These groups are required to report annually, filing complete membership lists, the names of their officers, and the details of their financing. The act also created the Subversive Activities Control Board (SACB) to determine which groups are, in fact, subject to the law. It also forbade members of communist organizations to hold government jobs or to be employed by labor unions.

The Communist Control Act declares the Communist Party in this country to be "a conspiracy to overthrow the Government of the United States." It declares that the party's "role as the agency of a hostile power" makes it "a clear, present, and continuing danger" to the nation's security. The act denies to the party any of the rights or privileges commonly held by political parties in either federal or State law. (Several States have similar laws.)

The Supreme Court first upheld the constitutionality of the Smith Act in *Dennis* v. *United States,* 1951. Eleven of the Communist Party's top leaders had been convicted of teaching and advocating violent overthrow. They appealed to the Court, arguing that the Smith Act violates the 1st Amendment's speech and press guarantees. They also argued that no act of theirs

---

[17] *Espionage* is the practice of spying in behalf of a foreign power. *Sabotage* involves an act of destruction intended to hinder a nation's war or defense effort. *Treason* is specifically defined in Article III, Section 3 of the Constitution as consisting only of levying war against or adhering to the enemies of the United States (see page 170). *Sedition* is the incitement (prompting, urging, fomenting) of resistance to lawful authority; it does not necessarily involve acts of violence or betrayal.

posed a clear and present danger to this country. The Court disagreed, declaring:

> An attempt to overthrow the government by force, even though doomed from the outset because of inadequate numbers or power of the revolutionists, is a sufficient evil for Congress to prevent. . . . We reject any principle of governmental helplessness in the face of preparation for revolution, which principle, carried to its logical conclusion, must lead to anarchy.

After *Dennis*, Smith Act charges were filed against many lesser party leaders. They, too, were accused of teaching and advocating violent overthrow and with organizing the Communist Party to that end. Nearly all of them were convicted.

But 14 of these convictions were upset in *Yates* v. *United States*, 1957. There the Supreme Court voided the teaching and advocating convictions with this holding: Merely to urge one to *believe* something, in contrast to urging one to *do* something, cannot be made illegal. That is, the Court held that the Smith Act could be applied only to those who, singly or with others, teach or advocate *action* to bring about a forcible overthrow—not to those who teach or advocate only a belief in the desirability of such action.

In *Yates* the Court also reversed each defendant's conviction on the organizing count. It found that the Communist Party was fully "organized" in this country by no later than 1945. But these defendants had not been charged until 1951. Therefore, the Court ruled, a three-year statute of limitations barred any trial on a charge of organizing the party if that charge were brought any time after 1948.[18]

---

[18] A *statute of limitations* is a law which limits the time period within which a crime may be prosecuted. The time limit on federal prosecutions varies according to the specific crime involved but in most cases it is three years. The purpose of such statutes is not to permit a crime to go unpunished (though this sometimes happens). Rather, it is to prompt the "speedy trial" guarantee of the 6th Amendment and prevent endless harassment of individuals; see pages 163–164.

The "knowing membership" clause of the Smith Act was upheld in *Scales* v. *United States*, 1961. There the Court sustained the conviction of a party member. But it also ruled that it is those who are active, not passive or merely paper-affiliated, members of the Communist Party and those with a specific and clear intent to overthrow the government that the Smith Act intends to punish.

The end result of these major Smith Act cases was that, while the Court upheld the constitutionality of the law, it so construed its provisions as to make successful prosecutions extremely difficult.

The McCarran Act has proved to be an even less effective sedition law than the earlier Smith Act. The Court did uphold the law's requirement that communist-action organizations register when ordered to do so by the SACB, in *Communist Party* v. *United States*, 1961. The SACB had first ordered the party to register in 1953. The Court's 5–4 decision upholding the registration requirement came only after a lengthy legal battle in which the party argued that the act deprived it and its members of freedom of expression.

Subsequent efforts to force the party to register failed, however—largely for this reason: Any person who came forward to register the party, as required by the McCarran Act, could then be charged as a "knowing member" under the Smith Act. In 1965 the Supreme Court held that no person could be forced into such a position—for to do so would contradict the 5th Amendment's guarantee against self-incrimination (*Albertson* v. *United States*).

One practical effect of this decision was to leave the SACB with no real functions to perform. The board finally passed out of existence when Congress refused to fund it in 1974.

The Supreme Court further limited the effectiveness of the McCarran Act by declaring other portions of the law unconstitutional. Thus, it voided a provision denying members of communist organizations the right to obtain or use passports. In *Aptheker* v. *Rusk*, 1964, it found the passport section of the act so broadly and vaguely worded as to violate the 5th Amendment's Due Process Clause. And in *Robel* v. *United States*, 1967, it struck down the act's ban on the employment of those persons in defense industries. It did not find that Congress could not bar such employment; rather, it held that that section of the law was so loosely drawn as to be "an unconstitutional abridgment of the right of association protected by the 1st Amendment."

The net effect of court response to the McCarran Act has been to leave it a virtual hollow shell. That result was far from unexpected. The several court decisions have paralleled President Truman's veto that Congress overrode in enacting the law in the first place.[19]

No portion of the Communist Control Act has ever been tested in the courts. But, since its enactment, and despite the lack of success under the Smith and McCarran Acts, the party has all but disappeared as an active and open political movement in this country. It has all but abandoned the nomination of candidates for office. In fact, in 1968 it nominated its first presidential candidate since the elections of 1940. The Communist Party's 1980 candidate (Gus Hall) received fewer than 70,000 popular votes—only 0.0008 percent of the total vote.

Two factors have made the issue of internal subversion a less prominent one today than it was only a few years ago. One is the over-all ineffectiveness of the sedition laws. The other, the fact that U.S.-Soviet relations, while still strained, are not nearly so tense as in the Cold War period of the 1950's and 1960's.

ADVERTISING. Until recently, it was thought that "commercial speech"—advertising—was not covered by the 1st and 14th Amendments' protection of free speech. But in *Bigelow* v. *Virginia*, 1975, the Supreme Court held unconstitutional a State law prohibiting newspaper advertising of abortion services. And in 1976 it struck down another Virginia law, forbidding the advertisement of prescription drug prices (*Virginia State Board of Pharmacy* v. *Virginia Citizens Consumer Council*).

It made similar rulings in two 1977 cases. In *Carey* v. *Population Services International* it voided a New York law banning the advertisement of contraceptives; and in *Bates* v. *Arizona Bar* it invalidated regulations forbidding attorneys to advertise their services and fees.

In *Wooley* v. *Maynard*, 1977, the Court held that a State cannot require its citizens to act as "mobile billboards"—not, at least, when the words involved conflict with their religious or moral beliefs. The Maynards, Jehovah's Witnesses, objected to displaying the New Hampshire State motto, "Live Free or Die," on their automobile license plates. They found the words repugnant to their belief in "everlasting life," and so covered them over with tape. For this, Maynard was arrested and prosecuted on three separate occasions, fined, and jailed for 15 days. On appeal, the Supreme Court sided with the Maynards and ordered the State of New Hampshire to take no further action against them.

PICKETING. Picketing is the patrolling of a business site by workers who are on strike. It is an attempt by one of the parties to a labor dispute to inform the public of the controversy and to persuade customers and others not to deal with the firm involved. It is, then, a form of expression. So long as it is peaceful, it is protected by the 1st and 14th Amendments.

In the leading case, *Thornhill* v. *Alabama*,

---

[19] State sedition laws have met a generally similar fate in the courts. The leading case here is *Pennsylvania* v. *Nelson*, 1956. The Supreme Court held in that case that Congress, by enacting the Smith Act in 1940, the McCarran Act in 1950, and the Communist Control Act in 1954, had preempted the field of sedition; that is, it held that federal law so encompasses that field as to leave no room for State law on that subject.

1940, the Supreme Court struck down a State law making it a crime for one to loiter about or picket a place of business in order to influence others not to trade or work there. The Court declared:

> In the circumstances of our time, the dissemination of information concerning the facts of a labor dispute must be regarded as within the area of free discussion that is guaranteed by the Constitution.

But picketing which is "set in a background of violence" or is conducted for an illegal purpose may be prevented; see pages 144–145.

SYMBOLIC SPEECH. Ideas, views, opinions are usually communicated in one of two ways: either orally, as in a conversation or a speech, or in some published form, as in a newspaper, a handbill, a book, a recording, or a film.

But notice that conduct—the way in which one behaves or does something—can also be a means of expression. We have just seen an illustration of this fact in the discussion of picketing.

When is expression by conduct—so-called "symbolic speech"—protected by the 1st and 14th Amendments? Although there is not much case law on the point, the answer seems to be this: When the conduct involved is not of the sort that government may lawfully restrict or prohibit. To state it another way: When government cannot show a "sufficiently compelling interest"—a substantial and justifiable need—to regulate the conduct.

Two of the few symbolic speech cases thus far decided by the Supreme Court arose out of Vietnam war protests. *United States* v. *O'Brien,* 1968, involved four young men who had burned their draft cards at a protest meeting. They had then been convicted of violating a federal law which made it a crime to destroy or mutilate the cards. O'Brien argued that the 1st Amendment protects "all modes of communication of ideas by conduct." But the Court rejected that view and upheld the convictions.

Chief Justice Earl Warren, speaking for the majority, said: "We cannot accept the view that an apparently endless variety of conduct can be labelled 'speech' whenever the person engaging in the conduct intends thereby to express an idea." The Court held the use of draft cards to be an essential part of the administration of the selective service system. It held that acts of dissent can be punished if government has "a substantial and constitutional interest in forbidding them, the incidental restriction of expression is no greater than necessary, and the government's real interest is not to squelch dissent."

In the other case, *Tinker* v. *Des Moines School District,* 1969, the Court upheld the symbolic speech argument. It ruled that local school officials had violated the Constitution when they suspended two students who had defied the principal by quietly and passively wearing black armbands to school to protest the war. The Court found this conduct to be "closely akin to pure speech." And it noted that this conduct had not produced any substantial disruption of normal school activities.

In Chapter 8 we shall take a look at *Buckley* v. *Valeo,* 1976. There the Court upheld most of the provisions of federal campaign finance laws but also held some sections to be unconstitutional. In sustaining limits on campaign contributions, the Court said that the limits permit "symbolic expression of support evidenced by contributions" but do not "infringe the contributor's freedom to discuss candidates and issues." See page 204.

Freedom of Assembly and Petition. The 1st Amendment also guarantees:

> . . . the right of the people peaceably to assemble, and to petition the government for a redress of grievances.

And the 14th Amendment's Due Process

Clause extends the protection against the States and their local governments—as the Court first held in *DeJonge* v. *Oregon,* 1937. In that case DeJonge had been convicted of violating the State's law prohibiting "criminal syndicalism"—which the law defined as "the doctrine which advocates crime, physical violence, sabotage, or any unlawful acts . . . as means of accomplishing . . . industrial or political change or revolution."

DeJonge's only offense, for which he had been sentenced to seven years in prison, was that he had assisted in the conduct of and spoken at a public meeting advertised and sponsored by the Communist Party. The Court unanimously overturned his conviction, declaring:

> The greater the importance of safeguarding the community from incitements to the overthrow of our institutions by force and violence, the more imperative is the need to preserve inviolate the constitutional rights of free speech, free press, and free assembly in order to maintain the opportunity for free political discussion to the end that government may be responsive to the will of the people and that changes, if desired, may be obtained by peaceful means. Therein lies the foundation of constitutional government.

The Constitution here protects the right of the people to assemble and discuss public questions. It protects the right to organize in order to influence public policy, as in political parties and pressure groups. It protects the right of people to express their opinions—favorable or unfavorable—to public officials by such varied means as formal petitions, letters, news coverage, and lobbying.

But notice that it is the rights of *peaceable* assembly and petition that are guaranteed. No person or group may "use" these rights to incite a riot, block a public street, close a school, or otherwise endanger life, property, or public order. And government

The rights of peaceful assembly and petition, both important ways of influencing public policy, are protected by the 1st and 14th Amendments.

may make reasonable regulations concerning the time, place, and manner of assemblies in order to preserve the public peace.

Thus, the Supreme Court has upheld a city ordinance making it unlawful for persons on grounds adjacent to a school to make a noise or create any other diversion which would interfere with normal school activities, *Grayend* v. *City of Rockford,* 1972. It has also sustained a State law prohibiting demonstrations in or near a courthouse in order to interfere with court proceedings; *Cox* v. *Louisiana,* 1965.

But regulations designed to preserve the public peace must be precisely drawn, reasonable, and fairly administered. Thus, in *Coates* v. *Cincinnati,* 1971, the Court struck down, as too vague and loosely drawn, a city ordinance making it a crime for three or more persons to assemble on a public sidewalk and conduct themselves in a manner annoying to passersby. It also voided an ordinance which banned all picketing around school buildings except picketing involved in a labor dispute. The Court did so because the ordinance went beyond the neutrality of time-and-place regulation and dealt with the *content* of an assembly (*Police Department of Chicago* v. *Mosley,* 1972).

FREEDOM TO DEMONSTRATE. Organized demonstrations—mass meetings, parades, "sit-ins," or whatever form they take—are, of course, assemblies. They are a means of communicating ideas and opinions. And thus they fall within the scope of the 1st and 14th Amendments.

Demonstrations almost always occur in *public* places—streets, sidewalks, parks, public buildings, and the like. They do because it is the *public* the demonstrators want to contact. They want to bring their message to those who are not aware of their position and, too, to those who may not agree with them. Inevitably, there is some degree of conflict present—in terms both of ideas and of the normal use of the streets or other public facilities involved. And sometimes the antagonisms rise to very serious levels.

Given all of this, the Supreme Court has often upheld State or local regulations requiring advance notice and permits for the staging of demonstrations in public places. In an early leading case, *Cox* v. *New Hampshire,* 1941,[20] it unanimously approved such a statute, declaring:

> The authority of a municipality to impose regulations in order to assure the safety and convenience of the people in the use of public highways has never

been regarded as inconsistent with civil liberties but rather as one of the means of safeguarding the good order upon which they ultimately depend. . . . The question in a particular case is whether that control is exerted so as to deny . . . the right of assembly and the opportunity for the communication of thought and the discussion of public questions. . . .

The Court has faced a number of "right to demonstrate" cases in recent years. Several of them have raised such basic and thorny questions as these: How and to what extent can demonstrators and their demonstrations be regulated? Does the Constitution require that police officers protect unpopular groups when their activities excite others to violence? When, in the name of public peace and safety, may the police properly order demonstrators to disperse?

Among these cases, *Gregory* v. *Chicago,* 1969, remains typical. Dick Gregory and several others had been arrested by Chicago police and charged with disorderly conduct. They had marched, under police protection, singing and chanting and carrying placards, from city hall to the mayor's home, some five miles away. At the mayor's home, they continued to demonstrate. Marching in the streets, they demanded the ouster of the city's school superintendent and an end to *de facto* segregation in the schools.

A crowd of several hundred onlookers and residents of the all-white neighborhood had quickly gathered. Soon, insults and threats, rocks and eggs, and other missiles were hurled at the marchers. The police attempted to maintain order but, after about an hour, they concluded that serious violence was imminent. They then ordered the demonstrators to leave the neighborhood. When Gregory and the others failed to do so, they were arrested.

The Court unanimously reversed their convictions. It noted that the demonstra-

---

[20] One of the several Jehovah's Witness cases referred to on page 133. Cox and several other Witnesses were convicted of violating a State law requiring a license for the holding of any parade or procession on the public streets.

tors had done no more than exercise their constitutional rights of assembly and petition. The disorders which had occurred had been caused by the neighborhood residents and others, not by the marchers. No matter how reasonable the police request or laudable the police motives, said the Court, so long as the demonstrators acted peacefully, as they did, they could not be punished.

But, recall, there are reasonable limits to the exercise of the rights of assembly and petition. Thus, in *Adderly* v. *Florida,* 1966, a large group of black students had marched to the jail in Tallahassee to protest segregation within the jail. The sheriff ordered them away from the jail entrance and off the driveway and other jailhouse property. When they did not leave, 32 of them were arrested. They were later convicted for "trespass with a malicious and mischievous intent."

The Supreme Court, 5–4, upheld their convictions. The majority emphasized that jails are built for security purposes and are not open to the general public. "The United States Constitution does not forbid a State to control the use of its own property for its own lawful nondiscriminatory purpose," said the Court. And it expressly

LePelly in *The Christian Science Monitor* © TCSPS

STEP CAREFULLY

rejected the notion "that people who want to propagandize protests or views have a constitutional right to do so whenever and however and wherever they please."

SUMMARY

Because ours is a democratic government, it is limited, not all-powerful. It is most severely limited in power and in action in the area of civil rights.

All civil rights are *relative,* not absolute. No one has an absolute right to do as he or she pleases; each person must respect the rights of others. With minor exceptions, aliens enjoy the same civil rights as citizens.

The fact that we have a federal system complicates our system of civil rights somewhat, but the effects of this complication have been lessened by the Supreme Court's interpretation and application of the Due Process Clause of the 14th Amendment.

The provisions of the Bill of Rights apply *only* against the National Government. But the Court has held that the 1st and 4th

Amendments, the 5th Amendment's ban of compulsory self-incrimination and of double jeopardy, the 6th Amendment's guarantees of the right to counsel, of confrontation, to compel witnesses, to jury trial, and to a speedy trial, and the 8th Amendment's ban against cruel and unusual punishment are extended against the States through the Due Process Clause of the 14th Amendment.

No all-inclusive listing of civil rights' guarantees is possible; the seldom-noted 9th Amendment assures this. The fundamental freedoms included in the 1st Amendment guarantee *freedom of expression,* which includes freedom of religion, speech, press, assembly, and petition. Freedom of religion means both the right to freedom of belief and a ban on the establishment of any state religion. There is another group of rights that deals with *fair and equal treatment under the law,* and we shall consider those rights in Chapter 7.

Concept Development

Questions for Review

1. Why, according to the Declaration of Independence, are "Governments . . . instituted among Men"?

2. How do civil rights guarantees illustrate the concept of limited government?

3. What was the immediate cause for the addition of the Bill of Rights to the Constitution?

4. Why do the courts stand as the principal guardian of our individual liberties?

5. Why does no one possess an absolute right to do as he or she pleases in this country?

6. In what ways does federalism complicate our civil rights system?

7. Why does the 2nd Amendment not prevent the States from regulating the right to keep and bear arms?

8. In what sense has the Supreme Court "nationalized" many of the rights guaranteed against the National Government in the Bill of Rights?

9. What are the two basic purposes of the guarantee of freedom of expression?

10. Does the 1st Amendment provide for an absolute separation of church and state?

11. How did the Court's decision in *Reynolds* v. *United States,* 1878, indicate the basic shape of the guarantee of the free exercise of religion?

12. What are some of the restrictions that may properly be laid against the freedoms of speech, press, and religion?

13. What is the "clear-and-present-danger" rule?

14. What are the basic purposes of the guarantee of the rights of assembly and petition?

15. What are some of the restrictions that may properly be laid against the rights of assembly and petition?

For Further Inquiry

1. The Constitution contains a Bill of Rights but no "Bill of Obligations." If it did contain the latter, what would you have it include?

2. Woodrow Wilson once wrote:

We have learned that it is pent up feelings that are dangerous, whispered purposes that are revolutionary, covert follies that warp and poison the mind; that the wisest thing to do with a fool is to encourage him to hire a hall and discourse to his fellow citizens. Nothing chills folly like exposure to the air; nothing dispels folly like its publication; nothing so eases the machine as the safety valve.

Do you agree or disagree with Wilson's thought? Why?

3. Explain this statement: "One man's liberty ends where the next man's liberty begins."

4. Throughout this chapter the phrases "civil rights" and "civil liberties" are used interchangeably to mean the same thing; and they are customarily used in this manner. Some authorities, however, insist on drawing a distinction between them. On what basis do you think they do so?

5. Would you favor making each, or any, of the 1st Amendment freedoms absolute guarantees? Explain.

6. Do you agree or disagree with the proposition that the law of libel and slander should be more tolerant of criticisms of public officials than of private persons? Explain.

Suggested Activities

1. Invite a judge, attorney, or newspaper editor to speak to the class on a topic in the general area of civil rights.

2. Select one or more of the several Supreme Court cases cited in this chapter and, using the school or other library and/or the help of a local attorney, prepare a report to the class, indicating the facts and the holding in the case.

3. Prepare a report on the meaning and application of one of the provisions of the Bill of Rights.

4. For two or more of the civil rights guaranteed in the Constitution, draw up three hypothetical cases in which you think the Supreme Court would hold that a person's civil rights have been violated.

5. Write a report tracing the recent history of the civil rights movement.

6. Stage a debate or class forum on the question: *Resolved,* That all civil rights are privileges, since none are absolute.

Suggested Reading

Corwin, Edward S. and Peltason, J.W., *Understanding the Constitution.* Holt, Rinehart and Winston, 8th ed., 1979.

Cushman, Robert F., *Cases in Civil Liberties.* Prentice-Hall, 3rd ed., 1979.

Haiman, Franklyn S., *Freedom of Speech.* National Textbook Co., 1977.

Lofton, John, *The Press as Guardian of the First Amendment.* University of South Carolina Press, 1980.

Mendelson, Wallace, *The American Constitution and Civil Liberties.* Dorsey, 1981.

Murphy, Paul L., *World War One & the Origin of Civil Liberties in the United States.* Norton, 1980.

Oddo, Gilbert L., *Freedom and Equality: Civil Liberties and the Supreme Court.* Goodyear, 1979.

Pritchett, C. Herman, *The American Constitutional System.* McGraw-Hill, 5th ed., 1980.

The Public's Right to Know. Editorial Research Reports, 1980.

Sandoz, Ellis, *Conceived in Liberty: American Individual Rights Today.* Duxbury, 1978.

Shapiro, Martin and Tressolini, Rocco J., *American Constitutional Law.* Macmillan, 5th ed., 1979.

7

Civil Rights: Equal Justice Under Law

I have a dream that one day this nation will rise up and live out the true meaning of its creed: "We hold these truths to be self-evident, that all men are created equal."

MARTIN LUTHER KING, JR.

■ Which should be the principal concern in criminal justice: that the innocent be protected or that the guilty be punished?

■ Which should have the highest priority in the making and administration of law: justice, fairness, or equality? Are these values ever in conflict with one another?

■ Why must government never be permitted to violate the law as it goes about the business of enforcing the law?

Many contrasts may be drawn between democratic and dictatorial government. But the single, most profound one involves the extent to which government may exert its authority over the individual. In a democratic system that authority is severely limited and the rights of the people are purposefully safeguarded and promoted. But in a dictatorial regime governmental authority is virtually unlimited and the rights of the people are subordinated to the interests of the state.

In Chapter 6 we were especially concerned with the constitutional guarantees of freedom of expression—with those "fundamental freedoms" which lie at the very heart of democratic belief and practice. Now we turn to those constitutional guarantees intended to ensure fair and equal treatment for all under the law.

Whatever its many successes, the American democratic system has not succeeded in extending the guarantees of fair and equal treatment to *all* persons in the United States, particularly not to blacks. At least, it has not *yet* succeeded in doing so; and none of our public problems is a more compelling one today.

Due Process of Law

The Constitution contains two Due Process of Law Clauses. In the 5th Amendment the National Government is forbidden the power to "deprive any person of life, liberty, or property, without due process of law." And the 14th Amendment places the same restriction upon each of the States and, very importantly, upon all of their local governments, as well).

It has often been suggested that these two provisions, and their meanings, are more difficult to understand than any other portion of the Constitution. This may be so. But the fact remains that a thorough grasp of them is absolutely essential to an understanding of the American scheme of civil rights.

It is impossible to define due process of law in precise and all-embracing terms. Indeed, the Supreme Court has quite consistently, and quite purposefully, refused to give the concept an exact definition.[1] But, in broad terms, these two constitutional guarantees insist that government, in whatever it does, must *act fairly* and *in accord with established rules*, that it may not act arbitrarily, capriciously, or unreasonably.

Procedural and Substantive Due Process. As the two Due Process Clauses have been interpreted and applied by the Supreme Court, the concept of due process of law has developed along two lines: one *procedural*, the other *substantive*.

PROCEDURAL DUE PROCESS. The concept of due process originated and was developed in English and then in American law as a procedural concept. That is, it developed as—and it continues to be—a requirement that government employ fair procedures, that it act fairly, in enforcing the law.

SUBSTANTIVE DUE PROCESS. But *fair procedures* are of little value if they are employed to administer *unfair laws*. The Supreme Court recognized this fact in the

From *Straight Herblock* (Simon & Schuster, 1964)

"YOU KNOW WHAT? THOSE GUYS ACT LIKE THEY REALLY BELIEVE THAT"

latter part of the last century. It began to hold that due process demands that *both* the ways in which government acts *and* the laws under which it acts be fair.

That is, to the original notion of procedural due process the Court added that of substantive due process. In short, it may be said that procedural due process involves the *how* (the methods) of governmental action and that substantive due process involves the *what* (the policies) of governmental action.

Any number of cases may be used to illustrate these two basic aspects of due process. But, to illustrate procedural due process let us look at *Rochin* v. *California*, 1952. Rochin was a suspected narcotics pusher. Acting on a tip, three Los Angeles County deputy sheriffs went to his rooming house. Finding the outside door open, they entered and then forced their way

---

[1] Rather, it has relied on finding the meaning of due process on a case-by-case basis. The Court first described this approach a century ago, in *Davidson* v. *New Orleans*, 1878, as the "gradual process of judicial inclusion and exclusion, as the cases presented for decision shall require"— and it has maintained that approach ever since.

into Rochin's room. They found him sitting on a bed and spotted two capsules lying on a night stand beside the bed. When one of the deputies asked "Whose stuff is this?" Rochin seized the capsules, popped them into his mouth, and, although all three officers jumped him, managed to swallow them.

Rochin was handcuffed and taken to a hospital where his stomach was pumped. The capsules were recovered and found to contain morphine. Rochin was then prosecuted for violating the State's narcotics laws. The capsules proved to be the chief evidence against him and he was convicted and sentenced to 60 days in jail.

The Supreme Court reversed his conviction, holding that the deputies had violated the 14th Amendment's guarantee of procedural due process. Said the unanimous Court:

> This is conduct that shocks the conscience. Illegally breaking into the privacy of the petitioner, the struggle to open his mouth and remove what was there, the forcible extraction of his stomach's contents—this course of proceeding by agents of government to obtain evidence is bound to offend even hardened sensibilities. They are methods too close to the rack and the screw . . .

Take a case we cited earlier, *Pierce* v. *Society of Sisters,* 1925, to illustrate substantive due process—that is, the requirement that government *proceed under fair laws.* In 1922 the voters of the State of Oregon adopted a statute requiring that all children between the ages of eight and sixteen who had not completed the eighth grade attend *public* schools. The law was purposefully designed to destroy the private (and especially the parochial) schools in the State.

A Roman Catholic order challenged the constitutionality of the statute and brought suit against the governor to prevent its enforcement. On appeal, the Supreme Court unanimously found that the statute violated the 14th Amendment's Due Process Clause. The Court did *not* find that the State had enforced the law in an unfair manner. Rather, it found that the law itself "unreasonably interferes with the liberty of parents to direct the upbringing and education of children under their control." It also held that the law denied to private school teachers and administrators their liberty to practice a vocation "long regarded as useful and meritricious."

The 14th Amendment and the Bill of Rights. Recall that on pages 124–126 we made the point that the Supreme Court has held that the 14th Amendment's Due Process Clause includes *within its meaning* many (most) of the provisions of the Bill of Rights. That is, in a series of decisions dating from 1925 the Court has *incorporated* those basic civil rights guarantees into the 14th Amendment and has thus "nationalized" them. By holding that these rights exist against the *States* through the 14th Amendment, as well as against the *National Government* through the Bill of Rights, the Supreme Court has made their basic meaning uniform throughout the land.

Does all this seem complicated? It is. But an understanding of the point is crucial to an understanding of the meaning and importance of the 14th Amendment's Due Process Clause—and, indeed, to most of our civil rights law. The key cases in which the Supreme Court found various of the Bill of Rights guarantees to be included within the meaning of the 14th Amendment are set out in the table on the next page.[2]

Due Process and the Police Power. Prominent among the reserved powers of the States is the very broad *police power*—the authority to promote and protect the

---

[2] We considered the pertinent 1st Amendment cases in Chapter 6 and we shall consider those involving the guarantees of the 4th through the 8th Amendment in succeeding pages in this chapter.

THE NATIONALIZATION OF THE BILL OF RIGHTS

Year	Amend-ment	Provision	Case
1925	1st —	Freedom of speech	*Gitlow v. New York*
1931	1st —	Freedom of press	*Near v. Minnesota*
1937	1st —	Freedom of assembly, petition	*DeJonge v. Oregon*
1940	1st —	Freedom of religion	*Cantwell v. Connecticut*
1947	1st —	Establishment Clause	*Everson v. Board of Education*
1961	4th —	Protection from unreasonable searches, seizures	*Mapp v. Ohio*
1962	8th —	Prohibition of cruel and unusual punishment	*Robinson v. California*
1963	6th —	Right to counsel in criminal cases	*Gideon v. Wainwright*
1964	5th —	Protection from self-incrimination	*Mallory v. Hogan*
1965	6th —	Right to confront witnesses	*Pointer v. Texas*
1967	6th —	Right to speedy trial	*Klopfer v. North Carolina*
1967	6th —	Right to obtain witnesses	*Washington v. Texas*
1968	6th —	Right to trial by jury in criminal cases	*Duncan v. Louisiana*
1969	5th —	Prohibition of double jeopardy	*Benton v. Maryland*

public health, safety, morals, and welfare.[3] It is, at base, the power of State governments to safeguard individual well-being.

The extent of the police power—what the States can and cannot do in exercising it—is determined by courts as they decide actual cases in which exercises of the power come into conflict with personal liberties. As they decide most police power-civil rights cases, courts must strike a balance between the needs of society, on the one hand, and the rights of an individual, on the other hand.

Any number of cases arising out of any number of situations can be used here. Take, for example, a matter often involved in drunk-driving cases to illustrate the point:

Driving while under the influence of intoxicating liquor is a crime in each of the States. And every State prescribes one or more tests that may be used to determine whether one arrested and charged with the offense was in fact drunk at the time of the incident. These tests include, for example, requiring the accused to perform some exercise of physical dexterity, such as attempting to walk a straight line or touch the tip of his or her nose. They also include somewhat more sophisticated checks—notably, the use of the "breathalyzer test" or the drawing of a blood sample to measure the level of alcohol in a person's system. (In most States, one accused of drunk driving who then refuses to submit to the breath or the blood test is subject to the

[3] As the National Government is a government of delegated powers, it does not possess a general police power. Many federal statutes enacted by Congress under the commerce and postal powers—*e.g.*, those prohibiting the shipment of such items as obscene materials, lottery tickets, or illicit drugs in interstate commerce or through the mails are, however, examples of what is sometimes called the "federal police power."

automatic suspension of his or her driver's license.)

Question: Does the requirement that one submit to such a test violate that person's rights under the 14th Amendment? Does such a test involve an unconstitutional search for and seizure of evidence? Does it amount to an unconstitutional compulsory self-incrimination? Or, is such a requirement a valid exercise of the police power?

Both the State and federal courts have regularly come down on the side of the police power here. That is, they have regularly upheld the right of society to protect itself and rejected the individual rights argument. In the leading case, *Schmerber* v. *California*, 1966, the Supreme Court found no constitutional objection to a situation in which a police officer had directed a physician to draw blood from a man he had arrested for drunk driving. The Court stressed that the drawing of the blood sample occurred in a hospital and in accord with accepted medical practice, that the police officer had reasonable grounds to believe that the suspect was drunk, and that the officer had not had sufficient time to secure a warrant.

Again, any number of examples may be cited here to illustrate how legislators and judges have found the public health, safety, morals, and/or welfare to be of overriding importance. For example:

To promote health, States have been permitted to forbid or restrict the sale of intoxicants and dangerous drugs, forbid the practice of medicine or dentistry without a license, require the compulsory vaccination of school children, and require residences to be connected to sanitary sewers.

To promote safety, States have been permitted to forbid the carrying of concealed weapons and to require adequate braking systems, horns, lights, and shatter-proof glass on automobiles. And States may prohibit tall shrubbery at street intersections and require snow to be shoveled from sidewalks.

To promote morals, States have been permitted to forbid all or certain forms of gambling, forbid the sale of obscene materials, and outlaw prostitution; they may use zoning laws to forbid such establishments as adult theaters or bookstores and taverns in certain locations. And,

To promote welfare, States have been permitted to enact minimum wage and maximum hours laws and to restrict public utilities to reasonable profits. They may forbid the operation of oil and gas wells in a wasteful manner and forbid the operation of certain businesses on Sundays.

Again, note the fact that though the States can regulate many activities through the valid exercise of the police power, they cannot use that power in an unreasonable or unfair manner. Thus, a police officer may not use unnecessary force to compel a person accused of drunk driving to submit to a blood test. A city could not forbid a street demonstration by a group simply be-

In exercising their police powers, some States have imposed strict auto-emission controls on motor vehicles. Here, New Jersey's auto-emission control law is enforced by an employee of the Inspection Bureau; an exhaust tester is used to see if the vehicle is "clean."

cause the mayor opposes its political aims. Nor could a State ban the operation of private schools or the sale of all foreign-made automobiles.

The Right to Freedom and Security of the Person

Slavery and Involuntary Servitude. The 13th Amendment was added to the Constitution in 1865. Section 1 declares:

> Neither slavery nor involuntary servitude, except as a punishment for crime, whereof the party shall have been duly convicted, shall exist within the United States, or any place subject to their jurisdiction.

And, *importantly,* Section 2 gives Congress the expressed power "to enforce this article by appropriate legislation."

Prior to the adoption of the Amendment, each State decided for itself whether or not to permit slavery within its borders. With its ratification, that power was denied to them, and to the National Government, as well.

Section 1 of the Amendment is self-executing. That is, it required no action by Congress to make it effective.[4] Nonetheless, Congress has passed several laws to implement it; and a violation of them can result in a fine of up to $5000 and/or as much as five years in prison. There have been few, but occasional, cases of slavery since 1865. Thus, as recently as 1980, a federal court in Louisiana sentenced a man to five years in prison for holding two Mexican aliens as his slaves.

Most of the controversies that have arisen under Section 1 have turned on the question of "involuntary servitude"—that is, forced labor. The Antipeonage Act of 1867 makes it a federal crime for any person to hold another in *peonage*—a condition of servitude in which a person is bound to work in order to fulfill a contract or satisfy a debt. It is still vigorously enforced to protect debtors.

On several occasions, the Supreme Court has struck down State laws making it a crime, punishable by imprisonment, for any person to fail to work after having received money or other benefits by promising to do so. In destroying one of these State peonage laws, the Supreme Court said:

> The undoubted aim of the 13th Amendment as implemented by the Antipeonage Act was not merely to end slavery but to maintain a system of completely free and voluntary labor throughout the United States.[5]

The 13th Amendment does not forbid *all* forms of involuntary servitude, however. Thus, in 1918 the Court drew a distinction between "involuntary servitude" and "duty" in upholding the constitutionality of the selective service system (the draft).[6] Nor does imprisonment for crime violate the Amendment, as its own terms declare. And note that its guarantee, unlike any other in the Constitution, applies against *private* as well as public actions.

SECTION 2. Shortly after the Civil War, Congress enacted several civil rights laws, based on the 13th Amendment and applicable to *both* public officials *and* private parties. But in several cases (especially the *Civil Rights Cases,* 1883) the Supreme Court narrowly restricted the scope of federal authority. In effect, the Court held that racial discrimination against blacks by private persons did not impose upon blacks the "badge of slavery" nor keep them in servitude.

Congress soon repealed most of the statutes; and federal enforcement of the

---

[4] It is also one of the two provisions in the Constitution that an individual can violate by his or her own act; the other is Section 2 of the 21st Amendment.

[5] *Pollock* v. *Williams,* 1944; but note that the fact that a person cannot be forced to work in order to satisfy a debt does *not* relieve that person of the legal obligation to pay the debt.

[6] *Selective Draft Law Cases (Arver* v. *United States),* 1918. The Court held military conscription to be a proper exercise of the power of Congress "to raise and support armies," Article I, Section 8, Clause 12; see pages 447, 455.

CIVIL RIGHTS GUARANTEED IN THE FEDERAL CONSTITUTION

Against the National Government

1. Writ of *habeas corpus* not to be suspended except in rebellion or invasion. *Art. I, Sec. 9, Cl. 2.*
2. No bill of attainder. *Art. I, Sec. 9, Cl. 3.*
3. No *ex post facto* laws. *Art. I, Sec. 9, Cl. 3.*
4. Treason specifically defined and punishment limited. *Art. III, Sec. 3.*
5. No establishment of religion. *1st Amendment.*
6. No interference with religious belief. *1st Amendment.*
7. No abridging of freedom of speech and press. *1st Amendment.*
8. No interference with right of peaceable assembly and petition. *1st Amendment.*
9. No interference with right of people to keep and bear arms. *2nd Amendment.*
10. No quartering of soldiers in private homes without owners' consent. *3rd Amendment.*
11. No unreasonable searches and seizures; no warrants issued but upon probable cause. *4th Amendment.*
12. No criminal prosecution but upon grand jury action. *5th Amendment.*
13. No double jeopardy. *5th Amendment.*
14. No compulsory self-incrimination. *5th Amendment.*
15. No persons to be deprived of life, liberty, property, without due process of law. *5th Amendment.*
16. Speedy and public trial. *6th Amendment.*
17. Trial of crimes by impartial jury. *Art. III, Sec. 2, Cl. 3; 6th Amendment.*
18. Persons accused of crimes must be informed of charges, confronted with witnesses, have power to call witnesses, have assistance of counsel. *6th Amendment.*
19. Jury trial of civil suits involving more than $20. *7th Amendment.*
20. No excessive bail or fines. *8th Amendment.*
21. No cruel and unusual punishments. *8th Amendment.*
22. No slavery or involuntary servitude. *13th Amendment.*

Against the States and Their Local Governments

1. No bills of attainder. *Art. I, Sec. 10, Cl. 1.*
2. No *ex post facto* laws. *Art. I, Sec. 10, Cl. 1.*
3. No slavery or involuntary servitude. *13th Amendment.*
4. No denial of privileges and immunities of citizens of other States. *Art. IV, Sec. 2, Cl. 1; 14th Amendment, Sec. 1.*
5. No denial of equal protection of the laws. *14th Amendment, Sec. 1.*
6. No person to be deprived of life, liberty, property, without due process of law. *14th Amendment.*
7. Guarantees of freedom of religion, speech, and press and the right of peaceable assembly and petition. *Through Due Process Clause in 14th Amendment.*
8. No unreasonable searches and seizures; no warrants issued but upon probable cause. *Through Due Process Clause in 14th Amendment.*
9. No cruel and unusual punishments. *Through Due Process Clause in 14th Amendment.*
10. Right of the accused to counsel. *Through Due Process Clause in 14th Amendment.*
11. No compulsory self-incrimination. *Through Due Process Clause in 14th Amendment.*
12. Right of the accused to confront witnesses against him or her. *Through Due Process Clause in 14th Amendment.*
13. Right of those accused to call witnesses in their favor. *Through Due Process Clause in 14th Amendment.*
14. Right of the accused to a speedy trial. *Through Due Process Clause in 14th Amendment.*
15. Right of the accused to trial by jury in serious criminal cases. *Through Due Process Clause in 14th Amendment.*
16. Prohibition of double jeopardy. *Through Due Process Clause in 14th Amendment.*
17. Guarantee of all freedoms "basic or essential to the American concept of liberty." *Through Due Process Clause in 14th Amendment.*

★　　　★　　　★

That to secure these rights, Governments are instituted among Men. . . . July 4, 1776.

---

few that remained was, at best, unimpressive. For decades it was generally believed that Congress lacked the authority under the 13th (or 14th) Amendments to deal directly with private parties who practice racial discrimination.

But, in *Jones* v. *Mayer*, 1968, the Supreme Court breathed new life into the 13th Amendment. The case involved one of the post-Civil War acts Congress had not repealed. Enacted in 1866, it provided in part that:

> All citizens of the United States shall have the same right, in every State and Territory, as is enjoyed by white citizens thereof to inherit, purchase, lease, sell, hold, and convey real and personal property.

Jones had sued Mayer because the latter had refused to sell him a home in St. Louis County, Missouri, solely because he was black. Mayer argued that the 1866 law was unconstitutional, as it sought to prohibit *private* racial discrimination.

The Court, 7-2, decided for Jones. It upheld the law, declaring that the 13th Amendment abolished slavery *and* gives to Congress the power to abolish "the badges and the incidents of slavery," as well. Said the Court:

> At the very least, the freedom that Congress is empowered to secure under the 13th Amendment includes the freedom to buy whatever a white man can buy, the right to live wherever a white man can live. If Congress cannot say that being a free man means at least this much, then the 13th Amendment made a promise the Nation cannot keep.

Since that decision the Court has several times reaffirmed it.[7] For example, it did so in *Tilman* v. *Wheaton-Haven Recreation Assn.*, 1973, when it disallowed the guest policy of a private swimming club that discriminated against blacks.

And—of widespread import—it did so in *Runyan* v. *McCrary*, 1976. Here, the Court held that private schools may not refuse to admit black students solely because of their race. In its ruling the Court applied another provision of the 1866 law:

> All persons within the jurisdiction of the United States shall have the same right in every State and Territory to make and enforce contracts . . . as is enjoyed by white citizens . . .

Two black students had been refused admittance to two private schools in Virginia. In doing so, the schools had refused to enter into a contract of admission which the schools advertised to the general public. The Court held that, by refusing to admit

---

The Open Housing Act of 1968 makes it illegal for newspapers to knowingly accept advertising for the sale or rental of housing which is discriminatory.

the black students, the schools had violated the century-old civil rights law.

In effect, the 13th Amendment, as it is now applied, gives Congress the power to enact whatever legislation is necessary and proper to overcome any of "the badges and the incidents of slavery," from whatever source they may arise.

"A Man's Home Is His Castle." In several of its provisions the Constitution enshrines the storied maxim that "a man's home is his castle."

The 3rd Amendment forbids the quartering of soldiers in private homes in peacetime. It also prohibits the practice in time of war except "in a manner to be prescribed by law." The guarantee was added to the Constitution to prevent what had been British practice in colonial days. Recall that one of the specific grievances cited in the Declaration of Independence was "Quartering large bodies of troops among us." The amendment has had little importance in our history, and so we may follow

---

[7] While *Jones* v. *Mayer* was before the Court, Congress enacted the Civil Rights (Open Housing) Act of 1968; see pages 175, 540.

the still apt comment of Mr. Justice Samuel F. Miller of the Supreme Court who, in 1893, wrote:

> This amendment seems to have been thought necessary. It does not appear to have been the subject of judicial exposition; and it is so thoroughly in accord with all our ideas, that further comment is unnecessary.

The 4th Amendment also grew out of colonial practice. It was designed to prevent the use of *writs of assistance*—that is, blanket search warrants, with which customs officials had invaded private homes to search for smuggled goods. Unlike the 3rd Amendment, it has proved a highly significant guarantee. It reads:

> The right of the people to be secure in their persons, houses, papers, and effects, against unreasonable searches and seizures, shall not be violated, and no warrants shall issue, but upon probable cause, supported by oath or affirmation, and particularly describing the place to be searched, and the persons or things to be seized.

Each of the State Constitutions contains a similar provision. And, recall, the guarantee applies to the States through the 14th Amendment's Due Process Clause.

The general rule laid down by the 4th Amendment is that police must obtain a proper warrant before making a lawful search for and seizure of evidence. *But*, notice, only *unreasonable* searches and seizures are prohibited. There are some situations in which lawful searches and seizures may occur *without* a warrant.

As one fairly common example: no warrant is necessary when police are in "hot pursuit" of a suspect. Thus, in *United States* v. *Santana*, 1976, the Supreme Court upheld the arrest, accompanying search and seizure, and subsequent conviction of a woman whom police officers had first spotted standing outside her home. The officers, who were there to arrest her on a heroin charge, pursued and captured her

just inside. There they arrested her. In searching her, they found both heroin and the marked bills with which an undercover agent had only minutes earlier made a buy. Because all of this had occurred without a warrant, she contended that her arrest and the search conducted in her home was prohibited by the 4th Amendment.

An arrest is the "seizure" of a person. When a lawful one is made, officers do not need a warrant to search "the arrestee's person and the area within his immediate control"—that is, "the area within which he might gain possession of a weapon or destructible evidence."[8]

Nor do police need a warrant to search an automobile, a boat, an airplane, or other vehicle they have good reason to believe contains evidence of crime or is being used to commit one—because such a "movable scene of crime" could disappear while the warrant was being sought.[9] *But*, notice, police cannot stop a motorist "at random," simply because they choose to do so—to check the driver's license or the car's registration, for example. They must *first* have good reason to believe that a law is being broken, *Delaware* v. *Prouse*, 1979.

Nor is a warrant required to seize evidence "in plain view"—for example, a bag of marijuana found during the routine inventory of a car's contents after it had been impounded for parking violations, *South Dakota* v. *Opperman*, 1976.

But, again, the general rule is this: ". . . searches and seizures conducted without any warrant are condemned by the plain language of the 4th Amendment," *Payton* v. *New York*, 1980.

---

[8] The Supreme Court has had much trouble with setting the limits to which a search incident to a lawful arrest can be carried. The present rule, quoted here, was first laid down in *Chimel* v. *California*, 1969.

[9] But in the leading case on the point, *Carroll* v. *United States*, 1925, the Court emphasized that "where the securing of a warrant is reasonably practicable it must be used . . . In cases where seizure is impossible except without a warrant, the seizing officer acts unlawfully and at his peril unless he can show the court probable cause."

Case Study

In *Brown* v. *Texas*, 1979, the Supreme Court held that police cannot stop someone and ask for identification simply because that person "looked suspicious."

The case arose in El Paso, where two policemen were patrolling "an area with a high incidence of drug traffic." They saw Brown and another man in an alley. One of the officers later testified that things "looked suspicious and we had never seen [Brown] in that area before."

The policemen stopped Brown and asked him to identify himself. He refused. Instead, he insisted that they had had no right to stop him. He was then told that he was "in a high drug problem area." He still refused to identify himself.

Brown was then arrested. He was charged with violating a Texas law under which it is a crime not to give one's identity to an officer "who has lawfully stopped him and requested the information."

At his trial, the officer who testified that the situation in the alley had "looked suspicious," could not point to any facts to support that conclusion. Nonetheless, Brown was convicted and fined $45.

On appeal, the Supreme Court reversed that conviction. It found the State law to be "designed to advance a weighty social objective: prevention of crime." But it held that when, as in this case, police have no specific basis upon which to believe that a person is involved in crime, the 4th and 14th Amendments require that "the balance between the public interest and [a person's] right to personal security and privacy tilts in favor of freedom from police interference."

■ Do you agree with the Supreme Court's reversal of the conviction in this case? Why, or why not?
■ Here the Court did not weigh the constitutionality of the Texas law. Had it done so, how do you think it should have decided the matter?

Michigan v. *Tyler,* 1978, illustrates the general line between those warrantless searches which are lawful and those which are not. There, the Court set aside the arson convictions of two furniture dealers. Much of the evidence against them had come from two separate sets of searches. One series had occurred as the fire department fought the blaze in their store and immediately thereafter. The other searches were conducted some three weeks later.

The Court found that a burning building presents an emergency—one in which a warrantless entry is clearly reasonable. And it held that the firefighters, once inside the store, could properly seize any evidence in plain view.

But it also held that the subsequent searches, made well *after* the emergency, and also made without warrants, violated the 4th and 14th Amendments.

THE WEEKS DOCTRINE. The real heart of the search and seizure guarantee lies in the answer to this question: *If an unlawful search and seizure does occur, what use can be made of the evidence thus obtained?*

If it can be used in court, the 4th Amendment's guarantee provides no real protection for one accused of crime. The officers who committed the illegal act might be punished. But this punishment would provide no particular help to the person being tried on the basis of the evidence they had turned up.

To make the guarantee truly effective, the federal courts have long followed the *Weeks Doctrine*—the "exclusionary rule," first laid down by the Court in *Weeks* v. *United States,* 1914. By the rule, any evidence obtained from an unlawful search or seizure by federal agents cannot be used in a federal court. Until 1960, however, the federal courts did admit evidence illegally gained by State or local police and then handed to federal agents, as "on a silver platter." The Supreme Court finally outlawed the Silver Platter Doctrine in *Elkins v. United States,* 1960.

Then, in a historic decision in 1961, *Mapp* v. *Ohio,* it extended the Weeks Doctrine against the States. It held that the 14th Amendment forbids unreasonable searches and seizures by State and local officers, just as the 4th Amendment bars such actions by federal officers. *And* the Court held, as well, that the fruits of an illegal search or seizure cannot be used in a *State* court.

In the case, Cleveland police officers had gone to Dollree Mapp's home to search for gambling materials. They entered the house over her objections, forcibly, and without a warrant. Although they conducted a widespread search, they turned up no gambling evidence. But they did find some obscene books, the possession of which Ohio law prohibited. Miss Mapp was later convicted of possession of the books and sentenced to jail. On appeal, the Court overturned her conviction—because the evidence against her had been obtained without a search warrant.

In short, the 4th and 14th Amendments generally forbid the use of evidence secured by any unlawful search or seizure in *any* court in the land.[10]

To apply all of this, look again at *Michigan* v. *Tyler.* There the Court ordered that the two furniture dealers be retried in the State courts—and that, at their new trial, all evidence seized during the second set of searches be excluded.

WIRETAPPING, ELECTRONIC EAVESDROPPING. Wiretapping, electronic eavesdropping, and other even more sophisticated means of "bugging" are now fairly commonplace and widely used. And they present difficult problems in applying the ban on unreasonable searches and seizures.

In its first wiretapping case, in 1928, the Supreme Court held that intercepting telephone conversations did not constitute an unreasonable search and seizure. But in 1967 it reversed that decision holding such communications to be within the 4th Amendment's protection.

In the earlier case, *Olmstead* v. *United States,* 1928, federal agents had tapped telephone conversations over a five-month period. Thus the agents had gained evidence against a large ring of bootleggers. A bare majority of the Court upheld a conviction based on that evidence. It held that no warrant was needed because the agents had made no physical entry into the premises of the accused; the intercepting and recording of his telephone calls had occurred *outside* his home and his office.[11]

Congress reacted to *Olmstead* in one section of the Federal Communications Act of 1934. Referring to radio, telegraph, and telephone communications, the law prohibited any person to "intercept any communication and divulge or publish" its contents. In several subsequent cases the Supreme Court then held that the statute effectively banned the use of wiretap evidence in federal courts. (But note that what the 1934 law prohibited was to intercept *and* divulge; thus interception could and did go on. In the opinion of many, that interception constituted a most serious and unjustifiable invasion of privacy. And, that view is supported by the widespread bugging activities of the FBI and the CIA in the

[10] Of late, the Supreme Court has been narrowing the scope of the Weeks Doctrine, however. For example, it has held that evidence against a defendant that was gained by an unlawful search of *another* person's property is not "tainted,"—i.e., can be used, *United States* v. *Payner,* 1980. In that case a man was convicted of tax evasion on the basis of evidence found because an IRS agent had stolen some related documents from a banker's briefcase.

[11] In a vigorous dissent, strongly critical of federal agents acting without a warrant, Justice Holmes castigated "such dirty business." He remarked: "For my part I think it a less evil that some criminals should escape than that the government should play an ignoble part."

1960's and early 1970's.)

The Supreme Court expressly over-ruled *Olmstead* in *Katz* v. *United States,* 1967. The case involved a conviction under the federal anti-gambling statutes. Katz had been found guilty of transmitting betting information across State lines, from a public phone booth in Los Angeles to his contacts in Boston and Miami. Much of the evidence against him had come from an electronic listening and recording device FBI agents had attached to the outside of the booth. The Court of Appeals, applying the rule from *Olmstead,* held that there had been no need for a warrant because there had been "no physical entrance into the area occupied" by the defendant.

But the Supreme Court reversed the conviction and, in doing so, overruled *Olmstead.* It held, 7–1, that the 4th Amendment protects *persons* and not just places. The Court noted that "the reach of that Amendment cannot turn on the presence or absence of a physical intrusion into any given enclosure." Even though Katz was in a public, glass-enclosed booth, he was constitutionally entitled to the making of a *private* telephone call. Said the Court:

> What a person knowingly exposes to the public, even in his own home or office, is not a subject of 4th Amendment protection. . . . But what he seeks to preserve as private, even in an area accessible to the public, may be constitutionally protected.

The Court went on, however, to note that the requirements of the 4th Amendment could be satisfied in such situations if law-enforcement officers secured a proper warrant before placing a listening device.

Congress reacted to *Katz* in certain sections of the Omnibus Crime Control Act of 1968. Those sections amended the Communications Act of 1934. They make it illegal for any unauthorized person to tap telephone wires or use or sell electronic bugging devices in interstate commerce. But they also provide that federal or State police officers may secure warrants "to search and seize" evidence by electronic means in circumstances closely controlled by court orders.

Under the 1968 law, if officers present reliable evidence that a law is being violated, a judge may issue a warrant authorizing a bugging operation. Such a warrant can run for a maximum of 30 days, but it can also be renewed. In certain "emergency" situations involving national security or organized crime, the Attorney General may also authorize eavesdropping by federal agents for up to 48 hours without prior court approval. But a warrant *must* be sought during that period.

The Court has ruled that the 1968 law does not authorize—and the 4th Amendment prohibits—any eavesdropping without a warrant in cases where *domestic* subversion is suspected, *United States* v. *United States District Court,* 1972. (Here, the Court distinguished such cases from those involving foreign powers or their agents.)

In an organized crime case, the Court ruled that federal agents, with a warrant authorizing a bug, do not have to have a second warrant authorizing them to make a "covert entry" in order to plant it, *Dalia* v. *United States,* 1979.

Right to Keep and Bear Arms. The 2nd Amendment, quoted on page 124, is a widely misunderstood part of the Bill of Rights. It was added to the Constitution *solely* to protect the right of the States to maintain and equip a militia. It was intended to preserve the concept of the citizen-soldier—the "minuteman," as its text clearly indicates. It does *not* guarantee to any person the "right to keep and bear arms" free from any restrictions by government—nor was it written to do so.

The Amendment has no real significance today—*except* for its propaganda clout in arguments over gun control.

The Supreme Court rendered its only significant decision involving the 2nd Amendment some four decades ago. In

United States v. *Miller,* 1939, the Court upheld the constitutionality of the National Firearms Act of 1934. That act makes it a crime to ship a sawed-off shotgun, machine gun, or silencer across State lines unless one first registers the weapon and pays a virtually prohibitive tax. The Court could find no evidence that such weapons have any relevance to "the preservation of a well-regulated militia."

Congress enacted the most far-reaching gun-control law in our history in 1968. Generally, the measure bans the mail-order or other interstate retail sale of firearms and ammunition. It also generally prohibits the across-the-counter sale of guns or ammunition to persons who do not live in a dealer's State. The law further forbids the sale of rifles, shotguns, and their ammunition to persons under age 18 and the sale of handguns and ammunition to persons under 21. The measure also prohibits the importing of foreign-made surplus military weapons.

The law—the Gun Control Act of 1968—does not require registration of all privately-owned firearms. But it does require that certain guns—for example, all machine guns—must be registered with the Treasury Department.

As a provision in the Bill of Rights, the 2nd Amendment applies only against the National Government. The Supreme Court has never found it to be included within the meaning of the 14th Amendment. Thus, it has no application against the States. They may—and all of them do—limit the right to keep and bear arms. In most States, for example, it is a crime to own or use various automatic weapons or to carry a concealed weapon without a proper license.

Fair Treatment for Persons Accused of Crime

Both the Constitution of the United States and the various State constitutions contain numerous guarantees of fair treatment for those accused of crime. And, as we have noted, the 14th Amendment's Due Process Clause reinforces the federal guarantees against unfair treatment by the States.

As we consider these rights, bear in mind that each of them is rooted in the concept that any person accused of crime is presumed to be innocent unless or until proved guilty by fair and lawful means.

Writ of Habeas Corpus. The *writ of habeas corpus*—sometimes called the "writ of liberty"—is designed to prevent arbitrary arrest and unlawful imprisonment.[12] It is a court order directed to an officer holding a prisoner. It requires that that prisoner be brought before the court and that the detaining officer show cause why he or she should not be released. If good cause cannot be shown, the court will then order the prisoner freed. (Such cases are rare, but the writ may also be used in disputes between private parties.)

The right to the writ of *habeas corpus* is guaranteed against the National Government in Article I, Section 9 of the Constitution. It is guaranteed against each of the States in their own constitutions.

The right to the writ cannot be suspended, says the Constitution, "unless when in cases of rebellion or invasion the public safety may require it."[13] But the

---

[12] The phrase *habeas corpus* is from the Latin, meaning "you should have the body"—and these are the opening words of the writ.

[13] President Lincoln, acting without congressional authorization, suspended the writ in 1861 in various parts of the country, including areas in which war was not then being waged. Chief Justice Roger B. Taney, sitting as a circuit judge, held Lincoln's action unconstitutional in *Ex parte Merryman,* 1861. Taney declared that the power to suspend the writ was vested exclusively in Congress. Congress then passed the Habeas Corpus Act of 1863, specifically authorizing the President to suspend the writ whenever and wherever, in his judgment, such action was necessary. Whether the writ may be suspended in areas not the scene of actual fighting, or not in serious danger of becoming so, was considered by the Supreme Court in *Ex parte Milligan,* 1866. The full Court agreed that the President could not do so, and a majority of five of the justices also held that even Congress did not have such power.

Constitution does not make clear whether the right may be suspended *only* in those areas immediately involved in the rebellion or invasion. Nor does it indicate which branch of the National Government—Congress, the President, or the courts—possesses the power of suspension.

The right to the writ has been suspended only once over the past century—in Hawaii during World War II. And the Supreme Court held in 1946 that that action had been illegal.[14]

Bills of Attainder. A *bill of attainder* is a legislative act which inflicts punishment without court trial. Neither Congress nor the States may enact such measures.[15]

The prohibition of bills of attainder is both a guarantee of individual freedom *and* a part of the system of separation of powers. A legislative body may decide what conduct is to be deemed a crime, and it may pass laws to prohibit that conduct. But it *cannot* exercise the *judicial* function; it cannot decide that an individual is guilty of a particular crime and then impose a punishment upon that person.

The Supreme Court has held that the prohibition is aimed at all legislative acts which apply "to named individuals or to easily ascertainable members of a group in such a way as to inflict punishment on them without a judicial trial," *United States* v. *Lovett*, 1946.

The ban on bills of attainder was included in the Constitution because both Parliament and the colonial legislatures had passed many of them in the colonial period. They have been quite rare in our own history, however.

United States v. *Brown*, 1965 is one of the few cases, and the most recent, in which the Court has voided a law as a bill of attainder. There it struck down part of the Landrum-Griffin Act of 1959—a section which made it a federal crime for a member of the communist party to serve as an officer of a labor union.

Ex Post Facto Laws. An *ex post facto* law is a *criminal* law which is applied to an act committed *before* the law was passed and which works to the disadvantage of the accused. Neither the Congress nor the State legislatures may pass such laws.[16]

The guarantee means, for example, that a State law making it a crime to sell marijuana cannot be applied to one who sold it *before* the act was passed. It could, however, be applied to one who sold marijuana *after* the law was enacted. Nor could a law increasing the penalty for murder from life imprisonment to death be applied to a person convicted of a murder committed prior to the increasing of the penalty. The penalty could be applied only to a person who committed a murder after the act was passed.

Notice that for a law to be *ex post facto*—and hence unconstitutional—it must meet *all* three requirements previously mentioned. That is, the law must be (1) a criminal law, (2) applied to an act committed before enactment of the law, and (3) disadvantageous to the accused. Thus, a retroactive *civil law* is not forbidden. For example, an income tax law enacted in November can impose a tax upon one's income for the entire year, including the preceding ten months.

---

[14] The Hawaiian Islands were placed under martial law by order of the territorial governor immediately after the Japanese attack on Pearl Harbor, December 7, 1941. His order, issued with the approval of President Roosevelt, not only suspended the writ of *habeas corpus* but also provided for the supplanting of the civil courts by military tribunals. Martial law was not ended, by presidential proclamation, until 1944—long after the danger of invasion had passed. While it was in force, civilians were tried for crimes before military courts without benefit of jury or similar processes. In 1946, in *Duncan* v. *Kobanamoku*, the Supreme Court held that the governor's order had been too sweeping in character. Its decision was not based upon the constitutional provision, however. Rather, the Court found that in the Hawaiian Organic Act of 1900, under which the governor had acted, Congress had not intended to authorize so drastic a subordination of civil to military authority.

[15] Article I, Sections 9 and 10.

[16] Article I, Sections 9 and 10.

Right to a Fair Trial. The Bill of Rights contains several guarantees relating to fair trial in the federal courts.[17] A fair trial is guaranteed in the State courts by a State's own constitution and by the 14th Amendment's Due Process Clause.

DOUBLE JEOPARDY. The 5th Amendment says, in part, that no person shall be "twice put in jeopardy of life or limb." The taking of a life or the cutting off of an arm, leg, ear, or some other "limb" was a common punishment in ancient times. The old English phrase "life or limb" was carried into our Constitution.

Today, the provision means, in plain language, that once a person has been tried for a crime he or she may not be tried again for that same crime. This requires some elaboration, however.

A single act may violate both a national *and* a State law—for example, kidnapping or peddling narcotics. The accused may be tried for the federal crime in a federal court and for the State crime in a State court.

A single act may also result in the commission of several different crimes. One who breaks into a store at night, steals liquor, and later resells it, can be tried for at least three separate offenses—the crimes of illegal entry, theft, and selling liquor without a license.

In a trial in which a jury cannot agree on a verdict, there is no "jeopardy." It is as though no trial had been held, and the accused may be retried. Nor is double jeopardy involved when a case is appealed to a higher court.

Recall that in *Benton* v. *Maryland,* 1969, the Court held the 5th Amendment's ban on double jeopardy applies against the States through the 14th Amendment.

GRAND JURY. The 5th Amendment also provides that:

No person shall be held to answer for a capital, or otherwise infamous, crime, unless on a presentment or indictment of a grand jury. . . .

The grand jury is, then, the formal device by which a person may be accused of a serious federal crime. It is a body of from 16 to 23 persons drawn from the area of the federal district court which it serves. The votes of at least 12 of the grand jurors are necessary to return an indictment or make a presentment.[18] An *indictment* is a formal complaint laid before a grand jury by the prosecutor (the United States Attorney). It charges the accused with the commission of one or more federal crimes. If the grand jury finds that there is sufficient evidence to warrant a trial, it returns a "true bill of indictment." The accused is then held for prosecution. If the grand jury refuses to make such a finding, the charge is dropped.

A *presentment* is a formal accusation brought by the grand jury on its own motion—rather than at the instance of the United States Attorney. It is little used in federal courts.

As a grand jury's proceedings are not a trial, and unnecessary harm could come if they were held in public, its sessions are secret. And they are also one-sided (in the law: *ex parte*). That is, they are one-sided because only the prosecution, not the defense, is present.

The 5th Amendment's grand jury provision is the only portion of the Bill of Rights relating to criminal prosecution which the Supreme Court has not brought within the coverage of the 14th Amendment's Due Process Clause. Indeed, the Court specifically rejected this notion in *Hurtado* v. *California,* 1884. There it held

---

[17] See the 5th, 6th, 7th, and 8th Amendments and also Article III, Section 2, Clause 3. The practice of excluding evidence obtained in violation of the 4th Amendment (see page 157) is also intended to guarantee a fair trial.

[18] Congress has provided that one may *waive* (put aside) the right to grand jury if he or she chooses. When, as increasingly, this happens, the trial proceeds on the basis of an accusation (an *information*) filed by the United States Attorney.

that the States may provide for whatever fair method of accusation they choose.

The right to grand jury is intended as a protection against over-zealous prosecutors. But its use long has been the subject of criticism. Its critics contend that it is too time-consuming, too expensive, and too prone to follow the dictates of the prosecutor. It has been abolished in England, where it originated. And in most of the States today most criminal charges are not brought by grand juries, but rather by an information—an affidavit in which the prosecutor swears that there is sufficient evidence to justify a trial; see page 733.

SPEEDY AND PUBLIC TRIAL. The 6th Amendment commands that:

> In all criminal prosecutions, the accused shall enjoy the right to a speedy and public trial. . . .

However much the accused may—or may not—"enjoy" a trial, this guarantee is a vital part of the Constitution's insistence that *all* who are accused be treated fairly.

The guarantee of a speedy trial is meant to insure that one accused of crime will be tried in a reasonable time, without undue delay. It seeks to prevent the accused from being forced to languish in jail while awaiting trial. And it is intended to prevent delays that could hinder the ability to mount an adequate defense.

The 6th Amendment's guarantee is of a prompt trial in *federal* cases. The Supreme Court first declared the right to apply against the States through the 14th Amendment in *Klopfer* v. *North Carolina,* 1967.

A trial must occur promptly, without undue delay. But how long a delay is too long? The Supreme Court has long recognized that there can be no pat answer to that question. Cases differ, and each must be considered in its own light. In *Barker* v. *Wingo,* 1972, the Court did list four considerations which must be taken into account. They were: the length of the delay; the rea-

Hesse in *St. Louis Globe Democrat*

"GOING DOWN FOR THE THIRD TIME."

sons for it; whether the delay did in fact harm the defendant; and whether or not the defendant demanded a prompt trial. (Notice that a delay can work to the *advantage* of a defendant. For example, witnesses for the prosecution might die or for some other reason become unavailable, or their memories might fade or become faulty.)

However inexact the 6th Amendment's word "speedy" may be, the Court has destroyed a number of State prosecutions because the delays involved were too lengthy. Thus, in *Smith* v. *Hooey,* 1969, it ordered Texas to dismiss a theft charge against a man because the State had failed for six years to bring him to trial. It had not acted even though he had repeatedly asked to be tried. And it had failed to act even though he was more or less readily available for trial—as a prisoner serving a term in a federal penitentiary.

Congress has recently attempted to implement the speedy trial guarantee in federal prosecutions. The Speedy Trial Act of

1974 provides that the period from an arrest to the commencement of a trial must be progressively shortened. The period between arrest and trial was set from an outside limit of 250 days beginning in 1976 to not more than 100 days in 1980 and thereafter. The law does permit a judge to make some reasonable exceptions—for example, in those cases where a lengthy mental examination is necessary or where the defendant or a key witness is ill. Otherwise, if the deadline is not met, the judge is to dismiss the charge against the accused.

A "speedy" trial must also be a "public" trial. "The guarantee has always been recognized as a safeguard against any attempt to employ our courts as instruments of persecution." So said the Court in *In re Oliver*—the 1948 case in which it held the right to a public trial to be guaranteed against the States.

A trial must be neither *too* speedy nor *too* public, of course. Thus, in *Moore* v. *Dempsey*, 1923, the Court voided an Arkansas murder conviction in which the trial had lasted but 45 minutes while a threatening mob thronged the courtroom.

A court may limit, within reason, both the number and the kind of spectators who may be present at a trial. For example, the boisterous or those who seek to disrupt orderly proceedings may be excluded. Or, a courtroom may be cleared when delicate testimony embarrassing to a witness or to someone else not a party to the case is to be given.

Many of the hard questions concerning how public a trial should be involve the news media. Fairly often, the guarantees of fair trial and of free press come into conflict. And, when they do, a judge must find the proper balance between them. The Supreme Court insists that "trial judges must take strong measures to ensure that the balance is never weighed against the accused," *Shepard* v. *Maxwell*, 1966.

Champions of the public's "right to know" often argue for the broadest possible coverage of court proceedings—and especially of sensational criminal trials. But the Supreme Court has often held that newspaper, radio, and television reporters have only the same rights as the general public in a courtroom.

The federal courts—and nearly all State courts—prohibit the broadcasting, televising, or photographing of court proceedings. In a leading case, *Estes* v. *Texas*, 1965, the Court reversed the conviction of a man who had been found guilty of swindling on a massive, multi-million-dollar scale. It did so because it found that television and radio reporting, which had been permitted from within the trial courtroom, was so disruptive that a fair trial was made impossible. And, in its opinion, the Court emphasized the point that the right to a public trial belongs to the defendant, not to the news media.

TRIAL BY JURY. The 6th Amendment also requires that those accused of crime be tried "by an impartial jury." And it adds that the jury panel must be drawn from "the State and district wherein the crime shall have been committed." The provision reinforces a similar guarantee set out earlier in the Constitution, in Article III, Section 2, Clause 3.

The right to trial by jury is also binding on the States through the 14th Amendment's Due Process Clause—as the Supreme Court first declared in *Duncan* v. *Louisiana*, 1968.[19]

The trial jury is often called the "petit jury"—*petit*, from the French, "small" or "smaller." The term is used to distinguish it from the grand jury. We shall return to the role of the trial jury in Chapter 31. But, for now, these points:

The accused may *waive* (put aside, relinquish) the right to a jury trial. If the

---

[19] The 7th Amendment also preserves the right to jury trial in civil cases "where the value in controversy shall exceed twenty dollars." This guarantee has *not* been incorporated into the 14th Amendment's Due Process Clause.

This jury was the first all-black jury to sit in the history of Houston County, Alabama. It found the defendant guilty of second-degree murder.

right is waived, a "bench trial" is held— that is, the case is heard by the judge alone. (Of course, one can plead guilty to a crime and so avoid a trial of any kind.)

In federal practice the jury consists of 12 persons, as it does in most of the States; but several States now provide for juries with fewer, frequently six, members. Federal trial juries may convict only by a *unanimous* vote. That is, all 12 jurors must agree before a guilty verdict can be returned. Most of the States also follow the unanimity rule.[20]

The Supreme Court has held, in a long series of cases, that a jury must be "drawn from a fair cross section of the community," must be "a body truly representative of the community . . . and not the organ of any special group or class." In short, no person may be excluded from jury service because of race, color, religion, national origin, or sex.

To put it the other way, a defendant is denied the right to an impartial jury if tried before a jury from which any of these classes of persons has been deliberately excluded. But, interestingly, the Court did not finally forbid the States to exclude women from juries until quite recently—in *Taylor* v. *Louisiana*, 1975.

RIGHT TO AN ADEQUATE DEFENSE. Every person accused of crime has the right to offer the best possible defense that circumstances will permit. Thus, the 6th Amendment specifies that a defendant is entitled: (1) "to be informed of the nature and cause of the accusation"; (2) "to be confronted with the witnesses against him" and question them in open court; (3) "to have compulsory process for obtaining witnesses in his favor"; and (4) "to have the assistance of counsel for his defence."

As provisions in the Bill of Rights these key safeguards apply in *federal* courts. But if a State fails to honor any of them in its own courts, a conviction may be appealed on grounds that the 14th Amendment's guarantee of due process has been violated. Recall that the Supreme Court held that these protections are assured in State courts by the 14th Amendment. The Court

[20] The 14th Amendment does not dictate juries of no less than 12 members, *Williams* v. *Florida*, 1970; but it does not permit juries of less than six members, *Ballew* v. *Georgia*, 1978. Nor does it prevent a State from providing for convictions upon a less than unanimous jury vote, *Apadaca* v. *Oregon*, 1972; but if the jury consists of only six persons, it may convict only by a unanimous vote, *Burch* v. *Louisiana*, 1979.

protected the right to counsel in *Gideon* v. *Wainwright,* 1963; the right of confrontation in *Pointer* v. *Texas,* 1965; and the right to call friendly witnesses in *Washington* v. *Texas,* 1967.

These guarantees are designed to see that the "cards" in the court contest will not be "stacked" in favor of the prosecution. A leading right-to-counsel case, *Escobedo* v. *Illinois,* 1964, illustrates the point:

Danny Escobedo had been taken into custody by Chicago police on suspicion of murder. Both on the way to the police station and later while being questioned there, he asked several times to see his lawyer. These requests were denied—even though his attorney was in the police station, was seeking to see him, and the police knew that he was there. While he was being questioned, by the police and without the help of his lawyer, Escobedo made several damaging statements. These statements implicated him in the murder and were ones which later contributed to his conviction. The Supreme Court reversed that conviction on grounds that Escobedo's

right to counsel had been improperly denied.

SELF-INCRIMINATION. The 5th Amendment declares that no person

> . . . shall be compelled in any criminal case to be a witness against himself.

This protection against self-incrimination applies with equal force in federal *and* State proceedings, *Malloy* v. *Hogan,* 1964.

In a criminal case, the burden of proof is always on the prosecution. That is, a defendant need not prove his or her innocence. Rather, it is up to the prosecution to show, if it can, that the criminal charge it has brought against the defendant is true. The ban on self-incrimination prevents the prosecution from shifting that burden to the defendant. As the Court put it in *Malloy* v. *Hogan,* the prosecution cannot force the accused to "prove the charge against" him "out of his own mouth."

The language of the 5th Amendment suggests that the guarantee applies only to criminal cases. But, in fact, it applies to *any*

Two cartoonists comment on the right of suspects to remain silent and to have an attorney present when questioned by the police.

From *Herblock Gallery* (Simon & Schuster, 1968)

G. G. Wallmeyer in *Independent Press-Telegram,* Long Beach, Calif.

governmental proceeding in which a person is legally compelled to answer any question the answer to which could later be used as the basis of a criminal charge. For example, one may claim the right ("take the Fifth") in a divorce proceeding (which is a *civil* case), or before a legislative committee, or in a disciplinary hearing held by a local school board.

The courts determine when the right may be properly invoked—and not those individuals who claim it. If the plea of self-incrimination is pushed too far, one may be held in *contempt.* That is, he or she may be punished by a court for obstructing the lawful processes of government.

The privilege against self-incrimination is a personal right. One can claim it only for himself or herself.[21] It cannot be invoked in someone else's behalf; a person *can* be compelled to "rat" on another. Nor can it be used to protect an "artificial person," as a corporation or a partnership.

The privilege covers only evidence given as testimony—required answers to lawful questions. It does not offer any protection against a requirement to be fingerprinted or photographed, submit a handwriting sample, or appear in a police lineup. Nor does it protect one from having to submit to a blood test, as we saw in *Schmerber* v. *California* on page 152.

Confessions, and other incriminating statements obtained under duress are prohibited by the two Due Process Clauses, of course. And the Supreme Court has voided a number of State prosecutions based on "third degree" methods. Such methods are those in which confessions are obtained by such "shockingly unjust" procedures as beatings or the threat of them, starvation, prolonged sleeplessness, or other forms of physical and/or psychological mistreatment.

---

[21] With this large exception: a husband may refuse to testify against his wife or a wife against her husband; although either can testify voluntarily, neither can be compelled to do so, *Trammel* v. *United States,* 1980.

Thus, in *Ashcraft* v. *Tennessee,* 1944, it threw out the conviction of a man accused of hiring another to murder his wife. The confession, on which his conviction rested, had been secured only after some 36 hours of continuous, abusive, and threatening interrogation. The prolonged questioning took place in a jail room under high-powered lights and was conducted by officers who worked in relays because, they said, they became so tired they had to rest.

The gulf between what the Constitution provides and what does in fact occur at times in some police stations can be wide, indeed. As a result, the Supreme Court has in recent years borne down hard in cases involving the protection against self-incrimination and the closely related right to counsel. In a series of decisions it has insisted upon strict police compliance with the commands of the Constitution.

Recall the Court's decision in *Escobedo* v. *Illinois.* There, it held that a confession cannot be used against a defendant if it was obtained by police who refused to permit the accused to see an attorney and did not advise the accused of the right to refuse to answer their questions.

In a truly historic case two years later, *Miranda* v. *Arizona,* 1966, the Court refined and extended its holding in *Escobedo.* It laid down what is now often referred to as the *Miranda Rule.* Henceforth, said the Court, no convictions will be upheld unless, prior to any police questioning, suspects have been:

(1) Informed of their right to remain silent;

(2) Warned that any statements they make may be used against them;

(3) Informed that they have the right to have an attorney present during questioning;

(4) Told that if they cannot afford to hire an attorney, one will be provided; and

(5) Notified that they may terminate the questioning at any time.

The *Miranda* precedent has been applied in several later cases. As but one example, the Court ordered a new trial for a convicted murderer in *Brewer* v. *Williams,* 1977, despite the fact that the murderer had admitted his guilt and even led the police to his victim's body. It did so because the police, who had promised not to do so, had interrogated their suspect and persuaded him to admit his guilt at a time (during an automobile ride) when his attorney could not be present.

Many police officials, and others, have opposed the *Miranda Rule* because they see it as a serious obstacle to effective law enforcement. But many others applaud it. They insist that criminal law enforcement is most effective when it relies on independently secured evidence, rather than confessions secured by questionable means and in the absence of counsel.

EXCESSIVE BAIL AND FINES.   The 8th Amendment prohibits the requiring of "excessive bail" and the imposing of "excessive fines." Each of the State constitutions contains similar restrictions.

These guarantees have had little judicial exposition. But the general rule is that the bail or fine in a case must bear a reasonable relationship to the gravity of the offense involved. In the leading case on bail, *Stack* v. *Boyle,* 1951, the Court observed that the purpose of bail is to ensure that the accused will appear for trial. And, it held that bail must not be set so high that the accused cannot give it and so be unable to be at liberty to prepare for the trial.

CRUEL AND UNUSUAL PUNISHMENTS.   The 8th Amendment also forbids "cruel and unusual punishments." The 14th Amendment extends the prohibition against the States, *Robinson* v. *California,* 1962; and each of the State constitutions includes a similar restriction.

The punishments the Constitution originally intended to prohibit were those barbaric and bloody penalties fancied a

few centuries ago—burning at the stake, drawing and quartering, dismemberment, and the like. Those particular punishments which are today "cruel and unusual," and so prohibited, is a matter for the courts to determine. Only a comparative handful of pertinent cases has been decided by the Supreme Court thus far. As a result, the general content of the law of the matter is still being developed.

The Court's first "cruel and unusual" case was that of *Wilkerson* v. *Utah,* 1879. In that case the Court affirmed the view that "torture . . . and all other [punishments] in the same line of unnecessary cruelty are forbidden" by the 8th Amendment. But in that case it also upheld a sentence of death by firing squad that a territorial court had imposed on a convicted murderer.

More often than not, the Court has upheld those punishments which have been challenged, finding them not to be "cruel and unusual." Thus, in *Louisiana* v. *Resweber,* 1947, it found that it was not unconstitutional to subject a convicted murderer to electrocution a second time because the chair had failed to function properly on the first occasion.

The Court has adopted a somewhat more liberal view of the guarantee in some later cases. Thus, in *Trop* v. *Dulles,* 1958, it held that to denaturalize a person who fled the country to avoid wartime military service constituted a cruel and unusual punishment; see page 116. Denaturalization, said the Court, involves

> no physical mistreatment, no primitive torture. There is instead the total destruction of the individual's status in organized society.

And in *Robinson* v. *California,* 1962, a State law defining narcotics addiction as a crime to be punished—rather than as an illness to be treated—was held to be cruel and unusual punishment and so prohibited by the 8th and 14th Amendments.

CAPITAL PUNISHMENT.   Is the death pen-

Even though a person may be serving a sentence in jail, the right to counsel does not cease. Here, a lawyer meets with her client.

alty a cruel and unusual punishment and thus forbidden by the Constitution? The Court was for years reluctant to face that highly charged issue. In fact, it did not provide a direct answer to that question until as recently as 1976.

The Court did meet the issue more or less directly in *Furman* v. *Georgia*, 1972.[22] There it struck down all of the then existing State laws allowing the imposition of

the death penalty. A divided Court found all of them to be repugnant to the 8th and 14th Amendments—but *not* because capital punishment *as such* is cruel and unusual. Rather, they were voided because they gave almost unlimited discretion to judges or juries in deciding whether or not to impose a death sentence. A majority of the Court agreed that, of all of those who committed capital crimes, only "a random few," most of them black or poor or both, were "capriciously selected" for execution. The death penalty was "cruel and unusual in the same way that being struck by lightning is cruel and unusual."

Following the decision in *Furman*, 35 of the States enacted new capital punishment laws. Essentially, these new statutes took one of two forms:

Several States removed *all* discretion from the sentencing process, by making the death penalty *mandatory* for certain specified crimes—for example, the killing

---

[22] The Court managed to avoid a direct ruling on the constitutionality of the death penalty in several cases prior to 1972. As we have seen, it did hold that neither death by firing squad (*Wilkerson* v. *Utah*) nor by a second electrocution (*Louisiana* v. *Resweber*) are unconstitutional. But in neither of those cases, nor in others, did it deal with the question of the death penalty *as such*. It had also avoided the point in *Witherspoon* v. *Illinois*, 1968. There it held that the death penalty had been unconstitutionally imposed upon the defendant—but *not* because that punishment was cruel and unusual. Rather, because those opposed to capital punishment had been excluded from the jury which tried him, it held that Witherspoon had been denied the right to trial by *impartial* jury.

John Brown, moments before his execution for treason against the State of Virginia in 1859.

of a police officer or murder done while committing rape, kidnap, or arson.

Others provided for a two-stage process in capital cases: *first*, a trial to settle the issue of guilt or innocence; then a *second*, separate hearing to fix the appropriate sentence, with closely drawn standards to guide judges or juries in deciding when and upon whom to impose a sentence of death.

The Supreme Court has now (1981) considered scores of challenges to those newer State laws—with these principal results, thus far:

The mandatory death penalty laws were found to be unconstitutional. They were "unduly harsh and rigidly unworkable," and simply attempts to "paper over" the decision in *Furman*, said the Court in

Woodson v. *North Carolina*, 1976. Capital punishment laws "must allow for whatever mitigating circumstances" may be present in a case, *Roberts* v. *Louisiana*, 1977.

But the two-stage approach to capital punishment is constitutional. In *Gregg* v. *Georgia*, 1976, the Court held, for the first time, that the "punishment of death does not invariably violate the Constitution." And it ruled that the two-stage laws practically eliminate "the risk that [the death penalty] will be inflicted in an arbitrary or capricious manner."

TREASON. Treason against the United States is the only crime which is defined in the Constitution. The Framers provided a specific definition of the crime because they knew that the charge of treason is a favorite weapon in the hands of tyrants. Examples of its use to eliminate political opponents in recent times are not hard to find. It was a common practice in Nazi Germany, and it still is in several Latin American dictatorships and in the communist nations of Eastern Europe and Asia.

Treason, says Article III, Section 3, can consist of but two things: either (1) levying war against the United States or (2) "adhering to their enemies, giving them aid and comfort." And, the Constitution adds, no person may be convicted of the crime "unless on the testimony of two witnesses to the same overt act, or on confession in open court." The penalty for treason can be imposed only on the traitors themselves; it may not be extended to their families.

The law of treason covers all American citizens, at home or abroad, and all permanent resident aliens. The maximum penalty for treason against the United States is death, but no person has ever been executed for the crime. In fact, the death penalty was not imposed in a federal treason case until as recently as 1942. Then four German-born American citizens were sentenced to be hanged for aiding a group of Nazi saboteurs who had been landed on the East Coast by a German submarine. But their sentences were never carried out.[23]

Note that treason may be committed only in wartime. But Congress has also made it a crime, in either peace or wartime, to commit espionage or sabotage, to attempt to overthrow the government by force, or to conspire to do any of these things; see pages 138–139.

Most of the State constitutions also provide for treason. John Brown was hanged as a traitor to Virginia after his raid on Harpers Ferry in 1859. He is believed to be the only person ever to be executed for treason against a State.

Equality Before the Law

Nothing—not even a constitutional command—can make all people equal in the literal sense, of course. Individuals differ in strength, intelligence, height, weight, health, and countless other factors. But the democratic ideal demands that, insofar as governmental actions are concerned, all persons are entitled to be treated equally.

The equality of all persons—so prominently asserted in the Declaration of Independence—is not proclaimed in so many words in the Constitution. Still, all of the document is permeated by the concept.

The Equal Protection Clause. The closest approach to a literal statement of equality is to be found in the 14th Amendment's Equal Protection Clause. It declares that

> No State shall . . . deny to any person within its jurisdiction the equal protection of the laws.

And the Supreme Court has often held that the National Government is similarly bound to provide "equal protection" by the 5th Amendment's Due Process Clause.

The Equal Protection Clause was originally intended to benefit the newly freed slaves. In practice, however—and especially in recent decades—it has become a much broader guarantee. In effect, it forbids States (and local governments) to draw *unreasonable* distinctions between different classes of persons.

REASONABLE CLASSIFICATION. Government must have the power to classify—to draw distinctions between, discriminate among persons and groups. Otherwise, it would be impossible for it to regulate any aspect of human behavior.

That is to say, the States may and do discriminate. Thus, those who rob banks fall into a special class and are subject to a special treatment by the law. This sort of discrimination is an obviously reasonable one. Or, the States may legally prohibit marriage by those under a certain age, or by those currently married to other persons. Again, these are reasonable discriminations (classifications).

But the States may not discriminate unreasonably. Every State now levies a sales tax on cigarettes—and so taxes smokers, but not nonsmokers. But no State could lay a tax only upon *blonde* smokers or only upon *males* who buy cigarettes. Nor for example, may a State make *women* eligible for alimony in divorce actions but provide that *men* are not—as the Court ruled in a case from Alabama, *Orr* v. *Orr*, in 1979.

The Court has upheld many State and local governmental actions as *not* in conflict with the Equal Protection Clause. But it has also voided several on that ground. We shall consider a number of them in a moment—and we treat several others elsewhere; *e.g.,* too-lengthy residence requirements for voting, on page 214, and the malapportionment of State legislatures, on page 693.

---

[23] The sentence of one was commuted to life in prison; he was later denaturalized and then deported. The other three appealed their convictions and won new trials. One of them was again convicted of treason but this time sentenced to life imprisonment; the other two pleaded guilty to reduced charges and received five-year prison terms.

A massive public demonstration—the March on Washington—was arranged by civil rights leaders in August of 1963. Congress was then at work on the early stages of what was to become the Civil Rights Act of 1964.

Ordinarily, when a State's law is challenged under the Equal Protection Clause, the Supreme Court upholds the law. And this is especially true when the State can shown some *rational basis* for the classification it has made—that is, can show that that classification is "reasonably related" to the achieving of some proper public purpose.

A recent New York case, *Ambach* v. *Norwick*, 1979, illustrates the usual outcome. In New York an alien who is eligible but has not applied for American citizenship cannot be hired as a public school teacher. The Court found that teachers play a critical role in the shaping of their students' attitudes toward the society, government, and the political process. And the Supreme Court held, therefore, that it is reasonable for a State to exclude this class of aliens ("persons who have not become a part of the process of self-government")

from the teaching role.

But the Court does not always sustain the judgment a State legislature makes when it enacts a law which draws distinctions between persons or groups. And this is especially true when the law deals with either (1) such "fundamental rights" as the right to vote, the right to travel between the States or the rights guaranteed in the 1st Amendment, or (2) such "suspect classifications" as those which are based upon race, sex, or national origins.

In these instances the Court has said, repeatedly, in recent years that the *rational basis test* is not enough. Rather, the law is "subject to strict judicial scrutiny"—any classification it makes will be examined very closely. And, for the law to survive that scrutiny—that is, be upheld, the State must be able to show that some "compelling public interest" justifies the distinction it has drawn.

Among many recent cases, take *Orr* v. *Orr*, 1979—the Alabama alimony case we cited on page 171—to illustrate the Court's application of the *strict scrutiny test.* There the Court declared that need, not sex, must be the basis upon which the award of alimony hinges.

THE SEPARATE-BUT-EQUAL DOCTRINE. Beginning in the latter 1800's, nearly half of the States adopted racial segregation laws. These "Jim Crow" laws were aimed primarily at blacks. But they often affected such other groups as those of Mexican or Oriental descent and American Indians, as well. In the main, they required segregation by race in the use of both public and private facilities in such areas as transportation, education, housing, recreation, and the service of meals.

The Supreme Court provided a constitutional basis for these segregation laws— the "separate-but-equal" doctrine—in 1896. It did so in *Plessy* v. *Ferguson,* in which it upheld a Louisiana law requiring the segregation of blacks and whites in rail coaches. It held that the requirement did not violate the Equal Protection Clause as long as the *separate* facilities for blacks were *equal* to those provided for others.

The "separate-but-equal" doctrine was soon extended to other fields as a constitutional justification for racial segregation. And the doctrine stood for nearly 60 years. Indeed, until the late 1930's little serious attempt was made by the courts—or by any other arm of government—to insist even that the separate accommodations for blacks were, in fact, equal to those reserved to whites. And, more often than not, they were not.

BROWN V. TOPEKA BOARD OF EDUCATION, 1954. The Supreme Court began to "chip away" at the separate-but-equal doctrine in a series of cases decided in the late 1930's and 1940's. It did so for the first time in *Missouri ex rel. Gaines* v. *Canada* in 1938. Lloyd Gaines had applied for admission to the law school at the all-white State

university. Gaines was wholly qualified for admission except in one particular: he was black. The State did not maintain a law school for blacks. However, it did offer to pay his tuition at the law school maintained by any one of the four adjacent States—that is, at the Universities of Illinois, Indiana, Kansas, or Nebraska, where blacks were admitted on equal terms with whites. But Gaines insisted on a legal education in his home State. The Supreme Court held that the separate-but-equal doctrine left the State of Missouri with but two choices here. It could either (1) admit Gaines to the State's law school or (2) establish a separate-but-equal one for him. Needless to say, the State gave in.

Over the next several years the Supreme Court took an increasingly stern attitude toward the doctrine's requirement of equal facilities for blacks.

Finally, in a historic decision in 1954, the Court reversed *Plessy* v. *Ferguson.* In *Brown* v. *Topeka Board of Education* it struck down the laws of four States requiring or permitting separate public schools for white and black students.[24]

Holding segregation of the races in public education to be unconstitutional, Chief Justice Earl Warren said for a unanimous Court:

> . . . Does segregation of children in public schools solely on the basis of race, even though the physical facilities and other "tangible" factors may be equal, deprive the children of the minority group of equal educational opportunities? We believe that it does.
>
> . . . To separate them from others of similar age and qualifications solely because of their race generates a feeling of inferiority as to their status in the community that may affect their hearts and minds in a way unlikely ever to be undone. . . . We conclude that in the field of

---

[24] Kansas, Delaware, South Carolina, and Virginia.

public education the doctrine of "separate but equal" has no place. Separate educational facilities are inherently unequal.

On the same day that it announced its decision in *Brown,* the Court also decided a closely similar case from the District of Columbia—where a racially segregated school system operated under *federal* law. In *Bolling* v. *Sharpe* the Court found the existence of segregated public schools in the nation's capital in conflict with the 5th Amendment's Due Process Clause.

The Court recognized in *Brown* that implementing its decision presented a "problem of considerable complexity." The observation proved to be a monumental understatement. After extensive hearings, a year later it issued an implementation order. The States were directed to make "a prompt and reasonable start toward full compliance" with the 1954 decision and to end school segregation "with all deliberate speed." And the federal district courts were ordered to supervise the process of desegregation.

A "reasonable start" was made in several places. Thus, in Washington, D.C., Baltimore, Louisville, and St. Louis, and in several other places, substantial steps were taken. But in most of the Deep South what came to be known as "massive resistance" soon developed. State legislatures passed numerous and voluminously detailed statutes to block integration. Most of them were clearly unconstitutional, but the process of attacking them in the federal courts was both slow and costly. Many school boards and administrators, urged on by the white community, worked to thwart progress. And, until the 1960's, neither Congress nor the President gave either support or leadership to the integration movement.

The pace of desegregation was quickened considerably after Congress enacted the Civil Rights Act of 1964. Among its many provisions, that law forbids the use of federal funds to aid any State or local

activity in which segregation is practiced. The law also authorized the Justice department to file suits to prompt desegregation actions.

And the pace was further quickened in 1969. In that year the Supreme Court finally ruled in *Alexander* v. *Holmes County Board of Education* that, after 15 years, the time for "all deliberate speed" had run out. In this case from Mississippi it unanimously held that "the continued operation of segregated schools under a standard allowing for 'all deliberate speed' . . . is no longer constitutionally permissible."

DE JURE AND DE FACTO SEGREGATION.[25] By the fall of 1970 *de jure* segregated school systems had everywhere been abolished. That is *not* to say that desegregation had been fully and finally accomplished by that time—far from it. All that is meant by that statement is that, by then, nowhere in the country was there a public school legally identified as one reserved either for whites or for blacks. The process of achieving a complete integration of the nation's schools continues yet today, of course.[26]

For years, segregation was viewed by most as a problem peculiar to the South. But the events of recent years have shown that the problem is, and long has been, of *nationwide* dimensions. Many of the recent integration controversies have come in areas where the schools have never been segregated *by law.* Rather, they have come from areas where *de facto* segregation has long existed, and continues.

De facto segregation exists where, although no law required it, circumstances in fact produced it. Housing patterns have

---

[25] *De jure*—by law, with legal sanction; *de facto*—by fact, in reality.

[26] Note that most of the legal and political controversies surrounding desegregation have involved *public* schools. Some States, several school districts, and many parents have sought to thwart integration or avoid integrated schools through established or, often, newly-created *private* schools. But see page 155 and *Runyan* v. *McCrary,* 1976, where the Court held that private schools cannot refuse to admit students because of their race.

been the principal cause of *de facto* segregation. The concentration of black populations in one or more sections of several cities inevitably produced local school systems in which some schools are predominately black and others largely white. The condition is strikingly apparent in many *northern* as well as southern communities.

Efforts to desegregate these school systems have taken several forms. They have included the redrawing of school district boundaries, pupil assignment programs, and the use of busing to transport students out of racially segregated neighborhoods. These efforts have often produced strong reactions, including mass demonstrations and even violence—most prominently in Boston and Detroit, but in other places, as well.

The Supreme Court first sanctioned busing to achieve racial balance in local schools in a North Carolina case, *Swann* v. *Charlotte-Mecklenburg Board of Education,* in 1971. There it held that "desegregation plans cannot be limited to walk-in schools." Since then, busing has been utilized to increase the racial mix in many school districts across the country—in some by court order, in others voluntarily.

The whole matter of school integration is packed with legal questions. And it is just as obviously packed with highly charged political and emotional issues. The point is, indeed, sharply underlined in the ongoing national dispute over busing.

SEGREGATION IN OTHER FIELDS. The elimination of the constitutional sanction for segregation in public education came in 1954, as we have seen. Today—more than a quarter of a century later—the final goal of realizing that legal fact in actual practice remains to be achieved—in all sections of the country.

Meanwhile, the abandonment of legally-enforced racial segregation in other fields has been virtually realized. Many State laws and local ordinances have been repealed, and many have been struck

down by the courts. Thus, the Supreme Court found racial segregation in public recreational facilities (*Dawson* v. *Baltimore,* 1955), local transportation (*Gayle* v. *Browder,* 1956), and in State prisons and local jails (*Lee* v. *Washington,* 1968) to be as unconstitutional as in the schools. And in *Loving* v. *Virginia,* 1967, it voided all *miscegenation* laws—State statutes prohibiting interracial marriages.

Recent Civil Rights Legislation. For more than 80 years—from the 1870's to the latter 1950's—Congress was unable to enact a single piece of meaningful civil rights legislation. The use of the filibuster in the Senate, and the threat of its use, were a major factor in that long dearth; see page 324.

That logjam was finally broken in 1957, however. Congress has since enacted the Civil Rights Acts of 1957, 1960, 1964, and 1968, and the Voting Rights Acts of 1965, 1970, and 1975. Each of them is designed to implement the Constitution's insistence upon the equality of all before the law.

The Civil Rights Acts of 1957 and 1960 deal largely with the right to vote.[27] Together with several related provisions of the 1964 Act and the Voting Rights Acts of 1965, 1970, and 1975, they are discussed in Chapter 9.

The Civil Rights Act of 1968 is often called the Open Housing Act. With limited exceptions, it forbids anyone to refuse to sell or rent a dwelling to any person on grounds of race, color, religion, or national origin. See page 540.

The Civil Rights Act of 1964 is a much broader statute than the others. In addition to its voting rights provisions, its other major sections outlaw discrimination in a number of other areas. With its later

---

[27] The 1957 law created the *Civil Rights Commission.* Its six members oversee the application of the various civil rights statutes, investigate cases of alleged discrimination, and report its findings and recommendations to the President, Congress, and the public.

amendments, the law now:

(1) Provides that no person may be denied access to, or be refused service in, various "public accommodations"—including restaurants, hotels, motels, theaters, and the like—on grounds of race, color, religion, or national origin (Title II; see page 535).

(2) Prohibits discrimination against any person on grounds of race, color, religion, national origin, sex, or physical handicap in any program which receives federal funds (Title VI).

(3) Forbids discrimination by employers against any person on grounds of race, color, religion, national origin, sex, physical handicap, or age (40 to 65) in hiring and all other conditions of employment (Title VII).

The 1964 law also established the *Equal Employment Opportunity Commission.* Its six members are appointed by the President and Senate for five-year terms. The EEOC's major charge is the enforcement of Title VII—that is, the law's prohibitions of discrimination in employment.

The Commission seeks to promote voluntary compliance with the law. But, where those efforts fail, it may bring federal court suits to halt discriminatory practices in hiring, pay, promotion, and all other job-related situations.

AFFIRMATIVE ACTION. The several recent statutes and court decisions we have just reviewed all come down to this: Those discriminatory practices which are based upon such arbitrary factors as race, color, religion, or sex are illegal.

But, notice, that very important fact begs this equally important question: What of the *present* and *continuing* effects of *past* discrimination? The fact that the law *now* prohibits discrimination does almost nothing to overcome the consequences of the discriminatory practices of the past.

As but one of many illustrations of the point, consider the black man who, for no reason of his own making, did not get a decent education and so today cannot get a decent job. Of what real help to him are all of those laws and court decisions which make illegal *today* what was done to him years ago?

Thus far, the Federal Government's chief response to this troubling question has been a policy of *affirmative action.* It now requires that most employers take positive steps (affirmative action) to remedy the effects of past discriminations against women and the members of various minority groups.

All public and private employers who receive federal funds are required to adopt and implement affirmative action programs. Thus, the requirement applies to all of the agencies of the Federal Government itself, to all of the States and their local governments, and to all other employers who hold federal contracts (including, then, both business and industrial firms and public and private universities).

In short, the policy covers most of the nation's major employers and many of its smaller ones. And it applies to *each* of them—including even those who have *never* engaged in discrimination.

In effect, these employers must strive to make their work forces reflect the general composition of the population—with so many women, so many blacks, so many Latinos, and so on. And their affirmative action programs must include steps to correct (or prevent) inequalities in such job-related matters as pay, promotion, and fringe benefits. For most of them, this has meant that they must hire (and/or promote) more women and more persons from various minority backgrounds. And for most of them it has also meant that they must take these job actions even in situations in which better qualified white males are available for consideration.

The affirmative action approach is supported by those who insist that some form of preferential treatment is necessary to break down the long-standing patterns of discrimination against women and minorities in the job market. Its critics contend that, however good its intentions, the policy amounts to "reverse discrimination"—that is, it requires that preference be given to females and/or nonwhites, solely on the basis of sex or race. They also insist that affirmative action programs necessarily involve the use of quotas—and so necessarily contradict the concept of equality of opportunity for each individual based upon his or her own merits.

The Supreme Court has now decided three major affirmative action cases:

(1) Regents of the University of California v. *Bakke*, 1978. The *Bakke* case involved the admissions policies of the University's medical school at Davis. The school had set a quota to ensure minority representation in its student body; at least 16 of the 100 seats in each year's entering classes were to be filled by nonwhite students.

Allan Bakke, a white male, had twice been denied admission. But, both times, minority applicants, with admissions test scores significantly lower than his, had been accepted by the school.

Bakke sued, charging the University with reverse discrimination. The State Supreme court agreed. It found that Bakke had been denied admission because of his race and so had been denied his 14th Amendment right to equal protection. It ordered the school to admit him and it directed the University not to use race as a factor in its admission policy.

The State appealed to the United States Supreme Court—where the decision was not nearly so clear cut. By a 5-4 majority, the Court did uphold the order to admit Bakke. And, 5-4, it did hold that quotas are illegal—at least when they are used by a recipient of federal funds (here, the medical school) to discriminate against individuals. *But* that holding was based on the

provisions (Title VI) of the 1964 Civil Rights Act. Thus, the Court stopped short of deciding the constitutional question of quotas versus the Equal Protection Clause.

The Court did not say that quotas can *never* be used in affirmative action decisions. Rather, it held that race cannot be used, as it was here, as the *sole* factor in such actions. But it also indicated that race can be used as *one among several* factors in such situations.

In short, the Court held: *Quotas* are not legal, at least not when used by schools receiving federal funds; but *race* can be one of the several factors used in the making of affirmative action decisions.

(2) Kaiser Aluminum & Chemical Corporation v. *Weber*, 1979, involved an affirmative action plan agreed to by Kaiser and the United States Steelworkers in a labor contract. That plan set up on-the-job training programs at 15 Kaiser aluminum plants. The programs were specifically designed to increase the number of blacks in skilled jobs in Kaiser's workforce.

Each of the training programs was open to both black and white Kaiser workers, on a one-to-one basis. To ensure that each training group included an equal number of blacks and whites, the trainees were selected from each racial group by seniority (length of employment by the company).

Brian Weber, a white male working at the Kaiser plant in Gramercy, Louisiana, was rejected for training on three occasions. Each time, several blacks with less seniority were selected, however.

Weber then went to court. He claimed that, by agreeing to and conducting the programs, the company and the union had subjected him to reverse discrimination—and, so, had violated Title VII of the 1964 law. The lower federal courts agreed with him. Both the company and the union appealed those decisions.

The Supreme Court was then faced with this question: Does Title VII of the 1964 law forbid private parties—here the company and the union—to voluntarily establish such an affirmative action plan? (Notice the contrasts with *Bakke*—which had to do with Title VI and, because a State was involved, the applicability of the 14th Amendment's Equal Protection Clause. *Weber* did not involve an action taken by any public agency; and it called for the interpretation of a statute, not a provision in the Constitution.)

The Court ruled 5-2 for the company and the union. It held that a voluntarily adopted affirmative action program, even one containing numerical quotas which give special preferences to black workers, does not automatically violate the law. The Court did concede that a literal reading of Title VII might suggest otherwise—might suggest that any job distinctions made on the basis of race are illegal. But, said the Court, such a reading contradicts the very purpose of the law—"a law triggered by a nation's concern over centuries of racial injustice" and intended to speed "the integration of blacks into the mainstream of American society."

The Court did not hold that any and all job plans which give special preferences to blacks are legal. Rather, it held that the Kaiser-USWA plan is a lawful one. But there are many similar affirmative action plans in force today—and they are conducted by hundreds of companies employing millions of workers in this country.

(3) Fullilove v. *Klutznick,* 1980, centered on one section of the Public Employment Act of 1977. Congress had passed the law to combat unemployment in the construction industry. It authorized the Secretary of Commerce to make $4 billion in federal grants to State and local governments for various public works projects.

The section at issue in the case was the law's "minority set-aside" provision. It directed that at least 10 percent of the grant monies be spent with (set aside for) minority businesses.

E. Earl Fullilove, a white contractor, challenged the set-asides. He claimed that they were quotas—and unconstitutional because they denied to white contractors an equal chance to compete with black contractors for all of the available funds.

Fullilove lost in the lower federal courts and then in the Supreme Court. The High Court held, 6-3, that the law did not violate the 5th Amendment's Due Process Clause (by setting aside federal funds) nor the Equal Protection Clause (in directing State and local governments to spend those funds with minority businesses).

Rather, the Court found that Congress had properly exercised its constitutional powers to spend and regulate interstate commerce. In short, it held that the law was a permissible attempt to overcome the effects of long-standing discrimination in the construction industry.

Some insist that the decisons in *Weber* and *Fullilove* have destroyed the reverse discrimination argument as an effective legal challenge to affirmative action programs. At the very least, that remains to be seen. What is certain is that the Supreme Court will hear several more affirmative action cases in the next few years.

SUMMARY

The Constitution contains two Due Process Clauses: in the 5th Amendment restricting the National Government and in the 14th Amendment restricting the States. Due Process has a double meaning: *Procedural due process* guarantees fair procedures by government; *substantive due process* guarantees that government will act under fair laws. A State law that can be justified as a valid exercise of the police power does not violate the 14th Amendment's Due Process Clause.

The rights to freedom and security of the person include freedom from slavery and involuntary servitude and from unreasonable searches and seizures. They also include the virtually meaningless protection against the quartering of troops in private homes and the insignificant guarantee of the right to keep and bear arms.

The rights of those accused of crime include the protection of the writ of *habeas corpus;* prohibitions against bills of attainder, *ex post facto* laws, double jeopardy, self-incrimination, excessive bail and fines, and cruel and unusual punishments; guarantees of grand jury indictment, trial by jury, speedy and public trial, and an adequate defense; and a specific definition of the crime of treason.

The rights to equality before the law center around the 5th Amendment's Due Process Clause and, especially, the 14th Amendment's Equal Protection Clause.

Concept Development

Questions for Review

1. Where in the Constitution are the two Due Process Clauses found? What is the chief distinction between them?

2. What are the two basic meanings of *due process?*

3. What is the *police power* of the State?

4. Why does the 13th Amendment not prohibit *all* forms of involuntary labor? What is peonage?

5. How has the Supreme Court lately breathed new life into the 13th Amendment?

6. What particular type of searches and seizures does the 4th Amendment prohibit?

7. Will the federal courts admit evidence obtained by an unlawful search or seizure? The State courts? Why? What is the "exclusionary rule"?

8. What is a writ of *habeas corpus?* When may it be suspended?

9. What is a bill of attainder? An *ex post facto* law?

10. What constitutes double jeopardy?

11. What is the major function of a grand jury?

12. Why is an accused person entitled to a speedy and public trial?

13. Why is an accused person entitled to a trial by an impartial jury?

14. What are the 6th Amendment's guarantees to the right to an adequate defense?

15. Why is compulsory self-incrimination forbidden? What did the Supreme Court hold in *Miranda* v. *Arizona?*

16. What bail or fine is "excessive"?

17. Do the 8th and 14th Amendments outlaw capital punishment?

18. Why does the Constitution contain a specific definition of treason?

19. Does the 14th Amendment's Equal Protection Clause forbid the States to discriminate?

20. What did the Supreme Court hold in *Brown* v. *Topeka Board of Education?*

21. What is the difference between *de jure* and *de facto* segregation?

22. With particular reference to discrimination, what does the Equal Protection Clause forbid?

23. What is the basic purpose of the several civil rights laws lately enacted by Congress over the past two decades?

For Further Inquiry

1. What did the late Justice Robert H. Jackson mean when he wrote: "Liberty is advanced only by the rule of law"? And the late Justice Felix Frankfurter when he observed: "The history of liberty is largely the history of the observance of procedural safeguards"?

2. Many parents, educators, and others insist that busing is not the best, or at least not always the best, way to achieve racial balance in local schools. They advocate other measures to overcome the results of *de facto* segregation. What other means can you suggest? What is your own view in this matter?

3. In an article written for a London newspaper in 1958, an Englishman confessed to a particularly brutal murder committed eight years earlier. He had been tried at that time and acquitted by the jury. As in our law, double jeopardy is prohibited in English law. Thus, a confessed murderer cheated the law. Do you think it should have been possible to retry him?

4. Discuss this statement: "It is better that the law allows one hundred guilty persons to go free than that it punishes one innocent man."

5. What is your view of affirmative action programs? Can you suggest another approach to the remedying of the present effects of past discrimination?

Suggested Activities

1. Stage a debate or class forum on one of the following topics: (a) *Resolved,* That the Constitution should be amended to forbid forced busing in school integration cases; (b) *Resolved,* That the proposed Equal Rights Amendment should be ratified; (c) *Resolved,* That the constitutional ban of compulsory self-incrimination should be repealed.

2. A great many United States Supreme Court decisions are cited in this chapter. Read one or more of them and prepare a class report. (A librarian can lead you to the volumes of the *United States Reports* or the *Supreme Court Reporter.*)

3. Now that you have read the discussion of civil rights guarantees in this and the preceding chapter, prepare an oral or written reaction to Judge Learned Hand's comment on page 122.

Suggested Reading

Abraham, Henry J., *Freedom and the Court: Civil Rights and Liberties in the United States.* Oxford, 3rd ed., 1977.

Barker, Lucius J. and Barker, Twiley W., *Civil Liberties and the Constitution: Cases and Commentaries.* Prentice-Hall, 3rd ed., 1978.

Cary, Eva and Peratis, Kathleen W., *Women and the Law.* National Textbook Co., 1977.

Corwin, Edward S. and Peltason, J.W., *Understanding the Constitution.* Holt, Rinehart and Winston, 8th ed., 1979.

Cushman, Robert F., *Cases in Constitutional Law.* Prentice-Hall, 5th ed., 1979.

Editorial Research Reports, *The Rights Revolution.* Congressional Quarterly, 1979.

Gill, Gerald R., *The Meanness Mania: The Changed Mood.* Harvard University Press, 1980.

Lerner, Gerda (ed.), *The Female Experience: An American Documentary.* Bobbs-Merril, 1978.

Okin, Susan M., *Women in Western Political Thought.* Princeton University Press, 1980.

Pritchett, C. Herman, *The American Constitutional System.* McGraw-Hill, 5th ed., 1980.

Sicherman, Barbara and Green, Carol H. (ed.), *Notable American Women: The Modern Period.* Harvard University Press, 1980.

Walker, Samuel, *Popular Justice: A History of American Criminal Justice.* Oxford, 1980.

THE POLITICS OF AMERICAN DEMOCRACY

Politics is the term we use to describe the conduct of public affairs. It embraces *all* aspects of the governing process: the making of public policies, the execution of those policies, the selection of those who make and of those who execute those policies, and all else included within the realm of government. Taken in this sense, the term *politics* covers an almost infinite variety of things, from the most routine and commonplace to those of the greatest moment—from such matters as a city council's enactment of an amendment to a local zoning ordinance to the ratification of an amendment to the Constitution of the United States; from a legislative committee's hearings on a bill to increase civil servants' salaries to a congressional declaration of war; from the nomination of a candidate for the office of county sheriff to the impeachment of the President; and much, much more.

Politics may also be described, very usefully, as the "pursuit and exercise of power." That is, it may be viewed in terms of the ability of some persons and groups to influence or control the political behavior of other persons and groups, in terms of the ability of some to acquire and exercise the power to make policies and to set rules which others are required to follow.

Of course, there are some who view *politics* in quite another, narrower and meaner, sense—as something evil or, at the very least, as a "dirty business," something with which "good people" have as little as possible to do. It should take only a moment's reflection to expose the sheer nonsense of this view. Government cannot possibly exist without *politics.* It is at the very core of any government, whatever its form and whatever its time or place. (Notice that those who use the term in this derogatory sense frequently do so only when they are referring to some acquisition or use of power for a purpose to which they are opposed. When something they agree with is involved they are inclined to use such more honorific descriptions as "statesmanship" or "reflecting the people's will" to cover the situation. If we disregard the value judgments being expressed, it is apparent that it is the same form of behavior that is being talked about in both instances.)

Unfortunately, it is true that at some times and in some places in the United States the level of *politics* is not all that it might be. It is also true, however, that *at all times* and *in all places* in this country the people themselves are responsible for the quality of the political atmosphere. It is this that Elihu Root—distinguished statesman, Cabinet officer, Senator, and Nobel Peace Prize winner—had in mind when he declared: "Politics is the practical exercise of the art of self-government, and somebody must attend to it if we are to have self-government. . . . The principal ground for reproach against any American citizen should be that he is not a politician."

Over the course of the next four chapters we shall explore the "Politics of American Democracy," building our consideration of that exciting topic about the broad headings of political parties, the right to vote and voter behavior, nominations and elections, and public opinion and pressure groups.

8

Government by the People: Political Parties

No America without democracy,
no democracy without politics,
no politics without parties,
no parties without compromise
and moderation. . . .

CLINTON ROSSITER

■ Are political parties necessary to democratic government?

■ Why is the phrase "power-seeking structures" useful to an understanding of the nature of political parties?

■ Should our two-party system be redesigned to provide two new major parties—one distinctively liberal and the other distinctively conservative?

Popular participation in the political process is the very definition of democratic government. And the extent to which democratic government is able to function effectively is the direct result of both the willingness and the ability of the people to participate in politics.

We Americans can and do take part in politics in many different ways. We can join a political party, join other organizations which support candidates or take stands on public issue questions, and become actively involved in political campaigns. We can attend political meetings. We can express political opinions by taking part in demonstrations or by writing letters to public officials and to newspapers. We can do so by appearing before such public bodies as city councils, school boards, and legislative committees, and by "talking politics" with friends and neighbors. And we can vote in elections and even run for public office.

In this chapter we are concerned with one of the major vehicles of popular participation, political parties. We shall treat the other means of participation in succeeding chapters. As we turn to parties, bear in mind the comments we made on page 181. And bear this in mind, too: Those who participate in politics—whatever the form that participation may take—are involved in the pursuit and the exercise of power.

Nature and Functions of Parties

What Is a Party? A political party may be defined as a group of persons who seek to control government through the winning of elections and the holding of public office.

This definition is purposefully broad and may be applied to *any* political party—including the two major parties in American politics, of course.[1]

A somewhat more specific definition may be applied to *most* political parties, both here and abroad: A group of persons joined together on the basis of certain common principles for the purpose of controlling government and securing the adoption of certain policies and programs.

But—and the "but" is crucial—any definition laid upon basic principles and public policy positions will *not* fit the two major parties in the United States.[2]

Certainly, most of the members of our two major parties *do* share with one another a dedication to certain basic principles—for example, to popular sovereignty and to limited government. But, notice, *not only* do Republicans agree with Republicans and Democrats with Democrats here; Republicans *and* Democrats also agree *with one another* in their support of these principles. And, at the same time, many Republicans *and* many Democrats often find that they have little in common with many other members of *their own* party. Thus, Republicans often disagree with other Republicans, and Democrats with Democrats, in such vital areas as foreign policy, national defense, taxation, social welfare—in fact, in all areas of public policy consideration.

To make the point, compare on the one hand, these leading Republicans: Senators Paul Laxalt of Nevada and Barry Goldwater of Arizona with Senators Mark Hatfield of Oregon and Lowell Weicker of Connecticut. Or, on the other hand, these well-known Democrats: Senators Sam Nunn of Georgia and John Stennis of Mississippi with Senators Edward Kennedy of Massachusetts and Gary Hart of Colorado.

Actually, as we shall see, our two major parties are composed of a great many persons who, broadly speaking, hold *rather similar* views on public questions.

What Do Parties Do? We know from our own history—and from that of other peoples, as well—that political parties are absolutely essential to the successful operation of democratic government. They are the vital link between the people and the government in a democracy—between the governed and the governors. They are the principal means by which the will of the people is made known to government and by which government is held responsible for what it does. Their pivotal place can be best seen by examining the major functions they perform in politics.

THE NOMINATING FUNCTION. A party's *major* function and, indeed, its chief reason for existence is to nominate candidates and present them to the electorate. There must be some device for finding and sifting the candidates for public office. And, there must be some device for concentrating strength (votes) behind those candidates, especially when we insist on majority rule. Parties are the best device we have yet found for these purposes. In fact, parties are generally the only groups which make nominations in American politics.[3]

THE INFORMER AND STIMULATOR FUNCTION. A party helps to inform the people and to stimulate their interest and participation in

[1] State election laws regularly define political parties; but these legal definitions are very narrow and tell us virtually nothing about the nature of parties. These definitions are intended only to identify the object to which the laws regulating political parties and their activities apply.

[2] Note that the discussion here is chiefly concerned with the two *major* parties in the United States. The various minor parties in American politics are considered on pages 193-195.

[3] Except in nonpartisan elections and in those infrequent situations in which an independent candidate enters a partisan contest. We shall deal with the nominating process at length in Chapter 10.

public affairs in a variety of ways. It does this, especially, by campaigning for its candidates, taking stands on issue questions, and criticizing the candidates and stands of the opposition. Of course, each party attempts to inform the people in the ways it thinks they *should* be informed—to the party's advantage. This "educational" process is carried on in several ways. Pamphlets, signs, and newspaper advertisements, speeches on radio and television and in person at rallies and conventions, and virtually every other means available are used in this process.

By taking at least *some* kind of stand on public issues, parties and their candidates offer the voters alternatives from which to choose. But the major parties usually do not take *too* firm a stand on controversial issues. Recall, each party's primary aim is to win elections. It attempts to do this by attracting as many voters as possible while, at the same time, offending as few as possible.

THE BONDING AGENT FUNCTION. A party serves as a "bonding agent" to insure the good performance of its candidates and officeholders. In choosing its candidates, a party attempts to see that they are persons who are both qualified and of good character—or, at least, that they are not unqualified and that they have no serious blemishes on their records. It also attempts to see that those of its candidates who win elections "toe the line" while they are in office. When it fails to do these things, the party runs the serious risk that it and its candidates will suffer in future elections—especially where vigorous two-party competition exists. The damage Watergate did to Republican candidacies, especially in the elections of 1974 and 1976, provide a strong case in point.

THE WATCHDOG FUNCTION. Parties act as "watchdogs" over the conduct of the public's business. This function is primarily that of the party out of power. The "out" party performs the role as it criticizes

Drawing by Brian Savage, from Look Magazine

"SOONER OR LATER, LARRY, YOU'RE GOING TO HAVE TO TAKE A STAND ON SOMETHING."

the party in power, attempting to convince the voters that the "outs" should become the "ins" and the "ins" the "outs." Its attacks tend to make the "ins" more careful of their public charge and more responsive to the wishes of the people. In effect, it is the function of the party out of power to serve as "the loyal opposition."

THE GOVERNMENTAL FUNCTION. From several different standpoints, government in the United States may be quite accurately described as government by party. Or, to put it another way, parties provide a basis for the conduct of government in this country. Thus, public officeholders—those who govern—are regularly chosen on the basis of party. Congress and the State legislatures are organized and conduct much of their business on the basis of party. And, appointments to executive offices, both federal and State, are usually made on a partisan basis.

In yet another sense parties provide a basis for the conduct of government: Under our system of separation of powers the party is usually the principal agent through which the legislative and executive branches cooperate with one another. And, in this connection, recall our discussion of the process of "informal amendment" of the Constitution. Political parties have played a prominent role in the development of the American constitutional system. As a leading illustration of the point, the curious and cumbersome electoral college system works because the parties have transformed it into what it is and have made it work; see pages 65, 73; 375–384.

The Two-Party System

Ours is basically a *two-party system.* That is, in the typical election in the United States, only the candidates of the Republican and/or the Democratic Parties have a reasonable chance of winning public office. There have been and are other parties—*minor* or *third parties*—in American politics, of course; and we shall consider them shortly. But only seldom does one of them make a serious bid for power, and then usually only at a local level. Their existence does not alter the basic fact that the party system is dominated by two major parties.

Why a Two-Party System? Several factors tend to explain the existence, and the retention, of a two-party system in this country. Each of them, taken separately, is a useful explanation of the phenomenon. In combination, they are quite persuasive.

THE HISTORICAL BASIS. The two-party system is rooted in the formation of the country itself. The Founding Fathers were opposed to political parties and hoped to discourage their development. But, as we noted in Chapter 2, their hope was a futile one.[4] The debates over the ratification of the Constitution saw the emergence of our first two parties—the Federalists led by Alexander Hamilton and the Anti-Federalists who followed Thomas Jefferson. In short, our party system *began* as a two-party system.

THE FORCE OF TRADITION. Once established, human institutions tend to be self-perpetuating—and so it has been with our party system. The very fact that we began with a two-party system has been, in itself, an important cause for the retention of it. And it has been an increasingly important cause over time. To a very meaningful extent, most Americans accept the idea of a two-party system simply because it has always been with us. And, conversely, they tend to reject challenges to it—third party efforts—for the same reason.

THE ELECTORAL SYSTEM. Several major features of the American electoral system tend to promote the existence of but two major political parties. Among the most prominent of them is the *single-member district* arrangement.

Nearly all elections in the United States, from the presidential election down to those at the most local levels, are conducted in single-member districts. That is, they are elections in which only one candidate is to be chosen to each office on the

---

[4] The Framers of the Constitution hoped to create a *unified* country; they sought to bring order out of the chaos of the Critical Period of the 1780's. To them, parties were "factions," agents of divisiveness and disunity. George Washington reflected the prevailing view when, in his Farewell Address in 1796, he warned the new nation against the "baneful effect of the spirit of party." In this light, it is hardly surprising that the Constitution made no provision for political parties. The Founding Fathers could not foresee the various ways in which the governmental system they created would develop, of course. Thus, they could not possibly know that two major political parties would emerge as prime instruments of government in the United States. Nor could they foresee that these two parties would tend to be moderate, to adopt middle-of-the-road positions, and so help to unify rather than divide the country.

ballot.[5] The winning candidate is the one who receives a *plurality* (the largest number) of the votes for the office he or she seeks.[6]

When there are but two candidates for an office, one or the other of them is bound to win an absolute plurality, a majority of the votes (barring the unlikely tie, of course). Thus, from a very practical standpoint, it has seemed wise to us to limit election contests to two principal contenders. Put another way, the fact that our election system is dominated by the single-member district pattern has been very persuasive to the establishment and the maintenance of a two-party system.

The single-member district scheme rather clearly works to discourage third-party efforts. Because only one winner can emerge from each contest, voters usually face only two practical choices: One is to vote for the candidate of the party holding the office; the other is to vote for the candidate of the party with the best chance to replace the incumbent. In effect, most voters regard a vote for a third-party candidate as a "wasted" one.

Another important—and too seldom noted—aspect of the electoral system works in the same direction. Much of American election law is purposefully written to discourage third parties. Or, to put it the other way around, much of it is intentionally framed to preserve and protect the two-party system. Thus, for example, in most States it is much more difficult for the minor parties to nominate their candi-

dates—get them on the ballot—than it is for the major parties to do so.

The 1980 presidential election furnishes a striking illustration of the point. Both of the major party candidates, Jimmy Carter and Ronald Reagan, were on ballots of all 50 States and the District of Columbia. But only two of the ten or more other, and serious, presidential aspirants were also listed everywhere—only Libertarian Party nominee Ed Clark and independent candidate John Anderson.

Both Clark and Anderson were forced to spend critical amounts of time, effort, and money to gain what was virtually automatic for the major party candidates. And notice this, too: By gaining the ballots everywhere, Clark and Anderson became the first nonmajor party contenders to do so in more than 60 years—since the Socialist Party nominee, Allan L. Benson, appeared on the ballots of all the then-48 States in 1916.

THE GENERAL HOMOGENEITY OF THE ELECTORATE. Another leading reason for the two-party system can be seen in the overall character of the American electorate. The nation's voters constitute an essentially *homogeneous* group—as, indeed, do all of our people. That is, we are all essentially alike, quite similar to one another, in virtually all significant respects.

As a people, we are not plagued by sharp cleavages based upon economic, religious, nationality, or ideological factors. Those conditions which might prompt the appearance of several, and sharply distinguishable, parties do not exist in this country—in sharp contrast to the situation, say, in Western Europe. The late Adlai Stevenson made our point very well in 1952. Congratulating Dwight Eisenhower on election night in 1952, the defeated Democratic candidate said:

> It is traditional for Americans to fight hard before an election. It is also tradition to close ranks after an election. We vote as many, but we pray as one.

---

[5] A comparatively few *multi-member district* elections are held in the United States, notably for some seats in a few State legislatures. But the principal offices—*especially* the Presidency, which is the "grand prize" in American politics, all of the seats in both houses of Congress, each of the governorships, and most of the seats in the State legislatures—are filled from single-member districts.

[6] A candidate who wins a *plurality* of the votes wins more than does any other candidate. A candidate who wins a *majority* of the votes wins more than half of all the votes cast in the election. Thus, a majority is *always* a plurality, but a plurality is not necessarily a majority.

The general homogeneity of the electorate is also a leading reason why our two major parties are so generally similar to one another. Both seek the same prize: the support (votes) of a majority of the electorate. To do so, they must vie with one another—in the same market for the same votes at the same time. Inevitably, each takes stands fairly close to those taken by the other side. Neither one can afford to be extreme or even very different from the other. And neither can long afford to concentrate its chief appeal on any one specific segment of the electorate—to farmers, or to the business community, or to organized labor, and so on. Nor, by the same token, can either ignore such groups.

The Multi-Party Alternative. There are some who argue that the American two-party system should be scrapped. They would replace it with a *multi-party* arrangement—one in which several major and many lesser parties would exist, as in most other Western democracies today.

In the typical multi-party system, the several parties are each based on some particular and distinctive interest—as, for example, economic class, religious belief, sectional attachment, or political ideology. Those who advocate such an arrangement claim that it would be more representative and more responsive to the people. They insist that it would give voters a truly meaningful choice among candidates and policy alternatives.

The practical effects of two of the factors we have just cited—*i.e.,* the single-member district system and the general homogeneity of the nation's electorate—seem to make such an arrangement an impossibility, however. Beyond that, the multi-party system tends to promote instability in government. One party is seldom able to win the support of a clear majority of the voters. The power to govern must, therefore, be shared among a number of parties. Several of the multi-party nations of Western Europe have long been plagued by governmental crises and frequent shifts in party control. Italy furnishes an almost nightmarish example: It has had a new government on the average of once every nine months ever since the end of World War II.

One-Party Systems. In most dictatorships, as in the Soviet Union and the People's Republic of China, opposition to the regime is not tolerated. Only one party, that of the ruling clique, is permitted. For all practical purposes, it would be just as accurate to say that in such circumstances a "no-party system" exists.

In quite a different vein, notice that in a number of States and in several locales in this country one or the other of the two major parties is (or has been at some time) overwhelmingly dominant. To describe these States or locales in "one-party" terms is to shift the frame of reference altogether, of course.

"IT IS *A SUPERB VISION OF AMERICA, ALL RIGHT, BUT I CAN'T REMEMBER WHICH CANDIDATE PROJECTED IT.*"

Drawing by Ed Fisher; (c) 1976
The New Yorker Magazine, Inc.

Party Membership. Membership in either of the major parties is purely voluntary. A person is a Republican or a Democrat—or belongs to a minor party or is an independent—simply because he or she chooses to be, on his or her own terms.[7] There are no dues to be paid; party membership costs nothing, unless one chooses to contribute to a party's coffers. There are no chores a party member must perform; but one may volunteer to work for the party and its candidates, of course.

We have already noted that the two major parties are very broadly based—that is, that they are multi-class in nature. Each of them has always represented, in greater or lesser degree, a cross-section of the nation's population. Each is made up of Protestants, Catholics, and Jews; whites, blacks, and other minorities; professionals, farmers, employers, and union members. Each has the young, the middle-aged, and the elderly; city-dwellers, suburbanites, and small-town and rural residents in its ranks. Members of these and of all of the many other groupings which make up American society are to be found in both Republican and Democratic ranks.

It is true that the members of certain segments of the electorate tend to align themselves more solidly with one party than the other, at least for a time. Thus, blacks, Catholics and Jews, and members of labor unions have tended to vote far more often for Democrats than for Republicans in recent years, especially in presidential elections. Similarly, white males, Protestants, and those from the business community have tended to support the Republican Party. Yet, never have all of the members of one race, one creed, or one economic group attached themselves permanently, indivisibly, to one major party.

Individuals identify themselves with a particular party for a variety of reasons. Family is almost certainly the most important determinant of party preference. Several studies of voter behavior show that approximately two out of every three Americans follow the party allegiance of their parents. Better than nine out of ten married couples share the same partisan preference and vote alike. They do so usually in the belief that to do otherwise would cancel the effect of their votes.

Dramatic events can have a substantial influence on party choice. Of these, the Civil War and the Great Depression of the 1930's have been the most significant in American political history, as we shall see in a moment.

Economic status is also a major factor in the individual's selection of party. Generalizations are risky here—as they are in all other matters. But there is a clear tendency of those in the higher income groups to regard themselves as Republicans and for those in the lower income ranges to think of themselves as Democrats.

The section of the country in which one lives—for example, the South—often has an effect on party membership and voting behavior, too. National origin is sometimes a consideration, as well. As a general rule, descendants of Northern Europeans are inclined to be Republicans while those of Southern and Eastern European extraction tend to be Democrats. The effects of religious affiliation are highly debatable, but it is true that the larger share of Protestants regularly support Republicans for office and Roman Catholics and Jews back Democrats.

Again, generalizations are risky here. These and the many other factors involved in the process of party choice may conflict in the case of any one individual—and, indeed, they often do. Thus, for example, a young person from a strongly Democratic

---

[7] In several States voters must declare a party preference when registering to vote in order to participate in a party's primary. This is often described as "declaring party membership," or as making one a "registered Republican (or Democrat)." But the requirement is a mechanical one and wholly a matter of individual choice. See pages 239–240.

family in a southern State may move to a high income suburb near a large northern city and, sooner or later, switch his or her allegiance to the Republican ticket.

For a more specific discussion of partisan preferences and voting behavior, see pages 225–230.

The History of the Two-Party System

The Nation's First Parties. Today is the product of yesterday—with political parties as with all else.[8] As we have seen, the origins of political parties in this country may be traced to the controversies surrounding the adoption of the Constitution. The conflicts of the time, centering around the proper form and role of government in the United States, were not stilled by the ratification of the Constitution. Rather, they were carried over into the early years of the Republic, and they led directly to the formation of the nation's first full-blown parties.

The Federalist Party was the first to appear. It was created by Alexander Hamilton, the Secretary of the Treasury in the new government organized by President George Washington. The Federalists were the party of "the rich and the well-born." Many of them had been staunch supporters of the adoption of the new Constitution. They advocated a stronger national government, vigorous executive leadership, and policies beneficial to the nation's financial, manufacturing, and commercial interests. And they urged a liberal interpretation of the new Constitution to support the expansion of national power.

Thomas Jefferson, Washington's first Secretary of State, marshalled the opposi-

tion to Hamilton and the Federalists. He and his followers were more sympathetic to "the common man." They favored a limited and decentralized federal government, legislative supremacy, governmental policies for the benefit of workers, small shopkeepers, farmers, and planters, and a strict construction of the Constitution. Jefferson resigned from Washington's Cabinet in 1793 to devote his energies to the formation of his party. The new party first took the name Anti-Federalists; then it was variously known as the Jeffersonian Republicans or the Democratic-Republicans, and finally (by 1828) as the Democratic Party.

These first two parties clashed in the elections of 1796. John Adams, the Federalist candidate to succeed Washington, defeated Jefferson by a scant three electoral votes. During the Adams administration, Jefferson and James Madison worked tirelessly to organize the Democratic-Republicans throughout the country. Their efforts paid huge dividends in the elections of 1800. Jefferson won the Presidency, defeating the incumbent Adams, and the Democratic-Republicans captured control of the Congress. Federalist control of the National Government was ended.

The Eras of One-Party Domination. The history of the American party system since 1800 may be conveniently divided into three major periods. During each of them, one or the other of the two major parties has regularly held the Presidency, and with it, usually, both houses of Congress, as well.

In the first of these periods, from 1800 to 1860, the Democrats won 13 of 15 presidential elections, losing the office only in the elections of 1840 and 1848. In the second era, from 1860 to 1932, the Republicans were dominant; they won 14 of 18 elections, losing only in 1884, 1892, 1912, and 1916. The third period began with the Democrats' return to power and Franklin Roosevelt's first election to the Presidency

---

[8] The several charts, tables, maps, and graphs on pages 191, 222, 226–227, 230, 241, 286, 360, and 376 should be consulted as you read this brief summary of party history.

in 1932. Since 1932, the Republicans have won the Presidency with but three of their candidates: Dwight Eisenhower in 1952 and 1956; Richard Nixon in 1968 and 1972; and Ronald Reagan in 1980.

There are many who insist that the 1980 elections mark the beginning of a new era in American politics. At the very least, we must wait and see on that score.

THE ERA OF THE DEMOCRATS, 1800–1860. Jefferson's election in 1800 marked the beginning of a period of Democratic domination that was to last until the Civil War. The Federalists, shattered in 1800, offered only weak and declining opposition; by 1816 they had disappeared altogether.

For a time, through the Era of Good Feeling, the Democratic-Republicans were unopposed in national politics. The party began to split into factions by the mid-1820's, however. By Andrew Jackson's administration (1829–1837) a new and potent National Republican (Whig) Party had arisen to challenge the Democrats. The major issues of the time—conflicts over the distribution of public lands, the Second Bank of the United States, the high protective tariff, and the slave question—all had made new party alignments inevitable.

The Democrats, led by Jackson, were a coalition of small farmers, debtors, frontiersmen, and slaveholders. Their main strength lay in the South and West, with some support from the poorer elements of the populations of the North and East. The years of Jacksonian democracy saw the coming of universal white male suffrage and a large increase in the number of elective offices at the State and local levels of American politics. And they brought, too, shorter terms of office for public officials and the spread of the spoils system.

The Whig Party was led by the widely popular Henry Clay and the great orator, Daniel Webster. It was a loose coalition of eastern bankers, merchants, and industrialists, and southern planters—all opposed to the precepts of Jacksonian democracy

and dedicated to the high tariff. The Whigs' electoral victories were few. As the other major party from the mid-1830's to the 1850's, they were able to elect only two Presidents, both of them war heroes—William Henry Harrison in 1840 and Zachary Taylor in 1848.

By the 1850's the growing crisis over slavery sundered both major parties. Left leaderless by the deaths of Clay and Webster, the Whig coalition fell apart. The Democrats split into two sharply divided camps, North and South. Through the decade the nation drifted toward civil war.

Of the several groupings which arose to compete for supporters, the Republican Party was the most successful. Born in 1854, it attracted many Whigs and anti-slavery Democrats. The Republicans nominated their first presidential candidate, John C. Fremont, in 1856 and elected their first President, Abraham Lincoln, in 1860. The Republican Party thus became the only party in the history of American politics to move from the ranks of third-party to major-party status.

THE ERA OF THE REPUBLICANS, 1860–1932. The Civil War signalled the beginning of a new era in American politics. For nearly three quarters of a century, the Republicans—supported by business and financial interests, and by farmers, laborers, and newly-freed blacks—were to dominate the national scene.

The Democrats, crippled by the war, were able to survive mainly through their hold on the Solid South. For half a century they slowly rebuilt their electoral base. In all of that time they were able to place only one of their candidates in the White House—Grover Cleveland in 1884 and again in 1892. Those elections marked only brief interruptions in Republican supremacy, however. Riding the crest of both popular acceptance and unprecedented prosperity, the GOP remained the dominant party well into the 20th century.

The election of 1896 was especially

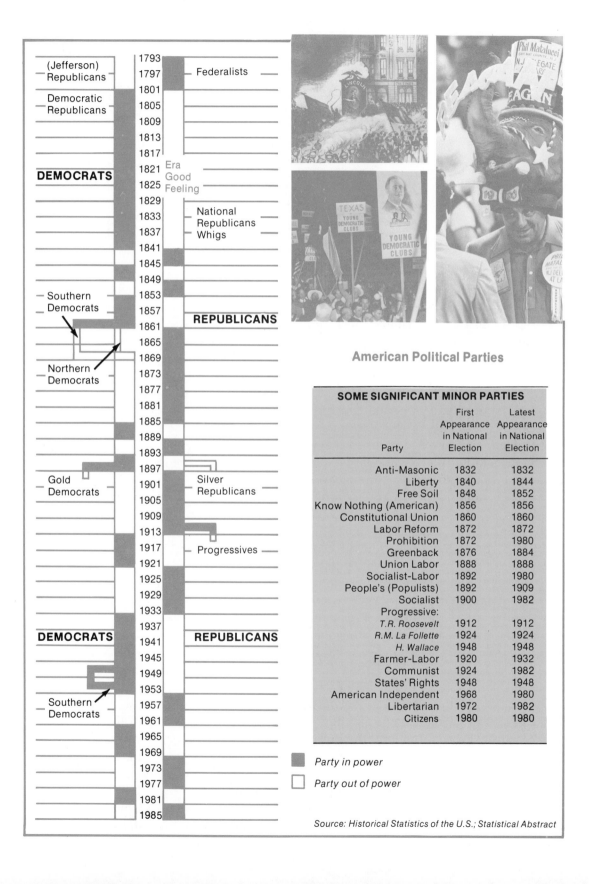

American Political Parties

SOME SIGNIFICANT MINOR PARTIES		
Party	First Appearance in National Election	Latest Appearance in National Election
Anti-Masonic	1832	1832
Liberty	1840	1844
Free Soil	1848	1852
Know Nothing (American)	1856	1856
Constitutional Union	1860	1860
Labor Reform	1872	1872
Prohibition	1872	1980
Greenback	1876	1884
Union Labor	1888	1888
Socialist-Labor	1892	1980
People's (Populists)	1892	1909
Socialist	1900	1982
Progressive:		
T.R. Roosevelt	1912	1912
R.M. La Follette	1924	1924
H. Wallace	1948	1948
Farmer-Labor	1920	1932
Communist	1924	1982
States' Rights	1948	1948
American Independent	1968	1980
Libertarian	1972	1982
Citizens	1980	1980

■ *Party in power*

□ *Party out of power*

Source: Historical Statistics of the U.S.; Statistical Abstract

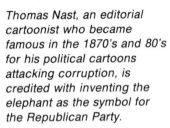

Thomas Nast, an editorial cartoonist who became famous in the 1870's and 80's for his political cartoons attacking corruption, is credited with inventing the elephant as the symbol for the Republican Party.

Library of Congress

critical in the development of the party system. It climaxed years of protest by small businessmen, farmers, and the emerging labor unions against big business and financial monopolies and the railroads. The Republicans regained the Presidency with William McKinley and, in the process, they were able to gather new support from several segments of the electorate—new strength that enabled them to maintain their majority role in national politics for another three decades. Although the Democratic nominee, William Jennings Bryan, lost the election, he championed the "little man"—and so helped to push the nation's party politics back toward economic, rather than sectional, dividing lines.

The Republicans suffered their most serious setback of the era in 1912, when they renominated incumbent President William Howard Taft. Former President Theodore Roosevelt, denied the nomination, bolted the party to become the candidate of his "Bull Moose" Progressive Party. With Republican support divided between Taft and Roosevelt, the Democratic nominee, Woodrow Wilson, captured the Presidency. And Wilson retained the office by a very narrow margin four years later.

But, again, the Democratic successes of 1912 and 1916 proved only an interlude. The Republicans won each of the next

three presidential elections—with Warren Harding in 1920, Calvin Coolidge in 1924, and Herbert Hoover in 1928.

THE RETURN OF THE DEMOCRATS, 1932 TO . . . ? The Great Depression, which began in 1929, had a massive impact upon nearly all aspects of American life and politics. The landmark election of 1932 brought Franklin D. Roosevelt to the Presidency and the Democrats back into power at the national level. The long period of Republican domination was ended. A Democratic reign was begun—a reign which has lasted, almost uninterrupted, to the present day. And, of fundamental importance, that 1932 election marked a basic shift in the American people's attitudes toward the proper role of government in the spheres of economic and social policies.

Franklin Roosevelt and the Democrats engineered their victory in 1932 with a new coalition of electoral support—built largely of southerners, small farmers, organized labor, and big city political organizations. The economic and social welfare programs, which formed the heart of the New Deal of the 1930's, cemented that coalition; and it soon began to attract increasing support from blacks and other minorities in the electorate.

President Roosevelt won overwhelming reelection in 1936. And he secured an unprecedented third term in 1940 and yet another term in 1944, both times by convincing majorities. Harry S Truman succeeded FDR upon the latter's death in 1945 and completed the fourth term. Mr. Truman then earned a full term of his own, turning back the Republican challenge of Thomas E. Dewey, in a close contest in 1948.

Since 1932, the GOP has won only five presidential elections. They regained the White House, for the first time in 20 years, in 1952, marching behind the candidacy of World War II hero Dwight D. Eisenhower. General Eisenhower repeated his triumph in 1956. In both elections he vanquished Democrat Adlai Stevenson.

The Republican return to power was short-lived, however. John F. Kennedy recaptured the Presidency with a razor-thin plurality over the Republicans' Vice President Richard M. Nixon in 1960. Lyndon Johnson took office following President Kennedy's assassination in 1963. In 1964, he virtually annihilated his Republican opponent, Senator Barry Goldwater.

Richard Nixon staged a dramatic comeback in 1968. He defeated Vice President Hubert Humphrey, the candidate of a Democratic Party badly torn by conflicts over the war in Vietnam, civil rights, and social welfare issues. The Republican victory margin was only a bare plurality over Humphrey and the strong third-party effort of the American Independent Party nominee, Governor George Wallace. Mr. Nixon remained in power by routing the choice of the still-divided Democrats, Senator George McGovern, in 1972.

But, once again, the GOP hold was only temporary. President Nixon's role in the Watergate scandal forced him from office, in disgrace, in 1974. Gerald Ford filled out the balance of the presidential term.

Beset by problems in the economy, by the continuing effects of Watergate, and by his pardon of former President Nixon, Mr. Ford lost the Presidency to Jimmy Carter and the resurgent Democrats in 1976.

A steadily worsening economy and his own inability to establish himself as an effective President spelled the defeat for Mr. Carter in 1980, however. The Republicans recaptured control of the executive branch with Ronald Reagan's sweeping victory in the most recent Presidential election.

Minor Parties

Two major parties dominate our politics. But that fact should not blind us to the existence, nor to the importance, of minor parties.[9] A large number of them have flashed across that scene over the years. Only a few of them have achieved any degree of permanence—for example, the Prohibition Party, founded in 1869. But all of them have left a collective and continuing imprint on the American political system.

Types of Minor Parties. The number and variety of these parties makes it somewhat difficult to classify them. Some have limited their activities to a particular locale, others to a single State, some to a particular region of the country, and still others have sought support throughout the nation. As we have already noted, most minor parties are short-lived but some have existed for decades. Then, too, most minor parties have existed moth-like around the flame of a single issue or idea while others have had broader and more practical bases.

No method of classification of minor parties is completely satisfactory. But most minor parties do fall fairly neatly into one of two categories: They have either been parties of "the great idea" or parties of "the great personality."

The "great idea" parties have each been built upon a special set of concepts or

---

[9] Some authorities attempt to distinguish between *minor parties* and *third parties* by using the former term to label those parties with little or no influence on elections or other aspects of the governing process and reserving the latter term for the more consequential groups. But here, as in most commentaries, the terms are used interchangeably.

issues—for example, the Anti-Masonic, Know-Nothing, Greenback, Populist, and States' Rights Parties of the past, and the Socialist, Socialist-Labor, Prohibition, and Libertarian Parties of today. The Progressive Parties of 1912 and 1924, on the other hand, were each founded and lived upon the appeal of a dominant personality— Theodore Roosevelt and Robert M. LaFollete, respectively.

The "great idea" parties have regularly collapsed, or faded to impotence, as either: (1) their central theme has failed to appeal to any significant portion of the electorate, or (2) one or both of the major parties has adopted their key issue as one of its own. Similarly, the "great personality" parties have passed into the limbo of history when their leaders have stepped aside. This happened, for example, to the "Bull Moose" Progressives when Theodore Roosevelt returned to the Republican Party after the election of 1912.

The Republican Party was originally one of the "great idea" parties, born in the cause of anti-slavery in 1854. The Whig Party, unable to embrace the new party's burning issue, passed into oblivion. The Republicans became the major party in opposition to the Democrats.

Some minor parties have been—and some are today—successful at the State or local level. They have, at times, elected a few members of Congress and occasionally gained some electoral votes, but none has ever captured the Presidency.

Importance of Minor Parties. Despite the general unwillingness of most Americans to support them, minor parties have had a very significant impact upon our political history and upon the major parties. Thus, it was a minor party, the Anti-Masons in 1831, that introduced the national convention as a device for nominating presidential candidates. The Democrats and the Whigs seized upon the method for the elections of 1832. Ever since it has been the means by which the major parties have picked their presidential candidates.

A strong third-party candidacy *can* play a decisive role in an election contest. This is true at any level in our politics, national, State, or local—and it is especially true where the two major parties compete on roughly equal terms. The point was dramatically illustrated in the presidential election of 1912. A split in the Republican Party and the resulting third-party candidacy of Theodore Roosevelt that year produced these results:

Party and Candidate	Popular Vote	%	Electoral Vote
Democrat — Woodrow Wilson	6,293,152	41.8	435
Progressive — Theodore Roosevelt	4,119,207	27.4	88
Republican — William H. Taft	3,486,333	23.2	8
Socialist — Eugene V. Debs	900,369	6.0	—
Prohibition — Eugene Chafin	207,972	1.4	—

Historically, the most important roles the minor parties have played have been those of critic and innovator. Unlike the major parties, most of them have been ready, willing, and able to take quite specific stands on difficult issue questions. In doing so they have often drawn attention to controversial issues the major parties have preferred to ignore or straddle.

Many of the more important issues in American politics over the years were first brought to prominence by a minor party. For example, the progressive income tax, prohibition, woman suffrage, railroad and banking regulation, old-age pensions, and farm relief were presented by minor parties. But this very important function of minor parties has also been a major source of their frustration. When their proposals have gained any significant public support, one and then shortly both of the major parties have adopted and presented them

The "Bull Moose" Progressives nominated Theodore Roosevelt to run for the Presidency in 1912. When he returned to the Republican fold after his defeat in 1912 by Woodrow Wilson, the Progressive Party passed into limbo.

as their own. The late Norman Thomas, six times the Socialist Party candidate for President, often complained that "the major parties are stealing from my platform."

The Presidential candidates of at least ten minor parties appeared on ballots of various States in 1980—and there will likely be at least that number in 1984. The 1980 nominees were those of the American, American Independent, Citizens, Right to Life, Libertarian, Socialist, Socialist Workers, Communist, Workers World, and Prohibition parties. Then, too, there was the very active independent effort made by Congressman John Anderson of Illinois. Some 300 minor party nominees sought seats in Congress, as well.

Party Organization

Organization is essential to the accomplishment of any purpose—in politics just as certainly as in all other areas of human behavior. Before we turn to the details of party organization, however, we must rec-

ognize a vitally important feature of the American party system.

The Two Major Parties Are Highly Decentralized. We often refer to the major parties in terms that suggest that they are highly organized, closely-knit, well-disciplined groups. Despite such descriptions—and despite their "on-paper" appearances, too—neither of them is anything of the sort. Rather, they are *highly decentralized* structures—fragmented, and often beset by factional strife.

Federalism is a principal cause of this condition. Because the purpose of each party is to gain control of government by winning elections, party organization is built around the electoral system. And, in the American federal system, elective offices are scattered over a broad political landscape. That is, elective offices are widely distributed at the national, the State, and the local levels of government. In short, because the governmental system is decentralized, so, too, is the organizational framework of the major parties.

The *making of nominations* is another major factor here. Recall the central role of the nominating function in the life of the major parties—a matter we discussed on page 183. We shall turn to nominations at some length in Chapter 10. But, for now, let us consider two highly significant and important aspects of the candidate selection process.

First, it takes place *within* a party; and, secondly, it can be (and often is) a *divisive* process. Whenever a fight over a nomination occurs, it pits members of the same party against one another—Republicans compete with Republicans, Democrats do battle with other Democrats. In short, the prime function of the major parties, the making of nominations, is a prime contributor to their highly fragmented, disjointed character.

Again, both major parties are highly decentralized structures. It is quite misleading to think of them in terms of a cohesive or disciplined organizational pattern. There is no "chain of command" running from the national through the State to the local level in either of them. Each of the State party organizations is only loosely tied to the party's national structure. And, too, local party organs are frequently quite independent of their parent State organizations. The various party units regularly cooperate with one another, of course—but they don't always do so.

The President's party is usually more solidly united, more cohesively organized, than is the opposition. The President is automatically the party leader. There are a number of weapons with which that leadership can be asserted—including, for example, the President's own popularity and power to make appointments to federal office.

The other party, the party out of power, has no one in an even remotely comparable position. Indeed, in our party system it is virtually impossible to find anyone in the opposition party who can be called, in fact, that party's leader.[10]

Rather, there are a number of personalities in the opposition party—frequently in competition with one another—who form a loosely identifiable leadership group.

National Party Machinery. There are four major elements in the hierarchy of both parties at the national level.

THE NATIONAL CONVENTION. The national convention is often described as the party's national voice. It meets only every fourth year, in the summer, to select the party's candidates for President and Vice President and to proclaim the party's platform. Beyond these functions it has little or no authority. It has literally no control over such matters as the nomination of candidates for other offices and cannot force anyone to support its candidates or its platform. We shall return to the convention in Chapter 15, where we consider the presidential selection process.[11]

THE NATIONAL COMMITTEE. Between conventions, party affairs are managed, at least in theory, by the national committee and national chairperson.

For decades, the national committee in each of the major parties consisted of a committeeman and committeewoman chosen by the party organization in each of the States and several of the territories. Both parties have recently enlarged the committee's membership, however.

---

[10] Except the party's presidential candidate from the time of nomination until the election is held. The defeated presidential candidate is often called the "titular leader" of the party. This label is quite apt—the losing candidate is the party's leader in title, by custom, but not in fact.

[11] In 1974 the Democrats (then the party out of power) held the first mid-term convention ever staged by a major party. That "mini-convention," which met in Kansas City, Missouri, adopted a national charter (set of by-laws) for the party, recommended an economic program to Congress, and suggested several planks for inclusion in the party's 1976 platform. A second mid-term conference, this one carefully programmed to emphasize President Carter's role as the party's leader, was held in Memphis in late 1978.

Today, the Republican National Committee includes a committeeman and -woman from each State and, as well, several State chairpersons. The latter come from those States which were won by the Republican presidential candidate or which elected a Republican Senator, or a majority of Republicans to the House, or a Republican as governor in the preceding election.

The Democratic National Committee has been extensively reorganized in the last few years. It now has more than 300 members. Besides the committeemen and -women, the DNC includes the party's chairperson and vice-chairperson from each State, several additional members from the larger States, and 25 members chosen by the committee itself. And it now includes, as well, four members of Congress, three governors, several mayors, and representatives from the Young Democrats.

PARTY ORGANIZATION

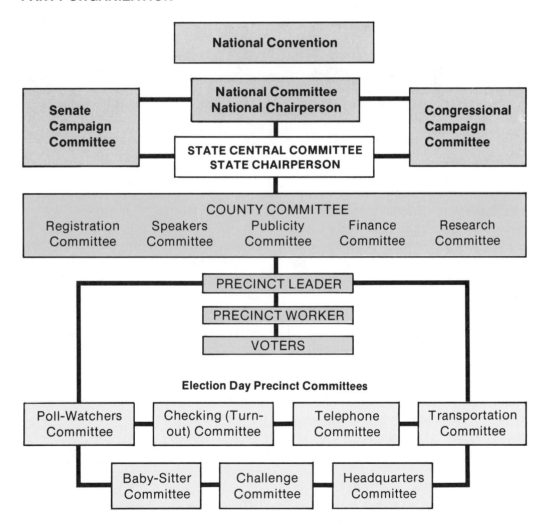

A political action group readies pro-Reagan literature, posters, stickers, and other campaign materials for distribution.

On paper, the national committee appears to be a powerful organ within each party. In fact, it is not. It is chiefly concerned with the problems involved in the staging of the national convention every fourth year.

THE NATIONAL CHAIRPERSON. The national chairperson heads up the national committee in both of the major parties. In form, he or she is appointed to a four-year term by the national committee at a meeting held immediately after the adjournment of the national convention. In actual practice, the choice is made by the party's just-nominated presidential candidate and then ratified by the committee.

The Democrats selected the first woman ever to serve in either major party as national chairperson, Mrs. Jean Westwood of Utah, in 1972. But she was replaced in 1973—and so paid the price usually exacted of the head of the losing party's national committee. The first woman to chair the RNC—Mrs. Mary Louise Smith of Iowa—served in the post from 1974 to 1977.

The chairperson directs the work of the party's headquarters in Washington, D.C., and is assisted by a small staff. The staff is assigned to such tasks as publicity, research, fund-raising, and attracting support from such groups as women, labor, new voters, farmers, ethnic minorities, and the like. In presidential election years, the focus is on the national convention and the ensuing campaign. In between, the chairperson and the national committee attempt to strengthen the party. They seek to do this by promoting unity among its members, raising funds, attracting new voters, and otherwise preparing for the next presidential season.

THE CONGRESSIONAL CAMPAIGN COMMITTEES. Both parties also maintain a campaign committee in each house of Congress. Each of these groups works to reelect incumbents. Where the prospects seem to justify it, the committees also work to help challengers unseat members from the other party.

The Republican National Congressional Committee consists of one GOP Representative from each State with party representation in the House. It selects its own head and appoints a staff to carry on its work. The Democratic Congressional Campaign Committee is similarly organized.[12]

The Republican Senatorial Campaign Committee consists of a chairperson and several other GOP Senators (usually eight of them) selected by the Republican Conference (caucus) in the Senate. The Democratic Senatorial Campaign Committee is chaired by a Senator appointed by the party's Floor Leader. The appointed chairperson selects the other Senators who constitute this five-to-nine member group.

In both parties, and in both houses, the members of these congressional campaign committees serve for two-year terms—that is, for the term of a Congress.

State and Local Party Machinery. National party organization is largely the product of custom and of the rules adopted by the national convention every fourth year. At the State and local levels, on the other hand, party structure is largely determined by State law.

THE STATE CENTRAL COMMITTEE. A State central committee, headed by a State chairperson, supervises the party's machinery in each of the States. The committee varies in composition and powers rather widely across the country. Its members are chosen from congressional or legislative districts or counties within the State—and in a crazy-quilt-like variety of methods: by a

State convention, in the primaries, or by the local party units.

State chairpersons are usually selected by the central committees. Occasionally, these officials are important political figures in their own right. But more often they front for the governor, one of the State's U.S. Senators, or some other potent leader or faction in their party. With members of the State central committees, they work to promote their party and its fortunes. Their efforts are especially directed to trying to build and maintain effective State organizations, promoting party harmony, and raising campaign funds. They also recruit candidates and assist them in their bids for office.

LOCAL UNITS. Local party structure varies so widely among the States that it almost defies brief description. The typical organization follows the lines of the electoral districts. That is, there is usually a party committee for each congressional and legislative district and county, town, borough, precinct, and ward in the State. In the more populous cities party organization is also broken down by residential blocks and often apartment buildings. In some locales, party organizations are active year-round; but, generally, they are lifeless save in the few hectic months before election day.

The Three Basic Elements of the Party. Looking at the two major parties from another angle—the roles of their members, rather than their institutional structure—provides some useful insights. From this vantage point, the major parties are composed of three basic elements:

(1) The Party Organization—the leaders, the activists, and the hangers-on who control and operate the party machinery—"all those who give their time, money, and skill to the party, whether as leaders or followers."[13]

---

[12] Each State without a Democrat in its House delegation is represented by someone chosen for that purpose by the campaign committee's chairperson.

[13] Frank J. Sorauf, *Party Politics in America*, Little, Brown, 4th ed., 1980, p. 8.

the small society   by Brickman

(2) The Party in the Electorate—the party's voters: its loyalists who vote the straight party ticket and those other voters who call themselves party members and usually support its candidates at the polls.

(3) The Party in Government—the party's officeholders, those who occupy elective and appointive offices in the executive, legislative, and judicial branches of the Federal, State, and local governments.

We shall look at the party in the electorate in the next chapter and the party in government in several later chapters.

Party Finance

Money plays a key role in politics. Political activities, and especially election campaigns, cost money—and often a great deal of it.

There is ever present the threat that some candidates will try to buy their way into public office and that certain special interests will attempt to buy favored treatment from those who make public policy.

Certainly, these dangers must be guarded against. But how? Parties and their candidates *must* spend in order to inform the electorate and attract support. Yet, the spending of money can corrupt the entire political process.

Expenditures. No one really knows exactly how much is spent in any election year in the United States. But we do know that elections are expensive and that election costs have risen sharply in recent years. Reliable *estimates* of total campaign spending in the last several presidential years—for all offices at all levels, including nominations and general elections—show this:

Year	Estimated Spending	Votes Cast for President	Cost per Voter
1952	$140,000,000	61,551,118	$2.28
1956	155,000,000	62,025,372	2.50
1960	175,000,000	68,828,950	2.54
1964	200,000,000	70,644,510	2.83
1968	300,000,000	73,211,875	4.10
1972	425,000,000	77,727,590	5.47
1976	540,000,000	81,603,346	6.62
1980	790,000,000	84,899,739	9.31

The presidential election consumes by far the largest share of campaign dollars. For 1980, total spending—for all the pre-convention primaries, the national party conventions, the campaign itself, and for all third-party and independent efforts—was at least $250 million. For 1976, that spending was $160 million.

The totals for all of the U.S. Senate and House races in 1980 reached $200 million, up from $140 million in 1976.[14]

Radio and especially television time, paper, printing, newspaper advertisements, campaign buttons, posters, and stickers, paid staff, office rent, furniture, and equipment, travel expenses—these and a host of other items account for party spending. Television is by far the most costly item in the typical campaign budget today. A single half hour of TV network time can run to as much as $300,000.

The specific amounts spent in particular campaigns vary, of course. More, or less, is spent depending on a number of factors. They include, for example, the office involved, the candidate, whether he or she is the incumbent or not, the opposition, and the availability of funds.

Sources of Funds. Only about one in every ten voters in the United States ever makes a money contribution to a political party or to its candidates. Because of this, both parties and their candidates have traditionally relied on five other principal sources for their funding.

These major sources are: (1) wealthier individuals and families—the so-called "angels" or "fat cats"; (2) the candidates themselves, incumbents, and those who hold appointive government positions; (3) non-party organizations—special interest groups with a major stake in the making and content of public policy, most notably organized labor and business groups; (4) *ad*

hoc committees formed for the immediate purposes of a campaign, including fund-raising; and (5) a variety of special fund-raising events, including marathon television appeals ("telethons"), direct-mail campaigns, and such social-electioneering affairs as $100- and $1000-a-plate dinners, picnics, concerts, and rallies.

To these traditional sources a newer one—public subsidies—has lately been added, especially at the presidential level, as we shall see.[15]

Campaign Finance Regulation. Congress first began to regulate the use of money in the federal election process in 1907. In that year it made it unlawful for any corporation or national bank to make "a money contribution in any election" of candidates for federal office. Since then, it has enacted a number of statutes intended to regulate various aspects of the use of money in federal campaigns. Today, these regulations are contained in three extensively detailed laws: the Federal Election Campaign Act of 1971, the Federal Election Campaign Act Amendments of 1974, and the Federal Election Campaign Act Amendments of 1976.[16]

---

[14] Principal sources for the data in this section are: Herbert E. Alexander, Director, Citizens' Research Foundation; *Congressional Quarterly;* and the Census Bureau.

[15] Several States also provide for some form of public financing for parties and/or candidates—including Hawaii, Idaho, Iowa, Kentucky, Maine, Maryland, Massachusetts, Michigan, Minnesota, Montana, New Jersey, North Carolina, Oklahoma, Oregon, Rhode Island, Utah, and Wisconsin.

[16] The previous statutes were often described as "more loophole than law"; they were loosely drawn, seldom obeyed, and almost never enforced. The 1971 law, which became effective in 1972, replaced them. The 1974 law marked the major legislative response to the Watergate scandal; it tightened many of the provisions and substantially broadened the coverage of the 1971 statute. The 1976 law was enacted in direct response to the Supreme Court's decision in *Buckley* v. *Valeo,* 1976; see below. A number of minor amendments were added to these laws in 1980.

Congress does not have the constitutional power to regulate the use of money in State and local elections; that matter lies within the reserved powers of each of the States. The election laws of every State now contain provisions dealing with at least some aspects of campaign finance; but, unfortunately, in some States those provisions are either inadequate or are only haphazardly enforced, or both.

THE FEDERAL ELECTION COMMISSION. All of federal law relating to campaign finance is now administered by the Federal Election Commission. The FEC was created by Congress in the 1974 law and began functioning in 1975. It is an independent agency in the executive branch and its six members are appointed by the President, subject to confirmation by the Senate.[17]

The statutes which the Commission enforces cover four general areas. They (1) require the disclosure of campaign finance data; (2) place limitations on campaign contributions; (3) place limitations on campaign expenditures; and (4) provide for the public funding of several aspects of the presidential election process.

DISCLOSURE REQUIREMENTS. Congress first began to require the reporting of certain campaign finance information in 1910. The present-day law is quite detailed. It requires any political committee which expects to receive or spend more than $5000 in the calendar year in behalf of one or more candidates for federal offices to file a statement describing its purposes and organization with the FEC. Each of these committees must have a treasurer, and it can make only those expenditures that that person authorizes. The treasurer must keep an accurate and detailed account of all the committee's income and spending.

Much detail must be disclosed to the FEC. The principal reporting requirements today include:

(1) All campaign committees or candidates must report any expenditure of more than $200—including those which, although made in separate and lesser amounts, total more than $200 in the calendar year.

(2) All committees or candidates must report all contributions, including loans, which exceed $50. The names and addresses of the contributors and the dates of their contributions must also be reported. Any contribution in excess of $5000 must be reported within 48 hours of its receipt; so, too, must any contribution of $1000 or more received in the last 20 days of a campaign.

(3) Any person or committee which spends more than $250 in behalf of a candidate, and does so without that candidate's approval, must: (a) publicize the fact that it operates independently, without the candidate's authorization, and (b) swear, subject to perjury, that its spendings were not made in collusion with that candidate or his/her organization.

(4) All committees or candidates must report the total proceeds realized from any fund-raising events, including the sale of any of its campaign materials.

(5) Each political party which holds a presidential nominating convention must file a detailed report of the convention's financing within 60 days of its conclusion.

(6) All committees or candidates must file the required reports quarterly and also 12 days before and not more than 30 days after an election.

(7) Copies of all reports which must be filed with the FEC must also be filed with the chief election officer (usually secretary of state) of the State in which the elect-involved was held.

LIMITS ON CONTRIBUTIONS. Congress first began to regulate campaign contributions in 1907—when, as we have seen, it outlawed contributions by corporations. A similar ban was first applied to labor unions in 1943. Individual contributions first became the subject of legal regulation in 1939.

---

[17] The FEC was originally created with two members appointed by the President, two by the Speaker of the House, and two by the President *pro tem* of the Senate, and with the Clerk of the House and the Secretary of the Senate as *ex officio* members. However, the Supreme Court found this selection process unconstitutional in *Buckley* v. *Valeo,* 1976. It held that, because the FEC is an *executive* agency, the arrangement violated both the doctrine of separation of powers and Article II, Section 2, Clause 2, which grants the appointing power to the President. Congress reconstituted the FEC in 1976. The Clerk of the House and the Secretary of the Senate remain as *ex officio* (by virtue of office), non-voting members of the Commission.

Ed Vattman in the *Hartford Times* © 1972

*'THE BEST POLITICS, OF COURSE, IS TO INVEST IN
BOTH SIDES—YOU'LL NEVER BE A LOSER'*

Neither corporations nor labor unions may make contributions today. But the *officers* of a corporation and the *members* of a union may give from their own funds if they choose, of course—and many of them do. Corporations are often able to make indirect contributions. For example, they do so by paying higher salaries or giving "bonuses" to corporate officers with the understanding that they will then give to the campaigns of friendly candidates. And labor unions regularly behave in similar fashion—for example, by maintaining "political action committees," which operate with funds contributed to them by union members. Both practices are legal.

No individual may now contribute more than $1000 to a single federal candidate in any primary, run-off, or general election. And no individual may give more than $5000 in a year to any political action committee, or $20,000 to the national committee of a political party. The *overall* total of any one person's contributions to federal candidates and committees cannot exceed $25,000 in any one year.

Clearly, these limits, which were first applied in 1976, have finally curbed the long-standing, very substantial influence of wealthy contributors in *federal* campaigns.[18] (But, remember, they do *not* apply to campaigns for State or local office.)

---

[18] The limits may seem generous; in fact, they are very tight. In past elections, many individuals made contributions far in excess of those amounts. For example, in 1972, W. Clement Stone, a Chicago insurance executive, contributed more than $2 million and Richard Mellon Scaife, heir to oil, aluminum, and banking fortunes, gave more than $1 million to the campaign to reelect President Richard Nixon. In that same year, Stewart R. Mott, heir to a General Motors fortune, gave more than $820,000—nearly all of it to Democratic candidates, including $400,000 to the party's presidential nominee, Senator George McGovern. In all, the top ten individual contributors in 1972 provided a total of at least $7.4 million, most of it to presidential candidates.

Organizations—such as the American Medical Association or the National Education Association—cannot give more than $5000 to a candidate in a federal election. The same limit applies to "political action committees," set up by labor unions to represent their members and by companies to represent their officers and stockholders. But neither organizations nor political action committees are subject to any overall ceiling on their political giving.

No contribution may be made by any person or group in the name of another. Cash contributions of more than $100 are absolutely prohibited. So, too, are contributions from any foreign source. No person or business firm holding a contract with any federal agency may make or promise a contribution to any federal candidate, nor may any person knowingly solicit campaign funds from them.

All newspaper, radio, and television ads, billboards, circulars, and all other campaign materials promoting a candidate for a federal office must carry the names of the persons or groups which sponsor them.

LIMITS ON EXPENDITURES. Congress first began to limit federal campaign spending in 1925. Most of the limitations now in the law apply only to the presidential election process.[19]

---

[19] In *Buckley* v. *Valeo* the Supreme Court struck down several restrictions the 1974 law had placed on spending in federal campaigns. The Court held each of them to be contrary to the 1st Amendment's guarantees of freedom of expression. In effect, said the Court, in politics "money is speech." The voided provisions: (1) placed strict limits on House and Senate campaign expenditures; (2) placed strict limits on how much of their own money candidates could put into their own campaigns; and (3) prohibited any person or group to spend more than $1000 in behalf of a candidate without that candidate's authorization. The Court also struck down limits on presidential campaign spending—*but only* as applied to a candidate who does not accept subsidies from the FEC. To this point, Congress has not found any constitutionally acceptable way to reimpose any of those limits.

"HE'S SWORN TO REFUSE ANY CONTRIBUTION OVER ONE HUNDRED DOLLARS, BUT NOBODY'S OFFERED HIM THAT MUCH YET."

Drawing by Donald Reilly; © 1974
The New Yorker Magazine, Inc.

A presidential aspirant may spend no more than a certain amount in his/her pre-convention campaign, including the various presidential primaries. For 1976 that lid was set at $10.9 million, and for 1980 it was $14.7 million. There is also a limit on the amount that may be spent in each of the primaries; it is based upon the number of eligible voters in the given State.

Once nominated, a presidential candidate can spend no more than a fixed sum in the general election campaign—$21.8 million in 1976 and $29.4 million in 1980. And there is also a limit in the spending for each party's national convention—$2.1 million in 1976, and $2.9 million in 1980.

PUBLIC FUNDING OF PRESIDENTIAL CAMPAIGNS. Congress first began to provide for the public funding of presidential campaigns in the Revenue Act of 1971. It enlarged upon the pertinent sections of that law in the Federal Election Campaign Act Amendments of 1974 and 1976.

The 1971 law created the Presidential Election Campaign Fund. It also provided that each person who files a federal income tax return may designate ("check off") $1 of his or her tax payment (or $2 on a joint return) as a contribution to the Fund. The monies channeled to the Fund are then to be used to underwrite campaign costs in the succeeding presidential election.

The "check-off system" became effective with the filing of tax returns in 1973. Thus, the monies in the Fund had their first impact on the presidential election of 1976.[20] As the law now stands, it provides for the public funding of presidential primary campaigns, of presidential nominating conventions, and of presidential election campaigns.

---

[20] The Revenue Act of 1971 also attempted to stimulate and broaden the base of campaign giving. As amended in 1978, the law allows an income tax payer to take a *credit* (a subtraction from the total tax due) of up to $50, or $100 on a joint return, for political contributions. The tax laws of more than half of the States now contain similar provisions.

PRESIDENTIAL PRIMARIES. The primary campaigns of presidential contenders are now financed with a mixture of private and public funds. That is, they are funded from a combination of private contributions a contender raises and public money he or she receives from the Federal Election Commission.

To be eligible for the public funds, a presidential aspirant must first raise at least $100,000 from private sources—*and* must do so in accord with a specific formula. He or she must gather at least $5,000, in individual donations of not more than $250 each, in each of at least 20 States. This rather complicated requirement is meant to demonstrate that the aspirant has at least some base of popular support and is not a hopeless or a frivolous candidate.

For each contender who passes that test, the FEC matches the first $250 of each private contribution he or she can raise—up to as much as half of the overall limit on primary spending. Recall that for 1980 that ceiling was set at $14.7 million for each qualified candidate.

These primary subsidies had a number of significant effects on the nominating process in 1976 and again in 1980. And their impact was felt in both major parties. As but one of the many illustrations of that point, notice this very large consequence: The mere fact that the money was available prompted a much larger than usual number of presidential hopefuls to enter the preconvention struggle—in both of the major parties and in both election years.

According to the FEC, presidential primary spending in 1980 totalled more than $115 million—including some $25 million that it paid out to seven Republican and four Democratic contenders.

NATIONAL CONVENTIONS. If a major party applies for the money—as both did in 1976 and again in 1980—it automatically receives a grant to defray the costs of its national convention. And, recall that is all

Case Study

In 1974 Congress imposed strict limits on the amounts of their own or their families' money congressional and presidential candidates could spend on their own campaigns. For House races the ceiling was $25,000, for the Senate $35,000, and for the Presidency, $50,000.

In *Buckley* v. *Valeo*, 1976, however, the Supreme Court found these limitations unconstitutional. It held, 7–2, that they were in conflict with the 1st Amendment. "The candidate," said the Court, "no less than any other person, has a 1st Amendment right to engage in the discussion of public issues . . . and advocate his own election." And, it noted, "the use of personal funds reduces the candidate's dependence on outside contributions and thereby counteracts the coercive pres-

sures and attendant risks to which the act's contributions limits are directed."

In the Federal Campaign Finance Act Amendments of 1976 Congress re-imposed the $50,000 limit on presidential contenders, if they accept public financing.

■ What prompted Congress to enact the original limits?
■ Why do you think the original ceiling set for candidates for Senate races was set at a higher figure than that for House races?
■ Do you agree with the Court's holding here?
■ What factor appears to make the 1976 limit constitutionally acceptable?

---

that the law permits it to spend for that purpose.

PRESIDENTIAL CAMPAIGNS. Each major party presidential nominee automatically qualifies for a public subsidy to cover the costs of the general election campaign. For 1980, then, Ronald Reagan and Jimmy Carter each received $29.4 million.[21]

In addition, each major party national committee received $4.6 million for its presidential campaign efforts. All told, then, each of the major party campaigns was financed with $34 million in public funds in 1980.

A candidate, or a national committee, can refuse to accept the public money. If either one does so, it can then raise its

campaign funds from private sources.

Both the Republican and the Democratic candidates, and their national committees took the money in 1976 and again in 1980. By doing so, each of them was automatically: (1) limited to spending no more than the amount of the subsidy for the presidential campaign, and (2) prohibited from accepting campaign funds from any other source.

A minor party candidate may also qualify for public funding—but not automatically. To be eligible, the minor party must either (1) have won at least five percent of the popular vote in the last presidential election or (2) win at least that number of votes in the current election.[22]

---

[21] The 1974 law set this subsidy at $20 million, but it also allowed for an inflation factor. Thus, the 1976 subsidy figure was actually $21.8 million. The same inflation-triggered increase was also built into each of the other subsidies the law provides for—*i.e.*, for presidential primary campaigns, for each party's national convention, and for each national committee's presidential campaign work. The FEC fixes the exact amount of each subsidy in each election year.

[22] In which case the public money would be received *after* the election and could not possibly be of help to the candidate in that election. Again, as we noted on page 186, many provisions of election law are purposely drawn to discourage minor party efforts. No minor party candidate received five percent of the presidential vote in 1976 or in 1980. But independent candidate John Anderson won 6.6 percent in 1980, and, presumably, he will be eligible for public funding in 1984.

SUMMARY

With particular reference to our two major parties, a political party may be defined as a group of persons who seek to control government through the winning of elections and the holding of public office.

Parties perform five vital functions in American politics. They (1) nominate candidates and present them to the electorate, (2) inform the voters and stimulate interest in public affairs, (3) act as a "bonding agent" to insure the good performance of their candidates, (4) act as a "watchdog" over the conduct of public business, and (5) provide a basis for the conduct of government.

Our two-party system is principally the result of historical factors, the force of tradition, the nature of the electoral system, and the generally homogeneous character of the nation's population. Membership in the two major parties is purely voluntary and multi-class in nature. A variety of factors—including family influence, economic status, and place of residence—influence party choice.

From its beginnings with the Federalists and the Anti-Federalists, the history of parties in the United States may be traced through three broad periods: The era of the Democrats, 1800–1860, the era of the Republicans, 1860–1932, and the return of the Democrats, 1932 to 1980.

Minor (or third) parties have been and are of two general types: parties of "the great idea" or parties of "the great personality." They have been notable forces in American politics, especially in prompting the major parties on issue questions.

Each major party is highly-decentralized, principally as the result of federalism and the potentially divisive nature of the nominating process. At the national level, both are organized around four major elements: the national convention, the national committee, the national chairperson, and the congressional campaign committees. State and local organization is typically built on a geographic-electoral base. Each of the major parties may also be viewed, quite usefully, as a three-part structure: the party as an organization, the party in the electorate, and the party in government.

Money is of key importance in politics and poses serious problems for democratic government. The major sources of campaign funds are: (1) individual or family contributors; (2) officeholders and office-seekers; (3) non-party groups; (4) temporary campaign committees; and (5) party fund-raising social functions—and, now, public subsidies. Federal laws dealing with campaign finance—most especially the Federal Election Campaign Act of 1971 and the Federal Election Campaign Act Amendments of 1974 and 1976—are now administered by the Federal Election Commission. Generally, these laws: (1) require the disclosure of campaign finance data, (2) place limits on contributions, (3) place limits on expenditures, and (4) provide for public funding of several aspects of the presidential election process.

Concept Development

Questions for Review

1. Why is a definition emphasizing principle and issue inappropriate to our two major parties?

2. What five major functions do parties perform in the United States? Which of them is the key function?

3. How did the American two-party system originate? What role has tradition played in its retention?

4. Why is the single-member district pattern an important factor with reference to the two-party system?

5. Why can neither major party long neglect any significant group in the electorate?

6. What is the chief factor which typically influences a person's choice of party?

7. What are the two basic types of minor parties in American politics? Of what particular value have minor parties been in our politics?

8. Why is it misleading to describe party organization in terms of a national-to-local-level pyramid?

9. Why is it proper to describe the two major parties as highly decentralized structures?

10. What are the major elements of national party organization?

11. On the basis of what particular factor is the typical State party organization built?

12. Why does it seem necessary that campaign finances be regulated by law?

13. What is the Federal Election Commission? What is its mission?

14. With what four major areas of campaign finance do federal laws now deal?

For Further Inquiry

1. What advice would you give to a person who wanted to make politics his or her career?

2. In Great Britain the party out of power is known as Her Majesty's Loyal Opposition and its leader is paid an official salary. Why has it been said that the phrase "Her Majesty's Loyal Opposition" is "one of the most illustrative of terms in the democratic dictionary"? Do you think the leader of the party out of power in the United States should be paid an official salary?

3. After his defeat for the Presidency in 1940, Wendell Willkie said:

> A vital element in the balanced operation of a democracy is a strong alert, and watchful opposition. Ours must not be an opposition against—it must be an opposition for—an opposition for a strong America, a productive America. For only the productive can be strong and only the strong can be free.

How would you phrase Mr. Willkie's thought in your own words? How would you compare Mr. Willkie's comments with Adlai Stevenson's, quoted on page 186?

4. Which of the following proposals do you consider to be the most important? (a) Pay the costs of all political campaigns from public funds. (b) Outlaw party organizations. (c) Encourage the growth of a strong third party. (d) Compel all citizens to vote. (e) Reduce the number of elective offices in the United States. Why?

Suggested Activities

1. Invite local political party officials and public officeholders to class to discuss their conceptions of a political party.

2. Stage a debate or class forum on the question: *Resolved,* That the two major parties should be completely redesigned so that each one truly reflects sharp differences of opinion in American society.

3. Secure copies of the most recent platforms of the Republican and Democratic Parties. Hold a panel discussion on how they differ from one another, in what ways they are quite similar, and in what ways they are more vague than specific.

4. Write a report on one of the following topics: (a) party organization in your State; (b) the history of one of the "great idea" parties; (c) campaigning for local office.

5. Prepare a bulletin board display depicting eventful happenings in the history of each of our two major parties.

6. Examine copies of the campaign finance reports filed by various candidates in the most recent elections in your State or locale. Compare the reports of competing candidates in terms of the sources and totals of the contributions they received and the objects and the totals of the expenditures they made. Relate your findings to the results of the elections involved.

Suggested Reading

Adamany, David W. and Agree, George E., *Political Money: A Strategy for Campaign Financing in America.* Johns Hopkins University Press, 1980.

Barone, Michael, *et al.* (eds.), *The Almanac of American Politics.* Dutton, 1981.

Blank, Robert H., *Political Parties.* Prentice-Hall, 1980.

Bollens, John C. and Schmandt, Henry J., *Political Corruption: Power, Money, and Sex.* Palisades Publishers, 1979.

Clem, Alan T., *American Electoral Politics.* Van Nostrand, 1980.

Crotty, William, *Party Reform.* Longman, 1981.

Crotty, William (ed.), *The Party Symbol: Readings in Political Parties.* Freeman, 1980.

Fishel, Jeff (ed.), *Parties and Politics in an Anti-Party Age.* Indiana University Press, 1978.

Hinkley, Barbara, *Coalitions and Politics.* Harcourt Brace Jovanovich, 1981.

Jacobson, Gary C., *Money in Congressional Elections.* Yale University Press, 1980.

Ladd, Everett C., *Where Have All the Voters Gone?* Norton, 1978.

McCarthy, Eugene J., Kilpatrick, James J., and McNulty, Jeff, *A Political Bestiary.* McGraw-Hill, 1978.

Maisel, Louis and Cooper, Joseph (eds.), *Political Parties: Development and Decay.* Sage, 1979.

Malbin, Michael (ed.), *Parties, Interest Groups, and Campaign Finance Laws.* American Enterprise Institute, 1979.

Politics in America. Congressional Quarterly, 1979.

Pomper, Gerald M. (ed.), *Party Renewal in America.* Praeger, 1980.

Safire, William, *Safire's Political Dictionary.* Random House, 1978.

Sorauf, Frank, *Party Politics in America.* Little, Brown, 4th ed., 1980.

9

Government by the People: Voters and Voter Behavior

No right is more precious in a free country than that of having a voice in the election of those who make the laws under which, as good citizens, we must live. Other rights, even the most basic, are illusory if the right to vote is undermined.

CHIEF JUSTICE EARL WARREN,
WESBERRY V. SANDERS, 1964.

■ Is the "right to vote" most properly viewed as a right, a privilege, or a duty?

■ Should there be a single, national set of voter qualifications uniformly applicable to *all* elections in the United States?

■ Can one in fact express an opinion in an election by *not* voting?

We have observed several times that democratic government is, for us, representative government. It is self-government conducted through the medium of elected representatives. These representatives are the agents of the people—responsible to the people for the day-to-day conduct of government. And they are held accountable to the people at elections.

It is at these elections, through the exercise of the *suffrage*[1]—the right to vote—that the typical citizen can most directly affect the course of government and of public events at all levels in this country. Clearly, then, no right can be more precious to the people than the right to vote. It is, as the poet Oliver Wendell Holmes wrote, "the vote that shakes the turret of the land."

Suffrage a Political Right. The use of the word "right" in the phrase "the right to vote" should be clearly understood. No one possesses the right to vote in the same sense that he or she possesses the right to free speech, to a fair trial or to any of the other *civil* rights guaranteed by the Constitution. The right to vote is *not* a civil right—one belonging to all persons. Rather, it is a *political* right—one belonging to those who qualify, those who can meet certain requirements set by law.

The right to vote is sometimes described as a privilege—to distinguish it

---

[1] The word comes from the Latin *suffragium*—literally, "a vote."

The women suffragists' struggle for the right to vote was finally won in 1920 when the 19th Amendment was ratified.

from a civil right.[2] But it most certainly is *not* a privilege in the sense that government may grant or withhold it from particular individuals or certain groups as it pleases. If voting is to be described as a privilege then it must be noted that it is a privilege that democracy demands be made available to all persons on the same terms.

In this chapter we first consider the matter of suffrage qualifications—*who* may vote in elections in the United States. Then we turn to non-voting—to the fact that, and reasons why, millions of potential voters do *not* go to the polls in this country. And, finally, we look at voter behavior—at "how" and "why" the many millions more who *do* vote actually cast their ballots as they do in American elections.

Suffrage and the Constitution

The overall size of the American electorate today is truly impressive. More than 160 million persons—virtually all of our citizens who are at least 18 years of age—can qualify to vote. That large number, the size of the electorate, is a direct result of the legal definition of the right to vote. That is, it is the product of those laws which set suffrage qualifications—those laws which provide who may and who may not vote. And it is also the product of nearly two centuries of continuing, often contentious, and sometimes violent struggle.

Historical Development of the Suffrage. Largely because the Framers could not agree upon specific requirements, the Constitution left the power to determine suffrage qualifications almost entirely to the States.[3]

When the Constitution became effective in 1789 probably not more than one man in 15 could vote in elections in the various States. The long history of the development of the suffrage since then has

---

[2] In law, a *privilege* is a particular benefit, advantage, or favor that one enjoys beyond, in addition to, those which are held by all citizens.

[3] Originally, the Constitution contained only two provisions relating to the right to vote: (1) Article I, Section 2, Clause 1 requires each State to permit those persons qualified to vote for members of the "most numerous branch" of its legislature to vote as well for members of the national House of Representatives. And, (2) Article II, Section 1, Clause 2 provides that presidential electors be chosen in each State "in such a manner as the legislature thereof may direct." (The "most numerous branch" restriction was subsequently extended to voting for members of the United States Senate, by the 17th Amendment, ratified in 1913.)

been marked by two long-term trends:

First, by the gradual elimination of a number of restrictive requirements based on such factors as religious belief, property ownership, tax payment, race, and sex; and

Second, by the transfer of an increasingly substantial amount of authority over the suffrage from the States to the National Government.

The growth of the American electorate to its present size and scope has occurred in five fairly distinct stages—and those two trends are woven through them:

The first stage of the struggle to extend voting rights came in the early 1800's. Religious qualifications, born in the colonies, rather quickly disappeared; no State has imposed a religious test since 1810. Property ownership and tax payment requirements then began to fall one by one among the States. By mid-century, universal white adult male suffrage had been largely achieved.

The second major effort to broaden the electorate followed the Civil War. The 15th Amendment, ratified in 1870, was intended to guarantee that no citizen would be denied the right to vote because of race or color. Despite the amendment, however, black Americans have until quite recently constituted the largest single group of disfranchised citizens.

The third expansion culminated in the ratification of the 19th Amendment in 1920. That amendment prohibited the denial of the right to vote on account of sex. Wyoming, while still a territory, first gave women the right to vote in 1869. By 1920 more than half of the States had followed that lead.

A fourth major extension spanned the 1960's, as federal legislation and court decisions focused on securing to blacks a full role in the electoral process in all States. With the enactment and implementation of the Voting Rights Act of 1965, especially, racial equality finally became a virtual

fact in polling booths throughout the nation. The 23rd Amendment, added in 1961, added the voters of the District of Columbia to the presidential electorate. The 24th Amendment, added in 1964, eliminated the poll tax, or any other tax, as a condition for participation in federal elections.

The fifth and most recent broadening of the electorate came with the adoption of the 26th Amendment in 1971. It set the minimum age for voting in all States at 18.

Power to Establish Voter Qualifications. The Constitution does *not* give to the National Government the power to establish suffrage qualifications. Rather, that matter is reserved to the States. But the Constitution does place five restrictions on the States in the exercise of that power. It provides that:

(1) Any person whom a State permits to vote for members of "the most numerous branch" of its own legislature it must also permit to vote for Representatives and Senators in Congress.[4] This restriction is of little real significance today. With only minor exceptions, each of the States commonly permits the same voters to vote in *all* elections within the State.

(2) No State may deprive any person of the right to vote on account of race, color, or previous condition of servitude.[5]

(3) No State may deprive any person of the right to vote on account of sex.[6]

(4) No State may require the payment of a poll tax, or of any other tax, as a condition for participation in the nomination

---

[4] Article I, Section 2, Clause 1; 17th Amendment.

[5] 15th Amendment. Note that this amendment does *not* guarantee the right to vote to blacks, or to anyone else. Instead, it prohibits the States the power to discriminate against any person on these grounds in the setting of suffrage qualifications.

[6] 19th Amendment. Note that this amendment does *not* guarantee the right to vote to females, as such. Rather, it is cast on terms of *sex.* Technically, it prohibits a State from discriminating against either males *or* females in the setting of suffrage qualifications.

With the implementation of the Voting Rights Act of 1965, racial equality came closer to becoming a reality at polling places throughout the nation.

or election of any federal officeholder. That is, no State may do so in any process held in connection with the selection of the President, Vice President, or members of Congress.[7]

(5) No State may deprive any person who is 18 years of age or older the right to vote on account of age.[8]

In addition to these five restrictions, which relate expressly to the right to vote, no State may violate any other provision in the Constitution in the setting of suffrage qualifications, of course. Thus, for example, no State may write into its election code any provision which excludes any persons or groups from the electorate on arbitrary or unreasonable grounds. To do so would be to violate the Equal Protection Clause in the 14th Amendment; see pages

171–178. A case decided by the United States Supreme Court in 1975, *Hill* v. *Stone*, illustrates the point. The Court struck down a section of the Texas State constitution providing that *only* those persons *who own taxable* property could vote in city bond elections. It found the drawing of such a distinction for voting purposes to be an unjustifiable classification, prohibited by the Equal Protection Clause.

But, notice, so long as a State does not violate any provision in the Constitution of the United States, it may determine who may and who may not vote. That is, within those limits, it may set suffrage qualifications as it chooses.

Suffrage Qualifications Among the States

Qualifications Imposed by All States. Each of the 50 States today requires all voters to meet qualifications based on two factors: (1) citizenship and (2) residence.

---

[7] 24th Amendment.

[8] 26th Amendment. Note that this amendment does not forbid any State the power to permit persons *younger* than age 18 to vote in any election. But it does prohibit a State from establishing a *maximum* age for voting.

CITIZENSHIP. No alien may vote in any public election held anywhere in the United States. Still, nothing in the Constitution prohibits voting by aliens, and any State could permit them to do so if it chose. Many States, especially in the West, did so in the nineteenth century. Arkansas, the last State in which it was possible for aliens to vote, established a citizenship requirement in 1926.

Only one State now draws any distinction between native-born and naturalized citizens with regard to suffrage. The Minnesota constitution requires that one have been a citizen for at least three months in order to vote.

In actual practice a few aliens do vote—though in what number no one knows, of course. Those who do either mistakenly believe that they are citizens or unlawfully pose as citizens.

RESIDENCE. Each State requires that a potential voter live within the State for at least some period of time in order to qualify to vote. The residence requirement rests on two principal justifications, one historical and the other of continuing significance. The first justification is that of preventing a political machine from importing a group of non-residents to vote in the locale and thus effect the outcome of elections. The second one is to insure that every voter has had at least some chance to become familiar with the candidates and issues in an election.

The actual period of time that a voter must have lived within any of the States is now quite brief. The specific details vary somewhat—but only slightly—among the 50 States. And the fact that the residence requirement is a fairly uniform one today is a direct result of a 1972 decision of the United States Supreme Court.

Today 17 of the States[9] require that a voter live within the State for at least 30 days before an election. In two others the minimum period is slightly longer: 32 days in Colorado, 50 days in Arizona.

Ten States require shorter periods: 29 days in California and West Virginia; 28 days in Massachusetts; 20 days in Kansas, Minnesota, Oregon, and Tennessee; and 10 days in Alabama, New Hampshire, and Wisconsin.

The other 21 States[10] have set no fixed number of days. They simply require that a voter be a legal resident of the State.

Until quite recently, every State required a much longer period of residence—typically, a year in the State, 60 or 90 days in the county and 30 days in the ward or precinct.[11] But in the Voting Rights Act Amendments of 1970 Congress prohibited any requirement of more than 30 days for voting in presidential elections. And, in *Dunn* v. *Blumstein,* 1972, the Supreme Court found Tennessee's requirement of a year in the State and three months in the county to be in conflict with the 14th Amendment's Equal Protection Clause. It held such a lengthy requirement to be an unsupportable discrimination against new residents. While the Court did not specify just how lengthy an acceptable period might be, it did suggest that "30 days appears to be an ample period of time." Election law and practice among the 50 States rather promptly accepted that standard.

When Congress acted against lengthy State residence requirements for voting in the 1970 law it provided that no State could deny any person the right to vote in

---

[9] Alaska, Illinois, Indiana, Michigan, Mississippi, Montana, Nevada, New Jersey, New York, North Carolina, North Dakota, Ohio, Pennsylvania, Rhode Island, Texas, Utah, Washington.

[10] Arkansas, Connecticut, Delaware, Florida, Georgia, Hawaii, Idaho, Iowa, Kentucky, Louisiana, Maine, Maryland, Missouri, Nebraska, New Mexico, Oklahoma, South Carolina, South Dakota, Vermont, Virginia, Wyoming.

[11] The *precinct* is the basic, smallest unit of election administration; for each precinct there is a polling place. It is also the basic unit in party organization; see page 199. The *ward* is a unit into which cities are often divided for the election of members of the city council.

Most States permit college students to vote in their campus communities if they claim legal residence there. The college students here are soliciting support for a presidential contender.

a presidential election if that person met two requirements. If that person: (1) had resided within the local precinct (or similar unit) for at least 30 days immediately prior to the election and (2) was otherwise qualified to vote in that State, he or she could not be denied the right to vote. The provision was upheld by the Supreme Court in *Oregon* v. *Mitchell* in 1970. Speaking for the Court, Justice Hugo Black said:

> Acting under its broad authority to create and maintain a national government, Congress unquestionably has power under the Constitution to regulate federal elections. The Framers of our Constitution were vitally concerned with setting up a national government that could survive.
>
> Essential to the survival and to the growth of our national government is its power to fill its elective offices and to ensure that the officials who fill these offices

are as responsive as possible to the will of the people whom they represent.

Nearly every State prohibits *transients,* persons in the State only for a limited time for a specific purpose, from gaining a legal residence there. Thus, a member of one of the armed services or an out-of-State college student is often unable to vote in a State where he or she has only a *physical* residence.

In several States, however, the courts have now held that college students who claim the campus community as their legal residence must be allowed to vote there. And they have held this to be so *regardless* of where a student's parents may live or where his or her "permanent" home may be.

AGE. As we know, the 26th Amendment sets a uniform voting age of 18 for all elections in all States. It declares:

The right of citizens of the United States, who are 18 years of age or older, to vote shall not be denied or abridged by the United States or by any State on account of age.

Prior to its adoption in 1971, 21 was the generally accepted minimum age for voting.

In fact, up to 1970 only four States had set the minimum voting age below that figure: Georgia had permitted 18-year-olds to vote since 1943 and Kentucky since 1955. Alaska entered the Union in 1959 with the age set at 19 and Hawaii later the same year with the age set at 20. The latter two States set the voting age slightly above 18 in order to avoid whatever problems might be caused by high school students voting in local elections. But, whatever their fears on this score, they certainly have not been borne out by the experiences thus far under the 26th Amendment.

Qualifications Imposed by Some States. A few other suffrage qualifications—notably registration—are found in several States.

REGISTRATION. Forty-nine States—all except North Dakota—today (1981) require that all voters, or at least most of them, be *registered* to vote. Registration is simply a device intended to provide election officials with a list or record of those persons who are legally entitled to vote in an election. That is, registration is a device of voter identification—one designed to prevent fraudulent voting.[12] (In some States voter registration is known, instead, as "enrollment.")

Without a registration system, it is often difficult to determine whether a person who claims to be eligible is actually entitled to vote. It may have been true that in earlier times election officials commonly knew most of the residents of their local areas. But, obviously, a much different situation prevails in many places today.

Most States require *all* voters to register; but in a few States—in Wisconsin, for example—only those who reside in urban areas must do so. Typically, a prospective voter must "register" his or her name, age, place of birth, present address, length of residence, and similar pertinent facts with a local registration officer.[13]

Every State (except North Dakota) now has some form of permanent registration. That is, a voter once qualified remains a registered voter unless something occurs to void that registration. Typically, a voter remains registered unless or until he or she moves, dies, is convicted of a serious crime, is committed to a mental institution, or fails to vote within a certain number of years or elections. For example, a voter who fails to vote in at least one election in a two-year period in Florida, Indiana, Pennsylvania, or South Carolina must reregister in order to vote again. And the same holds true for anyone who did not vote in the most recent general election in Alaska, Colorado, Nebraska, or Wyoming.

The registration requirement has become quite controversial in recent years. Some favor the elimination of voter registration altogether. They cite the requirement as a bar to voter turnout, especially among the poor and the less educated.

Others favor retaining registration but want to make it more convenient. To that end, two States (Maine and Oregon) now permit voters to register at any time, including registration on election day. In each of the other States, however, one must register at some time before an election—usually at least 30 days before it is held.

---

[12] Several States also use their registration systems to identify voters in terms of party preference and, hence, eligibility to participate in closed primaries; see page 239. In a few States the registration requirement is not imposed as a prerequisite to voting in *all* elections—*e.g.,* it is not required of voters in some school districts in Minnesota.

[13] Most often with an officer known as the *registrar of elections,* or with the county clerk. In some States party officials and even candidates are allowed to register new voters.

Nearly half of the States now provide for the conduct of the entire registration process by mail.

LITERACY. In the Voting Rights Act Amendments of 1970 Congress suspended for five years the use of a literacy requirement as a qualification for voting in any election held anywhere in the United States. Congress made the ban a permanent one in 1975. Hence, none of the States may impose a literacy qualification today.

Until 1970, some form of a literacy requirement was found in 18 of the States. In some of them merely the ability to read was required; in others, to read and write. And, in still others, the ability to read, write, and "understand" a piece of printed material was required—usually a passage from the State or National Constitution.

The first literacy requirements were adopted by Connecticut in 1855 and then Massachusetts in 1857 and were aimed specifically at Irish Catholic immigrants. Mississippi adopted a literacy qualification in 1890 and, shortly thereafter, most of the other Southern States followed suit, usually with an "understanding clause."[14]

A number of States outside the South also adopted literacy qualifications of various sorts. Wyoming did so in 1889, California in 1894, Washington in 1896, New Hampshire in 1902, Arizona in 1913, New York in 1921, Oregon in 1924, and Alaska (while still a territory) in 1949.

The literacy requirement could be—and in many places was—used to insure

Copyright ©, 1962, St. Louis Post-Dispatch, reproduced by courtesy of Bill Mauldin

"BY THE WAY, WHAT'S THAT BIG WORD?"

that a qualified voter had at least some capacity to cast an informed ballot. But it could also be—and in many places was—administered unfairly, to prevent or discourage certain groups from voting. The device was used in precisely that way for many years in some parts of the South.

Its unfair use finally led Congress to destroy it as a suffrage qualification. Congress did so first temporarily in 1970 and then absolutely in 1975, as we have noted. Upholding the congressional ban on literacy tests, the Supreme Court noted, in *Oregon* v. *Mitchell,* that:

> In enacting the literacy ban . . . Congress had before it a long history of discriminatory use of literacy tests to disfranchise voters on account of their race.

TAX PAYMENT. Property ownership—as evidenced by the payment of property taxes—was once a common suffrage re-

---

14 A "grandfather clause" was added to the Louisiana constitution in 1895, and six other States (Alabama, Georgia, Maryland, North Carolina, Oklahoma, and Virginia) soon added them, as well. These clauses provided that any person, or his male descendants, who had voted in the State at some time prior to the adoption of the 15th Amendment (1870) could become a legal voter without regard to a literacy or taxpaying qualification. The basic purpose was to enfranchise those whites who were otherwise disqualified by such requirements. The Supreme Court found the Oklahoma provision, the last to be adopted (1910), in conflict with the 15th Amendment in *Guinn* v. *United States* in 1915.

quirement. It has now all but disappeared. In the few States in which the qualification still exists it is used only as a prerequisite to voting on such questions as bond issues and special assessments. And, it is of doubtful constitutionality today; see page 213. (Until the ban on literacy tests, South Carolina exempted property taxpayers from the application of that State's literacy requirement.)

The *poll tax*, once found throughout the South, has now disappeared altogether as a suffrage qualification.[15] Beginning with Florida in 1889, each of the 11 Southern States had by 1902 provided for it as a part of the concerted effort to disfranchise the Negro. The device proved to be of only limited effect, however. That fact, combined with opposition to its use—from within the South as well as elsewhere in the country—led to its abandonment by most of those States. By 1966—the final year in the life of the poll tax as a suffrage qualification—it was still being used by but four States: Alabama, Mississippi, Texas, and Virginia.[16]

The 24th Amendment, ratified in 1964, outlawed the payment of a poll tax—or of any other tax—as a condition for voting in any federal election. But, recall, its provisions do not apply to State and local elections.

The Supreme Court wrote *finis* to the poll tax as a qualification for participation in *any* election—State or local as well as federal—in 1966. In *Harper* v. *Virginia State Board of Elections* the Court held the Virginia tax to be in conflict with the Equal Protection Clause of the 14th Amendment. Said

---

[15] A few States still levy a poll tax—also known as a "head" or "capitation" tax—today; but they do so for revenue-raising purposes, *not* as a suffrage qualification; see page 775.

[16] Seven States had abandoned the poll tax several years earlier: North Carolina in 1920, Louisiana in 1934, Florida in 1937, Georgia in 1945, South Carolina in 1950, Tennessee in 1951, and Arkansas in 1964 (shortly after the ratification of the 24th Amendment).

the Court:

> . . . once the franchise has been granted to the electorate, lines may not be drawn which are inconsistent with the Equal Protection Clause. . . . Voter qualifications have no relation to wealth nor to paying or not paying this or any other tax. Wealth, like race, creed, or color, is not germane to one's ability to participate intelligently in the electoral process.

Suffrage Disqualifications. Every State bars certain groups from voting. Thus, no State permits those who are confined to mental institutions to vote. Nor does any State allow to vote those who, though not confined, have been legally judged to be mentally incompetent. Nearly all of the States also disqualify those who have been convicted of certain types of crimes, the most common being felonies and election offenses. A few States also forbid voting by anyone dishonorably discharged from the armed forces. And in some such odd groups as duelists, vagrants, and polygamists are also disqualified.

Civil Rights Laws and the Suffrage. The 15th Amendment was ratified in 1870. It prohibits the denial of the right to vote on account of race, color, or previous condition of servitude. The Amendment is not self-executing, however; to make it effective, Congress had to act. And for almost 90 years the Federal Government paid little attention to the problem of black voting.

Over that period, blacks were quite generally and systematically kept from the polls in much of the South. White supremacists employed a number of tactics to that end. Violence and threats of it were a major weapon. So, too, were more subtle intimidations and social pressures—for example, firing a black man who did try to vote, or denying his family credit in local stores.

More formal—"legal"—devices were used, as well. Of these, the most effective were the literacy tests, which we considered on page 217. They were regularly manipulated by white election officials to disfranchise black citizens.

Registration requirements often served the same purpose. On the surface, those requirements applied to all potential voters, black or white. But in practice they were administered to prevent blacks from qualifying to vote. Poll taxes, gerrymandering, white primaries, and various other devices were used, as well.[17]

---

[17] *Gerrymandering* is the practice of drawing electoral district lines to the advantage of a particular party or faction; see pages 290-291. The Supreme Court finally destroyed gerrymandering for purposes of racial discrimination in a case from Alabama, *Gomillion* v. *Lightfoot,* 1960.

The *white primary* arose out of the near-complete and decades-long Democratic Party domination of the politics of the South. Almost invariably, only the Democrats nominated candidates for office—and usually in primaries. In several southern States, political parties were defined by law as "private associations." As such, they could admit (or exclude) members as they chose; and the Democrats regularly refused to admit blacks. Because only party members could vote in a party's primary, blacks were thus effectively excluded from *the* critical step in the public election process. The Supreme Court finally outlawed the white primary in a case from Texas, *Smith* v. *Allwright,* 1944. There it held that, because nominations are an integral part of the election process, when a political party holds a primary it is performing a *public* function and is bound by the 15th Amendment.

Led by decisions of the Supreme Court, the lower federal courts began to strike down many of these practices in the 1940's and 1950's. But those courts could react only when suits were filed by those who claimed to be the victims of discrimination. And this case-by-case approach was, at best, agonizingly slow.

Finally, Congress was moved to act—and very largely in response to the civil rights movement led by Dr. Martin Luther King. It has enacted several civil rights measures since the late 1950's. Recall that we discussed many of their provisions in Chapter 7. And there we noted that those statutes contain a number of sections specifically designed to implement the 15th Amendment.

The first of them, the *Civil Rights Act of 1957,* created the United States Civil Rights Commission (page 175). One of its major duties is to inquire into claims of voter discrimination. It reports its findings to Congress and the President and, through the media, to the public at large. The Act also gave to the Attorney General the power to seek federal court orders (injunctions) to prevent interferences with any person's right to vote in federal elections.

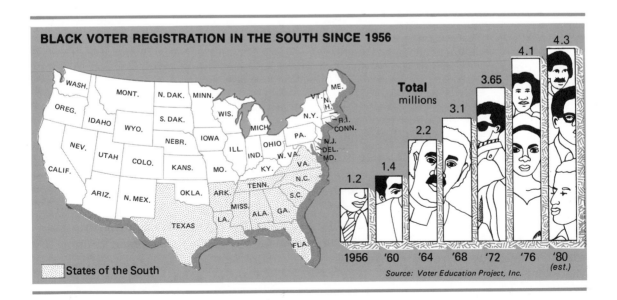

BLACK VOTER REGISTRATION IN THE SOUTH SINCE 1956

States of the South

Total millions

1956: 1.2
'60: 1.4
'64: 2.2
'68: 3.1
'72: 3.65
'76: 4.1
'80 (est.): 4.3

Source: Voter Education Project, Inc.

The *Civil Rights Act of 1960* added an additional safeguard. It provided for the appointment of federal voting referees. These officers were to serve in any locale in which a federal court found that voter discrimination was present. They were empowered to assist qualified persons to register and to vote in federal elections.

The *Civil Rights Act of 1964* is a much more extensive civil rights law than either of its predecessors, a point we noted on page 175. With regard to voting rights, its most important section forbids the application of any registration requirement in an unfair and discriminatory manner.

The 1964 law continued a pattern set in the two earlier measures. In the main, it relied on judicial action to overthrow racial barriers. It emphasized the use of federal court orders—injunctions, backed by the power of the courts to punish for contempt those public officials and others who refused to obey them.

Dramatic events in Selma, Alabama, soon demonstrated the shortcomings of this approach, however. Dr. King had mounted a voter registration drive in that city in early 1965. He and his supporters hoped that they could focus national attention on the issue of black voting rights— and they most certainly did. Their registration efforts were met with unbridled abuse and violence—by local whites, by city and county police, and then by State troopers. The nation saw much of the drama on television and was shocked. An outraged President Johnson urged Congress to adopt new and stronger legislation to ensure the voting rights of black Americans. And an equally offended Congress was quick to respond.

The *Voting Rights Act of 1965* made the 15th Amendment, at long last, a truly effective part of the Constitution. Unlike its predecessors, its provisions apply to *all* elections held anywhere in this country— State and local as well as federal.

The original version of the law has now been extended, and strengthened, twice— by the *Voting Rights Act Amendments of 1970* and again by the *Voting Rights Act Amendments of 1975*. In its present form, the statute will expire in 1982.

As it was first enacted, the principal sections of the law:

(1) Ordered the Attorney General to contest the constitutionality of the remaining State poll tax laws. (This section led directly to *Harper* v. *Virginia Board of Elections,* 1966; see page 218.)

(2) Suspended the use of literacy tests and all similar voting requirements in any State or county where less than half of the voting-age population had either been registered or had actually voted in the 1964 elections.

(3) Authorized the appointment of federal voting examiners to register voters and oversee the conduct of future elections in those States or counties.

(4) Provided that no new election laws could become effective in those States unless first approved by a three-judge panel of the United States District Court for the District of Columbia.

(5) Contained a "bail-out" process, by which any State or county affected by the voter examiner and the pre-clearance provisions can be removed from coverage. This relief may come if the State is able to satisfy the three-judge court that it has not applied any of its voting procedures in a discriminatory manner for at least the past five years.

The section triggering the law's application immediately affected the election processes in six entire States: Alabama, Georgia, Louisiana, Mississippi, South Carolina, and Virginia. And a number of counties in North Carolina were covered, as well. In the 1970 Amendments Congress added the year 1968 to the triggering formula. And that added several counties in six more States to the list: in Alaska, Arizona, California, Idaho, New York, and Oregon.

The constitutionality of the Voting Rights Act was upheld by the Supreme Court in 1966. In *South Carolina v. Katzenbach* the Court ruled that Congress had chosen both "rational and appropriate" means to implement the provisions of 15th Amendment.

Congress continued its assault on literacy as a suffrage qualification in 1970. The 1970 Amendments provided that for a period of five years *none* of the States could use literacy as the basis for any voting requirement.

Recall that the 1970 law also eased residence requirements for voting in presidential elections. And it also set 18 as the minimum age for voting in *all* elections. The 18-year-old vote provision became a part of the Constitution with the adoption of the 26th Amendment in 1971, of course. And the new law's literacy ban and its residence provision were upheld by the Supreme Court in *Oregon v. Mitchell* in 1970—points we dealt with on pages 215 and 217.

Congress finally destroyed the use of literacy as a suffrage qualification altogether in 1975. In the most recent voting rights measure it replaced the five-year ban on such qualification with a *permanent* prohibition of them.

The 1975 law also made a significant addition to the voting examiner and the pre-clearance sections of the law. It brought within their coverage any State or county in which more than five percent of the voting-age population belongs to certain "language minorities." Those minorities are defined to include persons of Spanish heritage, American Indians, Asian Americans, and Alaskan Natives. This addition spread the law's coverage to all of Alaska and Texas, and to various counties in 24 more States, as well.

The 1975 law requires that in each of the language-minority areas all ballots and other official election materials be printed both in English *and* in the particular minority language involved.

Non-Voting

We began this chapter with a comment on the critical relationship between the suffrage and democratic government. We also observed that "clearly, . . . no right can be more precious to the people than the right to vote." But, despite the obvious truth of this remark, there are literally millions of persons who, for one reason or another, do not vote.

Scope of the Problem. The table on page 222 lays out the major features of the non-voter problem in American elections. Notice, for example, that on election day in 1980 there were an estimated 160,491,000 persons of voting age in the United States. Yet, only some 84.9 million persons—only 52.9 percent of them—actually voted in the presidential election. That is to say, some 76.6 million—very nearly half—did not vote.

Also in 1980 there were some 77.2 million votes—48 percent—cast in the elections held across the country to fill the 435 seats in the House of Representatives. That is, *more than half* of the potential electorate did not vote in the congressional elections of 1980.[18]

LITTLE-RECOGNIZED ASPECTS OF THE PROBLEM. The fact that we do have a non-voter problem of considerable proportions in this country is widely recognized, of course. The figures just presented—and those in the accompanying table—simply detail the fact.

But there are several aspects of the problem which are not widely recognized at all. For example, few recognize the fact that there are literally millions of non-voters *among those who vote.* Look again at the 1980 figures: more than 7 million persons who *did* vote in the presidential election

[18] Except for the District of Columbia, the 435 congressional districts altogether occupy the same geographic area and involve the same voters as does the presidential election.

VOTER TURNOUT, 1920–1978

Year	Population of Voting Age[a] (Estimated)	Vote Cast for President		Vote Cast for U.S. Representatives	
		Number	Percent	Number	Percent
1920	61,495,000	26,753,788	43.5	25,080,000	40.8
1922	63,598,000	—	—	20,409,000	32.1
1924	66,195,000	29,135,859	44.0	26,884,000	40.6
1926	68,550,000	—	—	20,435,000	29.8
1928	70,993,000	36,790,364	51.8	33,906,000	47.8
1930	73,623,000	—	—	24,777,000	33.7
1932	75,768,000	39,739,382	52.4	37,657,000	49.7
1934	77,997,000	—	—	32,256,000	41.4
1936	80,174,000	45,642,503	56.9	42,886,000	53.5
1938	82,354,000	—	—	36,236,000	44.0
1940	84,728,000	49,840,443	58.8	46,951,000	55.4
1942	86,465,000	—	—	28,074,000	32.5
1944	89,996,000	47,794,819	53.1	45,103,000	50.1
1946	92,659,000	—	—	34,398,000	37.1
1948	95,573,000	48,692,432	50.9	45,933,000	48.1
1950	98,134,000	—	—	40,242,000	41.1
1952	99,929,000	61,551,118	61.6	57,571,000	57.6
1954	102,075,000	—	—	42,580,000	41.7
1956	104,515,000	62,025,372	59.3	58,426,000	55.9
1958	106,447,000	—	—	45,818,000	43.0
1960	109,674,000	68,828,950	62.8	64,133,000	58.5
1962	112,958,000	—	—	51,261,000	45.4
1964	114,085,000	70,644,510	61.9	65,886,000	57.8
1966	116,638,000	—	—	52,900,000	45.4
1968	120,285,000	73,211,875	60.9	66,109,000	55.0
1970	124,498,000	—	—	54,173,000	43.5
1972	140,068,000	77,727,590	55.5	71,188,000	50.8
1974	144,928,000	—	—	52,397,000	36.2
1976	150,041,000	81,603,346	54.4	74,259,000	49.5
1978	155,500,000	—	—	54,592,000	35.1
1980	160,491,000	84,899,739[b]	52.9	77,196,000	48.1[b]

[a] Defined by Census Bureau as resident population 18 years and over since ratification of 26th Amendment in 1971. Prior to 1971, 21 years and over in all States, except: 18 years and over in Georgia since 1943 and Kentucky since 1955, 19 years and over in Alaska and 20 years and over in Hawaii since 1959.

[b] Preliminary figure.

Sources: Bureau of the Census; *Statistical Abstract of the United States; Congressional Quarterly.*

did *not* vote, at the same election, for a candidate for the House of Representatives.

The "non-voting voter" aspect of the problem is not confined to federal elections, of course. In fact, the problem is a much larger one at the State and local levels. As a general rule, the further down the ballot an office is the lesser the number of votes that will be cast for it. This phenomenon, sometimes described as "ballot fatigue," occurs regularly throughout the country. Some quick illustrations of the point: More votes are regularly cast in the presidential than in the gubernatorial election in every State. And, more votes are usually cast in the contest for the governorship than for such other Statewide offices as lieutenant-governor and attorney general. And, too, more votes are cast in a county for the governorship and for other Statewide offices than for such county offices as coroner or sheriff, and so on.

Dedicated to stimulating an active and informed electorate, the League of Women Voters sponsored the nationally televised 1980 Carter-Reagan debate. It was held in Cleveland's Public Hall six days before the presidential election.

There are other little-recognized facets of the non-voter problem, too. Notice that voter turnout in congressional elections is consistently higher in the presidential years than it is in the "off years." And the same pattern holds true among the States in terms of primary, special, and general elections. More voters regularly participate in general elections than in either primaries or special elections; and, more people vote in the primaries than in special elections.

Reasons for Non-Voting. Why do we have so many non-voters? Why, even in a presidential election, do nearly one half of all of the potential voters stay away from the polls?

To begin with, it should be noted that the group of approximately 76 million persons of voting age who did not vote in 1980 includes several million who, in fact, *could not vote.* Thus, that figure includes some four million aliens who, legally, cannot vote. It also includes some five million citizens who were so ill or otherwise physically handicapped that they could not go to the polls on election day. And it includes another two to three million persons who were travelling, either for business or pleasure, and so were absent from their home precincts on election day.

Then, too, some 500,000 adults were confined to mental institutions and another 250,000 were in prison—and so could not vote. And perhaps as many as 100,000 persons do not (cannot) vote because of their religious beliefs.

Discrimination still plays a large role here, too. This happens despite the many recent federal statutes, court cases, and enforcement actions designed to eliminate practices aimed at preventing or discouraging voting by blacks and other minorities. Perhaps as many as five million persons could not vote in 1980 because of (1) laws purposefully drawn or administered to disfranchise them, and/or (2) "informal" local pressures applied to the same end.

There are also many who do not vote because they are convinced that it really makes no difference to them who holds public office and makes public policy. Of course, this group of non-voters includes those who are relatively content with their lives and the course of public events. *And* it includes those who feel *alienated*—those who do not trust, or fear or scorn, political institutions and processes.

And there are many who do not go to the polls because of the real, or imagined,

Case Study

A large number of studies of voting behavior indicate that between one fourth and one third of the American electorate switch their votes from party to party often enough to be classed as independents, rather than as Republicans or Democrats. That is, these studies show that a sizable slice of the electorate either votes a "split ticket"—balloting for several Republican and several Democratic candidates at the same election—or else changes party allegiance, as measured by voting behavior, from election to election.

Many of these same studies report that only about one tenth of all eligible voters,

and about 15 percent of those who actually do vote, are well-informed, sensitive to issues, and make conscious choices for individual candidates who appear to favor the voters' own perceived interests.

■ What questions about rationality of voter behavior do these findings raise in your mind?

■ What characteristics do you think would identify the "independent voter"?

■ Before answering that question, would it be necessary first to distinguish between or among different types of independent voters?

absence of meaningful contests or issue differences between candidates. Others may not vote because of cumbersome election procedures, long ballots, overcrowding at the polls, or inclement weather on election day.

But all of the reasons just cited do not constitute the *chief cause* for non-voting. The reason why some 76 million persons did not go to the polls to vote in 1980 is a quite simple one: *lack of interest.*

Those people who lack sufficient interest to vote—who are indifferent and apathetic, who just cannot be bothered—are usually uninformed. They are often unaware of even the basic and relatively simple facts concerning an election, and ignorant of the significance of the right to vote. The fact that such persons often do stay away from the polls might well be counted among our blessings. Surely, elections are not intended to be polls of the indifferent, the lazy, the apathetic, or the ignorant.

The table on the next page demonstrates a number of factors associated with voter turnout. As you can see, the profile of those persons most likely to vote includes such characteristics as: higher levels of income, education, occupational status,

and ethnic prestige. In sociological terms, such persons are fairly well integrated into community life—that is, long-time residents who are active in civic groups. Psychologically, they have a strong sense of party identification, have faith in the effectiveness of voting, and are subject to relatively few cross pressures that might discourage participation. And, in the legal and political spheres, they reside in those States where laws, customs, and interparty competition all tend to promote turnout. The opposite characteristics produce a profile of persons least likely to vote, of course.

A few of the factors listed in the table are so weighty as to influence turnout even when they are *not* supported by other factors. For example, the turnout of men is greater than that of women in every category: income, education, race, age, religion, section, and so on. Similarly, the presence or absence of vigorous two-party competition has the same across-the-board effect. That is, the greater the competition which exists between two or more candidates, the greater the voter turnout, regardless of other factors.

Despite these exceptions, notice that it is a complex of various factors, rather than

FACTORS AFFECTING VOTER TURNOUT IN AMERICAN ELECTIONS

High Turnout	Lower Turnout
High income	Low income
High education	Low education
Occupation:	Occupation:
Businessman	Unskilled worker
White-collar employee	Servant
Government employee	Service worker
Commercial-crop farmer	Subsistence farmer
White	Non-white
Second- or third-generation American	First-generation immigrant
Catholic or Jew	Protestant
Male	Female
Urban resident	Rural resident
Northeastern, Middle West, Far West region	Southern region
35 years of age or older	Younger voter
High degree of exposure to political stimuli	Little exposure to political stimuli
Long-time resident in locale	Newcomer to locale
Member of voluntary groups	Isolated individual
Married person	Single person
High political interest in work group	Low political interest in work group
Crisis political situation	Normal political situation
Strong party identification in family	Weak or no party identification in family
Holds strong party identification	Holds weak or no party identification
Strong sense of political effectiveness	No sense of political effectiveness
Strong sense of civic duty	Little sense of civic duty
Perceives personal stake in election	Perceives no personal stake in election
Few cross pressures	Many cross pressures
Lack of cumbersome registration and other election procedures	Restrictive, cumbersome election procedures
National election	State or local election only
Two-party competition	One-party constituency
Absence of community pressures against participation	Community pressures against participation

any one of them alone, that prompts an individual's decision to vote or not.

Voter Behavior

Although many millions of potential voters do *not* go to the polls, many millions more quite obviously do. *How* do those who do vote tend to cast their ballots? *Why* do they vote as they do? That is, what factors tend to prompt some voters to vote most often for Republican candidates? What factors tend to persuade other voters to support Democrats?

Unfortunately, these questions cannot be answered with absolute certainty. But several useful observations *can* be made—

and especially because extensive studies of voting behavior have produced a vast amount of information about those factors that: (1) *tend* to persuade people to vote, and (2) *tend* to influence them to support one party and its candidates rather than the other.[19]

A mass of factual data on *how* voters have cast their ballots can be and has been drawn from the careful study of election

---

[19] The study of voting behavior is still an infant science. Much research and refinement of technique remain to be done before questions such as these can be answered in more than generalized and highly qualified terms. Much of the most useful work on voter behavior has been and is being done through the Center for Political Studies at the University of Michigan.

SELECTED PRESIDENTIAL ELECTIONS

| | Popular Vote (in Millions) | Electoral Vote |

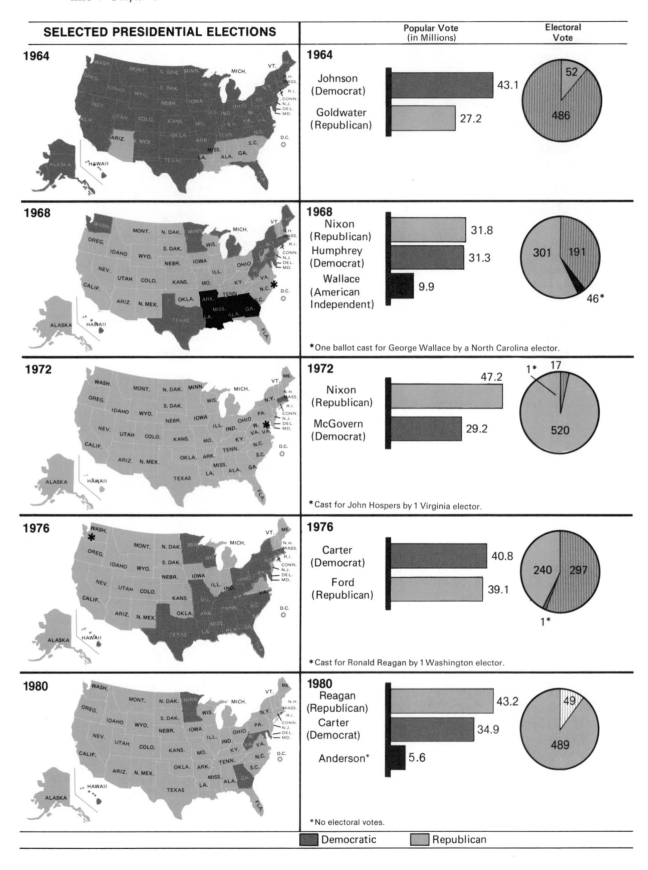

1964

1964

Johnson (Democrat) 43.1

Goldwater (Republican) 27.2

Electoral: 52 / 486

1968

1968

Nixon (Republican) 31.8

Humphrey (Democrat) 31.3

Wallace (American Independent) 9.9

Electoral: 301 / 191 / 46*

*One ballot cast for George Wallace by a North Carolina elector.

1972

1972

Nixon (Republican) 47.2

McGovern (Democrat) 29.2

Electoral: 1* / 17 / 520

*Cast for John Hospers by 1 Virginia elector.

1976

1976

Carter (Democrat) 40.8

Ford (Republican) 39.1

Electoral: 240 / 297 / 1*

*Cast for Ronald Reagan by 1 Washington elector.

1980

1980

Reagan (Republican) 43.2

Carter (Democrat) 34.9

Anderson* 5.6

Electoral: 49 / 489

*No electoral votes.

Democratic ▮ Republican ▯

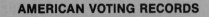

AMERICAN VOTING RECORDS

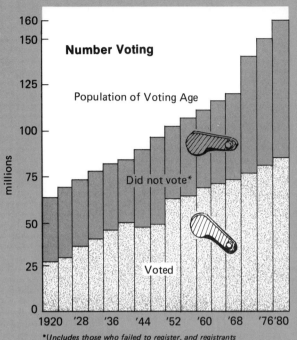

Number Voting

Population of Voting Age

Did not vote*

Voted

millions

1920 '28 '36 '44 '52 '60 '68 '76'80

(Includes those who failed to register, and registrants who did not vote.)

Voting by Various Groups in 1980

Group	Reagan %	Carter %
SEX		
Male	54	37
Female	46	45
RACE		
White	55	36
Black	14	82
Hispanic	36	54
AGE		
18-21	43	44
22-29	43	43
30-44	54	37
45-59	55	39
60 and over	54	40
RELIGION		
Protestant	56	37
Catholic	51	40
Jewish	39	45
OCCUPATION		
Prof./Business	56	33
White-collar	48	42
Blue-collar	47	46
Agriculture	66	29
FAMILY INCOME		
Over $25,000	59	31
$15,000-$25,000	53	38
$10,000-$15,000	42	47
Under $10,000	41	50
UNION MEMBERSHIP		
Yes	44	47
No	55	35
PARTY		
Republican	84	11
Democratic	26	66
Independent	84	11

(The above data is drawn from CBS-New York Times surveys.)

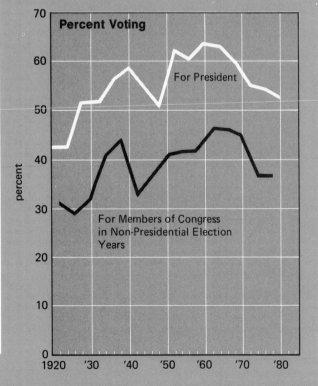

Percent Voting

For President

percent

For Members of Congress in Non-Presidential Election Years

1920 '30 '40 '50 '60 '70 '80

Source: Bureau of the Census

returns. For example, an analysis of the returns from areas populated largely by blacks or by Catholics or by high-income families will show *how* those particular groups voted. The reasons *why* the particular groups voted as they did can then be sought by interviewing a representative cross-section (sample) of the voters involved.

Political Socialization. The attempt to understand and explain political behavior has led many social scientists to focus their research and investigative efforts on the process of *political socialization.* That is, they have studied the highly complex process by which individuals acquire their political attitudes and opinions.

Political socialization is the process by which the young in any society come to know the values, structures, and procedures that govern behavior within that society. As one pioneering study put it:

> Political socialization is the process of induction into the political culture. Its end product is a set of attitudes—cognitions, value standards, and feelings—toward the political system. . . . Thus in . . . the United States, family, church, peer group, community, school, work group, voluntary associations, media of communications, political parties, and governmental institutions all share in the function of political socialization, and the associations, relationships, and participations of adult life continue the process.[20]

The first and most potent agent of political socialization is the family. Numerous studies have confirmed this view. They show that the enormous influence of the family on the development of political opinion is due largely to the family's almost exclusive access to the child as the child develops and begins to mature. They also show that:

The orientations acquired in early childhood tend to be the most intensely and permanently held of all political views. They serve as the base on which later political learning is built.[21]

The start of formal schooling marks the first break in the force of family influence. For the first time the child becomes involved in activities beyond the family circle. The family's role in the socializing process is then gradually taken over by a second major agent of political socialization—the peer group.

Certain peer groups exert greater influence on an individual than do others. Moreover, the groups to which an individual belongs will change as he or she grows to adulthood. Those peer groups which most influence the child are usually classmates, neighborhood chums, and school social organizations. As one becomes an adult, these early peer groups give way to other groups—most notably such others as a church group, a political party, an ethnic group, a labor union, and the like.

Following the peer group, a number of secondary agents play a significant part in the continuing process of socialization to politics. Among them are a person's occupation, level of education and of income, ethnic identity, and place of residence. Then, too, the individual's exposure to television and the other mass media, and its influence on his or her awareness of events, issues, and candidates, can become important contributors to the socializing process.

It should be quite clear from what has been said to this point that the mechanics of political learning—the means of political socialization—are very complex. They involve the interaction of a variety of psychological, emotional, intellectual, and

[20] Gabriel A. Almond and James S. Coleman (eds.) *The Politics of Developing Areas.* Princeton, N.J.: Princeton University Press, 1960, page 27.

[21] Richard E. Dawson and Kenneth Previtt, *Political Socialization.* Boston: Little, Brown and Co., 1969, page 133.

other factors on the development of the individual. It should also be noted that political socialization involves more than the simply passive assimilation of the views expressed by families, friends, organized groups, and the mass media. At an early age individuals begin to express their own ideas and opinions, and through one or more channels of participation, too.

These channels of participation are many, as we suggested on page 182. Here, however, we are concerned with the principal method by which most persons express themselves politically—voting.

Party Preference and Voting Behavior. However it may have been acquired, *party preference* appears to be the single most significant, durable, and predictable factor in prompting voters to vote as they do. That is, if a person regards himself or herself as a Democrat (or a Republican), then that person is very strongly inclined to vote for the Democratic rather than the Republican candidates in an election (or vice versa).

As we noted on page 188, the acceptance by voters of the political attachments of their parents is a dominant fact of American political life. Indeed, approximately two out of every three voters inherit their choice of party. They adopt the partisan label worn by their parents and then vote much as their parents do or did. Recall, too, that better than nine out of every ten married couples share the same partisan preference.

But, as we also noted earlier, many other factors—such as economic status, place of residence, work relationships, and social contacts—can also affect the choice of party. Indeed, when family-born loyalties conflict with one's contemporary social or economic status, a change in party allegiance is quite likely to occur. And so it is with voting. Family influence plays a very significant role, but other forces also enter the mix to determine the manner in which people vote.

James Dobbins in Boston *Herald-Traveler*

A cartoonist comments on the "courtship" by office seekers of the independent voter—the voter with no firm allegiance to a single political party.

Demographic Factors. Among these other forces, several *demographic factors*—that is, population characteristics—are quite important. The leading studies of voting behavior indicate a quite close general correlation between these characteristics and how those who possess them *tend* to vote. The table on the next page summarizes the relationship of these characteristics to voting behavior.

Note that the table indicates *only* that various groups *tend* to vote in certain ways. It would be a serious mistake to assume that any given election can be predicted on the basis of the findings that it summarizes. Many of the factors it takes into account are closely interrelated, and frequently they act in combination with one another to affect the voting decision.

For example, the table indicates that women *as a whole* tend to vote Republican—but, of course, many do not. In fact, *black* women and *Catholic* women tend to vote most often for Democratic candidates, and so, too, do a majority of women under age 35. As yet another indication of the point, the table shows that residents of urban areas tend to vote Democratic. But, many do not; thus, business owners who live in cities usually support Republican candidates. In short, it should be clear that the demographic factors reported in the table cannot be regarded as mutually exclusive in terms of their effect upon voter choices.

Other Factors. Any one of a number of additional factors may—and often do—exert a determining influence on voter behavior. Included among them are such things as the personalities of the opposing candidates, economic conditions at the time, local, national, or international events, the ability of a candidate to use television as an effective campaign device, sensational campaign charges, and even the marital status of a candidate. These examples can be multiplied many times over. But to illustrate the point: The election of Franklin D. Roosevelt to the Presidency in 1932 was decisively influenced by the Great Depression which plagued the nation at the time. Dwight D. Eisenhower's election in 1952 was strongly influenced by his role as a military hero. And, it is highly doubtful if Richard Nixon could have been reelected if all or even much of the facts of the Watergate affair had been known by election day in 1972.

Far more women than ever before now seek and hold elective offices. Senator Nancy Landon Kassebaum (R., Kansas) typifies the recent and ongoing changes in attitudes about women in American politics. Senator Kassebaum, the first woman to be elected to a full term in the Senate whose husband did not precede her in Congress, won her seat in 1978.

Demographic Factors	Voting Tendency	
	Republican	Democratic
Sex		
Male		x
Female	x	
Race		
White	x	
Black		x
Religion		
Protestant	x	
Catholic		x
Jewish		x
Age		
Under 35		x
Over 55	x	
Education		
Grade school		x
High school		x
College	x	
Income		
Low		x
High	x	
Occupation		
Business, professional	x	
Other white collar	x	
Skilled, semi-skilled		x
Unskilled		x
Farm operator	x	
Type of Community		
Urban, metropolitan		x
Rural, small town	x	
Labor Union Affiliation		
Member		x
Non-member	x	

SUMMARY

No right is more precious to an American than the right to vote. It is, however, a political, not a civil right.

The development of American suffrage law has been marked by two long-term trends: (1) a gradual relaxation of restrictive requirements, and (2) increasing federal authority in the field. Voting qualifications are set by the States, subject to five specific limits imposed by the Constitution: (1) "the most numerous branch" proviso in Article I (and the 17th Amendment); (2) the 15th Amendment's prohibition of denial of the right to vote on grounds of race or color; (3) the 19th Amendment's prohibition of denial of the right to vote on grounds of sex; (4) the 24th Amendment's prohibition of any tax-paying qualification in order to participate in the federal election process; and (5) the 26th Amendment's prohibition of denial of the right to vote on account of age to any citizen at least 18 years of age.

All States now impose suffrage qualifications based on two factors: (1) citizenship and (2) residence. The Voting Rights Act Amendments of 1970 forbids States to impose more than a 30-day residence requirement for voting in presidential elections. In 1972 the Supreme Court held lengthy residence qualifications for State and local elections to violate the 14th Amendment's Equal Protection Clause; it suggested a 30-day requirement would be constitutionally acceptable, however. In the Voting Rights Act Amendments of 1975 Congress decreed a permanent ban on the use of literacy as a suffrage qualification by any State.

Every State, except North Dakota, has a voter registration system to prevent fraudulent voting. The once-common property requirement has all but disappeared as a suffrage qualification; and in 1966 the Supreme Court held the imposition of a poll tax as a qualification for voting in State or local elections to be unconstitutional. Mental incompetents, felons, and some others are commonly barred from voting by the State.

Congress has enacted several significant statutes in recent years to implement the 15th Amendment's guarantee: the Civil Rights Acts of 1957, 1960 and 1964, and the Voting Rights Act of 1965 and its substantial amendments in 1970 and 1975.

Millions of potential voters fail to vote for a variety of reasons—but, chiefly, out of lack of interest. Among the millions who *do* vote, party preference exerts a strong influence on the way in which they vote. A large number of other factors also shape voting behavior.

A wealth of data on how votes have been cast has led to some general notions of voter behavior related to demographic characteristics and other factors. The study of *why* votes are cast in certain ways requires more sophisticated, in-depth analysis. Research has shown that much adult voter behavior is a product of the process of political socialization.

Concept Development

Questions for Review

1. What is the distinction between a *civil* and a *political* right?

2. Are the terms *citizenship* and *suffrage* synonymous?

3. Does the Constitution guarantee the right to vote to any group?

4. What five specific restrictions does the Constitution place upon the States in the setting of suffrage qualifications?

5. What two bases for suffrage qualifications are common to all 50 States?

6. How have residence requirements for federal elections been changed by the legislation passed by Congress in 1970? For State and local elections by the Supreme Court's decision in *Dunn* v. *Blumstein*, 1972?

7. Which amendment to the Constitution lowered the voting age to 18?

8. What is the essential purpose of a registration system?

9. Why do some urge the elimination of voter registration while others urge that the process be made more convenient?

10. What was the legitimate purpose of a literacy requirement?

11. On what constitutional basis did Congress first (1970) suspend and then (1975) permanently ban the use of literacy as a voting qualification?

12. Why may the States not impose a poll tax as a suffrage qualification in federal elections?

13. Why may the States not impose a poll tax as a suffrage qualification in State or local elections?

14. How many times has the Constitution been amended in ways that have expanded the electorate?

15. What is the principal purpose of the voting provisions in the several recent civil rights statutes enacted by Congress?

16. Approximately how many persons voted in the last presidential election? How many potential voters did not vote?

17. Approximately how many persons voted in the last congressional elections? How many potential voters did not?

18. What is the major cause for nonvoting in American elections?

19. What appears to be the most significant factor in prompting people to vote as they do in elections?

20. What is *political socialization?*

For Further Inquiry

1. What are the specific provisions of your State's registration law? Does it make registration comparatively easy? What changes, if any, do you think might be made in the law?

2. What are the specific suffrage provisions contained in your State's constitution and election laws? What qualifications, if any, do you think should be added? Deleted? Modified?

3. How should suffrage be viewed—as a right, a privilege, or a duty?

4. Why would you favor or oppose a compulsory voting law?

5. What do you think the late historian and novelist H. G. Wells meant by the following statement? "Until a man has education, a vote is a useless and dangerous thing for him to possess." Do you agree?

6. Some people criticize the American election system for putting too much emphasis upon the *quantity* as opposed to the *quality* of the electorate. Do you think this is a valid criticism?

Suggested Activities

1. Invite the registrar, county clerk, or other local election official to discuss your State's suffrage requirements and registration system.

2. Stage a debate or class forum on one of the following questions: (a) *Resolved,* That the voting age in all States should be raised to 21; (b) *Resolved,* That a maximum age for voting should be set; (c) *Resolved,* That voting qualifications should be uniform throughout the United States.

3. Secure copies of the returns for the most recent general election in your State (usually readily available in the State's manual or bluebook or from the Secretary of State). Analyze the returns in terms of the text's discussion of voter turnout and nonvoting (pages 221–225).

4. Write a report on one of the following topics: (a) voter apathy, (b) the history of the suffrage in the United States, and (c) methods of disenfranchisement used against various minority groups.

5. Prepare a report on the ways in which you feel political socialization ought to be handled in a free society. Contrast these methods with examples of methods used in other countries.

Suggested Reading

Barone, Michael, *et al., The Almanac of American Politics.* Dutton, 1981.

Bollens, John C. and Schmandt, Henry J., *Political Corruption: Power, Money, and Sex.* Palisades Publishers, 1979.

Campbell, Bruce A., *The American Electorate: Attitudes and Action.* Holt, Rinehart and Winston, 1979.

Clubb, Jerome, Flanagan, William and Zingale, Nancy, *Partisan Realignments: Voters, Parties, and Governments in American History.* Sage, 1980.

Flanigan, William H., *Political Behavior of the American Electorate.* Allyn and Bacon, 4th ed., 1978.

Greenfield, Jeff, *Playing to Win: An Insider's Guide to Politics.* Simon & Schuster, 1980.

Grimes, Alan P., *Democracy and the Amendments to the Constitution.* Heath, 1979.

Hill, David B. and Luttbeg, Norman R., *Trends in American Electoral Behavior.* Peacock, 1980.

Ladd, Everett C., *Where Have All the Voters Gone?* Norton, 1978.

Nie, Norman H., *et al., The Changing American Voter.* Harvard, rev., 1979.

Politics in America. Congressional Quarterly, 1979.

Wolfinger, Raymond and Rosenstone, Steven J., *Who Votes?* Yale University Press, 1980.

10

Government by the People: The Electoral Process

As citizens of this democracy, you are the rulers and the ruled, the lawgivers and the law-abiding, the beginning and the end.

ADLAI STEVENSON

■ Which of the two basic steps in the electoral process—nomination or election—is the more important?

■ Why is the nominating process a potentially divisive one? Why is this a significant matter?

■ Is popular election the most satisfactory way in which to choose those who hold public office?

In a representative democracy there must be some method by which the people are able to choose those who govern—those who represent the people in the conduct of the people's business. There must, as well, be some method by which those who govern with the consent of the people can be held accountable to the people for their conduct. The only device we know which satisfies these needs is that of popular election.

In the United States we elect far more public officeholders than most people realize—*more than 490,000* of them, in fact. And we hold elections far more often than most realize, too. Indeed, Sundays and national holidays are about the only days in any year in which people do not go to the polls somewhere in this country.

In this chapter we deal with the two basic stages of the electoral process: (1) the nomination of candidates for office, and (2) the selection of officeholders from among the candidates who have been nominated. As we do, you might ponder this rather pungent observation by Adlai Stevenson: "Your public servants serve you right."

The Nominating Process

The importance of the first stage of the electoral process—nomination—cannot be overstated. It is as fundamental to the fabric of democracy as is the final election itself.

At the 1876 Republican National Convention held in Cincinnati, Ohio, Rutherford B. Hayes was nominated for President.

The making of *nominations* is the selecting of those who will run for office. It provides the answer to the question: Between or among whom will the voters be permitted to choose?

The fact that ours is a two-party system means that in the typical election in this country the voters must choose between *two* candidates for a given office in the final election. Clearly, those who make nominations thereby place very drastic limits upon the practical exercise of the right to vote. In those areas in which one party regularly wins elections, the nominating stage is the only point at which there is usually any real contest for office. Theodore Roosevelt had our point in mind when he observed:

> The right of popular government is incomplete unless it includes the right of the voter not merely to choose between candidates when they have been nomi-

nated but also the right to determine who these candidates shall be.

Authoritarian systems provide abundant proof of the crucial importance of nominations. In the Soviet Union, for example, general elections are conducted in much the same manner as in the United States. The comparison is only a superficial one, however. In the Soviet Union, as in most other one-party states, only those candidates *acceptable* to the ruling party are *nominated*. Most often only one candidate (the nominee endorsed by the Communist Party) is permitted to run for each office on the ballot. It is hardly surprising that in such a system the successful candidates regularly win with majorities of 98 to 100 percent of the vote.

No one single method is used for the making of nominations in American politics. Rather, a variety of different methods is found across the country. In broad terms, the various methods employed can be grouped under five general headings: (1) self-announcement; (2) the caucus; (3) the delegate convention; (4) the direct primary; and (5) petition.

Self-Announcement. Self-announcement, sometimes labelled "self-nomination," is the oldest form of the nominating process in American politics. It was first used in colonial times and is still quite commonly found at the small town and rural levels in many parts of the country.

The method is a quite simple one: a person who wishes to run for an office simply announces that fact. Modesty or local custom may dictate that someone else make the candidate's announcement, but even so the process is essentially that of self-nomination.

The process is sometimes used by a candidate who sought but failed to win a regular party nomination, or by someone who is otherwise dissatisfied with the nominee chosen by the party. Notice that whenever a "write-in" candidate appears in an election the process of self-announcement has been used.

Self-announcement is not altogether unknown at the more rarified levels in our politics. Three prominent presidential contenders have been self-nominated in recent years: George Wallace, the candidate of the American Independent Party in 1968, and independent candidates Eugene McCarthy in 1976 and John Anderson in 1980.

The Caucus. As a nominating device,[1] a *caucus* is a group of like-minded persons who meet to select—that is, nominate—the candidates they will support in an election.

The first caucus nominations in American politics were made in the later colonial period, in informal meetings of influential citizens. The practice probably originated in Boston. One of the earliest descriptions of a caucus can be found in John Adams' diary, in an entry for February, 1763:

> This day learned that the Caucus club meets at certain times in the garret of Tom Dawes, the Adjutant of the Boston regiment. He has a large house, and he has a movable partition which he takes down, and the whole club meets in one room. There they smoke tobacco till you cannot see from one end of the garret to the other. There they drink flip, I suppose, and they choose a moderator who puts questions to the vote regularly; and selectmen, assessors, collectors, firewards, and representatives are regularly chosen before they are chosen in the town.[2]

In its early form the caucus was an informal, private meeting, attended only by a select and influential few. The growth of party organizations tended to regularize the caucus and also to modify its closed character.

Independence brought with it the need to make nominations for offices above the local level. The *legislative caucus*, a meeting of a party's members in the legislature to nominate candidates for the governorship and other State offices, developed quickly and rather naturally out of the local caucus system. By 1800 both the Federalists and the Democratic-Republicans were selecting their presidential candidates in *congressional caucuses.*

---

[1] Generally, the term *caucus* is used to describe any private meeting at which party members decide upon some course of political action. Most often, it is used in connection with a legislative body. The *legislative caucus* is a meeting of a party's members in the legislature to decide upon such questions as legislative organization, committee assignments, the party's position on pending bills, and the like. See page 309.

[2] Quoted in M. I. Ostrogorski, *Democracy and the Organization of Political Parties,* New York: Macmillan, 1902, Vol. 11, p. 4. The origin of the term *caucus* is obscure. Some authorities suggest it is derived from the Algonquin Indian word *kaw-kaw-was,* meaning "to talk," "to talk over," "to give advice." Others suggest that the term is derived from the word *caulker,* because the Boston Caucus club at times met in a room formerly used as a meeting place by the caulkers in the Boston shipyards.

A 1916 campaign van. In that year, President Woodrow Wilson was renominated by delegates at the Democratic National Convention, which met in St. Louis.

The legislative and congressional caucuses were quite practical devices in their day. Transportation and communication were difficult at best, and legislators were regularly assembled at a central place. The spread of democracy produced increasing criticism of their use, however. They were widely condemned as closed, unrepresentative gatherings in which only a very few could participate.

Opposition to the caucus reached its peak in the early 1820's. The supporters of the three leading contenders for the Presidency in 1824—Andrew Jackson, Henry Clay, and John Quincy Adams—boycotted the Democratic-Republican party's congressional caucus that year. In fact, Jackson and his supporters made "King Caucus" a leading campaign issue. The other major aspirant, William H. Crawford of Georgia, became the caucus nominee—at a meeting attended by fewer than a third of the party's members in Congress.

Crawford ran a poor third in the electoral college balloting, and the reign of "King Caucus" at the national level was ended. With its demise at the presidential level, the caucus system soon withered at the State and local levels, as well.

Caucuses are still used to make local nominations in some places—especially in New England, where they are open to all of the party's members and bear only a faint resemblance to the original device.

The Delegate Convention. As the caucus method collapsed, it gave way to the *delegate convention* system. The first national convention to nominate a presidential candidate was held by a minor party, the Anti-Masons, in Baltimore in 1831. Both the Democrats and the Whigs picked up the practice in 1832, and all major party presidential nominees have been chosen in conventions since that time. By 1840 the convention method had become the major means for the making of nominations at every level in American politics.

On paper the system seems ideally suited to representative government. Under it, a party's members meet in a local caucus to pick candidates for local office and, at the same time, to select delegates to represent them at a county convention.[3] At

[3] The meetings at which delegates to local conventions are selected are frequently called *caucuses*. Earlier, they were also known as *primaries*—that is, the first meetings. The use of the latter term gave rise to the term *direct primary* to identify that newer nominating method and to distinguish it from the convention process; see the next page.

the county convention the delegates nominate candidates for the various county offices and also select delegates to the next rung on the convention ladder, usually the State convention. There, the delegates chosen at the county conventions pick the party's candidates for governor and for other Statewide offices and also select delegates to the national convention. And at the national convention, the party's delegates from all of the State conventions nominate the party's presidential and vice presidential candidates.

In the theory of the convention system, the will of the party's rank and file membership is supposed to be channeled upward through each of its representative levels. Actual practice soon demonstrated the shortcomings of the theory, however. The system easily proved to be subject to control by party bosses. By manipulating the selection of delegates, especially in county conventions, they were able to control the system quite handily.

The caliber of conventions at all levels deteriorated, especially in the late 1800's. The depths to which some declined is shown by this description of the delegates to a Cook County convention held in Chicago in 1896:

Of the delegates those who had been on trial for murder numbered 17; sentenced to the penitentiary for murder or manslaughter and served sentence, 7; served terms in the penitentiary for burglary, 36; served terms in the penitentiary for picking pockets, 2; served terms in the penitentiary for arson, 1; . . . keepers of gambling houses, 7; keepers of houses of ill fame, 2; convicted of mayhem, 3; ex-prize fighters, 11; poolroom proprietors, 2; saloon keepers, 265; . . . political employees, 148; . . . no occupation, 71; Total delegates, 723.[4]

The convention system was originally hailed as a vast improvement on and a democratization of the caucus. It proved a poor substitute, however. Its evils were a major target of the reforms which swept much of the country at the turn of the century, and it was soon replaced as the principal nominating method by the direct primary.

The convention device has been abandoned for the making of all or at least most nominations in most of the States. It is still used fairly extensively in some, however—in Connecticut, Delaware, Michigan, and Utah, for example—where it is closely regulated by State election law.

No adequate substitute for the conven-

---

[4] R. M. Easley, "The Sine-qua Non of Caucus Reform," *Review of Reviews,* September, 1897, p. 322.

Small Society   By Brickman

tion has yet been found at the presidential level—as we shall see in Chapter 15.

The Direct Primary. The direct primary is the most widely used method for the making of nominations in American politics today. It is an *intra-party nominating election.* That is, it is an election held within the party at which the voters choose the party's candidates.

The origins of the primary are obscure, but the first one was apparently held by the Democratic Party in Crawford County, Pennsylvania, in 1842. Its use spread gradually to other locales in other parts of the country through the latter decades of the last century. Wisconsin enacted the first Statewide direct primary law in 1903, and several other States soon followed that lead.

Today every State makes some provision for its use. In most of them, State law requires that the major parties use the primary to select their candidates for seats in the United States Senate and House, for the governorship and all other State offices, and for most local offices as well.[5] In a few States, however, various combinations of convention and primary are employed for the nomination of candidates for the major offices.[6]

Although the primary is a party nominating election, it is closely regulated by law in most of the States. The State usually sets the date on which primaries are to be held. It conducts them, as well, furnishing

ballots, providing election officials, using its official registration lists, and otherwise policing the process.

Two basic forms of the direct primary are in use among the States today: (1) the *closed primary* and (2) the *open primary.* The critical distinction between the two forms lies in the answer to this question: Who may vote in a party's primary—*only* those qualified voters who are *also* party members or *any* qualified voter, regardless of party preference?

The Closed Primary. Thirty-eight States[7] now use the closed primary—a party nominating election in which *only* those voters who are avowed party members may vote. It is *closed* to all others.

In most of the closed primary States, party membership is established by registration (see page 216). When voters appear at the polling places on primary election day, their names are checked against the poll books (the lists of registered voters for each precinct). The voters are then handed the primary ballot of the political party in which they are registered.

In several of the southern States party membership is established by the "challenge system," rather than by registration. In this arrangement, any voter who doubts the party loyalty of another may challenge the right of the latter to vote in the party's primary. The challenged voter must then pledge that he or she will support the party's candidates in the upcoming election.

[5] In most States minor parties are required to make nominations by convention or by petition.

[6] The convention is still used to select the major party candidates for one or more of the principal offices in Connecticut, Utah, and Virginia. However, in Connecticut any unsuccessful aspirant who receives at least 20 percent of the convention vote may demand a primary which must then be held to make the final selection of a nominee for the office involved. In Utah any person who receives a majority of at least 70 percent of the votes of the convention's delegates is thereby nominated and no primary is then held for that office. In those contests in Utah in which no one secures the required majority the two top contenders in the convention's balloting face one another in a primary.

In Indiana and Michigan the major party candidates for the U.S. Senate and House and for governor and lieutenant governor are nominated by primary vote; the nominees for other Statewide offices are selected by convention.

In New York candidates for all Statewide offices are picked by the party's State central committee. The committee may authorize the making of any such nomination at a primary, however. And, any person who receives at least 25 percent of the committee members' votes for a nomination may demand a primary. Both parties have regularly used the primary route in recent years.

[7] All of the States except those listed in note 8.

In any of the closed primary States, those who do not wish to declare a party preference may nonetheless register to vote. And, as registered voters they may vote in general and special elections and in nonpartisan primaries. But they cannot vote in the party primaries—which, again, are *party* nominating elections *closed* to all but party members.

THE OPEN PRIMARY. Although it was the original form of the direct primary, the open primary is now used in only 12 of the States.[8] It is a party nominating election in which any qualified voter may participate. That is, it is *open to any qualified voter*—without reference to party affiliation or preference.

No voter is required to declare a party preference at registration or at any other time. When the voters appear at the polling places on primary election day, they are handed either the ballots of *all* of the parties holding primaries or one large ballot containing the separate ballots of the various parties. (Usually only the two major parties are involved but occasionally one or more minor parties appear.) In the privacy of the voting booth the voters then pick the party in whose primary they want to participate and mark that ballot.

A differing version of the open primary is used in Alaska and in Washington, where it is known as the "wide open" or "blanket" primary. There, the voter receives a single large ballot containing the ballots of each of the parties holding primaries. The voter may vote in a single party's primary, as in the typical open primary—or the voter may switch back and forth, office to office, among the parties. Thus, one may vote to nominate a candidate for the United States Senate in the Republican primary, then switch over to the Democratic primary to nominate a can-

didate for governor, and so on, back and forth, down the ballot.

Louisiana inaugurated yet another version of the open primary in 1975. Its so-called "open election" law provides for what is in fact a combination primary and general election. In this unique process, the names of *all* persons who seek office are listed on a single primary ballot.[9] Any candidate who wins a majority of the votes in the primary then runs unopposed in the general election. In effect, he or she is elected at the primary. Otherwise, the two top vote-getters in each primary race—regardless of party—face one another in the general election.

PRO AND CON: THE CLOSED V. THE OPEN PRIMARY. Those who favor the closed rather than the open form of the primary usually advance three arguments supporting the closed primary: *First,* that it prevents the members of one party from raiding the other's primary in the hope of nominating weak candidates.[10] *Second,* that it tends to make candidates more responsive and responsible to the party and its members. And *third,* that it tends to make voters more conscious of their role because they must choose between the parties in order to participate in the primaries.

The critics of the closed primary argue that it: (1) compromises the secrecy of the ballot to the extent that it forces the voter to declare publicly his or her party preference; and (2) tends to exclude the independent voter from the partisan nominating process.

The major arguments advanced in favor of the open primary are, in effect, those most often heard against the closed form:

---

[8] Alaska, Hawaii, Idaho, Louisiana, Michigan, Minnesota, Montana, North Dakota, Utah, Vermont, Washington, Wisconsin.

[9] That is, a lengthy bipartisan ballot—one containing the names of *all* who seek office, regardless of party. Each candidate's party identification is, or is not, indicated on the ballot—as the candidate chooses.

[10] The practice of "raiding" became so common in the early years of the direct primary that the closed form was developed to prevent it; the tactic is still known in some of the present-day open-primary States.

Case Study

Quite regularly, the party in power—that is, the party which holds the Presidency—loses seats in Congress in the "off-year" congressional elections (those held between the presidential elections). The elections of 1978 followed the general pattern, as the table below indicates. The table details the seat gain (+) or loss (−) for the President's party in the 20 off-year elections thus far held in this century.

Year	Party in Power	House	Senate	Year	Party in Power	House	Senate
1902	R	+9	+2	1942	D	−45	−10
1906	R	−28	+3	1946	D	−55	−12
1910	R	−57	−10	1950	D	−29	−6
1914	D	−59	+5	1954	R	−18	−1
1918	D	−19	−6	1958	R	−47	−13
1922	R	−75	−8	1962	D	−4	+4
1926	R	−10	−6	1966	D	−47	−3
1930	R	−49	−8	1970	R	−9	+1
1934	D	+9	+10	1974	R	−43	−4
1938	D	−71	−6	1978	D	−11	−3

■ Why do you think that this general pattern of presidential party loss is repeated election after election through the off-years?

■ How important a phenomenon is this in our national politics? Does it lend support to those who argue that we should replace the presidential system with a parliamentary system of government?

■ Would the historic pattern continue if the Constitution were amended to provide that all members of the House and Senate be elected for four-year terms and at the same election at which the President is chosen?

■ Would it remain the same if the present four-year term, two-term limit on presidential tenure were changed to a single six-year arrangement?

that is, the claims that it (1) protects the secrecy of the ballot and (2) makes it possible for an independent to vote in the primary of his or her choice.

The major arguments made against the use of the open primary are that it: (1) permits primary raiding; and (2) subverts the concepts of party loyalty and responsibility.

THE RUN-OFF PRIMARY. In most States candidates need only a *plurality* of the votes cast in the primary to win their party's nomination.[11] In 10 States,[12] however, an absolute majority is required. If no one receives a majority in a particular race, a sec-

ond or "run-off" primary is held a few weeks later. In the run-off, the two top contenders face one another, and the winner becomes the party's nominee.

THE NONPARTISAN PRIMARY. In most of the States today all or nearly all of the elec-

---

[11] Iowa and South Dakota require a candidate to win at least 35 percent of the votes cast in the primary contest; if no aspirant wins that many votes in a given race, the party must then nominate a candidate for that office by convention.

[12] Alabama, Arkansas, Florida, Georgia, Mississippi, North Carolina, Oklahoma, South Carolina, Texas—and Louisiana under its unique "open election" law.

tive school and municipal offices are filled in nonpartisan elections. And, in over a third of the States, judges are chosen on nonpartisan ballots, as well.

The nomination of candidates for these offices occurs on a nonpartisan basis, too—frequently by nonpartisan primaries.

Those who seek these offices usually gain a place on the primary ballot by submitting petitions containing a required number of signatures of qualified voters or by paying a filing fee, or both.

Typically, a contender who gains a clear majority in the nonpartisan primary then runs unopposed in the general election—but subject to write-in opposition, of course. In many States, however, a candidate who wins a majority of the votes cast in the nonpartisan primary is declared elected at that point. If there is no majority winner in the primary, the names of the two top contenders are placed on the general election ballot.

EVALUATION OF THE PRIMARY. The direct primary, whether open or closed, is an *intra-party nominating election.* It was developed in reaction to the convention system, and was intended to take the nominating function out of the hands of the party organization and place it in the hands of the rank-and-file party membership.

But these basic facts about the primary have never really been very well understood by most voters. Thus, many resent having to divulge their party choice in closed primary States. And where the open primary is used many are annoyed because they cannot nominate in more than one party (except in Alaska and Washington). Many voters are also annoyed by the "bedsheet ballot," not realizing that the use of the primary almost automatically dictates a long ballot.

It is fairly clear, too, that a large segment of the electorate does not recognize the critical importance of the nominating process. Thus, the turnout in primaries in most States is usually less than half of that in the general election.[13]

Where nominations are contested the primary can become a quite expensive process. And the fact that the successful contender must mount (and finance) yet another campaign, for the general election, compounds the problems of party finance (see pages 200–206). It is unfortunately true that some well-qualified persons are discouraged from seeking public office by the financial facts of political life.

The nominating process, whatever its form, can have a very divisive effect upon a political party. It is an *intra*-party operation

An important step in gaining a place on a primary ballot is the gathering of signatures of qualified voters on petitions.

---

[13] Notice that this frequently means that there are two quite different constituencies involved in the electoral process—one in the primaries, the smaller of the two, dominated by those persons and groups most likely to vote, and the other and larger one in the general election. To amplify the point, consult the discussion of voter turnout on pages 221–225.

in which most conflicts which arise occur *within* the party—that is, between members of the *same* party. The direct primary magnifies this characteristic of the nominating process because it is so *public* a matter. A bitter contest in the primaries can so wound and divide a party that it cannot bind its wounds in time for the general election. Many a primary fight has cost a party the election.

Because many voters are not always well informed, the primary places a premium on "name-familiarity." That is, it gives an advantage to the aspirant who has a well-known name, or has a name that sounds much like that of another person who is widely known in the constituency— and all of this with no particular reference to that candidate's ability or, for that matter, lack of it.

The direct primary has not remedied all of the evils of the old convention system. Still, it does offer the party voters an *opportunity* to defeat a conspicuously unfit candidate or to nominate a conspicuously well-qualified one. No electoral machinery can take the place of intelligent and informed participation, however.

The Presidential Primary. The presidential primary developed as an offshoot of the direct primary. It is *not* a nominating device, however. It is, rather, an *election.*

A presidential primary is one or both of two things. It is a process in which a party's voters elect some or all of a State party's delegates to the party's national convention. *And/or* it is a preference election—in which voters may choose (express a preference) among various contenders for a party's presidential nomination.

The presidential primary first appeared in the early years of this century, as part of the reform movement aimed at the boss-dominated convention system. Wisconsin adopted the first presidential primary law in 1905, with a statute providing for the popular election of national convention delegates. Several States quickly followed

that lead. And in 1910 Oregon added the preference feature.

By 1916 nearly half of the States had enacted presidential primary laws. Many of them later abandoned the device, however. Indeed, as recently as 1968, it was to be found in only 16 States and the District of Columbia.

Efforts to reform the presidential nominating process, undertaken by both major parties in recent years, rekindled interest in the presidential primary. As a result, some version of it was used in 23 States and in the District of Columbia in 1972; and six more States were added to the list for 1976.

In 1980 some form of the presidential primary was provided for in the election laws in 33 States[14] and in the District of Columbia and Puerto Rico. (In the other States—*i.e.*, those without presidential primaries—national convention delegates are chosen by party conventions or party committees, or by a combination of these two methods; see page 369.)

Again, a presidential primary is either or both of these things: a delegate selection process and/or a preference election. But once that much has been said about it, the device becomes extremely difficult to describe—except on a State-by-State basis. The difficulty here comes largely from two

---

14 Alabama, Arkansas, California, Connecticut, Florida, Georgia, Idaho, Illinois, Indiana, Kansas, Kentucky, Louisiana, Maryland, Massachusetts, Michigan, Montana, Nebraska, Nevada, New Hampshire, New Jersey, New Mexico, New York, North Carolina, Ohio, Oregon, Pennsylvania, Rhode Island, South Dakota, Tennessee, Texas, Vermont, West Virginia, Wisconsin. Four of these States (Connecticut, Kansas, Louisiana, and New Mexico) and Puerto Rico did not hold such primaries in 1976. North Dakota voters approved a presidential primary law in 1980 and that State will hold its first one in 1984.

On occasion, a State party organization stages a presidential primary even though one is not provided for by State law. Thus, the Republicans (but not the Democrats) did so in both Mississippi and South Carolina in 1980.

Also, in a few States—in Arkansas and Texas, for example—the presidential primary law is only permissive. That is, it permits either major party to hold a primary but does not require them to do so.

sources. One is the fact that the details of the process vary from State to State, and sometimes very considerably. The other is the ongoing effects of the reform efforts of both major parties. In recent years the Republicans and, most especially, the Democrats have written and rewritten rules to stimulate grass-roots participation in their delegate selection processes. And those rules, promulgated by the national committees, have prompted many and frequent changes in State election laws.

Even so relatively simple a matter as the date on which a State holds its presidential primary illustrates the crazy-quilt pattern involved here. Traditionally, New Hampshire holds the first of these primaries every four years. And it guards that first-in-the-nation distinction quite jealously. For 1980, New Hampshire scheduled its primary on February 26th. All of the others were then scattered over the next three months. The last ones (eight, altogether) were scheduled on June 3rd.

Until recently, most presidential primaries were *both* delegate selection *and* preference exercises. And several of them were also "winner-take-all" primaries. That is, they were contests in which the presidential aspirant who won the preference vote automatically won the support of all of the delegates chosen at the primary. In 1972, for example, Oregon's Republican voters cast a very substantial majority for then-President Richard Nixon. Thus, all 18 of the convention delegates they elected were bound to support his renomination at the Republican convention. At the same time, the State's Democrats preferred Senator George McGovern, and the 34 delegates to their national convention were pledged to his support.

The winner-take-all contests have now all but disappeared, however. They have because of one of the reforms adopted by the Democrats for their 1976 and 1980 conventions. They have imposed a "proportional representation" rule on the delegate

selection process. In brief, the rule requires that, no matter how Democratic delegates are chosen, they (and their votes at the national convention) must be apportioned among the party's presidential contenders in line with the amount of support each of them has in the particular State.

As a practical matter, the several States with winner-take-all primaries have had to amend their presidential primary laws to accommodate the Democrats' rule. And most of them have done so by simply abolishing the winner-take-all feature.[15]

The Democrats' proportional representation rule has had another major impact on the structure of the presidential primary system. It has persuaded several States to abandon the popular election of convention delegates—among them, both Oregon and Wisconsin, the two States which pioneered the presidential primary idea.

In fact, more than half of the States which currently provide for the device now schedule *only* a preference primary. The national convention delegates from those States are not chosen by the party's voters at the primary. Instead, they are picked by the party organization—in conventions and/or by committees. Take Oregon as a fairly typical example here: At the primary, each party's voters express a preference among the contenders for their party's presidential nomination. Then, after the primary, each party holds conventions, one in each of the State's congressional districts. There the party's delegates to the upcoming national convention are chosen. And those delegates are picked in accord with the results of the primary preference

---

[15] Not all have done so, however. Although most States treat the two major parties alike in their election laws, a few States changed their presidential primary laws to abolish the winner-take-all arrangement for the Democrats but allowed the Republicans to retain it if they choose. Thus, in California in 1976 and again in 1980 the Democrats held a proportional representation primary while the Republicans staged a winner-take-all contest.

The contest for the presidential nomination in the Democratic Party in 1980 featured three major contenders. Top left: President Jimmy Carter, shaking hands with young suporters. Left: Senator Edward Kennedy of Massachusetts. Above: Governor Jerry Brown of California.

vote—in 1980, so many for Carter, so many for Kennedy; so many for Reagan, so many for Bush, and so on.

Some of the States in which a preference vote is held now use a mixed delegate selection process. That is, some delegates are elected at the primaries and the others are picked by some other means. In both Pennsylvania and Tennessee, for example, a part of each party's national convention delegation is chosen by the party's voters and the balance of it is selected by party conventions.

Until fairly recently, each State with preference primaries allowed each of the contenders for a presidential nomination to decide whether to enter the State's preference contest or not. And, of course, the various aspirants picked and chose among the primaries. They ran in those in which they expected to win or at least do reasonably well; and they purposefully avoided the others.

Now, however, more than half of those States hold "all-candidate" primaries. That

is, they now require that the names of all of the generally recognized aspirants for a party's presidential nomination be placed on that party's preference ballot. In effect, they have taken the enter-or-not decision out of the contenders' hands. And, by doing so, they have given the voters a full range of choice among the various possibilities.

In most of these States, however, any person whose name is placed on the preference ballot may have it removed. Usually, this requires only the filing of a declaration of non-candidacy. That is, a statement is filed to the effect that he or she is not now and does not intend to become a candidate for the party's presidential nomination. Only a few of these States—Idaho, Nevada, and Oregon, for example—make it impossible for one who has been listed as a generally recognized contender to have his or her name removed from the State's primary ballot.

EVALUATION OF THE PRESIDENTIAL PRIMARY. No one who surveys the presidential primary system, as we have, needs to be told that it is very complicated. Nor do they need to be reminded that there are many—and sometimes too many and too confusing—variations among the States.

Nonetheless, the presidential primaries play a very significant role in the presidential nominating process. Overall, they are important for two major reasons: *First,* they tend to democratize the delegate selection process. *Second,* they usually force would-be presidential nominees to test their candidacies in actual political combat.

Some presidential hopefuls have used the primaries as an effective route to nomination by the convention. John Kennedy did so in 1960, George McGovern in 1972, and Jimmy Carter in 1976 in the Democratic Party. But there is no one-to-one relationship between success in the primaries and victory at the convention. Thus, Barry Goldwater's 1964 primary record was at best mediocre; yet he won the nomination with comparative ease on the first ballot at the Republican convention that year. And Hubert Humphrey, the Democratic nominee in 1968, did not enter a single primary held that year.

Hard-fought presidential primary contests seldom occur within the ranks of the party in power. This tends to be true either because the incumbent President (1) is himself seeking reelection or (2) has groomed a successor. In either case, the President is usually able to use his power within the party to gain the desired end.

Both 1976 and 1980 provided exceptions here—but not altogether. Ronald Reagan made a stiff run at President Ford in the Republican Party in 1976. And Senator Edward Kennedy gave President Carter a hard challenge in the Democratic Party in 1980. But one very useful way of looking at both of these contests is to begin with the fact that the incumbent *did* win the nomination.

The primaries are frequently "knock-down, drag-out" affairs in the other party, however. Without the unifying force of the President as party leader, the several rival leaders and factions of that party vie with one another, vigorously, for the presidential nomination. Here one of the prime functions of the presidential primaries can usually be seen—that of screening, winnowing out the lesser contenders to the point where only one or a few are really available for the nomination.

Take the situation in the Republican Party in 1980 as a typical illustration of the point. Several leading personalities sought the GOP nomination. Among them were Senators Howard Baker, Robert Dole, and Larry Pressler; Congressmen John Anderson and Philip Crane; former GOP national chairman George Bush; and former Governors John Connally and Ronald Reagan. All of them pursued primary votes and convention delegates, and chased one another, from one end of the country to the other.

Altogether, there were 37 presidential primaries in 1980. That was an all-time record, seven more than the 30 held four years earlier. Over three-fourths of the delegates to both major party conventions were selected in the primary States. The recent "explosion" of presidential primaries has any number of consequences. Not the least of them revolve about the candidates and their problems of time, effort, finance, scheduling, and fatigue—to say nothing of voter fatigue. Adlai Stevenson once remarked, in a day when there were only half as many primaries: "The hardest thing about any political campaign is how to win without proving you are unworthy of winning."

Many have long urged the selection of *all* convention delegates by primaries. And the problems produced by the present multiplicity and variations of presidential primaries have prompted new interest in the holding of a single, nationwide presidential primary in each of the major parties.

The contest for the GOP nomination in 1980 featured several leading personalities. Top left: *George Bush, former GOP National Chairman.* Top right: *Ronald Reagan (seated at right), former Governor of California.* Center left: *John Anderson, Representative from Illinois.* Left: *Howard Baker, of Tennessee, Senate Minority Leader.* Above: *John B. Connally, former Governor of Texas.*

In fact, many have long argued for the elimination of the national conventions altogether—except, perhaps, for platform purposes. They would replace the conventions with a national primary to nominate the presidential and vice presidential candidates. Indeed, Woodrow Wilson urged the Congress to propose a constitutional amendment to that end back in 1913.

We shall return to the notion of a national primary—and the presidential primary, in general—in Chapter 15.

Nomination by Petition. One other nominating method is fairly widely used in American politics today—nomination by petition. Where it is used, the practice is a relatively simple one: Candidates are nominated via petitions signed by a certain number of qualified voters in the election district involved.[16]

Nomination by petition is found most widely at the local level—and there chiefly for elective school offices and for municipal offices in middle-sized and smaller communities.

---

[16] The petition device is employed in several other aspects of the election process. Thus, it (and/or a filing fee) is the usual method by which an aspirant's name is placed on the direct primary ballot. It is also a prominent part of the recall (page 712) and the initiative and referendum processes (see page 705).

the small society   by Brickman

HOO-BOY!

SOMETIMES I THINK WE ELECT A MAN JUST TO HAVE A SCAPEGOAT—

Washington Star Syndicate, Inc.

10-3   BRICKMAN

Most of the States provide that the direct primary can be used only by the major parties. The petition method (and/or conventions) is frequently the alternative open to minor party candidates. It is also the usual device by which independents may get their names on the general election ballot.

The details of the petition procedure vary from State to State, and even from city to city within the same State. As a general proposition, the higher the office and/or the larger the constituency the greater the number of signatures required.

Elections

Once candidates have been nominated they must face their opponents, and the voters, in the general election—in what H. G. Wells once called democracy's "feast, its great function."

There are elections in which the outcome is never in doubt. Most often and in most places this is not the case. But it is especially in one-party constituencies—in areas where one of the parties is so dominant, so regularly and heavily supported by the voters, that its candidates are virtually assured of election. There, as we noted on page 235, the nominating stage is more significant than final election.

The Administration of Elections. Democratic government cannot succeed unless elections are free, honest, and accurate exercises. Too many regard the details of the election process as too complicated and too legalistic—as too dry and boring—to worry about. But those who take this attitude miss the vital part these details play in the effort to make democracy work.

How something *can* be done regularly has a striking effect on what *is* done—and this is certainly true in the conduct of elections. The often lengthy and closely detailed provisions of election law are designed to protect the integrity of democracy itself. And election laws frequently have a telling impact on the outcome of elections, as well.

We've seen the point demonstrated several times. Recall, for example, our discussion of campaign finance laws, on pages 201-206. The critical importance of how much money is spent and of how it can be spent need hardly be restated here.[17]

The Extent of Federal Control. Nearly all elections in this country are held to choose the more than 490,000 persons who hold public offices in the nearly 80,000 units of government at the State and local levels. It is quite understandable,

---

[17] The same point can be made with regard to a number of other matters—including suffrage qualifications (pages 213-221), voter registration systems (pages 216-217), and the form of the primary (pages 239-247), for example.

then, that the overwhelming bulk of election law in the United States is State law.

There is a body of federal election law, however. The Constitution gives to Congress the power to fix "the times, places, and manner of holding elections" of members of Congress.[18] And Congress also has the power to determine the time for the choosing of presidential electors, to set the date for the casting of their electoral votes, and to regulate other aspects of the presidential election process.[19]

Congress has set the date for the holding of congressional elections as the first Tuesday following the first Monday in November of every even-numbered year. It has set the same date every fourth year for the presidential elections. Hence, the next off-year congressional elections will be held on November 2nd, 1982, and the next presidential election will occur on November 6th, 1984.[20]

Congress has also required the use of secret ballots and sanctioned the use of voting machines in federal elections. It has prohibited various corrupt practices and regulated campaign finance in federal elections. It has provided public subsidies for presidential primary and general election campaigns, as we noted on pages 201–206. And it has also enacted several statutes to protect the right to vote, which we considered on pages 218–221.

All other matters relating to national elections, and the entire process of choosing the many thousands of State and local officials, are dealt with in the laws of the individual States.

A local election official watches as a voter places his ballot in a ballot box on election day in a New Hampshire village.

When Elections Are Held. Most of the States hold their general elections to fill State offices on the same date Congress has set for national elections—in November of every even-numbered year.[21]

Some States do fix other dates, for at least some offices. Thus, Kentucky, Mississippi, New Jersey, and Virginia elect the governor, other executive officers, and State legislators in November of the *odd-*numbered years—and Louisiana, in December of those years. Other local election dates vary from State to State. Where these elections are not held in November they usually occur in the spring.

---

[18] Article I, Section 4, Clause 1; see pages 289–290.

[19] Article II, Section 1, Clause 4; see pages 375–378.

[20] Congress has made an exception for Alaska which may, if it chooses, elect its congressional delegation and cast its presidential vote on a different date. Thus far, however, Alaska has followed the regular November date. Up to 1960 Maine was also allowed to hold its congressional elections on another date, early in September; the practice gave rise to the often-quoted, but not-too-often-accurate, saying: "As Maine goes, so goes the nation." See page 289.

---

[21] The formula-like "Tuesday-after-the-first-Monday" is purposeful. It prevents election day from falling: (1) on Sundays, to maintain the principle of separation of church and state, and (2) on the first day of the month, which is often payday and peculiarly subject to campaign pressures.

THE COATTAIL EFFECT. Strong candidates running for major offices can produce what is often called the "coattail effect." Those candidates, with their wide appeal to the electorate, can help to pull voters to other candidates on the party's ticket. In effect, the lesser known office-seekers "ride the coattails" of the more prestigious personalities.

The coattail effect has been most dramatically apparent in certain presidential elections.[22] But a prominent candidate for senator or governor can have the same kind of pulling power.

There are some who believe that all State and local elections should be held on a date other than the one set for federal elections. If this were done, they argue, voters would pay more attention to State and local candidates and issues—be less subject to the coattail effect.

The Polling Place. For each precinct (voting district) into which a county or city is divided, there is a polling place. State law typically requires that local election officials—usually the county clerk or board of elections—draw precinct lines (and provide polling places) to make voting as convenient as possible. For example, the size of precincts is commonly restricted to an area containing no more than a certain number of qualified voters—often no more than 500 or 1000 of them, in order to prevent the delays and frustrations of long lines on election day. And the polls must be open during certain prescribed hours to accommodate the electorate—typically, from 7 or 8 A.M. to 7 or 8 P.M.

Each polling place is supervised by an election board which administers the election in that precinct. The board must open and close the polls, make certain that ballots and ballot boxes, or voting machines, and voting booths are available. The board must see that only qualified voters cast ballots, must count the votes which are cast, and must certify the results of the precinct voting to the proper officials (usually the county clerk or board of elections).

A "poll watcher" from each party is permitted to be present at the polling place. They may challenge any person whom they have reason to believe is not qualified to vote, attempt to see that as many as possible of their own party's members do vote, and watch the entire process (including the counting of the ballots) to insure its fairness.

The Ballot. The ballot[23] is the physical device by which a voter registers a choice in an election. It can take a number of different forms. But whatever the form, it is an obviously vital and sensitive part of the electoral process.

Each of the States now provides for a *secret ballot*. That is, each provides for the casting of ballots in such manner that others cannot know how a particular voter has in fact voted—unless, of course, the voter volunteers that information.

Voting was a *public* process through much of our earlier history. Although paper ballots were used in some colonial elections, voting was commonly by voice *(viva voce)*. Voters simply stated their choices to election officials. With suffrage restricted to the privileged few, oral voting was frequently defended as the only "manly" way in which to participate. Whatever the merits of that view, the expansion of the electorate brought with it various intimidations, vote-buying, and other corruptions of the voting process.

[22] There can be a *reverse* coattail effect, too. It occurs when the candidate at the head of the ticket tends to prejudice voter attitude against the party and its other nominees—as, for example, Barry Goldwater as the Republican presidential candidate in 1964 and George McGovern as the Democratic nominee in 1972.

[23] The term is derived from the Italian word *balla*—"ball" (more precisely, *ballota*—"little ball") and reflects the practice of dropping tokens (commonly black or white balls) into a box to indicate a choice. The term "blackball" comes from the same practice.

Paper ballots came into general use in the middle years of the 19th century. The first ones were unofficial—slips of paper which voters prepared themselves and deposited in the ballot box. Soon candidates and parties began to compose ballots and hand them to voters to cast—sometimes paying them to do so. These party ballots were printed on distinctively colored paper and any observer could tell for whom voters casting them actually voted.

Machine politicians, reaping their harvest from the unofficial ballots, fought all attempts to make voting a more secure process. The political corruption of the post-Civil War years brought widespread demand for ballot reforms, however.

THE AUSTRALIAN BALLOT. A new voting arrangement was devised in Australia, where it was first employed in elections in Victoria in 1856. Its successes there led to its adoption in other countries. It found its way to elections here via Great Britain.

The Kentucky legislature first authorized its use in municipal elections in Louisville in 1888, and later that same year Massachusetts adopted it for all elections in that State. By the turn of the century nearly all of the States had made provisions for it, and it remains the basic form of the ballot in all of them today.

The Australian ballot has four essential features: (1) It is printed at public expense. (2) It lists the names of all of the candidates in an election. (3) It is distributed only at the polls, one to each qualified voter. (4) It is voted in secret.

Two basic types of the Australian ballot are now in use among the States. Nearly half of them provide for the "office-group" ballot and slightly more than half for the "party-column" ballot.

A portion of a specimen ballot displayed in polling places in Massachusetts in the 1980 general elections.

ELECTORS OF PRESIDENT and VICE PRESIDENT
Vote for ONE

ANDERSON and LUCEY ++++++++++++++++ The Anderson Coalition	**3** ▶
CARTER and MONDALE +++++++++++++++++++++Democratic	**4** ▶
CLARK and KOCH +++++++++++++++++++++++ Libertarian Party	**5** ▶
DEBERRY and ZIMMERMAN +++++++++++ Socialist Workers Party	**6** ▶
REAGAN and BUSH +++++++++++++++++++++++ Republican	**7** ▶

REPRESENTATIVE IN CONGRESS
Twelfth District **Vote for ONE**

GERRY E. STUDDS 16 Black Horse Lane, Cohasset ++++++++++Democratic	**11** ▶
	Candidate for re-election
PAUL V. DOANE 3 Witchwood Lane, Harwich +++++++++++++ Republican	**12** ▶

COUNCILLOR
Fourth District **Vote for ONE**

PETER L. ELEEY 69 Forbes Hill Rd., Quincy ++++++++++++++Democratic	**21** ▶
WILLIAM J. ROBINSON 109 Beach Ave., Hull ++++++++++ Republican	**22** ▶

SENATOR IN GENERAL COURT
Norfolk & Plymouth District **Vote for ONE**

ALLAN R. McKINNON 78 Cottage Ln., Weymouth ++++++++++Democratic	**26** ▶
	Candidate for re-election
PAUL C. BARBER 122 Powder Point Ave., Duxbury ++++++++++ Republican	**27** ▶

REPRESENTATIVE IN GENERAL COURT
Third Plymouth District **Vote for ONE**

MARY JEANETTE MURRAY 30 Margin St., Cohasset +++++++ Republican	**32** ▶
	Candidate for re-election
THEODORE M. FORD 573 Jerusalem Rd., Cohasset +++++++++Democratic	**33** ▶

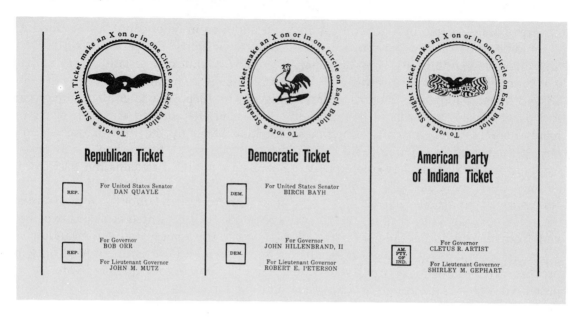

A portion of Indiana's sample ballot. Note that the candidates are listed under their respective party's name.

THE OFFICE-GROUP BALLOT. The office-group ballot is the original form of the Australian ballot. It is also sometimes called the Massachusetts Ballot because of its early use there. On it, the candidates for each office are grouped together. Originally, the names of the candidates were listed in alphabetical order. Most of the States now rotate the names because of the psychological advantage of having one's name at the top of the list.

THE PARTY-COLUMN BALLOT. The party-column ballot is also known as the Indiana ballot, from its early (1889) use in that State. On it, the names of each party's candidates are listed in a vertical column under the party's name. Usually there is a square or circle at the top of each party column where, by marking an "X," a voter may vote for all of that party's candidates. Politicians tend to favor this form because it encourages and simplifies "straight-ticket" voting—especially when the party has a strong candidate at "the head of the ticket." On the other hand, students of the political process tend to favor the office-group ballot—because it encourages voter judgment and "split-ticket" voting.

SAMPLE BALLOTS. Sample ballots, clearly marked as such, are commonly available in most States. In some they are mailed to all voters before an election and they are usually printed in the newspapers. They cannot be cast, of course—but they do help voters prepare for an election.[24]

THE LONG AND THE SHORT OF IT. The ballot in a typical American election is a lengthy one—often and aptly described as a "bed-sheet ballot" and sometimes as a "jungle ballot." It frequently contains so many offices, so many candidates, and so many measures that even the most conscientious and well-informed voters have difficulty casting intelligent votes.

The long ballot came to American politics in the era of Jacksonian Democracy in

---

[24] First in Oregon, and now in several States, an official Voter's Pamphlet is mailed to all voters before an election. It lists all candidates and measures which will appear on the ballot. In Oregon each candidate is allowed space to present his or her qualifications, and proponents and opponents of measures are allowed space to present their arguments on each measure.

1 For Electors of President and Vice-President (Vote Once)	4 UNITED STATES SENATOR (Vote for One)	5 JUSTICE OF THE SUPREME COURT (Vote for One)	6 REPRESENTATIVE IN CONGRESS (Vote for One)	7 STATE SENATOR (Vote for One)	8 MEMBER OF ASSEMBLY (Vote for One)	9 / 10 COUNTY JUDGE (Vote for any Two)		11 JUDGE OF THE FAMILY COURT (Vote for One)
1 A DEMOCRATIC Presidential Electors for **Jimmy Carter / Walter F. Mondale**	4 A DEMOCRATIC Elizabeth **Holtzman**	5 A DEMOCRATIC Thomas J. **O'Toole**	6 A DEMOCRATIC Richard L. **Ottinger**	7 A DEMOCRATIC Arthur **Goodman**	8 A DEMOCRATIC Richard E. **Upton**	9 A DEMOCRATIC Carmine C. **Marasco**	10 A DEMOCRATIC Jules N. **Bloch**	11 A DEMOCRATIC H. Hawthorne **Harris**
1 B REPUBLICAN Presidential Electors for **Ronald Reagan / George Bush**	4 B REPUBLICAN Alfonse M. **D'Amato**	5 B REPUBLICAN Matthew F. **Coppola**	6 B REPUBLICAN Joseph W. **Christiana**	7 B REPUBLICAN Mary B. **Goodhue**	8 B REPUBLICAN Jon S. **Fossel**	9 B REPUBLICAN J. Radley **Herold**	10 B REPUBLICAN James R. **Cowhey**	11 B REPUBLICAN Adrienne Hofmann **Scancarelli**
1 C CONSERVATIVE Presidential Electors for **Ronald Reagan / George Bush**	4 C CONSERVATIVE Alfonse M. **D'Amato**	5 C CONSERVATIVE Matthew F. **Coppola**	6 C CONSERVATIVE Joseph W. **Christiana**	7 C CONSERVATIVE Mary B. **Goodhue**	8 C CONSERVATIVE Jon S. **Fossel**	9 C CONSERVATIVE J. Radley **Herold**	10 C CONSERVATIVE James R. **Cowhey**	11 C CONSERVATIVE Adrienne Hofmann **Scancarelli**
1 D RIGHT TO LIFE Presidential Electors for **Ellen McCormack / Carroll Driscoll**	4 D RIGHT TO LIFE Alfonse M. **D'Amato**	5 D RIGHT TO LIFE Matthew F. **Coppola**	6 D RIGHT TO LIFE Joseph W. **Christiana**	7 D RIGHT TO LIFE Joseph P. **Jennings**	8 D RIGHT TO LIFE Theresa A. **Weth**	9 D RIGHT TO LIFE J. Radley **Herold**	10 D RIGHT TO LIFE James R. **Cowhey**	11 D RIGHT TO LIFE H. Hawthorne **Harris**
1 E LIBERAL Presidential Electors for **John B. Anderson / Patrick J. Lucey**	4 E LIBERAL Jacob K. **Javits**	5 E LIBERAL Thomas J. **O'Toole**	6 E LIBERAL Richard O. **Reyes**			9 E LIBERAL Carmine C. **Marasco**	10 E LIBERAL Jules N. **Bloch**	11 E LIBERAL H. Hawthorne **Harris**

A portion of a sample ballot mailed to voters in New York before the 1980 general elections. The names are arranged as they will appear in a voting machine.

the 1830's. The prevailing view of the time was that the greater the number of elective offices the more democratic the governmental system. The notion remains a widely accepted one today. As a consequence, and as we've noted before, there are nearly *half a million* elective offices in the United States.

National elections involve a short ballot. At most, the voter is called upon to cast but three votes: one for the Presidency (and Vice Presidency), one for a Senator, and one for a Representative. Some of the States have also achieved a shorter ballot at that level—notably, Alaska, Hawaii, New Hampshire, New Jersey, Tennessee, and Virginia. Essentially, they've done so by reducing the number of elective State offices.

Typically, the longest ballots are found at the local level, and especially among the nation's 3000-odd counties. At the county level it is not unusual to find such popularly elected officials as commissioners, a clerk, a sheriff, one or more judges, a prosecutor, a coroner, a treasurer, an auditor, an assessor, a surveyor, a school superintendent, an engineer, a sanitarian, and, in some places, even a dog-catcher.

Critics of the long ballot reject the argument that the more you elect the more democratic you are. They believe that quite the reverse is true. They argue that, with a smaller number of elected offices to fill, the voter can better know the candidates and their qualifications. They also point to "voter fatigue"; the drop-off in voter turnout can run as high as 20 to 30 percent for offices at and near the end of the ballot.

There seems little, if any, good reason to elect such local officials as clerks, coroners, surveyors, and engineers. Their jobs, and many others commonly filled by popular election, do not involve basic policy-making responsibilities. Rather, they administer policies made by others. For good government the rule should be: *elect* those who make public policies; *appoint* those who only administer them.

Voting Machines. Thomas Edison secured the first American patent for a voting machine and his invention was first used in an election held in Lockport, New

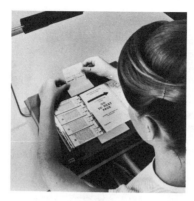
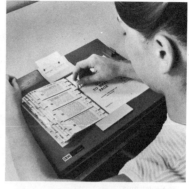
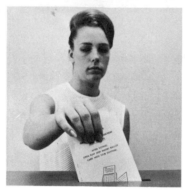
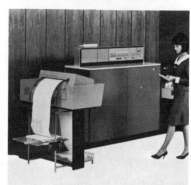

EDP (electronic data processing) voting systems are designed to speed up and reduce the costs of conducting elections. Upper left: A voter inserts a specially-designed card in the vote recorder. Upper right: Voter selections are recorded by using a pen-like stylus to punch holes in the ballot card. Lower left: The card, now inside an envelope, is placed in a ballot box. Lower right: After the polls close, cards are taken to a data processing center, where they are quickly counted by computer.

York, in 1892. Over the years since, the use of similar voting devices has spread to the point where their use is now sanctioned by the laws of every State.

Only a handful of States make the use of voting machines mandatory. The devices are often used in some (and usually the more populous) areas but not in others within the same State. All told, however, more than half of all of the votes cast in national elections today are cast on them.

The typical voting machine serves as its own booth. The voter pulls a lever to close the curtain and simultaneously unlocks the machine. The ballot appears on the face of the machine, and the voter indicates his or her choices by pulling down the levers over the names of the candidates he or she favors. In most of the States using the party-column ballot the voter may pull a master lever to vote a straight ticket.

Space is provided for measures, as well as candidates, with *yes* and *no* levers for each. The machine is programmed to prevent the casting of more than one vote per contest. Once all of the levers are in the desired position, the voter opens the curtain. That action simultaneously records the votes cast and clears the machine for the next voter.

The use of voting machines eliminates the need for manual vote counting, reduces the number of persons required to administer elections, and speeds the voting process. It also increases the number of voters who can be handled per precinct, makes ballot spoilage impossible, and minimizes the possibilities of counting errors and of fraud.

The machines in common use today are rather expensive, costing several thousand dollars apiece. Although they pay for themselves over time, the initial expense sometimes discourages their purchase. Then, too, they are quite bulky and present storage, moving, and maintenance problems. Some voters, especially older ones and residents of sparsely populated rural areas, claim that the machines are too complicated and confusing. Clearly, voting machines are most useful in densely populated areas.

ELECTRONIC VOTE COUNTING. Electronic data processing techniques have been applied to the voting process in recent years—first in California and Oregon and now, to at least some degree, in over half of the States.

To date, EDP applications have followed two general lines: (1) the use of cards as ballots which are punched by voters and then tabulated by highspeed computers; and (2) the use of optical scanners to read marked paper ballots.

SUMMARY

Both the nomination and the election process are fundamental to democracy.

Five different methods of nomination have been and are used in the United States: (1) *self-announcement*, the earliest method used, was developed in colonial times, widely used in the early years of our national history, and used at the local level today in some parts of the country; (2) the *caucus*, developed in colonial times, widely used in the early years of our national history, and used at the local level in some parts of the country; (3) the *delegate convention*, which replaced the caucus in the 1830's in national politics and is yet used to select presidential and vice presidential candidates and for some offices in a few States; (4) the *direct primary*, which developed at the turn of the century as a substitute for the ills of the convention system and is the most widely used method today; and (5) *nomination by petition*, which is used in many local areas and by independent and minor party candidates at the State level and local levels.

There are two forms of the direct primary: (1) the *closed primary*, in which only party members may participate, and (2) the *open primary*, in which any qualified voter may participate. *Nonpartisan primaries* are used to nominate candidates for nonpartisan offices. *Run-off primaries* are commonly used in Southern States where a nominee must have a majority of votes for party nomination.

Some form of the *presidential primary* is used in most of the States and the District of Columbia and Puerto Rico. At base, a presidential primary is: (1) a national convention delegate selection process, and/or (2) a preference election where voters may indicate a choice for their party's presidential nomination.

The National Government exercises only limited control over the election process. It is very largely regulated by State law.

National elections are held on the Tuesday following the first Monday in November in even-numbered years. Most States hold their general elections at the same time; local elections are commonly held then, too, or in the spring. The elections are conducted in precincts (voting districts), for each of which there is a polling place.

In all States today the voter casts the Australian ballot, which is of either the office-group or the party-column type. Voting machines and/or electronic data processing to count ballots are now used in the more populous areas of nearly all States. Most ballots used in American elections are much too long and tend to confuse and discourage the voter and lead to blind voting.

Concept Development

Questions for Review

1. Why is the nominating stage so crucial an aspect of the democratic process?

2. What is the oldest method for the making of nominations in American politics?

3. What aspect of the nominating caucus made it subject to heavy criticism?

4. Why may it be said that in theory the convention system seems ideally suited to representative government?

5. What is the most widely used nominating method in American politics today?

6. What is the chief distinction between the open and the closed primaries? What feature of the open primary led to the development of the closed primary?

7. What are the two basic aspects of the presidential primary?

8. Why are the details of the electoral process so vital to the success of democratic government?

9. Why is the large bulk of election law in this country State rather than federal law?

10. When are national elections held? Most State general elections? Why do many favor separate dates for national and for State and local elections?

11. What is the "coattail effect"?

12. What are the four essential features of the Australian ballot?

13. How do the office-group and party-column ballots differ? Why do most students of government favor the former?

14. Why is the typical ballot so lengthy? Why do some favor the long ballot? Others a short ballot?

15. Why is the use of some type of voting machine usually held to be an improvement over the use of paper ballots, at least in more populous areas?

16. What have been the two general lines followed in the application of electronic data processing techniques to the voting process?

For Further Inquiry

1. What did the Nazi political scientist Ernst Huber mean when he wrote that "it is not decisive for the character of an elected representative body who possesses the suffrage, but, to a much higher degree, who determines the candidates put up before the electorate"?

2. Would you favor or oppose a nationwide presidential primary? Why?

3. What offices are elective in your State, county, and city? Do you think any of them should be made appointive instead? If so, why?

4. H. G. Wells once wrote: "Until a man has an education, a vote is a useless and dangerous thing for him to possess." Does the fact that one has a formal education necessarily mean that one will vote intelligently? Is the vote actually a "useless thing" in the hands of the uneducated?

5. Why do party professionals usually favor the use of the party-column rather than the office-group form of the ballot? Which form is used in your State?

6. Why does the fact that we have a federal system of government in the United States mean that our election system is a very complex one?

7. What arguments can you present in opposition to the author's contention (on page 253) that: "For good government the rule should be: *elect* those who make public policies; *appoint* those who only administer them"?

8. What did the late Robert M. Hutchins mean when he remarked: "The death of democracy is not likely to be an assassination from ambush. It will be a slow extinction from apathy, indifference, and undernourishment"?

Suggested Activities

1. Prepare a bulletin board display of sample ballots from elections held in your State. (The ballots can usually be obtained from local election officials or from the office of the Secretary of State.)

2. Invite the clerk or another election official to speak to the class on the conduct of elections in your locale.

3. From your State's election code, draw a flow chart of the steps involved in the casting and counting of ballots in elections in your State.

4. Write a report on one of the following topics: (a) a recent State nominating convention; (b) the history of the caucus; or (c) historical highlights of national conventions.

5. Invite a recent candidate (either a successful or an unsuccessful one) to describe her or his campaign experiences to the class.

6. Stage a class forum or debate on one or more of the following topics: (a) *Re-*

solved, That this State should (adopt or abandon) the direct primary as its basic nominating device; (b) *Resolved,* That this State should adopt the (open or closed) primary; (c) *Resolved,* That this State should (provide for or abandon) the recall of public officers; or (d) *Resolved,* That this State should adopt the (office-group or party-column) ballot for use in all partisan elections.

Suggested Reading

Asher, Herbert B., *Presidential Elections and American Politics.* Dorsey, rev. ed., 1980.

Barone, Michael, *et al.,* The Almanac of *American Politics.* Dutton, 1981.

Campbell, Bruce A., *The American Electorate: Attitudes and Actions.* Holt, Rinehart and Winston, 1979.

Crotty, William J. (ed.), *Paths to Political Reform.* Heath, 1980.

David, Paul T. and Ceaser, James W., *Proportional Representation in Presidential Nominating Politics.* University of Virginia Press, 1980.

Fishel, Jeff (ed.), *Politics and Parties in an Anti-Party Age.* Indiana University Press, 1978.

Grimes, Alan P., *Democracy and the Amendments to the Constitution.* Heath, 1979.

Kessel, John H., *Presidential Campaign Strategies and Citizen Response.* Wiley, 1980.

Ladd, Everett C., *Where Have All the Voters Gone?* Norton, 1978.

Langton, Stuart (ed.), *Citizen Participation in America.* Heath, 1978.

Politics in America. Congressional Quarterly, 1980.

Pomper, Gerald and Lederman, Susan S., *Elections in America.* Longman, 2nd ed., 1980.

Scott, Ruth K. and Hebenar, Ronald J., *Parties in Crisis.* Wiley, 1979.

Watson, Richard A., *The Presidential Contest.* Wiley, 1980.

11

Government by the People: Public Opinion and Pressure Groups

Our government rests on public opinion. Whoever can change public opinion can change government.

ABRAHAM LINCOLN

■ In a democracy are there any "right" answers to public policy questions?

■ Do public opinion polls enhance or do they threaten the effectiveness of representative government?

■ Are pressure groups inevitable in a democratic government? Are they indispensable to democratic government?

The concept of popular sovereignty is fundamental to the American scheme of government. In this country we believe that the people *should* and *do* rule. We believe that the people are the only legitimate source for any and all government power and that the primary task of government is that of translating the public will into public policy. Government in the United States is, as Lord Bryce observed, "government by public opinion." Thus, the process by which the public will is expressed, and by which it is translated into public policy, lies at the heart of the governmental system. In a large sense, this entire book concerns itself with that process. In this chapter we are directly concerned with two particular aspects of it: the nature and role of public opinion and the nature and tactics of pressure groups.

Public Opinion

Nature of Public Opinion. What is *public opinion?* At first glance this question may seem an easy one—for, after all, few terms are more widely used in American politics. Public officials, candidates, and lobbyists are especially fond of the phrase and tend to use it often. Editorial writers use it; press, radio, and television commentators use it; and even the fabled "man in the street" uses it frequently, too.

Few who use the phrase ever pause to define it, however. Those who do quickly discover that it is not readily definable. Even such authorities on the subject as public opinion pollsters and political scientists find it a vague and somewhat ambiguous thing, hard to pin down in terms of precise meaning.

THE "PUBLIC." To illustrate how vague and difficult the term is to define, consider this question: *Who is* to be included within the "public" which has an "opinion" upon which public policy is to be based?

Clearly, the "public" here does *not* include *all* of the people. A great many people have *no* opinion on a great many issues. They do not either because they have no interest in those issues or because they know nothing about them.

Does the "public" include all voters, then? Again, many who vote have no opinion on a great many issues, including issues involved in elections in which they vote. And, recall, 40 percent and more of the electorate does not vote, even in presidential elections. Then, too, government does many things (and there are many issues) upon which the voters, as such, never express an opinion.

Does the "public" include, then, only those persons who hold opinions which arise out of a direct interest they have in a particular issue? Surely this cannot be so— for there are a great many people who are directly *affected* by a given issue but who are never *aware* of that fact. Indeed, it is probably true that on most issues there are more who do *not* realize that they are affected by the matter than there are those who *do*. To eliminate from the "public" those who do not perceive the ways in which they are affected by an issue would be to contradict the whole notion of democracy and to substitute for it rule by the minority.

Then *who does* comprise the "public" upon whose opinion public policy is supposed to be based? The most realistic an-swer is: *several different groups*, with memberships which vary from *issue to issue*. That is to say, there is no *one* public which does or can hold *the* dominant opinion in our society; instead, there are *many* "publics." Each "public" consists of those persons who hold the same or similar views on some particular issue of public policy. Each of these groups is a "public" with regard to that issue, and the view the group shares distinguishes it from all other "publics." For example, all persons who believe that capital punishment ought to be abolished belong to the "public" which holds that view. Or, all persons who believe that the smoking of marijuana should be legalized belong to the "public" which shares that

"HOW WOULD YOU LIKE ME TO ANSWER THAT QUESTION? AS A MEMBER OF MY ETHNIC GROUP, EDUCATIONAL CLASS, INCOME GROUP, OR RELIGIOUS CATEGORY?"

Drawing by D. Fradon; © 1969 The New Yorker Magazine, Inc.

view. But note, there are many persons who belong to *one* of these "publics" but *not* to the other.[1]

"OPINION." Just as we must analyze "public," so we must define "opinion" in order to understand the term *public opinion.* As used here, the word "opinion" refers to a judgment made and expressed with regard to a public issue. Thus, it involves three elements.

First, an opinion is something more than a guess, a hunch, or a mere impression. It is a consciously reached conclusion, a *judgment.* To serve as a sound basis for public policy an opinion *should* be the result of a judgment made after a careful examination of all relevant facts. But, unfortunately, many judgments are not made in this fashion.

Second, an opinion must be *expressed* in some way. A view which is *not* expressed cannot be called an "opinion" in the *public* sense. If it is not expressed, it cannot be known by others; and if it cannot be known by others, it cannot be identified with any public.

Third, an opinion which forms a part of a public opinion must deal with a *public issue,* not a private matter. A woman may be unhappy with the color of her hair or a man may be disturbed by his increasing weight. But the attitudes they have in these instances are ones they hold on *private* matters. An opinion is a *public* one only when the matter on which it is held is a subject of general concern, one of interest to a significant portion of the population.

Of course, *many* matters are of general interest to the public. For example, the antics of various popular entertainers attract public attention; so do the World Series, the Rose Bowl, the Super Bowl, and other athletic events. On each of these matters public opinions exist. Thus, the activities of a television personality may be admired by many while condemned by others. Or, the New York Yankees may be favored over the Los Angeles Dodgers and vice versa in the World Series. But our concern here is with public opinion *as it relates to public issues*—that is, with *political* matters, matters of *public policy.*

DEFINITION. With what has been said, then, *public opinion* is used here to refer to a view pertaining to a matter of public policy which is held (shared) by a significant portion of the population. Public opinion is a compound of the points of view of many individuals; it consists of expressed group attitudes on questions of public policy.

Formation of Public Opinion. Social scientists have given a vast amount of study to public opinion in recent years. As a result, we know far more about the subject today than ever before. Still, we have much to learn, and there are many questions about it which can be answered only in relatively broad terms. Not the least of these are such questions as: How is public opinion formed? What are its roots? What factors shape and influence it?

In broad terms, public opinion is formed out of *all* of the factors that influence human thought and action. That is, opinion-making is a very complex process, and the various factors involved in it are practically without number.

No single factor, alone, shapes any person's opinion on any matter. Some factors do play a much larger role than others, however. For example, a person's family and occupation are regularly much more

---

[1] Notice too, that because there is never unanimous agreement on any issue, there is always *more than one* "public" on a given issue. In fact, there are regularly *several* "publics" on a single issue. For example, on the question of capital punishment one "public" may hold the view that the death penalty ought not be imposed for *any* crime. Another "public" may take the position that the death penalty should be imposed for *several* crimes, including murder, criminal assault, kidnapping, and treason. Yet another "public" may share the view that this penalty ought to be imposed only for a *few specific* crimes, such as murder committed by one serving a life sentence for a previous murder or for the killing of a police officer, and so on.

significant in the shaping of that person's opinions than is, say, the climate of the area in which he or she lives.

Take this question to illustrate the point: Should daylight saving time be abolished? (On daylight time and the law, see page 557.) Several different factors will affect one's opinion on this issue. But, for now, look at the three we've just mentioned—that is, age, occupation, and climate.

Family-related factors might well have a large effect on one's judgment here. Does the family include small children? If so, one might take a dim view of daylight saving—because small children are usually awake in the early morning hours and they usually go to bed in the early evening hours.

Occupational considerations may have a similar weight. Does one's job demand that he or she be at work early in the day? If so, daylight saving may mean that that person must get up and go to work in the dark. On the other hand, if a person must work late in the day, the elimination of daylight saving would mean less daylight time available after work.

And climate has an obvious impact here, too. How much and what kind of daylight is being "saved" by daylight saving time? If it is often chilly or windy in the late spring, summer, or early fall afternoons, a person may take a much different view of the matter than would be the case if it is usually balmy at that time of day.

Many of the factors that go into the mix that produces an opinion *interact* upon one another. That is, some factors tend to complement or reinforce others, while some tend to have a contradicting or a weakening affect.

For example, add another element to the daylight saving time illustration we've just used: recreational interests. A family with small children may go to drive-in movies frequently. For them, daylight sav-

Reprinted by permission of the Chicago Tribune–New York News Syndicate

"45% OF ME SAYS YES, 38% NO, AND 15% MAYBE . . ."

ing time involves some obvious inconveniences but, perhaps, the family prefers to go on picnics or do something else outdoors in the late afternoons and early evenings. For them, the time change is a boon. Or, the family's leisure interests may center around reading or the television set. The time change would have little or no effect on their recreational interests.

The most important factors influencing opinion formulation appear to be the family, school, church, political party affiliation, labor union or business association, and other organized groups to which an individual belongs and from which ideas are drawn. One's age, sex, race, vocation, and social contacts contribute strongly, too. So do newspapers, books, magazines, radio and television, motion pictures, advertising, and all of the other means by which

DUNAGIN'S PEOPLE

*"I'M FOR THE FRONT-
RUNNER...WHO IS IT THIS
WEEK?"*

DUNAGIN'S PEOPLE by Ralph Dunagin.
© 1980 Field Enterprises, Inc.
Courtesy of Field Newspaper Syndicate.

*Television stations often bring
together people of varying
backgrounds and with different views and ask them to
comment on some matter of
public interest.*

ideas and information on public affairs are disseminated.

The views expressed by opinion leaders also bear heavily upon the opinions held by most persons. An *opinion leader* is any person who, for any reason, has a more than usual influence over the opinions of others. Such persons are a distinct minority in the total population, of course; but they appear at every level in society, and they follow many different vocations. They include, for example, high-ranking public officials; political party, pressure group, business, and labor union leaders; and newspaper editors and radio and television commentators. And, they include the members of certain professions—especially those such as teachers, ministers, doctors and lawyers who deal closely with the public. Whoever they may be—the President of the United States, a prominent person in business, an active leader of a club, or the neighborhood barber—opinion leaders are persons to whom others listen and from whom others draw their ideas and convictions. Whatever their political, economic, or social standing or outlook may be, they play a very significant role in opinion formulation.

Measurement of Public Opinion. If public policy is to be based on the dictates of public opinion, there must be ways in which it is possible to discover the answers to these questions: What is the *content* of public opinion on a particular issue? Approximately *how many persons* share a given opinion in the matter? *How firmly* do those who express an opinion actually hold it? This is to say, it must be possible to "measure" public opinion.

MEANS OF EXPRESSION. The *general* content of public opinion—what various groups of people say they want—may be determined in a very obvious way: by consulting the means by which public opinions are expressed in our society. These means are both many and varied. Those most commonly used include voting, lobbying,[2] books, pamphlets, magazine and newspaper articles, paid advertisements, editorial comments in the press and by radio and television, letters to editors, legislators, and other public officials, and direct personal contacts with public agencies. These and other means of expression are the devices through which the content of public opinion becomes known. But most of the *means* tell little—and often nothing reliable—about the *size* of the group holding a particular opinion or the depth of *conviction* with which that opinion is held.

MEASUREMENT THROUGH ELECTIONS. In a democracy the voice of the people is supposed to be heard through the ballot box. Election results are regularly taken as indicators of public opinion. The votes cast for rival candidates are regarded as evidences of the people's approval or rejection of the stands taken by the candidates and of the platforms offered by the parties which nominated them. A party and its victorious candidates frequently claim to have been given a mandate to carry out their campaign promises.[3]

In actual practice, election results provide an *accurate* measure of public opinion only in rare instances, however. Voters make the choices they do in elections for any of several reasons, as we have already seen (pages 225-230). Some of the votes received by candidates are votes cast *for them*, while others are votes cast *against their opponents*. And some of these votes were actually cast *for their party*, or *against the other party*, rather than for them. Candidates often disagree with some, and occasionally even with many, of the planks of their party's platform. The stands taken by candidates and their parties frequently are purposely vague and general, as we have noted.

Thus, a vote cast for a candidate may express little more than a vague and general approval of his or her campaign image or the party's traditional record. Also, voters often vote a "split ticket," voting for the Democratic candidates for some offices and Republican candidates for other offices *at the same election*. Thus, those who do support one party and its candidates at a given election include a bewildering variety of interests which agree with one another on some issues and disagree, sometimes sharply, on others.

All of this suggests that to call a typical election a "mandate" for much of anything in terms of public policy is to be on very shaky ground. Elections are, at best, *useful indicators* of public opinion. Votes cast for a candidate cannot be interpreted accurately as votes cast for all of the candidate's views.[4]

MEASUREMENT THROUGH PRESSURE GROUPS. A *pressure group* is an organization composed of persons who share certain views

---

[2] See pages 275-278.

[3] The term "mandate" comes from the Latin *mandare*—literally, to place in one's hand or to commit to one's charge. In American politics the term refers to the instructions or commands a constituency gives to its elected officials.

[4] Elections at which voters approve or reject measures—State constitutional amendments, statutes, local ordinances, or such other proposals as bond issues—are elections in which public opinion is registered directly upon a public policy question. The usefulness of such an election as a reflection of public opinion depends in large part upon the proportion of the electorate participating in it, of course.

and objectives and who actively seek to influence the making and content of public policy. We shall consider them at some length in a moment (pages 267–279). But, for now, notice that though they vary considerably in their size, power, and objectives, all pressure groups seek to influence public policy. And, in the process of doing so, they serve as a chief means by which public opinion is made known. They convey information and the views of their members through the efforts of their lobbyists, by letter and telegram campaigns, through electioneering, and by a variety of other methods. But, in dealings with pressure groups, public officials often find it very difficult to determine two things: How many people does each group actually speak for? And, just how intensely do those people hold the views which are attributed to them?

MEASUREMENT THROUGH THE MEDIA. The press, radio, and television are often described as "mirrors" as well as "molders" of public opinion. The peculiar importance of these media is reflected by these impressive statistics: More than 9,800 newspapers, including some 1750 dailies, are currently published in this country; they have a combined circulation of nearly 150 million copies per issue. Some 7000 commercial radio and more than 700 commercial television stations are on the air. Their programs can be received by at least 150 million television sets in the United States. The Census Bureau reports that there is at least one radio set and at least one television set in 99.9 percent of the more than 76 million households in this country—and there are two or more of each in several million of them, of course.

Editorial pages and news commentators are commonly believed to be fairly good indicators of majority opinion on public issues. Whether they are or not is in fact unknown. That they may not be as reliable as many think seems to be indicated by this fact: By a wide margin, most daily newspapers have supported the Republican candidate for President in every election save one from 1932 through 1980. The one exception was in 1964, when most newspapers did not back Barry Goldwater. Yet, the Democrats won eight of the 13 presidential elections held in that 48-year span. The Republicans won only with Dwight Eisenhower as their candidate in 1952 and 1956, Richard Nixon in 1968 and 1972, and Ronald Reagan in 1980. The truth of the matter appears to be this: Newspapers are more influential in terms of public attitudes on issue questions than they are on candidates—and more influential in terms of State and local rather than national candidates.

MEASUREMENT THROUGH PERSONAL CONTACT. Public officials regularly attempt to sound out and assess public opinion on the basis of direct contacts with the people. These contacts are of many varied types. Thus, the President—or more often a Cabinet member or other major figure in the administration—will make a speaking tour of the country. Various aspects of the administration's program may be discussed, while, at the same time, an attempt is made to gauge public sentiment. Members of Congress return home to talk to the voters between sessions and frequently during a session. They receive huge quantities of mail from their constituents and many visitors from home. Governors, State legislators, and other public policymakers utilize the same techniques, of course.

The success of these attempts to measure public opinion depends in good part upon the shrewdness with which a public official interprets what is seen and heard. The possibility that officials will glean only what they *want* to find—only that which supports the positions they themselves favor—is an ever-present trap.

MEASUREMENT THROUGH PUBLIC OPINION POLLS. Public opinion polls have been used "to take the public pulse" in this country for more than a century. They are widely used today to discover sentiment on public questions and to forecast election results.

Most early polling attempts were of the "straw vote" variety. That is, they were polls in which accuracy was sought simply by asking a certain question of the largest possible number of persons. Straw votes are still fairly common today. Local newspapers occasionally run "ballots" for their readers to "clip out and mail in," and radio stations pose questions to which listeners may respond by postcard. But this polling method is notoriously unreliable. It rests on the fallacious assumption that a relatively large response will tend to produce a fairly accurate picture of the public view on a given question. Nothing in the process insures that those who do respond—no matter how numerous—in fact represent an accurate sample (cross-section) of the population. The emphasis is upon *quantity* rather than upon the *quality* of the sample to which the question is posed.

Even an extraordinarily large sample can produce a highly inaccurate result if the sample itself is faulty. The most spectacular failure of a straw vote poll occurred in connection with the presidential election of 1936. During that campaign the *Literary Digest* mailed ballots to several million persons whose names had been drawn from telephone directories and automobile registration lists. Each person who received a ballot was asked to indicate his or her preference between the Republican candidate, Governor Alfred Landon of Kansas, and the Democratic candidate, President Franklin D. Roosevelt. Some two million ballots were returned, and on the basis of the results, the *Digest* predicted an overwhelming victory for Governor Landon. But in the election itself, President Roosevelt won in a landslide. Roosevelt carried every State except Maine and Vermont and received 27,751,597 popular votes to Governor Landon's 16,597,583. The magazine had managed to forecast the winners in the presidential elections of the 1920's.

President Truman chuckles over his victory that upset pollsters in 1948, when an overwhelming victory was predicted for his opponent, Thomas E. Dewey.

But its failure in 1936 was so colossal that it ceased publication almost immediately thereafter. The problem, of course, was that a far larger number of Republicans had telephones and owned cars than did Democrats in that mid-Depression year.

Since the 1930's, serious public opinion polling has been based on the concept of "scientific sampling." That is, it has been based on efforts to reach a carefully drawn sample of the population. Most responsible pollsters now attempt to tap an accurate cross-section of the population to be surveyed either by:

(1) Drawing a *quota sample,* in which several characteristics of the population—such as age, sex, place of residence, occupation, and income level—are represented in the sample in the same proportion as they exist in the total population. Thus, if 51.3 percent of the population is female, females will make up 51.3 percent of the sample, and so on.

Or, (2) drawing a *random sample* (also known as a *probability sample*), in which a limited number of clusters of people—in blocks, precincts, or other small districts—is selected with infinite care. Most major pollsters use this method, choosing the particular areas for their interviews in mathematically random fashion.

Among the best-known polling organizations today are the American Institute of Public Opinion (the Gallup Poll) and Louis Harris & Associates (the Harris Survey), both nationally syndicated. These, and many other national and regional pollsters, who use rigorous scientific polling techniques, have not developed foolproof methods for the measuring of public opinion. But—with the exception of the presidential election of 1948—they have produced generally useful and increasingly reliable results.

Still, several problems continue to plague public opinion pollsters. The drawing of accurate samples—an extraordinar-

ily complex mathematical and sociological exercise—needs (and is receiving) constant refinement. Several factors affect the reliability of the responses to pollsters' questions, and many of those factors are difficult or even impossible to control. For example, an interviewer's physical appearance, dress, or accent or voice inflections may affect an answer.

Then, too, there are unsolved problems in the wording of questions intended to tap opinions on issues. Clearly, questions must be very carefully phrased in order to avoid prejudicing the answers that will be given to them. For example, many persons will answer "yes" to a question put in these terms: "Should taxes be reduced?" But many of the same persons will also answer "yes" to such questions as: "Should the city's police department be expanded in order to combat the rising crime rate?" "Should the local schools be upgraded?"—both of which would almost certainly require more tax dollars.

One of the major weaknesses of scientific polls is that they do not accurately measure either the depth of knowledge or the strength of feeling behind the opinions they report. Answers given to pollsters' questions are sometimes nothing more than snap judgments. Others are ill-considered emotional reactions or answers of the sort the person interviewed thinks "ought" to be given. Some answers are those that the person thinks will please (or offend) the interviewer, rather than accurate indications of opinion. Lack of interest or knowledge often warps responses, too.

Public opinion polls are sometimes accused of helping to *shape* the opinions they are *supposed* to measure. The charge is most often levied against polls which appear in syndicated columns in newspapers across the country.

Even with these problems, it is clear that scientific polls have proved of real benefit in the difficult task of measuring public opinion. They can be—and *are*—

used much more frequently and conveniently than formal elections. Though they may not be *precisely* accurate, they do offer reasonably reliable guides to public thought. They tend to focus attention on public questions and to stimulate discussion of them. Their value is underscored by the widespread and growing use of them by candidates running for office and by public officials.

Constitutional Limitations on Majority Opinion. A final word is necessary before we turn to pressure groups. Public opinion is supposed to serve as the *principal guiding force* behind public policy in the United States. But its power is tempered. Our system of constitutional government is *not* designed to give free, unrestricted play to public opinion—and, especially, it is not designed to give such force to *majority* opinion. The doctrines of separation of powers and of checks and balances, and the constitutional guarantees of civil rights are intended to protect minority interests against excesses of majority action.

Pressure Groups

A *pressure group* is an organization composed of persons who share one or more opinions or objectives and who seek to promote their common interests by influencing the making and the content of public policy.[5]

In every society there are many persons with common aims and concerns in economic, religious, racial, sectional, and other social matters. It is only natural that they should join together to promote their interests. Whatever they may call themselves—whether clubs, leagues, unions, committees, or something else—the groups they form become pressure groups whenever they seek their ends by attempting to influence government.

Political Parties and Pressure Groups. People learned long ago that there is strength in both numbers and unity. The existence of political parties and pressure

[5] Pressure groups are also known, less widely but somewhat more accurately, as *interest groups* or *special interest groups*.

Concerned that Congress was considering making major changes and/or cuts in the revenue-sharing program (see pages 90-91), hundreds of county representatives marched near the Capitol in late 1980 to show their support for continuation of the program.

"WELL, IF YOU FEEL SO LEFT OUT, WHY DON'T YOU JOIN ONE OF THOSE CITIZENS CONCERNED ABOUT SOMETHING GROUPS?"

Drawing by Whitney Darrow, Jr.; © 1968 The New Yorker Magazine, Inc.

groups are both reflections of that fact. While each of these types of organizations overlaps in many ways, there are three vital differences between them.

NOMINATIONS. Parties nominate candidates for office; pressure groups do *not*. As we noted on page 183, the making of nominations is *the* principal function of a political party. If a pressure group were to nominate candidates, it would, in effect, become a political party.

PRIMARY INTEREST. Parties are primarily interested in winning elections and maintaining control of government. Pressure groups are especially concerned with controlling or influencing the policies of government. That is, parties are primarily interested in public offices, while pressure groups are primarily interested in public policies.

SCOPE OF INTEREST. Parties are (and must be) concerned with the *general range* of public affairs. Pressure groups, however, are usually concerned *only* with those particular public questions that *directly* affect their members.

Scope of Pressure Groups. Pressure groups may have many thousands or even millions of members, or they may consist of only a handful of people. They may be long-established and permanent organizations or new and even temporary in char-

acter. But whatever the length of their membership rosters or the strength of their political muscle, they are found in virtually every field of human activity.

The largest number of pressure groups has been formed on the basis of economic interest. Many exist on a variety of other bases, however. Thus, many are formed out of a particular geographic area, such as the South, the Columbia River Basin, or the State of Ohio. Others are based upon a common cause or idea, such as prohibition, governmental reform, or civil rights. Still others exist to promote the welfare of certain groups, such as veterans, the aged, racial minorities, or the handicapped.

Most persons, even if they are not conscious of the fact, are members of several different pressure groups. Mr. Jones, who owns an automobile agency, for example, may belong to a car dealers' association, a veterans organization, the local chamber of commerce, a particular church, a parent-teacher association, and several other local, regional, and national organizations. Mrs. Jones may belong to some of these groups, as well, including the church and the parent-teacher association. And, she may be a member of still others, including a local voters league and the auxiliary of her husband's veterans organization. All of these are, in one degree or another, pressure

Case Study

The following table is drawn from data reported in several recent Gallup polls. It indicates, by age groups and also by the size of the community of residence, the percentage of poll respondents who knew certain political facts.

	Age			Size of Community				
	21 -29	30 -49	50 and Over	Under 2500	2500- 49,999	50,000- 499,999	500,000- 999,999	1,000,000 and over
Name of Representative in Congress	44	55	54	51	60	55	57	44
Name of State Senator	17	30	31	31	42	22	23	23
Name of State Representative	14	26	28	26	43	16	17	18
Name of Mayor	57	72	73	55	74	76	74	84
Name of County Clerk	18	30	32	44	49	20	11	8
Whether Representative in Congress Is a Republican or Democrat	54	63	64	59	68	62	62	60
Mean	34	46	47	45	56	42	41	40

■ Why are those persons in the 50-and-over age group and those who reside in communities in the 2500 to 49,999 population range apparently the best informed?

■ What other conclusions can you draw? Do you find any contradictions here?

groups, even though Mr. and Mrs. Jones may never think of them in that light. For example, churches often express views on such public issues as the regulation of drinking, curfew ordinances, and Sunday store closures. And, churches often seek to influence public policy on these matters, too. When they do so, they are pressure groups.[6]

---

[6] Not *every* group to which individuals belong can be properly described as a pressure group. Thus, a garden club or a chamber music group may or may not be one, depending on whether or not it attempts in some way to influence public policy. The garden club might, for example, attempt to persuade the city to upgrade the public parks—and it would thus become a pressure group. The most striking illustration of an unorganized interest in American politics is the consumer. All Americans are consumers, of course; but we have chosen to organize as *producers* rather than as consumers.

GROUPS BASED ON ECONOMIC INTERESTS. Most pressure groups in the United States are formed on the basis of *economic interests.* That is, they are formed on the basis of the manner in which men and women make their living and the ways in which they acquire and use the property they hold. Among those groups the most active, and certainly the most effective, are those representing business, labor, and agriculture.

BUSINESS GROUPS. Business has long looked to government for the promotion and protection of its interests. Recall that merchants, creditors, and property owners were the groups most responsible for the calling of the Constitutional Convention of 1787. The concept of the protective tariff was fought for and won in the earliest years of the Republic, and business interests have worked to maintain it ever since. One of the oldest active pressure groups is the United States Brewers' Association, created when Congress levied a tax on beer in 1862. The association was established to insure "the brewing trade that its interests be vigorously and energetically prosecuted before the legislative and executive departments."

A vast number of business associations operate at the national, State, and local levels today. The National Association of Manufacturers (NAM) and the Chamber of Commerce of the United States are among the most potent of them. Both organizations speak for the interests of business in general. The NAM does tend to represent the views of the larger industrial concerns, however. The Chamber of Commerce, on the other hand, tends to speak for the thousands of smaller businesses across the country and is organized into hundreds of local chambers.

Various segments of the business community also maintain their own specialized pressure groups, and their number is legion—*e.g.,* among hundreds of them, the American Trucking Association, Inc., the Southern States Industrial Council, the National Association of Electric Companies, the Association of American Railroads, and the National Association of Real Estate Boards.

Despite a common impression, groups based upon a particular economic interest do not always present a solid front in their attempts to influence public policy. In fact, the competition among them is often very intense. For example, the trucking industry regularly bends every effort to promote funds for federal aid for highway construction. But the railroads are less than happy with such "special favor" to their competition. At the same time, the railroads regard taxes on gasoline, oil, tires, and other "highway user levies" as valid and necessary sources of national revenue. But the

truckers take quite another view.

LABOR GROUPS. The interests of organized labor are also promoted by a host of pressure groups. The most potent of them is, of course, the AFL-CIO (the American Federation of Labor-Congress of Industrial Organizations). Its more than 16.6 million members belong to some 130 separate unions—such as the United Steel Workers, the United Shoe Workers, and the International Association of Machinists. Each of its constituent unions, like the AFL-CIO itself, is organized on a national, State, and local basis. There are also a number of powerful independent unions— that is, labor organizations not affiliated with the AFL-CIO. They include, for example, the Brotherhood of Locomotive Engineers, the International Brotherhood of Teamsters, and the United Mine Workers.

We shall come back to the subject of the organization and functions of labor unions later (pages 587–589). But for now notice that organized labor is relatively united in promoting such positions as higher minimum wages, the closed shop, and increased unemployment compensation coverage and benefits. Labor groups also generally unite in opposing such matters as "right to work" laws.

But, as with business and other groups, there are several areas in which labor opposes labor. For example, there are different points of view between "white collar" and "blue collar" workers and between skilled and unskilled union members. Sectional differences and interests arising out of the particular commodities that union members produce frequently split labor's forces, too. Thus, it is not uncommon to find labor groups opposing one another on such issue questions as higher or lower tariffs, public or private power developments, or subsidies for various transportation industries.

AGRICULTURAL GROUPS. Farm interests are served by a number of politically pow-

Pressured by mounting operating costs and rising prices for fuel, hundreds of farmers took part in a "Farmers March on Washington" in 1979, seeking to influence the National Government to take steps to resolve some of their problems.

erful associations. The most important are the National Grange, the American Farm Bureau Federation, and the National Farmers' Union. The Grange was established in 1867 and is the oldest and most "conservative" of the three major national farm organizations. The Farm Bureau, which dates back to 1920 and has some 1.8 million family-members, is the largest and generally the most effective of the three. It works closely with the so-called "farm bloc" in Congress, and it tends to favor governmental programs to promote agriculture more enthusiastically than does the Grange. The smaller Farmers' Union is more "liberal" than either of the older farm organizations and frequently disagrees with them. It generally supports programs designed to regulate the production and marketing of farm products.

A number of other agricultural groups—based upon the interests of the producers of such specific commodities as dairy products, grain, fruit, peanuts, livestock, cotton, wool, and corn—also operate as pressure groups. For example, the National Association of Wheat Growers, the American Cattlemen's Association, and the National Wool Growers Association each represents particular groups of farmers.

And, as with business and labor groups, various farm organizations sometimes find themselves at odds with one another. Thus, dairy farmers and cotton, corn, and soybean growers often compete with one another as each group attempts to influence State laws regulating the sale of margarine and similar products.

PROFESSIONAL GROUPS. The professions are generally organized for political purposes, too; but, most often, they are not nearly as influential as the business, labor, and farm groups. Among the several and most influential professional organizations are the American Medical Association, the National Education Association, and the American Bar Association. There are also hundreds of less well-known and less politically active professional groups, such as the American Society of Civil Engineers, the American Genetic Association, and the American Library Association. Much of the effort of professional groups is directed to such internal matters as the standards of the profession, the holding of professional meetings, and the publication of scholarly journals and other papers. But each organization, in varying degrees, functions as a pressure group bent on promoting the welfare of its members.

GROUPS BASED ON NON-ECONOMIC INTERESTS. There are many groups based upon the promotion of a particular cause or idea, the interests of a specific geographic region, and the welfare of such groups as veterans, the aged, racial minorities, and immigrants. Several of these organizations have a considerable amount of political muscle. Although they are essentially noneconomic in character, they often become very actively involved in public issue questions which are *distinctly* economic in character.

Among the many groups formed to promote a *cause* or an *idea* are such influen-

tial ones as the Women's Christian Temperance Union, a vocal advocate of prohibition; the American Civil Liberties Union, interested in the promoting and safeguarding of political and civil rights; and Common Cause, working for major changes in the political process and called by its supporters "the citizen's lobby." Another is the League of Women Voters of the United States, dedicated to stimulating more active participation in and greater public knowledge about governmental affairs. And the National Reclamation Association, the National Wildlife Federation, and the Sierra Club are all pledged to the cause of

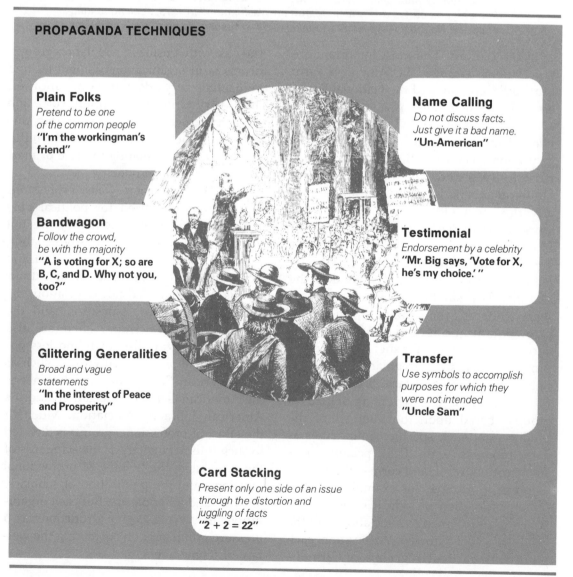

PROPAGANDA TECHNIQUES

Plain Folks
Pretend to be one of the common people
"I'm the workingman's friend"

Bandwagon
Follow the crowd, be with the majority
"A is voting for X; so are B, C, and D. Why not you, too?"

Glittering Generalities
Broad and vague statements
"In the interest of Peace and Prosperity"

Name Calling
Do not discuss facts. Just give it a bad name.
"Un-American"

Testimonial
Endorsement by a celebrity
"Mr. Big says, 'Vote for X, he's my choice.'"

Transfer
Use symbols to accomplish purposes for which they were not intended
"Uncle Sam"

Card Stacking
Present only one side of an issue through the distortion and juggling of facts
"2 + 2 = 22"

conservation and environmental protection.

Several pressure groups work to promote the *welfare* of certain segments of the population. Among the best organized and most powerful are the American Legion and the Veterans of Foreign Wars, both actively engaged in advancing the interests of the nation's veterans. Older Americans, Inc., is active in public policy areas related to the welfare of the aged, especially old-age pensions, medical care for the aged, and other retirement-related programs. Several organizations—for example, the National Association for the Advancement of Colored People, and the National Urban League—are closely concerned with governmental policies which are of special interest to blacks.

A number of church-related organizations attempt to influence public policy from the standpoint of their separate religious positions. Thus, many individual Protestants and their local and national churches work through the National Council of Churches; Roman Catholics maintain the National Catholic Welfare Conference, and Jewish communicants have the American Jewish Congress and B'nai B'rith's Anti-Defamation League.

Pressure Group Tactics. Because pressure groups are vitally concerned with influencing the formation of public policy, they operate (exert their "pressures") wherever public policy is made or influenced. This means, of course, that they are to be found at *all* levels of government in the United States. Although Lord Bryce's classic comment may be somewhat indelicate, it is quite descriptive: "Where the body is, there will the vultures be gathered."

PROPAGANDA AND PUBLIC OPINION. As difficult as it may be to determine, public opinion is the most significant long-term force in American politics. That is, over the long run, no public policy can be followed successfully without the support of a con-

siderable element within the population. Pressure groups are quite aware of this fact, of course. Because they are, they frequently seek to create a favorable—or at least a neutral—reception for their positions in the general public.

Pressure groups attempt to create the public attitudes they want through the use of *propaganda.*[7] Propaganda, much like public opinion, is a vague and somewhat inexact term. Its objective is to create a particular popular belief. That objective may be "good" or "bad," depending upon who assesses it. It may be factually true, false, or distorted. But as a *technique,* it is neither moral nor immoral; it is amoral. It does not employ objective logic; rather, it begins with a conclusion and proceeds to marshall the arguments that will support it. Propaganda and objective analysis sometimes arrive at the same conclusion, but their methods are vastly different. In short, propagandists are not teachers; they are advertisers, persuaders, brainwashers.

Propaganda techniques have been developed to a high level in the country—especially in the field of commercial advertising. In large measure, they depend for their success upon appeals to emotions and to preconceived prejudices. The major propagandistic techniques are summarized in the chart on the opposite page.

In opposing a policy, the talented propagandist seldom attacks its logic. Rather, name-calling is often employed. The skilled practitioner uses some uncomplimentary term such as "communist," "fascist," "extremist," or "radical." The policy supported is labeled with some term designed to evoke a favorable response—a

---

[7] The term has been a widely used part of the American political vocabulary since the 1930's. It is derived from the Latin verb *propagare*—to propagate, spread, disseminate. Almost certainly, it acquired its present-day shape, as a noun in our language, from the *Congregatio de Propaganda Fide*—the Congregation for Propagating the Faith, a missionary organization of the Roman Catholic Church, established by Pope Gregory XV in the 17th century.

glittering generality, such as "American," "sound," "fair," or "just."

Propagandists often use symbols in an attempt to transfer to their cause the favorable reactions those symbols can produce. For example, such symbols as Uncle Sam and the flag are frequently used to convey the idea that a particular policy is patriotic. Testimonials (supporting statements, endorsements) may be secured from famous personalities such as television entertainers and professional athletes to prompt a favorable response. They may identify their subject with "plain folks" through pictures and stories. As a last resort, propagandists may even utilize "card-stacking"—that is, presenting material selectively, attempting to make something appear to be that which, in fact, it is not.

The means by which propaganda is broadcast include the press, radio, television, movies, billboards, books, magazines, pamphlets, and speeches—in fact, every device of mass communication. Pressure groups frequently use them all. The more controversial a particular position is, the more necessary the propaganda campaign becomes—for competing interests will likely be conducting campaigns of their own.

ELECTION TACTICS.   We know that pressure groups and political parties are significantly different creatures (page 268). This does not mean, however, that pressure groups are indifferent either to parties or to election results. Indeed, quite the opposite is true. Pressure groups are very much aware that it is through parties that those who make public policy are selected and through them that the policy-making machinery is organized. And they recognize the fact that if people favorable to their special interests are chosen to office, their task is a much easier one than it would otherwise be. Thus, pressure groups often attempt to work within one or both of the major parties.

A few organizations are able to work actively to influence public policy and, at the same time, maintain a neutral position in relation to parties and their candidates. For example, the League of Women Voters has walked the tightrope of neutrality with considerable success for more than half a century. But such feats are relatively rare today.

Many pressure groups campaign actively for candidates partial to their views. Most groups prefer to operate "behind the scenes," but some of them do openly align themselves with and actively support one or the other of the major parties. Many contribute to the campaign funds of "good" candidates; and a few even contribute to the treasuries of both parties, just to play it safe. Occasionally, members of pressure groups work their way up in party organizations in order to advance the aims of their group.

Of course, the election tactics a pressure group uses may involve some very delicate questions and finely-made decisions. For example, if a group supports a Democratic candidate for the United States Senate, it may not want to help by attacking the Republican opponent. It may not because the Republican might stand a good chance of winning. Or the victorious Republican candidate for the House of Representatives or some other office may be offended by attacks upon a colleague even if sympathetic to the group's aims. The pressure group must always remember that its first concern is with the making of public policy; its interest in the election process is only secondary to that objective.

LOBBYING TACTICS.   Lobbying is usually defined as the process by which group pressures are brought to bear upon the legislative process. Certainly it is this—but it is also much more. Realistically, lobbying is the process by which group pressures are applied to all aspects of the public policy-making process. Lobbying occurs in legislative bodies, of course; and it frequently

Senior citizens from Michigan meet with their Senator, Don Riegle (standing). They have asked him to support a national health insurance bill.

has significant effects upon legislative action. But it also occurs in relation to administrative agencies, and on occasion even the courts.

What happens in a legislative body is often of vital concern to several different—and often competing—interests. The provisions of a particular measure, not to mention whether it will be passed or not, can be critically important to them. For example, a bill to regulate the sale of firearms and require licenses for all who own them excites many persons and groups. Those firms which make firearms, those which sell them, and those which produce or sell such related items as ammunition, targets, and hunting apparel have a clear stake in the bill's contents and its fate. So, too, do law enforcement agencies and peace officers, hunters, wildlife conservationists, and the members of the National Rifle Association and various civil rights organizations.

But, notice, public policy is made by more than the words in a statute. What happens *after* a law has been passed is often of vital concern to interest groups, too. How is a statute interpreted and how vigorously is it applied by the agency responsible for its enforcement? And what atti-

tude do the courts take if the statute is challenged on some legal ground? These questions demonstrate the point that pressure groups often have to carry their lobby efforts *beyond* the legislative arena—into one and sometimes several agencies in the executive branch and occasionally into the courts, as well.

Practically all of the more important organized interests in this country—business, labor, agriculture, the professions, veterans, the aged, churches, and a host of others—maintain *lobbyists* in Washington.[8]

Lobbyists themselves often prefer to be known by some other title—for example, "legislative counsel" or "public representative." But, whatever they call themselves, the lobbyists' major task is that of working for those matters of benefit to their clients and against those that may harm them.

---

[8] Of course, many lobbyists are also stationed in the various State capitals, particularly when the legislature is in session. The lobby is actually an ante-room or the main corridor or some other part of the capitol building to which the general public is admitted. The word has lent itself to the identification of those who attempt to influence the decisions of legislators and other policymakers, and to the activities of those who attempt to do so.

Senator Alan Cranston (D., Calif.) meets with children who testified as witnesses before his Labor and Human Resources Committee as part of a "Save the Children Day" observance.

The competent lobbyist is thoroughly familiar with government and its ways, with the facts of current political life, and with the techniques of "polite" persuasion. Some lobbyists are former members of Congress (or of a State legislature). They know the "legislative ropes" and have many intimate contacts among present-day members. Others are frequently lawyers, former journalists, public relations experts, or specialists in some field.

Lobbyists at work employ any number of techniques. They regularly attempt to persuade individual members to adopt their points of view. They see that pamphlets, reports, and other information favorable to their cause are placed in legislators' hands. Often, they offer testimony before committees. When a committee is considering a bill on agriculture, for example, representatives of the Grange, the Farm Bureau, and other farm organizations are certain to be asked or to request permission to present their views. The information a lobbyist provides is "expert"; but, of course, it is couched in terms favorable to the lobbyist's client.

Frequently, lobbyists bring pressure to bear through campaigns designed to create favorable public opinion. They may call upon their organizations to drum up support at the "grass-roots" level. They may urge that letters, post cards, and telegrams be sent by the "folks back home." A legislator's local newspaper may run an editorial urging what amounts to support for a lobbyist's position, and a delegation from the home district may even call upon their Representative in Washington. Favorable news stories, magazine articles, advertisements, endorsements by noted personalities, radio and television appeals, and many other weapons of publicity are all within the arsenal of the lobbyist.

The typical lobbyist of today is a far cry from those of an earlier day—and from those still found in many television portrayals, novels, and other pieces of fiction. The once fairly common practice of bribery and the heavy-handed uses of "wine, women, and song" are now virtually unknown. Most present-day lobbyists work in the open, and their major techniques come under the headings of friendliness, persuasion, and helpfulness.

Lobbyists are ready to buy lunches and

CONGRESSIONAL PARKING LOT

BIG BUSINESS   LABOR   DAIRY   MEDICAL

Garner in *Memphis Commercial Appeal*

dinners, to provide information, to write speeches, and to prepare bills in proper form. The food is good, the information usually quite accurate, the speeches forceful, and the bills well drawn. Lobbyists know that to behave otherwise—to falsify information, for example—would be to risk damage, and perhaps even the destruction, of their credibility and thus their effectiveness.

Lobbyists work hard to influence debate and the final vote in a legislative body. If they fail in one house they carry their fight to the other. If beaten there, too, they may turn their efforts to the executive branch in the hope of gaining some favorable action at that stage.[9] And, recall, they may carry their cause to the courts.

---

[9] Notice that various governmental agencies often act as pressure groups do in their relations with Congress or the State legislature. They do this, for example, when they press for appropriations or for or against a particular measure.

REGULATION OF LOBBYING. Lobbying abuses do occur now and then, of course. False or misleading testimony, unethical pressures, and even bribery are not completely unknown. But, again, instances of these shady tactics are uncommon today.

To keep lobbying within bounds, Congress enacted the Federal Regulation of Lobbying Act in 1946. Each of the States now has a somewhat similar statute.

The federal law requires lobbyists to register with the Clerk of the House and the Secretary of the Senate. More precisely, the law requires the registration of any person who is employed and of any organization which collects and spends money for the "principal purpose" of influencing legislative actions.

Individual lobbyists must disclose the names and addresses of their employers and the amounts of salary and expense monies they are paid for their services. In addition, they must file quarterly reports with the Clerk of the House listing all of the funds they have received and the purposes for which they were spent during the period. They must also report the names of any publications in which they cause articles or editorials to be printed.

Organizations covered by the law must also file quarterly reports with the Clerk of the House. In them, they must account for all of the funds they receive and all expenditures made. This accounting must include the names and addresses of all persons or groups who contributed $500 or more to them and of all to whom they paid $10 or more, and for what purpose.

The law also directs that all of the data reported is to be published at quarterly intervals in the *Congressional Record.* Any failure to comply with the law may lead to very stiff penalties: a fine of up to $10,000, a prison term of up to five years, and/or suspension of the right to lobby for a period of as long as three years.

The constitutionality of the law was attacked in the courts as a violation of the 1st Amendment's guarantees of freedom of speech, press, assembly, and petition. Although it was declared unconstitutional by a United States District Court, the Supreme Court upheld the law in 1954. In its opinion in the case (*United States* v. *Harriss*) the Court declared:

> Congress has not sought to prohibit these pressures. It has merely provided for a modicum of information from those who for hire attempt to influence legislation or who collect or spend funds for that purpose.

On balance, the statute has proved to be a quite inadequate one over the past 30 years—and, unfortunately, Congress has not been disposed to strengthen it. Its vague phrase "principal purpose" has provided a huge loophole through which many active organizations have purposefully avoided the registration requirement. They do this either on the grounds that lobbying is only "incidental" to their main objectives or that monies collected have been spent for "research" and "public information" rather than lobbying. Some of the groups that do register thereafter report no expenditures. No agency checks the accuracy of the reports which are filed and no public officials analyze or interpret them for public use. And, to compound the problem, Congress did not establish any agency to enforce the law. Lobbying aimed at executive agencies is not covered by the law, nor is testifying before congressional committees.

Thus far, over 15,000 registrations have been filed under the law, involving more than 8,000 different individuals and groups. Several hundred new filings are made each year. The records of the Clerk of the House also show that lobbyists now spend—or, at least, report the spending of—more than $5 million a year on their activities.

Value of Pressure Groups. Lobbying and other pressure group activities involve the expression of the views of organized groups. As such, they are a part of the democratic process. But just *how* valuable a part they are has long been debated.

Pressure groups, especially through their lobbyists, perform a distinct and necessary service. They provide for representation on the basis of *functional* interests rather than geographic areas. That is, they provide for the representation of interests which arise out of occupational and other economic or social factors.

Representation in Congress (and the State legislatures) is based upon geography, of course. But the interests which unite many persons and groups today are at least as much related to *how* they make a living as to *where* they live. Thus, the interests of a labor union member in Chicago may be much more like those of a person who works at the same type of job in Seattle than those of a business owner in Chicago or a farmer in another part of Illinois.

"SO FAR, MY MAIL IS RUNNING THREE TO ONE IN FAVOR OF MY POSITION."

Drawing by Robt. Day; © 1970 The New Yorker Magazine, Inc.

One's Representative and Senators in Washington can represent the interests of one's *local area* and State; but they may not be willing or able to represent an *economic* or *social* group. Pressure groups do provide this kind of representation—and this is especially why lobbyists are often referred to as members of "the third house of Congress."

The "third house" is certainly not a perfect mirror of the many and diverse interests out of which our society is composed, however. The strength of a pressure group is not a valid indication of the number of people it speaks for or the degree of popular support it may, or may not, enjoy. Nor is it a valid indication of its relative importance to the nation's welfare.

Many of the most effective lobbies in Washington speak for only a small fraction of the American people. Nearly all segments of the business community are well represented. So, too, is organized labor. But the great mass of consumers is not. Thus, who speaks for those who travel on trains and in airplanes against those who own or those who work for the railroads and the airlines? Who represents the interests of those who use electricity against the interests of the owners of the utilities or those who work in the electric power industry? Public agencies—as the Interstate Commerce Commission, the Federal Aviation Administration, or the Federal Trade Commission—do sometimes support the general consumer interest. But these agencies are themselves the targets of pressure group tactics, and sometimes they lose sight of the "public interest."

The whole point here is that the representation of special interests is valuable; but so, too, is the representation of the general public interest. And sometimes the general public interest tends to get lost in the competition between the many special interests.

If there is a solution to the problem of representing the general public interest, it would seem to be with the voters at the ballot box. In the final analysis, public policies are made by the elected representatives of the people. If the voters perform their task as the democratic system intends they should, the voice of the public interest should be heard with controlling force.

SUMMARY

In this country we believe that the primary task of government is that of translating the public will into public policy. Both public opinion and pressure groups are vital aspects of the process by which that is accomplished.

Public opinion is a vague and somewhat ambiguous term. As used here, it refers to a view pertaining to a matter of public policy held by a significant portion of the population. Many "publics" hold separate "opinions" on nearly all public issues. Public opinion arises out of all of the factors which influence thought and action; but some factors have a more substantial effect than others. The most potent of them appear to be the family, school, church, political party, labor union or business association, and other organized groups to which an individual belongs, and the mass media.

The general content of public opinion may be determined by considering the many and varied means by which it is expressed. Determining the extent and intensity with which a given opinion is held is far more difficult; for this purpose we must rely on such rough indicators as elections, the claims of pressure groups, the press, radio, and television, citizen contacts with public agencies and officials, and public opinion polls.

Pressure groups are organizations composed of persons who share one or more opinions or objectives and seek to promote their common interest by influencing the making and content of public policy. They overlap with political parties in several ways, but they do not nominate candidates. They are chiefly concerned with affecting policies rather than controlling offices, and each of them is primarily concerned with one or a few specific areas of public policy rather than the total range of public affairs.

Most pressure groups arise out of an economic interest; among them, the most potent are those representing business, labor, agriculture, and the professions. Pressure groups are also formed on several other bases, including sectionalism, racial and religious factors, a cause, and the welfare of a given group.

Pressure groups apply their pressures wherever public policy is made or can be influenced. They do so by attempting to influence public opinion (especially with propaganda), the use of electioneering techniques, and lobbying. They are a means for the expression of views in the democratic process and provide an avenue of functional representation. But all interests are not equally represented by pressure groups. The public interest is, at best, insufficiently represented.

Concept Development

Questions for Review

1. What is the primary task of government in the United States?

2. Who comprises the "public" upon whose opinion public policy is to be based in this country?

3. What three elements are involved in the term "opinion," as it occurs in the phrase "public opinion"?

4. As the term is used in this book, what is "public opinion"?

5. Out of what factors is public opinion formulated?

6. In what ways do many of these factors interact upon one another?

7. Why are opinion leaders significant in opinion formulation?

8. Why must public opinion be measured?

9. How may the general content of public opinion be determined?

10. Why are election results seldom accurate measures of public opinion?

11. Through what other devices may public opinion be measured?

12. What is the basic difficulty with the "straw vote" as an indicator of public opinion?

13. What is the basic thesis of scientific sampling?

14. Why do pressure groups exist?

15. What are the significant differences between political parties and pressure groups?

16. The largest number of pressure groups arise on the basis of what common interest?

17. Why do pressure groups attempt to influence public opinion?

18. What is propaganda?

19. Why do pressure groups participate in the election process?

20. Why is it erroneous to conceive of lobbying only with reference to the legislative process?

For Further Inquiry

1. Alexander Hamilton once wrote: "All governments, even the most despotic, depend, in a great degree, on public opinion." What did he mean? Do you agree?

2. In what respects might one argue that public opinion polls pose a threat to the continued success of representative democracy?

3. In what particular ways can the typical citizen best go about the business of becoming as fully informed as possible in the realm of public affairs?

4. Why may political parties and pressure groups be described as "unofficial agencies of politics"? Are they more vital to the success of democracy than such institutions as federalism, separation of powers, and checks and balances?

5. How does the general structure of the American political system contribute to the strength and importance of pressure groups in our politics?

6. Writing in the *North American Review* in 1878, Horatio Seymour observed: "It is necessary for those who have charge of public affairs to learn what men have in their minds, what views they hold, at what ends they aim. . . . The follies of fanatics frequently teach wisdom better than the words of the wise." How would you expand upon this comment? Who was Seymour?

7. Do you agree with the observation that pressure groups are inevitable in a political system such as ours? Why?

8. Can you cite an example of a government in the United States either *influencing* or *creating* public opinion (as opposed to responding to it)? Do you think this is a proper function of government?

9. Why is the great mass of consumers *not* well represented in Washington, D.C., while nearly all segments of the business community *are*?

Suggested Activities

1. Invite a local newspaper editor to discuss with the class the role the paper plays in relation to public opinion.

2. Invite a representative of a local pressure group to describe to the class the group's organization and its aims and methods.

3. Conduct a sample poll on a current local issue, using scientific sampling methods as best you can.

4. Write a report based upon an analysis of a newspaper editorial's use of propaganda techniques.

5. Stage a debate or class forum on one of the following questions: (a) *Resolved,* That Congress should enact a new regulation-of-lobbying act to require that *all* professional lobbyists be publicly registered; (b) *Resolved,* That lobbying be prohibited except in direct connection with the legislative process.

6. Invite a lobbyist, local legislator, or other knowledgeable person to discuss the subject of group pressures on the political process.

7. Attempt to list the number of ways in which your own behavior and attitudes are influenced by the propaganda efforts of both public and private agencies.

Suggested Reading

Barone, Michael, *et al., The Almanac of American Politics.* Dutton, 1981.

Bennett, W. Lance, *Public Opinion and American Politics.* Harcourt Brace Jovanovich, 1980.

Campbell, Bruce A., *The American Electorate: Attitudes and Action.* Holt, Rinehart and Winston, 1979.

Comstock, George, *Television in America.* Sage, 1980.

Erikson, Robert S., *et. al., American Public Opinion: Its Origins, Content, and Impact.* Wiley, 2nd ed., 1980.

Graber, Doris, *Mass Media and Congress.* Congressional Quarterly Press, 1980.

Halloway, Harry and George, John, *Public Opinion: Coalitions, Elites, and Masses.* St. Martin's Press, 1979.

Ippolito, Denis S. and Walker, Thomas G., *Political Parties, Interest Groups, and Public Policy.* Prentice-Hall, 1980.

Nimmo, Dan and Rivers, William, *Watching American Politics.* Longman, 1981.

Saldich, Anne R., *Electronic Democracy: The Impact of Television on the American Political Process.* Praeger, 1979.

Washington Lobby. Congressional Quarterly Press, 3rd ed., 1979.

CONGRESS: THE FIRST BRANCH

The American system of government—the ways in which it is organized, the ways in which it is controlled by the people, and the ways in which it functions—is, as we said on the very first page, what this book is all about. To this point, through 11 chapters and for more than 280 pages, we have focused on that theme in a primary sense. That is, we have considered our governmental system in terms of its origins and development, the fundamental principles upon which it is based, and the basic means by which it is limited and by which it may be made to do the bidding of the people.

Now we turn our attention to the structure of the Federal Government, to that vast and complex mechanism through which the governmental system operates at the national level. Over the course of the next 16 chapters and for some 390 pages, we shall examine the organization, powers, procedures, and functions of each of its three great branches.

We begin our examination with the Congress—in part because it is the branch of the National Government for which the Constitution first provides. But we do so, too, because the Congress is, in James Madison's phrase, "the First Branch of the Government" for other reasons as well. As the legislative body for the nation it is the central institution of our representative democracy. Its members are chosen *by* the people and they are chosen to *represent* the people; it is, both constitutionally and practically, the organ of government *closest* to the people. And it is also the body to which the Constitution gives the bulk of the powers held by the

National Government. The executive and the judicial branches each play an important part in the making of the public policies of the United States; but it is to the Congress that the Constitution assigns major responsibility for the performance of that supremely important task.

"Anyone who is unfamiliar with what Congress actually does and how it does it, with all of its duties and all of its occupations, with all of its devices of management and resources of power," wrote Woodrow Wilson, "is very far from a knowledge of the constitutional system in which we live." The next three chapters are devoted to an attempt to satisfy Mr. Wilson's demand.

The Congress exists and it plays its vital role within a framework established by the Constitution, of course—*and* one established, as well, by a myriad of legislative statutes, rules, traditions, and usages. We must look, and in some detail, at its structure and organization, at its complicated modes of operation, and at both its legislative and its nonlegislative powers. If at times the detail seems overwhelming, be patient and determined—for, again in Wilson's words: "Like a vast picture thronged with figures of equal prominence and crowded with elaborate and obtrusive details, Congress is hard to see satisfactorily and appreciatively in a single view and from a single standpoint. Its complicated form and diversified structure confuse the vision and conceal the system which underlies its composition. It is too complex to be understood without an effort, without a careful and systematic process of analysis."

12

The Congress

■ Why is the legislative power of such pivotal importance in democratic government?

■ Does the concept of representative government require that legislators be chosen by popular vote?

■ On which of these bases should members of Congress cast their votes: the views of a majority of their constituents or their own informed judgment?

A responsible, responsive, and effective legislative body is an indispensable necessity to democratic government.

In the absence of such an agency, "talk" of democratic government is only that. Nearly all governments in the world today maintain elected assemblies of some kind. But many of them are shams, facades to mask the real location and exercise of the public-policy-making power. The Supreme Soviet in the USSR stands as a prime example. Its members are chosen by popular vote, but in elections in which no opposition candidates are permitted. It observes many of the procedures of democratic assemblies, but its members are not there to exercise independent judgment. Rather, they meet to be told and to approve—not to propose, argue, and decide.

In the American democratic system, Congress is the legislative branch of the National Government. Its basic function is to make law. It, then, is charged with *the* basic governmental function in a democratic system: that of translating the public will into public policy in the form of law.

How profoundly important the Framers considered that function to be, can be seen in the fact that the *first* and the lengthiest of the Articles of the Constitution is devoted to it. Article I, Section 1 reads:

All legislative powers herein granted shall be vested in a Congress of the United States, which shall consist of a Senate and House of Representatives.

A rare photograph, taken during President Lincoln's first inauguration, shows the Capitol's dome under construction in 1861. (It wasn't until 1863 that work on this dome was completed, replacing a smaller dome made of wood and sheathed in copper.) During the Civil War, Union troops were sometimes quartered in the adjoining Senate and House chambers, as well as in the rotunda, located beneath the dome.

Bicameralism. The Constitution immediately establishes a *bicameral* Congress—that is, one composed of two houses; and it does so for a number of reasons:

Historically, the British Parliament, with which all of the Framers and most other Americans were quite familiar, had consisted of two houses for nearly 500 years. Most of the colonial assemblies, and all but two of the State legislatures in 1787, were also bicameral.[1]

Practically, a two-chambered legislature was dictated by the compromise struck between the Virginia and New Jersey Plans at the Philadelphia Convention. By design, a bicameral Congress reflects federalism: The States are represented equally in the Senate and in terms of their populations in the House.

Theoretically, the Framers favored two houses in order that one might act as a check on the actions of the other. The leading authority on the framing of the Constitution reports:

Thomas Jefferson, who possessed great faith in "the voice of the people," was in France when the Constitution was framed. Upon his return, while taking breakfast with Washington, he opposed the two-body form of legislature, and was disposed to twit Washington about it. At this time Jefferson poured his coffee from his cup into his saucer. Washington asked him why he did so. "To cool it," he replied. "So," said Washington, "we will pour legislation into the Senatorial saucer to cool it."[2]

Some argue that the equal representation of the States in the Senate ought to be scrapped as undemocratic.[3] They frequently cite the two extremes to make their case: Alaska has the smallest population today, only some 420,000 residents. California, on the other hand, now has a population of more than 22 million. Yet, each State has two Senators.

---

[1] Only Georgia and Pennsylvania had had wide experience with *unicameral* colonial and State legislatures. Georgia adopted bicameralism in 1789 and Pennsylvania in 1790. Among the 50 States today, only Nebraska (since 1937) has a unicameral legislature.

[2] Max Farrand, *The Framing of the Constitution.* New Haven: Yale University Press, 1913, p. 74.

[3] The prospects for any such change are so slim as to be nonexistent. Article V of the Constitution provides, in part: ". . . that no State, without its consent, shall be deprived of its equal suffrage in the Senate." In the face of this, the impossibilities of securing a change are obvious.

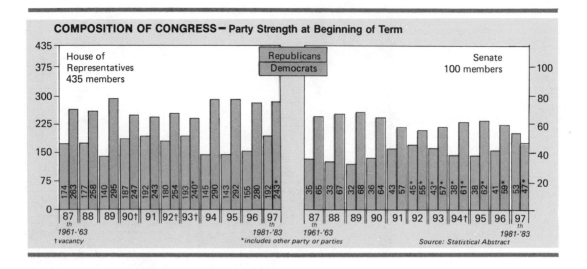

COMPOSITION OF CONGRESS — Party Strength at Beginning of Term

House of Representatives 435 members

Republicans
Democrats

Senate 100 members

House: 87th 1961-'63 | 88 | 89 | 90† | 91 | 92† | 93† | 94 | 95 | 96 | 97th 1981-'83

174 263 | 177 258 | 140 295 | 187 247 | 192 243 | 180 254 | 193 240* | 145 290 | 143 292 | 155 280 | 192 243*

† vacancy   *includes other party or parties

Senate: 87th 1961-'63 | 88 | 89 | 90 | 91 | 92 | 93 | 94† | 95 | 96 | 97th 1981-'83

35 65 | 33 67 | 32 68 | 36 64 | 43 57 | 45* 55* | 43* 57* | 38* 61* | 38 62* | 41 59* | 53 47*

Source: Statistical Abstract

Those who argue against State equality in the Senate ignore a large and critical fact: The Senate was very purposefully created as a body in which the States would be represented as co-equal members and partners in the Federal Union. And recall, had not the States been equally represented in the Senate there might well never have been a Constitution.

Terms of Congress. Each *term* of Congress lasts two years[4] and is numbered consecutively from the first term, which began on March 4, 1789. The date for the commencing of each term was reset by the 20th Amendment in 1933 and is now "noon on the 3d day of January" of every odd-numbered year. Thus, the term of the 97th Congress began at noon on January 3, 1981, and will end at noon on January 3, 1983.

Sessions of Congress. There are two *regular sessions* to each term of Congress—that is, one each year. Section 2 of the 20th Amendment provides that:

The Congress shall assemble at least once in every year, and such meeting shall begin at noon on the 3d day of January, unless they shall by law appoint a different day.

Congress adjourns each regular session as it sees fit. Before World War II a typical session ran for perhaps four or five months. But the many and pressing issues since then have forced Congress to remain in session through most of each year. The Constitution forbids either house to adjourn *sine die*—i.e., finally, ending a session—without the consent of the other. Article I, Section 5, Clause 4 reads in part:

Neither House . . . shall, without consent of the other, adjourn for more than three days, nor to any other place than that in which the two Houses shall be sitting.[5]

---

[4] Article I, Section 2, Clause 1 dictates a two-year term for Congress by providing that Representatives shall be chosen "every second year."

[5] Article II, Section 3 empowers the President to adjourn a session, but *only* when the two houses cannot agree upon a date for adjournment. No President has ever been called to exercise this power. The Legislative Reorganization Act of 1946 requires each regular session of Congress to adjourn no later than July 31—unless Congress should decide otherwise or a national emergency exists. But Congress has met this deadline only twice in the past 30 years, in 1952 and 1956. Both houses recess for brief periods during a session. The "spring recess" of about ten days in April has been a regular occurrence for several years. A "Labor Day recess," of about two weeks in election years and a month in the off years, now appears to be a permanent feature, too.

Special Sessions. Only the President may call special sessions of Congress.[6] Only 26 such sessions have ever been held. The most recent one was called by President Truman in 1948—to consider a number of anti-inflation and welfare measures. The fact that Congress now meets in nearly year-round sessions obviously reduces the likelihood of special sessions—and also diminishes the importance of the President's power to call one.

The House of Representatives

Size. The House of Representatives is the larger of the two chambers of Congress. Its exact size—today, 435 members—is not fixed by the Constitution. Rather, the Constitution provides that the total number of seats, however many that may be, shall be *apportioned* among the States on the basis of their respective populations.[7]

Each State is guaranteed at least one seat in the House, regardless of its population. Today (1981), six States—Alaska, Delaware, Nevada, North Dakota, Vermont, and Wyoming—have only one Representative apiece.

The District of Columbia, Guam, the Virgin Islands, and American Samoa are represented by a Delegate, and Puerto Rico by a Resident Commissioner. Although they are not *members* of the House, each is accorded the salary and privileges of one—but does not have the right to vote.

Terms. The Constitution provides that "Representatives shall be . . . chosen every second year"[8]—that is, for two-year terms. This relatively short term is purposefully intended to make the House more immediately responsive to popular pressures than the Senate. As all of the 435 seats in the House go before the voters at each biennial election, the entire body is reconstituted every two years.

Reapportionment. The Constitution directs Congress to *reapportion* the seats in the House—that is, redistribute them among the several States—following a census to be taken every 10 years.[9]

Until a first census could be taken, the Constitution set the temporary size of the House at 65 seats. That figure remained in effect for the 1st and 2nd Congresses (1789-1793). The Census of 1790 put the nation's population at 3,929,214 persons. That was a far larger number than the Framers had anticipated. And that first census also indicated that the Framers had made some very poor guesses about the number of persons living in each of the 13 States. So, in 1792, Congress increased the size of the House to 106 members.

As the nation's population grew, and as the number of States increased, so did the size of the House: to 142 seats after the Census of 1800, to 186 after the Census of 1810, and so on.[10] By 1912—following the Census of 1910 and the admissions of Arizona and New Mexico—the House had grown to 435 seats.

With the Census of 1920, Congress found itself faced with an extraordinary and painful dilemma. The House had long since grown too large for effective floor action. To increase its size still further would only compound the difficulty. Yet, if the House were to be reapportioned without such an increase, some States would have to lose seats if each State were to be represented on the basis of its population. But Congress was unable to find a satisfactory solution to the problem. So, despite the

---

[6] Article II, Section 3 provides that the President may "convene both Houses or either of them" in a special session. The Senate has been called into special session alone on 46 occasions, to consider treaties and appointments; the House has never been called alone.

[7] Article I, Section 2, Clause 3.

[8] Article I, Section 2, Clause 1.

[9] Article I, Section 2, Clause 3.

[10] Except after the Census of 1840, when it was decreased from 242 to 232 seats.

Constitution's command, nothing was done. There was *no* reapportionment on the basis of the Census of 1920.

THE REAPPORTIONMENT ACT OF 1929. With the approach of the Census of 1930, Congress moved to avoid a repetition of its earlier lapse. It did so with the passage of the Reapportionment Act of 1929, which provides for what may be called an "automatic reapportionment." The law, with the few amendments made to it since 1929, now provides that:

(1) The "permanent" size of the House of Representatives shall be 435 members. Of course, that figure is "permanent" only so long as Congress decides not to change it. (When Alaska and then Hawaii were admitted to the Union in 1959, each was given one seat in the House—thus, membership rose to 437. But the increases were only temporary. In admitting the two

States Congress declared that the size should revert to 435 after the Census of 1960—that is, with the elections of 1962.)

(2) Following each census, the Census Bureau is to determine the number of seats to which each State is entitled according to its population.

(3) When the Census Bureau's plan is available, the President is to send it to Congress via a special message.

(4) If, within 60 days of its receipt from the President, neither house rejects the Census Bureau's plan, it becomes effective.

The scheme set out in the 1929 law has worked quite well through the past five reapportionments—and most recently in 1971. The next one, drawn from the 1980 census, is slated this year (1981). The arrangement leaves with Congress its constitutional responsibility to apportion the seats in the House, but gives to the Census

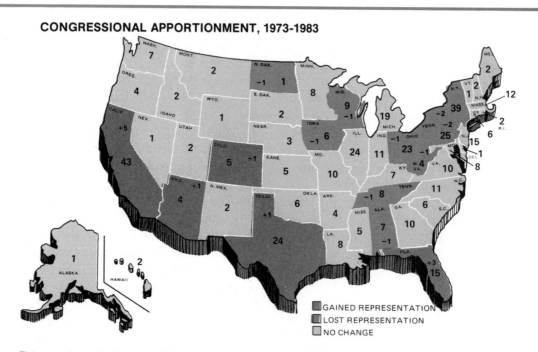

CONGRESSIONAL APPORTIONMENT, 1973-1983

This map shows the changes in State representation due to the reapportionment of the House after the 1970 Census, and effective from January 3, 1973 to January 3, 1983. Large numbers = State's seats in the House; small numbers = seats gained or lost. The next apportionment, following the 1980 Census, will occur in 1981 and become effective with the congressional elections in 1982.

When this print was made in 1848, the House Chamber seated 236 Representatives from the then 30 States. Today, it seats 435 members from 50 States.

Bureau the mechanical chores (and political blame) involved in the task.

Today (1981), each House seat represents an average of some 500,000 persons.

Election. The Constitution commands that all persons a State permits to vote for members of the "most numerous branch" of its own legislature are qualified to vote in congressional elections.[11] It also declares that:

> The times, places, and manner of holding [congressional] elections . . . , shall be prescribed in each State by the legislature thereof: but the Congress may at any time, by law, make or alter such regulations. . . .[12]

In 1872 Congress declared that congressional elections should be held on the same day in every State—on the Tuesday following the first Monday in November of each even-numbered year.[13] The same law declared that Representatives be chosen by written or printed ballots. Voting machines were sanctioned in 1899.

VACANCIES. According to the Constitution, a vacancy in a House seat may be filled in only one way: by a special election, which may be called only by the governor of the State involved.[14]

DISTRICTS. For more than half a century Congress left to each State the question of whether its Representatives should be chosen from districts within the State or by the general ticket system. Most of the States established congressional districts, with the voters in each district electing one member of the House. Several States, however, employed the *general ticket* system. Under that arrangement, all of a State's seats in the House were filled *at-large*—that

---

[11] Article I, Section 2, Clause 1; see page 212.

[12] Article I, Section 4, Clause 1; see pages 249–250.

[13] Congress has made an exception for Alaska, which may, if it chooses, hold its elections in October. To date, however, Alaskans have gone to the polls on the same November date as voters in each of the other 49 States. Through 1958 Congress permitted Maine to hold its congressional elections in September, but an amendment to the Maine Constitution now provides that the State's congressional and other elections are to be held on the regular November date. Maine's early voting in congressional (and presidential) elections gave rise to the oft-recited, but not always accurate, comment: "As Maine goes, so goes the Nation."

[14] Article I, Section 2, Clause 4.

THE GERRY-MANDER!

ALL that we can learn of the natural history of this remarkable animal, is contained in the following learned treatise, published in the newspapers of March, 1812, embellished by a drawing, which is pronounced by all competent judges, to be a most accurate likeness.

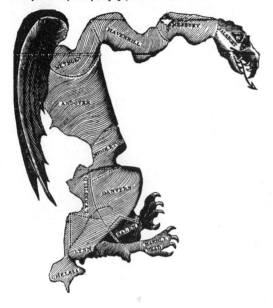

This 1812 drawing of a gerrymandered district in Massachusetts is discussed in some detail in footnote 16 at the bottom of this page.

is, representatives were chosen by all of the voters in the *entire* State.

The general ticket system was grossly unfair. Under it, a party with a plurality in the State, no matter how slight, could elect all of the State's Representatives in Congress. Congress finally eliminated the general ticket arrangement in 1842. It did so by providing that thereafter all seats in the House of Representatives were to be filled from districts within the State.[15] And, it made each State legislature responsible for the drawing of the congressional districts within its own State.

The 1842 law also required that each district be composed of "contiguous territory." In 1872 Congress added the command that the districts contain "as nearly as practicable an equal number of inhabitants." And in 1901 it directed that the districts be of "compact territory."

These requirements of contiguity, population equality, and compactness were often disregarded by the States, and Congress made no serious effort to enforce them. They were omitted from the Reapportionment Act of 1929; and in 1932 the Supreme Court held (in *Wood* v. *Broom*) that they had thus been repealed. Historically, then—and notably since 1929—many districts have been of very peculiar geographic shapes. And in many of the States they have also been of widely varying populations.

GERRYMANDERING. Districts which on a map appear much like a shoestring, a dumbbell, or the letter Y—or some other odd form—have generally been *gerrymandered*.[16] That is, they have been drawn to the advantage of the party or faction in power. Gerrymandering can be, and often is, accomplished in several ways. One way, for example, is by collecting as many of the minority party's voters as possible in one district, thus leaving the other districts comfortably safe for the ruling party. Or, the same end can be accomplished by drawing the districts to spread the minority party's voters as thinly as possible through all of the districts.

POPULATION VARIATIONS. Through much of our history, congressional districts in most States have varied widely in terms

---

[15] Except, of course, in States with but one Representative; in those States the one seat is filled at-large. Under the Reapportionment Act of 1929, whenever a State *gains* one or more seats and the legislature does not redistrict to account for the additional representation, the new seat or seats *must* be filled at-large until such time as the legislature performs its duty. And, the Act provides that whenever a State *loses* one or more seats after a census, *all* the remaining seats must be filled at-large if the legislature fails to redistrict.

---

[16] The practice takes its name from Elbridge Gerry (1744–1814). In 1812, while Gerry was governor of Massachusetts, his supporters in the legislature redrew the State's legislative districts to favor the Democratic-Republicans. It is said that a noted artist added a head, wings, and claws to Essex County on a district map which hung over the desk of a Federalist editor. "That will do for a salamander!" he said. "Better say Gerrymander," the editor growled.

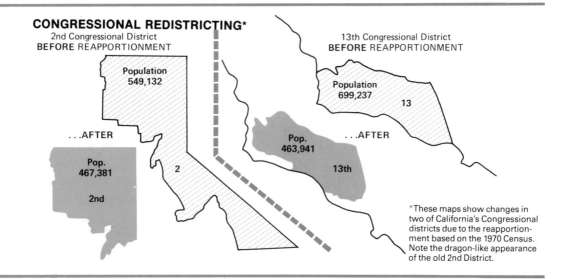

CONGRESSIONAL REDISTRICTING*
2nd Congressional District
BEFORE REAPPORTIONMENT

Population
549,132

...AFTER

Pop.
467,381

2nd

2

13th Congressional District
BEFORE REAPPORTIONMENT

Population
699,237   13

Pop.
463,941   ...AFTER

13th

*These maps show changes in
two of California's Congressional
districts due to the reapportionment based on the 1970 Census.
Note the dragon-like appearance
of the old 2nd District.

of population. For example, the 1960 Census showed Michigan's 12th District (the Western Peninsula) to be the least populous in the nation, with only 177,431 residents. Yet, the districts in and around Detroit were among the nation's largest (the 16th had 802,994 residents, the 18th had 690,259, and the 7th had 664,556). In Texas, at the same time, the 5th District (Dallas) included 951,527 persons, but the neighboring 4th District had only 216,371 residents.

Obviously, the State legislatures were responsible for this condition. In several States the legislature gerrymandered the districts on a strictly partisan basis—and, in the process, produced wide variations in population. In most States, however, the legislature did so on behalf of the State's *rural* interests—for, until quite recently, the typical State legislature has been controlled by the less populous, over-represented rural areas of the State.[17]

[17] The long-standing pattern of rural over-representation and urban under-representation in the State legislatures has largely disappeared—as a consequence of the Supreme Court's enunciation of the "one-man, one-vote" rule. In the leading case, *Reynolds* v. *Sims* (1964), the Court held that *both* houses of a State's legislature must be apportioned on the basis of population equality. See Chapter 29.

WESBERRY v. SANDERS, 1964. Suddenly, and quite dramatically, the traditional patterns of wide population variation and of rural over-representation changed in the 1960's. In State after State congressional district lines were redrawn to provide districts containing approximately equal numbers of persons.

This abrupt change came as a consequence of a 1964 decision by the Supreme Court. In *Wesberry* v. *Sanders* the Court held, 6-3, that the population variations among Georgia's congressional districts were so great as to violate the Constitution.

In reaching its historic decision, the Court noted that Article I, Section 2 declares that Representatives shall be chosen "by the people of the several States" and shall be "apportioned among the several States . . . according to their respective numbers." These words the Court held, especially when viewed in the light of what the Founders intended, mean that:

. . . as nearly as practicable one man's vote in a congressional election is to be worth as much as another's.

And the Court added:

While it may not be possible to draw congressional districts with mathematical precision, that is no excuse for ignoring our Constitution's plain objective of making equal representation for equal numbers of people the fundamental goal for the House of Representatives. That is the high standard of justice and common sense which the Founders set for us.

The results of the Court's decision were immediate and dramatic. Legislatures in State after State drew new districting plans to meet the new "one-man, one-vote" standard. Indeed, over half of the States had taken some action in the matter by the time of the 1966 congressional elections, and more redistricting followed.

The Supreme Court has refined the focus of its original decision in several later cases. Thus, in *Kirkpatrick* v. *Preisler,* 1969, it rejected a plan drawn by the Missouri legislature in which no district varied from the average population for all districts in the State by more than 3.1 percent. The Court held that any variation, no matter

"THUMBS OFF!"

© 1964 by Herblock, from *Straight Herblock* (Simon and Schuster, 1964)

how slight, had to be justified, that the State must "make a good faith effort to achieve precise mathematical equality"— and that Missouri had not. And the Court repeated that holding in *White* v. *Weiser* in 1973—a case where the variation between the largest and smallest of the districts in Texas was only 4.1 percent. Quite clearly, the Court will not accept such traditional reasons for variations as political boundaries, geographic features, compactness, or population trends or forecasts.

The importance of the "one-man, one-vote" decisions, in terms of their effects on the makeup of the House, on public policy, and on electoral politics in general, is hard to overstate. The nation's cities and suburbs now speak with a much stronger voice in Congress than ever before. *But,* notice the Court has ruled *only* on the matter of population equality. It has done nothing to prevent a legislature from drawing congressional districts in accord with the principle of "one-man, one-vote" while, at the same time, gerrymandering the State to favor one faction or party over any or all others.

Qualifications. The Constitution demands that a Representative be at least 25 years of age, have been a citizen for at least seven years, and be an inhabitant of the State from which he or she is chosen.[18]

Political custom, not the Constitution, dictates that a Representative also reside in the district. The district custom dates from colonial times and is based on the feeling that a Representative should be thoroughly familiar with the locale and its problems. It often means, notice, that members of Con-

---

[18] Article I, Section 2, Clause 2. Article I, Section 6, Clause 2 further provides that neither a Senator nor Representative "shall, during the time for which he was elected, be appointed to any civil office under the authority of the United States, which shall have been created, or the emoluments whereof shall have been increased, during such time; and no person holding any office under the United States [a federal office] shall be a member of either House during his continuance in office."

gress are regarded by many of their constituents as "errand boys"; see page 296. Some claim that the district custom also means that the voters cannot always select the best possible person for the job. Whatever the merits of the custom, it is rare that one who does not live in a district is chosen to represent it.

The Constitution makes the House "the judge of the elections, returns, and qualifications of its own members."[19] Thus, when the right of a member-elect to be seated is occasionally challenged, the House itself has the power to decide the matter. Challenges are rarely upheld.

The House may refuse to seat (*exclude*) a member-elect by majority vote. It may also "punish its own members for disorderly behavior" by majority vote, and "with the concurrence of two-thirds, expel a member."[20]

Historically, the House has viewed its power to judge the qualifications of any member-elect as the power to impose additional, informal qualifications. But in 1969, in *Powell* v. *McCormack,* the Supreme Court held that the House was "without power to exclude . . . from its membership" any member-elect who meets the constitutionally prescribed standards of age, citizenship, and residence.[21]

The House has expelled only four of its members—three for their "support of re-

bellion" in 1861 and Michael Myers (D., Pennsylvania) for bribery in 1980. Myers was ousted after his court conviction for taking a $50,000 bribe from undercover FBI agents who had posed as the representatives of an oil-rich Arab sheikh.

Punishments for "disorderly behavior" are infrequent, but not nearly so rare as expulsions. The most recent case occurred in 1980 when the House voted to "censure" Charles H. Wilson (D., California). He was disciplined for financial misconduct. The House found that Wilson had converted some $25,000 in campaign funds to his own use and had accepted $10,500 in "gifts" from a man with a direct interest in a matter before the House. (Prior to the censure vote, Wilson was defeated for renomination in the primaries and he is no longer a member of Congress.)

The Senate

Size. The Senate is a much smaller body than the House. It "shall be composed of two Senators from each State," declares the Constitution.[22] As there are now 50 States, there are, of course, 100 Senators.

Election. Until the adoption of the 17th Amendment in 1913, Senators were chosen by the several State legislatures.[23] But, from 1914 on, they have been chosen by the people every other November. Newly elected Senators take office when the new Congress assembles in January.

Each Senator is elected from the State-at-large. All persons whom the State permits to vote for members of "the most numerous branch" of its legislature are qualified to vote in Senate elections.

---

[19] Article I, Section 5, Clause 1.

[20] Article I, Section 5, Clause 2.

[21] The House had over the years excluded several members-elect on extra-constitutional grounds. Thus, in 1900 it refused to seat Brigham H. Roberts of Utah because he was a practicing polygamist. The late Representative Adam Clayton Powell of New York, re-elected to a 12th term in 1966, was barred in 1967. A special committee had recommended that Powell be seated but then be censured for "gross misconduct." It found that he had misused public funds, had defied the courts of his State, and was "contemptuous" in refusing to cooperate with the committee's investigation of him. The House voted instead to exclude him. The Court held, 7-1, that, as Powell had been "duly elected by the voters of the 18th Congressional District of New York and was not ineligible to serve under any provision of the Constitution, the House was without power to exclude him from its membership."

[22] Article I, Section 3, Clause 1; 17th Amendment. Only one Senator is elected from a State at any one election, except when the other Senate seat has been vacated by death, resignation, or expulsion. The 17th Amendment provides that a vacancy may be filled by a special election called by the governor, or that the State legislature may authorize the governor to make a temporary appointment until the voters fill the vacancy at the next general election. Most states follow the latter practice.

[23] Article I, Section 3, Clause 1.

WHEN SENATORS ARE ELECTED

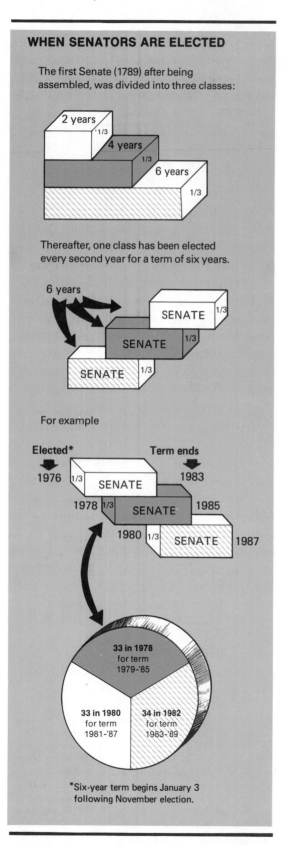

The first Senate (1789) after being assembled, was divided into three classes:

2 years ·1/3
4 years 1/3
6 years 1/3

Thereafter, one class has been elected every second year for a term of six years.

6 years

SENATE 1/3
SENATE 1/3
SENATE 1/3

For example

Elected*   Term ends

1976 1/3 SENATE 1983
1978 1/3 SENATE 1985
1980 1/3 SENATE 1987

33 in 1978
for term
1979-'85

33 in 1980
for term
1981-'87

34 in 1982
for term
1983-'89

*Six-year term begins January 3 following November election.

Terms.   Senators are chosen for 6-year-terms—three times the length of that for which members of the lower house are elected.[24] The terms are so staggered that only one-third (today 33 or 34) of them expire every two years[25]—hence, the Senate is known as a "continuous body."

The six-year term makes members of the Senate less susceptible to the pressures of public opinion and to the demands of organized interests than their colleagues in the House. And the larger size and the geographic scope of their constituencies tends to have the same effect.

Qualifications.   A Senator must meet a higher set of qualifications than those the Constitution sets for a Representative. He or she must be at least 30 years of age, must have been a citizen for at least nine years, and must be an inhabitant of the State from which elected.[26]

The Senate, like the House, may judge the qualifications of its members and may exclude a member-elect by a majority vote.[27] And the Senate, too, may "punish"

---

[24] Article I, Section 3, Clause 1.

[25] Article I, Section 3, Clause 2.

[26] Article I, Section 3, Clause 3. Under the inhabitant qualification, a Senator need *not* have resided in the State for any prescribed period. Typically, of course, Senators-elect have been long-time residents of their States; the only contrary case in modern times is that of the late Senator Robert F. Kennedy, elected from New York in 1964. Note, too, that Senators may not hold any other federal office while serving in Congress (Article I, Section 6, Clause 2).

[27] Article I, Section 5, Clause 1. As has the House, the Senate has on occasion refused to seat a member-elect. Presumably, the Court's holding in *Powell* v. *McCormack* applies with equal force to the Senate. The closest contest in Senate history occurred in New Hampshire in 1974. The first official count in that election indicated the winner to be the Republican candidate, Louis C. Wyman, by a margin of 335 votes out of the more than 220,000 cast. However, a recount awarded the seat to the Democrat, John A. Durkin, with a ten-vote margin. But a second recount favored Wyman by two votes, and the State then certified him as elected. Durkin appealed that action to the Senate and, when the body convened in 1975, it seated neither claimant. After months of debate, the Senate resolved the dispute by declaring the seat vacant. The governor of New Hampshire then called a special election from which Durkin finally emerged the winner with a 27,711-vote margin (53.6% of the total).

House	Senate
Larger body (435 members)	Smaller body (100 members)
Shorter term (2 years)	Longer term (6 years)
Smaller constituencies (elected from districts)	Larger constituencies (elected from entire State)
Younger membership	Older membership
Less prestige	More prestige
More centralized organization; power less evenly distributed	Less centralized organization; power more widely shared
More rigid rules	More flexible rules
More committees	Fewer committees
Acts more quickly	Acts more slowly
More "conservative"	More "liberal"

its own members for "disorderly behavior" by majority vote, and "with the concurrence of two-thirds, expel a member."[28]

Fifteen members of the Senate have been expelled by that body—one in 1797 and 14 during the Civil War—but no such action has been taken since 1862.[29]

Cases of discipline "for disorderly behavior" have also been rare. The most recent one occurred in 1979, however. Then, the Senate voted 81-15 to "denounce" the financial misconduct of one of its senior members. Herman Talmadge (D., Georgia) had mishandled large amounts of Senate expense monies and campaign funds. The Senate found his conduct to be "reprehensible," tending "to bring the Senate into dishonor and disrepute." (Senator Talmadge, first elected to the Senate in 1956, was defeated for re-election in 1980.)

---

[28] Article I, Section 5, Clause 2.

[29] Senator William Blount of Tennessee was expelled in 1797 for conspiring to lead two Indian tribes, supported by British warships, in attacks on Spanish Florida and Louisiana. The 14 Senators ousted in 1861 and 1862 were all from States of the Confederacy and were expelled for supporting secession.

Members of Congress and Their Jobs

The Members. Whatever else they may be, the 535 members of Congress are *not* a representative cross-section of the people they represent.

Rather, the "average" member is a white male in his latter 40's. The median age in the House is now just about 48 and in the Senate 50. There are only 21 women in Congress—19 in the House and two, Nancy L. Kassebaum (R., Kansas) and Paula Hawkins (R., Florida), in the Senate. And there are but 18 blacks—all of them in the House.

Nearly all members of Congress are married, a few are divorced, and they have, on the average, two children. Only a very few claim no church affiliation. Just over 70 percent of them are Protestants, nearly a fourth are Roman Catholics, and just over five percent are Jewish.

Over half of the members of each house are lawyers. Following the legal profession, the major occupational fields represented are business and banking, education, agriculture, and journalism. Nearly all of them have gone to college; better than four out of five have college degrees and some have several.

Most of them were born in the States they represent, and only a bare handful were born outside of the United States. Sprinkled among the 535 members are several millionaires, but a surprisingly large number must depend upon their official salaries as their major source of support.

Most members of Congress have had considerable political experience. The average Senator is now in the midst of a second term in the Senate, and the average Representative has served four terms in the House. Nearly a third of the Senate once sat in the House. Several Senators are former governors and a few of them once held Cabinet or other high posts in the executive branch. The House includes a large number of former State legislators and prosecuting attorneys.

Congress clearly is not a representative cross-section of the nation's population. Rather, it is composed largely of upper-middle class Americans who, on the whole, are able and hard-working people.

Their Job. The primary job of the 535 members of Congress is to make law, of course. That is to say, they are legislators.

As legislators, they play several vital and closely related roles. They do (1) make law. But they also function (2) as representatives of their constituents, (3) as servants of their constituents, (4) as committee members, and (5) necessarily, as politicians.

We have already looked at some aspects of these roles—in this and earlier chapters. And we shall consider other pieces of them here and in the next two chapters. But, for now, ponder this job description, offered only half-facetiously by former Representative Luther Patrick of Alabama:

A Congressman has become an expanded messenger boy, an employment agency, getter-outer of the Navy, Army, Marines, ward heeler, wound healer, trouble shooter, law explainer, bill finder, issue translator, resolution interpreter, controversy oil pourer, gladhand extender, business promoter, convention goer, civil ills skirmisher, veterans' affairs adjuster, ex-serviceman's champion, watchdog for the underdog, sympathizer with the upper dog, namer and kisser of babies, recoverer of lost luggage, soberer of delegates, adjuster for traffic violators, voters straying into Washington and into toils of the law, binder up of broken hearts, financial wet nurse, good samaritan, contributor to good causes—there are so many good causes—cornerstone layer, public building and bridge dedicator, ship christener—to be sure he does get in a little flag waving—and a little constitutional hoisting and spread-eagle work, but it is getting harder every day to find time to properly study legislation—the very business we are primarily here to discharge, and that must be done above all things.

THE "ERRAND-BOY" CONCEPT. Members of Congress are elected to represent the people, of course. But some of the people take this to mean that Senators and Representatives are in Washington especially to do favors for them. The average member is plagued with requests—as Mr. Patrick points out—from the moment he or she takes office. The range of those requests is almost without limit—everything from help in securing a government contract or an appointment to West Point to cadging a free sight-seeing tour of Washington or even a personal loan. Most members of Congress know that to refuse—or, at least not to respond in some way to most of these requests—would mean to lose votes at the next election.

Compensation. Members of Congress, unlike the other officials and em-

The House Committee on Merchant Marine and Fisheries hears testimony on an energy-related matter.

ployees of the Federal Government, fix their own salaries and other compensation. The only limits in the matter are the President's veto and voter reaction. The Constitution provides that:

> The Senators and Representatives shall receive a compensation for their services, to be ascertained by law, and paid out of the Treasury of the United States. . . .[30]

Today (1981) each member is paid an annual salary of $60,663. (The Speaker's

salary equals that of the Vice President, now $79,125 a year; the Senate's President *pro tem* and the majority and minority floor leaders in each house are paid $65,000 a year.)

In addition to the salary, each member also receives a number of "fringe benefits," some quite substantial. Thus, each has a $3000 tax deduction to help carry the burden of maintaining two residences, one at home and another in Washington. Liberal travel allowances cover the costs of several round trips between his or her home State and the capitol each year. Each member pays only modest amounts for a $45,000 life insurance policy and for health insurance coverage, regardless of age or physical condition. A medical staff provides free care at the Capitol and full care is available, at very low rates, at any military hospital. There is also a generous pension plan (to which members contribute); it

---

[30] Article I, Section 6, Clause 1; from 1789 to 1795 members of each house were paid $6 per day. In 1795 Senators received $7 per day and Representatives $6. From 1796 to 1816 the salary for both was again $6 per day. In 1816 it was raised to $15 per day, but it reverted to $6 in 1817. From 1818 to 1856, $8 per day; 1856 to 1866, $3000 per year; 1866 to 1873, $5000; 1873, $7500; 1874 to 1907, $5000; 1907 to 1925, $7500; 1925 to 1933, $10,000; 1933 to 1936, $8663; 1936 to 1946, $10,000; 1946 to 1955, $12,500 plus $2500 "expense account"; 1955 to 1965, $22,500; 1965 to 1969, $30,000; 1969 to 1975, $42,500; 1975 to 1977, $44,625; 1977–1979, $57,500.

is based on years of service and can produce a retirement income of as much as $47,054 a year.

Each member is also provided with a suite in one of the Senate or House office buildings and with allowances for offices in the member's State or district. Then, too, each is granted funds to hire administrative assistants and other office staff, for stationery, office equipment and furnishings, and for telephone and telegraph services and special delivery postage. All of a member's official mail goes free under the "franking privilege."

And, beyond all that, members are entitled to free publication and distribution of their speeches and much other material, including radio and television tapes at reduced cost. They are entitled to free parking, plants for their offices, the research help of the Library of Congress, and to a great deal more, as well—including the use of several fine restaurants and two modern gymnasiums (with swimming pools and saunas).

With the salary and all the many allowances, the typical member's compensation amounts to about $100,000 a year. Even so it doesn't seem reasonable to argue that members of Congress are overpaid. Their responsibilities are so immense and the demands made upon them so many and varied as to defy any attempt to fix an "adequate" salary.

In fact, many Senators and Representatives insist that their "day-to-day expenses" regularly exceed their allowances. Senator Robert Packwood (R., Oregon) estimates that just two items—trips to his home State and newsletters to his constituents—push his expenses some $40,000 above his allowances each year. Add such items as the costs involved in campaigning, in meeting the high cost of living in or around Washington, in maintaining two homes, and in coping with the many other "extras" imposed by the office, and it is easy to appreciate the point.

The fear—and certainty—of political repercussions has made members of Congress historically reluctant to raise the salary figure. They have much preferred to give themselves such "fringe benefits" as a special tax deduction and a generous pension plan. Such items are much less apparent to the voters than a pay increase.

Congress has tried to avoid the political pitfalls of a pay raise in recent years—but without much success. Since 1967, it has provided that every fourth year a panel of private citizens should recommend to the President an appropriate salary for members of Congress, for top-level executive officials, and for all federal judges. After reviewing the panel's report, the President makes salary recommendations to Congress. These recommendations then become law if neither house rejects them within 30 days. The present congressional salary figure was a product of this process in 1979—but was fixed amidst much political controversy and criticism.

Higher salaries, alone, will not attract the most capable men and women to Congress, or to any other public offices; but, certainly, they can make public service much more appealing.

Privileges of Members of Congress. The Constitution commands that Senators and Representatives

> shall, in all cases, except treason, felony, and breach of the peace, be privileged from arrest during their attendance at the session of their respective Houses, and in going to, and returning from, the same; . . .[31]

The provision dates from colonial days when the king's officers arrested legislators on petty grounds to prevent them from performing their official duties. It has been of little importance in our national history, but it does save a member of Congress from a minor traffic ticket now and then.

---

[31] Article I, Section 6, Clause 1.

Case Study

Each of the 435 members of the House and the 100 members of the Senate is called upon to cast literally hundreds of votes on legislative questions over the course of each annual session of Congress. Many of those votes involve routine and relatively unimportant matters. But, of course, a goodly number of them are cast on very important public policy questions, on measures of far-reaching impact.

Few questions relating to the nature and operations of Congress can be more vital, then, than this: On what basis do (or should) the members cast their votes?

In broad terms, four options are available to them: they can vote as *trustees,* as *delegates,* as *partisans,* or as *politicos.*

Those who see their role as that of trustee view each measure on its merits. They exercise an independent judgment on each question, regardless of any conflicts that may exist with the views held by their constituents or by any other group which attempts to influence their decisions. The classic statement of this mode of legislative behavior was made two centuries ago by the English statesman and political theorist Edmund Burke. Speaking to his constituents in the city of Bristol in 1774, he declared that a representative should give weight to the wishes of his constituents and should have a high respect for their opinions; but "his unbiased opinion, his mature judgment, his enlightened conscience, he ought not to sacrifice to you, to any man, or to any set of men living."

Those who act as delegates see themselves as the agents of those who elected them. That is, they vote in accord with the wishes of their constituents, at least insofar as they are able to discover them. If need be, they suppress their own feelings, ignore the dictates of their party, turn deaf ears to their legislative colleagues, and act contrary to the arguments of special interests outside their constituencies. They do these things in order to express the views of those who elected them. They see their function not as that of law-giver but as that of a mirror to reflect the wishes of "the folks back home."

To legislators who perceive their role as that of a partisan, first allegiance is owed to the programs of their political party. In deciding how to vote on a matter they feel duty-bound to support the party's platform and the policy positions adopted by the party's leaders. (Most studies of legislative voting behavior indicate that party membership is the leading factor influencing legislators' votes on most important measures.)

Those representatives who see themselves as politicos attempt to combine, as best they can, the basic elements of each of the other three roles. That is, in deciding how to vote on a measure, they try to balance their own views of what is best for their constituents and for the country as a whole, their appreciation of the demands of representative democracy, and their sense of party loyalty.

■ If you were a member of Congress, which of these options would you choose as a guide to your voting behavior? Why?
■ Why would you reject each of the others?

A longtime member of the House, the late Adam Clayton Powell (D., New York), once expressed this view of how a member of Congress should vote:

> The primary and overriding duty and responsibility of each Member of the House and the Senate is to get reelected. . . . It would be ridiculous for anyone to think otherwise or for a Member to do otherwise, for if a Member was not interested in reelection, there would be no point in his starting in the first place to seek the public office. . . .

■ What do you think of Mr. Powell's view? In which category—trustee, delegate, partisan, or politico—would you place him?

Another and much more important privilege is provided in the same place in the Constitution:

... and for any speech or debate in either House, they shall not be questioned in any other place.

This protection against being "questioned in any other place"—that is, in the courts—is intended to throw a *cloak of legislative immunity* about members of Congress. It protects them against suits for libel or slander arising out of their official conduct. The Supreme Court has held that the immunity applies "to things generally done in a session of the House [or Senate] by one of its members in relation to the busi-

ness before it."[32] The protection extends, then, beyond floor debate, to include reports, resolutions, committee proceedings, and to all things generally done in Congress by members in relation to congressional business. But a member is not free to defame another person in a public speech, an article, a conversation, or otherwise. The very important and necessary object of the provision is to encourage freedom of legislative debate.

---

[32] The leading case is *Kilbourn* v. *Thompson,* 1881; the holding has been affirmed many times since. In *Hutchinson* v. *Proxmire,* 1979, however, the Court held that members of Congress may be sued for libel for statements they make in news releases or in newsletters sent to constituents.

SUMMARY

Congress is the *legislative* (lawmaking) branch of the National Government. It is composed of two houses—the House of Representatives and the Senate. Congress is *bicameral* for several reasons: because of the familiarity of the Framers with the bicameral British Parliament, the fact that all but two of the State legislatures in 1787 were bicameral, the Connecticut Compromise, and the belief that one house could act as a check on the other.

A *term* of Congress lasts for two years. There are two *regular sessions* to each term, one a year. Special sessions may be called only by the President.

Members of the House of Representatives serve a two-year term and are popularly elected. The Congress reapportions the seats in the House among the States on the basis of their respective populations after every decennial census, but each State is guaranteed at least one Representative. The House now consists of 435 members elected from districts drawn by the legislature in each State. The districts must contain approximately equal populations (*Wesberry* v. *Sanders,* 1964), but may be *gerrymandered.*

A Representative must be at least 25 years old, seven years a citizen of the United States, and an inhabitant of the State from which chosen. The Senate and House each have the power to decide contests over the seating of members-elect. Each house may refuse to seat a member-elect or may censure or expel a member. But, in 1969, the Supreme Court held that the House could not properly exclude a member-elect who met the age, citizenship, and residence qualifications set by the Constitution.

Each State has two seats in the Senate. Senators serve a six-year term. One-third of the Senate terms regularly end every two years. Since 1913 (the 17th Amendment), Senators have been popularly elected. They must be at least 30 years old, nine years a citizen of the United States, and an inhabitant of the State from which chosen.

Members of Congress fix their own salaries by law. Today they receive $60,663 a year along with various other compensations. They enjoy freedom from arrest for petty offenses during sessions of Congress and immunity in debate and other official remarks.

Concept Development

Questions for Review

1. Why is a representative legislative body indispensable in a democracy?

2. Which Article in the Constitution deals especially with Congress? Is there significance to this?

3. What does each house of Congress represent?

4. Why did the Framers create a bicameral Congress?

5. How long is a term of Congress?

6. How often are regular sessions held?

7. Who may call special sessions of Congress?

8. How is the size of the House fixed? How many members does it have?

9. The Constitution directs what body to reapportion the House every 10 years?

10. Do any States have more seats in the Senate than in the House? If so, why?

11. By whom are congressional districts drawn?

12. What did the Supreme Court hold in *Wesberry* v. *Sanders?*

13. What is gerrymandering?

14. When are the members of the House elected? Senators? How long is it after the election until they take their seats? What are their terms of office?

15. What are the qualifications for membership in the House of Representatives? In the Senate?

16. What did the Supreme Court hold in *Powell* v. *McCormack?*

17. Of how many members does the Senate consist? How is its size fixed?

18. What salary do members of Congress receive? What further compensation?

19. What is the primary job of a member of Congress?

20. What special privileges does a member of Congress have?

For Further Inquiry

1. It may seem at times that popularity is the only requisite for members of Congress aside from age, citizenship, and residence in the State. What additional qualifications for this office might be listed?

2. Members of Congress are said by some to be overpaid, underworked, and ineffective. Will Rogers was not the first, and far from the last, to make this sort of comment: "Suppose you were an idiot. And suppose you were a Congressman. But I repeat myself." He also once said: "It can

probably be shown that there is no distinctly American criminal class except Congress."

Similar assessments can be found in many places—for example in editorial cartoons. Yet, on page 296, the author of this book says that members of Congress are "on the whole, . . . able and hard-working people." And that judgment is supported by any number of academic, journalistic, and other studies and commentaries. Can you explain the apparent contradiction here?

3. In an election speech in 1774, the British statesman Edmund Burke told his constituents: "Your representative owes you not his industry only, but his judgment; and he betrays, instead of serving you, if he sacrifices it to your opinion." Do you agree or disagree with that view?

4. Would you favor or oppose a constitutional amendment to lengthen (or shorten) the elected term of Representatives? Of Senators? Why?

5. If members of Congress are to do what the people want them to do, they must know what it is the people want. How can they best discover that? How can a private person best inform his or her Representative and Senators of his or her views on public matters?

6. Should the gerrymandering of congressional districts be prohibited by statute? How else might it be prevented?

Suggested Activities

1. Invite your Representative or Senator to speak to the class or to the entire student body on his or her role as a representative of the people or on another topic of his or her choosing.

2. Prepare a biographical study of your Representative and Senators. (Consult such sources as *Who's Who* and *The Congressional Directory.*)

3. Stage a debate or class forum on

one or more of the questions: (a) *Resolved,* That former Presidents should automatically become lifetime members of the Senate; (b) *Resolved,* That Senators should receive a higher salary than Representatives; (c) *Resolved,* That no member of either house should be permitted to serve more than three consecutive terms in office.

Suggested Reading

Baker, Ross, *Friend and Foe in the United States Senate.* Free Press, 1979.

Barone, Michael, *et al.,* *The Almanac of American Politics.* Dutton, 1981.

Cohen, William S., *Power and Privilege: One Year in the United States Senate.* Simon & Schuster, 1981.

Congressional Directory, 97th Congress, 1st Session. Government Printing Office, 1981.

Congressional Ethics. Congressional Quarterly, 1980.

CQ *Weekly Report.* Congressional Quarterly, Inc. Weekly.

Davidson, Roger H. and Oleszek, Walter J., *Congress and Its Members.* Congressional Quarterly Press, 1981.

Dodd, Lawrence and Oppenheimer, Bruce J., *Congress Reconsidered.* Congressional Quarterly Press, 2nd ed., 1981.

Drew, Elizabeth, *Senator.* Simon and Schuster, 1979.

Green, Mark, *Who Runs Congress?* Bantam Books, rev. ed., 1979.

Inside Congress. Congressional Quarterly Press, 2nd ed., 1979.

Jones, Rochelle and Woll, Peter, *The Private World of Congress.* Free Press, 1979.

Keefe, William J., *Congress and the American People.* Prentice-Hall, 1980.

Mann, Thomas E. (ed.), *Unsafe at any Margin: Interpreting Congressional Elections.* American Enterprise Institute, 1979.

Oleszek, Walter J., *Congressional Procedures and the Policy Process.* Congressional Quarterly Press, 1978.

Congress
in Action

*For this reason the laws are made:
that the strong shall not have power
to do all that they please.*

OVID

■ What do the details of legislative organizations, procedure, and practice tell us about the overall character of a governmental system?

■ How can such practices as the seniority rule and the filibuster be fitted into the rationale of representative democracy?

■ Is Congressional organization, procedure, and practice "out of touch with the times"? If so, what changes should be made?

We have just considered the general structure of the Congress, the selection and terms of its membership, and the shape of the lawmakers' role. Now we turn to Congress in action—to its internal organization, procedures, and practices. How—and how well—is Congress equipped to perform the lawmaking function? With what machinery and by what devices does it play its pivotal part in the democratic process?

The answers to these questions are of fundamental importance. They are, of course, because of the central place of the legislative branch in democratic government. But they are also important because they determine how power is distributed within Congress, in each of its houses. Their answers point to who has and can exercise major influence and control over the making of law, and who gets "what, when, and how."

Woodrow Wilson once observed that "the making of laws is a very practical matter." In addition to being very practical, and very important, it is also a very complicated matter, as we shall see.

Convening of a New Congress

As we know, a new term of Congress commences every two years—on the 3rd day of January in every odd-numbered year, following the regular November elections.

Speaker of the House, Thomas P. O'Neill of Massachusetts, swears in members of the House of Representatives as Congress begins a new term.

Opening Day in the House. When the 435 men and women who have been elected to the House assemble at the Capitol on January 3, they are, in effect, just so many Representatives-elect. Because all of its 435 seats are refilled every two years, the House has no sworn members, no rules, no organization until its opening day ceremonies are held.

The Clerk of the House in the preceding term presides at the beginning of the first day's session. He calls the roll of the members-elect as furnished by the several States. They then choose a Speaker to serve as the permanent presiding officer.

The Speaker is always a member of the majority party, and election on the floor is a mere formality. The majority party *caucus* (conference of party members) has in fact chosen the Speaker beforehand.

The new Speaker is then sworn in by the "Dean of the House," the member-elect with the longest record of service in the House of Representatives.[1] Once that oath has been administered, the Speaker swears in the rest of the members as a body. The Democrats then take their seats to the right of the center aisle and the Republicans to the left.

The House then proceeds to elect its Clerk, Sergeant at Arms, Doorkeeper, Postmaster, and Chaplain. Their elections, too, are a formality—the majority party caucus has already determined who these non-member officers are to be.

Next, the House adopts the rules that will govern its operations through the term. The rules of the House have been developed over a period of more than 190 years and are contained in a volume of several hundred pages. They are regularly re-adopted, with little change, at the beginning of each term—though they are occasionally, and sometimes extensively, amended during a term.

Finally, the members of the various standing committees of the House are appointed by a vote of the chamber and the House of Representatives is organized.

Opening Day in the Senate. The Senate is a continuous body. That is, it has been continuously organized since its first session in 1789. As we have seen, only one-third of its seats are up for election every two years. From one term to the next, then, there is a regular carry-over of two-thirds of its membership.

The Senate thus does not have the problems the House faces on opening day. Unless the most recent elections produced a change in party control—as they did for 1981—its proceedings are usually brief and largely routine. Newly elected and re-elected members must be sworn in, vacancies in its organization and on committees must be filled, and a few other details attended to. Then the Senate is ready to deal

---

[1] The "Dean of the House" today (1981) is Representative Jamie L. Whitten (D., Mississippi) who has been a member of the House since January 3, 1941.

Case Study

The late Sam Rayburn (D., Texas) served in the House for nearly half a century and for more than 17 of those years he was the Speaker of the House.

Reflecting on his long years of service, he once remarked: "I haven't served *under* anybody. I have served *with* eight Presidents."

A small sign in his office carried a piece of advice he regularly drew to the attention of new members of the House. The sign read: "If you want to get along, go along."

■ What does Mr. Sam's long tenure in the House, and as Speaker, tell us about the Speakership? What did the sign suggest? His comment about serving *with* rather than *under* eight Presidents?

■ Why do you think that, although neither the Constitution nor its own rules demand it, the House of Representatives has always selected its Speaker from among its own members?

---

with those matters which will come before it.

The President's State of the Union Message. When the Senate is notified that the House is organized, a joint committee of the two is appointed and instructed:

> . . . to wait upon the President of the United States and inform him that a quorum of each House is assembled and that the Congress is ready to receive any communication he may be pleased to make.

Within a few days the President delivers his annual State of the Union Message. The members of the two houses, together with the members of the Cabinet, the Supreme Court, the foreign diplomatic corps, and other dignitaries and guests assemble in the House chamber to receive him.

From Woodrow Wilson's first message in 1913, the President has usually delivered this annual assessment in person. In the speech, the Chief Executive reports on the state of the nation in all its concerns, foreign and domestic. And the address often contains a number of specific legislative recommendations. The message is followed closely both at home and abroad—for in it the President indicates the shape of administration policies and the course charted for the nation.

At the conclusion of the President's speech the joint session is adjourned, and each house returns to the legislative business before it.

The Organization of Congress

The national legislature is a far larger operation than most realize. Congress has appropriated more than $1 billion to fund itself in the current fiscal year. Only $32,454,705—about three percent of that huge sum—is spent to pay the salaries of the 535 members. More than $200 million now goes to hire staff assistants for members, and the annual postage ("franking) bill runs to well over $50 million a year.

There are, all told, some 38,000 congressional employees. We have mentioned a few of them, the Clerk of the House, for example. There are hundreds of committee aides, legislative and administrative assistants, office clerks, secretaries, guards, maintenance personnel, groundskeepers, and so on. And each of them, in his or her own way, is important to the workings of the legislative machinery.

The Presiding Officers. The Constitution provides for the presiding officers of each house of Congress.

The Speaker of the House is by far the most important and influential member of the House of Representatives. The Speakership was created by the Constitution and, as the Constitution commands, the post is filled by a vote of the House at the beginning of each of its two-year terms.[2] As a matter of *practical fact,* however, the Speaker is the leader of the majority party in the House—and so is actually selected by the members of that party.

Although neither the Constitution nor its own rules require it, the House has invariably selected the Speaker from among its own members. Typically, they have been longtime members who have risen in stature and influence through years of service. The present incumbent, Representative Thomas P. O'Neill (D., Mass.), has been in the House since 1953 and became Speaker in 1977.[3]

At base, the immense power wielded by the Speaker arises from this fact: the Speaker is, at one and the same time, the elected presiding officer of the House *and* the acknowledged leader of its majority party. Speakers are expected to preside in a fair and judicial manner, and they regularly do so. But they are also expected to aid the fortunes of their own party and their party's legislative goals—and they regularly do that, too.

Nearly all the Speaker's specific powers revolve about two duties: to preside and to maintain order. The Speaker presides over all sessions of the House, or appoints a temporary presiding officer to do so. No member may speak unless and until the member is "recognized" by the Speaker. The Speaker interprets and applies the rules, refers bills to the standing committees, decides points of order (questions of procedure raised by members), puts questions to a vote, and determines the outcome of most of the votes taken.[4]

The Speaker also appoints the members of all special and conference committees and must sign all bills and resolutions passed by the House. The presiding officer may order the galleries cleared if such an action is deemed necessary. If a member is speaking and strays from the subject, the Speaker may rule the member out of order and force the member to yield the floor.

Whenever the House is in session, the *mace* (the symbol of the Speaker's authority) rests in a stand to the Speaker's right. If the Speaker cannot maintain order, the Sergeant-at-Arms may be directed to approach an unruly member with the mace to demand it. If necessary, the Speaker may order the arrest of a defiant member.

As a member, the Speaker may debate and vote on any matter before the House; but to do so, a temporary presiding officer must be appointed and the chair vacated by the Speaker. Although a Speaker may vote on *any* question, the rules require such a vote only to break a tie. (In the House a tie vote results in the defeat of a question. Thus, the Speaker can occasionally *cause* a tie and so defeat a measure.)

The Speaker follows the Vice President in the line of succession to the Presidency—a considerable testimony to the power and importance of both the office and its occupant.

The *President of the Senate*, by constitutional command, is the Vice President of the United States.[5] The Vice President is a

---

[2] Article I, Section 2, Clause 5.

[3] Speaker O'Neill succeeded Carl Albert (D., Okla.). Mr. Albert, who sat in the House from 1947, served as Speaker from 1971 until his retirement from Congress, January 3, 1977. The late Sam Rayburn (D., Texas) served as Speaker for a record 17 years, 62 days. Except for two terms in which the Republicans controlled the House (1947-1948 and 1953-1954), "Mr. Sam" held the post from September 16, 1940, until his death November 16, 1961. The first Speaker, elected at the first session of Congress in 1789, was Frederick A. C. Muhlenburg, a Federalist from Pennsylvania. Speaker O'Neill is the 47th person to serve in the post.

[4] On most matters the House takes a *voice vote:* The Speaker puts the question, those in favor respond (shout) "Aye," then those opposed respond "Nay," and the Speaker decides and declares the result; see page 321.

much less potent presiding officer than the Speaker in the House. The Vice President does not come to preside over the Senate by dint of long service in the upper house—but, rather, out of a strikingly different process, as we shall see in Chapter 15. In fact, the Vice President may be from the party with a minority of the seats in the Senate.

As the President of the Senate the Vice President does have the ordinary powers of a presiding officer—to recognize members, put questions to a vote, and so on. The Vice President, who is not a member of the Senate, cannot take the floor to debate a measure—and may, but is not required to, vote *only* to break a tie.

Whatever influence the Vice President may have in the Senate comes largely from the personal ability to generate it. Several recent Vice Presidents—Harry Truman

(1945), Alben Barkley (1949-1953), Richard Nixon (1953-1961), Lyndon Johnson (1961-1963), Hubert Humphrey (1965-1969), and Walter Mondale (1977-1981)—served in the Senate before reaching the Vice Presidency. And each of them was able to enhance the power of the position out of that experience.

The Senate does have another presiding officer, the *President pro tempore*, who presides in the Vice President's absence. The President *pro tem* is elected by the Senate itself and, as a leading member of the majority party, is always a potent figure. The Senate's President *pro tem* today (1981) is Senator Strom Thurmond (R., S. Carolina). He was elected to the Senate for the first time in 1954 and was chosen its President *pro tem* in 1981.

The Vice President is occasionally absent from the Senate because of other duties—a more frequent occurrence in late years because recent Presidents have made

---

5 Article I, Section 3, Clause 4.

Two months before inauguration day (January 20, 1981), President-elect Ronald Reagan and Vice President-elect George Bush met with Speaker of the House, Thomas P. O'Neill (center) in the Speaker's office. To the right is Representative Jim Wright of Texas, Majority Leader of the House.

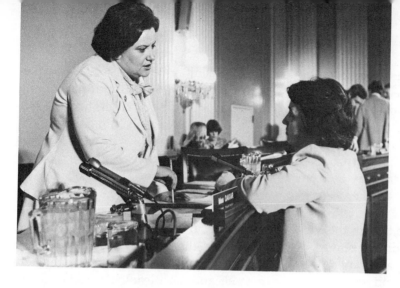

As do most members of the House, Representative Mary Rose Oaker of Ohio (at left) serves on two standing committees and on several subcommittees, as well.

increasing use of their Vice Presidents. And, recall that nine times, thus far, fate has suddenly made the Vice President the President of the United States.

Various other members of the Senate also preside over the chamber; newly-elected Senators are accorded this "honor" early in their terms.

Floor Leaders and Other Party Officers. Congress is distinctly a *political* body. That it is is inevitable for two leading reasons: *first,* because it is the nation's central *policy-making* organ; and, *secondly,* because of its *partisan* make-up. And, reflecting its political complexion, both houses are organized along party lines.

THE FLOOR LEADERS. Next to the Speaker, the most important officers in Congress are the *majority* and *minority floor leaders* in the House and Senate. These officers are the managers of their party's interests on the floor in each chamber. They do not occupy *official* posts in the organization of either house; rather, they are *party* officers chosen by their party caucuses.

The floor leaders are their party's legislative strategists. They attempt to control floor action to the party's benefit. To do so, they must keep in close touch with the party's members as a whole, with key committee members, and with the leaders of the various State delegations. And they must keep in touch with such unofficial but pivotal coalitions as the Black Caucus or the Democratic Study Group. They try to persuade the members of these groups to act in committee and vote on the floor in accord with the wishes of the party leadership—often a difficult task.

The majority leader's post is the more important of the two in each house—for the obvious reason that the majority party has more seats (more votes) than does the minority leader's. In consultation with the presiding officer and the minority leader, the majority leader in each house plans the order of business on the floor. This function is shared in the House with the Rules Committee, as we shall see.

The two floor leaders are assisted by *party whips* in each house. The whips serve, in effect, as assistant floor leaders. They are chosen by the party caucus, usually upon the recommendation of the floor leader. There are also several assistant whips in each party in both houses.

The whips canvass party members and advise the floor leader of the number of votes that can be counted upon in any particular matter. Of course, they attempt to see that members vote with the party leadership and that they are present when important votes are to be taken. (If a member must be absent for some reason, the whip sees that that member is "paired" with a member of the other party—one who is also absent or who agrees not to vote on certain measures.)

The *party caucus* is a closed meeting of the members of each party in each house. It meets just before Congress convenes in January, and occasionally during a session. In recent years the Republicans have referred to their caucus in each house as the *party conference;* the Democrats now use this term only in the Senate.

The party caucus decides such questions as the candidate for Speaker and who the floor leaders shall be, and it attempts to secure united party action on certain measures. Neither party attempts to force its members to follow its caucus decisions— nor can it. The *policy committee,* composed of the party's principal leadership, acts as an "executive committee" for the caucus.[6]

Committee Chairmen.[6a] The large bulk of the work of Congress—especially in the House—is actually done in committee. Thus, those members who head the standing committees in each chamber—the *committee chairmen*—also occupy very strategic posts in the scheme of congressional organization. The chairman of each committee is chosen by the majority party caucus and is always a ranking member of that party.

Committee chairmen regularly have the power to decide when their committees will meet, which bills they will consider, whether public hearings are to be held, and what witnesses are to be called. And when a committee's bill has been reported to the floor, they manage the debate and attempt to steer it to final passage.

In a moment we shall see how the committees operate in the legislative process and return to the chairman's role. But, first, we must examine the *seniority rule.*

The seniority rule is, in fact, an *unwritten custom.* It first emerged in congressional practice in the latter part of the last century and, despite some recent relaxations, is still closely followed in both houses today. Under the rule, the most important posts in the formal and in the party organization of each house are awarded to the "ranking members." That is, important posts go to those party members with the longest record of congressional service.

The rule is applied most strictly in the case of those who chair committees. The head of each committee is almost invariably the member of the majority party who has served for the longest period of time on that particular committee.

Critics of the rule are legion, and they do make a strong case. They insist that it ignores ability, puts a premium on mere length of service, and discourages younger members. They also note that the rule means that a committee head almost always comes from a "safe" constituency— that is, chosen from a State or district where, election after election, a single party dominates and there is little or no effective opposition. They argue that because the play of fresh and contending forces is almost nil, those who head committees are often out of touch with current public opinion.

Defenders of the rule argue that it means that a powerful and experienced member will head each committee, that it is easy to apply, and that it virtually eliminates intraparty feuds.

Opponents of the rule have gained some vital ground in recent years. Since 1971, for example, the House Republican conference (caucus) has chosen the ranking GOP members of House committees by secret ballot; and in 1973 the Democrats in the House agreed to use secret ballots to pick committee chairmen whenever 20

---

[6] Until recently, both parties in each house referred to the policy committee as its *steering committee;* the older title is still used by the Democrats in the House.

[6a] We use the title *chairman,* rather than *chairperson,* advisedly: first, because this is the form used in both houses of Congress, both officially and unofficially, and secondly, because no woman now (1981) chairs a standing committee in either house. Only three women have ever done so: the most recent, Leonor K. Sullivan (D., Mo.), who chaired the House Merchant Marine and Fisheries Committee from 1973 until her retirement in 1977.

STANDING COMMITTEES OF CONGRESS

House Committees

Agriculture	Government Operations	Public Works and
Appropriations	House Administration	Transportation
Armed Services	Interior and Insular Affairs	Rules
Banking, Finance and Urban	Interstate and Foreign	Science and Technology
Affairs	Commerce	Small Business
Budget	Judiciary	Standards of Official
District of Columbia	Merchant Marine and Fisheries	Conduct
Education and Labor	Post Office and Civil Service	Veterans' Affairs
Foreign Affairs		Ways and Means

Senate Committees

Agriculture, Nutrition, and	Commerce, Science, and	Foreign Relations
Forestry	Transportation	Governmental Affairs
Appropriations	Energy and Natural	Judiciary
Armed Services	Resources	Labor and Human
Banking, Housing and Urban	Environment and Public	Resources
Affairs	Works	Rules and Administration
Budget	Finance	Veterans' Affairs

percent of their caucus requests such an action. And, in 1975 the House Democrats actually removed three long-tenured, "autocratic" committee heads.

Despite the weight of arguments against the rule and the recent breaches of it, prospects for its abolition remain at best dim. Those who have the real power to abolish it are the ones who benefit the most from its retention.

The Committee System

Both the House and the Senate are so large and the volume of their business is so great that each relies heavily upon its committee system.

Standing Committees. In 1789 the House and Senate each adopted the practice of appointing a special committee to consider each bill as it was introduced. The situation soon got out of hand, however. By 1794 there were more than 300 committees functioning in each chamber. Each house then began to create permanent groups—*standing committees*—to which all similar bills could be referred.

The number of standing committees has varied over the years. By 1946 there

were 48 in the House and 33 in the Senate. Many members were forced to spend practically all of their time in committee work. On the average, each Representative was serving on two committees and each Senator on five. Several members held even more assignments, and some were serving on two or more of the most important (and work-laden) groups. So, by the Legislative Reorganization Act of 1946, the number of committees was sharply reduced.

Today (1981) there are 22 standing committees in the House and 15 in the Senate. The size of each of these committees varies from 12 to 54 members in the lower house and from 10 to 28 in the upper chamber. The rules of the House limit Representatives to service on only one major committee and the Senate allows its members to serve on only two.

The Speaker and the President of the Senate refer bills to the appropriate standing committee. For instance, the Speaker refers tax bills to the House Ways and Means Committee and the President of the Senate refers them to the Senate Finance Committee. A bill dealing with enlistments in the Army goes to the Armed Services Committee in either chamber, and so on.

HOUSE LEADERSHIP, 1981

Position	Name	Age*	Year Entered House	State	% of Vote in Last Election
Leadership					
Speaker	Thomas P. O'Neill, Jr.	69	1953	Massachusetts	78
Majority Leader	James C. Wright, Jr.	59	1955	Texas	62
Majority Whip	Thomas S. Foley	52	1965	Washington	52
Minority Leader	Robert H. Michel	58	1957	Illinois	62
Minority Whip	Trent Lott	40	1973	Mississippi	74
Committee Chairmen					
Agriculture	Thomas S. Foley	52	1965	Washington	52
Appropriations	Jamie L. Whitten	71	1941	Mississippi	63
Armed Services	Melvin Price	76	1945	Illinois	64
Banking, Finance and Urban Affairs	Fernand J. St. Germain	53	1961	Rhode Island	68
Budget	James R. Jones	42	1973	Oklahoma	58
District of Columbia	Ronald V. Dellums	46	1971	California	56
Education and Labor	Carl D. Perkins	69	1949	Kentucky	Unopposed
Foreign Affairs	Clement J. Zablocki	69	1949	Wisconsin	70
Government Operations	Jack Brooks	59	1953	Texas	Unopposed
House Administration	Augustus F. Hawkins	74	1963	California	86
Interior and Insular Affairs	Morris K. Udall	59	1961	Arizona	58
Interstate and Foreign Commerce	John D. Dingell	55	1956	Michigan	70
Judiciary	Peter W. Rodino, Jr.	72	1949	New Jersey	86.4
Merchant Marine and Fisheries	Walter B. Jones	68	1966	North Carolina	Unopposed
Post Office and Civil Service	William D. Ford	54	1965	Michigan	68
Public Works and Transportation	James J. Howard	54	1965	New Jersey	50
Rules	Richard Bolling	65	1949	Missouri	70
Science and Technology	Don Fuqua	48	1963	Florida	71
Small Business	Neal Smith	61	1959	Iowa	54
Standards of Official Conduct	Charles E. Bennett	71	1949	Florida	77
Veterans' Affairs	Gillespie V. Montgomery	60	1967	Mississippi	Unopposed
Ways and Means	Dan Rostenkowski	53	1959	Illinois	84

* As of birthdate in 1981.
Source: Congressional Directory, with additional data from the Clerk of the House.

SENATE LEADERSHIP, 1981

Position	Name	Age[a]	Year Entered Senate[b]	State	% of Vote in Last Election
Leadership					
Majority Leader	Howard Baker, Jr.	56	1967	Tennessee	56
Majority Whip	Ted Stevens	58	1968	Alaska	76
Minority Leader	Robert C. Byrd	63	1959 (1963)	West Virginia	Unopposed
Minority Whip	Alan Cranston	67	1969	California	59
Committee Chairmen					
Agriculture, Nutrition, and Forestry	Jesse A. Helms	60	1973	North Carolina	55
Appropriations	Mark O. Hatfield	59	1967	Oregon	62
Armed Services	John G. Tower	56	1961	Texas	50
Banking, Housing and Urban Affairs	Jake Garn	49	1975	Utah	74
Budget	Pete V. Domenici	49	1973	New Mexico	53
Commerce, Science, and Transportation	Bob Packwood	49	1969	Oregon	52
Energy and Natural Resources	James A. McClure	57	1973 (1967)	Idaho	68
Environment and Public Works	Robert T. Stafford	68	1971 (1961)	Vermont	52
Finance	Robert Dole	58	1969 (1961)	Kansas	64
Foreign Relations	Charles H. Percy	62	1967	Illinois	54
Governmental Affairs	William V. Roth	60	1971 (1967)	Delaware	56
Judiciary	Strom Thurmond	79	1955	South Carolina	56
Labor and Human Resources	Orrin G. Hatch	47	1977	Utah	56
Rules and Administration	Charles McC. Mathias	59	1969 (1961)	Maryland	66
Veterans' Affairs	Alan K. Simpson	50	1979	Wyoming	62

[a] As of birthdate in 1981.

[b] Date in parentheses indicates first year of prior service in House of Representatives.

Source: Congressional Directory, with additional data from the Secretary of the Senate.

The Senate Banking Committee hears testimony on the fiscal problems of New York City. City officials and public and private financial experts were invited to testify at the hearing.

We have already seen how the head of each committee is selected according to the seniority rule. The rule is also generally followed in each house when it elects the other members of its committees.[7]

The majority party controls each committee, but the minority party always has a substantial representation on each of them.[8] In fact, party membership on each committee is proportional to the party's strength in each house. Thus, if the Re-publicans have 220 seats in the House and the Democrats 215, the party split in committee seats is also very close. Thus, on a 25-member committee the division would be 13 Republicans and 12 Democrats.

Except for the House Committee on Rules and the Senate Committee on Rules and Administration, each of the standing committees is a "subject-matter committee." That is, each deals with bills relating to particular subject matters—for example, the House Committee on the Judiciary or the Senate Committee on Finance.

We shall discuss the committees again shortly. But for now a special note must be made of one of them.

The House Committee on Rules. Until 1880, the House Rules Committee was a special (temporary) committee created at the beginning of each term of Congress. Its function was to propose the adoption of the rules of the preceding House and to offer whatever changes, if any, the committee might think necessary. It became a standing committee in 1880. Over the years since, it has acquired a virtual life-and-death power in the legislative process.

---

[7] Though the committee members are *formally* elected by floor vote in each house, they are *actually* chosen in a much different manner. In the House, the Democrats receive their committee assignments from the Steering Committee of their party's caucus; the Speaker chairs that committee and is closely assisted by the majority floor leader. The Republicans in their House caucus select a Committee on Committees consisting of one member from each State with Republican representation. Each member of this group has as many votes as there are Republican Representatives from his or her State. Each party in the Senate has a Committee on Committees chosen by the party caucus.

[8] The only exception here is the House Committee on Standards of Official Conduct, with 12 members—six Democrats and six Republicans. It investigates allegations of misconduct by members and makes appropriate recommendations to the full chamber. (In the Senate a six-member bipartisan group, the Select Committee on Ethics, plays a similar role.)

So many measures are introduced in the House each term—an average of some 20,000 now—that some sort of screening process is obviously necessary. Most bills die in the committees to which they are referred. But many more than the House can possibly handle are reported out. So, before most bills can reach the floor, they must first clear the Rules Committee.

This potent 16-member group may bring in a *special rule*—a rule to consider a bill out of its regular order, or to limit floor debate on it, or to prohibit any amendments to it on the floor. In short, the Rules Committee has the power to hasten, to delay, or even to prevent floor action.

When a special rule is granted, the minority often cries "gag rule!" But each party and faction tries to use the device to its own advantage.

In theory, the committee works closely with the House leadership. In fact, however, it has been dominated for most of the period since the late 1930's by a Republican-Southern Democratic coalition—a combination which has often blocked or delayed "liberal" legislation.

In the smaller Senate, with its less stringent rules, the Committee on Rules and Administration is but a shadow of its counterpart in the House.

Select Committees. At times, each house finds need for a *select committee*—that is, a special group created for some specific purpose and (most often) for a limited time. Usually, the members of a select committee are chosen by the majority and the minority party floor leaders.

Most select committees have been charged with the investigation of some particular and current matter. The congressional power to investigate is essential to the lawmaking function. Congress must inform itself on matters before it. It must determine the need for new legislation and the adequacy of legislation previously enacted. And it must exercise its "oversight" function. That is, Congress must determine whether executive agencies are functioning effectively and in accord with the policies Congress has set by law. Congress frequently investigates, as well, to focus public attention on certain topics.

Most congressional investigations—the usual and routine as well as those which capture the headlines—are conducted by standing committees or by their subcommittees.

Select committees are also used for that purpose, however—for example, the Senate's Select Committee on Presidential Campaign Activities, popularly titled the

The Senate Select Committee on Presidential Campaign Activities held its extensive, televised, widely followed hearings in 1973 and 1974.

Watergate Committee. As the Watergate Scandal unfolded in 1973, as virtually day to day new and spectacular disclosures tumbled one upon another, the Senate responded by creating the committee. Chaired by Senator Sam Ervin (D., N.C.), the committee's mission was to investigate "the extent, if any, to which illegal, improper, or unethical activities were engaged in by any persons . . . in the presidential election of 1972." Its lengthy, often televised, and frequently sensational hearings fascinated the nation for months. They were a major link in the chain that led to the demise of the Nixon Presidency.

Most congressional investigations are not nearly so visible—nor so historic. Their much more usual shape can be seen when the House Committee on Agriculture takes a look at some aspect of the farm price support system, or when the Senate Armed Services Committee inquires into the need to upgrade housing facilities for military dependents abroad.

Joint Committees. A joint committee is one composed of members of both houses. Some are established as special (select) committees to serve some temporary purpose. But most are regular, permanent groups serving the two chambers on a continuing basis. To date, except for the Joint Committee on Atomic Energy, such committees have usually dealt with routine and less important matters—for example, the Joint Committee on Printing and the Joint Committee on the Library. Because the standing committees often duplicate one another's work, many have long urged a wider use of the joint committee device.

Conference Committees. Before a bill may be sent to the President, it must be passed in *identical form* by each house. Sometimes the two houses pass differing versions of the same bill, and the first house will not agree to the changes the other house has made. When this happens, a temporary "conference committee" is appointed.

A conference committee is composed of a varying number of members of each house appointed by the respective presiding officers. Its members attempt to iron out the differences in the House and Senate versions of a measure, aiming at a compromise both houses will accept. We shall come back to the role of the conference committees shortly, on page 325.

How a Bill Becomes a Law

More than 20,000 bills are now introduced during each term of Congress. Fewer than 10 percent of them ever become law. Where do these measures originate? Why do so few become law? What steps are involved in the House and the Senate in the making of law?

To answer these questions we shall first trace a bill through the House, from introduction to final passage. And then, because the process is quite similar, we shall note the major differences to be found in the Senate.

Authorship and Introduction. Most of the bills introduced in either house do *not* originate with members of Congress themselves. Most of the more important measures—and the more routine ones, too—originate in the executive agencies. Business, labor, agriculture, and other pressure groups frequently draft measures. Some, or at least the idea for them, come from private citizens who think "there ought to be a law . . ." And many are born in the standing committees of the House and Senate.

The Constitution declares that all bills for the raising of revenue must originate—be first introduced—in the House.[9] Measures dealing with any and all other topics may be introduced in either chamber. And once the lower house has passed a revenue measure the Senate may amend it in the same manner as it may any other bill.

9 Article I, Section 7, Clause 1.

Only a member may introduce a bill in the House—and does so in a somewhat less than formal manner, by dropping the bill in the "hopper."[10]

Types of Bills and Resolutions. The thousands of measures—*bills* and *resolutions*—Congress considers each session take several different forms:

Bills are proposed laws, drafts of laws presented to the House or Senate for enactment. Each bill's enacting clause reads: "Be it enacted by the Senate and House of Representatives of the United States of America in Congress assembled, That . . ." and the content of the measure follows.

Public bills are measures of general application, applying to the nation as a whole, as, for example, a tax measure, an amendment to the copyright laws, or an appropriation of funds for the armed forces.

Private bills are those measures which apply to specific persons or places rather than to the nation generally. For example, a few years ago Congress passed an act to pay a man in Wyoming $1229.52. This was the amount he would have made on a government contract had a local post office handled his mail promptly.

Joint Resolutions differ little from bills and when enacted have the force of law. The style of the enacting clause is: "Resolved by the Senate and House of Representatives of the United States of America in Congress assembled, That. . . ." They usually deal with unusual or temporary matters. For example, they may appropriate funds to finance the presidential inauguration ceremonies, or correct an error in a previously passed statute. Recall, too, that they are used to propose constitutional amendments (see page 68) and have also been used for territorial annexations.

Concurrent Resolutions deal with matters in which joint action of the House and Senate is necessary but for which a law is not needed. They usually begin in this form: "Resolved by the Senate, the House of Representatives concurring, That . . ." They are used most often to express a position, an opinion, by Congress on some matter—for example, in foreign affairs.

Resolutions deal with matters concerning either house alone and are considered only by that house. A simple resolution regularly begins: "Resolved by the Senate [or House], That . . ."

A bill or resolution usually relates to a single subject, but sometimes a *rider* dealing with an entirely unrelated matter is included. A rider is a provision, not likely to pass on its own merit, attached to an important measure certain to pass. Its sponsors hope that it will "ride" through the legislative process on the strength of the other measure. Thus, some years ago all barrooms in the Capitol were abolished by a short sentence "tucked into" an annual appropriations bill. (Riders have provided a means for getting a controversial matter enacted into law. Presidents sometimes veto a bill because of an objectionable rider.)

Reference to Committee. The Clerk of the House gives each bill a short *title* (a *very* brief summary of its principal contents). Each bill is also assigned a number; thus, "H.R. 3410" would be the 3410th bill introduced in the House during the congressional term.[11]

---

[10] The hopper is a large box hanging at the edge of the Clerk's desk. Puerto Rico's Resident Commissioner and the Delegates from Guam, the Virgin Islands, and the District of Columbia may also introduce bills. Only a Senator may introduce a bill in the upper house; the Senator does so by addressing the chair.

[11] Bills originating in the Senate receive the prefix "S."—as "S. 210." Resolutions are similarly identified in each house in the order of their introduction. Thus, "H.J. Res. 106" would identify the 106th joint resolution introduced in the House during the term and, similarly, "S.J. Res. 106" in the Senate. Concurrent resolutions are identified as "H. Con. Res. 321" or "S. Con. Res. 23" and simple resolutions as "H. Res. 237" or "S. Res. 2173."

HOW BILLS BECOME LAWS

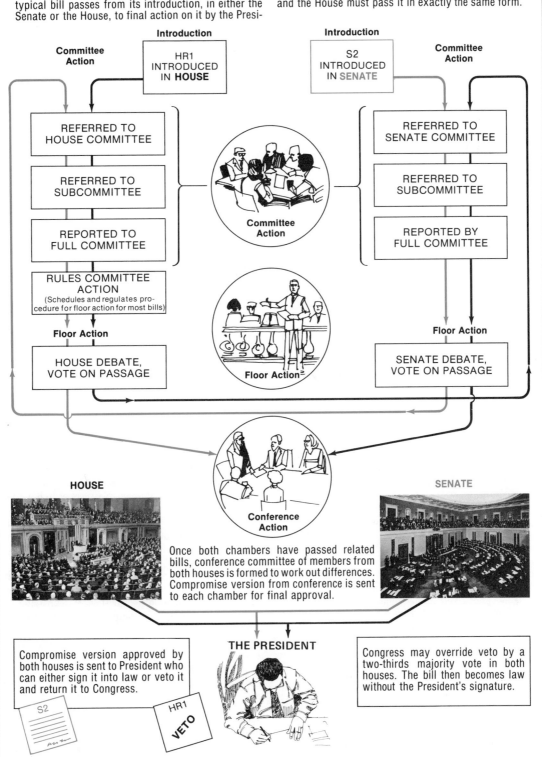

The diagram shows the major steps through which a typical bill passes from its introduction, in either the Senate or the House, to final action on it by the Presi-dent. Before a bill is sent to the White House, the Senate and the House must pass it in exactly the same form.

Introduction

HR1 INTRODUCED IN **HOUSE**

Introduction

S2 INTRODUCED IN SENATE

Committee Action

REFERRED TO HOUSE COMMITTEE

REFERRED TO SUBCOMMITTEE

REPORTED TO FULL COMMITTEE

RULES COMMITTEE ACTION
(Schedules and regulates pro-cedure for floor action for most bills)

Committee Action

Floor Action

HOUSE DEBATE, VOTE ON PASSAGE

Floor Action

Committee Action

REFERRED TO SENATE COMMITTEE

REFERRED TO SUBCOMMITTEE

REPORTED BY FULL COMMITTEE

Floor Action

SENATE DEBATE, VOTE ON PASSAGE

Conference Action

HOUSE

SENATE

Once both chambers have passed related bills, conference committee of members from both houses is formed to work out differences. Compromise version from conference is sent to each chamber for final approval.

Compromise version approved by both houses is sent to President who can either sign it into law or veto it and return it to Congress.

THE PRESIDENT

Congress may override veto by a two-thirds majority vote in both houses. The bill then becomes law without the President's signature.

S2

HR1 VETO

Having received its number and short title, the bill is then entered in the House *Journal* and in the *Congressional Record* for the day.[12]

With these actions the bill has received what is known as its *first reading.* Each bill that is finally passed in either house receives three "readings" along the legislative route. In the House, the *second reading* comes during floor consideration, if the measure gets that far. And the *third reading* occurs just before the final vote on the measure.[13]

Each of these readings is usually by title only: "H.R. 3410, A bill to provide . . ." However, the more important or controversial bills are read in full and considered line by line, section by section, at second reading—that is, during consideration on the floor. Occasionally, the full reading of a measure is demanded by its opponents, as a delaying tactic.

With first reading accomplished, the Speaker refers the bill to the appropriate standing committee—that is, the regular committee with jurisdiction over the subject matter of the bill.

The Committee Stage. The standing committees have been described as "sieves," sifting out most bills and considering and reporting only those they judge to be the more important or worthwhile ones. As Woodrow Wilson once wrote, "Congress in its committee rooms is Congress at work."

Most bills die in committee. They are *pigeonholed,*[14] and never see the light of day. Many of the bills killed in committee certainly deserve their fate. Occasionally, however, for personal or political reasons, a committee majority will pigeonhole a measure that the majority of the House wishes to consider. In that circumstance, the bill can be "blasted out" of committee through the use of the *discharge rule.*[15] But this is seldom a successful maneuver.

The bills that a committee, or at least the chairman, does wish to consider are discussed and considered at times indicated by the chairman. Most committees work through *subcommittees,* which are actually "committees within committees." When more important measures are involved, committees may decide to hold public hearings on them. Interested persons, private organizations and pressure groups, and various government officials are invited to give testimony at these hearings.[16]

---

[12] The *Journal* contains the minutes of the daily proceedings and the *Journal* for the preceding day is read at the opening of each day's session, unless dispensed with (as usually happens). The *Congressional Record* is a voluminous record of the daily proceedings (speeches, debates, other comments, votes, disposition of bills, etc.) in each house. The *Record* is not a verbatim account, however. Members have five days in which to alter the temporary *Record.* They frequently insert long speeches that were never in fact given, reconstruct "debates," and delete thoughtless or inaccurate remarks. The *Record* is, nonetheless, extraordinarily valuable, both politically and historically.

[13] All bills introduced are immediately printed and distributed to the members. The three readings, an ancient practice in parliamentary law, are intended to ensure careful consideration of all bills and to prevent any measure from sneaking by with little or no notice. The practice, really unnecessary now, was quite important in the day when, quite literally, some members of Congress could not read.

[14] The term comes from the old-fashioned roll-top desks with pigeonholes into which papers were often put and promptly forgotten. A great number of "by-request" bills are regularly killed in the committees. These are bills that members introduce only because some person or group at home has asked them to do so.

[15] Under the rule, after a bill has been in committee at least 30 days (seven days in the Rules Committee) a petition signed by a majority (218) of the House membership can force a floor vote on the question of discharging the bill—that is, bringing it to the floor for action. Once the required signatures have been obtained, a seven-day delay occurs. If the committee does not report the bill during that period, any member who signed the petition may (on the second or fourth Monday of the month) move that the committee be discharged. Debate on a discharge motion is limited to 20 minutes. If the motion carries, the House turns to floor consideration of the discharged bill immediately.

[16] If necessary, a committee has the power to *subpoena* a witness. A subpoena is an order compelling one to appear or produce evidence under penalty of contempt for failure to comply.

Occasionally, subcommittees make *junkets* (trips) to particular areas affected by a measure. Thus, some members of the House Agriculture Committee may journey to the Southwest to look into drought conditions. Or, members of the Senate Energy and Natural Resources Committee may visit the Pacific Northwest to gather information on a public power bill.

These junkets are made at public expense, and members of Congress are sometimes criticized for taking them. But an on-the-spot investigation often proves to be the best way a committee may inform itself.

After examining a bill, the full committee may do one of several things. It may:

(1) Report the bill favorably, with a "do pass" recommendation. It is then the chairman's job to steer the bill through debate.

(2) Refuse to report the bill—pigeonhole it. Again, this is the fate suffered by most measures, and in both houses.

(3) Report the bill in amended form. Many bills are changed in committee, and several bills on the same subject may be combined before they are reported out.

(4) Report the bill with an unfavorable recommendation. This does not often happen. But sometimes a committee feels that the full body should have a chance to consider a bill or does not want to take the responsibility for killing it.

(5) Report a "committee bill." In effect, this is an entirely new bill which the committee has substituted for one or more referred to it. The chairman reports this new bill, and it goes on from there.

The Rules Committee and the Calendars. Before it goes to the floor for consideration, a bill reported by a standing committee is placed on one of several calendars. A *calendar* is a schedule of the order in which bills will be considered on the floor. There are five of these calendars in the House:

(1) *The Calendar of the Committee of the Whole House on the State of the Union,* com-

monly known as the *Union Calendar*—for all bills relating to revenues, appropriations, or government property.

(2) *The House Calendar*—for all other public bills.

(3) *The Calendar of the Committee of the Whole House,* commonly called the *Private Calendar*—for all private bills.

(4) *The Consent Calendar*—for all bills from the Union or House Calendar which are taken up out of order by unanimous consent of the House of Representatives. These are usually minor bills to which there is no opposition.

(5) *The Discharge Calendar*—for petitions to discharge bills from committee.

Theoretically, bills are taken from the calendars on a first-come-first-served basis. As we have seen, however, the Rules Committee has the power to bring in a special

"LISTEN—IF I HEAR ANY MORE COMPLAINTS, I MAY STOP HURRYING"

From Herblock's *State of the Union* (Simon & Schuster, 1972)

rule to consider a bill out of its regular order, and this is often done. The Rules Committee also can prevent a bill from getting to the floor by failing to bring in a special rule. It is no wonder that the Rules Committee is sometimes known as the "traffic cop of the House."

The Rules Committee is often criticized, and it is true that some members use their powers as members of this Committee for personal or political advantage. But it must be remembered that despite the number of bills that die in committee, many more bills than the House can possibly consider are reported.

For certain bills, definite days are assigned by the House rules. Bills from the Consent Calendar are considered on the first and third Mondays of each month. District of Columbia measures are considered on the second and fourth Mondays, and private bills each Friday. On "calendar Wednesdays" the various committee chairmen may call up any bills their committees have acted on.

None of these arrangements is followed too closely, however. What generally happens is rather complicated. Some bills are "privileged." That is, they may be called up at almost any time, interrupting other business less privileged. Privileged bills include general revenue and appropriations measures, reports of conference committees, and special rules. On some days, often the first and third Mondays, a two-thirds vote of the House may suspend all rules. When this happens, the House departs so far from its established rules that a major bill can go through all the necessary steps for enactment in a single day.

The House calendars and the complicated order of business developed over the years for several reasons. They developed especially because of the large size of the House and the number and variety of bills introduced. And, they developed because of the fact that no one member could hope to know the contents, to say nothing of the

merits, of each bill to be considered. As we have seen, custom, too, has played a large part in the development of the procedures as they exist today.

Consideration on the Floor. When a bill finally manages to reach the floor it receives its second reading. It is this part of House procedure that is usually seen by the visitors in the galleries.

Many of the bills the House passes are minor ones to which there is little or no opposition. Bills of this kind are usually called from the Consent Calendar, get their second reading by title only, and are quickly disposed of. Nearly all of the more important measures are dealt with in a much different manner, however. They are considered in *Committee of the Whole,* an old parliamentary device for speeding business.

The Committee of the Whole[17] is the House of Representatives sitting not as itself but as one large committee of itself. Its rules are much less strict, and debate is freer. A *quorum* (majority of the full membership, 218) must be present to permit the House to do business; but, when measures are considered in Committee of the Whole only 100 members are needed.

When the House resolves itself into Committee of the Whole, the Speaker steps down, and the mace is removed, for the House is not legally in session. Another member takes the chair and presides.

General debate is held, and then the bill receives its second reading, section-by-section. As each section of the bill is read, amendments may be offered. Under the

---

[17] Technically, there are two committees of the whole: the Committee of the Whole House, which considers private bills, and the Committee of the Whole House on the State of the Union, which considers public bills. But both these committees are simply the House of Representatives sitting as a committee of itself. The device has not been used in the Senate, except to consider treaties, since 1930. Because of the Senate's smaller size, many types of committees are somewhat less necessary than in the larger House.

"five-minute rule," the supporters and opponents of each amendment have just five minutes to present their case. Votes are taken on each section and its amendments as the reading proceeds.

When the entire bill has been gone through—and some run to many pages—the Committee of the Whole has completed its work. It adjourns, the House is back in session, and the committee's work is formally adopted.

DEBATE. Because of the large size of the House, debate must, as a practical matter, be severely limited. A rule adopted in 1841 limits each member to no more than one hour on any point unless unanimous consent to speak for a longer time has been granted. Since 1880 the rules have provided that if a member strays from the subject the Speaker may force that member to relinquish the floor—in short, to stop talking and sit down.

The majority and minority floor leaders usually decide in advance how much time will be spent on a bill. At any time, however, a member may "move the previous question." That is, a vote may be called for. If the motion is adopted, the Speaker may then allow each side another 20 minutes of debate. After the 40 minutes a vote must be taken. The "previous question" is the only motion used in the House to *close* (end) debate, but it is a very effective device.

VOTING. A single bill may be—and often is—voted upon several times before it is finally approved or rejected by the House. Thus, a vote is taken on the rule for the bill—for example, whether to take it up out of calendar order and/or to place a time limit on floor consideration of it. If amendments are offered, and they frequently are, these must be voted up or down, as well. (The voting on amendments is often a more illuminating test of a bill's support than the final tally. Members of Congress sometimes support a measure after having backed amendments to it which,

"ON THE WAY HOME, WE CAN READ SOME OF THIS STUFF WE'VE BEEN VOTING ON"

if adopted, would have in fact scuttled it.)

Then, too, various motions may interrupt floor consideration—for example, any member may move the previous question, or offer a motion to adjourn. These, too, must be voted upon.

The House now (1981) uses three methods for the taking of floor votes:

(1) *Voice votes* are the most common, with the members answering "aye" or "no" in chorus.

(2) If any member thinks the Speaker may have erred in judging which side has the most voice votes, he or she may call for a *standing vote*, technically known as "a division of the House." All in favor, and then all opposed, stand and are counted by the Clerk.

(3) A *roll-call vote,* also known as a *record vote,* may be demanded by one-fifth of the members present.[18]

The House began using a computer-operated electronic voting system in 1973. It is now used for all quorum calls and record votes, and replaced the traditional roll-call by the Clerk. Under the new arrangement, House members may vote at any one of 44 stations located about the floor. Each member votes by inserting his or her personal computer card in a small box and

---

[18] The Constitution (Article I, Section 7, Clause 2) requires a record vote on the question of overriding a presidential veto. The House rules also require a record vote whenever any member objects to a non-record vote (a voice or standing vote) taken when a quorum was not present. Until 1973 the House also used yet another method: the *teller vote.* Whenever one-fifth of the members present demanded one, each member voting passed between two tellers, one from each party, and was counted for or against. The new electronic voting system effectively eliminated the practice, however.

"LISTEN, IT ISN'T EASY MAKING LAWS FOR OTHER PEOPLE TO LIVE BY!"

"Grin and Bear It," by Lichty & Wagner, Courtesy of Field Newspaper Syndicate

then pushing one of three buttons—"Yea," "Nay," "Present." (When a vote of "present" is cast, it means that that member does not wish to vote on the bill. In some instances, a "present" vote is not allowed, as on the question of overriding a veto.) Each computer card is punched with a pattern of holes to identify the member. Representatives who wish to change their votes may do so by simply reinserting their card and pushing another button.

A master board, listing all House members, is situated on four large panels on the front wall high above the chamber. Beside each name are three colored lights to indicate the type of votes cast—green for "yea," red for "nay," and amber for "present."

Smaller summary boards are attached to the balcony ledges on either side of the chamber, showing the vote totals and the amount of time remaining for the casting of votes. The leadership tables on either side of the aisle are also equipped with consoles, permitting the majority and minority floor leaders to follow voting patterns and the behavior of each member.

The House rules now allow members 15 minutes in which to answer quorum calls or to cast record votes. Under the old roll-call system, it took anywhere from 25 to 45 minutes to complete the process. In previous sessions, all of the roll-calls taken occupied about *three months* of House floor time per session. Voting now ends when the Speaker locks the vote totals into the machine.

In addition to its vote-recording chores, the computer is also used to keep track of the legislative history of measures in both the House and Senate through an information retrieval system.

Voting procedures are quite similar in the Senate. But the upper house has not felt the need for an electronic scoreboard system. Only six or seven minutes are required for taking a roll-call vote in the Senate.

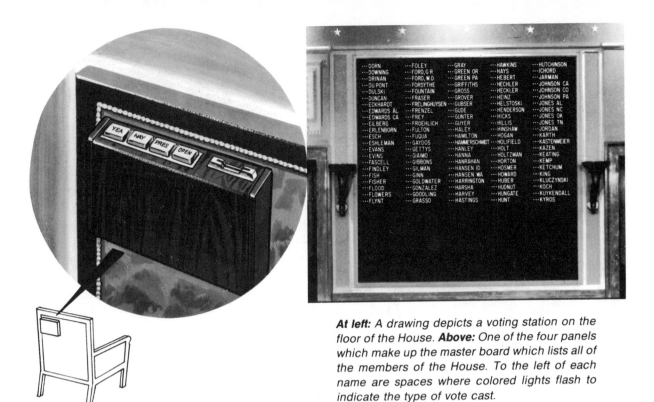

At left: *A drawing depicts a voting station on the floor of the House.* **Above:** *One of the four panels which make up the master board which lists all of the members of the House. To the left of each name are spaces where colored lights flash to indicate the type of vote cast.*

Final Steps in the House. Once a bill is approved at second reading, it is *engrossed*; that is, the bill is printed in its final form with all changes made. Then it is read a third time, by title, and the final vote is taken. If the bill is defeated, it must begin all over again if it is ever to pass the House. If it is approved, as most bills which reach this stage are, it is signed by the Speaker and taken to the Senate by a page who places it on the Vice President's desk.

The Bill in the Senate

The steps in the legislative process are quite similar in each house. Thus, we need not trace a bill through the Senate in the detail with which we have just viewed the actions of the House. Rather, we shall consider the major contrasts to be found in the upper house.

Bills are introduced by Senators, who are formally recognized for that purpose. A measure is then read twice, given a number and short title, and then referred to committee—where measures are dealt

with much as they are in the House.

The Senate has only one calendar for all bills and they are called up at the discretion of the majority floor leader. Proceedings are generally less formal and the rules less strict than in the much larger House.

Debate. The major differences in House and Senate procedures involve debate. It is strictly limited in the House of Representatives but almost unfettered in the Senate. Most Senators are proud of belonging to what is often called "the greatest deliberative body in the world."

As a general matter, Senators may speak on the floor for as long as they please. No rule requires that they speak only on the measure under consideration. And, unlike the House, the Senate's rules do not permit the moving of the previous question.

The Senate's consideration of most major bills is brought to a close by *unanimous consent* agreements. That is, discussion ends and a final vote is taken at a fixed time previously agreed to by the majority and

minority leaders. But if any Senator objects to that agreement—prevents unanimous consent—the device fails. Again, however, it is the procedure regularly used.[19]

The Senate's dedication to freedom of debate is well-nigh unique among modern legislative bodies. It is intended to encourage the fullest possible discussion of matters on the floor, of course. But the great latitude it permits can be, and has been, abused by the *filibuster*.[20]

---

[19] The Senate's rules do contain a "two-speech rule." Under it, no Senator may speak more than twice on a given question on the same legislative day. By *recessing* rather than *adjourning* a day's session the Senate can prolong a "legislative day" indefinitely. Thus, it can limit, to some extent at least, the length of time it devotes to a single item of business.

[20] The term comes from the Dutch *vrijbuiter*—literally, "free booter," and was first used to describe pirates in the Caribbean in the 16th century. In French, the Dutch word became *filibustier*, in Spanish *filibustero*, and then in English, *filibuster*. It acquired its present meaning in American politics well over a century ago. See William Safire, *Safire's Political Dictionary* (New York: Ballentine Books, 1978), pages 226–227.

THE FILIBUSTER. A filibuster is an attempt to "talk a bill to death." One or more Senators filibuster by so monopolizing the floor and the time of the Senate, talking on and on, that the Senate must either drop the bill before it or change it in some manner acceptable to the filibusterers.

Talk is the filibusterers' major weapon. But time-consuming roll calls, points of order, and other motions are often used, as well. Indeed, anything to obstruct or delay is grist for the minority's attempt to thwart the majority of the upper house.

The history of the Senate is liberally dotted with filibusters—many of them prolonged and dramatic. Most have been team efforts, in which a small group of Senators speak in relays and are thus able to hold the fort indefinitely.

Among the many notable efforts, Senator Huey Long (D., Louisiana) spoke for more than 15 hours in 1935. He stalled along by reading from the Washington telephone directory and a mail-order catalog and regaled his colleagues with his recipes for "pot-likker," corn bread, and turnip greens. In 1947 Glen Taylor (D., Idaho) consumed eight and a half hours, talking of his children, Wall Street, baptism, and fishing.

The current filibuster record is held by Strom Thurmond (R., South Carolina). He held the floor for 24 hours and 18 minutes in an unsuccessful effort against what later became the Civil Rights Act of 1957. Maurine Neuberger (D., Oregon) became the first woman filibusterer when she spoke for more than four hours against a communications satellite bill in 1962.

Over the past century, well over 200 measures have been killed by filibusters. And the *threat* of a filibuster has resulted in the Senate's failure to consider a number of bills and the amending of many more. Most, but by no means all, filibusters in recent years have been staged by Southern Senators.

The Senate often tries to beat a filibuster with lengthy, even day-and-night, sessions to wear down the participants. At times some little-observed Senate rules are strictly enforced—including, for example, the requirement that members stand, not sit or lean on their desks or walk about as they speak; or that they not use "unparliamentary language." But these techniques seldom work.

THE CLOTURE RULE. The Senate's ultimate antifilibuster weapon is the Cloture Rule. It was first adopted in 1917, after a filibuster which had outraged public opinion. Twelve Senators had managed to kill a bill which would have permitted the arming of American merchant ships in order to protect them against marauding German submarines.

The Cloture Rule does not regularly apply, however, and it is difficult to bring into play. As it now (1981) stands, a vote to invoke *cloture* (limit debate) must be taken two days after a petition calling for it has been submitted by at least 16 Senators. If at least 60 members—three-fifths of the full Senate—then vote for the motion, each Senator is limited to not more than *one hour* of debate on the pending bill. After debate ends, the measure *must* be brought to a final vote.[21]

How difficult it is to invoke cloture can be seen in the fact that over the life of the rule—from 1917 to 1981—157 attempts to do so have occurred, and only 49 of them have succeeded. But the recent record indicates that the Senate is now more willing to combat filibusters by attempting to invoke tne rule than was the case only a few years ago. Two-thirds of all the attempts to close debate—110 of them—have been made over the past ten years in the Senate (1971 thru 1980). And nearly all of the successful tries—42 of them—have come in that same period.

The Final Stages

The Conference Committee. Before a bill may be sent to the White House, it *must* be passed by both houses in *identical* form. Occasionally, the House and the Senate do pass differing versions of the same legislation, and the first house will not agree to the changes the other has made. If this happens, a *conference committee*—a temporary joint committee—is appointed. It seeks to "iron out" the differences and produce a compromise bill which will be acceptable to both houses.

Each conference committee is composed of a varying number of Representatives and Senators appointed by the respective presiding officers. Almost invariably the conferees ("managers") from each house are leading members of the standing committee which originally handled the disputed measure. In fact, the chairman and the ranking minority member of that committee are usually appointed, along with others conspicuous on each side in the consideration of the bill. The majority position in each house is always represented by a majority of the conferees from that chamber; but the minority is also represented.

The rules of each house restrict a conference committee to the consideration of those points in a bill upon which the two houses have disagreed. The rules also prohibit the inclusion of new material in a compromise version. In practice, however,

---

[21] The Cloture Rule (Rule 22 in the Standing Rules of the Senate) was liberalized somewhat in 1975. Until then, it became operative only if a cloture motion were approved by two-thirds of the members *present and voting*. Under the 1975 revision, the three-fifths requirement applies to all matters *except* proposals to change any of the Standing Rules; cloture may be invoked with regard to any proposed rule change only if approved by two-thirds of the members present and voting.

the conferees possess a large amount of discretion. They meet in secret, almost never hold public hearings or invite outside testimony, and keep no record of their proceedings. And, very often, their product contains provisions not previously considered in either house.

A conference committee's report—the compromise bill it has hammered out—must be considered as a whole in each house. It cannot be amended on the floor. It must be accepted or rejected as it comes from the committee. Neither house very often rejects a conference committee's work. This is not surprising, given the potent membership of the typical conference committee, and, too, the fact that its report is usually made toward the end of a congressional session.

In short, the conference committee stage is an extraordinarily strategic step in the legislative process. It is a point at which many important legislative decisions may be made. Indeed, the late Senator George Norris of Nebraska once aptly described conference committees as "the third house of Congress."

The President's Action. The Constitution requires that "every bill which shall have passed the House of Representatives and the Senate" and "every order, resolution, or vote, to which the concurrence of the Senate and House of Representatives may be necessary (except on a question of adjournment) shall be presented to the President" for subsequent approval or disapproval. [22]

Once a measure has cleared both houses in identical form, then, it is sent to the President. The Constitution presents the President with four options at this point:

First, the President may sign the bill. The bill then becomes law.

Second, the President may veto the bill. The measure must then be returned to the house in which it originated, together with the President's objections to it. Although it usually does not, Congress may then enact the bill over the President's veto by a two-thirds vote in each house.

Third, the President may allow the bill to become law without signature—by not acting upon it (neither signing nor vetoing) within 10 days (not counting Sundays) of its receipt from Congress.

The *fourth* option is a variation of the third. Here, if Congress adjourns its session within 10 days of submitting a bill to the President and the Chief Executive does not act upon it, the measure dies—the "pocket veto" has been applied to it.

We shall return to the President's veto and other legislative powers in Chapter 16.

---

[22] Article I, Section 7, Clauses 2 and 3. Although the Constitution seems to provide otherwise, practice has it that neither concurrent resolutions (which, recall, do not have the force of law) nor those joint resolutions proposing constitutional amendments are submitted to the Chief Executive. (See page 409.)

SUMMARY

Opening day in the House of Representatives is filled with ceremony. A Speaker must be chosen, the members sworn in, employees selected, the rules adopted, and committee and other organizational posts filled. The Senate's first day is a much simpler matter for it is a continuous body and thus does not require such extensive reorganization.

After organizing, the two houses await the President's State of the Union Message, in which the Chief Executive reports on the condition of the nation and makes many specific legislative recommendations and other policy pronouncements.

The Speaker is the most powerful member of the House of Representatives. The Speaker's chief duties are to preside and to maintain order, and Speakers use their powers in a partisan manner. The Vice President (or, when absent, the President *pro tem*) presides over the Senate.

The majority and minority floor leaders, assisted by their party whips, manage their parties' programs on the floor. The party caucus consists of the party's members in either house and has an "executive committee" known as its Policy or Steering Committee.

Those who head committees have virtual life-and-death power over bills referred to their committee. It is in the committees where much of the actual work of Congress is, in fact, done.

Congress does a great deal of its work in committees, especially in the House. Standing committees are permanent ones, and bills introduced are referred to them for consideration. One, the House Rules Committee, is "the traffic cop of the legislative process." Select committees are temporary, while joint committees (composed of members of both houses) are usually permanent bodies. Conference committees are formed to "iron out" differences in bills passed by the two chambers.

Bills may be introduced only by Representatives in the House and Senators in the upper chamber—but they usually originate in some other source, the executive branch or a pressure group, for example. After bills are introduced, they are referred to committee, where most of them die. Bills reported out of committee go on one of the five calendars used by the House and are brought to the floor for consideration through the Rules Committee. There is but one calendar for bills in the Senate, and they are called up by the majority floor leader.

Bills are debated in the House at the second of the three readings. The House, but not the Senate, considers most important bills in Committee of the Whole. Debate is severely limited in the House, but not in the Senate. A filibuster, the practice of talking a bill to death, may be prevented in the Senate by the difficult process of invoking cloture.

Bills passed by the two houses which differ in form go to a conference committee. Then a bill goes to the President, who may sign it, veto it, allow it to become law without signing it, or apply a pocket veto to it. Congress may override a President's veto by a two-thirds vote in each house.

Concept Development

Questions for Review

1. Why is the opening day of a term a much simpler matter in the Senate than in the House?

2. Who presides over the House of Representatives? How is this officer chosen?

3. Who presides over the Senate? How is this officer chosen?

4. Why does the Senate have an alternate presiding officer?

5. Who selects the floor leaders? The whips? What are their major jobs?

6. On what basis are committee chairmen selected? By whom are they chosen? Why are they so powerful?

7. May the party caucus bind its members to follow its decisions?

8. How many standing committees are there in the House of Representatives? The Senate?

9. What role does the Rules Committee play in the House?

10. Why is it essential that Congress have the power to investigate?

11. Who may introduce bills in each house? About what proportion of those introduced actually become law? Where are many of the most important bills actually prepared?

12. Who refers bills to committee in the House? The Senate?

13. What is the function of the various calendars in the House?

14. Why is the Committee of the Whole a much more important and widely used device in the House than in the Senate?

15. Why is debate more limited in the House than in the Senate?

16. What three methods of voting are used in the House? Which is used most often?

17. What is a filibuster? How may one be ended?

18. What is the function of a conference committee?

19. What four options are available to the President in considering a bill passed by Congress?

20. By what vote may a presidential veto be overridden? What is a "pocket veto"?

For Further Inquiry

1. Many members of Congress are reluctant to vote on certain roll calls. Why? The new electronic voting system now used in the House provides a permanent voting record for each member. What significance can this have for a member of Congress in his or her home district?

2. One of the most famous filibusters in Senate history occurred in February and March of 1917. President Wilson had asked Congress to enact a law authorizing him to arm merchant vessels for protection against German submarine attacks. The bill passed the House of Representatives by a vote of 403 to 12. Nearly all members of the Senate favored it. But a small handful of Senators managed to kill it by filibustering. The public was outraged. President Wilson wrote: "A little group of willful men, representing no opinion but their own, have rendered the great Government of the United States helpless and contemptible." As a result of this episode, the Senate passed the Cloture Rule. The rule is a relatively weak one, however. What is your own attitude toward filibusters? Should they be prohibited? What would be valid arguments in support of the opposite stand?

3. The daily sessions of the House of Representatives are now carried by many cable TV systems around the country. If these broadcasts are available in your area, you can learn much about the House, the legislative process, and a good deal more by watching them, of course. Do you think that the sessions of the House, or the Senate, or both sould be televised? Why, or why not?

4. Many urge that the Senate abolish the filibuster and that both houses abandon the seniority rule. What is your stand on each of these practices? What other reforms in congressional organization and procedure do you think should be made?

5. Explain the meaning of this statement: "Ideally, a member of Congress should be both *responsive* and *responsible.*" Are both of these characteristics desirable? Are they necessary? Is either of them more important than the other?

6. Why do conference committees meet in executive (*i.e.,* closed) session? What would likely be the effect of open sessions on their work?

7. Why do you think the Founding Fathers provided that: (a) "All bills for raising revenue shall originate in the House of Representatives" (Article I, Section 7, Clause 1); and (b) ". . . but no appropriation of money to that use [to raise and support armies] shall be for a longer term than two years" (Article I, Section 8, Clause 12)?

Suggested Activities

1. Stage a class forum or debate on one of the following questions: (a) *Resolved,* That the seniority rule should be abolished in both houses of Congress; (b) *Resolved,* That filibusters should be prohibited in the Senate; (c) *Resolved,* That congressional committees should be denied the power to make investigations; (d) *Resolved,* That Republican and Democratic Party members in each house should be required to vote in accord with the decisions of their respective party caucuses.

2. Trace a current bill as it goes through the legislative mill in Congress.

Write to your Representative and Senators to learn their positions on it. Ask them if they would kindly forward to you the committee reports and other materials relating to the measure. Then, give an oral report to the class.

3. Write a report on one of the following topics: (a) the work of the House Rules Committee; (b) the office of Speaker; (c) the seniority rule; (d) congressional reform; or (e) the Library of Congress.

Suggested Reading

Baker, Ross K., *Friend and Foe in the U.S. Senate.* Free Press, 1979.

Congressional Directory, 97th Congress, 1st Session. Government Printing Office, 1981.

Edwards, George C., *Presidential Influence in Congress.* Freeman, 1980.

Goehlert, Robert, *Congress and Law-Making.* ABC—Clio Press, 1979.

Green, Mark, *Who Runs Congress?* Bantam Books, rev. ed., 1979.

Inside Congress. Congressional Quarterly Press, 2nd ed., 1979.

Keefe, William J. and Ogle, Morris S., *The American Legislative Process.* Prentice-Hall, 5th ed., 1981.

Kingdon, John W., *Congressmen's Voting Decisions.* Harper & Row, 2nd ed., 1981.

Malbin, Michael J., *Unelected Representatives: Congressional Staff and the Future of Representative Government.* Basic Books, 1980.

Oleszek, Walter J., *Congressional Procedures and the Policy Process.* Congressional Quarterly Press, 1978.

Olson, David M., *The Legislative Process.* Harper & Row, 1979.

Ornstein, Norman J. and Elder, Shirley, *Interest Groups, Lobbying and Policymaking.* Congressional Quarterly Press, 1978.

Schwab, Larry M., *Changing Patterns of Congressional Politics.* D. Van Nostrand, 1980.

Vogler, David J., *The Politics of Congress.* Allyn and Bacon, 1977.

The Powers of Congress

All legislative power herein granted shall be vested in a Congress of the United States. . . .

ARTICLE I, SECTION 1
CONSTITUTION OF THE UNITED STATES

■ What is *the* basic function of the Congress?

■ Why has Congress *only* those powers delegated to it by the Constitution?

■ Is the concept of implied powers a corruption of the concept of federalism?

As the opening words of Article I of the Constitution declare, the basic function of the Congress is to legislate, to make law. As we have suggested several times, that function is of pivotal importance to democratic government: it is the function of translating the public will into public policy in the form of law.

In this chapter we are concerned with the two basic categories of power possessed by Congress: *First,* its *legislative powers*—those constitutional powers upon the basis of which Congress can and does make law. And, *secondly,* its *nonlegislative powers*—those constitutional powers upon the basis of which Congress can and does perform other functions closely related to its role as the lawmaking branch of the National Government.

The Scope of Congressional Powers. At this point it would be well to recall two fundamentally important facts: *First,* that government in the United States is *limited* government. And, *secondly,* that the governmental system in the United States is a *federal* system.

The Constitution imposes a great many restrictions and prohibitions upon Congress—as it does upon the National Government as a whole. Large areas of power are denied to Congress. They are denied in so many words by the Constitution, because of that document's silence on many subjects, and because of the very nature of the federal system itself.

In short, Congress possesses *only* those

The Capitol in 1800, the year the North Wing was completed. The Congress met for the first time in its new quarters on the Potomac on November 21, 1800.

powers delegated to it by the Constitution. It cannot do a great variety of things. For example, it cannot create a national public school system, require that all eligible voters cast ballots on election day, nor insist that all persons attend church. It cannot enact a uniform marriage and divorce law, regulate city transit systems, nor prohibit trial by jury. These and many other things it cannot do because it has not been granted power to do so.

Recall, too, that Congress *is* granted the power to do many things. The Constitution delegates specific powers to Congress in three distinct ways. It does so: (1) Expressly, in so many words (the *expressed powers*). (2) By implication—that is, by reasonable deduction from the expressed powers (the *implied powers*). And (3) by virtue of the fact that it creates a *national* government for the United States (the *inherent powers*).

Strict Versus Liberal Construction.
Hardly had the Constitution come into force when a dispute arose as to just how broad the powers it granted to Congress actually were. The *strict-constructionists,* led by Thomas Jefferson, favored retaining as much power as possible in the States. They agreed with Jefferson that "that government is best which governs least." In essence, they wanted to restrict Congress to those powers actually stated in the Constitution. The *liberal-constructionists,* led by Alexander Hamilton, favored a stronger National Government and, therefore, favored a liberal or broad interpretation of the Constitution in order to widen the powers of Congress.

As we shall see in a moment (on page 343), those who favored a liberal interpretation prevailed. They established a pattern which has been generally followed to the present day. They set a precedent from

332 / Chapter 14

which, over the years, the powers wielded by the National Government have grown to a point immeasurably beyond their base in 1789.

Several factors, working in combination with a liberal construction of the Constitution, have been responsible for this marked growth in national power. Wars, economic crises, and other national emergencies have been very prominent causes. The spectacular industrial and technological advances we have made—most notably in the fields of transportation and communication—have also had a significant effect. And so have the demands of the people themselves for more and still more governmental services.

Congress has been led by these and other factors to view its powers in broadening terms. In the same sense, most Presidents have regarded and exercised their powers in this fashion. The Supreme Court in deciding cases involving the powers of the National Government has generally adopted a like position. And the American people have been in general agreement with a liberal rather than a strict interpretation of the Constitution. This agreement has prevailed even though our political history has been regularly punctuated by controversy over the proper limits of national power.

The Expressed Powers

Most, but not all of the expressed powers of Congress are found in Article I, Section 8 of the Constitution. There, in 18 separate clauses, some 27 different powers are explicitly granted to Congress.[1]

-----

[1] Several of the expressed powers of Congress are set out elsewhere in the Constitution. Thus, Article IV, Section 3 grants it the power to admit new States to the Union (Clause 1) and to manage and dispose of federal territory and other property (Clause 2). The 16th Amendment gives Congress the power to levy an income tax. And, importantly, the 13th, 14th, 15th, 19th, 24th, and 26th Amendments each vest in Congress the "power to enforce" the provisions of the particular Amendment "by appropriate legislation."

These grants of power are quite brief. What they do—and do not—permit Congress to do often cannot be discovered merely by reading the few words involved. Rather, their content is to be found in the ways in which Congress has in fact exercised its various powers since 1789. And, as well, their content is found in scores of Supreme Court decisions in cases arising out of many of the actions taken by Congress.

To illustrate the point, take the Commerce Clause (Article I, Section 8, Clause 3). It gives to Congress the power "to regulate commerce with foreign nations, and among the several States, and with the Indian tribes." The words of the provision are both brief and general. And both Congress and the Court have had to answer literally hundreds of questions involving its scope and content. For example, what does "commerce" include? Does it include persons? Radio and television broadcasts? Air transportation? Business practices? Labor-management relationships? Does the Commerce Clause empower the Congress to do such things as fix minimum wages and maximum hours and determine other labor conditions? Does it allow Congress to prohibit the shipment of certain goods, regulate banks and other financial institutions? Can Congress act to prohibit discrimination, or provide for the construction of multi-purpose dams? What commerce is *foreign* and what *interstate*? What commerce is neither, and thus *intrastate* and not subject to congressional regulation?

In providing the answers to these and to many other questions involving this *one* brief provision, Congress and the Court have spelled out, and are still spelling out, the meaning of the Commerce Clause. And so it is with each of the other portions of the Constitution which vest power in Congress.

Before we review the various congressional powers, remember this: Each of these powers has its historic significance.

And most of them have a very substantial and continuing, present-day, importance. It should be fairly obvious that such powers as those to tax, to borrow, to declare war, and to regulate foreign and interstate commerce are of that order. A few of them are of little real moment, however—most notably, the power to grant letters of marque and reprisal, a power that Congress has not exercised in well over a century; see page 342.

The Power to Tax. The Constitution gives to Congress the power:

> To lay and collect taxes, duties, imposts and excises, to pay the debts and provide for the common defence and general welfare of the United States. . . .[2]

As we observed in Chapter 2, the fact that the Articles of Confederation did not equip the Congress with the power to tax was among the major weaknesses of that document. Without it Congress was virtually impotent. And its absence was among the prime causes for the coming of the Constitution.

We shall deal with the taxing power and its exercise at length in Chapter 20. But for now notice several things about it.

The Federal Government will take in some $600 billion in fiscal year 1981—and that gargantuan sum will almost certainly be exceeded in fiscal 1982. Most of that huge amount of money—well over 95 percent of it—will be received as a direct result of the various taxes levied by Congress.

The basic purpose of the exercise of the power to tax is, of course, to raise the revenues necessary to finance the operations of government. Dictionaries tell us that "a tax" is "a charge laid by government upon persons or property to meet the public needs." Taxes *are* most often imposed in order to raise revenue—that is, in order "to meet the public needs."

But notice that the usual dictionary definition is an *incomplete* one. It is because taxes may be imposed for purposes *other* than the raising of revenue—and they often are. Illustrations of the use of the taxing power for non-financial purposes are many. The *protective tariff* is probably the oldest example one may cite. Although such levies do bring in some revenue, their primary object is that of "protecting" domestic industry against foreign competition. Or, as another illustration, notice that a tax may be levied in order to protect the public health and safety. For example, the bulk of federal regulation of the use of narcotics is carried on through taxation—in this instance, licensing for legitimate dealing in narcotics.

The power to tax is not an unlimited one. As with all of the other powers of the National Government, it must be exercised

2 Article I, Section 8, Clause 1.

Case Study

Taxes stir deep emotions, produce many conflicting opinions, and generate a vast amount of political heat. Most Americans seem to accept their federal tax burdens resignedly, even fatalistically. They recognize and accept the fact that a large share of the money raised goes for national defense purposes; and, although they obviously favor the lowest practicable level of taxation, they tend to agree with Justice Holmes that with taxes we "buy civilization." But there are also many Americans who regard taxes as, at best, onerous deprivations of personal property and freedom. In this context, Senator Barry Goldwater has written:

We have been led to look upon taxation as merely a problem of public financing: How much money does the government need? We have been led to discount, and often to forget altogether, the bearing of taxation on the problem of individual freedom. . . .

One of the foremost precepts of natural law is man's right to the possession and use of his property. And a man's earnings are his property as much as his land and the house in which he lives. Indeed, in the industrial age, earnings are probably the most prevalent form of property. . . . How can a man be truly free if he is denied the means to exercise freedom? How can he be free if the fruits of his labor are not his to dispose of, but are treated, instead, as part of a common pool of public wealth? Property and freedom are inseparable: the extent government takes the one in the form of taxes, it intrudes on the other. *The Conscience of a Conservative*, 1960.

■ Which of these two general attitudes toward taxation do you tend to accept? Why?
■ Do you think that a taxing system ought to be based upon the concept of ability to pay or, instead, upon the concept of benefits received?

in accord with all of the other provisions of the Constitution. Thus, Congress could not lay a tax on the conduct of church services. Such a levy would be a patent violation of the 1st Amendment's guarantee of religious freedom.

More specifically, the Constitution imposes four explicit limitations on the use of the taxing power. *First,* Congress may tax only for *public purposes,* not for private benefit. Recall that Article I, Section 8, Clause 1 provides that taxes may be levied only "to pay the debts, and provide for the common defence and general welfare of the United States." *Secondly,* Congress may not tax exports. Article I, Section 9, Clause 5 provides:

No tax or duty shall be laid on articles exported from any State.

Thus, customs duties (tariffs, which are taxes) may be applied only to imports.

Thirdly, direct taxes must be apportioned equally among the States, according to their respective populations. Article I, Section 9, Clause 4 declares:

No capitation, or other direct tax, shall be laid, unless in proportion to the census or enumeration herein before directed to be taken.

A *direct tax* is one which must be borne by the person upon whom it is imposed—for example, a tax on the ownership of land or buildings, or a *capitation* (head or poll) tax. An income tax is also a direct tax. But, notice, it may be laid without regard to population because of the 16th Amendment:

The Congress shall have power to lay and collect taxes on incomes, from whatever source derived, without apportionment among the several States, and without regard to any census or enumeration.

Finally, Article I, Section 8, Clause 1 provides that:

. . . all duties, imposts, and excises shall be uniform throughout the United States.

That is, all indirect taxes must be levied at the same rates in all parts of the country. It is very difficult to draw a precise line between direct and indirect taxes. In effect, the question of whether a particular tax is a direct or an indirect one rests with Congress and the Supreme Court. As a general rule, however, an *indirect tax* is one which, although it is actually paid by one person, is in fact passed on to another and is therefore indirectly paid by that second person. For example, the federal excise tax on each pack of cigarettes is paid by the tobacco company which produces the cigarettes. But the producer passes the tax on along the retail chain until, ultimately, it is in fact paid by the person who purchases the cigarettes.

Again, we shall return to the taxing power, and at greater length, in Chapter 20, Government and Finance.

The Commerce Power. The commerce power is as indispensable to the existence and the welfare of the nation as is the taxing power. As we have noted, it, too, played a vital role in the formation of the Union. The weak Congress under the Articles of Confederation had no power to regulate commerce among the States and but very little authority over foreign trade. The Critical Period of the 1780's was marked by intense commercial rivalries, jealousies, and foolish bickerings among the newly independent States. High trade barriers and spiteful State laws created chaos and confusion in both interstate and foreign commerce.

These conditions prompted the Framers to write the commerce power into the Constitution. Once they had reached compromises on such issues as the levying of import duties and the regulation of the slave trade, they agreed unanimously to Article I, Section 8, Clause 3. This clause grants to Congress the power:

To regulate commerce with foreign nations, and among the several States, and with the Indian tribes.

We shall deal with the commerce power and its exercise by Congress at length in several later chapters, especially in Chapters 21 through 25. But for now notice several things about it.

The Commerce Clause has done more to develop a loose confederation into a strong Union of States than has any other provision in all of the Constitution. It has permitted the development in the United

"INCOME TAX GUIDES?
YES, SIR—THEY'RE OVER IN SECTION R,
BETWEEN OUR GREEK MANUSCRIPTS
AND OUR BOOKS ON INTEGRAL CALCULUS."
Salt and Pepper, *The Wall Street Journal,* by James Estes. Reprinted by permission of *The Wall Street Journal.*

States of the greatest unrestricted market area in the world. And, along with the power to lay and collect taxes, it has contributed most to the vast growth in the power and authority of the National Government.

The very first case to reach the Supreme Court involving the Commerce Clause and its meaning was *Gibbons* v. *Ogden,* in 1824. We shall look at that landmark case in greater detail later, on page 530. But here, the vital point is this: In that case, the Court, siding with Congress, read the Commerce Clause in extremely broad terms. Wrote Chief Justice John Marshall:

> Commerce undoubtedly is traffic, but it is something more—it is intercourse. It describes the commercial intercourse between nations, and parts of nations, in all its branches, and is regulated by prescribing rules for carrying on that intercourse.

This view of the scope of the commerce power has permitted the reach of federal authority into many areas beyond the anticipation of the Framers of the Constitution. We cited several of those areas a moment ago, on page 332—and there are a great many others, as we shall see.

As another of any number of examples of the point: It is on the basis of the commerce power that the Civil Rights Act of 1964 prohibits discrimination in access to or service in hotels, motels, theaters, restaurants, and other public accommodations on grounds of race, color, religion, or national origin.[3]

It is on the basis of the expressed power to regulate commerce, and to tax, that Congress and the courts have built nearly all of the field of implied powers. Put another way: The vast bulk of what the Government of the United States does, day to day and year to year, it does as the result of legislation enacted by Congress in the exercise of these two powers.

The commerce power is not an unlimited one, of course. It, too, must be exercised in accord with all other provisions in the Constitution. Thus, Congress could not provide that only those firms with ten or more employees could conduct business in more than one State. Such an arbitrary and unreasonable regulation would be a clear violation of the 5th Amendment's Due Process Clause.

More specifically, the Constitution imposes four explicit limitations on the exercise of the commerce power. *First,* as we have seen, Article I, Section 9, Clause 3 forbids Congress the power to levy duties on exports. *Second,* Article I, Section 9, Clause 6 prevents Congress from favoring the ports of one State over those of any other in the regulation of trade. Thus, all ports of entry in the United States must be treated with an even hand. *Third,* the same constitutional provision forbids Congress the power to require that "vessels bound to, or from, one State, be obliged to enter, clear, or pay duties in another."

The *fourth* limitation is the curious "slave trade compromise" reached at the Philadelphia Convention and embodied in Article I, Section 9, Clause 1. As we noted on page 54, it is of course obsolete—and has been for more than 170 years now.

Again, we shall return to the commerce power, and at length, in several later chapters.

The Currency Power. The Constitution gives to Congress the power "to coin money [and] regulate the value thereof."[4]

---

[3] The Supreme Court upheld this use of the commerce power in *Heart of Atlanta Motel, Inc.* v. *United States,* 1964. In doing so, the unanimous Court noted that there was "overwhelming evidence of the disruptive effect [of] racial discrimination . . . on commercial intercourse." See pages 535–536.

[4] Article I, Section 8, Clause 5; see pages 513–516.

And the States are forbidden the power to do so.[5]

Until the Revolutionary War, the English shilling was the recognized unit of value. The restraining hand of Great Britain kept issues of depreciated paper money within bounds. With the coming of independence, however, the legislatures of several States printed the States' names on paper and called it money. As always happens, bad money drove good money from circulation. With each State's money unstable and declining in value, local business was at best uncertain and interstate trade practically intolerable.

The Framers gave Congress the power to *coin* money. But the Constitution says nothing of paper money, except to forbid to the States the power to issue it.

From the beginning, the United States has issued coins—in gold (until 1933), silver, and other metals. Congress chartered the First Bank of the United States in 1791, but the *notes* (paper money) it issued were not made legal tender. Congress did not create a national paper currency and make it legal tender until 1863.[6]

At first the new national notes ("greenbacks") could not be redeemed for coin at the Treasury and their worth fell to less than half their face value on the open market. In 1870 the Supreme Court held their issuance to be unconstitutional. Said the Court, in *Hepburn* v. *Griswold,* "to coin" meant to stamp metal and, hence, the Constitution did not authorize paper money.

The Bureau of Engraving and Printing designs, engraves, and prints all paper currency. Here, paper money is inspected for flaws.

The Court soon reversed itself, however. It did so first in 1871 in the *Legal Tender Cases,* and again in 1884 in *Julliard* v. *Greenman.* In each instance it held the issuing of paper money as legal tender to be a proper exercise of the power to coin money and of the borrowing and war powers.

The Borrowing Power. The Constitution gives to Congress the power "to borrow money on the credit of the United States."[7] The power permits the Government to face both short- and long-term problems with the funding necessary to meet them. Thus, the borrowing power was used extensively in World War II, as it had been during the economic crisis of the 1930's. And it has been much used to help

---

[5] Article I, Section 10, Clause 1 forbids the States the power to coin money, to emit bills of credit (paper money), or to make anything but gold and silver coin legal tender. (Legal tender is any kind of money a creditor is required by law to accept in payment of a monetary debt.)

[6] Although they could not issue paper currency, the States chartered private banks whose notes did circulate as money. As these notes interfered with the new national currency, Congress imposed a 10% tax on their issuance in 1865, and they soon disappeared. The Supreme Court upheld the 1865 law as a valid exercise of the taxing power in *Veazie Bank* v. *Fenno,* 1869.

[7] Article I, Section 8, Clause 2; see pages 509–512.

Postal Service workers now handle more than 90 billion pieces of mail each year.

finance the extraordinary costs of war and defense over the past three decades.

There is no constitutional limit on the amount, but Congress has placed a ceiling on the public debt—one which it raises or lowers as conditions demand, however. At the start of fiscal year 1981 the nation's outstanding public debt stood at $907.7 billion.

The most common method of governmental borrowing is through the sale of bonds. Government bonds are much like the *promissory notes* ("IOU's") given by individuals when they borrow—a promise to pay a certain sum at a specified time.

Government bonds are issued and sold as either short-term or long-term obligations. These bonds pay interest at a rate competitive with that being charged in the private financial markets. They are purchased as investments by individuals, businesses and other groups, and especially by insurance companies and banks and other financial institutions. The Government could conceivably borrow all of the money that it needs from banks, or it could simply print enough money to satisfy its wants. But to do either, and especially the latter, would be highly inflationary.

The fact that the Constitution gives

Congress the power to borrow makes borrowing a national function. Thus, federal bonds cannot be taxed by the States—which makes them quite attractive to investors, of course. The borrowing power also implies the power to create the Federal Reserve System and regulate the nation's banking and other financial institutions; see pages 516–524.

Bankruptcy. Congress has power to make "uniform laws on the subject of bankruptcies, throughout the United States."[8] *Bankruptcy* is a legal proceeding for the distribution of a debtor's assets among creditors when a debtor is unable to pay the bills in full. When a person has been declared a bankrupt, that person is no longer legally responsible for any debts made before becoming bankrupt.

The National Government and the States both have power in the field of bankruptcy. It is, then, a concurrent power. Except for three brief periods, Congress left the matter entirely under State control for more than 100 years. In 1898, however, Congress passed a general bankruptcy law, and today the law is so all-inclusive that it

---

[8] Article I, Section 8, Clause 4.

practically excludes the States from the field.

Bankruptcy proceedings are usually handled by the United States District Court in the district in which the bankrupt lives. A court-appointed *referee* usually handles the details of the case and advises the judge in the matter.

Today, any individual or corporation, except railroads, banks, building and loan associations, insurance companies, and cities, may voluntarily begin bankruptcy proceedings. Creditors may begin proceedings against any individual or corporation, except those just listed and wage earners.

A bankrupt may keep certain property—especially an interest of up to $7500 in a home and $1200 in a motor vehicle, and $200 in such personal effects as clothing and household items. Thus, those who are bankrupt can support themselves and their families. In some instances, it is possible for one to be declared a "debtor" and have debts adjusted downward without actually becoming a bankrupt.

Naturalization. Naturalization is the process by which citizens of one country become citizens of another. Article I, Section 8, Clause 4 gives Congress the exclusive power "to establish a uniform rule of naturalization." We treated the details of the naturalization process in Chapter 5.

The Postal Power. Congress has power "to establish post offices and post roads."[9] Here Congress is given the power to provide for the carrying of the mails. The clause also grants, in effect, the power to protect the mails and seek their quick and efficient distribution. And it carries with it the power to prevent the mails from being used for fraud or the carrying of outlawed materials.

The United States Postal Service traces its history to the early colonial period and presently functions on the basis of the Postal Reorganization Act of 1970. There are now some 30,000 post offices across the country and they do about $15 billion in business annually. The more than 650,000 postal workers now handle more than 90 billion pieces of mail a year.

Congress has made it a federal crime to obstruct the passage of the mails "knowingly and willfully." Thus, a person who purposefully wrecks a train on which mail is being carried commits a federal as well as a State offense.

The States cannot unreasonably interfere with the mails. For example, they cannot require trains carrying mail to make an unreasonable number of stops. Nor can they require a license for mail vehicles owned by the United States, or tax the gas they use. The States can tax those who carry mail on contract, however.

Articles which are banned by a State's laws, such as whiskey or firecrackers, cannot be sent into a State through the mails. A great many other items—including such things as fraudulent investment offers, obscene literature, and lottery tickets—are also prohibited.

Copyrights and Patents. Congress is given the power "to promote the progress of science and useful arts, by securing, for limited times, to authors and inventors, the exclusive right to their respective writings and discoveries."[10]

A *copyright* is the exclusive right of an author to reproduce, publish, and sell his or her literary, musical, artistic, or other creative work. That right can be assigned (transferred by contract) to another—for example, to a publishing firm.

Copyrights are issued by the Copyright Office in the Library of Congress. Under present law they are valid for the life of the

---

[9] Article I, Section 8, Clause 7. *Post roads* are all postal routes, including railroads, airways, and waters in the United States during the time that mail is being carried thereon.

[10] Article I, Section 8, Clause 8; see pages 547–548.

author plus 50 years. They cover a wide range of creative efforts—books, magazines, newspapers, musical compositions (and lyrics), dramatic works, paintings, sculptures, cartoons, maps, photographs, motion pictures, sound recordings, and much else.

The Copyright Office does not enforce the protections of a copyright. If a copyright is infringed, the owner of the right may sue for damages in the federal courts.

Internationally, copyrights are safeguarded by treaties, and we have several of these agreements with other countries. Unfortunately, we do not have them with all other nations, however; and "pirating" of the works of American authors, composers, and artists is a quite serious problem in many places abroad.

A *patent* is a grant of the exclusive right to manufacture, use, or sell "any new and useful art, machine, manufacture, or composition of matter, or any new and useful improvement thereof." A patent is good for a varying period of years—today 17 on a patent of invention. The term of a patent may be extended only by a special act of Congress. The patent laws are enforced by the Patent and Trademark Office in the Department of Commerce.

Weights and Measures. The Constitution gives Congress power to "fix the standard of weights and measures."[11] The clause reflects the absolute need for both accurate and uniform gauges of time, distance, volume, weight, and the like.

In 1838 Congress established the English system (of pound, ounce, mile, foot, gallon, quart, and so on) as the legal standards of weights and measures in the United States. In 1866 it also legalized the use of the metric system (gram, meter, liter, and so on). The original standards by which all other measures in the United States are tested and corrected are maintained by the National Bureau of Stan-

dards. This agency was created by Congress in 1901 and is now located in the Department of Commerce.

In 1975 Congress created the U.S. Metric Board to prompt on-going efforts for the increased use of and voluntary conversion to the metric system in this country.

Power Over Territories and Other Areas. Congress has power to acquire, govern, and dispose of various federal areas.[12] Of course, the power relates to the District of Columbia and to the several federal territories, including the Virgin Islands, Puerto Rico, and Guam. It also involves much more, however—including the hundreds of military and naval installations, arsenals, dockyards, post offices, courthouses, prison facilities, park and forest preserves, and other federal holdings throughout the country.

The Federal Government may acquire property in several ways. It may do so by purchase or gift, of course. It may do so, too, through the exercise of the power of *eminent domain*—the inherent power to take private property for public use.[13] Territory may also be acquired from a foreign state as a result of the power to admit new States, the war powers, and the President's treaty-making power.[14] Under international law, any sovereign state may acquire unclaimed territory by discovery.

Judicial Powers. As an integral part of the principle of checks and balances, Congress possesses several judicial powers. Thus, it has the expressed power to create

---

[11] Article I, Section 8, Clause 5; see page 547.

[12] Article I, Section 8, Clause 17; Article IV, Section 3, Clause 2; see pages 486–489.

[13] The 5th Amendment restricts the National Government's exercise of the power with the words, "nor shall private property be taken for public use, without just compensation." Each of the State constitutions contains a similar provision. Private property may be taken by eminent domain only: (1) for a public use, (2) with proper notice to the owner, and (3) for a fair price. What in fact constitutes a public use, proper notice, or a fair price often becomes a matter for judicial determination.

[14] Article IV, Section 3, Clause 1; Article I, Section 8, Clauses 11-16; and Article II, Section 2, Clauses 1 and 2.

Congress alone has the power to declare war. It took such action in December of 1941 against Japan, Germany, and Italy. Here, President Franklin D. Roosevelt requests Congress to declare war following the attack on Pearl Harbor.

all federal courts below the Supreme Court and to provide for the organization and composition of the federal judiciary.[15] The federal court system is discussed in Chapter 26.

Congress also has the power to define and provide for the punishment of federal crimes,[16] and the power to impeach and remove any civil officer of the United States.[17]

Powers over Foreign Relations. The National Government has greater power in the field of foreign relations than it has in any other. Congress shares this power with the President, who is primarily responsible for the conduct of our relations with other states. The States in the Union are not sovereign and are, hence, unrecognized in international law. The Constitution forbids them to participate in foreign relations.[18]

Authority for the power over foreign relations arises from two sources. *First*, from several of the delegated powers, including the powers to make treaties, to regulate foreign commerce, to send and receive diplomatic representatives, and to define and punish piracy and other crimes committed on the high seas and offenses against the law of nations. The war powers and the power to acquire and govern territories are also the basis for action in the

---

[15] Article I, Section 8, Clause 9; Article III, Section 1.

[16] The Constitution explicitly mentions only four types of crimes—counterfeiting, felonies committed on the high seas, and offenses against the law of nations (in Article I, Section 8, Clauses 6 and 10), and treason (in Article III, Section 3). But Congress has the implied power to define and provide punishment for many other offenses; see page 345.

[17] Article I, Section 2, Clause 5; Article I, Section 3, Clauses 6 and 7; and Article II, Section 3, Clause 4. The impeachment power is one of the nonlegislative powers to which we shall turn shortly; see page 346.

[18] Article I, Section 10, Clauses 1 and 3; see pages 84–85, 447.

To provide for the national defense and security, Congress has the power to appropriate funds for the raising and support of the armed forces. Here, infantrymen stand inspection.

field of international relations. *Second,* power to act in this field arises from the fact that the United States is a sovereign member of the world community. Thus, it has the inherent power to deal with any matter affecting the security of the nation.

War Powers. Several of the powers provided for in Article I, Section 8 deal exclusively with war and national defense. Although the President is Commander in Chief of the Armed Forces, Congress has power to declare war, to grant letters of marque and reprisal, and to make rules concerning captures on land and water.[19] It

has power to raise and support armies, to provide and maintain a navy, to make rules governing the land and naval forces. It also has power to provide for calling out the militia and for the organizing, arming, and disciplining of it.

Congress is forbidden to appropriate funds for "armies" for longer than a two-year period.[20] The restriction does not apply to the Navy,[21] but is intended to insure that the Army will always remain subordinate to civilian authority. (And, with the War Powers Resolution of 1973, Congress may act to restrict the use of American forces in combat in areas where a state of war does not exist. See page 408.)

---

[19] Article I, Section 8, Clauses 11-16. *Letters of marque and reprisal* are commissions authorizing private persons to fit out vessels to capture or destroy in time of war. They are forbidden in international law by the Declaration of Paris, 1856, to the principles of which the United States subscribes.

---

[20] Article I, Section 8, Clause 12.
[21] Nor, on the basis of a 1948 opinion of the Attorney General of the United States, to the Air Force.

The Implied Powers

The Necessary and Proper Clause. Clause 18, the final clause in Article I, Section 8, is the dramatically important Necessary and Proper Clause:

> The Congress shall have power: . . . To make all laws which shall be necessary and proper for carrying into execution the foregoing powers, and all other powers vested by this Constitution in the Government of the United States, or in any department or officer thereof.

Much of the vitality and adaptability of the Constitution can be traced directly to this provision—and, more particularly, to the manner in which both Congress and the Supreme Court have read and applied it over the years. For good reason, the Necessary and Proper Clause is frequently called the "Elastic Clause."

Liberal Versus Strict Construction. The Constitution had barely come into force when the meaning of Clause 18 was tested. In 1790 Alexander Hamilton, as Secretary of the Treasury, urged Congress to establish a national bank. That proposal touched off one of the most important disputes in all of our political history.

Opponents of Hamilton's plan insisted that nowhere did the Constitution give to Congress the power to establish such a bank. These "strict-constructionists," led by Thomas Jefferson, contended that the new Government had no powers beyond those that were expressly granted by the Constitution.

Hamilton and the "liberal-constructionists" relied upon Clause 18. They argued that it gave to Congress the power to do anything that might be reasonably "implied" from any of the expressly delegated powers. And they insisted that a bank was necessary and proper to the execution of the taxing, the borrowing, the commerce, and the currency powers.

The Jeffersonians rejected this claim of "implied powers." In their view, it would give the new Government almost unlimited powers and practically destroy the reserved powers of the States.[22]

Logic and practical necessity carried the day for Hamilton and the liberal-constructionists. Congress established the Bank of the United States in 1791. Its charter (the act creating it) expired in 1811. Over those 20 years, the constitutionality of the Bank—and with it the constitutionality of the concept of implied powers—went unchallenged in the courts.

McCulloch v. Maryland, 1819. In 1816 Congress created the Second Bank of the United States. And its chartering came only after another hard-fought debate over the extent of the powers of Congress.

Several States attempted to limit the new bank's authority in various ways. In 1818 Maryland imposed a tax upon all notes issued by any bank doing business in that State which was not chartered by the State legislature. This tax was aimed directly at the Second Bank's branch in Baltimore. McCulloch, the bank's cashier, purposely issued notes on which no tax had been paid in order to challenge the Maryland law. The State sought and won a judgment against him in its own courts. Acting for McCulloch, the United States then appealed to the Supreme Court.

Maryland took the strict-construction position before the High Court, arguing that the creation of the Bank had been an unconstitutional act. In reply, the United States took a two-fold position: (1) a defense of the concept of implied powers,

---

[22] In 1800, a bill was introduced in Congress to incorporate a company to mine copper. Jefferson, as Vice President, ridiculed the proposal with this sarcastic comment: "Congress is authorized to defend the nation. Ships are necessary for defense; copper is necessary for ships; mines necessary for copper; a company necessary to work the mines; and who can doubt this reasoning who has ever played at 'This Is the House That Jack Built'?" While Jefferson himself was President (1801–1809), he and his party were many times forced to reverse their earlier position. For example, it was only on the basis of the implied powers doctrine that the Louisiana Purchase in 1803 and the embargo on foreign trade in 1807 could be justified.

THE POWERS VESTED IN CONGRESS BY ARTICLE I, SECTION 8 OF THE CONSTITUTION

Expressed Powers

I. Peace Powers

1. To lay taxes.
   a. Direct (not used since the War Between the States, except income tax).
   b. Indirect.
      customs = tariffs.
      excises = internal revenue.
2. To borrow money.
3. To regulate foreign and interstate commerce.
4. To establish naturalization and bankruptcy laws.
5. To coin money and regulate its value; to regulate weights and measures.
6. To punish counterfeiters of federal money and securities.
7. To establish post offices and post roads.
8. To grant patents and copyrights.
9. To create courts inferior to the Supreme Court.
10. To define and punish piracies and felonies on the high seas; to define and punish offenses against the law of nations.
17. To exercise exclusive jurisdiction over the District of Columbia; to exercise exclusive jurisdiction over forts, dockyards, national parks, federal buildings, and the like.

II. War Powers

11. To declare war; to grant letters of marque and reprisal; to make rules concerning captures on land and water.
12. To raise and support armies.
13. To provide and maintain a navy.
14. To make laws governing land and naval forces.
15. To provide for calling forth the militia to execute federal laws, suppress insurrections, and repel invasions.
16. To provide for organizing, arming, and disciplining the militia, and for its governing when in the service of the Union.

Implied Powers

18. To make all laws necessary and proper for carrying into execution the foregoing powers.
    For example—To define and provide punishment for federal crimes.
    To establish the Federal Reserve System.
    To improve rivers, harbors, canals, other waterways.
    To fix minimum wages, maximum hours of work.

and (2) the contention that no State could lawfully impose a tax on any agency of the Federal Government.

Chief Justice John Marshall delivered one of the Supreme Court's most important and far-reaching decisions in this case. Here, for the first time, the Court was squarely faced with the 30-year-old question of the constitutionality of the implied powers doctrine. The Court upheld the constitutionality of the Second Bank as a necessary and proper step in the execution of such expressed powers as to borrow, to coin and regulate the value of money, and

to tax. But, far more important, the Supreme Court thereby upheld the doctrine of implied powers. The decision is so important that we quote its central passage:

We admit, as all must admit, that the powers of the government are limited, and that its limits are not to be transcended. But we think the sound construction of the Constitution must allow to the national legislature that discretion, with respect to the means by which the powers it confers are to be carried into execution, which will enable that body to perform the high duties assigned to it, in the manner most beneficial to the people. Let the end be legitimate, let it be within the scope of the Constitution, and all means which are appropriate, which are plainly adapted to that end, which are not prohibited, but consist with the letter and spirit of the Constitution, are constitutional.[23]

This broad interpretation of the powers granted to Congress has become firmly fixed in our constitutional system. Indeed, it is impossible to see how our nation could have developed as it has under the Constitution without it.

Examples of Implied Powers. As we have suggested several times, there are literally thousands of examples of the application of the doctrine of implied powers. Decisions of the Supreme Court and the manner in which Congress has regarded and used its power have made Article I, Section 8, Clause 18 truly the Elastic Clause. Today the words "necessary and proper" really read "convenient and useful," especially when applied to the power to regulate commerce and to tax.

The original Constitution gave the National Government the express power to punish only four specific crimes—counterfeiting, felonies committed on the high seas, offenses against the law of nations, and treason.[24] But many other laws Congress has the expressed power to enact—for example, tax laws—would be worthless if they could not be enforced. Congress has the *implied* right to define and provide the punishment for all offenses against the United States.

The Constitution does not expressly

A Coast Guard ensign inspects the log of a Russian trawler, checking for violations of the fishing law. Illegal catches are subject to impoundment.

provide for river and harbor improvements, but the power is *implied* from the expressed powers to regulate commerce and maintain a navy. The words *Air Force* do not appear in the Constitution. But should anyone ever question its constitutionality, the courts could imply the power to create the Air Force from the war powers.

A list illustrating the use and importance of the implied powers could be carried on and on; there are many throughout this book. But, *remember,* the basis for *any* implied power must *always* be found among the expressed powers.

The Nonlegislative Powers of Congress

Although the basic function of Congress is to make law, the Constitution also assigns it certain nonlegislative powers and duties.

---

23 The decision also invalidated the Maryland tax. Because "the power to tax involves the power to destroy," said the Supreme Court, Maryland could not be permitted to tax the United States or any of its instrumentalities. See page 770.

24 Article I, Section 8, Clauses 6 and 10; Article III, Section 3.

FAC-SIMILE OF TICKET OF ADMISSION TO THE IMPEACHMENT TRIAL.

A ticket similar to this one admitted a person to the Senate trial of President Andrew Johnson in 1868.

Electoral. On rare occasion, the House of Representatives may be called upon to elect a President. If no candidate receives a majority of the electoral votes for President, the House, voting by States, must choose one from among the three highest candidates. Similarly, the Senate may be called upon to choose a Vice President when no candidate for that office receives an electoral college majority.[25]

The House of Representatives elected Thomas Jefferson in 1801 and John Quincy Adams in 1825. The Senate chose Richard M. Johnson as Vice President in 1837.

Recall, too, that the 25th Amendment provides that, in case of a vacancy in the Vice Presidency, the President shall nominate a successor, subject to a majority vote of both houses of Congress. The Congress has been called upon to take such action twice recently. It did so for the first time in confirming Gerald Ford as Vice President in 1973. Then, in 1974, it acted on Nelson Rockefeller's nomination as Vice President.

We shall consider the presidential and vice-presidential selection process in Chapter 15.

Constituent. As we have seen, Congress may propose amendments to the Constitution by a two-thirds vote in each house. And it may call a national conven-

tion to propose amendments if such action is requested by two-thirds of the State legislatures.[26]

Impeachment. The Constitution provides that the President, Vice President, and all civil officers of the United States may be removed from office "on impeachment for, and conviction of, treason, bribery, or other high crimes and misdemeanors."[27] The House of Representatives has the sole power to *impeach* (bring charges) and the Senate the sole power to *judge* (sit as a court to try) in impeachment cases.[28]

A two-thirds vote of the Senators present is necessary for conviction, and the Chief Justice of the United States presides when a President is being tried. The penalty for conviction is removal from office. If it desires, the Senate may add a provision against the holding of any future federal office. Although judgment in cases of conviction of impeachment extends only to the removal from office, the accused official can also be indicted, tried, convicted, and

---

[25] 12th Amendment; see pages 366, 375–378.

[26] Article V; see pages 67–70.

[27] Article II, Section 4. Military officers are not "civil officers" and are removed by court-martial. Nor are members of Congress. When the House impeached Senator William Blount of Tennessee in 1798, the Senate refused to try the case on grounds that it had the power to expel one of its own members if it saw fit. Blount was later expelled, and the precedent thus set has been followed ever since.

[28] Article I, Section 2, Clause 5, and Section 3, Clause 6.

On July 30, 1974, the House Judiciary Committee reported three articles of impeachment against President Richard Nixon. It urged the House to impeach him for obstruction of justice, abuse of power, and contempt of Congress.

punished according to law by the regular courts.[29]

To date there have been but twelve impeachments and four convictions. On several other occasions officers have resigned under the threat of impeachment—most notably, of course, Richard Nixon who resigned the Presidency in 1974. When the House of Representatives impeached President Andrew Johnson in 1868, the Senate failed by a single vote to convict him.[30]

Executive. The Constitution grants two "executive powers" to the Senate, one relating to appointments and the other to treaties made by the President.[31]

All major appointments made by the President are subject to confirmation (or rejection) by the Senate by majority vote. Each nomination of a presidential appointee is referred to the appropriate standing committee. When the committee's recommendation is brought to the floor it may be (but seldom is) considered in executive (secret) session.

The appointment of Cabinet officers and other top members of the President's "official family" are only very rarely rejected by the Senate.[32] But the unwritten rule of "senatorial courtesy" applies to the appointment of federal officers who serve in the various States—for example, United States attorneys and federal marshals. The Senate will not approve the appointment of such an officer if a Senator, who is of the President's party and from the State involved, objects. This practice means in fact that some Senators often dictate certain presidential appointments.[33] We shall return to this whole matter in Chapter 16.

[29] Article I, Section 3, Clauses 6 and 7.

[30] The four persons removed were all judges. One other judge resigned after the House impeached him but just before the Senate began his trial, and the case was dropped. Four other judges were acquitted. Aside from Senator Blount and President Johnson, W. W. Belknap, who was President Grant's Secretary of War, was impeached and acquitted in 1876 on the ground that the Senate no longer had jurisdiction because Belknap had resigned. See page 660.

[31] Article II, Section 2, Clause 2.

[32] All told, only nine of the more than 500 Cabinet appointments have been rejected by the Senate.

[33] Those who criticize the practice often overlook the fact that a Senator is much more likely to be better informed about affairs in his or her own State than is the President.

Case Study

As a part of its broad power to investigate, Congress exercises what is often called its "oversight function." That is, it oversees—scrutinizes—the activities of the several agencies within the executive branch. Essentially, it does so in order to insure that those agencies are operating (1) effectively and efficiently and (2) in accord with the policies that Congress has set by law.

This watchdog function is regularly performed by most of the standing and many of the select committees of both houses. The performance of the function is most readily apparent in the course of formal committee investigations (see page 315). These proceedings are sometimes dramatic, sometimes not. Regularly, they are attempts to focus public attention on the behavior of certain federal officials and agencies charged with the conduct of the public's business.

The oversight function is also performed in a variety of other contexts—for example, when a Senate committee holds confirmation hearings to determine the fitness of a presidential appointee, and when House and Senate committees review agency budget requests.

Many have long urged that Congress equip itself with yet another oversight procedure—the "question hour." In its usual shape, their proposal would permit members of the President's Cabinet and other top executive officers to speak and be questioned on the floor of either house, at regularly scheduled times.

Over the years, a number of bills have been introduced in both chambers to establish the practice. And the device has long been used in other national legislative bodies—most notably in the British House of Commons.

■ Is the oversight function an indispensable aspect of the legislative power? Does the existence of a separation of powers heighten or diminish its importance?

■ Should the House or Senate, or both, provide for the "question hour"? Why has neither ever done so? Do presidential press conferences accomplish the purpose such a practice would serve?

Treaties are made by the President "by and with the advice and consent of the Senate . . . provided two-thirds of the Senators present concur."[34] For a while after the adoption of the Constitution the advice of the Senate was asked before the President prepared a treaty. But now the President merely consults with the Senate Foreign Relations Committee and with influential members of both parties. The Senate may reject a treaty in full or may suggest amendments, reservations, and understandings to it. Treaties may be considered in executive (secret) session. Because the House of Representatives has a hold on the governmental purse strings, influential House members are frequently consulted, too. See pages 405–406.

Investigative. Congress, through its committees, has the power to investigate matters for three purposes: *First,* to gather information that may be of use to Congress in the making of law. *Second,* to see how laws already enacted are working out and whether they need changing. And *third,* to determine whether or not programs are actually being administered in the way that Congress intended they should be. See pages 314–315.

---

[34] It is often said, erroneously, that the Senate "ratifies" a treaty. It does not. According to the Constitution, Article II, Section 2, Clause 2, the Senate may give (or withhold) its "advice and consent" to a treaty made by the President. After having secured senatorial approval, the President ratifies a treaty by exchanging the "instruments of ratification" with the other party or parties to the agreement.

SUMMARY   Congress may exercise only those powers (1) *expressly* granted to it in the Constitution, (2) that may be reasonably *implied* from the expressed powers, and (3) that are *inherent* in the existence of the National Government.

Most of the expressed powers of Congress are set out in Article I, Section 8, Clause 1–18 of the Constitution, but several are also to be found elsewhere in the document.

Early in our history the question of whether the powers granted to the National Government were to be strictly or liberally interpreted became an issue. It was finally resolved by the Supreme Court decision in *McCulloch* v. *Maryland,* 1819. The Supreme Court ruled that the powers were to be liberally construed, thus upholding the doctrine of implied powers. It is difficult to see how the nation could have developed as it has under the Constitution without the idea of implied powers.

Congress performs several nonlegislative functions—electoral, constituent, judicial, executive, and investigative.

Concept Development

Questions for Review

1. Where in the Constitution are most of the *expressed powers* to be found?

2. Upon what clause is the doctrine of *implied powers* based?

3. What are the *inherent powers?*

4. What was the nature of the dispute between the liberal-constructionists and the strict-constructionists?

5. What are the two most important expressed powers of Congress?

6. Why was Congress given the exclusive power to coin money?

7. How did Congress get its right to issue paper money?

8. Why is the congressional power over bankruptcy classed as a *concurrent power?*

9. Is the postal power a *concurrent* or an *exclusive power?*

10. What is the chief distinction between a *copyright* and a *patent?*

11. Why may it be said that the National Government has greater power in the field of foreign relations than in any other? With whom does Congress share authority in the field of foreign relations?

12. What are the *war powers?* With whom does Congress share authority in this field?

13. What are the implied powers?

14. Why is the Supreme Court's decision in *McCulloch* v. *Maryland* of such outstanding importance in the development of our governmental system?

15. What are the nonlegislative powers of Congress?

For Further Inquiry

1. Great Britain has no written constitution, and Parliament may enact any law it believes is necessary. Why has Congress only the expressed, implied, and inherent powers?

2. In his decision in *McCulloch* v. *Maryland* Chief Justice Marshall wrote that

"the power to tax involves the power to destroy." What did he mean by this?

3. Cite illustrations of this comment, made by Woodrow Wilson in his classic *Congressional Government*, published in 1885:

> The Constitution itself is not a complete system; it takes none but the first steps in organization. It does little more than lay a foundation of principles . . . The growth of the nation and the consequent development of the governmental system would snap asunder a constitution which could not adapt itself to the new conditions of an advancing society. . . . There can be no question that our Constitution has proved lasting because of its simplicity.

4. Would commercial progress in the United States be promoted if each of the States had its own monetary system? Weights and measures?

5. Why must the source for each and every exercise of an implied power be found in an expressed power?

6. How do the several nonlegislative powers of Congress illustrate the principle of checks and balances? (Richard Nixon, faced with almost certain impeachment by the House and conviction by the Senate, resigned as President on August 9, 1974. How can this event be used as an illustration here?)

Suggested Activities

1. Write a report explaining why Congress was given each of the expressed powers it possesses.

2. Identify the major legislation thus far enacted or still being considered in the present session of Congress. In a report indicate those bills which are based on the expressed powers and those which are applications of the doctrine of implied powers.

3. Stage a debate or class forum on one of the following questions: (a) *Resolved,* That the National Government should be permitted to do only those things expressly provided for in the Constitution; (b) *Resolved,* That the federal monopoly over the postal system ought to be abolished; (c) *Resolved,* That the metric system should, by law, be the sole standard of weights and measures in the United States.

4. Prepare a bulletin board display to indicate the meaning, scope, and importance of one of the powers held by Congress.

Suggested Reading

Congressional Directory, 97th Congress, 1st Session, Government Printing Office, 1981.

CQ Weekly Report. Congressional Quarterly, Inc. Weekly.

Corwin, Edward S. and Peltason, J. W., *Understanding the Constitution.* Dryden, 8th ed., 1979.

Havemann, Joel, *Congress and the Budget.* Indiana University Press, 1979.

Keefe, William J., *Congress and the American People.* Prentice-Hall, 1980.

LeLoup, Lance T., *The Fiscal Congress: Legislative Control of the Budget.* Greenwood, 1980.

McKenna, George and Feingold, Stanley (eds.), *Taking Sides.* Dushkin, 1978. Part II.

Oleszek, Walter J., *Congressional Procedures and the Policy Process.* Congressional Quarterly Press, 1978.

Powers of Congress. Congressional Quarterly Press, 1976.

Ripley, Randall B. and Franklin, Grace A., *Congress, the Bureaucracy, and Public Policy.* Dorsey, rev. ed., 1980.

Schick, Allen, *Congress and Money: Budgeting, Spending, and Taxing.* The Urban Institute, 1980.

THE PRESIDENCY: THE NATIONAL ADMINISTRATION AND PUBLIC POLICY

In Part Five we turn our attention to the vast, complex, sprawling, and critically important executive branch of the National Government. Here we are involved with more chapters—11 of them, covering more than 290 pages—than in any other section of this book: a manifestation of the decisive role the President and his Administration play in the government and politics of the American democracy. As we proceed, you might weigh these continuingly appropriate comments made more than four decades ago by a panel of distinguished authorities, the President's Committee on Administrative Management:

The Government of the United States is the largest and most difficult task undertaken by the American people, and at the same time the most important and the noblest. Our Government does more for more men, women, and children than any other institution; it employs more persons in its work than any other employer. It covers a wider range of aims and activities than any other enterprise; it sustains the frame of our national and our community life, our economic system, our individual civil rights and liberties. . . . [Its] goal is the constant raising of the level of the happiness and dignity of human life, the steady sharing of the gains of our Nation, whether material or spiritual, among those who make the Nation what it is.

Governments may operate without either legislatures or courts; but *no* government, whatever its form, can exist without some type of executive authority. Both the legislative and the judicial functions can be performed by the executive. Laws may be made by executive order, and public and private disputes can be settled in the same fashion. Obviously, a government with neither legislature nor courts could not be a democratic one—but it would be a government, nonetheless. Our governmental system, like any other, demands an executive authority. And, perforce, it demands a *strong* one, as Alexander Hamilton noted in *The Federalist* No. 70, in 1788:

Energy in the Executive is a leading character in the definition of good government. It is essential to the protection of the community against foreign attacks; it is not less essential to the steady administration of the laws; to the protection of property against those irregular and high-handed combinations which sometimes interrupt the ordinary course of justice; to the security of liberty against the enterprises and assaults of ambition, of faction, and of anarchy. . . . A feeble Executive implies a feeble execution of the government. A feeble execution is but another phrase for a bad execution; and a government ill-executed, whatever it may be in theory, must be, in practice, a bad government.

15

The Presidency

He is the vital center of action in the system, whether he accepts it as such or not, and the office is the measure of the man,—of his wisdom as well as of his force.

WOODROW WILSON

■ Why is the Presidency "the vital center" in the American political system?

■ What might American government be like today had not the Framers of the Constitution abandoned their early inclination to provide that the President be chosen by Congress?

■ Why have nearly all the Presidents of the United States been experienced professional politicians?

On April 30, 1789, George Washington placed his left hand on the Bible, raised his right hand, and swore that he would "preserve, protect, and defend the Constitution of the United States." As he did so, at New York which was then the temporary capital, he became the first President of the United States. Over the long course of 190 years, each of his successors has repeated that ceremony and recited the words of the constitutional oath. Most of them have done so in Washington, D.C., as Thomas Jefferson did for the first time in 1801. And, most of them have done so on the steps of the Capitol, as James Madison did for the first time in 1817.

Ronald Wilson Reagan recited the solemn words of the Constitution in the wintry chill of noon in the nation's capital on January 20, 1981—and so became the 40th President of the United States.

As the nation's Chief Executive, Mr. Reagan holds what is without question the most important and the most powerful office known to history. His powers are vast, his responsibilities are well-nigh immeasurable, and his functions are many.

When he announced his candidacy for the Democratic nomination in 1900, Admiral George Dewey declared that "the office of President is not such a very difficult one to fill, his duties being mainly to execute the laws of Congress." Let us proceed here, and later, to see why that assessment of the office—one still held by some—is a far-

Right: *Representing the United States as its Chief Diplomat, President Truman (center) met in Berlin in 1945 with Britain's Prime Minister Clement R. Atlee (at left) and Generalissimo Josef Stalin (right) of the Soviet Union.* Below: *Ronald Reagan speaks in Boston, Massachusetts.*

from-accurate measure of its present-day shape.

The President's Many Roles. At any given time, only one person is President of the United States, of course. The office of the Presidency and all of its powers and duties are held and exercised by that single individual.[1] But, whoever that person may be, the President must fill a number of different and varied roles—and all of them simultaneously.

The President is, to begin with, *Chief of State,* the ceremonial head of the government of the United States. The President is, then, the symbol of all of the people of the nation—in President William Howard Taft's words, "the personal embodiment and representative of their dignity and majesty."

In many countries, the chief of state

reigns but does not rule. This is most certainly true of the Queens of England, Denmark, and the Netherlands, the Kings of Norway, Sweden, and Belgium, the Presidents of Italy and West Germany, and the Emperor of Japan. It is just as certainly *not* true of the President of the United States, who both reigns *and* rules.

The President is the nation's *Chief Executive,* vested by the Constitution with *"the executive power of the United States."* And the President is also the *Chief Administrator* of the Federal Government—heading one of the largest governmental machines ever created. Today, the President directs an administration which includes some 2.9 million civilian employees and spends well over $600 billion a year.

The President is also the nation's *Chief Diplomat,* the chief formulator of American foreign policy and the nation's chief spokesman to the rest of the world. "I make foreign policy," President Harry Truman once asserted—and he did. The

---

[1] Although all of the Presidents have thus far been men, nothing in the Constitution precludes the possibility of the selection of a woman to that office.

Top to bottom: *President Roosevelt with General Eisenhower; President Carter meets with Nigeria's President Shagari; President Ford signs a bill.*

President's words and actions are carefully followed, not only in this country but everywhere abroad.

In close concert with that role in foreign affairs, the Constitution makes the President Commander in Chief of the nation's armed forces. Two million men and women in uniform, and all of the incalculable power in the nation's military arsenal, are thus made subject to the President's direct and immediate control.

Importantly, the President is also the nation's *Chief Legislator,* the chief architect of its public policies. It is the President who sets the overall shape of the congressional agenda—initiating, suggesting, requesting, supporting, insisting, and demanding that Congress enact most of the major legislation that it does.

These six presidential roles—those of Chief of State, Chief Executive, Chief Administrator, Chief Diplomat, Commander in Chief, and Chief Legislator—are all imposed by the Constitution. In addition to them, the President must fill still other vital roles.

Thus, the President is *Chief of Party,* the acknowledged leader of the political party in control of the executive branch. No matter what the record of previous political experience, whether much or little, the President becomes, automatically, the leader of that party. And a great deal of the real power and influence wielded by the Chief Executive depends upon the manner in which this critical role is played.

The office also automatically makes of its occupant the nation's *Chief Citizen.* The President is expected to be "the representative of *all* of the people," the one to work for and represent the *public* interest against the many different and competing private interests. "The Presidency," said Franklin Roosevelt, "is not merely an administrative office. That is the least of it. It is preeminently a place of moral leadership."

Again, the President performs each of these several roles. And it is useful and convenient to describe the Presidency by enumerating them. But it is important to recall, too, that they are *all* played *simultaneously*. The powers and duties of the presidential office are, in fact, indivisible.

Each of these presidential roles is inseparable from and closely interrelated with each of the others. None of them is, or can be, performed in isolation. The manner in which the President plays any one of them can have a very decided effect upon the ability to play another or several or all of them.

As but two illustrations from the recent past, take the experiences of Presidents Lyndon Johnson and Richard Nixon. Each was a strong and a relatively effective President in the first years of his tenure. But the agonizing and increasingly unpopular war in Vietnam persuaded Mr. Johnson not to run for reelection in 1968. In effect, the manner in which he acted as Commander in Chief seriously eroded his stature and effectiveness in the White House. And the many-sided and sordid Watergate affair—and the manner in which he filled the roles of party leader and chief citizen— so destroyed his Presidency that Mr. Nixon was forced to leave office in disgrace in 1974.

Surely, enough has been said to this point to confirm our description of the Presidency as "the most important and the most powerful office known to history." And enough has been said, too, to dismiss Admiral Dewey as, at best, a naive commentator. We shall return to the various roles of the President shortly. But for now let us look to the constitutional structure of the office and then the presidential election process.

Qualifications, Term, Compensation

Whatever else one must be to gain this highest of offices, the Constitution requires that the President: (1) be a "natural-born citizen," (2) be at least 35 years of age, and (3) have resided in the United States for at least 14 years.[2]

The Framers of the Constitution considered several different limits upon the length of the presidential term. Most of their debate centered around a four-year term, with the incumbent eligible for reelection, versus a six- or seven-year term without reeligibility. They finally settled upon a four-year term.[3] They agreed, as Hamilton explained in *The Federalist,* that this was a sufficient period of time for a President to demonstrate abilities, gain experience, and institute stable policies.

Until 1951, the Constitution placed no limit upon the number of terms a President might serve. Several Presidents, beginning with George Washington, refused to seek more than two terms, however. Soon the "no-third-term tradition" became an unwritten rule of presidential politics. After Franklin D. Roosevelt broke the tradition by winning a third term in 1940, and then a fourth in 1944, the unwritten custom became a part of the written Constitution. The 22nd Amendment, adopted in 1951, reads in part:

> No person shall be elected to the office of the President more than twice, and no

---

[2] Article II, Section 1, Clause 5. Under the doctrine of *jus sanguinus* (page 111) it is apparently possible that a person born abroad might someday become President. Martin Van Buren, who was born December 5, 1782, was the first President actually born in the United States; each of his seven predecessors (and his immediate successor) was born prior to the Declaration of Independence. John F. Kennedy was, at 43, the youngest ever elected to the office; Theodore Roosevelt reached it by succession at age 42. Only five others (Polk, Pierce, Grant, Garfield, and Cleveland) became President at less than age 50. Ronald Reagan is the oldest man ever elected, at age 69; William Henry Harrison became President at age 68. Dwight Eisenhower, who left the White House at age 70, was the oldest person ever to hold the office (but Mr. Regan acquires that distinction as of May 21, 1981). Given particularly Herbert Hoover's election in 1928 and Eisenhower's in 1952, the 14-year requirement involves *any* 14 years in a person's life, not the just 14 immediately preceding election.

[3] Article II, Section 1, Clause 1.

Case Study

The most telling of comments upon the Presidency have come from the most authoritative source of all—from Presidents themselves. Despite the fact that Calvin Coolidge once said that "the Presidency does not yield to definition," each President has given us descriptions of the office.

What do you think Woodrow Wilson meant when he described the Presidency as "one thing at one time, another at another"? And when he declared that "the President is at liberty, both in law and in conscience, to be as big a man as he can"?

Why did George Washington face his first inauguration in 1789 feeling, as he later said, much like "a culprit who is going to the place of his execution"? And what did Thomas Jefferson mean when he called the Presidency a place of "splendid misery"?

Why did William Howard Taft think of the office as "the loneliest place in the world" and why did Warren Harding regard it as "a prison"?

What did Harry Truman have in mind when he wrote that being President "is like riding a tiger"? And why did he often observe that the major work of the President consists in "trying to persuade people to do things they ought to have sense enough to do without my persuading them"? And why did Woodrow Wilson say that the President must have "the constitution of an athlete, the patience of a mother, the endurance of an early Christian"?

And what did these two Presidents tell us of the office?

John Kennedy, when he said, "The problems are more difficult than I had imagined them to be. The responsibilities placed on the United States are greater than I imagined them to be, and there are greater limitations upon the ability to bring about a favorable result than I had imagined there to be. And I think that is probably true of anyone who becomes President, because there is such a difference between those who advise or speak or legislate, and . . . the man who must select from the various alternatives and say that this shall be the policy of the United States."

Lyndon Johnson, when he wrote: "No one can experience with the President of the United States the glory and agony of his office. No one can share the majestic view from his pinnacle of power. No one can share the burden of his decisions or the scope of his duties. A Cabinet officer, no matter how broad his mandate, has a limited responsibility. A Senator, no matter how varied his interests, has a limited constituency. But the President represents all the people and must face up to all the problems. He must be responsible, as he sees it, for the welfare of every citizen and must be sensitive to the will of every group. He cannot pick and choose the issues. They all come with the job. So his experience is unique among his fellow Americans."

Finally, what do you think of this view of the Presidency, offered by Mr. Truman?

"When the Founding Fathers outlined the Presidency in Article II of the Constitution, they left a great many details out and vague. I think they relied on the experience of the nation to fill in the outlines. The office of chief executive has grown with the progress of this great republic. It has responded to the many demands that our complex society has made upon the government. It has given our nation a means of meeting our great emergencies. . . . Justice Holmes' epigram proved true. He said a page of history is worth a volume of logic. And as the pages of history were written they unfolded powers in the Presidency not explicitly found in Article II."

■ What common themes seem to run through these presidential observations?
■ Which of these comments is the most intriguing to you? Why?

During his third term in office, President Roosevelt led a nation at war. Here, he reads the declaration of war against Italy.

person who has held the office of President, or acted as President, for more than two years of a term to which some other person was elected President shall be elected to the office of the President more than once.

As a general rule, then, each President is now restricted to a maximum of two full terms—eight years—in office. *But* a President, who has *succeeded* to the office *beyond the midpoint* in a term to which another was originally elected, may serve for more than eight years. But, at the very outside, a President may not serve more than 10 years. Gerald Ford may be used to illustrate the point. He succeeded to the Presidency on August 9, 1974, with nearly two-and-a-half years remaining in what had originally been Richard Nixon's second term. Had Mr. Ford won a full term in 1976 he would not have been eligible to seek yet another term in 1980. That four-year term, beginning in early 1981, would have extended his tenure beyond the ten-year maximum

permitted by the Amendment.

Several Presidents—and most recently Jimmy Carter—have urged a single, six-year term for the office. Significantly, they have each come to this view at some point *after* having won the office.

Compensation. The President's salary is fixed by Congress, and it can neither be increased nor decreased during a presidential term.[4] The salary was originally set at $25,000 in 1789. It was raised to $50,000 in 1873, to $75,000 in 1909, and to $100,000 in 1949. Congress increased the figure to its present level—$200,000—in 1969. Since 1949 the President has also received a $50,000-a-year expense account—which is

---

[4] Article II, Section 1, Clause 7. At the Constitutional Convention, Benjamin Franklin argued that, since money *and* power might corrupt a man, the President ought to receive nothing beyond expenses. Franklin's suggestion was never put to a vote. The present salary was set by the first measure passed by Congress in 1969; it was signed by President Johnson on January 17—three days before the new presidential term, President Nixon's first, began.

Noted performers and performing groups are sometimes invited to perform at the White House.

taxable and is, in effect, really a part of the President's pay.

The Constitution forbids the President "any other emolument from the United States, or any of them."[5] But this does not prevent the President from being provided with the White House, a magnificent and priceless 132-room mansion set on an 18.3-acre (7.8-hectare) estate in the heart of the nation's Capital; a sizable suite of offices and a large staff; a 92-foot (28-meter) yacht and a 60-foot (18-meter) cruiser, a fleet of automobiles, three lavishly fitted Boeing 707 jets, and several other planes and helicopters; Camp David, the resort hideaway in the Catoctin Mountains in Maryland; the finest medical, dental, and other health care available; liberal travel and entertainment funds; and a great many other perquisites.

Many of the services and facilities made available to the President cannot be measured in dollar terms, of course. Who, for example, could possibly put a price-tag on the White House? Just to *operate* the mansion now requires more than $3 million a year. But, to have available all of the material benefits the Chief Executive receives, it has been estimated that a private

citizen would have to have an annual after-taxes income of more than $10 million. And to generate that amount of "take-home pay" would require a gross income of about $35 million a year.

Since 1958 each former President has received a lifetime pension, now $69,630 a year; and each presidential widow is entitled to a pension of $20,000 a year.

Presidential Succession

Section I of the 25th Amendment provides that:

> In case of the removal of the President from office or his death or resignation, the Vice President shall become President.

In strictest terms, then, before the adoption of the 25th Amendment in 1967, the Constitution *did not* provide that in such situations the Vice President should succeed to the Presidency. Rather, it declared that the *powers and duties* of the office (*not* the office itself) were to "devolve on the Vice President."[6] But practice—begun by John Tyler in 1841—had dictated that

---

[5] Article II, Section 1, Clause 7.

[6] Article II, Section 1, Clause 6. On removal of the President by impeachment, see Article I, Section 2, Clause 5; Article I, Section 3, Clauses 6 and 7; Article II, Section 4; and page 346.

should the office become vacant the Vice President succeeds to it. The effect of the ratification of the 25th Amendment was to make what had been one of the many *informal amendments* of the Constitution a part of the written document.

Congress fixes the order of succession following the Vice President.[7] The present law on the matter is the Presidential Succession Act of 1947. By its terms, the Speaker of the House and then the President *pro tem* of the Senate are next in line. They are followed, in turn, by the Secretary of State and each of the other 12 heads of Cabinet departments in order of precedence.[8]

Presidential Disability. Until adoption of the 25th Amendment, serious gaps existed in the succession arrangements under the Constitution. Neither that document nor the Congress made any provision for determining *when* a President was so disabled that presidential duties could not be performed. And, there was no provision to indicate *by whom* such a determination was to be made.

For nearly 180 years, then, the nation played with fate. President Dwight D. Eisenhower twice suffered temporarily disabling illnesses—a heart attack and ileitis—during his tenure. Two earlier Presidents were incapacitated for much longer periods of time. James Garfield lingered between life and death for 80 days before finally succumbing to an assassin's bullet in 1881. During that entire period he

Shortly after the death of President Kennedy, victim of an assassin's bullet, Lyndon B. Johnson is sworn in as the nation's President.

was able to perform only one official act: to sign an extradition warrant. Woodrow Wilson suffered a paralytic stroke in 1919 and was largely incapacitated for the remainder of his second term. He did not attend a meeting of his Cabinet until seven months after the attack. Meanwhile, his Vice President, Thomas R. Marshall, humbly refused to assume any of the presidential duties.

Sections 3 and 4 of the 25th Amendment fill the constitutional gap in detail. They provide that the Vice President shall become Acting President (1) if the President informs Congress, in writing, of an inability to perform in office; or (2) if the Vice President and a majority of the Cabinet (or a body authorized by law) inform Congress, in writing, that the President is incapacitated. In either case, the President may resume the powers and duties of office by notifying Congress that no inability

---

[7] Article II, Section 1, Clause 6.

[8] That is, the order in which their departments were created by Congress; see page 394. A Cabinet member is to serve only until a Speaker or President *pro tem* is available and qualified to assume the Presidency. But notice that Section 2 of the 25th Amendment provides for the filling of any vacancy which might occur in the Vice Presidency. In effect, that provision makes the Presidential Succession Act a law with little real significance—except in the quite unlikely event of simultaneous vacancies in the Presidency and Vice Presidency. The 25th Amendment almost certainly guarantees that the line of presidential succession will never pass below the Vice President.

PRESIDENTS OF THE UNITED STATES

Name	Party	State[a]	Born	Died	Entered Office	Age on Taking Office	Vice Presidents
George Washington	Federalist	Virginia	1732	1799	1789	57	John Adams
John Adams	Federalist	Massachusetts	1735	1826	1797	61	Thomas Jefferson
Thomas Jefferson	Dem.-Rep.[b]	Virginia	1743	1826	1801	57	Aaron Burr
							George Clinton
James Madison	Dem.-Rep.	Virginia	1751	1836	1809	57	George Clinton
							Elbridge Gerry
James Monroe	Dem.-Rep.	Virginia	1758	1831	1817	58	Daniel D. Tompkins
John Q. Adams	Dem.-Rep.	Massachusetts	1767	1848	1825	57	John C. Calhoun
Andrew Jackson	Democrat	Tenn. (S.C.)	1767	1845	1829	61	John C. Calhoun
							Martin Van Buren
Martin Van Buren	Democrat	New York	1782	1862	1837	54	Richard M. Johnson
William H. Harrison	Whig	Ohio (Va.)	1773	1841	1841	68	John Tyler
John Tyler	Democrat	Virginia	1790	1862	1841	51	. . . .
James K. Polk	Democrat	Tenn. (N.C.)	1795	1849	1845	49	George M. Dallas
Zachary Taylor	Whig	La. (Va.)	1784	1850	1849	64	Millard Fillmore
Millard Fillmore	Whig	New York	1800	1874	1850	50	. . . .
Franklin Pierce	Democrat	New Hampshire	1804	1869	1853	48	William R. King
James Buchanan	Democrat	Pennsylvania	1791	1868	1857	65	John C. Breckinridge
Abraham Lincoln	Republican	Illinois (Ky.)	1809	1865	1861	52	Hannibal Hamlin
							Andrew Johnson
Andrew Johnson	Democrat[c]	Tenn. (N.C.)	1808	1875	1865	56	. . . .
Ulysses S. Grant	Republican	Illinois (Ohio)	1822	1885	1869	46	Schuyler Colfax
							Henry Wilson
Rutherford B. Hayes	Republican	Ohio	1822	1893	1877	54	William A. Wheeler
James A. Garfield	Republican	Ohio	1831	1881	1881	49	Chester A. Arthur
Chester A. Arthur	Republican	N.Y. (Vt.)	1830	1886	1881	50	. . . .
Grover Cleveland	Democrat	N.Y. (N.J.)	1837	1908	1885	47	Thomas A. Hendricks
Benjamin Harrison	Republican	Indiana (Ohio)	1833	1901	1889	55	Levi P. Morton
Grover Cleveland	Democrat	N.Y. (N.J.)	1837	1908	1893	55	Adlai E. Stevenson
William McKinley	Republican	Ohio	1843	1901	1897	54	Garret A. Hobart
							Theodore Roosevelt
Theodore Roosevelt	Republican	New York	1858	1919	1901	42	. . . .
							Charles W. Fairbanks
William H. Taft	Republican	Ohio	1857	1930	1909	51	James S. Sherman
Woodrow Wilson	Democrat	N.J. (Va.)	1856	1924	1913	56	Thomas R. Marshall
Warren G. Harding	Republican	Ohio	1865	1923	1921	55	Calvin Coolidge
Calvin Coolidge	Republican	Mass. (Vt.)	1872	1933	1923	51	. . . .
							Charles G. Dawes
Herbert Hoover	Republican	Calif. (Iowa)	1874	1964	1929	54	Charles Curtis
Franklin D. Roosevelt	Democrat	New York	1882	1945	1933	51	John N. Garner
							Henry A. Wallace
							Harry S Truman
Harry S Truman	Democrat	Missouri	1884	1972	1945	60	. . . .
							Alben W. Barkley
Dwight D. Eisenhower	Republican	N.Y.-Pa. (Tex.)	1890	1969	1953	62	Richard M. Nixon
John F. Kennedy	Democrat	Massachusetts	1917	1963	1961	43	Lyndon B. Johnson
Lyndon B. Johnson	Democrat	Texas	1908	1973	1963	55	. . . .
							Hubert H. Humphrey
Richard M. Nixon	Republican	N.Y. (Calif.)	1913		1969	55	Spiro T. Agnew[d]
							Gerald R. Ford[e]
Gerald R. Ford	Republican	Michigan (Neb.)	1913		1974	61	Nelson A. Rockefeller[f]
James E. Carter	Democrat	Georgia	1924		1977	52	Walter F. Mondale
Ronald W. Reagan	Republican	Calif. (Ill.)	1911		1981	69	George H. W. Bush

[a] State of residence when elected; if born in another State that State in parentheses.
[b] Democratic-Republican. [c] Johnson, a War Democrat, was elected Vice President (as Lincoln's running mate) on the coalition Union Party ticket. [d] Resigned October 10, 1973. [e] Nominated by Nixon, confirmed by Congress December 6, 1973. [f] Nominated by Ford, confirmed by Congress December 19, 1974.

exists. If the Vice President and a majority of the Cabinet (or other body authorized by law) dispute the President's ability to resume office, Congress is given 21 days in which to resolve the matter. If two-thirds of both houses decide that the President's incapacity still exists, the Vice President then continues to serve as Acting President. Otherwise, the powers and duties of the office are returned to the President, of course.

The Vice Presidency

"I am Vice President. In this I am nothing, but I may be everything." So said John Adams, the first Vice President of the United States. His remark could have been repeated, very appropriately, by each of the Vice Presidents who have followed him in that office.

The Constitution pays only scant attention to the Vice President, who is assigned but two formal duties. They are: (1) to preside over the Senate,[9] and (2) to help decide the question of presidential disability and, if a disability is found, to serve as Acting President.[10] Beyond those formal roles, the Constitution makes the Vice President a "President-in-waiting"—to become "everything" should the President die, resign, or be removed from office.

Through much of our history the Vice Presidency has been slighted—treated as an office of little real consequence and, often, as the butt of jokes.

Several—in fact, nearly all—Vice Presidents have themselves had a hand in this matter. John Adams described his post as "the most insignificant office that ever the invention of man contrived or his imagination conceived." And Thomas Jefferson,

who succeeded Adams, saw the office as "honorable and easy," "tranquil and unoffending."

Theodore Roosevelt, who had come to the White House from the Vice Presi-

The more recent Presidents, from Eisenhower to Reagan, have made greater use of their Vice Presidents. Today, the Vice President takes part in Cabinet meetings, is a member of the National Security Council, and performs various diplomatic, political, and administrative chores for the President. Vice President Walter Mondale, while on a diplomatic mission to the Far East in 1979, talked with refugees from Viet Nam at a refugee camp in Hong Kong.

---

[9] Article I, Section 3, Clause 4.

[10] 25th Amendment, Sections 3 and 4. The 12th Amendment provides that the Vice President must meet the same formal qualifications as those required for the Presidency.

dency, was annoyed by the tinkling of the prisms of a chandelier in the presidential study. He ordered it removed, saying: "Take it to the office of the Vice President. He doesn't have anything to do. It will keep him awake." The handsome fixture has graced the Vice President's office, just off the Senate floor, ever since.

John Nance Garner, who served for two terms as Franklin Roosevelt's Vice President, once declared: "The Vice Presidency isn't worth a warm pitcher of spit." And Alben Barkley, who served during Harry Truman's second term, often told the story of a woman who had two sons. One of them, he said, went away to sea and the other one became Vice President, "and neither of them was ever heard of again."

Despite these—and many other— slightings, the Vice Presidency is significant, of course. It is because its occupant is, literally, "only a heartbeat away from the Presidency." Recall, eight Presidents have died in office[11]—and one, Richard M. Nixon, was forced to resign in 1974.

Much of the blame for the low state of the Vice Presidency belongs to the two major parties and the process by which they regularly nominate their candidates for the post. Traditionally, each national convention selects the hand-picked choice of the just-nominated presidential candidate. And, almost invariably, the presidential candidate picks someone who will "balance the ticket." That is, a running mate is picked who will enhance the electability of the presidential nominee. Vice presidential candidates are seldom picked with an eye to fate and the Presidency. Rather, they are chosen to help carry a doubtful State or appeal to a particular section of the country, to appease a disappointed faction in the party, or to reward a faithful party work horse. They may be selected to attract support from some segment of the electorate where the presidential candidate's own appeal is weak. Or they may be picked for some other distinctly election-oriented reasons.

The Vice Presidency has been vacant 18 times thus far—nine times by succession to the Presidency, twice by resignation, and seven times by death.[12] Yet, not

---

[11] William Henry Harrison contracted a cold at his inauguration and died of pneumonia one month later (April 4, 1841); Zachary Taylor succumbed after an attack of acute gastroenteritis (July 9, 1850); Abraham Lincoln (April 15, 1861), James Garfield (September 19, 1881), and William McKinley (September 14, 1901) each died of an assassin's bullets; Warren Harding succumbed to a sudden and undisclosed illness (August 2, 1923); Franklin Roosevelt suffered a fatal cerebral hemorrhage (April 12, 1945); and John Kennedy was also assassinated (November 22, 1963).

[12] John C. Calhoun resigned to become a Senator from South Carolina in 1832; Spiro T. Agnew resigned in 1973, following a conviction for income tax evasion and in the face of serious allegations of extortion and bribery dating from his tenure as a county executive and then as Governor of the State of Maryland. The seven Vice Presidents who died in office were George Clinton (1812), Elbridge Gerry (1814), William R. King (1853), Henry Wilson (1875), Thomas H. Hendricks (1885), Garret A. Hobart (1899), and James S. Sherman (1912). The eight who succeeded to the Presidency on the death of a President were John Tyler (1841), Millard Fillmore (1850), Andrew Johnson (1865), Chester A. Arthur (1881), Theodore Roosevelt (1901), Calvin Coolidge (1923), Harry S Truman (1945), and Lyndon B. Johnson (1963). Gerald Ford succeeded to the Presidency upon Richard Nixon's historically unique resignation in 1974.

until the 25th Amendment did the Constitution treat the problem. Section 2 provides that:

> Whenever there is a vacancy in the office of the Vice President, the President shall nominate a Vice President who shall take office upon confirmation by a majority vote of both houses of Congress.

The provision was first implemented in 1973—when President Nixon selected and Congress confirmed Gerald Ford to succeed Spiro Agnew as Vice President. And it came into play again in 1974 when President Ford named and Congress approved Nelson Rockefeller as Mr. Ford's successor in the Vice Presidency.

Many have long urged that the Vice President play a larger role in the executive branch. The more recent Presidents—from Eisenhower to Reagan—have, in fact, made greater use of their Vice Presidents. Today, the Vice President participates in Cabinet meetings and is a member of the critically important National Security Council. The Vice President also performs various social, political, diplomatic, and administrative chores for the President.

But, at least thus far, no President has "upgraded" the Vice President to the role of a true "Assistant President." The major reason: Of all of the President's official family, only the Vice President is not subject to the ultimate discipline of removal from office by the President.

Presidential Nomination and Election

In strictly formal terms, the President is chosen in accord with the provisions of the Constitution.[13] In actual practice, however, the President is elected through an altogether extraordinary process. The process has developed over the span of now 49 presidential elections. It is a composite of constitutional provisions, a few State and federal laws, and—in largest measure—a number of practices born of and applied by the nation's political parties.

No other election—here or abroad—can match its color, drama, or suspense. None can match the tremendous popular interest and participation it attracts. Nor can any match the high level of party activity it involves, or the huge amounts of time, effort, and money it consumes.

Original Constitutional Provisions. The Constitutional Convention devoted more of its time to the method for choosing the President than to any other matter. It was, said James Wilson of Pennsylvania, "the most difficult of all on which we have had to decide." The matter was a difficult one largely because most of the Framers were opposed to selecting the President by either of the obvious alternatives: by Congress or by a direct vote of the people.

Early in the Convention, most of the delegates favored selection by Congress. Nearly all of them later abandoned that position, however. They came to the view that it would destroy the concept of separation of powers—that it would put the President "too much under the legislative thumb."

Only a few of the Framers favored choosing the President by popular vote. Nearly all agreed that that would lead, as Alexander Hamilton put it, "to tumult and disorder." Most of them also felt that the people, scattered over so vast an area, could not possibly know enough about the available candidates to make a wise and informed choice. George Mason of Virginia spoke for most of his colleagues when he said on the floor of the Constitutional Convention:

> The extent of the country renders it impossible that the people can have the req-

---

13 Article II, Section 1, Clauses 2 and 4; 12th, 20th, and 23rd Amendments.

uisite capacity to judge of the respective contentions of the candidates.

After weeks of debate and 30 separate votes, the Framers finally adopted a plan first suggested by Hamilton. Under it, the President was to be chosen by a special body of electors. Briefly, they agreed that:

(1) Each State would have as many presidential electors as it has Senators and Representatives in Congress;

(2) These electors would be chosen in each State in whatever manner the State legislature directed;

(3) The electors, meeting in their own States, would each cast two votes—each for a different person;

(4) The electoral votes from the several States would be opened and counted before a joint session of Congress;

(5) The person receiving the largest number of electoral votes, provided that total was a majority of all of the electors, would become President;

(6) The person with the second highest number of electoral votes would become Vice President;

(7) If a tie occurred, or if no one received the votes of a majority of the electors, the President would then be chosen by the House of Representatives, voting by States;

(8) If a tie occurred for the second spot, the Vice President would then be chosen by the Senate.[14]

The Framers of the Constitution thought and spoke of the electors as "the most enlightened and respectable citizens" from each State. They were to be "free agents" who would "deliberate freely" as they sought to choose the persons best qualified to fill the nation's two highest offices.

As curious as it may seem today, the electoral college system was one of the few major features of the proposed Constitu-

tion to escape widespread debate and criticism in the struggle over the ratification of that document.

Impact of the Rise of Parties. The electoral college system worked as the Framers intended only for as long as George Washington consented to seek and hold the Presidency. He was twice, and unanimously, elected President. That is, in 1789 and again in 1792, each elector cast one of his two ballots for the great Virginian.

Flaws began to appear in the system in 1796, however. By then, political parties had begun to form. John Adams, the Federalist candidate, was elected to the Presidency. Thomas Jefferson, an archrival and Democratic-Republican, who trailed Adams by but three votes in the electoral balloting, became his Vice President.

The system collapsed in the election of 1800. By then, two well-defined parties had emerged—the Federalists, led by Adams and Hamilton, and the Democratic-Republicans, headed by Jefferson. Each of these parties nominated presidential and vice presidential candidates. And each of them also nominated elector-candidates in the various States. Those elector-candidates were picked with the distinct understanding that, if elected, they would then vote for their party's presidential and vice presidential candidates.

Each of the 73 Democratic-Republicans who won posts as electors voted for that party's nominees: Jefferson and Aaron Burr. In doing so, they produced a tie for the Presidency. Recall that the Constitution equipped each elector with two votes, each to be cast for a different person but each to be cast for someone *as President*. Although popular opinion clearly favored Jefferson for the Presidency, and the party had intended Burr for the Vice Presidency, the House of Representatives had to take 36 separate ballots before finally selecting Jefferson as third President of the United States.

---

[14] Article II, Section 1, Clauses 2, 3, and 4.

THE PATH TO THE PRESIDENCY

CANDIDATE

Two main paths are taken to win delegates at the national nominating convention of a candidate's party — one in States that choose delegates through primaries, the other in States that choose delegates by party conventions.

PRESIDENTIAL PRIMARIES

In States with presidential primaries, party's voters select some or all of the national convention delegates and/or express a preference among various contenders for party's presidential nomination.

LOCAL CAUCUSES

Party voters in local meetings choose delegates to conventions at the congressional district and / or State levels.

DISTRICT CONVENTIONS

Conventions held in the several congressional districts select some or all of the State's delegates to the party's national convention.

STATE CONVENTIONS

Convention held at the State level picks some or all of the State's delegates to the party's national convention.

NATIONAL CONVENTIONS

Delegates choose the nominee of each major party — with the convention of both major parties held in mid-summer.

ELECTION DAY

Voters, in choosing between candidates, actually pick presidential electors, known as the Electoral College — people expected to support a specific candidate. Election Day is Tuesday following the first Monday in November.

ELECTORAL COLLEGE

Presidential electors meet in State capitals on the Monday following the second Wednesday in December to cast their electoral votes, to be officially counted in Washington on Jan. 6. A majority of electoral votes — 270 out of 538 — is needed for election as President. The winner is sworn in on Jan. 20.

Note: This outline indicates general procedures; many states vary them.

The 1980 Republican National Convention opens in Detroit's Joe Louis Arena. Three nights later, Ronald Reagan was nominated for the presidency by acclamation.

The spectacular election of 1800 left a lasting imprint on the presidential election process. It marked the introduction of three new elements into that process: (1) party nominations for the Presidency and Vice Presidency; (2) the nomination of candidates for presidential electors pledged to vote for their party's presidential ticket; and (3) the automatic casting of the electoral votes in line with those pledges. Gone forever was the notion that the electors would be chosen as "free agents" to "deliberate" over the selection of a President to lead the nation.

THE 12TH AMENDMENT. The election of 1800 also produced another notable result. The 12th Amendment was added to the Constitution to prevent a repetition of the fiasco of 1800. Although the amendment is a lengthy one, it provided for only one major change in the original electoral college system. It *separated* the presidential and vice

presidential elections: "The Electors . . . shall name in their ballots the person voted for as President, and in distinct ballots the person voted for as Vice President."[15]

With the emergence of political parties, the election of 1800, and the adoption of the 12th Amendment, the constitutional setting was laid for the development of the presidential election system as we know it today. What has developed is, indeed, a far cry from that designed in 1787.

---

[15] Not only does the amendment preclude a repetition of the circumstances that produced the tie of 1800; it almost certainly guarantees that the President and Vice President will always be elected from the same political party. With the adoption of the amendment, too, the character of the Vice Presidency underwent an unintended change. Ever since the adoption of the 12th Amendment, the two major parties have regularly nominated their vice presidential candidates with an eye to augmenting the electability of their presidential candidates, and with too little consideration of their capacity for the Presidency.

National Conventions. The Constitution made—and still makes—no provision for the nomination of candidates for the Presidency. As the Framers designed the system, the electors would, out of their own knowledge, select the "wisest and best man" as President. Nominations, therefore, were unnecessary. But, as we have seen, the rise of parties altered the system drastically. It brought with it the need for nominations.

The first method the parties developed to nominate presidential candidates was the congressional caucus. As we noted on page 236, this method was regularly used in the elections of 1800 to 1824. But, as we know, the closed and unrepresentative nature of the caucus brought about its downfall in 1824. For the election of 1832, both major parties adopted the national convention as their nominating device. It has continued to serve the two major parties ever since.

EXTENT OF CONTROL BY LAW. Through the convention process the final choice for the Presidency is, for all practical purposes, narrowed to one of two persons—the Republican or the Democratic nominee. Yet, there is virtually no legal control of that vital process.

We have already noted that the Constitution is completely silent on the subject of presidential nominations. There is, as well, almost no statutory law on the matter. The only provisions in federal law relate to the financing of conventions; see page 205. And only a very small body of State law deals with a few aspects of convention organization and procedure—for example, the selection of delegates and the manner in which they may cast their votes; see pages 369-370. Otherwise, and in very large part, the convention is a creature and a responsibility of the political parties themselves.

CONVENTION ARRANGEMENTS. In both parties the national committee is charged with making the plans and arrangements for the national convention, held every four years; see page 196. As much as a year before it is held, the committee meets (usually in Washington, D.C.) to set the time and the place for the extravaganza. July is the typically favored month, but each party's convention has been held as early as mid-June and as late as the latter part of August.

Where the national convention is held is a matter of prime importance. For the party, there are two major considerations. First, the site must satisfy certain physical requirements. For example, there must be an adequate convention hall, sufficient hotel accommodations, plentiful entertainment outlets, and convenient transportation facilities. Political considerations are also brought to bear. Thus, for example, a city in a doubtful State—one which might be expected to go either way in the election—is usually chosen. Such a choice is made in the obvious hope of influencing the election outcome, of course. Where the meeting is held can have a bearing on its outcome, too. Aspirants for the party's nomination regularly lobby for the selection of a city in a section of the country in which they have a strong base of popular support.

Many of the nation's larger cities bid for the "honor"—and the financial return to local business—of hosting a national convention. For 1980, the Republicans chose Detroit. They met in that city's new and spacious Joe Louis Arena, beginning on July 14th. And the Democrats picked New York City (as they had in 1976), and their convention opened in Madison Square Garden on August 11th.

Both of the major parties have met in Chicago more often than in any other city—a fact which reflects that city's central location and other physical attractions. The city's selection points up, as well, the significance of Illinois as a doubtful or "pivotal" State. The Democrats held each of their first six conventions—from 1832

A Ronald Reagan supporter at the 1980 Republican National Convention.

City	Republicans	Democrats
Atlantic City		1964
Baltimore	1864	1860, 1872, 1912
Chicago	1860, 1868, 1880, 1884, 1888, 1904, 1908, 1912, 1916, 1920, 1932, 1944, 1952, 1960	1864, 1884, 1892, 1896, 1932, 1940, 1944, 1952, 1956, 1968
Cincinnati	1876	1856, 1880
Cleveland	1924, 1936	
Detroit	1980	
Denver		1908
Houston		1928
Kansas City, Mo.	1928, 1976	1900
Los Angeles		1960
Miami Beach	1968, 1972	1972
Minneapolis	1892	
New York		1868, 1924, 1976, 1980
Philadelphia	1856, 1872, 1900, 1940, 1948	1936, 1948
St. Louis	1896	1876, 1888, 1904, 1916
San Francisco	1956, 1964	1920

through 1852—in Baltimore. Since 1856—when the Republicans held their first convention, in Philadelphia, and the Democrats moved to Cincinnati—the two major parties have met in the principal cities indicated in the accompanying table.[16]

APPORTIONMENT OF VOTES. Once the date and location have been set, the national committee issues a "call" to each of the State party organizations. The call names the time and place and also indicates the number of convention votes to which each State is entitled.

Traditionally, both parties have allotted to each State a number of convention votes based on that State's electoral votes. Over the past several conventions, however, both parties have concocted complicated apportionment formulas to give bonus delegates to those States which have supported the party's candidates in recent elections.[17]

For 1980 the Republican Party apportioned 1994 votes among its State organizations while the Democrats allotted 3331. (Each party's total includes delegates assigned to the District of Columbia, Guam, Puerto Rico, and the Virgin Islands, and for the Democrats, the former Canal Zone.)[18] Given the size factor, it is clear that neither

[16] As the table indicates, the two parties have met in the same city in a given election year on only six occasions: Chicago four times, in 1884, 1932, 1944, and 1952; Philadelphia in 1948; and Miami Beach in 1972.

[17] The number of convention *votes* per State is a more realistic indication of the size of each State's convention delegation than the number of *delegates* per State, at least insofar as the Democrats are concerned. In several States the Democrats select more delegates than their quota of convention votes; in such instances, some delegates cast half-votes. The Republicans do not permit fractional voting; each delegate casts one full vote.

[18] Beginning in 1980, the Democrats provide for a number of "automatic" delegates. Each State's basic allotment of delegates is increased by 10 percent, to include the State's top party officials and those Democrats who hold major public offices. First in 1976 and again for 1980, the Democrats also allotted convention votes (three) to yet another category: Democrats Abroad. Each party also provides for alternate delegates, with approximately as many alternates as there are regular delegates.

party's convention can be fairly described as a "deliberative body."

SELECTION OF DELEGATES. State law and/or party rules determine how each State's convention delegation is to be selected.[19]

Thirty-four States,[20] the District of Columbia, and Puerto Rico now provide for some form of the presidential primary. In many of them, some or all of the delegates are selected by that device, as we noted on page 243. The details of the primary vary widely among those States. But, as we have noted, a large majority of the delegates to both parties' conventions now comes from the primary States.

In the other States, the delegates are chosen by party conventions or committees, or by a combination of them.

THE CONVENTION AT WORK. Each party's national convention meets in a huge auditorium lavishly bedecked with flags, bunting, and various party symbols. Portraits of great figures from the party's past adorn the hall. The front of it is dominated by a large platform and the speaker's rostrum from which the proceedings are managed. The floor itself is jammed with row upon row of hundreds of chairs. Standards and placards mark the seating reserved for each State delegation. Microphones and telephones, including one for the chairperson of each delegation, are spotted at strategic points. Extensive facilities are provided for the veritable army of press, radio, and television reporters, commentators, camera operators, technicians, and all their equipment. The surrounding galleries seat the thousands of spectators who come from all over the nation to see the "greatest political show on earth." They come to see a spectacle H. L. Mencken once described this way:

> . . . [T]here is something about a national convention that makes it as fascinating as a revival or a hanging. It is vulgar, it is ugly, it is stupid, it is tedious, it's hard upon both the cerebral centers and the *gluteus maximus,* and yet it is somehow charming. One sits through long sessions wishing heartily that all the delegates were dead and in hell—and then suddenly there comes a show so gaudy and hilarious, so melodramatic and obscene, so unimaginably exhilarating and preposterous that one lives a gorgeous year in an hour.

Amidst all of this—and the turbulence and confusion that accompanies nearly all

---

[19] The Republicans have few rules relating to the selection of national convention delegates. To a large extent, they leave the details of that process to their State party organizations and to State law.

But the Democrats have added several such rules in recent years. In effect, they have nationalized much of the delegate selection process. Those rules are a direct result of the reforms undertaken by the Democrats after their divisive convention in Chicago in 1968 and their subsequent defeat in the presidential elections that year. Most of them are aimed at prompting broader involvement in the choosing of delegates (especially by the young, blacks, other minority groups, and women) and at the democratization of other aspects of convention organization and procedure. The rules have been adopted by the Democratic National Committee and are enforced by it.

Thus, for 1976 and 1980 the DNC imposed a proportional representation rule on the delegate selection process—a matter we discussed on page 244. (The Republicans have no such rule and permit winner-take-all primaries.) Also, beginning in 1980, the DNC requires that each State party organization choose an equal number of men and women as convention delegates. (The RNC "requests" their State parties to do so.) Another DNC rule now provides that *only* Democrats may participate in the party's delegate selection processes. Thus, Democratic delegates cannot be chosen in an open primary (page 240) nor by any other method in which Republicans or others might be involved. (The GOP has no such rule.)

[20] Alabama, Arkansas, California, Connecticut, Florida, Georgia, Idaho, Illinois, Indiana, Kansas, Kentucky, Louisiana, Maryland, Massachusetts, Michigan, Montana, Nebraska, Nevada, New Hampshire, New Jersey, New Mexico, New York, North Carolina, North Dakota, Ohio, Oregon, Pennsylvania, Rhode Island, South Dakota, Tennessee, Texas, Vermont, West Virginia, Wisconsin. Four of these States (Connecticut, Kansas, Louisiana, New Mexico) and Puerto Rico did not hold such primaries in 1976 but did so in 1980. North Dakota will hold its first presidential primary in 1984. On occasion, a State party stages a presidential primary even though one is not provided for by State law—*e.g.,* the Republicans (but not the Democrats) in Mississippi and South Carolina in 1980. In a few States—*e.g.,* Arkansas and Texas—the presidential primary law is only permissive; it permits but does not require either major party to hold one.

that it does—the convention meets to accomplish two principal ends. First, the adoption of the party's platform and, second, the nomination of its presidential and vice presidential candidates.

THE OPENING SESSION. Each party's convention usually spans four, sometimes five, days, and the order of business is much the same in both.

The opening session is called to order by the chairperson of the party's national committee. The official call is read, prayer is offered, and the temporary roll of delegates is called. Welcoming speeches are made by the national chairperson and a number of other party dignitaries.

The national chairperson then announces a slate of temporary officers for the convention, including the temporary presiding officer—all named by the national committee. The delegates promptly elect these officials.

The temporary chairperson then takes the rostrum to deliver the convention's first major speech. Both it and the *keynote address* which follows run to a predictable pattern: the party is eulogized, the opposition is assailed, a plea for party harmony is made, and rousing success at the polls is forecast.

Following the keynoter's oratorical efforts, the delegates routinely elect the convention's standing committees. There are four major committees at every convention: rules and order of business, permanent organization, credentials, and platform and resolutions. Each State delegation now has two members (a man and a woman) on each of them. With the selection of these committees, the first session generally ends.

THE SECOND AND THIRD SESSIONS. The next two or three, and sometimes four, sessions of the convention are devoted to more speeches by leading party figures and to the receipt of committee reports. They usually consume the second and third days. Over the past few conventions, both parties have slated these sessions on a late afternoon and/or early evening basis—angling for prime time on network television, of course.

Typically, the committee on rules and order of business reports first. It regularly recommends the adoption of the rules of the preceding convention with, perhaps, a few changes.[21] Its report, which also presents an agenda for the rest of the convention, is usually adopted with little or no dissent. But vigorous rules fights have occurred in both parties at various times. The credentials committee prepares the permanent roll of delegates entitled to seats and votes in the convention. Occasionally, contests develop over the seating of particular delegates and even entire delegations. When this occurs, it usually involves a State in which the party is faction-ridden and where the delegates are chosen by local conventions. The credentials committee must decide such disputes. Its decisions may be appealed to the convention floor, but the committee's report is customarily upheld.

The committee on permanent organization nominates the permanent convention officers. When elected, they succeed their temporary counterparts and direct the remaining sessions of the convention. The committee's principal job is to name the permanent chairperson. The selection of this officer is often a test of the strength of the rivals for the presidential nomination.[22] Upon election, the permanent chairperson delivers another of those lengthy speeches in which the party is praised, the opposition party is attacked, unity is prayed for, and a smashing victory in November is foreseen.

---

[21] In both parties the convention rules are largely based on those of the House of Representatives.

[22] Except for the temporary and the permanent chairpersons, the convention's officers are regularly members of the national committee.

Above: *Republican delegates stage a floor demonstration.* Right: *Balloons float downward from the ceiling of Madison Square Garden, signalling the end of the 1980 Democratic National Convention.*

Left: *Delegates wave placards and posters as Jimmy Carter is renominated at the 1980 Democratic National Convention.* Below: *Reagan supporters from Nebraska.*

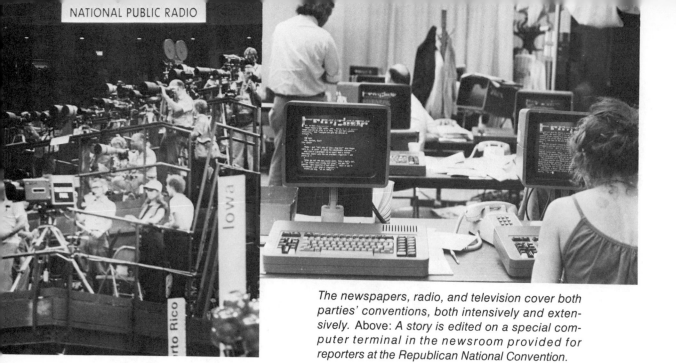

The newspapers, radio, and television cover both parties' conventions, both intensively and extensively. Above: A story is edited on a special computer terminal in the newsroom provided for reporters at the Republican National Convention.

The report of the committee on platform and resolutions—in the form of a proposed platform—usually reaches the floor by the third session. The committee frequently holds informal sessions before the convention assembles—where representatives of various interests and viewpoints urge their positions on the platform-makers.

Much of the party's platform emerges from a preliminary draft drawn up by party leaders or, for the party in power, by the President and his advisors. A struggle may—and often does—develop within the committee, and the fight occasionally spills over to the convention floor.

Platform-writing is a fine art. The document is supposed to be a basic statement of the party's principles and its stands on major policy matters. But it is also a campaign statement—intended to win as many votes as possible, while alienating none. As a result, both parties tend to produce somewhat generalized, less than specific comments on many of the hard issues of the day. The platforms may reflect the compromise nature of our politics and of the two major parties, but their value is open to serious question.

THE FINAL SESSIONS. By its fourth, sometimes the fifth, session, the convention comes to its real reason for being: the nomination of the party's presidential candidate.

At the Republican convention, the names of the contenders for the presidential nomination are presented to the convention in a format which both parties used until 1972. The secretary reads the roll of the States alphabetically, beginning with Alabama. As it is called, each State may place a name in nomination, yield to another State further down the line, or simply pass.

The Democrats now use a petition process to schedule their nominations. The supporters of a contender must submit a petition, endorsing that person and signed by at least 50 delegates, to the convention secretary by the day before the nominating session. The order in which the contenders' names are presented to the convention is then determined by lot.

Most nominating speeches are lavish hymns of praise, extolling the virtues of "The man who. . . ." Although the name of the person to be offered is well-known before the nominator begins to speak, tradition has it that the name not be mentioned until the very end of the speech. Its final announcement triggers a lengthy, wild, noisy demonstration on the floor. These "spontaneous" demonstrations—supposed to show widespread support for aspirant, whether real or not—are carefully planned, of course.[23]

After all of the nominating speeches, and their seconds, have been made, the balloting begins. The secretary calls the States alphabetically and each chairperson announces the vote of his or her delegation. Each complete roll call is known as a "ballot." In both parties a majority vote is required to select the presidential candidate, and succeeding ballots are taken until an aspirant receives the requisite number.

Most often, the first ballot produces a choice. In the 21 conventions each party has held in this century (1900-1980), the Republicans have made a first-ballot nomination 17 times and the Democrats 16.[24]

Once the presidential nomination has been decided, the choice of a running mate comes as an anti-climax. The vice presidential nominee is almost invariably the choice of the just-nominated presidential candidate.[25]

With the candidates named, the convention's presiding officer appoints two special committees, each composed of several delegates, to notify the candidates of their selection—something they knew the instant it happened, of course. These committees used to meet the candidates at their homes, or nearby where large audiences could gather, and each nominee would then deliver an "acceptance speech." Franklin Roosevelt broke this tradition in 1932 by flying to Chicago to make his acceptance speech to the convention itself. Since then, each candidate has followed that practice. In fact, today each of the party's hopefuls is at hand throughout the convention.

WHOM DOES THE PARTY NOMINATE? If an incumbent President wants another term, the answer is almost always easy—the President is virtually assured nomination, and usually with no real opposition from within the party.[26] Indeed, each time in this century that the incumbent has sought the nomination he has received it.[27] The incumbent's advantages are immense: the majesty and publicity of the office and close control of the party machinery.

But when the incumbent President is not in the field, from two or three to a dozen or so more-or-less serious contenders surface in the preconvention period. At least two or three of them usually survive to contest the prize at the convention.

---

[23] Some of the candidates offered to a convention have no real chance of becoming the party's presidential nominee, but are put forward for some other reason. Thus, a "favorite son" may be offered because a State delegation wants to honor one of its own. The delegation usually votes for its favorite son on the first ballot, especially when there is a close race among leading contenders. The tactic permits a State to judge the relative strength of the real contenders and puts it in a position to "jump on the bandwagon" of the apparent winner at the opportune moment.

[24] From 1832 until 1936 the Democrats required a two-thirds vote for nomination. The practice often produced deadlocks in the convention and the nomination of "darkhorse" candidates—those who did not appear to be prospects before the convention. The most spectacular deadlock occurred in the Democratic convention of 1924, when nine days and 103 separate ballots were needed to nominate John W. Davis. The Republicans have required a simple majority for nomination from their first convention in 1856. Until 1968 the Democrats permitted any State delegation to follow the "unit rule" under which all members of the delegation had to cast their votes for the aspirant favored by a majority of them. The Republicans have never allowed the unit rule.

[25] See page 362.

[26] Assuming, of course, the President's eligibility according to the 22nd Amendment.

[27] The Republicans renominated William McKinley in 1900, William Howard Taft in 1912, Herbert Hoover in 1932, Dwight Eisenhower in 1956, and Richard Nixon in 1972, and nominated successors Theodore Roosevelt in 1904, Calvin Coolidge in 1924, and Gerald Ford in 1976. The Democrats renominated Woodrow Wilson in 1916, Franklin Roosevelt in 1936, 1940, and 1944, and Jimmy Carter in 1980, and nominated successors Harry Truman in 1948 and Lyndon Johnson in 1964. In fact, only four sitting Presidents have ever been denied nomination—all in the 19th century: successor John Tyler, by the Whigs in 1844; successor Millard Fillmore, by the Whigs in 1852; Franklin Pierce, by the Democrats in 1856; and successor Chester Arthur, by the Republicans in 1884.

President Carter waves to delegates assembled to hear him accept the Democratic Party's nomination for another term in the White House.

Who among them will win the nomination? The record of our presidential politics to date argues this answer: the one who is, in the jargon of politics, the most *available*—the one who is the most nominatable and electable. The nominating process strives to produce candidates who can *win*, candidates with the broadest possible appeal within the party and electorate.

Most presidential candidates have come to their nominations with substantial and well-known records in public office. *But* those records have not been studded with controversies in which they have antagonized important elements within the party or among the voting public. And, usually, they have served in *elective* office, where they have shown a considerable vote-getting ability. Seldom does one step from the business world or from the military directly into the role of candidate, as did Wendell Willkie in 1940 or Dwight Eisenhower in 1952.

Historically, the governorships of the larger States have been the most prominent source of presidential candidacies. Eleven of the 20 men nominated by the two major parties between 1900 and 1956 were either then serving or had previously served as a governor.

For a time, the Senate became the prime source, however. In the four elections from 1960 through 1972, each of the major party nominees had been a Senator;

and none had ever been a governor.

But the old pattern now seems to have been restored. Jimmy Carter, the former governor of Georgia, was nominated by the Democrats in 1976 and 1980; and Ronald Reagan, former governor of California, was the GOP choice in 1980.

Despite the few exceptions, most notably Democrats Alfred E. Smith in 1928 and John F. Kennedy in 1960, most of the leading contenders for major party presidential nominations have been Protestant in their religious preferences. And most have also come from the larger and doubtful States—those as likely to go one way as the other in the election. Thus, candidates from such "pivotal" States as New York, Ohio, Illinois, or California are more available than those from smaller States likely to be won by one of the parties but not the other. From this standpoint, the nominations of Senator Goldwater of Arizona by the Republicans in 1964 and Senator George McGovern of South Dakota by the Democrats in 1972 were more than just a little exceptional—and so, too, was the Democratic nomination of Jimmy Carter from Georgia in 1976.

Neither party has, at least to this point, seriously considered a woman as its candidate for the Presidency—or for the Vice Presidency, for that matter. Nor has either party seriously contemplated a black for either role.

Presidential candidates usually present a pleasing and healthy appearance, are apparently happily married, and have an attractive (and exploitable) family. Adlai Stevenson, the Democratic nominee in 1952 and 1956, and Ronald Reagan, the GOP candidate in 1980, are the only major party nominees ever to have been divorced.

A well-developed speaking ability has always been a major factor of availability. And, of course, the ability to project well over television has become an absolute must for candidates in recent elections.

The Presidential Campaign. For a brief period after the conventions, the opposing candidates rest and map campaign strategies. Then the presidential campaign—the grueling effort to win voter support—begins in earnest. Every means to put the candidates and their ideas before the voters, and in the most favorable light, is used. Radio and television speeches, "whistle-stop" tours, press conferences, press releases, public rallies, party dinners, newspaper, radio, and television advertisements, campaign stickers and buttons, placards and pamphlets, billboards and matchcovers—all bombard the voters in behalf of each party's nominees. The can-didates pose for hundreds of photographs, shake thousands of hands, and strive to convince the electorate that a victory for the opposition would mean hard times for the country. Whether the campaign changes a significant number of votes or not—and the point is debatable—the massive efforts continue right up to election eve.

The Electoral College System Today. The presidential campaign ends with election day. The voters go to the polls in the 50 States and the District of Columbia to make their choice. Technically, of course, the voters do not vote on the presidential candidates directly. Rather, they vote to elect the members of the electoral college.

As we noted on page 364, the Framers of the Constitution intended the electors would exercise their own judgment in the selection of a President. But for more than 180 years now, the parties have nominated slates of electors who are, in effect, automatons—"rubber stamps" for their party's choices. The electors go through the *form* prescribed by the Constitution in order to meet the *letter* of the Constitution's requirements—but their actual behavior is a far cry from its *original intent.*

Accepting the cheers of the Republican National Convention in 1980 are (left to right): former President Gerald Ford and Betty Ford; Nancy Reagan and the presidential nominee, Ronald Reagan; vice presidential nominee George Bush and Barbara Bush.

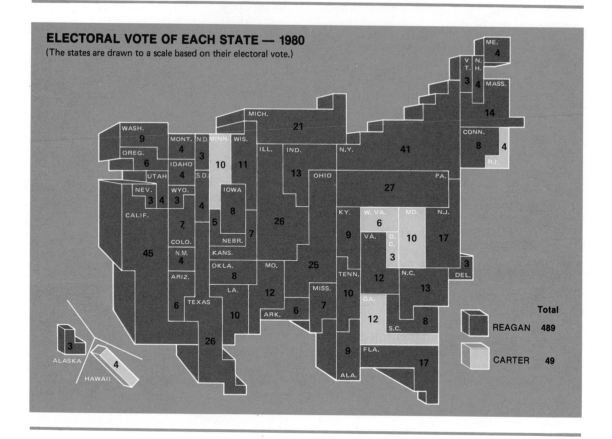

ELECTORAL VOTE OF EACH STATE — 1980
(The states are drawn to a scale based on their electoral vote.)

Total	
REAGAN	489
CARTER	49

The electors are chosen by popular vote in every State,[28] and on the same day throughout the country—the Tuesday following the first Monday in November every fourth year. In 1980 the presidential election fell on November 4th; in 1984 it will be held on November 6th.

The electors are chosen at-large—from the entire State—in every State now except Maine.[29] That is, the electors are chosen on a "winner-take-all" basis. The presidential candidate (technically, the slate of elector-candidates) receiving the largest popular vote in a State wins *all* of that State's electoral votes. (The names of the individual elector-candidates now appear on the ballot in less than a fourth of the States. Only the names of the presidential and vice presidential candidates are usually listed—

---

[28] The Constitution (Article II, Section 1, Clause 2) provides that the electors are to be chosen in each State "in such manner as the legislature thereof may direct." In several States, the legislatures themselves chose the electors in the first several presidential elections. By 1832, however, every State except South Carolina had provided for popular election; electors were chosen by the legislature in South Carolina through the election of 1860. Since then, all presidential electors have been chosen by popular vote in every State, with but two exceptions: the State legislature chose the electors in Florida in 1868 and in Colorado in 1876.

[29] Beginning with the 1972 election, Maine now uses the "district plan." Two of that State's four electors are chosen from the State at-large and the other two from each of the State's congressional districts. The district plan was used by a number of States in the first several presidential elections; but every State legislature (except South Carolina's) had provided for the election of presidential electors from the State at-large—that is, by the "general ticket" or "winner-take-all" system—by 1832. Since 1836 the district plan has been used only by Michigan in 1892 and by Maine in 1972, 1976, and 1980.

they stand as "shorthand" for the elector slates.)

Let us illustrate the process. If a voter in Ohio wishes to vote for the 25 Democratic elector-candidates, he or she does so by marking a ballot with an X in the box beside the names of the Democratic presidential and vice presidential candidates. Or, in many places in the State, the voter accomplishes the same thing by pulling the appropriate lever on a voting machine or by making the proper punch on a ballot card.

The secretary of state waits to receive the returns from all of the county boards of election. If it is found that the Democratic slate has received more than the Republican or any other set of elector-candidates, the secretary of state then certifies (officially declares) the 25 Democratic candidates to have been elected as Ohio's presidential electors.

The electors then assemble at the capitol in Columbus on the date set by Congress—the Monday following the second Wednesday in December.[30] There they each cast their electoral votes—one for President and one for Vice President. Having done so, they sign their ballots which are then sealed and sent by registered mail to the President of the Senate in Washington.[31]

Which party has won a majority of the electoral votes—and who, then, will be the next President of the United States—is usually known by midnight of election day, more than a month before the electors cast their ballots. But the *formal* election of the President and Vice President *finally* takes place on January 6th.

On that date, the President of the Senate opens the electoral votes from each State and counts them before a joint session of Congress.[32] The candidate who receives a majority of the elector's votes for President is declared elected—as, too, is the one with a majority of the votes for Vice President.

If no one has a majority for President (at least 270 of the 538 electoral votes), the election is thrown into the House of Representatives. This happened, as we saw, in 1800, and again in 1824. The House chooses a President from among the top three candidates in the electoral college. Each State delegation has one vote, and it takes a majority of 26 to elect. If the House fails to choose a President by January 20, the 20th Amendment provides that the newly elected Vice President shall act as President until it does.[33]

If no person receives a majority for Vice President, the Senate decides between the top two candidates. It takes a majority of the whole Senate to elect. The Senate has had to choose a Vice President only

---

[30] Article II, Section 1, Clause 4 provides that the date Congress sets "shall be the same throughout the United States." The 12th Amendment provides that the electors "shall meet in their respective States." Congress has provided that they meet "at such place in each State as the legislature of such State shall direct," and every State legislature has directed that they meet at the State capitol.

[31] Two copies of the ballots are also sent to the Archivist of the United States in the General Services Administration, two to the State's secretary of state, and one to the local federal district court. If neither the President of the Senate nor the Archivist receive a State's votes by the fourth Wednesday in December, and they cannot be obtained from the secretary of state by that date, the President of the Senate sends a special messenger for the votes filed with the federal court.

[32] The 12th Amendment commands the President of the Senate to open and count the returns in the presence of both houses. Hence, on January 6, 1961, Vice President Richard Nixon performed this constitutional duty and then declared John F. Kennedy, rather than the Republican candidate, Richard Nixon, the winner of the 1960 presidential election. But on January 6, 1969, Vice President Hubert Humphrey absented himself; the Senate President *pro tem*, the late Senator Richard B. Russell (D., Ga.), opened and counted the ballots and declared Nixon, not the Democratic candidate Humphrey, the winner of the 1968 election.

[33] The 20th Amendment further provides that "the Congress may by law provide for the case wherein neither a President-elect nor a Vice President-elect shall have qualified" by inauguration day. Congress has done so in the Succession Act of 1947; see page 359. In such an event, the Speaker of the House would "act as President . . . until a President or Vice President shall have qualified."

once. It elected Richard M. Johnson in 1837.

Defects in the Electoral College System. Criticisms of the electoral college system have been heard almost from the beginning—and so, too, have proposals for its reform. There are three major weaknesses in the present arrangement.

THE FIRST MAJOR DEFECT. There is the ever-present threat that the electoral vote result will contradict the outcome of the popular election. That is, there is always the possibility that the apparent winner, the winner of the popular vote, will *not* win the Presidency.

This continuing threat is largely the result of two factors:

The most important of them is the "winner-take-all" feature of the system—the fact that in each State the winning candidate customarily receives *all* of that State's electoral vote. The other major party candidate's popular votes count for nothing in terms of the final outcome. In 1976, for example, Jimmy Carter carried the State of Ohio by a wafer-thin margin—by only 9,333 votes, less than three-tenths of one percent. Despite the fact that more than two million Ohioans voted for Gerald Ford, Carter received all 25 of the State's electoral votes.

The other major culprit here is the way in which the electoral votes are distributed among the States. Recall that each State has two electors because of its Senate seats, regardless of its population. The Senate-based electors seriously distort the picture. Because of them, the distribution of electoral votes cannot possibly match the facts of population (and voter) distribution. Take the extreme case to illustrate this situation: California, the largest State, has 45 electoral votes—or one for each 443,402 persons, based on its 1970 population of 19,953,134. Alaska has three electoral votes—or one for each 100,724, based on its 1970 population of 302,173.

The popular vote winner has, in fact,

failed to win the Presidency on three occasions—in 1824, 1876, and 1888. In 1824, Andrew Jackson won the largest share (a plurality, but not a majority) of the popular votes—151,174, or 40.3 percent of the total. His nearest rival, John Quincy Adams, received 113,122 votes, or 30.9 percent. Ninety-nine of the 261 electors then voted for Jackson—again a plurality but far short of the constitutionally required majority. The election thus went to the House of Representatives and, early in 1825, it elected Adams to the Presidency.[34]

In the election of 1876, Rutherford B. Hayes, the Republican candidate, received 4,034,311 popular votes while his Democratic opponent, Samuel J. Tilden, garnered 4,288,548. Tilden, with a popular plurality of 254,237, received 184 electoral votes. Hayes won 185 electoral votes and so became President.[35]

In 1888 incumbent President Grover Cleveland won 5,534,488 popular votes—90,596 more than his Republican opponent, Benjamin Harrison. But Harrison received 233 electoral votes to Cleveland's 168—and so succeeded Cleveland as the nation's 23rd President.

Although the system has not "misfired" to produce a distorted result since 1888, it *could* have happened on *several* oc-

[34] Both Adams and Jackson were Democratic-Republicans; recall that the election of 1824 occurred during the one-party Era of Good Feeling; see page 190. Popular votes were cast in only 18 of the 24 States in 1824; the electors were chosen by the legislatures in Delaware, Georgia, Louisiana, New York, South Carolina, and Vermont. The popular vote figures cited here are only approximately correct; vote counts were neither well-kept nor -recorded in 1824. These figures, as most of the popular vote results cited in this book, are drawn from the authoritative *Guide to U. S. Elections*, Congressional Quarterly, Inc., 1975.

[35] The election of 1876 is often referred to as "the Stolen Election." Two conflicting sets of electoral votes were received from Florida (4 votes), Louisiana (8 votes), and South Carolina (7 votes), and the validity of one vote from Oregon was disputed. Congress created an Electoral Commission—composed of five Senators, five Representatives, and five Supreme Court Justices—to decide the matter. The Commissioners—eight Republicans and seven Democrats—voted on strict party lines, awarding all of the disputed votes, and so the Presidency, to Hayes.

Election night excitement and jubilation at the President-elect's headquarters in Dixon, Illinois, one of the towns in which Ronald Reagan lived as a youth.

casions. Take the close election of 1976 to illustrate the point. Jimmy Carter defeated his Republican opponent, Gerald Ford, by 1,678,069 popular votes—and won only a bare majority of the total popular vote.[36]

	Popular Vote	%	Electoral Vote	%
Carter	40,825,839	50.03	297	55.2
Ford	39,147,770	47.97	240	44.6
Others	1,629,737	2.00	1	0.2

If only a handful of voters in a few States had voted for Ford, instead of Carter, Ford would have had a majority of the

[36] To this point, 13 Presidents have been elected although they did not win a majority of the popular vote: John Quincy Adams won in the House in 1824, and Rutherford B. Hayes in 1876 and Benjamin Harrison in 1888 each won the electoral vote count while losing the popular vote contest, as we have noted. The other 10 all were elected with a plurality, but not a majority, of the popular vote. These "minority Presidents": James K. Polk (1844), Zachary Taylor (1848), James Buchanan (1856), Abraham Lincoln (1860), James A. Garfield (1880), Grover Cleveland (1884 and 1892), Woodrow Wilson (1912 and 1916), Harry Truman (1948), John F. Kennedy (1960), Richard Nixon (1968).

electoral votes, and so kept the Presidency. Combinations involving several different States can be used to play this game, but the simplest one involves Ohio and Hawaii. If only 4667 of the 2,009,959 Carter votes in Ohio (25 electoral votes) and only 3687 of the 147,375 Carter votes in Hawaii (4 electoral votes) had gone to Ford instead, Ford would have received a total of 270 electoral votes. Thus, Ford would have had a bare majority of the electoral votes and so won the election.

Several other presidential elections can be used to illustrate the point, as well. Thus, in 1960, John F. Kennedy won a popular plurality of 114,673 votes over the Republican candidate, Richard M. Nixon— less than two-tenths of one percent of all of the votes cast:

	Popular Vote	%	Electoral Vote	%
Kennedy	34,221,334	49.7	303	56.4
Nixon	34,106,671	49.6	219	40.8
Byrd	—	—	15	2.8
Others	500,945	0.7	—	—

from *The Herblock Gallery*
(Simon & Schuster, 1968)

*"YOU GO FIRST, SONNY,
THEN POINT ME TOWARD HIM"*

results in the 1980 race demonstrate the point:

	Popular Vote	%	Electoral Vote	%
Reagan	43,201,220	50.9	489	90.9
Carter	34,913,322	41.1	49	9.1
Anderson	5,581,379	6.6	—	—
Others	1,203,818	1.4	—	—

THE SECOND MAJOR DEFECT. There is no provision in the Constitution, nor in any federal statute, *requiring* the electors to vote for the candidate favored by the popular vote in their States. (Several States do have such laws but they are of highly doubtful constitutionality, and none has ever been enforced.)

The electors are expected to vote for the candidate who carries their State and, as loyal partisans, they almost always do. Thus far, electors have "broken their pledges"—voted for someone other than their party's presidential nominee—on only eight occasions: in 1796, 1820, 1948, 1956, 1960, 1968, 1972, and 1976. In the most recent case, one Republican elector from Washington voted for Ronald Reagan; the eight other electors from that State each voted for Gerald Ford, who had turned back Reagan's bid for the GOP nomination in 1976.

In no instance has the behavior of a "faithless elector" had a bearing on the outcome of a presidential election—but the potential is certainly there.

THE THIRD MAJOR DEFECT. In any presidential election it is possible that the contest will be decided in the House of Representatives. This has happened only twice, as we know—and not since 1824. But in several other elections a strong third party bid has threatened to win enough electoral votes to make it impossible for either major party candidate to win a majority of the electoral votes—especially in

If only a comparatively few voters in a few States had voted for Nixon rather than Kennedy—for example, 4430 in Illinois (27 electoral votes in 1960) and 23,122 in Texas (24 electoral votes), Nixon would have won the Presidency. And, like Carter in 1976, Kennedy would still have been the popular vote winner.

In short, the "winner-take-all" factor produces an electoral vote result which is, at best, only a very distorted reflection of the popular vote result. Even the lopsided

1912, 1924, 1948, and 1968. The 1968 election stands as a good example:

	Popular Vote	%	Electoral Vote	%
Nixon	31,785,148	43.4	301	55.9
Humphrey	31,274,503	42.7	191	35.5
Wallace	9,901,151	13.5	46	8.6
Others	242,568	0.4	—	—

George Wallace, the American Independent Party's candidate, won five States and received 46 electoral votes, as the map on page 226 indicates. If Democrat Hubert Humphrey had carried Alaska, Delaware, Missouri, Nevada, and Wisconsin—States where Richard Nixon's margin was thin and in which Wallace also had a substantial vote—Nixon's electoral vote total would have been 268 and Humphrey's 224. Neither would have had the necessary majority. The House would then have had to choose among Humphrey, Nixon, and Wallace.[37]

Three serious objections can be raised to election by the House: (1) The voting in such cases is by States, not by individual members. A small State—for example, Alaska or Nevada—would have as much weight as even the most populous States, California and New York. (2) If the Representatives from a State were so divided over the question that no candidate were favored by a majority of them, the State would lose its vote. (3) The Constitution requires a majority of the States for election in the House—today 26, of course. If a strong third party candidate were involved, it could prove to be almost impossible for the House to make a decision by inauguration day.[38]

Proposed Reforms. The defects in the electoral college system have long been recognized, of course. Constitutional amendments to revise the process have been introduced in every term of Congress since 1789. Most of the reforms which have been offered can be grouped under three headings:

(1) THE DISTRICT PLAN. Under this arrangement, the electors would be chosen in each State as are members of Congress. That is, two electors would be chosen from the State at-large and the others would be elected from each of the State's congressional districts.[39]

The district plan would eliminate the "winner-take-all" problem in the present system, of course. And its proponents—including former Presidents Johnson and Nixon—argue that it would therefore make the electoral vote a more accurate reflection of the popular returns.

The strongest argument against the district plan is that it would *not* eliminate the possibility that the loser of the popular vote would nonetheless win the electoral vote. In fact, if the plan had been in effect

---

[37] In 1968 Wallace received more popular votes than any other third-party presidential candidate, before or since; but Theodore Roosevelt in 1912 and Robert M. La-Follette in 1924 each received a *larger share* of the popular vote, 27.4 percent and 16.6 percent, respectively; see page 194. In 1948 the States Rights (Dixiecrat) candidate, Strom Thurmond of South Carolina, carried four States and received 39 electoral votes. Although President Truman won the election with 303 electoral votes to Thomas E. Dewey's 189, he won several States by very slim margins. A switch of fewer than 21,000 votes in two large States—16,807 in Illinois and 3,554 in Ohio—would have given those State's electoral votes to Dewey, reduced Truman's total to 250, and thrown the election into the House.

[38] In such an event, Section 3 of the 20th Amendment provides that "the Vice President-elect shall act as President until a President shall have qualified"; and if no Vice President-elect is available, the Presidential Succession Act (page 359) would come into play. Notice that it is even mathematically possible for the minority party in the House to have control of a majority of the individual State delegations. That party could then elect its candidate—even though he or she may have run second (or even third) in both the popular and the electoral vote contests.

[39] Maine now uses the district plan, and it has done so since 1972, as we noted on page 376. Any other State could adopt it if it chose to, of course. A constitutional amendment would be necessary to make its use mandatory in all States, however.

in 1960, Richard Nixon would have received 278 electoral votes and he, not John Kennedy, would have won the presidency.

Further, the results under the district plan would depend very heavily upon the particular way in which the congressional districts were drawn in each State. That is, it would put a premium on gerrymandering (see page 290).

(2) THE PROPORTIONAL PLAN. Under this arrangement, each presidential candidate would receive the same share of a State's electoral vote as he or she received of that State's popular vote. If, for example, a candidate won 40 percent of the votes cast in a State with 20 electoral votes, he or she would automatically receive eight electoral votes from that State.

Obviously, this plan would cure the "winner-take-all" problem. And, because it would do away with the electors, it would also eliminate the "faithless elector" possibility. And, as its backers claim, it would most certainly produce an electoral vote result more nearly in line with the popular vote—at least *for each State.*

But it would not necessarily produce such a result on a *national* basis. Because each of the smaller States is overweighted by its two Senate-based electors, the proportional plan still leaves open the possibility that the loser of the popular vote will nonetheless win the Presidency in the electoral vote. In fact, this would have occurred in 1896 if the plan had been in effect for that election. William Jennings Bryan would have defeated William McKinley,

even though McKinley had a comfortable popular vote margin of 596,985 (5.1 percent).[40]

Many who oppose the proportional plan worry about its consequences for the two-party system—and, therefore, for the whole fabric of the American political system. The adoption of the plan would almost certainly signal a substantial increase in both the number and the vigor of minor parties. Various minor party candidates would regularly receive at least some share of the electoral vote. And the chance that one or more of them might be able to force a presidential election into the House would be heightened considerably, too.[41]

(3) DIRECT POPULAR ELECTION. The proposal most often made—and most widely supported—is the most obvious one. It is: to abolish the electoral college system altogether and provide for the direct popular election of the President.

The principal arguments for direct election seem overpowering. The strongest of those contentions is that it would implement the democratic ideal: each vote would count, and equally, in the national result. The winner would always be the majority or plurality choice. And the dangers and confusions of the existing system would be ended—replaced by a simple and easily understood process. Opinion polls have long indicated overwhelming public support for direct election.

The House of Representatives did approve a direct election amendment in 1969. But the measure died, the victim of a Senate filibuster in 1970. A similar measure

---

[40] And, in the closest of all presidential elections, Winfield S. Hancock would have defeated James A. Garfield in 1880—even though Garfield had a popular plurality (of only 1898 votes, 0.0213 percent). But, on the other hand, there would have been no "Stolen Election" in 1876 and Cleveland would have defeated Harrison in 1888 (see page 378). Both the district and the proportional plans would tend to benefit the Republicans rather than the Democrats. This is chiefly because each would magnify the effect of the popular votes cast in smaller communities and rural areas (where, at least outside the South, the GOP is traditionally the stronger of the two major parties).

[41] Most of the plan's backers recognize that an increase in minor party clout would mean that the popular vote winner would often fail to gain a clear majority of the electoral vote. In 1976, for example, Jimmy Carter would have received 261.148 electoral votes to Gerald Ford's 258.860. (The typical proportional plan would carry the arithmetic involved out to three decimal points.) Hence, they would reduce the majority requirement to that of a plurality of at least 40 percent. If no candidate won at least 40 percent of the electoral votes, a second election, involving only the two front runners, would be held.

In the election of 1876 – the "Stolen Election" – there were two sets of conflicting electoral votes from three States and one disputed vote from another State. An Electoral Commission was created and directed to pass on the conflicting returns and to say which set from each of the doubtful States was to be received. The case was decided on partisan terms – eight of the 15 commissioners were Republicans. Here, the results of the count are handed to the Senate's President pro tempore in a joint session of Congress in March of 1877. The final electoral vote count – 185 for Rutherford Hayes and 184 for Samuel Tilden – meant victory for Hayes, the Republican candidate.

was brought to a floor vote and rejected by the Senate in 1979.

Although the closeness of the 1976 election stimulated new interest, there seems little real chance that the proposal can be successfully revived. Several "practical" obstacles stand in its way.

The constitutional amendment process itself is a major impediment. Recall two things here. *First,* there are three built-in minority vetoes in the amendment process. Two of them are in Congress, where one-third plus one of the members of *either* house can block the proposal of an amendment. And one-fourth plus one of the State legislatures (or conventions) can defeat an amendment once it is proposed. *Sec-*

ond, the smaller States are vastly overrepresented in the electoral college, and they would lose that advantage in a direct election plan. In short, it is likely that enough Senators, *or* Representatives, *or* small States, would oppose a direct election amendment, and so kill it.[42]

In addition to those who take the small State view here, many others oppose the reform. Some argue that it would undermine federalism—because the States, as *States,* would lose their role in the choice of a President. Others claim that direct election would put a virtually intolerable load

[42] Altogether, 30 States and the District of Columbia were over-weighted in the allocation of electoral votes for the 1972, 1976, and 1980 elections.

"MIDDLE MAN"

Hesse in *St. Louis Globe-Democrat*

on the election process. They argue that because *every* vote cast in *each* State would figure in the *national* result, parties and their candidates would have to campaign strenuously in *every* State. The consequences, they argue, would be very significant in terms of campaign time, effort, and, especially, financing.[43]

Some insist that direct election would be an added spur to ballot-box stuffing and other forms of vote corruption. Inevitably, they say, it would mean lengthy, bitter, highly explosive post-election challenges.

And they fear that those disputes could tear the nation apart.

In many States, the outcome of a State-wide election often hinges on the behavior of some particular minority in the electorate. The result frequently depends on how those voters cast their ballots or, of even greater importance, on how heavily they do or do not turn out to vote. Thus, for example, the black vote in Chicago is often decisive in the presidential election in Illinois. But in a direct election these groups would not hold the balance of power, the clout, they now have—and so many of them oppose direct election.

All in all, given these objections, there seems little real possibility of the adoption of the direct election proposal within the foreseeable future. Little real possibility, that is, *unless* the electoral college system malfunctions in another presidential election. Should that happen, a direct election amendment would very likely be adopted, and in short order.

---

[43] Under the existing "winner-take-all" system, the candidates naturally focus their campaigns on the larger States—those with the largest blocs of electoral votes. In fact, it is possible for a candidate to win the Presidency by carrying only the 11 largest States—because they have a total of 272 electoral votes, 2 more than the minimum of 270 needed to win. The 11 States (and their electoral votes) are California (45), New York (41), Pennsylvania (27), Texas (26), Illinois (26), Ohio (25), Michigan (21), Florida (17), New Jersey (17), Massachusetts (14), and North Carolina (13); Indiana also has 13 electoral votes.

SUMMARY

The Presidency is the most important and the most powerful office known to history. The President's many roles include those of chief of state, chief executive, chief administrator, chief diplomat, commander in chief, chief legislator, party chief, and chief citizen. The problems of the Presidency are as many and difficult as its powers are vast.

The Constitution provides that the President must be a natural-born citizen, at least 35 years of age, and must have resided in the United States for at least 14 years. The Chief Executive is chosen to a four-year term and is limited to serving two full terms or not more than ten years. The President receives a salary of $200,000 a year and many other compensations, as well.

A vacancy in the Presidency is filled by the Vice President who succeeds to the office. The line of succession passes to the Speaker of the House, the President *pro tem* of the Senate, and the now 13 Cabinet Department heads. The problems of presidential disability are treated by the 25th Amendment.

The Vice President, long regarded as a "fifth wheel," occupies a most significant office, particularly because of the possibility of succession. The Vice President's one constitutional duty is to preside over the Senate. Recent Presidents have "upgraded" the office. The 25th Amendment provides for filling a vacancy in the Vice Presidency.

In strictly formal terms, the President is elected in accord with the Constitution's provisions for the electoral college system. Actually, the President is chosen through a largely extralegal process which is chiefly the product of party practices. Presidential candidates are nominated by the parties in huge, boisterous, and complex national conventions. Technically, the President is elected by the presidential electors chosen by the voters in each State; but the electors have long since become rubber stamps for their parties, reflecting the popular election results in their States.

The electoral college system suffers several shortcomings. The most serious are that: it can produce a President who has won a majority of the electoral votes even though losing the popular vote contest; the electors can break their pledges; and, a presidential contest can be decided in the House of Representatives. Most of the proposed reforms have called for presidential selection by a district or proportional electoral vote system or by direct election. None of the proposed reforms, including direct election, seems likely to be approved in the near future.

Concept Development

Questions for Review

1. What are the formal constitutional qualifications for the Presidency?

2. For what term is a President elected?

3. To how many terms may a President be elected?

4. What is the maximum length of time any person may serve as President?

5. Who fixes the President's salary, and how much is it now?

6. By virtue of what does the Vice President succeed to the Presidency?

7. If the President is unable to do so, who then determines the question of presidential disability?

8. Why are the formal qualifications for the Vice Presidency identical with those for the Presidency?

9. Why has no President made the Vice President a true "Assistant President"?

10. What three events combined to lay the constitutional setting for the present-day presidential election system?

11. What body handles arrangements for a party's national convention?

12. By what method are a majority of the delegates to both parties' conventions now chosen?

13. Around what four committees is much of the work of a national convention organized?

14. Why are party platforms usually written in such vague, general terms?

15. What is *the* major purpose of a national convention?

16. Why are incumbent Presidents virtually certain to win the nomination of their party if they want it? What does the term *availability* mean in our presidential politics?

17. Why may the selection of presidential electors be described as a "winner-take-all" system?

18. A minimum of how many electoral votes will be necessary to win the Presidency in 1984?

19. What are the three most serious weaknesses of the present electoral college system?

20. Under what three major headings can most of the proposed electoral college reforms be grouped?

21. What are the principal arguments made for each of the major reform proposals? The major arguments advanced against them?

For Further Inquiry

1. Beyond the formal constitutional qualifications, what characteristics do you think a President ought to possess?

2. What arguments can be made *for* and *against* limiting a President to two terms?

3. What would the Presidency be like today if the Constitutional Convention had maintained its early position in favor of selection by Congress?

4. A noted French observer once characterized the national convention system as a "colossal travesty of popular institutions." Do you agree with this assessment? On what grounds can you *defend* the continued use of the national convention as the device for presidential nominations?

5. Why is it well that the 25th Amendment has finally added to the Constitution a procedure for filling a vacancy in the Vice Presidency?

6. Maine now employs the district system to choose its presidential electors. Why would you favor (or oppose) the adoption of a similar arrangement by your State?

Suggested Activities

1. Construct a diagram or poster to illustrate (perhaps with newspaper clippings and photographs) the various roles of the President noted on pages 353–355.

2. Stage a debate or class forum on one of the following questions: (a) *Resolved,* That the 22nd Amendment should be repealed. (b) *Resolved,* That the Vice Presidency should be abolished. (c) *Resolved,* That the major parties should be required to nominate their presidential candidates in a nationwide primary. (d) *Resolved,* That the President should be elected by direct popular vote.

3. Invite a recent delegate to a national convention of either major party or a presidential elector to speak to the class on her or his role in the nominating or electing of a President.

4. Prepare a report on one of the following topics: (a) the "Stolen Election" of 1876; (b) reform of the electoral college; (c) the presidential campaign and election of 1980; (d) the proposal and adoption of the 25th Amendment; (e) the "youth vote" in 1976 and 1980; and (f) the effect of the new federal campaign finance acts on the 1976 and 1980 elections.

Suggested Reading

Asher, Herbert B., *Presidential Elections and American Politics.* Dorsey, rev. ed., 1980.

Barber, James D., *The Presidential Character: Predicting Performance in the White House.* Prentice-Hall, 2nd ed., 1977.

————, *the Pulse of Politics: Electing Presidents in the Media Age.* Norton, 1980.

Cronin, Thomas E., *The State of the Presidency.* Little, Brown, 2nd ed., 1980.

Davis, Vincent (ed.), *The Post-Imperial Presidency.* Transaction Books, 1980.

Diclerico, Robert, *The American President.* Prentice-Hall, 1979.

Foley, John, *et al.* (eds.), *Nominating a President.* Praeger, 1980.

Hill, David B. and Luttbeg, Norman R., *Trends in American Electoral Behavior.* Peacock, 1980.

Hodgson, Godfrey, *All Things to All Men: The False Promise of the Modern American Presidency.* Simon & Schuster, 1980.

Kessel, John H., *Presidential Campaign Strategies and Citizen Response.* Wiley, 1980.

Moore, Jonathan and Fraser, Janet (eds.), *Campaign for President: The Managers Look at '76.* Ballinger, 1977.

National Party Conventions, 1831–1976. Congressional Quarterly, 2nd ed., 1979.

Neustadt, Richard, *Presidential Power: Politics of Leadership from FDR to Carter.* Wiley, 1980.

Patterson, Thomas E., *The Mass Media Election: How Americans Choose Their Presidents.* Praeger, 1980.

Pious, Richard M., *The American Presidency.* Basic Books, 1979.

Polsby, Nelson W. and Wildavsky, Aaron, *Presidential Elections.* Scribner's, 5th ed., 1980.

Politics in America. Congressional Quarterly, 1980.

Presidential Elections Since 1789. Congressional Quarterly, 2nd ed., 1979.

Ranney, Austin (ed.), *The Past and Future of Presidential Debates.* American Enterprise Institute, 1979.

Schlesinger, Arthur M., *et al., Winner Take All: Report of the Twentieth Century Fund Task Force on Reform of the Presidential Election Process.* Holmes & Meier, 1978.

Strum, Philippa, *Presidential Power and American Democracy.* Goodyear, 2nd ed., 1979.

Watson, Richard A., *The Presidential Contest.* Wiley, 1980.

Wayne, Stephen J., *Road to the White House: The Politics of Presidential Elections.* St. Martin's Press, 1980.

16

The Presidency in Action

When I ran for the Presidency . . . I knew this country faced serious challenges; but I could not realize—nor could any man who does not bear the burdens of this office—how heavy and constant would be those burdens.

JOHN F. KENNEDY

■ Is it true, as some argue, that the Presidency has become too powerful an office?

■ Does the President have too much power in some areas and not enough in others?

■ Why has the Presidency become so powerful an office?

■ Can any of the President's many roles be properly called "the most important"?

Article II of the Constitution begins:

> The executive power shall be vested in a President of the United States of America.

With these few words the Founding Fathers established the Presidency. And with those few words they laid the basis for the vast power and influence the nation's chief executive now possesses.

The Constitution does contain several other, and somewhat more specific, grants of presidential power—for example, to command the armed forces, to make treaties, to approve or veto acts of Congress, to send and receive diplomatic representatives, to grant pardons and reprieves, and to "take care that the laws be faithfully executed."[1]

But notice that the Constitution sets out the powers of the Presidency only in very sketchy fashion. Article II reads almost as an outline. It has been described as "the most loosely drawn chapter" in the nation's fundamental law.[2] It does not define "the executive power," and the other

---

[1] Most of the specific constitutional grants of presidential power are found in Article II, Sections 2 and 3. A few are found elsewhere—for example, the veto power in Article I, Section 7, Clause 2.

[2] Edward S. Corwin, *The President: Office and Powers.* New York: New York University Press, 1940, page 2. "To those who think that a constitution ought to settle everything beforehand it [Article II] should be a nightmare; by the same token, to those who think that constitution makers ought to leave considerable leeway for the future play of political forces, it should be a vision realized." *Ibid.* This volume is *the* classic study of the Constitution's treatment of the Presidency.

President Lyndon Johnson reviews an honor guard. In the background is the Washington Monument.

grants of presidential power are couched in similarly broad terms.

Much has been added to the constitutional outline of the Presidency over the past 19 decades. Thus, the manner in which the stronger Presidents have used their powers has done much to shape the office and the scope of its powers. The most notable contributors to that process have been Washington, Jefferson, Jackson, Lincoln, Wilson, the two Roosevelts, and Truman. A large number of acts of Congress and several court decisions have also helped to define and extend the powers of the Presidency. And, importantly, the way in which the public has viewed the presidential office has also been a prime factor in its development.

The Executive Office of the President

Every officer, employee, and agency in the huge and sprawling executive branch is legally subordinate to the Chief Executive. All exist to aid the President in the exercise of the executive power. But the President's chief right arm is the Executive Office of the President—a complex of several separate agencies staffed by most of the President's closest advisers and assistants.

The Executive Office was established by Congress in 1939 and has been reorganized in each administration since then—including President Reagan's Administration.

The White House Office. The White House Office is the "nerve center" of the entire executive branch. It houses the President's key personal and political staff, including a score of senior advisers and other top aides and several hundred professional and clerical people. Most of them have offices in the two wings extending to either side of the White House. They occupy most of the crowded West Wing, which is seldom seen by the public and where the fabled Oval Office and the Cabinet Room are located; and some are housed in the East Wing of the White House, where the public tours of the Executive Mansion begin.

Ronald Reagan's key aides include the Counsellor to the President and a number of Assistants and Special Assistants to the President. They serve the Chief Executive in such areas as foreign policy, national defense, the economy, congressional relations, White House appointments, schedules, and management, and contacts with the news media and with the public at large. The Counsel to the President is the Chief Executive's principal legal adviser.

Among the more important of them, too, are the Personal Assistant/Secretary to the President, the Physician to the President, and the Chief Speechwriter. Then, too, there are a number of aides to the President's wife—among them a Staff Director, a Personal Assistant, and a Press Secretary to the First Lady.

Altogether, the White House staff now numbers about 350 men and women who, quite literally, work for the President.

The National Security Council. The NSC counsels the President in all matters—domestic, foreign, and military—relating to the security of the nation. The President chairs the Council. Its other members include the Vice President and the Secretaries of State and Defense. The Chairman of the Joint Chiefs of Staff and the Director of the Central Intelligence Agency attend all Council meetings. Other officials also participate at the direction of the President. A highly competent professional staff functions under the direction of the Assistant to the President for National Security Affairs.

The super-secret *Central Intelligence Agency* operates under the Council. It gathers and evaluates information bearing on the nation's security and makes reports and recommendations to the Council. And, it performs whatever other tasks the Council assigns to it.

The Domestic Policy Staff. The Domestic Policy Staff serves the President as the home-front counterpart of the foreign-policy oriented National Security Council. It both shapes and melds domestic policy recommendations for the Chief Executive. The Staff is headed by one of the leading members of the White House family, the Assistant to the President for Domestic Affairs and Policy.

The Office of Management and Budget. The OMB is the largest, and after the White House Office, the most influential unit within the Executive Office. It is the President's budget-making agency. It directs the preparation of the federal budget which the President must submit to Congress in January each year.

The budget-making function is far more than a routine bookkeeping chore. It is, in a very real sense, the preparation of an annual statement of the public policies of the United States—translated into dollar terms.

The federal budget is, at base, a financial document. It is an estimate of receipts and expenditures—an anticipation of federal income and outgo—during the next

President Carter confers with Shirley Hufstedler. She was sworn in as Secretary of Education in May of 1980; the first to hold that Cabinet post.

fiscal year.[3] And, very importantly, it is something more. It is a *plan*—a carefully drawn, closely detailed work plan for the conduct of government and the execution of its policies.

The budget-making process is a lengthy one. Initially, each federal agency must prepare detailed estimates of its anticipated expenditures in the upcoming fiscal year. These spending proposals are then reviewed by the OMB—usually in a series of budget hearings at which agency officials must defend their estimates. Fol-

lowing that review, the revised (and usually lowered) spending estimates are dovetailed into the President's overall program. They become a part of the budget document the Chief Executive submits to Congress—early in each of its annual sessions, as we shall see on page 409.

In addition to its role as the President's budget-making arm, the OMB also supervises the *execution* of the budget. That is, it monitors the spending of budgeted funds once they have been appropriated by Congress. The President's close control over both the preparation and the execution of the budget is a major tool with which the Chief Executive is able to manage the huge executive branch.

Beyond its budget chores, the OMB is a sort of presidential "handy-man" agency.

---

[3] A *fiscal year* is the 12-month period used by a government for its record-keeping, budgeting, revenue collecting, and other financial management purposes. The Federal Government's fiscal year now runs from October 1 through the following September 30; see page 492.

It makes continuing studies aimed at improving the organization and management of the executive branch. It keeps the President abreast of the ongoing work of all of the agencies under presidential control, and clears and coordinates agency stands on all legislative matters. It assists the President in the preparation of executive orders and veto messages. And it also aids other federal agencies with their fiscal, management, and other organizational problems.

The Council of Economic Advisers. The Council of Economic Advisers is composed of three eminent economists appointed by the President with the consent of the Senate. It is a prime source of information and advice to the President on all matters pertaining to the nation's economy.

The Council functions through a small staff of professional economists and statisticians. It makes continuing studies of the economy, keeps the President abreast of economic developments, and analyzes the economic impact of governmental programs and policies. It recommends to the President those programs and policies which it believes will best promote economic growth and stability.

The Council also assists the President in the preparation of the annual economic report to Congress. That report is usually accompanied by a message which the Chief Executive presents in person to Congress and by television to the nation. Both the report and the message regularly detail various economic proposals first broached by the President in the State of the Union address.

"OH, WASHINGTON HIMSELF IS ALL RIGHT. IT'S THE MEN AROUND HIM LIKE JEFFERSON AND ADAMS AND..."

The Council on Wage and Price Stability. The Council on Wage and Price Stability is an inflation monitoring agency. Its prime mission is to publicize—expose to public view—those wage and price actions by labor or management which it regards as excessive in an inflation-plagued economy. It also conducts studies to isolate the causes of inflation.

The Council supplanted the mandatory wage and price control programs pursued by the Nixon Administration from 1971 to 1974. These programs proved to be, at best, ineffective. A Chairman, appointed by the President, several members of the Cabinet, the Chairman of the Council of Economic Advisers, The Director of the OMB, and the President's Assistant for Domestic Affairs all serve on the Council. The agency's ongoing, day-in, day-out work is performed by a Director and a small staff of professional economists.

Other Units in the Executive Office. There are several other agencies within the Executive Office. As with those we've just noted, they house key presidential assistants—men and women upon whom the President must, and does, rely for the advice and information necessary to the performance of the executive function.

The Council on Environmental Quality advises the Chief Executive in all policy matters relating to the environment and in the composition of the annual report to Congress on the quality of the nation's environment. The Council's three members are appointed by the President, with Senate consent. They work in close concert with the Environmental Protection Agency; see page 607.

The Office of the United States Trade Representative assists the President in all matters of foreign trade policy. Its head, the Trade Representative, is appointed by the President and Senate, carries the rank of ambassador, and represents the President in trade negotiations with other countries.

The Office of Science and Technology Policy is the President's principal adviser in all scientific, engineering, and other technological matters as they bear on national policies and programs. Its Director, who is chosen by the President and Senate, is regularly drawn from the upper reaches of the nation's scientific community.

The Intelligence Oversight Board is a watchdog agency. It oversees—and keeps the President informed of—the work of the CIA and the several other federal agencies involved in the foreign intelligence field. One of its principal missions is to insure that these agencies never again abuse their powers or exceed their legal authority.

The Cabinet

The Cabinet is an informal and extralegal advisory body assembled by the President to serve his needs. The Constitution makes no reference to it,[4] nor did Congress create it. Rather, it is the product of custom and usage developed over the years since George Washington's first administration.

At its first session in 1789, Congress established four executive posts: Secretary of State, Secretary of the Treasury, Secretary of War, and Attorney General. By his second term, President Washington was regularly seeking the counsel of the outstanding personalities he had named to those offices—Thomas Jefferson in the Department of State, Alexander Hamilton at the Treasury, Henry Knox in the War Department, and Edmund Randolph, the Attorney General. And so the Cabinet was born.

---

[4] The closest approach is in Article II, Section 2, Clause 1, in which the President is given the power to "require the opinion, in writing, of the principal officer in each of the executive departments, upon any subject relating to the duties of their respective offices." The Cabinet was first mentioned in an act of Congress in 1907, well over a century after its birth.

Today the Cabinet is composed of the heads of the 13 executive departments, as the table to the right indicates.

Certain other officials are occasionally accorded Cabinet rank. Thus, every recent President has included the United States Representative to the UN among the full-fledged members of the Cabinet. And the Vice President regularly participates in all of its sessions.

THE SELECTION OF CABINET MEMBERS. The President appoints the head of each of the now 13 executive departments. This is another way of saying that the President appoints the members of the Cabinet. Each of these appointments is subject to confirmation by the Senate, but rejections have been exceedingly rare. Of the more than 500 such appointments the various Presidents have made thus far (1981), only nine have ever been rejected.[5]

Many different factors influence the President in the choice of Cabinet members. Party considerations are invariably important. Democratic Presidents seldom appoint Republicans, and vice versa. And, one or more of a new President's appointees regularly come from the ranks of those who had a large hand in the recent presidential campaign.

Professional qualifications and practical experience are also taken into account, of course—most especially in the selections of the Secretary of State and the Attorney General. Geography plays a part, too. In

---

[5] The most recent rejection of a Cabinet appointee occurred in 1959 when the Senate refused to approve President Eisenhower's selection of Lewis Strauss as Secretary of Commerce. The Senate also refused to confirm Andrew Jackson's appointment of Roger B. Taney as Secretary of the Treasury in 1834; John Tyler's appointment of Caleb Cushing and then James Green as Secretary of the Treasury in 1843 and 1844, respectively, David Henshaw as Secretary of the Navy in 1844, and James M. Porter as Secretary of War in 1844; Andrew Johnson's appointment of Henry Stanberry as Attorney General in 1868 and Alexander Stewart as Secretary of the Treasury in 1869; and Calvin Coolidge's appointment of Charles B. Warren (rejected twice) as Attorney General in 1925.

THE PRESIDENT'S CABINET

Cabinet Post*	Year Created
Secretary of State	1789
Secretary of the Treasury	1789
Secretary of Defense[a]	1947
Attorney General[b]	1789
Secretary of the Interior	1849
Secretary of Agriculture	1889
Secretary of Commerce[c]	1903
Secretary of Labor[c]	1913
Secretary of Health and Human Services[d]	1953
Secretary of Housing and Urban Development	1965
Secretary of Transportation	1967
Secretary of Energy	1977
Secretary of Education	1979

*The Cabinet posts are listed in order or precedence—i.e., the order in which each originated. This ranking is followed for formal and ceremonial purposes (protocol) and also is the order in which the Cabinet officers rank in the line of presidential succession; see page 359.

[a] Congress created the National Military Establishment, as an executive department headed by the Secretary of Defense, in 1947. It was renamed the Department of Defense in 1949. Since 1947 it has included the former Cabinet-level Department of War (1789) and Department of the Navy (1798) and the Department of the Air Force (1947). The Secretaries of Army, Navy and Air Force do not hold Cabinet rank.

[b] Although the post of Attorney General was created in 1789, the Department of Justice was not established until 1870.

[c] The Secretary of Commerce was originally the Secretary of Commerce and Labor. The Department of Commerce and Labor, created in 1903, was replaced by the separate Departments of Commerce and of Labor in 1913.

[d] The Secretary of Health and Human Services was originally the Secretary of Health, Education, and Welfare. The Department of Health, Education, and Welfare was created in 1953. HEW's education functions were transferred to a separate Department of Education in 1979 and HEW was renamed at that time.

The Postmaster General, who headed the Cabinet-level Post Office Department, was a regular member of the Cabinet from Andrew Jackson's first year in the Presidency (1829) until Congress replaced the Department with an independent agency, the United States Postal Service, in 1971.

President Washington, with members of the first Cabinet, left to right: George Washington; Henry Knox, Secretary of War; Alexander Hamilton, Secretary of the Treasury; Thomas Jefferson, Secretary of State; Edmund Randolph, Attorney General.

broad terms, each President attempts to give some sectional balance to the Cabinet. Thus, in more specific terms, the Secretary of the Interior almost always comes from the West—where most of the department's work is carried out.

Various special interest groups are especially interested in certain departments and have an influence on some of the choices. Thus, the Secretary of Agriculture is usually a farmer or at least has a background closely related to agriculture. The Secretary of the Treasury regularly comes from the financial community and the Secretary of Commerce from the ranks of business. The Secretary of Labor must be acceptable to labor, and the Secretary of Housing and Urban Development almost always has a "big-city" background.

Considerations of sex and of race,[6] a prospective appointee's civil rights record, management abilities and experiences, and other personal characteristics—these and innumerable other factors enter the mix of presidential Cabinet selections. Indeed, the matters that must be weighed, and the influences that operate on a President, in the making of these appointments—as well as hundreds of others—are so many and varied that they defy cataloging.

THE CABINET'S ROLE. Cabinet members have *two* principal jobs: *Individually,* each is the administrative head of one of the executive departments. *Collectively,* they serve as advisors to the President.

To what extent the President *uses* the Cabinet—how vital, then, its role really is—is a matter to be determined by each of the Presidents. William Howard Taft once put the Cabinet in its proper light:

> The Constitution . . . contains no suggestion of a meeting of all the department heads in consultation over general governmental matters. The Cabinet is a mere creation of the President's will. It is an extra-statutory and extra-constitutional body. It exists only by custom. If the President desired to dispense with it, he could do so.[7]

The Cabinet meets at the President's

---

[6] Franklin Roosevelt named the first woman to a Cabinet position: Frances T. Perkins, who served as Secretary of Labor from 1933 to 1945. Olveta Culp Hobby, the first Secretary of Health, Education, and Welfare, served in the Eisenhower Cabinet from 1953 to 1955. Lyndon Johnson appointed the first black to the Cabinet when he named Robert C. Weaver as the first Secretary of Housing and Urban Development in 1966. Gerald Ford became the first President to name both a woman (Carla Hills, Secretary of HUD) and a black (William T. Coleman, Secretary of Transportation); both were appointed in 1975. Jimmy Carter's first Cabinet selections included two women: Juanita M. Kreps as Secretary of Commerce and Patricia R. Harris, the first black woman ever to hold Cabinet rank, as Secretary of HUD (and, in 1979, Secretary of Health and Human Services); and he picked Shirley Hufstedler to head the new Department of Education in 1979.

---

[7] *Our Chief Magistrate and His Powers.* New York: Columbia University Press, 1916, pages 29–30.

President Franklin Roosevelt confers with a member of his "Brain Trust," Professor Raymond T. Moley (left) of Columbia University.

call. Usually, it assembles once a week in a room in the executive offices which adjoin the White House. Proposals and reports are made and advice is offered to the Chief Executive. That advice need not be taken, of course. Abraham Lincoln once laid a proposition he favored before his Cabinet. Each member opposed it, whereupon Lincoln declared: "Seven nays, one aye; the ayes have it."

Cabinet meetings are usually closed to the press and public, but other public officials often do attend them. Thus, each of the most recent Vice Presidents, from Alben Barkley to George Bush, has been a regular participant. The heads of several of the more important non-Cabinet agencies—for example, the Office of Management and Budget, the Environmental Protection Agency, and the Council of Economic Advisers—are frequently present, too.

Several Presidents have leaned upon other, unofficial advisory groups—and sometimes more heavily than upon the Cabinet. Andrew Jackson formed the first such group. It usually met in the kitchen at the White House and, inevitably, it came to be known as "the Kitchen Cabinet."

Franklin Roosevelt's "Brain Trust" of the 1930's and Harry Truman's "Cronies" of the late 1940's are other illustrations of the same practice. Each of these groups had substantially greater influence on the President than did the regularly established Cabinet.

One or a few individuals have often become trusted presidential advisers, working with the President on a strictly confidential and personal basis. These "President's Men" have had differing titles with each administration but they have regularly been a potent force in the shaping of White House decisions.

The Powers of the President

Again, Article II, Section 1 of the Constitution vests "the executive power" in the President of the United States. But, as we noted on page 388, the powers of the Presidency are set out in only very sparse fashion. Nowhere does the Constitution spell out the content of "the executive power."

The Growth of Presidential Power. Much of the story of the development of the American system of government can be told in terms of the growth of the Presidency and of presidential power. Much of our political history, that is, has revolved about a continuing struggle over the definition of the constitutional phrase "executive power." That struggle has pitted the advocates of a weaker Presidency, subordinate to Congress, on the one hand, against those who have pressed for a stronger, independent and coequal Chief Executive, on the other.

This contest, which has never ceased, began at the Philadelphia Convention. The Framers were divided on the matter. Several of them agreed with Roger Sherman of Connecticut who, according to Madison's *Notes:*

> . . . considered the executive magistracy as nothing more than an institution for carrying the will of the legislature into effect, and that the person or persons [occupying the Presidency] ought to be appointed by and accountable to the legislature only, which was the depository of the supreme will of the Society.

As we have seen, however, the advocates of a stronger executive authority—led by Alexander Hamilton, James Wilson, and James Madison—carried the day. They persuaded the Convention to establish a single executive, to be chosen independently of Congress, and with its own distinct field of powers.

The debate over the nature and extent of "the executive power" has continued now for more than 190 years. Over that period, and for many reasons, the champions of a stronger Presidency have prevailed.

One of the leading reasons involved here is the *unity* of the Presidency—that is, the office and its powers are held by *one* person. The President is the *single,* commanding head of the executive branch. By contrast, the Congress—although its powers are many and substantial—consists of *two* houses. And those two houses must agree on a matter before the Congress can act. Further fragmenting its power to act,

one of those two houses is composed of 100 separately-elected members and the other of 435.

Several other factors have worked to strengthen the role and the powers of the Presidency, and thus to enhance the scope of "the executive power." One outstandingly important one we have referred to a number of times—the influence the Presidents themselves, especially the stronger ones, have had upon the office.

Yet another of these factors has been the pressures generated by the increasingly complex nature of the nation's social and economic life. As the United States has become more and still more highly industrialized and technologically oriented, the people have demanded that the Federal Government play a larger and still larger role in a growing list of areas of public concern—in transportation, communications, labor-management relations, education, welfare, housing, civil rights, health, environmental protection, and a host of other fields. And it has been to the Presidency that the people have generally looked for leadership in these matters.

Congress itself has been a major contributor to the strengthening of the role and powers of the Presidency. This has been especially true as it has enacted the thousands of pieces of legislation necessary to the growth of the scope of the activities of the Federal Government. Congress has neither the time nor the technical knowledge to do much more than establish the basic outlines of public policy in many new fields. Hence, it has been literally forced to delegate substantial authority to the President—a point we shall return to in a moment.

Yet another of these closely related factors has been the frequent need for extraordinary and decisive action in times of national emergency, and—most notably—in time of war. The ability of the President—of the *single,* commanding Chief Executive—to act in such situations has done much to strengthen "the executive power." The history of the growth of presidential power cannot be graphed as a steadily ascending line. Rather, such a graph would show several periods of gradual increase, a few periods of decline, and, interspersed, a few periods of spectacular increase. And, to the point, the sharp upward leaps would appear on that historical graph during such periods as Abraham Lincoln's Presidency and the Civil War, during Woodrow Wilson's Presidency and the First World War, and during Franklin Roosevelt's Presidency and the Great Depression and World War II.

A number of other factors have entered into this mix, the growth of "the executive power." Among them have been the President's roles as chief legislator, party leader, and chief citizen, to which we referred on page 354. Another is the vast amount of staff support with which a President is provided, as we noted on page 390. And yet another is the unique position from which the President may attract and hold the public's attention, and so mobilize support

Case Study

The question of presidential tenure has been a matter of concern, and of controversy, at several points in our history. The Framers of the Constitution wrestled with the subject on and off for weeks at Philadelphia. Most of their debate centered on two rival proposals: one to provide a four-year term with no limit on re-eligibility and the other a single six- or seven-year term.

As we know, they finally settled on the relatively brief four-year term and, left the hard question of re-eligibility to the future.

Almost immediately that question was resolved through the informal amendment process. First George Washington, and then Thomas Jefferson, James Madison, and James Monroe each served only two terms, and each declined longer service. By Andrew Jackson's Presidency (1829–1837) the two-term limit had become a firm, albeit unwritten, constitutional rule.

Through the 19th century, strong support developed for lengthening the presidential term and then forbidding any President ever to hold the office again. The Senate actually approved such an amendment in 1913, soon after Theodore Roosevelt's bid for another term. That measure would have provided a six-year term and made any President ineligible to reelection. But the House, viewing the move as a slap at TR, refused to agree to it.

Franklin Roosevelt's election to a third term in 1940, and then a fourth in 1944, brought the matter into sharp public focus again. In 1947 a Republican-dominated Congress responded with a proposed amendment to limit presidential tenure. Ratified in 1951, the 22nd Amendment restricts a President to two full terms or, at the very outside, 10 years in office.

Making the unwritten custom an integral part of the written Constitution has quieted neither the concern nor the controversy, however. Up to 1981, more than 150 amendments have been offered in Congress to limit the President to a single six-year term. Several Presidents, from Andrew Jackson to Jimmy Carter, have supported the proposition.

■ Why do you favor or oppose the six-year term/no re-eligibility idea?
■ What effect might it have on the President's role as Chief Administrator?
■ Does experience under the 22nd Amendment offer any guide here?
■ What other observations, pro or con, can you make?

for policies and actions. Each of the most recent Presidents, from Franklin Roosevelt through Lyndon Johnson to Ronald Reagan, have very purposely used the press, radio, and television to that end.

PRESIDENTIAL VIEWS OF PRESIDENTIAL POWER. Before we turn to the specific powers of the Presidency, ponder this point: What the Presidency is at any given time depends, in no small part, upon the manner in which the President views the Presidency and exercises its powers.

Over the course of our history two general and contrasting views of the Presidency have been held by the men who have occupied the office. The stronger, and the more effective and successful of them, have taken a broad view of the scope of their powers. Theodore Roosevelt expounded their position in what he called the "stewardship theory":

My view was that . . . every executive officer in high position, was a steward of the people bound actively and affirmatively to do all he could for the people, and not to content himself with the negative merit of keeping his talents undamaged in a napkin. I declined to adopt the view that what was imperatively necessary for the Nation could not be done by the President unless he could find some specific authorization to do it. My belief was that it was not only his right but his duty to do anything that the needs of the Nation demanded unless such action was forbidden by the Constitution or by the laws . . . I did not usurp power, but I did greatly broaden the use of executive power. In other words, I acted for the public welfare, I acted for the common well-being of all our people, whenever and in whatever manner was necessary, unless prevented by direct constitutional or legislative prohibition.[8]

Ironically, the most cogent presidential statement of the opposing view was made

---

[8] *Theodore Roosevelt: An Autobiography.* New York: Macmillan, 1913, page 389.

Theodore Roosevelt, the 26th President, delivers a speech in San Francisco.

by Roosevelt's handpicked successor in the office, William Howard Taft. Looking back upon his Presidency, Taft had this to say about Roosevelt's view and about the office and its powers:

> My judgment is that the view of Mr. Roosevelt, ascribing an undefined residuum of power to the President, is an unsafe doctrine. . . . The true view of the executive function is, as I conceive it, that the President can exercise no power which cannot be fairly and reasonably traced to some specific grant of power or justly implied and included within such express grant. . . . Such specific grant must be either in the Federal Constitution or in an act of Congress passed in pursuance thereof. There is no undefined residuum of power which he can exercise because it seems to be in the public interest.[9]

Gerald R. Ford, the 38th President of the United States, behind his desk in the Oval Office. From this fabled room in the West Wing of the White House, the nation's Chief Executive exercises the vast powers and shoulders the awesome responsibilities of the Presidency.

At the beginning of the last chapter we suggested one useful standpoint from which to view the Presidency and the scope of its powers. We noted on pages 353–354 that the President plays a number of different roles, "wears several different hats." The President must be, at one and the same time, each and all of these vital things: Chief of State, Chief Executive, Chief Administrator, Chief Diplomat, Commander in Chief, Chief Legislator, Chief of Party, and Chief Citizen.

Another and convenient way to describe presidential powers is to group them under five broad headings: the President's executive, diplomatic, military, legislative, and judicial powers.

Executive Powers. As the nation's Chief Executive, the President's primary duty is to execute—to enforce, put into effect, carry out—the provisions of federal law. The power to do so rests upon two brief constitutional provisions. The first of them is the oath of office the President must take:

> I do solemnly swear (or affirm) that I will faithfully execute the office of President of the United States, and will, to the best of my ability, preserve, protect, and defend the Constitution of the United States.[10]

---

[9] *Our Chief Magistrate and His Powers.* New York: Columbia University Press, 1916, pages 139–140, 144.
[10] Article II, Section 1, Clause 8.

The other is the command that the President "shall take care that the laws be faithfully executed."[11]

The power to execute and enforce the law may be thought of in terms of criminal law enforcement, of course. This power does encompass such matters as those involved in the activities of the various federal police agencies, such as the FBI and the Secret Service. But it involves much more than this. It covers the application of *all* federal laws. It covers laws on such diverse subjects as flood control, social security, the armed services, housing, civil rights, environmental pollution, taxation, monopolies, collective bargaining, farm price supports, immigration, public health, and scores of others.

As with the Congress and the Courts, the President, and the President's subordinates, have much to say about the meaning of the law. That is, in executing and enforcing law, the executive branch also *interprets* it. The Constitution requires the President to execute *all* federal laws, regardless of the Chief Executive's own views of any of them. But the President may (and does) exercise some discretion as to how vigorously and in what particular manner any given law will be applied in practice.

To examine the point more closely: most of the laws enacted by Congress are written in fairly broad terms. In them, Congress sets out the basic policies and standards to be followed. The specific details necessary to the actual, day-to-day administration of the law are usually left to the President or presidential subordinates. Thus, the immigration laws require that all immigrants seeking permanent admission to this country must be able to "read and understand some dialect or language." But what does this literacy requirement mean in actual practice? What words must be

known, and how many of them? How well must the alien be able to read? What kind of test should be given to determine these matters? The law does not say. Rather, the answers to these and an unending number of similar questions are provided within the executive branch—specifically, in this case, by the Immigration and Naturalization Service in the Department of Justice.

DIRECTION OF ADMINISTRATION. From what has just been said, it should be clear that the President deserves the title Chief Administrator as well as Chief Executive. The actual day-in and day-out job of administering and applying most federal law is accomplished through the many departments, bureaus, offices, boards, commissions, councils, and other agencies that make up the mammoth executive branch. All of the some 2.9 million men and women who staff these agencies are subordinate to the President. They work under the President's control and direction.

THE ORDINANCE POWER. The President possesses the power to issue *executive orders* which have the effect of law. The power to do so, the *ordinance power,* arises from two sources: the Constitution and acts of Congress.

Although the Constitution does not expressly mention the ordinance power, it is clearly intended. In conferring certain powers on the President the Constitution anticipates their use. In order to exercise those powers, the President must have the power to issue the necessary orders—directives, rules, regulations—and to implement them. And the President must have, as well, the power to authorize subordinates to issue such orders, too.[12]

As the number, the scope, and the

---

11 Article II, Section 3; the provision gives to the President what is often referred to as the "take care power."

12 All executive orders are published in the *Federal Register,* which appears five times a week. At least annually, all orders currently in force are published in codified form in the *Code of Federal Regulations.* Both publications are compiled by the National Archives and Records Service in the General Services Administration.

complexity of governmental problems has grown, it has become increasingly necessary for Congress to delegate more and still more discretion to the President in the execution of the laws it enacts—more and more necessary for Congress to allow the President, and presidential subordinates, to spell out the many details of the policies and programs established by law. Members of Congress are not, and cannot be expected to be, experts in all of the fields with which they must deal—nor are they equipped with all-seeing crystal balls.

In delegating authority to the executive branch, Congress cannot give away its constitutional power to legislate, to make basic policy. Rather, it must, and does, set out the broad standards within which the President and other executive officers and agencies must operate. Examples are legion. We have just noted an illustration involving the literacy of immigrants. Or, Congress has provided for the payment of subsidies to support the prices of certain farm products, as we shall see in Chapter 24. It has specified 12 particular commodities to be supported. And Congress has given the Secretary of Agriculture the authority to add farm commodities to that list. The additions are made by executive order.

POWER OF APPOINTMENT. A President cannot hope to succeed without loyal subordinates who support the policies of the President's administration. No matter how able a President, no matter how wise those policies, a President cannot function successfully without such loyalty and support.

The Constitution provides that the President:

> by and with the advice and consent of the Senate, shall appoint ambassadors, other public ministers, and consuls, judges of the Supreme Court, and all other officers of the United States whose appointments are not otherwise herein provided for; but the Congress may by law vest the appointment of such inferior officers, as

they think proper, in the President alone, in the courts of law, or in the heads of departments.[13]

Acting alone, the President appoints only a relative handful of the approximately 2.9 million federal civilian employees. Many of those the Chief Executive alone selects are members of the immediate staff of the White House Office.

With Senate consent, the President appoints most of the top-ranking officers of the Federal Government. These appointees include ambassadors and other diplomats, Cabinet members and their chief assistants, heads of the various independent agencies such as the Environmental Protection Agency and the Veterans Administration, all officers in the armed forces, federal judges, and United States attorneys and marshals.

When the President makes one of these appointments, the "nomination" is sent to the Senate. There it is referred to the appropriate standing committee. Thus, for example, the appointment of a federal judge is sent to the Judiciary Committee and the selection of an Assistant Secretary of State to the Foreign Relations Committee. If a majority of the committee endorses the appointment, it reports that fact to the Senate. The Senate then votes, with a majority of those present necessary to confirm a presidential nominee.

The unwritten rule of *senatorial courtesy* plays an important part in the selection of many of those officers whose appointments are subject to Senate confirmation. It applies to the approval of those federal appointees who will serve within one of the States—for example, a federal district judge or prosecuting attorney. The rule holds that the Senate will approve only those appointees who are acceptable to the

---

[13] Article II, Section 2, Clause 2. Those whose appointments are "otherwise provided for" are the Vice President, Senators, Representatives, and presidential electors.

President Carter witnesses the swearing in of Patricia Harris to the Cabinet post of Secretary of Health and Human Services. From 1977 to 1979, Patricia Harris served as Secretary of Housing and Urban Development. Associate Justice Thurgood Marshall, of the Supreme Court, administers the oath.

Senator or Senators of the President's party from the State involved. The practical effect of this custom, which is closely followed in the Senate, is to place a meaningful part of the appointment power in the hands of particular Senators.

Well over half of all the federal civilian work force is selected on the basis of competitive civil service examinations. Today, the Office of Personnel Management examines applicants for some two million positions; see pages 433–436.

REMOVAL POWER. The power to remove is the other side of the appointment coin—and it is as critically important to presidential success. Except for the cumbersome and little-used impeachment process,[14] however, the Constitution is silent on the matter. It does not say how or by whom appointed officers may be dismissed—for incompetence, for opposition to presidential policies, or for any other cause.

The question was the subject of intensive debate in the first session of Congress in 1789. Several members of Congress argued that for those offices for which the

concurrence of the Senate was necessary for appointment, Senate consent should also be required for removal. They insisted that this restriction on presidential authority was essential to congressional supervision (oversight) of the executive branch. Others contended that the President could not "take care that the laws be faithfully executed" without a free hand to dismiss those regarded to be incompetent or otherwise undesirable in the Chief Executive's administration.

The latter view prevailed. The 1st Congress gave to the President the power to remove any officer whom he appointed, except federal judges. Over the years since then, Congress has on occasion attempted to restrict the President's freedom to dismiss—but with little success.

One notable instance occurred in 1867. Locked with Andrew Johnson in the fight over Reconstruction, Congress passed the Tenure of Office Act. The law's plain purpose was to prevent President Johnson from removing several principal officers in his administration—especially the Secretary of War, Edwin M. Stanton. The law provided that any person holding an office by presidential appointment with Senate consent should remain in that office until a

14 Article II, Section 4; see pages 346–347.

President Andrew Johnson refused to adhere to the provisions of the Tenure of Office Act of 1867. He removed a number of appointed officers, including the Secretary of War, Edwin M. Stanton, and Congress initiated impeachment proceedings against him. Here, a print depicts the Senate impeachment trial.

successor had been confirmed by the Senate. The President vetoed the statute, charging that it was an unconstitutional invasion of executive authority. The veto, overridden by Congress, sparked the move for Johnson's impeachment. The law was ignored in practice and never challenged in the courts; it was finally repealed in 1887.

The question of the President's removal power did not reach the Supreme Court until *Myers* v. *United States,* 1926. In 1876 Congress had enacted a statute requiring Senate consent before the President could dismiss any first-, second-, or third-class postmaster. In 1920 President Woodrow Wilson removed Frank Myers as the postmaster at Portland, Oregon, and did so without consulting the Senate. Myers then sued for the salary he claimed due for the remaining portion of his four-year term. He based his claim on the point that he had been removed in violation of

the 1876 law. The Court found the law unconstitutional, however. The opinion was delivered by Chief Justice William Howard Taft, himself a former President. The Court held that the power of removal was an essential part of the executive power, indispensably necessary to the President's faithful execution of the laws.

The Supreme Court did limit the President's removal power somewhat in 1935 in *Humphrey's Executor* v. *United States.* President Herbert Hoover had appointed William Humphrey to a seven-year term on the Federal Trade Commission in 1931. When President Franklin D. Roosevelt entered office in 1933, he found Humphrey in sharp disagreement with many of his policies. He asked Humphrey to resign, saying that the purposes of his administration could be better realized with someone else on the FTC. Humphrey refused, and Roosevelt then removed him. Humphrey challenged the legality of the President's action but died before a case could be brought. His heirs then filed a suit for back salary. The Supreme Court upheld their claim. It based its decision on the act creating the FTC. The law provided that a member of the Commission may be removed only for "inefficiency, neglect of duty, or malfeasance in office." President Roosevelt had cited none of these reasons. Rather, he had dismissed Humphrey because of political disagreements. The Court further held that Congress does have the power to set the conditions under which a member of the FTC and similar agencies might be removed by the President. It did so because the agencies, the independent regulatory commissions, are not purely executive agencies; they are, instead, *quasi-legislative* and *quasi-judicial* in character.[15]

As a general rule, however, the President may remove those whom the President appoints. Although removals are sometimes cloaked as resignations, the Chief Executive finds the power a continuingly necessary one.

Diplomatic Powers. The Constitution makes the President the nation's Chief Diplomat. It does so by giving the President the power to make treaties (with the consent of two-thirds of the Senate) and to appoint ambassadors to other nations and other diplomatic officers (subject to Senate confirmation). It also gives Presidents the power to receive foreign diplomatic representatives (that is, to *recognize* foreign governments).[16]

THE TREATY POWER. A treaty is a formal agreement between two or more sovereign states. The President, usually acting through the Secretary of State, negotiates these international agreements. The Senate must give its approval, by a two-thirds vote of the members present, before a treaty made by the President can become effective.[17]

The Framers considered the Senate—with, originally, only 26 members—a suitable council to advise the President in foreign affairs. Secrecy was thought to be necessary and was regarded as an impossibility in a body as large as the House. The two-thirds requirement helped to compensate the House for its exclusion from the treaty process.

Turn the two-thirds rule around and it becomes a one-third-plus-one veto rule. That is, only one more than a third of the Senators present and voting may defeat a treaty—no matter how vital it might be to the nation's interests. Hence, many have long criticized the requirement and urged a change to a simple majority for approval.

In 1919 the Senate rejected the Versailles Treaty, the general peace agreement to conclude World War I. The pact included provisions for the creation of the League of Nations. Forty-nine Senators voted for the pact and only 35 against—but the favorable vote was seven short of the necessary two-thirds. More than once a President had been forced to bow to the

[15] That is, their duties are partly legislative and partly judicial; they *make rules* and *decide controversies*. The prefix *quasi-* is from the Latin, meaning "in a certain sense, resembling, seemingly." See pages 423–425. *Malfeasance* is wrongful conduct, especially by a public officeholder.

[16] Article II, Section 2, Clause 2; Section 3; see also Chapter 18.

[17] Despite a widespread belief, the Senate does *not* "ratify" treaties. The Constitution requires Senate "advice and consent" to a treaty made by the President. *After* Senate approval, the President ratifies a treaty by the exchange of formal notifications with the other parties to the agreement. Treaties have the same legal standing as do acts passed by Congress. Congress may repeal *(abrogate)* a treaty by passing a law contrary to its provisions, and an existing law may be repealed by the terms of a treaty. When a treaty and a statute conflict, the courts consider the latest enacted to be the law, *The Head Money Cases,* 1884. The terms of a treaty cannot conflict with the higher law of the Constitution, *Missouri v. Holland,* 1920; but the Supreme Court has never found a treaty provision to be unconstitutional. Money cannot be appropriated by a treaty. But in practice, whenever the Senate has approved a treaty requiring an expenditure, the House has agreed to a bill providing the necessary funds.

views of a small minority in the Senate in order to secure passage of a treaty—even when this involved concessions opposed by the majority.

On occasion, a President has had to resort to roundabout methods. When a Senate minority defeated a treaty to annex Texas, President Tyler accomplished annexation in 1845 by a joint resolution—a move which required only a majority vote in each chamber. And President McKinley persuaded both houses to annex Hawaii with a joint resolution in 1898, again after a treaty had failed in the Senate.

EXECUTIVE AGREEMENTS. Agreements between the United States and a foreign state do not always take the form of treaties. More and more, international agreements, especially the more routine ones, are made as *executive agreements*. These are pacts concluded between the President and the head of a foreign state, or their respective subordinates. They do not require Senate consent.

Most executive agreements flow out of legislation previously enacted by Congress or implement treaties the Senate has agreed to. But the President can make these agreements without prior (or subsequent) congressional action.[18]

Dozens of executive agreements are made each year, most of them of a fairly routine sort. But on occasion they have been used for extraordinary purposes. They were used, for example, to establish the "Open Door" policy in China in 1899 and 1900 and the "Gentleman's Agreement" of 1907 by which Japanese immigration to this country was long regulated. An executive agreement was used in the "Destroyer-Bases Deal" of 1940 in which the United States gave the hard-pressed British 50 "overage" destroyers during World War II. In exchange for the destroyers, the United States received 99-year leases to several island bases extending from Newfoundland to the Caribbean.

POWER OF RECOGNITION. When the President receives the diplomatic representatives sent to the United States by another sovereign state, the President exercises the power of *recognition*. That is, the President, acting for the United States, acknowledges the legal existence of that country and its government. In doing so, the President signifies that the United States accepts that country as an equal in the family of nations and is prepared to conduct relations with it.[19] Recognition does not necessarily indicate that one government approves of the character and conduct of another. The United States recognizes several governments about which we have serious misgivings, most notably those of the USSR and China. The facts of life in world politics make it necessary for us to maintain relations with these regimes.

Recognition is often used as a weapon in foreign relations, too. Prompt recognition of a new state or government may do much to guarantee its life. By the same token, the withholding of recognition may have a serious effect on its continued existence. President Theodore Roosevelt's quick recognition of the Republic of Panama in 1903 provides one of the classic examples of American use of the power as a diplomatic weapon. He recognized the new state less than three days after the Panamanians had begun a revolt against Colombia. His prompt action guaranteed the success of that revolt.

---

[18] The Supreme Court has held executive agreements to be as binding as treaties and a part of the supreme law of the land, *United States* v. *Belmont*, 1937; *Pink* v. *United States*, 1942. Some authorities argue that executive agreements can be used instead of treaties in any and all cases.

[19] Sovereign states normally recognize one another through the exchange of diplomatic representatives. Recognition may be accomplished in any of several other ways, however. For example, it may be accomplished by proposing to negotiate a treaty, since under international law only sovereign states are capable of making such agreements.

In 1940, President Franklin Roosevelt made an executive agreement with Prime Minister Winston Churchill whereby 50 "overage" destroyers were given to Great Britain in exchange for 99-year leases to island bases in Atlantic waters.

The President may indicate United States displeasure with the conduct of another country by requesting the recall of that nation's ambassador or other diplomatic representatives in this country. (The official recalled is declared to be *persona non grata*.) And the same point can be made by the recalling of an American diplomat from a post abroad. The withdrawal of recognition is the sharpest diplomatic rebuke one government may give to another and has often been a step to war.

Military Powers. The Constitution makes the President the Commander in Chief of the nation's armed forces.[20] Congress also possesses a series of important war powers. They include, especially, the power to declare war, to provide for the raising and maintaining of the armed forces, to make the rules by which they are governed, and to appropriate the funds necessary to the nation's defense.[21]

Even though Congress shares the war powers, the President's position in military affairs is as dominant as it is in the field of foreign affairs. In fact, it does not stretch the matter too far to say that the President's powers as Commander in Chief are almost without limit. Thus, in 1907 Theodore Roosevelt sent the Great White Fleet around the world. He did so partly as a training exercise for the Navy, but especially to impress other nations with America's naval strength. Several members of Congress objected to the cost and threatened to withhold the necessary appropriation. In response to this threat, TR replied: "Very well, the existing appropriation will carry the Navy halfway around the world and if Congress chooses to leave it on the other side, all right."

Presidents usually delegate most of their command authority to military subordinates, but they are not required to do so. George Washington actually took command of federal troops and led them into Pennsylvania in the Whiskey Rebellion of 1794. And, Abraham Lincoln often visited

---

[20] Article II, Section 2, Clause 1; see also Chapter 18.
[21] Article I, Section 8, Clauses 11–17; see also pages 72, 342.

President Lincoln meets with General McClellan and a group of officers at headquarters of the Army of the Potomac in 1862.

the Army of the Potomac and instructed his generals in the field during the Civil War.

Most Presidents have not become so directly involved in military operations, however. Still, the President always retains the ultimate authority over and responsibility for any and all military matters. And the most critical decisions are invariably the President's—as, for example:

—President Truman's decision to use the atomic bomb against Japan in the waning days of World War II.

—President Johnson's decision to commit massive air and then ground forces in Viet Nam in 1965.

—President Nixon's decisions to bomb targets in Cambodia (in secret) in 1969, to send American troops into that country in 1970, to resume bombing North Viet Nam and mine its seaports in 1972, and to bomb Cambodian targets again in 1973.

—And President Ford's use of the Navy and Marines to recover the *Mayaguez* and its crew, seized by the Cambodians in 1975.

Almost from the beginning, Presidents have used the armed forces abroad and in combat without a declaration of war by Congress. John Adams was the first to do so in 1798. He ordered American warships into action against French naval vessels harassing American merchant ships on the high seas.

Various Presidents have since followed the Adams precedent—and on no fewer than 150 separate occasions. Jefferson did so against the Barbary Coast pirates in 1801. Polk brought on the Mexican War by ordering troops across the Nueces River in 1846, and Buchanan sent troops across the border to punish Mexican bandits in 1859. More recently, President Truman sent the armed forces into action in Korea in 1950, as did Eisenhower in Lebanon in 1958 and Johnson in the Dominican Republic in 1965. And, most recently, the war in Southeast Asia—the longest in the nation's history—was prosecuted in the absence of a declaration of war by Congress.

In today's world there can be no doubt that the President must have the capacity to respond rapidly and effectively to threats to this nation's security. But many have long warned of the dangers inherent in the President's power to involve the nation in "undeclared wars." They have insisted that the Constitution never intended that the President should have the power to do so.

The nation's frustrations and increasing anguish over the war in Viet Nam finally moved Congress to enact the War Powers Resolution of 1973. It is designed to place severe limits on the President's war-making powers. President Nixon vetoed the measure, branding it "both unconstitutional and dangerous to the best interest of our nation." But Congress overrode the veto. The Resolution's central provisions require that:

—Within 48 hours after committing American forces to combat abroad, the President must report to Congress, detailing the circumstances and the scope of his actions.

—The use of American forces in combat must end within 60 days, unless Congress authorizes a longer commitment. But the deadline may be extended 30 days if the President certifies the extension necessary to the safe withdrawal of the forces involved.

—American forces engaged in combat abroad without a declaration of war or other specific congressional authorization must be withdrawn immediately should Congress pass a concurrent resolution to that effect.

The constitutionality of the War Powers Resolution remains in dispute. A determination of the question must await a situation—should one ever arise—to which it would apply.

The President's military powers are far greater in war than in peacetime, of course. During a war Congress grants the President vast powers in addition to the authority given by the Constitution. In this day and age, the President's wartime authority extends far beyond the traditional military field. In World War II, for example, the President was given the power to do such things as ration food, control wages and prices, and seize industries vital to the war effort.

Presidents may use their military powers to preserve domestic peace, as we saw in Chapter 4.[22] The President also has the power to call a State's militia into federal service when necessary,[23] and may use the armed forces to enforce federal law anywhere in the United States.

Legislative Powers. As part of its system of checks and balances, the Constitution grants certain legislative powers to the President. With these—and the skill to put to telling use the role of Chief of Party—the President can exert a considerable influence over the actions of Congress. The President is in effect, then, the nation's Chief Legislator.

POWER TO RECOMMEND LEGISLATION. The Constitution requires that the President:

shall, from time to time, give to the Congress information of the state of the Union, and recommend to their consideration such measures as he shall judge necessary and expedient.[24]

Soon after the beginning of each congressional session, the President delivers the State of the Union Message to Congress. This is quickly followed by the proposed budget and the annual Economic Report. The President also submits occasional special messages on particular subjects. In all of these the President calls upon the legislators to enact those laws the President considers to be necessary.

THE VETO POWER. The Constitution requires that "every bill" and "every order, resolution, or vote to which the concurrence of the Senate and House of Representatives may be necessary (except on a question of adjournment) shall be presented to the President" for his action.[25]

Recall our discussion of the legislative process in Chapter 13. As we noted there, the Constitution presents the President with four options when the Congress sends a measure to the White House:

First, the President may sign the bill—thus making it law.

---

22 See page 88 and Article IV, Section 4.
23 Article I, Section 8, Clause 15; Article II, Section 2, Clause 1.
24 Article II, Section 3; see also page 305.
25 Article I, Section 7, Clauses 2 and 3. We have already noted (page 326) that practice has it that joint resolutions proposing constitutional amendments and concurrent resolutions, which do not have the force of law, are not sent to the President.

Second, the President may veto[26] the bill—and then must return it to the house in which it originated, together with a written statement of objections. Although it seldom does so, Congress may override a presidential veto by a two-thirds vote in each chamber.

Third, the President may allow the bill to become law without signature—by not acting upon it, neither signing nor vetoing it, for 10 days (not counting Sundays). This rarely occurs.

The *fourth* option, the "pocket veto," is available only at the end of a congressional session. If Congress adjourns within 10 days of submitting a bill to the President and the Chief Executive does not act upon it, the measure dies. Thus, the "pocket veto" has been applied.

The veto power enables the President, who is the only representative of *all* of the people, to act as a check on Congress. Often, the mere *threat* of a veto is enough to defeat a bill or to prompt its modification before final passage by Congress.

The historical record of presidential vetoes—and the fact that they are rarely overridden by Congress—is shown in the table on page 411.

Bills must be vetoed in their entirety. The President does not have the power to veto only certain items in a measure. That is, the President has no "item veto," as do most State governors. With that power, needless or wasteful projects might be eliminated from an appropriations measure, or an objectionable provision in a bill the President might otherwise prefer to see become law. But, on the other hand, the power might be used as a weapon to punish or pressure the President's opponents in Congress. Every President since Woodrow Wilson has favored a constitutional amendment to add the item veto to the President's legislative arsenal.

OTHER LEGISLATIVE POWERS. Only the President may call special sessions of Congress, as noted on page 287. And the President also has the power to adjourn *(prorogue)* Congress. But this power can be used only when the two houses are unable to agree upon an adjournment date (which has never happened).

Judicial Powers. The Constitution declares that the President: shall have the power to grant reprieves and pardons for offenses against the United States, except in cases of impeachment.[27]

A *reprieve* is the postponement of the execution of a sentence. A *pardon* is legal (though not moral) forgiveness of a crime.

The President's power to grant reprieves and pardons is absolute, except in cases of impeachment where they may never be granted. These powers of *clemency* (of mercy, leniency) may be applied only in cases involving federal offenses, however. The President has no such authority with regard to those who violate State laws.

Presidential pardons are usually granted to persons accused of federal crimes *after* they have been convicted in court. But the President may pardon a federal offender *before* that person is tried, and even before the offender has been formally charged.

Pardons in advance of a trial or charge have been rare. The most noteworthy pardon, by far, occurred in 1974. In that year, President Gerald Ford granted "a full, free and absolute pardon unto Richard Nixon for all offenses against the United States which he . . . has committed or may have committed or taken part in during the period from January 20, 1969, through August 9, 1974."

To be effective, a pardon must be accepted by the person to whom it is granted. When one is granted before charge or conviction—as in Mr. Nixon's case—its ac-

---

[26] *Veto,* from the Latin, literally "I forbid."

[27] Article II, Section 2, Clause 1.

PRESIDENTIAL VETOES

President		Regular	Pocket	Total	Vetoes Overridden
		Vetoes			
Washington	1789–97	2	–	2	–
Madison	1809–17	5	2	7	–
Monroe	1817–25	1	–	1	–
Jackson	1829–37	5	7	12	–
Van Buren	1837–41	–	1	1	–
Tyler	1841–45	6	4	10	1
Polk	1845–49	2	1	3	–
Pierce	1853–57	9	–	9	5
Buchanan	1857–61	4	3	7	–
Lincoln	1861–65	2	4	6	–
Johnson	1865–69	21	8	29	15
Grant	1869–77	45	48	93	4
Hayes	1877–81	12	1	13	1
Arthur	1881–85	4	8	12	1
Cleveland	1885–89	304	110	414	2
Harrison	1889–93	19	25	44	1
Cleveland	1893–97	42	128	170	5
McKinley	1897–01	6	36	42	–
Roosevelt	1901–09	42	40	82	1
Taft	1909–13	30	9	39	1
Wilson	1913–21	33	11	44	6
Harding	1921–23	5	1	6	–
Coolidge	1923–29	20	30	50	4
Hoover	1929–33	21	16	37	3
Roosevelt	1933–45	372	263	635	9
Truman	1945–53	180	70	250	12
Eisenhower	1953–61	73	108	181	2
Kennedy	1961–63	12	9	21	–
Johnson	1963–69	16	14	30	–
Nixon	1969–74	24	18	42	5
Ford	1974–77	48	18	66	12
Carter	1977–80	7	13	20	–
		1372	**1006**	**2378**	**90**

Source: *Congressional Reference Service, Library of Congress. Presidents not listed vetoed no measures.*

Of the 66 bills vetoed by President Ford, 12 of them were overridden by a Democratic Congress.

ceptance is regularly interpreted as an admission of guilt by the person to whom it is given.

Nearly all pardons are accepted, of course—and usually gratefully. But there have been instances in which they were rejected. A leading case is *Burdick* v. *United States,* 1915. Burdick, a New York newspaper editor, had refused to testify before a federal grand jury concerning the sources for certain news stories printed in his paper. He invoked the 5th Amendment, claiming that his testimony would tend to incriminate him. President Wilson then tendered him "a full and unconditional pardon for all offenses against the United States" which he might have committed in obtaining material for the news stories. But Burdick refused to accept the pardon and continued to refuse to testify. The federal District Court then fined and jailed him for contempt. It held that the pardon was fully effective with or without his acceptance and that there was, therefore, no basis for his continued defense of self-incrimination. The Supreme Court unanimously overruled the lower court and ordered Burdick's release.

The pardoning power includes the power to grant *conditional* pardons, provided the conditions are reasonable. It also includes the power of *commutation*—that is, the power to commute (reduce) the length of a sentence and/or the fine to be paid.

It also includes the power of *amnesty*—in effect, a general pardon offered to a group of law violators. Thus, in 1889 President Benjamin Harrison issued a proclamation of amnesty forgiving all Mormons who had violated the antipolygamy laws in the federal territories.

Most amnesties have been conditional. For example, in 1974 President Ford offered amnesty to those who deserted from the military or evaded the draft during the Viet Nam conflict. That amnesty—often described as an "earned re-entry" program—offered deserters and draft evaders an opportunity to clear their records by swearing allegiance to the United States and then performing up to two years of some form of alternate service.

The Pardon Attorney in the Department of Justice advises the President on all matters relating to the exercise of executive clemency; see pages 669–670.

SUMMARY

Every officer, employee, and agency of the executive branch is subordinate to the President and aids the President to perform the executive function. The President's chief right arm is the Executive Office of the President—a complex of agencies staffed by key advisers and assistants. The Cabinet, composed of the heads of the 13 executive departments, is also a major source of advice to the President.

The President's powers arise from the Constitution, acts of Congress, and usage. The nature of the President's powers has been most tellingly shaped by the manner in which the stronger Presidents have actually used their powers. The President's powers include:

(1) *Executive powers:* to execute and enforce the law, to direct administration, to issue executive orders, and to appoint and remove major officers.

(2) *Diplomatic powers:* to make treaties, to make executive agreements, and to send and receive diplomatic representatives.

(3) *Military powers:* to act as Commander in Chief and to preserve domestic peace.

(4) *Legislative powers:* to recommend legislation, to approve or veto acts of Congress, to call special sessions of Congress, and to adjourn Congress when the two houses cannot agree on an adjournment date.

(5) *Judicial powers:* to exercise executive clemency (pardons, reprieves, amnesties, commutations).

Concept Development

Questions for Review

1. In whom does the Constitution vest *the* executive power?

2. From what sources has the sketchy outline of the President's powers in Article II been filled out?

3. Why may the Executive Office of the President be called the Chief Executive's "right arm"?

4. What agencies compose the Executive Office of the President?

5. On what basis does the Cabinet exist? Who are its members?

6. Around what two competing concepts of "the executive power" can much of our political history be written?

7. Cite at least three leading reasons for the historical growth of presidential power.

8. What two general and contrasting views of the Presidency have been taken by its various occupants?

9. Why is it true that in executing and enforcing the law the President also has much to say about its meaning?

10. Why may the President be called the Chief Administrator as well as the Chief Executive?

11. From what sources does the President's ordinance power arise?

12. Why must the President possess the ordinance power?

13. Why is the President's power of appointment so critically related to the success of an administration?

14. What is the general rule regarding the President's removal power?

15. By whom are treaties made?

16. By whom are treaties ratified?

17. How does the President ordinarily exercise the power of recognition?

18. What is the President's major military power?

19. Why does the Constitution vest certain legislative powers in the President?

20. For what crimes may a President grant pardons?

For Further Inquiry

1. What do you think President Eisenhower meant by the following observation? "The duties of the President are essentially endless. No daily schedule of appointments can give a full timetable—or even a faint indication of the President's responsibilities. . . . In Washington, on a weekend absence, indeed even at a ceremonial dinner, the old saying is true: 'A President never escapes from his office.' "

2. On what basis do you think the line should be drawn between those appointments made by the President that require senatorial confirmation and those made by the President that do not?

3. Which of the contrasting views of the nature of "the executive power" (page 399) do you favor, Theodore Roosevelt's or William Taft's? Explain your answer.

4. While he was President, Mr. Truman had on his desk a small sign which read: "The buck stops here." Can you explain the meaning of that sign? Why do you suppose that President Carter had that same sign on his desk?

5. Each of the President's powers is limited in one or more important ways—by constitutional provision, by congressional action, by court decision, by custom, and/or by political realities. What illustrations can you cite to document this statement?

Suggested Activities

1. Prepare a bulletin board or other display illustrating the various powers exercised by the President.

2. Stage a debate or class forum on one of the following questions: (a) *Resolved,* That the President should be granted the item veto. (b) *Resolved,* That the President as Commander in Chief should not have the power to use the armed forces in combat without a declaration of war by Congress. (c) *Resolved,* That all presidential appointments to office be made for a fixed term.

3. Prepare a report on the manner in which one (or more) of the Presidents viewed the office and exercised its powers.

4. Give a talk to the class explaining why a particular President was, in your estimation, the "best" or most capable one in our history.

Suggested Reading

Berman, Larry, *The Office of Management and Budget and the Presidency.* Princeton, 1979.

Caraley, Demetris, *The Making of American Foreign and Domestic Policy.* Dabor, 1979.

Corwin, Edward S. and Peltason, J.W., *Understanding the Constitution.* Holt, Rinehart and Winston, 8th ed., 1979.

Cronin, Thomas E., *The State of the Presidency.* Little, Brown, 1980.

Davis, Vincent (ed.), *The Post-Imperial Presidency.* Transaction Books, 1980.

Diclerico, Robert, *The American President.* Prentice-Hall, 1979.

Goldhammer, Herbert, *The Adviser.* Elsevier, 1977.

Gully, Bill, *Breaking Cover.* Simon & Schuster, 1980.

Hodgson, Godfrey, *All Things to All Men: The False Promise of the Modern American Presidency.* Simon & Schuster, 1980.

Ippilito, Dennis S. *The Budget and National Politics.* Freeman, 1978.

Neustadt, Richard E., *Presidential Power: The Politics of Leadership from FDR to Carter.* Wiley, 1980.

Pechman, Joseph A. (ed.), *Setting National Priorities: The 1981 Budget.* Brookings, 1980.

Pious, Richard M. *The American Presidency.* Basic Books, 1979.

Shull, Steven A., *Presidential Policy Making.* King's Court, 1979.

Soafer, Abraham, *War, Foreign Affairs and Constitutional Power.* Ballinger, 1977.

Strum, Philippa, *Presidential Power and American Democracy.* Goodyear, 2nd ed., 1979.

United States Government Manual, 1981–1982. Government Printing Office, 1981.

The National Administration

Government is a trust, and the officers of the government are trustees; and both the trust and the trustees are created for the benefit of the people.

HENRY CLAY

■ Why is a large and complex bureaucracy an apparently necessary feature of modern government?

■ Is "big government" incompatible with democracy's insistence upon the sanctity and dignity of the individual?

■ Can (or should) a valid distinction be drawn between the phrases "public servant" and "public employee"?

The Constitution gives *the* executive power of the United States to the President, and it charges the President "to take care that the laws be faithfully executed."[1] In doing so, it makes the President the *Chief Administrator* of the Federal Government. We have already noted the many and different roles the President must and does play. Each of them are vitally important, of course—and none of them more so than this.

The great powers of the Presidency, and the awesome responsibilities of that Office, necessitate a *bureaucracy*—a large and complex administrative structure within the executive branch. A number of other factors work in the same direction— that is, to make the federal bureaucracy the huge and complicated thing that it is. The size of the nation's population, ongoing scientific, technological, and industrial developments, and economic growth are all major contributors here. So, too, are government's increasing concern with social welfare and social justice, the need to protect and refurbish the environment, and the state of other peoples and of the world at large.

In this chapter we look at the shape, the organization, of that administrative structure. We also look at its staffing, that is, at the civil service.

As we turn to these matters, bear this in mind: A large and extensive executive branch—often called "the administration"

---

[1] Article II, Section 1, Clause 1 and Section 3.

415

or "the bureaucracy"—is a common feature of modern governments, both here and abroad. One of the central problems for democracy is the need to keep that bureaucracy responsive to the law and to the elected representatives of the people. The growth in number, reach, and power of administrative agencies makes effective control of them absolutely necessary. Controls are needed lest they obstruct rather than promote the policies, the interests, and the wishes of "government by the people." Reflecting on this point nearly 200 years ago, James Madison wrote, in *The Federalist No. 51:*

> In framing a government, which is to be administered by men over men, the great difficulty lies in this: You must first enable the government to control the governed; and in the next place, oblige it to control itself.

The Federal Bureaucracy

The Constitution makes only the barest mention of the organization of the executive branch of the National Government. It does provide for the offices of President and Vice President, of course. Article II also suggests the existence of various executive departments—in giving to the President the power to "require the opinion, in writing, of the principal officer in each of the executive departments."[2] And it suggests the existence of two departments in particular, for military and for foreign affairs. It does so by making the President the "commander in chief of the army and navy," and by giving him the power to make treaties and to appoint "ambassadors, other public ministers, and consuls."[3]

Beyond these few, quite general references, the Constitution is silent on the matter. The Framers obviously intended that administrative agencies be created, however—as, indeed, they have.

As the chart on the next page shows, the executive branch is composed of three major groups of administrative agencies: (1) the Executive Office of the President, (2) the 13 Cabinet departments, and (3) a large number of independent agencies.[4]

We discussed the Executive Office, and the several agencies within it, in Chapter 16. We shall look at the other two groups in a moment. But, first, a word on two matters: What is sometimes called the "name game" and the distinction between *staff* and *line* agencies and functions.

THE NAME GAME. The titles given to the various units of the executive branch vary considerably. That variation complicates the task of understanding the organization of the federal bureaucracy. The name *department* is reserved to identify the major operating agencies of Cabinet rank. Beyond that, there is not very much in the way of standardized use of names, however—and this can be confusing.

The term *agency* is frequently used to refer to any governmental body. In the federal structure it is sometimes used to identify a major unit headed by a single executive and of near-Cabinet status. For example, the title is used for the Environmental Protection Agency and the United States Arms Control and Disarmament Agency. But so, too, is the title *administration*—as in the case of the National Aeronautics and Space Administration and the Veterans Administration.

The name *commission* is usually given to

---

[2] In Section 2, Clause 1. There is also a reference to "heads of departments" in Clause 2, and to "any department or officer" of the government in Article I, Section 8, Clause 18, the Necessary and Proper Clause.

[3] In Section 2, Clauses 1 and 2.

[4] The chart is adapted from the current edition of the *Government Manual,* published annually by the Office of the Federal Register in the General Services Administration. It contains a brief description of the creation, authority, and functions of each of the agencies presently operating in each of the three branches of the Government. The bulk (over 90 percent) of its now more than 900 pages is devoted to the executive branch.

THE GOVERNMENT OF THE UNITED STATES

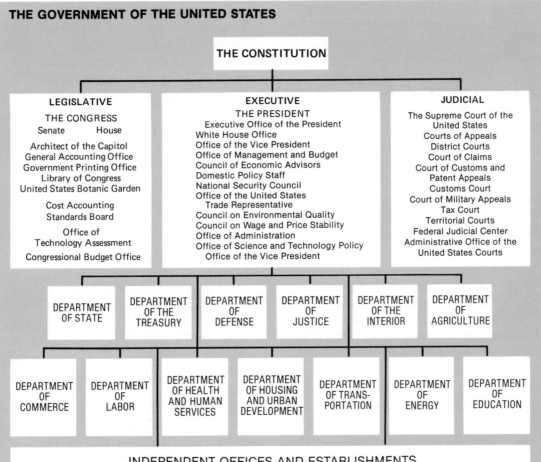

THE CONSTITUTION

LEGISLATIVE

THE CONGRESS
Senate   House

Architect of the Capitol
General Accounting Office
Government Printing Office
Library of Congress
United States Botanic Garden

Cost Accounting
Standards Board

Office of
Technology Assessment

Congressional Budget Office

EXECUTIVE
THE PRESIDENT
Executive Office of the President
White House Office
Office of the Vice President
Office of Management and Budget
Council of Economic Advisors
Domestic Policy Staff
National Security Council
Office of the United States
  Trade Representative
Council on Environmental Quality
Council on Wage and Price Stability
Office of Administration
Office of Science and Technology Policy
  Office of the Vice President

JUDICIAL
The Supreme Court of the
United States
Courts of Appeals
District Courts
Court of Claims
Court of Customs and
Patent Appeals
Customs Court
Court of Military Appeals
Tax Court
Territorial Courts
Federal Judicial Center
Administrative Office of the
United States Courts

DEPARTMENT OF STATE

DEPARTMENT OF THE TREASURY

DEPARTMENT OF DEFENSE

DEPARTMENT OF JUSTICE

DEPARTMENT OF THE INTERIOR

DEPARTMENT OF AGRICULTURE

DEPARTMENT OF COMMERCE

DEPARTMENT OF LABOR

DEPARTMENT OF HEALTH AND HUMAN SERVICES

DEPARTMENT OF HOUSING AND URBAN DEVELOPMENT

DEPARTMENT OF TRANS-PORTATION

DEPARTMENT OF ENERGY

DEPARTMENT OF EDUCATION

INDEPENDENT OFFICES AND ESTABLISHMENTS

Administrative Conference of the U.S.
Board for International Broadcasting
Civil Aeronautics Board
Commission on Civil Rights
Commodity Futures Trading Commission
Community Services Administration
Consumer Product Safety Commission
Environmental Protection Agency
Equal Employment Opportunity Commission
Export-Import Bank of the U.S.
Farm Credit Administration
Federal Communications Commission
Federal Deposit Insurance Corporation
Federal Election Commission
Federal Home Loan Bank Board
Federal Labor Relations Authority
Federal Maritime Commission
Federal Mediation and
  Conciliation Service
Federal Reserve System, Board of
  Governors of the
Federal Trade Commission
General Services Administration
FOOD & DRUG ADMINISTRATION

International Communications Agency
Interstate Commerce Commission
Merit System Protection Board
National Aeronautics
  and Space Administration
National Labor Relations Board
National Mediation Board
National Science Foundation
National Transportation Safety Board
Nuclear Regulatory Commission
Office of Personnel Management
Pension Benefit Guaranty Corporation
Postal Rate Commission
Railroad Retirement Board
Securities and Exchange Commission
Selective Service System
Small Business Administration
Tennessee Valley Authority
U.S. Arms Control and
  Disarmament Agency
U.S. International Trade Commission
U.S. Postal Service
Veterans Administration

Note: This chart seeks to show only the more important federal agencies.

those agencies involved in the regulation of business activities—as the Interstate Commerce Commission and the Securities and Exchange Commission. These units are seldom headed by a single administrator; rather, they are composed of a varying number of top-ranking officers (commissioners). The same title is often given to investigative, reporting, advisory, and other bodies, however—for example, the Civil Rights Commission and the Federal Election Commission.

Either *corporation* or *authority* is the title most often assigned to units headed by a board and manager which conduct business-like activities in the insurance, lending, and development fields—as the Federal Deposit Insurance Corporation, the Overseas Private Development Corporation, and the Tennessee Valley Authority.

Within each major agency the same pattern of lack of uniformity and confusion is common. Although *bureau* is the name most often applied to the major elements (sub-units) within a department, *service, administration, office, branch, division,* and other titles are frequently used for the same purpose. Thus, the major elements within the Treasury Department now include the Internal Revenue Service, the Customs Service, the Bureau of the Mint, the Bureau of Engraving and Printing, and the Office of the Comptroller of the Currency.

Many federal agencies, of various rank, are regularly referred to by their initials rather than their full titles. EPA, IRS, VA, FBI, CIA, FCC, and TVA are but a few of dozens of familiar examples of the practice.[5] And a few are more often known by

a nickname. Thus, the Federal National Mortgage Association is very often called "Fannie Mae"; and the National Railroad Passenger Corporation is much better known by its popular tag, Amtrak.

STAFF AND LINE. The several units of any administrative organization can be categorized as either staff or line agencies. *Staff* agencies and their personnel serve in a support capacity. They aid the chief executive and other administrators by furnishing advice and other assistance in the management of the organization. *Line* agencies, on the other hand, are directly involved with, actually perform, the basic task for which the organization exists.

Take, as two quick illustrations of this distinction, the several agencies in the Executive Office of the President and, in contrast, the Environmental Protection Agency.

The agencies which make up the Executive Office—the White House Office, the National Security Council, the Office of Management and Budget, and so on—each exist as staff support to the President. Their primary mission is to assist the President in the exercise of the executive power and in the overall management of the executive branch. They are *not* operating agencies; that is, they do not operate, administer, public programs. Recall, they do such things as keep the President informed of important domestic and international developments; manage the preparation and execution of the budget; perform scheduling, speech-writing, research, and similar chores; aid the President in his contacts with Congress, the news media, and the public; and so on.

The Environmental Protection Agency has a quite different mission. It is responsible for the actual, day-to-day enforcement of the several federal anti-pollution laws. It operates "on the line," where the action is.

This distinction between staff and line can help us to understand the complexities

---

[5] The *Government Manual* carries a list of some 300 more or less well-known initial-designations (acronyms) for federal agencies. The use of acronyms can cause occasional problems. When the old Bureau of the Budget, in the Executive Office, was reorganized in 1970, its name was changed to the Office of Management and Budget (OMB). Until almost the very moment of its creation, however, it was slated to be known as the Bureau of Management and Budget (BOMB).

of the federal bureaucracy. But, a word of caution: it can be oversimplified or pushed too far. For example, most line agencies do have staff units of their own—to assist them in their line operations. Thus, the Office of Legislation in the EPA assists the agency's Administrator in the all-important matter of liaison with Congress, its appropriate committees, and its individual members.

The Executive Departments

Much of the work of the Federal Government is conducted by the 13 executive departments. They are the traditional units of federal administration, and each of them is built around a broad field of governmental activity.

The 1st Congress established three of these departments, in 1789: State, Treasury, and War. As the size and the workload of the Federal Government grew, new departments were added. Some of the later ones took over various duties originally assigned to older departments, and they gradually assumed new functions, as well.

THE EXECUTIVE DEPARTMENTS TODAY

Department	Created
State	1789
Treasury	1789
Defense[a]	1949
Justice[b]	1870
Interior	1849
Agriculture	1889
Commerce[c]	1913
Labor[c]	1913
Health and Human Services[d]	1953
Housing and Urban Development	1965
Transportation	1967
Energy	1977
Education[d]	1979

[a] Created out of unification of Departments of War (established in 1789), Navy (1798), and Air Force (1947).
[b] Post of Attorney General created in 1789.
[c] Both departments created out of original Department of Commerce and Labor (1903).
[d] Education functions transferred from Department of Health, Education, and Welfare (1953), and HEW renamed, in 1979.

Another Cabinet agency, the Post Office Department, was abolished by Congress in 1971. Originally established in 1789, it was made an executive department in 1872; it was transformed into a government corporation, the United States Postal Service, in 1971.

To keep informed of developments at home and abroad, the President and his staff must draw upon a wide range of information sources. Not the least of these are the daily newspapers from different parts of the country, a number of which are shown on a table in President Lyndon Johnson's White House office.

And a few departments have been created and later abolished by Congress.

The head of each department is known as the Secretary—with the exception of the Attorney General who directs the work of the Justice Department, of course. Each of them is appointed by the President subject to Senate confirmation.

Together, the departmental secretaries serve as members of the President's Cabinet—a matter we discussed in the last chapter. Their duties as the chief officers of their own departments usually command their major attentions, however. Each of them serves as the primary link between presidential policy and his or her own agency. But, just as importantly, each represents, and attempts to promote and pro-tect, the interests of his or her department with the President, congressional commit-tees, the rest of the bureaucracy, and the public.

To aid the secretary in this many-faceted role there are regularly an under secretary or deputy secretary and several assistant secretaries. They, too, are appointed by the President and Senate. Staff assistance to the secretary is provided by various assistants and other aides in such areas as personnel, planning, law, public relations, and budgeting.

Each department is organized in a number of sub-units, both staff and line. As we noted a moment ago, these agencies are known variously as bureaus, offices, services, divisions, and so on. And each of

The approximately 2.9 million civilians currently employed by the National Government work in each of the 50 States, in the territorial possessions, and abroad. Note that less than 10 percent of the total federal work force is actually located in Washington, D.C.

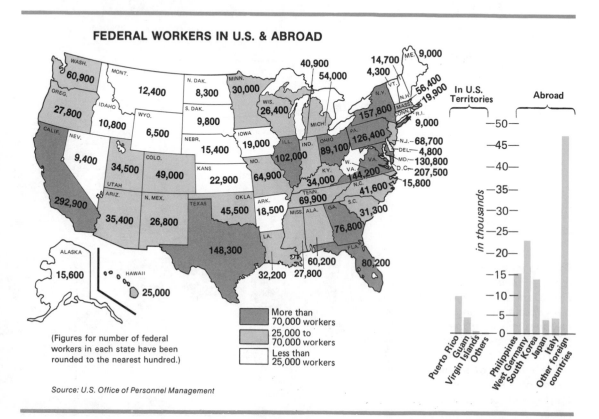

FEDERAL WORKERS IN U.S. & ABROAD

(Figures for number of federal workers in each state have been rounded to the nearest hundred.)

More than 70,000 workers
25,000 to 70,000 workers
Less than 25,000 workers

Source: U.S. Office of Personnel Management

them is divided into smaller units.[6] About 80 percent of the office and bureau chiefs, the "middle-management" personnel, are career people.

The internal structure of most of the departments is also arranged on a geographic basis. That is, its activities are conducted through regional offices which direct the work of agency employees in the field. For example, the Treasury Department's Internal Revenue Service is headquartered in Washington. But most of the IRS's tax collection and enforcement work is carried out through seven regional offices, 58 district offices, and some 200 local offices throughout the country. Altogether, about 90 percent of all federal civilian employees live and work outside the nation's capital. (See opposite page.)

We shall discuss each of these departments and their many functions in the chapters to follow.

The Independent Agencies

Until the 1880's, nearly all of the activities of the Federal Government were carried out by the regular Cabinet departments. Over the years since then, however, Congress has established a large number of agencies—the *independent agencies*—located outside of any of them. Many have come, and some have gone. Today, they number close to 200. Their functions range from the fields of transportation and communications through labor-management relations and finance to veterans affairs, nuclear energy, and natural resources. Forty-

odd of the more important of them are shown in the chart on page 417.

Several of these independent agencies administer programs which cannot be very easily distinguished from the major responsibilities of the various executive departments. There is a very close affinity between the work of the Veterans Administration and that of a number of agencies within the Department of Health and Human Services. And, the concerns of the VA are not very far removed from those of the Defense Department, either.

Neither the size of its budget nor the number of its employees provides a good dividing line between a number of these agencies and the executive departments, either. Thus, the VA has some 200,000 employees today—more than those of any of the departments except Defense. And its budget now runs to more than $21 billion a year—more than that of any of the departments except Defense, Labor, and Health and Human Services.

The reasons for the separate existences of these agencies are nearly as many as the agencies themselves. But a few major ones stand out. Some have been set up outside the regular departmental structure because they simply do not fit well within that scheme. A prime example is the Office of Personnel Management, the hiring agency for nearly all other federal agencies, as we shall see later in this chapter. The General Services Administration illustrates the point, too. Created in 1949, it is the general "house-keeping" agency for the entire executive branch. Its major chores include the management of buildings, furnishing of supplies and other equipment, storage of records, and a host of similar services to all executive departments and agencies.

Some agencies have an independent status to protect them from the play of partisan politics and from pressure group influences. Again, the Office of Personnel Management can be cited and, too, the Civil Rights Commission (page 175) and

---

[6] Thirty years ago the first Hoover Commission (the Commission on the Organization of the Executive Branch) recommended standard titles for the agencies within a department: service, bureau, division, branch, section, and unit. The bureaus would be the principal operating agencies; if several bureaus had very closely related functions they would be grouped into a service. The bureaus would be divided into division, branch, section, and unit levels. This arrangement is now in effect in some agencies, and in some to a greater extent than others; and it is sometimes followed as new agencies are created.

the United States International Trade Commission (page 501). Conversely, on occasion pressure groups have persuaded the Congress to place some agencies outside of any of the entrenched departments—and the protections they might afford against group pressures. Thus, the Veterans Administration might logically be housed within either Defense or Health and Human Services. But, several veterans organizations were responsible for the separate identity of the VA, and they have fought to maintain that situation for years.

Still other agencies have been born as independent entities largely by accident. That is, they were created to meet a specific need with no particular thought given at the time to the structural hodge-podge that inevitably followed. The Small Business Administration (pages 552–553) illustrates the point.

Finally, some agencies are independent because of the peculiar and sensitive nature of their functions. This is notably true of what are often called the "independent regulatory commissions"—a breed we shall look at in a moment.

The label "independent agencies" is a catch-all one. Most of them are independent only in the sense that they are not located within any of the Cabinet departments. They are *not* independent of the President and the executive branch. Some of them are independent in a much more realistic way, however. For most intents and purposes, they *do* lie outside the executive branch and are largely free of presidential control.

Perhaps the best way to get a good grasp on all of these agencies is to group them into three main categories: (1) the independent executive agencies, (2) the independent regulatory commissions, and (3) the government corporations. Again, we look at the work of these many agencies elsewhere in the book. What we are concerned with now is their place in the sprawling federal bureaucracy.

The Independent Executive Agencies. This group includes most of the independent agencies. Some of them are large, with thousands of employees, multi-million or even billion-dollar budgets, and highly imposing public tasks to perform. The VA, the National Aeronautics and Space Administration, the Environmental Protection Agency, and the General Services Administration are all leading examples. They are organized very much like the major departments, headed by a single administrator, with sub-units operating on a regional basis, and so on. The most significant difference between them and the 13 executive departments is, quite simply: they do not have Cabinet status.

Some of the agencies in this group are not administrative and policy giants. They do perform important tasks and occasionally attract public notice. For example, the Civil Rights Commission, the Farm Credit Administration, the Federal Election Commission, and the Small Business Administration fall into this category.

But most of them exist in near limbo. They have only a few employees, small to minuscule budgets, and almost never attract any attention. The American Battle Monuments Commission, the Board on Geographic Names, the Statistical Policy Coordination Committee, the Joint Board for the Enrollment of Actuaries, and the Migratory Bird Conservation Commission are rather typical of the dozens of these seldom-seen-or-heard public bodies.

The Independent Regulatory Commissions. The independent regulatory commissions stand out among the independent agencies. Not only are they not housed within any of the Cabinet departments, they are very largely beyond the reach of presidential direction and control.

There are 11 of these agencies today, each created to regulate important aspects of the nation's economic life. Their vital statistics are set out in the chart on page 424.

John A. Wagner; Sentinel Newspapers, Denver

"MIND IF WE BROWSE AROUND?"

Their large measure of independence from the White House is mainly a result of the way in which Congress has structured each of them. Each is headed by a board or commission composed of from five to 11 members—not more than a bare majority of whom may be drawn from the same political party. Their members are appointed by the President with Senate consent. They are appointed, however, for terms of such length—as long as 14 years in the case of the Federal Reserve Board—that the President is unlikely to gain control over any of these agencies through the appointing power during a single term in the White House. Furthermore, the terms of the commissioners are staggered so that the term of only one member on each commission expires in any one year. Their independence of presidential control is shown in another way: they are subject to removal *only* for those causes specified by Congress, not at the President's pleasure.[7]

As with the other independent agencies, the regulatory commissions possess administrative powers to carry out the functions Congress has assigned to them. But, unlike the other independent agencies, the regulatory commissions also exercise what are known as *quasi-legislative* and *quasi-judicial* powers.[8]

The regulatory commissions exercise their quasi-legislative powers when they issue rules and regulations. These rules and regulations have the force of law. They implement (spell out the details of) those statutes Congress has entrusted to their enforcement. For example, Congress has provided that railroad rates must be "just and reasonable." The Interstate Commerce Commission exercises control over the *actual* rates charged in particular situations and establishes them by issuing appropriate regulations.

The regulatory commissions exercise their quasi-judicial powers when they conduct hearings and decide disputes in those fields in which Congress has given them regulatory authority. For example, if a rail-

---

[7] SEC, FCC, CPSC, NRC, and CFTC commissioners are exceptions here; Congress has provided for their removal at the President's discretion. On these agencies and the President's removal power, see page 403.

[8] The prefix *quasi* is from the Latin, meaning, "in a certain sense, resembling, seemingly."

THE INDEPENDENT REGULATORY COMMISSIONS

Agency	Created	Members	Term	Function	Agency	Created	Members	Term	Function
Interstate Commerce Commission (ICC)	1887	11	7	Regulates rates, other aspects of commercial transportation by railroad, highway, waterway.	National Labor Relations Board (NLRB)	1935	5	5	Administers federal labor-management relations laws; settles labor disputes; prevents unfair labor practices.
Board of Governors, Federal Reserve System	1913	7	14	Supervises banking system; controls use of credit in economy.	Federal Maritime Commission (FMC)	1936	5	5	Regulates waterborne foreign commerce.
Federal Trade Commission (FTC)	1914	5	7	Administers antitrust laws prohibiting unfair competition, price-fixing, deceptive practices.	Civil Aeronautics Board (CAB)	1938	5	6	Regulates rates, other aspects of air transportation; allocates domestic air routes, and oversees routes (subject to presidential approval).
Securities and Exchange Commission (SEC)	1934	5	5	Regulates securities markets; administers laws prohibiting false, misleading, fraudulent investment practices.	Consumer Product Safety Commission (CPSC)	1972	5	5	Establishes, enforces safety standards for consumer products.
Federal Communications Commission (FCC)	1934	7	7	Licenses, regulates all radio and TV stations; regulates interstate telephone, telegraph rates and service.	Nuclear Regulatory Commission (NRC)	1974	5	5	Licenses, regulates all civilian use of nuclear materials and facilities.

Agency	Created	Members	Term	Function
Commodity Futures Trading Commission (CFTC)	1974	5	5	Regulates agricultural commodity exchanges, trading in commodity futures.

road requests ICC permission to raise its rates for carrying goods between two points, that request may be opposed by shippers. The ICC would then conduct hearings to determine the merits of the matter and render a decision, much as a court would. Appeals from decisions made by the regulatory commissions may be taken to the United States Courts of Appeals (see page 651).

In effect, Congress has created the regulatory commissions to act in its stead. Congress could, if it chose, hold hearings and set freight rates, license radio and TV stations, check trade practices, and perform the many other tasks it has assigned to the regulatory commissions. But these are complex and time-consuming matters which demand constant and expert attention. If Congress itself were to do these things, it would have no time for the other important legislative business to which it must attend.

Because these agencies exercise all three of the basic governmental functions—executive, legislative, and judicial—they provide an exception to the principle of separation of powers. Several authorities, and most recent Presidents, have urged that at least their administrative functions be assigned to regular Cabinet agencies. Even larger questions are asked about these regulatory bodies, and prompt proposals to abolish or redesign them. The most troublesome are: Have some of them been captured by the special interests they were created to control? And to what extent do the huge volumes of detailed rules and regulations these commissions have adopted add to the consumer's burden and unnecessarily stifle commercial activity and competition?

Back to our basic point here: the "location" of these agencies in the federal bureaucracy. Notice that they really should not be grouped with the other independent agencies, as they are in the chart on page 417. Rather, they should (somehow) be located somewhere between the executive and legislative branches. And, at the same time, they should be placed somewhere between the executive and judicial branches, too.

The Government Corporations. Several of the independent agencies are *government corporations* or *authorities*. That is, they are agencies established especially to perform certain commercial or business-like activities.

Congress established the first government corporation nearly 200 years ago, when it chartered the First Bank of the United States in 1791.[9] The device was little used until the First World War and then the Depression of the 1930's, however. In both those periods Congress set up dozens of corporations to carry out "crash" programs. Most of those agencies have long since disappeared.[10] But several of them are still with us—among them, for example, are the Federal Deposit Insurance Corporation, which insures bank deposits (page 519), and the Export-Import Bank, which helps finance the export and sale of American goods around the world (page 553).

There are at least 60 government corporations operating today. They have been formed to conduct a highly diverse list of business-like operations. That list includes: the generation and distribution of electric power (the Tennessee Valley Authority), the construction and operation of canal systems (the Saint Lawrence Seaway Development Corporation), intercity passenger trains (the National Railroad Passenger Corporation—Amtrak), mail service (the United States Postal Service), the insurance of savings accounts (the FDIC, the Federal

[9] See pages 343, 516.
[10] Among the best known of them, the Reconstruction Finance Corporation. The RFC was at one time the nation's largest lender, public and private, and was the center of intense controversy throughout its existence, from 1932 to 1954. It was replaced by the Small Business Administration; see page 553.

Savings and Loan Insurance Corporation), the guarantee of pension benefits due persons covered by private plans which fail (the Pension Benefit Guaranty Corporation), and many more.[11]

The typical government corporation is organized much like its private counterpart. It is run by a multi-member board of directors, and a general manager directs its operations in line with the policies set by the board. Most of them produce revenues which are plowed back into the "business."

There are several striking differences between government and private corporations, however. Among the major ones: Congress determines the purposes for which the public agencies exist and the functions they may perform. The officers of a government corporation are *public* officers. At the top level, these officers are usually appointed by the President with Senate confirmation. And a large difference exists in terms of both financing and stockholders. The public agencies are financed (capitalized) by congressional appropriations of public money, not by the funds of private investors; and the Government owns the stock in its corporations.

The major advantage usually claimed for the use of the corporation device is its flexibility. That is, it is argued that the public agency—freed of the overhead controls of the regular departmental organization—can conduct business-like activities with the incentive, efficiency, and ability to experiment that often characterizes private concerns. Whether the claim is valid or not is at least debatable.

The degree of independence, and flexibility, the various government corporations

actually enjoy varies quite a bit. In fact, some of them are not independent at all. They are attached to executive departments, and so are subject to the control of the secretary of the particular department. The Commodity Credit Corporation, for example, is the Government's principal crop-loan and farm-subsidy agency. It is located within the Department of Agriculture, and the Secretary of Agriculture chairs its seven-member board. Then, too, it carries out most of its functions through the personnel and facilities of another line agency in the USDA, the Agricultural Stabilization and Conservation Service. This agency is also subject to the direct control of the Secretary; see pages 619–620.

Some of these agencies do have a considerable measure of independence, however. The Tennessee Valley Authority (TVA) is a notable case in point. It operates within the framework of very broad statutory provisions. Congress has given it considerable discretion over its policies and programs. Although its budget is subject to review by the Office of Management and Budget and the President, and then by Congress, it has a large say in the uses of the revenues it generates. Moreover, the TVA even has its own civil service system.

Once more, as with the Cabinet departments and the other independent agencies, we shall consider the work of several government corporations in the following chapters. As we do, perhaps you will recall that each of them poses a very "sticky" question: How can the corporation's need for flexibility in its operations be squared with democratic government's requirement that all public agencies be held responsible and accountable to the people?

Reorganization of the Executive Branch

We have just dealt with the overall shape of the huge, sprawling executive branch—and we shall continue to examine it over

---

[11] State and local governments maintain many such corporations, most often called "authorities." They include those which operate airports, turnpikes, harbors, power plants, and the like. Of them all, the Port of New York Authority is probably the best known.

Case Study

The word "bureaucracy" is both much used and much abused in American politics. In its "unloaded" sense, it is regularly used to identify the whole of the administrative structure—all of the agencies, personnel, and procedures involved in the day-to-day machinery of government. In dictionary-like terms, it refers to a formal organization characterized by: (1) a hierarchical—i.e., a ranked—structure, (2) personnel with specialized assignments, and (3) the vesting of legal authority in positions rather than in particular persons.

But the term is also frequently used in an uncomplimentary or derisive sense. It is often applied to governmental agencies and personnel whom their critics see as pompous, too much involved in "red-tape" and precedent, unimaginative, overly dedicated to routine, and unreasonably opposed to change. To those who see and use the word in this light, bureaucrats are "empire builders," too powerful, too impersonal, insensitive to public needs, and unresponsive to public opinion.

To some of these critics, the growth of bureaucracy is a symptom of the moral degradation of the American people of today in contrast to Americans of an earlier time. And some of them see that growth as an insidious plot to destroy individual freedom—a plot hatched by power-hungry politicians and/or social theorists who think that they know what is best for everyone.

But it should be noticed that many of those who use "bureaucracy" as a "snarl word" are quite selective in the targets to which they apply it. In short, "the bureaucracy" is responsible for those public policies they dislike. Those governmental programs they support are regularly identified by such phrases as "responsible actions to meet urgent public needs" or "matters of top national priority."

Whatever the color one gives to the word, it is plain that "big government" has never been widely popular in this country. And for many Americans "big government" is simply another way of saying "bureaucracy." Much of the hostility many people now display toward the bureaucracy and bureaucrats developed in the wake of the war in Viet Nam and then Watergate. But an anti-government attitude has always been a prominent feature of American political thought and behavior. Recall that it was Thomas Jefferson who first said that "that government is best which governs least."

Each of the governments of all modern-day nations has equipped itself with a large and complex administrative organization—that is, with a bureaucracy. It is one of the continuing imperatives of democratic government that it keep its public servants responsible to the law and, at the same time, responsive to the will of the people and the dictates of their elected representatives. Consider once more James Madison's comment, in *The Federalist, No. 51,* which we quoted on page 416. And ponder, too, this comment by his colleague, Alexander Hamilton, in *The Federalist, No. 70:*

> Energy in the Executive is a leading character in the definition of good government . . . A feeble Executive implies a feeble execution of the government. A feeble execution is but another phrase for a bad execution; and a government ill-executed, whatever it may be in theory, must be, in practice, a bad government.

■ Is the existence of a bureaucracy an inescapable fact of life for modern-day government? If so, is its continued growth inevitable, as well?

■ Are there various safeguards—various beliefs, institutions, procedures, and the like—which tend to preclude the growth of irresponsible bureaucracy in this country? If so, what are some of them? And how effective are they?

the next several chapters. By now, you can see that there is a good deal of rhyme and reason to the structure of the federal bureaucracy. But, too, some of it is best described as confusingly complex—or as a hodge-podge, a disjointed jumble, even a hopeless mess.

Why? One very important answer to that question lies in this: The government of the United States is dynamic, not static; it is a constantly changing and growing thing. The march of time, fresh circumstances, the adoption of new policies and programs, and the expansion—or deemphasis or even abandonment—of existing ones all call for changes. These factors prompt the creation, reshuffling, and elimination of agencies. Wars, depressions and recessions, and other crises have a particularly hefty impact on the shape of governmental organization. In short, the tale of the structure of the executive branch can be told in good part as a *continuing* story of organization and *re*organization.

Basic responsibility for the structure of the executive branch rests with Congress. It has created nearly all of the complex of agencies beneath the President.[12] But Congress has been traditionally slow to react to the continuing need for change.

Because of this, and beginning with President Taft in 1911, every Chief Executive has asked Congress for the authority to reorganize the executive branch. Since the Depression years of the 1930's, Congress has responded with several statutes. The earlier ones usually provided for the creation of a commission to study the problems involved and make appropriate recommendations. One of the most notable of such groups was the President's Committee on Administrative Management, which reported in 1937. Two others

were the Commissions on the Organization of the Executive Branch, the first and second Hoover Commissions, which reported in 1949 and 1955, respectively.

As a result of the work of these groups, several changes and improvements have occurred over the past few decades. Thus, the 1937 (Brownlow) Committee's report led to the creation of the vastly important Executive Office of the President. And the first Hoover Commission prompted a number of important steps, including the creation of the Department of Health, Education, and Welfare. HEW brought dozens of scattered agencies under one more or less manageable roof. And it also led to the passage of the Reorganization Act of 1949, the forerunner of the present statute.

The Reorganization Act of 1977. First in 1949, and most recently in 1977, Congress has delegated to the President substantial authority to create, reshape, and abolish executive agencies.[13]

As the law now stands, the President may submit reorganization plans to Congress. If neither house rejects a plan within 60 days, it becomes effective.

There is always the possibility of the "legislative veto" of a plan, of course. But of the 93 reorganization plans submitted by five Presidents from 1949 to 1973, 74 were accepted by Congress. And, through 1980, President Carter's batting average was even higher: 10 for 10.

Several major federal agencies have been created by this process—among them: the Office of Management and Budget and the Environmental Protection Agency (both in 1970) and the Office of Personnel Management (in 1979).

---

[12] Except for those it has specifically authorized the President to create and those created, as we shall note in a moment, by presidential reorganization plans.

[13] The present statute is a slightly modified version of the original 1949 law. When that law expired in 1953 it was periodically extended thereafter, until 1973. Each President, from Harry Truman through Richard Nixon, used the law extensively. As the Watergate scandal grew, Congress refused to give President Nixon further reorganizational authority. The present law reinstated the power after a four-year lapse; it is scheduled to expire in April of 1981 but likely will be extended at that time.

Beyond the "legislative veto," there are only three significant restrictions on the Chief Executive's authority here: (1) No plan may create, merge, or abolish entire Cabinet departments or independent regulatory commissions. (2) No plan may abolish a function the performance of which Congress has required by law, or extend the legal time limit on or expand agency functions. (3) No more than three plans may be pending before Congress at any one time.

President Carter gave strong support to the passage of the new law. As he signed it, he reiterated his intention to:

> . . . reorganize and streamline the executive branch of our Government. This is one of the ways in which I plan to fulfill my commitment to the American people to make government more responsive, efficient, and open.

Almost immediately he began to send reorganization proposals to Congress. The first of them dealt, appropriately enough, with the Executive Office—and is reflected in our treatment of it in Chapter 16. A number of subsequent reorganization plans have reshaped various other elements of the executive branch—among them, the Government's personnel system, as we shall see in a moment.

The Civil Service

The Federal Government is the largest single employer in the United States. Some 2.9 million people now staff the federal bureaucracy.[14] Of this huge number, only 537—the President and Vice President, and the 535 members of Congress—are elected. All of the others are appointed.

It is upon the shoulders of these appointees, the federal "civil servants," that most of the burden of the day-to-day work of the Government rests. The quality of these appointees determines in very large measure the quality of the National Government itself. No matter how wisely Congress and the President may formulate public policies, the people and the country cannot benefit unless those policies are properly and successfully executed. For, as Woodrow Wilson once observed, the administration of governmental policy is "government in action."

Development of the Civil Service. The Constitution says very little about the personnel of the federal bureaucracy. In-

---

[14] Another two million wear the uniforms of the armed services; see pages 447–452. Altogether, there are now (1981) nearly 16 million civilian government employees in this country, including some 3.5 million who work for the States and another 9.5 million employed by their local governments, including school districts.

the small society   by Brickman

HOO-BOY!

IN THIS TOWN A MAN'S DESK IS HIS CASTLE—

7-16

Washington Star Syndicate, Inc.

BRICKMAN

deed, the only directly pertinent provision is to be found in Article II. Section 2, Clause 2 provides that the President:

> shall nominate, and, by and with the advice and consent of the Senate, shall appoint ambassadors, other public ministers, and consuls, judges of the Supreme Court, and all other officers of the United States whose appointments are not herein otherwise provided for, and which shall be established by law; but the Congress may by law vest the appointment of such inferior officers, as they think proper, in the President alone, in the courts of law, or in the heads of departments.

A GOOD BEGINNING. As our first President, George Washington knew that the success or failure of the new government under the Constitution would hinge in large measure upon those whom he appointed to office. He declared his policy to be that of selecting "such persons alone . . . as shall be the best qualified." He demanded that his appointees be loyal to the Constitution. But, he did not insist that they be loyal to him personally or to those who supported him politically.

As the party system developed, however, Washington's successors began to give weight to political considerations in the making of appointments. John Adams followed Washington's policy rather closely in that he insisted upon competence. But Adams was also careful to see that none of his political enemies gained appointive office.

When Thomas Jefferson entered the White House in 1801, he found that most posts were held by men who were both politically and personally opposed to him. Jefferson agreed in principle with Washington's concept of "fitness for office." Still, he combined it with "political acceptability," replacing many Federalists with his own Democratic-Republicans. Even so, not many offices were involved. When the national capital was moved to the new city of Washington in 1800, there were only about 1000 federal employees. The Treasury Department employed 69 persons; War, 18; Navy, 15; and State and Post Office, nine each.

Jefferson's immediate successors—James Monroe, James Madison, and John Quincy Adams—found little occasion to remove anyone for partisan reasons. They did insist, however, on party loyalty by their appointees.

JACKSON AND THE SPOILS SYSTEM. By the latter 1820's the number of federal employees had risen well into the thousands. When Andrew Jackson came to the Presidency in 1829, he dismissed many officeholders and replaced them with his own supporters.

Jackson is often cited as the father of the *spoils system*—the practice of giving offices and other favors of government to those who have supported the party.[15] This is not altogether fair. Jefferson had laid its foundations in the National Government in 1801, and it was used among the States and their local governments long before Jackson became President.

Jackson looked upon his appointing policy more as a "democratic" one than as a system for rewarding friends and punishing enemies. In his first message to Congress he explained and defended his program on four grounds. He held that: (1) Since the duties of public office were essentially simple, any normally intelligent person was capable of holding office. (2) There should be a "rotation in office" in order that a wider number of persons might have the privilege of serving in the National Government. (3) Long service by any person would promote tyranny and intolerance. And (4) the people were entitled to have the party which they placed in power control all of the offices of government from top to bottom.

---

[15] The famous comment "To the victors belong the spoils of the enemy" was first made by Senator William L. Marcy of New York on the floor of the Senate in 1832.

Whatever Jackson's high purposes and "democratic" concepts may have been, there were others who saw the spoils system as a means for building and holding power. For the next half-century the spoils system held sway. Every change in administration brought a new round of rewards and punishments. And, as governmental activities and agencies increased, so did the spoils.

Competent persons were squeezed out of the public service, or, more often, refused to "soil their hands" by entering it. Efficiency was mostly an idle dream of a few reformers. Huge profits were made on public contracts at the people's expense. Much of the nation's natural wealth was stolen. Political power was centered in the horde of officeholders and others who owed their livelihood to the party in power.

THE MOVEMENT FOR REFORM. Congress made feeble attempts to correct matters in 1851 and 1853. It required several thousand clerkships to be filled on the basis of examinations given by department heads. This minor reform produced no significant results. Nor did an 1871 law which established the first national civil service commission and introduced the idea of *competitive* examinations.

Able people pressed for major reform. Civil service reform was debated in every session of Congress after 1865. Men like William Cullen Bryant and Carl Schurz spoke out for it, and leading journals like *Harper's Weekly* and *The Nation* took up the cry. Groups like the National Civil Service Reform League,[16] which was founded in 1881, fought for it.

It finally took a tragedy to transform talk and hope into the reality of action. The assassination of President James A. Garfield by a disappointed officeseeker

roused the nation in 1881. Garfield's successor, Chester A. Arthur, pushed vigorously for reform, and Congress passed the Civil Service Act of 1883.

THE PENDLETON ACT. The Civil Service Act of 1883, better known as the Pendleton Act, established the present federal civil service system. It has been amended several times over the past nine decades, of course. Still, its major features remain in effect—even with the extensive changes which were made in 1978.

The Act created an independent agency, the *United States Civil Service Commission*, to administer its provisions. And the Commission did so for over 95 years—until it was replaced by two new agencies, the Office of Personnel Management and the Merit System Protection Board, on January 1, 1979.

The Act established two categories of employment in the executive branch: one, the *classified* and the other the *unclassified* service. And it gave to the President the key power to determine into which of those categories most agencies (and, hence, their personnel) were to be placed.

All hiring for the classified service was to be done on the basis of merit; and that qualification was to be determined by "practical" examinations administered by the Civil Service Commission. The Commission was directed to draw up lists (*registers*) of qualified persons based upon examination standings; and all appointments were then to be made from those registers.

Its emphasis upon merit was diluted by two other features of the law, however. One was the stipulation that classified appointments be geared to geography. That is, the number of persons hired from any particular State was to correspond approximately to that State's share of the total population. The other dilution was in the law's provisions for veterans preference; all veterans, and especially disabled ones and the widows of veterans, were accorded a preferred ranking in all federal hiring.

---

[16] Renamed the National Civil Service League in 1945, this organization is still one of the most influential groups promoting the merit system today.

To further its basic purpose, the law denied to classified employees the right to participate in partisan politics. And it expressly barred attempts by members of Congress to influence any civil service actions involving classified employment.

EXTENSION OF THE CLASSIFIED SERVICE. The Pendleton act was designed to erase the spoils system at the federal level—and, to do so, it created the classified service. But the Act itself brought fewer than 14,000 of the then 131,000 federal workers into those ranks. Any future expansions of the classified service were to be made by the President.

There were several fits and starts—many additions to and removals from the merit system—under Presidents Cleveland, Harrison, Cleveland again, and McKinley—and those early ups and downs were closely tied to partisanship.

Theodore Roosevelt firmly supported the merit principle. He had headed the Civil Service Commission in the Harrison and second Cleveland administrations. In his own Presidency, he shifted more than 115,000 positions to the classified service. When he left office in 1909, nearly two-thirds of the federal workforce had been brought under the classified umbrella.

Each of TR's successors generally followed his example. Today, roughly 90 percent of the men and women who work in executive branch agencies are covered by the civil service merit system.[17]

Congress has taken an occasional hand in the spread of the merit concept. Its major input has come as part of the grant-in-aid process. In 1939 it began to require that all State and local government agencies receiving funds from the Social Security Administration follow the merit principle in their own employment practices. Today nearly all federal grant programs carry that stipulation.

Civil Service Today. The first goal of civil service reform—eliminating the spoils system—was largely realized in the early decades of this century. And, as a consequence, efforts to shape the civil service system gradually shifted to a newer goal—to that of recruiting and retaining the best available persons for the federal workforce.

Over the years, those efforts sometimes stumbled over themselves, however. That is, they tended to emphasize job *security;* too often, they neglected the equally vital matters of job *performance* and *quality.* To put it another way, as civil service critics often have: not enough attention was paid to merit in the merit system.

President Carter summarized the situation this way in 1978:

The Pendleton Act . . . established the Civil Service Commission and the merit system it administers. These institutions have served our nation well in fostering the development of a federal workforce which is basically honest, competent, and dedicated. . . .

But the system has serious defects. It has become a bureaucratic maze which neglects merit, tolerates poor performance, and mires every personnel action in red tape, delay, and confusion.

Most civil service employees perform with spirit and integrity. Nevertheless, the public suspects that there are too many government workers, that they are underworked, overpaid, and insulated from the consequences of incompetence.

Such sweeping criticisms are unfair; but we must recognize that the only way to restore public confidence in the vast majority who work well is to deal effectively with the few who do not.

---

[17] That is, 90 percent not including the employees of the United States Postal Service and a few other federal agencies. The Postal Service is the largest agency not covered by the civil service system. It is now a government corporation (see pages 419, 425); and it is the only federal agency in which employment policies are governed by a collective bargaining process. The other major civilian agencies not included in compounding the 90 percent figure are the FBI, CIA, and TVA; each of those agencies has its own merit system.

"GO THROUGH THIS DOOR, TAKE A LEFT, THEN A RIGHT, THEN A LEFT, A RIGHT, A LEFT, ANOTHER LEFT, A RIGHT..."

REORGANIZATION. Large changes were made in the civil service system in 1978 and became effective in 1979. They were accomplished by both a presidential reorganization plan and an act of Congress.

The Civil Service Commission was replaced by two independent agencies:

The *Office of Personnel Management* is now the Federal Government's central personnel agency. It is headed by a director, appointed by the President and Senate, and administers most of the basic features of the civil service system. Thus, OPM examines and recruits new employees, conducts extensive training programs for career civil servants, sets position classifications, and manages the salary and other job benefit arrangements for some 2.1 million of the men and women who work for Uncle Sam.

The *Merit System Protection Board* now performs the balance of the functions once vested in the Civil Service Commission. It is a bipartisan, three-member panel and its members are chosen by the President and Senate for staggered six-year terms. As its title suggests, it is *the* agency which polices and protects the merit principle in federal employment practices.[18]

POSITION CLASSIFICATION. An effective government personnel program must be firmly based upon a logical system of *position classification*. That is, it must be based upon a breakdown of the service into related classes or groups of positions. Under this arrangement all positions with similar duties and responsibilities are grouped together into a single class. For example, all clerk-typists are put into a single class re-

---

[18] Another new agency, the *Federal Labor Relations Authority,* now manages labor-management relationships in federal employment. It, too, is a bipartisan, three-member body, appointed by the President and Senate. The Director of the OPM is the Government's principal representative in shaping its labor-management relationships.

gardless of the agency in which a clerk-typist may work. The clerk-typist job is essentially the same in all government agencies.

Position classification is necessary to the handling of the other basic problems of the personnel system, including recruitment, appointment, pay, promotions, retirement, and the like. For example, the exact nature of a particular job to be filled must be known in order that the best available person can be sought to fill that job.

RECRUITMENT. The phrase "government worker" often conjures up an image of file clerks, mailmen, typists, messengers, telephone operators, janitors, and the like. Of course, the Federal Government employs thousands of people for these jobs—and their work is absolutely essential to its effectiveness. But the federal civil service also includes nearly all of the other occupations to be found in private life—doctors, nurses, lab technicians, dentists, lawyers, chemists, botanists, biologists, political scientists, social workers, teachers, skilled mechanics, carpenters, plumbers, electronics technicians, draftsmen, photographers, physicists, pilots, psychologists, and so on. Altogether more than 2000 different occupational specialties are included in the civil service.

How does the Federal Government go about the important task of attracting people to its ranks? Until recently, recruitment was carried on almost entirely by the Civil Service Commission. Today, recruitment is primarily the responsibility of the various operating agencies themselves. Job announcements are usually posted in public buildings, especially in post offices. They are also placed in the classified advertisements sections of newspapers and sent to schools and radio and television stations. Until recently, however, most applicants learned of federal job opportunities more by chance than through any real effort on the part of the National Government.

There has been improvement in recent years, but still much more could be done to dramatize the opportunities that are available.

APPLICATION. When a person does learn of an opening in which he or she is interested, an application form must be filed. Forms are available at most post offices and many other public places.

The usual application form is a small card. It seeks such basic information as age, sex, social security number, current address, and the like. It does *not* ask an applicant's race or religion; neither of these factors may be considered in the hiring of any federal employee.

The small card is actually a preliminary application. Sooner or later, applicants are asked to file a two- or four-page statement of personal qualifications.

EXAMINATIONS. If the position is one that requires a written test, the applicant is informed (either by mail or in the original announcement) of the time and place for that examination. For many positions, written tests are not required. Rather, applicants are rated on the basis of training and experience. Where they are called for, the written tests are "practical." That is, they are designed to discover the applicant's ability to fill the particular job involved or his or her ability to learn how to do so.

Entry into the federal service today is regarded as more than the taking of a temporary job. It is looked upon as the beginning of a permanent career with promotion through the ranks to higher posts. In line with this, the whole federal civil service testing program now lays much stress on general all-round ability.

THE REGISTERS. All those applicants who pass the required examinations—a score of 70 is a passing grade on most—have their names placed on a *register*. A register is a list of "eligibles"—those persons qualified for appointment to a particular position or class of positions. Each

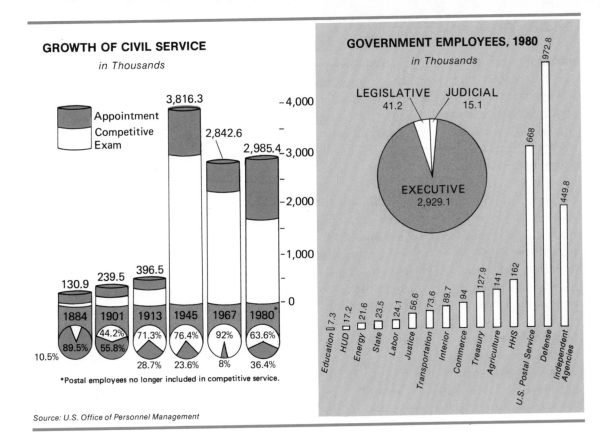

GROWTH OF CIVIL SERVICE

in Thousands

Appointment

Competitive
Exam

3,816.3

2,842.6

2,985.4

130.9   239.5   396.5

| 1884 | 1901 | 1913 | 1945 | 1967 | 1980* |

10.5%
89.5%

44.2%
55.8%

71.3%
28.7%

76.4%
23.6%

92%
8%

63.6%
36.4%

Postal employees no longer included in competitive service.

Source: U.S. Office of Personnel Management

GOVERNMENT EMPLOYEES, 1980

in Thousands

LEGISLATIVE   JUDICIAL
41.2   15.1

EXECUTIVE
2,929.1

Education 7.3
HUD 17.2
Energy 21.6
State 23.5
Labor 24.1
Justice 56.6
Transportation 73.6
Interior 89.7
Commerce 94
Treasury 127.9
Agriculture 141
HHS 162
U.S. Postal Service 668
Defense 972.8
Independent Agencies 449.8

---

applicant is ranked on an appropriate register according to his or her examination score. The registers are used by appointing officers among the various agencies; when one is exhausted or becomes obsolete, new examinations are held.

APPOINTMENT. The Office of Personnel Management does *not* appoint anyone to a federal job—except the employees of the OPM itself. Appointments (other than presidential) are made by the agency in which there is a vacancy.

Separate registers are kept for many agencies. Only the more common positions—clerks, stenographer, messenger, and the like—are now placed on central registers. An appointment must be made accordingly to the "rule of three"—that is, from among the top three eligibles on the appropriate register.

Veterans' preference in the making of civil service appointments antedates the Pendleton Act. In fact, it goes back to the beginnings of the Republic. Today an automatic

five extra points on an examination are given to any honorably discharged veteran. A total of ten points is added to the score of a disabled veteran, the wife of a disabled veteran unable to work, or the widow of a veteran who has not remarried. Some federal jobs, such as messengers and guards, are reserved especially for disabled veterans.

Nearly one-half of all federal jobs are now held by those with veterans' preference. Nearly all State and local civil service systems also give preference to veterans. The granting of this privilege to those who have served their country can be easily justified. Notice, however, that it is a departure from the principle of appointment on the basis of individual merit.

Geographical distribution in the making of appointments also complicates the process somewhat. Ever since the Pendleton Act, the number of persons in the civil service from any State is supposed to bear a close relation to that State's share of the total national population. Thus, if a State has six percent of our total population, approximately six percent of the total number of federal workers must come from that State. This geographic barrier often complicates the appointing process and hardly promotes the hiring of workers on the basis of merit alone.

After appointment, the civil servant must serve a period of *probation* (trial period) up to six months. If by the end of this period the employee is found suitable, the appointment becomes permanent. *Temporary appointments* may be made without examination for the filling of short-term jobs.

COMPENSATION. Recruiting well-qualified public servants and persuading them to remain in government service, is *very* obviously and importantly affected by the matter of compensation. Generally, the salaries paid by government at the middle and lower levels of federal employment compare favorably with those available in similar private jobs. The same cannot be said at the higher levels, however.

Salaries. Salaries paid in the classified service are set forth in the *General Schedule.* It provides for basic pay grades, with the lowest grade designated GS-1 and the highest designated GS-18. Within each grade there are currently (1981) 10 "steps" (pay levels). For those starting at the GS-1 level today, the pay ranges from $7960 to $9954 a year, and GS-2 salaries range from $8951 to $11,265. At the GS-17 level, the salary scale contains only five steps, from $53,849 to $58,500. The GS-18 salary is $58,500, with no steps. (But these latter figures are quite misleading. For several years now, Congress has set a *much lower* figure as the *maximum* salary that may be paid to any classified employee. For 1981 that ceiling is $50,112.)

An employee need not begin a government career at the very bottom of the General Schedule. In the position classification scheme, each job is classed according to its nature, and suitable pay is one of the bases

for classification. Thus, a job requiring some training and ability might be ranked GS-9. A person appointed to it would now start at $18,585 a year.

Government can never hope to compete with private industry on a dollar-for-dollar basis in the upper grades. For example, an agency head whose federal salary is $50,112 a year might well command a significantly higher salary in a similar position outside the government. How government service can attract and keep better people for the higher positions is a major headache in the civil service system.

Other Compensation. Several "fringe benefits" are provided to federal workers—but these generally lag behind those common in private industry. Most civil servants are covered by retirement, disability, and survivor insurance programs. As the civil service retirement program operates, the employee's contributions are matched by the Government and, at compound interest, produce a relatively generous retirement pension. The usual retirement age is 62 but one may retire on the full annuity at 55 after 30 years of service. Some fringe benefits are also available to federal workers during working years: for example, overtime and sick pay, paid vacations and group life, health, accident, and unemployment insurance.

PROMOTION. The question of promotion· is extremely important. If civil servants know that their chances for promotion are good, their morale and efficiency are likely to be higher than if they know they are not.

As we know, there is an opportunity for promotion within each salary grade. These promotions are made largely on the basis of seniority (length of service), but every employee is also rated on the basis of efficiency by his or her superior. Merit does play a part in these promotions. Merit plays its biggest role in the promotion from one job to a higher one. When there is a vacancy in a higher position, it is supposed to (and usually does) go to the person who has best demonstrated his or her abilities to do the job.

RESTRICTIONS ON POLITICAL ACTIVITY. One of the basic purposes of the merit system has always been to protect federal workers from political pressures. Thus, ever since 1883, the Civil Service Act has prohibited the dismissal or the disciplining of a classified worker for failure or refusal to make a campaign contribution.

At the same time, various statutes and voluminous OPM regulations closely restrict the partisan political activity of federal workers. They may vote at elections, attend party meetings, voice their opinions on political matters, make voluntary con-tributions to a party treasury, and even hold office in a political organization. But they may not take an active part in any campaign for public office. They cannot do such things as serve as delegates to party conventions, distribute campaign literature, and collect funds for a party or candidate. To do any of these things provides grounds for dismissal. These restrictions apply to all federal personnel covered under the classified service and, as well, to all but the top-most officials outside the merit system. The Hatch Act of 1939 extended these same curbs to all State and local government employees who work on programs financed, even in part, with funds from the Federal Government.

SUMMARY

The Constitution makes the President the Chief Administrator of the Federal Government. The great powers and responsibilities of the Presidency necessitate a bureaucracy—a large and complex administrative structure within the executive branch.

The Constitution makes little mention of the organization of the executive branch. Nearly all of it has been created by Congress. As it is now structured, it is composed of three major groups of administrative agencies: (1) the Executive Office of the President (discussed in Chapter 16), (2) the 13 Cabinet departments, and (3) the many independent agencies.

The several units of an administrative organization can be categorized as either (1) *staff* agencies, which serve in a support capacity, or (2) *line* agencies, which perform the basic tasks for which the organization exists. Below the department level, there is little uniformity in the use of such designations as bureau, service, office, and so on in the federal bureaucracy.

The 13 Cabinet departments are the traditional units of federal administration; each is built around a broad field of governmental activity.

The many independent agencies, located outside any of the Cabinet departments, have been created for a variety of reasons. They are of three main types: (1) independent executive agencies, (2) independent regulatory commissions, and (3) government corporations.

The Federal Government, with now some 2.9 million employees, is the largest single employer in the nation. Nearly all the public servants are appointed, not elected, and the day-to-day operations of the Government are largely in their hands.

George Washington inaugurated "fitness for office" as a qualification for federal employment; but in later administrations "political acceptability" also became a qualification. Andrew Jackson brought the full-blown "spoils system" to the National Government. The spoils system reigned until the passage of the Pendleton Act of 1883, which created the federal civil service system—now managed by two independent agencies: the Office of Personnel Management and the Merit System Protection Board.

Concept Development

Questions for Review

1. What is the federal bureaucracy?

2. What does the Constitution provide with regard to the organization of the executive branch?

3. What three major groups of administrative agencies compose the executive branch?

4. What is the "name game" in terms of titles given to government units?

5. What are *staff* agencies? *Line* agencies?

6. Which agencies are the traditional units of federal administration? How many exist?

7. What collective role do the heads of the Cabinet departments have? Separately?

8. Distinguish the three general types of independent agencies. Why have they been created?

9. For what general purpose has Congress established the independent regulatory commissions? How many now exist?

10. What is the major advantage claimed for the use of the government corporation?

11. What does the Reorganization Act of 1977 provide?

12. Approximately how many civilians now work for the Federal Government?

13. What major standard did George Washington set for the federal civil service?

14. How did Washington's immediate successors modify that standard?

15. On what bases did Andrew Jackson justify his version of the spoils system?

16. What event finally prompted the passage of the Pendleton Act?

17. What is the essential difference between the classified and the unclassified service?

18. Who determines which federal jobs are to be included within the classified service? Approximately what proportion of federal jobs are in the classified-service category today?

19. The primary goal of civil service has shifted from what original target to what concern today?

20. What is position classification? Why is it important?

21. What portion of the federal civilian workers work outside the nation's capital?

For Further Inquiry

1. On page 422 we suggested that the dynamic character of the Government is a leading reason for the confusing nature of some aspects of the organization of the executive branch. What other reasons can you suggest?

2. What was Thomas Jefferson suggesting when, in 1807, he remarked to Baron von Humboldt: "When a man accepts a public trust, he should consider himself as public property"? On what basis might one *disagree* with Jefferson here?

3. In what specific ways might the Federal Government make a civil service career more attractive to young people?

4. Some argue that the restrictions placed on the political activities of federal employees are necessary protections of them and of the integrity of the political process. But others argue that the restrictions make federal employees "second-class citizens" and that the general political health of the nation suffers because of them. With which position do you agree? Why?

5. Why do you think it is true that, with only a few notable exceptions, civil service systems based upon merit have been much slower to develop at the State and local levels than in the Federal Government?

Suggested Activities

1. Invite a representative of some federal agency operating in your locale to discuss that agency and its functions with the class.

2. Prepare a report comparing the personnel system of your city or that of another local government in your locale with the federal civil service system.

3. Attempt to prepare a chart of the organization of the executive branch of the Federal Government that places the independent regulatory commissions in their proper relationship to the President and to Congress and to the courts.

4. Stage a debate or class forum on one of the following topics: (a) *Resolved,* That the independent regulatory commissions be abolished and their functions assigned to the regular Cabinet departments; (b) *Resolved,* That federal employees be guaranteed by law the right to strike.

Suggested Reading

Barkley, George E., *The Craft of Public Administration.* Allyn and Bacon, 2nd ed., 1978.

Caraley, Demetris (ed.), *The Making of American Foreign and Domestic Policy.* Dabor, 1979.

Dye, Thomas R., *Understanding Public Policy.* Prentice-Hall, 4th ed., 1981.

Edwards, George C., *Implementing Public Policy.* Congressional Quarterly Press, 1980.

Gordon, George J., *Public Administration in America.* St. Martin's Press, 1978.

Henry, Nicholas, *Public Administration and Public Affairs.* Prentice-Hall, 1980.

Lasson, Kenneth, *Private Lives of Public Servants,* Indiana University Press, 1978.

Lineberry, Robert L., *American Public Policy: What Government Does and What Difference It Makes.* Harper & Row, 1978.

Miewald, Robert, *Public Administration: A Critical Perspective.* McGraw-Hill, 1978.

Nigro, Felix and Lloyd G., *Modern Public Administration.* Harper & Row, 5th ed., 1979.

Rose, Richard, *What Is Governing? Purpose and Power in Washington.* Prentice-Hall, 1978.

Seidmann, Harold, *Politics, Position, and Power: The Dynamics of Federal Organization.* Oxford, 1980.

United States Government Manual, 1981–82. Government Printing Office, 1981.

Wildavsky, Aaron, *The Politics of the Budgetary Process.* Little-Brown, 3rd ed., 1979.

18

Foreign Affairs and National Defense

Observe good faith and justice toward all nations. Cultivate peace and harmony with all.

GEORGE WASHINGTON

■ Why do the President and Congress share power in the field of foreign affairs? Which should be pre-eminent?

■ Does the fact that the United States possesses such tremendous military power pose any serious threat to the nation's democratic political system?

■ Should the Constitution be amended to require that before the United States can make war, such action must be approved in a national referendum?

It would be impossible to overstate the importance of our foreign relations and of the manner in which they are conducted. The United States is the most powerful nation on earth and the leader of the free nations of the world in the struggle against tyranny. The ways in which the might and influence of the United States are used—how we conduct our foreign affairs—affects the fate of all peoples, everywhere.

The ways in which other nations conduct themselves today is of vital concern to us, too. For more than 150 years American foreign policy was characterized by a refusal generally to become involved in the affairs of the rest of the world. Our policy of *isolationism* demanded that we steer clear of "entangling alliances" and similar international commitments.

The past four decades have been marked by a profound change in American foreign policy, however. World War II taught us that we cannot live in isolation in the modern world. We have learned that, in many ways and whether we like it or not, we live in "one world."

The inescapable fact is that this is "one world." That our own peace and security are intimately bound up with that of the rest of the world can be seen in any number of ways. As but one of them, inventive genius has produced an age of ultra-rapid travel and instantaneous communication, and has made the entire world almost a neighborhood. It took the *Mayflower* 60

The United States was the first nation to ratify, in 1945, the UN Charter—a striking example of our shift from isolationism to full participation in international affairs. Here, President Truman addresses the San Francisco Conference shortly after the delegates to that meeting had approved the UN Charter.

days to cross the Atlantic in 1620; that trip can now be made in a few hours by air.

Wars and political upheavals anywhere on the globe vitally affect the interests of the United States. Four times in this century we have become involved in wars thousands of miles from home. Numerous other times our security has been threatened by lesser events thousands of miles away. A flareup in Korea, an outbreak in the Middle East, an incident in Berlin, a revolution in Latin America, and strife in Southern Africa all have an impact on—and in—the United States.

Economic conditions abroad make themselves felt quite directly in the United States, too. Cheaper labor costs in Europe's steel mills and Japanese factories, a coffee shortage in Brazil, a shutdown in the oil fields of Iran all are reflected in our domestic markets.

In these and many other ways, then, we live in "one world." In some ways, how-

ever, we do not. The communist world, especially the Soviet Union and the People's Republic of China, and the free world, led by the United States, confront one another on many issues and in many places. Most of the newer nations of Africa and Asia compose yet another grouping, a "non-aligned" or neutralist bloc of growing importance in world politics. In this other—divided—world of today, we have come to realize that only through a foreign policy designed to promote and protect the security and well-being of *all* of the nations of the world can the security and well-being of the United States ever be finally and fully achieved.

A nation's foreign policy is actually many different policies on many different topics. It is made up of all the stands that a nation takes on a wide variety of problems arising out of a large number of situations. Insofar as the United States is concerned, the term *foreign policy* refers to the official

American positions on such matters as international trade, disarmament, national defense and collective security. It embraces our position on nuclear weapons testing, freedom of the seas, military aid, and fishing rights in Atlantic and Pacific waters. It involves aid to developing countries, colonialism, nationalism, the United Nations, arms limitations, and space exploration. It involves oil prices and imports, grain shipments, cultural exchanges, immigration, and positions, and actions, on a great many other matters, as well.

Obviously, some of our policies remain fixed (largely unchanged) year in and year out. For example, an insistence on freedom of the seas has marked American foreign policy from the very beginning. Other policies are flexible, liable to change as circumstances change. Thus, barely a generation ago, opposition to the German and Japanese dictatorships was a basic aspect of American foreign policy. But, today, West Germany and Japan are among our closest and staunchest allies in the world community.

Sometimes we are able to take the initiative in international relations. We are able to introduce new policies and programs that win friends for the United States and heighten American prestige abroad. Take, for example, the decision to help rebuild the war-torn countries of Europe and restore their shattered economies after World War II (the Marshall Plan). It was a bold and effective step at that critical point in history, and it was a major signal of American intentions in the postwar world.

Very often, American policy must also be defensive in nature. It must be adjusted to meet a change in the policy of some other country. Thus, our decision to "contain" the spread of communism was initiated by the Truman Doctrine more than 30 years ago, in 1947. It came in reaction to the U.S.S.R.'s aggressive policy of expansion after World War II.

In this chapter, we explore the governmental organization for the conduct of foreign affairs and then the way in which our government provides for the nation's defense and security. In Chapter 19, we shall review the content of American foreign policy from its early days to the present and explore, as well, the manner in which the international community is organized for the pursuit of peace and security.

The Department of State

The President, as we saw in Chapter 16, is the nation's chief diplomat. Congress does share power with the President in the field of foreign affairs. It does so particularly through its powers of the purse and through the Senate's roles in the treaty and appointment processes. But it is the President who bears primary responsibility, under the Constitution and by tradition, for the formulation of foreign policy and the conduct of the nation's foreign affairs.

In performing this immense task, the Chief Executive is assisted by a number of components of the sprawling Executive Branch. Here we are concerned with those agencies—especially with the Departments of State and Defense, and then with several others.

The State Department, headed by the Secretary of State, is the President's principal arm in the formulation and the implementation of the foreign policy of the United States. The Secretary is appointed by the President, subject to confirmation by the Senate.

The Secretary of State ranks first among the 13 members of the President's Cabinet—in part, because of the vital importance of the post, but especially because the Department of State was the first executive department created by Congress in 1789.

In the earliest days, foreign affairs were conducted by the Second Continental Congress through its Committee of Secret Correspondence (1775-1777). Then they were conducted by the Committee for Foreign Affairs (1777-1781). Under the Articles of Confederation, the Congress created the Department of Foreign Affairs. The latter was reconstituted by an act of Congress in 1789; later the same year its name was changed to the Department of State.

The duties of the Secretary of State relate chiefly to foreign affairs—to the framing and conduct of foreign policy and, too, serving as the "caretaker" of American interests abroad. The Secretary does have some formal and procedural domestic responsibilities, however—for example, attending to all official correspondence between the President and the governors of the several States. Thus, if a President should call a State's Guard units into federal service, the process is conducted through the Secretary's office. And, when Richard Nixon resigned the Presidency on August 9, 1974, it was to the Secretary of State that he was required to submit his formal certification of that action.

But, again, the Secretary's prime responsibilities are in the field of foreign affairs and the management of the work of the Department, its far-flung foreign posts,

and its more than 22,000 employees. Some Presidents have entrusted the conduct of foreign affairs largely to the Secretary of State. Other Presidents have preferred to hold the reins rather tightly in their own hands. But, in either case, the Secretary of State has been an important and influential officer in each presidential administration.

The Secretary's major assistant is the Deputy Secretary of State. The other top aides include three Under Secretaries—for Political Affairs, for Economic Affairs, and for Security Assistance—and several special assistants. The Deputy Under Secretary for Management oversees the internal administration of the Department and of the embassies and other posts abroad.

There are now (1981) 14 Assistant Secretaries who head "bureaus"—for example, the Bureau of Economic Affairs and the Bureau of African Affairs. Each bureau is, in turn, organized in "offices"—for example, the Office of Soviet Union Affairs in the Bureau of European Affairs, and the Passport Office and Visa Office in the Bureau of Consular Affairs.

The Department of State is organized along *geographic* and *functional* lines. Some of its agencies deal with a particular country

Secretary of State Edmund Muskie (1980-81) met with U.S. Ambassador to the United Nations, Donald McHenry (at right) in New York to discuss an outbreak of fighting between Iran and Iraq in the Persian Gulf.

Case Study

Many distinguished Americans have held the post of Secretary of State. The entire list reads like a roll-call of the nation's great. Among the outstanding personalities who have served in the office are Thomas Jefferson, John Marshall, James Madison, James Monroe, John Quincy Adams, Henry Clay, Daniel Webster, John C. Calhoun, William Seward, John Hay, Elihu Root, William Jennings Bryan, Charles Evans Hughes, and Cordell Hull.

The most recent Secretaries of State have been George C. Marshall (1947–1949), Dean Acheson (1949–1953), John Foster Dulles (1953–1959), Christian Herter (1959–1961), Dean Rusk (1961–1969), William P. Rogers (1969–1973), Henry A. Kissinger (1973–1977), Cyrus R. Vance (1977–1980), and Edmund S. Muskie (1980–1981).

Each of these several men has had his own unique relationship with the President. Some Presidents have entrusted their Secretaries with a fairly large measure of control over both the formation and the execution of foreign policy. Others have held the reins much more closely in their own hands. Among the more recent occupants of the post, only Secretaries Herter and Rogers played a minor-key role. Secretary Kissinger, on the other hand, played a near dominant part. Through his nearly four years in the office it was clear that the vital center of American foreign policy was located in the State Department rather than at the White House.

■ What characteristics should a President seek in the selection of a Secretary of State?

■ How might a President's policy of reliance on the Secretary affect the latter's ability to perform in the foreign arena?

■ How might it affect the President's relationships with the Congress? With the American people?

or region in the world. Others are concerned with particular subjects such as legislation and congressional relations, planning and research, or relations with international organizations. Because it is so organized, the Department of State is able to keep abreast of developments in many areas simultaneously; and this structure allows it to move quickly whenever new problems arise, whether in some particular country or involving some functional question.

The Foreign Service. More than 3400 men and women represent the United States abroad as members of the Foreign Service.

Under international law[1] every nation has the *right of legation*—the right to send and receive diplomatic representatives. The practice is ancient; history indicates that it was followed by the Egyptians at least 6000 years ago. Benjamin Franklin became our first foreign service officer when he was elected by the Continental Congress as our minister to France in 1778.

AMBASSADORS. Today the United States is represented by an ambassador stationed at the capital of each of the states with which we maintain diplomatic relations—that is, which the United States *recognizes.*[2] By 1981, American embassies were located in 143 different countries around the world.

---

[1] *International law* consists of those rules and principles followed by states in their dealings with one another. Its sources include treaties, decisions of international courts, reason, and custom, with treaties the most important source today.

[2] See page 406. An ambassador's official title is *Ambassador Extraordinary and Plenipotentiary.* When there is a vacancy in the office, or the ambassador is absent, the post is usually filled by a lesser-ranking foreign service officer. That officer, temporarily in charge of embassy affairs, is known as the *charge d'affaires.*

Anne Cox Chambers, U.S. Ambassador to Belgium, converses with two Belgians – an artist (at right) and a film critic (center). She had just accepted, as the President's representative in Belgium, an award for the naming of an American documentary film as the Film of the Year.

Ambassadors are appointed by the President, with Senate consent, and serve at the President's pleasure. Some of the posts are much-sought political plums; and there are many new appointments whenever there is a shift in the party in power in Washington. Too often, amateurs have been selected—usually because of their record of service in the President's party. Now, fortunately, most American ambassadors are career Foreign Service officers.

President Truman appointed the first woman as an ambassador, to Denmark, in 1949. And President Johnson named the first black (also a woman), as ambassador to Luxembourg in 1965. Now, several women, blacks, and other minority persons hold high rank in the Foreign Service.

Each American ambassador is the personal representative of the President of the United States, and reports to the President through the Secretary of State. Each must keep the President fully informed of events in the host country, negotiate diplomatic agreements, protect the rights of American citizens abroad, and do whatever else the best interests of the United States requires.

To perform these duties effectively, an ambassador must be on terms of friendly intimacy with the leaders of the country to which he or she is sent. An ambassador must be able to maintain cordial relationships with the peoples of that land, as well. A well-grounded knowledge of the language, history, customs, and culture also helps, of course.

At each embassy a *counselor* advises the ambassador on matters of international law and diplomatic practice and one or more *diplomatic secretaries* assist the ambassador. His or her staff also consists of several technical experts, clerks, interpreters, and others. The more responsible of these aides are drawn from the Foreign Service, but some are alien employees recruited on the scene. One or more *military attaches,* assigned from the Army and Air Force, are stationed at each embassy. In those nations which are sea powers, *naval attaches* are assigned, as well.

DIPLOMATIC IMMUNITY. In international law, every sovereign state is supreme within its own boundaries, and all persons and things found within its territory are subject to its jurisdiction.

Nonetheless, and as a major exception to that rule, ambassadors are regularly granted *diplomatic immunity.* That is, they are not subject to the laws of the state to which they are accredited. They cannot be arrested, sued, or taxed. Their official residences (embassies) cannot be entered or searched without their consent; and their official communications, papers, and other properties are similarly protected. This same immunity is normally extended to all other embassy personnel and to their dependents, as well.

The granting of diplomatic immunity is

intended to enhance the ability of each nation to conduct its foreign affairs—and, in turn, of all nations to do so. The practice does imply that diplomats will not abuse their privileged status, of course. If a host government finds a diplomat's conduct unacceptable, that diplomat may be declared *persona non grata* and expelled from the country. The mistreatment of diplomats can lead to a serious rupture in the relations between the countries involved.

Diplomatic immunity is a generally accepted and regularly honored practice. But there are occasional exceptions. The seizure of the American embassy in Iran in late 1979, and then the holding of 52 Americans as hostages for more than a year, is an outrageous illustration of that fact.

SPECIAL DIPLOMATS. In addition to the ambassadors regularly stationed in foreign capitals, those who hold certain other diplomatic posts are also given the rank of ambassador. For example, the American member of the North Atlantic Treaty (NATO) Council holds this rank; so, too, does the United States Representative to the UN in New York. On various occasions, individuals are appointed to the *personal* rank of ambassador to undertake special assignments from the President.

CONSULAR SERVICE. The Consular Service, part of the Foreign Service, is made up of officers who oversee the commercial interests of the United States abroad. We maintain about 130 consular offices in major cities throughout the world. Consular officers promote American trade and commerce abroad. They also enforce customs regulations of the United States, assist those who seek to enter this country, and help Americans who are abroad and in need of legal advice or other assistance.

Passports. *Passports* are certificates issued by states to identify their citizens who travel or reside abroad. They entitle their holders to the privileges accorded by international custom and treaty. Few states will admit persons who do not hold passports. No American may travel abroad without a valid passport—except to Mexico, Canada, and a few other nearby places.

The State Department's Passport Office issues some 3.5 million passports to American citizens each year. (Passports should not be confused with *visas.* The latter are permits to enter another state, and must be obtained from the country one wishes to enter. Most visas to enter this country are issued at American consulates abroad.)

The United States Embassy in Tehran, Iran, shortly after its unprecedented occupation by Iranian student militants early in November of 1979. The takeover of the Embassy, and the holding of U.S. personnel as hostages there, was in violation of the internationally accepted law of diplomatic immunity.

The Department of Defense

Just as the foreign policy of the United States is designed to preserve the nation's security, so, too, is its defense policy. Indeed, foreign policy and defense policy are but two sides of the same coin, each inseparably linked with the other.

The Framers of the Constitution stressed the importance of national defense by listing it in the Preamble as among the purposes for which the Constitution was written. And they placed additional emphasis upon it by mentioning it more often in the body of the Constitution than any other governmental function.

The War Powers. The Constitution makes defense a *national* function and virtually excludes the States from the field.[3] In several of its provisions it grants specific war powers to the Congress and to the President. Thus, Congress has the power to "declare war . . . and make rules concerning captures on land and water." It also possesses the power to "raise and support armies," to "provide and maintain a navy," and to "make rules for the government and regulation of the land and naval forces." And, as we know, the President is made "Commander in Chief of the army and navy of the United States, and of the militia of the several States, when called into the actual service of the United States."[4]

Civil Control of the Military. The Framers of the Constitution recognized the necessity for making provision for the nation's defense. But they also appreciated the dangers inherent in military power. Hence, they built into the Constitution a firm commitment to the rule of civilian control of the military. Thus, they gave extensive war powers to the Congress and made the President the Commander in Chief. By vesting "the power of the purse" in Congress they reinforced the insistence on civilian control. With its powers over money, Congress determines such basic military matters as the size of the armed forces, the funding available to them for pay purposes, training, equipment, and all other matters.[5]

We have adhered to the principle of civilian control throughout our history. It has been a dominant factor in the formulation of defense policy and, as well, in the establishment and staffing of the various agencies directly responsible for the execution of that policy. The point is clearly illustrated in a statutory restriction on the President's selection of a Secretary of Defense. That official cannot have served on active duty in any of the armed forces for a period of at least 10 years prior to assuming that office.

The nation's military forces are organized within the Department of Defense. The Department was created by Congress in 1947 and was originally known as the National Military Establishment. It was given its present title in 1949 and is the present-day successor to two long-established Cabinet-level departments—the

---

[3] Article I, Section 10. Clause 3 provides: "No State shall, without the consent of Congress . . . keep troops or ships of war, . . . or engage in war, unless actually invaded, or in such imminent danger as will not admit of delay." Each State does have a *militia* which it may use to keep the peace within its own borders. Each State's militia is legally separate from that of any other, but all are collectively "the militia of the United States." Congress has the power (Article I, Section 8, Clauses 15, 16) to "provide for calling forth the militia to execute the laws of the Union, suppress insurrections, and repel invasions," and to provide for organizing, arming, and disciplining it. Congress first delegated to the President the power to call the militia into federal service in 1795. In the National Defense Act of 1916 it defined the militia of the United States to include all able-bodied males between 17 and 45 years of age; it also declared the *organized* portion of the militia to be the *National Guard,* which is financed largely by federal funds and supervised by the Department of the Army.

[4] Article I, Section 8, Clauses, 11, 12, 13, and 14; Article II, Section 2, Clause 1.

[5] Congress is forbidden to appropriate funds for the Army for periods of longer than two years at a time (Article I, Section 8, Clause 12). Curiously, the Constitution does not apply the same kind of restriction to naval appropriations.

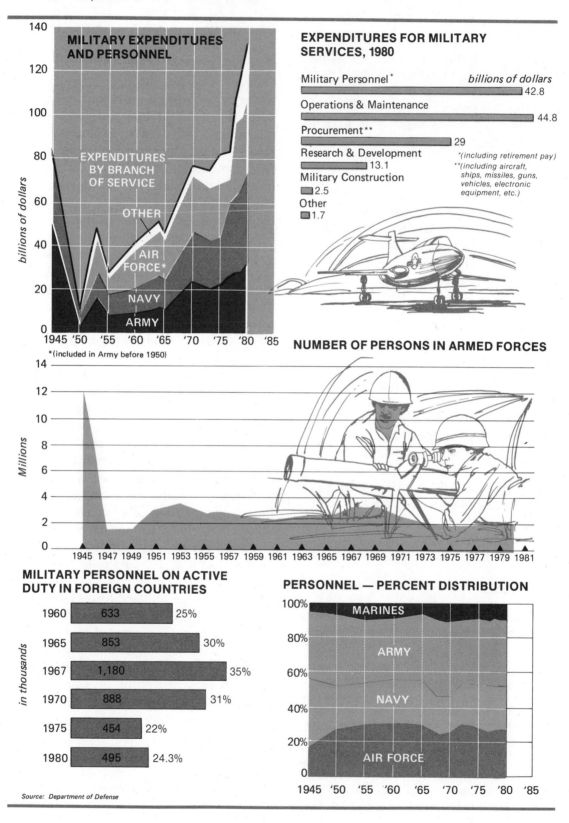

MILITARY EXPENDITURES AND PERSONNEL

billions of dollars

EXPENDITURES BY BRANCH OF SERVICE

OTHER

AIR FORCE*

NAVY

ARMY

1945 '50 '55 '60 '65 '70 '75 '80 '85

*(included in Army before 1950)

EXPENDITURES FOR MILITARY SERVICES, 1980

	billions of dollars
Military Personnel*	42.8
Operations & Maintenance	44.8
Procurement**	29
Research & Development	13.1
Military Construction	2.5
Other	1.7

*(including retirement pay)

**(including aircraft, ships, missiles, guns, vehicles, electronic equipment, etc.)

NUMBER OF PERSONS IN ARMED FORCES

Millions

1945 1947 1949 1951 1953 1955 1957 1959 1961 1963 1965 1967 1969 1971 1973 1975 1977 1979 1981

MILITARY PERSONNEL ON ACTIVE DUTY IN FOREIGN COUNTRIES

in thousands

Year	Number	Percent
1960	633	25%
1965	853	30%
1967	1,180	35%
1970	888	31%
1975	454	22%
1980	495	24.3%

Source: Department of Defense

PERSONNEL — PERCENT DISTRIBUTION

MARINES

ARMY

NAVY

AIR FORCE

1945 '50 '55 '60 '65 '70 '75 '80 '85

War Department, created by Congress in 1789, and the Navy Department, created in 1798. Within the Defense Department today are the three sub-Cabinet Departments of the Army, the Navy, and the Air Force.

Year after year, the Defense Department (DOD) accounts for a substantial slice of the federal budget. For fiscal year 1981, the nation's defense spending is expected to reach a record $160 billion—and total at least $170 billion in the following year.

The Secretary of Defense. The vast Department of Defense is headed by the Secretary of Defense. The Secretary is appointed from civilian life by the President, with the advice and consent of the Senate, and is always a prominent member of the President's official family.

Acting at the direction of the Commander in Chief, the Secretary has two major areas of responsibility: (1) the formulation and execution of the nation's defense policies and (2) the management of DOD.

The Secretary sits as a member of the critically important National Security Council, as we noted on page 390. And, of course, the Secretary of Defense is in virtually constant touch with the President, the Secretary of State, and all of the other top-level elements of the Government's national security structure.

CHIEF CIVILIAN AIDES. The Secretary of Defense's principal civilian assistant is the Deputy Secretary, who directs the day-to-day administration of the Department and becomes Acting Secretary in the Secretary's absence. Other top aides include several Assistant Secretaries; a General Counsel; the Secretaries of the Army, Navy, and Air Force; the Under Secretary for Policy, and the Under Secretary for Research and Engineering, who is the Secretary's scientific adviser and directs all space and other scientific research conducted by the armed forces.

CHIEF MILITARY AIDES. The Secretary of Defense's principal military advisers are the top-ranking officers in the armed services—the members of the Joint Chiefs of Staff. This group is composed of: the Chairman of the Joint Chiefs, the Army Chief of Staff, the Chief of Naval Operations, and the Air Force Chief of Staff. The Marine Corps Commandant attends all meetings of the Joint Chiefs and serves as a member whenever Marine Corps matters are considered.

THE ARMED FORCES POLICY COUNCIL. All of the Secretary of Defense's topmost advisers form the Armed Forces Policy Council. It consists of the Deputy Secretary, the Secretaries of the Army, the Navy, and the Air Force, the Under Secretaries for Policy and for Research and Engineering, and the members of the Joint Chiefs of Staff. As a group, the Council advises the Secretary of Defense on matters of broad policy relating to the armed forces and considers and reports on such other matters as the Secretary directs.

The Department of the Army. Among the three major services, the United States Army has primary responsibility for all military operations on land. Its major duties are to defend the United States against attack, defeat enemy land forces, seize and occupy enemy territory, train and equip its forces, and perform other missions assigned to it by the Commander in Chief.

DEPARTMENTAL ORGANIZATION. The Department of the Army is headed by the *Secretary of the Army*. The Army Secretary is subject to the direction and control of the President, directly subordinate to the Defense Secretary, selected by the President and Senate, and must be a civilian. The Under Secretary and four Assistant Secretaries are the Army Secretary's principal civilian aides. The key military adviser to the Secretary is the *Chief of Staff*, the Army's highest ranking officer. This officer commands the Army Staff and is directly responsible for the planning and execution of all Army operations.

THE ARMY. The Army of the United States includes all of the elements of the Regular Army, the Army National Guard, the Organized Reserves, and the Reserve Officers Training Corps (the ROTC).

The Regular Army is the nation's standing army and the heart of the land forces. Today, its strength is approximately 770,000 officers and enlisted personnel—professional soldiers and volunteers. The Regular Army is organized around a series of major commands, each of which involves either a broadly defined general function or a geographic area of operations.

Units of the Army. The infantry, artillery, and armored cavalry are the combat units of the land forces. The infantry's foot soldiers engage the enemy in direct small arms combat and hold conquered ground. The artillery supports the infantry, smashes enemy concentrations with its heavier guns, and provides antiaircraft cover. The armored cavalry also supports the infantry, using its tanks, other armored vehicles, and helicopters to spearhead assaults and breakthroughs and to oppose enemy counteroffensives.

Other units provide the services and supplies essential to the combat units. The infantry, artillery, and armored cavalry forces could not fight without the support of the signal, ordnance, chemical, quartermaster, engineer, intelligence, transportation, military police, and medical corps. Modern combat conditions often require that members of these units fight at a moment's notice alongside the regular combat troops.

The Department of the Navy. The United States Navy has primary responsibility for sea warfare and defense. Its major duties are to defend the nation through prompt and sustained combat at sea, defeat enemy naval forces, train and equip its own forces, furnish support for the opera-

tions of the other services, and perform other missions that may be assigned to it.

DEPARTMENTAL ORGANIZATION. The Department of the Navy is headed by the *Secretary of the Navy*—who, like the other service secretaries, is appointed by the President, is directly subordinate to the President and the Defense Secretary, and must be a civilian. The Under Secretary and three Assistant Secretaries are the other top civilians in the Department of the Navy.

The Chief of Naval Operations is the Secretary of the Navy's top naval adviser. The CNO is the Navy's highest ranking officer and is responsible for its use in war and its preparations and readiness for war. The Chief of Naval Operations has direct command of both the seagoing forces and the related shore units and facilities. The only naval unit not under the CNO's direct command is the Marine Corps.

THE NAVY. The United States Navy is composed of the Regular Navy (including the WAVES), the Marine Corps, the Naval Reserve, the Naval Air Reserve, the Marine Corps Reserve, and the Naval Reserve Officers Training Corps (NROTC). The Coast Guard, although at all times a part of the armed forces, operates within the Department of Transportation. For administrative purposes, the Navy has divided the nation and its possessions into seven naval districts. Today (1981), there are some 530,000 officers and enlisted personnel in the United States Navy.

THE MARINE CORPS. The United States Marine Corps is a part of the Navy but does not operate under the command of the Chief of Naval Operations. Rather, it serves under the Commandant of the Marine Corps who is directly responsible to the Secretary of the Navy for the efficiency, readiness, and performance of the Corps and its reserve.

The 185,000 Marines act as a land force for the Navy, secure and fortify land bases from which the fleet and the Navy and

Keeping military equipment in good running condition is a continual and vital function, one which is essential to the movement of army supplies and personnel.

Marine air arms can operate, and provide detachments for service on armed naval vessels. While the Marine Corps is organized much like the Army, it is almost entirely a combat force. For example, it does not have its own medical units; the doctors and others who provide medical aid to the Marine combat units are naval personnel assigned to that duty.

The Department of the Air Force. The United States Air Force has primary responsibility for military air operations. Its major duties are to defend the United States against air attack, defeat enemy air forces, strike military and related targets deep within enemy territory, provide combat and transport support for land and naval operations, train and equip its forces, and perform other missions assigned by the President.

DEPARTMENTAL ORGANIZATION. The Department of the Air Force is headed by the *Secretary of the Air Force.* This official serves under the President and the Secretary of Defense, is appointed by the President with Senate consent, and must be a civilian. The Secretary's top civilian aides are the Under Secretary and three Assistant Secretaries.

The Air Force *Chief of Staff* is the Secretary's principal adviser in all military matters, commands the top-level Air Staff and is directly responsible for the planning and execution of all Air Force operations.

THE AIR FORCE. The United States Air Force includes all military aviation not assigned to the other services. It is composed of the Regular Air Force (including the WAF), the Air Force Reserve, the Air Force ROTC, and the Air National Guard. The USAF performs its duties through twelve operational commands in this country and elsewhere across the globe. Its aircraft include heavy, light, dive, and attack bombers; conventional and jet fighters and interceptors; and transport, hospital, weather, and reconnaissance planes. The Regular Air Force has a strength of approximately 560,000 today, including officers and enlisted personnel.

THE USAF TODAY. The nation's overall defense strategy places its major emphasis on air power. This is not to say that the Army and the Navy are relegated to minor roles—far from it. But it is the Air Force we look to as the first line of defense against sudden enemy attack. No matter where the attack may occur, the Air Force will almost certainly strike the first counter blows against the aggressor and the aggressor's home bases.

The striking power of the Air Force today is truly awesome, and it is being added to and improved upon constantly. Very few of its combat planes currently on the line were in use as recently as the Korean War. The mammoth, eight-engined B-52's are the backbone of its strategic—long-range—bomber fleet today. Just *one* of these planes carries a nuclear bomb load with more destructive power than that packed by *all* the bombs that were dropped by both sides throughout all of World War II. The immense, incalculable striking power of these planes is spread across the globe in a state of constant combat readiness.

All American fighter and interceptor aircraft are now armed with air-to-air missiles for use against enemy planes and missiles. All tactical (short-range attack and dive) bombers also carry missiles for use against enemy ground targets.

Like the other services, the Air Force has several types of surface-launched missiles. It has the major responsibility for developing and firing military missiles, espe-cially the long-range intercontinental (ICBM) and intermediate-range (IRBM) ballistic missiles. Many of its newest missiles can seek out and destroy fast flying targets even hundreds of miles away.

Other Agencies with Responsibilities in Foreign Affairs

We have already suggested that several federal agencies in addition to the Departments of State and Defense, are involved, to a greater or lesser degree, in the field of foreign affairs. A few quick illustrations of this point: The Immigration and Naturalization Service, in the Department of Justice, deals with those who come here from abroad. The Customs Service, in the Treasury Department, deals with goods imported from other nations and combats international smuggling operations. The Coast Guard, in the Department of Transportation, maintains an iceberg patrol in the North Atlantic to protect the shipping of all nations. The Public Health Service, within the Department of Health and Human Services, works with a number of UN agencies and other governments on disease and other health problems in many parts of the world. With just these few illustra-

Cadets in class at the Air Force Academy. Upon completing a demanding course of study and training, they will become commissioned officers in the Air Force.

tions it should be fairly obvious that such a listing could be extended for several pages.

In fact, it does not stretch the point too much to say that *all* federal agencies are in some way or another involved with our foreign affairs. This is so because it has become increasingly difficult over recent years to draw clear and distinct lines between the nation's foreign affairs, on the one hand, and matters purely domestic, on the other.

But for now we will turn our attention to a number of independent government agencies with the most direct involvements in the nation's foreign (including its defense) concerns.

The International Communications Agency. The International Communications Agency is essentially a propaganda agency. It operates the "Voice of America" and a number of other projects to promote the image of this country abroad. In cooperation with the State Department it broadcasts the official views of our Government, presents news and feature programs on the American way of life, and attempts to promote our friendship with other peoples. Its shortwave broadcasts go out from New York in some 40 languages through transmitters in the United States and relay stations in Manila, Honolulu, and Munich. It also operates a floating transmitter to help beam broadcasts to people behind the Iron Curtain.

Motion pictures, libraries, information centers, personal contact, publications, and the exchange of persons also are used to promote international understanding and good will. For example, we are engaged in a vast international student exchange program. Thousands of foreign students are now studying in American colleges and observing various phases of our national life. At the same time, thousands of Americans are studying abroad.

The Central Intelligence Agency. The super-secret CIA is the nation's chief "cloak-and-dagger" agency. It was created by Congress in 1947 and functions under the direction of the National Security Council (page 390). It coordinates the intelligence-gathering activities of all of the many agencies which operate in the areas of national security and foreign policy. The CIA is also responsible for analyzing and evaluating the data collected by these other agencies.

The CIA is far more than simply a vehicle of coordination and evaluation, however. Its Director is appointed by the President with Senate consent, and its top-level staff operates at the very heart of the foreign policy-making process. It provides the President with regular briefings and advises the chief executive and the NSC on the most secret and sensitive of matters involved in the nation's foreign relations.

The CIA conducts its own intelligence-gathering operations and its covert activities reportedly span the full range of espionage. Among its more notable—*known*—involvements, it sponsored a successful revolution in Guatemala in 1954 and the abortive Bay of Pigs invasion of Cuba in 1961. It was extensively involved in Southeast Asia long before any American troops were committed there and it has been reputedly involved in many other places and events, before and since, throughout the world.

But the nature of its work, its methods, the results it achieves, and the contents of its reports are shrouded in deepest secrecy. Even the Congress has generally shied away from more than a cursory check on its activities and only a few key members are closely informed about them. Indeed, its annual operating funds—which are apparently well over the $2 billion level today—are camouflaged somewhere in the federal budget each year.

When Congress established the CIA it recognized the need for such an organization in today's troubled world. But at the same time it recognized the dangers inherent in the existence of such an agency. It saw the dangers of an agency operating in closely guarded secrecy, shielded from visibility and public scrutiny, freed from the usual congressional oversight to which other federal agencies are subject. Therefore, it expressly denied to the CIA *any* authority to conduct any police or intelligence activities within the limits of the United States itself.

That the CIA has not always obeyed that command has become all too clear in the past few years. Responding to widespread allegations in 1975, President Ford appointed the Commission on CIA Activities within the United States. Chaired by Vice President Rockefeller, the Commission conducted a five-month probe. Its report documented several instances of illegal domestic activity—extending back for years, and involving such matters as mail intercepts, wiretapping, the improper use of federal income tax returns, break-ins, and the infiltration of civil rights, antiwar, and other protest groups. And the Commission's findings were reinforced and enlarged upon by two congressional committee investigations.

Those airings of "the Company's" work and its methods were no doubt long overdue. Many share the hope that the agency has now been pushed back within its proper—and its quite necessary—sphere, and will never again overstep its bounds. The CIA has often insisted that that hope has now become fact.

The National Aeronautics and Space Administration (NASA). Since the days of ancient Greece, people have dreamed of conquering space. However, it was not until October 4, 1957, that the Soviet Union formally opened the space age with the launching of the first satellite, Sputnik I. The first United States satellite, Explorer I, was catapulted into orbit on January 31, 1958. From that date on, all kinds of satellites—many including men (and one woman)—have been thrust into outer space by the two superpowers.

The list of space accomplishments became long and fantastic in the 1960's, topped by the landing on the moon made by the American astronauts, Neil A. Armstrong and Colonel Edwin E. Aldrin, on July 20, 1969. The military importance of space endeavors can hardly be exaggerated. But other purposes, such as weather forecasting, communications, scientific discoveries, and the mapping of the earth's surfaces have been significantly advanced through space activities.

NASA, an independent executive agency, was established by Congress in 1958. It is headed by an Administrator appointed by the President and Senate and directly responsible to the Chief Executive. It conducts a wide range of programs at its research centers and laboratories throughout the country. For example, the training of astronauts and the development, testing, and flight operations of manned spacecraft are directed by the Lyndon B. Johnson Space Center located in Houston. Propulsion and power plant research is concentrated at the Lewis Research Center in Cleveland. Most of the work on the guidance and control of space vehicles is conducted at the Ames Research Center at Moffett Field, near San Francisco. Flight evaluation tests of such research aircraft as the X-15 are carried on at the Dryden Research Center located at Edwards, California. The development of launch vehicles, the missiles necessary to thrust payloads into space, is conducted at the George C. Marshall Space Flight Center at Huntsville, Alabama. Most of NASA's missile and satellite launchings occur at Cape Kennedy in Florida, although some also occur at Vandenberg Air Force Base in California and the Wallops Station on Wallops Island, a rocket and missile testing site which is situated off the coast of Virginia. Deep space flight operations—for example, the Mars probes—are the particular responsibility of the Jet Propulsion Laboratory, located near Pasadena.

The United States Arms Control and Disarmament Agency. For nearly a generation now, the world has lived with the continuing threat of a nuclear holocaust which could, quite literally, destroy all forms of life on this planet. That awesome fact has given new and compelling urgency to the ancient hope for the day when, in the words of Isaiah, people:

> shall beat their swords into plowshares, and their spears into pruning hooks;

and the day when:

> nation shall not lift up sword against nation, neither shall they learn war any more.

The USACDA is responsible for the preparation and management of American participation in international arms limitation and disarmament negotiations. Its Director also serves as the President's princi-

pal adviser in all matters involved in those areas.

A major share of the Agency's work to date has centered on nuclear test ban and disarmament negotiations which have been proceeding intermittently since 1958. We shall return to this critical subject in the next chapter.

The Selective Service System. Through most of our history, as today, the armed forces have relied on voluntary enlistments to fill their ranks. But over most of the past generation, from 1940 to 1973, a system of military conscription was a major source of military personnel. Today (1981) the personnel needs of the armed forces are again being met on an all-volunteer basis. The draft, administered by the Selective Service System, exists only on a standby basis.

Conscription has a long history in this country. Several of the colonies and later at

At left: *Space Shuttle Orbiter* Enterprise *first cleared its 747 carrier aircraft high above the California desert in 1977.*

At bottom: *The* Enterprise *after it completed its first free flight.*

least nine States required all able-bodied males to serve in their militia. However, proposals made by the first Secretary of War, Henry Knox, and endorsed by George Washington, for a national draft were rejected by Congress.

Both the North and the South did use a limited conscription system during the Civil War. It was not until 1917, however, that a system of national conscription was used in this country, even in wartime. More than 2,800,000 of the 4,700,000 men who served in World War I were drafted under the terms of the Selective Service Act of 1917.

The nation's first peacetime draft was begun under the Selective Service and Training Act of 1940, as World War II raged in Europe. Although voluntary enlistments were accepted after the United States entered the war, 10,022,000 of the 16,353,000 Americans who were in uniform in World War II entered the service under the terms of the 1940 draft law.

The World War II draft was ended in 1947. Almost immediately, however, the crises of the postwar period persuaded Congress to revive it, in the Selective Service Act of 1948. The present version of the law is the Military Selective Service Act of 1971. Altogether, from 1948 to 1973, nearly 5 million young men were drafted for service in the armed forces—most notably during the Korean War and, later, the war in Viet Nam.

Mounting criticisms of compulsory military service, fed by increasing opposition to Viet Nam policy, led many Americans to demand an end to the draft in the latter 1960's. Fewer than 30,000 men were drafted by the armed forces in 1972, and the draft was suspended entirely in 1973.

But the draft, and its administrative arm, the Selective Service System, are still on the books for reactivation if, at any time, the nation's security should demand that such action be taken.

The law imposes a military obligation on all males in the United States between ages 18½ and 26. Over the years in which the draft in fact operated, it was largely conducted through local selective service boards—hundreds of them, throughout the country. All young men were required to register for the draft at age 18, and those local draft boards then "selected" those who were to serve in the armed forces.

The registration requirement is now back in place. President Carter reactivated it in 1980. All young men—but not women—are required to sign up as they reach their 18th birthdays.[6]

The Veterans Administration. More than 30 million men and women—one out of every seven Americans—are veterans of the nation's armed forces. In gratitude for their service, Congress now appropriates approximately $23 billion a year for a vast array of veterans benefit programs.

A generous concern for veterans has long been an established part of the nation's public policy. From its first session in 1789 Congress has enacted literally hundreds of statutes reflecting that concern. In fact, the history of veterans benefits dates back to early colonial days. In 1636 the Pilgrim Fathers decreed:

> If any man shalbee sent fourth as a souldier and shall return maimed, he shalbee maintained completely by the Collonie during his life.

The colonies and later the States provided pensions to disabled militiamen, and most made grants of land to veterans, as well. The Second Continental Congress and then the Congress under the Articles enacted legislation to provide pensions to veterans of the Revolutionary War.

By 1819 the scope of federal veterans programs had reached such proportions

---

[6] The President's power to order the induction of men into the armed forces expired June 30, 1973. If the draft is ever to be reactivated, Congress must first act to renew that presidential authority.

The veteran population today numbers more than 30 million men and women, largely the result of World War II and the conflicts in Korea and Viet Nam. Shown here are landing craft used in D-Day operations during World War II.

that Congress found it necessary to create an agency—the Pension Bureau—to administer them. That agency has been continued in some form ever since. Its present-day descendant is the Veterans Administration.

The VA is an independent agency headed by an Administrator appointed by the President and Senate. With a workforce of a bit more than 200,000 doctors, dentists, nurses, lawyers, counselors, accountants, and other personnel, it is the third largest of all federal agencies today—ranking behind only the Defense Department and the Postal Service.

The VA provides medical, dental, and hospital care to needy veterans and to those with service-connected disabilities. To do so, it maintains more than 170 hospitals and also operates a nationwide system of clinics, domiciliaries, and other facilities.

More than half of the VA's annual budget—that is, over $12 billion a year—is spent for various kinds of pensions and compensations to veterans and their dependents or survivors. The VA also operates the world's largest life insurance business, with the total value of policies in force today in excess of $35 billion.

World War II produced a huge growth in the veteran population, of course. Some 16,353,000 persons served in the armed forces during that conflict, more than in all of the nation's other wars combined. And it brought a vast expansion in veterans aid programs, as well. To the traditional programs centering around pensions, compensations, medical hospitals, and domiciliary care, the Congress added a whole new series of aids: "readjustment benefits." Their purpose was to help *all* veterans, including those who were neither disabled nor destitute, to make a successful transition back into civilian life. These benefits were also intended to make up for the occupational, educational, and other opportunities veterans had missed because of their military service.

The Servicemen's Readjustment Act of 1944, popularly known as the GI Bill of Rights, provided four new major benefits for World War II veterans. They provided: (1) special assistance in seeking a job in civilian life, (2) a maximum of twelve months of unemployment compensation, (3) a maximum of thirty-six months of college or other educational or vocational training at government expense, and (4) VA-guaranteed loans for the purchase of a home, farm, or business.

These programs were later extended to veterans of the Korean War under the terms of the Korean GI Bill. And, in the Cold War GI Bill of 1966, they were made available to all those persons who served in the armed forces for more than 180 days at any time after January 31, 1955. Included, of course, were veterans of the conflict in Viet Nam.

SUMMARY

The importance of our foreign relations and of the manner in which they are conducted cannot be overstated. The ways in which the might and influence of the United States are used in today's "one world" affect the fate of people everywhere.

Although Congress has important foreign policy powers, it is the President who is the nation's chief diplomat; the Secretary of State and the Department of State are the President's "right hand" in the formulation and conduct of foreign policy. Under the Secretary of State, the State Department is organized on a geographic and functional basis. Our diplomatic agents abroad look to the Secretary of State and the staff in Washington for information and instructions. The Foreign Service, from ambassadors, ministers, and consular officers down to the lowliest clerks, represent the goals and serve the interests of the United States in other countries.

Today we maintain huge and powerful defense forces both at home and abroad in order to (1) defend the nation against foreign attack and (2) deter aggression. The Constitution makes defense a national function and excludes the States from the field, except to the extent of maintaining militia. Civilian control of the military is maintained through Congress, with its several war powers, and the President, who is Commander in Chief of the Armed Forces.

The Department of Defense is headed by the Secretary of Defense, who is assisted by a number of civilian aides, including the Secretaries of the Army, the Navy, and the Air Force, and by the Joint Chiefs of Staff and the Armed Forces Policy Council. Included within the Department of Defense are the three non-Cabinet Departments of the Army, the Navy, and the Air Force. The Army has primary responsibility for all military operations on land, the Navy (including the Marine Corps) on the sea, and the Air Force in the air.

Many governmental departments and agencies have foreign policy responsibilities in addition to the Departments of State and Defense. The International Communications Agency conducts programs to inform people in other nations of the American way of life and attempts to promote friendship with other nations. The Arms Control and Disarmament Agency works with other countries in the pursuit of arms reductions and disarmament treaties. The Central Intelligence Agency has the responsibility of securing information from many sources, which is necessary to the shaping of foreign policies. The National Aeronautics and Space Administration directs most of the federal government's nonmilitary aeronautical and space research and exploration. The Selective Service System is now a standby agency, maintaining the nation's draft machinery. The present array of benefit programs for the nation's veterans is administered by the Veterans Administration.

Concept Development

Questions for Review

1. In what ways may it be said that today we live in "one world"?

2. In what ways may it be said, on the other hand, that we do not?

3. What is the Secretary of State's primary responsibility?

4. Why is the State Department organized along geographic and functional lines?

5. What are the principal duties of an ambassador?

6. Of what in overall terms is a nation's foreign policy composed?

7. Why is it an error to conceive of the formulation and execution of foreign policy only in terms of the President and the State Department?

8. For what two basic purposes does the United States maintain its defense forces?

9. Who is directly responsible under the President for the formulation and execution of the nation's defense policies?

10. What are the major functions of each of the subordinate departments within the Defense Department?

11. Who is the top-ranking military officer in each of the armed services and what role does that officer play?

12. What is the status of the Selective Service System today?

13. What is the primary function of each of these agencies: the ICA, CIA, NASA, USACDA?

14. What has been and is the general character of the nation's concern for the welfare of its veterans?

For Further Inquiry

1. It has often been noted that the only checks upon the exercise of power by the National Government in the field of foreign affairs are political, not legal, in character. Do you think that this is either wise or proper in a nation with a governmental system founded upon the principles of popular sovereignty and limited government?

2. Constitutionally, the executive and legislative branches share power in the field of foreign affairs. What factors have led, in fact, to presidential supremacy in the field?

3. While he was President, Dwight D.

Eisenhower remarked: "Americans, indeed all free men, remember that in the final choice a soldier's pack is not so heavy a burden as a prisoner's chains." How would you explain his comment?

4. What basic arguments can be advanced in defense of and in opposition to the present "all-volunteer military manpower policy"?

5. It has been estimated that the NASA program that resulted in the moon landings of 1969 cost the nation at least $25 billion. Do you think that that huge sum should in fact have been spent for such a purpose? Should it have been spent for some other purpose instead?

Suggested Activities

1. Write a report on our foreign relations during the term of a particular Secretary of State.

2. Invite a person in the Foreign Service or a former Foreign Service officer to speak to the class on career opportunities in the Foreign Service. (Descriptive material, including sample questions from the Foreign Service entrance examination, can be obtained from the Director, Office of Public Programs, Bureau of Public Affairs, Department of State, Washington, D.C., 20520.)

3. Draw up a list of as many examples as you can of the ways in which the content and conduct of the nation's foreign policies are reflected in the everyday life of your community.

4. Invite a qualified veteran or present member of the United States Armed Forces to speak to the class on the general subject of military service.

5. Write an essay on one of the following themes: military service as an obligation of citizenship, the significance of civilian control of the military in a democracy, or the assets and liabilities of interservice rivalries.

6. Stage a debate or class forum on one of the following questions: (1) *Resolved,* That the Congress should reactivate the selective service system. (2) *Resolved,* That Congress should provide for universal military training.

Suggested Reading

Bobrow, David B., *et al., Understanding Foreign Policy Decisions: The Chinese Case.* Free Press, 1979.

Caraley, Demetrius (ed.), *The Making of American Domestic and Foreign Policy.* Dabor, 1979.

Clarke, Duncan L., *Politics and Arms Control.* Free Press, 1979.

Hughes, Barry B., *The Domestic Content of American Foreign Policy.* Freeman, 1978.

Kegley, Charles W. and Wittkopf, Eugene R., *American Foreign Policy: Pattern and Process.* St. Martin's Press, 1979.

Korb, Lawrence J., *The Fall and Rise of the Pentagon: American Defense Policies of the 1970's.* Greenwood, 1979.

Lefever, Ernest W. and Godson, Roy, *The C.I.A. and the American Ethic: The Unfinished Debate.* Ethics and Public Policy Center, 1980.

Spanier, John and Uslaner, Eric M., *How American Foreign Policy Is Made.* Praeger, 1978.

Stoessinger, John G., *Crusaders and Pragmatists: Movers of American Foreign Policy.* Norton, 1979.

Thompson, W. Scott (ed.), *National Security in the 1980s: From Weakness to Strength.* Institute for Contemporary Studies, 1980.

Yost, Ambassador Charles, *History and Memory: A Statesman's Perceptions of the 20th Century.* Norton, 1980.

American Foreign Policy

Today, we are faced with the preeminent fact that, if civilization is to survive, we must cultivate the science of human relationships—the ability of all peoples, of all kinds, to live together and work together, in the same world, at peace.

FRANKLIN DELANO ROOSEVELT

■ How can the United States best provide for and maintain its own security?

■ Has American foreign policy served well the national interests of the United States?

■ Why has not the United Nations played a more direct role in advancing international peace and security during the post World War II era?

■ Why should (or should not) the United States grant political independence to all of its territorial possessions as rapidly as that goal can be accomplished?

Today—as, indeed, through all of our history—the foreign policy of this country is directed toward one constant and overriding end: the maintenance of the security of the United States. Surely, then, no matter can be of greater moment to the American people than the nature and the content of American foreign policy. In this chapter we survey that policy—in terms both of its historical development and its contemporary shape.

The Early Years

From its beginnings and for a period of 150 years this nation's posture in international affairs was characterized by a policy of *isolationism*—by a refusal to become generally involved in the affairs of the rest of the world. Isolationism was born in the earliest years of our history. President George Washington, in his Farewell Address in 1796, reminded Americans that:

Europe has a set of primary interests, which to us have none, or a very remote relation. Hence she must be engaged in frequent controversies, the causes of which are essentially foreign to our concerns. Hence, therefore, it must be unwise in us to implicate ourselves, by artificial ties, in the ordinary vicissitudes of her politics, or the ordinary combinations or collisions of her friendships or enmities.

He advised the young republic to have "as little political connection as possible" with foreign nations—"to steer clear of permanent alliances with any portion of the foreign world." In 1801 Jefferson added to Washington's admonition his own warning against "entangling alliances."

At the time, and for decades to come, isolation seemed a wise policy: the United States was a new and relatively weak nation, with problems of its own, a continent to explore and settle, and two oceans to separate it from the rest of the world. The policy did not demand a *complete* insulation, however. From the first, the United States accepted the fact of its existence as a member of the family of nations—exchanging diplomatic representatives, making treaties, building an extensive foreign commerce, and otherwise participating in world affairs.

We began our westward expansion, and at the same time the elimination of European influence from this continent, almost at once. The Louisiana Purchase in 1803 embraced all of the vast area drained by the Mississippi and at a stroke doubled the size of the country. With the Florida Purchase of 1819 we completed our continental expansion to the south.

The *Monroe Doctrine,* proclaimed by James Monroe in a message to Congress in 1823, gave new expression to the policy of isolationism. A wave of revolutions had swept Latin America, destroying the old Spanish and Portuguese empires. The prospect that other European powers would seek to aid those nations to recover their lost possessions posed a threat to our own security and a challenge to our economic interests.

President Monroe declared the American intention to remain out of the affairs of Europe. But he also warned the nations of Europe—including Russia, then in control of Alaska—that the United States would regard:

> any attempt on their part to extend their system to any portion of this hemisphere as dangerous to our peace and safety.

The Monroe Doctrine is not law; rather, it is a self-defense policy—a policy of "America for the Americans." It is a policy that opposes any non-American encroachment on the independence of any country in the Western Hemisphere. It has been supported by each Congress and every President for a century and a half. At first, most Latin Americans paid little attention to the Monroe Doctrine. They knew that it was the Royal Navy and Great Britain's interest in their trade rather than the influence of the United States and Monroe's paper pronouncement that protected them. Later, as the United States became more powerful, Latin Americans came to regard it as a selfish policy. They felt that we were more concerned with our own security and commercial fortune than with their independence. Happily, matters have taken a brighter turn in recent decades, as we shall see.

Continued Territorial Expansion

While the United States remained aloof from the affairs of Europe, we continued to fill out the continent. Texas was annexed in 1845. We obtained the Oregon Country by treaty with Great Britain in 1846. Mexico ceded California and the land between after its defeat in the Mexican War of 1846–1848. The southwestern limits of the United States were rounded out by the Gadsden Purchase in 1853. In that year we bought from Mexico a strip of territory, in what is now the southern parts of Arizona and New Mexico, as the best rail route to the Pacific.

In 1867 we purchased Alaska from Russia to become a colonial power. In that same year the Monroe Doctrine got its first real test. While we were beset with conflict at home, Napoleon III had enthroned Prince Maximilian of Austria as Emperor of Mexico. We backed the Mexicans in forcing the withdrawal of France and the downfall of the Maximilian regime.

By W. A. Rogers in *New York Herald*, December, 1902

"THAT'S A LIVE WIRE, GENTLEMEN!"

United States Becomes a World Power

The United States emerged as a first-class world power just before the end of the nineteenth century. American feeling against Spain's mistreatment of its colonial possessions in the Caribbean had produced an explosive situation. When the *U.S.S. Maine* was mysteriously sunk in Havana Harbor on February 15, 1898, the United States and Spain went to war. The actual fighting of the Spanish-American War lasted only four months. With Spain decisively defeated, we gained the Philippines and Guam in the Pacific and Puerto Rico in the Caribbean. Cuba became independent, under American protection. We also annexed the Hawaiian Islands.

By 1900, the United States had become a colonial power with interests extending across the continent, to Alaska and the Arctic, to the tip of Latin America, and clear across the Pacific to the Philippines.

The Good Neighbor Policy

Our relations with Latin America have ebbed and flowed. The Monroe Doctrine has always served two purposes: (1) it has guaranteed the independence of Latin America, and (2) it has protected our position in the New World.

The threat of European intervention, which gave rise to the doctrine, declined in the last half of the nineteenth century. It was replaced by problems within the hemisphere. Political instability, revolutions, unpaid debts, and injuries to citizens and property of the United States and other countries plagued Latin America.

Under the Roosevelt Corollary of 1904 the United States began to police the Western Hemisphere. For example, in 1902 British and German ships blockaded the Venezuelan coast to force that country to pay debts it owed. The United States stepped in and forced a settlement. Carrying a "big stick," the United States used

464 / *Chapter 19*

marines to police customhouses and trouble spots throughout Central America. We stabilized political and financial conditions, settled boundary disputes, protected foreign lives and property, paid off foreign debts through customs collection, and generally maintained order. In 1903 Panama revolted and became independent of Colombia, with our blessings. In the same year we gained the right to construct a canal across the Panamanian Isthmus, which opened in 1914. In 1917 we purchased the Virgin Islands from Denmark to help guard the Panama Canal. Latin Americans were resentful and suspicious of our actions, even though they benefited greatly. They complained about "Yankee imperialism" and "dollar diplomacy."

In the late 1920's and early 1930's our Latin-American policies took a decisive turn. We began a conscious effort to "win friends and influence people" to the south. The Roosevelt Corollary was replaced with Franklin Roosevelt's Good Neighbor Policy. New life was breathed into the Pan American Union, first formed in 1890 and now known as the Organization of American States (OAS).

Today we and most of our Latin-American neighbors are partners in "hemispheric solidarity." The central proviso in the Monroe Doctrine—the warning against foreign encroachments in this hemisphere—is now enshrined in the Rio Treaty and is enforced by both the United States *and* the OAS. That the principle remains a vital part of American foreign policy was made abundantly clear to the Soviet Union during the Cuban missile crisis in 1962.

The Open Door in China

While American foreign policy interests were directed primarily toward Europe and Latin America in the first century of the nation's history, we were also concerned in the Far East. Forty-five years before the United States acquired territory in the far Pacific, Admiral Matthew C. Perry had opened Japan to American trade (1854). In 1899 we found our commercial interests in the Orient seriously threatened. Great Britain, France, Germany, and Japan were on the verge of grabbing slices of the coast of China as their own private trading preserves. Secretary of State John Hay announced American insistence on an "open door" to all nations trading with China and, at the same time, our insistence that

Theodore Roosevelt salutes the American flag from the platform of a railroad car during an inspection-tour of work underway in the Panama Canal Zone.

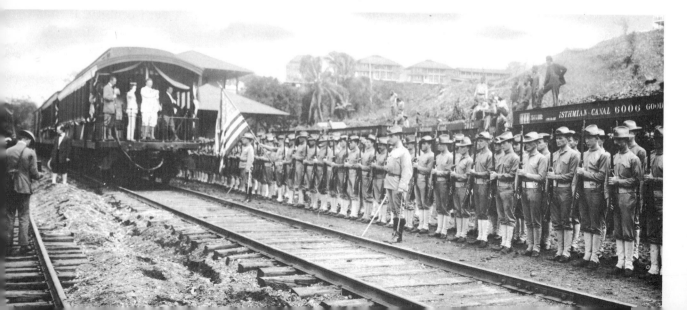

China's independence and sovereignty over its own territory be preserved.

The other powers came to accept the American position, although our relations with Japan worsened from then until the climax at Pearl Harbor in 1941. Strong Sino-American ties developed over the years through World War II. But when the communists came to power in 1949 relations plummeted. For nearly 30 years the United States and the People's Republic of China refused to recognize one another.

However, the People's Republic undertook a new role in world affairs when it assumed China's seat in the UN in 1971. And with President Nixon's historic visit to Peking in 1972 it became clear that the two nations were seeking a new relationship. Preliminary diplomatic contacts were begun with the exchange of "liaison officers" in 1973.

At last, the realities of world politics have led the two powers to a full-fledged relationship. The United States and the People's Republic formally recognized one another on January 1, 1979.

World War I and the Return to Isolationism

Germany's submarine campaign against American shipping forced the United States out of its isolationist cocoon in 1917. We entered World War I to "make the world safe for democracy."

After the defeat of Germany and the Central Powers, however, we retreated from the involvements brought on by the war. We refused to join the League of Nations, conceived by President Woodrow Wilson. Europe's problems and those of the rest of the world, so many Americans thought, were no concern of ours.

The rise of Mussolini in Italy, of Hitler in Germany, and of the militarists in Japan cast a dark cloud on the horizon. But for 20 years following World War I we continued to "wrap our two oceans around us."

World War II

It took the coming of World War II to awaken us finally and fully to the fallacies of isolationism in the modern world. Most Americans were pro-Ally at the start of the war in 1939, but our policy was to stay out of the war if at all possible. While the official position of the United States was one of neutrality, large scale aid was nonetheless provided to the Allies through such devices as the Lend-Lease Act. Under that 1941 law the President was authorized to "sell, transfer title to, exchange, lease, lend, or otherwise dispose of defense articles" to any countries judged vital to our own security.

With the sudden Japanese attack on Pearl Harbor, December 7, 1941, all thoughts of neutrality vanished. From then until the war ended in 1945, we fought side by side with our Allies in Europe and the Pacific. Our forces fought and defeated the Axis Powers (Germany, Italy, and Japan) on battlefields around the world. During the war we were the "arsenal of democracy." Through Lend-Lease our allies received nearly $50 billion in food, munitions, medicines, clothing, and other supplies.

American Foreign Policy Today

The years since 1945 have seen a fundamental change in the place and the role of the United States in world affairs. And that historic shift has been marked by major changes in the content of this nation's foreign policy.

Within the span of only a few years, the United States grew from a position as *one* of the world's major powers to its present place as *the* responsible leader of the free nations of the world. From the isolationism of former years, the basic thrust of American foreign policy has become one of global, full-scale participation in international affairs. But the continuing, overall goal of our foreign policy remains as it has throughout our history: the maintenance of our national security. We hope, pray, and work for peace. But we recognize the inescapable fact that there can be no lasting peace for us unless and until there is a just and lasting peace between all nations and for all people.

While we strive for peace, we also recognize another inescapable fact. The years since World War II have taught us that we can remain free and we can work for a just and lasting peace only so long as we remain strong. The aspects of our foreign policy now to be outlined are aimed at achieving the overall goal of that policy.

The Policy of Deterrence. One of the basic planks in current American foreign policy is that of *deterrence*—that is, the policy of making ourselves and our allies so strong that our very strength will deter aggression. President Reagan has put that policy in these words:

> We are not a warlike people. Quite the opposite. We always seek to live in peace. We resort to force infrequently. . . . But neither are we naive or foolish. We know only too well that war comes not when the forces of freedom are strong, but when they are weak. It is then that tyrants are tempted.

In effect, we have taken a page from our own revolutionary history: "Put your trust in God, my boys, but keep your powder dry."

Peace through Collective Security and the United Nations. We live in "one world" in the sense that no nation can live in peace and prosperity while others are at war or in want. Hence, *collective security*—the preserving of international order through the united efforts of free nations—has become a cornerstone in our foreign policy. Therefore, in 1945 we were determined not to repeat the basic error of 1919–1920 when we refused to join the

League of Nations. We took the lead in creating the United Nations, dedicated "to save succeeding generations from the scourge of war . . . and to maintain international peace and security."

Through every available means, we have sought and seek ways to lessen international tensions and to bring the world closer to peace. Thus, we have proposed steps to strengthen the UN. We have made continuing efforts to achieve an effective disarmament agreement, one which contains effective provisions for inspection and control to insure that it will be observed by all nations. We have given wholehearted support to the improvement of international law. We have promoted cultural exchange programs with the Soviet Union, the People's Republic of China, and other nations. We have pioneered the development and sharing of the peaceful uses of the atom.

In our search for collective security we have also made a number of *regional alliances* (mutual defense pacts) with several friendly nations around the world. See the map on page 473.

Resisting Communist Aggression. Another pillar of our policy is that of resistance to communist aggression. As President, General Eisenhower stated the root of our policy:

> The threat to our safety, and to the hope of a peaceful world, can be simply stated: It is communist imperialism.

We had hoped to work with the Russians through the UN to build the peace after World War II. It was soon clear, however, that the Communists had not abandoned their plans of world domination. At the Big Three conferences at Yalta and Potsdam in 1945, Stalin had guaranteed free elections in occupied East Germany and the nations of Eastern Europe. Instead, puppet communist regimes were quickly established, and an "iron curtain" was clamped tight around an empire of Soviet-dominated satellites. By 1949, when the Chinese Communists succeeded in over-running the mainland of China, postwar communist aggression had brought 700 million people and 7.5 million square miles (19.4 million square kilometers) of territory under its control.

THE TRUMAN DOCTRINE. The critical turning point in American policy toward the designs of the Soviet Union came in the early months of 1947. Greece and Turkey were in desperate straits. Without immediate and substantial assistance from the United States, both nations were certain to fall under Soviet control. The response was immediate. At President Truman's request Congress quickly provided for economic and military aid. In his message to Congress, President Truman declared that it was:

> the policy of the United States to support free peoples who are resisting attempted subjugation by armed minorities or outside pressures.

This statement and the actions which followed it came to be known as the *Truman Doctrine*. It is clear now that its enunciation, March 12, 1947, marked the beginning of the policy we have followed ever since: opposing communist aggression.

The Truman Doctrine has been applied many times and in many places over the years since 1947. Our military effort and other aid in support of South Viet Nam furnishes a leading (but unsuccessful) illustration, of course. But there are many others—including, for example, the substantial commitment of American land, naval, and air forces to the defense of Western Europe, our continuing military presence in South Korea, and American military intervention in such places as Lebanon in 1958 and the Dominican Republic in 1965.

COMMUNIST AGGRESSION. Each of the major clashes during the Cold War period—in Korea, Cuba, and Viet Nam—fur-

The Berlin Wall was erected in 1962 to prevent defections to the West; it remains in place today, a telling comment on Soviet policies.

nish prime examples of collective security and resistance to communist aggression.

Korea. The Korean War began on June 25, 1950, when Communist North Korea attacked the UN-sponsored Republic of South Korea. The UN immediately called upon its members to aid in repelling the invaders, and American forces went into action at once. The war pitted the UN Command (largely American and South Korean forces, but with contingents from 15 other nations[1]) against Soviet-trained and -equipped North Korean and Commu-

---

[1] Australia, Belgium, Canada, Colombia, Ethiopia, France, Great Britain, Greece, Luxembourg, the Netherlands, New Zealand, the Philippine Republic, Thailand, Turkey, and the Union of South Africa.

nist Chinese forces. The fighting ended with an armistice signed on July 27, 1953. Final peace terms have not yet been agreed to, however; and American and South Korean troops still stand guard against any renewed aggression.

The bitter Korean conflict did not end in a clear-cut UN victory in the sense that the enemy was beaten to his knees. The war cost the United States 157,530 casualties, including 33,629 combat deaths, and more than $20 billion. South Korea suffered hundreds of thousands of casualties, and nearly all of Korea was laid to waste.

Still, much was accomplished. The enemy was repulsed, and with far heavier losses. *For the first time in history* armed forces fought under an international flag to resist aggression. In the hope of preventing World War III, communist encroachment had to be stopped somewhere, and soon.

More than 5.7 million men and women served in the armed forces during the Korean War. Here, an infantry company is about to attack a North Korean position.

There is no telling how far the communist tide might have carried had South Korea not been defended. Only history can judge how effective the war was in preventing another global conflict. But the Korean War did furnish the spark which finally aroused and united the free world.

Cuba. The United States and the Soviet Union have faced one another often, and in many places, since World War II— but nowhere more forcefully than in the Cuban missile crisis in 1962.

Cuba slipped into the Soviet orbit not long after the Castro dictatorship gained power in 1959. The United States severed diplomatic relations with that regime in early 1961. The action came after a series of provocations, including the seizure of American properties, mass executions of anti-Castro Cubans, and vicious propaganda attacks on this country. The island was drawn even deeper into the Soviet sphere after an abortive invasion attempt by American-trained Cuban exiles, at the Bay of Pigs in April of 1961. The invaders, lacking air support, were quickly crushed.

By mid-1962 huge quantities of Soviet arms and thousands of Soviet "technicians" were being sent to Cuba. The Soviet Union insisted that the military buildup was purely defensive, intended to protect Cuba from a supposed threat of American invasion.

Suddenly, in October, the already massive buildup became unmistakably offensive in character. Despite repeated Soviet assurances to the contrary, aerial photographs revealed missile installations capable of launching nuclear strikes against this country and much of Latin America.

With this development, President Kennedy moved quickly. On October 22, he declared that the United States would not "tolerate deliberate deception and offensive threats by any nation, large or small." He ordered a quarantine to prevent further deliveries of offensive weapons to Cuba and demanded the withdrawal of those already there. He also directed that a close aerial inspection of the island be continued.

For several days the world seemed perilously close to all-out war. On October 28, however, with UN prompting, but especially through an exchange of letters between President Kennedy and Premier Khrushchev, the Soviet Union began to back down. Rather than risk all, so far from home, the missile installations were dismantled, and the weapons were returned to the USSR.

South Viet Nam. The policy of resisting communist aggression was the basic reason for the American presence in South Viet Nam. There—for the second time since the end of World War II—the armed forces of the United States became involved in a direct military confrontation with a communist enemy. Our massive participation in the Vietnamese war began in the early 1950's. American involvement rose sharply in the early 1960's, and especially in the period 1964 to 1968.

The United States became involved in South Viet Nam for several reasons. As President Johnson once declared:

We have learned that to yield to aggression brings only greater threats and more destructive war. To stand firm is the only guarantee of lasting peace.

The United States took the position that South Viet Nam was critical to the security of Southeast Asia. That is, if South Viet Nam fell to the Communists, that whole region could become prey to the forces of communism. Moreover, the Southeast Asia Treaty (page 475) was purposefully drawn to protect South Viet Nam, Cambodia, and Laos, as well as the members of SEATO.

Our presence was also based upon our insistence upon the rule of law in world affairs. The long record of communist aggression in Viet Nam was a direct violation of international law. Specifically, it violated

the ban of the use of force in the UN Charter and in the Geneva Accords of 1954. Then, too, the United States became involved in the conflict in Viet Nam at the request of the leaders of South Viet Nam itself.

President Eisenhower first responded to that request in 1954 when he pledged:

to assist the Government of Viet Nam in developing and maintaining a strong, viable state, capable of resisting attempted subversion or aggression through military means.

At the President's direction, American military advisers and aid were sent to bolster the South Vietnamese armed forces in their fight with the Viet Cong. The Viet Cong consisted of communist guerrilla elements in South Viet Nam trained, supplied, and directed from North Viet Nam with the support of the Communist Chinese.

The Viet Cong effort had become a full scale guerrilla war by 1961. It was a war replete with bombings, kidnappings, torture, assassinations, and other terrorist activities. The communists saw the conflict as a "war of national liberation"—in their idiom the term for any war which furthers the communist design for world conquest.

President Kennedy reaffirmed the pledge to preserve the security of South Viet Nam in 1961. The military aid and adviser programs were expanded. American advisers began to accompany South Vietnamese troops in combat and Air Force helicopters were directed to fly South Vietnamese units into battle.

President Johnson ratified the policy of his predecessors immediately after taking office in late 1963. But, despite the expansion of American support in the early 1960's, the communist forces continued to make substantial gains.

Several events brought a change in the course of the war beginning in 1964. With these events came a radical alteration in the nature of the United States' role in it. A series of governmental crises had weakened South Viet Nam's ability to carry the war to the enemy. North Viet Nam had stepped up its infiltration of men and supplies to aid the Viet Cong in the south. Direct attacks on American forces and installations began to occur. As a result, American combat units were ordered to South Viet Nam in growing numbers in 1965. Almost immediately, Army and Marine Corps forces began operations.

The United States soon took over from the South Vietnamese primary responsibility for the prosecution of the war, and fierce fighting punctuated the next several years. By 1968 more than 500,000 American troops were involved.

Even as the pace of the war was accelerated, the United States made efforts to prompt a settlement of the conflict. These endeavors were two-pronged: by *diplomatic* means to *persuade* the Hanoi regime to a peaceful settlement and by *military* means to *force* them to one.

President Johnson made a dramatic bid to prompt the North Vietnamese to negotiate in early 1968. To that end, he ordered a drastic reduction in the air attacks on factories, bridges, and other strategic targets in the North. He later ordered a total halt to bombing in North Viet Nam.

Hanoi then did agree to peace talks. Negotiations—involving the United States, South Viet Nam, North Viet Nam, and the NLF (Viet Cong)—began in Paris in May of 1968, and lasted for nearly five years.

In 1969 President Nixon adopted a policy of "Vietnamization" of the war—a policy Mr. Nixon thus described:

> The primary mission of our troops is to enable the South Vietnamese forces to assume the full responsibility for the security of South Viet Nam. . . . We have adopted a plan in cooperation with the South Vietnamese for the complete withdrawal of all U.S. combat ground forces,

and their replacement by South Vietnamese forces on an orderly scheduled timetable. This withdrawal will be made from strength and not from weakness.

During the spring of 1972, Vietnamization was tested most severely as the North Vietnamese and the Viet Cong launched a major offensive in South Viet Nam. The United States retaliated by mining North Vietnamese harbors and launching a massive bombing attack. The "blitz-blockade" was coupled with the continued withdrawal of American ground forces.

Viet Nam Critics and Hopes for Peace. As our participation in the war mounted, Americans became increasingly divided over the question of our involvement in South Viet Nam. A major controversy stemmed from disagreement over the importance of the North Vietnamese invasion of South Viet Nam. Critics of official government policies argued—with increasing intensity—that no major American interest was at stake, that the fight was primarily a civil war, and that the United States should withdraw from it. Meanwhile, most Americans hoped for a settlement that would end the nation's involvement in this long, costly, increasingly unpopular, and debilitating conflict.

THE CEASE-FIRE AGREEMENT. The protracted Paris peace talks finally produced an agreement to end the war early in 1973. President Nixon announced what he called the "peace with honor" pact on January 23, 1973.

In accord with its terms, an uneasy, internationally supervised truce became effective four days later. The last elements of the American military presence in Viet Nam were withdrawn from that devastated land over the next 60 days and a prisoner exchange program was completed in the same period.

The cease-fire and the subsequent withdrawal of our forces did not bring to a complete end the American presence in Southeast Asia, however. The United

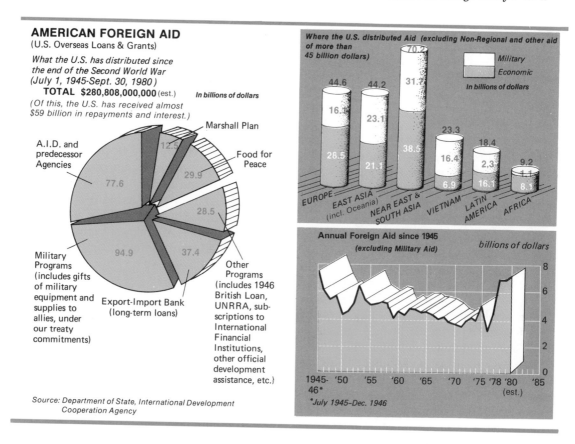

AMERICAN FOREIGN AID
(U.S. Overseas Loans & Grants)

What the U.S. has distributed since the end of the Second World War (July 1, 1945-Sept. 30, 1980)

TOTAL $280,808,000,000 (est.)
(Of this, the U.S. has received almost $59 billion in repayments and interest.)

In billions of dollars

- Marshall Plan — 12.5
- A.I.D. and predecessor Agencies — 77.6
- Food for Peace — 29.9
- 28.5
- Military Programs (includes gifts of military equipment and supplies to allies, under our treaty commitments) — 94.9
- Export-Import Bank (long-term loans) — 37.4
- Other Programs (includes 1946 British Loan, UNRRA, subscriptions to International Financial Institutions, other official development assistance, etc.)

Source: Department of State, International Development Cooperation Agency

Where the U.S. distributed Aid (excluding Non-Regional and other aid of more than 45 billion dollars)

Military / Economic
In billions of dollars

Region	Total	Economic	Military
EUROPE	44.6	28.5	16.1
EAST ASIA (incl. Oceania)	44.2	21.1	23.1
NEAR EAST & SOUTH ASIA	70.2	38.5	31.7
VIETNAM	23.3	6.9	16.4
LATIN AMERICA	18.4	16.1	2.3
AFRICA	9.2	8.1	1.1

Annual Foreign Aid since 1945
(excluding Military Aid) — *billions of dollars*

1945-46* '50 '55 '60 '65 '70 '75 '78 '80 '85 (est.)

8 6 4 2 0

*July 1945–Dec. 1946

States continues to maintain substantial air and ground units, at the ready, in the Philippines and elsewhere in the Far East.

The cease-fire agreement did bring to an end the longest war in our history. During the more than eight years of American participation, the United States spent a staggering $200 billion of its national treasure and, irreplaceably, nearly 60,000 American lives. Only history can render a final judgment as to the ultimate value of those tremendous sacrifices.

THE FALL OF SOUTH VIET NAM. The "uneasy truce" of 1973 proved to be short-lived. North and South Viet Nam resumed the conflict almost immediately. And, despite the continued, massive input of American economic and military assistance South Viet Nam was completely overrun in 1975.

Foreign Aid. The granting of aid to other nations has been a basic feature of

American foreign policy for more than 30 years now. It began with a number of emergency programs at the end of World War II. Thus, we lent $3.75 billion to Great Britain in 1946, and the next year we began the program of economic and military aid to Greece and Turkey.

Foreign aid became a permanent part of our foreign policy with the launching of the Marshall Plan in 1948. Through it, we played a major role in the recovery of war-ravaged Europe. Since World War II, we have now provided nearly $300 billion in aid to other nations.

Our aid policy has undergone many changes over the years. In the early years the bulk of it was economic in form, in the 1950's and 1960's much of it was military. More recently, most of it has become once again economic. Until the mid-1950's Europe received the lion's share of our help; in recent years the largest amounts have

Case Study

"Detente"—a French word meaning relaxation of tensions—has long been used in international affairs. In recent years it has been used to describe the overall shape of recent American foreign policy toward the Soviet Union.

Supporters of a policy of detente see it as a recognition of the realities of world politics today. They argue that the Cold War—the period of intense conflict between the two superpowers from the end of World War II to the 1970's—is all but over. Both sides, they say, have finally realized that a nuclear war would be so massively destructive that neither could emerge the victor and that all of humankind would be the loser. They foresee continuing differences in political ideology and economic systems and, as well, big-power rivalries in various parts of the world. But, as the prospect of nuclear confrontations has diminished, both nations have had the opportunity to become more involved with one another in such areas as scientific, cultural, and trade relations. They urge that these opportunities be exploited and suggest that the end result could well be a long period of peace for the world.

Critics of detente see the present as but an interlude in the continuing struggle between communism and the free world—brought on by a Soviet desire to lull the West into a relaxation of its strong defensive posture. They cite the invasion of Afghanistan in 1980 as hard evidence of long-range Soviet intentions. They insist that our foreign policy stances should be extended and reinforced, rather than relaxed or abandoned.

■ Which of these positions do you believe to be the correct one? What consequences might there be for the United States, internally as well as externally, should either view dominate American policy over the next several years?

■ Is it possible that within the foreseeable future some other matter—such as the population explosion—will replace the Soviet Union and/or the Middle East as our major concern in world affairs?

gone to nations in Asia and nations in Latin America.

From the beginning our aid policy has sought to advance our interests by winning friends and influencing peoples—in both military and humanitarian terms. President Eisenhower put the case for the policy on a quite practical level:

We need allies, and these allies must be bound to us in terms of their own enlightened self-interest, just as in like terms we are bound to them.

A new and immediately successful aid program was launched in 1961: the Peace Corps. It consists of a group of carefully selected and trained volunteers with special skills in such fields as engineering, teaching, and agriculture. These volunteers work with and help better the lot of underdeveloped peoples. The Peace Corps undertook its first mission, a road project, in Tanganyika in 1961. Today its volunteers work on projects in some 70 countries.

Regional Security Treaties. Security treaties help to spell out collective security and our resistance to communism. They are based on the realization that distance and oceans are no longer guarantees against foreign attack. Nuclear weapons, missiles, and other modern devices of mass destruction have pushed our defensive frontiers to the far corners of the earth. Because of this the United States now has eight separate "regional security" treaties with 43 nations. All of these agreements are defensive in nature. They pledge the parties to aid one another in the event either (or any) of them is attacked. The objective of each treaty is clear: security for us and for the rest of the free world.

THE UNITED STATES AND ITS COLLECTIVE DEFENSE ARRANGEMENTS

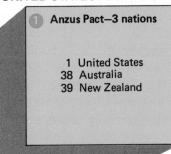

① Anzus Pact—3 nations

1 United States
38 Australia
39 New Zealand

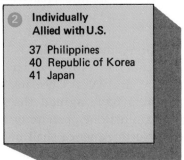

② Individually Allied with U.S.

37 Philippines
40 Republic of Korea
41 Japan

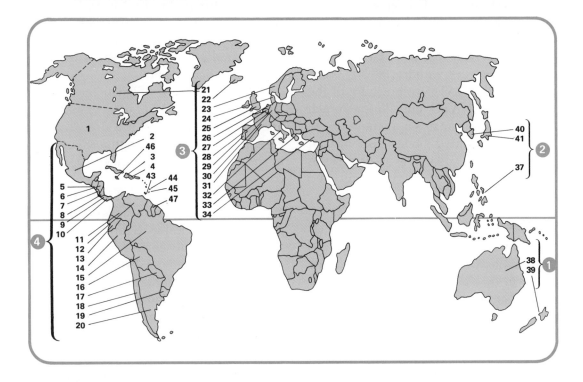

③ North Atlantic Treaty (NATO)—15 nations

1 United States	29 Portugal
21 Canada	30 Federal
22 Iceland	Republic
23 Norway	of Germany
24 Denmark	31 France
25 United Kingdom	32 Italy
26 Netherlands	33 Greece
27 Belgium	34 Turkey
28 Luxembourg	

④ Rio Pact—25 nations

1 United States	14 Peru
2 Mexico	15 Brazil
3 Haiti	16 Bolivia
4 Dominican Republic	17 Paraguay
5 Guatemala	18 Chile
6 Honduras	19 Uruguay
7 El Salvador	20 Argentina
8 Nicaragua	43 Trinidad
9 Costa Rica	& Tobago
10 Panama	44 Barbados
11 Colombia	45 Grenada
12 Venezuela	46 Jamaica
13 Ecuador	47 Surinam

THE NORTH ATLANTIC TREATY. Signed in 1949, the North Atlantic Treaty set up an alliance which now includes the United States, Canada, Great Britain, France, Italy, Portugal, Belgium, the Netherlands, Luxembourg, Denmark, Norway, Iceland, Greece, Turkey, and West Germany. The member nations have agreed that "an armed attack against one or more of them in Europe or North America shall be considered an attack against them all." The pact's object is mutual defense—particularly against the USSR, of course. France, long an uneasy partner, cracked NATO's solidarity in 1966. France's General De Gaulle ordered the withdrawal of French forces from the NATO command and the removal of all NATO units from French soil. Still, France remains a member of the alliance. The United States also has an agreement with Spain giving us air bases in that country in return for economic and military aid.

THE RIO PACT. Signed in 1947, the Inter-American Treaty of Reciprocal Assistance (the Rio Pact) binds the United States and 24 Latin American nations to aid one another in case of an attack in this hemisphere. Our neighbors to the south are es-

sential to our own defense; they are, in effect, our own backyard. We cannot afford to have enemies, or even unfriendly states, so close at hand. When President Kennedy moved against the Soviet missile buildup in Cuba in 1962, he did so under the terms of the Rio Pact. And, each of the other American republics immediately supported the position taken by the United States.

Similarly, President Johnson's use of American troops to effect a cease-fire between the rebel and government forces in the strife-torn Dominican Republic in 1965 represented a move to preserve the security of this hemisphere.

THE ANZUS PACT. Signed in 1951, the Anzus Pact unites Australia, New Zealand, and the United States in a defensive alliance. If any of the three nations is attacked in the Pacific area, the other two agree to come to its aid.

THE JAPANESE PACT. First signed in 1951, the Japanese Pact was revised and extended between Japan and the United States in 1960. After six years of military occupation we and our World War II allies (not the Soviet Union, however) concluded a peace treaty with Japan. At the same time

the small society   **by Brickman**

King Features Syndicate, Inc.

we also signed a mutual defense pact with the Japanese. In return for American protection, we are permitted to maintain land, sea, and air forces in and about Japan. We have added to our own security by converting a former foe into a friend.

THE PHILIPPINES PACT. Signed in 1951, the Philippines Pact serves notice on any potential aggressor that the United States and the Philippines will stand together in the Pacific area.

THE KOREAN PACT. Signed in 1953, the Korean Pact pledges the United States to come to South Korea's aid should it be attacked again.

THE SOUTHEAST ASIA TREATY. Signed in 1954, the SEATO pact is patterned after the NATO pact. It pledges seven nations— the United States, Great Britain, France, Australia, New Zealand, the Philippines, and Thailand—to insure the security of one another (and of South Viet Nam, Laos, and Cambodia) in Southeast Asia. (However, the member-states are now agreed that the "new realities of the region" have made the compact obsolete. The treaty remains in force—but it is of little or no real import or practical importance in the post–Viet Nam War era.)

THE US–TAIWAN PACT. From 1954 to 1980 another one of these agreements was in force, with the government of Nationalist China on Taiwan. It pledged American support should the People's Republic of China ever attempt to conquer Taiwan.

The United States and mainland China established full diplomatic relations in 1979. At the same time, the United States withdrew recognition of the Nationalist government. And the 1954 agreement was terminated a year later.

We continue to maintain relations with "the people of Taiwan," however— through a unique agency, the American Institute. It is a "private, non-profit, tax-exempt corporation," created Congress and financed by contracts with the State Department and other federal agencies.

The United Nations

As we have noted, a decisive change in the basic pattern of American foreign policy took place during and after World War II. This change—the shift from isolationism to full participation in international affairs—is strikingly illustrated by our membership in and support of the United Nations.

Birth of the UN. On January 1, 1942, less than a month after Pearl Harbor, 26 of the nations then at war with the Axis Powers met at Washington, D.C. They met to sign and proclaim the Declaration of the United Nations. In that document, each of the signatories committed itself to an all-out effort to win the war and pledged that it would not seek a separate peace with the enemy. The Declaration—signed by another 23 states later in the war—marked the first official use of the phrase "the United Nations."[2]

In 1943 both houses of Congress gave overwhelming approval to resolutions urging creation of an organization to preserve the peace in the postwar world. Later that same year, in Moscow, Secretary of State Cordell Hull pledged American cooperation in establishing "at the earliest practicable date a general international organization for the maintenance of international peace and security." In 1944, representatives of the United States, Great Britain, China, and the Soviet Union met at Dumbarton Oaks, an estate just outside Washington, to prepare a general plan for such an organization. Then, in February, 1945,

---

[2] The original signatory nations: the United States, Australia, Belgium, Canada, China, Costa Rica, Cuba, Czechoslovakia, the Dominican Republic, El Salvador, Great Britain, Greece, Guatemala, Haiti, Honduras, India, Luxembourg, the Netherlands, New Zealand, Nicaragua, Norway, Panama, Poland, the Soviet Union, the Union of South Africa, and Yugoslavia. Those which signed later were: Argentina, Bolivia, Brazil, Chile, Colombia, Denmark, Ecuador, Egypt, Ethiopia, France, Iran, Iraq, Lebanon, Liberia, Mexico, Paraguay, Peru, San Marino, Saudi Arabia, Syria, Turkey, Uruguay, and Venezuela.

President Roosevelt, British Prime Minister Churchill, and Soviet Premier Stalin, meeting at Yalta in the Crimea, called for a United Nations Conference on International Organization to be convened at San Francisco on April 25, 1945.

THE SAN FRANCISCO CONFERENCE. Delegates from 50 nations gathered at San Francisco to draft a charter for the United Nations. Although much preliminary work had been done, the conference still confronted a number of difficult problems— including such thorny ones as finding ways in which economic pressures and military force might be used to preserve peace, the voting strengths of the large and the small powers in the new organization, and the administration of former enemy territories. On these and several other issues the United States and Great Britain stood on one side and the Soviet Union on the other. Despite difficulties, however, the delegates of the assembled nations were able to forge a charter and give it their unanimous approval on June 26, 1945.

The United States became the first nation to ratify the UN Charter. The Senate agreed to it by the overwhelming vote of 89-2 on July 28, 1945. It was then ratified in quick order by Great Britain, France, China, the Soviet Union, and then 24 other states and went into force on October 24, 1945. Within a very short time, all of the states which had participated in the San Francisco Conference had approved the document. The world organization's first formal meeting, a session of the UN General Assembly, was convened in London on January 10, 1946.

The UN Charter. The UN Charter opens with an eloquent preamble which declares that the UN exists in order "to save succeeding generations from the scourge of war." The body of the document begins in Article I with a statement of the organization's purposes. These purposes are proclaimed to be: the maintenance of international peace and security, the development of friendly relations among all nations, and the promotion of justice and cooperation in the solution of international problems.

MEMBERSHIP. The United Nations is now composed of its 51 original members (those which drafted and first ratified the charter) plus the many other states admitted by the organization since its creation. According to the UN Charter, membership is open to those "peace-loving states" which accept the obligations of the charter and which will, in the UN's judgment, carry out those obligations. New members may be admitted by a two-thirds vote of the General Assembly on the recommendation of the Security Council. The UN now (1981) has 154 members. The General Assembly may suspend or expel any member, by a two-thirds vote, whenever the Security Council recommends that such an action be taken.

BASIC ORGANIZATION. The charter creates six "principal organs": the General Assembly, the Security Council, the Economic and Social Council, the Trusteeship Council, the International Court of Justice, and the Secretariat.

The General Assembly. Each member of the United Nations is represented in the General Assembly, hence, it now has 154 members.

SESSIONS AND VOTING. The General Assembly meets in regular session once each year, normally in September. Although the General Assembly may meet in other places, most of its sessions are held at the site of the UN's permanent headquarters in New York.

The General Assembly is organized on the basis of the equality of all of its members. Each nation has one vote in its proceedings, regardless of size. On important issues, such as those involving elections or finances, the Charter requires that decisions be made by a two-thirds vote. On lesser matters, a simple majority vote is sufficient.

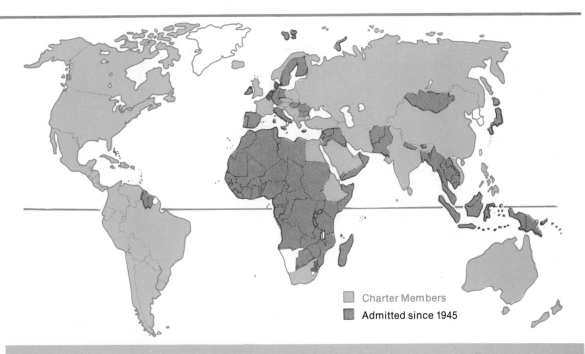

Charter Members

Admitted since 1945

U. N. MEMBERSHIP, 1945 AND NOW

51 Charter Members (in alphabetical order)

Argentina	Iraq
Australia	Lebanon
Belgium	Liberia
Bolivia	Luxembourg
Brazil	Mexico
Byelorussian S.S.R.	Netherlands
Canada	New Zealand
Chile	Nicaragua
China	Norway
Colombia	Panama
Costa Rica	Paraguay
Cuba	Peru
Czechoslovakia	Philippines
Denmark	Poland
Dominican Republic	Saudi Arabia
Ecuador	South Africa
Egypt	Syria
El Salvador	Turkey
Ethiopia	Ukranian S.S.R.
France	Union of Soviet
Greece	Socialist Republics
Guatemala	United Kingdom
Haiti	United States
Honduras	Uruguay
India	Venezuela
Iran	Yugoslavia

Admitted since 1945

Afghanistan	Hungary	Romania
Albania	Iceland	Rwanda
Algeria	Indonesia	St. Lucia
Angola	Ireland	St. Vincent and
Austria	Israel	The Grenadines
Bahamas	Italy	Samoa
Bahrain	Ivory Coast	São Tomé
Bangladesh	Jamaica	and Principe
Barbados	Japan	Senegal
Benin	Jordan	Seychelles
Bhutan	Kampuchea	Sierra Leone
Botswana	(Cambodia)	Singapore
Bulgaria	Kenya	Solomon Islands
Burma	Kuwait	Somalia
Burundi	Laos	Spain
Cameroon	Lesotho	Sri Lanka
Cape Verde	Libya	Sudan
Central African	Madagascar	Suriname
Republic	Malawi	Swaziland
Chad	Malaysia	Sweden
Comoros Islands	Maldives	Tanzania
Congo	Mali	Thailand
Cyprus	Malta	Togo
Dominica	Mauritania	Trinidad and
Djibouti	Mauritius	Tobago
East Germany	Mongolia	Tunisia
Equatorial Guinea	Morocco	Uganda
Fiji	Mozambique	United Arab
Finland	Nepal	Emirates
Gabon	Niger	Upper Volta
Gambia	Nigeria	Vietnam
Ghana	Oman	**West Germany**
Grenada	Pakistan	Yemen Arab Rep.
Guinea	Papua-New Guinea	Yemen Dem. Rep.
Guinea-Bissau	Portugal	Zaire
Guyana	Qatar	Zambia
		Zimbabwe

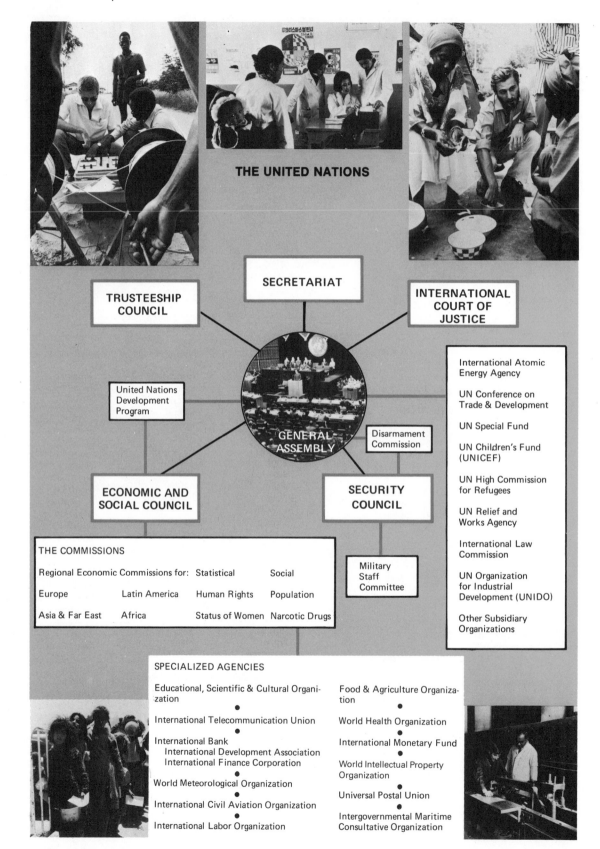

THE UNITED NATIONS

SECRETARIAT

TRUSTEESHIP COUNCIL

INTERNATIONAL COURT OF JUSTICE

United Nations Development Program

GENERAL ASSEMBLY

Disarmament Commission

International Atomic Energy Agency

UN Conference on Trade & Development

UN Special Fund

UN Children's Fund (UNICEF)

UN High Commission for Refugees

UN Relief and Works Agency

International Law Commission

UN Organization for Industrial Development (UNIDO)

Other Subsidiary Organizations

ECONOMIC AND SOCIAL COUNCIL

SECURITY COUNCIL

THE COMMISSIONS

Regional Economic Commissions for:	Statistical	Social
Europe	Latin America	Human Rights	Population
Asia & Far East	Africa	Status of Women	Narcotic Drugs

Military Staff Committee

SPECIALIZED AGENCIES

Educational, Scientific & Cultural Organization
●

International Telecommunication Union
●

International Bank
   International Development Association
   International Finance Corporation

World Meteorological Organization
●

International Civil Aviation Organization
●

International Labor Organization

Food & Agriculture Organization
●

World Health Organization
●

International Monetary Fund
●

World Intellectual Property Organization
●

Universal Postal Union
●

Intergovernmental Maritime Consultative Organization

POWERS AND FUNCTIONS. The Assembly is frequently called the "town meeting of the world." It may consider and debate any matter within the scope of the Charter,[3] and may make such recommendations as it deems appropriate to the Security Council, the other UN organs, and the member-states. Its recommendations to member-states are not legally binding, but they do carry substantial weight since they have been sanctioned by a significant number of the governments of the world.

The Assembly elects the 10 nonpermanent members of the Security Council, all of the members of the Economic and Social Council, and the elective members of the Trusteeship Council. With the Security Council, it also selects the Secretary-General and the judges of the International Court.

The Assembly shares with the Security Council the power to admit, suspend, or expel members. It alone may propose amendments to the Charter. And the Assembly supervises much of the work of the other UN organs. It provides for the staffing of the Secretariat, requires both annual and special reports from the other organs, and creates the relationships which exist with the several Specialized Agencies.

The Assembly controls the UN's finances. It enacts the biennial budget and sets the share of it that each member is obligated to provide. The UN's regular budget for 1980–1981 runs to approximately $1.2 billion. The United States provides one-fourth of that total. The minimum share for any member, paid by many of the smaller states, is now set at one one-hundredths of one percent of the budget—only some $90,000.

The Security Council. The Security Council is composed of 15 members. Five

of them—the United States, Great Britain, the Soviet Union, France, and China—are *permanent members* of the Security Council. The 10 *nonpermanent members* are chosen by the General Assembly, with five being elected each year. The Council is in continuous session, and its members must be represented at the UN seat at all times.

VOTING AND THE VETO. On *procedural* questions—that is, routine or relatively unimportant matters—decisions of the Security Council may be made by an affirmative vote of any nine members. On more important matters—*substantive* questions—nine affirmative votes are also required; *but* in such cases the nine *must* include the votes of each of the permanent members. Thus, on substantive questions, each of the permanent members of the Security Council has a *veto* it can use to prevent Security Council action.

Because of the veto power, the Security Council can function effectively only when the Big Five cooperate. The Soviet Union has often relied on the veto to thwart UN action; to date, it has cast more than 130 vetoes. The other permanent members have used it much less frequently. The United States did not find occasion to exercise the veto until 1970, and has now used it 22 times (to 1981).

POWERS. The Security Council is the UN organ especially responsible for maintaining international peace and dealing with threats to or breaches of that peace. Many of its powers concern the peaceful settlement of disputes. It may call on disputing parties to settle their difficulties by peaceful means. If it chooses to, it may investigate a dispute and recommend terms for its settlement. Sometimes the Security Council finds that a threat to or breach of the peace exists or an act of aggression has been committed. When it does, it may call upon the nations involved to take steps to ease the tensions or to take steps to halt the spread of hostilities.

In order to make its decisions and rec-

[3] Except matters currently under consideration by the Security Council. This restriction is intended to prevent the confusion that might result from the simultaneous consideration of matters by the UN's two major agencies.

ommendations effective, the Security Council may call on all members to sever economic and diplomatic relations with an offending state. If these measures prove inadequate, it may call on all members to take military action against the offender, as was done when the North Koreans invaded South Korea.[4]

ACTIONS AGAINST AN AGGRESSOR. Those who framed the UN Charter clearly intended the Security Council as the organ to take action against an aggressor whenever such action became necessary. But the Security Council may be paralyzed by a veto cast by any one of the Big Five; it can act only when one of the permanent members does not object.

Because of this (and because of the Soviet Union's frequent use of the veto), the United States proposed and the General Assembly adopted the "Uniting for Peace" Resolution in late 1950. Under its terms, whenever the Security Council cannot act in a case in which there "appears to be a threat to the peace, breach of the peace, or act of aggression," the matter may be considered by the General Assembly immediately. The General Assembly may *recommend* that the members take steps, including military action, to preserve or restore peace. Remember, *there is no veto power in the General Assembly.*

The Resolution has provided the basis for several of the UN's peace-keeping actions, notably in the Middle East.

The Economic and Social Council. Each member of the UN has pledged itself to cooperate with other nations to achieve several broad social objectives. These objectives aim at the fostering of friendlier relations among all nations and the producing of a more stable international community. According to the UN Charter,

these objectives include the promotion of: (1) higher standards of living, full employment, and other conditions for social and economic progress; (2) the solutions of economic, social, and health problems; (3) international cultural, and educational cooperation; and (4) universal respect for human rights and fundamental freedoms.

Acting under the direction of the General Assembly, the Economic and Social Council is the organ especially responsible for implementing these goals. Its 27 members are chosen by the Assembly for three-year terms, nine new members being elected each year.

ECOSOC does its work chiefly through conferences, studies, and recommendations in the economic, social, cultural, educational, scientific, and health fields. It maintains several commissions, as the chart on page 478 indicates.

THE SPECIALIZED AGENCIES. One of ECOSOC's most important functions is that of coordinating the work of the UN's Specialized Agencies. These are independent international bodies which, by special agreement, function under the UN's general supervision. Much of the UN's efforts to eliminate the causes of war by raising the level of world economic and social conditions is actually done by these agencies. There are presently 14 Specialized Agencies:

The *International Labor Organization* (ILO) was first established under the League of Nations in 1919. It was the only major body of the League of Nations to which the United States belonged. ILO works to promote the health and welfare of workers everywhere. The *World Health Organization* (WHO) seeks to improve health conditions throughout the world. The *Food and Agriculture Organization* (FAO) conducts projects to improve and increase world food production. The *United Nations Educational, Scientific, and Cultural Organization* (UNESCO) is the agency through which members exchange ideas and infor-

---

[4] When, on June 25, 1950, the Security Council called upon all UN members to aid South Korea to repel the North Korean aggressor, the Soviet delegate was boycotting sessions of the Security Council: hence, he was not present to veto the action.

mation; it works to raise the level of international understanding. The *International Civil Aviation Organization* (ICAO) promotes international cooperation in the interests of expanded commercial air traffic. The *Universal Postal Union* (UPU) is the oldest of the Specialized Agencies. It was first established in 1875 and has long been successful in facilitating international communications by mail. The *International Telecommunications Union* (ITU) promotes international communication by wire, radio, and similar means. The *World Meteorological Organization* (WMO) seeks to improve meteorological activities around the globe. The *Intergovernmental Maritime Consultative Organization* (IMCO) attempts to promote safety at sea and the expansion of the world's maritime trade.

The *International Monetary Fund* (IMF) encourages trade and prosperity by stabilizing the value of the currencies of member-states. The *International Bank for Reconstruction and Development* (World Bank) makes or insures loans for the development of the productive facilities of its members. The *International Finance Corporation* (IFC) and the *International Development Association* (IDA) are affiliates of the World Bank and assist it in the performance of its function. The *World Intellectual Property Organization* (WIPO) encourages nations to cooperate in the protection of such "intellectual properties" as literary and artistic works and scientific inventions.

The Trusteeship Council. The UN Charter requires each member to promote the interests and well-being of the people of all "non-self-governing territories" as a "sacred trust." It sets guidelines for the government of all dependent areas and makes rules for the administration of all UN trust territories.[5]

The Trusteeship Council is composed

---

[5] There were originally 11 trust territories; today (1981) there is but one: the Trust Territory of the Pacific Islands (administered by the United States).

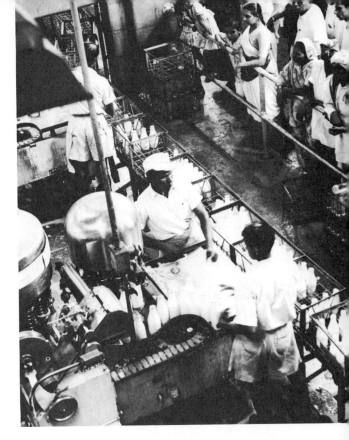

Established with help and advice of WHO experts, the bottling plant here near Bombay, India, produces some 750,000 bottles of milk taken each day from some 78,000 buffaloes.

of all UN members administering trust territories, as well as those Big Five members which do not. In addition, there are enough other members (elected by the General Assembly) on the Council to provide an equal balance of members which administer trust territories and members which do not. The Council receives reports from all states with non-self-governing possessions, oversees the administration of the trust territories, and seeks to encourage self-government for all dependent peoples.

The International Court of Justice. The ICJ is the judicial arm of the United Nations. It is dealt with only briefly in the UN Charter. However, it is the subject of a lengthy and detailed Statute appended to that document. The ICJ is composed of 15 judges selected for nine-year terms by the General Assembly and the Security Council. No two judges may come from the same country. It holds regular sessions at The Hague in the Netherlands. Only states (both members and nonmembers of the UN, but not individuals) may be parties in cases before the court. It deals with cases involving the interpretation of treaties, questions in international law, and any other legal matters brought before it. Its decisions are made by a majority vote.

The ICJ cannot hear a case unless both parties to a dispute agree to accept its jurisdiction. A nation may agree to the court's jurisdiction over a specific case. Or, a nation can agree in advance to ICJ jurisdiction over a general class of cases.

Under the aforementioned Statute, any nation may sign that document's "optional clause." By so doing, it agrees to the ICJ's jurisdiction in any legal dispute it may have with any other nation which has also signed the clause. About one-half of the UN's members have signed the optional clause. Several of these acceptances, however, have been accompanied by reservations. For example, the United States made several reservations to its acceptance in 1946. One declares that the ICJ shall not have the right to hear and decide "disputes which are essentially within the jurisdiction of the United States as determined by the United States." Such reservations have severely limited the ICJ's usefulness.

Thus far the ICJ has played only a minor role in settling international disputes. The problem has not been a lack of international law that might be applied in specific cases. Instead, it has been that most of the serious disputes have been treated as "political" rather than "judicial" questions. Hence, the nations involved have not been willing to submit those disputes to the Court for settlement.

The Secretariat. The Secretariat is the civil service branch of the UN. It is headed by the Secretary-General—chosen by the General Assembly, upon recommendation by the Security Council, for a five-year term. The staff of the Secretariat, numbering some 15,000, has been drawn from most of the UN's member-states.

The Secretary-General has a wide variety of functions. The Secretary-General is responsible for the administrative work of the principal organs of the UN, except for the International Court of Justice, and prepares annual reports to the General Assembly on the workings of the UN. The UN Charter gives the Secretary-General the power to bring to the attention of the Security Council any matter which is a threat to international peace and security.

The United Nation's Security Council votes on a resolution to extend the mandate of the United Nations Disengagement Observer Force, a multination peacekeeping/observation force serving in "trouble spots" in the Middle East.

The Secretary-General was originally looked upon as little more than the UN's chief clerk. Four men have occupied the office thus far, and have made much more of the office. They are, in order of their service, Trygve Lie of Norway, Dag Hammarskjöld of Sweden, U Thant of Burma, and Kurt Waldheim of Austria. Working in the extraordinarily sensitive realm of international politics, they transformed the office into an important channel for the negotiated settlement of international disputes. They did so by relying on their own persuasive diplomatic talents.

The Charter stipulates that all treaties concluded between or among member-states must be recorded with and published by the Secretariat. And, the Charter further decrees, no unrecorded treaty may be invoked in any matter pending before any organ of the UN.

The UN and Disarmament. The world has lived for three decades with the continuing threat of World War III—with the spectre of a nuclear holocaust in which humanity could, literally, be wiped out.

Over this period, the costs have been staggering—indeed, well-nigh incalculable. Just in monetary terms alone, the United States has spent almost *$2 trillion* on its armed forces *since the end* of World War II. President Eisenhower once attempted to point up the costs of this conflict-ridden world in terms of human value in these words:

Under the cloud of threatening war, it is humanity hanging from a cross of iron. . . . Every gun that is made, every warship launched, every rocket fired signifies—in the final sense—a *theft* from those who hunger and are not fed, those who are cold and are not clothed. The world in arms is not spending money alone. It is spending the sweat of its laborers, the genius of its scientists, the hopes of its children.

Certainly, one of the surest ways to end this tragic waste and to prevent another global war would be a general international disarmament plan, agreed to and honored by all nations. Just as certainly, any such plan would have to provide the most stringent controls over the use of nuclear energy for military purposes.

The United States unleashed the horror of atomic weapons in 1945. The war against Japan was ended in August of that year with two awesomely destructive atomic bombs. The first one was dropped on Hiroshima on August 6th. The second one fell on Nagasaki three days later. The Hiroshima bomb produced an explosion equivalent to that of 20,000 tons of TNT, leveling some 13 square kilometers (5 square miles) of Hiroshima. The bomb that hit Nagasaki was equally devastating.

Since 1945, the United States has been producing and stockpiling atomic and hydrogen bombs and other nuclear weapons, all with incredible destructive power. Today our supply of them exceeds by many times the explosive equivalent of *all* bombs and *all* shells that came from *every* plane and *every* gun in *every* theater of war through *all* the years of World War II.

The Soviet Union exploded its first atomic device in 1949; and it, too, has been stockpiling nuclear weapons ever since. Several other nations are also nuclear powers today: Great Britain made its first tests in 1952, and France joined the "nuclear club" in 1960. The People's Republic of China first demonstrated its nuclear capabilities in 1964 and India exploded its first nuclear device in 1974.

THE UN DISARMAMENT COMMISSION. The UN Charter empowers the General Assembly to recommend general principles of disarmament to the Security Council. The Council, in turn, is charged with formulating a specific disarmament plan for all nations. Most of the postwar effects to achieve arms control and disarmament have therefore centered in the UN.

Early in 1946 the UN created an Atomic Energy Commission, and the next year it created a Commission on Conventional Armaments. In 1952 these bodies were combined to form the Disarmament Commission, now composed of all members of the UN. From 1946 on, disarmament efforts have aimed at an agreement:

—outlawing the production or use of weapons of mass destruction;
—providing for the reduction of armaments and of armed forces to the minimum levels necessary for domestic policing; and
—providing for the maintenance of peace through the UN.

THE DISARMAMENT STALEMATE. Almost immediately in 1946 the United States presented a plan for international control of atomic power. The American proposal (the Baruch Plan) called for an International Atomic Energy Development Authority with broad powers to own and control all atomic production and materials. Although favored by most of the members of the United Nations, the plan floundered—largely on Russian opposition to its provisions for strict international inspection and enforcement.

The years since 1946 have seen a long series of disarmament conferences, focusing on both nuclear and conventional weaponry. But, despite them, the topic remains a major, unresolved, and contentious problem for the world community.

A few bright spots have appeared, however. One came with the creation, at Vienna in 1957, of the International Atomic Energy Agency. Its now more than 100 member-nations are pledged to "seek to accelerate and enlarge the contribution of atomic energy to peace, health and prosperity throughout the world."

A general disarmament conference was begun at Geneva in 1958 and has met periodically ever since. Thus far, the UN's continuing disarmament efforts have produced three major international agreements:

The Limited Test Ban Treaty, 1963. In 1963 the United States, the Soviet Union, and Great Britain agreed to a partial ban on nuclear testing. Their accord, in the form of a treaty, was registered with the UN and, immediately, the General Assembly called upon all states to ratify it. Under its terms, each signatory nation agrees not to conduct nuclear test explosions in the atmosphere, underwater, or in outer space. Underground tests, which are extremely difficult to detect, are permitted. But such tests are permitted only so long as they do not spread radioactive debris beyond the territory of a nation conducting such tests. Since then, more than 120 states have signed the agreement—but neither France nor China has done so.

The Outer Space Treaty, 1967. In 1967 the United States, the Soviet Union, and Great Britain signed an agreement to promote the peaceful exploration and use of outer space. The treaty outlaws in outer space and on all celestial bodies: all claims of national sovereignty, the stationing or orbiting of nuclear or other weapons of mass destruction, military bases or maneuvers, and all weapons testing. It calls for international cooperation in space activities and the reporting of their results. It guarantees to all states unrestricted access to all celestial bodies, and requires prompt aid for astronauts who accidentally land in another state or on the high seas. The treaty also requires all countries to avoid all space activities that might contaminate outer space or harm the earth's environment.

The Nuclear Nonproliferation Treaty, 1968. In 1968 the United States, the Soviet Union, Great Britain, and 60 other nations signed an agreement to prevent the spread of nuclear weapons and explosives to those nations not already possessing them. Since then, more than 100 states—but, again, not including France or China—have ratified the treaty.

THE SALT TALKS. The Strategic Arms Limitation Talks (SALT) are a series of ongoing negotiations between the United States and the Soviet Union. They were

The first hydrogen bomb was exploded in a test conducted in the South Pacific in 1952. Nuclear devices developed since then are even more destructive.

begun in Geneva in 1969. In effect, they amount to a continuing search for agreements to limit and/or reduce both nation's strategic (*i.e.*, their long-range) nuclear weaponry.

The first round of these talks (SALT I) resulted in two agreements in 1972. In one of them, the ABM Treaty, the superpowers agreed that each of them would maintain not more than 200 anti-ballistic missiles and that these *defensive* weapons would be deployed at but two sites in each country. That pact is of unlimited duration. The other, the Interim Agreement, related to *offensive* weapons. It placed a five-year freeze (to 1977) on each nation's arsenal of intercontinental ballistic missiles (ICBM's), missile-launching submarines, and submarine-launched missiles (SLBM's). Each side was limited to the possession of those weapons which were actually on station or actually under construction as of 1972. (When the agreement expired in 1977 both nations agreed to continue to honor its terms, at least until the completion of the SALT II process.)

The second round of these negotiations—SALT II—were begun in 1972. They produced two noteworthy accords in 1974. One of them amended the 1972 defensive missile treaty to limit each nation to a single site for the deployment of its ABM's. The other imposed a partial ban on underground testing of nuclear devices for military purposes. (That treaty has not gained the approval of the Senate. Nonetheless, both the United States and the Soviet Union have observed its provisions in practice.)

The United States and the Soviet Union signed another major pact in 1979. It is commonly known as the SALT II Treaty. Essentially, it would place fixed limits on the number of offensive strategic vehicles—*i.e.*, long-range missiles and bombers—that each of the superpowers may deploy through 1985.

The SALT II Treaty became deeply enmeshed in our domestic politics in 1980. To this point (1981), the United States has not ratified it—and it appears likely that it will not be approved, at least in its present form.

Evaluating the UN. The UN seems fairly well designed to accomplish the social, economic, and other humanitarian goals set by its Charter. It has served as the meeting place for airing international grievances and molding worldwide public opinion. It has been able to settle or bring about the settlement of several disputes between smaller nations.

The UN has been much less successful in controlling the conduct of the major powers and in settling disputes in which they are involved, however. Unless the Big Five members cooperate, the organization is virtually paralyzed in such cases—as in the Viet Nam situation. Unfortunately, in international politics the power of "might" is often at least as important as the power of "right."

Because the UN has not brought an end to world tensions and the threat of a third world war, some say that it is a failure. But those who do overlook a most important fact: the UN is *not* a world government. Like water which can rise no higher than its source, the UN can be no more effective than its members are willing to make it.

Then, too, one should not overlook the UN's many accomplishments. Among other things, it prevented the Soviet Union from seizing the oil fields of northern Iran in 1946. It halted the Arab-Israeli war of 1948 which erupted when Israel gained its independence. It helped to settle the Berlin Blockade dispute in 1948-1949. It arranged a truce between India and Pakistan in their disputes over Kashmir in 1949 and 1965.

In 1950, the Security Council called upon its members to help meet a North Korean attack upon South Korea. Sixteen nations responded. *For the first time in history an international organization met aggression with armed force.*

The UN brought an end to the fighting in Egypt in late 1956 and forced the withdrawal of the Israeli and Anglo-French forces from Egyptian soil. The General Assembly created the United Nations Emergency Force, *the first international police force in history,* to guard the truce. Although

UNEF's withdrawal in 1967 was followed by yet another Arab-Israeli war, the Security Council was soon able to obtain another cease-fire supervised by the UN. And the UN helped to stop the most recent Arab-Israeli war in 1973. The continued UN presence in the Mid-East is clearly a major reason why the two sides have not made even more frequent resorts to force to settle their outstanding differences.

Much has been done by the Specialized Agencies, whose work may seem unspectacular yet is very important. International peace can hardly become a lasting reality when millions of the world's people are hungry, lack shelter, suffer from disease, and live in ignorance. WHO stopped a cholera plague in Egypt, is spearheading a worldwide drive against malaria which has reduced the incidence of the disease by more than 50 percent throughout Central America, and is conducting massive attacks on disease through spraying, vaccination, and other programs. FAO found vast reservoirs of underground water in Saudi Arabia, and has sent agricultural experts, seeds, and machinery to aid millions in the world's underdeveloped areas. UNESCO is fighting illiteracy all over the world, helping to establish school systems and building schools in backward areas.

In these and other ways, the United Nations has served the interests of world peace. The organization is far from perfect, but, at the very least, it is helpful.

The American "Empire"

Let us turn to one final aspect of this nation's role in the world community: the territorial possessions of the United States.

The original thirteen States emerged from the Revolutionary War as a loose Confederation stretching some 1780 kilometers (1300 miles) along the Atlantic seaboard. By the Treaty of Paris, which officially ended the war in 1783, the new nation also held all of the territory from

THE AMERICAN EMPIRE

Principal Territories	Date Acquired	Prior Status	How Acquired	Area (Square Kilometers)	(Square Miles)	Population (1970)
Guam	1898	Spanish possession	Conquest and Treaty, Spanish-American War	549	212	84,996
Puerto Rico	1898	Spanish possession	Conquest and Treaty, Spanish-American War	8,897	3,435	2,712,003
Panama Canal Zone	1904	Panamanian territory	Treaty with Panama; returned to Panama by treaty in 1979; Canal now under joint administration	1,432	553	44,198
Virgin Islands	1917	Danish possession	Treaty with Denmark, purchased for $25 million	344	133	62,468
Trust Territory of the Pacific Islands	1947	Japanese mandate	Conquest in World War II and UN Trusteeship	21,987	8,497	90,940
District of Columbia	1791	Portion of Maryland	Donated by Maryland, accepted by acts of Congress, 1790–91	174	67	756,510

the Great Lakes on the north to Spanish Florida on the south and westward to the Mississippi.

At the close of the Revolution, then, the United States held title to a vast domain—to 2,301,694 square kilometers (888,685 square miles) of some of the richest of lands in all of the world.

This proved but a beginning, however. From it, the United States has now grown to 50 States embracing more than four times its original area—to 9,363,166 square kilometers (3,615,122 square miles). The Louisiana Purchase in 1803, the annexation of Florida in 1819 and of Texas in 1845, the Oregon Treaty in 1846, the cessions from Mexico in 1848, the Gadsden Purchase in 1853, the Alaska Purchase in 1867, and the annexation of Hawaii in 1898 all added to the territory which now forms the United States; see the map on page 95.

Today the American flag flies over other territory, as well—over a far-flung insular "empire," if indeed it may be called that, unlike any other the world has ever known.

Power to Acquire Territory. No clause of the Constitution contains an *expressed* grant of power to acquire territory. But the Supreme Court has often held that, as with other sovereign states, the United States has the *inherent* power to do so. Thus, in 1856 Congress authorized the President to take jurisdiction over any guano islands discovered by American citizens. The Supreme Court found the law to be constitutional in *Jones* v. *United States,* 1890, holding that:

> By the law of nations, recognized by all civilized states, dominion over new territory may be acquired by discovery and occupation, as well as by cession or conquest.

In addition to its basis in international law, the power to acquire is implied by three of the expressed powers. The *power to make treaties*[6] implies the power to gain territory by treaty. The *power to make war*[7] implies

---

[6] Article II, Section 2, Clause 2.
[7] Article I, Section 8, Clause 11.

From 1898 to 1934, the Philippines was governed by the United States as a territory. In 1934, Congress granted the Philippines a commonwealth status and established a ten-year transitional period, at the end of which the island-nation would be given complete independence. Pictured here is the inaugural ceremony held in 1935 when the first President of the Philippine Commonwealth was sworn into office. In 1946, the Philippines was given its independence, as decreed in the act passed by Congress in 1934.

the right to make conquests. And the *power to admit new States*[8] implies the power to gain territory from which States might be made. The United States has, at one time or another, relied on each of these bases in acquiring its territorial holdings.

Power to Govern Territories. While the Constitution is silent on the power to acquire, it *does* give to Congress the expressed power to govern territories. Article IV, Section 3, Clause 2 provides:

> The Congress shall have power to dispose of and make all needful rules and regulations respecting the territory or other property belonging to the United States.

And, in time of war, the President, as Commander-in-Chief,[9] governs territory occupied by the armed forces.

Notice that Article IV provides for the *disposal* as well as for the governing of the territories. Thus, the United States has agreed to cede complete control of the Panama Canal to the Republic of Panama no later than December 31, 1999, and has promised independence to Puerto Rico

whenever the Puerto Ricans themselves decide they are ready to accept it.

The "Empire" Today. Each of our territorial possessions today is legally classed as *unincorporated.* That is, each *belongs to* the United States but is not *a part of* (has not been *incorporated* into) the nation, as have each of the 50 States.

Congress has never provided a uniform pattern of territorial government. Rather, governmental arrangements vary as widely among the possessions as do such factors as size, location, and importance. Some—Puerto Rico, Guam, and the Virgin Islands—have been given a considerable measure of self-government. But in the other overseas possessions, which are held largely for military reasons, little self-government exists.

In recent years, though, some measure of self-government has come through the efforts of the Department of the Interior. Today, its Office of Territorial Affairs is charged with promoting the social and economic development of our overseas possessions—especially, Guam, the Virgin Islands, American Samoa, and the Pacific Trust Territory.

---

[8] Article IV, Section 3, Clause 1.
[9] Article II, Section 2, Clause 1.

The Office furnishes advice and assistance to the various territorial governments and is the major link between them and other federal agencies. It also administers Canton, Enderbury, Wake, Palmyra, Baker, Jarvis, and Howland Islands in the Western Pacific.

THE DISTRICT OF COLUMBIA is *not* a "possession" or "territory" of the United States. It is, rather, a federal district within the continental United States. It is an area set aside as the site of the nation's capital, and specifically provided for by the Constitu-tion, in Article I, Section 8, Clause 17.

For most of its history the District was governed directly by Congress. It was without local government, without representation in Congress, and without a role in presidential elections. Dramatic changes have occurred in recent years, however. The 23rd Amendment, ratified in 1961, added the District to the electoral college system. Congress gave its delegate a seat in the House in 1971. And an elected local government was finally created in 1967 and expanded in 1973.

SUMMARY

American foreign policy has always been directed toward one overriding end: the maintenance of the security of the United States. We began our history with a policy of isolationism dictated by our relative weakness, internal problems, and geographic position. From the beginning we also pursued a policy of continental expansion and warned Europe through the Monroe Doctrine not to interfere in Western Hemisphere affairs. As we expanded, we grew more powerful and became a first-class power in the world with the Spanish-American War. By 1900 our interests extended throughout this hemisphere and across the Pacific.

World War I brought the United States out of its isolationism for a brief period, but we returned to it until the coming of World War II. That conflict convinced us of the fallacy of isolationism in the modern world and wrought a basic transformation in American foreign policy. Today—through our own might, collective security agreements, the United Nations, and aid to the free world—we oppose communist aggression, work to prevent World War III, and seek a just and lasting peace for all nations.

The UN dramatically illustrates the postwar transformation of American foreign policy. Formed at San Francisco in 1945, it is intended "to save succeeding generations from the scourge of war." Under its Charter, it functions through six principal organs: the General Assembly, in which all of its 154 members are represented; the Security Council, composed of the Big Five and 10 nonpermanent members, which is intended as the organization's major peace-keeping arm but is sometimes crippled by the veto power; the Economic and Social Council, composed of 27 members, which is designed to attack the world's economic and social problems; the Trusteeship Council, which oversees the trust territories; the International Court of Justice, which is the UN's judicial arm; and the Secretariat, headed by the Secretary-General, which is the UN's civil service.

On balance, the UN is far from perfect but, at least, has been more than helpful in advancing the cause of world peace. It has had several notable successes in promoting the humanitarian goals set by the UN Charter and in resolving disputes among the smaller nations. It has been much less successful in regulating the conduct of the Big Five powers.

The major possessions which comprise America's insular "empire" are Guam, Puerto Rico, the Virgin Islands, and the Pacific Trust Territory. The District of Columbia is not one of the territorial possessions; rather, it is a federal district specifically provided for by the Constitution.

Concept Development

Questions for Review

1. What has been and is the constant aim of American foreign policy?

2. What basic self-defense policy was proclaimed in 1823 and has been supported by each Congress and each President since its announcement?

3. Why did the Good Neighbor Policy mark a decisive turn in our relations with Latin America?

4. What basic transformation did the coming of World War II bring in American foreign policy?

5. What is the policy of deterrence?

6. How do the UN and our regional security treaties illustrate the concept of "collective security"?

7. The enunciation of what doctrine inaugurated the policy of resistance to communist aggression?

8. What have, thus far, proved to be the major clashes of the Cold War?

9. The United States has given how much in economic and military aid to other nations since the end of World War II?

10. When and where was the UN Charter drafted?

11. What, according to the UN Charter, are the UN's basic purposes?

12. The UN had how many original members? How many members today?

13. What are the major functions and powers of the UN's six principal organs?

14. In which of the UN's organs are all of the organization's members equally represented?

15. What is the veto power?

16. What are the Specialized Agencies?

17. Who may be parties to cases before the International Court of Justice?

18. Who heads the Secretariat?

19. How effective has the UN been in its efforts to achieve the goal of general world disarmament?

20. Which territories have been granted a measure of self-government?

21. What kind of representation does the District of Columbia now have in Congress?

For Further Inquiry

1. Some critics have argued that the history of the United States demonstrates that we are not a "peace-loving people." How would you answer such critics?

2. The United States refused to join the League of Nations after World War I but took a leading role in the formation of the United Nations at the end of World War II. How do you explain this sharp reversal of policy?

3. The United States insisted upon the veto power when the UN was founded and does not favor its abolition today. Why might the United States take this position?

4. Articles 9 and 18 of the UN Charter provide that all member-states shall be represented equally in the General Assembly and that each shall have one vote in that body. Thus, the United States and the UN's smallest member (Seychelles, with an estimated population of 62,000 in 1978) each casts one vote in the General Assembly. Do you think this is either fair or realistic? Why does the United States not press for a change in this arrangement?

5. Why was American opinion so sharply divided on the issue of our involvement in the Viet Nam War in the late 1960's and early 1970's? Does it remain so today?

6. Some say that it should be the policy of the United States to take a "hard line" against communism both abroad and at home, while others feel that such a policy would in the end be self-defeating. What is meant by taking a "hard line"? Which view do you support? Why?

7. How might the following slogan relate to such matters as taxation, foreign policy, or military expenditures: "Put your trust in God, my boys, but keep your powder dry"?

8. Why does the Constitution provide for the location of the national capital outside the jurisdiction of any State?

Suggested Activities

1. Stage a debate or class forum on the following question: *Resolved,* That the United States should withdraw immediately from the United Nations and all other "entangling alliances."

2. Present a brief report to the class on a problem in our current foreign relations—for example, our policy toward China, the OPEC nations, the sale of arma-

ments to foreign nations, or the proliferation of nuclear weapons.

3. Write an essay on the necessity of preventing World War III.

4. Write a report on the history, government, and people of a U.S. territory.

Suggested Reading

Ambrose, Stephen E., *Rise to Globalism: American Foreign Policy, 1938–1980.* Penquin Books, 1980.

American Foreign Policy for the '80s: A Guide for the Facts and Issues. Foreign Policy Association, 1980.

Bailey, Thomas A., *A Diplomatic History of the American People.* Prentice-Hall, 10th ed., 1980.

Brewer, Thomas L., *American Foreign Policy: A Contemporary Introduction.* Prentice-Hall, 1980.

Brown, Seyom, *The Crisis of Power: Foreign Policy in the Kissinger Years.* Columbia, 1979.

Calvocoressi, Peter, *World Politics Since 1945.* Longman, 3rd ed., 1979.

China: U.S. Policy Since 1945. Congressional Quarterly, Inc., 1980.

Coplin, William D., *Introduction to International Politics.* Prentice-Hall, 3rd ed., 1980.

Cottrell, Alvin J., et. al., *The Persian Gulf States: A General Survey.* Johns Hopkins University Press, 1980.

Editorial Research Reports, *U.S. Foreign Policy: Future Directions.* Congressional Quarterly, 1980.

Frankel, Joseph, *International Relations in a Changing World.* Oxford, 1979.

Legum, Colin, *Continent in Crisis: Africa in the Coming Decade.* McGraw-Hill, 1979.

Luaard, Evan, *The United Nations: How It Works and What It Does.* St. Martin's Press, 1979.

Schaller, Michael, *The United States and China in the Twentieth Century.* Oxford, 1980.

Wendzel, Robert L., *International Relations.* Wiley, 2nd ed., 1980.

Government and Finance

Money is, with propriety, considered as the vital principle of the body politic; as that which sustains its life and motion, and enables it to perform its most essential functions.

ALEXANDER HAMILTON

■ Why did the Framers of the Constitution list the taxing power first among the powers granted to Congress?

■ What should be the objectives of the nation's tax policies?

■ To whom are the functions performed by the various federal banking and lending agencies most beneficial?

For fiscal year 1981—the 12-month period beginning October 1, 1980, and ending September 30, 1981—the Federal Government now expects to collect, from all sources, over $600 billion. And it expects to spend several billions more on all of its many programs and functions.

Among other things, these stupendous figures tell us that it now costs every man, woman, and child in the country, on the average, well over $2600 a year to support the Federal Government. And, if nothing else, that fact should tell us that the subject of governmental finance is a matter of vital importance to everyone.

In this chapter we turn first to that subject and then to a brief look at the Federal Government's banking and lending activities. As we do so, recall that we have already taken note of the fiscal powers exercised by Congress—especially the powers to tax, spend, and borrow. And, too, we have noted the President's authority in fiscal matters—exercised principally through the annual federal budget and his fiscal right-arm, the Office of Management and Budget.

As you read these pages, bear this important point in mind: The dollars involved in public finance—those which are collected and spent, borrowed or lent—are all *symbols* for *public policy decisions.*

How much money is collected? From what particular sources does it come? How much is spent? For what particular purposes does it go? How much more (or less)

THE
UNITED STATES
BUDGET
IN BRIEF

FISCAL YEAR
1981

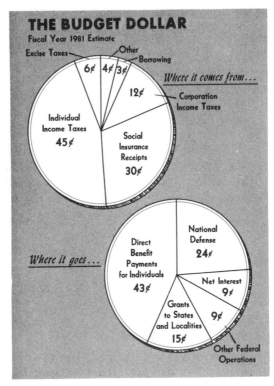

THE BUDGET DOLLAR

Fiscal Year 1981 Estimate

Excise Taxes — Other — Borrowing

6¢ 4¢ 3¢

Where it comes from...

12¢ — Corporation Income Taxes

Individual Income Taxes 45¢

Social Insurance Receipts 30¢

Where it goes...

Direct Benefit Payments for Individuals 43¢

National Defense 24¢

Net Interest 9¢

Grants to States and Localities 15¢

9¢

Other Federal Operations

The federal budget is developed within guidelines set by the President. It contains estimates of income and outgo for a fiscal year. Responsibility for its preparation falls mostly on the Office of Management and Budget.

is spent for what particular purposes now than in some earlier period?

These and a host of similar questions can all be answered in *dollar* terms, of course. They can also be answered in *public policy* terms. To put the point another way, the dollar signs and numbers involved in public finance are much more than simply arithmetic indicators. How many dollars are spent for what says a great deal about both the content and the general direction of public policy. And how many dollars are spent for certain programs in contrast to those spent for others is similarly indicative in public policy terms. Again, dollar signs = policy decisions.

The Power to Tax

The cardinal importance of the taxing power is underscored by the fact that the Constitution places it first among the pow-

ers it grants to Congress. Article I, Section 8, Clause 1 gives to Congress the power

> To lay and collect taxes, duties, imposts and excises, to pay the debts, and provide for the common defense and general welfare of the United States . . .

Congress exercises the taxing power in order to raise the revenues necessary to finance the operations of the Government, of course. But, recall, it also taxes for certain *non*-revenue purposes, as well (see page 503).

Limitations on the Taxing Power. The power to tax is *not* an unlimited one. As with all of the other powers possessed by the National Government, it must be exercised within the confines of *each* and of *all* of the limitations the Constitution places on the use of governmental power. Thus, for example, Congress could not lay a tax on membership in a political party.

Clearly, such a levy is prohibited by the 1st Amendment's guarantee of freedom of expression. Nor could it impose a tax upon a person as punishment for some act. Such a tax would amount to a bill of attainder and is forbidden by Article I, Section 9.

In more specific terms, the Constitution imposes four *expressed* limitations and one *implied* limitation on the taxing power.

(1) TAXES FOR PUBLIC PURPOSES ONLY. Article I, Section 8, Clause 1 declares that taxes may be levied only "to pay the debts, and provide for the common defence and general welfare of the United States." That is, says the Constitution, Congress may tax only for public purposes, not for private benefit.

To illustrate the point, it was on this ground that the Supreme Court in 1936 invalidated one of the major pieces of the New Deal program, the Agricultural Adjustment Act of 1933. That law provided for a broad range of controls on agricultural production. Among other things, it levied a tax on the processors of farm commodities. The proceeds from the tax were used to pay subsidies to farmers who agreed to reduce their production of those commodities. This, said the Court, amounted to the taxing of one private group (the processors) for the benefit of another (the farmers) and was prohibited by the Constitution.[1]

(2) EXPORT TAXES PROHIBITED. Article I, Section 9, Clause 5 provides:

> No tax or duty shall be laid on articles exported from any State.

Thus, customs duties (tariffs) may be applied only to imports; Congress may not levy duties on any goods exported from

the United States. This restriction was written into the Constitution at the insistence of the Southern States. They were fearful that Congress, controlled by the larger Northern States, would attempt to choke off their profitable cotton trade with Great Britain and divert it to mills in the New England States.

While Congress cannot tax exports, it can and does prohibit the export of certain items—usually for reasons of national security, and acting under its expressed power (in Article I, Section 8, Clause 3) to regulate foreign commerce.

(3) EQUAL APPORTIONMENT OF DIRECT TAXES. Article I, Section 9, Clause 4 provides:

> No capitation, or other direct tax, shall be laid, unless in proportion to the census or enumeration hereinbefore directed to be taken.

This restriction was a part of the curious three-fifths compromise at the Philadelphia Convention; see page 54. In effect, Northern delegates insisted that if slaves were to be counted in the populations of the Southern States, then those States were going to have to pay for them.

A *direct* tax is one that must be borne by the person upon whom it is levied—as, for example, a tax on land or buildings, which must be paid by the owner of the property; or a capitation tax (a head or poll tax), laid on each person.

Other taxes are *indirect* taxes. That is, they are levies which may be shifted to another for payment—as, for example, the taxes on whiskey or cigarettes. They are laid initially on the distiller or on the manufacturer of the cigarettes but are passed along to and ultimately paid by the purchaser of the commodity.

This provision means, in effect, that any direct tax levied by Congress must be apportioned among the several States according to their populations. That is, such a tax must produce from each State the

---

[1] In the case, *United States* v. *Butler,* the Court also struck down the law on another, and broader, base. It held the control of agricultural production to be a matter within the reserved powers of the States and thus beyond the reach of Congress. The Court soon reversed itself on this point, however; see page 617.

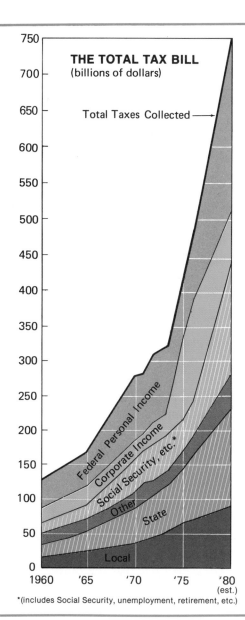

THE TOTAL TAX BILL
(billions of dollars)

Total Taxes Collected →

Federal Personal Income

Corporate Income

*Social Security, etc. ***

Other

State

Local

750
700
650
600
550
500
450
400
350
300
250
200
150
100
50
0

1960　'65　'70　'75　'80 (est.)

*(includes Social Security, unemployment, retirement, etc.)

The Average Taxpayer's Burden

Based on a man (with wife and 2 children) who had income of $20,000 in 1980 (estimates).

Federal Income Tax	$2,114
Social Security Tax	$1,226
Other Federal Taxes	$2,111
State Income Tax	$ 400
Local Property Tax on Home (includes School Tax)	$ 810
State and Local Sales Taxes	$ 330

TOTAL (est.) BASE TAXES $6,991

In addition some or all of these approximate taxes will be paid

On cigarettes at 21¢ a pack, a pack a day	$76.65
On gasoline at 14¢ a gallon, 13 gallons a week	$94.64
A substantial tax on all spirits (including wine and beer)	

Plus varying rates per dollar on toll telephone calls, air-travel, fishing equipment, and other items.

. . .So more than 35 cents of each dollar is taken by Federal, State and Local taxes

Sources: Bureau of the Census; Tax Foundation, Inc.

same share of the total tax take as that State's share of the total national population. A direct tax which raised $1 billion, for example, would have to produce nearly $100 million from California and nearly $10 million from Oregon. It would because California has nearly 10 percent of the nation's population and Oregon approximately one percent.

Wealth is not evenly distributed among the States, of course. Some are richer, or poorer, than others. Therefore, a direct tax laid in proportion to population would be quite unjust; it would fall more lightly, or heavily, upon the residents of some States than those in some others. As a result, Congress has seldom levied a direct tax (except for the income tax). In fact, Congress has not levied a direct tax outside the District of Columbia in more than a century, not since 1861.

An income tax is a direct tax. But it may be laid without regard to population because of the 16th Amendment:

The Congress shall have power to lay and collect taxes on incomes, from whatever source derived, without apportionment among the several States, and without regard to any census or enumeration.

Congress first levied an income tax from 1862 to 1872. The Supreme Court found it to be constitutional as an excise tax (that is, an indirect rather than a direct tax). But a later income tax law, enacted in 1894, suffered a different fate; it was declared unconstitutional in *Pollock* v. *Farmers' Loan and Trust Co.*, 1895. There the High Court found that taxes levied on incomes derived from land or other property were direct taxes. The tax law, the Court held, was invalid because it did levy taxes on such incomes but did not apportion them among the States as the Constitution required. The obvious impossibility of taxing incomes fairly in accord with any plan of apportionment led, finally, to the adoption of the 16th Amendment in 1913.

(4) INDIRECT TAXES MUST BE UNIFORM. Article I, Section 8, Clause 1 concludes with these words:

> . . . but all duties, imposts, and excises shall be uniform throughout the United States.

It is very difficult to draw a precise line between direct and indirect taxes. In the final analysis, the distinction with regard to any particular tax rests with Congress and the Supreme Court. But, as a general rule, indirect taxes are those which, although paid by one person, are actually passed on to another and ultimately (indirectly) paid by the latter. We used taxes on liquor and cigarettes to illustrate the point a moment ago. Customs duties are another good example. They are initially paid by the importer but then passed on to the wholesalers and distributor who, in turn, pass them on to the retailer. The retailer includes the duties in the price charged for, say, French perfume, Danish ham, or Japanese television sets—and the purchaser actually pays the tax.

The limitation here means that all indirect taxes must be levied at the same rate in all parts of the country. Thus, the federal excise tax on gasoline or beer or firearms must be the same in New York as it is in New Mexico. Or, the duty on cut diamonds or automobiles must be the same at the port of New York as it is at the port of New Orleans, and so on.

THE IMPLIED LIMITATION—TAXATION OF STATE AND LOCAL GOVERNMENTS. The National Government may *not* tax the States or any of their local governments in the exercise of their governmental functions. As the Supreme Court declared in *McCulloch* v. *Maryland* in 1819, "the power to tax

THE TAXING POWER

Congress may "lay and collect taxes, duties, imposts, and excises," subject to:

Expressed Limitations

1. Taxes must be levied "to pay the debts, and provide for the common defense and general welfare of the United States." *Article I, Section 8, Clause 1.*
2. No tax may be laid on exports. *Article I, Section 9, Clause 5.*
3. Direct taxes must be apportioned among the States on the basis of population. *Article I, Section 9, Clause 4.* But the *16th Amendment* permits the levying of an income tax without regard to this limitation.
4. Indirect taxes must be levied at a uniform rate throughout the United States. *Article I, Section 8, Clause 1.*

Implied Limitation

Congress may not tax the basic governmental functions of the States or their local governments. *Implied from the nature of the federal system.*

THE FEDERAL GOVERNMENT'S INCOME, BY SOURCE
(In Billions of Dollars)

Source	1970	1975	1979	1980	1981 (est.)
Individual income tax	$ 90.4	$122.4	$217.8	$244.1	$278.2
Corporation income tax	32.8	40.6	65.7	64.6	66.4
Social insurance taxes and contributions	45.3	86.4	141.6	160.7	184.5
Excise taxes	15.7	16.6	18.7	24.3	48.7
Estate and gift taxes	3.6	4.6	5.4	6.4	6.3
Customs duties	2.4	3.7	7.4	7.2	7.5
Miscellaneous receipts	3.4	6.7	9.2	12.8	12.4
Total Receipts	$193.7	$281.0	$465.9	$520.1	$604.0

Source: Office of Management and Budget

involves the power to destroy." If Washington could tax the governmental activities of the States or their local units it could conceivably tax them out of existence—and so destroy the federal system.

The National Government *may* tax those State and local functions which are of a *non-governmental* (or *corporate*, businesslike) character, however. That is, it may tax those activities which are not necessarily or ordinarily engaged in by the States or their local subdivisions. For example, in 1893 South Carolina created a State monopoly to sell liquor and then claimed exemption for each of the stores from the federal saloon license tax. But in *South Carolina* v. *United States*, 1905, the Supreme Court held that the State had to pay the tax because the sale of liquor is not a necessary or usual governmental activity. The Court ruled in a similar way in *New York and Saratoga Springs Commission* v. *United States*, 1946. Here, it held that spring water bottled and sold by a State is subject to the same federal taxes as those imposed on private bottlers and distributors. The various States (and many of their local governments) are involved in a large number of such businesslike activities, as we shall see in Chapter 33.

Current Federal Taxes. "Taxes," said

Oliver Wendell Holmes, "are the price we pay for civilized society." Society does not appear to be very much, if at all, more civilized now than it was when the great jurist made that remark in 1927. But "the price

". . . PLUS CITY TAX, PLUS COUNTY TAX, PLUS STATE TAX, PLUS THE NEW FEDERAL TAX—LET'S SEE, HAVE I LEFT ANYTHING OUT . . . ?"

CITIZEN SMITH, by Dave Gerard. Reprinted courtesy of The Register and Tribune Syndicate.

we pay" has certainly gone up over the past half century. A glance at the tables on page 497 and on pages 495 and 511 will confirm the point.

THE INCOME TAX. The income tax is the largest single source of federal revenue today. It first became the major source during the war years 1917 and 1918. Except for a few years during the Depression of the 1930's, it has remained so ever since.

Several factors suit the income tax to this dominant role. It is flexible; its rates can be readily adjusted to the current needs of the Government. It is easily adapted to the principle of ability to pay. The rates have always been progressive— that is, the higher the income the higher the tax rate. Then, too, the tax falls directly on those who must pay it—and so tends to make the taxpayer more aware of both the

costs and the range of the many services government provides.

Ever since 1913 the tax has been levied on the incomes of both individuals and corporations.

THE INDIVIDUAL INCOME TAX. The tax on individual incomes regularly produces the larger amount. The first year's returns under the 16th Amendment (fiscal year 1914) came to only $28 million. For the year ending September 30, 1981 (fiscal year 1981), the tax is expected to produce approximately $278 billion.

The tax is levied upon a person's *taxable* income—that is, one's total income minus certain personal exemptions and deductions. An exemption of $1000 is allowed to each taxpayer and each of his or her dependents. Thus, the exemptions for a family of five would amount to $5000. An additional $1000 exemption is allowed for each person over age 65 or blind. Deductions may be taken for several items—*e.g.*, medical and hospital care and insurance expenses, most State and local taxes, mortgage and other interest payments, charitable contributions, business or professional expenses, and so on.

By April 15th all persons who received taxable income in the preceding calendar year must file income tax returns—declarations of that income and of the exemptions and/or deductions claimed.[2] A husband and wife may file a joint return, even if one of them had no income in the previous year. The rates applied to joint returns are somewhat lower than those applied to returns filed by single persons.

The income tax returns are mailed to

"YOU'VE BEEN UTTERLY CHARMING,
MR. DANVERS, BUT I AM STILL
GOING TO DISALLOW YOUR HI-FI."

Drawing by Handelsman; © 1977
The New Yorker Magazine, Inc.

[2] Currently (1981) single persons with incomes of less than $3300 (married couples, $5400) are in the "zero bracket"—*i.e.*, they owe no taxes and so need not file. But those who had any income from which taxes were withheld should nonetheless file—to claim a refund.

The rates and other details of the various federal taxes dealt with in these pages are accurate as of January 1, 1981. At President Reagan's urging, Congress is expected to act sometime in 1981 to reduce the rates at which at least several of them are levied.

one of 10 regional Internal Revenue Service offices.[3]

The rates applied to income earned in 1980—and reported in 1981—range from 14 percent of the taxable income between $2300 and $3400 for single persons ($3400 to $5500 for married couples) on up to a maximum of 70 percent on incomes above $108,300 ($215,400 for married couples).

THE CORPORATION INCOME TAX. All of a corporation's earned income above the expenses of the business is taxable. On this income the progressive tax now runs as high as 46 percent on all corporate earnings in excess of $100,000.

Nonprofit organizations, such as churches, colleges, fraternal lodges, cooperatives, and labor unions, are exempted from the income tax. The corporation income tax was expected to produce some $66 billion in fiscal year 1981.

ENFORCEMENT OF THE TAX LAWS. The overwhelming number of taxpayers are honest, of course. Some people quite honestly under-figure their taxes; others often over-figure. The Treasury has a "conscience fund" into which goes all the money—several thousands a year—that people send to ease their consciences over past "mistakes." Not long ago a retired businessman sent in $5000 *just in case* he had made any mistakes through the years. After checking his returns the Internal Revenue Service not only returned the $5000 but an additional $17,000 for overpayments he had made in the past.

There are always a few cheaters, however, and the law provides for them. Those who intentionally fail to report part or all of their taxable income may be fined up to $10,000, imprisoned for as long as five years, charged a penalty of 50 percent of the amount not reported, or all three. Honest mistakes are excused if not found within three years but the IRS has six years in which to discover and bring criminal charges (tax-evasion) against those who make false returns or none at all.[4]

IRS files are filled with cases of tax evasion. A woman in Alabama claimed her mule "William" as a dependent for three years before agents caught her. A man in California claimed nine children on five annual returns when he actually had none. An Internal Revenue Service agent heard a man voicing some especially low opinions of income tax laws and, on a hunch, decided to check his returns. He had never filed any. In the end the complainer paid $76,000 in penalty and interest.

SOCIAL INSURANCE TAXES. The Federal Government now collects huge sums to finance three major social welfare programs: OASDI (the old-age, survivors, and disability insurance program), Medicare (health care for the elderly), and the unemployment compensation program.

OASDI and Medicare are supported by a tax levied on most employees, their employers, and the self-employed. At present, this social security tax is pegged at 6.65 percent of the first $29,700 of an employee's annual salary or wages plus an identi-

---

[3] There are actually two basic tax returns. If one's income was less than $20,000 and came only from salary, wages, tips, dividends, annuities, or interest, he or she may file the "short form." It is the front page of the famous (or infamous) *Form 1040*. On it, the taxpayer enters his or her total income, the number of exemptions, and the amount of tax, if any, already withheld. High speed computers process the return and allow a standard deduction in figuring the tax. The IRS then sends the taxpayer a bill for any tax still owed or, more often, a refund. If one's income was more than $20,000, he or she must file the more complicated "long form." That is, he or she must complete the second page of Form 1040, attach one or more additional forms (schedules), itemize his or her deductions, figure the tax from the accompanying tables, and send any amount due along with the form or apply for a refund for overpayment. A person with less than a $20,000 income *may* file the long form—and should if he or she can claim unusually high deductions. More than half of the approximately 90 million returns now filed each year are short-form filings.

[4] There is no statute of limitations concerning civil prosecutions. So, although after six years one may not be charged with a *crime* for falsifying a tax return, the Government may take steps to recover the taxes due plus penalty and interest.

cal levy on the employer. The employer deducts the employee's tax from his or her pay check and sends the combined contributions to the Treasury. Those who are self-employed pay an 9.3 percent tax on the first $29,700 of their annual incomes.

The unemployment compensation program is a joint federal-State operation. It is largely funded by federal grants which are paid out of a 3.4 percent tax on the payrolls of businesses with one or more employees.

These "payroll taxes" will bring in a projected $185 billion in fiscal 1981. The receipts are credited to trust accounts maintained by the Treasury, and Congress appropriates the funds for the various programs as they are needed. We shall take a look at the programs themselves later; see pages 584 and 626.

EXCISE TAXES. *Excises* are taxes laid on the manufacture, distribution, sale or consumption of goods and the performance of services. They have been imposed ever since Congress acquired its taxing power in 1789; among the first targets were carriages, liquor, snuff, sugar, and auction sales.

Today, excise taxes are imposed on many items, including gasoline, oil, tires

Case Study

The table here is drawn from the Budget for Fiscal Year 1981, submitted to Congress by the President and more current data supplied by the Office of Management and Budget. It shows the receipts, expenditures, and public debt of the Federal Government for selected recent years and relates them to the gross national product.

The gross national product (the GNP) is the total output of all goods and services in the country, expressed in terms of their market (*i.e.*, dollar) value. The GNP is a major device (analytical tool) for the measurement of the nation's overall economic well-being.

Among other things, the table demonstrates the important role of federal financing in the nation's economy and, too, its extraordinary impact on the nation's economic health.

Fiscal Year	GNP	Receipts Amount	Receipts % GNP	Outlays Amount	Outlays % GNP	Public Debt Amount	Public Debt % GNP
1955	$380.0	$65.5	17.2	$68.5	18.0	$274.4	72.2
1960	497.3	92.5	18.6	92.2	18.5	290.9	58.5
1965	657.1	116.8	17.8	118.4	18.0	323.2	49.2
1970	959.0	193.7	20.2	196.6	20.5	382.6	39.9
1975	1,457.3	281.0	19.3	326.2	22.4	544.1	37.4
1979	2,369.0	465.9	19.7	493.6	20.8	826.5	34.8
1980	2,557.0*	520.1	20.3	579.0	22.6	907.7	35.5
1981	2,821.0*	604.0*	21.4	633.8*	22.5	939.4*	33.3

Note: Dollar amounts expressed in billions.   *OMB estimates.

■ What conclusions can be drawn from the data presented here?

■ What general effect does a significant increase in the level of taxation have on the nation's economy? A significant increase in the rate of public spending?

■ What of the reverse: a reduction in taxes, or a decrease in spending?

■ What is the effect of an increase in the public debt? A decrease?

■ Is there a realistic prospect of a reduction in the debt in the foreseeable future?

the small society   by Brickman

and tubes, cigars, cigarettes, pipe and chewing tobacco, liquor, wine, beer, firearms, airline tickets, local and long-distance telephone service, and more. Those levied on the production or distribution of various items (tires, for example) are regularly figured into the price of those items and are frequently called "hidden taxes." Those laid on the sale of various items or services (airline tickets, for example) are, in effect, selective sales taxes. Because they are often levied on goods or services not usually considered to be necessities (liquor, for example) they are also sometimes known as "luxury taxes."

All of the various excises are expected to produce some $49 billion during fiscal year 1981.

CUSTOMS DUTIES. *Customs duties*—import duties, tariffs—are taxes on goods brought into the United States from abroad. Congress has the constitutional authority to impose these duties, of course. In doing so, it decides (1) which imports will be taxed and which will not and (2) the rates to be applied to those which are.[5]

Tariff rates vary on the almost 30,000 items now subject to duty; some run as high as 80 percent. Those articles which

may be imported without duty are said to be on the "free list"—included among them now are Bibles, raw silk, bananas, coffee, and farm implements. Those taxed at low rates are dutied "for revenue only"—for example, chamois skins, diamonds, and raw hair. And those taxed at high rates are dutied "for protection"—for example, wheat at 21¢ a bushel, wool at 11 to 28¢ a pound, and shoes at 20 percent *ad valorem* (of their value).

Many customs duties are set purposefully high to protect home industry. They produce little or no revenue, of course. But, purposefully, they affect the ability of foreign goods to compete in the domestic market. In short, they allow American manufacturers to sell their goods at prices somewhat higher than those they could otherwise charge. The *protective* tariff has been a prominent feature of the nation's tariff policy since the beginning of the Republic. And the basic concept of the protective tariff is strongly supported by most business, labor, and farm groups today.[6]

---

[5] Since 1922 Congress has authorized the President to raise or lower any tariff rate by as much as 50 percent. The President acts by executive order and on the basis of recommendations made by the United States International Trade Commission, see note 6.

[6] The extent to which the domestic economy is affected by tariff rates, and imports generally, is the subject of continuing study by the United States International Trade Commission. The Commission reports its findings and recommendations to the President and Congress. It was originally established by Congress in 1916 as the United States Tariff Commission and was renamed in 1974. It is an independent agency composed of six members appointed by the President and Senate for nine-year terms. Not more than three of the commissioners may be from the same political party and they are not eligible for reappointment.

Customs agents check the baggage and personal effects of incoming travelers in the Customs Area at Kennedy Airport.

Tariffs were the major source of federal revenue for more than a century. Now they produce only a minor fraction of the total receipts. The amount is still a very substantial sum, however—an estimated $7.5 billion in fiscal 1981.

ESTATE AND GIFT TAXES.   An *estate tax* is a levy imposed on the assets (the estate) left by one who dies.[7] A *gift tax* is one imposed on the making of a gift by a living donor. The estate tax has been a permanent part of the federal tax structure since 1916. The gift tax was first added in 1924—in order to catch wealth that would otherwise escape the estate tax by being given away by its owner before death.

Although the point might not be immediately apparent, these two taxes are quite similar and closely related ones. Both are levies on the transfer of property from one person to another. Estates are properties to be transferred (by will) *after* death; gifts are properties transferred (given, presented) *before* death.

Because of this basic similarity, Congress now subjects both estates and gifts to the same set of tax rates. These progressive rates range from a minimum of 32 percent on the net value of an estate or a gift up to a high of 70 percent of that portion of an estate or gift valued at more than $5 million.

Only one's *net* estate is taxable—that is, the total estate left at death minus certain deductions. The deductions allowed are for such things as debts, bequests to religious or charitable institutions, costs of administration, and State death taxes. Then, too, there is a marital deduction—of $250,000 or half of the value of the estate, whichever is larger. All of this means that most modest estates are not, in fact, taxed.

Nor are all gifts taxed. Those which a giver makes to any one person and which do not amount to more than $3000 within the year are tax-exempt. And here, too, there is a hefty marital deduction. The first $100,000 of gifts one spouse makes to the other is exempt, and so, too, is half of the value of all such gifts totaling more than $200,000.

Beyond all this, each person has a permanent credit of $40,000 to be applied against these taxes. One may use none, some, or all of that credit to offset any taxes on gifts made during his or her lifetime. Any portion of the credit left at death is then automatically applied against any estate tax that may be due.

Even with all of these complicated exemptions and deductions and the credit, however, the estate and gift taxes still bring over $6 billion into the federal treasury each year.

---

[7] An *inheritance tax* is another form of the so-called "death tax." It is not levied on the entire net estate but, instead, on each portion of it inherited by each heir. Most of the States impose inheritance, not estate, taxes; most of them also impose gift taxes. See page 774.

Taxation for Non-Revenue Purposes. As we've noted before, the power to tax may be, and often is, used for purposes other than the raising of revenue.

Usually, the non-revenue purpose is a regulatory one—to control or suppress those activities which Congress considers harmful or dangerous to the public. We have already cited several illustrations of this—among them the need for a license (a tax permit) for legitimate dealing in narcotics (page 333) or certain firearms (page 160) and the taxation of notes issued by State-chartered banks (page 337).

In upholding the tax on State banknotes, in *Veazie Bank* v. *Fenno*, 1869, the Supreme Court declared:

> Having in the exercise of undisputed constitutional powers, undertaken to provide a currency for the whole country, it cannot be questioned that Congress may, constitutionally, secure the benefits of it to the people by appropriate legislation.

Assured of the constitutionality of the technique, Congress has frequently used the taxing power as a regulatory weapon. As another of the many examples, in 1912 it levied a tax of 2¢ per hundred on the manufacture of white or yellow phosphorous matches. It did so because the highly poisonous phosphorous caused serious harm to workers in the match factories in which it was used. The immediate effect of the tax was to make phosphorous matches prohibitively expensive, and that section of the match industry was destroyed.

But Congress cannot use the power to tax in order to regulate in *any* manner it chooses. Here, as in all other matters, it is bound by *all* of the provisions of the Constitution.

To illustrate the point, consider those provisions of the Revenue Act of 1951 aimed at professional gamblers. The statute imposed a $50-a-year occupations tax (an excise) on bookies, levied other taxes on their activities and required them to register and render detailed reports to the IRS each year. The law brought in a small amount of revenue. But its *real* purpose was twofold: (1) to force those gamblers into the open, and especially to the attention of State and local police and prosecutors, and (2) to set a federal tax evasion trap for those who failed to comply with the law.

The Supreme Court held those provisions unconstitutional in *Marchetti* v. *United States* in 1968. It did *not* hold that the taxes had been imposed for an improper purpose. Rather, it voided the law because its application forced gamblers to furnish evidence against themselves—in violation of the 5th Amendment's ban on self-incrimination. (Note that the Court did not rule that Congress cannot tax such matters as gambling. Rather, it held that here Congress had chosen an unconstitutional *means* of doing so.)

Taxation may be used to accomplish any number of other ends, as well. For example, a tax may be levied on chain stores in order to improve the competitive position of independent retail outlets. Or, it may be used to influence consumer buying habits. Thus, in 1978 Congress levied a tax on the sale of "gas-guzzling" cars, beginning with 1980 models—to discourage their purchase and promote energy savings. Earlier (1965) it had repealed taxes on a long list of items, ranging from jewelry and furs through radio and television sets to lighters, matches, and playing cards—to encourage their purchase and so stimulate the nation's economy.

Among the many other purposes the use of the power to tax can serve, consider these: The relatively high rates at which large incomes and estates are taxed tends to equalize the distribution of wealth in the population. The raising of income taxes can reduce purchasing power and thus help to keep a lid on inflation. Or, alternatively, the lowering of income taxes can increase consumer spending and so help to reduce high levels of unemployment.

Nontax Revenues. Large sums of money reach the federal treasury from a multitude of nontax sources. Altogether, these miscellaneous receipts now come to about $12 billion a year.

These monies come from literally dozens of sources. The earnings of the Federal Reserve System, most in interest charges, produce a major portion of the total. The interest on loans made by several other agencies, canal tolls, fees for such things as passports, copyrights, patents, and trademarks generate large sums of money. The premiums on veterans life insurance policies, the sale or lease of public lands, the sale of surplus property, fines imposed by the courts—these and many other federal activities generate millions of dollars in nontax receipts.

One little-known source is *seigniorage,* the profit obtained from the minting of coins. It is the difference between the value of the metals used and the other costs of production and the monetary (face) value of the minted coins. And it is a tidy little sum—over $500 million in most years. The Philatelic Sales Branch of the Postal Service sells upwards of $100 million in mint stamps each year, and untold millions more are bought by collectors at local post offices. Few of these stamps are ever used on mail.

The Department of The Treasury

The Treasury Department was established by Congress in 1789 to "supervise and manage the national finances"—and that has remained its primary mission for nearly two centuries now.

The Department is headed by the Secretary of the Treasury. The post, like each of the other Cabinet offices, is filled by presidential appointment, subject to Senate confirmation, and the Secretary serves at the President's pleasure. George Washington selected Alexander Hamilton to be the first Secretary. His now 66 successors have often been men of outstanding abilities—among them, the historic figures: Albert Gallatin, Roger B. Taney, Salmon P. Chase, William G. McAdoo, Carter Glass, Andrew Mellon, Henry P. Morgenthau, Jr., and Fred M. Vinson.

Ten major and a number of lesser agencies now comprise the Department and employ the more than 110,000 men and women who work for it today.

The *Internal Revenue Service* is certainly the best known among them. It collects most of the tax monies that flow into the federal treasury—most prominently, income tax receipts. The IRS is also responsible for the enforcement of most of the tax laws. It is headed by a Commissioner of Internal Revenue and is organized on a geographic basis. Seven regional commissioners supervise the work of 58 district offices located across the country.

The *Bureau of Alcohol, Tobacco, and Firearms* administers the tax laws relating to liquor, tobacco products, firearms, and explosives, and collects the federal revenues from those sources. It also enforces the criminal provisions of the present federal gambling statutes. It functions under a Director and its organization is also decentralized. Most of its collections and its regulatory and enforcement activities are handled through seven regional offices which blanket the country. Its "revenooers" pursue moonshiners and others who flaunt the liquor laws in widely scattered places.

The *United States Customs Service* assesses and collects import duties, guards against smuggling and other fraud, and tracks down violators of the customs laws. All articles imported into the United States must be brought in through designated *ports of entry.* There are now some 300 of them. Most are located along the Atlantic, Pacific, and Gulf Coasts and the Canadian and

Mexican borders; but there are several inland, including Chicago, Cleveland, and St. Louis. The Commissioner of Customs directs the work of customs agents stationed at these ports and elsewhere in the country and abroad.

The *Office of the Treasurer of the United States* was created by Congress in 1789 to receive, hold, and pay out federal funds. The Treasurer is *the* officer personally responsible for every cent of all of the tens of billions of dollars involved in the finances of the National Government. By custom, the President usually appoints a woman to the post. By law, she is charged with the receipt, custody, and disbursement of the public monies and with keeping account of the sources, locations, and disposition of all of it. Funds are paid out by the Treasurer upon the presentation of a *warrant* (an order to pay, as a check) drawn by the Secretary and approved by the Comptroller

General. Her signature, and that of the Secretary, appears on all of the paper money of the United States.

The *Bureau of the Public Debt* supervises massive, complex, and continuing borrowing and other debt transactions of the Government of the United States. We shall turn to that subject, and the multi-billion-dollar public debt, in just a moment.

The *Bureau of Government Financial Operations* is the Federal Government's central bookkeeper and also its principal financial reporting agency. As the Constitution requires,[8] it publishes a daily, monthly, and annual *Statement of Receipts and Outlays of the United States Government.* All of the data in

---

[8] Article I, Section 9, Clause 7 reads: "No monies shall be drawn from the Treasury, but in consequence of appropriations made by law; and a regular statement and account of the receipts and expenditures of all public money shall be published from time to time."

Federal agents and Coast Guardsmen unload bales of confiscated marijuana from a fishing boat detected and seized off the coast of California.

RECEIPTS AND OUTLAYS OF THE UNITED STATES GOVERNMENT

For Fiscal Years 1979 and 1980, in millions of dollars*

	Fiscal 1979	Fiscal 1980
Receipts, By Source		
Individual Income Taxes	$217,841	$244,069
Corporation Income Taxes	65,677	64,600
Social Insurance Taxes, Contributions	141,591	160,741
Excise Taxes	18,745	24,329
Estate and Gift Taxes	5,411	6,389
Customs	7,439	7,174
Miscellaneous Receipts	9,252	12,742
Total Receipts	**$465,955**	**$520,050**
Outlays, By Major Agency		
Legislative Branch	$ 1,091	$ 1,218
Judicial Branch	480	564
Executive Office of the President	80	95
Funds Appropriated to the President (principally for Disaster Relief and Foreign Economic and Military Aid)	7,538	2,631
Department of Agriculture	20,636	24,555
Department of Commerce	3,756	4,072
Department of Defense—Military	115,013	132,840
Department of Defense—Civil	2,887	3,298
Department of Education	10,885	13,124
Department of Energy	7,889	6,457
Department of Health and Human Services	170,297	194,691
Department of Housing and Urban Development	9,222	12,576
Department of the Interior	4,087	4,377
Department of Justice	2,522	2,632
Department of Labor	22,650	29,751
Department of State	1,549	1,912
Department of Transportation	15,486	18,963
Department of the Treasury:		
Interest on the Public Debt	59,837	74,860
General Revenue Sharing	6,848	6,829
Other	−1,697	−5,047
Environmental Protection Agency	4,800	5,602
National Aeronautics and Space Administration	4,187	4,850
Office of Personnel Management	12,655	15,052
Small Business Administration	1,631	1,899
Veterans Administration	19,887	21,135
Other Independent Agencies	12,473	17,980
Deductions (undistributed offsetting receipts):		
Contributions to federal employees retirement	−5,271	−5,786
Interest received by various trust funds	−9,950	−12,045
Rents, royalties on Outer Continental Shelf	−3,267	−4,662
Total Outlays	**$493,067**	**$579,011**
Surplus (+) or Deficit (−)	**−$27,652**	**−$58,961**

* Figures may not add to totals due to rounding.

Source: Bureau of Government Financial Operations, Department of the Treasury.

the table on page 506 is drawn from the annual *Statement* for fiscal year 1980.

One of the Bureau's little-known functions is that of currency redemption. Every year thousands of banks, other organizations, and individuals bring batches of multilated paper money to the Treasury for replacement. The Bureau's "money surgeons" examine it and redeem as much as possible. Its files are filled with intriguing cases. A few years ago, a man brought in a large stack of bills that had rotted underground. Experts were able to reclaim $53,000 of this buried treasure. But $48,000 of it had to go to the tax collector, for he was a professional gambler and had not reported his winnings. A man in North Carolina put $600 in an electric heater for "safekeeping." He forgot about it and months later the Bureau was able to identify $570 from the ashes. It was also able to save $8500 out of a $9000 lump of black char belonging to a South Dakota farmer who didn't trust banks.

The Comptroller of the Currency supervises the operations of national banks. The Comptroller's office is an integral part of the nation's banking system, which we shall consider on pages 516–524.

The *Bureau of Engraving and Printing* produces the paper money, bonds, bills, notes, postage stamps, and food coupons issued by the Government. The bulk of its work involves the paper currency and we shall treat that subject in a few pages.

The *Bureau of the Mint* produces the nation's coinage, and we shall turn to that matter shortly, too.

The *United States Secret Service,* created by Congress in 1865, is today the oldest of the various federal police agencies. It was originally established to suppress the counterfeiting of United States currency. A number of additional functions have been added to that assignment over the years— most notably, of course, the protection of the person of the President. The Service is headed by a Director and its agents operate

Coins are bagged at the U.S. Mint in Philadelphia. Coins are produced in two other Mints—in Denver and in San Francisco.

out of Washington and from 61 district offices which blanket the country, and from an office in San Juan, Puerto Rico, and another one housed in the American embassy in Paris.

By any reckoning, the most important duty of the Secret Service is to protect the President of the United States. It has had the responsibility since the assassination of President McKinley in 1901. Today, no matter where he goes nor what he does, the President is under 'round-the-clock surveillance by the unobtrusive agents of the White House detail. Even the food that he eats is prepared and served under their supervision.

All of the members of the President's immediate family, no matter where they may live or travel, are kept under the same watchful eye. So, too, are the Vice President, the President- and Vice-President-

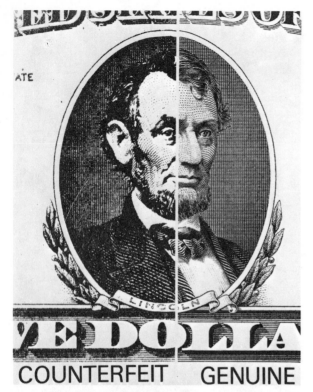

COUNTERFEIT   GENUINE

The fine detail in the portrait on a genuine note stand out prominently when compared to the portrait on a counterfeit bill.

elect, and their families. Agents also protect former Presidents and their wives, the widows of former Presidents, and the visiting heads of foreign governments.

The same protective shield now covers several other persons during the presidential campaign every four years. Congress has directed the Secret Service to guard the presidential and vice presidential nominees of the two major parties. And, before the nominations have been made, Secret Service agents guard any person who has qualified for federal election campaign subsidies.[9]

---

[9] See pages 205-206. Congress first ordered this protection following the assassination of Senator Robert Kennedy as he campaigned for the Democratic presidential nomination in Los Angeles in 1968. Congress then expanded this protection in 1972 after the wounding of Governor George Wallace as he campaigned for that nomination in Maryland.

Counterfeiters remain the special prey of the Secret Service. Most of those it apprehends have forged or otherwise trafficked illegally with the monies of the United States. But it also collars those who counterfeit foreign monies here or forge any of the obligations or securities of the United States; and it tracks down those who use false government travel authorizations, make false claims to federal lending agencies, or commit any of several similar federal offenses. All told, Secret Service agents handle some 5000 counterfeit and forgery cases each month. And, they destroy hundreds of thousands of dollars in bogus bills and coins each year.

Before we leave the administrative structure of the Treasury Department we must deal with one other piece of federal fiscal machinery:

The *General Accounting Office,* headed by the *Comptroller General of the United States,* is often described as "the watchdog of the Treasury." Its prime function is to check (audit) all expenditures of federal money to determine that those spendings are made as and for the purposes which Congress intended.

The GAO conducts both *pre-audits* and *post-audits.* That is, it checks upon the legality of expenditures both *before* and *after* they are made.

The GAO is *not* located within the Treasury, nor elsewhere in the executive branch. Rather, it is a legislative agency. When it was established in 1921, Congress attempted to assure its independence by placing it under its own wing. The Comptroller General *is* appointed by the President subject to Senate confirmation. But, again, to safeguard the agency's independence, the appointment is made for a 15-year term. Moreover, the incumbent cannot be reappointed and can be removed from office only by joint resolution of Congress.

Beyond its watchdog functions, the GAO also designs and oversees (and so standardizes) the accounting systems used by all federal agencies and supervises the recovery of debts owed to the United States. It reviews the information-gathering practices of the independent regulatory agencies. And, too, where it is appropriate, it recommends prosecutions to the Justice Department.

The Public Debt

The cost of government has mounted rapidly, and to well-nigh astronomical heights, in recent decades—as you can see in the graph on page 511. In 1900 the Federal Government spent less than $500 million. By 1940 its spending had risen to nearly 20 times that amount, to just over $9 billion. Over the years since then, federal expenditures have gone up, and up, and up. . . . Indeed, the Government now spends more every *three months* than it spent in all of the first *150 years* of our history.

Perhaps this comparison will give some useful impression of the mind-boggling size of present federal spending: If, on the day that Christ was born, a machine had begun to grind out a dollar bill every second of every hour of every day of every year, it would by now have produced about a tenth of the amount the Federal Government will spend in fiscal year 1981.

When government spending exceeds its income, it must borrow and so go into debt. The Framers of the Constitution recognized both the necessity for and the inevitability of a public debt. Thus, they gave to Congress the expressed power "to borrow money on the credit of the United States."[10]

Today (1981) the public debt is close to $925 billion—or about $4000 for every man, woman, and child in the country. This huge sum is primarily the result of World War I, the Great Depression of the

1930's, World War II, and defense and social welfare programs over the years since then. Interest on that debt amounted to almost $75 billion in fiscal year 1980, a rate of just over eight percent.

Over the period since 1930, the Government's expenditures have exceeded its receipts in all but six fiscal years. Only in fiscal years 1947, 1948, 1951, 1956, 1957, and 1969 did it take in more than it paid out. For selected, significant fiscal years, the gross public debt has been:

1916, pre-World War I	$ 1.3 billion
1919, post-World War I	25.5 billion
1930, start of Depression	16.2 billion
1940, decade of Depression	43.0 billion
1941, pre-World War II	48.9 billion
1946, post-World War II	269.4 billion
1950, pre-Korean War	256.1 billion
1954, post-Korean War	271.3 billion
1964, pre-Viet Nam buildup	308.1 billion
1974, post-Viet Nam with- drawal	474.2 billion
1980, latest fiscal year	907.7 billion

The Government borrows on both a "short-term" and a "long-term" basis. For short-term purposes, *notes, bills,* and *certificates of indebtedness* are issued; they run anywhere from 30 days to seven years. *Bonds* are issued to secure long-term loans, and they usually mature in 10 or, more often, 20 or 30 years.

The Government can and does get money at lower rates than those paid by private borrowers. Essentially, this is true because an investor can find no safer security than a federal note or bond. If the Government cannot pay its debts, neither can anyone else. At present (1981), the Treasury is paying interest rates in the range of 12 to 14 percent on both its short- and long-term borrowings.

The Treasury issues both *bearer* and *registered* bonds. Bearer bonds are *negotiable;* that is, they may be passed around like money. The interest on them is collected every six months by clipping and cashing

---

[10] Article I, Section 8, Clause 2; see pages 337-338.

OUR NATIONAL ECONOMY

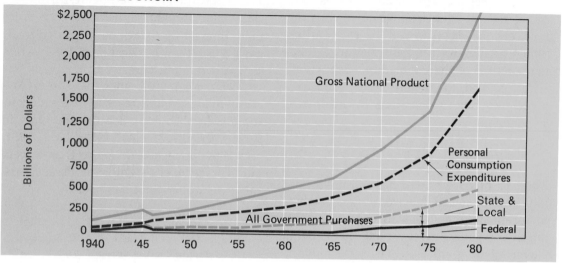

Gross National Product

Personal Consumption Expenditures

All Government Purchases

State & Local

Federal

Billions of Dollars

$2,500 2,250 2,000 1,750 1,500 1,250 1,000 750 500 250 0

1940 '45 '50 '55 '60 '65 '70 '75 '80

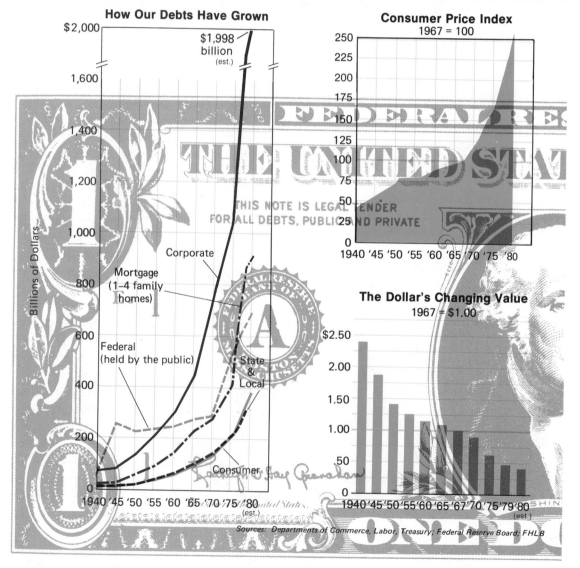

How Our Debts Have Grown

$2,000

$1,998 billion (est.)

1,600

1,400

1,200

1,000

800

600

400

200

0

Billions of Dollars

Corporate

Mortgage (1–4 family homes)

Federal (held by the public)

State & Local

Consumer

1940 '45 '50 '55 '60 '65 '70 '75 '80 (est.)

Consumer Price Index
1967 = 100

250 225 200 175 150 125 100 75 50 25 0

1940 '45 '50 '55 '60 '65 '70 '75 '80

The Dollar's Changing Value
1967 = $1.00

$2.50 2.00 1.50 1.00 .50 0

1940 '45 '50 '55 '60 '65 '67 '70 '75 '79 '80 (est.)

Sources: Departments of Commerce, Labor, Treasury; Federal Reserve Board; FHLB

THE FEDERAL BUDGET

Fiscal year ending September 30, 1980

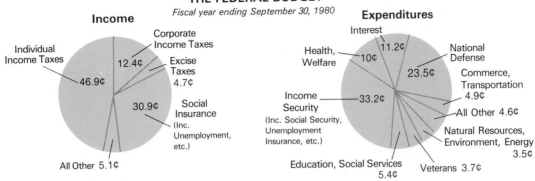

Income

- Individual Income Taxes 46.9¢
- Corporate Income Taxes 12.4¢
- Excise Taxes 4.7¢
- Social Insurance (Inc. Unemployment, etc.) 30.9¢
- All Other 5.1¢

Expenditures

- Interest 11.2¢
- Health, Welfare 10¢
- National Defense 23.5¢
- Income Security (Inc. Social Security, Unemployment Insurance, etc.) 33.2¢
- Commerce, Transportation 4.9¢
- All Other 4.6¢
- Natural Resources, Environment, Energy 3.5¢
- Veterans 3.7¢
- Education, Social Services 5.4¢

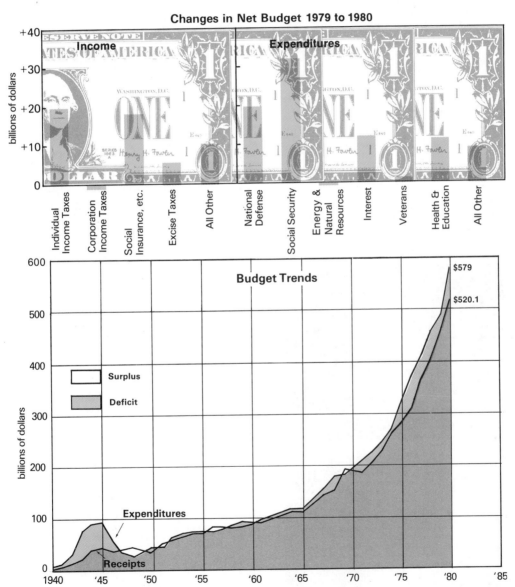

Changes in Net Budget 1979 to 1980

billions of dollars

Income

- Individual Income Taxes
- Corporation Income Taxes
- Social Insurance, etc.
- Excise Taxes
- All Other

Expenditures

- National Defense
- Social Security
- Energy & Natural Resources
- Interest
- Veterans
- Health & Education
- All Other

Budget Trends

billions of dollars

- Surplus
- Deficit

$579

$520.1

Expenditures

Receipts

1940 '45 '50 '55 '60 '65 '70 '75 '80 '85

Source: Office of Management and Budget.

at any bank the coupons attached to the bottom of each bond. Registered bonds are registered at the Treasury in the name of the owner. They can be circulated only by transferring ownership to another party. The interest is paid by checks from the Treasury.

The *Series EE Savings Bonds* are now the Treasury's most popular offerings. (They were first issued in 1980, succeeding the long popular *Series E Bonds*.) They are purposefully aimed at the small investor and many of them are purchased through payroll savings plans. EE Bonds now mature in 11 years and pay 8 percent interest if held to maturity. They are issued in face-value denominations ranging from $50 on up to $10,000. The face value of each bond is exactly one-half of its initial purchase price and the amount it will be worth if held for the full term—*i.e.*, 11 years.

This $5 gold piece was minted in 1834. The United States first began to issue paper money in the midst of the Civil War, in 1863; it has not minted any gold coins since 1933.

THE DEBT CEILING. The Constitution places no ceiling on the amount of the public debt, but Congress does. For fiscal year 1981, the limit was set at $925 billion—however, Congress may and often does change that figure.

The National Currency System

The Articles of Confederation gave to Congress the power to coin money and regulate its value. But the States were not prohibited from doing so. As we have seen, the lack of a stable and uniform national currency was one of the prime economic difficulties of the 1780's.

The Currency Power. Nearly all of the Founders were agreed on the need for a "hard" currency for the nation. Therefore, the Constitution gives to Congress the power "to coin money [and] regulate the value thereof." And it forbids the States the power to coin money, issue paper money, or make anything but gold or silver legal tender.[11] In effect, Congress is given the power to establish a *national* currency system.

Development of the Currency System. Congress first provided for a national currency system in the Mint Act of 1792. Both gold and silver were selected as the base for the nation's money, with coins minted of each metal to circulate side by side. The content of the silver dollar was fixed at 371.25 grains and that of the gold dollar at 24.75 grains.

The ratio between the two, 15 to 1, reflected the market price of the two metals at the time. But the fact that the law said that one ounce of gold was worth fifteen ounces of silver had little or no effect upon

---

[11] Article I, Section 8, Clause 5, and Section 10, Clause 1. *Legal tender* is any kind of money a creditor is required by law to accept when offered in payment of a monetary debt.

their actual market prices, and their respective values fluctuated constantly. Attempts to adjust the ratio between the two metals—by re-fixing the gold and the silver content of the nation's dollars—were a continuing source of bitter, often violent, political controversy throughout the 19th century.

As silver declined in value, silver dollars became "cheaper" than gold dollars, and the latter were hoarded by many people. To counteract this, Congress reduced the gold content of the dollar in 1834, establishing the ratio at 16 to 1. Of course, this made gold dollars worth more than they had been. Silver dollars were virtually driven out of circulation because those with debts to pay or who bought almost anything quite naturally preferred gold to silver money.

When Congress suspended the coinage of silver dollars altogether in 1873, it stirred one of the sharpest fights in all of American political history. Opponents, especially in the agricultural Middle West and the mining areas of the West, battled fiercely for the "free coinage of silver." That is, they fought for the resumption of the minting of silver at 16 to 1. The issue dominated the nation's politics for the next quarter of a century, with the Democrats generally supporting silver and the Republicans gold. The presidential campaign of 1896 was waged on this one question to the exclusion of nearly all else.

The Republican victory in 1896 led to the enactment of the Gold Standard Act of 1900. Congress made the gold dollar, pegged at 23.22 grains, *the* monetary standard. And, Congress required that all other money (silver and paper currency) be kept at a parity with gold. That is, it provided in law what had been true in fact for years: the nation was declared to be on the gold standard. The *bimetallic* (two-metal) base (gold and silver) established in 1792 was abolished. Henceforth, all currency was to be backed by gold, and all silver and paper

money could be redeemed at the Treasury for its face value in gold. The law also required the Treasury and national banks to maintain reserves sufficient to back all other money in circulation.

The gold standard was abandoned in 1933-34, however.[12] The Depression which began in 1929 brought severe business and financial crises. The public lost confidence in the security of bank deposits and the value of paper money. Gold began to disappear from circulation as millions of dollars' worth were hoarded and millions more were shipped abroad.

President Roosevelt moved to maintain the nation's gold reserves soon after taking office in 1933. He ordered the Treasury to halt its gold payments (the redemption of silver and paper currency in gold). Congress voided the "gold clauses" in all long-term bonds and contracts. These were provisions requiring the payment of both principal and interest in gold dollars.

Congress also authorized the President to reduce the gold content of the dollar—which he promptly did, from 23.22 grains to 13.7 grains. The action was especially intended to give a boost to the depressed economy. It had the effect of making gold dollars worth more than before and thus meant that there was now more money in circulation.[13]

In the Gold Reserve Act of 1934 and a number of other statutes Congress made several other significant changes in the currency system. Gold coinage was suspended, and it has not been resumed. All

---

[12] That is to say, it was abolished because gold coins and gold certificates were no longer allowed to circulate. From 1934 to 1968, the nation's money was backed by the gold bullion held by the Government. In effect, a *gold bullion standard* replaced the former gold standard.

[13] The legal price of gold was thus raised from the $20.67 per ounce price set in 1900 to $35 per ounce—and the dollar was thus "devalued." The price was pegged at that level until 1972 when Congress approved another increase (another devaluation of the dollar), to $38 per ounce. The price was raised again in 1973 to $42.22 per ounce; it remains at that level today.

holders of gold coin and of *gold certificates* (paper money redeemable in gold) were required to turn them in to the Treasury in exchange for paper money. In effect, gold was nationalized; the National Government became the sole owner of all gold in the country. Private transactions in gold were prohibited; mere possession was made subject to heavy penalty.[14]

When gold was withdrawn from domestic circulation in 1934, Congress directed the Treasury to accumulate a supply of gold sufficient to support (back) the nation's hugely expanded paper currency system. Specifically, it required the Treasury to maintain a gold reserve equal to at least 25 percent of the amount of paper money in circulation.

That gold reserve was then built up over the next several years—on through World War II and the immediate postwar period. By 1950 it had reached more than $24 billion. And, at that point, the United States Treasury held more than half of all the monetary gold in the world.

The nation's gold supply began to decline in the latter 1950's, however; by 1968 it had fallen by more than half, to just over $10 billion. It has risen somewhat since; it now stands at about $12 billion (measured at the legal price, $42.22 an ounce; but about $180 billion at the market price.)

The "outflow" of gold in the latter 1950's and the 1960's was the result of a number of factors. Chief among them was an unfavorable balance in our international trade (a *balance-of-payments deficit*). That is, the gold drain was due largely to the fact that the United States was spending more abroad than it was selling there. American exports regularly exceeded imports during that period. But economic and military aid to other countries, the costs of

maintaining American military forces abroad, and the spending of American tourists more than made up the difference.

In recent years—from 1973 on to the present, our ongoing balance-of-payments deficits have been the direct result of yet another factor: our heavy reliance on increasingly expensive foreign oil supplies.

The United States had made a number of attempts to counter the effects of the decline in the gold supply. Two of them are particularly important to our concern here—that is, are especially pertinent to the shape of the nation's currency system. The first of them came in 1968, when Congress suspended the requirement that gold be held to back the paper money supply. And the other came in 1971, when Congress suspended indefinitely the payment of gold to other nations in exchange for their U.S. dollars.

In effect, those actions signalled the end of any form of gold standard for the American monetary system. In short, even though the Treasury still holds a huge supply of gold, American paper money is now backed by American paper money.

Present Forms of Currency. Exercising its currency power, Congress has provided for the issuance of money in two basic forms: one metallic, the other paper.

METALLIC CURRENCY. All United States coins are stamped by the Bureau of the Mint. There are now three United States Mints—located in Philadelphia, Denver, and San Francisco. The Bureau also operates a Bullion Depository for gold at Fort Knox and another one for silver at West Point.

The coins of the United States in circulation today are one-, five-, ten-, twenty-five-, and fifty-cent pieces and dollars. They are the familiar pennies, nickels, dimes, quarters, and half-dollars and the not-so-familiar cartwheels. The metals from which they are produced are purchased through competitive bidding at the various Mints.

---

[14] Except for such strictly limited purposes as jewelry, industrial, or dental use or in coin collections. The private ownership of gold is now legal, however, and has been since 1975.

Until recently, all dimes and higher value coins contained a high percentage of silver—90 percent or more. In the Coinage Act of 1965, however, Congress directed that thereafter all of these coins were to be minted from copper and nickel.[15]

The change to the silverless "clad" coins came largely because of two factors: First, because of a marked increase in the use of coins in this country.[16] And, second, because of a steadily rising worldwide demand for silver for coinage and for many industrial and other uses. Virtually all of the older silver coins have disappeared—into collections, investment holdings, and the Mint's smelters where their silver content has been reclaimed.

The nation's demand for coins has produced occasional coin shortages in various parts of the country in recent years. Several factors have been responsible. Population growth and the rise in small-item prices above the penny and nickel range are among them, of course. And the demand for silver has outpaced its supply for several years. But there are a number of other and more specific causes, too. They include the spread of State and local sales taxes, the widespread use of parking meters, and the spectacular increase in vending machines to dispense an almost endless variety of goods and services. Then, too, coin collectors and speculators hoarding against a sharp rise in the market price of silver have added to the problem.

For decades the Treasury maintained a huge reserve of silver. As recently as 1967 it held more than 500 million ounces of the metal. Only a minor portion of that stockpile was used to mint new coins. Most of it was held to control the world price of silver—to keep it below the point (approximately $1.40 an ounce) at which it would be profitable to melt down United States coins.

The Treasury stopped buying silver and abandoned its stockpiling policy in 1967, however. It thus freed the price of the metal, and it jumped immediately and substantially. Today (1981) it is well above the $20-an-ounce level. All of this produced no real threat to the nation's coinage for three principal reasons: (1) the shift to the newer silverless coins, (2) the Treasury's policy of systematically withdrawing the older silver coins from circulation, begun in 1968, and (3) the fact that it is unlawful for anyone to melt down or otherwise deface any United States currency.

PAPER CURRENCY. Most of the money we see and use today is paper money. The Treasury's gold supply no longer stands as security for it. But, much more importantly, the Government *itself* does.

Recall that the Constitution gives to Congress the power to *coin* money; but it says nothing about *paper* money—except prohibit the States from issuing it.[17] As we noted on page 337, the Supreme Court finally upheld the right of Congress to authorize the printing of paper currency and to make it legal tender in *Julliard* v. *Greenman* in 1884. All paper currency issued by the United States today is legal tender.[18] That is, it must be accepted by a creditor when it is tendered (offered) in payment of a money debt.

Better than 95 percent of all paper currency in circulation today (some $100 billion) is in the form of *federal reserve notes*. These are bills issued by each of the 12 Federal Reserve Banks in denominations

---

[15] Pennies are minted of bronze (19 parts copper, one part zinc); all other coins are now faced with a copper-nickel alloy (three parts copper, one part nickel) bonded to a core of pure copper.

[16] Our voracious appetite for coins can be seen in the continuing climb in the dollar value of all coins in circulation: 1950, $3.9 billion; 1960, $4.9 billion; 1970, $6.5 billion; 1975, $9.1 billion.

[17] Article I, Section 8, Clause 5 and Section 10, Clause 1; see pages 336–337.

[18] But, notice, coins are *not* legal tender. They may be accepted for payment, of course; but creditors may refuse to accept them and demand that a debt be paid in paper currency instead.

from $1 to $100.[19] They are direct obligations on the United States Government. In effect, they are "warehouse receipts" against the Government's good faith and its intent; recall, they cannot be redeemed for anything except other Government money. The Federal Reserve Board's power to increase or decrease the amount of these notes in circulation has a fundamental effect on the nation's economy—as we shall see in a moment.

Several other forms of paper currency are in circulation, but only in very limited and steadily decreasing amounts. The once very common *silver certificate,* issued by the Treasury until 1964 and mostly in the form of $1 bills, has been almost entirely replaced by federal reserve notes. They were backed by the silver bullion held by the Treasury, but were discontinued to free the silver for coinage and other purposes. Treasury notes of 1890 and a few other forms of currency still show up occasionally but they are retired whenever they are deposited in banks.

All federal paper currency—that is, today, all federal reserve notes—are designed, engraved, and printed by the Bureau of Engraving and Printing. The Bureau produces all of the Treasury's bonds, notes, bills, and certificates of indebtedness. And it also produces all postage, revenue, customs, and savings stamps, food coupons, military and civilian award certificates, commissions of office, and a host of other items for several other federal agencies.

The Federal Government and The Banking System

Early National Regulation. The economic ills of the 1780's had been one of the chief causes for the drafting and adoption of the Constitution. Two years after

the Constitution went into force, Congress created the Bank of the United States. It did so largely at the urging of Alexander Hamilton. As the first Secretary of the Treasury, Hamilton had proposed the bank as a major step toward righting the financial chaos of the Critical Period.

As we saw earlier, Hamilton's proposal touched off one of the most momentous debates in all of our constitutional history. Hamilton and his supporters (the liberal constructionists) were pitted against Thomas Jefferson and his followers (the strict constructionists) over the extent of the powers of the new National Government.

THE FIRST BANK OF THE UNITED STATES. Logic and practical necessity convinced Congress of the need for a centralized national banking system. Thus, the Bank of the United States was created in 1791. It was granted a 20-year charter. The National Government held 20 percent of its capital stock of $10 million; the other 80 percent was subscribed by private individuals. The bank issued notes which circulated as paper money.

With its eight branches located in principal cities, the bank proved of great value to both business and the National Government. It aided in the collection of revenue, made loans to the National Government, and served as a depository for public funds. Although many continued to oppose the bank after its creation, its constitutionality was not challenged in the courts. When its charter expired in 1811, the Congress simply did not renew it.

THE SECOND BANK OF THE UNITED STATES. The financial crisis brought on by the War of 1812 led Congress to re-charter the Bank of the United States in 1816. It was quite similar to the first bank but was established on a much larger scale. Its capital stock was $35 million. The division of stock between private holders and the National Government, however, remained the same.

[19] Those bills previously issued in larger denominations—of $500, $1000, $5000, and $10,000—are now being withdrawn from circulation.

The chaos and confusion created by lack of a national banking system was a cause of a number of bank failures and panics in the 1800's. Here, an artist depicts New York's Wall Street during a bank panic in 1884 that swept that city's financial district.

The Second Bank had a much more stormy career than its predecessor. The constitutionality of its charter was attacked, but it was upheld by the Supreme Court in 1819 in the landmark case of *McCulloch* v. *Maryland*.[20] The Second Bank was not as well managed as its predecessor, and it was opposed by State-chartered banks which resented its competition. The bank became an issue in the presidential election of 1828. Andrew Jackson and his supporters charged that the bank was being used to support the re-election of President John Quincy Adams. With Jackson's victory, the fate of the "monster," as he called it, was sealed. As President, Jackson vetoed a bill to extend the bank's charter in 1832 and crippled it by withdrawing all federal funds. The bank finally died when its charter expired in 1836.

Period of State Bank Monopoly. From 1836 to 1863 *State banks* (private banks chartered under State law) held a monopoly of the banking business. State banking laws were generally lax.

The Constitution forbids the States to issue paper money, but the Supreme Court had held that the States were *not* forbidden from authorizing private banks to do so.[21] Some States permitted banks to issue only as much in notes as they could redeem in gold. Most States, however, allowed their banks to issue any amount that they pleased. Inevitably, the country was flooded with a bewildering variety of paper money. The value of the private bank notes varied from being "as good as gold" to being worth "next to nothing," depending upon the bank of issue. Two of the most spectacular banking crises in our history, those of 1837 and 1853, came during this period of "wildcat banking."

20 The case is especially important, recall, because the Court here for the first time upheld the doctrine of implied powers (see pages 80, 86, 343–345), and also ruled that the States could not tax the instrumentalities of the Federal Government (see page 770).

21 Article I, Section 10, Clause 1; *Briscoe* v. *The Bank of Kentucky*, 1837.

The National Banking System. The chaos brought on by the lack of a centralized banking system led many to argue for renewed federal control. The difficult problem of financing heavy wartime expenditures (those of the Civil War) finally forced Congress to act. A national banking system was created by the National Banking Acts of 1863 and 1864.

The new laws did not create another Bank of the United States; instead, they provided for the chartering of private banks by Congress. These *national banks* (private banks chartered under federal law) were each permitted to issue notes up to the amount of their capital stock. But these notes had to be secured by federal bonds owned by the bank and deposited with the United States Treasury. Each member bank had to agree to periodic inspection to insure its sound condition and to protect its depositors. And, each member bank was limited as to the amount of loans it might have outstanding at any one time. Any private bank could become a part of the national banking system by meeting these same conditions.

In 1865 Congress destroyed the power of the State banks to issue paper money by imposing a 10 percent tax on the notes issued by any bank that was not a part of the new national system. The Supreme Court upheld the move as a valid use of the taxing power in 1869, as we noted on page 503. The national banking system brought a marked improvement in the condition of the nation's banking and currency. And that system remained largely unchanged for 50 years, until Congress created the Federal Reserve System in 1913.

Two Systems of Banks Today. There are two principal systems of banks in the United States today: *State* and *national.* State banks are chartered under State law and national banks under federal law. Both kinds of banks are subject to extensive regulation by the States in which they do business. Most are also subject to extensive federal regulation.[22]

Of course, State banking regulations vary from State to State. Nevertheless, State and federal authorities cooperate well in safeguarding the public interest without disrupting the American principle of private enterprise. In particular, the creation of the Federal Reserve System in 1913 and the Federal Deposit Insurance Corporation in 1933 has produced considerable uniformity in the regulation and supervision of banks in general to safeguard the funds of depositors.

All national banks and the majority of State banks do the general business of *commercial banks.* That is, they receive deposits for safekeeping, accept savings accounts, perform trust functions. They also use their funds to make loans and investments, and render various other services to individuals and groups.

One group of State banks, the mutual savings banks, however, usually restrict their business exclusively to the receipt and investment of small savings deposits. Today there are approximately 500 mutual savings banks, located chiefly in New England and other Eastern States. Although they comprise only a small portion of the some 15,000 banks in the nation, they have impressive deposits that today total approximately $180 billion.

With the passage of the National Banking Act of 1863, State banks all but disappeared. Most State banks at the time became national banks in order to be able to continue the issuing of notes. Then, the number of State banks began to increase again. This increase came as the use of checks increased, as mutual savings banks

---

[22] A relatively small number of State banks are not members of the Federal Reserve System and so are not as closely regulated by federal law as are other State banks and all national banks. A national bank must have the word "national" in its corporate title: for example, the First National Bank.

the small society   **by Brickman**

WITH THE CURRENT INFLATION, HAVE YOU BEEN ABLE TO PUT ANYTHING ASIDE FOR RETIREMENT?

SURE. ALL THOUGHTS OF RETIREMENT —

Washington Star Syndicate, Inc.

7-6

BRICKMAN

began to grow, and as trust companies began to do general banking business. Today there are more State banks (about 9000) than there are national banks (about 4700).

National banks came into being to provide a sound control of bank note currency. When the currency-issuing Federal Reserve Banks were set up in 1914, national banks lost the power to issue notes. National bank notes are now retired whenever deposited in banks, and there are few such notes in circulation today. National banks today are merely federally-controlled commercial banks much like the State-chartered commercial banks.

Organization and Functions of National Banks. With the approval of the Comptroller of the Currency, any five or more persons may secure a charter of incorporation for a national bank. They must have a capital stock varying from $50,000 in places of less than 6000 inhabitants to $200,000 in cities of more than 50,000 inhabitants.

These banks receive deposits from individuals and corporations and lend money to them. They must be examined by federal examiners at least three times every two years. They must also make reports to the Comptroller of the Currency at least four times a year. Reports must be made *anytime* the Comptroller requests a bank to do so.

INSURANCE OF DEPOSITS. All national banks, and State banks which are members of the Federal Reserve System, must insure their deposits up to $100,000. State banks not members of the Federal Reserve System may also qualify for this insurance, however.[23] Insured banks pay an annual premium in proportion to their average deposits. In return each bank depositor's account is insured up to $100,000.

The insurance program is administered by the *Federal Deposit Insurance Corporation*, created when the insurance program was set up by Congress in 1933. It is an independent agency composed of the Comptroller of the Currency and two members appointed by the President with Senate consent for six-year terms.

Congress makes no appropriations to the FDIC. Its entire income consists of the premiums paid by insured banks and returns on investments. Its insurance fund now amounts to more than $10 billion. The FDIC has the authority to borrow up to $3 billion from the United States Treasury in order to cover its insurance commitments. As yet, the FDIC has never had to call upon the Treasury—largely because the nation's banks are in such sound condition and the Federal Reserve System and the insurance program have worked so well.

When a national bank is closed, the FDIC is appointed receiver. A new bank is

---

[23] Unsound practices cause a nonmember bank to lose its insurance privileges, a State bank to lose its membership, and a national bank to be closed.

organized and assumes the liabilities of the closed bank. If stock in the new bank can be sold, the new bank will continue. If not, the assets may be sold to another bank. If neither of these arrangements is possible within two years, the bank will be liquidated (abolished).

BRANCH BANKS. National banks may establish branch banks in their home cities if those cities have 25,000 or more inhabitants and also in foreign countries. Those with $500,000 or more capital may, with the consent of the Comptroller of the Currency, establish branches within the State to the extent that State banks are permitted to create branches.

EXAMINATIONS. In general, national banks are subject to unannounced examinations by specially trained examiners. These examiners check to see that the banks are in sound condition and are being properly run.

The Federal Reserve System

The banking reforms of the 1860's did much to cure the abuses of the earlier "wildcat banking" period. Still, the system was far from perfect, and crises continued to occur. The Panics of 1873 and 1893 were especially severe.

The chief defect of the banking system after 1863 lay in the fact that national banks were each separate institutions with no direct ties to one another. Financial reserves could not be shifted quickly from bank to bank to meet a credit emergency. Thus, in the Panic of 1907 several sound banks were forced to close their doors, simply because they did not have the ready cash at hand to meet a "run" by their depositors.

The Federal Reserve Act. Congress acted to remedy this weakness and to give national banks the strength of unity. It did so in 1913 when it passed the Federal Reserve Act which established the Federal Reserve System—"the Fed." The Act has been amended several times since, most notably in 1933 and 1935.

Organization. The United States is divided into 12 *Federal Reserve Districts*. A *Federal Reserve Bank* is located in a principal city in each of the districts.[24] Each of the 12 Federal Reserve Banks is supervised by a nine-member Board of Directors. Six of the nine members are chosen by the member banks: three must be bankers and three must represent industry, commerce, and agriculture in the district. The other three members are appointed by the *Board of Governors of the Federal Reserve System* and represent the public.

The Federal Reserve Banks do not carry on regular private banking operations. Instead, they perform central banking functions for their member banks.

Member Banks. Every national bank *is* a member of the Federal Reserve System. As such, it is required to purchase a share of the capital stock of the Federal Reserve Bank in its district. State banks and trust companies may also become member banks by meeting the same conditions imposed on national banks.

Board of Governors. The entire Federal Reserve System is supervised by a seven-member Board of Governors appointed by the President with Senate consent. No two members of the Board may come from the same district. Each member serves a single 14-year term, with one member retiring every second year. The President selects one of the Board's members to chair the Board for a four-year term.

POWERS OF THE BOARD. The principal duties of the Fed are to: (1) supervise the operations of the Federal Reserve Banks and member banks and (2) control the use and effect of credit in the nation's economy.

---

[24] In Boston, New York, Philadelphia, Cleveland, Richmond, Atlanta, Chicago, St. Louis, Minneapolis, Kansas City, Dallas, and San Francisco.

Supervision of Banks. The Board has general control over the operations of all banks within the system. In exercising this control, it decides whether or not a bank may become a member, may suspend a bank, or may even remove its officers if a situation warrants such action. It examines all member banks periodically and requires them to submit regular reports on their condition.

The Reserve Requirement. The Board sets the "reserve requirement" for the member banks. That is, it requires each member bank to deposit a certain percentage of its funds with its Federal Reserve Bank. By varying the reserve requirement, the Board can expand or contract the lending capacity of member banks. When there is a threat of inflation, the Board helps to check it by upping the reserve requirement to reduce risky or speculative borrowing and spending. By doing this, it creates what is known as a "tight money" condition. When, on the other hand, economic conditions seem to justify it, the Board can relax its reserve requirements and thus make more money available to stimulate business activity.

Rediscounting. The Board also controls the amount of credit in the economy by varying the "rediscount rate." When a member bank makes a loan, the borrower gives the bank his or her note. The bank may carry the loan itself, or it may "rediscount" the note. That is, it may borrow on it from the Federal Reserve Bank and thus receive additional funds with which to make still more loans. The interest that member banks pay on such loans (the rediscount rate) is set by the Board of Governors. The lower the rediscount rate the more member banks will be encouraged to make loans. The higher the rate the less anxious banks will be to make loans.

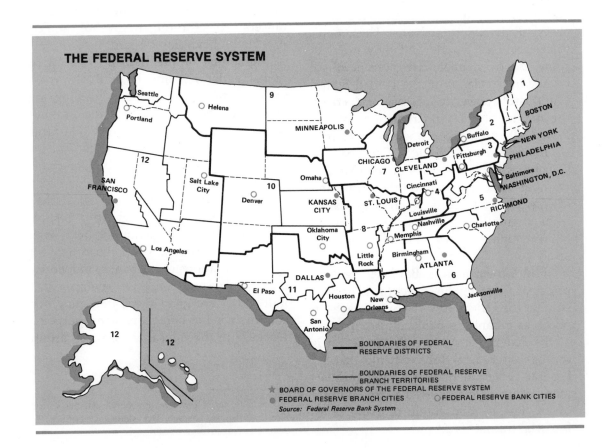

THE FEDERAL RESERVE SYSTEM

BOUNDARIES OF FEDERAL RESERVE DISTRICTS

BOUNDARIES OF FEDERAL RESERVE BRANCH TERRITORIES

★ BOARD OF GOVERNORS OF THE FEDERAL RESERVE SYSTEM
● FEDERAL RESERVE BRANCH CITIES   ○ FEDERAL RESERVE BANK CITIES

Source: Federal Reserve Bank System

"Open-Market" Operations. Still another important control over the amount of credit arises out of the functioning of the Federal Reserve System's Open Market Committee. The committee is composed of the seven members of the Board of Governors and five representatives of the Federal Reserve Banks. It controls the buying and selling of government securities by the Federal Reserve Banks. If an expansion of credit is desired, the committee authorizes the Federal Reserve Banks to purchase government securities on the open market. In taking this action, more money is put into business channels; it also helps to keep the price of government bonds up. If the committee wants to restrict credit, it may authorize the sale of a certain amount of government obligations held by the Federal Reserve Banks to drain money away from regular investment channels.

Federal Reserve Notes. Under the supervision of the Board of Governors any Federal Reserve Bank may issue paper currency—Federal Reserve Notes. These notes (bills) are legal tender, and they now account for over ninety-five percent of all money in circulation in the United States. The Board's power to increase or decrease the amount of notes in circulation also has a vital effect on the economy, of course.

Interest Rates on Deposits. The Board of Governors limits the rates of interest that member banks may pay on their time and savings deposits. Thus, it prevents banks from attempting to attract depositors by offering higher interest rates than they can safely pay.

The Government's Banker. By the principal functions just listed, it is easy to see that the Federal Reserve System acts, in effect, as a banker's bank. It also operates as the Federal Government's banker. It is through the Federal Reserve Banks that the Federal Government makes and receives many of its payments, sells a large portion of its "IOU's," and conducts many other financial transactions.

Federal Home Loan Bank System

The *Federal Home Loan Bank System* was created by Congress in 1932 to provide a credit reserve for local institutions involved in home financing. It is composed of several regional banks from which its member institutions may borrow to meet local home financing needs and withdrawal demands by their investors.

Organization. The system is managed by the *Federal Home Loan Bank Board.* It is an independent agency composed of three members appointed by the President with Senate consent for four-year terms. The Board supervises the operations of 12 regional *Federal Home Loan Banks* located in principal cities across the country.[25] Each of these banks is, in turn, managed by from 14 to 16 directors—some appointed by the central board and some elected by its local member institutions. The directors of each bank elect a president and other officers subject to the approval of the Federal Home Loan Bank Board.

Functions of the Banks. The 12 regional Federal Home Loan Banks make loans to savings and loan, building and loan, and homestead associations, savings and cooperative banks, and insurance companies. These member institutions make direct loans to home builders; most of them are of the savings-and-loan type.

Federal savings and loan associations can be organized by any group of responsible persons who make application to their regional Federal Home Loan Bank. In these associations (local banks) individuals may earn interest on their savings. Or, if individuals are good risks, they may borrow money for home financing purposes. Deposits in these local associations are in-

---

[25] In Boston, New York, Pittsburgh, Atlanta, Cincinnati, Indianapolis, Chicago, Des Moines, Little Rock, Topeka, San Francisco, and Seattle.

Under the supervision of the Farm Credit Administration, Federal Land Bank Associations make loans to farmers and ranchers at low rates of interest for terms as long as 40 years. Loans are made for such purposes as the purchase of land, equipment, or the construction of farm buildings, as the barn under construction here.

sured up to $100,000 by the *Federal Savings and Loan Insurance Corporation*—a federal agency operating under the supervision of the Federal Home Loan Bank Board.[26] There are over 5000 of these associations today, and they have assets totalling more than $500 billion.

System of Farm Credit Banks

The first piece of federal farm credit legislation was enacted by Congress more than 60 years ago: the Federal Farm Loan Act of 1916. It came as a response to two basic—

and continuing—facts of agricultural economics: (1) farming is usually, at best, a highly risky venture; and (2) farmers often need large amounts of credit, frequently on a long-term basis.

The Farm Credit System. Most federal agricultural loan programs today are supervised by the *Farm Credit Administration.*[27] It was created by Congress in 1933 to coordinate the various farm loan programs established since 1916.

The FCA's policies are made by a part-time member *Federal Farm Credit Board.* Twelve of its members are appointed by

---

[26] Other federal agencies in the field of home financing, most of them within the Department of Housing and Urban Development, are discussed in Chapter 22.

[27] Several farm credit programs are administered through the Department of Agriculture; see pp. 613–615.

the President and the 13th by the Secretary of Agriculture. The Board selects a governor who directs the agency's work.

The FCA is *not* itself a lending agency. It supervises the operations of the *Federal Land Banks* and the other banks in the Farm Credit System.[28]

The Federal Land Banks were created in 1916 to give the farmer an opportunity to borrow money at low rates against a long-term mortgage on his land. There is a Federal Land Bank in a principal city in each of 12 farm credit districts.[29] The Federal Land Banks make loans to local *Federal Land Bank Associations* which, in turn, make loans to their farmer-members. The stock of each of the approximately 550 associations is held by its members. These groups hold the stock of the Federal Land Banks. Thus, the whole system is completely farmer-owned.

The Federal Land Banks raise money through the sale of bonds to the investing public. They use the notes and mortgages put up by their farmer-borrowers, together with their other assets, as collateral for the bonds.

The associations make long-term loans to farmers and ranchers for such purposes as the purchase or improvements of land, buildings, and equipment. The loans are made for terms of from 5 to 40 years and in amounts up to 85 percent or the value of the real estate on which a mortgage is taken. Payments are usually due in annual or semi-annual installments.

An indication of the size and importance of the operations of the Farm Credit Administration can be seen in this fact: Farmers and their cooperatives now borrow some $20 billion a year from the banks and associations under its supervision. The bulk of this huge sum is borrowed by many of the approximately 350,000 individual members of the local Federal Land Bank Associations.

[28] They are: (1) The 12 *Federal Intermediate Credit Banks,* which make loans to more than 400 *Production Credit Associations.* These associations, in turn, make short-term loans to their farmer-members and to such other lending bodies as commercial banks and livestock-loan associations which also make loans to farmers. And (2) the *Central Bank for Cooperatives* and its 12 district banks which make loans to farm cooperatives in which farmers act together to market their products, purchase farm supplies, furnish farm business services, and the like.

[29] In Springfield (Massachusetts), Baltimore, Columbia (South Carolina), Louisville, New Orleans, St. Louis, St. Paul, Omaha, Wichita, Houston, Berkeley, and Spokane.

SUMMARY

The cardinal importance of the taxing power is underscored by the fact that it is listed first among the powers the Constitution grants to Congress.

Its exercise is subject to four expressed limitations: (1) Taxes must be levied for a public purpose; (2) Congress cannot tax exports; (3) Direct taxes except for the income tax, must be apportioned among the States on the basis of population; and (4) Indirect taxes must be uniform throughout the nation. The power is also subject to one implied limitation: Congress may not tax the governmental functions of the States or their local units.

A direct tax is one that is borne by the person upon whom it is laid, as a head tax or an income tax. An indirect tax is one that may be shifted to another for payment, as a tax on gasoline or cigarettes.

The *income tax* is the principal source of federal revenue today. It is levied on *personal* and *corporate* income. *Social insurance taxes,* "payroll taxes," support various welfare programs. *Excise taxes* are those laid on the manufacture, distribution, sale, or consumption of goods and the performance of services. *Customs duties* (tariffs) are taxes on imports. *Estate taxes* are imposed on the assets of those who die. *Gift taxes* are levies on gifts made by living donors. The Treasury also realizes large sums from a wide variety of nontax sources.

The basic function of taxation is revenue-raising; but the power can be, and is used, for various regulatory and other purposes.

The Treasury Department was established in 1789 to "supervise and manage the nation's finances"—and that remains its basic function today. It is headed by the Secretary of the Treasury. Most of its revenue collection and enforcement activities are the responsibilities of the Internal Revenue Service, the Bureau of Alcohol, Tobacco, and Firearms, and the United States Customs Service. Its other major components include the Treasurer of the United States, the Bureau of the Public Debt, the Bureau of Government Financial Operations, the Comptroller of the Currency, the Bureau of Engraving and Printing, the Bureau of the Mint, and the United States Secret Service. The General Accounting Office, headed by the Comptroller General, is a legislative agency, often called "the watchdog of the Treasury."

The public debt is now beyond $907 billion. It is largely the result of World War I, the Depression of the 1930's, World War II, and the defense and social welfare programs of the years since then.

The Constitution gives to Congress the power to establish a national currency (monetary) system. Currency circulates today in two forms, metallic and paper.

The First Bank of the United States (1791–1811) and the Second Bank (1816–1836) were the forerunners of the system of national banks first established by Congress in 1863. Today there are two principal banking systems in the United States: State banks, chartered under State law, and national banks, federally-chartered.

The Federal Reserve System was created by Congress in 1913 to give the nation's banking system the strength of unity. The "Fed" is both the Government's bank and bankers' bank. The Federal Deposit Insurance Corporation insures deposits up to $100,000 in eligible banks.

The Federal Home Loan Bank System was created in 1932 to provide a credit reserve for savings and loan institutions. The system of Farm Credit Banks was established in 1933 to manage various lending programs to aid farmers.

Concept Development

Questions for Review

1. Approximately how much are the Federal Government's annual receipts and expenditures today?

2. What expressed limitations does the Constitution place on the exercise by Congress of its power to tax? What implied limit?

3. Why has Congress not levied a direct tax, except for the income tax, outside of the District of Columbia in more than a century?

4. Why is the income tax, which is a direct tax, constitutional even though it is not apportioned among the States on the basis of population?

5. What is the primary distinction between a direct and an indirect tax?

6. Which federal tax produces the largest amount of revenue each year?

7. What three major social welfare programs are now supported by "payroll taxes"?

8. Why are some excises called "hidden taxes" and others "luxury taxes"?

9. What is the difference between customs duties and tariffs?

10. What is an estate tax? A gift tax? How are they closely related?

11. List five of the nontax sources of federal revenue.

12. Give three examples of congressional use of the taxing power for other than revenue-raising purposes.

13. Who heads the Treasury Department? How is that officer selected?

14. Most federal tax collections are made by what three agencies?

15. When and why was the Secret Service established? What is its most important duty today?

16. Why is the GAO often called the "watchdog of the Treasury"? Why is it a legislative agency?

17. To what particular causes is the nation's public debt largely due? Approximately how large is it today?

18. In what two forms is the nation's currency issued today?

19. What is the meaning of the term *legal tender*?

20. Why is *McCulloch* v. *Maryland*, 1819, one of the major landmark cases in our constitutional history?

21. What are the two principal systems of banks in the nation today?

22. What are the two principal duties of the Board of Governors of the Federal Reserve System?

23. What banks are members of the Federal Reserve System?

24. What is the Federal Home Loan Bank System?

25. What is a Federal Land Bank?

For Further Inquiry

1. Commenting on the high rates of federal taxation during World War II, Congressman Robert L. Doughton (D., North Carolina), said: "You can shear a sheep once a year; you can skin him only once." What did he mean?

2. Do you think it fair to require employers, acting at their own expense, to col-

lect (by withholding) federal income and social security taxes from their employees' paychecks?

3. What arguments can you advance for and against the use by Congress of its power to tax as a regulatory device?

4. Why were each of the Secretaries of the Treasury listed on page 504 singled out for mention there? Who is the Secretary today? What are his or her background and qualifications? The Chairman of the Board of Governors of the Federal Reserve System?

5. Which are most just, direct or indirect taxes? Which are easier to collect?

6. Do you agree or disagree with Mr. Justice Holmes' comment, quoted on page 497?

7. Should the Constitution be amended to require that the federal budget be balanced each year? Present at least two useful arguments *against* your view.

Suggested Activities

1. Write an editorial on the subject of the temptations and the morality of tax evasion.

2. Stage a debate or class forum on one or more of the following: (a) *Resolved,* That the Federal Government should adopt a general sales tax. (b) *Resolved,* That the Federal Government should conduct a regularly scheduled lottery to finance its operations. (c) *Resolved,* That all other federal taxes should be abolished and the Government be henceforth financed exclusively from the proceeds of the income tax.

3. Invite a local banker or an officer of another financial institution to speak to the class on a topic related to his or her work— *e.g.,* the making of sound investments, home financing, fluctuations in interest rates, commercial banking operations, etc.

4. Invite a local representative of a Treasury agency (*e.g.,* IRS, Customs Service, Secret Service) to speak to the class on that agency's history and functions.

5. Write a report on one of the following topics: the public debt, counterfeiting, the nation's gold supply, the principles of fair taxation, tax law enforcement, the role of the Federal Reserve System.

Suggested Reading

Davidson, James D., *The Squeese.* Simon & Schuster, 1980.

Facts and Figures on Government Finance. Tax Foundation, Inc., 20th ed., 1979.

Havemann, Joel, *Congress and the Budget.* Indiana University Press, 1978.

Heidensohn, Klaus (ed.), *The Book of Money.* McGraw-Hill, 1979.

Holtzman, Robert S., *A Survival Kit for Taxpayers.* Macmillan, 1979.

Horvitz, Paul M., *Monetary Policy and the Financial System.* Prentice-Hall, 4th ed., 1979.

Hutchinson, Harry D., *Money, Banking, and the U.S. Economy.* Prentice-Hall, 1980.

Luckett, Dudley, *Money & Banking.* McGraw-Hill, 2nd rev. ed., 1980.

McCarty, Marilu H., *Dollars and Sense: An Introduction to Economics.* Scott, Foresman, 2nd ed., 1979.

Musgrave, Richard and Peggy, *Public Finance in Theory and Practice.* McGraw-Hill, 3rd ed., 1980.

Myers, Henry, *Reduce Your Tax Bite.* Dow Jones, 1979.

Reese, Thomas J., *The Politics of Taxation.* Greenwood, 1980.

Schick, Allen, *Congress and Money: Budgeting, Taxing, and Spending.* The Urban Institute, 1980.

Schnepper, Jeff A., *Inside IRS.* Stein and Day, 1979.

Also: Office of the Assistant Secretary (Public Affairs), Treasury Department, Washington, D.C. 20220.

Office of Public Affairs, Board of Governors, Federal Reserve System, Washington, D.C. 20551.

Government and Business: Regulation and Promotion-I

A nation's prosperity rests fundamentally on the enterprise of individuals seeking to better themselves, their families, and their communities. It depends far more on what individuals do for themselves than on what government does or can do for them.

ARTHUR F. BURNS

■ Why is the American economic system often described as a "mixed" system?

■ Why is the Commerce Clause a prime illustration of the concept of "the living Constitution"?

■ Does government have an obligation to promote the health of the business community?

In Chapter 1 we considered the basic shape of the American economic system. We described it as a system of private enterprise, based upon the concepts of private ownership, individual incentive, competition, and profit. And we also noted that it is a *mixed* system, in which private enterprise is combined with a substantial amount of governmental regulation and promotion.

Government has been closely involved with the nation's economic life—and, more specifically, with its business life—from the very beginnings of the Republic. Recall, as we first noted in Chapter 2, the commercial conditions in this country in the 1780's were a leading reason for the writing of the Constitution.

In this chapter, and the one to follow, we turn to the place of government in the nation's business life. In this chapter we focus on the twin governmental roles of regulator and promoter; and, necessarily, we shall look at several segments of the business community. In Chapter 22 we shall extend our consideration to several other major segments of that realm.

In both chapters we shall be particularly concerned with the activities of the Federal Government in the world of business. As we do so, keep this important point in mind: Government at *all* levels in this country—national, State, and local—is, and long has been, so involved. Indeed, the range of State and local governmental activity in the field is even more extensive than that of the Federal Government. It runs the alphabetical scale, literally, from A to Z—ranging from the regulation of accounting and banking practices and the abatement of pollution, through the promotion of housing and industrial development and of recreation and tourism, to the control of public utilities and zoning.

The Commerce Power

The principal constitutional source of federal authority in the field of economic activities is the Commerce Clause.[1] It grants to Congress the extraordinary commerce power, the power:

> To regulate commerce with foreign nations and among the several States, and with the Indian tribes.

Certain other of the expressed powers also provide a basis for national authority in economic affairs. This is especially true of the taxing power, as we saw in the preceding chapter. A number of the other powers set out in Article I, Section 8 are relevant, too—including the postal, currency, bankruptcy, copyright, and patent powers; and, recall, we outlined their shape in Chapter 14. But it is the commerce power which serves as the bedrock here.

The broad interpretation of the Commerce Clause by the Supreme Court has stretched congressional authority into a great many areas not anticipated by the Framers. As but one of many illustrations of the point: Recall that Congress, in enacting the several recent civil rights laws, has relied heavily upon the commerce power to outlaw racial and other forms of discrimination in this country.

The Meaning of "Commerce." As it is used in the Constitution, the word "commerce" cannot be precisely defined. Rather, what it means—what it includes

Established by Congress in 1975, the Nuclear Regulatory Commission licenses and regulates the uses of nuclear energy to protect the public health and safety and the environment. Here, an exposure rate meter is used in checking the radiation levels near a nuclear generation station.

and does not include—is being determined continuously, by: (1) Congress as it exercises the commerce power and (2) the Supreme Court as it decides cases involving that exercise.

AN EVER-BROADENING INTERPRETATION. The chief and perhaps the only purpose in the minds of those who wrote the Commerce Clause was to prevent the States from interfering with the free flow of goods among themselves. To the Framers, the word "commerce" meant the exchange of goods by purchase and sale—the *articles* to be traded, not the *means by which* they are traded.

Like so many other parts of the Constitution, however, the meaning of the Commerce Clause has changed and expanded over the years. This has been especially true because of: (1) the spectacular improvements that have been made in transportation and communication in this country since 1789; and (2) the revolutionary

[1] Article I, Section 8, Clause 3; see pages 54, 335–336.

change in our economy from one based on simple local agriculture in 1789 to one geared to the industrialism and technology of today. Remember, the horse and sailing ship were the principal means of transportation *and* communication in 1787.

To appreciate the vast change that has occurred in the meaning of "commerce," one need glance at a list of only *some* of the things Congress has done under the commerce power. It has enacted, quite literally, thousands of statutes dealing with such subjects as radio and television broadcasting, the telephone and telegraph, railroads, steamships and nuclear-powered vessels, aircraft, automobiles, trucks, buses, bridges, ferries, rivers, harbors, canals, and pipelines. It has provided for the regulation of the transmission of electric energy, the building of dams, and the setting of freight and passenger rates. It has regulated the transporting of firearms, firecrackers, stolen goods of various kinds, kidnapped persons, alcoholic beverages, foods, drugs, cosmetics, agricultural sprays, and an almost endless list of other things.

Furthermore, it has restricted or forbidden the importing and exporting of many articles. It has provided for minimum wages, maximum hours, and safety conditions in many industries; guaranteed the rights of employees to join unions and bargain collectively; and regulated monopolistic business practices. It has provided sub-sidies for farmers; built highways and aided the States to build others; and Congress has done a veritable host of other things under the Commerce Clause.

GIBBONS V. OGDEN, 1824. The very first case to reach the Supreme Court involving the Commerce Clause set the stage for the vast expansion the clause has undergone.

In 1807 Robert Fulton's steamboat, the *Clermont*, made its first successful run up the Hudson from New York to Albany. The New York legislature then gave Fulton and his partner, Robert Livingston, an exclusive long-term grant to navigate the waters of the State by steamboat. From that monopoly, Aaron Ogden secured a permit for steam navigation between New York City and the New Jersey shore.

Thomas Gibbons, operating under a coasting license granted by the United States Government, began a competing line. Upon Ogden's petition, the New York courts ordered Gibbons to discontinue his business. Gibbons appealed to the Supreme Court. He claimed that the New York grant conflicted with the congressional power to regulate commerce.

The decision in this case was bound to have far-reaching effects. It was the first case involving the Commerce Clause to come before the Supreme Court. Even Congress itself had not been able to agree upon the extent of its powers over commerce.

The regulatory power of Congress extends to all waters which are used for navigation for commerce between the States. It requires, for example, that vessels used in interstate commerce – as the oil barge and towboat on the Ohio River – meet certain standards of seaworthiness and carry life preservers and other safety devices.

THE COMMERCE POWER AND THE CONSTITUTION

"The Congress shall have power . . . to regulate commerce with foreign nations, and among the several States, and with the Indian Tribes."

Article I, Section 8, Clause 3

BUT Congress is forbidden to:
1. Regulate the slave trade prior to 1808. *Article I, Section 9, Clause 1* (obsolete)
2. Levy duties or taxes on articles exported from any State. *Article I, Section 9, Clause 5*
3. Give preference to ports of one State over those of another. *Article I, Section 9, Clause 6*
4. Require vessels bound to or from ports of one State to enter, clear, or pay duties in another. *Article I, Section 9, Clause 6*
5. Deprive any person (including artificial persons: corporations) of life, liberty, or property without due process of law. *5th Amendment*

AND the States are forbidden to:
1. Lay imposts or duties on imports or exports. *Article I, Section 10, Clause 2*
2. Lay any duty on tonnage. *Article I, Section 10, Clause 3*

Except with the consent of Congress[a]

3. Place an unreasonable burden upon interstate or foreign commerce—by virtue of the Constitution's grant to Congress of the expressed power to regulate commerce. *Article I, Section 8, Clause 3*

[a] *Article I, Section 10, Clause 2* permits a State to levy "imposts or duties on imports or exports [if] absolutely necessary for executing its inspection laws" but "the net produce of all [such charges] shall be for the use of the treasury of the United States; and such laws [levying these charges] shall be subject to the revision and control of the Congress."

The Supreme Court ruled unanimously in favor of Gibbons. It held the New York law in violation of the Constitution's grant of the commerce power to Congress. In reply to Ogden's argument that "commerce" should be narrowly defined as "traffic" or the mere buying and selling of goods, Chief Justice Marshall wrote:

Commerce, undoubtedly, is traffic, but it is something more—it is intercourse. It describes the commercial intercourse between nations, and parts of nations, in all its branches, and is regulated by prescribing rules for carrying on that intercourse.

The Supreme Court's decision was immensely popular because it dealt a death blow to the steamboat monopolies. But it had a much broader significance, which became apparent only with the passage of time. The Court in giving a sweeping definition of commerce had greatly increased the regulatory powers of Congress. Freed from restrictive State regulation, steam navigation increased at an amazing rate on all the country's waterways. And in a few years, the railroads, similarly freed, revolutionized domestic transportation.

THE MEANING OF "REGULATE." Just as the meaning of the word "commerce" has undergone a great transformation, so has the constitutional meaning of "regulate." Originally, to regulate meant *to restrict, to restrain, to prohibit.* Over decades now, it also has come to mean *to protect, to promote, to encourage.* For example, in regulating commerce Congress has protected the people against misbranded foods and from such crimes as auto theft and kidnaping. It has promoted commerce by aiding railroads, trucking and bus companies, airlines, and steamship companies. It has encouraged agriculture by aiding farmers and done an almost countless number of similar things.

Foreign Commerce. The Commerce Clause gives to Congress the power "to regulate commerce with other nations"—that is, *foreign commerce.* The foreign commerce of the United States includes any trade which begins, passes through, or ends in any foreign country. The States have no power whatever in the field. Hence, the power of Congress to regulate foreign commerce is even broader than the power to regulate interstate trade.

Acting under this authority, Congress has absolutely prohibited the importation of many items. Here are but a few of them: diseased animals and plants, narcotics and other dangerous drugs except for medical or scientific purposes, obscene materials, or literature advocating the forceful opposition to any law of the United States. Among the many other items it has banned are lottery tickets, adulterated or misbranded foods, the skins of any animals classed as endangered species, and any article with a brand name or symbol simulating a domestic trademark.

It has also forbidden the export of certain commodities and restricted the shipment of others abroad.[2] Thus, since the end of World War II the exportation of weapons, other war materiel, and heavy equipment has been controlled by a strict licensing system.

PROTECTION FROM STATE INTERFERENCE. In *Brown* v. *Maryland,* 1827, the Supreme Court first announced the *original package doctrine,* which is generally followed to this day. The rule forbids any State to exercise its regulatory powers over imports until the original package has *come to rest*—that is, has reached the importer in this country

and is broken open, sold or used by that recipient. Thus, if a shoe store orders sandals from Mexico or dress shoes from Italy, a State cannot interfere with the sale of those items until the retailer opens the shipping cartons or sells the shoes while they are still in the original package. If it were not for this rule, a State could effectively close off some or all foreign trade for its residents. Or, similarly, a coastal State could erect various barriers to prevent imports from reaching inland States.

Interstate Commerce. The Commerce Clause gives to Congress the power "to regulate commerce . . . among the several States"—that is, *interstate commerce.* Interstate commerce includes any and all trade between and among the States and the means by which it is conducted. Trade which is carried on wholly *within* one State is known as *intrastate commerce* and is subject to State regulation.

What commerce is interstate in character and thus subject to congressional control? What is only intrastate and thus beyond the power of Congress? These seemingly simple questions are indeed quite complicated.

Although there is no simple test for distinguishing *inter*state and *intra*state commerce, this much can be said: Any transaction or movement that crosses a State line is interstate in character; so, too, is any transaction or movement that is *a part of* such an action. More and more as the country has grown, commerce once regarded as only intrastate has come to be viewed as interstate by both Congress and the courts.

Whenever State regulation of intrastate commerce conflicts with federal regulation of interstate commerce, the State regulation must yield. The historic *Shreveport Case (The Houston, East and West Texas Railway Company* v. *United States),* decided in 1914, illustrates this point.

Shreveport, Louisiana, is located near the Texas border. Shreveport merchants

---

[2] Recall, Congress cannot tax exports, Article I, Section 9, Clause 5; see page 494. But it can and does control them in other ways.

and those in Dallas, Texas, competed for the trade of the Texas towns between them. The freight rates from Dallas to these towns had been fixed by the Texas Railway Commission. They were much lower per mile than the rates from Shreveport, set by the Interstate Commerce Commission. The Shreveport merchants complained that they were being discriminated against simply because they were located across a State line. The ICC held that the intrastate rates from Dallas were too low, and it ordered those rates raised to a par with the interstate rates from Shreveport.

The ICC's order was appealed to the Supreme Court, which upheld it. The Court ruled that the authority to regulate interstate commerce carries with it the right to regulate intrastate commerce whenever that action is necessary to the protection of interstate trade.

WHEN DOES COMMERCE BECOME INTERSTATE? At what point does the shipment of goods from one State to another actually enter the stream of interstate commerce? The answer to this question is vital: *Before* the goods reach that point they are subject only to *State* regulation; *after* they reach it they pass under federal control. The Supreme Court has regularly held that when goods are *started on a continuous journey* that will take them across a State line, or when they are delivered to a carrier for such a journey, they become interstate commerce, no longer subject to local control.

A case (*Coe* v. *Errol*, 1886) decided by the Supreme Court more than ninety years ago demonstrates the point very well. It also shows how important the point can be even in the most routine of situations. A New Hampshire lumberman, Coe, had refused to pay the property taxes the town of Errol had imposed on a large quantity of logs he had dragged to the river bank. The logs had remained on the bank for several weeks while Coe waited for the river ice to melt so that he could float them to a sawmill in Maine. They were still there on the annual property tax assessment day. Coe claimed that they could not be taxed by the town because they were in interstate commerce. The Supreme Court held that he was liable for the tax, however. It ruled that the interstate journey did not begin until the logs were actually rolled into the river. Hauling the logs to the river, said the Supreme Court, was a preparation for the journey, not a part of it.

WHEN DOES INTERSTATE COMMERCE END? Determining the point at which goods *leave* interstate commerce and again become subject to State control is equally important. As we noted on page 532, the point at which goods leave *foreign* commerce is determined by the Original Package Doctrine. In general, the same rule applies to

In a recent year, the Port of New York handled more than 122 million tons of cargo. Of this, almost one-half consisted of goods imported from other nations and some two-fifths consisted of cargo carried by ships engaged in coastal trade. Thus, a major portion of the cargo handled in this port is subject to federal regulation.

Reprinted by permission of Chicago-Tribune-New York News Syndicate, Inc.

interstate commerce. But, in some cases, the courts have held that the States may tax and otherwise regulate goods shipped in interstate commerce once they have reached the *consignee* (the party to whom they are shipped). But a State cannot regulate goods simply because they happen to have come from outside the State.

COMMERCE INCLUDES NAVIGATION. We saw a moment ago that the Supreme Court held commerce to include navigation in *Gibbons* v. *Ogden.* Thus, Congress has the power to regulate vessels in interstate trade and also the use of the waters in which these vessels navigate. Congress requires that the vessels be inspected as to seaworthiness and that they carry life preservers and other safety devices. It sets the number of passengers a ship may carry and minimum working conditions for its crew.

Congress appropriates money for dredging rivers and harbors, constructing canals, marking channels, and operating lighthouses. It forbids obstructions in navigable streams. Thus, a bridge, causeway, or dam cannot be built across navigable streams without the consent of the Secretary of the Army.

Without the express permission of Congress, foreign vessels cannot carry freight or passengers from one port in the United States to another. Thus, Congress has protected American shipping interests against competition from foreign vessels.

The regulatory power of Congress extends to all waters which are used for navigation or are "capable of being made navigable" for interstate commerce. Congress has authority over navigable streams running through two or more States. And, it has authority over streams located wholly within one State which connect with other navigable waters so as to form a continuous channel with other States.[3]

In some instances, federal authority also extends to navigable waters that are wholly within one State and are not connected with any exterior water. This is true

---

[3] Only those streams "navigable in their natural condition" were originally considered to be within the power of Congress. This interpretation has been greatly modified by a series of congressional actions and court decisions over the past century, however. In the *Daniel Ball Case* in 1871 the Supreme Court upheld the requirement of a federal license for a vessel operating only on the Grand River between Grand Rapids and Grand Haven, wholly within the State of Michigan, since the steamer carried goods on a part of its journey in interstate commerce. The Court held that "those rivers must be regarded as public navigable rivers in law which are navigable in fact. And they are navigable in fact when they are used, *or are susceptible of being used,* in their ordinary condition, as highways for commerce." In 1940 the Supreme Court, in *United States* v. *Appalachian Electric Power Co.,* upheld the requirement of a Federal Power Commission license for a dam on the New River, flowing through Virginia and West Virginia. The Court ruled that the river, although not *navigable in fact,* is *navigable in law* and thus subject to federal regulation because it is "capable of being made navigable" and because it flows into and affects another river which is navigable in both fact and law.

when those waters are actually navigated by vessels which connect with other interstate carriers—for example, a ferry plying a lake and connecting with rail or truck lines which extend to other States.

COMMERCE INCLUDES TRANSPORTATION BY LAND AND AIR. The first rail lines were built in this country in the early 1830's. Over the next generation their development was encouraged by both the States and the National Government. In the 1870's and 1880's, however, several States began to impose drastic regulations on the railroads, especially at the behest of the Granger Movement in the Middle West. The Supreme Court checked this interference with interstate commerce in 1886, and Congress created the Interstate Commerce Commission in 1887. As other forms of interstate transportation—including motor vehicles, aircraft, power lines, and pipelines—developed, they also came under federal control.

Today, acting for Congress, the ICC regulates the railroads, interstate motor carriers, most ships plying between coastal ports and on the nation's lakes and rivers, and all interstate pipelines except those carrying water or natural gas. The Civil Aeronautics Board and the Federal Aviation Administration regulate private and commercial air transportation. The Department of Energy regulates the transmission of electricity and natural gas from one State to another. We shall take a look at each of these agencies in the next chapter.

COMMERCE INCLUDES COMMUNICATIONS. The first telegraph line was built in 1842, and the first telephone was exhibited at the Centennial Exposition in Philadelphia in 1876. Both means of communication are regulated under the commerce power. So, too, are radio and television broadcasting. The Federal Communications Commission, created by Congress in 1934, regulates all interstate wire and wireless communications today; we shall consider the FCC shortly, too.

COMMERCE INCLUDES THE MOVEMENT OF PERSONS. The movement of persons across State lines, whether for business or pleasure, is also within the scope of the commerce power.

During the Depression of the 1930's several States passed "anti-Okie" laws, prohibiting nonresident indigents (poor persons) from entering the State. The Supreme Court struck them down in *Edwards v. California,* 1941. It held California's version to be invalid as an unconstitutional barrier to interstate commerce.

In the Mann Act of 1910, known as the "White Slave Act," Congress made it a federal crime for any person to transport a woman across a State line for an immoral purpose. Congress has since made many other actions involving interstate travel federal crimes. Thus, it is unlawful to transport a kidnap victim or a stolen automobile from one State to another, or to obstruct interstate commerce by the threat or use of violence. And it is unlawful to flee to another State to avoid arrest, imprisonment, or testifying in a felony case. The Civil Rights Act of 1964 makes it a federal crime to flee a State after bombing a church, school, or other structure.

A major portion of the Civil Rights Act of 1964 is based upon the commerce power. Title II of the act (Public Accommodations) provides that no person may be denied access to or service in various public establishments on grounds of race, color, religion, or national origin. Places covered by the law are those in which lodgings are provided to transient guests or in which interstate travelers are served, and those public places in which a substantial portion of the goods sold or the entertainment presented moves in interstate commerce. Such public accommodations include: restaurants, cafeterias, lunch counters, and other eating places; movie theaters, concert halls, and other auditoriums; gasoline stations; sports arenas and stadiums; and hotels, motels, and rooming houses (except owner-occupied units with less than six rooms for rent).[4]

The Civil Rights Act of 1968 makes it a federal crime for any person to travel in or use such facilities of interstate commerce as the telephone, telegraph, radio, or television with intent to incite, organize, or take part in a riot, or to assist others to do so.

ARTICLES BANNED FROM INTERSTATE COMMERCE. Congress has prohibited the shipment of many items across State lines. Among them are such things as lottery tickets, dangerous explosives, firearms carried by or shipped to unlicensed persons, switchblade knives, gambling devices or information, impure or misbranded foods and drugs, and many more.

Today, three federal agencies are especially concerned with these prohibitions: the Consumer Product Safety Commission, to be considered shortly; the Food and Drug Administration (pages 636-637); and the FBI (pages 670-671).

PROTECTION AGAINST UNREASONABLE STATE INTERFERENCE. A package in interstate commerce retains protection against State taxation until it is delivered to the consignee or comes to rest. Moreover, it is immune from other State regulation until the original package is once broken open, sold, or used.

Because the original package has this important protection, it is not surprising that many disputes have arisen over precisely what that package is in various situations. As a general rule, the courts have held that it is the one which the trade ordinarily uses for the shipment of goods. Thus, a box of 12 one-pound packages of

margarine is the original package; the individual one-pound packages are not.

If the States could tax or otherwise interfere with goods shipped in interstate commerce, the whole value of the Commerce Clause would be lost. In effect, we would find ourselves living in much the same conditions that plagued the States before the adoption of the Constitution.

Although the States may not directly, purposefully regulate interstate commerce, they may (and must) do so *indirectly*. Inevitably they do so in the ordinary course of the exercise of their police powers. As two common illustrations, take the regulation of highway speeds and various forms of gambling. The speed limits apply to *all* vehicles moving on the roads of a State—including those in interstate commerce, of course. And, similarly, the gambling laws apply to *everyone* in the State—including those who happen to be riding on trains or buses or staying overnight in a motel.

The general rule here is that the States may incidentally affect interstate commerce. But they may not discriminate against it, may not single it out for special treatment, may not impose an unreasonable burden upon it.

The Constitution does give each of the States an *unrestricted* right to regulate alcoholic beverages—without regard to the question of interstate commerce. Section 2 of the 21st Amendment provides:

> The transportation or importation into any State, territory, or possession of the United States for delivery or use therein of intoxicating liquors, in violation of the laws thereof, is hereby prohibited.

---

[4] The Supreme Court upheld the constitutionality of Title II and the use of the Commerce Clause as a basis for civil rights legislation—at least in the area of access to public accommodations—in 1964. In reaching its unanimous decision, in *Heart of Atlanta Motel, Inc.* v. *United States,* the Court noted that there was "overwhelming evidence of the disruptive effect [of] racial discrimination . . . on commercial intercourse."

Regulation of Business Practices

Protection Against Monopolies. By 1890 most of the major industries in this country were dominated by such combinations as the Sugar Trust, the Beef Trust, the

Whiskey Trust, and the Standard Oil Trust.[5] Many supposedly competing companies made agreements with one another to limit production or fix prices. Sometimes they agreed not to compete in certain sections of the country assigned to one or another of them. Often the same persons sat on the boards of directors of competing companies *(interlocking directorates)* and could thus control competition.

THE SHERMAN ANTITRUST ACT OF 1890. State regulation proved largely ineffective against these powerful interstate combinations; thus federal regulation became necessary. Acting under the commerce power, Congress passed the famous Sherman Antitrust Act of 1890. This act remains the basic law against monopolies today. It prohibits "every contract, combination in the form of a trust or otherwise, or conspiracy in restraint of trade or commerce among the several States, or with foreign nations." It also provides penalties for violations. (These penalties were stiffened by Congress in 1975; business firms may now be fined up to $1 million and individuals up to $100,000; and individuals who violate the law may also receive jail sentences of up to three years.)

The Sherman Act's very general language caused considerable difficulty in its enforcement. The Supreme Court attempted to give some direction to that enforcement in two cases involving major monopoly prosecutions in 1911. The two cases involved were: *United States* v. *Ameri-*

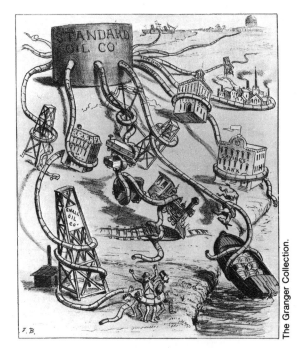

THE MONSTER MONOPOLY

An 1884 cartoon attacks the extent of the Standard Oil Trust's control over the oil industry.

The Granger Collection.

can Tobacco Company and *United States* v. *Standard Oil Company of New Jersey.* In forcing the dissolution of the two monopolies it announced the "rule of reason." Although the Sherman Act outlaws *every* agreement in restraint of trade, the Court interpreted the law to mean every *unreasonable* agreement—every agreement "unreasonably restrictive of competitive conditions."

In 1914 Congress passed the Clayton Act to supplement the Sherman Act. It makes four specific actions illegal. The Act made illegal: (1) the purchase by a corporation of the stock of any of its competitors, (2) interlocking directorates among competitors, (3) "exclusive agreements" requiring a dealer to handle only the products of one company, and (4) price-cutting, rebates, and similar practices designed to drive out competition. Over the years, Congress has specifically exempted certain groups from the terms of the Sherman and Clayton Acts. For example, the Transporta-

---

[5] The *trust* was originally a device by which several corporations engaged in the same line of business would combine to eliminate competition and regulate prices. This was done by creating a central board composed of the presidents or general managers of the different corporations and transferring to them a majority of stock from each of the corporations to be held "in trust" for the stockholders who thus assigned their stock. The stockholders received in return "trust certificates" showing that they were entitled to receive dividends on their assigned stock, though the voting power of it had been passed to the trustees. This enabled the trustees to elect all the directors of all the corporations and thus prevent competition and insure higher prices.

tion Act of 1920 permits railroads to agree to the division of traffic or earnings with the approval of the Interstate Commerce Commission. Labor unions have been exempted since the Clayton Act. Other statutes have permitted farmers to form cooperatives to market their products and various utilities (*e.g.,* electric power, natural gas, and telephone companies) to operate as monopolies.[6] Congress has also exempted professional baseball from coverage by the antitrust laws; but, curiously, it has not been similarly partial to such other professional sports as football and boxing.

Violators of the antitrust laws are dealt with in one or more of three ways: (1) criminal prosecutions, (2) civil suits for damages, brought either by the Government or by injured private parties,[7] and (3) corrective action by the Federal Trade Commission.

Criminal and civil cases brought by the Government are prosecuted by the "trustbusters"—the Antitrust Division of the Department of Justice. The largest antitrust case in the nation's history was decided in a federal district court in Philadelphia in 1961. The defendants were 29 electrical equipment concerns—including the nation's largest ones, General Electric and Westinghouse—and 45 of their executives. All were convicted of a huge price-fixing and market-dividing scheme to monopolize the sale of heavy electrical equipment in this country. Officers of the firms involved met secretly to agree on prices and

to rig the supposedly competitive bids each would then submit on contracts to supply their products. The companies took turns in submitting low bids in order that each of them would win a previously-agreed-to share of the multi-million dollar business. The convicted firms received very heavy fines and their officers served short jail terms.

The Federal Trade Commission. When Congress approved the Clayton Act it also created the Federal Trade Commission. It directed the new agency to enforce the prohibitions of the Clayton Act, and to prevent other "unfair methods of competition" and "unfair or deceptive acts or practices" in interstate and foreign commerce.

PRESENT FUNCTIONS. Over the years, the functions of the FTC have been expanded and strengthened. In fact, it has lately become a major federal consumer protection agency. In addition to its Clayton Act functions, it now is charged with enforcing a number of statutes which: (1) prohibit the false or deceptive advertisement of consumer products, (2) require the truthful labeling of textile and fur products, (3) regulate the packaging and labeling of various consumer products, (4) require truth and full disclosure in the lending practices of such lenders as finance companies and retailers who sell goods on the installment plan, and (5) police consumer credit agencies.

ORGANIZATION. The FTC is a fairly typical independent regulatory commission (see page 422). It is composed of five members appointed by the President and Senate for staggered seven-year terms. The President designates one of the commissioners to chair the agency. As a body, the commissioners select an executive director who supervises the work of the FTC's staff of some 1600 economists, lawyers, investigators, and other personnel.

PROCEDURES. The FTC works in close concert with the Antitrust Division in the

---

[6] For nearly 30 years Congress permitted so-called "fair trade laws." The Miller-Tydings Act of 1938 permitted any State to enact laws legalizing "price maintenance agreements." These were contracts in which retailers were bound to sell a manufacturer's products at not less than a stated "fair trade price," even if those products reached the retailer in interstate commerce. Most of the States enacted these "legalized price-fixing" laws. Heated controversy surrounded these laws until 1976, when Congress destroyed them by repealing the 1938 law.

[7] Since 1976 State attorneys general have been authorized to bring civil suits for damages on behalf of all of the citizens of their States.

Justice Department. Unlike the trust-busters, however, it is much more concerned with securing compliance with the law than it is with punishing violators. The Commission's enforcement efforts fall into two general categories.

(1) Voluntary and cooperative procedures. To meet the statutory command that it "prevent" unfair practices, the FTC makes extensive efforts to promote voluntary compliance with the law. To this end, the Commission's staff provides advice to business concerns, telling them what the law does or does not permit them to do. The Commission itself will furnish an advisory opinion on the legality of a proposed course of conduct by a particular business. It tells the business concern, in effect, what the FTC will or will not do if it pursues that course. It also publishes trade regulation rules as a guide to business practices. These rules are often developed in cooperation with the firms engaged in the particular areas of business covered by each set of rules.

(2) Formal enforcement procedures. In some situations voluntary compliance procedures will not work, of course. Then the FTC moves in formal, court-like fashion.

Complaints of unfair practices may be brought to the Commission by consumers, competitors, Congress, or other public agencies. Moreover, the Commission itself may initiate investigations to determine violations of the laws it administers. Two basic standards guide the FTC's decision as to whether a particular matter should be docketed for investigation: (1) the practical matter of its own resources, and (2) its twin goals of maintaining competition and protecting consumers.

Each FTC investigation is conducted by a trial examiner. The examiner reports his or her findings to the Commission which may then do one of three things. It may simply drop the matter, of course. Or it may propose a *stipulation* or issue a *cease-and-desist order.*

Where the Commission finds a complaint to be justified, it usually proposes a stipulation. This is a device that permits the offender to agree to "cease and desist forever" the challenged practice. If the accused party refuses to stipulate, a formal hearing is held. After that hearing the Commission either decides to dismiss the charges or issue a cease-and-desist order. The order becomes final after 60 days, unless the accused seeks a review of the case in the federal court of appeals. Violation of a cease-and-desist order causes the offender to be brought before a federal district court. There a penalty of not more than $10,000 for each violation can be imposed—and each day that a violation continues constitutes a separate offense.

Perhaps the real nature of the FTC's work can best be illustrated with an example. For years fur dealers in this country attempted to enhance their sales by giving imaginative and glamorous—but fictitious—names to common furs. Rabbit fur was sold under at least 30 different commercial aliases, including "French Chinchilla," "Electric Beaver," and "Baltic Fox." A trade practice conference proved unsuccessful and so, at the FTC's urging, Congress enacted the Fur Products Labeling Act. The law requires that all furs be sold under their actual common names and authorizes the FTC to issue regulations for its enforcement. Today rabbit must be called rabbit fur and a coat made of ordinary cat's fur must be labeled "domestic cat"; and a coat sold as "Persian lamb" must have been produced from that animal's fur and imported from the Middle East.

Protecting the Consumer. Historically, the free enterprise system developed with the notion that "competition polices competition." That is, it developed with the idea that vigorous competition among those who sell provides built-in protections for those who buy. The ancient rule of *caveat emptor*—"let the buyer beware"—has deep roots in our economic system.

Case Study

The Open Housing Act is the principal federal statute aimed at discrimination in the sale or rental of housing. It was enacted by Congress as a part (Title VIII) of the Civil Rights Act of 1968, and on the basis of the commerce power.

The law covers the sale or rent of approximately 80 percent of all housing—homes, rooms, apartments, and other dwelling units—in this country. It forbids the refusal to sell or rent any of those units to any person because of his or her race, color, religion, sex, or national origin.

It also prohibits discriminatory advertising and discriminatory practices by real estate agents or lending institutions. And it forbids "blockbusting"—the practice of pressuring someone to sell or rent property (usually below the market price) by suggesting that blacks or other minorities are about to move into the area.

The law does not apply to some 15 million housing units, however. Exempted are: (1) those houses owned by persons who do not own more than three houses and who sell or rent without the services of a real estate agent; (2) apartment or other dwelling places that contain no more than four separate units and in which the owner maintains his or her own residence; and (3) housing which religious organizations or private clubs provide for their own members on a nonprofit basis.

The law has few teeth. Its enforcement depends very largely on actions taken by private individuals. That is, it provides that any person who claims to be the victim of discrimination may file a complaint with HUD. If HUD does not resolve the matter, that person may then file suit, seeking an injunction (a court order) to halt the discriminatory practice. The suit may also seek money damages.

The Attorney General may initiate court actions to enforce the law, but only in locales where a "pattern of discrimination" is found.

■ Does this law represent a proper application of the commerce power?

■ Why are certain kinds of housing exempted from its coverage? Should it include *all* housing?

■ Should its enforcement provisions be strengthened? If so, how?

Most of us have long since recognized a pressing need for the complementary rule of *caveat vendor*—"let the seller beware." That is, we have come to see that—in an economy built largely upon huge business organizations, an organized workforce, and a national marketplace—the consumer operates at a serious disadvantage.

Public concern for the rights of consumers and demands for consumer protection have increased substantially in recent years. In fact, "consumerism" has lately become a significant political force—a fact perhaps best demonstrated by the activities and impact of Ralph Nader. Such phrases as "consumer protection," "consumer information," "consumer interest,"

and "the consuming public" have all become a stock part of the linguistic baggage of politicians, bureaucrats, and the news media.

At least a score of federal agencies have more or less important consumer protection functions today. Among the oldest of them is the FTC, as we've just seen. The Food and Drug Administration, now a part of the Department of Health and Human Services, is even older. It dates from 1906, and we shall look at it when we consider HHS in Chapter 25. Most of them are of more recent origin—for example, the National Highway Traffic Safety Administration in the Department of Transportation. It was established in 1970 and sets and enforces safety standards for cars, trucks, buses, motorcycles, and other vehicles—including bicycles.

The *Consumer Product Safety Commission* is the newest of the major consumer protection agencies. It was established in 1972. In creating it, Congress declared that "an unacceptable number of consumer products which present unreasonable risks of injury" are being sold in interstate and foreign commerce today.

Like the FTC, the Commission is an independent regulatory body. It has extensive quasi-legislative and quasi-judicial powers. Its five members are appointed by the President for staggered seven-year terms. The President designates one of the five members to chair the Commission.

Congress has given the CPSC broad authority to issue and enforce safety standards for consumer products. Those standards cover the design, construction, contents, performance, packaging and labeling of well over 10,000 separate items—from door and window glass, smoke alarms, and power tools to toys, stoves, ladders, and lawnmowers.

In setting mandatory standards, the Commission regularly invites advice from interested parties—representatives of the industry to be regulated, other public agencies, private citizens, and consumer organizations. Once a proposed standard has been developed, it is published in the Federal Register. The Commission then spreads word of the standard through the news media and industry and consumer groups.

Any interested party may submit written or oral comments on a proposed standard. After consideration of those comments the Commission may issue the standard. Anyone may then seek a review of it in the United States Court of Appeals for the District of Columbia. Unless that court intervenes, the standard becomes effective—becomes valid as law—60 days after its promulgation.

The Commission can ban the shipment or sale of hazardous products. Any product which presents the imminent hazard of death or serious injury or illness is subject to seizure by court order. Those who knowingly violate the Commission's rules can be prosecuted in a federal district court. Upon conviction, criminal penalties can be as stiff as a $50,000 fine and/or up to one year in a federal prison.

The CPSC cites some quite impressive statistics to dramatize the importance of its work. It estimates that 20 million persons are injured in and around the home each year. More than 110,000 of those injuries result in permanent disability, and 30,000 of them are fatal.

It has been quite active in its relatively brief life, too. Thus far, for example, it has banned some 1800 different children's toys because of electrical, mechanical, or thermal hazards. And it has issued several thousand detailed safety standards covering a multitude of items—for example, for power mowers. It has found that these machines are each year responsible for more than 50,000 injuries which are serious enough to require treatment in hospital emergency rooms.

Protecting Investors. Corporations are financed in large part through the sale of their securities to the public. Securities are usually sold through securities exchanges—that is, "stock markets." Millions of Americans own stock in most of the nation's larger and many of its smaller business concerns. And millions of investors have lent billions to business enterprises by purchasing their bonds and other securities. As we suggested in Chapter 1, it is impossible to see how our huge private enterprise system could have been financed—or be financed today—in any other way.

Without effective public regulation, investors can be misled—even if inadvertently by reliable brokers. Fraud is more than a mere possibility. The sale of bogus mining stocks became so widespread in the latter part of the last century that Mark Twain defined a mine as "a hole in the ground owned by a liar."

The States first began to regulate the traffic in securities more than a half century ago. Kansas and then Rhode Island passed the first "blue sky laws" in 1911.[8] The stock market crash of 1929, which signaled the beginning of the Depression, proved those State regulations inadequate, however. In fact, it demonstrated that the interstate character of corporate financing makes effective State control a practical impossibility. The losses suffered by gullible investors (many holding speculative and sometimes fraudulent securities) amounted to an estimated $25 billion as the country moved from the boom of the 1920's to the hard times of the 1930's.

The shattering impact of the Depression brought overwhelming public demand for effective national regulation of securities and of the exchanges through which they are sold. In response, Congress enacted the Securities Act of 1933, the Securities Exchange Act of 1934, and created the Securities and Exchange Commission in 1934. And it has since passed several other statutes designed to protect the nation's investors.

THE SECURITIES AND EXCHANGE COMMISSION. The SEC is another of the independent regulatory commissions. It is composed of five members appointed by the President with Senate confirmation for five-year terms. One of the commissioners heads the SEC by presidential designation. He or she and the executive director superintend the activities of the SEC's more than 2100 economists, attorneys, accountants, and other employees.

The SEC's primary task is to protect investors and the general public against fraud, misrepresentations, and other malpractices in the investment field. To this end it administers several statutes.

The *Securities Act of 1933* is sometimes called the "Truth-in-Securities Act." It requires a full disclosure of all of the material facts relating to the issuance of new securities. The essential purpose of the requirement is to give investors sufficient and reliable information on which to make purchase judgments. All persons and organizations[9] who issue securities, by mail or in interstate commerce, must register with and be licensed by the SEC. The law does not guarantee anyone a profitable investment. Rather, it seeks to insure adequate information upon which investors may base their decisions.

The *Securities Exchange Act of 1934* came as a logical follow-up to the 1933 law. Its provisions relate to the trading of securities *after* they have been issued. All national security exchanges—the best known of which is the New York Stock Exchange—must register with the Commission and adopt rules of practice approved by the SEC. The law also requires registration by

---

[8] The term originated with a Kansas legislator who claimed that dishonest promoters would sell "the bright blue sky above" if they could.

[9] With a few limited exceptions: *e.g.*, federal, State, or local government offerings and those which are not made to the public or are only intrastate in scope.

and periodic reports from all companies whose securities are listed on the exchanges and by companies with more than $1 million in assets and 500 or more shareholders.

Congress broadened the coverage of the 1933 and 1934 laws in the *Securities Acts Amendments of 1964*. Under the newer law those larger companies with stock issues which are not listed on the national exchanges but which are sold "over the counter" must also disclose the material facts about their security offerings.

The SEC also administers the *Public Utility Holding Company Act of 1935*. The statute was brought about by the activities of "holding companies." These are corporations chartered in one State and holding the controlling stock in operating companies scattered through several States. Because of their interstate character, these firms could evade State regulation.

The holding company device came to be widely used by electric power and natural gas companies. The financiers who controlled them argued that their holding companies promoted large-scale production and greater efficiency. Critics demonstrated that the very complexity of their operations made it possible to conceal profits that might otherwise be used to reduce electricity and gas prices.

The 1935 law directed the SEC to require full and fair disclosure of the corporate structure and operations of public utility (electric and gas) holding companies. It also gave the Commission the power to supervise the security transactions of these structures and to eliminate those it finds to be uneconomic.

Other statutes administered by the SEC include the *Investment Company Act of 1940*, which regulates the conduct of mutual funds and other investment firms. Another is the *Investment Advisers Act of 1940*, which covers the activities of investment counselors and their dealings with clients.

Each of these statutes contains provisions for its enforcement by the SEC. It may obtain court orders to halt fraudulent and other prohibited practices. It may revoke the registrations of firms or individuals who engage in fraudulent practices, and suspend or expel offenders from the national securities exchanges. And it may refer cases to the Attorney General for prosecution if this seems appropriate.

THE COMMODITY FUTURES TRADING COMMISSION. Brokers often buy and sell various commodities—especially agricultural products, but such others as timber and metals—long before those items actually reach the market. That is, they invest, speculate, and trade in "futures." Essentially, they do so in *futures contracts*—agreements in which one party agrees to sell and another to buy a specified quantity of a certain commodity at a stated price at some future date. Their operations serve a very

Trading is often fast and furious on exchanges where securities are bought and sold. Shown here is the Chicago Options Security Exchange.

useful purpose. They establish a known price for a commodity—corn or wheat or copper, say—*before* delivery. Establishing prices in this way gives some stability to the market for a commodity.

Dishonest trading practices could do serious harm to producers, retailers, and consumers, of course. For example, attempts to corner a market, price manipulations, or the dissemination of false crop or market information can have serious consequences.

Congress first provided for the regulation of trading in farm futures with the creation of the *Commodity Exchange Authority* in 1922. The Authority was replaced by the *Commodity Futures Trading Commission* in 1975. The newer agency has the authority to regulate futures trading in *all* commodities.

The Commission is an independent regulatory body. Its five members, appointed by the President and Senate, serve staggered five-year terms. Its chairman is named by the President, and it selects an executive director to manage the agency in accord with the policies it adopts.

The CFTC regulates the exchanges on which commodity futures may be traded, must approve all futures contracts traded on those exchanges, and licenses those firms and brokers who may buy or sell commodities for others or provide trading information.

Aids to Business

Just as government regulates the business community, so it promotes it, too—and in a great many ways. The maintenance of the monetary system and the supervision of banking, matters which we considered in Chapter 20, are outstanding illustrations of this fact. There are many others, as we shall see on through this chapter.

The Department of Commerce. Many of the Federal Government's activities to promote business are centered in the several agencies of the Department of Commerce. From its beginnings, Congress has charged it with this basic mission: "to foster, promote, and develop the foreign and domestic commerce of the United States."

The Department was originally created in 1903 as the Department of Commerce and Labor. Congress established the separate Department of Labor in 1913 and today's Commerce Department dates from that point. Many of its current functions originated well before that period, however. Thus, the forerunners of its census and patent programs were begun in 1790; the setting of weights, measures, and other physical standards began in 1836, and weather prediction first became a federal function in 1849.

The Secretary of Commerce usually comes to the President's Cabinet from a highly successful career in the world of business. Nearly all of the 27 persons who have thus far held the post fit that mold. The Secretary is a major presidential adviser in all matters relating to the business and industrial segments of the nation's economy. The Secretary is also responsible for making the services of the Department available to the business community and the general public.

Let us take a brief look at the activities of the principal agencies in the Department and of the more than 31,000 men and women who work for it.

THE CENSUS BUREAU. The Constitution requires that an "enumeration" of the nation's population be made every 10 years.[10] It does so, recall, in order that the seats in the House of Representatives and direct taxes may be apportioned among the States on the basis of their populations.

The First Census was taken in 1790 and the next one, the Twenty-first, is scheduled for April 1, 1990. The Census of 1790 reported a national population of 3,929,214

---

[10] Article I, Section 2, Clause 3.

TABLE 21. SECOND QUARTER--HOUSEHOLD TRIPS BY MAJOR MEANS OF TRANSPORTATION AND SELECTED TRIP CHARACTERISTICS--CON.

(IN THOUSANDS. FOR MEANING OF ABBREVIATIONS AND SYMBOLS, SEE INTRODUCTORY TEXT)

TRIP CHARACTERISTICS	TOTAL HOUSEHOLD TRIPS	MAJOR MEANS OF TRANSPORTATION								
		AUTO		TRUCK						DIFFERENT MEANS GOING AND RETURNING
		WITHOUT CAMPING EQUIPMENT	WITH CAMPING EQUIPMENT	WITHOUT CAMPING EQUIPMENT	WITH CAMPING EQUIPMENT	BUS	TRAIN	AIRPLANE	OTHER	
REGION OF ORIGIN										
NEW ENGLAND	3 551	2 162	28	196	42	184	33	808	29	69
EASTERN GATEWAY	6 738	4 087	65	124	51	392	213	1 606	56	145
GEORGE WASHINGTON COUNTRY	8 197	5 150	151	348	204	474	251	1 377	61	180
SOUTH	14 185	10 242	136	949	241	594	47	1 566	139	271
GREAT LAKES COUNTRY	18 277	12 548	296	897	737	632	133	2 516	216	301
MOUNTAIN WEST	4 312	2 764	56	373	258	165	26	447	115	109
FRONTIER WEST		7 842	170		449	411			132	225
FAR WEST		7 724	221		710	602			170	

The Bureau of the Census collects a wide variety of data, including those which relate to the production and consumption of energy. For example, its National Travel Survey provides estimates on the volume, means, and characteristics of how people travel when they take trips of a nonlocal nature.

persons; the most recent one, in 1980, produced an total of more than 226,000,000.

The earliest censuses were merely head counts. Little use of them was made beyond the reapportionment of the House. Beginning in 1810, and then increasingly, the questions asked by census takers were multiplied. Today they produce a great variety of useful and detailed information about the American people. Through the Twelfth Census in 1900, each decennial head count was made by a temporary agency set up for that purpose. Congress finally established the Census Bureau as a permanent agency in 1902.

The nation would be in dire straits without the mass of reliable statistical data the Census Bureau collects. Its reports have an almost unlimited number of uses. They show educators the levels of educational attainment in the population and school boards the numbers of children who will soon be of school age. They show the military how many of the nation's youth are of military age now or will be at some future date. Advertisers can find out how many radio and TV sets there are per household in each locality. Businesses searching for new plant locations can ascertain those places in which they might best recruit their labor forces, and so on.

The census volumes on manufactures and agriculture are especially valuable to the business community. For instance a firm which produces corn cutters, milk cans, or poultry feed may find them a useful market guide; they report how much corn is produced and the approximate number of cows and chickens there are in each county in the United States. A manufacturer of razors, blades, and shaving cream can discover those communities in which there are more men than women. A cosmetics firm can turn the process the other way. The statistics on birth rates and on the distribution of the population by age groups can be quite helpful to, say, a company which markets a line of children's clothes or toys. And a firm which handles luxury items can profit from the population break-downs by levels of income.

In fact, census figures are so vital that Congress has now provided for a mid-decade population survey. The first one is to be taken in 1985. Two major considerations prompted the move: (1) the increasing, wide-ranging and important uses made of census data and (2) the growing necessity that such data be as current as possible. (The regular decennial census will remain the basis for the allocation of congressional seats, of course.)

The Bureau conducts dozens of periodic and special censuses in addition to the regular population counts. For example, in five-year cycles it surveys and produces de-

POPULATION GROWTH, BY REGIONS

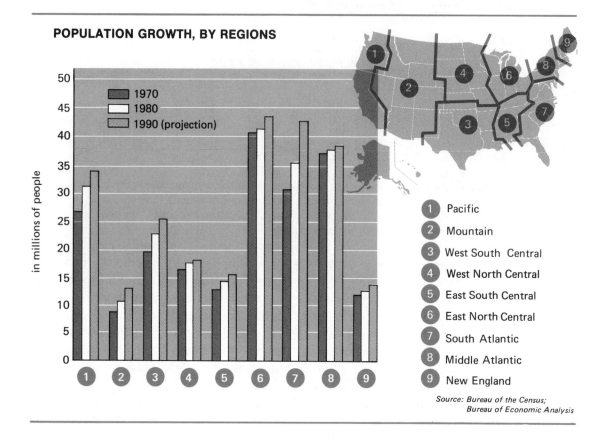

in millions of people

- 1970
- 1980
- 1990 (projection)

1 Pacific
2 Mountain
3 West South Central
4 West North Central
5 East South Central
6 East North Central
7 South Atlantic
8 Middle Atlantic
9 New England

Source: Bureau of the Census;
Bureau of Economic Analysis

tailed reports on agriculture, mineral industries, commercial fisheries, construction industries, transportation, and State and local governments. And it provides continuing current data on manufacturing, retail and wholesale trade, imports and exports, employment, and several other subjects. Special population surveys are often conducted for local governments. Although the Bureau charges for the counts, they can be winning propositions. They often are because most of the States make grants to their local governments from the funds collected from liquor, cigarette, and gasoline taxes—and those grants are usually based on population. (So, too, are most of the federal grants made to the States and their locales.)

Millions of persons were born in this country before birth records were universally kept. Proof of age or the location of one's birth are often important matters.

Such proof is important, for example, in getting a job, registering to vote, obtaining insurance, securing a driver's license, or applying for social security benefits. Thus far, some 4 million persons have been able to establish these vital facts with transcripts of information they or their parents once gave to a census taker.

The individual census report forms and the facts they contain are kept in the strictest confidence. The Bureau will furnish a summary of the data it has about the person who requests it and about that person's children or deceased parents. But it is forbidden to supply that information to anyone else. Not even the FBI or the IRS has access to its massive file. Each census enumerator must take an oath of secrecy. The revelation of any of the personal facts gathered is a federal crime, and conviction carries a penalty of as much as $1000 and/ or a year in jail.

THE NATIONAL BUREAU OF STANDARDS. The Framers of the Constitution recognized the absolute need for standardized physical measurements. Hence, Congress has the power to "fix the standards of weights and measures."[12]

Acting under this authority, Congress in 1836 established the English system (of pound, ounce, mile, foot, gallon, quart, and so on) as the legal standard of weights and measures in the United States. In 1866 it also legalized the use of the French metric system (gram, meter, liter, and so on) long so widely used in technical and scientific work.

In 1901 Congress created the National Bureau of Standards and made it responsible for the custody, maintenance, and development of the national standards of physical measurement. The originals, by which all other standards in the nation are tested, are kept in the Bureau's main laboratories in Gaithersburg, Maryland.

The Bureau was created as a scientific research and testing center for the Federal Government, and as an aid to American science and industry. Over the years it has become one of the world's truly great scientific institutions. Much of its activities are centered at its huge laboratory facilities in Maryland and at Boulder, Colorado. But the Bureau maintains field stations elsewhere in the country and abroad.

Its several thousands of scientists and highly skilled technicians perform a wide range of experimental and other testing functions. For example, they analyze all manner of materials, develop new and improved machines and measuring devices, and determine the resistance of products and substances to fire, cold, stress, and strain. To suggest the range of its activities, it has recently developed methods for testing the performance of solar energy collectors and storage units and developed criteria for checking the performance of residential smoke detectors. It has developed a portable atomic clock and made computer studies to predict the effect of aerosol propellants on the ozone layer. And, it has sponsored the first in-depth study of privacy in the keeping of computerized medical records.

Simply to list the Bureau's many significant accomplishments would more than fill this book. They range all the way from the standardization of clothing sizes to the very frontiers of nuclear physics.

THE PATENT AND TRADEMARK OFFICE. The Constitution grants Congress the power:

> To promote the progress of science and useful arts, by securing, for limited times, to authors and inventors, the exclusive right to their respective writing and discoveries.[13]

Acting under this authority, Congress has provided for both *copyrights* and *patents*. As we saw on page 339, these are licenses, grants of exclusive rights made to authors and to inventors. These legal devices protect the creations of those persons for certain periods of time; they safeguard the right to any benefits which may arise from the ownership of those creations.

The copyright laws are administered by the Copyright Office now located in the Library of Congress. The patent laws are the responsibility of the Patent and Trademark Office in the Commerce Department.

By law, a patent carries "the right to exclude others from making, using, or selling" the object of the patent "throughout the United States." The right may be assigned (sold or given to others), and it may be inherited as may other property.

Three different types of patents are now issued. *Patents of invention* are the most common. They are grants of the exclusive right to make, use, or sell "any new and

---

[12] Article I, Section 8, Clause 5; see page 340.

[13] Article I, Section 8, Clause 8.

useful art, machine, manufacture, or composition of matter, or useful improvement thereof." These patents are valid for 17 years. Patents of invention cannot be renewed except by special act of Congress—something quite rare.

Plant patents are issued to cover those who originate and develop new varieties of certain living plants—fruit and ornamental trees, roses, and the like. They, too, are good for 17 years. *Patents of design* cover ornamental designed articles of manufacture—fraternal insignia, automobile bodies, wallpaper patterns, and the like. They have a life of 3½, 7, or 14 years, at the patentee's option and, unlike other patents, they are sometimes extended by Congress.

If a patent is ignored, infringed, or challenged, the holder of the patent (not the Government) must act to protect it. The patentee's usual recourse is to the federal district courts.[14]

Some 70,000 patents are now issued each year and, altogether, more than 4 million have been granted so far. Among the earliest were those for Eli Whitney's cotton gin (1793) and Robert Fulton's steamboat (1809). Thomas Edison is credited with a record of 1,093 patents, among them those for the incandescent light bulb, the phonograph, the carbon transmitter which made the telephone commercially feasible, the motion picture camera, and the sound motion picture.

The Office also issues—that is, *registers*—*trademarks*. A trademark is a distinctive word, emblem, symbol, or other device used on goods sold in interstate or foreign commerce to identify the manufacturer or seller. Any individual or firm providing service but not making or selling goods may also register a certain mark to identify its particular service. Trademarks are registered for 20 years and may be renewed any number of times.[15]

About 30,000 trademarks are now registered each year and another 5000 are renewed annually. There would be little point in a firm's spending huge sums in advertising and using a distinctive symbol if others were allowed to imitate it. A trademark can be worth a very substantial sum to its owner.

THE NATIONAL OCEANIC AND ATMOSPHERIC ADMINISTRATION. Two long-established federal agencies—the *Coast and Geodetic Survey*, created in 1807, and the *Weather Bureau*, dating from 1890—were joined together to form the *National Oceanic and Atmospheric Administration* in 1970. The newer agency is often known by its rather apt acronym: NOAA.

NOAA's province is the environmental sciences and it would be difficult to imagine an agency with a broader mandate. It is charged by law "to describe, understand, and predict the state of the oceans, the state of the lower and upper atmosphere, and the size and the shape of the earth."

The activities of its Weather Service are of incalculable value. It receives countless daily reports—of heat, cold, clouds, rain, snow, wind direction and velocity, and similar conditions. These reports are received from hundreds of places across the country, from ships and aircraft, and from satellites orbiting the earth. From all of the data it collects, weather conditions are forecast with usually remarkable accuracy.

No one could possibly catalog the uses to which the reports of the Weather Service are put, nor the benefits derived from them. Here is but a sample: frost warnings allow fruit growers to protect their orchards; daily wind reports and storm advi-

[14] Appeals from actions taken by the Office—for example, its refusal to issue a patent—are taken first to the Board of Appeals within the Office and from there to the Court of Customs and Patent Appeals; see page 658.

[15] Although the Constitution does not mention trademarks, the Commerce Clause gives Congress the implied power to provide for their registration and protection.

NOAA administers and directs the National Sea Grant program which includes grants for marine research and education. Here, an electronic, highly complex sea-floor mapping instrument is inspected by engineers of the University of California's Scripps Institution of Oceanography.

sories aid pilots and fishermen; flood warnings, often a week in advance, allow cities some time to prepare for the high waters and enable farmers to save livestock that might otherwise be lost. The spotting and tracking of hurricanes save untold numbers of lives; freeze forecasts permit railroads to save perishables in transit and warn motorists to check the anti-freeze level; rain forecasts govern planting and harvesting and are watched very closely by building contractors, baseball players, picnickers, those who must fight forest fires, and thousands of others.

While NOAA's efforts in the fields of weather and atmospheric conditions—the work of the *National Weather Service*—are quite well-known, its other activities are not. The work of the *National Ocean Survey* is the present-day continuation of the functions of the historic Coast and Geodetic Survey. Its maps, charts, and other reports are indispensable to commercial and general aviation and to water-borne commerce. And they are of great value in any number of other fields including engineering, construction, and communications. Its seismological research is critical to an understanding of earthquakes, the reduction of damage from them, and the hoped-for ability to anticipate them. Among its several other functions, the Survey maintains a number of navigational and data-collecting buoys. Some of these buoys are stationary and many of them drift along the continental shelf. Some drift

farther out in the Atlantic and Pacific Oceans and in the Gulf of Mexico, and elsewhere in the international waters of the world.

Its *National Marine Fisheries Service* promotes both the conservation and development of marine resources. Thus its saltwater fish research has recently prompted a fast-growing salmon-farming industry in the Pacific Northwest. Its broad-ranging activities also include the enforcement of laws to protect whales, porpoises, turtles, and other threatened species of marine mammals. It inspects fish processing plants and provides financial help to commercial fishermen whose vessels are seized in the territorial waters of other nations.[16]

NOAA carries on much of its work with research ships, aircraft, and satellites. It maintains oceanographic, seismological,

---

[16] International law generally recognizes a nation's territorial jurisdiction seaward to the historic 3-mile limit. In recent years many nations, including the United States, have unilaterally extended their jurisdiction over fishing and other sea resources out beyond that point; see page 600. Some Latin American states have even claimed control out to a 500-mile limit. The situation is particularly troublesome for commercial fishermen; on occasion their vessels have been seized by other nations for violations of those extended limits. The problem has another side. In recent years Russian and Japanese fishing fleets have worked the waters immediately off our coasts. As a result, Congress extended the area of exclusive American fishing rights to 12 miles in 1966 and then to 200 miles in 1977. Foreign vessels may fish within the protected zones only with permits issued by the National Marine Fisheries Service. The Service and the Coast Guard police the coastal fishing zones.

and meteorological laboratories, observatories, and field stations in several places in this country and abroad—including a magnetic and seismological observatory at the South Pole. It also administers the *Sea Grant Program*, which provides funds to support oceanography schools, courses, and research at more than 120 of the nation's colleges and universities.

THE MARITIME ADMINISTRATION. From the earliest days of the Republic the nation's maritime policy has centered around a strong merchant marine—one adequate to carry our domestic water-borne commerce and the bulk of our foreign trade. And, it has been committed to maintaining a merchant marine capable of serving as a naval auxiliary in time of war, as well.

The Maritime Administration is the present descendant of a long line of merchant marine agencies dating back more than 60 years. A steady decline in the nation's merchant marine occurred in the years immediately before and after the turn of this century. It had been caused in large part by the lower construction and operating costs enjoyed by most foreign shipping concerns. It prompted Congress to create the *United States Shipping Board* in 1916. That agency and its successors were given powers with which to promote and regulate the nation's shipping efforts.

Many aids are provided to American shipping. Congress has long granted subsidies to shipbuilders, owners, and operators to help them meet overseas competition. Today the subsidy program is conducted by the Maritime Administration through its Maritime Subsidy Board. The Administration also guarantees loans to shipbuilders and pays the costs of defense features—such as troop-carrying facilities—built into vessels that are certified by the Navy as necessary for national defense. It conducts an extensive research and development program aimed at improving the quality and efficiency of the merchant marine. Thus it studies such varied problems

as ship design, safety, propulsion, and cargo handling.

In both World Wars the Government became directly involved in shipbuilding. Thousands of Liberty, Victory, and other ships were built in Government shipyards. The Maritime Administration keeps over a thousand of these vessels in a national defense reserve fleet for emergency use. Many of the ships are used by the Navy and other agencies; the rest have either been chartered or sold to private operators. A fully-equipped shipyard is kept on a stand-by basis at Richmond, California.

The Maritime Administration operates the United States Merchant Marine Academy at Kings Point, New York, to train officers for the merchant marine. Its graduates are licensed as ship's officers by the Coast Guard and are also qualified for commissions as ensigns in the Naval Reserve. The Administration also administers a grant program to aid the maritime academies operated by California, Maine, Massachusetts, Michigan, New York, and Texas. And the Administration offers marine specialty courses for merchant seamen in schools in San Francisco, New York, Seattle, Toledo, and New Orleans.

Over the years, Congress has given the several maritime agencies extensive powers to regulate the rates, services, and labor practices of American vessels engaged in foreign and offshore water commerce. Today that authority is exercised by an independent regulatory agency, the *Federal Maritime Commission.* The Commission's five members are appointed by the President and Senate for five-year terms.[17]

THE INDUSTRY AND TRADE ADMINISTRATION. The Industry and Trade Administration is the federal agency primarily responsible for the promotion of the foreign trade of the United States.

---

[17] Vessels operating on the inland waters of the United States are regulated by the Interstate Commerce Commission; see pages 562-564.

The ITA maintains detailed files on thousands of foreign firms engaged in international trade. These records, compiled with the aid of the Foreign Service, are readily available to American firms. Its weekly magazine, *International Commerce,* reports on business conditions and trade and investment prospects around the world. With local chambers of commerce, it holds "trade clinics" to acquaint business owners with the opportunities for marketing their products in other countries.

The agency sends trade missions abroad to make contacts for American firms. It conducts international trade fairs and maintains permanent trade centers in other countries to display American goods to potential foreign customers. It is also responsible for enforcing the Export Administration Act of 1969—the current law to prevent the export of strategic materials and data to any potential enemy nation.

The Administration also provides the working staff for the *Foreign Trade Zones Board.* The Board, an independent agency, creates and manages "foreign trade zones" at selected American ports of entry. These zones are small enclosed areas where foreign goods intended for transshipment to other countries may be stored and processed free of customs duties. Storage and processing facilities are also available for domestic goods destined for export. Trade zones are presently in operation at some two dozen coastal and inland cities.

OTHER AGENCIES. The six units in the Commerce Department we've just surveyed each conduct several programs purposefully designed to aid and promote the nation's business community. They do not exhaust the list; there are other Commerce agencies with the same basic mission.

The *Bureau of Economic Analysis* is a major economic research organization. It maintains a close and studious eye on the structure, condition, and prospects of the nation's economy. Quite importantly, it gauges and makes continuing reports on

the *gross national product*—the GNP, the total national output of goods and services. The information it provides indicates growth and recession trends in all segments of the economy. This, and the Office's other statistical data and analyses, are vital to other executive agencies, to Congress, and to the business community in charting the nation's economic course. Economists find its journal, *Survey of Current Business,* indispensable.

The *Economic Development Administration* identifies those locales which are economically depressed and so eligible for aid under the *Public Works and Economic Development Act of 1965.* EDA's primary function is to promote the long-range development of those communities. It makes loans and grants for public works projects, provides loans to businesses for plant construction and expansion, and guarantees private loans to business concerns. It also works with other federal agencies concerned with combatting severe unemployment in depressed communities, and furnishes help to State and local agencies engaged in economic development activities.

The *Office of Minority Business Enterprise* coordinates the efforts of the many different federal agencies with programs which may contribute to the formation or strengthening of businesses operated by the members of minority groups. It also seeks to prompt the efforts of State and local public and private organizations to the same end. The Office also serves as a focal point for information useful to minority businesses in establishing and running successful enterprises.

The *United States Travel Service* is a sort of super tourist agency. Its particular function is to attract tourists and other foreign visitors to this country—for study, business, recreation, and the like.

Other Aids to Business. We are frequently reminded that business enterprises pay hefty sums in taxes each year—and indeed they do. But we are not so repeatedly told that a very large share of governmental revenue finds its way back, directly and indirectly, to the coffers of the business community. The monies paid out by government go to many different places in the national economy, of course. But business is often the first, and frequently the chief, recipient of these funds. `

GOVERNMENT SPENDING. The Federal Government is far and away the nation's biggest spender. In fiscal 1981 it will spend well over $600 billion—and nearly all of that huge sum will be spent in the United States.

That vast public spending has a tremendous and stimulating effect upon the economy. Welfare and social insurance payments go immediately to the beneficiaries, of course—and we shall discuss that matter in Chapter 25. But for now notice this important point: Most who receive those payments almost immediately spend the money in supermarkets and other retail stores, with landlords, and so on.

Much the same point can be made with every other segment of the federal budget (and, incidentally, State and local governmental spending, too). Thus, of the more than $150 billion now spent for defense, about 47 billion goes as pay to military personnel—who are consumers in the national economy just as the rest of us are. And much of the rest of the defense budget goes to the manufacturers of guns, tanks, planes, and electronic equipment, to the construction industry, to the producers and processors of food and fiber, and to the dozens of other places in the business community which provide the goods and services needed by the defense establishment.

SUBSIDIES. Federal subsidies reach into virtually every part of the economy, too. We noted the direct support given to the shipping industry a moment ago, and shortly we'll encounter more such federal help in other areas of transportation, in housing, in agriculture, and elsewhere.

Many subsidies are indirect and so not very visible. Protective tariffs, imposed by law and paid for by consumers, are a leading example of them. So, too, are the annual postal deficits, federal aid for highway construction, grants for building and improving airports, and the operation of air traffic control systems.

The several billion dollars the Federal Government spends each year for research and development amount to a very substantial subsidy to private business. A significant amount of R & D work is done in and by federal agencies. But the larger share of R & D work is contracted to the private sector—for pay, of course. And, though much of it relates to aircraft, missiles, and other military hardware, much of it also produces results which have profitable commercial applications. Thus, for example, the space-age research done by and for NASA has spawned dozens of down-to-earth businesses and salable products.

Surprising though it may seem, the income tax laws are also a vehicle for business subsidies. The deductions allowed for the interest paid on home mortgages and other installment contracts are a boon to homebuilders, financial institutions, appliance manufacturers and dealers, and many others. Congress added another of these subsidies in 1978 when it provided a tax credit for those who install or add to the insulation of their homes. The immediate reason for the credit was to save energy, of course. But the tax credit also had a quick and healthy impact on the sale of storm windows, doors, and other insulating materials.

CREDIT PROGRAMS. Several federal agencies make or guarantee loans to a large number of businesses, and for many purposes. Again, we have just encountered the Federal Maritime Administration, and the Economic Development Administration, too. There are many others.

One of the most active is the *Small Busi-*

ness Administration. Since 1953 it has made loans to small business concerns to help them finance plant construction or expansion and buy machinery, supplies, or materials. It also makes or guarantees loans to smaller firms for a variety of other purposes—to help them meet federal water pollution standards or overcome the effects of the closure of a nearby military base or a change in the scope of some other federal program, or assist those firms that are adversely affected by energy shortages, for example.

Most SBA loans are relatively small, now averaging only about $50,000. The SBA can lend as much as $500,000 to a single borrower, however.

The SBA also administers an extensive disaster relief program for both individuals and businesses. The victims of floods, hurricanes, droughts, forest fires, and other catastrophes are helped with low-cost loans. They are used to repair, rebuild, or replace homes, businesses, or other properties. So,

too, are those small businesses injured by any federally-aided urban renewal, highway, or other construction project. In fact, the list of SBA loan activities goes on and on.

Another independent agency, the *Export-Import Bank* of the United States is also a major source of loan help to American business. Eximbank was established in 1934 to help stimulate our foreign trade which had sagged in the worldwide depression.

Its major purpose is to aid in financing the export of American-made goods and services. About 85 percent of those exports go abroad without Eximbank support. But many, large and small, cannot be financed by the private sector. Eximbank takes up the slack with direct loans to exporters, by guaranteeing portions of loans made by commercial banks, and with *discount loans.* The latter are Eximbank loans to commercial banks which, in turn, lend to private borrowers for export purposes.

SUMMARY

The Federal Government has been closely involved in the nation's economic life from the very beginnings of the Republic. The principal source of its authority in the field is the Commerce Clause, which grants to Congress the commerce power.

What, precisely, is included within the scope of the Commerce Clause is being determined, continuously, by: (1) Congress as it exercises its commerce power and (2) the Supreme Court as it decides cases involving that exercise. Historically, both Congress and the Court have given it an ever-broadening interpretation. *Gibbons* v. *Ogden,* 1824, set the pattern for that process.

The *foreign commerce* of the United States includes any trade which begins, passes through, or ends in any foreign country. As the States have absolutely no power in the field, the power to regulate foreign commerce is even broader than that to regulate interstate trade.

Interstate commerce includes all trade between and among the States and the means by which it is conducted. Trade conducted wholly within one State, *intrastate commerce,* is subject only to State regulation; however, much commerce once considered intrastate has come to be viewed as interstate in character by both Congress and the courts. In the exercise of their police powers the States may only incidentally affect interstate commerce; they cannot impose an unreasonable burden upon it.

Exercising its commerce power, Congress has provided for both the regulation and the promotion of business activities. In the Sherman Antitrust Act of 1890, strengthened by the Clayton Act in 1914 and by later statutes, it has outlawed various practices in restraint of trade. These laws are enforced particularly by the Justice Department and the Federal Trade Commission. It has also enacted a number of consumer protection laws, now enforced by several different federal agencies, including the Consumer Product Safety Commission. And it has enacted several statutes to protect investors; most of them are enforced by the Securities and Exchange Commission.

It has also provided for numerous aids to business. These promotional activities take many different forms—both direct and indirect subsidies, loans and other credit supports, informational programs, and several others. Various agencies within the Commerce Department and a host of other federal agencies administer these aids. The massive spending of the Federal Government is itself a huge stimulator for the business community.

Concept Development

Questions for Review

1. Where in the Constitution is the Commerce Clause found? What does it provide?

2. By whom is "commerce" being continuously defined?

3. Why is *Gibbons* v. *Ogden* a landmark case in our constitutional law?

4. What is foreign commerce? Interstate commerce? Intrastate commerce? By whom is each regulated?

5. Why is the power to regulate foreign commerce a broader one than the power to regulate interstate commerce?

6. May the commerce power be exercised so as to reach a carrier operating wholly within a single State? Why?

7. May the States impose regulations upon interstate commerce? If so, to what extent?

8. Why did Congress enact the Sherman Act of 1890? The Clayton Act of 1914?

9. What is the principal function of the Federal Trade Commission?

10. What is the ancient rule of *caveat emptor?* The newer rule of *caveat vendor?*

11. What is the principal function of the Consumer Product Safety Commission?

12. What are "blue sky" laws? What is the principal function of the Securities and Exchange Commission? The Commodity Futures Trading Commission?

13. What is the basic mission of the Commerce Department? Cite a specific program or function of each of three of its agencies which illustrates that mission.

14. Why may the fact that the Federal Government is the biggest spender in the United States be cited as an aid to business?

15. Cite three illustrations of direct federal subsidies to business. Three indirect subsidies.

For Further Inquiry

1. In enacting the Civil Rights Act of 1964 (see pages 175, 535), Congress declared Title II of the statute, dealing with access to public accommodations, to be based upon the Commerce Clause. Why did it not choose, instead, to rely upon the Due Process and the Equal Protection Clauses of the 14th Amendment as its constitutional authority?

2. A corporation is owned by its stockholders. As a rule, however, the stockholders have little real control over the management and policies of the corporation. Effective control is actually held by a board of directors or similar group. To what extent, if any, do you think that this separation of ownership and operating control of the modern corporation undermines the principle of individual initiative in the private enterprise system?

3. None of the 20 censuses so far taken has ever included a question relating to a person's religious preferences. Why would many church groups and others welcome the inclusion of questions concerning church membership and related matters? Why would many oppose them?

4. Do you think it fair for the Federal Government to provide subsidies to such special groups as ship owners and operators when these aids are financed by taxes levied upon the entire population?

5. Why can the copyright, patent, and trademark laws be cited as significant federal aids to business? The functions of the Federal Deposit Insurance Corporation? The postal system? Welfare programs? Defense activities?

Suggested Activities

1. Prepare a list of as many examples as you can find of the ways in which business activities in your locale are regulated by the Federal Government. By State and local governments.

2. Prepare a similar list of the ways in which those three levels of government aid businesses in your community.

3. Invite a local business owner to discuss with the class the ways in which government regulates and aids his or her particular business.

4. Invite a representative of one of the federal agencies cited in this chapter to discuss that agency and its functions with the class.

5. Prepare a chart or bulletin board display to illustrate the scope and importance of the commerce power.

Suggested Reading

Boskin, Michael J. (ed.), *The Economy in the 1980's: A Program for Growth and Stability.* Institute for Contemporary Studies, 1980.

Brugchey, Stuart W. (ed.), *Small Business in American Life.* Columbia University Press, 1980.

Gill, Richard, *Economics & the Public Interest.* Goodyear, 4th ed., 1980.

Halacy, Dan, *One Hundred Ninety Years of Counting America.* Elsevier-Nelson, 1979.

Heilbroner, Robert L., *The Making of Economic Society.* Prentice-Hall, 6th ed., 1980.

Samuelson, Paul A., *Economics.* McGraw-Hill, 11th ed., 1980.

Siegan, Bernard H. (ed.), *Government Regulation and the Economy.* Heath, 1980.

Also: Office of Communications, Department of Commerce, Washington, D.C. 20230

Directorate for Communications, Consumer Product Safety Commission, Washington, D.C. 20207

Office of Public Information, Federal Trade Commission, Washington, D.C. 20580

Office of Public Information, Securities Exchange Commission, Washington, D.C. 20549

Government and Business: Regulation and Promotion-II

The prosperity of commerce is now perceived and acknowledged by all enlightened statesmen to be the most useful as well as the most productive source of national wealth, and has accordingly become a primary object of their political cares.

ALEXANDER HAMILTON

■ Why has the Federal Government been so closely concerned with all forms of transportation from the very beginnings of the Republic?

■ To whom are the various federal housing programs most beneficial?

■ Why are not newspapers subject to the same federal regulatory authority as radio and television?

■ What is the basic shape of the nation's energy problem? What short- and long-term solutions are available?

In Chapter 21 we began to survey the very extensive topic: Government and Business. There we were especially concerned with three major aspects of the subject: (1) The principal constitutional basis for federal activities, the commerce power; (2) federal regulation of business practices; and (3) federal supports to the business community.

In this chapter we continue our discussion of that topic. Here, we focus on four major areas of federal activities: (1) transportation, (2) housing, (3) communications, and (4) energy. As we do so, ponder Abraham Lincoln's oft-quoted admonition:

The legitimate object of government is to do for the community of people whatever they need to have done, but cannot do so well for themselves, in their separate and individual capacities.

Government and Transportation

The history of the United States can be told in good part in terms of the development of its transportation system. The means of transportation at the time provided the physical basis for the political unification of the nation in the latter part of the 18th century. Our territorial expansion, growth in population, and vast accumulation of wealth and power have gone hand-in-hand with the means by which we move persons and goods—from the days

FEDERAL EXPENDITURES FOR TRANSPORTATION FACILITIES
For AIR*, WATER** and HIGHWAYS

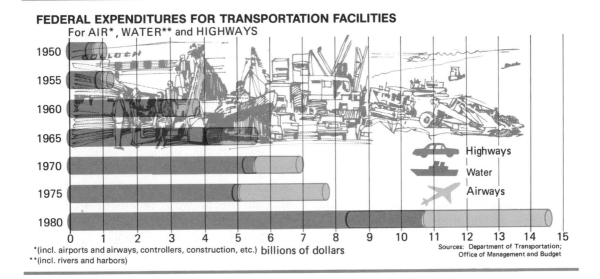

1950
1955
1960
1965
1970
1975
1980

Highways
Water
Airways

0 1 2 3 4 5 6 7 8 9 10 11 12 13 14 15

*(incl. airports and airways, controllers, construction, etc.) billions of dollars
**(incl. rivers and harbors)

Sources: Department of Transportation;
Office of Management and Budget

of the horse and rider, the stagecoach, the sailing ship, and the covered wagon through the development of the steamboat, the railroad, the automobile, and the airplane to the age of jet propulsion and supersonic travel.

In fact, it is not too much to say that the United States is a nation made by transportation. And it should not be surprising, then, that from its beginnings the Federal Government has been closely concerned with all forms of transportation.

As we turn to that concern bear these points in mind: The United States is the only major nation in the world that relies on *privately*-owned and operated transportation. As a people, we are generally agreed that private enterprise has served us well and that its predominant role should be continued.

But, at the same time, remember that private enterprise has succeeded as it has only through the use of *publicly* granted authority and an immense investment of *public* resources. Notice how indispensable to our transportation system have been and are such governmental contributions as the construction of channels, locks, dams, and canals on our rivers and other inland waterways, and the development of ports and harbors, the construction of a vast network of highways, the development of airports,

and huge grants of public lands.

In short, government has been a most useful and a willing partner with private enterprise in providing for the nation's transportation needs.

The Department of Transportation. The Department of Transportation was created by Congress in 1966 and began to operate the following year. It was built out of the combination of a number of agencies and functions previously scattered through several other Cabinet departments and several independent agencies.

Congress established it "to assure the coordinated, effective administration of the transportation programs of the Federal Government," and to develop "national transportation policies and programs conducive to the provision of fast, safe, efficient, and convenient transportation." DOT is headed by the Secretary of Transportation and operates through seven major line agencies.[1]

---

[1] The Secretary is responsible for fixing the standard time zones throughout the United States and also enforces the Uniform Time Act of 1966. That statute requires that daylight time be observed in all time zones from 2 A.M. on the last Sunday in April through 2 A.M. on the last Sunday in October each year. A State wholly within one time zone may exempt itself from the law only if the State legislature votes to keep the entire State on standard time. In a State split by time zones, the legislature may vote to exempt that portion of the State in the westerly zone.

THE FEDERAL RAILROAD ADMINISTRATION. The Federal Railroad Administration was born with DOT in 1967. It is now the major federal promotional, regulatory, and safety agency in the field of rail transport. It thus operates in the same general area as the Interstate Commerce Commission—and in fact acquired many of its functions by transfer from the ICC. The ICC continues to play its historic role as the economic regulator of the nation's railroads, however—as we shall see later in this chapter.

The FRA administers the rail safety provisions of the Interstate Commerce Act of 1887 and a host of other statutes enacted over the years since.

With private industry, it conducts an extensive research and development program to improve intercity ground transportation by conventional rail and more advanced means. It has recently opened a large Test Center near Pueblo, Colorado.

The FRA also operates the Alaska Railroad, a federally-owned rail system created by Congress in 1914 to encourage the settlement and the agricultural and industrial development of Alaska. The Railroad runs over some 771 kilometers (482 miles) of main line from its southern terminus at Seward through Anchorage and on to Fairbanks in the interior. It also operates a number of branch lines and a tug and barge service on the Tanana and Yukon Rivers.

THE FEDERAL AVIATION ADMINISTRATION. Congress first began to regulate civil air transportation with the passage of the Air Commerce Act of 1926. Over the years since, that regulation has evolved to the point where today three agencies are closely involved in it. Two of them are independent agencies and we shall discuss them in a moment. They are the National Transportation Safety Board, which is especially concerned with fixing the causes of air accidents, and the Civil Aeronautics Board, especially concerned with the economic regulation of air transport.

The other and major agency is the Federal Aviation Administration. It was first established as an independent agency in 1958 and became a part of DOT in 1967.

By law, the FAA is "empowered and directed to encourage and foster civil aeronautics and air commerce in the United States and abroad." It possesses very broad authority to discharge this mission, beginning at the drawing board-research level and extending throughout the realm of aviation. It licenses all civilian pilots and aircraft, both private and commercial. It makes and enforces safety rules for all air traffic—both private and commercial. And, it regulates the use of all navigable air space within the nation—for both civilian *and* military purposes.

The importance of the FAA's work can be underscored with some statistics. There are nearly 800,000 licensed private and commercial pilots and over 230,000 civilian aircraft in this country today. The FAA estimates that those pilots and planes now pile up more than 40 million hours of flight time each year. And the nation's commercial airlines now fly more than 275 million passengers a distance of nearly 230 billion passenger-miles each year.

The FAA is also responsible for the installation, maintenance, and operation of such air navigation devices as beacons, wind and directional signals, radar, and other and more sophisticated electronic aids to flight. It operates a nationwide air traffic communications system and equips and operates air traffic control towers and centers at hundreds of local airports. It promotes aviation research, maintains emergency landing fields, dispenses grants-in-aid for airport construction and maintenance. No federal funds may be spent on *any* civilian airport, nor may the military build or alter an airport or missile site, without FAA approval.

THE FEDERAL HIGHWAY ADMINISTRATION. The United States is literally a nation on wheels. There are now more than 140 million licensed drivers in the country. They operate some 120 million cars, 30 million trucks and buses, and 6 million motorcycles on 6.2 million kilometers (3.9 million miles) of road, traveling more than 2.2 trillion kilometers (1.4 trillion miles) a year. We have better than one automobile for every two persons, about 25 vehicles for every kilometer (40 per mile) of road, and more than a kilometer of road for every square kilometer in the country. Four of every five persons old enough to drive have licenses. The figures grow each year.

Congress passed the first federal road-building law at least as early as 1806. But, until the Age of the Automobile arrived, road construction and maintenance were almost exclusively State and local governmental responsibilities. And the major responsibility for these functions still resides at that level.

The Federal Aid Road Act of 1916 set the basic pattern followed in the development of the hefty federal highway programs ever since. That law provided for $15 million in yearly roadbuilding grants to the States and required each to match its allocation on a dollar-for-dollar basis. Grants-in-aid remain a basic feature of federal highway programs. But the sums now involved have grown astronomically.

The Federal Highway Administration is the principal federal roadbuilding agency today. It came into being with DOT in 1967 and is, in large part, the successor to the old Bureau of Public Roads. For decades the Bureau was located in the Commerce Department.

The FHWA has charge of most of the roadbuilding work done on federal lands—in the national forests and national parks and on Indian reservations, for example. It determines the reasonableness of any tolls charged on bridges across the nation's navigable waters and does extensive planning and research work on all phases of highway construction and maintenance. It

also administers the federal safety standards which apply to commercial vehicles (mostly trucks and buses) and their operators in interstate commerce—some 3 million vehicles and 4 million drivers. But, with all its other functions, its major task is the administration of the huge federal-aid highway program.

The Federal Aid Highway Act of 1956, now amended several times, is the basic federal road construction law today. Its passage inaugurated the largest public works program in history—the construction of the 68,000-kilometer (42,500-mile) National System of Interstate and Defense Highways. Soon, this herculean effort will have provided a coast-to-coast network of controlled-access, four-to-eight lane superhighways connecting all of the nation's larger and thousands of smaller cities.

The States now receive grants totaling nearly $4 billion a year to build and improve the freeways of the Interstate System. Monies for the grants come from the Highway Trust Fund—a special account in the Treasury fed by the federal excises on gasoline, tires, truck parts, and similar items. When it is finally completed, sometime in the early 1980's, the System will have cost about $105 billion—with federal funds covering 90 percent of the cost.

The States also receive grants for the improvement of the additional 1.4 million kilometers (872,000 miles) in the federal-aid network of *primary* (main), *secondary* (feeder, farm-to-market, and the like), and *urban* roads. These grants are financed by the Highway Trust Fund, too, and have now reached the $3 billion-a-year level. The States must match these federal aid funds on a 70 (federal)–30 (State) basis.

Altogether, federal grant monies now support the building or upkeep of nearly 25 percent of the nation's roads—and those roads carry about two-thirds of all of the nation's motor vehicle traffic.

THE NATIONAL HIGHWAY TRAFFIC SAFETY ADMINISTRATION. Last year some 50,000 persons were killed in traffic accidents, and many millions more were injured. Since the coming of the automobile, more Americans have been killed in traffic accidents than in all of the nation's wars and natural disasters put together.

Since the mid-1960's Congress has enacted several laws to protect drivers, passengers, and pedestrians and to promote the safety of motor vehicles. The first of these measures was the National Traffic and Motor Vehicle Safety Act of 1966—and its title suggests the tenor of the several which have followed it.

The Safety Administration enforces those laws. It prescribes safety standards for all new cars and motor vehicles produced or sold in this country, and runs an intensive testing program to insure compliance. It makes continuing reports to Congress and the public and can require car manufacturers to recall defective vehicles or take other corrective actions. It also administers a number of grant programs to support such activities as driver training courses, safety inspections, and campaigns to get the drunk driver off the road.

As horrifying as the current rate of highway slaughter is, it has actually declined in recent years. As recently as 1973, 55,000 persons died in traffic accidents. Three factors seem to be principally responsible for this rather remarkable turn of events: (1) sharp increases in fuel prices brought on by the energy crisis, (2) the 55 mile-per-hour speed limit mandated by Congress in 1974, and (3) the efforts of the Safety Administration and State and local traffic law enforcement agencies.

THE NATIONAL TRANSPORTATION SAFETY BOARD. The investigation of accidents in all fields of transportation—ground, sea, and air—is the special province of the National Transportation Safety Board. Originally located within DOT, the Board was restructured by Congress in 1975. It is now an independent agency. Its five members are appointed by the President and Senate to serve five-year terms; every two years the President selects its chairman.

The Board is, in effect, the overseer of transportation safety in this country. Its jurisdiction is quite broad. Congress has directed it to investigate and attempt to fix the causes of a number of accidents and mishaps. All civil aircraft accidents, such major marine mishaps as ship collisions and sinkings, and all accidents involving passenger trains are investigated by the Board. It also investigates any other rail or any pipeline accident in which someone is killed or in which there is substantial property damage. And the Board investigates any highway accident in which such peculiar factors as railroad crossings or school buses are involved.

The results of its investigations are broadcast in several ways. It reports to Congress and makes safety recommendations to other public agencies and to the various segments of the transportation industry. Its findings are regularly covered by the news media.

Beyond whatever impact its reporting activities may have, Congress has given it some other teeth. It evaluates and reports on the effectiveness of the safety efforts of other federal agencies. It also has an appellate function. It hears appeals taken from any action in which the FAA revokes or modifies a pilot's license or in which the Coast Guard takes similar steps with regard to merchant marine papers.

THE URBAN MASS TRANSIT ADMINISTRATION. The transportation systems within most American cities are much like Topsy—they just "growed" over the years.

The privately-owned rail lines were developed as parts of a national, intercity transportation system, not to serve transit needs *within* cities. The once-convenient location of train stations and tracks, usually in the heart of a city's downtown area, are reflections of that fact—and have been the source of vexing urban problems in recent years.

The large-scale development of intra-city transit systems began in the decades around the turn of the century. Streetcar lines, subways, and elevated trains appeared. In some places these systems were developed under private ownership, in others as public ventures, and in most places with little or no useful long-range planning. Taxis began to roam city streets in the early 1900's. Then buses, public or private, came along to supplement or displace other carriers. Finally, the private automobile took over the streets, dominating and congesting them—and adding such new problems as parking, demands for better roadways, and increased air and noise pollution.

Cities have been plagued with the consequences of those developments. Their inability to resolve the resulting problems, and of the States to help them, finally prompted Congress to act. It passed the Urban Mass Transportation Act of 1964. That law and several later ones provide grants and loans to acquire or upgrade mass transit facilities, either publicly or privately owned.

These programs are administered by the Urban Mass Transit Administration, a DOT agency since 1968. Congress has gradually increased UMTA funding to its current (1980) level of about $3.8 billion a year. UMTA works with other public agencies and private industry and research groups to improve existing transit modes, and to develop new ones. Those efforts, for example, have lately included such things as mini-buses, air-cushioned rail vehicles, and other "people movers," park-and-ride facilities, experiments with staggered working hours, and the like.

THE SAINT LAWRENCE SEAWAY DEVELOPMENT CORPORATION. The Saint Lawrence Seaway was built and is now operated as a joint venture of the United States and Canada. Work on the project, a dream for decades, was begun in 1955. It opened to its first deep-water traffic in 1959.

The Seaway is ice-free and navigable for about nine months a year. Its locks and canals link the inland ports of the Great Lakes to the Atlantic Ocean, and so to the rest of the world. It has given to the United States a fourth seacoast and transformed several midwestern cities into major seaports. By 1981 the Seaway was carrying some 65 million tons of raw materials and finished products to and from world markets.

The Saint Lawrence Seaway Development Corporation is a wholly-owned federal entity and has been a DOT agency since 1968. Today it operates that part of the seaway between Montreal and Lake Erie on the American side. It is financed by the tolls it charges for the use of its facilities. Those tolls and other details of its operations are set in cooperation with Canada's St. Lawrence Seaway Authority.

THE UNITED STATES COAST GUARD. The Coast Guard belies its name. It does guard the coasts of the United States, and it has for more than 190 years now. But it also operates in all of the 50 States. Its life-saving net encircles the globe; its ships ply all

DOT grants figured prominently in financing San Francisco's new rapid-transit system.

of the world's oceans, often far from any coast. And the Coast Guard has served with distinction in all of the nation's wars.

The Coast Guard was created as an arm of the Treasury Department in 1915 and was transferred to DOT in 1967. It traces its ancestry to 1790, however—to the Revenue Marine, a maritime law enforcement agency established by the 1st Congress.

The Coast Guard operates as a branch of the nation's armed forces. In time of war, or at the President's direction, it becomes a part of the Navy. Its Commandant is a career officer appointed to that post by the President, subject to Senate confirmation. Today the service has a total complement of more than 37,000 officers and enlisted personnel. In 1977 four of those officers and 20 from the enlisted ranks became the first women ever assigned to sea duty aboard an armed vessel of the United States.

The Coast Guard's primary mission is to enforce federal law on the high seas and the navigable waters of the United States. Its specific duties are numerous. It maintains inshore and offshore ships, aircraft, and radio stations to carry out search and rescue operations. Its six ocean stations—manned by four large cutters in the North Atlantic and two in the Pacific—transmit up-to-the-minute weather information, aid in search and rescue missions, furnish navigational aid to marine and air traffic, and collect oceanographic data.

It also polices the 200-mile fishing zone and maintains aids to navigation ranging from relatively simple river buoys and fog signals to the highly sophisticated Loran network that extends around the world. It clears ice-clogged channels and licenses merchant marine personnel. It inspects all classes of vessels, from the smallest pleasure boats to the largest supertankers, for seaworthiness and safety. It administers grants to support State safe-boating programs, and regulates pilotage on the Great Lakes. And it enforces several laws aimed at preventing, detecting, and controlling oil spills and other pollution of the navigable waters of the United States.

Coast Guard officers, detailed as captains of the port, are responsible for port security and regulate the anchorage and movement of vessels in American territorial waters. The Coast Guard's International Ice Patrol guards the shipping lanes of the North Atlantic, warning of dangerous conditions during the iceberg season. Not a single life has been lost from mishaps due to icebergs since the patrol went on station after the *Titanic* disaster in 1912.

The Interstate Commerce Commission. The Interstate Commerce Commission, established by Congress in 1887 to regulate the nation's railroads, was the first of the independent regulatory commissions to be created. Its creation was prompted by a number of factors, notably: the growth of the interstate character of railroads, the shortsighted character of many of their business practices, and a key Supreme Court decision.

In the early days of railroading, from the 1830's to the 1860's, the operations of the various lines were generally simple and sufficiently local to permit adequate State regulation. As early as the late 1830's, however, the rail companies had begun to extend their lines through several States. By the time the first transcontinental line was opened in 1869, some three-fourths of all rail traffic in the United States was interstate in character.

The early public attitude toward the railroads was distinctly favorable. Congress and several of the States made large grants of land and of monies to encourage them. But many of the railroads exploited their favored positions. Monopolies grew; finances were manipulated; rate gouging and the corruption of public officials became common. By the 1870's, these and similar abuses had worked a large change in the public's view of the railroads. Several State legislatures, especially in the

Middle West, responded to the complaints of farmers and other shippers by enacting "Granger laws"—statutes imposing strict regulations on the railroads.

State regulation was dealt a severe blow by the Supreme Court in 1886, however. In a case from Illinois, the Court held that State regulation of interstate railroad rates was unconstitutional—a prohibited infringement upon the power of Congress to regulate interstate commerce.[2]

The Court's decision finally prompted action by Congress. In 1887 it enacted the Act to Regulate Commerce—now known as the Interstate Commerce Act of 1887. Essentially, the statute prohibited excessive or discriminatory rates and banned other unfair practices. And the Act created the Interstate Commerce Commission to enforce its provisions.[3]

Today the ICC's authority covers not only the railroads but nearly all other surface carriers in interstate commerce—trucking companies, bus lines, freight forwarders, express agencies, and coastal and inland water carriers.[4]

The ICC's 11 members are appointed by the President, subject to Senate confirmation, for staggered seven-year terms; the President designates one of them to chair the Commission. A staff of some 2100 men and women assists them.

The ICC's regulatory powers are ex-

In this 1873 cartoon, a Granger warns the nation's people of the dangers of being crushed by the monopolistic practices of the railroads.

tremely broad—so broad in fact that its annual report to Congress is itself a fair-sized book. Here we touch upon the two major areas of its activities—rate-setting and service. Some indication of the breadth of its authority can be seen in the fact that it ranges from a requirement that all utilities subject to its regulation keep uniform accounts and render periodic reports to the regulation of the sale of any carrier and of the securities any of them issue.[5]

RATE-SETTING. The setting of the rates that may be charged by the carriers it regulates is key to the purpose and the work of the ICC. If rates are set too low, the carriers will lose money or, at the least, investors will not receive a fair return for the risks

---

[2] The Court decided the case, *Wabash, St. Louis, and Pacific Railway Co. v. Illinois,* as it did even though Congress had to that point enacted no legislation on the subject.

[3] Today the functions of the ICC are based on several later statutes enacted to meet other problems related to rail operations and by other and newer forms of transportation. These later statutes include, especially, the Hepburn Act of 1906, the Motor Carrier Act of 1935, the Interstate Commerce Act of 1942, and the Transportation Acts of 1920, 1940, 1958, and 1966. But the 1887 law remains at the core of the agency's authority.

[4] Until 1977 oil pipelines were also under ICC jurisdiction. They are now regulated by the Federal Energy Regulatory Commission in the new Department of Energy, which also regulates water and gas pipelines; see page 574. Air transportation is regulated by the FAA and the CAB and water-borne foreign commerce by the Federal Maritime Commission, as we have seen.

[5] Three types of carriers are regulated by the ICC: (1) *common carriers,* which offer their services for "common use," to the public generally, as regularly scheduled buses or passenger trains; (2) *contract carriers,* which offer to perform services under specific contract, as a charter bus or a truck hired to haul freight from one point to another; and (3) *private carriers,* sometimes called self-service carriers, which belong to the concerns which operate them and provide services only for them. The distinctions are important because regulations must vary to meet the different kinds of problems each type creates.

they have assumed. If they are too high, shippers and, in turn, the public will suffer. Fixing the proper balance is often a very complex and difficult process, but the law and the ICC require that rates be "reasonable" from both standpoints.

Carriers must publish their rates for public inspection. They may not give rebates or other preferential treatment to selected shippers; nor may they discriminate unreasonably among shippers and localities. The rates charged between points within the same State cannot be so low as to put points outside the State at an unfair disadvantage—as we saw in the *Shreveport Case,* on page 532.

Normally, carriers may not charge more for a short than a longer haul over the same route. But in some special instances the ICC may permit them to do so. Thus, rail rates from New York to the Rocky Mountain States are sometimes at least as high as those from New York to California or the Northwest. If the Pacific Coast rates were not given this preferential treatment, much more freight would be carried by water through the Panama Canal. The railroads, thus, would lose the business that their expensive roadbeds can carry at little additional cost.

The ICC is sometimes criticized because it often fixes bus and truck rates higher than necessary in order to help rail lines compete. Those who defend the policy argue that the railroads are essential to the nation's economic well-being and defense, and so must be kept in the healthiest possible condition.

SERVICE. Common carriers are required to furnish "reasonable service" to the public. Before a carrier may begin operations or extend an existing route, the ICC must grant it a *certificate of convenience and necessity.* Thus, uneconomic duplications of lines and services may be avoided; and, in the case of motor carriers, some highway congestion can be prevented.

The ICC may require a common carrier to extend its routes where that seems necessary and reasonable. And its consent must be obtained before rail lines may merge, and before a carrier can abandon an established route or eliminate a scheduled stop. Carriers may also be required to cooperate with one another in the interest of shippers or the public. For example, the ICC may order the transfer of freight cars from one rail line to another to meet such emergency situations as those involving perishable goods ready for shipment.

FINANCIAL PLIGHT OF THE RAILROADS. Most of the nation's railroads have been in serious financial straits for several years. Many of their present difficulties stem directly from the great increases in the amount of highway and air traffic in recent decades.

The rail lines' huge investments in rolling stock and in other capital equipment, and their high labor costs, made it increasingly difficult for them to compete with other carriers. And, in particular, nearly all of them found it virtually impossible to make their passenger operations pay out. In fact, until Amtrak relieved them of that burden in 1971, most of the lines were regularly losing vast sums on that part of their business each year.

The railroads once dominated the field of intercity transportation. They carried almost everyone and everything everywhere. Fifty years ago there were no fewer than 20,000 passenger trains linking the nation; now there are fewer than 300. Trains carry less than 1 percent of all intercity passenger traffic today; private automobiles carry nearly 90 percent of it. The airlines, buses, and inland waterways account for the rest of this traffic.

Although their freight business still operates in the black, the roads' share of all freight shipments has declined from over 75 percent in 1930 to less than 40 percent today. Trucks and pipelines each now carry over 20 percent of all freight. Water and air carriers account for the rest.

In a major effort to help bail them out, Congress established the *National Railroad Passenger Corporation* in 1970. Popularly known as Amtrak, its prime function is to operate, and revitalize, intercity rail passenger traffic.

Amtrak is a corporation and, as such, is intended to be a profit-making venture—at least eventually. More specifically, it is a *semi-public* corporation—as distinguished from a private one. It is, in part, federally-funded. The Secretary of Transportation and seven other presidential appointees make up a majority of its 15-member board of directors.

Amtrak began operations in 1971—with a $40 million appropriation from Congress, a long-term federal loan of $100 million, and nearly $200 million from the railroads (whom it then relieved of the burden of providing intercity passenger service). Despite such handsome financing, the corporation was on the verge of bankruptcy before its first year was out. Congress has had to administer huge injections of new funding to keep Amtrak alive each year since its creation—including the more than $970 million appropriated for fiscal year 1981.

Amtrak's prospects appear none too bright at this reading. It remains to be seen whether the Federal Government can, or will, save what many see as a dying industry. Nationalization of the country's railroads looms as a real, and perhaps an inevitable, next step.

THE CIVIL AERONAUTICS BOARD. Congress first began to regulate civil aviation in the Air Commerce Act of 1926. That statute applied to all interstate flying, but it left the regulation of local flights and facilities to the individual States. It created a Bureau of Air Commerce (later the Civil Aeronautics Administration) in the Commerce Department. That agency was given the power to license pilots, fix safety standards, and provide for regulating the increasing volume of air traffic.

As the entire field of civil aviation continued to grow, and in spectacular fashion, Congress broadened federal authority over it in the Civil Aeronautics Act of 1938. That law, as amended especially by the Federal Aviation Act of 1958, forms the basis of present-day regulation. Today two major agencies operate in the field: the Federal Aviation Administration (page 558) and the Civil Aeronautics Board.

The CAB was established by the 1938 law to promote and regulate the major aspects of civil aviation in this country. The President appoints its five members, with Senate consent, for staggered six-year terms. Each year the President designates one of the five to chair the board and direct the work of its staff of some 800 men and women. The CAB is one of the independent regulatory commissions—which means, recall, that its decisions are not subject to review or approval by the President or any other department or agency.

Today the CAB has two basic functions. It (1) assigns routes to the nation's airlines and other commercial air carriers and (2) supervises their rates and services.[6] Thus, passengers and freight may be carried in the public airways—at times and prices and by those carriers approved by the Board.

The CAB sets the sums to be paid by the Postal Service for the carrying of mail by air. It also administers subsidies to certain air carriers where those payments serve "the public convenience and necessity"—for example, subsidies to provide air service to communities which would otherwise be without it.

---

6 The CAB regulates three types of carriers: *air carriers,* who fly over established routes, carrying persons and property (and often mail) on a regularly scheduled or a nonscheduled (charter) basis; *indirect air carriers,* who do not themselves operate aircraft but are express agencies, freight forwarders, travel agents, and the like; and *fixed-base operators,* who operate airports, flying schools, crop-dusting services, etc., many of whom also carry persons or property on a "fly-anywhere-anytime" basis in the small aircraft used in their other activities.

Government and Communications

In most other countries the various means of communications—by telephone, telegraph, cable services, radio, and television—are largely or entirely government-owned and -operated. They have been developed and are generally owned and operated privately in the United States, however.

The Federal Government does maintain extensive communications facilities, especially in the armed forces. State and local governments do, too, especially for police purposes. But, by and large, the communications field is dominated by private ownership and operation—with, however, a considerable amount of federal regulation and control today.

There was comparatively little federal activity before 1934. The responsibility for that which did occur was shared by the ICC, the Post Office, and the Federal Radio Commission which had been created in 1927. In the Communications Act of 1934, however, Congress provided for very substantial federal regulatory authority—and placed it in the hands of a single independent agency, the *Federal Communications Commission.*

The FCC is a seven-member body. The commissioners are appointed by the President and Senate for staggered seven-year terms, and one of them chairs the agency by presidential designation.

The FCC regulates interstate and foreign communications by radio, television, wire, and cable. Its regulation of telephone, telegraph, and cable services is much like the ICC's control of land and water transportation. The communications companies are common carriers. The services they provide must be adequate and their rates fair and reasonable. Interstate rates can be changed only with FCC approval and all rates must be published for the information of clients. The carriers must secure *cer-*

tificates of convenience and necessity from the FCC before new interstate lines may be built or existing ones extended. Moreover, no existing service may be abandoned without the approval of the Federal Communications Commission.

The Commission's authority over telephone and telegraph is not quite so broad as that it exercises over cable services, radio, and television. This is the case for a quite practical reason: a large share of telephone and telegraph service is not interstate but purely local in character—and so it is subject only to State regulation.

Radio and television broadcasts do not respect State lines, of course; their signals range far and wide. The Communications Act specifically declares that radio and television stations are *not* common carriers. Hence, the FCC has no direct authority to regulate such matters as the rates charged to advertisers. *But* all radio and television stations and operators—commercial, amateur, and governmental—must be licensed by the FCC. Radio and television stations are licensed only after FCC investigations and public hearings; and operators are licensed on the basis of examinations.

When licensed, stations are assigned particular frequencies and often other limits are imposed, too—broadcasting power and the hours of use, for example. Licenses are issued for three years and may be revoked at the FCC's discretion. The Commission assigns licenses, wave lengths, periods of operation, and station power among the States and their local communities in order to provide, as the law directs, "a fair, efficient, and equitable distribution of service to each."

All stations and operators are subject to strict rules, closely policed by the FCC. Thus, when paid matter is broadcast the names of the sponsor must be announced, a station's call letters must be announced regularly, and the broadcast of obscene material is prohibited. The "equal time" rule requires that if a station permits a broadcast by or in behalf of a candidate for public office it must offer opposing candidates equal time on the same terms (see the Case Study). The "fairness doctrine" demands that broadcasters present all sides of important public issues.

Clearly, radio and television do not enjoy the same 1st Amendment protections as those afforded to newspapers and other print media—a point we raised in Chapter 6. Recall the basic reason for this: Unlike newspapers, both radio and television broadcasters use the airwaves—*public property*—to disseminate their materials.

The Supreme Court has several times upheld federal regulation of broadcasting as a proper exercise of the commerce power. Put the other way, it has regularly rejected the argument that the 1st Amendment prohibits such regulation. Essentially, it has held that the regulation of radio and television *implements* the constitutional guarantees of free expression. Thus, in a leading case, *Red Lion Broadcasting Company v. FCC*, 1969, the Court noted that without regulation "broadcast frequencies . . . would be of little use because of the cacophony of competing voices, none of which could be clearly and predictably heard." Failure to observe any of the FCC's rules can lead to the suspension or revocation of a license or a refusal to renew it.

Case Study

The FCC enforces Section 315, the "equal time" provision of the Communications Act of 1934. It provides that if a radio or television station or network makes air time available to one candidate for a public office it must offer it, on the same terms, to all other candidates for that office.

Until 1976, Section 315 was a major obstacle to the broadcasting of debates or other joint appearances by the major party presidential candidates. If broadcasters had made time available to them, equal time would also have had to be afforded to all of the minor party candidates for the Presidency.

Congress did provide a temporary solution to the problem in 1960. Then, and only for the presidential election that year, it suspended the application of Section 315. With that action, the major television networks were able to sponsor the four Kennedy-Nixon debates. Congress did not enact similar suspensions for the 1964, 1968, or 1972 campaigns, however.

A different solution made the Ford-Carter debates of 1976 possible. In late 1975 the FCC ruled that the equal time provision does not apply to debates or other joint appearances which (1) are sponsored by someone other than stations or networks and (2) do not occur in broadcast studios. In short, the FCC held that radio and television could cover candidate confrontations on the same terms as any other newsworthy event.

The three Ford-Carter debates (and the Dole-Mondale vice presidential session) were sponsored by the nonpartisan League of Women Voters.

Court challenges to the FCC's interpretation of Section 315 were brought by several minor party presidential candidates in 1976 and 1980. All were rejected.

In 1980, quite similar arrangements were made for the one debate between Reagan and Carter, as well as for several debates that took place among contenders for each major party's presidential nomination.

■ Do you think the FCC's current interpretation of Section 315 is a reasonable one? Why? What arguments can you present against your view?

■ On what bases can it be argued that an incumbent President should not engage in such appearances?

Government and Housing

The Federal Government did not enter the housing field until the nation became mired in the economic slough of the 1930's. From the early years of the Depression on, however, it has been deeply involved. Its first housing efforts came as part of the larger attempt to restore economic stability, and they were prompted by catastrophic conditions throughout the country. New home construction had all but ceased. Millions of Americans could not meet their mortgage payments, and many were losing their homes to foreclosures.

Congress began to respond to the crisis in 1932—with the creation of the Federal Home Loan Bank System, as we saw on page 522. The New Deal began in the following year, and with it came several major housing actions—several new measures which set the basic patterns the Federal Government has followed in the field of housing ever since.

Today nearly all of the many federal housing programs are centered in HUD— the Department of Housing and Urban Development, established in 1965.

Private Housing Programs. Since the 1930's several federal programs have been designed to make long-term mortgage credit more readily available to private home buyers. The year after the Home Loan Bank System was established Congress created the Federal Deposit Insurance Corporation (page 519). The FDIC insures savings deposited in lending institutions, now up to $100,000.[7] The money individual savers have thus been encouraged to deposit has provided most of the mortgage funds private lenders have loaned to private home buyers over the past 40 years.

The *Federal Housing Administration* was established in the National Housing Act of 1934. It is easily the best known HUD agency today. The FHA aids home financing in several ways. It does not itself make building loans but it operates insurance programs for those who do. It guarantees banks and other private lenders against loss on the housing loans they make.

FHA's principal function is to provide mortgage insurance on the purchase of new and existing one- to four-family homes. But it also provides such insurance for other purposes—including home improvements, cooperative housing, rental housing for the elderly, and nursing homes.

To 1981, FHA has insured some 15 million mortgages, totalling over $200 billion. Some 1.5 million new homes will be built in 1981, and nearly one in five will be purchased with FHA-backed loans. The independent Farm Credit Administration (page 523) and the USDA's Farmers Home Administration (page 614) operate similar programs for farmers and other rural residents; and the VA does so for veterans.

Public Housing Programs. The other major area of federal housing programs involves public housing. Ever since the Housing Act of 1937 the Federal Government has provided loans and subsidies to local authorities to aid them in the construction and operation of low-rent public housing projects.

Typically, the Government has made long-term, low-interest loans to local housing agencies—usually called "public housing authorities." Those loans cover up to 90 percent of housing project construction costs. And it has also granted subsidies to those local agencies, to permit them to op-

---

[7] As does a companion agency, the Federal Savings and Loan Insurance Corporation, set up in 1934; see page 523. Among other notable New Deal housing agencies was the temporary Homeowners Loan Corporation, formed in 1933. The HOLC was a direct loan agency; it made longterm, low-interest mortgage loans to persons in urgent need of funds to protect or recover their homes from foreclosure. It loaned some $3.5 billion and saved the homes of more than a million families in the years 1933–1936.

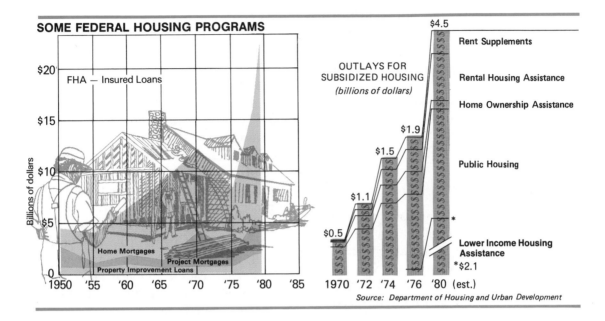

SOME FEDERAL HOUSING PROGRAMS

FHA — Insured Loans

Home Mortgages

Property Improvement Loans

Project Mortgages

Billions of dollars

$20
$15
$10
$5
0

1950 '55 '60 '65 '70 '75 '80 '85

OUTLAYS FOR SUBSIDIZED HOUSING
(billions of dollars)

$4.5
Rent Supplements
Rental Housing Assistance
Home Ownership Assistance

$1.9
$1.5
Public Housing

$1.1
$0.5

*
Lower Income Housing Assistance
*$2.1

1970 '72 '74 '76 '80 (est.)

Source: Department of Housing and Urban Development

erate with rents set at levels low-income tenants can reasonably afford. Nearly one million of the nation's approximately 80 million families live in public housing units today.[8]

Public housing efforts have not been nearly so successful as have the various federal programs to promote private home ownership. Many projects have become highrise slums, fostering the social ills they were intended to combat. Some have been poorly managed; funding has never been adequate. Tenants often do not like them and those who live nearby often resent them.

Some newer approaches have been tried in recent years. The most notable are the rent- and mortgage-supplement programs—in which HUD makes cash grants to cover a portion of the monthly rent or mortgage payments of low-income families. HUD is also pursuing a scatter-housing policy—scattering sites for public housing, rather than concentrating it in high-density projects.

It seems clear that effective public

housing—programs capable of making more than just a dent in needs—cannot come until a number of obstacles are overcome. That means changes must first occur in levels of funding, in stereotyped attitudes toward race and minority groups, in suburban resistance to public housing, and in the fragmented powers and the structure of governments at the local level. In short, it cannot come until the public is willing to make the necessary commitments of resources and political support.

Urban Renewal. For more than 40 years now, federal support for public housing has been accompanied by efforts to reclaim slums and other blighted urban areas. Since the enactment of the Housing Act of 1937 Congress has made billions of dollars available to cities for this purpose.

Today, several HUD programs provide loans and grants and offer technical advice to cities and other local governments for the planning and execution of urban renewal projects. Typically, cities acquire and clear slum properties, then sell or lease the land to private developers who agree to rebuild the area according to an approved plan. Nearly a thousand cities have undertaken such projects in the past 25 years.

---

[8] Approximately 65 percent of the nation's families own the homes they occupy; the remainder rent from private agencies or individuals.

We shall return to the cities and their problems later, in Chapter 32. But for now notice that urban renewal has made some substantial changes in the urban scene. However, some projects have been criticized for replacing the slum homes of the poor with housing that the poor cannot afford to rent or buy.

Government and Energy

The Energy Problem. The basic shape of the nation's energy problem can be put quite simply: *It is one of increasing demands versus dwindling supplies.* In short, we consume far more energy than we produce in this country—and the gap between needs and supplies is widening.

The problem itself is far from simple, however. It is, instead, extraordinarily complex. It reaches into virtually every aspect of the daily life of every person in this country. And it is an integral part of several other and crucial areas of public policy including, especially, foreign policy, defense, the health of the economy, and the quality of the environment.

President Carter stressed the gravity of the energy problem in these terms:

> With the exception of preventing war, this is the greatest challenge our country will face during our lifetimes. The energy crisis has not yet overwhelmed us, but it will if we do not act quickly.

HUGE DEMANDS. Our appetite for energy is enormous. With less than six percent of the world's population, the United States now consumes as much as 30 percent of the world's energy production. We lead all other nations in the consumption of oil, of natural gas, of coal, of nuclear energy, and of water-generated power. And, we use more electricity drawn from those basic energy sources than do the people of any other nation.

And, over time, we have used more and still more energy each year. The *rate* at which our consumption has increased has declined somewhat in the past few years. But, still, we continue to use more energy each year than we did the year before.

ENERGY SOURCES. Abundant, low-cost energy has been a decisive factor in the building of modern America. In historical terms, the United States has passed through three energy eras—three periods in which first *wood*, then *coal*, and today *oil* and *natural gas* have been our principal sources of energy. Put another way, the United States has made two major energy transitions in the past—first from wood to coal, then from coal to oil and natural gas. And we are now on the verge of yet another such change.

Until the latter 1800's, wood was the nation's primary energy source. Trees grew almost everywhere; and the forest seemed to stretch forever. After the Civil War, however, wood (and such secondary sources as waterwheels and windmills) gave way to coal. Wood remained abundant; but technological progress had made coal a better and a cheaper source of fuel—first for the railroads, and then in industry and for such other uses as home heating. From the 1880's to the 1940's, coal supplied more than half of our energy needs.

In the years since World War II, oil and natural gas have become the major sources of our energy supply. As with the earlier change from wood to coal, this second transition resulted from technological progress—and it was prompted, too, by the

the small society   by Brickman

WE BEGIN OUR NEWSCAST WITH THIS SPECIAL BULLETIN...

OIL PRICES WERE NOT INCREASED TODAY! LET ME REPEAT THAT...

Washington Star Syndicate, Inc.   9-25   BRICKMAN lower cost, the ease of handling, and the cleanness of oil and gas compared to coal.

Today we rely upon oil for about 45 percent of all our energy needs, and upon natural gas for just over 25 percent. Coal now furnishes nearly 20 percent, hydro-electric generation about four percent, and nuclear reactors barely three.

In terms of end uses, our energy demands break down this way: Manufacturing processes of all kinds take the largest share—approximately 40 percent of all the energy we consume. About 20 percent goes for the heating and cooling of residential, commercial, and industrial buildings—for regulating the temperatures in all of the structures in which we live, work, and play. Another 25 percent is taken by transportation—and especially by the private automobile, which accounts for half of all of the energy now used to move people and goods in this country. The other 15 percent goes for all other purposes: for lighting, heating water, and running the millions of appliances and mechanical aids found in homes and business places—from stoves, refrigerators, freezers, and electric mixers to telephones, cash registers, and electric typewriters.

DECREASING SUPPLIES. The United States produces neither enough oil nor enough natural gas to meet the current demands upon these prime energy sources. And our domestic reserves of both are diminishing rapidly.

Domestic production of oil has been declining since 1970, and natural gas production has been falling since 1973. Oil from Alaska's North Slope began flowing through the Trans-Alaska pipeline in 1977. Together with the output of new fields on the Outer Continental Shelf, and the yield from new recovery techniques in older fields, it should bolster domestic supplies for a few years—but not for long. And the same is true of the natural gas to be produced from these sources. Other major additions to domestic reserves seem unlikely.

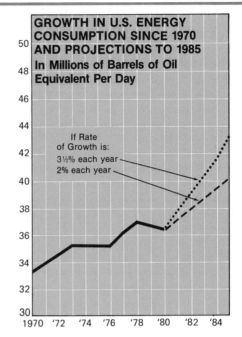

Source: U.S. Bureau of Mines and Federal Energy Administration.

In sum, there is a serious energy gap—a growing shortfall in domestic supplies of both oil and natural gas.

The most troublesome aspects of this energy gap involve oil. They do so inevitably, for America runs on oil. It is both the most widely used and the most widely usable of all of our energy resources. It is utilized for a multitude of purposes—in transportation, of course, *and* in all other sectors of the economy, as well. It is used to make plastic, synthetic fabrics, paints, and a host of other items. And it is used, too, to heat, to cool, to preserve, to lubricate, and to do scores of other things.

Inescapably, the United States has had to turn to foreign sources to supplement dwindling domestic oil supplies. And our dependence on those sources has risen dramatically in recent years. In 1970 we imported only about 20 percent of our total needs. By 1975 that figure had jumped to

35 percent, and today we import approximately 45 percent of the oil we consume.

Much of the oil we now import comes from the turbulent Middle East—a fact fraught with acute economic and foreign policy consequences. Its high cost has been and is a major contributor to ongoing inflation in this country. And the seething politics of that region mean that our dependence on its oil is at best a very chancy matter.

The pitfalls of our increased reliance on foreign supplies go beyond the flammable mixture of Arab oil and Arab politics. The reserves of the Middle East—and of Nigeria, Venezuela, and all other oil-producing countries—are not unlimited, of course. And our ability to draw from those sources is conditioned by the demands of other energy-hungry nations. Current estimates indicate that worldwide demands for oil will outstrip world production by the latter 1980's. They also suggest the real prospect that all of the world's recoverable oil resources will be exhausted within the next 40 years or so. In short, with even the best of diplomatic relationships, we cannot count on imported oil to overcome our own energy shortfall for much more than another bare handful of years.

PRIMARY CAUSE. It should be fairly obvious that our present energy difficulties are the result of one overriding root cause: our historic, voracious, and largely unthinking appetite for energy.[9]

Until the 1970's, most Americans—in business, in government, and the public at large—behaved as though this nation's energy resources were without limit. For decades, both private industry and public policy promoted ever-increasing uses of those resources. Most of us believed in and lived by the notion that "more is better" and "still more is better yet." Impending shortages and approaching crisis were seen by some, both in and out of government; but their warnings went largely unheard and regularly unheeded.

---

[9] The five-month Arab oil embargo of 1973-74 was not a cause but rather a harbinger of the current situation. Middle East oil-producing nations imposed the temporary ban on oil shipments to the United States, Western Europe, and Japan as a lever in their continuing conflict with Israel. When the embargo was lifted in the spring of 1974 the Arab states simultaneously *quadrupled* the price of their oil. This price increase substantially compounded the inflation-recession-unemployment problems of the United States and other countries. And later price increases also had similarly damaging effects. But a major point here: Our present and impending energy shortages would be with us today, Arab oil embargo and price increases or not.

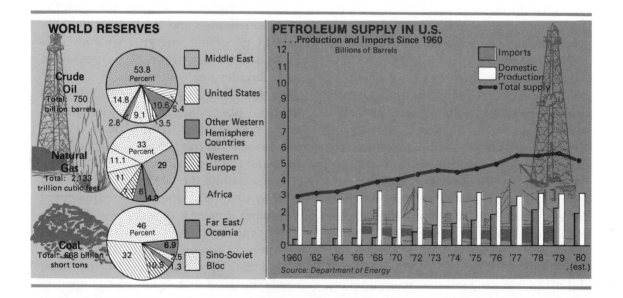

Put another way, the primary cause can be found in our mass-consumption lifestyle—built as it is around such high energy users as the automobile, television, neon lights, central heating, air conditioning, and the like. Electric toothbrushes, hair dryers, and carving knives may make only a minuscule dent in total consumption, but they most certainly symbolize the principal cause of the energy problem.

SHORT- AND LONG-TERM SOLUTIONS. The United States is now in the earliest phases of another historic energy transition—a third shift in terms of its basic sources of fuel. As we've noted, the nation's two earlier energy changeovers were prompted by new technologies—by the development of the railroads, for example, which spurred the move to coal, and by the mass production of automobiles, which inspired the age of oil.

Unlike the previous shifts, the present transition has been brought on by growing scarcities. It is the result of our current energy problem, the result of the crunch produced by our continuing demands for energy, on the one hand, and declining supplies of oil and gas, on the other.

How can this new changeover be accomplished? Nearly all who are closely familiar with the situation see the answer to that vital question in quite similar ways. With some differences over detail, they see it as a two-stage, three-part matter: In the *short term*, through the balance of this century, the United States must (1) increase its supplies and make greater use of presently available fuels. And, at the same time, it must (2) promote greater conservation in the use of those resources. Over the *long term*, this nation, and the rest of the world, must (3) develop renewable and essentially inexhaustible sources of energy.

(1) We must increase domestic supplies and make greater use of presently available fuels. While our stocks of oil and natural gas are shrinking, we do have other energy sources—other fuels which are now avail-

able and can be used to supplement and replace them.

Coal and nuclear energy are foremost among these alternatives.[10] Coal now provides only some 20 percent of the energy we consume. It could supply a much larger share, however. In addition to direct burning as an industrial fuel, there are excellent prospects for its use in gasified and liquefied form. Our reserves of this fossil fuel are so immense that, at the current rate of consumption, they could not be exhausted in 300 years. But this vast abundance is not an unmixed blessing—especially because coal scars the earth when mined and it pollutes the air when burned.

Nuclear reactors generate about three percent of present needs. They, too, could furnish a much more substantial share. But, despite its great promise, the accelerated use of atomic power also poses serious problems. Chief among them is the threat of accident. Most nuclear engineers insist that mishaps are extremely unlikely. But, however remote, the possibility does exist, and the results could be catastrophic. There is, as well, the vexing and unresolved question of the safe disposal of radioactive waste materials. Public concern over the safety and the environmental impact of nuclear generation has slowed the construction of new plants, dramatically.

(2) We must conserve present supplies. The need to conserve existing energy sources is both compelling and altogether practical. And conservation can be, in itself, a significant source of energy supply.

Reducing wasteful uses of energy could produce sizable savings. Fully 30 percent of the fuel now consumed in this country is squandered. Much of it goes unused—out of the window, out the exhaust pipe, and up the smokestack. Most homes, stores, factories, and other buildings are poorly

---

[10] Hydroelectric power meets about four percent of current needs; but its potential has been almost fully exploited at most available sites around the country.

insulated; many of them are overlighted, overheated in winter and overcooled in summer. The oversized and overfed automobile epitomizes our spendthrift use of energy. And many commercial and industrial uses are similarly extravagant and inefficient.

(3) We must develop additional, essentially inexhaustible resources. For the immediate future, for the next decade or so, the United States will have to rely upon those fuels now at hand. That is, it will have to rely upon oil, natural gas, coal, nuclear energy, and hydroelectric power. For the longer term, however, beyond the year 2000, we must develop other resources. The need to do so is made especially urgent by our dwindling supplies of oil and natural gas.

Quite apparently, these newer fuels must be both cleaner and safer than those upon which we now depend. And, too, they must be drawn from more secure sources and be available in virtually unlimited quantities.

Several promising options exist. There are a number of fuels which can be developed and which also appear to satisfy the requirements that they be cleaner, safer, more secure, and essentially inexhaustible. The sun's energy has already been captured to heat space and water in several places. Its use for these purposes should become much more common within the next few years. Other applications of solar power—for example, to generate electricity—are at various stages of the research and development process. So, too, are the uses of geothermal energy, the natural heat in the earth's crust; its potential is particularly large in the Western States. Other possibilities include the harnessing of wind force and tidal power and the conversion of solid wastes into liquid, gaseous, and solid combustibles.

The Department of Energy. Congress established the Department of Energy in 1977. Its Cabinet-level status is a reflection of both the importance and the urgency of the nation's energy problem.

The birth of the new Department marked a major reorganization of agencies within the executive branch. DOE absorbed and replaced three large independent agencies: the Federal Energy Administration, the Federal Power Commission, and the Energy Research and Development Administration. It also acquired a broad range of energy related functions and programs from some 50 other agencies scattered throughout the federal bureaucracy.

The Department is headed by the Secretary of Energy, appointed by the President and subject to confirmation by the Senate. The Secretary serves as the President's chief aide and principal adviser in all energy policy matters and directs the work of the Energy Department and its approximately 20,000 employees.

DOE came into formal being at the beginning of fiscal year 1978—that is, on October 1, 1977. Some of its agencies were born full-blown, transplanted from elsewhere in the executive branch. Others were established by Congress in quite skeletal fashion, given only very broadly defined responsibilities. Many of the functions and programs transferred to the new Department were assigned to the Secretary, who was given powers to shape them and flesh out the departmental structure.

The *Federal Energy Regulatory Commission* is the successor to the Federal Power Commission, an independent regulatory body originally established by Congress in 1920. By a wide margin, it is the most completely structured entity within DOE.

The FERC is a semi-autonomous agency. It both is and is not subject to the Secretary's control and direction. In fact, except for the role the Secretary may play in its operations, it could well be placed among the independent regulatory commissions we described in Chapter 17 (see pages 422–425). It is composed of five commissioners, each appointed by the President and Senate. They serve staggered four-year terms, and the President names one of them as the Commission's chairman. They may be removed from office only by the President and only, says the law, "for inefficiency, neglect of duty, or malfeasance in office."

As the FPC's heir, the Commission has three vitally important powers: *First*, it fixes the rates and otherwise regulates the interstate transportation and sale of electricity and natural gas.[11] *Second*, it issues permits and licenses for the construction and operation of hydroelectric power projects, gas pipelines, and related facilities. And *third*, it supervises mergers, the issuing of securities, and other economic transactions of electric power and natural gas firms.

The FERC exercises another key regulatory power, this one gained by transfer from the Interstate Commerce Commission. It sets the rates that may be charged for the interstate transportation of oil by pipeline. The Energy Secretary shares a piece of this oil-pricing authority, but only in extraordinary circumstances. The Secretary, acting alone, may fix the pipeline rates in those situations in which the President declares the existence of "an emergency of overriding national importance." Any such action is subject to congressional veto, however.

The Secretary may also prod the FERC to act—by exercising the power to fix a reasonable time limit for FERC action in any proceeding before it. And the Secretary also has the authority to intervene (become a party, make a presentation) in

any matter before the Commission.

The *Economic Regulatory Administration* is the Federal Government's other major arm in the field of energy regulation. It is responsible for all of the many and varied federal efforts to supervise the production, distribution, sale, and use of energy in the United States—except for those functions assigned to the FERC.

Among its several duties, the ERA operates a domestic oil price control program—which places a ceiling on the prices that may be charged for all crude oil produced in this country. And it conducts a number of allocations and export-import control programs—each of them intended to insure the availability of adequate supplies of crude oil, petroleum products, and natural gas to all sections of the country, and to a wide range of domestic users of them, at all times.

The Administration also oversees the "coal conversion" policy, put in place by the National Energy Act of 1978. Its aim is to wean industries and utilities away from the use of oil and natural gas, toward coal. The law decrees that, henceforth, all newly constructed industrial and utility plants are to be built to burn coal or other fuels. Those utilities which are now fired by oil or gas must switch fuels by 1990; and the ERA has the authority to order some industrial plants to convert to coal or to other fuels, as well.

The *Energy Information Administration* is essentially a data-gathering and -analyzing agency. Its prime function is to collect and evaluate comprehensive information on the nation's energy resources, demand, production, technology, use, and the like. Put another way, it assembles the basic facts upon which energy policy decisions are to be made.

The *Office of Energy Research* is an oversight and advisory agency. It monitors all of DOE's extensive research and development programs and related activities. Its Director, appointed by the President and

---

11 The National Energy Act of 1978 provides that the FERC's authority to regulate the price of natural gas will expire in 1985. Until then, the agency is directed to permit the prices charged for newly produced gas to increase approximately 10 percent each year. The law also granted to the FERC, for the first time, the power to regulate rates in the *intrastate* natural gas market; that is, now, and until 1985, the FERC has the power to fix the prices charged for gas which is sold within the State in which it is produced.

Senate, reports to and advises the Secretary with respect to those matters.

In effect, the Office is the Secretary's staff arm for the conduct of the functions the Department acquired from the Energy Research and Development Administration. ERDA had been set up in 1974 as the successor to the first major federal energy agency, the Atomic Energy Commission. Over its brief life span, ERDA was responsible for the conduct of the Government's now very extensive energy research and development efforts.

Four separate *Power Administrations*, formerly in the Interior Department, are now a part of DOE. The Bonneville Power Administration is the oldest and by far the largest of them. It was created in 1937 to market the power generated by the mighty Bonneville Dam on the Columbia River. The dam itself, which first began producing electricity in 1936, was constructed and is operated by the Army's Corps of Engineers. BPA also markets the power from several other federal projects along the Columbia River and in other parts of Oregon, Washington, northern Idaho, and western Montana. It sells the electricity at wholesale to local public agencies and private power companies, which then retail it, and to large industrial users.

The Southeastern and the Southwestern Power Administrations sell the power generated by Army Engineers' projects in their respective regions. In effect, they act as business agents for those projects outside the area in which most federal hydroelectric power production is concentrated, the Pacific Northwest.[12]

Nearly all of the land within the State of Alaska—more than 96 percent of it—is owned by the Federal Government. The Alaska Power Administration is charged with promoting the development of the water power and related resources of this huge domain. It operates the Eklutna Project, north of Anchorage. The Project supplies electricity to Anchorage, Alaska's largest city, and to the Matanuska Valley and several military installations.

The *Office of Inspector General* is DOE's watchdog agency. It is headed by an Inspector General appointed by the President and Senate. The Office conducts audits and runs other investigative checks in order to fulfill its principal charge: to promote economy and efficiency and prevent fraud or abuse in all of DOE's wide-ranging activities. As with most other presidential appointees, the Inspector General serves at the President's pleasure and may be removed from office at the President's discretion. However, if the President does dismiss the Inspector General, the law requires the Chief Executive to explain that action to Congress.

As we've noted, Congress inaugurated DOE with a great many of its powers and functions vested in the Secretary rather than in any of its subordinate agencies. As the Secretary builds the Department, most of them will almost certainly be assigned to particular places within its structure. But, at least for now, they are held and exercised by the Secretary.

Several of these powers and functions are of pivotal importance. They include, for example, the charting, direction, and enforcement of programs to stimulate competition in all phases of the energy production and supply industry, to promote conservation of the nation's energy resources, and the power to allocate and distribute fuels during periods of shortage. The Secretary is also directly responsible for such other highly critical matters as nuclear weapons research and development, nuclear waste management, and the protection of the environment in all aspects of energy production and use.

The authority to lease portions of the public domain to private individuals and

---

[12] The huge Tennessee Valley Authority is an independent agency and markets the power generated by its several facilities; see pages 607–608.

firms, and for various purposes, has long been held by the Secretary of the Interior; and it remains there (see pages 598–599). However, the Secretary of Energy now has the power to regulate the conduct of those who hold such leases for oil, gas, and other fuel exploration and development purposes. That mandate includes, for example, the authority to set production schedules for oil and gas wells on public lands, including those on the Continental Shelf. It also includes the power to set "diligence requirements"—that is, to set standards to insure that those who are granted federal leases do not hold them principally to keep portions of the public domain in a purposefully unexplored, unused, or undeveloped state.

SUMMARY

Transportation. From its beginnings the Federal Government has been both closely and necessarily concerned with all forms of transportation in this country. While we have relied primarily on privately owned and operated transportation, and continue to do so, government has been a most willing and active partner in the development of the nation's transportation system.

The Department of Transportation is the leading manifestation of that fact today. The list of its principal agencies is broadly descriptive of its promotional and regulatory responsibilities. They include the Federal Railroad Administration, the Federal Aviation Administration, the Federal Highway Administration, the National Highway Traffic Safety Administration, the Urban Mass Transit Administration, the Saint Lawrence Seaway Development Corporation, and the United States Coast Guard.

An independent regulatory body, the Interstate Commerce Commission, regulates the rate charges and other economic aspects of nearly all surface carriers in interstate commerce. The Civil Aeronautics Board exercises similar functions in the field of air transportation.

Communications. Unlike the situation in much of the rest of the world, the techniques and the means of communication by telephone, telegraph, cable, radio, and television have been largely developed and are generally owned and operated by private persons and companies in this country. Very substantial federal regulatory authority is exercised by the Federal Communications Commission, however.

Housing. The now very extensive federal role in the housing field dates from the Depression of the 1930's and is today centered in the Department of Housing and Urban Development. HUD operates several private housing programs designed to foster home ownership and public housing programs intended to meet the needs of low-income persons and families.

Energy. The United States is now faced with an energy problem of very serious and considerable dimensions. Its key elements are huge and increasing demands for energy, on the one hand,

and dwindling supplies of oil and natural gas, on the other. To overcome it, most authorities agree that, in the years immediately ahead, we must (1) increase domestic supplies and make greater use of presently available fuels and, at the same time, (2) make concerted efforts to conserve our energy resources. Over the longer term we must (3) develop additional, cleaner, and safer fuels and draw them from more secure and essentially inexhaustible sources. The new Department of Energy is charged with directing the Government's efforts to realize that prescription.

Concept Development

Questions for Review

1. Why may the nation's history be told in good part in terms of the development of its transportation system?

2. Why can our transportation system be fairly described as a "private-public partnership"?

3. When was the Department of Transportation created? What is its principal mission?

4. What are the principal functions of the Federal Railroad Administration? The Federal Aviation Administration? The Federal Highway Administration?

5. What is the National System of Interstate and Defense Highways? How is it financed?

6. What does the National Transportation Safety Board do?

7. Why does the text suggest that the Coast Guard "belies its name"?

8. When and why was the Interstate Commerce Commission established? What is the scope of its authority today? What is Amtrak?

9. What are the Civil Aeronautics Board's two main functions?

10. When and upon what constitutional authority did Congress establish the Federal Communications Commission? Why are radio and television broadcasting subject to more stringent federal regulation than are telephone and telegraph communications?

11. What circumstance prompted the Federal Government's entry into the housing field? What is the major federal agency operating in that field today?

12. Why do the functions of the FDIC and the FHA typify the Federal Government's private housing programs? What is the basic purpose of its public housing programs?

13. Briefly, what is the nation's energy problem? What is its primary cause?

14. Approximately what proportion of our present energy needs are met by oil? Natural gas? Coal? Nuclear energy? Hydroelectric power?

15. Why are oil imports at such much higher levels today than they were only a decade ago? Why is this disturbing?

16. What two-stage, three-part solution to the energy problem do most authorities agree must be pursued by the United States?

17. Why are our vastly abundant coal reserves not an unmixed blessing? What is the major impediment to increased reliance upon nuclear energy?

18. Why may the conservation of energy be described as itself a significant source of energy supply?

19. What newer sources of energy hold substantial promise for the future?

20. What agency is now the focal point for efforts to resolve the energy problem?

For Further Inquiry

1. When DOT was created in 1967, President Lyndon Johnson observed: "In a nation that spans a continent, transportation is the web of union." Can you expand upon and illustrate his comment? At the same time, the first Transportation Secretary, Alan S. Boyd, declared that DOT would make "an energetic effort to account for the social as well as the economic costs of transportation." What are some of the "social costs" of transportation?

2. Can the functions of the Federal Deposit Insurance Corporation, the Federal Savings and Loan Insurance Corporation, and the Federal Housing Administration be properly described as subsidies? If so, who benefits? If not, why not?

3. The syndicated columnist David Broder has written:

> "Television is a personal medium, and no other person looms so large on the television screen as the President. No one else can summon the cameras of all the networks simultaneously, in a setting and at a time of his own choosing to address the massive national audience that the President can command; no one else has so great an ability to keep the cameras turned off or at a distance when he does not want them."

Should this important fact of our national political life be of any concern to the FCC? If so, in what terms?

4. The nation's largest oil company regularly uses this advertising slogan: "Energy for a strong America." Beyond the commercial intent, what thoughts do those words prompt?

Suggested Activities

1. Invite a representative of some segment of the transportation system in your locale to discuss with the class the nature of his/her occupation and that segment of the transportation industry.

2. Using your locale as the basis, compose a list of examples of the functions of the several federal agencies mentioned in this chapter.

3. Invite an officer of a local bank or other home-financing institution or a homebuilder to speak to the class on housing conditions and related matters in your community.

4. Attempt to discover the extent to which the need to conserve energy is recognized and practiced in your community—and include your own behavior in that survey.

Suggested Reading

Cowan, Geoffrey, *See No Evil: The Backstage Battle Over Sex and Violence in Television.* Simon & Schuster, 1980.

Galbraith, John K., *The New Industrial State.* New American Library, 3rd ed., 1979.

Gordon, Sanford D. and Dawson, George G., *Introductory Economics.* Heath, 4th ed., 1980.

The National Academy of Sciences, *Energy in Transition, 1985–2010.* Freeman, 1980.

Schurr, Sam H., *et al., Energy in America's Future: The Choices Before Us.* Resources for the Future, 1979.

Starling, Grover, *The Politics and Economics of Public Policy: An Introductory Analysis with Cases.* Dorsey, 1979.

Also: Office of Public Affairs, Department of Energy, Washington, D.C. 20461

Public Information Office, Federal Communications Commission, Washington, D.C. 20554

Office of Public Affairs, Department of Housing and Urban Development, Washington, D.C. 20410

Public Information Office, Interstate Commerce Commission, Washington, D.C. 20423

Office of Public Affairs, Department of Transportation, Washington, D.C. 20590

23

Government
and Labor

Labor is prior to, and independent of capital. Capital is only the fruit of Labor, and could never have existed if Labor had not first existed. Labor is the superior of capital, and deserves much the higher consideration.

ABRAHAM LINCOLN

■ Should the basic shape of the Government's relationships with labor be largely promotional or essentially regulatory in character?

■ What is government's proper role in the labor-management relationship?

■ To whom are the various programs administered by the Department of Labor most beneficial?

Some type of labor system—that is, some basic pattern of labor-management relationship—exists in every society. That pattern may take any of a number of different forms—slavery, serfdom, forced state labor, free contract labor, or some other. Whatever the form, it determines the relationship between workers and their work and between workers and those who direct their work. Certainly, no aspect of the structure of a society can be more important to the nature of that society than its labor system.

In this country, both by tradition and by law, the system is that of *free contract labor*. And that system is embedded in the Constitution—most prominently so in the 13th Amendment; see page 153. No person is born to a master, to a job, or to a piece of ground he or she cannot leave. Nor—except for military purposes or as punishment for crime—can any person be forced to work against his or her will. Rather, each person is free to sell his or her services—free to contract for the use of those services in any lawful occupation—as he or she chooses.

We are firmly committed to the concept of the laborer's freedom of contract. And we are firmly committed, as well, to the belief that it is the duty of government to protect that freedom and, in protecting it, to promote and regulate its use.

The force of that commitment is more than aptly demonstrated by the existence, and the functions, of the Department of Labor.

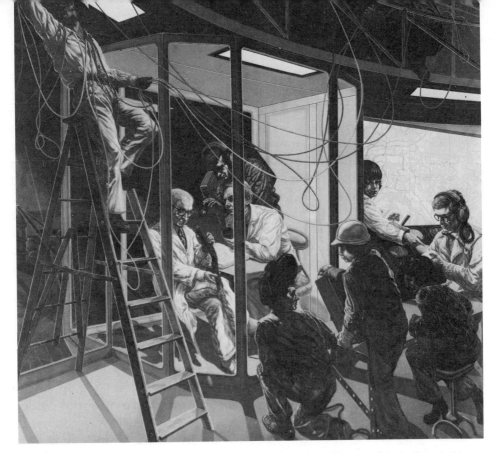

On view in the Grand Lobby of the Labor Department Building is this mural, which depicts the pervasiveness of technology in the work of the 20th-century American.

The Department of Labor

The Department of Labor was created as a separate Cabinet department in 1913. Congress had first established a Bureau of Labor in the Interior Department in 1884. That agency was later made an independent department, but without Cabinet status. Increasing concern for the problems of labor in a growing industrial economy led to the establishment of the Department of Commerce and Labor in 1903. Ten years later the separate Department of Labor was formed.

In the statute creating the Department, Congress directed the new agency to:

advance the public interest by promoting the welfare of the wage earners of the United States, improving their working conditions, and advancing their opportunities for profitable employment.

The Secretary of Labor is responsible for the management of the Department and all of its activities. As the Government's chief labor administrator, the Secretary also serves as the President's chief advisor in all labor matters.

The Labor Department employs only some 22,000 persons today and is among the smallest of the Cabinet-level departments. Its comparative size is *not* a useful indication of either the scope or the importance of its work, however.

Its work is essentially *promotional* in character. It is primarily concerned with the fostering of improvements in labor conditions, not with the settlement of labor disputes. It does lend a helping hand at times. But the settling of labor disputes is a function of other agencies with no formal ties to the Department, as we shall see.

Perhaps the best way to approach Labor's wide-ranging activities is to look at them in their organizational framework—that is, through its line agencies (see pages 418–419).

The Bureau of Labor Statistics. The BLS was first established as the Bureau of Labor in the Interior Department in 1884, and is the agency out of which the present-day Labor Department grew. Today it is the Government's principal fact-finding and reporting agency in the field of labor economics. It collects, analyzes, and publishes data on a number of related topics. The bulk of its work is focused on these areas: the size and characteristics of the nation's labor force, employment, unemployment, hours of work, productivity, wages, prices, labor-management relations, living conditions, and occupational safety.

BLS is headed by a Commissioner of Labor Statistics, a presidential nominee who must be confirmed by the Senate. The agency itself has no enforcement or other administrative functions. Practically all of the basic data it gathers are supplied to it voluntarily. Most of it comes from business and labor organizations and from other governmental agencies—all of them with an interest in and need for the analyses and reports that BLS provides. The information it collects and the results of its researches are reported in a number of periodic bulletins and in a major publication, the *Monthly Labor Review.*

The work of the Bureau gives real meaning to the phrase "cost of living." It makes continuing studies of the current wholesale and retail prices of thousands of commodities and reports its findings in daily, weekly, and monthly "price indexes." These indexes provide a measure of the purchasing power of the dollar and are, in effect, a barometer of the nation's economic health. Many labor contracts and other wage and salary agreements are tied to them. They are widely followed and reported in the news media.

The Bureau's surveys of employment trends can be of special interest and use to young people. All significant trends in employment and job opportunities are continually analyzed to determine which types of jobs are and will be most in demand. The findings are published in a series of "occupational outlook" pamphlets.

The Employment Standards Administration. Several related agencies are housed under the broad roof of the Employment Standards Administration.

The *Wage and Hour Division* administers the oft-amended Fair Labor Standards Act of 1938. That law placed a floor under wages and a ceiling over hours of work. That is, it sets a minimum wage and a maximum work week for those who hold jobs covered by its provisions.

Initially, the law covered employees of firms engaged primarily in interstate or foreign commerce or in the production of goods for that trade. Over the years it has been broadened to include most workers who are not self-employed—that is, more than 60 million persons today.[1]

Congress first set the minimum wage at 25¢ an hour in 1938. It has been raised a number of times in the past 40 years. The most recent hike, to $3.35 an hour, became effective January 1, 1981. Those covered by the statute *must* be paid *at least* that much—and must also be paid at least one-and-a-half times that rate ("time-and-a-half") for any work beyond eight hours a day or 40 hours in any week.

The law also prohibits the use of *child labor* by most firms engaged in or producing goods or services for interstate or foreign commerce. Such firms are prohibited from hiring any person under age 16 for most jobs and any person under 18 for those jobs classed as hazardous. Several

---

[1] State and local government employees are the only major category of workers not now covered. They were, for a time. Congress first brought State school and hospital workers under the law in 1966 and then all State and local employees in 1974. In *California* v. *Usery,* 1976, however, the Supreme Court found the 1974 law to be an unconstitutional invasion of the reserved powers of the States.

types of employment are exempted from the child labor prohibition, however—notably most agricultural work, newspaper delivery, acting, and jobs in which children work for their parents.

The Office also enforces the Equal Pay Act of 1963. Under its terms, some 30 million women—all of whom are covered by the Fair Labor Standards Act—must be paid the same amount as that paid to men who do comparable work. It also administers statutes aimed at discrimination in employment on account of age.

The *Office of Workers' Compensation Programs* administers several laws which provide injury and accident benefits to federal employees—similar to compensation laws for those who work in the private sector. It decides whether federal workers who are injured or disabled are entitled to benefits and, if so, how much their compensation should be. It has similar responsibilities toward certain non-federal employees, especially under the terms of the Longshoremen's and Harbor Workers Compensation Act and the "black-lung" provisions of the Coal Mine Health and Safety Act.

The *Office of Federal Contract Compliance Programs* is a watchdog agency. Its basic mission is to ensure that those who do any form of contract work with any federal agency comply with the anti-discrimination provisions of the several federal civil rights laws. It works closely with the Equal Employment Opportunity Commission; see page 176.

The *Women's Bureau* is especially concerned with working women—who now make up nearly half of the nation's total labor force. The welfare of these 45 million women is its special concern. It is a research and advisory agency. It studies such matters as the wages, hours, and working conditions of women; family and property law; and the care of working mothers' children. As the Bureau has described its work, it is concerned "with all women at work, or seeking work, and with their

training and skills; with women in all fields of employment; with the student selecting her career; with the girl on her first job and the older woman worker; and with women who are both homemakers and wage earners." It furnishes its reports and advice to Congress, other federal and State agencies, private groups and foreign governments.

The Employment and Training Administration. Another group of related agencies make up the Employment and Training Administration.

WORKING WOMEN

WOMEN IN LABOR FORCE

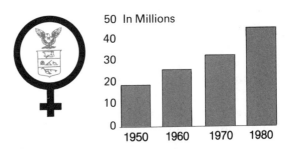

WOMEN AS A PERCENT OF TOTAL LABOR FORCE

MARRIED WOMEN

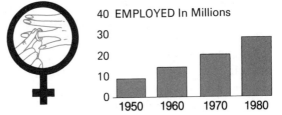

MARRIED WOMEN AS A PERCENT OF WOMEN IN THE LABOR FORCE

Source: U.S. Labor Department

The *United States Employment Service* was born during the Great Depression. Created in 1933, the USES was one of the first of the New Deal responses to the widespread unemployment of the time. Its original mission was to prompt the States to set up and maintain a system of local employment offices.

That remains its basic function today. For more than 40 years now, it has provided financial and other kinds of assistance to the States, and there are currently some 2500 local employment offices located throughout the country. These offices serve both employers and workers, seeking to bring jobs and job-seekers together through a variety of placement and counseling programs.

The *Unemployment Insurance Service* concentrates on the other side of the job coin—unemployment, and, in particular, unemployment compensation.

The problem of employment is most pressing in periods of national economic difficulty, of course—as it was during the Depression of the 1930's; and it has been a problem of considerable proportions over the past several years, as well. A certain amount of unemployment always exists—even in so-called "normal" times.

For idled workers and their families, unemployment can pose many very serious and difficult problems, of course. And this is true no matter when or why it occurs. And it can occur for any number of reasons: a general downturn in the national economy, automation, a shift in consumer buying habits, aging, seasonal demands, bad weather, plant relocation, and many more.

The mass unemployment of the 1930's brought the plight of the jobless into sharp national focus. The number out of work had leaped from some two million in 1929 to more than 13 million by 1933. Neither the private sector nor the few and limited State efforts could possibly cope with the problem.

The crisis prompted national action on a number of fronts. One of the most far-reaching of the steps taken at the time was the enactment of the Social Security Act of 1935 (see page 625). Along with several other relief and welfare programs, that omnibus law created an unemployment compensation program.

In strictest terms, there is no *national* unemployment compensation program. Rather, there exists a cooperative federal-State effort in which each State administers its own program under standards set by Congress and administered by UIS.

The heart of the unemployment compensation system is in its complex financing. Federal law imposes a payroll tax on employers—in 1981, 3.4 percent of the first $6000 of each employee's annual wages.[2] Proceeds from the tax are credited to each State's account in the Unemployment Compensation Trust Fund maintained in the federal Treasury. Unemployment benefits are paid by the States from this fund and from whatever additional funds they themselves make available for this purpose.

If a State's program meets the minimum federal standards, the National Government grants to the State the money necessary to pay the administrative costs of running its program. If a State's program fails to meet the minimum federal stan-

---

[2] Every State's law exempts some employers and their employees from coverage. Agricultural workers, domestic servants, and public employees are commonly excluded. In 1938 Congress established a separate program of unemployment compensation, health insurance, and retirement benefits for railroad workers. It is financed by a payroll tax and is administered by the independent Railroad Retirement Board. Congress enacted an unemployment compensation law for federal workers in 1954. No State *must* have an unemployment compensation program. But the 1935 law provided that any State tax an employer must pay to support such a program may be deducted from his federal tax—up to a maximum today of 2.7 points of the present 3.4 percent federal levy. Hence, an employer's *federal* tax may be reduced to as low as .7 percent, depending upon how much the State levies. This offset feature prompted each State to set up its own program.

dards, it not only is denied the administrative grant but it cannot draw from the Trust Fund, either. Among the standards that must be met are the requirements that States make benefit payments promptly and that all payments be made through a public employment service which has been approved by the Secretary of Labor, that workers have the right to an impartial hearing if their benefit applications are denied, and that no worker is to lose his or her benefits for not taking another but unsuitable job.

Unemployment compensation is *not* designed to take care of the sick, the disabled, or the aged. It is intended for those who are willing and able to work but who are involuntarily unemployed. An idle worker who refuses a suitable job offered through a State employment office can lose his or her right to further compensation.

The *Office of Comprehensive Employment Development* is the current descendant of a long line of federal work-training agencies dating back to the 1930's.

Through most of our history we have enjoyed a general and rising level of economic prosperity. Those relatively brief times on which this happy condition has not been so—for example, the recession of

1979–1980—have been few and far between. The most recent serious and prolonged period of severe economic hardship for the nation, the Great Depression of the 1930's, is some 40 years behind us.

That is not to say that we have not known other periods, nor that there are not continuing pockets, of economic distress in this country, however. Economic well-being has not been spread evenly throughout the nation, nor among all of our people. There are places, and there are segments of the population, in which long and persistent unemployment is altogether too well-known.

OCED conducts a host of programs aimed at those localities and groups most severely affected by chronic unemployment. It was created by the Comprehensive Employment and Training Act of 1973, the current statute on which most such efforts are based.

It administers a veritable catalog of grant programs to stimulate employment. Among the best known of them today is the CETA (Comprehensive Employment and Training) program—in which federal grants are made to finance a wide range of job-training projects. Another is PEP (the Public Employment Program)—in which

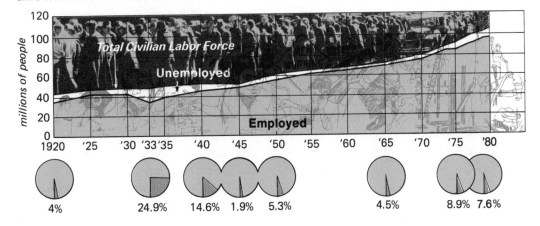

GROWTH OF THE LABOR FORCE

PERCENT UNEMPLOYED

A representative of the Labor Department (at right) inspects a factory to see if conditions for workers meet health and safety standards.

federal funds are used to help support jobs in many different State and local governmental agencies. A number of similar endeavors provide grant monies to support other public jobs and also for such related efforts as recruitment, testing, counseling, and classroom instruction in various occupational skills.

It also furnishes various job-related services (training, counseling, placement, and the like) to several segments of the population in particular need of them. Such services are furnished, for example, to migrant and seasonal farm workers, persons with limited English-language abilities, Viet Nam-era veterans, and American Indians.

OCED conducts many other programs, all built around the theme of stimulating jobs. Among them is the Job Corps, to provide up to two years of citizenship and occupational training, together with work experience, for disadvantaged youth. The Work Incentive Program (WIN) finances both training and placement programs for employable members of those families receiving aid-to-dependent-children payments from the Office of Human Development Services in the Department of Health and Human Services; see page 632.

OCED's efforts are aimed at a number of other targets, as well. Thus, it attempts to boost minority employment in the construction trades and seeks to help older workers find jobs in rural areas. It also makes follow-up studies to gauge its own effectiveness and see that those who have received its help remain in the work force.

The *Bureau of Apprenticeship and Training* seeks to promote the development of skilled workers through apprenticeships. It is armed with advice, good intentions, and, most importantly, grant monies. It works closely with State labor agencies, employers, labor unions, vocational schools and the like to bring labor and management together in the acceptance of apprenticeship standards in a variety of trades.

The Labor Management Services Administration. Several offices also constitute this umbrella agency.

The *Office of Pensions and Welfare Plan Reports* administers the Employee Retirement Income Security Act of 1974. That statute requires full public access to the terms and functioning of the many "fringe benefits" funds maintained under various labor-management contracts. The Act also directs the Secretary of Labor to police and administer these funds. The Secretary does so through this Office. The office also administers the provisions of the Labor-Management Reporting and Disclosure (Landrum-Griffin) Act of 1959 (page 592).

The *Office of Veterans Reemployment Rights* protects the job rights of men and women who return to civilian life after service in any of the armed forces. In several statutes, dating back to the Selective Service Act of

1940, Congress has guaranteed that draftees and others entering the military have a later right to return to their civilian jobs. The Office administers these statutes in close cooperation with the Defense Department, the Veterans Administration, and, when necessary, the Department of Justice.

The *Office of Labor-Management Relations Services* is both an advisory and clearinghouse agency and a sort of emergency first-aid team. Among its many tasks, it conducts continuing studies of the collective bargaining process and reports on current and potentially critical labor-management dispute situations. It provides staff assistance to presidential emergency boards appointed under the Taft-Hartley Act (page 592). It prepares information for immediate use in specific collective bargaining situations, and it attempts to help State and local governments with their labor-management problems.

The *Office of Federal Employee Organizations* performs in the field of the Federal Government's own labor-management relations the role that the NLRB plays in the private sector. Its role is a most important one, as we shall see in a moment.

The Bureau of International Labor Affairs. The Bureau of International Labor Affairs directs and coordinates all of the Department's activities in the international field. Thus, it furnishes advice and information to the State Department, other federal agencies, and to foreign governments. It supervises the work of the labor attachés who are assigned to most of our embassies abroad and is responsible for United States participation in the International Labor Organization (ILO); see page 480.

The Bureau's major purpose is that of fostering cooperation and the exchange of technical know-how in the international labor field. It supplies consultants for foreign assignments, provides technical materials for use abroad, and conducts training programs for labor leaders and officials from other countries. It also sponsors an exchange program under which American labor officials go abroad and union representatives of foreign nations visit the United States.

Labor-Management Relations

The Development of Labor Unions. In our early history the nation's economy was a relatively simple one in which most persons worked for themselves. Those who did work for others usually bargained with their employers on an individual basis. That is, the details of the labor contract—wages, hours, and working conditions—were settled by an employer and an employee as a personal, face-to-face matter between two persons well known to one another.

The coming of the industrial revolution, with the factory system and mass production, wrought a drastic change in the employer-employee relationship. Especially in the years following the Civil War, the small shop gave way to the huge corporation. Where the demand had once been for the services of "Tom Smith, skilled mechanic" it became a demand for "fifty precision machinists." To meet the growing power of corporate industry labor began to develop organizations of its own to protect the worker.

The history of union organization goes back almost to the days of the Revolution. Before 1800 mechanics and artisans in a few of the larger cities had joined together to form unions. The industrialization of the 1830's spurred local union growth, but unionization gained real momentum only in the latter three decades of the 19th century.

THE KNIGHTS OF LABOR. A number of attempts were made to combine various local unions into national groups in the 1850's and 1860's. The Knights of Labor, formed in 1869, was the most successful of the early national unions. The Knights sought to organize men and women of every craft, creed, and color, and it included both skilled and unskilled workers. By 1886 its membership reached 700,000. It advocated such policies as the prohibition of child labor, progressive income and inheritance taxes, and equal pay for men and women.

The Knights began to fade in the mid-1880's for a number of reasons. Several unsuccessful strikes discouraged many members. The union contained locals and individual members with widely differing views and was often torn by internal strife. The bloody Haymarket Riot in Chicago in 1886 produced splits within the union that threatened to destroy it completely. Several large unions, especially the Railroad Brotherhoods, refused to join the Knights of Labor. By 1917 the Knights of Labor had dissolved.

THE AMERICAN FEDERATION OF LABOR.   In 1881 a group of union officials, socialists, and dissatisfied members of the Knights of Labor formed the Federation of Organized Trades and Labor Unions. It was organized as a union of skilled workers in particular crafts. The Federation and the Knights became intense rivals, and in 1886 the Federation called upon all unions not members of the Knights of Labor to join together for protection against the Knights. Thus, in 1886, the American Federation of Labor (AFL) was born out of the Federation of Organized Trades and Labor Unions. This new organization soon led the field.

The AFL was formed as a federation of *craft unions*. A craft union is one which is composed only of those workers who possess the *same* craft or skill—for example, a plumbers, a carpenters, or an electricians union.

THE CONGRESS OF INDUSTRIAL ORGANIZA-TIONS.   The development of mass production industries in the United States created a large class of industrial workers not skilled in any particular craft. Many of these workers are organized into *industrial unions*. An industrial union is one which includes *all* workers, skilled or unskilled, in a single major industry—for example, the Textile Workers Union and the United Steel Workers.

The AFL, with its traditional craft-union organization, found it difficult to organize workers in the new mass-production industries. A majority of the craft unions opposed the admission of unions composed of unskilled workers into the AFL. Finally, after a long and bitter fight over craft versus industrial unionism, a group led by John L. Lewis was expelled from the AFL. In 1938 Lewis and his followers established the Congress of Industrial Organizations—the CIO.

THE MERGER OF THE AFL AND THE CIO. After nearly two decades of existence as separate and rival national unions, the AFL and the CIO combined into one huge labor organization in 1955. The huge new group took the name *American Federation of Labor and Congress of Industrial Organizations*—and is commonly referred to as the AFL-CIO. It chose as its first president George Meany, the former head of the AFL, and he continued to hold that post until 1979.

The AFL-CIO holds a national convention to shape its policies every two years. It is governed in the period between conventions by an executive council composed of nineteen leaders from the former AFL unions and ten from the old CIO. The combined organization is made up of 104 different affiliated unions.

Union Membership Today.   The Labor Department reports that some 22 million workers now belong to American labor unions. [3] The AFL-CIO has a membership of some 16.6 million. Several million other workers belong to various independent unions—that is, to unions not affiliated with the AFL-CIO.

---

[3] Including more than 550,000 who work outside the United States, most of them in Canada.

The largest of the independents are the International Brotherhood of Teamsters (expelled by the AFL-CIO in 1957), 1.9 million members; the United Auto Workers (who withdrew from the AFL-CIO in 1968), 1.3 million members; the United Steel Workers, 1.3 million members; and the International Brotherhood of Electrical Workers, 990,000 members.

By 1981 there were well over 105 million employable persons in the United States. Thus, only about one-fifth of our total national labor force is actually unionized today.

Government Regulation of Labor-Management Relations. Government has an obvious interest and obligation in the maintaining of industrial peace. A dispute between a small employer and one or two employees over wages, hours, safety, and other conditions of employment is quite important to the parties directly involved. The results of such a dispute may have widespread consequences, but they seldom do. Still, the rights of each party must be protected. A labor dispute which involves a large employer and hundreds or thousands of employees can, and frequently does, have a tremendous effect upon the health, the safety, or the economy of the entire nation.

COLLECTIVE BARGAINING. Collective bargaining is the process of negotiation between an employer and organized employees (that is, employees as a group rather than individually) to determine the terms of a labor contract. It is the cornerstone upon which the present-day system of labor-management relations in the United States is laid. It takes place when representatives of management and labor sit down to work out an agreement which sets forth the wages, hours, and other conditions of employment.

Collective bargaining is a two-way street. Management makes its proposals for a contract to govern employment. Labor makes its proposals, too. The two sides

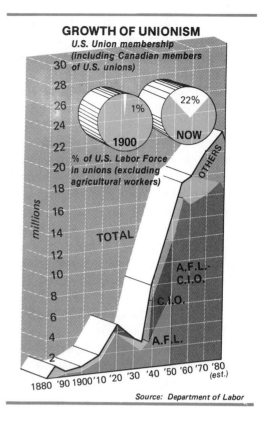

GROWTH OF UNIONISM

U.S. Union membership (including Canadian members of U.S. unions)

1% 1900

22% NOW

% of U.S. Labor Force in unions (excluding agricultural workers)

millions

TOTAL

OTHERS

A.F.L.-C.I.O.

C.I.O.

A.F.L.

1880 '90 1900 '10 '20 '30 '40 '50 '60 '70 '80 (est.)

Source: Department of Labor

then bargain (discuss and compromise) with one another in order to reach an agreement satisfactory to each side.

EARLY GOVERNMENTAL REGULATION. The right of workers to organize and bargain collectively is now recognized by all States and the National Government. In their early days, however, unions were commonly regarded with suspicion and disfavor. The common law, inherited from England, held combinations of workers to be criminal conspiracies. Unions were never declared to be illegal as such, but organized efforts to gain higher wages or better working conditions were often prosecuted as conspiracies.

The Supreme Court of Massachusetts pioneered the change in governmental attitude in 1842 when it expressly recognized the legality of unions and upheld their right to strike. Through the latter part of the 19th century and into the early decades of this one, government tolerated rather than encouraged and protected union organization. Being legal, unions were permitted to pursue their objectives, but only by what were then regarded as "lawful" means.

An employer was generally free to oppose unions, and the law paid little attention to the methods used to oppose them. "Yellow-dog" contracts were common. These were contracts in which, as a condition of employment, a worker agreed not to join a union. Company police and labor spies were used, and many workers who favored unions were "black-listed." Company unions were formed to stall the growth of legitimate labor unions. Injunctions[4] were used frequently to break strikes. And, in the early years of this century, courts often held union attempts to enforce labor contracts to be violations of the Sherman Anti-Trust Act (page 537).

Unions continued to grow despite the many obstacles raised against them. As they grew in number so did their political power through the votes of their members. By 1900 labor's political strength had become a force to be reckoned with in the halls of Congress. In the Clayton Act (page 537) of 1914 unions were specifically exempted from the provisions of antitrust laws. Other legislation designed to protect workers and to promote their interests in such matters as wages, hours, and working conditions began to appear on federal and State statute books.

The Depression which began in 1929 brought widespread unemployment and other hardship. It also produced a wave of new legislation favorable to labor, especially after the inauguration of the New Deal in 1933. Three statutes enacted by Congress in the 1930's are often referred to as "labor's bill of rights." These laws are the Norris-LaGuardia (Anti-Injunction) Act of 1932, the Wagner (National Labor Relations) Act of 1935, and the Fair Labor Standards Act of 1938. These statutes made collective bargaining a standard feature of labor-management relations, placed a number of restrictions on management, and otherwise strengthened the hand of organized labor.

The Taft-Hartley (Labor-Management Relations) Act of 1947 was passed by Congress later to provide a fairer balance between labor and management in the bargaining relationship.

Four particular statutes form the base of national regulation of labor-management relations today. They are the Norris-LaGuardia Act of 1932, the Wagner Act of 1935, the Taft-Hartley Act of 1947, and the Landrum-Griffin (Labor-Management Reporting and Disclosure) Act of 1959.

THE NORRIS-LAGUARDIA ACT OF 1932. The Norris-LaGuardia Act severely restricts the power of federal courts to issue injunctions in labor disputes. Before an injunction may be issued it must be shown that every reasonable effort has been made to settle the dispute peacefully, that specific unlawful actions have been threatened, and that police officers have not furnished apparently necessary protection. The Act also provides that no one may be prevented from joining a union, striking or urging others to strike, or engaging in other normal union activities.

THE WAGNER ACT OF 1935. The Wagner Act expressly recognizes the right of workers to organize and to bargain collectively. Employers in any industry engaged in interstate commerce are required to bargain with those unions favored by a majority of their employees. These employers are also prohibited from committing various "unfair labor practices."

The Act created the *National Labor Relations Board* (NLRB) to administer its provi-

---

[4] An *injunction* is a court order that prevents (enjoins) one from performing some act which would injure the personal or property rights of another.

sions.[5] The NLRB was given two broad functions: (1) to conduct elections among employees to determine which, if any, union they favored as their bargaining agent, and (2) to enforce the unfair labor practices provisions of the law.

The unfair labor practices listed in the Act are quite broad. Employers are especially forbidden: (1) to refuse to bargain collectively with recognized unions, (2) to interfere in union organization, (3) to exert undue influence on any employee with regard to union membership or activity, and (4) to discharge or otherwise punish an employee for union membership or activity. The Act set out no similar list of restrictions on workers or unions.

The Wagner Act was the subject of intense criticism from the moment of its passage. Most of its critics accepted the law's insistence on the principle of collective bargaining. But they argued that unions and union leaders were given great power without being made responsible for the manner of its exercise. That is, they objected to the fact that the law contained no list of unfair labor practices that unions were not to commit. For example, they objected to the law's failure to prohibit unions from preventing the use of labor-saving machines or from insisting on the practice of "featherbedding." (Featherbedding is the practice of forcing an employer to hire workers not actually needed.)

THE TAFT-HARTLEY ACT OF 1947. The Taft-Hartley Act was passed by Congress to meet the criticisms of the Wagner Act. As its proponents described it, the law was passed to "redress the balance between labor and management." Its provisions are a series of amendments to the Wagner Act.

The Taft-Hartley Act increased the size of the original NLRB from three to five members and added to it a general counsel. This officer's function is to prosecute cases involving alleged unfair labor practices before the Board. The unfair labor practices listed in the Wagner Act were expanded to include restrictions on the activities of labor unions. Like employers, unions may not refuse to bargain collectively. And, too, they are forbidden to coerce an employee or force an employer to coerce an employee to support union policies or activities.

Unions may not charge excessive or discriminatory fees or attempt to force an employer to accept featherbedding. "Secondary boycotts" are prohibited. That is, unions are forbidden to strike against one employer in order to force an employer not to do business with another employer who is involved in a labor dispute. Also, unions may not strike to force an employer to deal with one union when the NLRB has certified another as the employees' bargaining agent. And, strikes against the Federal Government are forbidden.

Union leaders must make periodic reports of union finances to the union members and to the Secretary of Labor. They must file sworn statements with the NLRB that they are not affiliated with the Communist Party or any other group that advocates the violent overthrow of government in the United States. Failure to file either the financial reports or the noncommunist affidavits bars a union from using the NLRB to advance or protect its interests under the law.

The Act outlaws the *closed shop* in any industry in interstate commerce.[6] It per-

---

[5] The NLRB is an independent regulatory commission composed of five members appointed by the President and Senate for five-year terms; see pages 422-425.

[6] A *closed shop* is one in which, as a condition of the labor contract, union membership is a prerequisite to employment—one in which, then, only union members may be hired. A *union shop* is one in which employees must join the union within a short time after being hired. Several of the States now have "right-to-work" laws, which ban *both* the closed and the union shops; they provide only for the *open shop*—a worker may join a union or not, as he or she sees fit. See the Case Study, page 593.

mits a *union shop* in such industries only: (1) where a majority of the workers agree to its establishment and (2) in those States where State law does not forbid it. No union may refuse to admit a worker to membership nor may a union expel a member except for nonpayment of union dues.

Unions and union leaders are legally responsible and may be sued for damages which result from engaging in unfair labor practices.

The Taft-Hartley Act also created the *Federal Mediation and Conciliation Service,* an independent executive agency which works to promote labor-management agreement. In effect, it seeks to prevent strikes or, when they occur, to facilitate settlements.

When a labor contract expires, or when a union wishes to change the terms of an existing one, the law prohibits the calling of a strike except with 60 days' notice. This "cooling-off period" is designed to allow time for continued bargaining. Sometimes a strike is called which endangers the national health or safety. In such a case, the President, acting through the Attorney General, may seek an 80-day injunction to halt the walkout. This additional "cooling-off period" allows time for further negotiation. It also allows time for congressional action in the event that it is needed.

No union may contribute funds to *any* campaign for *any federal* office. Of course, any individual union member may make a political contribution if he or she chooses to do so. And, unions may—and do—maintain political action groups to support candidates sympathetic to the views of organized labor. Among such groups, the most potent today is the AFL-CIO's Committee on Political Education (COPE). See pages 203, 270.

THE LANDRUM-GRIFFIN ACT OF 1959. The Landrum-Griffin Act was passed following a three-year investigation by a special Senate Rackets Committee. Its investi-gation documented a shocking record of corruption on the part of a few union leaders. It disclosed the misuse (even theft) of union funds, associations with known racketeers, fraud in union elections, perjury, bribery, extortion, falsification of union and tax records, and the use of threats and of violence to silence those members who dared to challenge the action of union officials.

The Act was passed to protect union members and the general public against such abuses. It is lengthy and quite detailed. But the Act's title—the Labor-Management Reporting and Disclosure Act—makes its chief purpose quite clear: to make union records and union proceedings public.

The statute strengthens many sections of the Taft-Hartley Act. For example, it broadens the definition and coverage of the ban on secondary boycotts. It forbids "hot-cargo contracts," in which an employer agrees not to do business with a firm that has been labeled as unfair by a union.

Those convicted of a felony are banned from holding a union office for at least five years after their conviction or imprisonment. Misuse of union funds and similar practices are federal crimes, and stiff penalties are provided for violations. Detailed annual reports of union finances and other activities and copies of all labor-management contracts must be filed with the Secretary of Labor (page 586).

This labor reform law also contains a "bill of rights" for union members. These provisions guarantee to members the right: to participate freely and to ballot secretly in union meetings; to nominate and vote for union officials; and to have access to all financial and other union records and contracts. Union members also may sue their union officers to prevent a violation of members' rights, a misuse of union funds, or a refusal of access by the members to union records.

Case Study

The Labor-Management Relations Act of 1947—the Taft-Hartley Act—expressly forbids any labor agreement which provides for the "closed shop." That is, the law prohibits those work situations in which only the members of a particular union may be hired.

The law does sanction the "union shop," however. That is, the statute allows for those contracts which require that all newly-hired workers must join the union soon after they have been employed. (Unlike the arrangement under a closed shop contract, then, a person need not be a member of the union in order to secure a job in a union shop. But that person must join the union within a specified period of time, usually within 30 days.)

But, in Section 14B, the Act also permits any of the States to outlaw the union shop, should they choose to do so. And a number of them have. That is, those States have enacted what are commonly called "right-to-work" laws—statutes which forbid the use of union membership either as a prerequisite to hiring or as a condition of continued employment.

Put the other way, right-to-work laws authorize only the "open shop"—in which a worker may join a union or not, as he or she chooses.

At the present time (1981), 20 States have right-to-work laws: Alabama, Arizona, Arkansas, Florida, Georgia, Iowa, Kansas, Louisiana, Mississippi, Nebraska, Nevada, North Carolina, North Dakota, South Carolina, South Dakota, Tennessee, Texas, Utah, Virginia, and Wyoming.

Most of the leaders of organized labor are bitterly opposed to right-to-work laws, and they have long argued for the repeal of Section 14B. They contend that those laws are purposefully misnamed and that their real object is to destroy unions (and, with them, the principle of collective bargaining). They insist that nonunion workers are "freeloaders"—that they receive the wages and other benefits gained by union action but do not bear any of the burdens of the unions' efforts.

The supporters of right-to-work laws, advocates of the open shop, are led by the National Right to Work Committee. They deny the allegation that those statutes are aimed at the destruction of unions. Indeed, they point to the fact that unions have gained in membership in those States in which those laws exist. They maintain that both the closed and the union shop amount to "compulsory unionism"—that they force all employees in a given work situation to belong to a union, without regard to their individual preferences in the matter.

■ Does your State now have a right-to-work law? If not, do you think one should be enacted? If so, should the statute be repealed?

■ Do you see any particular significance in either the geographic locations or the general economic character of the 20 States which now have right-to-work laws? With the single exception of Indiana (where it was repealed in 1965), none of the nation's major industrial States has enacted a right-to-work law. Why do you think this is so?

A number of labor-management contracts today provide for the "agency shop," as an alternative to the union shop. That is, they provide for work situations in which the employees are not required to join a union; but those who do not must pay a fee (make a continuing contribution) to help defray the costs of the union's bargaining efforts. Do nonunion workers in fact benefit from those union efforts?

■ None of the current State right-to-work laws authorize the agency shop. Do you think that they should do so?

SUMMARY

By both tradition and law, the United States is committed to the free contract labor system. The concept is embedded in the Constitution—most prominently in the 13th Amendment.

The Department of Labor was created as a separate Cabinet-level department in 1913. The principal line agencies within it today are: the Bureau of Labor Statistics, a fact-finding and reporting agency; the Wage and Hour Division, chiefly concerned with the administration of the minimum wage and maximum hours provisions of the Fair Labor Standards Act of 1938; the United States Employment Service, which prompts the States to operate employment services; the Unemployment Insurance Service, which supervises the federal-State unemployment compensation program; the Office of Comprehensive Employment Development Programs, which directs the PEP and CETA programs and a host of similar job-stimulation efforts; and the Labor-Management Services Administration, primarily concerned with facilitating labor-management agreements.

Labor unions existed in the United States before 1800, but their real growth began with the industrial revolution. About 22 million workers today belong to organized labor unions. The combined AFL–CIO has about 16.6 million members while several million belong to independent unions. Thus, about one-fifth of the well over 105 million employable persons belong to unions today.

Despite early opposition, unions grew, and as they did they gained political power through the votes of their members. Four particular acts form the base of federal regulation of labor-management relations today: the Norris-LaGuardia (Anti-Injunction) Act of 1932, the Wagner (National Labor Relations) Act of 1935, the Taft-Hartley (Labor-Management Relations) Act of 1947, and the Landrum-Griffin (Labor-Management Reporting and Disclosure) Act of 1959 which was passed to combat abuses by some labor leaders.

Concept Development

Questions for Review

1. What is the free contract labor system?

2. When was the Department of Labor established? What is this Department's basic function?

3. What does the BLS do?

4. For what did the Fair Labor Standards Act of 1938 provide? The Equal Pay Act of 1963?

5. What is misleading about the phrase "a national unemployment insurance program"?

6. What is the basic purpose of such programs as PEP and CETA?

7. What effect did the coming of the industrial revolution have upon labor management relations?

8. Which labor organization was the

most successful among the early attempts to form a national union?

9. Which is the major national labor union in the country today?

10. Approximately what portion of the total national work force is unionized today?

11. What is an independent union?

12. What federal statutes form the base of national regulation of labor-management relations today?

13. What two major functions does the NLRB perform?

14. What is a closed shop? A union shop? An open shop? Which of them are permitted in federal law today?

For Further Inquiry

1. Why do you agree or disagree with this comment by Abraham Lincoln:

Property is the fruit of labor; property is desirable, is a positive good in the world. That some should be rich shows that others may become rich, and hence is just encouragement to industry and enterprise. Let not him who is houseless pull down the house of another, but let him work diligently and build one for himself, thus, by example assuring that his own house shall be safe from violence when built.

Do you think that Lincoln would subscribe to the same views were he alive today?

2. Which, if any, of the present-day activities of the Labor Department do you think should be abolished? Why?

3. Do you agree with those who argue that Section 14-B of the Taft-Hartley Act, which permits States to adopt "right-to-work" laws which allow only the open shop, ought to be repealed? Why, or why not?

4. Why do you think that the total membership in labor unions today is such a comparatively small portion of the nation's total labor force?

Suggested Activities

1. Prepare as extensive a list as you can of the activities conducted by agencies of the Department of Labor in your locale.

2. Invite a local labor union representative to speak to the class on the subject of the union, its membership, organization, history, and policies.

3. Invite a spokesperson for a federal labor agency operating in your locale to speak to the class on that agency and its functions.

4. Stage a debate or class forum on one of the following questions: (a) *Resolved,* That all labor unions in the United States be abolished forthwith; (b) *Resolved,* That this State adopt a (or repeal its) "right-to-work" law.

Suggested Reading

Brody, David, *Workers in Industrial America.* Oxford, 1980.

Bureau of Labor Statistics, *Brief History of the American Labor Movement.* Department of Labor, 1977.

Chamberlain, Neil, *et al., The Labor Sector.* McGraw-Hill, 3rd ed., 1980.

Dubinsky, David and Raskin, A. H., *Dubinsky: A Life with Labor.* Scribner's, 1977.

Pinkstaff, Marlene A. and Wilkinson, Anna B., *Women at Work: Overcoming the Obstacles.* Addison-Wesley, 1979.

Rehmus, Charles M., *et al.,* (eds.), *Labor and American Politics.* University of Michigan Press, 2nd ed., 1978.

———, *Labor and American Politics: A Book of Readings.* University of Michigan Press, 2nd ed., 1978.

Summers, Clyde and Rabin, Robert, *The Rights of Union Members.* Avon Books, 1979.

Wilson, Graham K., *Unions in American National Politics.* St. Martin's Press, 1979.

Also: Office of Information, Publications, and Reports, Department of Labor, Washington, D.C. 20210.

Government and the Environment

Conservation means the wise use of the earth and its resources . . . for the greatest good of the greatest number for the longest time.

GIFFORD PINCHOT

When tillage begins, other arts follow. The farmers therefore are the founders of human civilization.

DANIEL WEBSTER

■ Should self-sufficiency be a major goal of the nation's natural resources programs? Why?

■ Do you perceive any conflicts between the goals of conservation and environmental protection, on the one hand, and those of economic security and development on the other?

■ Is the basic function of the Department of the Interior regulatory or promotional in character? The EPA? The USDA?

■ To whom are the programs administered by the Interior Department of the greatest value? The EPA? The USDA?

Nowhere on earth has nature been more generous than in the United States. The first Americans—the Indians—and then the first white settlers, and the millions who followed them, found a land of almost unbelievable natural wealth. They found an entire continent of vast forests, of mighty rivers and bountiful lakes, of grassy plains extending far beyond the distant horizons. Beneath the rich soil they found seemingly inexhaustible deposits of coal, iron, oil, copper, gold, and other minerals.

For nearly 300 years this great wealth was used with little or no thought for the future. There was a nation to be built, and nature's larder seemed boundless. Whole forests disappeared, grasslands were put to the plow, mineral deposits were overworked. The few who warned against exploitation and waste, who pleaded for conservation and wiser use, were seldom heard. Not until the turn of this century did many Americans begin to realize that the land's great natural wealth might not be inexhaustible after all.

The modern conservation movement was begun during the Presidency of Theodore Roosevelt (1901–1909). With the zeal of crusaders, the President and his Chief Forester, Gifford Pinchot, set out to make the nation "conservation conscious." Their battle has not been entirely won, even today. Exploiters and the selfish, the wasteful, and the ignorant are still with us. On the whole, however, most Americans—in

Farmland in Wisconsin—only one example of how the nation is blessed by nature and one reason why our productive farmlands are the envy of the world.

evergrowing numbers today—have come to realize the absolute necessity for conservation—for the wise use and restoration of our natural resources.

In this chapter we shall look at the three major federal agencies which are most directly involved with the conservation and use of the nation's natural resources and the quality of its environment. That is, we shall be particularly concerned with the work of the Cabinet-level Departments of the Interior and of Agriculture and the independent Environmental Protection Agency.

THE DEPARTMENT OF THE INTERIOR

Most of the National Government's activities in the field of conservation are conducted by agencies within the Department of the Interior.[1] The Department was established by Congress in 1849. Originally, it was assigned a wide range of functions: it contained the General Land Office, the Office of Indian Affairs, the Pension Office, and the Patent Office. It also had supervision of public buildings, the census, the District of Columbia's penitentiary, United States marshals, and enforced federal mining laws. Over the years, other functions were added to the Department's workload, including activities in such areas as education, health, commerce, and labor.

---

[1] The two major conservation agencies outside the Department are the Forest Service and the Soil Conservation Service, both within the Department of Agriculture (pages 611–613).

As new departments and other agencies were created, many of Interior's early functions were transferred to them. Gradually, the Department's role changed from that of general house-keeper for the National Government to its present one of general custodian of the nation's natural resources. Its principal concern today is with the management, conservation, and development of the public lands, water and mineral resources, forest holdings, fish and wildlife, and the national parks.

The Department's jurisdiction extends over some 190,000,000 hectares (500,000,-000 acres) of land in the 50 States, to islands in the Caribbean and the South Pacific and to lands in the Arctic Circle. It is responsible for mine safety, the protection of fish and wildlife, the preservation of scenic and historic areas, the reclamation of arid lands in the West, the management of hydroelectric power systems, and the welfare of over 200,000 persons in our territorial possessions and some 550,000 Indians residing on or near reservations.

The Secretary of the Interior. The Department is headed by the Secretary of the Interior. The Secretary is appointed by the President with the consent of the Sen-ate and, as a rule, comes from the West—the region in which the bulk of the Department's work is located.

The Bureau of Land Management

The Bureau of Land Management has charge of the management, survey, and disposition of large areas of public lands, and of the minerals these lands contain.

Federal Land Policy. Present-day mapping techniques fix the size of this country at 916.9 million hectares (2.264 billion acres). More than a third of that huge area (308.1 million hectares, 716 million acres) is now in the *public domain—i.e.,* is now owned by the Federal Government.

The building of the public domain was begun in the years 1781–1802, as the original States ceded their western land claims to the National Government. Other public lands were added as the nation expanded. At one time or another since 1781, over 80 percent of all land in the United States (some 744 million hectares, 1.8 billion acres) has been held by the Government—including nearly all of the land west of the original 13 States except Texas.

Over the years, the Federal Govern-

ACQUISITION OF THE TERRITORY COMPRISING THE 50 STATES

Acquisition	Date	Area Acres*	Hectares*	How Acquired
Original 13 States and the Western Lands	1775–1783	568.8	230.2	Revolutionary War and Treaty with Great Britain
Louisiana Purchase	1803	529.4	214.2	Treaty with France
Florida	1819	46.1	18.6	Treaty with Spain
Texas	1845	249.7	101.0	Admission of independent state
Oregon Country	1846	182.8	74.0	Treaty with Great Britain
Mexican Cession	1848	338.6	137.0	Conquest and Treaty with Mexico
Gadsden Purchase	1853	19.0	7.7	Treaty with Mexico
Alaska	1867	375.3	151.9	Treaty with Russia
Hawaii	1898	4.1	1.7	Annexation of an independent state

In millions

ment has disposed of large portions of its vast holdings—in fact, almost 60 percent of all of the land at one time or another within the public domain. Major chunks were either given away or sold at very low prices to encourage settlement of the West.

Much of it went to homesteaders in 160-acre lots. The attraction of free or very inexpensive land in the West was a major factor in the building of the nation. Large tracts were given to the railroads to encourage the building of lines across the country. The States were granted huge areas for the support of public education and of various institutions, for the construction of canals and roads, for river improvements and reclamation, and for many other purposes. Other grants were made to veterans, and much land was sold at very cheap prices to foster the reclaiming of desert lands.

Nearly all of the public land best suited for agriculture has long since been disposed of. Only within the past 40 years or so has Congress provided for the planned management and development of the remaining public lands—much of which no one wanted.

Today, the BLM controls about 167 million hectares (417 million acres), most of it in the West. Most of the public land is located in 12 western States.[2]

BLM practices "multiple use management" on the lands it administers. That is, it promotes the widest and wisest possible uses of those lands and of the resources they contain. In doing so, it engages in many varied and related activities.

It sells public lands and also grants leases or permits for mining and other types of mineral extraction and for livestock grazing. It works to conserve and develop the water, soil, and wildlife resources on its holdings and to provide for the sustained yield of its timber lands. It promotes the recreational use of public lands and also sells or leases to the States for that purpose. The land records it keeps are often vital in deciding disputes over property ownership in those States where there are large public land holdings.

The Continental Shelf Lands. There has been considerable legal and political controversy in the past several years over the ownership of the offshore coastal lands of the United States. Do they belong to the Federal Government or to the States?

The *tidelands*—those covered by the ebb and flow of the tides—have never been in dispute. Historically, they have been recognized as State-owned. Rather, the controversy has concerned the offshore *submerged lands*—those reaching out under the sea to the territorial limits of the United States. The importance (and value) of these lands lies in the resources they hold—especially the oil and natural gas deposits off the upper Atlantic, Gulf, and California coasts.

In *United States* v. *California*, 1947, the Supreme Court rejected State claims to ownership of the submerged lands. Said the Court: "In our constitutional system, paramount rights over the ocean waters and their seabed were vested in the Federal Government." And it repeated that holding in several later cases, most recently in *United States* v. *California*, 1978.

The Submerged Lands Act of 1953. Several years of often heated debate followed the 1947 court decision. Finally, Congress enacted a quitclaim bill—a law giving title to the disputed lands to the coastal States—in 1953.

---

2 While the BLM is the principal federal landlord, several other governmental agencies administer sizable parts of the public domain. The major ones include the Fish and Wildlife Service and the National Park Service (Interior), the National Forest Service (Agriculture), and the Army, Navy, and Air Force. The overwhelming bulk (95.8%) of all federal lands are located in 12 western States. In Alaska, 96.4% of all of the land in the State is held by the Federal Government; Nevada, 85.8%; Idaho, 66.8%; Utah, 64.9%; Oregon, 52.4%; Wyoming, 48.1%; California, 45.4%; Arizona, 43.6%; Colorado, 36.0%; New Mexico, 33.6%; Montana, 29.6%; and Washington, 29.1%. Only 4.2% of all of the rest of the country is taken up by federally-held lands today.

A backpacker crosses a mountain stream as he hikes a part of the Pacific Crest Trail.

The Submerged Lands Act gives each of the coastal States control over those lands out to its "historic boundaries." That is, a state's control extends out to the seaward limits as they existed when the State entered the Union. In no case, however, can those limits extend more than three miles (4.8 kilometers) into the Atlantic or Pacific Oceans or three marine leagues (10½ miles) into the Gulf of Mexico.[3]

In 1953 Congress also passed the *Outer Continental Shelf Lands Act,* and added major amendments in 1978. The law provides for federal control over all resources in the submerged lands on the Continental Shelf beyond the State limits.[4] The Shelf involves those lands beneath shallow water—usually less than 183 meters (600 feet)—out well beyond the territorial limits. In the Atlantic the Shelf extends as far out as 400 kilometers (250 miles); in some places in the Gulf it runs as far as 225 kilometers (140 miles). The BLM administers the Outer Continental Shelf Act and has leased many sites to private oil and natural gas concerns in recent years.

The Heritage Conservation and Recreation Service

A number of federal agencies administer programs that might be grouped under the general heading "outdoor recreation." Leading examples are the Forest Service and the National Park Service. The agency *primarily* involved in that field, however, is the Heritage Conservation and Recreation Service.

The Service is generally responsible for the development of recreational facilities and activities on federal lands. It also administers a number of programs to promote such developments on other public (State and local) and private holdings. As the Agency puts it, it seeks to enhance outdoor recreation for "the benefit and enjoyment of present and future generations."

Much of the Service's work today centers around three highly important conservation-recreation statutes:

Under the *Land and Water Conservation*

---

[3] In *United States* v. *Louisiana,* 1960, the Supreme Court held that the Submerged Lands Act sets the Texas and Florida boundaries at 10.5 miles while those of Alabama, Louisiana, and Mississippi reach out only 3 miles. The latter three States have ever since sought changes in the 1953 law to give them the maximum limits, too.

---

[4] International law generally recognizes the three-mile limit for territorial waters; historically, the United States has supported the three-mile rule. The assertion of federal control over the Shelf lands beyond that point raises questions that may ultimately lead to international complications. The United States has been careful *not* to claim that its boundaries extend to the limits of the Shelf, but only that its jurisdiction over the resources existing there does. In recent years both Russian and Japanese fishing fleets have regularly worked the waters immediately off our Pacific Coast. As a result, Congress extended the area of exclusive American fishing rights in 1966, from the previous three-mile limit out to 12 miles, and in 1977 to 200 miles.

Fund Act of 1965 the Agency administers a program of grants to the States and to local governments. These grants are for the acquisition and development of land and water recreation areas and facilities. The Fund also helps to finance similar efforts by the Service and by other agencies.

The Fund's monies come from four sources: the admission and user fees charged at several federal recreation areas, the sale of federal lands, the 2¢ federal tax on motorboat fuels, and congressional appropriations.

The *Wild and Scenic Rivers Act* of 1968 established the National Scenic Rivers System, to preserve stretches of some of the nation's rivers in their natural and unpolluted state. The statute placed segments of these rivers under the protection of the System: the Salmon and Clearwater Rivers in Idaho; the Rogue River, Oregon; the Feather River, California; the Eleven Point River, Missouri; the Rio Grande and the Red River in New Mexico; the Saint Croix River in Minnesota and Wisconsin; and the Wolf River in Wisconsin. It also directed the Secretaries of Interior and Agriculture to study other rivers for later inclusion in the System—and several have been added to it in recent years.

The *National Trails System Act* of 1968 established the National Trails System, to preserve scenic and recreational trails in various parts of the country for hiking and similar uses. Congress designated the 3200-kilometer (2000-mile) Appalachian Trail and the 3760-kilometer (2350-mile) Pacific Crest Trail as the first two in the System. It directed that several more be studied for later inclusion—giving attention first to routes near cities, with second priority to trails in remote areas.

The Water and Power Resources Service

Vast stretches of the western half of the United States are dry—either arid or semi-arid. In much of the region, productive agriculture is impossible. In much of the rest of it, successful farming and ranching must depend upon extensive water conservation and development efforts.

Congress first addressed the water problems of the West in the Reclamation Act of 1902. It directed the Secretary of the Interior to "locate, construct, operate, and maintain works for the storage, diversion, and development of waters for the reclamation of arid and semiarid lands." Immediately, a Reclamation Service was created to carry out the law. That agency was reshaped as the Bureau of Reclamation in 1923—and the Bureau became the Water and Power Resources Service in 1979.

Most of the agency's work is centered in the Western States—in the 17 States extending from the Dakotas and Texas on to the Pacific Coast. The bulk of that work centers around the original mission. That is, it involves the reclaiming of dry lands through the conservation and storage of water and its distribution to those lands to make them productive.

The 1902 law created the Reclamation Fund. It is a *revolving fund* which supplies money for the financing of most reclamation projects. The monies in the Fund are used to build dams, tanks, and other storage facilities and for pumping stations, canals, and other distribution systems. Reclaimed public lands are sold or leased to farmers and ranchers, on easy terms. The proceeds from these sales and leases go into the Fund, and they are used to finance future reclamation work.

In addition to its reclamation work on public lands, the agency supplies irrigation water to individual farmers and ranchers and to users' associations—usually on a long-term contract basis. It now delivers water to nearly 150,000 farms and ranches, to irrigate more than 3.6 million hectares (9 million acres). The crops now produced on those lands have a market value in excess of $4.5 billion a year.

Fertile fields line the San Juan River in New Mexico, one of many areas brought to life by Hoover Dam and the Boulder Canyon Project.

Multipurpose Projects. Originally, most of the agency's projects were relatively small ones. Their prime purpose, and usually their only one, was to gather and distribute the water necessary to reclaim parched lands. Many of the present-day projects still fit within that general description.

Since the 1930's, however, Congress has approved the construction of several multipurpose projects. These huge undertakings, with their gigantic dams, now dot the West. They do perform the traditional reclamation function—but they provide for many other things, as well. Their "other" major functions regularly include hydroelectric power generation, flood and erosion control, municipal and industrial water supply, and the provision of recreation sites.

Many of these projects, and their mammoth dams, reservoirs, canals, tunnels, and power plants, are truly "seventh wonders." Among the many of them are Hoover

Dam, which tamed the mighty Colorado River; the All-American Canal, which runs through the shifting sands along California's Mexican border; the Alva B. Adams Tunnel, which pierces the Continental Divide in Colorado; and Grand Coulee Dam, which houses the world's largest hydroelectric generators in Eastern Washington.

The National Park Service

The National Park Service was created in 1916 to promote and regulate the use of national parks and monuments. The various programs carried on by the Service stem primarily from the responsibility to provide areas for public recreation and to give protection to the nation's natural and historic resources.

The National Park System now contains some 320 parks, historic sites, memorials, monuments, recreation areas, and other properties of historic and archaeological significance. The Service oversees incalculably valuable lands which embrace some of the most breathtaking scenic beauty in the world.

Its 12-million-hectare (30-million-acre) domain stretches from the gleaming beaches and undersea splendors of the Virgin Islands to flamethrowing volcanoes in Hawaii. It soars as high as Alaska's 6197-meter (20,320-foot) Mt. McKinley and drops as low as Oregon's 600-meter (1966-foot) deep Crater lake. It includes many other towering peaks, massive glaciers, lakes, sand dunes, seashores, and deserts, giant sequoias over 3500 years old, cascading waterfalls and geysers, and caves and petrified forests.

These natural splendors are like magnets pulling American and foreign visitors. Each year now tourists, campers, hikers, skiers, canoeists, naturalists, and many others pay some 300 million visits to the national playgrounds maintained for their use and pleasure by the Park Service.

Government and the Environment / **603**

The Geological Survey

In 1879 Congress created a still little-known agency, the Geological Survey. It develops and publishes geographic and geologic facts for public use. It has made topographic and geologic maps which now cover over half of the country. Because of them, we know the heights of mountains, the volume of water which flows in streams, the areas where valuable minerals are most likely to be found beneath the surface, and a great many other vital and useful facts.

The Survey's varied work can best be described with a few illustrations. In World War II the Japanese launched some 9000 bomb-laden balloons intended to drift to our Pacific Coast to ignite forest fires. Examining only four cups of ballast, the Survey was able to pinpoint the tiny strip of beach southeast of Tokyo from which the balloons were being sent aloft. The Air Force then destroyed the launching sites.

A Survey research project found usable quantities of uranium in phosphate rock in Florida. From maps developed by the Survey, a mining company discovered zinc deposits worth $100 million in Tennessee. From its glacial maps, building contractors are able to find great stores of excellent sands and gravels, and well drillers are able to locate waters trapped in glacial rubble. Over and over again, the Survey's work has led to rich oil discoveries and other important finds. No wonder its scientists are called "Uncle Sam's treasure hunters."

The Fish and Wildlife Service

The Fish and Wildlife Service is the direct descendant of the oldest of all federal conservation agencies. It traces its ancestry back to the Bureau of Fisheries, created by Congress in 1871.

Today the Service is charged with conserving, restoring, and increasing the na-tion's fish and wildlife resources and with promoting their more effective use. It works closely with other federal and similar State agencies and with private organizations in the forestry, agriculture, and recreation fields.

The range of the Service's activities are quite broad. Currently, it operates 88 fish hatcheries on the coastal and inland waters and plants millions of eggs and fingerlings each year. It maintains 398 wildlife refuges on more than 13.7 million hectares (34 million acres and 13 major fish and wildlife research centers. Its research findings on the lives and habits of all manner of fish and game are quite valuable to conservationists, hunters, commercial concerns, and many others.

The Bureau of Indian Affairs

The Bureau of Indian Affairs was first established in 1824 as a part of the old War Department and was shifted to the Department of the Interior when that latter Department was created in 1849.

Our Indian policy has developed by fits and starts, and many of its pages are none too glorious. At first, the National Government treated the Indian tribes much as foreign nations and attempted to deal with them by treaty. As the nation moved westward and the Indians were pushed from their ancestral homes, remote lands were set aside as "reservations"—lands often barren and ill-suited to the Indians' way of life. Many of the treaties were violated by the thoughtlessness and greed of white people. Even the Congress, at times, broke the agreements.

By 1871 Congress stopped making treaties with the various tribes, and our policy soon became one of attempting to school the Indian to take a full and complete place in the general population. But sad experience proved this to be the wrong approach. For example, lands were allotted to individual Indians as private holdings. Most of these grants were soon squandered or lost to unscrupulous whites. In general, long years of neglect, mistreatment, and dishonesty by white people left the Indians ill-equipped to deal with white society.

Our Indian policy changed abruptly in 1933. Instead of trying to break down the tribal relationships and wipe out the distinctions between Indians and other people, the policy became one of developing the Indians within the framework of their own particular cultures and their own distinctive way of life.

Many Indians have bridged the gap between their own culture and the broader society. Large numbers live in tribal communities, but Indians in increasing numbers became urban dwellers during the 1960's.

Contrary to the trend of earlier years, our Indian population is growing rapidly today. Today there are more than 900,000 Indians in the United States.[5] Of these, the majority receive special services from the Government, and about 550,000 of them live on some 260 reservations, mostly in the Western States.

The Bureau has two major responsibilities in its work with the Indians: (1) assisting and encouraging the Indians in the wise and efficient use of their lands and resources, and (2) providing public services in education, public health, welfare, and community development.

In 1953 Congress declared that the Bureau should seek to end the Indians' status as wards of the government as rapidly as possible. Even with inadequate funds, much progress by the Bureau has been made in that direction. Significant work has been done in the field of education, particularly. Thus, just since the early

1950's the percentage of the number of Indians between ages six and eighteen attending school has jumped from 75 to 95 percent. Dormitories have been built or leased in communities near reservations to house Indian children so that they might attend the local public schools. Federal funds have been granted to local school districts to defray the increased costs involved. Suitable buildings have been converted into schools. Even trailer schools have been provided in sparsely populated areas. Some tribes have established scholarship programs to aid Indians who want to go on to college. An adult education program concentrating on English and basic arithmetic has been started; so has a vocational education program. The Federal Government's efforts at providing Indians with opportunities for educational advancement have been noteworthy. But the reality is that Indians in this country generally receive educational services of a comparatively inferior quality. Like other minority groups, they still struggle to realize the ideal of equal opportunity.

The Bureau works for the Indian in many other ways. For example, it is encouraging industries to locate near reservations, and it shares the costs of training unskilled Indians. It also helps Indians in urban areas to find jobs.

Still, with all of its efforts, the Indians' lot remains a far from happy one. This is especially true for those "Native Americans" who live on the reservations. After a lengthy, exhaustive survey of the Bureau's work in 1966, the Senate Interior Committee declared that "Indians remain at the bottom of the economic ladder, have the highest rate of unemployment, and suffer chronic poverty." It directed the Bureau to redouble its efforts in order that Indians may soon "take their long-awaited, rightful place in our national life." There have been any number of other public and private reports and exhortations. But, despite them, it seems abundantly clear that two

---

[5] The Bureau estimates that approximately one million Indians lived in what is now the United States when Columbus discovered America in 1492. By the late 1800's their number had dwindled to less than 250,000.

The director of a bilingual program (at far right) at San Juan, Mexico, explains some features of a class project model of San Juan Pueblo. At the chalkboard, a Tewa teacher works with a student in the language of that Indian tribe, as well as in English.

chief lacks—one of public concern and the other of public funding—lie close to the heart of the nation's continuing "Indian problem."

Other Interior Agencies

The Bureau of Mines, created in 1910, is now essentially a research and factfinding unit. It was, for several decades, one of the major resources conservation and development agencies. Many of its former functions have been transferred elsewhere in recent years, however. Thus, its once extensive research and development work in the field of energy resources is now the responsibility of the Department of Energy, and its early concerns with air pollution are within the province of the Environmental Protection Agency.

Still, its work remains vitally important. Most of its studies relate to the extraction, processing, use, and recycling of the nation's mineral resources. Some appreciation of the value of that work can be had from this mind-boggling fact: It now takes *20 tons* of mineral commodities—of stone, metals, coal, petroleum, and natural gas—to sustain each person in the United States each year.

The Office of Surface Mining Reclamation and Enforcement was established by Congress in 1977. It has the twin goals of protecting the nation's environment from the often harmful effects of coal mining operations while ensuring an adequate supply of coal to meet the nation's energy needs. It is charged with establishing minimum standards for regulating the surface effects of mining, assisting the States in developing and implementing regulatory programs, and promoting the reclamation of mined-over areas. Congress has given the Office inspection and investigative powers; it can levy penalties upon those who fail to adhere to its rules and regulations.

The Office of Water Research and Technology seeks to find new and improved approaches to the solution of the nation's many water resources problems. Much of its work involves grant and contract relationships with other research oriented agencies. Especially involved are the Water

Resources Research Institutes which have been established by several major State universities across the country.

The OWRT's own and promising efforts to find a practical and economical method of converting saline (salt) into usable fresh water are of major importance. It now operates test facilities in the search for such a process in several places, including Freeport, Texas; San Diego, California; Webster, South Dakota; Roswell, New Mexico; and Wrightsville Beach, North Carolina. If and when its efforts are successful, the benefits that will be realized literally defy the imagination.

The Office of Territorial Affairs is charged with promoting the interests of the nation's territories and other possessions; see page 488.

The Tennessee Valley Authority

The Tennessee Valley Authority, created in 1933, is a major independent agency. It grew out of a World War I project—Wilson Dam, at Muscle Shoals on the Tennessee River in Alabama. The dam had been built to provide electric power for the manufacture of explosives from rich nitrate and phosphate deposits.

The disposition of the project was the subject of stormy debate throughout the 1920's. Many proposed that its dam, two nitrate plants, and other facilities be sold to private interests. And at one point it nearly was, to Henry Ford. But others, led by Senator George Norris (R., Nebraska) urged that it be transformed into a huge multipurpose program for the entire Tennessee River Valley. Bills to begin such a plan were vetoed by both Presidents Calvin Coolidge and Herbert Hoover, however.

Finally, in 1933, Congress passed and President Franklin Roosevelt signed the Tennessee Valley Authority Act. That statute provided for the "orderly and proper physical, economic, and social development" of the Tennessee River Valley. It called for coordinated development and utilization of the natural resources of a huge geographic area—a region that today includes large parts of seven States: Tennessee, Kentucky, Virginia, North Carolina, Georgia, Alabama, and Mississippi.

TVA is headed by a three-member Board of Directors. The Directors are appointed by the President with Senate consent, each for a nine-year term. The agency's operations are supervised by a General Manager, chosen by and responsible to the Board. Its operations cover a broad range of activities. They include electric power development, flood control and navigation work, reforestation, soil conservation, fertilizer production, agricultural research and experiments, the development of recreational facilities, and the promotion of industrial growth in the Tennessee River Valley.

The Authority is organized as a *government corporation*—and it is a leading example of that form of federal agency, as we noted on page 425. Its financing comes principally from congressional appropriations; but a substantial amount of its funding is also generated by sales of electric power and fertilizer and from the agency's limited power to issue bonds.

TVA has had an extraordinary impact on the Valley and its now nearly four million residents. It has made the Tennessee River a navigable waterway from its mouth at Paducah, Kentucky, upstream some 1045 kilometers (650 miles) to Knoxville, Tennessee. Nine enormous dams span the mainstem of the river, and a series of power and storage dams dot its tributaries and the nearby Cumberland.

There has been no serious flooding in the Valley since the completion of the storage system, and the flood pressures on the Ohio and Mississippi Rivers have been reduced. Per capita income has risen dramatically with the advent of scientific farming and plentiful electric power. Much new industry has been attracted and sustained-yield forests now cover wide areas once denuded.

Measured by any standard, TVA is one of the major illustrations of government in business. And, for precisely that reason, it was for many years the subject of bitter opposition. The production and sale of electric energy, in direct competition with private industry, was—and for some still is—the most controversial of its many activities.

The constitutionality of the major elements of the TVA program were challenged early in its history. They were sustained by the Supreme Court in a landmark case, *Ashwander* v. *TVA*, in 1936. The Court held that Congress could authorize a federal agency to construct and operate multipurpose dam projects as a proper exercise of both the war and commerce powers. It sanctioned building transmission lines and the sale of electric power as a valid use of the congressional power, in Article IV, "to dispose of . . . the territory or other property belonging to the United States."

THE ENVIRONMENTAL PROTECTION AGENCY

Most of us have finally awakened to an absolutely compelling need. We know that we *must* repair the damages that we—and our vaunted industrial and technological progress—have done to our air, our land, and our water. The reminders of that need are at nearly every hand—in the smog-laden skies over many of our cities, in lakes and streams clogged with human and industrial waste, on fouled beaches, on once forested hillsides now barren, in once fertile pastures now eroded, and in many other places.

The Federal Government's efforts to redress our environmental sins are now centered in the Environmental Protection Agency. EPA is an independent unit in the executive branch. It is headed by an Administrator appointed by the President with Senate consent. Before its creation in 1970, at least 40 other federal agencies were involved with the problems of air, water, and solid waste pollution.

EPA works closely with the Council on Environmental Quality, in the Executive Office of the President. As we noted on page 393, the Council is the President's chief source of advice and information in all matters relating to the nation's environmental policies.

EPA describes its basic mission in these terms:

> . . . to control and abate pollution in the areas of air, water, solid waste, pesticides, noise, and radiation. . . . In all, EPA is designed to serve as the public's advocate for a livable environment.

While it has certainly not ignored pesticides, noise, and radiation, most of EPA's work has so far related to water, air, and solid waste pollution.

Water Pollution. The first expression of federal concern for the environment came in the Refuse Control Act of 1899. Although it lay dormant until 1970, that law did prohibit unlicensed dumping of pollutants into interstate waterways; and it stipulated a $2500 fine and/or a jail sentence for each offense.

More recent laws have taken another tack—notably, the Water Pollution Control Act of 1956 and the Clean Water Restoration Act of 1966. With their later amendments, they provide for comprehensive programs of water quality control on all navigable waterways. They also authorize sizable federal grants for the construction and upgrading of local sewage treatment systems.

The Water Quality Improvement Act

of 1970 forbids the discharge of harmful amounts of oil or other hazardous materials into navigable waters—from any source, including ships, onshore refineries, and offshore drilling platforms.

The Marine Protection, Research, and Sanctuaries Act of 1972 regulates the dumping of industrial and municipal wastes at sea. And the Safe Drinking Water Act of 1974 provides for minimum standards for the nation's drinking water.

EPA enforces each of these statutes and conducts the extensive research programs they authorize.

Air Pollution. Federal efforts to combat air pollution began, modestly, in the Federal Air Pollution Control Act of 1955. It authorized the Public Health Service to undertake a research program and offer technical advice to those State and local governments concerned about the problems of air quality.

Congress moved somewhat more boldly in the next several years—especially in the Clean Air Act of 1963 and the Air Quality Control Act of 1967. Those laws established several federal-State-local research and control programs. The 1967 law provided for the identification of those regions of the country with real or potentially serious problems of air contamination. It required the States to develop air quality standards for the designated regions and adopt acceptable plans for their enforcement.

These statutes, and the State and local efforts they sparked, focused public attention on the growing problems of air pollution. And, significantly, they paved the way for the passage of the historic Clean Air Act Amendments of 1970.

That 1970 law, with its later amendments, is the basic air pollution law today. It called for the establishing of national air quality standards for all major air pollutants. EPA has done so for several of them—including carbon monoxide, sulphur and nitrogen oxides, hydrocarbons,

particulates (such as dust and smoke), and photochemical oxides. The latter is the technical term for smog, the eye-stinging haze that often hangs over many cities. It is produced when nitrogen oxides combine with hydrocarbons in the presence of sunlight.

The law also required EPA to set emission standards for new motor vehicles and for such stationary sources as power plants, municipal incinerators, and industrial factories.

Each State is obligated to develop a specific program to achieve and maintain the clean air standards set by EPA. If a State fails to adopt, or enforce, one, EPA may then do so in its behalf.

The 1970 law, and several others, direct EPA to conduct extensive research into all phases of air pollution, including its effects upon health.

Automobile and other motor vehicle exhaust emissions are regularly blamed for more than half of all air contamination. The 1970 law required that by 1975 all new cars sold in this country emit approximately 90 percent fewer pollutants than did 1970 models. But Congress has several times relaxed the standards and backed away from the timetable it set in that law. It has for two major reasons: the economic and technical problems involved *and* the political influence of the automobile manufacturers and of the United Auto Workers. The statutory deadline for the attainment of the goals first set for 1975 has now been pushed into the 1980's.

Solid Waste. EPA estimates that our "throw-away" society now generates an astounding 4.5 billion tons of solid waste each year. That almost incomprehensible bulk includes 48 billion cans, 26 billion bottles and jars, seven million cars and trucks, seven million television sets, four million tons of plastic, and 30 million tons of paper. It puts the national trash bill at something over $5 billion a year.

For decades the most convenient means

of waste disposal seemed to be open dumping. But burning at most dumps fouls the air; and about half of all dumps are so situated that their drainage aggravates local water pollution. Then, too, open dumps attract rodents, flies, and many other such pests.

Many communities have now turned to "sanitary landfills"—dumps in which new trash deposits are regularly covered with layers of dirt. Once filled, these sites can be converted to other uses. But few of them have been designed to prevent seepage and, then, water pollution.

The Solid Waste Disposal Act of 1965 was the first significant indication of federal interest in the field. It directed HEW to research the problems of waste collection and disposal.

The Resource Recovery Act of 1970 emphasized recycling and the recovery of valuable waste materials. EPA has undertaken several experimental and demonstration projects under that law.

The Resource Conservation and Recovery Act of 1976 is now the major federal solid waste management law. It provides for substantial federal grants to aid State and local governments to plan and carry out disposal programs. All of the nation's open dumps are to be phased out over a five-year period, and it bans them entirely by 1983.

The 1976 law also orders EPA to set standards for the handling of hazardous wastes—which it defines as any waste that "because of its quantity, concentration, or physical, chemical or infectious characteristics" poses a threat to either health or the environment. The States must establish rules for the treatment, storage, and disposal of those materials. If a State fails to do so, the Environmental Protection Agency's own regulations then apply.

The antipollution efforts of recent years have accomplished much. But far more remains to be done. And several factors work to hinder the ongoing efforts: Many

pollution problems can be met only with very close federal-State-local cooperation. Many sources of pollution are privately owned. Many industrial and other polluters resist controls, calling them unnecessary, unreasonable, or too costly. Serious problems are often occasioned by the need to control pollution and conflicting demands for energy. And, finally, there are continuing pockets of public apathy and an oft-found attitude that clean-up is fine, but in the other fellow's backyard.

© 1979 by Herblock
in The Washington Post

*"IT FELL TO EARTH
I KNEW NOT WHERE"*

THE DEPARTMENT OF AGRICULTURE

The more than eight million Americans who live on the nation's 2.3 million farms grow the food upon which all of us must depend. And they produce food vital to millions elsewhere in the world and a goodly share of the raw materials which are essential to the nation's manufacturing industries.

We began our history as an agricultural people. For 300 years, from the very first of the settlements along the Atlantic seaboard until the dawn of the present century, *the* dominant theme in American history was westward agricultural expansion. The First Census in 1790 reflected the fact that 95 percent of the 3,929,214 persons who then lived in the United States lived in rural areas. Nearly all of them lived on farms. In fact, until about 1910, agriculture was the way of life for a majority of all the nation's people.

Governmental concern for agriculture dates from our earliest history. In 1622 James I promoted—though an unsuccessful venture—the growing of mulberry trees and the breeding of silkworms in the colonies. Parliament and the colonial legislatures also subsidized other farm products on various occasions. As early as 1776, the Second Continental Congress considered measures to aid agriculture. In his last annual message to Congress in 1796 President Washington urged the creation of boards of agriculture to provide information for farmers.

It was not until 1839, however, that Congress began to develop the present Department of Agriculture. In that year it appropriated $1000 to be used "to distribute seeds, conduct agricultural investigations, and collect agricultural statistics." A single clerk in the Patent Office administered the program. Then, in the period of a few short months in 1862, Congress passed three acts of lasting importance to farmers: (1) the act creating a Department of Agriculture (though not of Cabinet rank), (2) the Homestead Act, which made grants of 160-acre plots to people who would settle on and develop that land, and (3) the Morrill Act which made grants of land to the States to establish colleges of agriculture and mechanical arts.

From 1862 to 1889 the Department of Agriculture was administered by a Commissioner of Agriculture. Then in 1889 Congress enlarged the powers and duties of the Department. It was raised to Cabinet rank, and the Commissioner became the Secretary of Agriculture.

The Secretary directs the work of the more than 85,000 men and women who staff the several agencies of the Department. The major functions of the USDA may be grouped under four broad headings, those of: (1) research and education, (2) conservation and rural development, (3) marketing, and (4) crop stabilization and credit.

Research and Education Activities

The Science and Education Administration. The Department of Agriculture is heavily involved in both scientific research and in education—and it has been for decades. Today much of its work in those fields is centered in its Science and Education Administration.

The Administration is the present-day descendant of a long line of similar USDA agencies. And it would be well-nigh impossible to exaggerate their importance over time. Their dedicated scientists and other personnel have contributed much, and often, to the development of American agriculture—and so, in turn, to the general well-being of all of the rest of us in the United States.

To perform its work, The Science and Education Administration is organized into six major units. And a brief look at each of them demonstrates both the scope and the importance of that work.[6]

The *Agricultural Research* staff is one of those major units; and the scope of its work is broad, indeed. It conducts basic, applied, and developmental research in several fields: in animal and plant production; the use and improvement of soil, water, and air; the processing, storage, and distribution of farm products; food safety; and consumer services.

Much of the staff's work is carried on at the huge Agricultural Research Center at Beltsville, Maryland. It also operates some 140 other field locations—many in cooperation with State agricultural experiment stations, other federal agencies, and private organizations.

The *Human Nutrition Center* staff is chiefly concerned with foodstuffs. Its laboratory and field projects focus on several major areas. They include: human nutritional requirements; the nutrient composition of foods; and the effects that farming practices, handling, processing, and cooking have on foods and on their nutritional contents.

The *Cooperative Research* staff makes grants to support research in nearly all phases of agriculture. Its funds go to State agricultural experiment stations, land-grant institutions, and to various other State agencies. Its functions date back to 1888, when the Congress established an experiment station at each of the land-

grant colleges.[7] Today these stations exist in all 50 States, and they conduct thousands of experiments each year. Their findings are made available to farmers and to others in an ever-growing list of very useful bulletins.

The *The Higher Education* staff administers grants to promote education in the food and agricultural sciences at the college level throughout the country. It also makes grants to help the States establish schools of veterinary medicine.

The *Technical Information Systems* staff operates the prestigious National Agricultural Library, the largest storehouse of knowledge of its kind in the world. Its more than 1.5 million volumes and thousands of monographs and other pieces cover the field of agriculture, ranging through all of the natural sciences as well as blanketing agriculture in general.

The *Extension* staff is the USDA's half of a federal-State partnership in agricultural education. Together with each State's land-grant institution and nearly all county governments, it forms the Cooperative Extension Service. Ever since 1914, the Service has brought "beyond-the-classroom" education in agriculture to the public at large and especially to those who live in rural areas. It works through hundreds of specialists at state land-grant institutions and thousands of county extension agents, home demonstration agents, and 4-H Club agents.

Conservation and Rural Development Activities

The Department of the Interior is primarily responsible for the conservation of the na-

---

[6] SEA refers to each of these major elements in its organization as a "staff." And this use of that word provides a prime example of a point made in Chapter 17, where we considered the basic structure of the executive branch. To see the point, look again at the discussion of the "name game" on page 416 and of *staff* and *line* agencies and functions on page 418.

[7] The land-grant colleges are those State colleges and universities established as a result of the Morrill Act of 1862. This and later acts of Congress provided for the granting of land (altogether nearly 11 million acres, much of it very valuable) to the States for the establishing and maintaining of colleges to teach "without excluding other scientific and classical studies and including military tactics . . . such branches of learning as are related to agriculture and the mechanical arts."

A dust storm in Oklahoma in 1936, a State severely stricken by such storms in the 1930's. Loss of valuable topsoil through wind erosion prompted a massive tree-planting program to curtail such losses.

tion's natural resources. By improving farm products, promoting better farming methods, and in its other related work, the USDA also helps to conserve those resources. Two of the Department's major agencies—the Forest Service and the Soil Conservation Service—are directly engaged in the traditional field of conservation. The forest, water, range, and soil resources of the United States are foundation blocks in the nation's economic structure. From them come our food, the bulk of our municipal, industrial, and agricultural water supplies, most of our clothing, paper, and other fibers, much of our shelter, and a large part of the public's opportunities for outdoor recreation. How well these resources are protected and improved has a direct bearing on the income and the standard of living enjoyed by all Americans.

The impact of conservation measures have a direct bearing, as well, on the beauty of the environment in which we live.

The Forest Service. No one need be told of the importance of the forests and of wood products to our way of living. Our forests provide natural cover for wildlife. They act as great natural reservoirs to collect rainfall and, by releasing it gradually, help to prevent floods and droughts. Forests also help to hold the soil against erosion.

Over two-fifths of what is now the United States was once covered by forests. Much of this natural wealth, however, has disappeared through the clearing of farmlands and the cutting of timber for fuel and construction. Outright carelessness has also destroyed much of it.

In the early years of this century, the Congress authorized the setting aside of certain timberlands as national forests. The Forest Service administers the 154 national forests which now cover more than 76 million hectares (188 million acres) in 41 States and Puerto Rico. Its rangers are charged with promoting the conservation and best use of our forest lands.

The Forest Service provides fire protection, disease control, and recreational facilities in our public timberlands.

The forests are under careful management for the permanent production and use of their timber, water, forage, wildlife, and recreational resources. The Forest Service scientifically regulates livestock grazing on its lands, and it also controls the exploitation of minerals the lands may contain. New trees are constantly planted. Selective logging is practiced to clear out mature trees which would otherwise decay and to promote the growth of younger trees. Several experiment stations and laboratories maintained by the Service conduct continuing studies of all phases of forestry.

The Soil Conservation Service. Wasteful land-use practices have caused erosion which has ruined some 120 million hectares (300 million acres) of land in the nation, or an area twice the size of Texas. In earlier days farmlands in many parts of the East were "mined out." So long as new, fertile lands could be had to the west, no one seemed to be concerned about "over-cropping" and erosion. Once the good lands in the West had been taken up, however, the problems of proper soil care could no longer be ignored.

For many years the Department of Agriculture has attempted to promote soil conservation by educating the farmer in soil-saving practices. In 1935 the Soil Conservation Service was created to assist farmers and ranchers in soil conservation. Its principal duty is to assist farmers in locally organized and locally directed soil conservation districts. There are now some 3000 districts in the 50 States, Puerto Rico, and the Virgin Islands. They include 96 percent of the nation's farms and over 93 percent of its farmlands.

The SCS also administers the paying of subsidies to farmers and ranchers who will undertake supervised soil conservation projects under a broad federal-State program. Soil conservation scientists have helped over 2 million farmers and ranchers, with holdings of more than 810 million hectares (2 billion acres) plan and put into operation their own projects.

Soil abuse today is due mostly to old-fashioned methods of "square farming." Plowing in straight rows uphill and downhill has produced *sheet erosion*. In this kind of erosion, the top layer of soil is skimmed off the land and *gullies* are formed that eat away the earth in big chunks, leaving worthless subsoil. Other abuses include one-crop farming which exhausts and ruins the soil, *overgrazing* which destroys the grass and causes erosion, and the *wasteful use* of forests and woodlands.

AIR-CONDITIONING THE DUST BOWL. In the drought-ridden year of 1934, President Franklin D. Roosevelt promoted a program to plant some 300 million trees from the Canadian border to Texas to salvage the Dust Bowl area of the country. Some 40,000 windbreaks, each with about twenty rows of trees, some of them as high as a house, now cover this area. The original plantings were made by the Forest Service, but they are now managed by local farmers in soil conservation districts. The stately string of trees stands as a growing monument to an idea which was once a target of a barrage of doubts and jokes.

These windbreaks help to "condition" the air by slowing down the winds which blew thousands of tons of topsoil halfway across the continent in the early 1930's. Valuable topsoil and moisture are now held in place. The danger of uncontrollable prairie fires is lessened and insect-eating birds like pheasant and quail are again plentiful. The planting continues, and the trees are cheap, coming very largely as a gift from the National Government and the States.

The Rural Electrification Administration. When the REA was created in 1935, only 10 percent of all farms in the United States were receiving electricity. Today, 98 percent of the nation's farms are electrified. Private power companies have expanded their service in rural areas. Even so, more than half of the farms which today have electricity have it because of the REA.

The REA administers loan programs for two general purposes: rural electrification and rural telephone service. Electrification loans are made to provide electric distribution, transmission, and generation facilities in order to bring or improve service in rural areas. Some short-term loans are also made to finance wiring and the purchase of electrical and plumbing appliances. These loans are made in order to bring some of the taken-for-granted comforts of city living to our rural population.

More than 1000 REA-financed power systems, with some 3 million kilometers

Case Study

Early in the twentieth century, President Theodore Roosevelt spoke eloquently about the nation's resources:

We are prone to speak of the resources of this country as inexhaustible: this is not so . . .

All of the great natural resources which are vital to the welfare of the whole people should be kept either in the hands or under the full control of the whole people. This applies to coal, oil, timber, water power, natural gas. Either natural resources of this land should be kept in the hands of the people and their development and use allowed under leasing arrangements (or otherwise); or, where this is not possible, there should be strict governmental control over their use. . . . The farmer is a good farmer who, having enabled the land to support himself and to provide for the education of his children, leaves it to them a little better than he found it himself. I believe the same thing of a nation.

In a nation that prided itself on free enterprise, this was a strong statement. The President called for federal control over vital resources that are so essential to national well-being. However, most did not heed Teddy's call for conservation. Too few really felt they had an obligation to leave the land "a little better than [they] found it."

■ What has been the price of the nation's reluctance to view its resources as something of value to be enjoyed by each succeeding generation?

■ Is it the function of government to place limitations on how people use valuable resources?

■ Do you perceive any potential for conflicts between those who regard themselves as "conservationists" and those who see themselves as "environmentalists" today?

(1.9 million miles) of line serving 8 million rural customers, are now in operation. By 1981 Congress had authorized the lending of close to $12 billion for the electrification program. And, Congress has provided that, in the making of loans under the program, preference must be given to public bodies and cooperatives.

REA loans to finance rural telephone service are made to telephone organizations, with preference going to existing companies and cooperatives. Unlike the electrification program, telephone borrowers are required to provide a portion of the investment themselves. By 1980 REA had made more than $3 billion in telephone loans and thus helped to bring new or better service to some 4 million rural subscribers. Thousands more are being added each month.

The interest rate on most REA loans is now 5 percent, and the loans may be repaid in installments over a period extending for as long as 35 years. The agency and

its work stand as one of the many examples of how government can help people to help themselves.

Farmers Home Administration. By the mid-depression year 1935, two-fifths of the nation's farmers had slipped from farm ownership to farm tenancy. Today only one in eight of our farmers is a tenant. The Farmers Home Administration helps to keep the independent farmer solvent and assists tenants to buy farms by extending credit to those farmers who cannot obtain loans at reasonable rates elsewhere.

Farm ownership loans are made for the purchase of a family-type farm, to improve or enlarge a farm in order to make it an efficient family-type unit, or for such other purposes as the construction or repair of buildings. They are also made for improvement; water, forestry, and fish resources development; and the refinancing of debts. These loans are made in amounts up to $300,000 and for as long as 40 years at 5 percent interest. The payments may be ar-

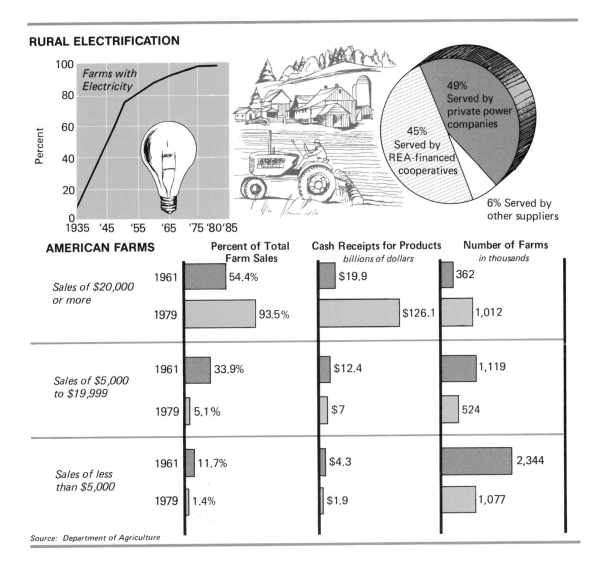

RURAL ELECTRIFICATION

Farms with Electricity

49% Served by private power companies

45% Served by REA-financed cooperatives

6% Served by other suppliers

AMERICAN FARMS

		Percent of Total Farm Sales	Cash Receipts for Products *billions of dollars*	Number of Farms *in thousands*
Sales of $20,000 or more	1961	54.4%	$19.9	362
	1979	93.5%	$126.1	1,012
Sales of $5,000 to $19,999	1961	33.9%	$12.4	1,119
	1979	5.1%	$7	524
Sales of less than $5,000	1961	11.7%	$4.3	2,344
	1979	1.4%	$1.9	1,077

Source: Department of Agriculture

ranged so that advance installments are paid in good years. In this way, the farmer is protected against falling behind in lean years.

Operating loans are made for the purchase of such things as livestock, seed, feed, equipment, and fertilizer. Not more than $100,000 will be lent to any one person. The interest rate is now about 8 percent; the repayment period can run as long as seven years.

Other loans are made to construct modest homes (especially for the elderly), to provide water facilities such as wells and pumps, and for such other purposes as disaster relief.[8] Practically all of the loans made by the agency are made with funds advanced by private lenders on an insured basis and from funds collected on loans previously made.

Marketing Activities

Farming is at best a risky business. One thing that makes it so is the weather. It is

___

[8] Another major farm loan agency, the Farm Credit Administration, operates independently of the USDA; see page 523.

Giant combines harvest ryegrass seed in Oregon's Willamette Valley. With such equipment, and when climate conditions are favorable, a single seed company has harvested more than 3,000 acres of grass seed. This seed is shipped throughout the nation and is used for millions of lawns, parks, and pastures.

often the farmer's friend, but the weather can be a mortal enemy, too. Too much sun, not enough sun, too much rain, not enough rain, too much wind can be a farmer's downfall. These and the other quirks of nature are natural hazards over which the farmer has no control. Another difficult factor is the market in which the farmer must deal—something, too, over which the farmer has little control.

As farming methods have improved, the annual output of farm products has naturally increased. When the supply of farm products exceeds the demand for them, the farmer suffers unless government steps in to take care of the surplus. As we shall see shortly, the National Government does step in to take care of a substantial amount of the annual farm surplus. It also provides aid to help farmers plan and market their crops to avoid surpluses.

The Agricultural Marketing Service. The Agricultural Marketing Service aids farmers in the orderly marketing and effective distribution of their products. The Service collects marketing information and releases regular up-to-the-minute reports on crop conditions, prices, and prospects at home and abroad. These releases are made available to the farmer in the press, by ra-

dio and television, and bulletins sent to farmers through the mail. Through such releases the farmer is able to learn the best marketing times and methods. The farmer is also able to plan ahead in selecting the best crops to plant.

The Food and Nutrition Service. The Food and Nutrition Service administers the USDA's several food assistance programs—most notably, the food stamp program and the school lunch program.

Under the food stamp program, the FNS, working through State and local welfare agencies, provides food stamps (actually coupons) to needy persons—to increase their food purchasing power and so enable them to feed their families properly. Eligibility for the coupons is based upon income. Those persons and families with net incomes at or below the official poverty line can secure them—in varying amounts, depending upon income and household size. These coupons may be used to buy food in any retail store which has been approved by the FNS.

Under the school lunch program, the FNS makes cash grants to both public and private schools to help them provide nonprofit school lunch programs. This arrangement is intended to make meals available to all students, and to serve meals free or at reduced rates to students from needy families.

The FNS conducts a number of other and similar programs. They include a school breakfast program and another which provides meals for children in day care centers in low income areas.

The Federal Crop Insurance Corporation. Some of the risks of farming are also reduced by the Federal Crop Insurance Corporation. The FCIC will insure farmers who raise several different crops[9] against losses from such causes as weather, insects, and diseases; but it will not protect farmers against the results of their own negligence or poor farming practices. Thus far, FCIC policies are available in just over one-half of the nation's agricultural counties, and the program is gradually being extended throughout the country. The costs of the indemnities paid out by the program are borne by the premiums paid by those who hold policies.[10]

The Foreign Agricultural Service. The Foreign Agricultural Service is constantly seeking new markets for our farm products abroad. With so much of the world hungry and in want, and with the productivity of our farms and farmers, the work of the Service can be of untold value in promoting friendships abroad and the cause of world peace.

Stabilizing Farm Prices

Following World War I there was a gradual decline in the general price level throughout the nation's economy. The decline in farm prices was much sharper than that in other fields. Wheat dropped from the wartime price of $2 a bushel to less than 40¢.

---

[9] Currently (1981), wheat, cotton, tobacco, corn, flax, dry beans, soybeans, barley, grain sorghums, oats, peanuts, peas, raisins, apples, sugarcane, grapes, rice, citrus fruit, peaches, tomatoes, sugar beets, sweet corn, forage, potatoes, and sunflowers.

[10] The independent Commodity Futures Trading Commission also works to safeguard the farmer's interests, especially in futures trading; see page 543.

Cotton skidded from 29¢ a pound in 1923 to less than 6¢ in 1933. Farmers found that their incomes were far below that of their city friends.

The First AAA, 1933. After trying several plans to rescue the farmer in the late 1920's, Congress passed the first Agricultural Adjustment Act in 1933. The act encouraged farmers to reduce production in order to force prices up. Those who did so were paid a subsidy out of funds collected by a processing tax levied on the commodities which were produced. Thus, a tax was levied on each bushel of wheat a miller processed. The proceeds went into a fund to pay farmers a subsidy for the wheat they did not grow.

The law met with considerable public opposition, but it did raise farm prices an average of more than 60 percent in three years. In 1936 the Supreme Court held the processing tax unconstitutional, however—in *United States* v. *Butler;* see page 494.

The Second AAA, 1938. After attempting for two years to accomplish crop reduction through payments under the soil conservation program, Congress enacted the second Agricultural Adjustment Act in 1938. Essentially, the new law provided what the first one had but without the processing tax.

It also provided for the "ever-normal granary." As Joseph in ancient Egypt stored up grain in years of plenty to use in years of famine, so the new law provided for storing surpluses against future shortages. The second AAA directed the *Commodity Credit Corporation* (CCC) to make loans to farmers to help them carry over their surpluses in government warehouses and elevators for sale in the short years.

War and the Farm Problem. World War II brought a sudden change in the nature of the farm problem. Instead of the need to *limit* farm production, it became necessary to expand it rapidly. Everything possible was done to increase the output of food products. The heavy demands of the

FARM PRICES AND COSTS

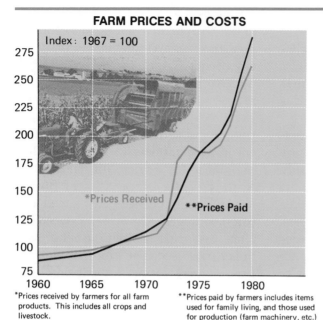

Index: 1967 = 100

*Prices Received

**Prices Paid

275
250
225
200
175
150
125
100
75

1960   1965   1970   1975   1980

*Prices received by farmers for all farm products. This includes all crops and livestock.

**Prices paid by farmers includes items used for family living, and those used for production (farm machinery, etc.)

FARMER'S SHARE OF THE CONSUMER'S FOOD DOLLAR

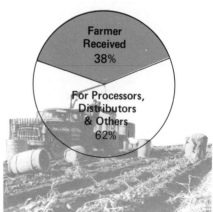

Farmer Received 38%

For Processors, Distributors & Others 62%

armed forces and the needs of millions abroad gave vital meaning to the wartime slogan "Food Is Ammunition."

A major shift in the price support program was made in 1942. To stimulate wartime production, Congress provided that farmers were to be guaranteed a minimum price for certain crops. That is, Congress inaugurated a program of *rigid price supports.* A floor was placed under the prices for certain crops. Thus, the farmer was to be guaranteed a minimum price for these crops no matter what the condition of the market might be. The Secretary of Agriculture was authorized to add crops to the list of supported commodities as the war effort demanded it.[11] The new support program was to continue for two years beyond the end of the war. Most farm prices stayed generally above the support level during the war. But the mere existence of supports encouraged expanded production. Farmers knew that no matter how much they produced they could sell their production, ei-

ther on the open market or to the Federal Government.

Postwar Development. With the expiration of the 1942 program, Congress provided for a system of *flexible price supports* in 1948. The Secretary of Agriculture was authorized to support basic crops at 60, 75, or 90 percent of parity, depending upon whether in a particular year the supply of a crop was unusually large, normal, or below normal. But the 1948 law proved immediately unpopular, especially among farmers. The presidential and congressional election of that year gave ample indication of the dissatisfaction. Congress then returned to the rigid price support program in 1949 with a statute setting the price support figure for most crops covered at a flat 90 percent of parity.

A flexible support policy was reintroduced in 1954 and has remained in effect since. Under the present law various crops are supported at from 65 to 90 percent of parity. The law provides that certain crops (the "basic crops") *must* be supported: corn, wheat, rice, barley, oats, rye, grain sorghums, tobacco, wool, cotton, peanuts,

---

[11] By the end of the war (1945), 165 different crops were on the support list.

tung nuts, mohair, honey, milk, and butterfat. Other items may be supported at the discretion of the Secretary of Agriculture.

PARITY. The support price guaranteed on a crop is figured in terms of *parity*. Parity means *equality*—and refers here to an equality between the purchasing power of farmers and that of city dwellers. Or, put another way, parity refers to a *ratio* between the prices farmers *receive* when they *sell* agricultural products and the prices they must *pay* when they *buy* nonagricultural items. Under the parity arrangement an attempt is made to ensure that the farmer's purchasing power today will be roughly comparable to the purchasing power of urban dwellers.

The parity price on a particular commodity is figured on the basis of some earlier period in which farmers enjoyed a favorable purchasing power. To illustrate, if during the earlier period the price of 142 liters (4 bushels) of wheat would buy a pair of shoes, then the parity price of wheat would be about the cost of the same pair of shoes on today's market. Until 1948 parity was figured on the base period 1909–1914, a period in which the farmer did hold a favorable position in purchasing power. In 1948 Congress provided that parity could be figured for each crop either on the "old" base period or on a "new" one: the 10 years immediately preceding the year in which the parity figure was being set. Since 1957, Congress has required the exclusive use of the "new" base period.

ACREAGE ALLOTMENTS. In order to prevent the depression of the prices of those crops under price support, the Federal Government also operates an acreage allotment program. It is administered by the *Agricultural Stabilization and Conservation Service*.

Each year the Service estimates the probable market demand for each support crop. The number of acres necessary to produce that amount is also determined.

This total acreage is then distributed among *(allotted to)* farmers. The actual allotment is done by a series of State and county farmer committees elected by the farmers themselves. Farmers are not *required* to observe their individual allotments, but those farmers who ignore their allotments can receive no support payments.

Congress modified the parity concept somewhat in the Agricultural Act of 1973. It did so with a system of "target prices" for cotton, wheat, and feed grains (and, in 1976, rice). For these commodities Congress now sets target prices—for example, for 1980, $3.40 a bushel for wheat, $2.20 a bushel for corn, and 51 cents a pound for cotton. These target prices are set below current market levels—but they are much higher than the prices farmers received for these crops before a sharp upward climb began in 1972. If market prices stay above the target prices, no subsidies are paid to those who produce these crops. But such payments will be made if and when oversupply again drags the market price below the target level.

Since 1973 Congress has imposed a ceiling on the amount of subsidy money any one farmer can receive for each of the price-supported crops that farmer raises—for 1981, $50,000.

MARKET QUOTAS. If, in spite of steps taken to prevent one, a surplus of a supported crop does occur, a *market quota* for that crop may be set. That is, a limit is set on the amount of the crop that may be sold. For this quota to go into effect, farmers producing this crop vote in a national referendum, with a two-thirds vote needed for approval. If rejected, no price supports are paid for that crop that year; if accepted, farmers who violate their quotas are subject to fines. Quotas are usually accepted by farmers in referendums by a comfortable margin.

CROP LOANS. If a farmer is unable to sell the allotted share of a crop at or above the parity level, the Commodity Credit Corporation will lend the farmer whatever the support price is on the crop. The CCC holds the crop as security for the loan.[12] If the market price rises above the support level, the farmer may sell the crop on the open market, repay the loan, and pocket the difference as his or her profit. If the price remains below the support level, the farmer lets the CCC have the crop.

THE "SURPLUS PROBLEM." The depression years of the 1930's saw a concerted effort to *restrict* farm production. The war years of the 1940's brought extraordinary demands to *increase* farm output. As a result, the price support program was not put to a real test in either period.

The return of more normal times, however—and the capacity of American farmers to overproduce—brought a major problem in the 1950's. Farm prices declined and government costs rose sharply as farmers became increasingly dependent on price supports rather than market forces to maintain their prices. Huge surpluses piled up in government storage facilities. By 1955 the CCC held commodities valued at

more than $4.5 billion; by 1960 that figure was over $6 billion.

Disposal of the surpluses posed tremendously difficult problems. If released to "flood the market" at home, prices would be depressed, forcing the Government to step in to shore them up. Selling them abroad could undermine world markets and seriously damage the economies of many other countries.

Even so, a substantial portion was used up in the 1960's—principally through such outlets as the school lunch program, aid to the needy and such public and private institutions as mental hospitals and juvenile homes, and disaster relief. Billions of dollars worth also went abroad through the "Food for Peace" program which channels surplus commodities overseas through direct sales, barter deals, famine relief, and other foreign assistance.

By the late 1970's, the CCC's holdings were down to minimal—virtually "cupboard bare"—levels. Our domestic needs, stimulated by prosperous times, and the importance of food as a weapon for peace in a hungry world, have transformed the "surplus problem" of the 1950's and early 1960's. Now, American agriculture is once again being asked to increase the production of many farm items.

---

[12] The CCC actually performs most of its functions through the staff and facilities of the Agricultural Stabilization and Conservation Service.

SUMMARY

For more than 300 years the vast natural wealth of America was used with little or no thought for the future. Today, however, the nation realizes the absolute necessity for conservation and wise use of its natural resources. The Departments of Interior and Agriculture, as well as agencies associated with these departments, shape and manage national resources policy as they seek to preserve and enrich what remains of America's natural resources.

Most of the federal conservation agencies are within the Interior Department. Headed by the Secretary of the Interior, the Department was created in 1849. The Department's principal work is that of acting as custodian of the nation's natural resources.

The Bureau of Land Management supervises much of the public domain and mineral resources. It also has jurisdiction over the Outer Continental Shelf lands, rich in oil and other mineral resources. The Heritage Conservation and Recreation Service promotes the development of recreational lands and facilities and administers the Land and Water Conservation Fund and National Scenic Rivers and National Trails Systems.

The Water and Power Resources Service is responsible for the reclaiming of arid lands, irrigation, and many of the huge multi-purpose dam projects.

The National Park Service has charge of the national parks and monuments and of other sites of national and historical interest. The Geological Survey develops and publishes facts about the geographic and geologic nature of the United States. The Bureau of Mines is concerned with the conservation and use of our mineral and fuel resources and with mine safety.

The Fish and Wildlife Service works to conserve, restore, and promote the more efficient use of those resources. The Bureau of Indian Affairs has primary responsibility for the welfare of Indians still living on reservations. A number of lesser agencies in the Department perform a wide range of tasks. The huge Tennessee Valley Authority, an independent agency, is responsible for the development of the physical, economic, and social resources of the Tennessee River Valley.

Agriculture is a, and perhaps *the*, basic industry in the United States. We began our history as an agricultural people, and agriculture has played a primary role throughout the nation's development. Although the Department of Agriculture did not achieve Cabinet status until 1889, governmental concern for agriculture dates back to the early colonial period.

The USDA's functions may be grouped under four broad headings: (1) research and education, conducted mainly through the Science and Education Administration (2) conservation and rural development activities, conducted through the Forest Service, the Soil Conservation Service, the Rural Electrification Administration, and the Farmers Home Administration; (3) marketing activities, conducted mostly through the Agricultural Marketing Service and the Food and Nutrition Service; and (4) crop stabilization and credit, conducted chiefly through the Agricultural Stabilization and Conservation Service and the Commodity Credit Corporation.

Since the 1920's the Federal Government has made determined efforts to raise the agricultural price level and to stabilize it at a relatively high point. Today those efforts center on parity price supports, acreage allotments, market quotas, and crop loans. These policies produced a huge surplus of several commodities, but that problem is now very largely a thing of the past.

Concept Development

Questions for Review

1. What is meant by "conservation"?

2. Under which President did the modern conservation movement begin?

3. When was the Department of the Interior created? What was the general nature of its original role?

4. What is the general nature of the Interior Department's role today?

5. For what major purposes was a huge portion of the public domain disposed of?

6. Where are most of the nation's public lands now located?

7. Why is the "tidelands controversy" misnamed? Why is ownership and control of the lands involved of such importance?

8. What is a "multipurpose" dam?

9. What is the basic function of the National Park Service?

10. What is the basic function of the Geological Survey?

11. What was the nature of the abrupt change in Indian policy in 1933?

12. From what original project did TVA develop? What are its broad purposes and functions?

13. Why has TVA been a center of controversy from its beginnings?

14. What is the EPA's basic mission? Cite three factors which work to hinder ongoing antipollution efforts.

15. What are the four main kinds of USDA activities?

16. Which agency carries out most of the physical, biological, chemical, and engineering research work of the USDA?

17. Why might the USDA be described as a conservation agency?

18. What factor is responsible for nearly all forest fires?

19. The REA administers loan programs for what two general purposes?

20. In what ways does the government help farmers market their crops?

21. Why was it necessary for Congress to enact a *second* Agricultural Adjustment Act in 1938?

22. What prompted Congress to abandon almost immediately the flexible price support program it provided for in 1948?

23. Who determines what crops are to be supported under the price support program?

24. What fact prompts most affected farmers to vote for market quotas?

25. What was in large measure responsible for producing the "surplus problem" of the 1950's and early 1960's?

For Further Inquiry

1. How would you expand on this statement: "Conservation is the wise use of our natural resources, not the refusal to use them."

2. Does the reclamation of arid lands increase or decrease the value of other arid lands not irrigated? Why is the reclamation of land becoming increasingly important today?

3. We have about one-third of the world's known copper reserves but are using them at a rapid rate. We have huge reserves of many other underground resources, but some are in short supply and others may be in the near future. Our supply of high-grade iron ore is no longer abundant. We have little or no chromium, manganese, or nickel. Bauxite, from which aluminum comes, is relatively scarce. Our zinc supply is diminishing steadily. Lead is still relatively plentiful, but it, too, is being used rapidly. In what ways could we conserve our supplies of these important minerals?

4. Is it wise that on the one hand the USDA aids farmers to produce bigger and

better crops while at the same time helps farmers restrict the volume of farm goods flowing to the market?

5. Labor unions have been far more effective in seeking and winning higher wages and better working conditions for their members than farm organizations have been in securing higher incomes for farmers. Why do you think this has been so?

6. Figured on the basis of sales, less than one-half of all of the farm production in the United States is covered by price supports, and most farmers do *not* receive price support subsidies. The price support program tends to help the larger producers and does little for the small farmers. Should, then, the price support program be abolished?

Suggested Activities

1. Ask a representative of one or more of the agencies discussed in this chapter to speak to the class on the nature of the work of that agency.

2. Prepare as extensive a list as you can of illustrations of the work of agencies of the Department of the Interior in your locale.

3. Write a brief essay or editorial on the relationship between conservation and the nation's security.

4. Stage a debate or class forum on the topic: *Resolved,* That the National Government should sell its hydroelectric power projects to private interests; or: *Resolved,* That the National Government should sell or otherwise transfer its hydroelectric power projects to the States.

5. Stage a debate or class forum on the question: *Resolved,* That the Federal Government should abandon, as rapidly as possible, its various programs designed to subsidize American agriculture.

6. If there is an REA, Soil Conservation Service, Agricultural Stabilization and Conservation Service, or other USDA agency in your locale, make a study of its operations and prepare a report on it.

7. Invite a member or representative of a national farm organization (such as the Farm Bureau or the Grange) or a representative of a local farm-related business to speak to the class on the general subject of federal agricultural policy.

Suggested Reading

Crane, John (ed.), *Environment 79/80.* Dushkin, 1979.

Fraenkel, Richard, Hadwiger, Don, and Browne, William P., *American Agriculture and U.S. Foreign Policy.* Praeger, 1979.

Gill, Richard, *Economics & the Public Interest.* Goodyear, 4th ed., 1980.

Gordon, Sanford D. and Dawson, George G., *Introductory Economics.* Heath, 4th ed., 1980.

Halcrow, Harold G., *Economics of Agriculture.* McGraw-Hill, 1980.

Lecomber, Richard, *Economics of Natural Resources.* Halsted Press, 1979.

McKenzie, Richard, *Economic Issues in Public Policy.* McGraw-Hill, 1979.

Smithsonian Institution, *This Generous Land: The Smithsonian Book of the American Environment.* Norton, 1979.

Sprout, Harold and Margaret, *The Context of Environmental Politics.* University of Kentucky Press, 1979.

Water for the West: The Bureau of Reclamation: 1902–1977. Public Works Historical Society, 1979.

Also: Office of Communications, Department of Agriculture, Washington, D.C. 20250.

Office of Public Affairs, Environmental Protection Agency, Washington, D.C. 20460.

Office of Public Affairs, Department of the Interior, Washington, D.C. 20240.

Information Office, Council on Environmental Quality, Washington, D.C. 20006.

Government and Human Resources

If a free society cannot help the many who are poor, it cannot save the few who are rich.

JOHN F. KENNEDY

■ What does the phrase "social welfare" mean?

■ What is the proper scope of governmental concern for social welfare?

■ Which is the more important goal for public policy: a sound and productive national economy or a decent quality of life for all of the nation's people?

In a very fundamental sense, the people are a nation's most important resource. And, especially, its young people are its foremost asset.

Most Americans would agree to this definition of the good society: one in which all are properly fed, adequately clothed, and comfortably sheltered; in which the health and safety of all are properly protected; and in which all are afforded the opportunity for a good education, the chance to earn a decent living and to live happy and productive lives, and the prospect of reasonable security in old age.

There is not now, nor has there ever been, such a society. But we have come closer to the creation of such a society—for at least the major share of our population—than has any other people on earth.

Today most Americans would also agree that it is a proper function of government to help to create such a society. We have come to recognize both the need for and the desirability of governmental responsibility for social welfare.

In earlier days, the States, and especially their local governments—and even before them, the colonies—did make some provision for the unfortunates in society. The "relief" they provided was quite limited, however. Mostly, it came in such forms as poor farms, almshouses, and orphanages.

Quite commonly, the problems of the poor, the sick, and the aged, the blind, the crippled, and the retarded, were looked upon as private matters. They were viewed as essentially the concern of the family and the church and other private charity. Education, the prevention of disease, and similar matters were looked upon in much the same light.

The picture is radically different today, of course. The States and the Federal Government spend literally billions of dollars each year on a host of social welfare programs. Over the past four decades or so—since the Great Depression of the 1930's—what amounts to a "national welfare system" has been created. In large part, it is based on a complex mixture of federal, State, and local governmental activity.[1] But it seems accurate to emphasize its *national* character—for the nation's welfare system is conducted largely under the leadership of *national* agencies in accord with policies and standards set at the *national* level and mostly at *national* expense.

In this chapter we shall look at that national welfare system—at programs of social insurance and public assistance and at federal activities in the fields of health and education. As we do so, bear this important point in mind. Most of us do live in fairly comfortable circumstances. We *do* have enough to eat; we *do* have sufficient clothing; we *do* live in clean and adequate homes; and so on. But there are some who do *not*—too many Americans who live in what has been called "the other America."[2] In the midst of plenty, too many are born and live in want and squalor. We

shall come back to them, and their plight, in a few pages.

Social Insurance

The passage of the *Social Security Act of 1935* highlighted the massive entry of the Federal Government into the field of public welfare in the 1930's.

The Great Depression, which began in 1929 and lasted for a decade, was a shattering national experience. Millions of persons—one of every four in the labor force—were thrown out of work, and millions more were impoverished. Hunger and poverty stalked the land. In 1929 there were some two million unemployed workers in the country. By 1933 the figure had leaped to 13.5 million. In 1935 there were some 18 million persons in this country—

A cartoonist depicts economic conditions during a Depression year, 1938.

ONE PERSON OUT OF EVERY TEN

Fitzpatrick in St. Louis Post-Dispatch

---

[1] The point here—the existence of a *federalized* welfare system—is demonstrated several times in this chapter, but we have encountered it before. For example, see the discussion of grants-in-aid on pages 89–90 and unemployment compensation on pages 584–585.

[2] This now oft-used phrase comes from the title of a forceful and graphic description of poverty in the United States in the 1960's: Michael Harrington's *The Other America* (New York: Macmillan, 1963). The book had a substantial impact on public thinking and policy in the period.

men, women, and children—wholly dependent upon emergency public relief programs; some 10 million workers had no employment other than that provided by temporary public projects.

Only a handful of States had made any provision to meet such a crisis; and those efforts, and the traditional private ones, soon proved to be pitifully inadequate. Almost overnight, need and poverty had become massive national problems.

The inauguration of Franklin D. Roosevelt as President in 1933 initiated the New Deal era. Almost at once Congress established temporary programs and appropriated billions of dollars for direct relief, and provided for dozens of public works projects intended to stimulate employment. These early steps to combat the nation's economic ills were stopgap in nature, however; they were intended to meet the immediate situation. What was clearly needed were permanent, long-range programs to help the country to right itself and to prevent such disasters in future years.

The *Social Security Act* was among the most important of the steps taken in that direction. The Act, which has been amended scores of times since 1935, created a number of different social welfare programs—including the unemployment compensation program (pages 584–585) and others we shall consider shortly. At its heart, however, the law created the *Old-Age and Survivors Insurance* plan (OASI)—or, as it has been called ever since its beginnings, "social security."

The original OASI program has been expanded a number of times over the past four decades. Today, it is the Old-Age, Survivors, and Disability Insurance program (OASDI)—reflecting the addition of a disability plan in 1956. And since 1965 it has also included a health care insurance program (Medicare), as well.

The Social Security Administration is responsible for OASDI. It manages the program from a huge headquarters complex in Baltimore and through some 1300 local offices around the country. Medicare is now run by the Health Care Financing Administration. Both of these agencies are major units within the Department of Health and Human Services.

OASDI. OASDI is a contributory insurance program. It is intended to provide a minimum income, a pension, to those persons who are covered by the program when they (1) retire or (2) become permanently disabled. It also provides benefits for the dependents of retired or disabled workers and for the dependents (survivors) of workers who die before or after retirement. In short, it is a program under which individuals make contributions during their working years to help build up a fund for their own protection and that of their families and survivors.

Coverage. Over the years, Congress has extended OASDI's coverage to virtually all employed persons—including the self-employed—in the United States.[3] For a few groups coverage is voluntary—the employees of State and local governments, for example. For most, however, inclusion within the system is mandatory. Some 120 million persons are expected to make OASDI contributions in 1981.

Financing. OASDI is financed by taxes levied on employees, their employers, and the self-employed. A major portion of the Medicare program is paid for in the same way.

To finance *both* programs, employees now (1981) pay a tax of 6.65 percent on the first $29,700 of their annual salary or wages (or a maximum of $1975.05 a year). Their employers pay a like tax—that is, an amount equal to that paid by each of their employees. The taxes levied on both employees and their employers are "payroll

---

[3] Federal civilian employees covered by the civil service retirement system (page 436) are the only sizable group of workers exempted today.

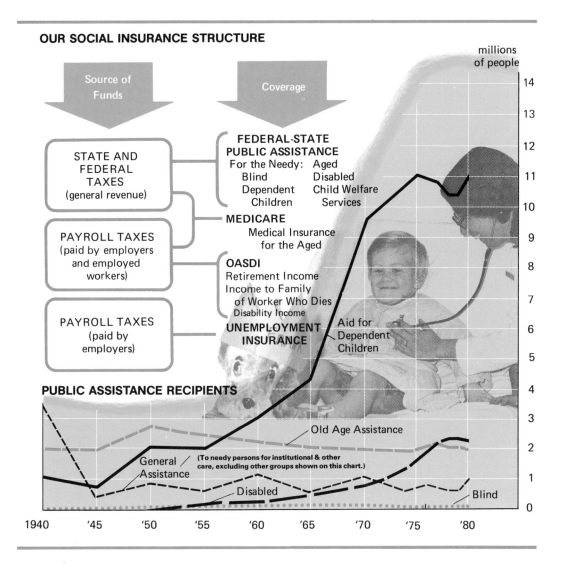

OUR SOCIAL INSURANCE STRUCTURE

millions of people

Source of Funds

Coverage

STATE AND FEDERAL TAXES (general revenue)

PAYROLL TAXES (paid by employers and employed workers)

PAYROLL TAXES (paid by employers)

FEDERAL-STATE PUBLIC ASSISTANCE
For the Needy: Aged
Blind   Disabled
Dependent   Child Welfare
Children   Services

MEDICARE
Medical Insurance for the Aged

OASDI
Retirement Income
Income to Family of Worker Who Dies
Disability Income

UNEMPLOYMENT INSURANCE

Aid for Dependent Children

PUBLIC ASSISTANCE RECIPIENTS

Old Age Assistance

General Assistance

(To needy persons for institutional & other care, excluding other groups shown on this chart.)

Disabled

Blind

1940   '45   '50   '55   '60   '65   '70   '75   '80

taxes" and are actually collected from employers. Self-employed persons now pay a tax of 9.3 percent on their annual income up to $29,700 (or as much as $2762.10 a year). [4]

The tax rates are fixed by Congress; and they are adjusted periodically, to meet the demands on the system. Thus, the current payroll taxes are now scheduled to go up sharply next year (1982)—to 6.70 on the first $31,800 of an employee's income. And further hikes are slated for future years, as we shall see in a moment.

The Internal Revenue Service collects the social security taxes. The receipts—some $150 billion in 1981—are credited to trust funds in the Treasury. Benefits are paid out of the monies in those accounts.

Essentially, OASDI operates on a pay-as-you-go basis. Benefits are paid out of current tax receipts. Put another way, the social security taxes paid by the current

---

[4] In strictest fact, the OASDI tax on employees and employers is 5.35 percent of the first $29,700 and on the self-employed 8.25 percent; the balance of the tax in each instance is the Medicare levy. The distinction between these separate taxes is hardly meaningful, however; those liable for the one must also pay the other.

working population support the payments made to the current beneficiaries of the program. Those who pay today have a moral commitment from Congress that, when they become eligible, they will in turn receive benefits paid for by the working population at that time.

Through most of its history, OASDI has operated with a comfortable surplus in its trust accounts. But that was not the case for a few recent years. Outgo exceeded income. The funds operated at a deficit, eating away the reserves.

That situation developed out of two major reasons: (1) Congress, moved by inflation and also some compassion, increased social security benefits more rapidly than the tax receipts, taken by themselves, could justify. And (2) largely as the result of birth rates, the number of workers paying social security taxes has not been increasing in recent years as rapidly, proportionally, as the number of people receiving social security payments.

The deficit problem became increasingly acute. By 1977 it was apparent that the trust funds would soon be exhausted. OASDI was literally approaching bankruptcy. Congress *had* to act to guarantee the integrity of the system.

It did so in 1977—by scheduling a series of hefty jumps in OASDI taxes over the next several years. The tax rate or the income base to which it is applied, or both, were raised for each of the next ten years, through 1987. The 1981 tax—6.65 percent on incomes up to $29,700 a year—is a product of that schedule. For 1982 the rate will remain the same, but it will be applied to a higher base—to incomes up to $31,800 a year.

BENEFITS. Monthly benefits go to those who are insured and either reach retirement age or die or are permanently disabled before then. And, they go to their spouses or survivors (widows or widowers, minor children, dependent parents).

Currently, some 36 million persons— 15 percent of the population—are paid benefits under the program. That total includes nearly 20 million retired workers and nearly 3 million disabled workers, and their more than 13 million dependents and survivors.

The *usual* retirement age is 65. A person *may* choose to retire at 62, but in that case the monthly benefits are less. No one is *forced* to retire at any age. But a person who chooses to work after 65 does receive reduced benefits if his or her earnings exceed a certain annual amount—$5,500 in 1981, $6,000 in 1982. (This restriction—reduction in benefits—does not apply beyond age 70, however.)

Benefits are fixed by a very complicated formula. Its chief ingredients are the in-

EXAMPLES OF MONTHLY OASDI PAYMENTS

Average Annual Earnings[a]	Worker, retired at 65	Worker, retired at 62	Disabled worker, any age	Wife or husband, at 65	Wife or husband, at 62	Widow or widower at 65, no child	Widow or widower, one child	Maximum family payment
$ 923 or less	153.10	120.30	153.10	76.60	57.50	153.10	229.70	229.70
$ 3,000	316.40	253.20	316.40	158.20	118.80	316.40	474.60	369.30
$ 4,000	372.20	297.80	372.20	186.10	136.60	372.20	558.30	636.00
$ 5,200	443.80	354.50	443.80	221.90	166.60	443.80	665.60	832.60
$ 6,000	487.80	390.30	487.80	244.00	183.00	487.80	731.70	940.60
$ 8,000	606.30	485.10	606.30	303.20	227.50	606.30	909.40	1061.00
$10,000	671.80	537.50	671.80	336.00	252.10	671.80	1007.70	1175.50

[a] Generally, average annual earnings are figured for the period beginning with 1951 until the covered worker reaches retirement age, is disabled, or dies. Up to 5 years of no or low earnings can be excluded from the computation. Monthly benefit payments are adjusted in June of each year to reflect increases in the cost of living.

Source: Social Security Administration

OASDHI COVERAGE

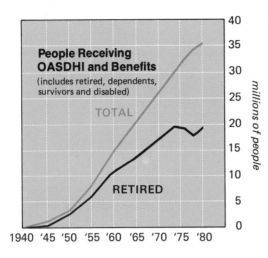

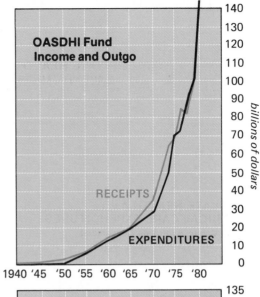

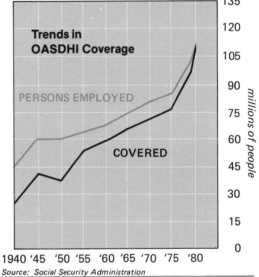

Source: Social Security Administration

sured person's (1) number of years spent and (2) average annual earnings in covered employment. The accompanying table provides examples of the benefits paid in the 12 months ending in June of 1981. At the time, the average monthly check for a retired worker came to $330 and for a couple $563.[5]

Medicare. Adequate medical care is both a necessity *and* expensive. The need is widespread. Nine out of 10 (more than 60 million) of the nation's families require some kind of medical care each year. One out of every six persons (some 37 million) becomes a patient in a general hospital during the same period.

The nation's total medical bill—payments for physicians, dentists, hospitalization, medicines, and all other health care goods and services—now runs to about $275 billion a year. That figure has more than quadrupled just since 1970, and its

upward climb continues. The annual health care bill comes to an average of more than $1100 for every person in this country.

Concern, prompted by these needs and costs, has mounted steadily in recent years. Many—including individual doctors, medical and hospital associations, public officials and agencies, and others—have sought the means by which adequate health care can be provided to all Americans on the basis of need.

One of the major results of that concern has been the extensive growth of *private* health insurance programs. Most of

[5] Those average amounts are at the low end of the range shown in the table for two major reasons: (1) the comparatively lower levels of income earned in their working years by persons now retired and (2) the lower taxable earnings base of previous years. The maximum amount of income to which OASDI taxes applied (that is, then, the maximum income creditable for benefit purposes) has been increased sharply in recent years. (It was only $3,600 until 1955, $4,200 until 1959, $4,800 until 1966, $6,600 until 1968, $7,800 until 1972, $10,800 in 1973, $13,200 in 1974, $14,100 in 1975, $15,300 in 1976, $16,500 in 1977, $17,700 in 1978, $22,900 in 1979, $25,900 in 1980. The base ($29,700) will go up to $31,800 in 1982.

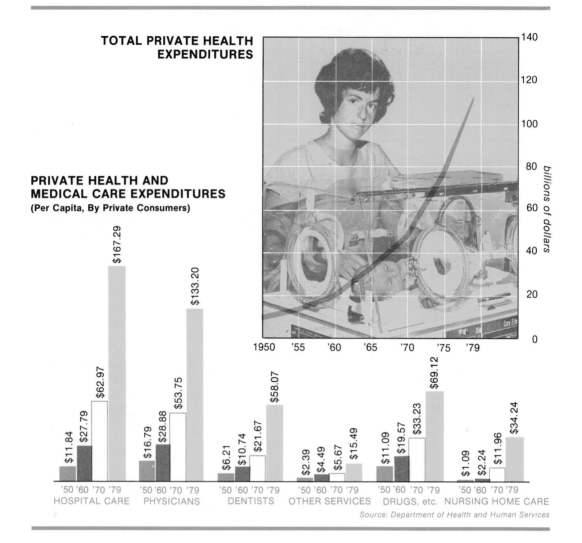

TOTAL PRIVATE HEALTH EXPENDITURES

PRIVATE HEALTH AND MEDICAL CARE EXPENDITURES
(Per Capita, By Private Consumers)

billions of dollars

140

120

100

80

60

40

20

0

1950 '55 '60 '65 '70 '75 '79

	HOSPITAL CARE	PHYSICIANS	DENTISTS	OTHER SERVICES	DRUGS, etc.	NURSING HOME CARE
'50	$11.84	$16.79	$6.21	$2.39	$11.09	$1.09
'60	$27.79	$28.88	$10.74	$4.49	$19.57	$2.24
'70	$62.97	$53.75	$21.67	$5.67	$33.23	$11.96
'79	$167.29	$133.20	$58.07	$15.49	$69.12	$34.24

Source: Department of Health and Human Services

them are built around the voluntary pre-payment of at least a portion of the sub-scribers' medical and/or hospital bills. Some 185 million Americans are now cov-ered by such arrangements, and they are a standard feature of labor-management agreements today.[6]

Many have long urged the creation of a national—that is, a *public*—health insur-ance program. Most who do so favor a compulsory pre-paid plan tied into the so-cial security system. President Truman rec-ommended one more than 30 years ago; it was rejected by Congress in 1950, how-ever. A number of similar proposals have been before Congress ever since.

Those who favor some form of national health insurance argue that it is made nec-

---

[6] Among the many such programs, the *Blue Cross Hospital Plan* is by far the most popular. Under it, the subscriber pays a monthly fee. In return, the Blue Cross Hospital Service pays a member hospital a scheduled fee to cover some or all of the costs of hospitalization for the subscriber or a dependent. Such special services as anesthetic and operating room costs are covered on a similar basis. Under the related *Blue Shield Plan*, Blue Cross members are usually able to cover a significant portion of their doctors' bills, as well.

essary by the fact that millions cannot afford adequate medical care today. They contend that a national program would reduce the per person cost of care and also encourage the upgrading of existing care and facilities. They insist that their proposals are not "radical" but simply an extension of the present and generally favored social security system.

The opposition to a national program of health insurance is led by the American Medical Association. The AMA and other opponents contend that such a program would lead to "socialized medicine." They urge, instead, the expansion of existing private voluntary programs like Blue Cross. They claim that a federal program is unnecessary and would require a huge and wasteful bureaucracy to administer it. They contend that such a program would destroy the traditional and confidential doctor-patient relationship, and would lower the present standards of medical care.

To this point, Congress has not been persuaded to enact a national program for the people as a whole. It has provided for such an arrangement—Medicare—for those over 65, however. Congress established it as part of a general expansion of the social security system in 1965.

As it now operates, Medicare involves two broad programs of health care for most persons age 65 and older:

THE BASIC PLAN. One of these—called the *basic plan*—provides for the coverage of at least the major portions of the costs of hospital, nursing home, and similar care for the nation's 25 million elderly.[7] It is financed by a portion of the compulsory taxes levied to support OASDI—as we noted a moment ago.

THE SUPPLEMENTARY PLAN. The other part of Medicare is voluntary. It helps pay

doctors' bills and similar charges—for X-rays, surgical dressings, artificial limbs, and so on. Those who choose to participate pay a flat monthly fee which is then matched by the Government. The fee was originally set at $3 a month but rising costs have forced it upwards—to $9.60 in 1981. All but about 100,000 of the 25 million elderly persons covered by the basic plan are now also enrolled in this plan.

Medicare's annual costs now run about $37 billion and will undoubtedly go up.

Public Assistance

The Social Security Act of 1935 inaugurated the Federal Government's *social insurance* programs—old-age-and-survivors insurance, and the later-added disability and Medicare features, and unemployment insurance. It also provided for a number of *public assistance* programs, to which others have been added in the years since.

The social insurance programs are financed by the contributions of employers and employees—by taxes paid by them. The public assistance programs—which are the ones usually referred to as "welfare programs"—are paid for out of general tax revenues.

Most public assistance programs are the modern-day version of what once were called "poor relief." They are especially intended to reach those who live in "the other America"—those who, in the midst of plenty, live in poverty. How successful those programs are is a matter of considerable debate.

How many Americans live in poverty today? The answer to that question must depend upon how the term is defined—and there is much disagreement on that score. But, as the term is most commonly used, it refers to conditions in which people live—subsist—below a generally accepted minimum standard. It refers to conditions in which people have little or no income, do not have enough to eat, are ill-clothed and

[7] And, since 1974, another group—the now approximately 2.8 million persons under 65 who have been eligible for OASDI disability benefits for at least 2 years.

poorly housed, have only sketchy educations and little or no skills, are unemployed or under-employed.

The Federal Government answers that question in terms of the number of people who have incomes below the "poverty level"—an income figure most recently set for 1980. For that year the official line was drawn at $7450 for a nonfarm family of four and at $6340 for a rural family of the same size. On that basis, some 25 million Americans, nearly 12 percent of the nation's population, live in poverty.

Who are the poor? The Census Bureau says that there are more than twice as many poor whites as poor blacks—about 17 million whites as compared with 7.5 million blacks. But a higher percentage of black Americans are poor—almost one out of every three blacks and only one out of every 11 whites.

More than a third of the families below the poverty line are headed by females—families in which the father has died, been disabled, been divorced, or has deserted. One half of the poor live in families where the breadwinner—male or female—has only an eighth-grade education or less. Only about a third are from families in which the breadwinner has been without a job for a lengthy period; 40 percent of poor families are headed by a full-time worker. Almost half of the poor are children.

Although poverty is usually thought of in terms of large inner cities and ghettos, only about a third of the poor live in inner cities. About 40 percent of the poor live in metropolitan, nonfarm areas and nearly 20 percent in the suburbs. Nearly half of all of the poor live in the South.

From this grim recitation, let us turn to several of the welfare programs aimed at the nation's poor.

Supplementary Security Income. SSI is a program of direct federal assistance to the needy aged, blind, and disabled.

At the time the Social Security Act was written, it was realized that a large number of older persons would not qualify for old-age insurance benefits. So a parallel old-age assistance program was established. It was set up as a joint federal-State operation. The Federal Government made grants to the States which then created their own programs for aid to the needy aged. At the same time, similar federal-State programs for aid to the blind and the disabled were also put in place.

These three separate programs were completely federalized in 1974. Under what is now known as the *Supplementary Security Income* program, the Social Security Administration makes direct assistance payments to the needy aged, blind, and disabled. SSI is not a contributory program; it is financed entirely by funds appropriated by Congress out of the general treasury—currently at the rate of about $7 billion a year.

The federalization of these programs has had some striking results. Before 1974—when the States administered their own programs, determined eligibility, set the level of payments, and so on—some 3.2 million persons received aid. Today almost 4.3 million receive SSI payments. And the level of those payments has increased substantially, too. Today (1981) a single person is paid $238.00 a month and a married couple $357.00.

Aid to Families with Dependent Children. AFDC is the most costly, and the most controversial, of the various public assistance programs. It, too, was born in 1935 as a joint federal-State plan. Unlike SSI, however, it has remained an undertaking in which the Federal Government makes substantial grants to the States to help them make welfare payments.

For AFDC purposes, a dependent child is one who: (1) is in need, (2) is under 18 years of age, (3) has been deprived of normal parental support by the death, incapacity, or continued absence of a parent, and (4) is living with the other parent, another close relative, or a foster family.

The federal funding for the AFDC program is now funneled through the Social Security Administration. The SSA pays a monthly amount per child; the States add matching monies and actually administer the aid. For 1981 AFDC payments total $13 billion—nearly $7 billion of it in federal funds. They help support some 11 million individuals, in 3.7 million families.

AFDC was originally conceived as a program for widows and orphans and for families who needed temporary help to meet special hardships. In its early years about 75 percent of those who received help were children of fathers who had died or been totally disabled. Less than 20 percent of AFDC children are in that category today, however. More than 80 percent of them have living and able-bodied fathers; but the fathers have either deserted their families or were never married to the mothers of the children.

This has led many critics to charge that AFDC, which began as a program to help fatherless and husbandless families, has become one which actually encourages their creation. Because AFDC payments hinge on the absence of a parent (usually the father), the program has what many see as built-in incentives for either (1) the father to desert the family or (2) illegitimate births.[8]

The Food Stamp Program. The food stamp program was begun in 1964 and, as we noted on page 616, it is administered by the Department of Agriculture's Food and Nutrition Service. Nearly all of the cost of the program is borne by the Federal Government; the States contribute only to local administrative costs.

Help for the disabled is an important feature of the Supplementary Security Income program.

The food stamp program's original purpose was two-fold: (1) to increase the food purchasing power of low-income families and so improve their diets and (2) to help dispose of surplus agricultural commodities. As we've seen (page 620), the once troublesome food surpluses have all but disappeared in recent years. So, today, only the first purpose remains.

Congress made extensive changes in the food stamp program in 1977. As it now operates, the stamps are available, free of charge, to persons or families with net incomes below the poverty line.

The stamps (actually coupons) are issued in monetary denominations. They may be exchanged—spent as money—for food items in supermarkets and other retail outlets. The amount (dollar value) any person or family receives depends upon net income and the size of the family unit.

---

[8] The problem of "runaway fathers" has become so acute (and so costly to both the Federal and State Governments) that Congress has erected the Office of Child Support Environment in the Department of Health and Human Services. It works with State and local police and welfare agencies to locate absent parents, enforce their support obligations to their children, and when necessary establish paternity.

In short, the lower the income, and/or the larger the family, the greater will be the dollar value of the stamps received.

The program has grown dramatically. In 1965 some 425,000 persons received food-stamp aid at a cost of $33 million to the Federal Government. By 1981 some 20 million persons were being aided and federal food stamp expenditures had reached nearly $10 billion.

There can be little doubt that the program has accomplished much good. It was originally intended to help the poor. It still is and it still does. But its hefty growth prompted many charges of mismanagement and fraud—and, especially, complaints of widespread use by large numbers of ineligible persons.

These criticisms persuaded Congress to overhaul the program in 1977. It tightened the eligibility standards considerably. It also liberalized the law at the same time, however. Until 1978 the stamps were available free only to the very poor—only to those with net incomes of less than $30 a month. All other recipients had to buy them. They could do so at a substantial discount; but they did have to pay at least something for the stamps they received.

Medicaid. When Congress added Medicare to the social security system in 1965, it also established another health care program, *Medicaid.* It is conducted by the Health Care Financing Administration in cooperation with each of the various State's own welfare agencies.

Medicaid grants are made to the States to help them help two segments of the population: (1) those who are covered by SSI and AFDC—that is, the needy aged, blind, and disabled and families with dependent children, and (2) others whom the law calls "the medically indigent." These are persons "whose income and resources are insufficient to meet the costs of necessary medical services."

The States set the specific rules which define the medically indigent and adminis-

ter Medicaid. The program has grown far beyond original expectations. More than 23 million persons now receive Medicaid-sponsored care—in most cases at no cost to themselves. The cost in federal funds is now over $15 billion a year, and the various States provide nearly that much from their own welfare funds.

This hard fact dogs Medicaid: With a third party (the public) paying the bill, neither the patient nor the doctor nor the hospital is encouraged to economize.

Other Welfare Programs. We have just taken a brief look at four of the major federal welfare programs. As large and as important as they are, they don't begin to exhaust the list of such efforts. Nor can we do so here; but we can cite some of the more important of them.

The USDA's Food and Nutrition Service, which handles the food stamp program, also manages efforts to make low- or no-cost breakfasts, lunches, and milk available to school children. It also administers a number of similar programs. For example, it administers programs to provide meals for children in day care centers in low-income areas and nutritious food supplements for new mothers, mothers-to-be, babies, and infants in low-income families. The largest of these is the school lunch program. It involves the serving of meals, free or at reduced prices, to some 26 million students in both public and private schools. All told, the several child nutrition programs now consume more than $3.5 billion in federal funds each year.

In such projects as *Headstart* and *Upward Bound,* the Department of Education tries to give special preschool opportunities to poorer children. It does so in an attempt to reach those children before the impact of poverty disables them. It attempts to give them at least a fighting chance to profit from formal education when they reach age five or six. The Department of Education and other federal agencies also administer a number of grant programs to support vocational, consumer, and other adult education. They also provide special help and training for the physically and the mentally handicapped.

The Office of Human Development Services distributes grants to aid the States with family planning and other counseling services for AFDC recipients and many other persons. It and a number of other federal agencies also work with State and local agencies and several private organizations to combat drug addiction, alcoholism, and a variety of other social ills.

The Economic Development Administration in the Commerce Department makes grants and loans to promote the resurgence of areas affected by severe and chronic unemployment. The independent *Appalachian Regional Commission* fosters and funds programs specifically targeted to meet the health and welfare needs of the people in that largely mountainous region.

VISTA is one of the several components of the umbrella agency, ACTION. VISTA volunteers—Volunteers in Service to America—constitute what is often called "the domestic Peace Corps." They are men and women of all ages who come from all walks of life—skilled craftspersons, doctors, engineers, architects, agronomists, teachers, and many others. They work in a broad range of projects designed to attack poverty and its causes. For up to two years, they live and work in such places as urban ghettos and pockets of rural poverty in Appalachia and elsewhere, with migrant farm workers, on Indian reservations, and in hospitals and mental and correctional institutions.

The list goes on and on. The Labor Department's Employment and Training Administration attempts to help people find jobs through the State employment programs prompted by the United States Employment Service. And it administers many other job-related programs.

Several HUD agencies work to better the housing of the poor—with low-cost public housing, rent subsidies, or slum clearance and urban renewal projects.

A number of other federal agencies conduct programs not often thought of in "welfare" terms, but which are at least closely related. Thus, the VA offers extensive help to veterans. The Small Business Administration aids minority businesses and the victims of natural disasters. The Rural Electrification Administration brings power and telephone service to many who live in rural areas. The Bureau of Indian Affairs works to improve the lot of Indians and natives of Alaska. Again, the list goes on and on.

Public Health

Protecting the public health—preventing and combating threats to the health of the community at large—is among the oldest of the functions of government. The origins of the function are lost in antiquity.

VISTA volunteers can be found in migrant farm workers camps, like this one in California, and in many of those other places that make up "the other America."

At least as early as the 3rd Century B.C., the Greeks enforced quarantines in order to prevent the spread of disease.

The public health activities of the Federal Government date back to 1798. In that year Congress enacted a statute authorizing the construction of hospitals to care for American merchant seamen. From that small beginning, federal health activities have grown to huge proportions.

For 1981, federal health outlays will be well over $60 billion—well over 10 percent of all federal expenditures. The bulk of that spending—about three fourths of it— is accounted for by the Medicare and Medicaid programs, as we have seen. Most of the other federal health activities are centered in the Public Health Service.[9]

The Public Health Service. The Public Health Service traces its history back to the act of 1798 in which Congress created the Marine Hospital Service. Today it describes its basic mission in these terms:

> . . . to promote and assure the highest level of health attainable for every individual in America.

It seeks to do so through a number of research, grant, and action programs and through six line agencies.

The work of the *Center for Disease Control* reflects the traditional public health function. The Center is *the* federal agency charged with protecting the nation's health through the prevention and control of diseases.

The Center is headquartered in Atlanta and operates on the time-honored notion that the best way to control a disease is to prevent it. Its major concerns are (1) communicable diseases—such as diphtheria, measles, the many strains of flu, venereal diseases, and so on, and (2) those which are vector-borne (spread by insects and other organisms)—hepatitis, malaria, typhus, and the like.

The Center fights disease with a variety of weapons. It conducts immunization programs, enforces quarantines in foreign and interstate commerce, and utilizes spraying and many other techniques of eradication. It inspects and licenses all clinical laboratories operating in interstate commerce. And it makes extensive efforts to inform, warn, and advise health authorities, and the general public with regard to threats and the treatment of disease.

Because diseases respect no boundaries, the Center works closely with such other federal agencies as the Immigration and Naturalization Service and the Customs Service, with foreign governments, and with the UN's World Health Organization.

The almost complete disappearance of such once dreaded scourges as smallpox and scarlet fever are monuments to the efforts of the Public Health Service over decades.

The *Food and Drug Administration* is a part of the same historic line, and its functions are absolutely vital to all of the people of the United States. When foods and drugs are mass produced, as are most of ours today, the consumer has little chance to check on their quality and purity. They may be "checked," perhaps, in terms of their effect on personal health, but that may come a bit late.

Toward the turn of the century, shocking practices in the food processing and the drug industries were brought to light by the "muckrakers"—the forerunners of Ralph Nader and other contemporary consumer advocates. Many foods were adulterated, misbranding was common, and

---

[9] Two other federal agencies conduct large-scale health care programs, both for a specialized clientele: The Defense Department now spends some $4 billion a year to provide medical and hospital care for some 3 million active and retired military personnel and their 4 million dependents. And, the Veterans Administration spends about $6 billion a year on its medical and hospital programs; see page 456. A few other federal agencies also furnish such care, but on a more limited basis—for example, the Bureau of Prisons; see page 669.

An FDA inspector takes a sample of frozen french fried potatoes in an Idaho processing plant to check for bacterial contamination.

Much of the FDA's scientific research is conducted at its headquarters in Rockville, Maryland. It also maintains regional offices and laboratories, staffed by chemists and other scientists, investigators, and other personnel. A significant share of its scientific work is also done by contract with several universities and other public and private research groups.

FDA agents regularly inspect food processing plants, pharmaceutical laboratories, and other locations to guard against unsanitary conditions and practices. They take samples of the materials used, and check the quality controls exercised in the compounding, processing, packaging, and labeling of goods destined for interstate commerce. They also survey drugstores and other retail outlets to prevent the dispensing of harmful drugs without prescription.

Thousands of samples are tested in FDA laboratories each year. Those products it finds adulterated, misrepresented, or otherwise dangerous are banned from interstate shipment. Labels must list the ingredients and quantity in any package.

unsanitary practices were widespread. False claims for cures for every known ache and pain led many unsuspecting sufferers to put both faith and money in useless and often harmful concoctions and contraptions.

Congress passed the Pure Food and Drug Act of 1906 to counteract these conditions. The present-day Food and Drug Administration has descended from that law. Today the FDA is charged with protecting the nation's health against hazards found in foods, drugs, cosmetics, medical devices, diagnostic and therapeutic products, veterinary preparations, and similar consumer items.[10]

---

[10] The Consumer Product Safety Commission operates in a closely related area. It is a five-member independent regulatory agency established in 1972 (page 541). Its principal function is to guard the public against unreasonable risks of *physical injury* from consumer products. Thus, it enforces several statutes and its own regulations which ban the manufacture, sale, or use of such things as poisonous packaging materials, unsafe flame retardants in clothing, refrigerators without door safety devices, childrens' toys with sharp edges, and the like.

Salt and Pepper, *The Wall Street Journal*, May 18, 1977 by Ray Morin. Reprinted by permission of the Wall Street Journal.

Narcotic drugs must be labeled "Warning—May Be Habit-Forming." Poisonous drugs and other preparations must be plainly tagged; instructions must be given for their safe use and antidotes for their misuse. Applications for the manufacture and distribution of new drugs, accompanied by the results of careful tests, must be approved by the FDA before any new drug can be marketed in this country.

The *Health Services Administration* is "the doctor" to several thousand patients a year. It provides comprehensive health care to American Indians and Alaskan natives, merchant seamen, personnel of the Coast Guard and the Public Health Service and their dependents, retired members of the regular armed forces, and others.

It maintains a number of hospitals—including eight general hospitals in various places around the country, a leprosarium, two hospitals for drug addicts, and a tuberculosis hospital.

Its National Health Service Corps promotes the development of medical care programs in areas critically short of service and facilities. It also assigns its own medical personnel to those programs. Through several Neighborhood Health Centers it offers a wide range of care to low-income families who lack adequate access to it from other sources. And the Administration operates a number of grant programs to encourage the States to develop and expand their own public health organizations and projects.

The *Health Resources Administration* is essentially a vehicle for the management of a number of grant and loan programs. It makes funds available to State and local governments, and to nonprofit organizations, for the development and strengthening of health care services and facilities. It also houses the National Center for Health Statistics. The Center is a primary source for data reflecting the state of the nation's health. It gathers and distributes data on births and birth rates, life expectancy, deaths and death rates, causes of death, and much else.

The *Alcohol, Drug Abuse, and Mental Health Administration* is primarily a research and grant agency. It studies biological, psychological, and sociological aspects of alcoholism, drug abuse, and mental health and illness. In addition to its own research activities, it administers grants to States and to local communities to support and strengthen their own efforts in these fields.

The *National Institutes of Health* constitute the major research arm of the Public Health Service. NIH conducts and also provides extensive grant funds for research into the causes, prevention, and cure of diseases.

There are 11 separate research institutes within NIH. Each specializes in a major field of human malady—for example, the National Heart, Lung, and Blood Institute, the National Cancer Institute, and the National Institute of Allergy and Infectious Diseases. Most new knowledge of diseases today comes from these NIH components—from the scientists who work in their laboratories and from those others whose work is funded by their grants. And the NIH National Library of Medicine is the nation's foremost medical information resource.

NIH also maintains a huge Clinical Center near Bethesda, Maryland. There patients, the doctors caring for them, and laboratory scientists researching their maladies are brought together. The Center's patients are all volunteers, referred by their own physicians and selected by the various research institutes.

Education

The providing of public education is one of the major reserved powers of the States in the American federal system—and in most of the States it is primarily a local responsibility. Still, the Federal Government is extensively involved in the field—typically through the grant-in-aid route, as we shall see.

Measured by any standards, public education is a huge enterprise today. In terms of expenditures, it heads the list of *all* public functions, including national defense. The States and their local governments now spend over $120 billion a year on their public school programs (including nearly $15 billion in funds from the Federal Government).

Today more than *one-fourth* of all of our people attend school. There are nearly 58 million students enrolled in the nation's public and private schools and colleges. More than four-fifths of them, some 50 million, attend publicly financed institutions. About 32 million are enrolled in elementary schools (through the 8th grade), almost 15 million in high schools, and almost 10 million in colleges and universities.

The nation's school population climbed at a rapid pace through the 1950's and 1960's; but it has plateaued in the 1970's. In fact, it has declined slightly in each of the past few years—as a result of the con-

tinuing annual drop in the nation's birth rate, of course.

The Federal Role. Federal aid to education dates back to before the adoption of the Constitution. Initially, it was directed to *institutions* and in recent decades it has gone to *individuals*, as well.

In the Ordinance of 1785 Congress directed that one section of land (one square mile) in each geographic township in the territories be set aside for the support of public schools. Beginning with Ohio in 1802, each of the newly admitted States was granted two townships of public land (72 square miles) for a public university. The *Morrill Act of 1862* provided each of the States with huge tracts of federal land—30,000 acres for each of its members of Congress—to establish "land grant" colleges.

FEDERAL EDUCATIONAL INSTITUTIONS. For decades the Federal Government itself has operated a number of educational institutions. The best known of them are the service academies, of course: the Military Academy at West Point, the Naval Academy at Annapolis, the Air Force Academy

Case Study

Median School Years Completed by Persons 25 Years Old and Over

	1940	1950	1960	1970
All Races	8.6	9.3	10.6	12.2
White	8.7	9.7	10.9	12.2
Male	8.7	9.3	10.7	12.2
Female	8.8	10.1	11.2	12.2
Black	5.8	6.8	8.2	9.9
Male	5.4	6.4	7.7	9.6
Female	6.2	7.2	8.6	10.2

This table is drawn from data reported by the Census Bureau. It indicates the level of educational attainment in the adult population for the census years 1940 through 1970. It also shows levels of educational attainment by race and by sex for that period. Among the several facts reflected is one major reason why the per-

centage of the nation's population attending schools did not drop, despite the fact that the nation's birth rate has declined since the mid-1960's: increasingly, more students stay in school more years.

■ What reasons can you suggest for the fact that, historically, the level of attainment for whites has been consistently far above that for blacks? That, at least over the past 30 years, the level of attainment for females has been consistently higher than that for males, white and black? In which category has the level risen most rapidly over the period? What explanations can you offer for this fact? What other conclusions can you draw from the table?

at Colorado Springs, and the Coast Guard Academy at New London. There are several others, less well-known. They include the National War College at Fort McNair in Washington, D.C.; the Naval Postgraduate School at Monterey, California; the Armed Forces Staff College at Norfolk, Virginia; and the Uniformed Services University of the Health Sciences, at Bethesda, Maryland, which expects to graduate its first class of military career doctors in 1982. Gallaudet College and Howard University, both in Washington, D.C., are "federally aided corporations." Schooling is also provided for many Indians and Alaskan natives, for the dependents of military personnel in many other parts of the world, and for students in the District of Columbia and the territories.

The Department of Education. Although the history of federal involvement is a lengthy one, Congress did not establish the Department of Education until 1979.

At base, the Department is a research, advisory, and grant-dispensing agency. The Secretary of Education heads a staff of some 6000 men and women and manages a 1981 budget of $13 billion. Most (but not all) of the massive federal contribution to education is funneled through it.[11]

AID TO ELEMENTARY AND SECONDARY EDUCATION. Congress has long provided money for the support of certain specific educational efforts at the elementary and secondary levels. It first did so in the Smith-Hughes Act of 1917, which established matching grants to the States for the teaching of courses in agriculture and home economics. Over the years it enacted a number of other statutes directed at spe-cific aspects of public education. Among the most important of them was the *Impacted Areas Act of 1950.* It provided for annual grants to the States to help cover school costs in those districts either (1) overcrowded ("impacted") by the nearby location of a military base or other federal activity or (2) deprived of local revenues because of the tax-exempt status of federal lands in those districts. (The impact-aid program is currently funded at more than $500 million a year.)

It was not until 1965, however, that Congress enacted a statute to provide for *general* federal aid to education. The *Elementary and Secondary Education Act of 1965* began an omnibus program of federal assistance. Amended a number of times since then, the law was most recently extended in 1978 and will undoubtedly be renewed again in 1983. It now supplies about $4 billion in elementary and secondary aid. Much of that funding is targeted for those areas (urban and rural) with a high percentage of students from low-income, poverty-level families. But substantial amounts are also provided for school purposes generally and for such other uses as textbooks, library resources, special education for the handicapped, and teacher training.

AID TO HIGHER EDUCATION. Federal aid to higher education began with the Morrill Act in 1862. That measure, and its later amendments, donated more than 11 million acres of public lands to the States for the support of institutions of higher learning.[12] The legislation is the basis for the

---

[11] In addition to the nearly $15 billion in federal aid to the States (most of it administered by the Department of Education), the Veterans Administration pays out more than $2 billion in educational benefits each year. Several other federal agencies spend hundreds of millions a year in the field of education, most of it for research purposes—most prominently, NIH, the Defense Department, NASA, and the Department of Energy.

[12] The law defined its "leading object" to be "without excluding other scientific and classical studies, and including military tactics, to teach such branches of learning as are related to agriculture and the mechanical arts . . . in order to promote the liberal and practical education of the industrial classes in the several pursuits and professions of life." Most historians regard the Morrill Act as among the most important of the statutes ever enacted by Congress. It marked the first commitment by any nation to make higher education available to the people at large rather than to only a small elite.

ENROLLMENT
(public and private)

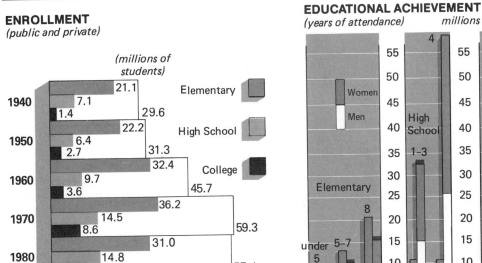

EDUCATIONAL ACHIEVEMENT
(years of attendance)   *millions*

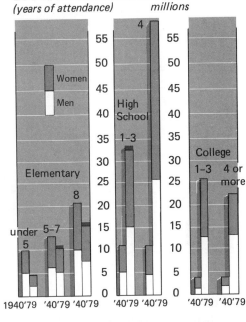

HOW OUR PUBLIC SCHOOLS ARE FINANCED
(elementary and secondary)

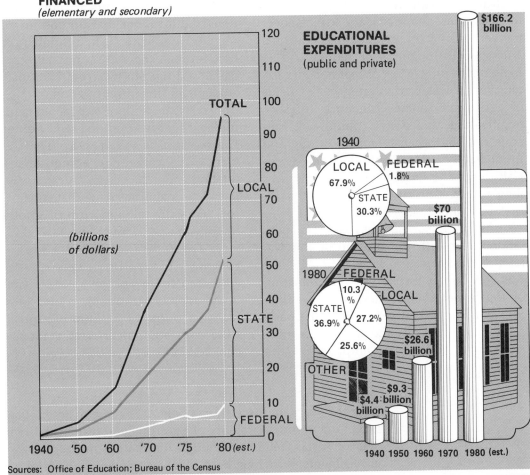

Sources: Office of Education; Bureau of the Census

The students here are receiving instruction in electrical circuitry and wiring, only one of the many aspects of vocational training programs which federal funds have substantially helped in financing.

land grant colleges and universities of each of the 50 States and Puerto Rico.

Much as with the assistance provided to elementary and secondary schools, over the years Congress provided for occasional and specific programs of federal aid to higher education. Most of that not very extensive aid was concentrated in the fields of agriculture, home economics, forestry, engineering, and ROTC training. Large-scale funding began to appear during and immediately after World War II—especially with the enactment of the Servicemen's Readjustment Act of 1944, the fabled GI Bill of Rights (see page 458).

The first major piece of *general* aid legislation came with the passage of the *National Defense Education Act of 1958*. The law was very largely inspired by the launching of the Soviet Union's first earth satellite, *Sputnik I*. For several years it was the basis for a battery of loans and grants to institutions and students; it emphasized the strengthening of offerings in the sciences, math, and foreign languages.

Construction grants to public institutions and loans for that purpose to private schools were featured in a number of statutes through the 1960's. However, the focus of aid has shifted from institutions to students in the current period.

Today the bulk of federal aid is funded under the oft-amended and -extended *Higher Education Act of 1965*. The Department of Education now administers grants totaling about $5 billion a year under that law. The major share of that money goes for "educational opportunity grants" to low-income students. The law also provides for student loans and a work-study program—to pay the wages of students with part-time jobs on or near campus. Some additional funding is also provided for such purposes as library acquisitions, laboratory equipment, and graduate student fellowships.

SUMMARY

Over the years the American people have come to accept both the need for and the desirability of governmental responsibility in the field of social welfare. Although the States, and especially local governments, have long been involved, large-scale federal participation dates from the Depression of the 1930's.

The enactment of the Social Security Act of 1935 inaugurated several major federal social insurance and public assistance programs. The principal social insurance programs today are OASDI—a contributory insurance plan financed by taxes levied on employees, their employers, and the self-employed; Medicare—which provides for hospitalization and other health care for the aged financed in part by payroll taxes and monthly fees; and unemployment compensation.

Most public assistance programs are the modern-day version of what once were called "poor relief." They are especially intended to reach those who live in "the other America." The principal public assistance programs today include Supplementary Security Income (SSI), Aid to Families with Dependent Children (AFDC), the food stamp program, and Medicaid.

Protecting the public health is among the oldest of governmental functions. The several agencies of the Public Health Service provide hospital, medical, and other health care for various classes of patients, administer several grant and research programs, work to prevent and control disease, and enforce the federal statutes which ban impure foods, drugs, and similar items from interstate and foreign commerce.

Education is a huge enterprise. It is the largest single object of governmental expenditure today and more than a fourth of all of the American people are enrolled in schools today. A substantial amount of federal aid is provided to the States for support of public education.

Concept Development

Questions for Review

1. What major occurrence in our history brought large-scale federal participation in the social welfare field?

2. What major statute highlighted federal involvement in social welfare?

3. What is OASDI? How is it funded?

4. Why did OASDI trust fund income fall behind outgo in recent years?

5. What is Medicare? How are the "basic" and "supplementary" plans funded?

6. How do public assistance programs differ from social insurance plans?

7. What is meant by the phrase "the other America"? Approximately how many Americans now live there?

8. What groups does SSI attempt to help? AFDC? Medicaid? How are these programs financed?

9. What was the original two-fold purpose of the food stamp program?

10. At base, what is the public health function?

11. What is the primary mission of the Center for Disease Control? The Food and Drug Administration? The National Institute of Health?

12. In the federal system, where does the basic responsibility for public education rest?

13. Approximately how much do the States now spend for education? How much federal aid is included in sum?

14. Approximately how many Americans now attend school?

15. For how long has the Federal Government been involved in the field of education?

For Further Inquiry

1. Why does the term "welfare" produce antagonistic reactions from many people? What is your reaction to this bumper-sticker reflection of an oft-expressed attitude: "I fight poverty; I work for a living."

2. On page 632 we drew a brief profile of the poor in America. How can you explain the several characteristics set out there—for example, that more than a third of the families below the poverty line are headed by females?

3. Do you agree that education is the "bulwark of democracy"?

4. To what extent do you think the Federal Government should be responsible for the quality of education in the public schools? For providing equal educational opportunities for all students?

Suggested Activities

1. Prepare an essay or stage a class discussion based upon one or more of the following quotations. *Henry Adams:* "They know enough who know how to learn." *John Milton:* "As good almost kill a man as kill a good book: who kills a man kills a reasonable creature, God's image; but he who destroys a good book kills reason itself." *Descartes:* "It is not enough to have a good mind, the main thing is to use it well."

2. Invite representatives of one or more local welfare programs to describe their work to the class.

3. Stage a debate or class forum on one of the following questions: (a) *Resolved,* That the Congress henceforth refuse to appropriate funds to the States in support of public education; (b) *Resolved,* That the Congress adopt immediately a general program of national health care insurance.

Suggested Reading

Aday, LuAnn, *et al., Health Care in the United States: Equity for Whom?* Sage, 1980.

Benet, James and Daniels, Arlene K. (eds.) *Education: Straitjacket or Opportunity.* Transaction Books, 1980.

Falkson, Joseph L., *HMO's and the Politics of Health System Reform.* American Hospital Assn., 1979.

Friedlander, Walter A. and Apte, Robert Z., *Introduction to Social Welfare.* Prentice-Hall, 5th ed., 1980.

Segalman, Ralph and Basu, Asoke, *Poverty in America: The Welfare Dilemma.* Greenwood, 1980.

Steiner, Elizabeth, *et al., Education and American Culture.* Macmillan, 1980.

Strauss, Anselm M., *Where Medicine Fails.* Transaction Books, 1979.

Struyk, Raymond J., *A New System for Public Housing: Salvaging a Natural Resource.* The Urban Institute, 1980.

Zigler, Edward and Valentine, Jeanette, *Project Head Start: A Legacy of the War on Poverty.* Free Press, 1979.

Also: Information Center, Department of Health and Human Services, Washington, D.C. 20201.

Information Center, Department of Education, Washington, D.C. 20202.

THE COURTS AND THE ADMINISTRATION OF JUSTICE

In the American system of separation of powers, we know, it is the prime function of the legislative branch to *make* the law, of the executive branch to *enforce* and *administer* the law, and of the judicial branch to *interpret* and *apply* the law. "It is," as the great Chief Justice Marshall declared in *Marbury* v. *Madison,* "emphatically the province and the duty of the judicial department to say what the law is."

As with the Congress and the Presidency, the federal "judicial department"—and, particularly, the Supreme Court of the United States—has played a major part in the building of the American constitutional system. We have seen any number of illustrations of the point throughout this book: for example, in *Marbury* v. *Madison,* 1803, in which the Supreme Court first established the power of judicial review; in *McCulloch* v. *Maryland,* 1819, in which the Court enunciated the doctrine of implied powers; in the many great civil rights cases (with which we dealt in Chapters 6 and 7); in *Baker* v. *Carr,* 1962, and its several succeeding cases, in which the Court laid down the "one-man, one-vote" rule; and in many, many more. Through our history, it has been—and it is today—true that, as Chief Justice Charles Evans Hughes once put it: "The Constitution means what the judges say it means."

Democratic government is limited government. The democratic ideal insists that there are areas of activity prohibited to government and into which government may not intrude. In the American frame of democratic government it is upon the courts that

major reliance is placed for the preservation of the concept of limited government. It is peculiarly the duty of the courts to see that government does not overstep the bounds of the powers the nation's people have granted to it.

One of the many distinctive features of the American legal system is its *dual* organization. There are two separate and distinct judicial structures, one for the Federal Government and the other(s) for the 50 States. Federalism does not demand such an arrangement. In fact, in most other federal systems in the world today, the principal courts are those of the states (or provinces) which make up the federation; the only significant federal court is a national supreme court which caps the judicial hierarchy as a court of last resort. Article III of the Constitution of the United States does allow for a similar arrangement. But the 1st Session of the 1st Congress in 1789 decided to construct a complete set of federal courts to parallel those of the States.

In Chapter 26 we shall be concerned with the structure, jurisdiction, and operations of the national judiciary. (We shall consider the State court systems later, in Chapter 31 in Part Seven.) And in Chapter 27, the other chapter in Part Six, we shall turn to the administration of the law—that is, to the organization and operations of the legal arm of the executive branch of the National Government, the Department of Justice. As you read these chapters, contemplate Daniel Webster's observation: "Justice, Sir, is the greatest interest of man on earth."

26

The Federal Court System

There is hardly a political question in the United States which does not sooner or later turn into a judicial one.

ALEXIS DE TOCQUEVILLE

■ What role or roles do the federal courts play in the American governmental process?

■ Why should (or should not) federal judges be appointed rather than elected to office?

■ Is the power of judicial review consistent with the basic principles of democracy?

We have referred to the Supreme Court and to various other courts in the federal judiciary often to this point. Finally, in this chapter, we shall take a systematic look at the judicial branch of the National Government.

Most of the authors of the Constitution saw the lack of a national judiciary as a major weakness in the government created by the Articles of Confederation. They were convinced that a national judiciary—a system of *national* courts—was essential to the success of the new government they had designed at Philadelphia.

Throughout the period the Articles were in force (from 1781 to 1789), the laws of the United States were interpreted and applied within each of the States as that particular State chose (or chose not) to do. Disputes between States were decided—if at all—by the courts of one of the States involved in the controversy.[1] And the same was true of disputes between residents of different States. Very often, the decisions of the courts of one State were neither accepted nor enforced in the others.

Alexander Hamilton spoke to the problem in *The Federalist No. 78*. He described "the want of a national judiciary" as "a cir-

---

[1] The Articles of Confederation did provide (in Article IX) a complicated procedure for the settlement of such disputes, but it was rarely used.

Over the entrance to the Supreme Court Building is the motto "Equal Justice Under Law." Here, Amishmen mount the steps that lead to the highest court in the land. They are on their way to listen to the arguments in Yoder v. Wisconsin—*a case in which the Supreme Court held Amish children to be exempt from State compulsory school attendance laws; see page 133.*

cumstance which crowns the defects of the Confederation." Arguing the need for a *national* court system, he added:

> Laws are dead letters without courts to expound and define their true meaning and operation.

To meet the need, the Framers wrote Article III into the Constitution. It creates the national judiciary in one sentence:

> The judicial power of the United States shall be vested in one Supreme Court, and in such inferior courts as the Congress may from time to time ordain and establish.

And Congress is given the expressed power "to constitute tribunals inferior to the Supreme Court" in Article I, Section 8, Clause 9.

A Dual Court System. Bear in mind as we proceed with this examination of the *national* court system that we have in this country what is often called "a dual court system." That is, there exist, side by side throughout the country, two entirely separate court systems. On the one hand there is the national judiciary, consisting of more than a hundred courts spanning the nation. On the other, each of the 50 States main-

tains its own system of courts, with the total number of them running well into the thousands. We shall consider the State court systems in Chapter 31.

Types of Federal Courts. As we have noted, the Constitution creates only the Supreme Court of the United States. It leaves to Congress the creation of the "inferior courts"—those beneath the Supreme Court. Congress has created two distinct types of federal courts: (1) constitutional courts and (2) special courts.

The *constitutional courts* are those Congress has created under Article III to exercise "the judicial power of the United States." Together with the Supreme Court, these tribunals—the Courts of Appeals, the District Courts, the Court of Claims, the Customs Court, and the Court of Customs and Patent Appeals—are often called the "regular courts."

The *special courts* do not exercise "the judicial power of the United States." Rather, they have been created by Congress to hear cases arising out of the exercise of certain of the legislative powers vested in Congress by Article I. For example, one of them, the Court of Military Appeals, hears only certain cases arising out of the courts-martial system in the armed forces. It was created by Congress in 1950 as an exercise of its power "to make rules for the government and regulation of the land and naval forces."[2] Today, these courts are often referred to as the "legislative courts." They include, in addition to the Court of Military Appeals, the United States Tax Court, the various territorial courts, and the courts of the District of Columbia.

The Constitutional Courts

Jurisdiction. Jurisdiction may be defined as the authority of a court to hear (to *try* and to *decide*) a case. The term means, literally, the power "to say the law." Under Article III the federal courts have jurisdiction over a case either because of: (1) the subject matter involved in the case, or (2) the parties involved in the case.

SUBJECT MATTER. In terms of subject matter, the federal courts may hear a case if it involves:

(1) a question of the interpretation and application of a provision in the federal Constitution or in any federal statute or treaty; or

(2) a question of admiralty or maritime law.[3]

Any case which falls into either of these categories can be brought in the proper federal court.

PARTIES. A case also comes within the jurisdiction of the federal courts if one of the parties (one of the *litigants*) involved in the case is:

(1) the United States or one of its officers or agencies;

(2) an ambassador, consul, or other representative of a foreign government;

(3) a State suing:
(a) another State,
(b) a citizen of another State, or
(c) a foreign government or one of its subjects;[4]

(4) a citizen of one State suing a citizen of another State;

(5) an American citizen suing a foreign government or one of its subjects; or

(6) a citizen of one State suing a citizen of that same State where both claim land under grants from different States.

Any case which falls within one of these categories can be brought in the proper federal court.

All of this may seem quite complicated—and it is. But notice that is a reflection of federalism and, so, of a dual system of courts in this country. To put the whole point of the jurisdiction of the federal courts the other way around: Those cases which are not heard by the federal courts are within the jurisdiction of the State courts.

Still more must be said on the federal courts' power to "say the law."

EXCLUSIVE AND CONCURRENT JURISDICTION. In several of the categories of cases we have just listed, the federal courts have *exclusive jurisdiction.* That is, such cases can be heard *only* in the federal courts. For example, a case involving ambassadors, other public ministers, and consuls *must* be tried in a federal court. Or, a case involving the application of the patent or copyright laws falls within the exclusive jurisdiction of the federal courts.

---

[2] Article I, Section 8, Clause 14, see page 342.

[3] *Admiralty law* relates to matters which arise on the high seas or the navigable waters of the United States. *Maritime law* relates to matters arising on land but directly related to the water—for example, a contract to deliver ship's supplies at dockside. The Framers purposefully gave the federal courts exclusive jurisdiction in all admiralty and maritime cases in order to assure national supremacy in the regulation of all waterborne commerce.

[4] Note that the 11th Amendment provides that a State may *not* be sued in the federal courts by a citizen of another State or of a foreign state. A State *may* be sued without its consent in the federal courts only by the United States, another State or a foreign state. If a citizen of the State, of another State, or of a foreign state wishes to sue a State he or she may do so only with that State's consent and only in that State's own courts. But, as above, a State may bring suit against a citizen of another State, an alien, or a foreign state in the federal courts.

Many cases, particularly those involving residents of different States, may be tried *either* in a federal *or* in a State court. In such instances, the federal and State courts have *concurrent jurisdiction*; that is, they share jurisdiction. Cases involving residents of different States are commonly referred to as cases in *diverse citizenship*. The principal reason why such cases may be heard in federal courts is to provide a neutral forum to decide the dispute involved. That reason reflects an early fear that State courts (and their juries) might be prejudiced against "foreigners" from another State. There seems little real likelihood of such bias today. And many judicial authorities urge the elimination of federal jurisdiction in such cases—in order to eliminate the heavy burden they impose on the federal courts.

Congress has provided that the federal District Courts may hear such cases *only* if the amount involved exceeds $10,000. In a diversity case, the plaintiff[5] may bring the suit in the appropriate State or federal court as he or she chooses. If brought before the State court, however, the defendant[6] may have the case transferred to the federal District Court.

ORIGINAL AND APPELLATE JURISDICTION. A court in which a case is heard first-hand is said to have *original jurisdiction* over it. A court which hears a case on appeal from a lower court exercises *appellate jurisdiction*. In the federal court system, the District Courts have only original jurisdiction, the Courts of Appeals have only appellate jurisdiction; the Supreme Court has both.

The District Courts. The United States District Courts are the federal trial courts. They now dispose of more than 180,000 cases a year—some 90 percent of all of the federal case load. As the Courts

"WE MIGHT AS WELL ABOLISH THE LOWER COURTS. ALL THE CASES ARE COMING TO US ANYWAY."

Copyright (c) 1974. Reprinted by permission of *Saturday Review* and Bob Schochet

of Appeals and the Supreme Court handle only some 20,000 cases annually, most federal cases not only begin but also end at the District Court level.

The District Courts were established by the First Congress in 1789. There are, altogether, 91 of these tribunals today. The 50 States are divided into a total of 89 federal judicial districts, with one court for each district. There is also a United States District Court for the District of Columbia and another for Puerto Rico.

Each State forms at least one federal judicial district, and the larger, more populous ones include two or more districts. This is because of the greater volume of judicial business arising in those States, of course. At least one judge is assigned to each district, but in many several judges preside over the same United States District Court. Thus, the State of New York is

---

[5] A *plaintiff* is one who commences a suit in law against another.

[6] A *defendant* is a party who must make answer, defend himself or herself, in a legal action.

FEDERAL JUDICIAL CIRCUITS AND DISTRICTS

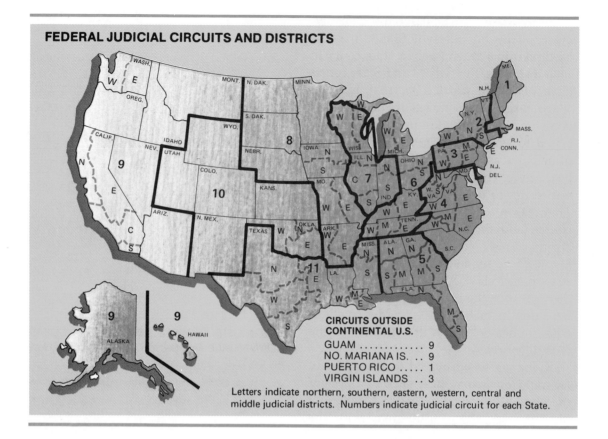

CIRCUITS OUTSIDE
CONTINENTAL U.S.

GUAM 9
NO. MARIANA IS. . . 9
PUERTO RICO 1
VIRGIN ISLANDS . . 3

Letters indicate northern, southern, eastern, western, central and
middle judicial districts. Numbers indicate judicial circuit for each State.

divided into four districts, one of them with 27 judges. All told, 507 federal district judges now preside over the 91 federal District Courts.

Cases tried in the District Courts are most often heard by a single judge, but an occasional case is tried before a three-judge panel.[7]

JURISDICTION. The District Courts have original jurisdiction over all federal cases except those within the original jurisdic-

tion of the Supreme Court and those which are tried in the Court of Claims, the Customs Court, the Court of Customs and Patent Appeals, or in the special courts.

Hence, they hear a wide variety of cases. They hear criminal cases ranging from bank robbery and kidnapping to counterfeiting and tax evasion. They hear civil cases arising under the bankruptcy, postal, tax, labor relations, public lands, civil rights, and other laws of the United States. They are the only federal courts that regularly employ *grand juries* (to indict) and *petit juries* (to try) defendants.

Cases decided in the District Courts may be appealed to the Court of Appeals for the judicial circuit in which it is located, as we shall see in a moment. And, in a few instances, they may be taken directly to the Supreme Court.

The Courts of Appeals. The Courts of Appeals were created by Congress in 1891

---

[7] Congress has directed that three-judge panels hear certain cases. Chiefly, these are cases involving congressional districting or State legislative apportionment questions, those arising under the Civil Rights Act of 1964 and the Voting Rights Acts of 1965, 1970, and 1975, and certain anti-trust actions. Until recently, three-judge courts also heard any case seeking an injunction (restraining order) to prevent the enforcement of a federal or State law on grounds of unconstitutionality. Congress repealed this requirement in 1976, however; such cases are now heard by a single judge.

to relieve the Supreme Court of much of the burden of appeals from the District Courts.[8] Those appeals had become so numerous that the High Court was three years behind its docket at that point.

There are now 12 Courts of Appeals. The United States is divided into 11 judicial circuits, and for each there is a Court of Appeals. There is also a Court of Appeals in the District of Columbia.

Today, 132 circuit judges sit on the 12 Courts of Appeals, and one Justice of the Supreme Court is also assigned to each of them. Thus, the Court of Appeals for the Seventh Circuit encompasses three States: Illinois, Indiana, and Wisconsin. It sits in Chicago and is composed of nine judges plus Justice John Paul Stevens of the Supreme Court. The Ninth Circuit covers nine States: Arizona, Nevada, California, Oregon, Washington, Idaho, Montana, Alaska, and Hawaii, and Guam and the Northern Mariana Islands. Its Court of Appeals has 20 judges, and Justice William H. Rehnquist is also assigned to it. The court regularly sits in San Francisco but holds sessions in several other cities within its jurisdiction, as well.

Each of the Courts of Appeals usually sits in panels of three judges. But, occasionally, and to hear an important case, one of them will sit *en banc*—that is, with all of the judges participating. One or more of the District Court judges from within the circuit may be assigned to sit with the appellate court when its docket of cases becomes particularly heavy.

JURISDICTION. The Courts of Appeals have only appellate jurisdiction. They hear appeals from decisions in the lower federal courts—most often from the District Courts but also from the United States Tax Court and the various territorial courts. They also hear appeals from the decisions of various federal regulatory agencies—from such *quasi-judicial* agencies as the Interstate Commerce Commission, the Civil Aeronautics Board, and the Federal Trade Commission, as we noted on page 425.

The Courts of Appeals now dispose of some 18,000 cases a year. Their decisions are final—except to the extent that the Supreme Court chooses to accept appeals from them.

The Supreme Court. The Supreme Court of the United States is the only court specifically created in the Constitution.[9] It is composed of the Chief Justice of the United States, whose office is also established in the Constitution,[10] and eight Associate Justices.[11]

It would be well-nigh impossible to overstate the significance of the role of the Supreme Court in the American system of government. Its role in both the historical development of the system and its present-day operations cannot be overstressed. The Framers of the Constitution purposefully placed it on a co-equal plane with the President and Congress and designed it as the apex of the nation's judicial system. As the highest court in the land, the Supreme Court stands as the court of last resort in *all* questions of federal law. That is, it is the final authority in *any* case involving *any* question arising under any provision in the Constitution, an act of Congress, or a treaty of the United States.

THE SUPREME COURT AND JUDICIAL REVIEW. As we have noted, most courts in this country, federal and State, may exercise

---

[8] These tribunals were originally known as the Circuit Courts of Appeals. Congress changed their title in 1948 but they are still frequently referred to as the Circuit Courts. Prior to 1891 Supreme Court Justices "rode circuit" to hear appeals from the District Courts.

[9] Article III, Section 1.

[10] Article I, Section 3, Clause 6.

[11] Congress determines the number of Associate Justices and thus the size of the Supreme Court. The Judiciary Act of 1789 established a Court of six justices, the Chief Justice and five Associate Justices. The Court was reduced to five members in 1801, increased to seven in 1807, to nine in 1837, and to 10 in 1863; it was reduced to seven in 1866 and then raised to its present size in 1869.

the critically important power of *judicial review*. That is, they have the extraordinary power to determine the constitutionality of a governmental action, whether executive, legislative, or judicial (see pages 86–87). The *ultimate* exercise of the power rests with the Supreme Court of the United States. That single fact makes the Supreme Court the final authority on the meaning of the Constitution.

The Constitution does not *in so many words* provide for the power of judicial review. But there is little room for doubt that the Framers intended that the federal courts, and especially the Supreme Court, should possess the power.[12] In *The Federalist No. 78*, Alexander Hamilton wrote:

> The interpretation of the laws is the proper and peculiar province of the courts. A constitution is, in fact, and must be regarded by the judges, as a fundamental law. It therefore belongs to them to ascertain its meaning, as well as the meaning of any particular act proceeding from the legislative body. If there should happen to be an irreconcilable variance between the two, that which has the superior obligation and validity ought, of course, to be preferred; or, in other words, the Constitution ought to be preferred to the statute, the intention of the people to the intention of their agents.

The Court first asserted its possession of the power of judicial review in the classic case of *Marbury* v. *Madison* in 1803.[13] The case arose in the aftermath of the stormy elections of 1800. Thomas Jefferson and his Anti-Federalists had won the Presidency and, as well, control of both houses of Congress.

The outgoing Federalists, stung by their defeat, then attempted to pack the judiciary with loyal party members. Several new federal judgeships were created by Congress in the early weeks of 1801. President John Adams promptly filled these new posts with Federalist appointees.

William Marbury had been appointed a justice of the peace for the District of Columbia. The Senate had confirmed his appointment and, late the night of March 3, 1801, the President had signed his and a number of other new judges' commissions of office. On the next day Jefferson became President—and found that Marbury's commission, and several others, had not been delivered.

Enraged by the Federalists' court-packing, Jefferson immediately instructed James Madison, the new Secretary of State, not to deliver those commissions to the "midnight justices." Marbury then sued Madison in the Supreme Court. He sought a *writ of mandamus*[14] to compel delivery.

Marbury brought his suit on the basis of a provision of the Judiciary Act of 1789, in which Congress had created the federal court system. That provision empowered the Supreme Court to hear such suits in its *original* jurisdiction, not on appeal from a lower court.

In a unanimous opinion written by Chief Justice John Marshall, the Court refused Marbury's request.[15] It did so be-

---

[12] Consult Article III, Section 2, setting out the Court's jurisdiction, and Article VI, Section 2, the Supremacy Clause.

[13] It is often said that the Court first *exercised* the power in this case; but, in fact, the Court did so at least as early as 1796. It did so when, in *Hylton* v. *United States*, it *upheld* the constitutionality of a tax Congress had levied on carriages. It held the tax not to be a "direct tax" and thus not one which would have to be apportioned among the States in accord with Article I, Section 2, Clause 3.

[14] A court order compelling an officer of government to perform an act which that officer has a clear legal duty to perform.

[15] Marshall was appointed Chief Justice by President Adams and assumed the office on January 31, 1801. He served in the post for 34 years, until his death on July 6, 1835. He also served as Adams' Secretary of State, from May 13, 1800 to March 4, 1801. Thus, he served *simultaneously* as Secretary of State *and* Chief Justice for more than a month at the end of the Adams Administration. Moreover, *he* was the Secretary of State who had failed to deliver Marbury's commission in timely fashion.

cause it found the pertinent section of the Judiciary Act in conflict with the Constitution and, therefore, void. Specifically, it found the statute to be in conflict with Article III, Section 2, Clause 2 which reads in part:

> In all cases affecting ambassadors, other public ministers and consuls, and those in which a State shall be a party, the Supreme Court shall have original jurisdiction. In all other cases before mentioned, the Supreme Court shall have appellate jurisdiction . . .

Marshall's powerful opinion supporting the Court's decision was based upon these three propositions: (1) The Constitution is, by its own terms, *the* supreme law of the land. (2) All legislative enactments, and all other actions of government, are subordinate to and cannot validly conflict with the supreme law. And (3) judges are sworn to enforce the provisions of the Constitution and are therefore obligated to refuse to enforce any governmental action they find to be in conflict with it.

As we have seen, the Court has exercised its power of judicial review thousands of times since 1803. Usually it has upheld, but sometimes denied, the constitutionality of federal and State actions.

The dramatic and often far-reaching effects of the Supreme Court's exercise of the power of judicial review tends to overshadow other aspects of its work. Each year it hears dozens of cases in which questions of constitutionality are *not* raised but in which federal law is nevertheless interpreted and applied. Thus, many of the more important statutes enacted by Congress have been brought to the Supreme

CHIEF JUSTICES OF THE UNITED STATES

Name	State From Which Appointed	President By Whom Appointed	Years Of Service	Life Span	Age When Appointed
John Jay	New York	Washington	1789–1795	1745–1829	44
John Rutledge[a,b]	South Carolina	Washington	1795	1739–1800	55
Oliver Ellsworth	Connecticut	Washington	1796–1800	1745–1807	51
John Marshall	Virginia	John Adams	1801–1835	1755–1835	46
Roger B. Taney	Maryland	Jackson	1836–1864	1777–1864	59
Salmon P. Chase	Ohio	Lincoln	1864–1873	1808–1873	56
Morrison R. Waite	Ohio	Grant	1874–1888	1816–1888	58
Melville W. Fuller	Illinois	Cleveland	1888–1910	1833–1910	55
Edward D. White[b]	Louisiana	Taft	1910–1921	1845–1921	65
William Howard Taft	Connecticut	Harding	1921–1930	1857–1930	64
Charles Evans Hughes[b]	New York	Hoover	1930–1941	1862–1948	68
Harlan F. Stone[b]	New York	F. D. Roosevelt	1941–1946	1872–1946	69
Fred M. Vinson	Kentucky	Truman	1946–1953	1890–1953	56
Earl Warren	California	Eisenhower	1953–1969	1891–1974	62
Warren E. Burger	Dist. of Columbia	Nixon	1969–	1907–	61

[a] Rutledge was appointed Chief Justice by President George Washington on July 1, 1795, while the Congress was not in session. He presided over the August 1795 term of the Supreme Court; but the Senate refused to confirm his appointment, rejecting it on December 15, 1795. Rutledge subsequently went insane.

[b] Four men served as Associate Justice before being appointed as Chief Justice: John Rutledge, from 1789 to 1791; White, 1894 to 1910; Hughes, 1910 to 1916; and Stone, 1925 to 1941. Rutledge was appointed an Associate Justice when the Supreme Court was first organized in 1789; but he resigned a year and a half later, having attended no sessions of the Court. Hughes resigned as an Associate Justice in 1916 to seek the Presidency. White and Stone each were serving as Associate Justice when elevated to Chief Justice.

Court repeatedly for decision. For example, the Interstate Commerce Act, the Sherman Antitrust Act, the Social Security Act, the National Labor Relations (Wagner) Act— and many of the lesser ones, as well, have reached the Court for decision. In interpreting these statutes and applying them to specific situations, the Supreme Court has had a considerable impact upon their meaning and effect.

As we have noted, the Court also plays a very significant role as the arbiter or referee in the federal system; see pages 86–87. It decides the legal disputes which arise between the National Government and the States and those which arise between or among the States.

JURISDICTION. The Supreme Court has both original and appellate jurisdiction. But it is primarily an appellate tribunal. Most of the cases it hears come to it on appeal from the lower federal and the State courts. Article III, Section 2 defines two classes of cases which may be heard by the Supreme Court under its *original* jurisdiction. They are: (1) those in which a State is

a party; and (2) those affecting ambassadors, public ministers, and consuls.

Congress cannot enlarge upon this constitutional grant of original jurisdiction. Recall that this is what the Supreme Court ruled in holding a portion of the Judiciary Act of 1789 unconstitutional in *Marbury* v. *Madison*. If Congress could do so, it would in effect be amending the Constitution. But Congress can *implement* the constitutional provision, and it has. It has provided that the Supreme Court shall exercise original *and exclusive* jurisdiction over: (1) all controversies between two or more States; and (2) all cases *against* ambassadors or other public ministers (but not consuls). The Court may take original jurisdiction over the other cases covered by the broad wording of Article III. But these cases usually are tried in the lower courts.

HOW CASES REACH THE COURT. Some 3500 to 4000 cases are now appealed to the High Court each year. Of these, only a few hundred are accepted for decision, however. In the large bulk of cases, then, the petitions for review are denied—usually

The Supreme Court Justices pictured here are (standing, left to right): William H. Rehnquist, Harry A. Blackmun, Lewis F. Powell, and John P. Stevens; seated (left to right): Byron R. White, William J. Brennan, Chief Justice Warren E. Burger, Potter Stewart, and Thurgood Marshall.

because all or at least most of the Court is in agreement with the decision of the lower court or it feels no significant point of law is involved.

More than half of the cases actually decided by the Court are disposed of in brief orders. For example, a case may be disposed of in an order *remanding* (returning) it to a lower court for reconsideration in the light of some other recent and related case decided by the Supreme Court. All told, the Court decides, after hearing arguments and with full opinions, only about 100 to 120 cases each year.

Generally, cases come to the Supreme Court either by *certiorari* or on *appeal.* Most cases reach the Court by *writ of certiorari* (from the Latin, "to be made more certain"). This is an order by the Court directing a lower court to send up the record in a given case because one of the parties alleges some error in the lower court's handling of that case. An *appeal* involves a petition by one of the parties to a case requesting the Court to review the lower court's decision in the case. A few cases do reach the Court in a third way, by *certificate.* The process is used when a lower court is unsure of the procedure or the rule of law that should apply in a case. The lower court asks the Supreme Court to certify the answer to a specific question in the matter.

Most cases which reach the Court do so from the highest State courts and the federal Courts of Appeals. Some do come, however, from the federal District Courts, as we have seen. Some also come from the Court of Claims, the Court of Customs and Patent Appeals, and the Court of Military Appeals.

Speaking of the appellate role of the Supreme Court, the late Chief Justice Fred M. Vinson once told a meeting of the American Bar Association:

> The Supreme Court is not, and never has been, primarily concerned with the correction of errors in lower court decisions. In almost all cases within the Court's appellate jurisdiction, the petitioner has already received one appellate review of his case. The debates in the Constitutional Convention make clear that the purpose of one supreme national tribunal was, in the words of John Rutledge of South Carolina, "to secure the national rights & uniformity of Judgmts." The function of the Supreme Court is, therefore, to resolve conflicts of opinion on federal questions that have arisen among lower courts, to pass upon questions of wide import under the Constitution, laws, and treaties of the United States, and to exercise supervisory power over lower federal courts. If we took every case in which an interesting legal question is raised, or our *prima facie* impression is that the decision below is erroneous, we could not fulfill the Constitutional and statutory responsibilities placed upon the Court. To remain effective, the Supreme Court must continue to decide only those cases which present questions whose resolution will have immediate importance far beyond the particular facts and parties involved.[16]

THE SUPREME COURT AT WORK. The Supreme Court sits for a term of about nine months each year—from the first Monday in October until some time the following July. Customarily, the Justices hear arguments in the cases before them for two weeks, then they recess for two weeks to prepare their opinions. While arguments are being heard, the Court opens at 10 A.M., Monday through Thursday.

Monday is usually "decision day"; the decisions ready for release are announced at the beginning of that day's session.[17] Once the decisions have been announced and the Justices have read their opinions which accompany them, the Court turns to the hearing of oral arguments in the next cases on the docket.

---

[16] Chief Justice Fred M. Vinson, "The Work of the Supreme Court," *Supreme Court Reporter,* Vol. 69, 1949, p. v.

[17] Since 1965, however, the Court has adopted the practice of releasing decisions on other days, as well.

Each of the parties to a case (the *litigants*) is normally allowed one hour in which to present oral arguments. The Justices often interrupt a presentation with questions. The litigants also submit written *briefs*, detailed and systematic arguments which often run to hundreds of pages. Regularly, the Justices rely very heavily upon these briefs in reaching their decisions.

On Friday of most weeks of a term the Justices meet in conference to discuss the cases they have heard and to determine their disposition. These conferences are held in the closest secrecy, and no formal report of their conduct is ever made. Fifty years ago, the late Chief Justice Harlan Fiske Stone wrote one of the very few first-hand descriptions which exist:

At Conference each case is presented for discussion by the Chief Justice, usually a brief statement of the facts, the question of law involved, and with such suggestions for their disposition as he may think appropriate. No cases have been assigned to any particular judge in advance of the Conference. Each Justice is prepared to discuss the case at length and to give his views as to the proper solution of the questions presented. In Mr. Justice Holmes' pungent phrase, each must be able to "recite" on the case. Each Judge is requested by the Chief Justice, in the order of seniority, to give his views and the conclusions which he has reached. The discussion is of the freest character and at its end, after full opportunity for each member of the Court to be heard and for the asking and answering of questions, the vote is taken and recorded in the reverse order of the discussion, the youngest, in point of service, voting first.

On the same evening, after the conclusion of the Conference, each member of the Court receives at his home a memorandum from the Chief Justice advising him of the assignment of cases for opinions. Opinions are written for the most part in recess, and as they are written, they are printed and circulated among the Justices, who make suggestions for their correction and revision. At the next succeeding Conference these suggestions are brought before the full Conference and accepted or rejected as the case may be. On the following Monday [usually] the opinion is announced by the writer as the opinion of the Court.[18]

Six Justices constitute a quorum for the decision of a case, and at least four must agree before a case can be decided. If (as usually happens) all nine Justices take part, a case may be decided by a 9-0, 8-1, 7-2, 6-3, or 5-4 vote. Although many cases are decided unanimously, several find the Court split.

As Chief Justice Stone indicated, a *majority opinion* regularly accompanies the deciding of a case. A Justice who disagrees with the majority's decision often writes a *dissenting opinion*. Indeed, two, three, or even four dissents are occasionally presented. A Justice who agrees with the Court's decision, but not with the reasoning by which it was reached, often prepares a *concurring opinion*. One or more of these opinions are often presented.

The Supreme Court is sometimes criticized because many cases are not decided by unanimous vote, but rather by "split decisions." But most of the cases the Court hears involve very difficult and controversial issues. The "easy" cases seldom get that far. In many of them, too, there have been contradictory lower court decisions.

Neither the majority nor the concurring or dissenting opinions are actually necessary to the decision of a case. In fact, decisions are occasionally handed down without opinion. But the opinions do serve valuable purposes. The majority opinions

---

[18] Justice Harlan F. Stone, "Fifty Years of Work of the United States Supreme Court," *Report of the American Bar Association*, 1928.

Case Study

The law, it has often been observed, must be stable, yet it cannot stand still. The dilemma of providing a known set of rules while, at the same time, adapting them to cope with changing times and circumstances makes the judicial decision-making process an inherently creative one.

Many court decisions are fraught with policy implications. Thus, inevitably, judges play a major role in the making of public policy—whether they wish to or not. Judges are not automatons, not dispassionate computers searching memory banks of established rules and cranking out the particular one to apply to the facts of a given case. Rather, they must often make choices among competing contentions and competing values in reaching a decision. And frequently they can exercise considerable discretion in choosing among the alternatives available to them.

Justice Benjamin Cardoza once offered this view of the judicial decision-making process:

My analysis of the judicial process comes then to this, and little more: logic, and history, and custom, and utility, and the accepted standards of right conduct, are the forces which singly or in combination shape the progress of the law. Which of these forces will dominate in any case must depend largely on the comparative importance or value of the social interest that will thereby be promoted or impaired. . . . If you ask how [the judge] is to know when one interest outweighs another, I can only answer that he must get his knowledge just as the legislator gets it; from experience and study and reflection; in brief from life itself.

■ Why must the law be simultaneously stable and adaptable? Are judges any more or less susceptible to the influence of those factors and events which have shaped their lives than are other human beings? Would a judge like William O. Douglas, who, as a young man, was nearly killed by a railroad detective, have seen a case involving alleged police brutality in the same light as a judge who was reared in a wealthy, socially prominent family environment?

■ If you were asked to appoint a judge, what characteristics would you seek? Would they vary, depending on the court over which the judge presided? If so, how?

---

stand as precedents to be followed in similar cases as they arise in the lower courts or reach the Supreme Court. The concurring opinions may prompt the Supreme Court to go beyond its present position in future cases. Chief Justice Hughes once described dissenting opinions as "an appeal to the brooding spirit of the law, to the intelligence of a future day." The minority opinion of the Supreme Court today might become its majority opinion in a case heard in the future.

The Other Constitutional Courts. Three other constitutional courts—each originally created by Congress as a special court—exist today.

THE COURT OF CLAIMS. The United States may not be sued by one of the States or by an individual without its consent.[19] If this were not the case, the courts would be flooded and the Government hamstrung by all manner of unfounded claims.

Originally, any person having a claim against the United States could secure *redress* (satisfaction of the claim, payment) only by special act of Congress. In 1855, however, Congress, acting under its power

---

[19] This immunity from suit comes down from the ancient principle of English public law summed up by the phrase: "The King can do no wrong."

THE NATIONAL JUDICIARY

Court	Created	Number of Courts	Number of Judges	Term of Judges	Judges Appointed By[a]	Salary of Judges
District Court	1789	91	507	Life	President	$57,528
Court of Appeals	1891	12	132	Life	President	$60,663
Supreme Court	1789	1	9	Life	President	$75,960[b]
Court of Claims	1855	1	7	Life	President	$60,663
Customs Court	1926	1	9	Life	President	$57,528
Court of Customs and Patent Appeals	1909 and 1929	1	5	Life	President	$60,663
Court of Military Appeals	1950	1	3	15 years	President	$60,663
United States Tax Court	1969	1	16	12 years	President	$57,528

[a] With Senate confirmation.   [b] Chief Justice receives $79,125.

to pay the debts of the United States,[20] created the Court of Claims as a special court. Congress established it as one of the constitutional courts in 1953.

The Court is composed of a chief judge and six associate judges. They hear claims for money damages against the Federal Government. When a claim is filed, testimony and evidence are taken by one of 16 trial judges. Then the case is submitted to the court itself for decision.[21]

Awards made by the Court of Claims cannot be paid unless and until Congress makes the necessary appropriations. The funds are provided almost as a matter of course, however. Occasionally, those who lose in the Court of Claims still manage to secure compensation. Some years ago, for example, a mink rancher lost a case in which he claimed that low-flying Navy planes had caused several of his female mink to become sterile. He asked $100 per mink, but the Government was able to

show that any one of several factors—including diet, weather, and fights and jealousies in the group—could have caused the condition. Even so, his Representative introduced a bill that eventually paid him $10 for each animal.

Appeals from decisions of the Court of Claims may be carried to the Supreme Court.

THE CUSTOMS COURT. The Customs Court was originally created in 1890 as the Board of United States General Appraisers. Congress renamed it in 1926 and made it one of the constitutional courts in 1956.

The Customs Court consists of nine judges, one of whom serves as chief judge. It hears disputes arising out of the administration of the tariff laws. Thus, most of its cases involve decisions made by customs officers in the Treasury Department. Its judges sit in divisions of three and hear cases at such principal ports of entry as New York, Boston, New Orleans, and San Francisco. Appeals from decisions of the Customs Court are taken to the Court of Customs and Patent Appeals.

THE COURT OF CUSTOMS AND PATENT APPEALS. The Court of Customs and Patent Appeals was established as a special court in 1909 and made a constitutional court in

---

[20] Article I, Section 8, Clause 1.

[21] Under the Federal Tort Claims Act of 1946 the District Courts also have jurisdiction over many claims cases, but their jurisdiction is limited to cases in which the redress sought does not exceed $10,000; the same statute also gives executive agencies the authority to settle claims under $1000.

1958. Its chief judge and four associate judges sit *en banc,* usually in Washington.

It hears appeals from cases decided in the Customs Court. It also decides those challenges brought to actions taken by two agencies in the executive branch: those of the Patent and Trademark Office relating to applications for or infringements on patents or trademarks, and the findings of the United States International Trade Commission involving unfair practices in the nation's import trade.

Appeals from the decisions of the Court of Customs and Patent Appeals may be taken to the Supreme Court.

The Special Courts

The special courts, often called the *legislative courts,* are those Congress has created to exercise jurisdiction only in certain cases— cases involving particular subjects included within the expressed powers of Congress. That is, they have not been created under Article III and vested with "the judicial power of the United States." Rather, they have each been established to hear certain cases arising out of the exercise of specific congressional powers.

The Territorial Courts. Acting under its authority to "make all needful rules and regulations respecting the territory . . . belonging to the United States,"[22] Congress has created local courts for the Virgin Islands, Guam, and the Northern Mariana Islands (in the Pacific Trust Territory). These territorial courts function in much the same manner as do the local courts in the 50 States. (Recall, there is a regular federal District Court in Puerto Rico.)

The Courts of the District of Columbia. Acting under its power to "exercise exclusive legislation in all cases whatsoever, over such District . . . as may . . . become the seat of Government of the United States,"[23] Congress has provided a judicial system for the nation's capital. Both the federal District Court and the Court of Appeals for the District of Columbia hear many local cases in addition to those they hear as constitutional courts. Congress has also established two *local* courts, similar to the courts of the various States: a Superior Court, which is the general trial court, and an appellate Court of Appeals.

The Court of Military Appeals. Acting under the power "to make rules for the government and regulation of the land and naval forces,"[24] Congress created the Court of Military Appeals in 1950. It is composed of a chief judge and two associate judges, appointed by the President and Senate for 15-year terms.

The Court is sometimes called the "GI Supreme Court." It reviews the more serious courts-martial convictions of members of the armed forces. That is, it is the court of last resort in the prosecution of offenses against military law.

The United States Tax Court. Acting under its power to tax, Congress established the Tax Court in 1969.[25] It is composed of 19 judges, one of whom serves as chief judge; they are appointed by the President and Senate for 12-year terms.

The Tax Court hears civil—not criminal—cases involving disputes over the application of the tax laws. Most of its caseload is generated, then, by the actions of the Internal Revenue Service and other Treasury Department agencies.

---

[22] Article IV, Section 3, Clause 2; see page 340.

[23] Article I, Section 8, Clause 17; see page 340.

[24] Article I, Section 8, Clause 14. This provision, and the 5th Amendment, permits Congress to regulate the conduct of members of the armed forces in a separate (non-civilian) code of military law. The Uniform Code of Military Justice, enacted in 1950, is the present, lengthy, and oft-amended statute designed to meet the special disciplinary needs of the military.

[25] Article I, Section 8, Clause 1. When it created this tribunal Congress abolished the Tax Court of the United States—which was not in fact a court but an independent agency in the executive branch.

The Judges

Appointment. The President appoints all federal judges, subject to Senate confirmation. The Constitution provides that the President "shall nominate, and, by and with the advice and consent of the Senate, shall appoint . . . judges of the Supreme Court."[26] And Congress has provided for the same procedure for the selection of all other federal judges. Hence the President is free to appoint to the federal bench whomever the Senate will confirm. Put another, and equally meaningful, way, the President and the Senate are partners in the process.

Most federal judges are drawn from the ranks of leading attorneys, legal scholars and law school professors, former members of Congress, and from the State courts. Judicial selections are shaped by the same sorts of considerations as other exercises of the Chief Executive's appointing power—which we considered on pages 402–403. In short, the judicial selection process involves a combination of inputs. The President and his closest political and legal aides—including, especially, the Attorney General—take leading parts, of course. But major roles are also played by influential Senators—most notably those from the nominee's home State; by the legal profession—especially the American Bar Association's Committee on the Federal Judiciary; and by various other personalities in the President's political party.

Term. Article III, Section 1 reads, in part:

> The judges, both of the Supreme and inferior courts, shall hold their offices during good behavior . . .

In effect, all judges of the constitutional courts are appointed for life—until they resign, retire, or die in office. They may be removed only through the impeachment process. Only nine federal judges have

ever been impeached—and none in more than 40 years. Of the nine impeached, only four were found guilty by the Senate.[27]

The provision of life tenure for judges is intended and works to insure the independence of the judiciary.

The judges of the territorial courts and those of the District of Columbia are appointed for terms varying from four to eight years. The judges of the Court of Military Appeals serve 15-year terms and those of the Tax Court 12 years.

Compensation. Article III, Section 1 also provides that federal judges:

> . . . shall, at stated times, receive for their services a compensation which shall not be diminished during their continuance in office.

Congress sets the salary scale for all federal judges. For the salaries federal judges receive today (1981), see the table on page 658.

Congress has provided a rather generous retirement arrangement for the judges of the constitutional courts. They may retire at age 70 and, if they have served for at least 10 years, receive their full salary for the remainder of their lives; or they may retire on full salary at age 65 after at least 15 years of service on the federal bench.

---

[26] Article II, Section 2, Clause 2.

[27] Judge John Pickering of the District Court in New Hampshire, for irregular judicial procedures, loose morals, and drunkenness in 1803; Judge West H. Humphreys of the District Court in Tennessee, for disloyalty in 1862; Judge Robert W. Archibald of the old Commerce Court, for improper relations with parties to cases in his court, 1913; and Judge Halstead L. Ritter of the District Court in Florida, for bringing his court into "scandal and disrepute" in 1936. Four other judges were impeached by the House but acquitted in the Senate: District Court Judges James H. Peck of Missouri in 1831; Charles Swayne of Florida, 1905; Howard Louderback of California, 1933; and Associate Justice Samuel Chase of the Supreme Court in 1804–1805. Mr. Justice Chase had been impeached for extreme partisanship and overzealous prosecution of sedition cases. A few District Court judges have resigned to avoid impeachment. One, Judge George W. English of the District Court in Illinois, was impeached in 1926 for partiality, tyranny, and oppression in his court; but he resigned before the Senate could try him. See page 347.

The Chief Justice may call any retired judge back to active service in the lower federal courts at any time, however.

Judicial Administration

Federal judges are today little involved in the day-to-day administrative operations of the courts over which they preside. Their primary mission is to hear and decide the cases brought before them. Other judicial personnel provide the support services necessary to permit them to perform that mission.

Court Officers. Each federal court appoints a *Clerk* who has custody of the seal of the court and keeps a record of the court's proceeding. The clerk is assisted by deputy clerks, stenographers, bailiffs, and such other attendants as are needed.

Each of the 91 federal District Courts now appoints at least one *United States Magistrate*. These court officers are chosen in whatever number they are needed and available funding will allow. They serve for eight-year terms and handle a variety of legal matters once dealt with by the judges themselves. Magistrates issue warrants for arrest, and they often hear evidence to determine whether or not a person who has been arrested on a federal charge should now be held for action by the grand jury. They also set bail in federal criminal cases and even have the power to try those who are accused of certain petty offenses.

The President appoints, subject to Senate confirmation, a *United States Attorney* for each federal judicial district. Attorneys and their assistants are responsible for the prosecution of all persons charged with the commission of federal crimes in the district, and they represent the United States in all civil actions to which it is a party in the district.

The President and Senate also appoint a *United States Marshal* to serve each District Court. Each federal marshal and the marshal's deputies perform duties much like those assigned to a county sheriff and the sheriff's deputies. They make arrests in federal criminal cases, keep accused persons in custody, secure jurors, serve legal papers, keep order in the courtroom, and execute court orders and decisions.

United States Attorneys and Marshals are each appointed for four-year terms. Although they are officers of the court, they serve under the direction of the Attorney General and are officials of the Department of Justice. See page 668.

"THESE STEPS ARE KILLING ME. I SAY WE SETTLE OUT OF COURT."

Drawing by Richter; © 1968 The New Yorker Magazine, Inc.

SUMMARY

The lack of a national judiciary was one of the most serious weaknesses in the Articles of Confederation. The Framers corrected this in Article III of the Constitution. There the Supreme Court is provided for and Congress is given the power to create whatever lower courts may be needed. The federal system gives rise to a "dual system of courts" in the United States; the federal and the 50 separate State court systems function side by side.

The Congress has created two types of federal courts: the constitutional courts and special courts. The constitutional courts are the District Courts, the Courts of Appeals, the Supreme Court, the Court of Claims, the Customs Court, and the Court of Customs and Patent Appeals. The special courts are the territorial courts, the courts of the District of Columbia, the United States Tax Court, and the Court of Military Appeals.

The constitutional courts, which exercise the judicial power of the United States, have jurisdiction over a case either because of the subject matter or the parties involved. Some cases are within their exclusive jurisdiction; those heard on appeal are within their appellate jurisdiction.

The 91 District Courts hear the bulk of federal cases. The 12 Courts of Appeals hear appeals from the District Courts and the independent regulatory commission.

The Supreme Court is the highest court in the land. The importance of the fact that the ultimate exercise of the power of judicial review rests with the Supreme Court of the United States cannot be overstated. The Supreme Court generally chooses the cases it will hear on appeal from the lower federal courts and the highest State courts. It has original jurisdiction over cases against ambassadors and other public ministers and over cases involving controversies between two or more States.

The Court of Claims hears cases involving claims against the United States. The Customs Court hears disputes involving the administration of the tariff laws. The Court of Customs and Patent Appeals hears appeals from decisions of the Customs Court, from patent and trademark decisions of the Patent and Trademark Office, and United States International Trade Commission findings of unfair practices in the import trade.

The special courts are those which Congress has created *not* under Article III. They do not exercise the judicial power of the United States but handle cases arising out of the exercise of particular congressional powers. The territorial courts and those of the District of Columbia are special courts. So, too, is the Court of Military Appeals, which reviews serious courts-martial convictions, and the Tax Court, which hears appeals in civil disputes arising out of the administration of the tax laws.

Concept Development

Questions for Review

1. Which of the Articles of the Constitution deals principally with the judiciary? What does it provide?

2. Why is there a "dual system of courts" in the United States?

3. What is the chief distinction between the constitutional courts and the special courts?

4. On what two general bases do federal courts have jurisdiction of cases? What does the term *jurisdiction* mean in this context?

5. Distinguish between the terms *exclusive jurisdiction* and *concurrent jurisdiction; original jurisdiction* and *appellate jurisdiction.*

6. Why are there more District judges than there are District Courts in the national judiciary?

7. Do the District Courts exercise appellate jurisdiction?

8. Why were the Courts of Appeals created?

9. Do the Courts of Appeals exercise original jurisdiction?

10. Which is the only federal court specifically created in the Constitution?

11. How is the size of the Supreme Court determined? What is it now?

12. What is the power of judicial review? Why is its exercise by the Supreme Court so vitally important to the nature of the governmental system?

13. Why is the case of *Marbury* v. *Madison* so important?

14. From what courts are cases appealed to the Supreme Court?

15. In what classes of cases does the Supreme Court have original jurisdiction? Exclusive jurisdiction?

16. How many men have thus far served as Chief Justice of the United States? Who holds this office today?

17. Why are many of the decisions of the Supreme Court split decisions?

18. Which of the constitutional courts were originally created as special courts?

19. Over what particular types of cases does the Court of Claims have jurisdiction? The Customs Court? The Court of Customs and Patent Appeals?

20. Which are the special courts in the national judiciary?

21. Over what particular types of cases do the territorial courts have jurisdiction? The courts of the District of Columbia? The Court of Military Appeals? The Tax Court?

22. Who appoints all federal judges? For what terms?

23. How may judges be removed from office?

24. What restriction does the Constitution place on Congress' power to set judicial salaries?

25. What are the major functions of the Clerks of the federal courts?

26. What are the major functions of the United States Magistrates? Attorneys? Marshals?

For Further Inquiry

1. The Constitution prescribes no qualifications for judicial office beyond the provision that those whom the President appoints must be acceptable to the Senate. What qualifications do you think a President should set in making appointments to the federal bench? Would you favor the popular election of federal judges?

2. Do courts, as they decide cases, "make law" when they interpret and apply provisions in statutes or in the Constitution? Explain.

3. The federal judicial salaries shown in the table on page 658 are those which are now (1981) provided by law. Congress set them in 1979. It did so out of a very peculiar chain of circumstances, however. On October 1 it allowed all federal judges a 12.9 percent increase in pay. But 11 days later it revised that action, providing for increases of only 5.5 percent. (The salaries set out in the table reflect that latter congressional action.) Why do many judges (and others) now argue that every federal judge who was in office October 1, 1979, is lawfully entitled to the higher salary the 12.9 percent increase would have provided? Why have Congress and the President refused to accept that view?

4. Do you agree or disagree with this observation: The principles of popular sovereignty and majority rule, on the one hand, and that of judicial review on the other, are clearly contradictory and cannot logically exist together in a governmental system. Explain.

Suggested Activities

1. Write a short essay based on this comment by Chief Justice Hughes:

Democracy will survive only as long as the quick whims of the majority are held in check by the courts in favor of a dominant and lasting sense of justice. If democratic institutions are long to survive, it will not be simply by maintaining majority rule and by the swift adaptation to the demands of the moment, but by the dominance of a sense of justice which will not long survive if judicial processes do not conserve it.

Compare this observation with Judge Learned Hand's, quoted on page 122.

2. If possible, attend a session of the nearest United States District Court and report your observations of the proceedings to the class.

3. Invite a local judge or attorney to speak to the class on the nature of the law, the legal profession, and our court system.

4. Hold a debate or class forum on the question: *Resolved,* That since Justices of the Supreme Court serve as the final arbitrators regarding the constitutionality of legislative and executive action, they should be selected by means other than presidential appointment, thus removing them from the sphere of politics.

Suggested Reading

Abraham, Henry J., *The Judicial Process.* Oxford, 4th ed., 1980.

Ball, Howard, *Courts and Politics: The Federal Judicial System.* Prentice-Hall, 1980.

Baum, Lawrence, *The Supreme Court.* Congressional Quarterly Press, 1981.

Corwin, Edward S. and Peltason, J.W., *Understanding the Constitution,* Holt, Rinehart and Winston, 8th ed., 1979.

Guide to the U.S. Supreme Court. Congressional Quarterly Press, 1979.

Hobber-Williams, Richard, *The Politics of the U.S. Supreme Court.* Allen and Unwin, 1980.

Pritchett, C. Herman and Murphy, Walter F. *Courts, Judges, and Politics: An Introduction to the Judicial Process.* Random House, 1979.

Schmidhauser, John, *Judges and Justices: The Federal Appellate Judiciary.* Little, Brown, 1979.

Simon, James F., *Independent Journey: The Life of William O. Douglas.* Harper & Row, 1980.

Stephens, Otis H. and Rathijen, Gregory, *The United States Supreme Court and the Allocation of Constitutional Power.* Freeman, 1980.

Woodward, Bob and Armstrong, Scott, *The Brethren: Inside the Supreme Court.* Simon & Schuster, 1980.

Also: Director, Administrative Office of United States Courts, U.S. Supreme Court Building, Washington, D.C. 20544.

The Administration of Justice

27

The United States wins its point whenever justice is done one of its citizens in the courts.

Inscription in the Rotunda
OFFICE OF THE ATTORNEY GENERAL
OF THE UNITED STATES

■ Are "law" and "justice" synonymous terms?

■ Must democratic government necessarily be just government?

■ Does the Constitution require that all elements of government in the United States act in accord with the concept of justice?

Justice is, must be, a fundamental concern to democratic government. To establish it, says the Preamble, is one of the high purposes for which the Government of the United States was created. To provide it, wrote Thomas Jefferson, is "the most sacred of the duties of government." Eliminate it, asked St. Augustine, "and what are Kingdoms but great robberies?"

What, precisely, is "justice"? The question is a far from simple one. It is far from simple because justice is a *concept.* Justice has no *physical* existence; it cannot be seen or touched, weighed or measured. Rather, like "truth," "good," and all other concepts, it is an invention of the human mind. And, because it is a product of human thought, it means what human beings *make* it mean.

As the concept has developed in the United States, it means that the law, both in its content *and* its administration, shall be reasonable, fair, and impartial.

We have suggested before that we have not always met our professed ideal of "equal justice for all." But we have also noted this vital point: Our history is replete with evidence that we do honor that goal, that we have constantly sought to achieve it, and that we continue to do so.

In the last chapter we were concerned with the judicial machinery through which the National Government seeks to do justice. Here, we turn to the Department of Justice—to the federal *administrative machinery* charged with that high task.

665

666 / Chapter 27

The Department of Justice

The Attorney General. The Department of Justice is headed by the Attorney General of the United States. The Department itself was not created until 1870. The post of Attorney General was established by the Congress in 1789, however; and the nation's first Attorney General, Edmund Randolph, was a member of President Washington's original Cabinet. Most of Randolph's now 73 successors have followed him in the role of intimate advisor to the Presidents they have served.

Prior to 1870, the Attorney General's only formal duties were to provide legal advice to the President and his aides and to represent the United States in court. Over the years, however, those duties have multiplied considerably.

Today the AG directs the work of an agency which has described itself as "the largest law firm in the nation."[1] Through its thousands of lawyers, investigators, agents, and other employees—today, some 55,000 in all—the Justice Department furnishes legal advice to the President and to the heads of the other executive departments; enforces most of the federal criminal laws; investigates violations of those statutes and arrests those who commit federal offenses; supervises the work of the United States attorneys and marshals throughout the country; represents the United States in court; operates the federal prison system; and enforces the nation's immigration, naturalization, and narcotics laws.

The *Deputy Attorney General* is the AG's top aide in the overall direction of the Department's activities. More than that, the Deputy AG heads the Executive Office of United States Attorneys and also coordinates all of the Government's activities during any civil disturbance that erupts anywhere in this country.

Another principal aide, the *Associate Attorney General,* handles all matters involved in the presidential appointment of federal judges and directs the hiring of the Department's legal staff.

The Solicitor General. The Attorney General heads the Justice Department and is almost always a well-known national figure. The Department's principal officer in its work in the courts, the Solicitor General of the United States, is seldom so visible. Even so, he (and perhaps someday she) is a key figure in both the development and the operations of the nation's legal system.

The Solicitor General is chosen by the President and confirmed by the Senate and deserves the title "the Government's chief lawyer." He represents the United States in all cases to which it is a party in the Supreme Court,[2] and may appear in the Government's behalf in any federal or State court.

The Solicitor General decides which cases the Government should ask the Supreme Court to review and what position the United States should take in cases before the High Court. In fact, he decides when the United States will, or will not, appeal any case it loses in the lower courts. The long and short of this is that the Solicitor General plays a great and a vital role in the continuing development of our constitutional law.

One measure of the importance of the office is in the fact that it regularly attracts attorneys of outstanding qualifications and reputation. Many of its incumbents have been elevated to the Supreme Court—the most recent of them, Mr. Justice Thurgood Marshall.

---

[1] Altogether, some 20,000 attorneys work for the Federal Government. They hold positions throughout the executive branch. The Treasury Department (especially the IRS) and the several independent regulatory commissions have large legal staffs; however, well over half of all federal attorneys are employed by the Justice Department.

[2] The Attorney General may argue the Government's position in any case before the Supreme Court, of course; this rarely occurs, however.

Thurgood Marshall, shown at left conferring with his aides while serving as Solicitor General in 1965, was appointed to the Supreme Court in 1967.

The Assistant Attorneys General. Much of the workload of the Justice Department is carried by the 10 Assistant Attorneys General. Like their counterparts in the other departments, the Assistant Secretaries, they are appointed by the President and confirmed by the Senate.

One of the Assistant AG's heads the Department's *Office of Legal Counsel* and acts as the Attorney General's chief aide in the latter's role as legal advisor to the President and all of the executive branch agencies. The Assistant AG for Administration supervises the Department's internal workings. And its *Office of Legislative Affairs* and *Office for Improvements in the Administration of Justice* are each headed by one of the Assistant Attorneys General.

Each of the other Assistant AG's heads a *division* within the Department:

THE ANTITRUST DIVISION. This division investigates complaints charging violation of the Sherman, Clayton, and other antitrust statutes. Whenever it finds enough evidence to justify a prosecution, the division's lawyers (the "trustbusters") handle the case in court. It also represents the United States in cases which arise under various statutes administered by the independent regulatory commissions. Its Consumer Affairs Section tries those cases referred to Justice by the federal agencies with responsibility for consumer protec-

tion activities—for example, cases involving unfair or deceptive trade practices sent over by the Food and Drug Administration or the Federal Trade Commission.

THE TAX DIVISION. This division handles all cases involving the internal revenue laws, except for proceedings before the Tax Court.[3] Its chief function is to act as in-court counsel for the Internal Revenue Service. Several of its cases are those which are brought against individuals and firms for tax evasion, failure to file returns, or the filing of false returns. They also involve any number of different disputes over the meaning of federal tax laws—for example, the definitions of income, deductible expenses, and charitable contributions. When the IRS challenges a tax return, the tax-payer must pay the full amount and then sue for a refund.

THE CIVIL DIVISION. This division is responsible for representing the United States in all civil (that is, non-criminal) cases to which the Government is a party—except for those assigned to another division within the Department. It defends the Government in all cases brought against it in the Customs Court and most such cases in the Court of Claims.[4] It also handles civil cases involv-

---

[3] See page 659; the Tax Division does handle appeals taken from decisions of the Tax Court.

[4] See pages 657, 658.

ing admiralty or maritime law;[5] damages arising out of fraud or misrepresentation; patent, copyright, and trademark laws; damage claims against the United States; veterans' benefits matters; and much more—including all actions by and against the United States in foreign courts.

THE LAND AND NATURAL RESOURCES DIVISION. This division has charge of all noncriminal cases relating to the public lands or other real property owned by the United States. Its case load includes such varied matters as the title to or acquisition, sale, or condemnations of lands, boundary disputes, water rights, oil reserves, and mineral leases. It represents the Government's interests in all civil cases involving Indians and Indian affairs. In addition, it handles both civil and criminal cases relating to the control of sources of pollution, the preservation of wetlands, and, generally, the protection of the environment.

THE CRIMINAL DIVISION. This division prosecutes most of those cases in which persons have been accused of committing federal crimes. The many federal crimes—those activities Congress has outlawed and provided punishment for—fill more than 270 pages in the *United States Code*. These crimes range from arson, aircraft hijacking, bank robbery, and counterfeiting through kidnapping, narcotics, and perjury to trespassing, treason, and white slavery. (The Internal Security Division was quietly abolished by the Nixon Administration in 1973. It had handled all cases involving such subversive activities as espionage, sabotage, and treason, and the violations of such statutes as the Internal Security (McCarran) Act; pages 139–140. Its functions were returned to the Criminal Division—out of which it had come during the "subversives-under-the-bed" era of the 1950's.)

THE CIVIL RIGHTS DIVISION. This division is responsible for all cases arising out of constitutional and statutory guarantees of civil and political rights. Thus, it handles such cases as those involving the denial of the right to vote, racial segregation or other forms of discrimination, election frauds, slavery, the conduct of unlawful searches and seizures, and the treatment of prisoners. And, it handles all other situations in which it appears that federal, State, or local authorities have misused their authority deliberately to deprive a citizen of his or her constitutional rights. The Division also handles legal matters relating to the sentencing, custody, or escape of federal prisoners.

United States Attorneys. There is one United States attorney for each of the 91 judicial districts of the federal court system (see page 661). Each of the United States attorneys represents the United States in the federal District Court of the attorney's particular judicial district. Each has as many assistants as the Attorney General thinks necessary and the departmental budget will allow.

These offices have long been viewed, and used, as patronage plums. The President regularly consults local party leaders before selecting an appointee (who must then be confirmed by the Senate).[6]

United States Marshals. There is also one United States marshal for each of the judicial districts. They, too, are chosen by the President, confirmed by the Senate, serve four-year terms, and are picked with an eye to politics.

A marshal's principal duties are to arrest those who violate federal laws, take charge of federal prisoners, and execute the orders of federal courts. Each marshal has several deputies and, in emergencies,

---

[5] On admiralty and maritime law, see page 648.

[6] The fact that partisan politics plays a large role in the selection of United States attorneys does *not* mean that those who are appointed are not competent lawyers; most are highly qualified. Most appointments to public office— National, State, and local—are made on the basis of politics. Recall, as we pointed out in Chapter 8 and elsewhere, politics is the very stuff of which government is made, and necessarily so.

may deputize as many citizens as are needed to enforce the law.

The Immigration and Naturalization Service. The immigration and nationality laws of the United States are administered by the Immigration and Naturalization Service in the Department of Justice. It is headed by a Commissioner appointed by the President and confirmed by the Senate. The Service and the statutes it enforces are treated at length in Chapter 5.

The Bureau of Prisons. The Bureau of Prisons is responsible for the custody of all federal prisoners—that is, for all persons convicted of federal crimes and sentenced to a term of imprisonment.

The Bureau is headed by a Director who is appointed by the President and Senate. It supervises all of the federal correctional institutions—which now include five penitentiaries and 44 other facilities in various places around the country.

The five federal penitentiaries are located at Atlanta, Georgia; Marion, Illinois; Terre Haute, Indiana; Leavenworth, Kansas; and Lewisburg, Pennsylvania. They take custody of the long-term and "hard-case" federal offenders.

Various other classes of prisoners are confined at other facilities. Thus, there are several reformatories for young first offenders. Several correctional institutions house those prisoners serving intermediate-length terms, and others hold those sentenced for shorter periods. Seven of the latter are work camps where inmates are assigned to road-building and other useful outdoor work. And nine "community treatment centers" supervise prisoners involved in "work-release," drug abuse aftercare, and similar programs. The Medical Center for Federal Prisoners, at Springfield, Missouri, cares for the seriously ill; each federal penal facility has its own medical staff, of course.

Federal prisoners awaiting trial, or post-conviction transfer, or serving very short terms are often "boarded" in local

Drawing by Handelsman; © 1970
The New Yorker Magazine, Inc.

"WHAT'S SO GREAT ABOUT DUE PROCESS? DUE PROCESS GOT ME TEN YEARS."

jails under contract by the Bureau with local governments.

The Parole Commission. Sole authority to grant, modify, or revoke paroles for all federal prisoners is vested in the Parole Commission. Its nine members are appointed by the President and confirmed by the Senate.

The Parole Commission has supervision over all federal parolees and over those prisoners who are released "with time off for good behavior." In imposing sentences, judges of the District Courts often specify that the date upon which a prisoner shall become eligible for parole is to be determined by the Commission.

The Pardon Attorney. The Constitution gives to the President the power to

Future special agents go through a 15-week training program at the FBI National Academy at Quantico, Viriginia.

grant pardons, reprieves, and amnesties.[7] The Pardon Attorney investigates each application for clemency and then recommends appropriate action to the President.

The Federal Bureau of Investigation. There is *no* single national police force. Rather, several agencies investigate violations of federal law and make the appropriate arrests. Among the more important and better-known of the federal law enforcement agencies today are the United States Customs Service, the Internal Revenue Service, and the United States Secret Service, all in the Treasury Department. There are many others. But the best known of all is the Federal Bureau of Investigation—the FBI.

[7] Article II, Section 2, Clause 1; see page 410.

The FBI was first established in 1908. Its spectacular crime-busting history dates from 1934, however. During the early years of the Great Depression a wave of kidnappings, bank robberies, and other violent crimes swept the country. To meet it, the FBI was reorganized under its late Director, J. Edgar Hoover. Moving swiftly and with almost frightening efficiency, he and his agents fought the racketeering and lawlessness of the 1930's.

Hoover was appointed as the first Director of the Bureau by President Coolidge in 1924, and he was reappointed by seven Chief Executives. He held the reins of the Bureau about as firmly as any head of a federal agency, and he dominated all activities of the FBI. Always a controversial figure, Hoover was outspoken on the necessity to cut down crime and to meet the threat of internal subversion. He passed away in 1972. But his monumental influence on law enforcement in this country will survive for decades to come.

Today the FBI has charge of investigating all violations of federal laws except those assigned to another federal law enforcement agency. Altogether, the FBI has jurisdiction over some 185 investigative matters. Simply to list a few of the more important of them is to dramatize the huge scope of its concerns: treason, espionage, sabotage, and other criminal matters relating to the nation's internal security; bank robbery, kidnapping, and extortion; interstate gambling violations; crimes committed on federal reservations; theft of government property; interstate flight to avoid arrest or imprisonment; fraud against the National Government; election law violations; civil rights matters; and the assaulting or killing of a federal officer. In fact, the only major federal criminal matters beyond the FBI's jurisdiction are counterfeiting; postal, customs, and internal revenue violations; and illegal drug traffic.

The Bureau is essentially an investigative, a fact-finding, agency. Its function is to develop the facts in a given matter. It leaves to others, especially to federal prosecutors and the courts, the conclusions to be drawn from facts it has developed.

The FBI operates out of its new headquarters building in Washington, D.C., and 59 field offices. It also maintains a number of offices abroad, for liaison with foreign police and intelligence agencies. Its annual budget is now well over half a billion dollars. It employs nearly 20,000 persons—nearly 40 percent of all of the Justice Department's work force. Some 9,000 of that total are special agents and most of the others are scientists, laboratory technicians, clerks, and secretaries.

FBI agents are carefully selected and highly trained. They use almost every device known to modern science in their crime detection work. They function very closely with State and local police forces and maintain a National Police Academy to give them advanced training. In addition, they make the Bureau's laboratories, extensive files, and other resources readily available to all legitimate law enforcement agencies. Today its Identification Division has more than 200 million fingerprint cards on file.

The existence—let alone the power and activities—of a secret police agency must raise profoundly disturbing questions in a free society. For nearly four decades the FBI enjoyed an extremely favorable public image. It was generally regarded as a tough, principled, highly professional, and extraordinarily competent law enforcement agency.

That image was badly tarnished in the recent past. Investigations in the wake of Watergate disclosed that, as with the CIA and the IRS, there are a number of unsavory chapters in the Bureau's record. Its misdeeds, extending over several years, included illegal break-ins, wiretaps, falsification of records, the blackening of personal reputations, the harassment of "radical" persons and groups, and much more.

There can be little doubt that the Bureau is both a necessary and a highly competent law enforcement agency. But there can be little doubt, too, that one of its major tasks today is that of reclaiming the respect and confidence it once enjoyed.

The Community Relations Service. The Community Relations Service was created by Congress in the Civil Rights Act of 1964 (see page 175). It is headed by a Director appointed by the President and the Senate. The Director and staff members are charged with an extraordinarily sensitive and important job. Their task is that of assisting local communities to resolve disputes and other difficulties arising out of discrimination based upon race, color, or national origin.

The Service may offer its help to any community in which peaceful relationships among its residents are threatened or have been disrupted. The Service may do so at the request of local officials, interested persons, or upon its own motion.

The Law Enforcement Assistance Administration. The job of preventing, combatting, and punishing crime in the United States is, in the federal system, primarily the responsibility of the States and, in particular, their local governments. Currently, they spend some $20 billion a year on their efforts to do so.

That those efforts have not been altogether successful is only too obvious. No one knows, with any real precision, how much crime there is in the United States. But it is clear that there is a great amount of it—and that it has increased, and at an alarming rate, over the past several years.

Most authorities agree that the solutions to the problem of crime in America require a massive two-pronged approach: (1) to identify and remove the root causes of crime and (2) to improve the capabilities of our judicial and law enforcement agencies.

The Law Enforcement Assistance Administration is the major federal response built around the second of these approaches. It was created by Congress in the Omnibus Crime Control and Safe Streets Act of 1968 and is headed by an Administrator appointed by the President.

LEAA channels hundreds of millions of dollars to State and local governments each year—nearly half-a-billion in fiscal year 1981 alone. These funds are targeted to aid State and local efforts to strengthen all aspects of their law enforcement and criminal justice efforts. They are made available for projects which run the gamut from the recruitment and training of police, through the development of new methods to prevent, detect, and reduce crime, to the upgrading of jails, prisons, and other correction facilities.

THE EXTENT OF CRIME IN AMERICA. Again, no one knows how much crime there is—how many crimes are committed—in this country. The best figures available are those reported by the FBI in its *Uniform Crime Reports.*[8]

According to the FBI, more than 288,000 murders, forcible rapes, aggravated assaults, and other violent crimes were reported to the police in 1960. That total, frightening in itself, increased every year through the decade, and in 1970 came to more than 738,000. By 1979, the latest year for which figures are available, the 1960 total had more than *tripled*, to well over one million.

The same shocking pattern is present for burglary, larceny-theft, motor vehicle theft, and other property crimes: 3.1 million were reported in 1960, 7.4 million in 1970, and nearly 11 million in 1979.

The more than 12 million serious crimes reported in 1979 are detailed in the accompanying table. As you can see, 21,460 persons were murdered in this

CRIME IN THE UNITED STATES, 1979

Crime	Estimated Number	Rate per 100,000 Inhabitants
Violent	1,178,540	535.5
Property	10,974,200	4,986.0
Murder	21,460	9.7
Forcible rape	75,990	34.5
Aggravated assault	614,210	279.1
Robbery	406,880	212.1
Burglary	3,299,500	1,499.1
Larceny-theft	6,577,500	2,988.4
Auto theft	1,097,200	498.5
Total	12,152,700	5,521.5

Source: Adapted from FBI, *Crime in the United States: Uniform Crime Reports, 1979.*

country in 1979. More than 3 million burglaries were committed, 64 percent of them in homes. And over one million cars were stolen. To put these statistics another way, 20 serious crimes were committed, on the average, during *every minute* of 1979. A violent crime was committed every 27 seconds, a murder every 24 minutes, a rape every 7 minutes, a robbery every 68 seconds, and a car stolen every 29 seconds.

But notice that these statistics, as startling as they are, do *not* reflect the full magnitude of crime in the United States. They are figures compiled by the FBI on the basis of crimes *reported* to police agencies.[9] The FBI and most other authorities agree that many crimes—at least half of them, of all types—are *not* reported.

---

[8] The data in this section are drawn largely from the FBI's *Crime in the United States: Uniform Crime Reports, 1979.* The report is published annually, in the fall following the year covered, and is widely covered by the news media.

---

[9] Many law enforcement authorities and criminologists dispute the precise rate at which crime has risen in the United States in recent years. Much of their questioning centers around the reliability of crime reporting procedures. The marked and continuing improvement in those procedures in the past 20 years, and such other factors as population increases, has led some to discount the rise in crime as a "statistical crime wave." Most authorities recognize the fact of dramatic increase, however, whatever its precise dimensions.

Case Study

The graphs and charts on this page are adapted from the most recent edition of the FBI's *Uniform Crime Reports.* Each of the annual *Reports* is an extensive statistical examination of the incidence of crime in the United States—quite literally, an "anatomy of crime."

For the past several years the document has emphasized the widespread use of firearms in the commission of violent crimes. Thus, those weapons were used to commit 63 percent of all murders, 23 percent of all aggravated assaults, and 40 percent of all robberies in 1979. (A knife or some other cutting instrument was used in the commission of 19 percent of the murders, 23 percent of the aggravated assaults, and 13 percent of the robberies. The other most often used weapons were clubs, poisons, and "personal weapons"—*i.e.,* hands, fists, and feet.)

Among many other things, the document also shows that police made some 10.2 million arrests in 1979—not counting traffic violations. Arrests of males outnumbered those of females by five to one. And almost exactly one of every four of those arrested were under 18 years old.

Of all persons arrested for the most serious crimes, the percentage of those who were under 18 was: murder, 9.3 percent; forcible rape, 15.9 percent; robbery, 31.5 percent; aggravated assault, 15.5 percent; burglary, 48.6 percent; larceny-theft, 40.4 percent; and motor vehicle theft, 49.2 percent.

■ Why does the FBI issue the *Uniform Crime Reports*? Why does it choose to emphasize the use of firearms?

■ What conclusions can you draw from the graphs and clocks?

■ From the data on the commission of serious crimes by those under 18?

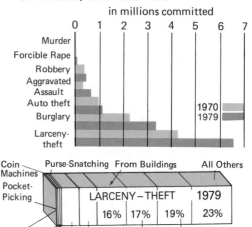

GROWTH OF NUMBER OF CRIMINAL OFFENSES, 1970 AND 1979

in millions committed

Murder
Forcible Rape
Robbery
Aggravated Assault
Auto theft
Burglary
Larceny-theft

1970
1979

Coin Machines — Pocket-Picking — Purse-Snatching — From Buildings — All Others

LARCENY—THEFT 1979

16% 17% 19% 23%

1% 1% 1% 11% 11%

Bicycles — Shoplifting — From Motor Vehicles — Motor Vehicle Accessories

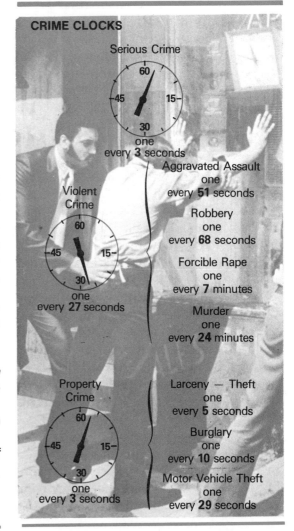

CRIME CLOCKS

Serious Crime
one every **3** seconds

Violent Crime
one every **27** seconds

Property Crime
one every **3** seconds

Aggravated Assault
one every **51** seconds

Robbery
one every **68** seconds

Forcible Rape
one every **7** minutes

Murder
one every **24** minutes

Larceny — Theft
one every **5** seconds

Burglary
one every **10** seconds

Motor Vehicle Theft
one every **29** seconds

People fail to report crimes for many different reasons, chief among them: a reluctance to "get involved," a low opinion of police, a doubt that anything can be done about the matter, or fear of reprisal by the criminal. Too, "crime" is a broad label. It covers many nonviolent offenses such as embezzlement, bribery, kickbacks, loan-sharking, and the like—the so-called "white-collar crimes" which often go unreported and even undetected.

The incidence of crime is spread quite unevenly, both geographically and within the population. Thus, more crimes are committed, and the rate of crime is higher, in larger cities than in medium- and small-sized communities. And, more crimes are committed in cities than in their suburbs, and more in urban than in rural areas. Similarly, more crimes are committed by the poor, and against the poor, than by other elements in the population. And by age groups, the largest number of serious crimes (those included in the table on page 672) are committed by younger persons. In 1979, 38.5 percent of all persons arrested for these crimes were under 18 years of age, 18.3 percent were 18 to 21 years old, and 14.5 percent were 21 to 25 years old.

In economic terms, the cost of crime is difficult to calculate. LEAA estimates put the current annual loss to crime at at least $140 billion—not counting the billions spent to combat it. The cost in social and human terms is beyond calculation.

The Drug Enforcement Administration. Illicit traffic in and use of narcotics and other dangerous drugs may well be the most serious of law enforcement problems in this country today.

An alarming share of all criminal activity can be traced directly to the problem. Many acts of violence are committed by persons under the influence of such illicit narcotics as opium, heroin, cocaine, or their many derivatives. Addicts often commit crimes in order to get the money with which to feed their cravings. And marijuana, LSD or other hallucinogenic drugs, or depressants or stimulants of uncountable variety are frequently present in criminal or otherwise irresponsible actions. The vicious parasites, the suppliers and peddlers who prey on addicts and other users, are often a part of organized operations also involved in such other nefarious activities as gambling, prostitution, and smuggling.

The regulation of narcotics and of other dangerous drugs is universally recognized as a proper and essential governmental function. Our law holds that the *only* legitimate uses for such drugs are in medicine and other scientific work; their sale and use are limited to those purposes.

Each of the 50 States has strict narcotics control laws. But purely local control is virtually impossible. Control is inadequate even at the national level because the major sources of supply are abroad, especially in India, Turkey, Indochina, China, Kuwait, and Mexico. The United States has joined with most other nations by treaty and through the United Nations to meet the problem.

The Drug Enforcement Administration directs the enforcement of the federal narcotics laws and our international obligations. Its Administrator is appointed by the President with Senate consent.

Working with the Public Health Service, the Administration determines the amount of narcotics to be allowed legal entry each year. Only those who have a valid federal license may lawfully deal in narcotics, and the penalties for violation are severe.

Most illegal drugs are smuggled into the country by ship or plane. Highly trained narcotics agents are stationed along the traditional routes of the illicit traffic, both in this country and abroad. The agency works closely with the FBI, the Coast Guard, the Customs Service, other federal agencies, and with State and local police. In one recent case, agents broke up a ring so highly organized that it had its own fleet of planes to supply peddlers and addicts in various parts of the country.

Of all persons now sentenced to federal prisons each year for offenses of *all* types, approximately one in every four is a drug-law violator. But even with vigorous enforcement huge problems remain.

SUMMARY

Justice is, must be, of fundamental concern to democratic government. As the concept has developed in American thought and practice, it means that the law, both in its content *and* its administration, shall be reasonable, fair, and impartial.

The Department of Justice is the federal administrative agency chiefly concerned with the administration of justice. It is headed by the Attorney General. The Department furnishes legal advice to the President and his chief aides, represents the United States in court, enforces most of the federal criminal laws, and administers the immigration, naturalization, and narcotics statutes.

The Solicitor General appears for the United States in the Supreme Court and ranks as the Government's chief lawyer. The several divisions within the Department and the 91 United States attorneys argue cases in the lower courts. United States marshals arrest criminals, handle prisoners, and execute court orders.

The Justice Department also includes these line agencies: the Immigration and Naturalization Service, the Bureau of Prisons, the Parole Commission, the Federal Bureau of Investigation, the Community Relations Service, the Law Enforcement Assistance Administration, and the Drug Enforcement Administration.

Concept Development

Questions for Review

1. Why is "justice" a difficult term to define? What has it come to mean?

2. When was the post of Attorney General created? The Justice Department? Who selects the Attorney General?

3. What are the principal functions of the Justice Department today?

4. Why is the Solicitor General called the "Government's chief lawyer"?

5. What are the six divisions within the Justice Department and their chief areas of work?

6. How many United States attorneys are there? What is their main function?

7. How many United States marshals are there? What are their main functions?

8. What does the Bureau of Prisons do? The Parole Commission? The Pardon Attorney?

9. When was the FBI originally established? Who served as its longtime Director? What are its principal duties today? Why must it rebuild its public image?

10. What is the principal mission of the Community Relations Service?

11. When and why was the Law Enforcement Assistance Administration established?

12. What two-pronged approach do most authorities agree must be taken to solve the problem of crime in America?

13. What is the most useful source of statistics on crime in this country today? Why are precise figures on the number and rate of crime difficult to report? Why do many people not report crimes?

14. What agency is charged with the administration and enforcement of federal narcotics laws?

For Further Inquiry

1. What did Benjamin Disraeli mean when he commented: "Justice is truth in action"? Do you agree or disagree with him?

2. What is meant by the phrase "the politicization of the Department of Justice"? Why have many proposed in the past few years that the Department and the Attorney General be removed from the executive branch and converted into an independent agency patterned along the lines of the General Accounting Office and the Comptroller General (page 508)? Do you think this would be a good idea?

4. The FBI reports that firearms are used to commit approximately two-thirds of all of the murders committed in this country each year. Do you think this is a valid argument for stricter federal gun control laws (page 159)? If so, what would you include within them? If not, why not?

5. If you found yourself in a situation in which you could steal $1000 and no one else could possibly ever know that you did so, would you steal the money? Why or why not?

Suggested Activities

1. Invite a local attorney or judge to speak to the class on the nature of justice and its role in a democracy.

2. Ask an FBI or other federal law enforcement agent to speak to the class on the nature of his or her work.

3. Stage a debate or class forum on one of the following questions: (a) *Resolved,* That the Congress establish a single national police agency to supplant all of the various agencies now responsible for the enforcement of federal law; (b) *Resolved,* That a single national police agency be established to replace all existing law enforcement agencies in this country; (c) *Resolved,* That the Congress outlaw the private ownership of all handguns in the United States.

5. From such sources as newspaper and news magazine files and the annual reports of the Attorney General discover what role the Department of Justice has played in enhancing minority group access to housing, jobs, education, and/or voting in this country (and/or your locale) in recent years.

Suggested Reading

Blumberg, Abraham S., *Criminal Justice: Issues and Ironies.* Franklin Watts, rev. ed., 1979.

Daudstel, Howard, *et al., Criminal Justice.* Holt, Rinehart and Winston, 1979.

Datesman, Susan K. (ed.), *Women, Crime, and Justice in America.* Oxford, 1980.

Felt, W. Mark, *The FBI Pyramid: From the Inside.* Putnam, 1980.

Glaser, Daniel, *Crime in Our Changing Society.* Holt, Rinehart and Winston, 1978.

Hanes, Joseph M. (ed.), *Law and Order in American History.* Kennikat, 1979.

Rember, Charles, *The Law of the Land: The Evolution of Our Legal System.* Simon & Schuster, 1980.

Schroeder, Richard, *Politics of Drugs.* Congressional Quarterly, 2nd ed., 1979.

Walker, Samuel, *Popular Justice: A History of American Criminal Justice.* Oxford, 1980.

Also: Office of Public Information, Department of Justice, Washington, D.C. 20530.

STATE AND LOCAL GOVERNMENTS

To this point in our study of the American system of government we have been very largely concerned with the constitutional basis of that system, the democratic processes by which it is controlled and operated, and the organization, powers, and functions of the National Government. Now we turn to an examination of the States and their local governments.

To a much greater extent than most of us realize, it is the States and their local governments which most directly, intimately, and regularly affect our daily lives. Nearly every citizen of the United States is a resident of one of the 50 States. And most of us are also, at the same time, residents of a county within that State and of one of its villages, towns, townships, boroughs, or cities. Each of us usually resides within the boundaries of a number of other units (special districts) of local government, as well.

Practically everything that we do, at any time of the day or night, is influenced—and frequently in quite important ways—by the laws of the State in which we live and by the ordinances of its local governments. That this is so can be illustrated by an almost limitless number of examples drawn from a great many fields—including, especially, public education, roads and highways, law enforcement, and public health and sanitation. The fact that we are not constantly or often consciously aware of them does not diminish the degree of their importance to us.

As we examine the governments of the States and their local units, it will become clear that the governmental arrangements in each State are much like those to be found in all States. Thus, each of the States has a written constitution which serves as its fundamental law. Under it the State is organized and the relationships of individuals with one another and with the State are regulated. In each State the powers of government are divided among three branches: executive, legislative, and judicial; and each branch possesses powers with which to check the other two to insure that no one of them will become all-powerful. And, similarly, the patterns of local government tend to resemble one another from State to State.

Variations do exist among the States, to be sure. As we shall see, for example, the legislature in Nebraska is unicameral while in each of the other States that body is bicameral. Only North Carolina does not give to its governor the power to veto acts of the legislature. Only Oregon does not permit its legislature to remove public officials by impeachment. County governments function in all of the States except Connecticut and Rhode Island. But these and the other modifications to be found are much more differences in degree than they are differences of kind. The American philosophy of government demands that government be conducted by and with the consent of the people. And, in essence, whatever the variations among them, the 50 States and their local governments are designed to accomplish that end.

State Constitutions

He that goeth about to persuade a multitude, that they are not so well governed as they might be, shall never want attention and favorable hearers.

THOMAS HOOKER

■ What is meant by this observation: "Constitutions govern governments"?

■ Are there any circumstances in which it should be possible for a provision in a State's constitution to override a provision in the United States Constitution?

■ As a general rule, should a State's constitution be relatively easy or relatively difficult to change?

Each of the 50 States has a written constitution—the State's fundamental law. Each of these documents determines the way in which the government of the State is organized and distributes powers among its various branches. State constitutions both authorize the exercise of power by government and place restrictions upon the exercise of governmental power.

Each of the State constitutions is the supreme law of the State. Its provisions are superior to all other forms of State (and local) law. *But,* recall, none of its provisions may conflict with any provision in the Constitution of the United States, nor with any other form of federal law.

The First State Constitutions

When the 13 colonies declared their independence in 1776, each was faced with the problem of establishing a new government. The Second Continental Congress, on May 15, 1776, had advised each of the new States to adopt:

> . . . such governments as shall, in the opinion of the representatives of the people, best conduce to the happiness and safety of their constituents in particular, and America in general.

Colonial Origins. Despite their several shortcomings, most of the colonial charters served as models for the first State constitutions. Indeed, in Connecticut and Rhode Island the old charters seemed so well adapted to the needs of the day that they were carried over as constitutions al-

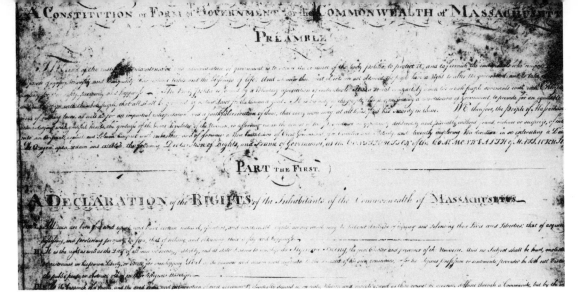

The Massachusetts Constitution of 1780 is the oldest written constitution in force in the world today.

most without change. Connecticut did not frame a new fundamental law until 1818, and Rhode Island not until 1842.

Adoption of the First Constitutions. The earliest of the State constitutions were adopted in a variety of ways. The people were given scant opportunity to approve or reject them anywhere. In Connecticut and in Rhode Island the legislature made the minor changes thought to be necessary in the charters, and no special action by the people was involved in either State.

In 1776 the Revolutionary legislatures in six States (Maryland, New Jersey, North Carolina, Pennsylvania, South Carolina, and Virginia) drew up new documents and proclaimed them in force. In none of these States was the new constitution submitted to the voters for ratification.

In Delaware and New Hampshire in 1776 and in Georgia and New York in 1777 constitutions were drafted by conventions called by the legislature. In each instance the new documents had to be approved by the legislature to become effective; but in none was popular approval required.

In 1780 a popularly elected convention drafted the Massachusetts constitution which was then submitted to the voters for ratification. Thus, Massachusetts set the pattern of popular participation in consti-

tution-making—a pattern followed generally among the States ever since.[1]

As new States have entered the Union, and as earlier State constitutions have been revised, popular participation has been the rule. All of the present State constitutions were drafted by assemblies representing the people, and most became effective only after popular approval.[2]

Congress has regularly required that those territories seeking Statehood hold a constitutional convention, composed of popularly elected delegates. It has also required that the convention's product be submitted to popular vote prior to admission; see pages 95–98.

Contents. While the first State constitutions differed in many of their details, they shared a number of general features. In each of them the people were recognized as the sole source of governmental authority. And in each the powers of the

---

[1] New Hampshire adopted its second and present constitution in 1784. It followed the Massachusetts pattern of popular convention and popular ratification of the convention's product in doing so. The Massachusetts constitution of 1780 and the New Hampshire constitution of 1784, both still in force, are the oldest of written constitutions now in effect anywhere in the world today.

[2] Only the present constitutions of Delaware (1897), Mississippi (1890), South Carolina (1895), and Vermont (1793) came into force without a popular vote.

new government were severely limited. Seven of the documents began with a lengthy bill of rights. All of them made it clear that the sovereign people held "certain unalienable rights" which government must always respect.

The doctrine of separation of powers was proclaimed in each of the new charters, and each branch was given powers with which to check the other two. In actuality, however, the doctrine was seriously strained. With the memories of the hated royal governors still fresh, the bulk of the authority each State possessed was given to the legislature.

In all States except Georgia (until 1789) and Pennsylvania (until 1790), the legislatures were *bicameral* (two-chambered).[3] At first, only Massachusetts and South Carolina gave the governor the power to veto acts of the legislature. The governor was generally limited to a one-year term, and he was chosen by the legislature in each of the States except for Massachusetts and New York.

For their time, the first State constitutions—products of the Revolutionary period—were quite democratic in character. Each, however, contained several provisions (and some important omissions) which today would be considered thoroughly undemocratic. Thus, none of them provided for full religious freedom, each set rigid qualifications for voting and for office-holding, all gave property owners a highly preferred status.

State Constitutions Today

The present-day State constitutions deal with a broad, and an increasing, range of matters. Each of them establishes a framework of government much like that to be found among the other States. And all 50 of them rest upon principles which are very nearly uniform. But there are unique provisions and considerable variations among them, as well.

Basic Principles. There is a striking similarity amongst the State constitutions from the standpoint of the principles upon which they are based. Each is founded upon the concepts of *popular sovereignty* and *limited government.* That is, each of them recognizes that the people are the ultimate source of any and all governmental authority. And, in each, the powers vested in government are confined with certain, often closely-detailed, boundaries.

In each of the State constitutions the powers and functions of government are distributed among the legislative, executive, and judicial branches, in accord with the principles of *separation of powers* and *checks and balances.* And each of the documents provides, either explicitly or by implication, for the power of *judicial review.*

Bill of Rights. Each of the documents contains a bill of rights—provisions setting forth the rights which individuals hold against the State and any of its officers and agencies. Most of them contain all or most of the guarantees set out in the first 10 amendments to the Constitution of the United States. And most usually contain a number of other guarantees, as well—for example, the right to self-government, to be secure from imprisonment for debt, to migrate from the State, and to join with others to bargain collectively.

Structure of Government. Any constitution is, in major part, a statement of the framework of government. Each of the State documents provides for the structure of government at both the State and the local levels. The major variations among them in this regard come largely in terms of the detail with which each treats the matter. A few State constitutions follow the national pattern by providing a more or less broad outline. But most State con-

---

[3] Vermont, which became the 14th State in 1791, had a unicameral legislature until 1836. Nebraska (since 1937) is the only State with a one-house legislative body today; see pages 691–692.

stitutions treat the subject of governmental organization in considerable and often quite specific detail.

Governmental Powers and Processes. Every State constitution deals with the powers and processes of government at some length. The powers vested in the governor and in other elements of the executive branch, the legislature, the courts, and units of local government occupy a large portion of each of them.

The powers to tax, spend, borrow, and provide for public education are especially prominent in terms of space and detail. So, too, are provisions relating to such processes as elections, legislation, and (in several States) the initiative, referendum, and recall, and to the matter of intergovernmental (State-local) relations.

Constitutional Change. Constitutions are the product of human effort. None are perfect. Sooner or later, changes become necessary, or at least desirable. Recognizing this, each of the State constitutions provides for the means by which it may be formally changed—that is, revised or amended.

As constitutions are *fundamental* law, they cannot be changed by those methods employed to change ordinary law. Rather, they require more complex procedures, somewhat more difficult to accomplish—as we shall see in a moment.

Miscellaneous Provisions. Every State constitution contains several sections of a miscellaneous character. Thus, most begin with a *preamble*—which has no legal effect but does serve as a statement of purpose by those who drafted and adopted the document originally.

Most also contain a *schedule*—a series of provisions for putting a new document into effect and avoiding conflicts with its predecessor. And most also contain a number of "dead letter" provisions—those with no current force and effect but which remain, nonetheless, a part of the constitution.

Constitutional Change

A constitution tends to reflect the goals, ideals, and concepts of those who framed and adopted it. That is, it is an expression of the time in which it was made. But human beings do not live in a static environment. Society is dynamic. Times change, circumstances are altered. Inevitably, a constitution—or, at least, some of its provisions—becomes outdated, lagging behind changes in outlooks, attitudes, and institutions.

In short, even the wisest of constitution-makers cannot build for all time. An essential part of any constitution, therefore, is the provision of methods by which the document may be altered.

As you can see from the table on page 687, some State constitutions have proved to be more durable than others.

Formal and Informal Amendment. As you recall from the discussion on pages 67–74, the Constitution of the United States has been changed over the years by both the *formal* and the *informal* amendment process. The State constitutions have been subjected to both processes, too.

But—and this is a very important *but*—the informal amendment process has not been nearly so significant at the State level as it has been nationally. For one thing, State constitutions have been and are much less *flexible*—are more rigid and detailed—than the national document. The structures, powers, and procedures of State government are usually treated at great length in a State's constitution—in marked contrast to the national document.

State courts have often proved a block to the more meaningful use of the informal amendment process. Unlike the federal courts, they have generally been quite strict in their roles as constitution-interpreters. In short, the States have had to rely principally on formal amendments as the major path to constitutional change and development.

As we turn to the methods of formal change, the distinct meanings of two sets of terms—"proposal-ratification" and "amendment-revision"—must be borne in mind. First, the process of formal change involves two basic steps: *proposal* and *ratification.* Proposals for change may be made by a constitutional convention, by the legislature, or by initiative petition. Ratification is accomplished by popular vote in every State except Delaware. As to the second set of terms, note that *amendment* usually refers to a limited change, involving only one or a few provisions in a constitution. The term *revision* is usually used to refer to changes of a broader scope—for example, an entire new document.

Constitutional Convention. The convention is the chief device by which new constitutions have been written and older ones revised. To this point, over 200 of them have been held among the States.[4]

In every State the legislature has the power to call a convention, and regularly the call is subject to voter approval.[5] In 14 States the question of calling a convention *must* be submitted to the voters at regular intervals.[6] Three elections commonly accompany a convention's work: (1) the vote at which the people authorize the calling of the convention, (2) the popular election of delegates, and (3) the vote by which the people ratify or reject the document framed by the convention.

Proposal of Amendments. Again, formal changes in a State constitution are most often made by amendment rather than revision. Among the States, amendments may be proposed by convention, by the legislature, or by initiative petition.

CONVENTION PROPOSAL. Although the convention is most often used for the broader purpose of revision, in several States it can be and sometimes is used to propose amendments. In fact, until 1965, it was the *only* means by which amendments could be offered in New Hampshire. But, because this approach is both expensive and time-consuming, it is seldom used for amendment purposes.

LEGISLATIVE PROPOSAL. Amendments are most often proposed by the legislature. The details of the process vary widely from State to State, as you can see in the accompanying table.

In some States the process is relatively simple, in others quite difficult. As a general rule, and as one might expect, the easier the process the more often are amendments proposed and adopted. Thus, the California constitution, which dates from 1879, has now been amended some 430 times (to 1981). But the Massachusetts document of 1780, in force for twice as long, has been changed only some 115 times.[7]

Only a few States limit the number of amendments which may be submitted to the voters at any one election. No more than four may be offered in Kentucky,

---

[4] In several States another body, a *constitutional revision commission,* may be used to propose extensive changes in the existing document or frame a new one. Only the Florida constitution expressly provides for one; there it must assemble every twentieth year and may itself submit unlimited changes directly to the voters. Elsewhere, a revision commission is usually created by and reports to the legislature, which may modify and send some or all of its proposals on to the voters. The present Georgia constitution, framed by a commission, went to the voters as a single amendment. The present North Carolina and Virginia documents were each drafted by a commission; in each case, the legislature modified that work and then submitted the constitution to the voters.

[5] In six States—Georgia, Louisiana, Maine, South Carolina, South Dakota, and Virginia—the legislature may call a convention without submitting the question to the voters. In Florida, Montana, and South Dakota a convention may be called by the initiative process.

[6] Every 20 years in Connecticut, Illinois, Maryland, Missouri, Montana, New York, Ohio, and Oklahoma; 16 years in Michigan, 10 years in Alaska, Iowa, New Hampshire, and Rhode Island, and nine years in Hawaii.

[7] The number of amendments which have been proposed (and added) to a State's constitution is the result of several other factors, too—most prominently, the *content* of the document (whether well-drawn or not, flexible or rigid and detailed, and so on) and its *age,* of course.

AMENDMENT BY LEGISLATIVE PROPOSAL

Legislative Vote Required	Popular Vote for Ratification	States
Majority vote, each house	Majority on amendment	Arizona, Arkansas, Missouri, New Mexico[a], North Dakota, Oklahoma, Oregon[b], Rhode Island, South Dakota
Majority vote, each house	Majority at election	Minnesota
Two-thirds vote, each house	Majority on amendment	Alaska, California, Colorado, Georgia, Hawaii[d], Idaho, Kansas, Louisiana, Maine, Michigan, Mississippi, Montana, South Carolina[e], Texas, Utah, Washington, West Virginia
Two-thirds vote, each house	Majority at election	Wyoming
Three-fourths vote, each house	Majority on amendment	Connecticut[c]
Three-fifths vote, each house	Majority on amendment	Alabama, Florida, Kentucky, Maryland, Nebraska[d], New Jersey[c], North Carolina, Ohio
Three-fifths vote, each house	Majority at election or three-fifths on amendment	Illinois
Three-fifths vote, each house	Two-thirds on amendment	New Hampshire
Majority vote, each house at two successive sessions	Majority on amendment	Connecticut[c], Hawaii[c], Indiana, Iowa, Nevada, New Jersey[c], New York, Pennsylvania[f], Virginia, Wisconsin
Majority vote in joint session, at two successive sessions	Majority on amendment	Massachusetts
Two-thirds vote, each house, two successive sessions	No popular vote required	Delaware
Majority vote, each house at one session; two-thirds vote each house at next session.	Majority of votes cast for governor	Tennessee
Two-thirds vote of senate, majority vote of house at one session; majority vote of each house at next session	Majority on amendment	Vermont

[a] Amendments relating to voting qualifications or to the guarantee of equal treatment of Spanish-speaking students in public schools may be proposed only by a three-fourths vote of each house, and must be approved by three-fourths of all voting in the election, including at least two-thirds of those voting in each county.

[b] By a two-thirds vote in each house, legislature may propose a revision of all or a part of the constitution.

[c] Either method may be used in these States (Connecticut, Hawaii, New Jersey).

[d] Majority for ratification must equal at least 35 percent of total vote cast in election.

[e] Subsequent majority vote of each house required to complete ratification.

[f] An "emergency amendment" may be proposed by two-thirds vote of each house at a single session; such an amendment must be ratified by a majority of voters who vote in election.

AMENDMENT BY INITIATIVE PROPOSAL

State	Number of Petition Signatures Required[a]	Distribution of Signatures	Popular Vote for Ratification
Arizona	15% of votes cast for governor	—	Majority on amendment
Arkansas	10% of votes cast for governor	Must be at least 5% in each of 15 counties	Majority on amendment
California	8% of votes cast for governor	—	Majority on amendment
Colorado	8% of votes cast for secretary of state	—	Majority on amendment
Florida	8% of votes cast for presidential electors	Must be 8% in each of one-half of congressional districts	Majority on amendment
Illinois[b]	8% of votes cast for governor	—	Majority at election, or three-fifths on amendment
Massachusetts[c]	3% of votes cast for governor	Not more than one-fourth from any one county	Majority on amendment[d]
Michigan	10% of votes cast for governor	—	Majority on amendment
Missouri	8% of votes cast for governor	Must be 8% in each of two-thirds of congressional districts	Majority on amendment
Montana	10% of votes cast for governor	Must be 10% in each of two-fifths of legislative districts	Majority on amendment
Nebraska	10% of votes cast for governor	Must be at least 5% in each of two-fifths of counties	Majority on amendment[e]
Nevada	10% of highest vote cast	Must be 10% in each of three-fourths of counties	Majority on amendment in two consecutive general elections
North Dakota	4% of the population	—	Majority on amendment
Ohio	10% of votes cast for governor	Must be at least 5% in each of one-half of counties	Majority on amendment
Oklahoma	15% of highest vote cast	—	Majority on amendment
Oregon	8% of votes cast for governor	—	Majority on amendment
South Dakota	10% of votes cast for governor	—	Majority on amendment

[a] Based on number of votes cast in most recent general election, except in North Dakota.

[b] Initiative process may be applied only to Article IV, The Legislature.

[c] Initiated measure must first be approved by at least one-fourth of all members of legislature, sitting in joint session, at two successive legislative sessions before submission to voters for ratification.

[d] Majority must equal at least 30% of all votes cast in election.

[e] Majority must equal at least 35% of all votes cast in election.

three in Arkansas, and five in Kansas. In Illinois no single session of the legislature may propose amendments to more than three articles in the constitution, and in Colorado to no more than six.

PROPOSAL BY INITIATIVE. The voters themselves may propose (initiate) constitutional amendments in 17 States. They may do so in those States by the *initiative*—a process in which a certain number of qualified voters must sign petitions supporting the proposal. If the required number of signatures is gathered the proposal then goes directly to the ballot—for popular approval or rejection.

The details of the process vary among these 17 States. And, as you can see in the accompanying table, two of them place large restrictions on its use. In Illinois *only* the legislative article may be the subject of an initiated amendment. And in Massachusetts such an amendment must *first* be submitted to the legislature; it then goes to the voters—but *only* if that step has been approved by the votes of at least one-fourth of the members of both houses at two successive sessions of the legislature.

Ratification of Amendments. In every State except Delaware amendments must be ratified by popular vote before they may become a part of the constitution.[8] As with the matter of proposal, the details of the ratification process vary somewhat from State to State—as, again, the tables on pages 683 and 684 indicate.

Typically, the approval of a majority of those voting on the amendment adds it to the State constitution. But a somewhat greater margin is required in some States.

And on many occasions amendments have been defeated in those States despite the fact that they actually received more *yes* than *no* votes. Usually this happens because, as we suggested on page 253, many voters fail to vote on ballot measures.

General Observations

The Need for Reform. Almost without exception, State constitutions are in urgent need of reform. The typical document today is sorely outdated—the product of an earlier and a simpler time. It is cluttered with unnecessarily detailed provisions, overly burdensome restrictions, and many obsolete sections. It contains much repetitious, even contradictory, material and is replete with clumsy, often confusing, terms and phrasings. And not least among its sins are those of omission—it fails to deal with many of the pressing problems State and local governments face in the latter part of the 20th century.

Unfortunately, this indictment may be read against even the newest, the most recently rewritten, documents.

The need for reform can be pointed up in several ways. As one approach, look at these two factors—the length and the age of State constitutions.

THE PROBLEM OF LENGTH. The original State constitutions were quite brief. They were intended as statements of basic principle and organization. Purposefully, they left to the legislature and to time and practice the task of providing the details as they became necessary.

The lengthiest of the original documents was the Massachusetts constitution of 1780; it contained some 12,000 words. The shortest was New Jersey's constitution of 1776, with only about 2500 words.

Through the years State charters have become longer and still longer. Today most of them range between 15,000 and 30,000 words. The briefest are those of Vermont (1793), only some 7000 words long, and Connecticut (1965), with fewer than 8000

---

[8] In Delaware if an amendment is approved by a two-thirds vote in each house of the legislature at two successive sessions of that body it then becomes effective. In South Carolina *final* ratification, after a favorable vote by the people, depends upon a majority vote in both houses of the legislature.

Both the Georgia and the South Carolina constitutions provide that an amendment of only local, as opposed to Statewide, application need be approved only by the voters in the affected locale.

words. At the other extreme, the Alabama document of 1901 runs to very nearly 100,000 words and the Georgia (1945) document an incredible 600,000.[9]

Why are the documents so lengthy—and, most of them, becoming even more so? The reasons are not difficult to find. A leading one: popular distrust of government, an historical and continuing fact of American political life. It has often led to quite detailed and restrictive constitutional provisions aimed at preventing the misuse of governmental power. And many provisions have been purposefully placed in the fundamental law where they can neither be ignored nor readily changed.

Pressure groups—veterans organizations, liquor interests, private utilities, and many others—long ago learned that public policies of benefit to them are much more secure in the constitution than in a mere statute. They have carved out their preserves in the constitutions of several States. Then, too, court decisions can be and often have been effectively overridden by constitutional amendments.

There has been a marked failure in nearly every State to distinguish *fundamental law* (that which is basic and of lasting import and ought to be included in the constitution) from *statutory law* (that which should be handled through ordinary law). There may be some gray areas in distinguishing that which is fundamental from that which is not. But, to pick but a few from dozens of examples: Who can seriously argue the fundamental character of New York's constitutional authorization of an exchange of 10 acres of State land for 30 acres held by the village of Saranac Lake, in order to provide the village with a site for a dump? Or the California provision exempting from property taxation all fruit and nut trees planted within the preceding four years? Or, too, Oregon's constitutional guarantee of the right to sell liquor by the glass?

Two additional reasons have been quite important: (1) State and local governmental functions have expanded greatly in the past few decades, and new powers and agencies have been called forth; and (2) the people have not been stingy in the use of the initiative in those States where it is available.

THE PROBLEM OF AGE. If you look again at the table on page 687, you will see that most of the State constitutions are comparatively ancient. Though most of them have been amended many times, those changes have, as often as not, compounded the clutter of the documents.

The Oregon constitution affords a *typical* example. It was written by delegates—most of them farmers—to a territorial convention in 1857 and became effective in 1859. It has now been amended more than 160 times, runs to some 30,000 words, and has two Articles VII and ten Articles XI!

Like most of the other State constitutions, it is overloaded with statutory material and in urgent need of reform. Thus, for example, one of the Articles XI devotes nearly 2000 closely detailed words to the subject of veterans' farm and home loans. And another section deals with retirement benefits of employees of any transportation system taken over by a public body.

And, again typically, it includes a number of obsolete provisions. One provision, for example, forever bars any person who engages in a duel from holding any public office in the State. Another provision forbids the legislature to tax, spend any money, or contract any debt for building of a capitol building prior to 1865.

From the table on page 687, you can see that the oldest of all of the fundamental laws in force today are those of Massachusetts (1780), New Hampshire (1784), and Vermont (1793). All told, 19

---

[9] But the Georgia constitution contains a vast amount of material applicable only to individual locales (see note 8, page 685); the printed version, which contains only provisions of Statewide applicability, is only some 50,000 words in length.

STATE CONSTITUTIONS

State	Present Constitution Became Effective in[a]	State Entered Union in	Number of Previous Constitutions	State	Present Constitution Became Effective in[a]	State Entered Union in	Number of Previous Constitutions
Alabama	1901	1819	5	Montana	1973	1889	1
Alaska	1959	1959	0	Nebraska	1875	1867	1
Arizona	1912	1912	0	Nevada	1864	1864	0
Arkansas	1874	1838	4	New Hampshire	1784	1788	1
California	1879[b]	1850	1	New Jersey	1948	1788	2
Colorado	1876	1876	0	New Mexico	1912	1912	0
Connecticut	1965	1788	3	New York	1895	1788	3
Delaware	1897	1788	3	North Carolina	1971	1789	2
Florida	1968	1845	5	North Dakota	1889	1889	0
Georgia	1977	1788	8	Ohio	1851	1803	1
Hawaii	1959	1959	0	Oklahoma	1907	1907	0
Idaho	1890	1890	0	Oregon	1859	1859	0
Illinois	1971	1818	3	Pennsylvania	1874	1788	3
Indiana	1851	1816	1	Rhode Island	1843	1790	1
Iowa	1857	1846	1	South Carolina	1895	1788	6
Kansas	1861	1861	0	South Dakota	1889	1889	0
Kentucky	1891	1792	3	Tennessee	1870	1796	2
Louisiana	1975	1811	10	Texas	1876	1845	4
Maine	1820[c]	1820	0	Utah	1896	1896	0
Maryland	1867	1788	3	Vermont	1793[c]	1791	2
Massachusetts	1780	1788	0	Virginia	1971	1788	5
Michigan	1964	1837	3	Washington	1889	1889	0
Minnesota	1858	1858	0	West Virginia	1872	1863	1
Mississippi	1890	1817	3	Wisconsin	1848	1848	0
Missouri	1945	1821	3	Wyoming	1890	1890	0

[a] Nineteen of the present-day State constitutions were actually ratified a year or more before they became effective: Alaska (1956), Arizona (1911), Georgia (1976), Hawaii (1950), Kansas (1859), Louisiana (1974), Maine (1819), Michigan (1963), Minnesota (1857), Montana (1972), New Jersey (1947), New Mexico (1911), North Carolina (1970), Oregon (1857), Pennsylvania (1873), Rhode Island (1842), Utah (1895), Virginia (1970), Wyoming (1889).

[b] California's constitution became effective July 4, 1879, for purposes of the election of officers, the beginning of their terms of office, and the meeting of the legislature. It became effective for all other purposes January 1, 1880.

[c] The Maine constitution in 1876 and the Vermont constitution in 1913 were rearranged by incorporating the amendments into the text itself.

States still retain their original constitutions. Twenty-two States have documents now at least 100 years old, and 15 others have constitutions which were written between 50 and 100 years ago. Several States have adopted new (revised) constitutions in recent years—Michigan in 1964, Connecticut in 1965, Florida in 1968, North Carolina and Virginia in 1970, Illinois in 1971, Montana in 1972, Louisiana in 1974, and Georgia in 1976. Even so, the average among them all exceeds 80 years.

SUMMARY

The State constitution is the State's fundamental law. It determines the way in which State government is organized and distributes power among its various branches. It both authorizes the exercise of power by government and places restrictions upon the exercise of governmental power.

Each of the State constitutions is superior to all other forms of State law; but none of its provisions may conflict with the Constitution of the United States, nor with any other form of federal law.

When independence came, 11 of the original States adopted new constitutions; in Connecticut and Rhode Island the old colonial charters were transformed into constitutions. Generally, the people had little to do with either the drafting or adoption of these early documents until 1780. In that year, the Massachusetts constitution was written by a convention composed of popularly elected delegates and then ratified by the people. Since then, popular participation in the constitution-making process has been the almost universal rule.

Despite many variations, the first State constitutions had several common features. Each manifested the principles of popular sovereignty, limited government, separation of powers, and checks and balances. In each State the legislature was relatively strong, the governor weak, and rigid suffrage qualifications were imposed.

The present-day constitutions also vary in many particulars, but all contain major sections making quite similar provision for certain basic principles, civil rights guarantees, the structure of State and local government, the powers and processes of government, and the methods of constitutional change.

The details of the process of formal constitutional change differ from State to State. The revision or replacement of a constitution is usually proposed by a convention. Amendments may be proposed by the legislature in every State, and in 17 of them by initiative petition. The ratification of a new constitution or the revision of an existing one commonly must be by popular vote. Amendments must be ratified by popular vote in every State except Delaware.

Nearly every one of the State constitutions is in urgent need of reform. Most are outdated, too lengthy and detailed, and overloaded with statutory material.

Concept Development

Questions for Review

1. What is a State constitution?
2. What is the relationship between a State constitution and the Constitution of the United States? Other forms of federal law? Other forms of State law?

3. Which of the State constitutions is the oldest written constitution in force anywhere in the world today?
4. What pattern of constitution-making did Massachusetts set?

5. Were the first State constitutions democratic documents?

6. What are the major features of the 50 State constitutions today?

7. Has the process of formal or of informal amendment been more significant in the development of State constitutions?

8. Why are provisions for formal change an essential part of a constitution?

9. What is the principal device used for the writing of a new constitution?

10. How are amendments to State constitutions usually proposed? Ratified?

11. What is the initiative?

12. Why have State constitutions typically become longer and still longer documents?

13. When was your State's constitution adopted?

For Further Inquiry

1. If each of the State constitutions were to be abolished would government then become more or less democratic?

2. From an analysis of your State's constitution, determine how well it meets this standard set by Alexander Hamilton in *The Federalist*, No. 57:

> The aim of every political constitution is, or ought to be, first to obtain men who possess most wisdom to discern, and most virtue to pursue, the common good of the society; and in the next place, to take the most effectual precautions for keeping them virtuous whilst they continue to hold their public trust.

3. Is the process by which your State's constitution may be amended too easy or too difficult to accomplish? Why? How many times has it been amended? What amendments (if any) were added at the most recent election? Rejected?

4. What provisions (if any) in your State's constitution would you class as statutory rather than fundamental? Outdated or obsolete? Repetitious or contradictory?

Suggested Activities

1. Secure a copy of your State's constitution (usually available from the secretary of state). Study its contents, outline its provisions, then answer these questions: (1) How long is the document? (2) How can it be amended? (3) How many times has it been amended? (4) Does it deal largely with basic principles and the framework of government, or does it contain much material that could be handled through ordinary legislation? (5) What changes (if any) would you recommend be made in it?

2. Invite a State legislator, judge, or some other public figure to discuss your State's constitution, its contents, and the changes they recommend be made in it.

Suggested Reading

Berkley, George and Fox, Douglas, *80,000 Governments: The Politics of Subnational America.* Allyn and Bacon, 1978.

Berman, David R., *State and Local Politics.* Allyn and Bacon, 3rd ed., 1981.

Dye, Thomas R., *Politics in States and Communities.* Prentice-Hall, 4th ed., 1981.

Henry, Nichola, *Governing at the Grassroots: State & Local Politics.* Prentice-Hall, 1980.

Maddox, Russell W. and Fuquay, Robert F., *State and Local Government.* Van Nostrand, 4th ed., 1981.

Morlan, Robert L. and Martin, David (eds.), *Capitol, Courthouse, and City Hall: Readings in American State and Local Government and Politics.* Houghton Mifflin, 6th ed., 1981.

Press, Charles and VerBurg, Kenneth, *State and Community Governments in the Federal System.* Wiley, 1979.

Stedman, Murray S., *State and Local Governments.* Winthrop, 2nd ed., 1979.

The Book of the States, 1980-81. Council of State Governments, 1980.

Ziegler, L. Harmon and Tucker, Harvey J., *The Quest for Responsive Government.* Duxbury, 1978.

State Legislatures

Representative government is in essence self-government through the medium of elected representatives of the people.

CHIEF JUSTICE EARL WARREN
REYNOLDS v. SIMS, 1964.

■ What is the basic function of a State legislature?

■ What is the basic function of a State legislator?

■ What extra-constitutional qualifications should a State legislator possess?

■ On what basis should legislators cast their votes: the views of their constituents or their own informed judgments?

The size of the legislature, the details of its organization, the frequency and the length of its sessions, and even the official name given to it vary among the States. But the basic reason for its existence is everywhere the same: the legislature is the law-making branch of State government. It is charged with the high duty of translating the public will into the public policy of the State.

The legislature has been described as "the powerhouse of State government." Through the exercise of its vast law-making powers, it creates the energy necessary to operate the governmental machinery of the State and its local units.

The "State legislature" is known officially by that title in 27 of the States. In 19 others it is the "General Assembly."[1] In North Dakota and Oregon it is known as the "Legislative Assembly," and in Massachusetts and New Hampshire as the "General Court."

Forty-nine of the 50 State legislatures are two-chambered (*bicameral*). The upper house in each of them is called the "Senate."[2] The lower house is known by several names among the States, most commonly as the "House of Representatives." But in California, Nevada, New York, and Wisconsin it is the "Assembly"; in New

---

[1] Arkansas, Colorado, Connecticut, Delaware, Georgia, Illinois, Indiana, Iowa, Kentucky, Maryland, Missouri, North Carolina, Ohio, Pennsylvania, Rhode Island, South Carolina, Tennessee, Vermont, Virginia.

[2] Nebraska applies that term to its single chamber.

The only unicameral body among the 50 State legislatures meets in Lincoln, Nebraska. Its 49 members are elected on a nonpartisan basis for four-year terms.

Jersey the "General Assembly"; and in Maryland, Virginia, and West Virginia, the "House of Delegates."

Bicameralism

With the exception of Nebraska, all of the State legislatures are bicameral today.[3] Bicameralism has been the dominant pattern of legislative organization among the States for two major reasons: (1) the influence of both English and colonial experience, and (2) the tendency among the newer States to follow the precedent set by both the original States and the National Government.

The first colonial legislatures were typically unicameral; the elected representatives commonly sat with the governor and his council in the making of colonial laws. As the popularly chosen legislators gained in political power in most of the colonies, the governor's council assumed the role of a second, or upper, chamber. Thus, well before the coming of independence, most of the colonies had created bicameral legislative bodies similar in their structure to that of the British Parliament. After independence, those States which had not already done so soon established two-chambered legislatures.

---

[3] Nebraska's voters approved the creation of a *unicameral* legislature in 1934 and the first session of that body was held in 1937. Georgia until 1789, Pennsylvania until 1790, and Vermont until 1836 also had unicameral bodies.

Unicameralism vs. Bicameralism.

Unicameralism is widely recommended today as one of the most significant steps that could be taken to upgrade the quality of State legislatures, their procedures, and their products.

Those who support bicameralism have long argued that one house may act as a check on the other, and thus prevent the enactment of unwise legislation. But the critics of bicameralism point to numerous examples to show that the theory has not worked altogether well in practice. It is regularly true that each house in a bicameral legislature fails to pass many bills passed and sent on to it by the other. But the major reason for this is that most of those bills never receive consideration in the second house. Typically, bills that pass both houses are seldom changed in any way by the second chamber. Too, many routine, noncontroversial measures pass *both* houses with little or no attention paid to them in *either*. Most often, the governor's veto, the news media, and public opinion have proved a better check against harmful or "hasty and ill-considered" legislation than has bicameralism.

The fact that bicameralism has worked well in Congress is often cited in support of it at the State legislative level. But a bicameral Congress is a reflection of the *federal* character of the Union; the States are not federal, they are *unitary* in character. Recall, too, that a bicameral Congress came out of the Connecticut Compromise—and, recall, without that agreement, the Philadelphia Convention may well have foundered; see pages 53–54, 285.

Until recently, many supported bicameralism at the State level because they favored a "little federal plan" for their own State's legislature. That is—despite the non-federal character of the States—they favored the existence of two houses, with one based upon area and the other upon population. Otherwise, they insisted, the more populous cities would so thoroughly dominate the State's law-making body that the small town and rural interests would be practically unrepresented. As we shall see in a moment, however, the Supreme Court destroyed their position in 1964—by holding that the 14th Amendment's Equal Protection Clause demands that *both* houses of a State's legislature *must* be apportioned on the basis of population.

Critics of bicameralism argue that in the complicated structure and procedures of a two-house system, special interests have more opportunities to block popular legislation. Significantly, the need for conference committees is eliminated in a unicameral arrangement; see pages 325–326.

The advocates of unicameralism also insist that with two chambers involved in the law-making process it is almost impossible to fix the responsibility for action, or inaction. With but one house to watch, the people can much more readily discover what the legislature is doing—and, they add, the legislature itself can much more readily monitor the activities (and lessen the influence) of lobbyists.

The Nebraska experience has not proved a cure-all for the shortcomings of State legislatures. But it does appear to have worked quite well for more than 40 years. Legislative costs have been reduced, greater efficiency has been achieved, and lobbyist influence has been lessened. A generally higher caliber of legislator has been chosen. And, too, the typical legisla-

tor has been more responsive to his or her constituents than under the previous two-house system.

Even so—despite the weight of the arguments for it and the Nebraska experience—unicameralism has made little or no headway among the other States. Both tradition and inertia stand on the side of bicameralism—and so, too, do a lack of interest and knowledge on the part of the general public.

Size and Apportionment

Size. As the table on page 698 indicates, the 50 State legislatures vary, often widely, in terms of size. None of them contains as many members as there are in Congress but several of them do run to more than 200 members. No precise figure can be cited as the ideal size of a legislative body, but two basic considerations are important. First, a legislature (and each of its houses) should not be so *large* as to hamper the orderly conduct of the people's business. Secondly, it should not be so *small* that the many views and interests within the State cannot be adequately represented.

The *upper house* in most States consists of from 30 to 50 members. But there are now (1981) only 20 seats in the Senate in both Alaska and Nevada and only 21 in Delaware. Minnesota's upper house is the largest with 67 members.

The *lower house* usually ranges between 100 and 150 members. However, there are only 40 seats in Alaska's and Nevada's lower chamber, and only 41 in Delaware's. In Pennsylvania, on the other hand, the lower house is composed of 203 seats and in New Hampshire 400.

Apportionment. Each State constitution makes some provision for the *apportionment* of legislative seats within the State. That is, it provides for the manner in which the seats will be allocated, distributed among districts, within the State.

On what particular basis should the

legislature be apportioned? Should the seats be distributed among legislative districts of substantially equal populations? Or should they be apportioned on the basis of area, with district lines drawn according to geographic and/or economic factors? Or should some combination of both population and area be used—with, for example, one house based upon population and the other upon area?

Clearly, these are vital questions. How they are answered plays a major part in determining which groups and regions within a State control its legislative machinery and, so, shape its public policies.

Each State constitution makes some provision for apportionment. Although there are wide variations among them, most have always provided for population as the only or at least the major basis for the distribution of legislative seats. And, as we shall see shortly, population is the only standard that may be used today.

REAPPORTIONMENT. Most State constitutions assign the task of reapportionment to the legislature itself. That is, they direct the legislature to make periodic readjustments in the distribution of its seats to account for increases, decreases, and shifts of population within the State. Usually, the constitution orders the legislature to reapportion itself every 10 years, in line with the most recent federal census.[4]

The "Reapportionment Revolution." Although the pattern has finally changed, most State legislatures were long con-

trolled by the rural, less populated sections of the State. In well over half of the States, and for decades, more lawmakers were elected from the rural than from the more heavily populated urban areas.

This general pattern of rural over-representation and urban under-representation persisted long after the United States became predominantly a nation of city-dwellers. Two practices accounted for this imbalance. *First*, the failure of many State legislatures to reapportion themselves, either fully or at all, despite constitutional commands or population changes. *Second*, the use of area as well as population as a basis for apportionment.

BAKER V. CARR, 1962. The long-standing fact of rural domination has now come to an end in nearly all of the States. This dramatic shift in the locus of political power occurred in the 1960's and early 1970's. It was prompted by an historic decision by the United States Supreme Court in a case from Tennessee in 1962. In *Baker v. Carr*, the Court held, for the first time, that federal courts could properly hear cases in which it is alleged that the way in which a State legislature is apportioned violates the Equal Protection Clause of the 14th Amendment.[5]

In *Baker v. Carr* the Supreme Court decided only a *jurisdictional* question. It did not decide this critically important constitutional (and political) question: On what particular factor(s) can a reapportionment be based? Rather, that question was left to future cases. But the handwriting was large on the constitutional wall, and those cases were not long in coming.

REYNOLDS V. SIMS, 1964. In a now lengthy series of cases, the Court has consistently applied the "one-man, one-vote" rule. That is, it has consistently held that

---

[4] In some States reapportionment is no longer a legislative function—a direct result of the "reapportionment revolution," which we consider in a moment. Thus, in Ohio the task is now performed by a commission composed of the governor, secretary of state, auditor, and a representative from each of the major political parties. In Pennsylvania the task is performed by a body which includes the majority and minority leaders in the two houses and a fifth commission member, a private citizen, chosen by the other four; and in Maryland by the governor. A few States now provide that if the legislature fails to reapportion itself, or does so inadequately, it will be done otherwise—in Maine, for example, by the State Supreme Judicial Court and in Oregon by the secretary of state.

---

[5] Prior to *Baker*, both federal and State courts regularly refused to hear cases involving the composition of legislative bodies. Such cases were held to involve "political questions," to be resolved by legislatures or voters, not by the courts.

population is the *only* valid basis for apportionment. Said the Court in the leading case, *Reynolds* v. *Sims,* from Alabama:

> Legislators represent people, not trees or acres. Legislators are elected by voters, not farms or cities or economic interests. . . . [T]he Equal Protection Clause requires that the seats in both houses of a bicameral State legislature must be apportioned on a population basis.

All other factors were rejected as bases for apportionment. The *only* constitutionally acceptable apportionments are those which rest upon the principle of population equality.[6]

The significance of the "reapportionment revolution," which began with *Baker* v. *Carr,* cannot be over-stated. Within only a couple of years, some redistribution of legislative seats occurred in each one of the 50 States. In a few States the impact was slight, only minor adjustments were necessary to satisfy the one-man, one-vote standard; but in many the redistricting was quite extensive. In a few the changes came more or less voluntarily; but in most they came only after hard-fought court, legislative, and ballot battles.

Today there is comparatively little malapportionment at the State legislative level. The struggle to achieve population equality does continue in a few places; but the one-man, one-vote standard is now the prevailing basis of representation among the State legislatures.

Reapportionment solely on the basis of population means that the majority of the seats in most State legislatures are now held by legislators chosen from metropolitan areas—from the cities and their suburbs. The days of rural domination through overrepresentation have, in effect, passed. Only in those few States with predominantly rural populations, and those in which the economy is primarily agricultural, has the "reapportionment revolution" had little effect.

To grasp the vital importance, and the practical meaning, of all of this, look at it in these terms: The *location* of political power, *where* that clout is based, has recently shifted in most of the States. And in several of them that shift has been quite dramatic. Most of the real muscle in State politics—and, with it, the shaping of public policies—has been relocated, from the once-dominant rural interests to the cities and suburbs.

Recall, the State legislatures draw the boundaries of *congressional* districts, too. And those districts must also be laid out in accord with the one-man, one-vote rule (*Wesberry* v. *Sanders,* 1964). Hence, the "reapportionment revolution" has also had a substantial effect upon Congress, as we noted on pages 291–292.

Qualifications, Elections, Terms, Compensation

Qualifications. Each of the State constitutions sets forth qualifications for membership in the legislature. These formal qualifications—of age, citizenship, and residence—can be met rather easily.

In most States a representative must be at least 21; but in several the minimum age for service in either house is now 18. Most States do set a higher minimum age for senators, usually 25; in some the standard is even higher—in Texas, for example, 26 and in New Jersey and Tennessee 30.

Each State requires that its legislators be citizens of the United States; but only four specify any particular period—Maine, five years; Alabama and California, three years; and New Jersey, two years for representatives and four years for senators.

---

6 In *Reynolds* v. *Sims* the Court voided an Alabama apportionment dating from 1901; by 1964 it had produced rural-urban population splits of as much as 43 to 1 among senate districts and 16 to 1 among house districts. When it decided *Reynolds* the Court also disposed of companion cases from 14 other States. In each of them, as in *Reynolds,* it held that the State legislature was unconstitutionally apportioned because of substantial violations of the one-man, one-vote standard.

Case Study

"Legislators represent people, not trees or acres," said the Supreme Court in *Reynolds* v. *Sims.* And, of course, they do. But State legislators do not "represent" the populations of their States in the sense that they are mirror-like cross sections of them.

Rather, the nearly 7500 men and women who now sit in the 50 State legislatures generally come from the better-educated, more prestigiously employed, and middle-to-upper-middle class segments of those populations.

Approximately three-fourths of all State legislators have attended college, a majority of them are college graduates, and many of them have advanced degrees. They come from nearly every significant occupational group. The fields of law, business, agriculture, finance, and education are most heavily represented,

however—and, in most States, usually in that order. Few legislators have occupations that demand only manual skills, and almost never does one come from an unskilled job.

Legislators do generally mirror their constituents in certain characteristics—especially race, religion, and ethnic and nationality backgrounds. But—and this is the basic point here—they generally do not have the same social backgrounds as those shared by most of their constituents.

■ Why do most State legislators come from the kind of background described?

■ Given that background, can they satisfactorily represent the interests of their constituents?

■ Does the answer to that question depend in large part on how the word "represent" is defined? Why?

A legislator must also be a legal resident of the State in every instance—typically for at least a year. And usually, either by law or custom, a lawmaker must also live in the district he or she represents.

Practical politics regularly imposes additional, *informal*—and more meaningful—qualifications upon those who seek seats in the legislature. The factors of *political availability* vary somewhat from State to State—and even from district to district within a State. They relate to a candidate's vote-getting abilities and are based on such characteristics as occupation, national origin, race, education, record of public service, party identification, and name familiarity. The "right" combination of these factors will help a candidate to win nomination and then election to the legislature. On the other hand, any "wrong" factor, or combination of them, can doom an aspirant's chances.

Elections. State legislators are elected by popular vote in every State. Typically, legislative elections are partisan in charac-

ter, with the opposing candidates nominated in their respective party primaries. But in a few States—Delaware, for example—the parties pick their legislative candidates by convention. And in one State, Nebraska, legislators are chosen on a nonpartisan basis; that is, candidates are nominated at nonpartisan primaries, and the opposing candidates are not identified by party label on the general election ballot.

In most of the States the lawmakers are elected in November of the even-numbered years. But this is not the case in four of them. In Mississippi, New Jersey, and Virginia legislative elections occur in November, and in Louisiana in December, of the *odd*-numbered years—in the hope of separating consideration of State candidates and issues from national politics.

Terms. As the table on page 698 indicates, State legislators serve either two- or four-year terms. Senators are usually elected for a longer term than their colleagues in the lower house. They are chosen for four-year terms in 38 States (in-

PARTY CONTROL OF GOVERNORSHIPS AND STATE LEGISLATURES

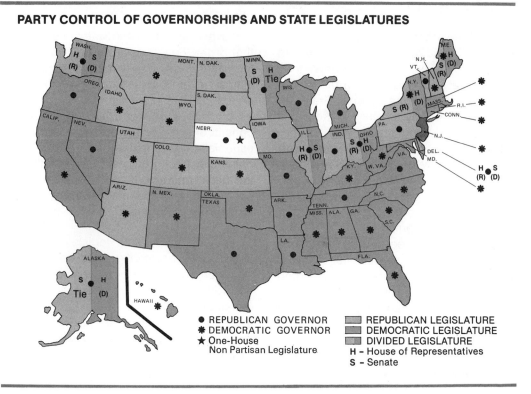

- ● REPUBLICAN GOVERNOR
- ✳ DEMOCRATIC GOVERNOR
- ★ One-House
  Non Partisan Legislature

- ▢ REPUBLICAN LEGISLATURE
- ▢ DEMOCRATIC LEGISLATURE
- ▢ DIVIDED LEGISLATURE
- H – House of Representatives
- S – Senate

cluding Nebraska) and for two-year terms in the other 12. Representatives serve two-year terms in 45 States and four-year terms in only four of them—Alabama, Louisiana, Maryland, and Mississippi.

The rate of turnover in legislative seats is fairly high, although it tends to vary from State to State and from time to time. Typically, there are more new members ("freshmen") in the lower house than in the senate in each State in each term. This is mostly the result of the larger size of the house, the longer term served by senators, and the fact that members of the lower house seek "promotion" to the upper chamber far more often than the reverse.

In any given year, more than *one-fourth* of all State legislators in the country are serving their first term in office. The major reasons for this high turnover seem to be low pay and political instability. The fact that legislators tend to remain in office

longer in those States paying the higher salaries and in which one party tends to dominate elections testifies to the importance of these reasons.

Compensation. How much legislators are paid is a very serious matter—and not alone to the legislators themselves. Some people seem to feel that it is payment enough for one to have the honor, to enjoy the supposed prestige, of sitting in the State legislature. And some people apparently feel that legislators are not really worth paying at all. But most people seem unaware of the problems involved.

The cold, hard facts are these: It costs money for legislators to live and to take time away from their normal occupations to serve the State. Far too often, capable, hardworking men and women refuse to run for the legislature; they feel that they cannot afford the financial (and other) sacrifices involved.

From the table on page 698 you can see the salaries now paid in each State. Most States also provide some sort of additional allowances. Oregon furnishes a fairly typical example. The basic salary is now $654 per month ($15,696 for the *biennium,* a two-year period). In addition, each member is paid an expense allowance of $44 for each day of the legislative session (which usually runs about 160 days) and for each day he or she attends interim committee meetings (between sessions). And each member also receives a $300 per month expense allowance for each month in which the legislature is not in session. The total compensation per member, including both salary and allowances, comes to about $15,000 a year. (Most of the State legislatures now grant fairly generous expense allowances to their members.)

Legislative pay is set by constitutional provision in a few States; in most the legislature itself determines the matter, however. (Lawmakers often hesitate to vote for higher salaries—usually because they fear voter reaction to such a step.)

Legislative Sessions

Regular Sessions. As you can see from the table on page 698, 37 States now (1981) hold their regular legislative sessions on an annual basis, and the California legislature meets in a continuous two-year session. In the other 13 States,[7] regular sessions are convened only every other year.

Most of the States have turned to the scheduling of annual sessions only within the past decade or so—as it has become increasingly apparent that the legislative workload cannot be handled on an every-other-year-for-a-few-months basis.[8]

As a general rule, regular sessions, whether annual or biennial, are becoming lengthier and lengthier affairs. As the table on page 698 indicates, some State constitutions limit the period for which a session may meet. But, again, because of the growing volume of State business, these restrictions are gradually disappearing.

Special Sessions. A special session of the legislature may be called by the governor in every State, and by the legislature itself in just over half of them.

As the term suggests, special sessions are held to permit the lawmaking body to consider urgent matters between its regular meetings. Special sessions are fairly common among the States today, especially in those still holding regular sessions only every other year. In five States—Connecticut, Hawaii, Louisiana, Missouri, and Washington—a special "veto session" is held soon after each regular session ends; it meets to consider those bills the governor vetoed following the adjournment of that regular session.

Powers of the Legislature

None of the 50 State constitutions contains a complete and detailed listing of all of the powers vested in the legislature. Rather, the legislature has all those powers which the State constitution does not grant exclusively to the executive or judicial branches or to local governments, and which neither the State nor the National Constitution specifically denies to it.

To put it another way, the legislature possesses all of those powers which are: (1) not granted elsewhere, and (2) not prohibited to it by some constitutional provision. In effect, *most* of the powers held by a State are vested in its legislature.

[7] Arkansas, Kentucky, Minnesota, Montana, Nevada, New Hampshire, North Carolina, North Dakota, Oregon, Tennessee, Texas, Vermont.

[8] In six of the annual session States—Colorado, Connecticut, Maine, New Mexico, Utah, and Wyoming—the second session is a budget session, limited entirely or mainly to the consideration of budget and related fiscal measures.

State	Year Held	Regular Sessions Limitations on Length*	Regular Sessions Month Convenes	Upper House No. of Members	Upper House Term of Members	Lower House No. of Members	Lower House Term of Members	Salary of Members[d]
Alabama	annual	30 L days	Feb	35	4	105	4	$10 per day
Alaska	annual	None	Jan	20	4	40	2	$11,750 ann.
Arizona	annual	None	Jan	30	2	60	2	$6000 ann.
Arkansas	odd[g]	60 C days	Jan	35	4	100	2	$15,000 bien.
California	f	None	Dec	40	4	80	2	$28,111 ann.
Colorado	annual[b]	None	Jan	35	4	65	2	$14,000 ann.
Connecticut	annual[b]	5 months[c]	Jan	36	2	151	2	$7500 ann.
Delaware	annual	June 30	Jan	21	4	41	2	$9630 ann.
Florida	annual	60 C days	Apr	40	4	120	2	$12,000 ann.
Georgia	annual	40 L days	Jan	56	2	180	2	$7200 ann.
Hawaii	annual	60 L days	Jan	25	4	51	2	$12,000 ann.
Idaho	annual	None	Jan	35	2	70	2	$4200 ann.
Illinois	annual	None	Jan	59	4	177	2	$28,000 ann.
Indiana	annual	61 L days / 30 L days	Jan	50	4	100	2	$6000 ann.
Iowa	annual	None	Jan	50	4	100	2	$12,800 ann.
Kansas	annual	None / 90 C days	Jan / Jan	40	4	125	2	$40 per day
Kentucky	even	60 L days	Jan	38	4	100	2	$75 per day
Louisiana	annual	60 L days	Apr	39	4	105	4	$50 per day
Maine	annual[b]	None	Dec	33	2	151	2	$3500 ann.
Maryland	annual	90 C days	Jan	47	4	141	4	$17,600 ann.
Massachusetts	annual	None	Jan	40	2	160	2	$21,050 ann.
Michigan	annual	None	Jan	38	4	110	2	$27,000 ann.
Minnesota	odd[g]	120 L days	Jan	67	4	134	2	$18,500 ann.
Mississippi	annual	90 C days[e]	Jan	52	4	122	4	$8100 session
Missouri	annual	6 months[c]	Jan	34	4	163	2	$15,000 ann.
Montana	odd	90 L days	Jan	50	4	100	2	$3195 session
Nebraska	annual	90 L days / 60 L days	Jan / Jan	49	4	—	—	$4800 ann.
Nevada	odd	60 C days	Jan	20	4	40	2	$80 per day
New Hampshire	odd	90 C days[a]	Jan	24	2	400	2	$200 bien.
New Jersey	annual	None	Jan	40	4	80	2	$18,000 ann.
New Mexico	annual[b]	60 C days / 30 C days[b]	Jan	42	4	70	2	$40 per day
New York	annual	None	Jan	60	2	150	2	$23,500 ann.
North Carolina	odd[g]	None	Jan	50	2	120	2	$6000 ann.
North Dakota	odd	80 C days	Jan	50	4	100	2	$5 per day
Ohio	annual	None	Jan	33	4	99	2	$22,500 ann.
Oklahoma	annual	90 L days	Jan	48	4	101	2	$12,948 ann.
Oregon	odd	None	Jan	30	4	60	2	$15,696 bien.
Pennsylvania	annual	None	Jan	50	4	203	2	$25,000 ann.
Rhode Island	annual	60 L days[a]	Jan	50	2	100	2	$5 per day
South Carolina	annual	None	Jan	46	4	124	2	$250 per day
South Dakota	annual	45 L days / 30 L days	Jan / Jan	35	2	70	2	$3600 session / $2400 session
Tennessee	odd[g]	90 L days[a]	Jan	33	4	99	2	$8308 ann.
Texas	odd	140 C days	Jan	31	4	150	2	$7200 ann.
Utah	annual[b]	60 C days / 20 C days[b]	Jan / Jan	29	4	75	2	$25 per day
Vermont	odd[g]	None	Jan	30	2	150	2	$9500 bien.
Virginia	annual	30 C days / 60 C days	Jan	40	4	100	2	$8000 ann.
Washington	annual	105 C days / 60 C days	Jan	49	4	98	2	$9800 ann.
West Virginia	annual	60 C days	Jan	34	4	100	2	$5136 ann.
Wisconsin	annual	None	Jan	33	4	99	2	$19,767 ann.
Wyoming	annual[b]	40 L days / 20 L days[b]	Jan / Jan	30	4	62	2	$30 per day

Legislative Powers. Because a legislature may enact any law not in conflict with either federal law or the State constitution, it is impossible to provide an all-inclusive list of any State legislature's powers. Even so, such powers as those to tax, appropriate and borrow money, regulate commercial activities within the State, establish courts and fix their jurisdictions, define crimes and provide for their punishment, and create and maintain public schools are commonly mentioned as legislative powers in State constitutions.

The powers of every State legislature include the extremely important *police power*—the State's power to act to protect and to promote the public health, safety, welfare, and morals, as we noted on pages 150–153. Although this broad power cannot be more precisely defined, it is the basis for literally thousands of State laws. Its vast scope can be illustrated by a *few* examples. Under it, laws may be (and are) enacted to require vaccinations and impose quarantines, restrict automobile exhaust emissions, forbid gambling, regulate the sale and consumption of alcoholic beverages, prohibit the ownership of dangerous weapons, fix highway speed limits, impose safety requirements in industrial plants, limit campaign contributions and spending, forbid the sale of soft drinks and other beverages in nonreturnable bottles or cans,

compel school attendance, set the minimum legal age for marriage, provide for food inspections, and bar immoral or indecent entertainments. Indeed, a list of this sort could be carried on for pages.

Nonlegislative Powers. Each of the State legislatures possesses certain nonlegislative powers—powers in addition to those it exercises in the making of law.

EXECUTIVE POWERS. Some of the powers vested in the legislature are *executive* in nature. For example, the governor's power to appoint certain high officials is frequently subject to the approval of the legislature, or at least the upper house. And in some States the legislature itself appoints various executive officers. Thus, the secretary of state, elected by the voters in most States, is chosen by the legislature in Maine, New Hampshire, and Tennessee. Similarly, the State treasurer is selected by the legislature in each of those States and in Maryland; and the lawmakers also pick the attorney general in Maine.

JUDICIAL POWERS. Each of the State legislatures also exercises certain *judicial* powers. The chief illustration is, of course, the power of impeachment. In every State except Oregon the legislature may impeach executive and judicial officers and, if convicted, remove them from office.

Each of the State legislatures possesses judicial powers with regard to its own

---

(Footnotes accompanying "THE STATE LEGISLATURES" table on page 698.)

⌐L = legislative (in-session) days; C = calendar days.

a Indirect limit; legislators' pay and/or expenses cease, but session may continue.

b Annual session every other year is budget session; budget session held in even-numbered years.

c Approximate length. In Connecticut, session must adjourn by the Wednesday after first Monday in June (odd years) and May (even years); in Missouri, session must adjourn by June 30 in odd-numbered years and by May 15 in even-numbered years.

d Most States also provide substantial expense allowances for legislators.

e Except 125 days every fourth year (the first year of a new gubernatorial term).

g Session may be (and in practice is) divided, so often meets in even year also.

Sources: State constitutions and statutes, and information furnished by appropriate State officials and Council of State Governments.

members. Thus, disputes involving the election or the qualifications of a member-elect are regularly decided by the house involved in the matter. Then, too, because legislators themselves are not liable to impeachment, each chamber has the power to discipline—and, in extreme cases, even expel—any of its own members.

CONSTITUENT POWERS. As we saw in Chapter 28, each State legislature plays a significant role in both constitution-making and in the constitutional amendment process. When it proposes an amendment to the State constitution, the legislature is not making law; rather, it exercises a nonlegislative power—the *constituent* power.

Organization of the Legislature

Presiding Officers. The lower house in each of the bicameral legislatures elects its own presiding officer, known everywhere as the *speaker*.

In 29 States the lieutenant governor serves as *president of the senate;* in the other 21 States the senate chooses its own presiding officer.[9] In those States where the lieutenant governor does preside, the senate elects a *president pro tempore* to serve in his or her absence. In actual practice, of course, the presiding officer in each house is selected by the majority party caucus—except for the popularly elected lieutenant governors, of course.

The presiding officers—and especially the speaker—are extremely potent figures in the legislature. And they regularly carry hefty clout in their own party and elsewhere in the politics of the State, as well.

Their chief duties—and prime sources of their power—include the recognition of members who seek the floor, interpretation and application of the rules, and reference of bills to committee.

Unlike the Speaker of the House in Congress, in nearly every State the speaker appoints the heads of committees and all other members of house committees.[10] The senate president or president *pro tem* has the same power in only slightly more than half of the States.[11] The presiding officers regularly use the power to name committees—and their other powers—to reward friends, punish enemies, and otherwise work their influence on the legislature.

The Committee System. The number of measures introduced at each session of the legislature runs from 500 or so in some of the smaller States to several thousand in many of the larger ones. This flood of proposed legislation makes the committee system as obviously necessary at the State level as it is in Congress. And, too, as in Congress, much of the work of each State legislature is accomplished in its committee rooms.

Committees make their most important contributions to the lawmaking process: (1) as they sift out those measures which merit floor consideration, and (2) when they inform the full house upon those measures they have handled.

The standing committees in each house are usually organized on a subject-matter

---

[9] In 13 States with the office, the lieutenant governor does not preside over the Senate. In Tennessee the senate elects its own presiding officer (known, uniquely, as the "speaker") and that officer is also, by statute, the lieutenant governor; in Utah the elected secretary of state is also, by statute, the lieutenant governor. The seven States in which there is no lieutenant governor are Arizona, Maine, New Hampshire, New Jersey, Oregon, West Virginia, Wyoming. See pages 711, 719.

[10] Another very considerable source of the speaker's power, of course. House committees are named by the respective party caucuses in Hawaii, by a committee on committees in Alaska, Kentucky, and Pennsylvania, and by the speaker and the minority floor leader in Colorado, Illinois, Nevada, and Wisconsin.

[11] Committees are picked by a committee on committees in the upper chamber in 15 States: Alaska, Arkansas, California, Georgia, Kansas, Kentucky, Michigan, Minnesota, Montana, Nebraska, New Mexico, North Dakota, Ohio, Vermont, and Wisconsin. They are picked by the majority party floor leader in Iowa, Rhode Island, and South Dakota, and by the majority and minority leaders in Colorado and Nevada. In Virginia, they are elected on the floor.

basis—*e.g.,* committees on highways, local government, elections, the judiciary, education, and so on. They occupy very strategic spots in the legislative process. It is to them that all bills are referred and it is in them that most bills are subjected to the closest attention they receive. A bill may be entirely rewritten in committee, amended in varying degree, or—as frequently happens—ignored altogether. Whether or not a bill is to be considered on the floor usually depends upon the actions taken by the committee to which it has been referred.[12]

There are, on the average, 15 to 20 standing committees in each house in the typical legislature. But, of course, the exact number varies State-to-State. In recent sessions, the number of committees in the lower house has ranged from as few as four in Massachusetts and six in Maryland and Rhode Island to as many as 49 in North Carolina; and in the senate, they have ranged from four in Massachusetts and five in Maryland to 32 in Mississippi.

There is no formula by which the ideal number of committees may be determined for any chamber, of course. But a relatively small number of them, each with well-defined areas of jurisdiction, seems the arrangement best-suited to accomplish a legislature's work. Strong support for this view can be found in this fact: In nearly all States most of the bills introduced during a session are referred to only a few of the committees.

The number of members per committee also varies considerably among the States. Ten to 12 is a fairly common size,

but in some States some committees have as many as 30 or even 40 or more members. And it is not uncommon for a legislator to serve on three or four committees simultaneously. In short, in too many States too little attention is given to the obvious relationship between the number and the size of committees on the one hand, and the effectiveness with which the legislature can and does function, on the other.

Joint committees—permanent groups composed of members of both houses—can produce substantial savings in terms of legislative time and effort. They have been used extensively in a few States for several years—most notably in Massachusetts, Maine, and Connecticut. In fact, the legislatures in the latter two States utilize *only* joint committees. Their use is now spreading. One or more joint committees function in approximately half of the State legislatures today.

The use of *interim committees*—which function *between* legislative sessions—is also on the increase. These groups make detailed studies of particular problems and then report their findings and recommendations to the next session.

The Legislative Process

The basic function of the State legislature is, of course, to make law. You can follow the major steps in the legislative process in a typical State in the diagram on page 703. Because that diagram is fairly descriptive, and because the lawmaking machinery in each State functions in much the same manner as it does in Congress (pages 315–326), we shall comment only briefly here.

Sources of Bills. Legally, only a member may introduce a bill in either house in any of the State legislatures. So, in the strictest sense, it may be said that the legislators themselves are *the* source for the thousands of measures introduced in legislatures each year. But, in the broader view,

---

[12] The "pigeon-holing" of bills is as well-known in the States as it is in Congress; see page 318. In fact, in most States one of the standing committees in each house is regularly the "graveyard committee"—a body to which a bill may be sent and never heard of again. The judiciary committee, to which bills may be referred "on grounds of doubtful constitutionality," most often fills the role. A striking illustration of the graveyard committee existed for several years in the landlocked State of Oklahoma: the Committee on Deep Sea Navigation.

"BEFORE WE VOTE, DID HE SAY 'MILLION' OR 'BILLION'?"

Reprinted with permission from THE SATURDAY EVENING POST. © 1977 The Curtis Publishing Company.

the lawmakers are the actual source for only a relative handful of bills.

A large number of bills come from *public sources*—various officers and agencies of State and of local government. The governor's office is regularly a principal source for legislation. Every governor has a legislative program of some sort—and, frequently, an extensive and ambitious one. Much of the legislature's agenda, much of what the lawmakers do, is shaped by proposals from the governor's office.

Many bills also come from other public sources. Take, for example, a measure authorizing the investment of surplus funds in short-term public securities. The bill may, in fact, have been drafted in the State treasurer's office. A proposed revision of the compulsory school attendance law may have been prompted by the superintendent of public instruction. An amendment

to the rules of criminal procedure may have come from the attorney general; and a bill relating to the use of the receipts of the State's gasoline tax may have been born in a city council or a city manager's office. And the legislature itself often produces legislative proposals, as well.

A substantial number of bills considered at each session arise from *private sources*. Indeed, the largest single source for proposed legislation in the States appears to be pressure groups. Recall that these groups, and the lobbyists who represent them, exist for one overriding purpose: To influence public policy to the benefit of their own particular interests. Of course, some bills also originate with private individuals—lawyers, businessmen and businesswomen, farmers, and other constituents who, for one reason or another, think that "there ought to be a law. . . ."

Voting. In most States votes on the floor may be taken in a variety of ways.[13] And they are taken for a variety of purposes, too.

The most important vote on a measure usually comes at the point at which the bill is either approved or rejected by the chamber—typically at second reading. But votes are taken at several other steps in the legislative process—for example, on amendments, on motions to limit or close debate, on motions to re-refer (send a measure back to committee), and so on.[14]

The methods we cite here are the principal ones used in the State legislatures:

VIVA VOCE. A voice vote is the method most often used in most States. Here, the presiding officer puts the question and then judges the outcome from the

---

[13] But in some States the constitution dictates the use of a particular method; thus in Oregon *all* floor votes must be by roll call.

[14] One of these other votes may in fact be *the* critical vote that determines the fate of a measure. For example, the real test of a bill may occur with the vote on a key amendment to it. Once that vote is taken, the question of final passage (or defeat) may be a mere formality.

THE COURSE OF A BILL

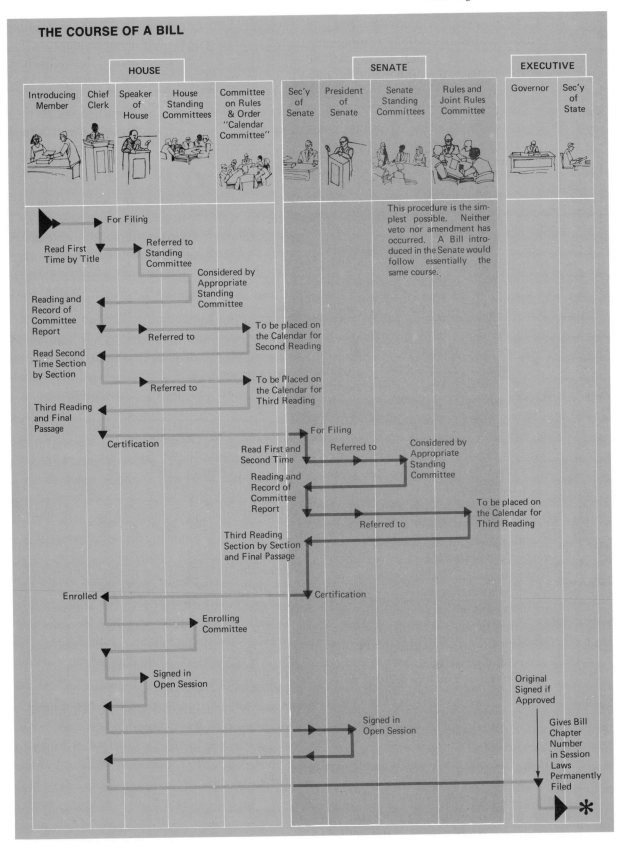

HOUSE

| Introducing Member | Chief Clerk | Speaker of House | House Standing Committees | Committee on Rules & Order "Calendar Committee" |

SENATE

| Sec'y of Senate | President of Senate | Senate Standing Committees | Rules and Joint Rules Committee |

EXECUTIVE

| Governor | Sec'y of State |

This procedure is the simplest possible. Neither veto nor amendment has occurred. A Bill introduced in the Senate would follow essentially the same course.

For Filing

Read First Time by Title

Referred to Standing Committee

Considered by Appropriate Standing Committee

Reading and Record of Committee Report

Referred to

To be placed on the Calendar for Second Reading

Read Second Time Section by Section

Referred to

To be Placed on the Calendar for Third Reading

Third Reading and Final Passage

Certification

For Filing

Read First and Second Time

Referred to

Considered by Appropriate Standing Committee

Reading and Record of Committee Report

Referred to

To be placed on the Calendar for Third Reading

Third Reading Section by Section and Final Passage

Enrolled

Certification

Enrolling Committee

Signed in Open Session

Original Signed if Approved

Signed in Open Session

Gives Bill Chapter Number in Session Laws Permanently Filed

*

volume of the response from those for and then those against. Its major advantage lies in the speed with which votes can be taken. But it does allow the presiding officer some very useful latitude in assessing the result.

DIVISION OF THE HOUSE. This method is often called a "standing vote," because those for and then those against a motion rise and are counted by the presiding officer. It is often used when the presiding officer's reading of a voice vote has been challenged.

TELLER VOTE. In this process members' votes are counted as they file past "tellers." Usually two tellers, one for and one against the question, stand in the front of the chamber and count the members' votes as they pass between them. Its use does provide a more accurate count than either the voice or division methods. But it does *not* provide a record of how the individual members cast their votes.

RECORD VOTE. Commonly called a "roll-call vote," a record vote is one in which each member is recorded in terms of "yea," "nay," "present" (not voting), or absent. Its use furnishes a permanent record of each legislator's vote on those questions for which it is used. But it is time-consuming—and a demand for a roll-call is often made as a delaying tactic.

The time a legislature spends in the voting process can be substantial over the course of a session—especially where roll-calls are involved. As a result, many States now use electronic devices ("scoreboards") to speed matters along.

The Governor's Veto. Once the legislature has completed action on a measure it must go to the governor. With the exception of North Carolina, the governor in every State has the veto power.

We shall consider the veto and the governor's other legislative powers in the next chapter. But, for now, these quick points. Unlike the President, the governors in 43 States have the "item veto"—the power to

veto specific items or sections of a bill without disapproving the entire measure.[15] The item veto power is usually restricted to action on appropriations measures. And, bear in mind the fact that the governor, like the President, can often use the *threat* of a veto as a lever to influence the actions of the legislature.

Improving State Legislatures

State legislatures are, of course, human creations. Like their creators, each of them exhibits some weaknesses and shortcomings. Quite happily, recent years have seen some substantial improvement. Several developments indicate that much-needed upgrading is well underway in many States; among the major improvements: the trend to annual sessions, significant pay increases, the increasing use of electronic data processing, and greatly expanded staff and research support for legislators.

Still, much remains to be done in many States. Several authorities—and especially the Council of State Governments and the Citizens Conference on State Legislatures—have long urged various actions to upgrade the 50 State lawmaking bodies. Their principal recommendations include:

(1) Restrictions on the length of regular sessions should be removed. The legislature should be able to meet as often and for as long as conditions require.

(2) Adequate salaries and allowances, sufficient to permit competent persons to serve as legislators should be provided.

(3) Legislative terms of office should be lengthened, and staggered to provide for continuity in membership.

(4) The lieutenant governor should be eliminated as a legislative figure.

(5) More effective regulation of lobbyists and of legislators' conflicts of interest should be enacted.

---

[15] In all States except Indiana, Maine, Nevada, New Hampshire, Rhode Island, Vermont, and North Carolina.

(6) Legislators and committees should be provided with adequate professional research, secretarial, and other staff aides and facilities.

(7) Legislative rules should be revised wherever necessary to expedite procedures, although with due regard for deliberation and for minority viewpoints.

(8) Committees should be reduced in number wherever practical; and they should be organized in terms of subject matter, equalization of workload, and cooperation between the two houses. Permanent and public records of committee action should be kept.

(9) Committees should operate "in the sunshine"—that is, hold open meetings; public hearings should be held on all major bills, with adequate notice of time and place.

(10) The legislature should control the auditing function, to insure that appropriated funds are spent in accord with the manner and the purposes for which the legislature provided them.

Direct Legislation

Beginning with South Dakota in 1898, several States permit the voters themselves to take a direct part in the lawmaking process—through the *initiative* and the *referendum*.

The Initiative. On page 685 we noted that the voters themselves may propose (initiate, by petition) constitutional amendments in 17 States. In 21 States they may initiate ordinary statutes.[16] The *initiative* is

a device by which interested individuals and groups may draft proposed laws (or constitutional amendments), and by securing a certain number of signatures of qualified voters, place their proposals before the electorate (or the legislature) for approval or rejection.

The number of voters who must sign the petitions proposing a statute varies. In North Dakota, for example, that number must equal two percent of the population of the State. In Arkansas, Michigan, and Washington, the requirement is eight percent of the number of votes cast for governor in the last election. In Arizona, the requirement is ten percent of all qualified voters.

When enough valid signatures have been collected, a proposed measure goes either directly to the ballot *or* to the State legislature. Where it goes depends upon whether the State provides for the *direct* or the *indirect* form of the initiative.[17]

The *direct initiative* is the most common form. Under it the proposed law goes directly to the voters at the next regular election. Under the *indirect initiative* the proposed law goes *first* to the legislature. Then, if the legislature does not enact the measure, it goes to the voters. As recent illustrations of the use of the initiative: In 1976 Utah voters approved a measure to prohibit the fluoridation of water systems without voter approval; similar proposals were defeated at the polls in Oregon and Washington. And in 1978 the California electorate approved fabled Proposition 13; that measure imposed a strict limitation on the levying of local property taxes and triggered similar ballot measures in several other States.

The Referendum. The *referendum* involves the submission (referral) of a legislative act to the voters. Three distinct

[16] Alaska, Arizona, Arkansas, California, Colorado, Idaho, Maine, Massachusetts, Michigan, Missouri, Montana, Nebraska, Nevada, North Dakota, Ohio, Oklahoma, Oregon, South Dakota, Utah, Washington, Wyoming. In each of these States a majority of the votes cast on the measure is required to enact an initiated statute. In Massachusetts that majority must equal at least 30 percent of the total number who vote in that election, and in Nebraska 35 percent. These 21 States also provide for the initiative at the local level; and it can be found in at least some cities or counties in most of the other 29 States, as well.

[17] Five States provide only for the indirect form: Maine, Massachusetts, Michigan, Nevada, South Dakota. Ohio, Utah, and Washington have both.

forms of the device are now used among the States—the mandatory, the optional, and the popular referendum.

The mandatory referendum is involved whenever the legislature *must* refer a particular measure to the voters. Thus, in every State except Delaware the legislature must submit proposed amendments to the constitution to the electorate. In several States some other measures must also go to the voters for final action; the calling of a constitutional convention and bond issues are common examples.

If a measure need not be but is *voluntarily* referred to the ballot by the legislature, it is said to be an *optional* (or legislative) *referendum*. Such referenda are relatively rare; they usually involve "hot potato" questions the lawmakers are reluctant to decide.

The *popular referendum* is the form most often associated with the notion of "direct legislation." It is now found in altogether 24 of the States—in the 21 States which use the statutory initiative (page 705), and three others—Maryland, New Mexico, and Kentucky (where it may be used *only* to refer measures relating to property taxes).

Under this form, the people may demand that a measure passed by the legislature be referred to them for final approval or rejection. That is, they may veto acts of the legislature.[18] The demand must be made by petitions signed by a certain number of qualified voters. For example, the number must be at least five percent of the vote cast for governor at the last election in California, Michigan, and South Dakota, and two percent of the State's population in North Dakota. Voters now face some 300 initiative and referendum measures among the States in each two-year span—most of them on the general election ballots every other November.

---

[18] Typically, a measure enacted by the legislature does not become effective immediately upon enactment. Rather, it does so at some prescribed time thereafter—usually 60 or 90 days after the legislature has adjourned. In the 24 States with the popular referendum, then, this delay permits time (and a deadline) for the circulation of referenda petitions. Some measures do need to become effective at once, however. To these "emergency measures" the legislature may attach an *emergency clause*—a provision which makes them immediately effective. To prevent the legislature from abusing the use of the emergency clause, most States allow the governor to veto such provisions; and one State, Oregon, absolutely forbids the inclusion of an emergency clause in *any* tax measure.

SUMMARY

The details of organization and procedure and even the official name of the legislature varies from State to State, but the legislature's basic function is everywhere the same: to make law.

Each of the State legislatures, except in Nebraska, is bicameral today. The size of the legislature, and each house, varies considerably among the States, but in each of them the apportionment of seats is a critical matter. The long-standing pattern of rural overrepresentation has now all but disappeared. The "reapportionment revolution" of the 1960's and early 1970's was triggered by the United States Supreme Court's decision in *Baker* v. *Carr,* 1962. In a now lengthy series of cases, beginning with *Reynolds* v. *Sims,* 1964, the Court has applied the "one-man, one-vote" rule to the apportionment problem.

Each State constitution sets out formal qualifications for membership in the legislature. The informal qualifications, those imposed by practical politics, are far more important, however. Legislators are elected by popular vote in every State. Senators serve four-year terms in 38 States and two-year terms in the other 12. Representatives are chosen for two-year terms in 45 States and for four-year terms in only four of them. Legislative pay and allowances are generally inadequate among the States and, as a consequence, many well-qualified men and women refuse to run for legislative office.

The steadily increasing volume of State governmental functions and responsibilities has prompted most of the States to provide for annual legislative sessions. Only 12 States today schedule regular sessions on a biennial basis. Special sessions may be called by the governor in every State and by the legislature itself in more than half of them.

The legislature possesses all of those powers which the State constitution does not exclusively grant to either the executive or the judicial branch or to local government and which neither it nor the National Constitution specifically denies to the legislature. Its extensive legislative powers include the police power, and it also exercises certain nonlegislative powers.

The organization and procedures of the typical State legislature are generally similar to those of Congress. The presiding officers are regularly potent figures within the legislature and their respective parties. As in Congress, a major share of the legislature's work is done in committees. Bills originate with both public and private sources. The governor holds the veto power in every State except North Carolina and also may apply the item veto in 43 States.

Through various forms of direct legislation—various forms of the initiative and the referendum—voters in several States may take an active role in the lawmaking process.

Concept Development

Questions for Review

1. What is the basic function of the State legislature?

2. By what official name is the legislature and each of its houses known in your State?

3. For what two major reasons has bicameralism predominated among the States?

4. How many members are there in each house in your State legislature?

5. Why is the basis upon which legislative seats are apportioned an important matter?

6. What did the Supreme Court hold in *Baker* v. *Carr*, 1962? Why was this so significant? What did the Court hold in *Reynolds* v. *Sims*, 1964?

7. What is the essential meaning of the phrase "one-man, one-vote"?

8. Why are the informal qualifications more important considerations in legislative elections than the formal ones?

9. For what term are the members of each house of your State legislature chosen?

10. What salary is paid to the members of your State legislature?

11. How frequently are regular legislative sessions held in your State?

12. What is the general scope of the powers possessed by each of the State legislatures? What is the *police power*?

13. What officer presides over the lower house of your State legislature? The upper house?

14. Why must and does the legislature rely so heavily upon its committees?

15. What are *joint committees? Interim committees?*

16. What appears to be the largest single source for legislative proposals in the States?

17. By what four methods are floor votes commonly taken in a State legislature?

18. What is the *initiative?* Distinguish the two basic forms of the device.

19. What is the *referendum?* Distinguish the three basic forms of the device.

20. Is either device available in your State? If so, in what form(s)?

Further Inquiry

1. What particular qualifications would you require of all candidates seeking election to the State legislature?

2. As the table on page 698 indicates, many State constitutions impose a limit on the length of the legislature's regular session. Why do most authorities recommend that such restrictions be eliminated?

3. How does your State legislature fare in terms of the major recommendations for legislative improvement summarized on pages 704–705?

4. On page 696 we noted that inadequate pay and political instability appear to be the major reasons for the relatively high rate of turnover in legislative seats in most States. What other reasons for this condition can you suggest?

Suggested Activities

1. Invite a State legislator to speak to the class on his/her role and functions.

2. If possible, arrange for the class to visit the legislature when it is in session.

3. Stage a debate or class forum on the subject: *Resolved,* That the legislature of this State be reorganized on a unicameral basis.

4. Prepare a chart to indicate the course of a bill through the various steps of the legislative process in your State. The chart on page 703 may be a useful model.

Suggested Reading

America's State Legislatures: Their Structures and Procedures. Council of State Governments, 1977.

Berman, David R., *State and Local Politics.* Allyn and Bacon, Inc., 3rd ed., 1981.

BeVier, Michael J., *Politics Backstage: Inside the California Legislature.* Temple University Press, 1979.

Jewell, Malcolm C. and Patterson, Samuel, *The Legislative Process.* Random House, 3rd ed., 1977.

Keefe, William J. and Ogul, Morris S., *The American Legislative Process.* Prentice-Hall, 5th ed., 1981.

Morlan, Robert L. (ed.), *Capitol, Courthouse, and City Hall.* Houghton Mifflin, 6th ed., 1981.

Rosenthal, Alan, *Legislative Life: People, Process, and Performance in the States.* Harper & Row, 1981.

Sharkansky, Ira, *The Maligned States.* McGraw-Hill, 2nd ed., 1978.

The Book of the States, 1980–81. The Council of State Governments, 1980.

The Governor and State Administration

Energy in the Executive is a leading character in the definition of good government.

ALEXANDER HAMILTON

The governor is the principal executive officer in each of the 50 States. He—or she[1]—is always a central figure in State politics.

The governor today occupies an office that is the direct descendant of the earliest public office in American politics—the colonial governorship, first established in Virginia in 1607.

Much of the colonial resentment that finally exploded into revolution was directed at the royal governors. Somewhat illogically, that attitude was carried over into the first State constitutions. The new State governors were given, for the most part, only meager authority. Most of the powers of State government were vested in the legislature. In every State except Massachusetts and New York, the governor was chosen by the legislature, and in most of them only for a one-year term. And only in Massachusetts and South Carolina did the governor have the veto power.

The early State governors were regularly described as "figureheads." Thus, James Madison, addressing the Philadelphia Convention in 1787, was able to say:

■ Can the governor be properly described as the State's "chief executive"?

■ What extra-constitutional qualifications ought a governor possess?

■ Is popular election the most satisfactory method for the selection of a governor? What other methods might be used?

---

[1] All 50 of the State governors are presently (1981) men. All told, only five women have ever been elected to a governorship: Nellie T. Ross (Wyoming, 1925-1927); Miriam A. Ferguson (Texas, 1925-1927, 1933-1935); Lurleen Wallace (Alabama, 1967-1968); Ella T. Grasso (Connecticut, 1975-1981); and Dixy Lee Ray (Washington, 1977-1981). Unlike Governors Grasso and Ray, the three earlier women governors followed their husbands in the office.

Governors often meet with one another—on a neighboring State, a regional, and a national basis—to discuss common problems and promote interstate cooperation.

"The executives of the States are little more than ciphers; the legislatures are omnipotent."

This original separation of powers soon proved unsatisfactory, however. Many of the State legislatures abused their powers and several became prey to special interests, and the weak governors were unable to respond. So, as new constitutions were written, and the older ones revised, the legislatures were curbed and the powers of the governors generally increased.

Through the early years of the last century the power to choose the governor was taken from the legislature and given to the people. The veto power was lodged in the governor and the gubernatorial powers of appointment and administration were increased, as well.

But, at the same time, new popularly elected executive officers, boards, and commissions were also created in several States. These executive officers, supposedly within the governor's administration, were in fact largely independent of the governor's control—because they, too, were elected by the voters. Many States are yet plagued by the consequences of this development, as we shall see.

The most dramatic developments in the nature of the governorship have occurred within the past half-century or so. Beginning with Illinois in 1917, most States have reorganized the executive branch to make

the governor the chief executive in something more than name. Of course, some States have gone further than others in the strengthening of the office. In all of them, however, the governor is a much more potent figure than at any time in the past. And, the trend to a stronger governorship is a continuing one.

The Office

Qualifications. Every State constitution sets out certain formal qualifications which must be met by any person who would be governor. Commonly, the governor must be a citizen of the United States, must have resided in the State for at least a certain period, and must be of at least a certain age. Those in the Texas constitution are typical. There the governor must (1) be an American citizen, (2) have lived in the State for at least five years, and (3) be at least 30 years of age.[2]

Of course, these formal qualifications are not too difficult to satisfy and are, in fact, met by hundreds of thousands of persons in each State. Far more important are the *informal* requirements imposed by the

---

[2] Only one State prescribes an age above 30—Oklahoma, where the governor must be at least 35. Texas and seven other States—Arkansas, Maryland, Mississippi, North Carolina, Pennsylvania, South Carolina, and Tennessee—bar atheists from the governorship. But the ban is almost certainly unconstitutional; see *Torcaso* v. *Watkins*, page 128.

politics of the State. Thus, an aspirant usually must reside in a populous area, have an acceptable record of accomplishment in politics, business, or some other field, be acceptable to various party factions or, at least, not have made too many enemies, and so on.

Selection. The governor is chosen by popular vote in every State. In all but four, only a plurality is required for election. But if no candidate wins a clear majority in Georgia or Louisiana, the two top vote-getters meet in a second (run-off) election. In Mississippi the winner is chosen by the lower house of the legislature; in Vermont the choice is made by both houses.

The major parties' gubernatorial candidates are usually nominated by primaries. But they are still picked by conventions in a few States, as we noted on page 239. In recent years, nearly half of the States have provided for the team election of the governor and lieutenant governor. That is, in those States each party's nominees for the two offices run jointly; the voter casts one vote to fill both offices.

Term. The one-year gubernatorial term has long since disappeared. Nearly everywhere the governor is now chosen for four years. Only four States—Arkansas, New Hampshire, Rhode Island, and Vermont—provide for a two-year term.

Half of the States still place some limit on the number of terms governors may serve. In four they cannot serve more than one term;[3] in 24 others they cannot serve more than two consecutive terms.[4] Interestingly, approximately two-thirds of all incumbent governors who do seek reelection are successful in doing so.

Succession. Every State constitution provides for a successor should the governor die, resign, be removed from office, or be physically unable to carry out the duties of the office. In 43 States the lieutenant governor is first in the line of succession; see page 719. In four States—Maine, New Hampshire, New Jersey, and West Virginia—the president of the senate succeeds. In the other three States—Arizona, Oregon, and Wyoming—the governorship passes to the secretary of state.

Governors are mortal, and occasionally one dies in office, of course. Most of them are also politically ambitious, and occasionally one of them resigns in mid-term—to take a seat in the United States Senate or accept a presidential appointment, for example. When a gubernatorial vacancy does occur, it often sets off a game of political musical chairs in the State.[5]

REMOVAL. The governor may be removed from office by the *impeachment* process in all but one State, Oregon. But such actions have been quite rare. Only four governors have been thrown out since Reconstruction days—and none over the past half-century.[6]

---

[3] Kentucky, Mississippi, New Mexico, Virginia.

[4] Alabama, Alaska, Delaware, Florida, Georgia, Hawaii, Indiana, Kansas, Louisiana, Maine, Maryland, Missouri, Nebraska, Nevada, New Jersey, North Carolina, Ohio, Oklahoma, Oregon, Pennsylvania, South Carolina, South Dakota, Tennessee, West Virginia. In Delaware, Missouri, and North Carolina the ban is an absolute two-term limit; in the others it is a two *consecutive* term limit.

[5] Thus, when Jimmy Carter became President in 1977 he named Governor Cecil Andrus of Idaho as Secretary of the Interior. Later the same year he appointed Governor Patrick Lucey of Wisconsin ambassador to Mexico and Governor Raul Castro of Arizona ambassador to Argentina; and in 1978 Governor Richard Kneip of South Dakota became ambassador to Singapore. And, in 1977, as well, Walter Mondale resigned his Senate seat to become Vice President, whereupon Governor Wendell Anderson of Minnesota appointed himself to the Senate vacancy. In all five instances, the incumbent lieutenant governor succeeded. And, as a consequence, the political plans, the timetables of ambition, of several public figures in each of these States were revised accordingly.

[6] William Salzer of New York, 1913; James E. Ferguson of Texas, 1917; J. C. Walton of Oklahoma, 1923; and Henry S. Johnston of Oklahoma, 1929. "Pa" Ferguson was later pardoned by the Texas legislature and then immediately announced his candidacy for the governorship. But the State Supreme Court held the legislature's pardon unconstitutional in 1920. Article XV, Section 4 of the Texas constitution provides that any officer removed by impeachment is thereafter forever barred "from holding any office of honor, trust, or profit" in the State. Most State constitutions contain a similar clause.

STATE GOVERNORS

State	Term in Years	Annual Salary
Alabama	4	$50,000 and residence
Alaska	4	$52,992 and residence
Arizona	4	$50,000
Arkansas	2	$35,000 and residence
California	4	$49,100 and residence
Colorado	4	$50,000 and residence
Connecticut	4	$42,000 and residence
Delaware	4	$35,000 and residence
Florida	4	$56,017 and residence
Georgia	4	$52,750 and residence
Hawaii	4	$50,000 and residence
Idaho	4	$40,000 and residence
Illinois	4	$55,000 and residence
Indiana	4	$42,500 and residence
Iowa	4	$55,000 and residence
Kansas	4	$45,000 and residence
Kentucky	4	$45,000 and residence
Louisiana	4	$50,000 and residence
Maine	4	$35,000 and residence
Maryland	4	$60,000 and residence
Massachusetts	4	$60,000
Michigan	4	$65,000 and residence
Minnesota	4	$62,000 and residence
Mississippi	4	$53,000 and residence
Missouri	4	$37,500 and residence
Montana	4	$37,500 and residence
Nebraska	4	$40,000 and residence
Nevada	4	$50,000 and residence
New Hampshire	2	$44,520 and residence
New Jersey	4	$65,000 and residence
New Mexico	4	$40,000 and residence
New York	4	$85,000 and residence
North Carolina	4	$50,085 and residence
North Dakota	4	$44,750 and residence
Ohio	4	$50,000 and residence
Oklahoma	4	$48,000 and residence
Oregon	4	$50,372
Pennsylvania	4	$66,000 and residence
Rhode Island	2	$42,500
South Carolina	4	$60,000 and residence
South Dakota	4	$37,000 and residence
Tennessee	4	$68,226 and residence
Texas	4	$71,400 and residence
Utah	4	$40,000 and residence
Vermont	2	$41,000
Virginia	4	$60,000 and residence
Washington	4	$58,900 and residence
West Virginia	4	$50,000 and residence
Wisconsin	4	$65,801 and residence
Wyoming	4	$55,000 and residence

Sources: State constitutions and statutes and information furnished by appropriate State officials.

The governor may be *recalled* by the voters in 15 States.[7] Only one has ever been so removed. Governor Lynn J. Frazier was recalled by the voters in North Dakota in 1921—but the very next year he was elected to the United States Senate.

Compensation. A glance at the table on this page will show that gubernatorial salaries now average just about $50,000 a year among the States. There is a fairly wide spread among them, however—from the few where the pay is comparatively low on up to as much as $85,000 in New York. Most States also provide the governor with an official residence and an expense account.

To the governor's salary and other compensation must be added the psychic income involved—the intangibles of honor and prestige which accompany the office. It is this factor, as well as a sense of public service, that often persuades many of our better citizens to seek the office. About a third of the members of the United States Senate are former governors, and a number of Senators have later served as governors. Former Chief Justice Earl Warren went to the High Court from the governor's chair in California. And several Presidents were governors of their respective States before entering the White House—including, in this century: Theodore Roosevelt, Woodrow Wilson, Calvin Coolidge, Franklin Roosevelt, Jimmy Carter, and Ronald Reagan.

The Governor at Work

The Many Roles. The powers and the duties of the governor of each State may be classified under three major headings: (1) executive, (2) legislative, and (3) judicial. And, a fourth and lesser category may be added here: miscellaneous and ceremo-

---

[7] Alaska, Arizona, California, Colorado, Georgia, Idaho, Kansas, Louisiana, Michigan, Montana, Nevada, North Dakota, Oregon, Washington, Wisconsin.

nial. A useful understanding of the nature of the office can be had from an examination of each of these categories—and we shall do that in a moment.

But, first, notice that the governor, like the President, plays many roles—wears many different hats. He or she is, simultaneously, an executive, an administrator, a legislator, a party leader, an opinion leader, and a ceremonial figure. What the office amounts to depends in no small part on the way in which the governor plays each and all of these roles. And the way in which he or she does so must depend, in turn, upon the strength of the governor's personality, political muscle, and overall abilities.

Some, often many, of the governor's formal powers are hedged with various constitutional restrictions. But the powers possessed, in combination with the prestige of the office, make it quite possible for a capable, persuasive, dynamic incumbent to be a "strong" governor, accomplishing much for the State and the public good.

Executive Powers. Although the Presidency and the governorship can be likened in several ways, the comparison can be pushed too far. This is most strikingly true in the area of executive powers. Recall that the Constitution of the United States makes the President *the* executive in the National Government. State constitutions, on the other hand, regularly describe the governor as merely the *chief* executive in State government.

This distinction between *the* and *chief* is a critical one. Most of the State constitutions distribute the executive power among several "executive officers"—and this, in effect, makes the governor only "first among equals." For example, Article IV, Section 1 of the Texas constitution declares:

> The Executive Department of this State shall consist of a Governor, who shall be the Chief Executive Officer of the State, a

Lieutenant Governor, Secretary of State, Comptroller of Public Accounts, Treasurer, Commissioner of the General Land Office, and Attorney General.

As we shall see, these other executive officers are usually popularly elected—and so they are very largely beyond the governor's immediate control.

In most States, then, executive authority is fragmented. It is lodged in several separate, and independently chosen, officers. Only a part of the executive authority is held by the governor. Yet, whatever the *realities* of power may be, it is the governor to whom the people look for leadership in State affairs—and hold responsible for their conduct and condition.

The basic legal responsibility of the governor is regularly contained in a constitutional provision directing the chief executive to "take care that the laws be faithfully executed." And, even though the executive authority may be fragmented among several executive officers, the governor is given several specific powers designed to that end.

APPOINTMENT AND REMOVAL. The governor can best perform the duty to execute—enforce and administer—the law with subordinates of his or her own choosing. Hence, the powers of appointment and removal are, or should be, among the most important in the arsenal of a State's chief executive.

A leading test of any administrator is the ability to select loyal and able assistants. Two major factors work to limit the governor's competence here, however. *First,* of course, is the existence of those other elected executives; the people choose them, and the governor cannot remove them.

Secondly, the State's constitution and statutes regularly place restrictions on the governor's power to hire and fire. Thus, for example, in most States the constitution requires that most of the governor's major appointees be confirmed by the State senate. And the legislature often attaches qualifications and other conditions that must be met by those appointed to the offices it creates by statute. In a vigorous two-party State, for example, it is fairly common for the law to require that not more than a certain number of the members of each board or commission be from the same political party. This means, of course, that the governor must appoint some members of the opposing party to posts in his/her administration.

State civil service laws also work to hinder the governor's discretion. The basic thrust of the civil service concept is appointment and promotion on the basis of merit and removal only for cause. It is now well-established in several States. And it has made large inroads in the time-honored spoils system in most of the others. But, whatever its advantages, it does place limits on the governor's authority to hire and fire subordinates.

Still, the governor must fill many important posts. Recent reorganization efforts have regularly stressed the consolidation of governmental functions in the hands of a relatively small number of departments—each headed by an administrator selected by and directly responsible to the governor.

SUPERVISION OF ADMINISTRATION. The governor is the State's chief administrator—again, not *the* and not the *only* but the *chief* administrator.

Alone and unaided, the governor cannot possibly "take care that the laws be faithfully executed." The day-to-day job of enforcing the State's laws, performing its many functions, and providing its many services is done by the various agencies and the thousands of men and women who make up the executive branch. The governor must supervise that work—must manage and oversee the administration.

That is, the governor must do so to the extent that he or she *can*. Many State agencies are subject to the governor's direct control. But, recall, many are not. They are headed by other elected officials. For example, the attorney general heads the department of justice, and the secretary of state usually administers the election laws.

At base, the governor's ability to supervise State administration depends, *first,* upon the extent to which the constitution and statutes make it possible. And, *second,* it depends upon the governor's ability to operate through such informal channels as party leadership, patronage, appeals to the public, and the like.

THE BUDGET. We shall look at the budget process in Chapter 33. But we must delve into the subject for a moment here.

As we've suggested before (page 493), a budget is more than a balance sheet, a dull recitation of dollars from here and dollars for that. It is a political document, a highly important policy statement. Its numbers reflect the struggle over "who gets what"— and who doesn't.

Public agencies, no less than private enterprises, can accomplish very little without money. And, obviously, those who control the purse-strings have much to say about the activities and the very life of a public agency and its programs.

In most States today the governor is responsible for the preparation of the annual (or biennial) budget to be submitted to the legislature. That is, the governor has the *power* to make the budget.

The legislature usually has the authority to make whatever changes it cares to in the governor's budget proposals. *But* the governor's recommendations regularly carry a great deal of weight.

In short, the governor's budget-making power can be—and often is—a highly effective tool with which he or she can control State administration. Although unable to appoint or remove the head of a particular agency, for example, the governor can use the budget power to affect that agency's programs. And this can have a signifi-

Case Study

In nearly every State the formal powers of the governor are surrounded by several constitutional restraints. In fact, this is so typical that one authority insists that the governors' real powers rest very largely on their talents of persuasion:

> Their power depends upon their ability to persuade administrators over whom they have little authority, legislators who are jealous of their own powers, party leaders who are selected by local constituents, federal officials over whom governors have little authority, and a public that thinks that governors have more authority than they really have. Thus, the role of governors is, above all, that of a persuader—of their own administrators, State legislators, federal officials, party leaders, the press, and the public.*

■ How closely does this comment fit the governorship in your State?

■ What resources are available to help a governor fill the role of persuader?

■ An earlier (1977) presentation of this same comment was cast in the male gender (governor/he). Why has the author changed that form in this version?

■ Why have only five women ever been elected State governors? Do you foresee any significant change in that fact in the near future? Why, or why not?

* Thomas R. Dye, *Politics in States and Communities* (Englewood Cliffs, N.J.: Prentice-Hall, 4th ed., 1981), p. 162.

cant impact upon the attitudes and conduct of the agency's administrator.

MILITARY POWERS. Every State constitution makes the governor the commander-in-chief of the State militia—effectively, of the State's units of the National Guard.

The National Guard is the *organized* part of the State militia. In the event of national emergency, it may be "called up"—ordered into federal service by the President.[8]

When the State's Guard units are not in federal service—which is most of the time—they are commanded by the governor. The governor's chief military aide, the adjutant general, serves as the Guard's highest-ranking uniformed officer.

On various occasions, the governor finds it necessary to call out the National Guard—for example, to deal with such emergencies as prison riots and strike disturbances, to aid in evacuation and relief work and to prevent looting during and after floods, violent storms and other natural disasters, and to augment State police and reduce holiday traffic mishaps.

Legislative Powers. The State's principal *executive* officer possesses three quite important formal legislative powers. Governors possess the power: (1) to send messages to the legislature, (2) to call the legislature into special session, and (3) to veto measures passed by the legislature. These, together with the governor's ability to rely upon informal sources of power, frequently make the governor, in fact, the State's chief legislator.

THE MESSAGE POWER. The message power is really the power to recommend legislation. Its importance depends very largely upon the governor's personality, popularity, and political strength—in short, on the governor's power to persuade. A strong governor can accomplish much with the power.

As we suggested earlier, much of what the legislature does is centered around the governor's legislative program. That program is transmitted to the lawmakers in

---

[8] All of the States' National Guards were federalized in 1940 and served as a part of the nation's armed forces throughout World War II. Many units also saw extensive combat duty in both Korea and Viet Nam. National Guard units are only rarely called into federal service in domestic crises; see page 88.

several messages—especially an annual State of the State address and the budget, but in several special messages, too. In all of them the governor recommends the enactment of legislation. Various informal tactics—appeals to the people, close contacts with legislative leaders, and a judicious use of the appointing power, for example—help the governor promote his or her legislative program, too.

SPECIAL SESSIONS. Every State constitution gives to the governor the power to call the legislature into special session (see page 697).[9]

Special sessions have become fairly common among the States, as both the volume and the complexity of State business has grown. This is especially true in those several States which still schedule regular sessions on a biennial basis, and even more so where the biennial sessions are limited as to length.

The basic purpose of the governor's power here is to permit the State to meet extraordinary situations, of course. But the power can also be an important part of the governor's legislative arsenal, too. Thus, the governor may persuade reluctant legislators to pass a particular bill—and many have—by threatening to call them back in a special session if they adjourn the regular session without having done so.

THE VETO POWER. With the single exception of North Carolina, the governor in every State has the power to veto measures passed by the legislature. This power, including the *threat* to use it, is often the most potent weapon the governor has to influence the actions of the legislative branch.

In most States the governor has only a few days in which to sign or veto a measure—most commonly five.[10] If no action is taken within the prescribed period—*and the legislature remains in session*[11]—the measure then becomes law.

THE POCKET VETO. Unlike the President, the governor does not have the *pocket veto* in most States. That is, those bills the governor neither signs nor vetoes *after* the legislature adjourns become law without his or her signature.

The governor does possess the pocket veto in 14 States, however.[12] Take Minnesota to illustrate the process. There the governor has three days (not counting Sunday) to act on a measure while the legislature remains in session. But if the legislative session ends during that three-day period the governor then has 14 days in which to act. If the governor neither signs nor vetoes the bill within that 14-day period, it dies—the pocket veto has been applied.

THE ITEM VETO. In 43 States[13] the governor's veto power includes the *item veto*. That is, unlike the President, the governors in most States may veto one or more provisions (items) in a bill without rejecting the entire measure.

The power is usually—but not always—restricted to items in appropriations

---

[9] In several States the constitution forbids a special session to consider any matters except those for which the governor has called it. But in a majority of States the lawmakers may deal with any subjects they choose. This latter fact frequently means that the governor in those States is reluctant to call a special session. Recall that, as we noted on page 697, the legislature may also call itself into special session in just over half of the States.

[10] Three days in Iowa, Minnesota, New Mexico, North Dakota, Wyoming; six days in Alabama, Maryland, Rhode Island, Wisconsin; seven days in Florida, Indiana, Virginia; 10 days in Colorado, Delaware, Hawaii, Kansas, Kentucky, Louisiana, Maine, Massachusetts, New Jersey, New York, Ohio, Pennsylvania, Texas; 12 days in California; 14 days in Michigan; 15 days in Alaska, Missouri; 60 days in Illinois; and five days in the other 19 States. In most States Sundays are excluded from the count.*

[11] The period *after* adjournment is somewhat longer in several States—for example, 20 days in Alaska, Arkansas, Oregon, and Texas; 30 days in Colorado, Georgia, Maryland, Pennsylvania; and 45 days in Hawaii and New Jersey. On "veto sessions" in some States, see page 697.

[12] Alabama, Delaware, Hawaii, Massachusetts, Michigan, Minnesota, New Hampshire, New Jersey, New Mexico, New York, Oklahoma, Vermont, Virginia, Wisconsin.

[13] All except Indiana, Maine, Nevada, New Hampshire, Rhode Island, Vermont, and North Carolina.

bills. It allows the governor to delete spending items he or she finds excessive or undesirable. (In some States the governor may reduce, as well as eliminate, money items.)

The item veto is regularly used to check extravagant legislative appropriations. But, notice, the fact that the governor has the power sometimes encourages legislators to vote for various spending proposals and "pass the buck" on balancing the State's budget to the governor. And, often, the governor finds the item veto a useful device with which to persuade or punish lawmakers who oppose the governor's own legislative program.

THE LEGISLATURES' POWER TO OVERRIDE. The governor does not have an absolute veto in any State—except where a pocket veto is involved. That is, the governor's veto is regularly subject to a vote to override it in the legislature.

The size of the vote necessary to override varies among the States, but two-thirds of the full membership in each house is the most common requirement.[13a]

In actual practice, not many bills are vetoed. Altogether, less than five percent of all measures enacted by the various State legislatures are rejected. But when the power is used it is quite effective. Less than ten percent of all vetoed bills are then enacted over the governor's veto.

Judicial Powers. In every State the governor has a variety of powers of a judicial nature. Most of them are usually re-

[13a] A majority of the full membership in each house in Alabama, Arkansas, Indiana, Kentucky, Tennessee, West Virginia; three-fifths of the full membership in Delaware, Illinois, Maryland, Nebraska, Ohio; three-fifths of the members present in Rhode Island; two-thirds of the members present in Florida, Idaho, Maine, Massachusetts, Montana, New Hampshire, New Mexico, Oregon, South Carolina, Texas, Vermont, Virginia, Washington, Wisconsin; and two-thirds of the full membership in the other 23 States. (But for appropriations bills, the required vote is three-fourths of the full membership in Alaska and two-thirds in West Virginia; and for a bill containing an emergency clause, three-fourths of the full membership in Oklahoma.)

ferred to as the powers of "executive clemency"—powers of mercy which may be shown toward those convicted of crime. They include:

The power to *pardon*—i.e., to release a person from the legal consequences of a crime. In most States, a pardon may be either full or conditional and cannot be granted until *after* conviction. And in most States a pardon cannot be granted in cases involving either treason or impeachment.

The power to *commute*—i.e., to reduce the sentence imposed by a court. Thus, for example, a death sentence may be commuted to life imprisonment or the commutation may be to "time served"—which means that the prisoner is then released.

The power to *reprieve*—i.e., to postpone the execution of a sentence. Reprieves are usually granted for a few hours or a few days—to allow additional time for an appeal or because of the discovery of some new piece of evidence in a case.

Governors may call out the National Guard to help deal with a natural disaster. Here, a Guardsman helps in filling sandbags which will be used to prevent a river from overflowing its banks.

Iowa's Governor Robert D. Ray and Mrs. "Billie" Ray welcome Pope John Paul II at the Des Moines airport.

The power to *remit*—i.e., to eliminate or reduce the fine imposed upon conviction.

The power to *parole*—i.e., to release a prisoner short of the completion of the term of a sentence. Paroles are usually conditional and supervised; and they are a regular—and often controversial—part of the criminal corrections process.

The governor may have some or all of these powers, but they are frequently shared with one or more boards—for example with a board of pardons and/or a parole board.

There is always a danger that a governor will use the powers of clemency too freely, of course. In her first term (1925-1927) Governor "Ma" Ferguson of Texas pardoned 3737 convicted felons—an average of more than five a day. The pardons came so thick and fast that several Texas newspapers ran "pardon columns" rather than separate news stories.[14]

The receipt of an extradition warrant from another State also casts the governor in a judicial role; see page 94.

Miscellaneous Duties. The governor regularly performs a number of other, and very time-consuming, duties. In every State he or she is an *ex officio* (by virtue of office) member of several boards and commissions. A governor must receive official visitors and welcome distinguished persons, open State fairs, dedicate new buildings, crown beauty contest winners, address an incredible number of organizations and public gatherings, and attend countless local celebrations. And, a governor must help settle labor disputes, support many worthy causes—indeed, the list is well-nigh endless.

Other Executive Officers

As we've noted several times, in most States the governor must share the control of "his" (or "her") administration with a number of other executive officers.

In only three States is the governor the only popularly elected executive officer—Maine, New Jersey, and Tennessee. And only in New Jersey does the governor have the power to appoint the other principal officers in the executive branch.[15]

The other executive officers most often found among the several States include the

---

[14] "Ma" sought and won the governorship after the State Supreme Court voided her husband's legislative pardon; see note 6, page 711. She vented her anger over the treatment "Pa" had received in several other ways, as well—for example, by refusing to honor any and all extradition requests from other States.

[15] In Maine the secretary of state, treasurer, and attorney general are selected by the legislature; in Tennessee the secretary of state and treasurer are chosen by the legislature and the attorney general by the State Supreme Court.

lieutenant governor, secretary of state, treasurer, auditor, attorney general, and superintendent of public instruction—and no useful treatment of the executive function can afford to overlook them.

The Lieutenant Governor. The office of lieutenant governor now exists in 43 States and is filled by the voters in 41 of them.[16]

The formal duties of the incumbent compare rather closely with those of the Vice President; that is, the lieutenant governor usually has little to do. He or she succeeds to the governorship in the event of a vacancy, and presides over the senate in most (but a declining number) of the States; see page 700.

The office is frequently looked upon as a stepping-stone to the governorship—by succession, of course, but often in terms of future election, too. Seven States seem to have survived quite well without the office, and many have long urged that the post be abolished everywhere. Former Governor Clyde Crosby of Nebraska, while serving as lieutenant governor, wrote a popular magazine article entitled "Why I Want to Get Rid of My Job."

The Secretary of State. The office of secretary of state exists everywhere except in Alaska and Hawaii. The post is filled by the voters in 38 States, by gubernatorial appointment in eight,[17] and by the legislature in the other three.[18]

The secretary of state is the State's chief clerk and records-keeper. He or she has charge of a great variety of public documents, records the official acts of the governor and the legislature, usually administers the election laws and is "the keeper of the great seal of the State." As with most of these other elected executive officers, little real discretion is lodged in the secretary of state; most of the duties of the office are closely detailed by law.

The Treasurer. The voters in 38 States elect a State treasurer. The governor appoints the treasurer in Michigan, New Jersey, New York, and Virginia; and the legislature does so in Maine, Maryland, New Hampshire, and Tennessee.[19]

The treasurer is the custodian of State funds, often the chief tax collector, and the State's paymaster. The treasurer's principal job is to make payments out of the State treasury. They are made mostly to meet the many agency payrolls and to pay the bills submitted by those who have furnished goods or services to the State. Here he or she must work closely with the auditor, as we shall see in a moment.

The State regularly has surplus monies, dollars not currently at work—funds not yet appropriated by the legislature, contributions to the public employees' retirement system, and the like. In most States the treasurer manages the investment of these funds—putting them in such places as the short-term notes of the Federal Government, bonds issued by local governments, and even the private stock and bond market. The interest on these investments usually returns a tidy little profit to the State's treasury.

In short, the Treasurer is the State's banker.

The Auditor and the Comptroller. Every State constitution forbids the spend-

---

[16] In Tennessee the presiding officer chosen by the Senate (the speaker) is, by statute, also the lieutenant governor, and in Utah the person elected secretary of state is also, by statute, the lieutenant governor; see page 700. The seven States in which the office does not exist: Arizona, New Hampshire, New Jersey, Oregon, Maine, West Virginia, Wyoming.

[17] Delaware, Maryland, New Jersey, New York, Oklahoma, Pennsylvania, Texas, Virginia. In Alaska and Hawaii the usual duties of the office are assigned to the lieutenant governor.

[18] Maine, New Hampshire, Tennessee.

---

[19] The duties elsewhere handled by the treasurer are assigned to the Commissioner of Revenue in Alaska, the Director of Fiscal Services in the Department of Administrative Services in Georgia, the Director of the Department of Budget and Finance in Hawaii, and the Director of the Department of Administration in Montana. In each case, these officials are appointed by the governor.

ing of any of the State's monies "except in consequence of an authorization made by law." That is, no money can be spent unless the legislature has appropriated it for that purpose.

Some official must perform the *pre-audit* function—must authorize the spending, *before* it is made. That official must be satisfied that the expenditure is in all respects legal—and will then issue a warrant, authorizing the treasurer to make payment.

Some official must also perform the *post-audit* function. That is, someone must examine and verify the accounts of all officers and agencies handling public funds, *after* expenditures are made. That official checks to ensure that the spending was, in fact, made in accord with the law.

Most experts in public finance agree that the pre-audit function should be performed by an officer (a comptroller) appointed by the governor. And they argue that the post-audit should be the responsibility of an officer (an auditor) selected by the legislature. In effect, the comptroller's job should be to keep public officers and agencies on the straight and narrow path as they spend the public's money. The auditor's job should be to police the books, weed out misdeeds and other unauthorized practices, and make both regular and special reports to the legislature.

The actual organization for these purposes varies widely among the States. Only 16 States presently give the pre-audit function to a gubernatorial appointee and the post-audit task to a legislative appointee.[20] In the other 34 States an elected official—often known as the auditor or the comptroller—is involved in one or both functions. Many States have both an elected auditor and an elected comptroller. In one

State, Oregon, both pre- and post-audits are made by the elected secretary of state.

Altogether, only 26 States now give the all-important post-audit responsibility to an official or agency chosen by and responsible to the legislature.[21] Putting the post-audit function in the hands of an officer in the executive branch runs the same sort of risks as those involved in asking the fox to guard the chicken coop.

The Attorney General. The attorney general, the State's chief legal officer, is now elected by the voters in 43 States. The post is filled by appointment by the governor in five States: Alaska, Hawaii, New Hampshire, New Jersey, and Wyoming; by the legislature in Maine; and by the supreme court in Tennessee.

The AG acts as the legal adviser to the governor and other State officers and agencies, and frequently to the legislature. The AG is the State's chief prosecutor, defends the State in actions brought against it, and institutes suits in its name.

Much of the power and importance of the office centers around the attorney general's *opinions*. These are formal written interpretations of constitutional and statutory law. They are rendered in response to questions posed by the governor, other executive officers, legislators, and local officials—regarding the lawfulness of their actions or proposed actions. These opinions have the force of law in the State unless and until they are successfully challenged in court.

The Superintendent of Public Instruction. Although known by a variety of titles among the States, a chief school administrator has general supervision of the public school system. The title is most often superintendent of public instruction or

[20] Alaska, Arizona, Colorado, Georgia, Hawaii, Kansas, Maine, Michigan, Minnesota, Montana, New Hampshire, New Jersey, Rhode Island, Tennessee, Virginia, Wisconsin.

[21] The 16 States listed in footnote 20 and Arkansas, Connecticut, Florida, Idaho, Illinois, Louisiana, Maryland, Nevada, South Dakota, Texas.

commissioner of education, and the occupant of the post usually shares authority with a board of education.

The voters still choose the chief school officer in 18 States, usually on a non-partisan ballot.[22] The position is filled by appointment by the governor in but five States,[23] and by the board of education in the other 27.[24]

Lesser Officers and Agencies. The offices we have just considered are the major ones to be found in all or most of the 50 States. There are, of course, many others. They vary in number, name, and function from State to State. Some have been created by constitutional provision, others by statute. Some are headed by officers chosen by the voters, others by appointed officials.[25]

In many of the States various functions are handled by boards or commissions—rather than by a single agency headed by a single administrator. Thus, the management of charitable, correctional, mental, and educational institutions is often in the hands of a several-member board—for example, the State Board of Prisons and Parole and the State Board of Education. The administration of the laws relating to such matters as agriculture, health, highways, and natural resources is usually the responsibility of such agencies as the Board

Jon Kennedy in the *Arkansas Journal*

"ONE OF US HAS GOT TO GO"

Governors are often dismayed over the lack of control they have over many State agencies.

of Agriculture, the Board of Health, the Highway Commission, or the Department of Natural Resources. Public utilities and other corporations are often regulated by such agencies as the Public Service Commission, the Commissioner of Insurance, and the Department of Commerce and Industry. And there are a number of licensing and examining bodies in every State—for example, the Board of Medical Examiners, the Board of Barber Examiners, the Department of Motor Vehicles, the Liquor Control Commission, and so on.

Administrative Reorganization. As one function after another was added to the work of State government, boards and commissions were frequently established to handle them. And, oftentimes, the new agencies were created in haphazard fashion. Usually, these agencies were made independent of one another, and often even

---

[22] Arizona, California, Florida, Georgia, Idaho, Indiana, Kentucky, Louisiana, Mississippi, Montana, North Carolina, North Dakota, Oklahoma, Oregon, South Carolina, Washington, Wisconsin, Wyoming.

[23] Maine, New Jersey, Pennsylvania, Tennessee, and Virginia.

[24] The members of the State board of education are themselves chosen by popular vote in 12 States today: Alabama, Colorado, Hawaii, Kansas, Louisiana, Michigan, Nebraska, Nevada, New Mexico, Ohio, Texas, Utah. Generally they are picked by the governor elsewhere in the country.

[25] These officers and agencies are so numerous and vary so much from State to State that it would be pointless to attempt to detail them here. Nearly every State publishes a *Blue Book* or other directory which at least lists—and often describes the organization and functions of—all State agencies.

of the governor. The inevitable result was confusion and, at times, chaos.

Overlapping and duplication of effort, waste and inefficiency, a lack of coordination—sometimes mingled with graft and frequently tinged with favoritism—came to characterize most State administrations. Yet today some States are still plagued by the jerry-built way in which the executive branch developed.

A general reform movement began in several States in the early part of this century. Over the course of the past half-century every State has made at least some progress in reorganization; and this activity has increased considerably in recent years. Among the most efficiently organized administrations today are those in Alaska, California, Hawaii, Michigan, Missouri, New Jersey, New York, and North Carolina. Much remains to be done in most States.

The basic guidelines of reorganization regularly advocated by authorities in the field of public administration have been conveniently summarized by the Council of State Governments:[26]

---

26 The Council, founded in 1935, is a research and reporting agency supported by each of the 50 States. It maintains a central headquarters at Lexington, Kentucky, and other offices in New York, Chicago, Atlanta, San Francisco, and Washington, D.C. It publishes a quarterly journal, *State Government*, and a biennial summary of current statistical and other material, *The Book of the States*, as well as the reports on the many matters it investigates.

(1) Consolidate all administrative agencies into a relatively small number of departments (usually 10 to 20), on the basis of function or general purpose. The number of such departments should be small enough so that the chief executive can exercise an effective "span of control."

(2) Establish clear lines of authority and responsibility running from the governor at the top of the hierarchy down through the entire organization.

(3) Establish appropriate staff (advisory, planning) agencies immediately responsible to the governor.

(4) To the greatest extent possible, eliminate the use of multi-headed agencies (boards and commissions) for administrative work.

(5) Establish an independent auditor, with authority for post-audit only.

There is an encouraging trend among the States to reorganize along departmental lines—that is, to place all similar and related activities under the direction of a single overall agency (a department). In the most thoroughgoing reorganizations, each department is headed by a single administrator, appointed by and responsible to the governor. The departments most commonly found today are: administration, agriculture, corrections, education, environmental protection, finance, health, insurance, justice, labor, military, natural resources, public works, transportation, and welfare.

SUMMARY

The governorship is the oldest executive office in America. The first State governors were given only severely limited powers, as a reaction against the abuses of colonial governors. Most of the powers of State government were vested in the legislature. Gradually, this original separation of powers was changed as legislatures tended to abuse their powers. The governorship has been strengthened, in greater or lesser degree, everywhere, and especially in recent decades.

The governor is elected by popular vote in every State. Each State constitution sets out formal qualifications for the office, but everywhere the informal qualifications are more meaningful.

Governors are now chosen for two-year terms in four States and for four years in the rest. Half of the States still place some constitutional limit on gubernatorial tenure.

The governor's salary ranges from $35,000 a year in several states up to $85,000 in New York. Most governors are also furnished with an expense allowance and an official residence.

The governor may be removed by impeachment in every State except Oregon and by recall in Oregon and 13 other States; few have ever been removed from office, and none in the past half-century. Succession falls first to the lieutenant governor in 43 States, to the president of the senate in four, and to the secretary of state in the other three.

The governor's powers are usually shared with several other elected executive officers over whom he or she has little or no control. The executive powers include those of appointment and removal, supervision of administration, command of the National Guard, and budget authority. The governor's legislative powers are those to send messages to the legislature, call special sessions, and (except in North Carolina) to veto bills (and specific items in 43 States). The governor's judicial powers are those of executive clemency. The governor must also perform a number of miscellaneous chores, many of a ceremonial nature. In most States, the governor's real power depends upon personality, popularity, political clout, and the talent of persuasion.

In every State there are several other major executive officers, usually elective. The principal ones are: lieutenant governor, secretary of state, treasurer, auditor, attorney general, and superintendent of public instruction. Recent years have seen a growing trend toward the reorganization of State administrations.

Concept Development

Questions for Review

1. Why were the governors given little power by the first State constitutions?

2. To what extent have the powers of the office been increased in most States?

3. How is the governor chosen in every State?

4. For what term is the governor elected in your State? Is gubernatorial tenure limited?

5. How may the governor be removed from office in your State?

6. Who succeeds to the governorship in case of a vacancy?

7. What salary is paid to the governor of your State?

8. What is meant by the observation that the governor "wears several different hats"?

9. In what major way is the executive power fragmented in most States?

10. What is the basic legal responsibility of the governor in every State?

11. Why are the governor's powers of appointment and removal so significant? The budget-making power?

12. What are the governor's principal legislative powers?

13. What is the item veto? What two objections are sometimes raised with regard to it?

14. What is the general character of the governor's judicial powers?

15. What other major executive officers exist in your State? How are they chosen?

16. What are the basic guidelines for State administrative reorganization identified by the Council of State Governments?

For Further Inquiry

1. On page 711 we noted that in recent years nearly half of the States have provided that each party's candidates for governor and lieutenant governor must run "in tandem." What prompted the States to provide for such an arrangement? Should your State do so?

2. In New Jersey the governor is the only executive officer elected by the voters, and he or she appoints all of the others and is responsible for their actions. No other State so completely concentrates executive authority and responsibility in the governor's office. Should a similar arrangement be instituted in your State?

3. Why have so few women ever been elected to the governorship?

4. Do you think the State constitution should or should not place a limit on the number of terms a governor may serve in office?

Suggested Activities

1. Prepare a short biography of the governor of your State.

2. Prepare a table of the successive governors of your State, the year in which each first took office, the manner in which each gained office (by election/succession), the political party to which each belonged, and such other facts as the number of years served and the years of birth and death of each.

3. From the State constitution and Blue Book prepare a list of the major executive offices in the government of your State. Outline each in terms of selection, term, powers and duties, and similar factors.

4. Invite a State executive official to describe his or her work to the class.

Suggested Reading

Adrian, Charles R., *Governing Our Fifty States and Their Communities.* McGraw-Hill, 4th ed., 1978.

Berkley, George and Fox, Douglas, *80,000 Governments: The Politics of Subnational America.* Allyn and Bacon, 1978.

Berman, David R., *State and Local Politics.* Allyn and Bacon, 3rd ed., 1981.

Hale, George E. and Palley, Marian L., *Politics and Federal Grants.* Congressional Quarterly Press, 1981.

Henry, Nicholas, *Governing at the Grassroots: State & Local Politics.* Prentice-Hall, 1980.

Morlan, Robert L. (ed.), *Capitol, Courthouse, and City Hall.* Houghton Mifflin, 6th ed., 1981.

Press, Charles and VerBurg, Kenneth, *State and Community Governments in the Federal System.* Wiley, 1979.

Sabato, Larry, *Goodbye to Good-Time Charlie: The American Governor Transformed, 1850–1975.* Heath, 1978.

Solomon, Samuel R., *The Governors of the American States, Commonwealths, and Territories: 1900–1980.* Council of State Governments, 1980.

Stedman, Murray S., *State and Local Governments.* Winthrop, 2nd ed., 1979.

The Book of the States, 1980–81. The Council of State Governments, 1980.

State Court
Systems

31

Where law ends, Tyranny begins.

JOHN LOCKE

■ What distinctions may be drawn between "a law" and "the law"?

■ How should judges be chosen? Should judicial tenure be limited?

■ Are there any circumstances in which one should be excused for disobeying the law?

Courts are tribunals established by the State for the administration of justice according to law. All of the courts of a State comprise its court system, the State *judiciary.*

The basic function of courts is to settle disputes between private persons, and between private persons and government. They protect the rights of individuals as guaranteed in both the federal and the State constitutions. They determine the innocence or guilt of those accused of crime. And they act as a check on the conduct of the executive and the legislative branches of government.

Recall that in the federal system there are two separate and distinct sets of courts in the United States. The national court system (which we considered in Chapter 26) makes up one set and those of the 50 States the other. The federal courts have jurisdiction over certain classes of cases, as we noted on pages 648–649. All other cases heard in courts in the United States—and by far the overwhelming number—are heard in State courts.

Organization of State Court Systems

The constitution of each of the States provides for the State's court system. Typically, detailed organization of the judiciary is left to the legislature, however. Thus, the Iowa constitution provides:

The judicial power shall be vested in a Supreme Court, District Courts and such

725

Law officers were scarce in parts of the West in 1900. Here, Judge Roy Bean, the "hanging judge" (seated at table), tries a horse thief in Langtry, Texas.

other Courts, inferior to the Supreme Court, as the General Assembly may, from time to time, establish.[1]

Over the next few pages we shall look at the structure of the State court systems—beginning with the lower courts and working our way up the judicial hierarchy.

Justice of the Peace. Justices of the peace stand at the base of the State judicial ladder. They preside over what are commonly known as *justice courts*. Once found in every State, the "JP" is gradually disappearing from the American judicial scene. The justice court has been abolished in many States and shorn of many of its already limited powers in several others. They are now found most often in smaller towns and rural areas.

Justices of the peace are usually popularly elected, on a partisan ballot, by the voters of a township or other district within a county—and regularly for a short term, commonly two or four years.

The jurisdiction[2] of a justice court usually extends throughout the county, but it is regularly confined to minor legal matters. Most JP's have jurisdiction of only minor civil cases[3] and misdemeanors.[4]

To illustrate, most cases heard by JP's involve such misdemeanors as traffic violations, breaches of the peace, disregard of health ordinances, drunkenness, and the like. JP's also hear such civil cases as those involving money demands (but seldom over $50 or $100), the ownership of personal property, and wrongs or injuries to property. They generally do not hear such civil cases as those involving titles to real estate, titles of office, and torts (wrongs) to the person.

JP's regularly have the power to issue warrants for the arrest of persons charged

---

[1] Article V, Section 1. Considerable attention is paid to the court system in some constitutions, however. Thus, Article V of the Texas constitution contains 30 sections, covering more than seven closely printed pages.

[2] The power of a court to hear and decide a case; literally, the term means "to say the law." See page 648.

[3] A *civil case* is a suit brought by one party against another for the enforcement or protection of a private right or the prevention or redress of a *tort* (a private wrong). It is distinguished from a *criminal case* which is brought by the State against one accused of committing a crime—a public wrong. The State is at times itself a party to a civil suit, but it *always is* (as prosecutor) in a criminal trial. In the strictest sense, the terms "suit" and "trial" may be and are used interchangeably in the law. In general usage, however, "suit" is commonly used to refer to civil actions and "trial" to criminal proceedings. A judicial proceeding which is neither a suit nor a trial is usually called a "hearing."

[4] Crimes are of two kinds: felonies and misdemeanors. A *felony* is the greater crime and may be punished by a heavy fine, imprisonment, or death. A *misdemeanor* is the lesser crime involving a small fine and/or a short jail term.

with even the most serious of crimes. They also hold *preliminary hearings*—at which they decide whether the evidence against a person is sufficient to hold the accused (bind that person over) for action by the grand jury or the prosecutor.

Police or Magistrates' Courts. The lowest courts in urban areas, especially in small- and medium-size towns and cities, are known as *police* or *magistrates' courts.* These courts are much like the justice courts, with practically the same jurisdiction. The judges are usually elected, and salaries are generally quite low.

These courts are sometimes criticized because, very often, their judges (as most JP's) are not trained in the law. Several years ago, a study in California indicated that that State's nonlawyer local judges included a number of ministers, real estate agents, contractors, truck drivers, school teachers, druggists, and grocers—including one whose wife held court whenever he went fishing. About half of the States, including California, now require that *all* judges be licensed attorneys.

Municipal Courts. Unhappy experience with police courts has led to the creation of municipal courts in many cities. The first was established for Chicago in 1906. Their jurisdiction is citywide, extending to civil cases involving several thousands of dollars, and misdemeanors.

Municipal courts are frequently organized into functional divisions. Each division regularly handles cases of a given type—for example, civil, criminal, juvenile, domestic relations, traffic, small claims, and probate. These divisions embrace the subject matter of cases most often heard in the municipal courts.

Take *small claims courts* as an example. Many people cannot afford to pay the costs involved in suing for the collection of a small debt. A paper carrier can hardly afford to hire an attorney to collect a month's subscription from a customer. An elderly widow may have the same problem with collecting a tenant's rent; and many merchants are forced to forget a bill or sell it to a collection agency.

Small claims courts have been created for just such situations. In them, a person can bring a claim for little or no cost. The proceedings are quite informal; the judge usually handles the matter without attorneys for either side.

General Trial Courts. Most of the more important civil and criminal cases heard in American courts are heard in the States' *general trial courts.*

Each of the 50 States is divided into a number of judicial districts. Each of these districts usually covers one or more counties. For each district there is a general trial court—known variously among the States as the circuit, district, county, common pleas, or superior court.

The judges who preside in these trial courts are popularly elected in two-thirds of the States—commonly for four-, six-, or eight-year terms. In the more populous districts (circuits), where the caseload is especially heavy, each of these courts frequently has several judges.

These general trial courts are courts of "first instance." That is, they exercise *original jurisdiction* over most of the cases they hear. When cases do come to them on appeal from some lower court (a municipal court, for example), a trial *de novo* (a new trial, as though the case had not been heard before) is usually held.

The cases heard in these courts are tried before a single judge. Most often, a *petit jury* (the trial jury) hears and decides the facts at issue. Criminal cases are presented for trial either by a grand jury or on motion of the prosecuting attorney.

The trial court is seldom limited as to the types of cases it may hear or the amount that may be in controversy in a civil case. Its decision is usually final insofar as the *facts* in a case are concerned; but disputes over questions of *law* may be appealed to a higher court.

In the more heavily populated districts of some States, cases involving such matters as the settlement of estates or the handling of the affairs of minors are heard in separate courts—often called surrogate, probate, or orphans' courts. In most States, and districts, these matters are handled as a part of the regular work of the trial courts, however.

Intermediate Appellate Courts. Well over half of the States today[5] maintain courts of appeals—intermediate appellate courts which stand between the trial courts and the State's highest court. They serve to ease the burden of the high court.

Like the trial courts, these appellate courts are known by a variety of names among the States—but, most often, the court of appeals.[6] The judges who sit on them are chosen by the governor in a few States—as in New York and New Jersey. Most often they are popularly elected, however—usually for terms of six or eight years, but for as long as 12 in both California and Missouri.

Most of the work of these courts involves the review of cases originally heard in the trial courts. That is, they exercise mostly *appellate jurisdiction.* Their original jurisdiction is quite limited; where it does exist it is confined to a few specific kinds of cases—for example, election contests. In exercising the appellate function, the judges do not hold trials. Rather, they hear oral arguments from attorneys, study the briefs they submit, and examine the record of the case in the lower court.

Ordinarily, a court of appeals does not concern itself with the *facts* in a case. Rather, its decision turns on whether the *law* was correctly interpreted and applied in the court below. Its decision *may* be reviewed by the State's high court—but, in practice, its disposition is usually final.

The State Supreme Court. The State's *supreme court* stands at the apex of its judicial system.[7] Its primary function is to review the decision of lower courts. It is the final interpreter of the State's constitution and laws.

The number of justices who sit on the high court is fixed by the constitution. The usual number is five or seven. In Delaware, only three justices form the court and nine sit on the high bench in seven States: Alabama, Iowa, Minnesota, Mississippi, Oklahoma, Texas, and Washington.

In 23 States the justices are appointed by the governor.[8] They are selected by the legislature in four States.[9] And they are chosen by the voters in the other 23 States (on a nonpartisan ballot in half of them).

A decision of a State supreme court *may* be reviewed by the United States Supreme Court. But, as we noted on page 654, a decision is reviewed *only* if (1) a "federal question" is involved—that is, only when the case turns upon the interpretation of some provision in the Federal Constitution, an act of Congress, or a treaty; *and* (2) the Supreme Court agrees to hear the case. Otherwise, review is not avail-

---

[5] Alabama, Arizona, Arkansas, California, Colorado, Florida, Georgia, Hawaii, Illinois, Indiana, Iowa, Kansas, Kentucky, Louisiana, Maryland, Massachusetts, Michigan, Missouri, Nevada, New Jersey, New Mexico, New York, North Carolina, Ohio, Oklahoma, Oregon, Pennsylvania, South Carolina, Tennessee, Texas, Washington, Wisconsin.

[6] In New York the general trial court is known as the Supreme Court; the intermediate appellate court is the Appellate Division of the Supreme Court; and the State's highest court is the Court of Appeals.

[7] The State's highest court is known as the supreme court in 45 States. But in Maine and Massachusetts it is styled the Supreme Judicial Court, in Maryland and New York the Court of Appeals, and in West Virginia the Supreme Court of Appeals. Two States maintain two top tribunals: In Oklahoma and in Texas the Supreme Court is the highest court (the court of last resort) in *civil* cases, but a separate Court of Criminal Appeals is the court of last resort in *criminal* cases.

[8] Arizona, Delaware, Hawaii, Maine, Massachusetts, New Hampshire, New Jersey—and, through some version of the Missouri Plan (page 731), Alaska, California, Colorado, Florida, Idaho, Indiana, Iowa, Kansas, Maryland, Missouri, Nebraska, New York, Oklahoma, Utah, Vermont, Wyoming.

[9] Connecticut, Rhode Island, South Carolina, Virginia.

able, and the State supreme court stands as the "court of last resort."[10]

Unified Court Systems. The typical State court system is structured on a *geographic* basis. The court system is compartmentalized according to the map rather than by *types of cases.* Thus, for example, the general trial courts are usually so organized that each of them hears those cases which arise within its own circuit, district, or county—regardless of the subject matter involved.

In these geographically-oriented systems, a judge must be prepared to render decisions in virtually all areas of the law. A backlog of cases may (often does) build up in some courts while judges sit in comparative idleness in others. And uneven interpretations and applications of the law may (often do) occur from one part of the State to another.

To overcome these difficulties, a number of States have abandoned the map in recent years. They have turned, instead, to a *unified court system*—one organized on a *functional* basis (see chart at right).

In the ideal unified court system there is technically only one court for the entire State, presided over by a chief judge or judicial council. Within this single court are a number of levels, including supreme, intermediate appellate, and general trial sections. And, within the sections, divisions are established to hear cases in various specialized or heavy-caseload areas of the law—criminal, juvenile, family relations, and other functional areas that seem to demand special attention.

---

[10] State law regularly provides that various lower courts have final jurisdiction in many types of minor cases. That is, review cannot be sought in a higher court; the lower court is the State "court of last resort" in the particular case. If any review is to be had it can only be in the Supreme Court of the United States. Such reviews are quite rare. The most recent one appears to be *Powell* v. *Texas,* 1968, in which the Court upheld a conviction for public drunkenness in a case decided by the County Court at Law in Travis County, Texas.

NEW JERSEY COURT SYSTEM

Supreme Court

Chief Justice and six Associates. Jurisdiction — final appeals in selected cases defined by the Constitution. First term — seven years, tenure on reappointment, retirement at 70.

Superior Court

Term, tenure, and retirement of judges same as Supreme Court. Court has State-wide jurisdiction and is divided into three divisions.

Law Division	Appellate Division Decides appeals from Law and Chancery Divisions, County Courts, and others as may be provided by law.	Chancery Division

County Court

Minimum of one judge in each county. Equity powers when complete determination of case so requires. Jurisdiction subject to change by law.

Inferior Courts

Either created prior to and not abolished by the Constitution or created by law subsequent to the Constitution. All subject to abolition or change by law.

District Court	Municipal Court	Juvenile and Domestic Relations Court	Surrogate's Actions (Partially Judicial)

Most judges are appointed by the Governor with Senate approval. Municipal judges are appointed by governing body unless serving in two or more municipalities, then appointed by the Governor. Surrogates are elected.

In a unified court a judge can be assigned to that section or division to which his or her talents and interests seem especially suited. Because judges may be shifted from one section or division to another, the delays and other problems caused by crowded dockets may be overcome. In short, the unified court system is a modern response to the old common law adage: "Justice delayed is justice denied."

The move to a unified arrangement was pioneered by New Jersey in the late 1940's. Today more than half of the States have taken major steps in that direction.

The Selection of Judges

Although there is much variation among the States, judges are most often chosen in one of three ways: by (1) popular election, (2) appointment by the governor, or (3) appointment by the legislature.[11]

Before independence, judges were regularly appointed by the colonial governor. During the Revolution and immediately after, selection by the legislature became common. The influence of Jacksonian democracy, which colored much of American political thought in the 19th century, persuaded most States to provide for the popular election of judges, however.

Selection Today.   In most States today only one or another of the major methods of judicial selection are in use—for all or at least most judgeships. But, again, there are many variations.

Popular election is by far the most common way in which State judges are picked around the country; and it has been the most widely used method for well over a century now. Approximately three-fourths of all judges sitting in American courts today are chosen by the voters. In fact, in 13 States popular election is the *only* means of judicial selection.[12] And in most of the other States most or at least some judges are chosen at the polls. Judicial elections are about as often partisan as they are nonpartisan today.

Selection by the legislature is now the least commonly used of the three major methods. The legislature chooses all or at least most of the judges in only four States today: Connecticut, Rhode Island, South Carolina, and Virginia.

The governor appoints nearly a fourth of all State judges today. In three States—Delaware, Massachusetts, and New Hampshire—all of them are named by the governor. In several others the governor also has the power to appoint all or at least many of the State's judges—but under a *Missouri Plan* arrangement, as we shall see in just a moment.

How Should Judges Be Selected?   Most of us are convinced that judges should be independent, that they should "stay out of politics." Whatever method of selection is used, then, should be designed to establish and preserve that independence.

Nearly all authorities agree that selection by the legislature is the most political of all of the methods of choice—and few favor it. So, the question really becomes: Which is better, popular election or gubernatorial appointment?

Those who advocate popular election usually make the democratic argument, of course. They insist that because judges "say the law," interpret and apply it, they

---

[11] In some States some judges are selected by other means. In Ohio, for example, all of the State's judges, except those who sit on the court of claims, are elected by the voters; the judges of the court of claims are appointed by the chief justice of the supreme court. And in Alabama, Michigan, Mississippi, Oregon, Texas, and Washington all judges are popularly elected except for municipal court judges; they are chosen in accord with city charter provisions, usually by the city council.

[12] Except that gubernatorial appointment is the usually prescribed method for filling judicial vacancies. The 13 States: Arkansas, Illinois, Kentucky, Louisiana, Minnesota, Montana, Nevada, New Mexico, North Carolina, North Dakota, Pennsylvania, West Virginia, Wisconsin. (Judicial vacancies are fairly common occurrences in every State; see the Case Study on the next page.)

Case Study

There are more than 15,000 judges in the United States today. Nearly all of them sit in the State and local courts. Only a comparative handful—fewer than 800—sit on the federal bench.

All federal judges are appointed—by the President, subject to confirmation by the Senate. Popular election is the most widely used device for selecting judges at the State and local levels, however.

Despite the prevalence of popular election, the appointment process does play a much larger role in judicial selection at the State and local levels than is generally realized. It does so for two related reasons: (1) gubernatorial appointment is almost always the method provided for the filling of judicial vacancies and (2) the rate of turnover in judicial offices is comparatively low. That is, most judges hold their offices for several years; once chosen, they tend to remain in office through several elections. When they finally do relinquish their posts, many do so either by retirement in mid-term or by death. In either case, their departures leave vacancies to be filled between elections—ones which are regularly filled by gubernatorial appointments.

Studies in several States indicate that, despite the provisions for popular election, most judges first reach office in fact by appointment.

■ Why do most students of the subject favor either direct gubernatorial appointment or some version of the Missouri Plan rather than popular election as the method of judicial selection? What method do you prefer? Why?

■ Why are few incumbent judges ever defeated when they seek reelection?

■ Why do many judges who retire do so in mid-term rather than at the conclusion of a full term?

---

should be chosen by and be held directly responsible to the people. They also frequently argue that the concept of separation of powers is undercut if the executive has the power to name the members of the judicial branch.

Those who support appointment by the governor argue that the judicial function is highly specialized and should be performed only by those who are qualified to do so. The mere fact that one has the support of a political party, or is a good vote-getter, does not mean that that person has the capacity to be a judge. They insist that executive appointment is the best way to ensure that those who preside in courts will possess the qualities most needed in that role—absolute honesty and integrity, a judicial temperament and independence, and the necessary training and ability in the law.

At best, it is difficult to decide between these two positions. The principal reason for the difficulty: The people have often made excellent choices, and governors have not always made wise and nonpolitical ones. Still, most authorities come down on the side of gubernatorial appointment—largely because those characteristics that make a good judge and those that make a good candidate are not too often found in the same person.

But popular election is very widespread, and attempts to abandon it have been stoutly resisted by party organizations. Hence, most moves to revise the method of judicial selection have retained at least some element of voter choice.

THE MISSOURI PLAN. For some 60 years now, the American Bar Association has sponsored an approach that combines the basic advantages of election and appointment. A version of the ABA plan was first adopted in California in 1934 and then in Missouri in 1940. Because its adoption in Missouri involved much political drama, and attracted wide attention, the method is often called the "Missouri Plan."

The operation of the plan in Missouri is more or less typical. There, the governor appoints the seven justices of the supreme court, the 31 judges of the court of appeals, and those who sit in certain of the State's trial courts.[13] The governor must make the appointment from a *panel* (list) of three names recommended by a judicial nominating commission. That body is composed of a sitting judge, members of the bar, and lay citizens.

Each appointed judge then serves until the first general election to occur after he or she has been in office for at least one year. At that election, the judge's name appears on the ballot, without opposition. The voters decide whether to retain the judge or not.

If the vote is favorable, the judge then serves a regular term. For trial court judges, the term is six years and for those who sit on the higher courts, 12 years. And the judge may seek additional terms in future retain-reject elections.

Should the voters reject the judge, the process begins again—the governor makes a new appointment from a list drawn by the commission, and so on.

Some version of the Missouri Plan is now in use for the selection of at least some judges in 18 States.[14] California and Missouri pioneered the device, and then stood alone for several years. But the list of States which use the plan has been growing fairly rapidly in recent years.

[13] Presently, the judges of the circuit and probate courts in St. Louis City and County, and Jackson, Platte, and Clay Counties, and the court of criminal corrections in St. Louis. All other judges are elected on a partisan ballot; but the plan may be adopted by the voters in any of the State's judicial districts.

[14] Alaska, California, Colorado, Florida, Hawaii, Idaho, Illinois, Indiana, Iowa, Kansas, Maryland, Missouri, Nebraska, New York, Oklahoma, Tennessee, Utah, Wyoming. In Vermont the governor appoints the judges of the supreme, superior, and district courts from the lists of candidates recommended by the Judicial Nominating Board; but, after an initial term, those judges are either retained or removed by vote of the *legislature*.

The Jury System

A jury is a body of persons selected according to law and sworn to declare the truth on the evidence laid before it. There are two basic types of juries in the American legal system: (1) the *grand jury* and (2) the *petit jury.*

The principal function of the grand jury is to determine whether the evidence against a person accused of crime is sufficient to justify a trial. Obviously, it is used only in criminal proceedings. The petit jury is the trial jury, and it is used in both civil and criminal cases.

The Grand Jury. The grand jury is composed of from six to 23 persons, depending on the State involved. Where larger juries are used, at least 12 jurors must usually agree that an accused person is probably guilty before a formal accusation can be made. Similarly, with juries which are smaller, an extraordinary majority is required to *indict* (bring the formal charge).[15]

When a grand jury is *impaneled* (selected), the judge instructs the jurors to find a true *bill of indictment* against any and all persons whom the prosecuting attorney brings to their attention and whom they think probably guilty. The judge also instructs them to bring a *presentment* (accusation) against any and all persons whom they, of their own knowledge, believe to have violated the State's criminal laws within that judicial district.

The grand jury meets in secret. To preside over its sessions, either the judge appoints or the jurors select one of their number to serve as the *foreman*. The prosecuting attorney presents witnesses and evidence against persons suspected of crime. The jurors may question those witnesses and summon others to testify against a suspect. No one is allowed in the

[15] A few States—Michigan, for example, employ "one-man grand juries."

DOOLEY'S WORLD

Panel 1: LOOK HERE— "Jury selection takes three months..." WHY IS THAT, PROFESSOR?

Panel 2: BECAUSE AN IDEAL JURY IS COMPOSED OF INTELLIGENT, FAIR-MINDED, WELL-EDUCATED FOLKS...

Panel 3: WHO HAVE NO OPINIONS ON-OR PRIOR KNOWLEDGE OF THE CASE; WHO DON'T KNOW THE DEFENDANT; AND WHO HAVEN'T READ OR BEEN INFLUENCED BY NEWSPAPERS, MAGAZINES OR TELEVISION

Panel 4: IT'S PRETTY HARD TO FIND 12 PEOPLE THAT SMART WHO DON'T KNOW ANYTHING

jury room except the grand jurors themselves, the prosecutor, witnesses, and, in some States, a stenographer. All are sworn to secrecy.

After receiving the evidence and hearing witnesses, the grand jury deliberates—with only the jurors themselves present. With the completion of their review they proceed to the courtroom where their report—including any indictments they may have returned—is read in their presence.

ACCUSATION BY INFORMATION. The grand jury is cumbersome and time consuming. It adds to the already considerable delay and expense of the criminal process. Hence, most States today rely more heavily upon a much simpler process of accusation—the *information.*

An information is a formal charge filed by the prosecutor, without the action of a grand jury. It is now regularly used for most minor offenses. And more than half of the States have substituted it for indictment by the grand jury in most of the more serious cases, as well.

The use of the information has much to recommend it. It is far less costly and time consuming. Then, too, since grand juries regularly tend to follow the prosecutor's recommendations, many of its proponents argue that the grand jury is really unnecessary.

The chief objection to the abandonment of the grand jury appears to be the fear that some prosecutors may be overzealous, that they may abuse their powers and harass defendants.

The Petit Jury. The *petit jury* is the trial jury. It hears the evidence in a case and decides the disputed facts. In some instances it may also have the power to apply the law, but this is almost always the function of the judge.

The number of trial jurors may vary. As it developed in England, the jury consisted of "12 men good and true"—and 12 is still the usual number. But a lesser number, often six, now fill jury boxes in several States. And women are everywhere qualified for jury duty.

In over a third of the States jury verdicts need not be unanimous in civil and minor criminal cases; rather, some extraordinary majority is required. In most of the States, however, verdicts must be unanimous in all cases. If a jury cannot agree on a verdict (a "hung jury"), either another trial (with a new jury) is held or the matter is dropped.

Misdemeanor cases and civil proceedings in which only minor sums are involved are frequently heard without a jury—that is, in a *bench trial,* by the judge alone. When they are heard before a jury it is usually because one of the parties has demanded it. In several States even the most serious of crimes may be heard without a jury—*if* the accused, fully informed of his or her rights, waives the right to trial by jury.

A GENERAL VIEW OF THE CRIMINAL JUSTICE SYSTEM

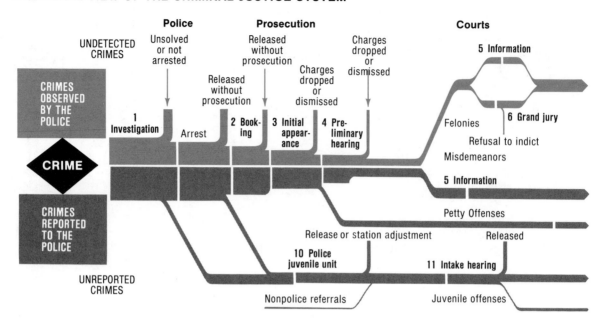

1 May continue until trial.

2 Administrative record of arrest. First step at which temporary release on bail may be available.

3 Before magistrate, commissioner, or justice of peace. Formal notice of charge, advice of rights. Bail set. Summary trials for petty offenses usually conducted here without further processing.

4 Preliminary testing of evidence against defendant. Charge may be reduced. No separate preliminary hearing for misdemeanors in some systems.

5 Charge filed by prosecutor on basis of information submitted by police or citizens. Alternative to grand jury indictment; often used in felonies, almost always in misdemeanors.

Source: The President's Commission on Law Enforcement and Administration of Justice

Selection of Jurors. In scarcely any two States are jurors chosen in exactly the same manner; but in most they are selected in a somewhat similar manner. Once a year, or oftener, some county official,[17] or special jury commissioners, prepare a list of persons eligible for jury service. The lists are usually quite long. Depending upon the State, the lists are drawn from the poll books or the tax assessor's rolls. When jurors are needed names are picked from these lists at random.

The sheriff serves each person chosen for jury service with a court order, a writ of *venire facias* (you must come). After elimi-

nating the names of those who, for good reason, cannot serve, the judge prepares a list of those who can serve—the *panel of veniremen.* Persons under 21 and those over 70 years of age, illiterates, those in poor health, and criminals are commonly excluded. In many States those engaged in occupations vital to the public interest—physicians, druggists, teachers, firefighters, and the like—are also excused. Those for whom jury service would mean real hardship are regularly excused, as well.

As with the grand jury, the trend is away from the use of the trial jury among the States. The greater time and expense in jury trials are leading reasons. The competence of the average jury and the impulses which may lead it to a particular verdict are frequently questioned, too.

But much of the criticism is directed not so much at the jury system itself as at its *operation.* And several other things

[17] Usually the clerk of the court, the sheriff, or the county governing body, and sometimes the presiding judge—and in New England officers of the town. In New Jersey the *chancellor* (chief justice) appoints for each county a jury commissioner who must be of the party opposed to that of the sheriff; together, these two officers select those eligible for jury duty.

This chart seeks to present a simple yet comprehensive view of the movement of cases through the criminal justice system. Procedures in individual jurisdictions may vary from the pattern shown here. The differing weights of line indicate the relative volumes of cases disposed of at various points in the system.

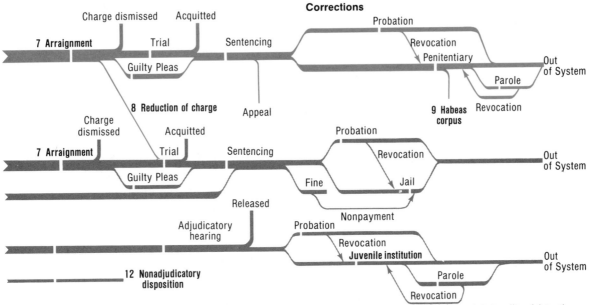

6 Reviews whether government evidence sufficient to justify trial. Some states have no grand jury system; others seldom use it.

7 Appearance for plea; defendant elects trial by judge or jury (if available); counsel for indigent usually appointed here in felonies. Often not at all in other cases.

8 Charge may be reduced at any time prior to trial in return for plea of guilty or for other reasons.

9 Challenge on constitutional grounds to legality of detention. May be sought at any point in process.

10 Police often hold informal hearings, dismiss or adjust many cases without further processing.

11 Probation officer decides desirability of further court action.

12 Welfare agency, social services, counselling, medical care, etc., for cases where adjudicatory handling not needed.

should be said for the jury system. It has both a long and an honorable place in the development of Anglo-American law. Its high purpose is to promote a fair trial, by providing an impartial body to hear the charges brought in either civil or criminal cases. It tends to bring the common sense of the community to bear upon the law and its application. It gives the citizen an opportunity to participate in the administration of justice, and it gives the people greater confidence in the judicial system.

Kinds of Law Applied by State Courts

The law—the code of conduct by which society is governed—is composed of various forms of law.[18] And, in dealing with the cases that come before them, the State courts apply these several different forms. Thus, they apply:

Constitutional law—the highest form of law, that based upon the provisions of the Constitution of the United States and the constitution of the State, and judicial interpretations of those provisions.

Statutory law—the law (statutes) enacted by legislative bodies, including the United States Congress, the State legislature, the people (through the initiative or referendum), and city councils and other local legislative bodies.

Administrative law—the rules, orders, regulations which are issued by federal,

---

[18] In its overall sense, *law* may be defined as the whole body of "rules and principles of conduct which the governing power in a community recognizes as those which it will enforce or sanction, and according to which it will regulate, limit, or protect the conduct of its members." *Bouvier's Law Dictionary*, 3rd revision, vol. II, pp. 1875–76. For us, "community" here refers to the United States, any of the States, and any unit of local government.

"I THINK WE SHOULD FIND HIM GUILTY AND LET THE SUPREME COURT WORRY ABOUT IT!"

Grin and Bear It by George Lichty © Courtesy of Field Newspaper Syndicate

State, or local executive officers, acting under proper constitutional and/or statutory authority.

The State courts also apply:

Criminal law—that portion of the law which defines public wrongs (offenses against the public order) and provides for their punishment.

Civil law—that portion of the law relating to human conduct, to disputes between private parties, and to disputes between private parties and government, not covered by criminal law.

We have dealt with each of these various forms of law at many places to this point, of course. The State courts also apply two other forms of law: *common law* and *equity*. And we must now pay some specific attention to them.

COMMON LAW. The common law comprises a large part of the law of each of the States, except Louisiana.[19] It is *unwritten,*

judgemade law. It has developed, over centuries, from those generally accepted ideas of right and wrong which have gained judicial recognition. It covers nearly all aspects of human conduct. Common law is applied by State courts—*except* when in conflict with written law, which takes precedence over it.

The common law originated in England. It grew out of the decisions made by the king's judges on the basis of local customs. It developed as judges, encountering situations similar to those found in previous cases, applied and reapplied the rulings from those earlier cases. Thus, gradually, the law of those cases became *common* throughout the land—and, eventually, throughout the English-speaking world.

That is to say, the common law developed as judges followed the *precedent* of earlier decisions—as they applied the rule of *stare decisis*, "let the decision stand."[20]

The common law is *not* a rigidly fixed body of rules controlled in every instance by a clear line of precedents which can be easily found and readily applied. Judges are regularly called upon to interpret and reinterpret the existing rules in the light of changing times and circumstances. Or, the point may be put this way: Most legal disputes in American courts are fought out very largely over the application of precedents. The opposing lawyers attempt to persuade the court that the precedents support their side of the case—or that the general line of precedents should not, for some reason, be followed. The judge must weigh the precedents—and their applicability—in reaching a decision.

The importance of the common law in the American legal system cannot be overstated. It forms the basis of legal procedure in every State, except Louisiana. Statutory

---

[19] Because of the early French influence, Louisiana's legal system is based upon French legal concepts which are derived from Roman law. Gradually, however, the common law has been working its way into Louisiana law.

[20] American courts generally follow the rule. A decision, once made, becomes a precedent—a guide to be followed in all later, similar cases, unless compelling reasons call for its abandonment and the establishment of a new precedent.

law does override common law, as we have noted. But many statutes are based on the common law. They are, in effect, common law translated into written law. And they are interpreted and applied by the courts according to common law tradition and meaning.

EQUITY. *Equity* is a branch of the law which supplements the common law. It developed in England to provide equity—"fairness, justice, and right"—when the remedies available under the common law fell short of that goal.

As the common law developed, it became somewhat rigid. Remedies were available only through various *writs* (orders) issued by the courts. If no writ was suited to the particular relief sought in a case, no action could be taken by the courts.

Those who were thus barred from the courts—for whom there was no adequate remedy at common law—appealed to the king for justice. These appeals became so numerous that they were usually referred to the *chancellor*, a member of the king's council.[21] By the middle of the 14th century a special court of *chancery*, or equity, was established. Gradually, a system of rules developed, and equity assumed a permanent place in the English legal system.

Perhaps the most important distinction to be drawn between common law and equity today is this: The common law is primarily *remedial* while equity is *preventive*. That is, the common law commonly applies to matters *after* they have happened; equity seeks to prevent threatened wrongs from occurring. To illustrate, suppose your neighbor plans to add a room to his house, despite your protest that the addition will encroach on your property and destroy a portion of your rose garden. You can prevent the construction of the addition by securing an injunction from a court of equity. The *injunction*—a court order prohibiting (enjoining) a specified action by a party named in the order—probably would be granted by the court for two reasons: (1) the immediacy of the threat to your property and (2) the law could provide no adequate remedy once your garden is destroyed. It is true that damages might be assessed under common law, but in a legal sense money could not restore the satisfaction and enjoyment you derived from the plants.

The English colonists brought both equity and the common law to America. At first, the two forms of law were administered by different courts. But, in time, most of the States provided for the administration of both forms by the same courts; and, in general, the procedural differences between the two are disappearing. Only four States—Arkansas, Delaware, Mississippi, and Tennessee—maintain separate equity (chancery) courts today.

Advisory Opinions. Ordinarily, a court will not act upon a question unless it is presented in a case actually before it. And, then, it will do so only when the issue is "ripe for decision." Among other things, this means that, as a general rule, courts will not issue advisory opinions.[22]

In 11 of the States, however, the supreme court is authorized to render *advisory opinions*. That is, in these States the high court may indicate its views on the constitutionality or the legal effects of a law. In each of these States these opinions

---

21 The chancellor was, until the Reformation, always a member of the clergy. With the assumption of the equity function, he became known as the "Keeper of the King's Conscience." The term *chancery*, a synonym for equity, derived from his title.

22 Court opinions do sometimes contain comments (*dicta*) on some point other than the precise issue involved in determining a case. The *dicta* in court opinions, and especially those of the higher courts, can be quite important—as indications of a court's views on related matters and as portents of future decisions.

are available to the governor and, in all except three, to the legislature, as well.[23]

There are a number of advantages in the use of advisory opinions. They can serve as useful guides to the legislature. For example, they are useful when it is considering a measure which appears to break new ground or about which serious constitutional questions have been raised. Similarly, they can be an aid to the governor—in deciding whether to sign or veto a bill or in determining whether a law already on the books is in fact enforceable.

As the term suggests, these opinions are *advisory* only. They do not have a binding effect upon the decision of later cases—except in Colorado. In that state they do

have the same legal force as the regular decisions of the high court. Most authorities on the judicial process do not favor the assignment of this function to the supreme court. Rather, they believe it should be performed by the attorney general; see page 720.

Declaratory Judgments. In nearly all of the States the principal courts may render *declaratory judgments*. These judgments are available *before* an actual case is instituted. The judgments are declarations of the legal rights and obligations of the parties to a controversy before a lawsuit is filed. They may be sought by any person involved in a controversy over his or her rights under any legal instrument, such as a statute, an ordinance, a will, or a contract.

Declaratory judgments are legally binding on the parties involved. They serve to prevent the doing of a wrong, to avoid loss or injury, or to forestall long and expensive legal entanglements.

---

[23] To both the governor and the legislature in Alabama, Colorado, Maine, Massachusetts, Michigan, North Carolina, Rhode Island; to the governor only in Delaware, Florida, South Dakota. Neither the Supreme Court nor any other federal court will render an advisory opinion.

SUMMARY

A court is a tribunal established by the State to administer justice according to law. The State courts hear most of the cases heard in American courts; only a very small proportion of cases are heard in the federal courts.

The details of the structure of the several State court systems are quite complicated, and there are many variations State to State. Justice courts, police or magistrates' courts, and/or municipal courts exist in all or most of the States to hear minor civil and misdemeanor cases.

The general trial courts, known by a variety of names among the States, are the principal courts of first instance. They hear most of the major civil and criminal cases tried in American courts.

The intermediate appellate courts, found in over half of the States today, stand between the general trial courts and the State supreme court. They hear appeals from the lower courts.

The supreme court stands at the pinnacle of the State's judicial system. Except for those cases which may be appealed to the United States Supreme Court, it is usually the court of last resort and the final interpreter of the State's constitution and laws.

Most State judges are selected in one of three ways: (1) popular election, (2) appointment by the governor, or (3) appointment by the legislature. Approximately three-fourths of all of them are chosen by the voters—about as often as not on a partisan ballot. The Missouri Plan is a widely recommended selection process which combines the advantages of popular election and executive appointment.

There are two types of juries: (1) the *grand jury*, which determines whether the evidence against a suspect is sufficient to warrant trial in a criminal case; and (2) the *petit* (trial) *jury*, which hears a case and decides the facts at issue in civil or criminal proceedings. In most States an *information* may be filed by the prosecutor as an alternative to accusation by the grand jury, and the process is frequently used today.

The State courts apply several different kinds of law: constitutional, statutory, and administrative law, civil and criminal law, and common law and equity. Eleven of the State supreme courts may render advisory opinions and the principal courts in most States also deliver declaratory judgments.

Concept Development

Questions for Review

1. What is a court?
2. What functions do courts perform?
3. What two separate judicial systems exist in the United States? In which are the largest proportion of cases heard?
4. What is meant by the *jurisdiction* of a court?
5. What distinguishes a *civil* from a *criminal* case?
6. What is the difference between a *felony* and a *misdemeanor*?
7. What courts are commonly the lowest in a State's judicial system?
8. Many cities now have what courts in place of the lower courts commonly found elsewhere? Why are these courts often organized in functional divisions?
9. In what type (or level) of courts are most of the more important civil and criminal cases heard? By what title are they known in your State?
10. Why do half of the States now maintain one or more intermediate appellate courts?
11. What is the primary function of the State's supreme court?
12. The United States Supreme Court will review a decision of a State supreme court only under what circumstances?
13. What is a unified court system? Why is it widely recommended?
14. What are the three principal methods now used for the selection of State judges? Which is the most widely used?
15. What is the *Missouri Plan?* Why is some version of it recommended by nearly all students of judicial administration?
16. What is the primary function of the *grand jury?* What device is often used as an alternative to it?
17. What is an *indictment?* A *presentment?* An *information?*
18. What is the *petit jury?*

19. Distinguish between the terms *constitutional law, statutory law,* and *administrative law.*

20. What is *criminal law? Civil law?* Is government ever a party to a civil case? A criminal case?

21. What is *common law?* How did it originate? What is meant by the term *stare decisis?*

22. Which takes precedence in case of conflict: common law or statutory law?

23. What is *equity?* How did it originate?

24. What is probably the chief distinction between common law and equity?

25. What are *advisory opinions? Declaratory judgments?*

For Further Inquiry

1. Are crimes more likely to be prevented by the *severity* of the punishments imposed or by the *certainty* that punishment will be imposed? How can crime be most effectively combatted?

2. How are judges selected in your State? What changes, if any, do you think should be made in the existing arrangement? Who might be expected to oppose such changes?

3. In some States justices of the peace are still paid out of the fines they collect; the more fines they impose, the higher their income. Why is this "fee system" vigorously condemned by virtually all students of judicial administration? Why is it sometimes said that "JP" really stands for "judgment for the plaintiff"?

4. If you had the power to select the judges of the courts of your State, what qualifications would you seek in those you appointed? Would the qualifications vary depending upon the court involved?

5. Are *justice* and *law* synonymous terms? Do you agree with Daniel Webster that "Justice . . . is the great interest of man on earth"?

Suggested Activities

1. Attend a session of a local court and prepare a report to the class describing the proceedings and your impressions.

2. Invite a judge, prosecuting attorney, or practicing lawyer to speak to the class on the courts, their functions and procedures, and their importance.

3. Construct a diagram of the courts in your State. Indicate the jurisdiction of the various types of courts and by whom and for how long judges are selected.

4. Prepare a report to the class on some case currently being tried in a court in your locale. Describe the nature of the dispute and the procedures involved in the court process. (Notice that a civil case can often be as interesting or exciting as a criminal case.)

Suggested Reading

Abraham, Henry J., *The Judicial Process.* Oxford, 4th ed., 1980.

Brody, David E., *The American Legal System: Concepts and Principles.* Heath, 1978.

Carter, Lief H., *Reason in Law.* Little, Brown, 1979.

Datesman, Susan K. (ed.), *Women, Crime, and Justice.* Oxford, 1980.

Daudstel, Howard, *et al., Criminal Justice.* Holt, Rinehart and Winston, 1979.

Gaynor, James K., *Profile of the Law.* BNA Books, 1978.

Hanes, Joseph M. (ed.), *Law and Order in American History.* Kennikat, 1979.

Jacob, Herbert, *Justice in America: Courts, Lawyers, and the Judicial Process.* Little, Brown, 3rd ed., 1978.

Pritchett, C. Herman and Murphy, Walter F., *Courts, Judges, and Politics: An Introduction to the Judicial Process.* Random House, 3rd ed., 1979.

Spurrier, Robert L., *Inexpensive Justice: Selfrepresentation in the Small Claims Court.* Kennikat, 1980.

Governing the Communities

How can a people unaccustomed to freedom in small affairs learn to use it temperately in great affairs?

ALEXIS DE TOCQUEVILLE

■ Is it really true that the local units of government are those governments "closest to the people" in the United States?

■ Upon what factors should the geographic size of a local unit of government depend?

■ Is the number of elected officials a useful measure of the democratic character of a governmental unit?

As we have suggested several times, it is the States and especially their local governments which most directly and continuously affect the daily business of living in this country.

As but one measure of their ever-present importance, consider the *sheer number* of local governments in the United States. In its most recent tabulation, the 1977 Census of Governments, the Census Bureau reported the existence of 79,913 separate units of government across the nation. As the following table indicates, 79,862 of these units—nearly all of them—are at the *local* level.

Type of Government	Number of Units
National Government	1
State Governments	50
Local Governments	79,862
Counties	3,042
Municipalities	18,862
Townships	16,822
School Districts	15,174
Special Districts	25,962

In this chapter we turn to these local units of government—to those governments so often described as the ones "closest to the people." As we do so, it seems wise to fix the place of these units in the structure of our federal system.

The Legal Status of Local Governments. Government in the United States is very often discussed in terms of three basic layers: national, State, and local.

741

LOCAL GOVERNMENTS IN THE UNITED STATES

State	All Local Governments	Counties	Local Governments, by Type			
			Munici-palities	Town-ships[a]	School Districts	Special Districts
US TOTAL	79,862	3,042	18,862	16,822	15,174	25,962
Alabama	935	67	419	—	127	336
Alaska	151	8	142	—	—	—
Arizona	423	14	70	—	230	106
Arkansas	1,349	75	467	—	380	424
California	3,824	57	413	—	1,109	2,227
Colorado	1,474	62	262	—	185	950
Connecticut	421	—	33	149	16	236
Delaware	206	3	55	—	25	127
District of Columbia	2	—	1	—	—	1
Florida	909	66	389	—	95	361
Georgia	1,264	158	530	—	188	387
Hawaii	20	3	1	—	—	15
Idaho	975	44	199	—	117	612
Illinois	6,643	102	1,274	1,436	1,063	2,745
Indiana	2,864	91	563	1,008	307	885
Iowa	1,853	99	955	—	464	334
Kansas	3,730	105	625	1,449	327	1,219
Kentucky	1,186	119	405	—	181	478
Louisiana	459	62	300	—	66	30
Maine	781	16	24	475	86	178
Maryland	423	23	151	—	—	252
Massachusetts	749	12	39	312	75	328
Michigan	2,639	83	531	1,245	606	168
Minnesota	3,424	87	855	1,792	440	263
Mississippi	838	82	283	—	166	304
Missouri	2,953	114	916	326	574	1,007
Montana	966	56	126	—	465	311
Nebraska	3,585	93	534	471	1,195	1,192
Nevada	184	16	17	—	17	132
New Hampshire	504	10	13	221	159	103
New Jersey	1,510	21	335	232	549	380
New Mexico	311	32	93	—	88	100
New York	3,312	57	618	930	740	964
N. Carolina	874	100	472	—	—	302
N. Dakota	2,712	53	361	1,000	346	587
Ohio	3,288	88	935	1,319	631	312
Oklahoma	1,687	77	567	—	625	406
Oregon	1,452	36	239	—	375	797
Pennsylvania	5,333	66	1,015	1,549	581	2,035
Rhode Island	118	—	8	31	3	78
S. Carolina	583	46	264	—	93	182
S. Dakota	1,730	64	311	1,010	194	148
Tennessee	911	94	326	—	14	471
Texas	3,914	254	1,066	—	1,138	1,425
Utah	490	29	216	—	40	207
Vermont	651	14	57	237	272	67
Virginia	389	95	229	—	—	65
Washington	1,670	39	265	—	302	1,060
W. Virginia	599	55	227	—	55	258
Wisconsin	2,520	72	576	1,270	412	190
Wyoming	382	23	90	—	59	217

[a] Includes "towns" in the six New England States, New York, and Wisconsin.

Source: Census Bureau, Census of Governments, 1977.

However convenient this may be, it is somewhat misleading. Recall, as we first noted on page 20, the basic components of the federal system are the National Government and the 50 States. Local governments, all of them, are parts (subunits) of State governments.

All local governments in the United States are creatures of their respective States. Each of the 50 States, either through its constitution or its laws, establishes (and may abolish) any or all of these units. To whatever extent any of them can provide services, regulate activities, collect taxes, or do anything else, they can *only* because the State has established and empowered them to do so. As they exercise the powers they possess, then, they actually exercise *State* powers—powers delegated to them by the State.

Another way of putting all of this is to remind you that each of the 50 States has a *unitary* form of government—a point we first made on page 20.

The Counties

The nation's 3,042 counties cover nearly all of the United States. And organized county governments exist in all of the States except Connecticut and Rhode Island. In Louisiana what are known elsewhere as counties are called *parishes,* and in Alaska they are known as *boroughs.*

There are a number of places, scattered across the country, where no organized county government exists, however. These places are identified in the table to the right. As you can see, they include several major metropolitan centers. Thus, some 10 percent of the nation's population today is *not* served by any separately organized county government.

Counties serve almost entirely as judicial districts in the New England States. In these States, *towns* perform most of the functions undertaken by counties elsewhere. The functions of rural local govern-

THE AREAS WITHIN THE UNITED STATES LACKING INDEPENDENTLY ORGANIZED COUNTY GOVERNMENT

Areas with governments legally designated as city-counties, operating primarily as cities:
  Alaska: City and Borough of Juneau, City and Borough of Sitka
  California: City and County of San Francisco
  Colorado: City and County of Denver
  Hawaii: City and County of Honolulu

Areas with certain county offices, but as part of another government (city or town):
  Florida: Duval County (Jacksonville)
  Indiana: Marion County (Indianapolis)
  Kentucky: Lexington-Fayette Urban County
  Louisiana: Orleans Parish (New Orleans), East Baton Rouge Parish (Baton Rouge)
  Massachusetts: Nantucket County (town of Nantucket), Suffolk County (Boston)
  New York: Bronx, Kings, New York, Queens, and Richmond Counties (all New York City)
  Pennsylvania: Philadelphia County (Philadelphia)

Areas designated as metropolitan government, operating primarily as a city:
  Tennessee: Metropolitan Government of Nashville and Davidson County

Cities completely independent of any county:
  Alaska: Anchorage
  District of Columbia: Washington
  Georgia: Columbus
  Maryland: Baltimore (distinct from Baltimore County)
  Missouri: St. Louis (distinct from St. Louis County)
  Nevada: Carson City
  Virginia: 41 "independent cities"

Unorganized areas with county designations:
  Connecticut: Fairfield, Hartford, Litchfield, Middlesex, New Haven, New London, Tolland, Windham Counties
  Rhode Island: Bristol, Kent, Newport, Providence, Washington Counties
  South Dakota: Shannon, Todd, Washabaugh Counties (attached to other counties for governmental purposes)

Other unorganized county-type areas:
  Alaska: 23 census divisions
  Montana: Area within Yellowstone National Park

ment are shared by counties and *townships* in the States extending from New York and New Jersey west to the Dakotas, Nebraska, and Kansas. In the South and the West counties are the predominant units of government in rural areas.

Number, Size, and Population. The number of counties varies widely among the States. They range from none in Connecticut and Rhode Island and three in Delaware and Hawaii to as many as 254 in Texas. And notice that there is no very close relationship between the size of a State and the number of counties it has.

In terms of area, San Bernardino County in Southern California is the largest; it sprawls across 52,304 square kilometers (20,117 square miles). Arlington County in Virginia, bordering the District of Columbia, is the smallest, covering only 67.6 square kilometers (26 square miles). And there is a marked difference in the area covered by each county within most of the States, too.

Counties also vary widely in terms of population—both within each State and across the nation. More than seven million persons now live in Los Angeles County in California. At the other end of the scale, only 164 residents were counted in Loving County, in western Texas, in the 1970 census. The large majority of counties (nearly 80 percent of them) serve populations of fewer than 50,000.

County Government—Organized (?) Chaos. County government has long been described as "the dark continent of American politics." Most people know very little about the government of the county in which they happen to live—and most don't care to know more, either.

It has often been said that if county governments in this country have any one principle of organization in common, it is that of confusion. In the typical county, no one official can be identified as the chief administrator. Rather, governmental authority is scattered among a number of elected officials and boards, each largely independent of the others. Several of these officials and boards often have executive, legislative, and even judicial powers. As a result, it is seldom possible to fix the responsibility for laxity, inefficiency, or inaction, or worse, in the conduct of county affairs.

In short, county government is in serious need of reform almost everywhere. Fortunately, recent years have seen some progress in that direction in a number of places—as we shall see in a moment. But much—indeed, a great deal—remains to be done in most places.

The structure of county government differs, often considerably, from place to

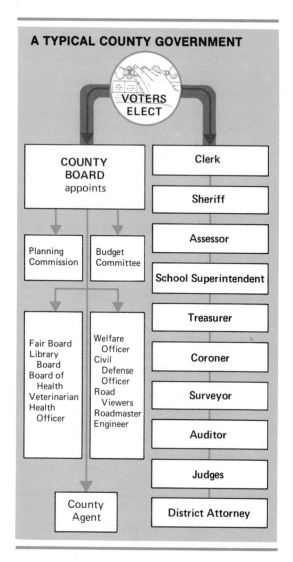

A TYPICAL COUNTY GOVERNMENT

VOTERS ELECT

COUNTY BOARD appoints	Clerk
	Sheriff
Planning Commission — Budget Committee	Assessor
	School Superintendent
	Treasurer
Fair Board, Library Board, Board of Health, Veterinarian, Health Officer — Welfare Officer, Civil Defense Officer, Road Viewers, Roadmaster, Engineer	Coroner
	Surveyor
	Auditor
	Judges
County Agent	District Attorney

place. But, as you can see from the chart on the opposite page, it typically contains four major elements:

(1) A governing body—frequently referred to as the "county board." This body is known by at least 20 other names among the States—among them, the board of commissioners, board of supervisors, county court, board of chosen freeholders, fiscal court, and police jury.

The members of the board, whatever its title, are almost always popularly elected. Their terms of office range from one to eight years, but four-year terms are the most common. They are usually chosen from districts within the county rather than on an at-large basis.[1]

Generally, county boards may be grouped into two distinct types: boards of commissioners and boards of supervisors.

The board of commissioners is the smaller and more common type. It is found everywhere in the South and West but is well known elsewhere, too. It usually has three or five, but occasionally seven or more, members. The members (usually called commissioners) are elected specifically to these bodies; normally, they hold no other public office.

The board of supervisors is typically a much larger body—composed of an average of about 15 members, but sometimes running to as many as 80 or more. The supervisors are elected from each of the several townships within the county—as in New York, Michigan, and Wisconsin. Each of them is usually an officer of his or her township as well as a member of the county-wide governing body.

The powers held by the county governing bodies are prescribed—and often very

narrowly defined—in the State constitution and acts of the State legislature. And, however restricted they may be, their powers are usually both executive *and* legislative in character, despite the American tradition of separation of powers.

Their most important legislative powers are those relating to finance. County boards levy taxes, appropriate funds, and incur limited debts. They also possess a number of lesser legislative powers, especially in the regulatory field. For example, county boards enact health and zoning ordinances and control amusement places located outside of incorporated communities, especially those where liquor is sold.

Subject to varying degrees of State control and supervision, most county boards perform a number of administrative functions. They supervise the road program and manage county property—including the courthouse, jails, hospitals, parks, and the like. County boards are often responsible for the administration of welfare programs and the conduct of elections. They also appoint certain county officers, deputies, and assistants of many kinds, as well as most other county employees. And they regularly fix the salaries of most of those who work for the county.

In nearly every county, however, the board shares its executive powers with a number of other elected officials. Because of this, efficiency and economy are difficult and often impossible to achieve.

(2) A number of separately elected officials with county-wide jurisdiction. Typically, these other officers (and their principal duties) include:

The *sheriff*—who keeps the jail, furnishes police protection in rural areas, carries out the orders of the local courts, and is often the tax collector.

The *clerk*—who registers and records such legal documents as deeds, mortgages, plats, birth and marriage certificates, and divorce decrees. The county clerk often administers elections within the county, and

---

[1] In *Avery* v. *Midland County*, 1968, a case from Texas, the U.S. Supreme Court held that the 14th Amendment's Equal Protection Clause "forbids the election of local officials from districts of disparate size." It thus extended the "one-man, one-vote" rule to the local level, and has followed that holding in several subsequent cases; see pages 693–694.

acts as secretary to the county board and as clerk of the local courts.[2]

The *assessor*—who appraises (determines the value of) all taxable property within the county.

The *treasurer*—who keeps county funds and makes authorized payments from them.

The *auditor*—who maintains financial records and authorizes payments to meet county obligations.

The *district attorney*—who is the prosecuting attorney, conducts criminal investigations and prosecutes law violators.

The *superintendent of schools*—who is responsible for the administration of all or many of the public elementary and secondary schools in the county.

The *coroner*—who conducts investigations of deaths that occur by violent means and certifies the causes of deaths unattended by a physician.

Many other county officers are often elected. They include: a *surveyor*, who conducts land surveys and determines boundary lines; an *engineer*, who supervises the construction of roads, bridges, drains, and other public improvements undertaken by the county; and one or more *judges* of the various local courts.

(3) A number of boards or commissions. These bodies, whose members are also sometimes elected, have authority over various county functions. They commonly include a fair board, a library board, a planning commission, a hospital board, a board of road viewers, a board of health, and, too infrequently, a civil service commission. And it is not at all unusual for members of the county governing body to serve *ex officio* on one or more of these other agencies.

(4) An appointed county bureaucracy. The nation's 3,042 counties now employ more than 1.8 million men and women. They perform the day-to-day work in all of the many areas in which the county has responsibilities.

Functions of Counties. Because counties are creatures of the State, they are responsible for the administration of State laws and such county laws (*ordinances*) as the State's constitution and legislature permit them to enact.

Historically, counties have been institutions of *rural* government. And the large majority of them remain rurally oriented today. Although there is some variation State to State, their major functions reflect that fact. The most common ones are to preserve the peace and maintain jails and other correctional facilities; assess property for tax purposes; collect taxes and expend county funds; build and repair roads, bridges, drains and similar public works; maintain schools; record deeds, mortgages, marriage licenses, and other legal documents; issue licenses for such things as hunting, fishing, and marriage; administer elections; care for the poor; and protect the health of the inhabitants of the county.

Many counties have undertaken additional functions in the past few decades. Indeed, a number of them have had to do so—as they have become more and still more urbanized. Perhaps this fact will make the point: More than two-thirds of all of the people who live in the United States today live within the boundaries of some 300 of the nation's 3,042 counties.

Several of the more heavily populated counties now furnish many of the public services and facilities usually found in cities. A number of them provide water and sewer service, have professionally organized police, fire, and medical units, and do such other things as operate airports and mass transit systems. Some enforce zoning and other land-use regulations; and many have built and operate auditoriums, sports stadiums, golf courses, and other recreational facilities.

---

[2] In several States a separate officer known as the *recorder* or the *register of deeds* has custody of those documents relating to property transactions.

Reform of County Government. Earlier, we suggested that the description of the county as the "dark continent of American politics" remains appropriate. And we also suggested that public apathy is a leading justification for that description. The several weaknesses of county government justify it, too, of course. Three major weaknesses can be readily seen:

(1) <u>Its chaotic and headless structure.</u> It is virtually impossible to locate responsibility in the jungle of independently elected officers, boards, and commissions so commonly found. Lax, inefficient, and wasteful government, unresponsive government, government by the "courthouse gang," favoritism in awarding public contracts, occasional instances of outright corruption—the list of indictments that structure invites goes on and on.

(2) <u>The large number of popularly elected offices.</u> Confronted by the long ballots that typify county elections, voters are at best hard put to cast the informed votes upon which good government must depend. Further, many elected county officials hold jobs which do not involve the making of basic public policy, but which do demand professional qualifications. Popular election is not the best way to fill those offices with the talented persons who should occupy them.

(3) <u>The size and the number of counties in most States.</u> Nearly every one of the counties that now exists was laid out in the days of the horse and the stagecoach. Then, it made good sense to draw county lines so that no resident lived more than a dozen miles or so from the county seat. But most of them are geographically ill-suited to the realities of today.

The need for thoroughgoing reform of county government has long been recognized. Some steps have been taken in that direction—in some places.

COUNTY HOME RULE. One of the many barriers to meaningful change in the structure of county government lies in the legal

As custodian of the public records of a county, a county clerk is kept busy with requests for licenses, copies of legal documents, and so on.

status of counties. Recall, they are creatures of the State. Thus, their structure and functions are usually closely defined by State constitutional provisions and legislative enactments.

Over half of the States have lowered that barrier in recent years—by providing for county *home rule.* That is, they have permitted some or all of their counties to determine the details of their own governmental structures—subject to approval by the local voters.[3]

Many reformers and students of local government see home rule as a significant

---

[3] County home rule is now provided for in the constitutions of Arkansas, California, Colorado, Florida, Hawaii, Illinois, Iowa, Kansas, Maine, Maryland, Michigan, Minnesota, Missouri, Montana, New Jersey, New York, Ohio, Oregon, Pennsylvania, South Dakota, Utah, Washington, and Wisconsin (where, uniquely, local voter approval is not required). The constitutions of Georgia, Indiana, Louisiana, and Tennessee also provide for county home rule. But, in those States, special action by the legislature is necessary in order for any county to utilize the process. In Kentucky the legislature has provided for county home rule by statute. We shall take a closer look at home rule later in this chapter, on page 756.

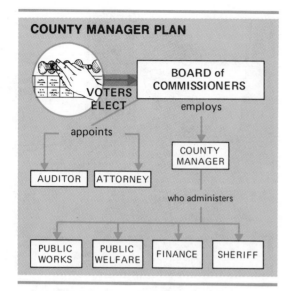

COUNTY MANAGER PLAN

VOTERS ELECT → BOARD of COMMISSIONERS

appoints

employs

AUDITOR   ATTORNEY

COUNTY MANAGER

who administers

PUBLIC WORKS   PUBLIC WELFARE   FINANCE   SHERIFF

avenue to the improvement of county government. But, at least to date, it has not been too widely used. There are nearly 1500 counties in those States where it is available. Yet, only about 100 of them have chosen to adopt home rule charters.[4]

Some useful changes have come in some of the States without home rule. Thus, in some States the legislature has offered counties an optional arrangement—permitting them to choose from different patterns of organization. Each pattern is set out in more or less detail in statutes. In North Dakota, for example, counties may select one of three different plans, and in Virginia they may pick from two or three, depending upon population.

And in a few places striking reforms have come by direct action of the State legislature. A very notable example exists in Tennessee. There, the legislature purposefully created a unique unit of government by combining a county and a major city—the Metropolitan Government of Nashville and Davidson County.

TREND TO A STRONGER EXECUTIVE. The

most prominent efforts to restructure county government have focused on county government's most prominent weakness: fragmented executive authority. Three newer patterns of organization have emerged, especially in urban counties in recent years. They are:

(1) The *county manager plan*—modeled along the lines of the council-manager form of city government now in wide use in middle-sized and smaller cities (see pages 760–761). Under this arrangement, the elected county board remains the legislative, policy-making, arm of county government. The executive function—the administration of county affairs—is in the hands of a manager, hired by and accountable to the board. In the ideal circumstances, the manager is a trained professional, a career administrator who appoints all of the other administrative officers of the county and directs their work.

The county manager plan separates the policy-making and policy-administering functions, concentrating administrative responsibility in a single and visible officer. It adds professional competence to county management and shortens the ballot. And it has the enthusiastic support of most students of local government.

The plan has not spread among counties to nearly the extent of its success at the city level, however. Only some 50 counties use it today—among them: Sacramento, San Mateo, and Santa Clara Counties in California; Dade County, Florida; Anne Arundel and Montgomery Counties in Maryland; Durham County, North Carolina; and McMinn County, Tennessee.

A leading reason why it has not been more widely adopted: Elective county officers are deeply entrenched—both constitutionally and politically—in so many places around the country.

(2) The *chief administrative officer* model—a less extensive reform than the manager plan, a limited version of it. Where it is found, a chief administrative officer (of-

---

[4] On the encouraging side, the list does include eight of the nation's most populous counties: Los Angeles, San Diego, and Alameda Counties in California; Erie, Nassau, Suffolk, and Westchester Counties in New York; and Dade County in Florida.

ten called the CAO) is also chosen by the board and is responsible to that body. But, unlike a manager, the CAO frequently has only very restricted or no authority in a number of important areas. For example, the CAO's powers are very limited in the making of appointments and the preparation of the budget.

In short, the CAO approach is a sort of compromise between the traditional multiple-executive arrangement and the stronger manager system. The CAO is the agent of the board, performing whatever functions that body may assign.

Los Angeles was one of the first counties to provide for a chief administrative officer. The post was established there in 1944. The plan has since spread to several other counties, in California and elsewhere. In fact, the number of counties with CAO's has grown rapidly in the past decade or so—to at least 500 today.

(3) The *elected chief executive* plan—patterned after the strong mayor-council form of city government (see pages 758–759). The plan features the county board and an elected chief executive—known as the county president, mayor, or supervisor.

The arrangement has several advantages. It separates the legislative and executive functions, focuses administrative responsibility in the chief executive, and cuts the length of the ballot. Although it is certainly an improvement on the traditional county structure, it does suffer the shortcomings found in the mayor-council form of city government. In brief, its success hinges upon the extent of the powers vested in the county president *and* that officer's personality and political clout.

The precise details of the plan vary from place to place. Cook County (Chicago), Illinois, was among the first counties to provide for an elected president. There the president is popularly chosen as a member of the county board, chairs its meetings, and has broad powers of appointment, budget-making, and veto.

Thirty years ago only three counties had an elected chief executive; today there are some 60 of them.

COUNTY CONSOLIDATION. As we noted earlier, the boundaries of most counties were horse-drawn. It seems clear that consolidating counties—combining two or more adjacent counties—would make them much more satisfactory units of government. Yet, despite serious studies and many proposals in several States, little has ever come of that notion. In fact, only two county consolidations have occurred in this century.[5] Local pride, politics, and economics stand as major impediments to any such effort.

COUNTY-CITY CONSOLIDATION. Consolidation of another sort has met with somewhat greater success—as you can see from the table on page 743. In several places, a major city and its surrounding county have been joined into a single unit of government. San Francisco, Denver, and the Metropolitan Government of Nashville and Davidson County are prime examples of the mergers.

COUNTY-CITY SEPARATION. The table on page 743 also lists those several situations in which a quite different path has been followed. Several cities and the counties around them have been separated from one another. St. Louis and Baltimore are the leading examples of these "independent cities" today.[6]

Towns and Townships

The *town* or *township* is found as a separate unit of local government in nearly half of the States. Generally, as you can see in the table on page 742, it is found in those States stretching from New England

---

[5] James County was joined to Hamilton County (Chattanooga), Tennessee in 1919, and Campbell and Milton Counties were merged with Fulton County (Atlanta), Georgia in 1923.

[6] A special situation exists in Virginia. There, whenever a city's population reaches 10,000 it automatically becomes an independent city—*i.e.*, a separate governmental unit, no longer a part of the surrounding county.

through the Middle West. It is little known in either the South or the West.[7]

The New England Town. The town is a major unit of local government in New England. With the exception of only a few cities, each of the six States in the region is divided into towns. Each town usually includes all of the rural *and* urban areas within its boundaries. And, the town is the unit which delivers most of the governmental services provided by cities and counties elsewhere in the country.

The roots of the New England town reach back to the earliest of colonial days. The Pilgrims landed at Plymouth Rock in 1620 as an organized congregation. They quickly established a close-knit community in which their church and their government were practically one. As other Puritan congregations settled in the region they followed the Pilgrims' pattern. The desire to be near the church, the real or imagined Indian threat, the severe climate, and the fact that the land was not suited to large farms or plantations all led them to form compact communities. Their settlements soon came to be known as "towns," after the English practice.[8]

At least in form, much of town government today is little changed from colonial times. The principal organ is the town meeting—long praised by political philosophers as the ideal vehicle of direct democracy. It is an assembly open to all of the town's eligible voters. It meets once a year,

and sometimes oftener, to levy taxes, make spending and other local policy decisions, and elect officers for the coming year.

Between town meetings the board of selectmen, chosen at the annual meeting, manage the town's activities. Typically, the board is a three-member body and has responsibilities in such areas as roads, schools, care of the poor, sanitation, and so on. The other officers regularly selected at the annual meeting include the town clerk, a tax assessor, a tax collector, a constable, road commissioners, and school board members.

The ideal of direct democracy is still alive in many smaller New England towns. But it has given way to the pressures of time, population, and the complexities of public problems in many of the larger towns. There representative government has largely replaced it. Members of the town meeting are frequently elected in advance of the yearly gathering. Many of the decisions once made by the assembled voters are now made by the selectmen. In recent years a number of towns have gone to a town manager system for the day-to-day administration of local affairs.

Townships. Outside of New England, townships exist as units of local government in those States bounded by New York and New Jersey on the east and the Dakotas, Nebraska, and Kansas on the west.[8a] In none of them do townships blanket the State, however. Where they exist, they are mostly county subdivisions.

In New York, New Jersey, and Pennsylvania townships were created as areas were settled and the people required the services of local government. As a result, the township maps of those States tend to resemble crazy-quilts. But from Ohio westward, township lines are much more regular.

---

[7] The term *town* is used in some States as the legal designation for smaller urban places; it is also sometimes used as a synonym for township. *Township* is also a federal public lands survey term, used to identify geographic units (often referred to as *congressional townships*) each containing exactly 36 square miles (36 *sections*).

[8] When a clan in England or Northern Europe settled in a particular place, it usually built a wall around it. In Old English, the wall was a *tun;* in time the space within the wall became known as the *tun,* then the town. As the New England towns grew in number and in population, it became necessary to survey their boundaries. The small and irregular areas that resulted were called "townships" (town shapes). The suffix *ship* comes from the Old English word *scip,* meaning "shape."

[8a] As the table on page 742 indicates, the other States are: Illinois, Indiana, Michigan, Minnesota, Missouri, Ohio, Pennsylvania, and Wisconsin.

They usually follow the lines drawn in federal public land surveys, and many are rectangles or perfect squares.

About half of these States provide for annual township meetings, patterned after those held in New England towns. Otherwise, most townships have rather similar governmental mechanisms. The governing body is a three- or five-member board, commonly called the board of trustees or board of supervisors. Often it is composed of members popularly elected to it for two- or four-year terms. But in many places the board's members serve because they hold other elected township offices—such as supervisor, clerk, and treasurer. Other township officers regularly include an assessor, a constable, one or more justices of the peace, and road commissioners.

Unlike the situation in New England, a municipality located within a township—especially one of any size—usually exists as a separate governmental entity. Thus, township functions tend to be rural—involving such matters as roads, cemeteries, noxious weed control, drainage, and minor law enforcement. In some States, however, the township is also the basic unit of public school administration.

Many believe that townships have outlived their usefulness. The fact that more than half of the States get along without them suggests that they are not altogether indispensable. Many rural townships have been abolished in the past few decades. They have been victims of declining populations, improvements in transportation and communication, school consolidations, and a host of other factors.

Some of the more densely populated townships appear to have brighter futures than their country cousins, however. This seems especially true in the suburban areas around some larger cities. In fact, some States—Pennsylvania, for example—now permit these townships to exercise many of the powers and furnish many of the services formerly reserved to cities.

Special Districts

As we first noted on page 741, there are now several thousand *special districts* throughout the country. These are independent local units which have been created to perform a single and occasionally a few related governmental functions at the local level. They exist in almost mind-boggling variety in every one of the States except Alaska.

The school districts are by far the most widely found examples of this type of governmental unit. Counting them, there are more than 41,000 special districts in the United States today. The first special districts—for school purposes—were established in New York as early as 1812. In the 1950's, there were more than 50,000 school districts. But continuing reorganizations have cut the number to some 15,000 today.

Most of the other special districts, which exist for a wide range of purposes, have been created since the onset of the Depression of the 1930's—and their numbers continue to increase. They are found most frequently—but by no means always—outside the boundaries of most cities, in rural and suburban areas. Among the most common of them are those created to provide water, sewage, or electrical service; to furnish fire, police, or sanitation protection; and to construct and maintain roads, bridges, airports, swimming pools, parking facilities, libraries, or parks. Others have been created for such purposes as soil conservation, housing, slum clearance, public transportation, irrigation, or reforestation. There are even, in many places, districts for dog control or for mosquito abatement purposes.

The reasons for the creation of these units are many. A leading one has been the felt need to provide some service in a wider (or a smaller) area than that covered by a county or a city. For example, stream pollution may very well be a problem in each of several counties through which a river flows. And (or) there might be a desire to develop recreational possibilities at several places along the river's course. In many cases, special districts have been formed because other local governments could not, or would not, provide the services desired. For example, police or fire protection might be provided in some remote locale by creating a special district.

And they have been created for a host of other reasons, too—for example, in order to sidestep constitutional limits on the size of a county's debt, to finance a service out of users' fees rather than from general tax revenues, to insulate a particular function from "politics," to facilitate the financing of an enterprise taken over from private ownership, or to take advantage of some federal grant or loan program.

An elected board is usually the governing body for a special district. It regularly has the power to levy taxes (usually on the property within the district) or impose fees. Of course, it has the power to spend and to perform the function or functions for which it was established.

The Cities

To this point we have dealt with those local governments which are, in the main, rural—in their functions and, very often, in their outlook. Now we turn to what are *the* principal units of local government in the United States: the cities.

Urban Growth. We are fast becoming a nation of city dwellers. Where once our population was small, predominantly rural, and agricultural, it is now huge, largely urban, and industrial.

The nation's cities have grown spectacularly—and particularly in the past 100 years. When the First Census was taken in 1790, there were only 3,929,214 persons

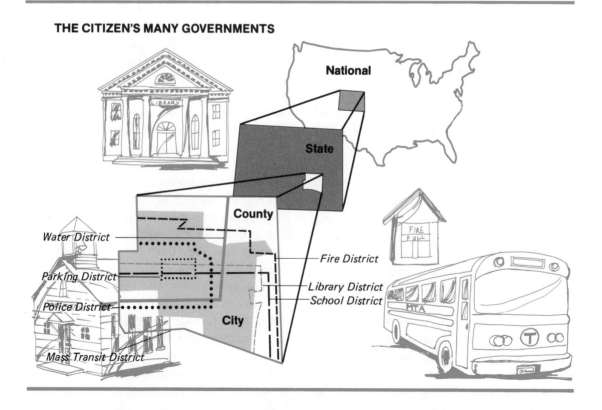

THE CITIZEN'S MANY GOVERNMENTS

National

State

County

City

Water District

Parking District

Police District

Mass Transit District

Fire District

Library District

School District

living in the United States. Of these, only 201,655—5.1 percent—lived in the nation's few cities. Philadelphia was then the largest, with a population of only 42,000; 33,000 persons lived in New York and only 18,000 in Boston.

A scant nine years before the First Census, James Watt had patented his double-acting steam engine—and so made large-scale manufacturing possible. Robert Fulton patented his steamboat in 1809 and George Stephenson his locomotive in 1829. These inventions made the transportation of raw materials to factories and, in turn, the wide distribution of manufactured goods readily possible. Almost overnight, the home manufacturing system gave way to industrial factories and populations began to concentrate in budding industrial and transportation centers. The nation's cities began to grow rapidly.

The invention of several mechanical farm implements reduced the labor required on farms. More was produced by fewer people, and the surplus farm population began to migrate to the cities. By 1860 the nation's population had increased more than seven-fold—and the *urban* population had multiplied *thirty* times. By 1900 nearly two-fifths of all our people lived in cities, and by 1920 more than half were residing in urban areas.

With the 1970 census, our urban population had grown to nearly 150 million, as the table on page 754 indicates. The final data from the 1980 census will almost certainly show that that figure has grown by another 25 million over the past 10 years. Today, then, three-fourths of all of our people live in the nation's cities and their surrounding suburbs.

The shift from a predominantly rural to a largely urban society in the United States is a matter of tremendous significance—and it has had dramatic consequences. When large numbers of people live in close proximity to one another, the relationships among them are far more complex than are those among people who live in less densely settled areas. The rules governing their behavior become more numerous and detailed. Their local governments must furnish them with a wide range of services. Water, police and fire protection, streets, sewers, traffic regulation, transportation, public health, schools, and recreation must be provided. The larger the population the more extensive—and expensive—these services become.

The Legal Status of Cities. Depending on local custom and State law, municipalities may be known as "cities," "towns," "boroughs," or "villages." The use and meaning of these terms varies among the States.[9] The larger municipalities are everywhere known as cities, and the *usual* practice is to apply that title only to those communities with a fair-sized population.

Ohio furnishes a somewhat typical example. There the State constitution declares that all municipalities with 5000 or more residents are to be known as cities and those with a lesser population as villages. But in some States the law provides that *all* municipalities, regardless of size, are cities. Thus, for example, Cleveland, with a 1970 population of 750,879, is legally a city; but so, too, is Granite, Oregon. Granite's population consisted of only four residents when the last federal head count was taken.

Cities Subordinate to the State. Recall that each of the 50 State governments is unitary in form. Consequently, each of them possesses complete authority and control over *all* of the units of local government within its borders. All of these

---

[9] Do not confuse the town (village) in the South and West with the New England town (township); nor the borough in Connecticut, New Jersey, and Pennsylvania with the borough in Alaska, where it is a substitute for the county; see pages 749-751. In the New England States villages have been created in only a very few instances. This is because the town is sufficiently organized to collect the necessary taxes and furnish the necessary services that villages (or towns or boroughs) provide elsewhere.

URBAN POPULATION GROWTH

Census	Total Population	Urban Population	Percent Urban
1790	3,929,214	201,655	5.1
1800	5,308,483	322,371	6.1
1810	7,239,881	525,459	7.3
1820	9,638,453	693,255	7.2
1830	12,866,020	1,127,247	8.8
1840	17,069,453	1,845,055	10.8
1850	23,191,876	3,543,716	15.3
1860	31,443,321	6,216,518	19.8
1870	28,558,371	9,902,361	25.7
1880	50,155,783	14,129,735	28.2
1890	62,047,714	22,106,265	35.1
1900	75,994,575	30,159,921	39.7
1910	91,972,266	41,998,932	45.7
1920	105,710,620	54,157,973	51.2
1930	122,775,046	68,954,823	56.2
1940	131,669,275	74,423,702	56.5
1950	150,697,361	96,467,686	64.0
1960	179,323,175	125,268,750	69.9
1970	203,235,298	149,377,944	73.5
1980	226,000,000*	169,500,000*	75.0*

* Preliminary figure.

units—including cities—are "creatures of the State." Each was created by the State, received its powers from the State, and is subject to a variety of limitations imposed by the State.

The State's authority over cities is reflected in provisions in the State constitution and in laws enacted by the legislature. In our early history State constitutions contained few provisions relating to cities. Practically all of the State's authority was exercised through the legislature. The degree of control the legislature possessed—and in many ways still does—is illustrated in this excerpt from an 1868 decision of the Iowa State Supreme Court:

[Cities] owe their origin to, and derive their powers and rights wholly from, the legislature. It breathes into them the breath of life, without which they cannot exist. As it creates, so it may destroy. If it may destroy, it may abridge and control. Unless there is a constitutional limitation on the right, the legislature might, by a single act, if we can suppose it capable of so great a folly and so great a wrong, sweep from existence all the municipal corporations in the State, and the corporations could not prevent it.

As cities grew in population and multiplied in number, this complete legislative domination produced many difficult situations. State legislatures, usually dominated by members from the rural areas, were often unfamiliar with the needs and problems of cities. Many of the laws they enacted were either grossly unfair or impractical. Many rural legislators were suspicious or jealous of cities (and their residents) and sought to restrict their growth.

Today, and in reaction to legislative abuse of power, most of the State constitutions contain a large number of provisions relating to municipal government and its problems. Generally, these provisions deal with incorporation, city charters, offices, elections, council meetings and procedures, and financial matters.

INCORPORATION. Cities are *incorporated* [10]—made into a legal body, by the

---

[10] The term comes from Latin *in* (into) and *corpus* (body). To say that cities are incorporated is another, and legal, way of saying that they are creatures of the State.

State. Each State prescribes, in its constitution or by statute, the conditions and the procedures under which a community may become an incorporated municipality. There are many variations. Generally, a State requires that at least a certain number of persons must reside within a defined area before incorporation can occur. This number is commonly 200 or 300 persons within a one-mile square.

In a few States an incorporated community may be created only by a special act of the legislature. In fact, this is the historic means by which most cities were established. But the usual process today demands that a petition signed by a certain number of the residents of a locale be submitted to a designated public officer. When that officer (usually a judge) is satisfied that the legal requirements have been met, he or she declares the defined area to be incorporated—to exist as a municipal corporation. In most States, however, that declaration cannot become finally effective until the qualified voters who live within the affected area approve that action at a special election.

The fact that cities, unlike counties, are incorporated highlights a very important difference between these two types of local government. Cities are called into being primarily because of concentrations of population, at the behest of their residents, to provide them with various public services. Recall that counties, on the other hand, exist primarily to serve the administrative needs of the State. Cities do act as agents of the State, of course—for example, in the fields of law enforcement and public health. But the *principal* reason for the existence of a city is the convenience of those who live within it.

The City Charter. The *charter* is the city's basic law, its constitution. Its contents may vary somewhat from city to city, but commonly the charter names the city, describes its boundaries, and declares it to be a *municipal corporation.*

As a municipal corporation, the city is a legal (artificial) person. As such, it has the right to sue and be sued in the courts, to have a corporate seal, to make contracts, and to acquire, own, manage, and dispose of property. It also enjoys the "right of perpetual succession." This means that a complete change in the city's population from generation to generation does not affect its status as a legal body.

Regularly, the charter also sets out the other powers vested in the city and outlines its form of government. It provides how and for what terms its officers are to be chosen and prescribes their duties, and deals with finances and other matters.

Broadly speaking, five distinct types of city charters have been or are presently found among the States.

THE SPECIAL CHARTER. In colonial days each city received its charter from the governor. With Independence, the State legislatures assumed the function—providing a charter for each city in the State by the passage of a special act. That practice is still followed in a few States today—Delaware, Maine, New Hampshire, and Vermont among them.

The special act arrangement does allow for flexibility. But it also means that each city is subject to direct, regular, continuing, and detailed supervision by the legislature. Any meaningful change in its organization, powers, or functions can come only if the legislature acts. And in those States where the practice still exists, the legislature spends much of its time in each session considering a great many bills of purely local concern.

THE GENERAL CHARTER. Many State legislatures abused the special charter system. Often, for example, those cities where the voters proved loyal to the majority party received better treatment than that accorded to others. In several States most city charters were hopeless reflections of the ignorance, jealousies, and suspicions of rural legislators.

Reactions to the special charter process grew to the point where, by the middle of the 19th century, some States went to the opposite extreme. They adopted a *general charter*—one for *all* cities in the State.

This newer arrangement did eliminate the practice of singling out one or a few cities for special treatment, good or bad. But it soon proved to be as inadequate as the special-act approach. It failed to take account of the many differences of needs, desires, and circumstances among cities— for example, those of a bustling industrial city and those of a small farm community.

No State today provides a single charter for all of its cities. But many cities still operate under a charter dating from the days when the legislature did.

THE CLASSIFIED CHARTER. The defects of both the special and the general charter approaches led to the development of the *classified charter* system. Under this arrangement, all of the municipalities within the State are classified according to population, and a uniform charter is granted to all of those within the same class.

The classified method minimizes discriminations among cities; and, at the same time, it permits flexibility in meeting the varying needs of cities of different sizes. Still, it leaves much to be desired. There may be very real differences between cities with approximately the same number of inhabitants. Take, for example, a coastal city where the population is growing and the economy is brisk. Its needs are very different from those of a mining community where the population is static or declining and business is depressed.

Where classification is used, the legislature can play games with the population ranges—and in some States it has. There may be only one city in the State with more than 500,000 residents, or only one with a population between 200,000 and 300,000. Where this happens, classification really amounts to the old special charter system in disguise.

Several States do provide for the classified charter arrangement—but most of them now do so in combination with the optional approach.

THE OPTIONAL CHARTER. Several States have turned to the *optional charter* system in recent decades.[11] Under this arrangement, the State offers all cities—or, frequently, those within each population group—a choice from among a number of charters. Usually each city's choice is made subject to the approval of its voters. In Massachusetts, for example, each city may pick from five different charters offered by the legislature, and in New Jersey a city may select from as many as 14.

The optional charter process has much to recommend it—especially where the legislature proffers a fairly broad range of different charters. Still, it does not allow for the fullest possible consideration of peculiar local circumstances or local preferences. In effect, it is a compromise between near-domination of cities through special charters and home rule for them.

THE HOME RULE CHARTER. Three-fourths of the States now provide for *municipal home rule*. That is, they provide—either by constitutional provision or by statute—that some or all cities may draft, adopt, and amend their own charters.

In most of these States—34 of them— municipal home rule has been established by constitutional provision.[12] In seven others, however, the grant rests on the basis of

---

[11] Cities operating under optional charters are most frequently found today in Illinois, Iowa, Kansas, Massachusetts, Minnesota, New Jersey, and Pennsylvania.

[12] Alaska (1959), Arizona (1912), California (1879), Colorado (1902), Connecticut (1965), Georgia (1950), Hawaii (1959), Illinois (1970), Iowa (1968), Kansas (1960), Louisiana (1946), Maine (1969), Maryland (1915), Massachusetts (1960), Michigan (1908), Minnesota (1896), Missouri (1875), Montana (1972), Nebraska (1912), Nevada (1924), New Mexico (1949), New York (1923), North Dakota (1966), Ohio (1912), Oklahoma (1908), Oregon (1906), Pennsylvania (1922), Rhode Island (1951), South Dakota (1962), Tennessee (1953), Texas (1912), Utah (1932), Washington (1889), West Virginia (1936), Wisconsin (1924), Wyoming (1972).

legislative enactment alone.[13] The distinction here—between *constitutional* and *legislative* home rule—can be a vital one. Legislative home rule is a much less secure grant of power to cities—since any subsequent legislature can retract the grant if it chooses to do so.

In some of these States *any* municipality may frame and adopt its own charter—in Hawaii, Michigan, Minnesota, Ohio, and Oregon, for example. But in many of them only *certain* cities may do so. For example, only cities of more than 3500 population may do so in Arizona and California, only those of more than 5000 in Missouri, Nebraska, and Texas, and only those of more than 10,000 in Washington.

Typically, home rule provisions grant to cities "the powers of local self-government" or all powers relating to "municipal affairs." But home rule is never complete or absolute, never creates a "free city." The State always retains at least some degree of control over its home rule cities—and frequently a considerable amount of it. There is always difficulty in distinguishing those matters which are of purely *local* concern from those of general, Statewide import. As routine examples of this: the setting of speed limits on city streets which are also State highways, or the regulation of a municipal sewage system that empties into a river flowing through the State. The questions, and the vexations, of city versus State authority in such cases must often be settled in the courts.

A home rule charter may be framed and proposed by the city council or by an elected charter commission. To become effective, it must be approved by the city's voters—and in some States by the legislature, as well. Once adopted, amendments may be made by council proposal and voter ratification. In many cities amendments can also be proposed by initiative petition.

Changing Municipal Boundaries. As a city's population grows, the areas surrounding it tend to grow, too. These fringe areas often create rather serious problems for the city itself. Shacks may present fire hazards, septic tanks may threaten the city's water system, and taverns and roadhouses may complicate law enforcement.

Methods for the *annexation* (adding) of territory to the city are usually provided by the State constitution or by act of the legislature. Compulsory annexation (that is, forcing an area into a city) is rare. Annexation usually requires a vote of the residents of the area to be annexed. In some places the voters in the city must also act on the question.

Suburbs often tend to resist annexation. Thus, most States give their cities *extraterritorial powers*. That is, cities are granted the power to regulate certain matters such as roadhouses, sanitation, or fire hazards in the thickly settled areas around them. Cities sometimes induce suburbs to annex by dangling a carrot—for example, an agreement not to raise taxes in the area for a certain number of years.

Forms of City Government. Which is the more important: a particular form of government or those who operate it? That question has been argued for centuries. In 1733 Alexander Pope penned this couplet:

> For forms of government let fools contest;
> Whate'er is best administer'd is best.

Certainly good people are essential to good government, and good men and women can make at least something of even the worst of forms. But the form is important, too. The better the form of government the more chance there is that capable people will be attracted to public service. And, too, the better the form the greater the likelihood that the public will receive the kind of government it wants and needs.

---

[13] Delaware, Florida, Indiana, New Hampshire, North Carolina, South Carolina, Vermont.

Every city charter, however adopted, provides for one of three general forms of municipal government. Although there may be variations and adaptations from this city to that, each has: (1) a mayor-council, (2) a commission, or (3) a council-manager form of government.

THE MAYOR-COUNCIL FORM. The *mayor-council* form is the oldest and still the most widely used type. It features an elected mayor as the city's chief executive and an elected council as its legislative body.

The council is almost always unicameral. In fact, only one city in the nation now has a two-chambered council—Everett, Massachusetts. The council regularly has five, seven, or nine members, but there are more in some larger cities. Chicago now has the largest council, with 50 members.

The members of the council are everywhere popularly elected. Terms of office range from one to as many as six years, but four-year terms are the most common. Council members are now most often elected from the city at-large, and the trend is in that direction. But a substantial number of cities, including several larger ones, choose council-members from *wards* (districts) within the city.

A move to nonpartisan city government began in the early part of this century. It was based on the belief that national and State politics and parties have little to do with municipal problems and local issues. Today, less than a third of the nation's cities still conduct their elections on a partisan basis.

The mayor is regularly elected by the voters, too—though in some places the office is filled by appointment by the council from among its own members. The mayor presides at council meetings, usually may vote only to break a tie, and may recommend and (usually) veto ordinances. In most cities the mayor's veto can be overridden by the council.

Mayor-council governments are often described as either of the *strong-mayor* or the *weak-mayor* type—depending upon the powers lodged in the mayor. This classification is useful for descriptive and analytical purposes. *But,* notice it tends to ignore or blur the importance of *informal* power in a city's governmental structure.

In the *strong-mayor* type the mayor heads the city's administration, usually has the power to hire and fire employees, and prepares the budget. And, typically, the mayor is otherwise able to exercise strong

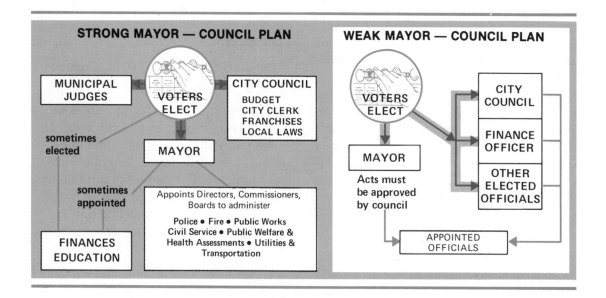

STRONG MAYOR — COUNCIL PLAN

MUNICIPAL JUDGES

VOTERS ELECT

CITY COUNCIL
BUDGET
CITY CLERK
FRANCHISES
LOCAL LAWS

sometimes elected

MAYOR

sometimes appointed

Appoints Directors, Commissioners, Boards to administer

Police • Fire • Public Works
Civil Service • Public Welfare &
Health Assessments • Utilities &
Transportation

FINANCES EDUCATION

WEAK MAYOR — COUNCIL PLAN

VOTERS ELECT

MAYOR

Acts must be approved by council

CITY COUNCIL

FINANCE OFFICER

OTHER ELECTED OFFICIALS

APPOINTED OFFICIALS

leadership in the making of city policy and the conduct of its affairs.

In the *weak-mayor* type the mayor has much less formal power. Executive duties are often shared with such other elected officials as the clerk, treasurer, city engineer, and police chief, and with the council. The powers of appointment, removal, and budget are shared with the council or exercised by that body alone, and the mayor seldom possesses a veto power.

Most mayor-council cities operate under the weak-mayor rather than the strong-mayor plan. But the latter form is usually found in larger cities.

Evaluation. The success of the mayor-council form depends in very large measure on the power, ability, and influence of the mayor. Especially in weak-mayor cities, responsibility for action or inaction is hard to fix.

The strong-mayor plan helps to solve the problems of leadership and responsibility. Still, it has three large weaknesses. First, it must rely very heavily on the capacities of the mayor. Recall, political *and* administrative talents are not often combined in the same person. Second, a major dispute between the mayor and the council can stall the workings of city government. But, notice, this is another way of saying that the form incorporates the principles of separation of powers and checks and balances. Finally, the form is somewhat complicated and so is often little understood by the average citizen—but whose fault is that?

THE COMMISSION FORM. Fewer than 10 percent of the nation's cities now have the commission form of government. Among the larger ones today are Portland (Oregon), St. Paul, Tulsa, Mobile, Lexington (Kentucky), and Jackson (Mississippi).

The *commission form* is rather simple and uncomplicated. Three to nine (usually five) commissioners are popularly elected. *Together*, they form the city council, pass ordinances, and control the purse strings.

Individually, they head the various departments of city government—police, fire, public works, finance, parks, and so on. Thus, both legislative and executive powers are centered in the one body.[14]

In some cities the voters and in others the commissioners themselves designate one of the commissioners to serve as the mayor. Like the other commissioners, the mayor heads one of the city's departments. He or she also presides over council meetings and represents the city on ceremonial occasions. The mayor seldom has any more authority than the other commissioners and rarely has the veto power.

The commissioners are usually elected for two- or four-year terms, and almost invariably from the city at-large and on nonpartisan ballots. Unlike their counterparts in both mayor-council and council-manager cities, they regularly serve as full-time officers.

Evaluation. The simplicity of the commission form, and especially its short ballot, attracted the support of municipal reformers in the first two decades or so of this century. However, experience with it disclosed serious defects and the popularity of the form declined rather rapidly—from a peak use in some 500 cities in 1920 to little more than 100 today.

Its chief defects: (1) The lack of a single chief executive (or, the presence of several chiefs-among-equals)—which makes it difficult to fix responsibility. This also means

---

[14] The commission form was born in Galveston, Texas, in 1901. A tidal wave had swept the island city the year before. Some 7000 persons, nearly a fifth of the city's population, lost their lives and much of the community was desolated. The old mayor-council regime was too incompetent (and corrupt) to cope with the emergency. The Texas legislature granted Galveston a new charter providing for five commissioners to make and enforce the law in the stricken city. Intended to be temporary, the arrangement proved so effective that it soon spread to other Texas cities and then elsewhere in the country. Its popularity has waned, however. In 1960 Galveston's voters approved a new charter establishing a council-manager government.

that the city usually suffers from a lack of effective political leadership. (2) A built-in tendency toward "empire-building"—or, usually, several separate empires, as each commissioner attempts to draw as much of the city's money and power as he or she can to his or her own department. And (3) a lack of overall coordination at the topmost levels of policy-making and administration. Each commissioner tends to equate the public good with the peculiar interests and ·functions of his or her department. Each tends to become jealous and protective of that department's turf. In short, the commission form tends to bear out the wisdom of the notion that "experts should be on tap, not on top."

THE COUNCIL-MANAGER FORM. *Council-manager* government is, in effect, a modification of the mayor-council form. The essential elements of the form include: (1) a strong council, of usually five or seven members, elected at large on a nonpartisan ballot, (2) a weak mayor, chosen by the voters, and (3) a manager, the city's chief administrative officer, appointed by the council.[15]

The council is the city's policy-making body. The manager executes the policies the council makes and is directly responsible to that body for the efficient administration of the city. The manager serves at the council's pleasure and, literally, may be dismissed at *any* time and for *whatever* reason the council deems appropriate.

Today most city managers are professionally trained, career administrators—and more and more women are now entering the field. As chief administrator, the manager directs the work of all city departments and has the power to hire and fire all city employees. The manager also prepares the budget for council consideration, and then controls the expenditure of the funds the council has appropriated.

Evaluation. The council-manager plan has the near-unanimous backing of students of municipal affairs, and its use has increased steadily throughout the country. It is now found in nearly 3000 communities, including about half of those with populations of 250,000 or more.

The *first* of the leading advantages of the form is its simplicity. The *second* is the fairly distinct clarification of responsibility for policy on the one hand and its application on the other. And the *third* is the use of trained experts who can adapt and employ modern techniques of budgeting, planning, computerization, and other administrative tools.

The theory of the form has it that the nonpolitical manager carries into practice the policies enacted by the council. And, in theory, the council will not bypass the manager to interfere in the details and routine of city administration. In fact, the sharp distinction between policy-making and its application seldom exists in practice. The manager is frequently the chief source for new ideas and fresh approaches to coping with municipal problems. *And,* too, a city council often finds it politically useful to share responsibility for controversial decisions with the "expendable" city manager.

Some critics of the plan contend that it is undemocratic, since the chief executive is appointed, not elected. Others claim that it does not provide for strong political leadership. This, they argue, is especially necessary in larger cities, where the makeup and interests of the population are often quite diverse and competitive. Some support for this view can be seen in the fact that only four of the nation's cities with more than half a million residents now

---

[15] The form was born in Staunton, Virginia, in 1908 when that city's council hired a general manager to direct the city's work. That step attracted the attention and then support of municipal reformers (most notably, that of Richard S. Childs and his National Municipal League) and was soon pushed throughout the country. The first charter to make specific provision for a council-manager form was the one granted by the South Carolina legislature to the city of Sumter in 1912.

Washington, D.C.'s new rail rapid-transit system began service in 1976. Scheduled for completion in 1984, the "Metro" will extend well into the suburbs of the District of Columbia, as well as throughout the city.

have manager government—Dallas, San Diego, San Antonio, and Phoenix.[16]

Municipal Functions. A city exists primarily to provide services to those who live within it. The scope and the variety of those services, which cities provide day in and year out, are so extensive that it is almost impossible to catalog them. Nearly all of our larger, and many smaller, cities issue annual reports, which summarize the city's condition and which now are often book-length publications.

Consider *some* of the many things that most or all cities do. To list a few, they: provide police and fire protection, and build and maintain streets, sidewalks, bridges, street lighting systems, parks and playgrounds, swimming pools, golf courses, libraries, hospitals, schools, correctional institutions, day-care centers, airports, public markets, parking facilities, auditoriums, and sports arenas. They furnish such public health and sanitation services as sewers and waste water treatment, rubbish and garbage collection and disposal, and disease prevention and eradication programs. They operate water, gas, light, and transportation systems. And they regulate traffic, building practices, noise pollution, and public utilities.

Then, too, many cities build and man-

age public housing projects, clear slums, provide summer youth camps, construct and operate docks and other harbor facilities, and maintain tourist attractions. Several have built their own hydroelectric power dams. Many operate farms in connection with their sewage disposal plants and have developed other recycling programs. The list, indeed, is endless.

CITY PLANNING. Most American cities, like Topsy, just "growed." With few exceptions, they developed haphazardly, without plan, and with no eye to the future. The results of this shortsightedness can be seen almost everywhere. And the most obvious, and damaging, examples can be seen in what is often called the "core city" or the "inner city"—the older and usually overcrowded central sections of larger cities.

Industrial plants were permitted wherever their owners chose to locate them. Rail lines were run through the heart of the community. Towering buildings shut out the sunlight from the too-narrow streets below. Main thoroughfares were laid out too close together and sometimes too far apart. Schools, police and fire stations, and other public buildings were squeezed onto cheap land or put where the local political organization could make a profit. Examples go on and on and on.

Fortunately, many cities have seen the need to create order out of their random growth. Most have established some sort of planning agency—usually a planning

---

[16] Several other major, but smaller, cities also use the manager form, including Cincinnati, Toledo, Oklahoma City, Austin, Fort Worth, Tucson, Oakland, Sacramento, and San Jose.

Case Study

Zoning ordinances can be used to control the make-up of an area's population. And they sometimes are, especially by high-income suburban communities. By setting various requirements—for example, establishing large minimum lot sizes and allowing only single-family dwellings—a suburb can practically guarantee itself that no minority, or low-income, or other "undesirable" persons will reside there.

The Supreme Court did not face a case which squarely posed these civil rights issues until *Arlington Heights* v. *Metropolitan Housing Development Corporation*, 1977.

Arlington Heights, a village near Chicago, had refused to rezone a parcel of land to permit construction of a racially integrated housing development for low- and moderate-income families. The federal Court of Appeals had found that refusal to be a violation of the Equal Protection Clause. It had held that the effect of that action was to deny to black families an opportunity to move into the community.

The Supreme Court, 5–3, reversed that decision, however. A majority of the justices could find no good evidence that the refusal to rezone was motivated by racial bias. Instead, said the Court, it appeared to be prompted by a legitimate desire to maintain the single-family dwelling character of the suburb and thus preserve its property values.

The Court ruled that a governmental "action will not be held unconstitutional solely because it results in a racially disproportionate impact. . . . Proof of racially discriminatory intent or purpose is required to show a violation of the Equal Protection Clause."

■ Why have many civil rights groups been very critical of this decision?
■ Why is the phrase "proof of racially discriminatory intent" so important here?
■ What is your reaction to this decision?

commission, supported by a trained professional staff.[17]

A number of factors have prompted this step. The need to correct past mistakes has often been an absolutely compelling one, of course. Then, too, many have recognized the values that can come, and the pitfalls that may be avoided, through well-planned and orderly development. *And,* importantly, they have been spurred on by the Federal Government. Most federal grant and loan programs require that cities which seek assistance must first adopt a master plan as a guide to future growth.

Washington, D.C., is one of the few cities in the nation that began as, and has remained, a planned city. Its basic plan was drawn before a single building was erected. In 1790 Congress decided to locate the nation's capital along the Potomac River. President Washington assigned the task of laying out the new city to an engineer, Major Pierre-Charles L'Enfant.

L'Enfant designed the city on a grand scale, with adequate parks and beautiful circles. Parallel streets, running in an east-west direction, were named according to the alphabet, and those running at right angles were numbered. Twenty-one avenues were provided to shorten distances by cutting diagonally through the city, and trees and shrubs were planted at the intersections. Wide streets were provided, and large areas reserved for public buildings.

The original plan has been followed fairly closely through the years. The National Capitol Planning Commission guides the city's development today.

---

[17] The first city planning commission was created in Hartford, Connecticut, in 1907. Only a handful of cities with populations of 10,000 or more do not have some kind of planning agency today.

Philadelphia also began as a planned city. It was first laid out by William Penn in 1682 much in the fashion of a checkerboard. Penn's simple scheme called for two main thoroughfares to cross one another at right angles, with an open place at the point of intersection. Other lesser streets were to crisscross the pattern at regular intervals. In his plan, the City of Brotherly Love was to cover some two square miles.

Philadelphia outgrew its founder's plan decades ago. It is now the nation's fourth largest city, with a population of nearly two million. It now sprawls over some 338 square kilometers (130 square miles). Much of its growth came in unplanned fits and starts, and with the inevitable consequences.

For the past several years, though, the city has been rebuilding itself. Whole blocks of old and decaying structures have been razed and replaced with attractive parks, modern expressways, and well-designed business and apartment buildings. The Pennsylvania Railroad's ancient Broad Street station, in the heart of the city, was torn down. To celebrate that event, the renowned Philadelphia Symphony Orchestra played a requiem in the train shed, and a large and enthusiastic crowd joined in the singing of *Auld Lang Syne.*

Pittsburgh accomplished a modern miracle by eliminating the industrial smog that only a few years ago blanketed its downtown area so completely that street lights often had to be turned on by 10 A.M. The heart of the business district, the Golden Triangle, has been rebuilt. So, too, has much of the surrounding area, with modern skyscrapers and landscaped parks which include several levels of underground parking.

In Dallas, Houston, Seattle, Detroit, and elsewhere new expressways and one-way street systems have eased downtown traffic congestion. San Francisco, Los Angeles, Boston, and other cities have put in underground garages with beautifully planned and kept parks right on top of them in the busiest districts.

The accomplishments in these and other communities in recent years are largely the result of the work of local planners and of public-spirited citizens, many of them prominent in business. Several cities have also been helped by loans, grants, advice, and other aid from a number of federal agencies.

CITY ZONING. *Zoning* is the practice of dividing a city into a number of districts (zones) and of regulating the uses to which property in each of them may be put. Usually, a zoning ordinance places each parcel of land within the city into one of three basic zones: residential, commercial, or industrial. Each of these is normally divided into sub-zones. For example, each or several of the residential zones may be broken down into several areas. One may be reserved exclusively for single-family residences. Another area may permit both one- and two-family dwellings. In still another area apartment houses and other multi-family units may be allowed.[18]

Zoning is really a phase of city planning—and an important device for assuring orderly growth. It began to come into general use only as recently as the 1920's. Zoning still meets opposition from many who object to this interference with their right to use their property as they choose. Even so, nearly every city of any size in the United States is zoned today; the only major exception is Houston, where zoning was rejected by popular vote.

Zoning ordinances must be *reasonable.* Recall that the 14th Amendment prohibits any State—including its cities, of course—the power to deprive any person of life,

---

[18] Zoning ordinances also regularly limit the height and area of buildings, determine the percentage of a lot that may be occupied by a structure. They often contain "set-back" requirements which prescribe that structures be located a certain minimum distance from the street and from other property lines, and several other such restrictions on land use.

liberty, or property without due process of law. Most of the State constitutions contain a similar provision.

Quite obviously, zoning *does* deprive a person of the right to use his or her property for certain purposes. Thus, if an area is zoned only for single-family dwellings, a person may not build an apartment house or a service station on property he or she owns within that zone.[19] And zoning *can* reduce the value of a particular piece of property, too. For example, a choice corner lot may be much more valuable with a drive-in restaurant rather than a house on it.

While zoning may at times deprive a person of liberty or property, the key question always is: Does it do so *without due process*? That is, does it do so *unreasonably*?

The question of reasonableness is one for the courts to decide. The Supreme Court first upheld zoning as a proper exercise of the *police power* in 1926. It did so in a case involving an ordinance enacted by the city council of Euclid, Ohio.[20]

Suburbanitis and Metropolitan Areas

Suburbanitis. Most larger cities, and many smaller ones, suffer from what has been called "suburbanitis." They are literally bursting at the seams, with their populations spilling over into the surrounding suburbs. Today over a third of our total population—and half of our urban population—live in suburban areas.

From 1950 to 1970 the nation's population grew by 35 percent—by more than 53 million persons. Most of that spectacular increase came in the suburban population.

It jumped some 35 million—about 85 percent—over those two decades. Many of the nation's larger cities actually *lost* population in the 1950's and 1960's, but, at the same time, their fringe areas grew by leaps and bounds. And the trend to suburbia has continued on into the 1980's.

This dramatic shift in population can be explained on several grounds. A plentiful number of quite understandable desires has helped to generate it—including desires for more room; cheaper land; less smoke, dirt, noise, and congestion; and greater privacy. At the same time, people wished for more neighborliness; less crime; newer and better schools, safer streets and playing conditions; lower taxes; and higher social status. Better means of transportation and communication have prompted the migration, too. The automobile and the freeway have transformed millions of once rooted city dwellers into highly mobile suburbanites.

Businesses have followed customers to the suburbs, of course—often clustering in modern and convenient shopping centers. Many industries have moved from the central city in search of cheaper land, lower taxes, and a more stable labor supply. Industries have also sought an escape from city building codes, health inspectors, and other regulations. And, in the process, these developments have themselves stimulated growth.

All of this has sharpened a great many problems for core cities. As many of the better-educated, high income families have moved out, they have taken their civic, financial, and social resources with them. They have left behind a central city which, in contrast to its suburbs, contains much higher percentages of older persons, low-income families, blacks, and other minorities, more older buildings and substandard housing, more unemployment, and higher crime rates. Thus, inevitably, both the need for and stress on city services have multiplied.

---

[19] However, nonconforming uses in existence *before* a zoning ordinance is enacted are almost invariably allowed to continue. And most ordinances permit the city council to grant exceptions (variances) in situations where property owners might suffer undue hardships.

[20] *Euclid* v. *Amber Realty Co.*, 1926. On the police power see page 150.

This is *not* to suggest that our larger cities are today made up entirely of poor, starving, and huddled masses, of course. As one noted authority argues, there is "another side to the matter. The plain fact is that the overwhelming majority of city dwellers live more comfortably and conveniently than ever before. They have more and better housing, more and better schools, more and better transportation, and so on. By any conceivable measure of material wealth, the present generation of urban Americans is, on the whole, better off than any other large groups of people have ever been anywhere."[21]

But most would agree with the judgment that "the central city has the problems and the suburbs the resources. . . . Central cities, like the Red Queen in *Through the Looking Glass*, must run very fast to stay in the same place."[22]

Metropolitan Areas. While the growth and sprawl of suburbia have raised many difficult problems for cities, those who live in the suburbs face their share of problems, too. Water supply, sewage disposal, health care, police and fire protection, transportation, traffic control, and planning for orderly development are only some of them. Duplication of functions by city and city, or city and county can be wasteful and even dangerous. More than one fire has burned on while neighboring fire departments quibbled over which of them was responsible for fighting it.

Attempts to meet the needs of metropolitan areas—that is, of the cities *and* their surrounding areas—have taken several forms. Historically, annexation has been the standard means; outlying areas have simply been brought within a city's boundaries. But, as we have already suggested, many suburbanites resist annex-

A cartoonist comments on the financial plight of most of the nation's cities.

ation. Moreover, cities, too, have often been reluctant to take on the burdens involved.

Another approach involves the creation of *special districts*, to which we referred on page 751. Although the best known and most common of these units are school districts, there are now more than 25,000 sanitary, water, fire protection, and other special districts across the country. Many of them have been established especially to meet the problems of heavily populated urban areas. Their boundaries frequently disregard county and city lines, and they are often called *metropolitan districts*.

These metropolitan districts are usually established for a single purpose. For example, they were established for park development in the Cleveland Metropolitan Park Development District and for sewage in the Metropolitan Sanitary District of Greater Chicago. There is no reason why a district's authority cannot be expanded to include other functions, however. The Metropolitan District Commission, created by Massachusetts, controls sewage, water

21 Edward C. Banfield, *The Unheavenly City Revisited.* (Boston: Little, Brown, 1974), pp. 1–2.

22 Robert L. Lineberry and Ira Sharkansky, *Urban Politics and Public Policy.* (New York: Harper & Row, 1971), p. 32.

supply, and park development for the City of Boston and several neighboring communities. And the MDC has a number of planning functions in the District as a whole. Boston itself accounts for only about a third of the District's total population; most of the balance lives within some 40 other municipalities.

City-county consolidation and, on the other hand, city-county separation, have also been tried in some places—including St. Louis, Denver, San Francisco, Baltimore, and Philadelphia, as we've noted on page 749.

Yet another, and more recent, approach to meeting the problems of large and rapidly growing urban areas is that of increasing the authority of counties. Among existing local governments around the country, counties are generally the largest in area

and are thus most likely to encompass those places demanding new and increased services.

The functions of many urban counties have been increased in recent years, as we noted on page 746. Dade County (Miami), Florida, has undertaken the nation's most ambitious approach to metropolitan problems. In 1957 its voters approved the first home-rule charter to be specifically designed "to create a metropolitan government." Under it, a county-wide metropolitan government ("Metro") is responsible for area-wide functions. These functions include fire and police protection; providing an integrated water, sewer, and drainage system; zoning; expressway construction; and the like. Miami and the other 26 cities within the county continue to perform the strictly local functions.

SUMMARY

There are more than 79,000 units of *local* government in the United States today. They include 3,042 counties, more than 16,000 townships, some 41,000 special districts (more than a third of them school districts), and nearly 19,000 municipalities.

Counties exist in all but two States—Connecticut and Rhode Island. They serve mainly as judicial districts in New England, share responsibility for rural government with townships in the northeastern and middle western sections, and are the predominant rural units in the South and West. Only a few places in the country do not lie within the boundaries of some county.

Counties vary widely in size, population, and number among the States. Legally, they are creatures of the State and administer State law and such ordinances as the State's constitution and legislature permit them to enact.

With a few exceptions, county government is in urgent need of reform across the country. Its major weaknesses include its headlessness, the existence of too many elective offices, and the failure to separate executive and legislative functions. The geographic size and number of counties in most States pose serious problems, as well. Reform has made little headway in most States.

Townships are also predominantly rural units, found from the New England States westward to the Dakotas. In New England the *town* is regularly the major vehicle of local government. Elsewhere, townships have been largely outmoded by modern means of transportation and communication and by urbanization.

Special districts are units of local government created to perform one or occasionally a few specific functions. They are found everywhere except Alaska. School districts are by far the most common example of the type.

The nation's cities have grown spectacularly, especially in the past century. Where our population was once predominantly agricultural and rural, it is now largely industrial and urban. Three-fourths of all our people live in urban areas.

Municipalities—known variously as cities, towns, villages, and boroughs—are creatures of the State. But, significantly, they also exist for the convenience of their residents. The range and variety of their functions and services virtually deny cataloging.

A city's *charter* is its fundamental law and may be *special, general, classified, optional,* or *home rule* in form.

Three major forms of city government are found in the United States: the *mayor-council* form (the most widely used), the *commission* form, and the *council-manager* form.

Most cities have developed haphazardly and with no eye to the future. Most have now recognized the need for effective planning, however. *Zoning* is a principal tool with which orderly growth can be obtained.

"Suburbanitis" has created many serious problems in and for central cities—and for the suburbs, as well. A number of *metropolitan districts* have been created and the functions of some urban counties have been increased to meet the problems raised by suburbanization.

Concept Development

Questions for Review

1. Approximately how many units of local government are there in the United States? How many of each type?

2. What is the basic nature of the relationship between each of the States and its several local governments?

3. Why is the county often called "the dark continent of American politics"?

4. What are the three major weaknesses in the typical county government?

5. What is county home rule?

6. Efforts to reform county government have been largely aimed at which of its major weaknesses?

7. What is the major unit of local government in the New England States? Why has the town meeting often been praised by political theorists?

8. What is the general condition of township government elsewhere in the country?

9. What are special districts? What is the most common example of this type of governmental unit?

10. What proportion of our population was urban in 1790? By 1980?

11. What is a city charter? What five distinct types have been or are being used?

12. What are the three major forms of city government?

13. Which of the three is the most widely used? Which is the one generally supported by students of local government? Why?

14. Why did city planning become so generally and vitally necessary?

15. What is meant by *zoning?*

16. What factors have been especially responsible for the spectacular growth of the nation's suburban population?

17. What sorts of problems has "suburbanitis" caused for cities? For the suburban areas themselves?

18. What is a metropolitan district? What newer approach has been tried in Dade County? What are the other major approaches attempted elsewhere?

For Further Inquiry

1. Do you think that every city should be permitted to frame its own charter? Every county?

2. What arguments may be made for and against the election of members of a city council (and/or a county governing body) from: (a) wards (districts) and (b) the city (or county) at large?

3. When was your city established? What particular factors led to its creation? Has its growth been generally orderly and well-planned? If so, why? If not, why not? What are the city's more acute planning problems today?

4. Why are bicameral city councils, once fairly common, now almost wholly unknown among American cities?

Suggested Activities

1. Prepare an organizational chart depicting the major features of the government of your county and/or city.

2. Invite one or more local officials— from the county, city, or other local unit— to discuss with the class his or her office and functions.

3. Stage a debate or class forum on one of these topics: (a) *Resolved,* That all counties in this State be abolished; (b) *Resolved,* That this city adopt (or abandon) the council-manager form of government; (c) *Resolved,* That this city's chief of police be hereafter selected by popular vote.

4. Obtain a copy of your city's zoning ordinance(s) and accompanying map(s). Examine and evaluate those documents. Do you recommend any changes in zoning laws? If so, why?

Suggested Reading

Berkley, George and Fox, Douglas, *80,000 Governments: The Politics of Subnational America.* Allyn and Bacon, 1978.

Berman, David R., *State and Local Politics.* Allyn and Bacon, 3rd ed., 1981.

Cooper, John L., *The Police and the Ghetto.* Kennikat, 1980.

Dye, Thomas R., *Politics in States and Communities.* Prentice-Hall, 4th ed., 1981.

Ellis, David M., *New York: State and City.* Cornell University Press, 1979.

Freed, Leonard, *Police at Work.* Simon & Schuster, 1981.

Hahn, Harlan and Levine, Charles (eds.), *Urban Politics: Past, Present, and Future.* Longman, 1980.

Henry, Nicholas, *Governing at the Grassroots: State & Local Politics.* Prentice-Hall, 1980.

Judd, Dennis R., *The Politics of American Cities.* Little, Brown, 1979.

Schnieder, Max, *Suburban Growth: Policy and Process.* King's Court, 1979.

Wright, Deil S., *Understanding Intergovernmental Relations.* Duxbury, 1978.

Ziegler, L. Harmon and Tucker, Harvey J., *The Quest for Responsive Government.* Duxbury, 1978.

Financing State and Local Governments

Finance is not mere arithmetic; finance is great policy.

WOODROW WILSON

■ What should be the objectives of State and local taxing policies? Spending policies?

■ Why is a budget a significant statement of public policy?

■ Should a government ever be permitted to spend more than it receives?

Government is an expensive proposition—and it is becoming more so year to year. Just as the costs of government at the national level have risen to astronomical heights in recent decades, so have its costs at the State and the local levels. Altogether, the 50 States and their thousands of local governments now (1981) take in and spend well over $400 billion a year.

State and local spending amounted to less than one billion dollars a year for *all* purposes at the turn of the century. It has grown more than 400 times over the years since, and it continues its upward climb. Even as recently as 1960, total State and local spending came to only about $61 billion a year. It is now running at a rate of more than seven times that amount.

This dramatic and continuing rise in the cost of State and local government can be traced to one overriding cause: As the nation's population has increased and has become more and more concentrated in urban and suburban areas, the people have demanded that more and still more services be provided by their governments.

Government can do little without money. Where does it come from? Where does it go? It is to these *vital* questions we now turn.

State and Local Revenues

The huge amounts of money consumed by State and local government come from

769

both tax and nontax sources. Today the States collect some $140 billion a year in taxes, and their local units take in more than $90 billion. And the 50 States and their local governments also receive another $170 billion or so from a variety of nontax sources.

Taxes are charges made by governments, compulsory exactions to raise money for public purposes.

Limitations on State and Local Taxing Powers. The power to tax is an essential part of the reserved powers possessed by each of the States. In the strictly legal sense, then, it is limited only by those restrictions imposed by the Federal Constitution and by its own fundamental law.[1] Every local unit acquires its taxing power from its parent State. Thus, its power to tax is limited by State constitutional *and* statutory provisions as well as by the restrictions contained in the Constitution of the United States.

FEDERAL LIMITATIONS. The Federal Constitution places only a few restrictions on State and local taxing powers.

(1) Interstate and Foreign Commerce. As we've already seen, the Constitution forbids the States the power to "lay any imposts or duties on imports or exports" and "any duty of tonnage."[2]

In effect, the States are here prohibited from taxing interstate and foreign commerce. The Supreme Court has often held that, because the Constitution gives to Congress the power to regulate that trade, the States are generally forbidden to do so. But they may and do tax property—buildings, trucks, aircraft, and much else—even though it is used in commerce.

(2) The National Government and Its Agencies. The States have been forbidden, ever since the Supreme Court's decision in Mc-

Culloch v. Maryland, 1819, to tax the National Government or any of its agencies or functions. They are because, as Chief Justice Marshall put it in that case, "the power to tax involves the power to destroy."

(3) The 14th Amendment. The Due Process and the Equal Protection Clauses of the 14th Amendment also limit the taxing abilities of State and local governments.

Essentially, the Due Process Clause requires that taxes: (1) be imposed and administered *fairly;* (2) *not* be so heavy as to actually *confiscate* (seize) property, and (3) be imposed only for *public* purposes.

The Equal Protection Clause forbids the making of *unreasonable* classifications for taxing purposes. Notice that most tax laws involve some form of classification. For example, an income tax involves classification, for it is applied only to that class of persons who have income. Likewise, a cigarette tax applies only to those who buy cigarettes, and a property tax only to those who own property. Of course, the Clause does not prevent these and similar classifications for they are *reasonable* ones. It does forbid tax classifications made on such bases as race, religion, nationality, political party membership, or similarly *unreasonable* factors, however.

STATE CONSTITUTIONAL LIMITATIONS. Each State's own constitution limits the taxing powers of the State and its local governments in a number of ways—and frequently in detail.

Most State constitutions provide that taxes shall be levied only for public purposes and that they be applied uniformly. Most provide that taxes be collected only within the geographic limits of the units of government which levy them, and that there be no arbitrary or unreasonable classifications made for tax purposes.

Most also exempt the properties of churches, private schools, museums, cemeteries, and the like from taxation. Many fix maximum tax rates. For example, many fix the State's sales tax at four percent and/or

---

[1] The power to tax is also limited by any number of *practical* considerations, too—*i.e.*, by a variety of quite important economic and political factors.

[2] Article I, Section 10, Clauses 2 and 3.

the local property tax at no more than so many *mills*[3] per dollar of assessed valuation. And some prohibit the use of certain kinds of taxes—for example, a sales tax or an income tax.

As local units possess no independent powers, the only taxes they may impose are those the State permits them to levy. The States have been notoriously reluctant in the matter. Even those units operating under home-rule charters are closely restricted in their taxing authority.

The Principles of Sound Taxation. Any tax, taken by itself, can be shown to be unfair. If all of a government's revenues were to come from but one tax—say, a sales, an income, or a property tax—its tax system would be grossly unfair. Some would bear a much greater burden than others, and some would bear little or none at all. Yet, each tax that is levied should be defensible as a *part* of a tax system.

More than 200 years ago, in his classic *The Wealth of Nations,* published in 1776, the English economist Adam Smith laid out four principles of a sound tax system. Most tax experts today cite the same four. Wrote Smith:

> 1. The subjects of every state ought to contribute towards the support of the government, as nearly as possible, in proportion to their respective abilities; that is, in proportion to the revenue which they respectively enjoy under the protection of the state.
> 2. The tax which each individual is bound to pay ought to be certain and not arbitrary.
> 3. Every tax ought to be levied at the time, or in the manner, in which it is most likely to be convenient for the contributor to pay it.
> 4. Every tax ought to be so contrived as to take out and to keep out of the pockets

Citizen Smith by Dave Gerard. Reprinted courtesy The Register and Tribune Syndicate Inc.

"NEVER MIND ABOUT DETOURS AND ROAD CONSTRUCTION. ROUTE ME THROUGH THE STATES WITH THE LOWEST SALES TAX AND THE CHEAPEST GASOLINE!"

of the people as little as possible over and above what it brings into the public treasury. . . .

Shaping a tax system—let alone any single tax—to meet these standards of *equality, certainty, convenience,* and *economy* is virtually impossible. That goal should be nonetheless pursued, always.

State and Local Taxes. Beyond the limits we have noted, a State may levy taxes as it chooses. The legislature determines what taxes the State will levy, and at what rates. It also determines what taxes the local units—counties, cities, school districts, and so on—may levy.[4]

THE SALES TAX. The sales tax is the single most important source of income among the 50 States today. It now accounts for approximately half of all of the tax monies collected by the States.

---

[3] A *mill* is one-thousandth of a dollar, or one-tenth of a cent. Thus, if the local property tax rate is 50 mills, one who owns property assessed at $10,000 would pay a property tax of $500.

[4] A State constitution sometimes grants certain taxing powers directly to local governments, but this is not at all common.

A *sales tax* is a tax applied to the sale of various commodities and is paid by the purchaser. It may be either general or selective in form. A *general sales tax* is one that is applied to the sale of most commodities. A *selective sales tax* is one applied only to the sale of certain commodities—such as cigarettes, liquor, or gasoline.

Today, 45 States[5] levy a general sales tax. The rate is most often three or four percent; but the rate varies from a low of two percent in Oklahoma on up to seven percent in Connecticut. In most States certain items are exempted from the tax—for example, all food, or certain food items such as milk or bread, drugs, newspapers, or sales under a certain amount.

---

[5] All except Alaska, Delaware, Montana, New Hampshire, and Oregon. Each of these States does impose various selective sales taxes, however.

In most States the tax is collected by the retailer as each taxable sale is made—that is, it is paid by customers as they buy taxable items. In a few States, however, the tax is not levied on each separate sale but, instead, on a retailer's total sales. In those States where this is the practice the sales tax is often called a *gross receipts tax*. In either case, it is the purchaser who pays the tax; and the retailer acts as the tax collector and turns the receipts over to the State at regular intervals.

Each of the 50 States now (1981) levies a selective sales tax on gasoline and other motor fuels, alcoholic beverages, insurance policies, and cigarettes and other tobacco products. And most of the States also levy a selective sales tax on such other things as hotel and motel accommodations, theater and other amusement admissions, restaurant meals, automobiles and parimutuel betting.

Case Study

Except in Hawaii, the public schools in every State are financed primarily by local property taxes. Some recent State court decisions foreshadow changes in this traditional pattern, however.

The California State Supreme Court triggered the matter in a case which it first decided in 1971 and then again, with the same result, in 1976. In *Serrano* v. *Priest* it held California's reliance on the local property tax for school purposes to be unconstitutional—as a violation of the equal rights guarantees in California's constitution.

It found that there are often very significant variations between and among school districts—especially in terms of the amount and the assessed values of taxable properties within each of them. The net result of these variations, it said, was flagrant inequalities, differences which made the quality of a child's educational experience "dependent upon the wealth of his parents and neighbors."

Similar decisions have now been made in several other States. And in many of them legislators, administrators, and educators are wrestling with the resulting complications.

The United States Supreme Court has come to a somewhat different conclusion here, however. In *San Antonio School District* v. *Rodriguez,* 1973, it held, 5–4, that the right to an education is not one of the fundamental rights covered by the 14th Amendment's Equal Protection Clause. In effect, it ruled that, whatever a State's own constitution may mean in this matter, the 14th Amendment does not prevent a State from relying on the local property tax as the principal source of financing for its public schools.

■ Which of these contrasting views of "equal rights" do you think is the proper one? Why?
■ How have the courts of your State ruled here?

There are two major reasons why the sales tax is so widely used among the States. *First,* the sales tax is relatively easy for the States to collect. And *second,* it is a fairly dependable revenue producer. But, notice, it is a *regressive* tax—that is, it is not geared to ability to pay and falls most heavily upon those with lower incomes.

Several larger and many smaller cities, and some counties, also levy a sales tax— usually as a "piggy-back" tax, added on to and collected with the State tax.

THE INCOME TAX. The income tax— levied on individuals and/or corporations—yields more than 35 percent of State tax revenues today. Forty-three States now levy an individual income tax; 46 have some form of the corporate income tax.[6]

The *individual income tax* rates are usually *progressive*—that is, the higher the income the higher the tax rate. The rates vary among the States, of course—from one or two percent on lower incomes in most on up to 15 percent or more on the highest incomes in some of them. Various exemptions and deductions are allowed in the figuring of one's taxable income. Over half of the States now provide that one's taxable income for State purposes is the figure reported on the federal return.

The *corporate income tax* rates are uniform, a certain fixed percentage of income. Only a few States fix the rates on a graduated (progressive) basis.

The progressive income tax is held by many to be the fairest (or least unfair) form of taxation—especially because it may be closely geared to ability to pay. If the rates are too high, however, the tax can discourage incentive. The high federal income tax rates tend to force the States to keep theirs relatively low.

---

6 Nevada, Texas, Washington, and Wyoming levy neither type of income tax. Alaska, Florida, and South Dakota impose only the corporate tax. Oil-rich Alaska abolished its tax on personal incomes in 1980.

Some cities also levy a small income tax. But local income taxes will never become significant revenue producers unless and until the federal and State rates are cut substantially. The prospects for any such action as that are dim, indeed.

THE PROPERTY TAX. The property tax is the chief source of income for local governments today. It now accounts for approximately 80 percent of their tax receipts today. Once the principal source of State income, it now brings in less than two percent of all State revenues.

The property tax may be levied on (1) *real property*—land, buildings, and improvements which go with the property if sold, or (2) *personal property*—either *tangible* or *intangible*. Tangible personal property includes all movable wealth which is visible and the value of which can be easily assessed. Tangible property, for example, includes farm implements, livestock, pianos, television sets, automobiles, and watches. Examples of *intangible personal property* include such things as stocks, bonds, mortgages, promissory notes, and bank accounts. Because intangibles can often be hidden from the tax assessor they are not taxed in some States. In others, intangibles are taxed at a lower rate than real or tangible personal property.

The process of determining the value of the property to be taxed is known as *assessment.* The task is usually performed by a popularly elected county, township, or city assessor. Only in a handful of States must he or she be a trained specialist, and in those States the assessor is usually appointed rather than elected. Most tax authorities believe that election is not likely to produce competent assessors. And, there is the possibility that elected assessors will under-assess in order not to antagonize the voters upon whom they depend for their office.

Where personal property is taxed, the assessment is regularly made each year. Real property is usually assessed less often, commonly every second or fourth year. The assessor is expected to visit the property and examine it in order to determine its value. In practice the assessment is often made simply on the basis of the previous year's figures, which were arrived at the same way.

Property is usually assessed at less than its true market value. Most property owners seem better satisfied if the assessment is set at, say, one half of its real value. Thus, a house assessed at $20,000 may actually be worth $40,000. If the tax rate is set at 20 mills (or two percent) the tax will be $400. In reality, of course, this is the same thing as a 10 mill (or a one percent) tax on the $40,000 house.[7]

Three major arguments are commonly made in support of the use of a property tax. They are: (1) because property is protected—and its value is often enhanced—by government it may logically be required to contribute to the support of government; (2) the rate at which the tax is levied may be readily adjusted to meet governmental needs; and (3) it is a dependable source of revenue.

Similarly, three major criticisms of the property tax are frequently heard: *First* is the claim that the tax is not geared to ability to pay—where the amount of real property one owns may in our earlier history have been a fair measure of one's wealth, it is not today. *Second,* it is argued that it is all but impossible, even with the most competent of assessors, to assess all taxable property on a fair and equal basis. And *third,* it is contended that personal property, especially intangible property, is often, and readily, concealed.

---

[7] Several reasons are advanced for assessing property at a fraction of its actual market value—none of them valid. Among them: the belief that full assessment means higher taxes; the wish to lessen the share of State or county taxes paid by an assessed area; political considerations, especially the desire of an assessor to be re-elected; the difficulty of making a fair full-value assessment.

INHERITANCE OR ESTATE TAXES. Every State except Nevada levies inheritance or estate taxes—so-called "death taxes." As we indicated on page 502, an *inheritance tax* is one levied on the beneficiary's share of an estate, and an *estate tax* is one levied directly on the full estate itself. Several States also impose *gift taxes*.

BUSINESS TAXES. A wide variety of business taxes, in addition to the corporate income tax, are imposed and are an important souce of revenue in most States.

Over half of the States impose *severance taxes*. Such taxes are levies imposed on the removal of such natural resources as timber, oil, gas, minerals, and fish from the land or water.

Every State has several different *license taxes*—fees which permit persons to engage in a business, occupation, or activity which is otherwise unlawful. All States require that corporations (artificial persons) be licensed to do business in the State. Certain kinds of businesses—especially chain stores, amusement houses, bars and taverns, and transportation lines—must also have an additional license to operate. Then, too, individuals who wish to engage in certain businesses or occupations must themselves be licensed. Most or all States require the licensing of doctors, lawyers, dentists, morticians, barbers, hairdressers, plumbers, engineers, electricians, and a host of others. Many local governments impose business license taxes, as well.

License taxes other than for business purposes are levied in all States, too—and are a significant revenue source. The most important are those required for motor vehicles and motor vehicle operators, of course; others include such permits as hunting, fishing, and marriage licenses.

Nearly half of the States have levies known as *documentary and stock transfer taxes*. These are charges made on the recording, registering, and transfer of such documents as mortgages, deeds, and securities. Some States also impose *capital stock taxes*, which are levied on the total assessed value of the shares of stock issued by a business concern.

POLL TAXES. Only New Hampshire now levies a poll tax—a head or capitation tax; in effect, a tax on the privilege of living and breathing. Recall that the poll tax was once widely used as a suffrage qualification in the Southern States; see page 218.

OTHER TAXES. A variety of other taxes are imposed by the States and/or their local governments. Thus, more than half the States levy amusement taxes—usually on the tickets of admission to theaters, sports events, circuses, and the like. *Payroll taxes* produce huge sums—altogether, some $40 billion among the States today. But these taxes produce money which is held in trust funds for such social welfare programs as unemployment, accident insurance, and retirement programs; see pages 584–585.

STATE-LOCAL TAX SHARING. The fact that the States tax so many different sources of revenue often makes it impractical for their local governments to do so. So, increasingly, the States now share with their local units portions of various taxes— either as they are collected or by appropriations made by the legislature.

For example, most States give a portion of the revenue from gasoline taxes and motor vehicle licenses to cities and counties. Where this is done the State can attempt to equalize the financial resources of local units—and can also attach some strings to the use of the money.

Nontax Receipts. State and local governments now take in approximately $170 billion a year from a wide range of nontax sources.

FEDERAL FUNDS. A sizable portion of all of the nontax monies received by both levels comes from the Federal Government. Federal grants-in-aid now total some $80 billion a year, and are provided for more than 100 different purposes. These funds provide for everything from prenatal and maternity care to aid for the elderly. And remember that revenue sharing provides another sizable chunk of federal money each year, too; see pages 89–91.

GOVERNMENT-OPERATED BUSINESSES. Each of the States and many of their local governments receive a handsome return from a large number of different publicly-operated business enterprises. Toll bridges and toll roads are found in many parts of the country. Several States—most notably Washington—are in the ferry business. North Dakota markets a flour sold under

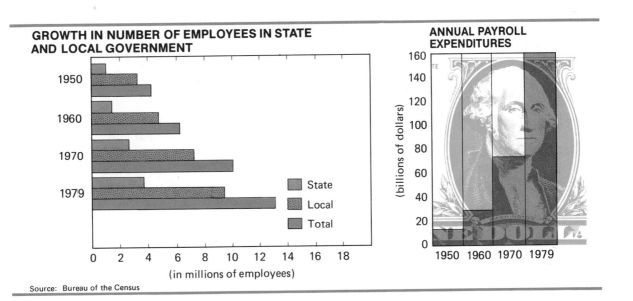

GROWTH IN NUMBER OF EMPLOYEES IN STATE AND LOCAL GOVERNMENT

State
Local
Total

(in millions of employees)

Source: Bureau of the Census

ANNUAL PAYROLL EXPENDITURES

(billions of dollars)

1950 1960 1970 1979

the brand-name "Dakota-Maid" and is also in the commercial banking business. Milwaukee produces and sells a plant fertilizer, "Milorganite." California operates a short railway line in San Francisco.

Eighteen States are in the liquor-dispensing business, selling it through State-operated stores.[8] For several years, Oregon and Washington jointly owned a distillery in Kentucky and marketed its product in their own outlets.

Many cities own and operate their water, electric power, and bus transportation systems. Some cities operate farmer's markets and rent space in office buildings, warehouses, and housing projects, own and operate dams and wharves, and so on. The receipts from these businesses (often including profits) go toward the support of the governments which own them.

Other nontax sources include such things as court fines, the sale or leasing of public lands, interest earned from investments, and the like. Fourteen States today—Connecticut, Delaware, Illinois, Maine, Maryland, Massachusetts, Michigan, New Hampshire, New Jersey, New York, Ohio, Pennsylvania, Rhode Island, and Vermont—conduct lotteries.

Borrowing. Borrowing may be classed as a source of nontax revenue. But, as the loans must be repaid, this source is hardly in the same category with other nontax receipts.

States and their local governments often must borrow money for unusually large undertakings, such as public buildings or bridges and highways, that cannot be paid for out of current revenues. The borrowing is most often done by issuing bonds, as is federal borrowing.

Generally, State and local bonds are easy to market because the interest from them is not taxed. That is, they are easy to market if the credit rating of the particular government is good.

Many State and local governments have, in times past, borrowed so heavily that they had to default on their debts. Thus, most State constitutions contain detailed limits on the power to borrow.

The total of all States' debts now amounts to more than $120 billion, and all local governments owe not quite twice that much today.

The State Budget

We have already suggested that a budget is much more than bookkeeping entries and dollar signs. It is a financial plan—a plan for the control and use of public money, public personnel, and public property. It is also a political document—a highly significant statement of public policy. Here, in its budget, the State establishes its priorities and decides who gets what, and who doesn't.

Until at least the 1920's, few if any of the State budgets could be dignified as a "plan." No officer or agency reviewed the needs of State government and its agencies and measured them against the available resources. No officer or agency pared them where necessary and, then, presented a carefully constructed and cohesive financial program to the legislature.

Instead, State budgets were jerry-built, the results of a haphazard and uncoordinated process centering in the legislature. Regularly, the various State agencies appeared before legislative appropriations committees, each seeking its own funding and often in fierce competition with one another. Their chances of success depended far less on either need or merit than upon the amount of political influence they could bring to bear. When the

---

[8] Alabama, Idaho, Iowa, Maine, Michigan, Mississippi, Montana, New Hampshire, North Carolina, Ohio, Oregon, Pennsylvania, Utah, Vermont, Virginia, Washington, West Virginia, Wyoming. North Carolina's stores are operated by the counties; Wyoming's liquor monopoly operates only at the wholesale level.

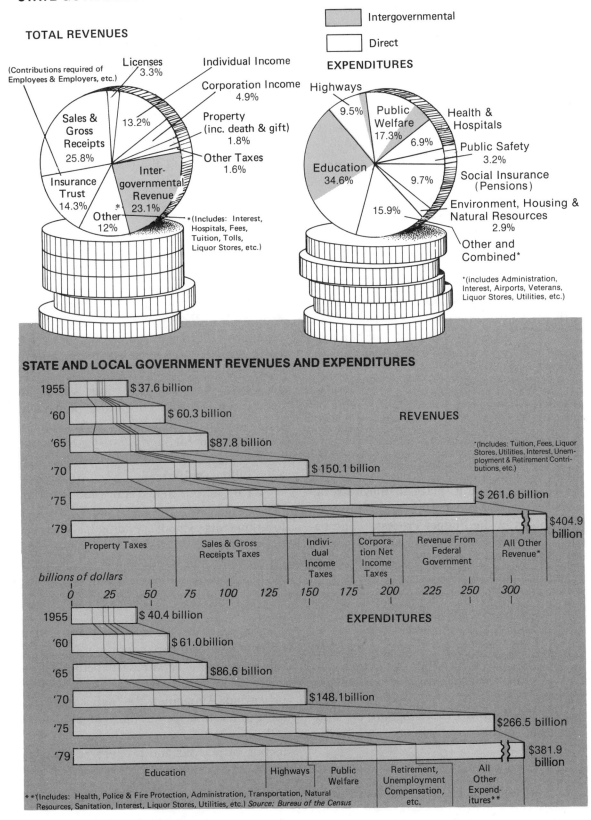

STATE GOVERNMENT FINANCES 1979

TOTAL REVENUES

Intergovernmental

Direct

EXPENDITURES

(Contributions required of Employees & Employers, etc.)

Licenses 3.3%

Individual Income 13.2%

Corporation Income 4.9%

Property (inc. death & gift) 1.8%

Other Taxes 1.6%

Sales & Gross Receipts 25.8%

Inter-governmental Revenue 23.1%

Insurance Trust 14.3%

Other 12%

*(Includes: Interest, Hospitals, Fees, Tuition, Tolls, Liquor Stores, etc.)

Highways 9.5%

Public Welfare 17.3%

Health & Hospitals 6.9%

Public Safety 3.2%

Education 34.6%

Social Insurance (Pensions) 9.7%

Environment, Housing & Natural Resources 2.9%

15.9%

Other and Combined*

*(includes Administration, Interest, Airports, Veterans, Liquor Stores, Utilities, etc.)

STATE AND LOCAL GOVERNMENT REVENUES AND EXPENDITURES

REVENUES

1955 — $37.6 billion

'60 — $60.3 billion

'65 — $87.8 billion

'70 — $150.1 billion

'75 — $261.6 billion

'79 — $404.9 billion

*(Includes: Tuition, Fees, Liquor Stores, Utilities, Interest, Unemployment & Retirement Contributions, etc.)

Property Taxes | Sales & Gross Receipts Taxes | Individual Income Taxes | Corporation Net Income Taxes | Revenue From Federal Government | All Other Revenue*

billions of dollars

0 25 50 75 100 125 150 175 200 225 250 300

EXPENDITURES

1955 — $40.4 billion

'60 — $61.0 billion

'65 — $86.6 billion

'70 — $148.1 billion

'75 — $266.5 billion

'79 — $381.9 billion

Education | Highways | Public Welfare | Retirement, Unemployment Compensation, etc. | All Other Expenditures**

**(Includes: Health, Police & Fire Protection, Administration, Transportation, Natural Resources, Sanitation, Interest, Liquor Stores, Utilities, etc.) *Source: Bureau of the Census*

legislature adjourned, no one had any real notion of how much it had appropriated or for what. Inevitably, extravagance and waste, problems unmet, debt, favoritism, and graft were all parts of the process.

State budgets are strikingly different today. They remain highly charged and vitally important documents, of course. But they are the end-products of what is, by and large, an orderly, systematic process.

Forty-seven States have now adopted the *executive budget*. That is, they have given the governor two vital powers: (1) the power to prepare the State budget, and (2) once the legislature has acted upon it, the power to execute that budget, and authority to administer the various funds the legislature has appropriated. And in most of them the governor has the assistance of a director and the professional staff of a budget agency, appointed by and responsible to the chief executive.[9]

The governor's key role in the budget process has been an important element in the strengthening of the office among the States, as we noted on page 714. And, recall, the executive budget is a key feature of council-manager government, and it has also been put into place in most strong-mayor-council cities.

Steps in the Budget Process. The basic steps in the budget process are much the same at the State and local levels as they are for the Federal Government:

(1) The preparation by each agency of estimates of its needs and expenditures in the upcoming fiscal period.

(2) The review of those estimates by the executive budget agency.

(3) The collection of the revised estimates and all supporting information into a consolidated financial program, the budget, for presentation by the governor to the legislature.

(4) The consideration of the budget, part by part, the appropriation of the necessary funds, and the enactment of the necessary revenue measures (if any) by the legislature.

(5) The supervision of the actual execution of the budget as approved by the legislature.

(6) An independent check (post-audit) of the execution of the budget.

Pattern of Expenditures

On page 769, we commented on the high rate of State and local government spending—currently at a level well above $400 billion a year.

Each of the 50 States, and their tens of thousands of local governments, spend for so many different purposes that it would be next to impossible to list them all. Another look at the graphs on page 777 will show that four major functions stand out as the most costly: education, highways, public welfare, public health and hospitals. They account for *nearly three-fourths* of all State and local spending today—more than $300 billion in 1981.

Of these four items, education is by far the most expensive entry in most State and local budgets. School spending has climbed ten-fold since 1950, and continues to increase year to year. Highways usually rank next each year, followed by welfare and by health and hospitals, but not always in that order.

The patterns of spending for other functions tend to vary considerably among the States. The variations depend largely upon the degree to which a given State is urbanized. Altogether, the States and their local units now spend approximately $100 billion annually for such items as the protection of persons and property, debt payments and interest, the development and conservation of natural resources, recreational facilities, correctional institutions, and general government.

---

[9] The preparation of the budget is a shared legislative and executive function in South Carolina and Texas; it is almost completely a legislative one in Mississippi.

SUMMARY

Money is just as essential to the existence of government at the State and local levels as it is to the National Government. And, just as the cost of government at the national level has increased markedly in the past few decades, so has the cost of State and local government.

Taxes are charges imposed by a legislative body upon persons or property to raise money for public purposes. The canons of sound taxation center around the four concepts of equality, certainty, convenience, and economy.

The United States Constitution, each State constitution, State laws, and city and county charters impose many limits on taxing powers.

The principal State and local tax sources include the property tax, the general and selective sales tax, the individual and corporation income tax, the inheritance or estate tax, and various business taxes and license taxes.

Nontax receipts come chiefly from federal grants and revenue sharing, government-operated businesses, and such other sources as court fines and the sale or leasing of public lands.

Borrowing, which is subject to strict limitations in most States, is only in a sense a nontax source of revenue.

Each State now has a budget system for the planned and more or less effective control of State finances. The budget-making process involves six steps: preparation of estimates, review of estimates, consolidation and presentation of the budget, consideration and adoption of the budget, execution of the budget, and a post-audit.

Approximately three-fourths of all State and local spending today goes for: education, highways, public welfare, and public health and hospitals. Of these, education is by far the most costly.

Concept Development

Questions for Review

1. State tax collections now come to approximately how much annually? Local tax collections?

2. Approximately how much do State and local governments receive from nontax sources annually?

3. The United States Constitution places what four major restrictions upon the taxing powers of the States and their local units?

4. What tax is the chief source of tax revenue among the States today?

5. What arguments are commonly made for and against the sales tax?

6. What two types of income tax are levied by the States today?

7. What tax is the chief source of income for local governments today?

8. Property taxes are commonly imposed on what two classes of property?

9. What arguments may be made for and against the property tax?

10. Why is the income tax widely regarded as the fairest possible tax by most authorities in the field?

11. Why do the States increasingly share their tax receipts with local units?

12. Approximately how great is the total amount of State indebtedness today? Local government indebtedness?

13. What is the purpose of a budget system?

14. What are the six major steps in a State's budget-making process?

15. What are the four costliest functions of State and local government?

For Further Inquiry

1. On page 771 we noted the fact that the sales tax is the single most important source of tax revenue among the 50 States today. It now accounts for approximately half of all of the tax monies the States now collect. But that is not the case in *each* of the States, of course. Most obviously, it is not the case in those five States which do not now levy a general sales tax. What are the major sources of tax revenue in your State? Which one of those taxes now produces the most income each year? Applying the four principles of sound taxation set out on page 771, how would you rate your State's tax structure?

2. Given the fact that both taxes are so regressive, why do the States continue to rely so heavily upon the sales tax and local governments upon the property tax?

3. What tax sources does your State allow to its cities? In what other ways does your State restrict the financial activities of cities?

Suggested Activities

1. Invite local tax officials to discuss their work with the class.

2. Stage a debate or class forum on the topic: *Resolved,* That this State abandon (adopt) the sales tax.

3. Identify and analyze each of the provisions of your State's constitution which relate to State and/or local finance.

4. Utilizing the six basic steps set out on page 778, detail the budget process in your State, county, and/or city. The most likely sources of useful information here will be the State budget director's office (the exact title and address can be obtained from the State Blue Book), the county courthouse, and city hall.

Suggested Reading

Berkley, George and Fox, Douglas, *80,000 Governments: The Politics of Subnational America.* Allyn and Bacon, 1978.

Berman, David R., *State and Local Politics.* Allyn and Bacon, 3rd ed., 1981.

Dye, Thomas R., *Politics in States and Communities.* Prentice-Hall, 4th ed., 1981.

Jarvis, Howard, *I'm Mad as Hell!* Times Books, 1979.

Lindblum, Richard W., *Financing and Managing State and Local Government.* Lexington Books, 1979.

Maxwell, James A. and Aronson, J. Richard, *Financing State and Local Governments.* Brookings, 3rd ed., 1977.

Palmer, Kenneth T., *State Politics in the United States.* St. Martin's, 2nd ed., 1977.

Press, Charles and VerBurg, Kenneth, *State and Community Governments in the Federal System.* Wiley, 1979.

Sharkansky, Ira, *The Maligned States.* McGraw-Hill, 2nd ed., 1977.

U.S. Bureau of the Census, *Compendium of State Government Finances, 1980.* Government Printing Office, 1981.

STOP THE PRESSES

Bury me on my face; for in a little while everything will be turned upside down.

DIOGENES

On this and the following page you will find a number of last-minute additions, changes, and corrections which, for reasons of timing, could not be included in the main body of the text itself.

■ ■ Some time during its 1981 term, the Supreme Court will decide *Chandler* v. *Florida.* It is yet another case involving a conflict between the constitutional guarantees of fair trial and of a free press. It poses this question: Does the televising of a criminal trial violate a defendant's 6th and 14th Amendment rights?

The case involves two Miami police officers who were convicted of burglary in 1977. Their prosecution attracted a high degree of public attention and was widely reported by the local news media. Over their objections, live television, radio, and still photographic coverage of courtroom proceedings was permitted.

Recall that the Court was faced with a similar case in *Estes* v. *Texas,* 1965. There it did reverse a swindler's conviction because it found that the in-court media coverage had been so disruptive as to make a fair trial impossible.

However, in deciding *Estes,* the Court did suggest the possibility that it might some day reach a different conclusion in a similar case: "the ever-advancing techniques of public communication and the adjustment of the public to its presence may bring about a change in the effect of telecasting upon the fairness of criminal trials."

The Court's decision in Chandler will have a broad impact. At least 28 States now permit at least some form of television coverage of courtroom proceedings—and that number has grown rapidly in the past few years. *Pages 162–168.*

■ ■ Another case before the Court in 1981 involves one of the Democratic National Committee's party reform rules. The case, *Democratic Party* v. *Wisconsin,* presents this question: Can a State require the Democratic Party to use an open primary as a part of the process of selecting its national convention delegates from that State?

As we note on page 369, one of the DNC's rules now provides that only Democrats may participate in the party's delegate selection processes. When the Wisconsin State legislature refused to change that State's presidential primary law to accommodate the new rule, the Democrats went to court.

The party lost in the State courts and appealed to the Supreme Court. In the meantime, the DNC granted the Wisconsin delegation an exemption to the rule and it was seated at the party's 1980 convention. *Pages 240, 243–246, 369–370.*

■ ■ Congress will reapportion the 435 seats in the House of Representatives among the 50 States in 1981. That redistribution will be made on the basis of the final results of the 1980 census and will become effective with the congressional elections to be held on November 2, 1982.

The Census Bureau's near-final figures indicate that 11 States will gain a total of 17 seats in the House and 10 others will lose that many.

Florida will pick up four new seats; Texas will gain three and California two; and Arizona, Colorado, Nevada, New Mexico, Oregon, Tennessee, Utah, and Washington, one apiece.

New York will lose five of its present seats; Illinois, Ohio, and Pennsylvania, two each; and Indiana, Massachusetts, Michigan, Missouri, New Jersey, and South Dakota, one apiece.

South Dakota's loss of one seat, and Nevada's gain of one seat, leaves the number of States with but one seat at six. *Pages 54, 287-292, 375-378, 544-545, 694.*

■ ■ Does the fact that television reports the results of presidential voting in the eastern States before the polls close in the West have an effect on voter behavior in the western States?

Many have long claimed that it does. Although there is little or no hard evidence to support their view, they insist that common sense suggests that the problem is real.

And they also insist that the networks' practice of making "projections" has the same impact. (Those projections are essentially predictions, made on the basis of partial returns. They are educated, computerized guesses as to the outcome of the presidential contest and other races on a State-by-State basis. Each of the networks relies on several factors when it makes those forecasts—principally, historic voting patterns, early returns, the results in pre-targeted precincts, and interviews of voters as they leave the polls.

The problem is far from new. It has been with us since the presidential election of 1960, at least. But it was brought to particular prominence on election night in 1980.

On the basis of their projections, the three major networks "declared" Ronald Reagan's victory shortly after 8:00 P.M., Eastern Standard Time. That was more than an hour before the polls closed in the Rocky Mountain States; and it was more than two hours before they closed in California, Oregon and Washington. And, to compound matters, President Carter conceded his defeat, on television, with more than an hour of voting time left on the West Coast.

An untold number of persons in the West, aware of those television reports, then did not vote. (And, of course, their failure to vote had an impact on other election contests being decided at the same time.)

Several bills aimed at this "time-zone fall-out problem" are now before Congress. Each of them proposes to meet it in one or more of three ways: (1) prohibit the broadcasting of presidential election results anywhere in the country until all polling places in all 50 States have closed; (2) forbid local election officials to release election results until all polling places everywhere have closed; (3) require that all polling places in all 50 States close at the same time.

Each of these approaches would produce its own problems. This is especially true of the first one, because it would raise serious 1st Amendment questions. *Pages 134-138, 221-224, 225-230, 248-250, 376-377, 566-567.*

The Declaration of Independence

In Congress, July 4, 1776

THE UNANIMOUS DECLARATION OF THE THIRTEEN UNITED STATES OF AMERICA

When in the Course of human events, it becomes necessary for one people to dissolve the political bands which have connected them with another, and to assume among the powers of the earth, the separate and equal station to which the Laws of Nature and of Nature's God entitle them, a decent respect to the opinions of mankind requires that they should declare the causes which impel them to the separation.

We hold these truths to be self-evident, that all men are created equal, that they are endowed by their Creator with certain unalienable Rights, that among these are Life, Liberty and the pursuit of Happiness. That to secure these rights, Governments are instituted among Men, deriving their just powers from the consent of the governed; That whenever any Form of Government becomes destructive of these ends it is the Right of the People to alter or to abolish it, and to institute new Government, laying its foundation on such principles and organizing its powers in such form, as to them shall seem most likely to effect their Safety and Happiness. Prudence, indeed, will dictate that Governments long established should not be changed for light and transient causes; and accordingly all experience hath shown, that mankind are more disposed to suffer, while evils are sufferable, than to right themselves by abolishing the forms to which they are accustomed. But when a long train of abuses and usurpations, pursuing invariably the same Objects evinces a design to reduce them under absolute Despotism, it is their right, it is their duty, to throw off such Government, and to provide new Guards for their future security.—Such has been the patient sufferance of these Colonies; and such is now the necessity which constrains them to alter their former Systems of Government. The history of the present King of Great Britain is a history of repeated injuries and usurpations, all having in direct object the establishment of an absolute Tyranny over these States. To prove this, let Facts be submitted to a candid world.

He has refused his Assent to Laws, the most wholesome and necessary for the public good.

He has forbidden his Governors to pass Laws of immediate and pressing importance, unless suspended in their operation till his Assent should be obtained; and when so suspended, he has utterly neglected to attend to them.

He has refused to pass other Laws for the accommodation of large districts of people, unless those people would relinquish the right of Representation in the Legislature, a right inestimable to them and formidable to tyrants only.

He has called together legislative bodies at places unusual, uncomfortable, and distant from the depository of their public records, for the sole purpose of fatiguing them into compliance with his measures.

He has dissolved Representative Houses repeatedly, for opposing with manly firmness his invasions on the rights of the people.

He has refused for a long time, after such dissolutions, to cause others to be elected; whereby the Legislative powers, incapable of Annihilation, have returned to the People at large for their exercise; the State remaining in the mean time exposed to all the dangers of invasions from without, and convulsions within.

He has endeavored to prevent the population of these States; for that purpose obstructing the Laws for Naturalization of Foreigners; refusing to pass others to encourage their migration hither, and raising the conditions of new Appropriations of Lands.

He has obstructed the Administration of Justice, by refusing his Assent to Laws for establishing Judiciary powers.

He has made Judges dependent on his Will alone for the tenure of their offices, and the amount and payment of their salaries.

He has erected a multitude of New Offices, and sent hither swarms of Officers to harass our people and eat out their substance.

He has kept among us in times of peace, Standing Armies, without the Consent of our legislatures.

He has affected to render the Military independent of, and superior to, the Civil power.

He has combined with others to subject us to a jurisdiction foreign to our constitutions, and unacknowledged by our laws; giving his Assent to their Acts of pretended Legislation:

For quartering large bodies of armed troops among us;

For protecting them, by a mock Trial, from punishment for any Murders which they should commit on the Inhabitants of these States;

For cutting off our Trade with all parts of the world;

For imposing Taxes on us without our Consent;

For depriving us, in many cases, of the benefits of Trial by Jury;

For transporting us beyond Seas, to be tried for pretended offenses;

For abolishing the free System of English Laws in a neighboring Province, establishing therein an Arbitrary government, and enlarging its Boundaries, so as to render it at once an example and fit instrument for introducing the same absolute rule into these Colonies;

For taking away our Charters, abolishing our most valuable Laws, and altering, fundamentally, the Forms of our Governments;

For suspending our own Legislatures, and declaring themselves invested with Power to legislate for us in all cases whatsoever.

He has abdicated Government here, by declaring us out of his Protection, and waging War against us.

He has plundered our seas, ravaged our Coasts, burned our towns, and destroyed the lives of our people.

He is at this time transporting large Armies of foreign Mercenaries to complete the works of death, desolation and tyranny, already begun with circumstances of Cruelty and perfidy scarcely paralleled in the most barbarous ages, and totally unworthy the Head of a civilized nation.

He has constrained our fellow Citizens taken Captive on the high Seas to bear Arms against their Country, to become the executioners of their friends and Brethren, or to fall themselves by their Hands.

He has excited domestic insurrections amongst us, and has endeavored to bring on the inhabitants of our frontiers the merciless Indian Savages whose known rule of warfare is an undistinguished destruction of all ages, sexes, and conditions.

In every stage of these Oppressions We have Petitioned for Redress in the most humble terms. Our repeated Petitions have been answered only by repeated injury. A Prince whose character is thus marked by every act which may define a Tyrant, is unfit to be the ruler of a free people.

Nor have We been wanting in attentions to our British brethren. We have warned them from time to time of attempts by their legislature to extend an unwarrantable jurisdiction over us. We have reminded them of the circumstances of our emigration and settlement here. We have appealed to their native justice and magnanimity, and we have conjured them by the ties of our common kindred to disavow these usurpations, which, would inevitably interrupt our connections and correspondence. They too have been deaf to the voice of justice and of consanguinity. We must, therefore, acquiesce in the necessity, which denounces our Separation, and hold them, as we hold the rest of mankind, Enemies in War, in Peace Friends.—

We, therefore, the Representatives of the United States of America, in General Congress, Assembled, appealing to the Supreme Judge of the world for the rectitude of our intentions, do, in the Name, and by the Authority of the good People of these Colonies, solemnly publish and declare, That these United Colonies are, and of right ought to be Free and Independent States; that they are Absolved from all Allegiance to the British Crown, and that all political connection between them and the State of Great Britain, is and ought to be totally dissolved, and that as Free and Independent States, they have full Power to levy War, conclude Peace, contract Alliances, establish Commerce, and to do all other Acts and Things which Independent States may of right do. And for the support of this Declaration, with a firm reliance on the protection of Divine Providence, we mutually pledge to each other our Lives, our Fortunes and our sacred Honor.

JOHN HANCOCK

New Hampshire

Josiah Bartlett
William Whipple
Matthew Thornton

Massachusetts Bay

Samuel Adams
John Adams
Robert Treat Paine
Elbridge Gerry

Rhode Island

Stephen Hopkins
William Ellery

Connecticut

Roger Sherman
Samuel Huntington
William Williams
Oliver Wolcott

New York

William Floyd
Philip Livingston
Francis Lewis
Lewis Morris

New Jersey

Richard Stockton
John Witherspoon
Francis Hopkinson
John Hart
Abraham Clark

Pennsylvania

Robert Morris
Benjamin Rush
Benjamin Franklin
John Morton
George Clymer
James Smith
George Taylor
James Wilson
George Ross

Delaware

Caesar Rodney
George Read
Thomas M'Kean

Maryland

Samuel Chase
William Paca
Thomas Stone
*Charles Carroll of
  Carrollton*

Virginia

George Wythe
Richard Henry Lee
Thomas Jefferson
Benjamin Harrison
Thomas Nelson, Jr.
Francis Lightfoot Lee
Carter Braxton

North Carolina

William Hooper
Joseph Hewes
John Penn

South Carolina

Edward Rutledge
Thomas Heyward, Jr.
Thomas Lynch, Jr.
Arthur Middleton

Georgia

Button Gwinnett
Lyman Hall
George Walton

An Outline of The Constitution of the United States

The Constitution of the United States of America

Preamble

We the People of the United States, in Order to form a more perfect Union, establish Justice, insure domestic Tranquility, provide for the common defence, promote the general Welfare, and secure the Blessings of Liberty to ourselves and our Posterity, do ordain and establish this Constitution for the United States of America.

Article I

LEGISLATIVE DEPARTMENT

SECTION 1. *Legislative Power; the Congress*

All legislative powers herein granted shall be vested in a Congress of the United States, which shall consist of a Senate and House of Representatives.

SECTION 2. *House of Representatives*

1. The House of Representatives shall be composed of members chosen every second year by the people of the several States, and the electors in each State shall have the qualifications requisite for electors of the most numerous branch of the State legislature.[1]

2. No person shall be a Representative who shall not have attained to the age of twenty-five years, and been seven years a citizen of the United States, and who shall not, when elected, be an inhabitant of that State in which he shall be chosen.[2]

3. Representatives and direct taxes[3] shall be apportioned among the several States which may be included within this Union, according to their respective numbers, [which shall be determined by adding to the whole number of free persons, including those bound to service for a term of years][4] and excluding Indians not taxed, [three-fifths of all other persons].[5] The actual enumeration shall be made within three years after the first meeting of the Congress of the United States, and within every subsequent term of ten years, in such manner as they shall by law direct. The number of Representatives shall not exceed one for every thirty thousand,[6] but each State shall have at least one Representative; [and, until such enumeration shall be made, the State of New Hampshire shall be entitled to choose three, Massachusetts eight, Rhode Island and Providence Plantations one, Connecticut five, New York six, New Jersey four, Pennsylvania eight, Delaware

---

[1] "Electors" means voters. Each State must permit the same persons to vote for United States Representatives as it permits to vote for the members of the larger house of its own legislature. The 17th Amendment (1913) extended this requirement to the qualification of voters for United States Senators.

[2] In addition, political custom requires that a Representative also reside in the district in which he or she is elected. The first woman to serve in the House, Jeannette Rankin (1881–1973), was elected from Montana in 1916; she did not seek re-election in 1918 but did run for and win a second term in 1940.

[3] Modified by the 16th Amendment (1913) which provides for an income tax as an express exception to this restriction.

[4] Altered by the 14th Amendment (1868).

[5] The phrase refers to slaves and was rescinded by the 13th Amendment (1865) and the 14th Amendment (1868).

[6] The Constitution does not set a specific size for the House; rather, Congress does so when it reapportions the seats among the States after each census. It fixed the "permanent" size at 435 members in the Reapportionment Act of 1929; see pages 287–289. Today (1981) there is one House seat for approximately every 500,000 persons in the population.

one, Maryland six, Virginia ten, North Carolina five, South Carolina five, and Georgia three].[7]

4. When vacancies happen in the representation from any State, the executive authority thereof shall issue writs of election to fill such vacancies.

5. The House of Representatives shall choose their Speaker[8] and other officers; and shall have the sole power of impeachment.[9]

SECTION 3. *Senate*

1. The Senate of the United States shall be composed of two Senators from each State [chosen by the legislature thereof][10] for six years; and each Senator shall have one vote.

2. Immediately after they shall be assembled in consequences of the first election, they shall be divided, as equally as may be, into three classes. The seats of the Senators of the first class shall be vacated at the expiration of the second year; of the second class, at the expiration of the fourth year; and of the third class, at the expiration of the sixth year; so that one-third may be chosen every second year; [and if vacancies happen by resignation, or otherwise, during the recess of the legislature of any State, the executive thereof may make temporary appointments until the next meeting of the legislature, which shall then fill such vacancies.][11]

3. No person shall be a Senator who shall not have attained to the age of thirty years, and been nine years a citizen of the United States, who shall not, when elected, be an inhabitant of that State for which he shall be chosen.

4. The Vice President of the United States shall be President of the Senate, but shall have no vote, unless they be equally divided.

5. The Senate shall choose their other officers, and also a President *pro tempore*, in the absence of the Vice President, or when he shall exercise the office of President of the United States.

6. The Senate shall have the sole power to try all impeachments. When sitting for that purpose, they shall be on oath or affirmation. When the President of the United States is tried, the Chief Justice shall preside; and no person shall be convicted without the concurrence of two-thirds of the members present.[12]

7. Judgment in cases of impeachment shall not extend further than to removal from office, and disqualification to hold and enjoy any office of honor, trust, or profit under the United States; but the party convicted shall, nevertheless, be liable and subject to indictment, trial, judgment, and punishment, according to law.

SECTION 4. *Elections and Meetings*

1. The times, places, and manner of holding elections for Senators and Representatives, shall be prescribed in each State by the legislature thereof: but the Congress may at any time, by law, make or alter such regulations, except as to the places of choosing Senators.[13]

2. The Congress shall assemble at least once in every year, [and such meeting shall be on the first Monday in December,][14] unless they shall by law appoint a different day.

SECTION 5. *Legislative Proceedings*

1. Each House shall be the judge of the elections, returns, and qualifications of its own members,[15] and a majority of each shall constitute a quorum to do business; but a smaller number may adjourn from day to day, and may be authorized to compel the attendance of absent members, in such manner, and under such penalties, as each House may provide.

---

[7] Temporary provision.

[8] Although the Constitution does not require it, the House always chooses the Speaker from among its own members.

[9] Impeachment here means *accusation*. The House has the exclusive power to *impeach* (accuse) civil officers; the Senate (Article I, Section 3, Clause 6) has the exclusive power to *try* those impeached by the House.

[10] Modified by the 17th Amendment (1913), which provides for the popular election of Senators.

[11] Modified by the 17th Amendment (1913), which provides for the filling of vacancies by election and (if a State chooses) by a temporary gubernatorial appointment to fill the vacancy until the election.

---

[12] Those who object on religious grounds to the taking of an oath (for example, Quakers) are permitted to "affirm" rather than "swear."

The required "two-thirds of the members present" must be at least a quorum (Article I, Section 5, Clause 1). A quorum (the number of members who must be present in order to conduct business) is 51 in the Senate and 218 in the House.

[13] In 1842 Congress required that Representatives be elected from districts within each State with more than one Representative. Alaska, Delaware, Nevada, North Dakota, Vermont, and Wyoming today (1981) have but one seat each. Beginning in 1983 (following the 1981 reapportionment and the 1982 elections), South Dakota will also have but one seat in the House. In 1842, Congress directed that Representatives and, in 1914, that Senators be chosen on the Tuesday after the first Monday in November of every even-numbered year. By special dispensation Maine was allowed to hold congressional elections in September but abandoned the practice beginning in 1960.

[14] Superseded by the 20th Amendment (1933), which fixes the date January 3rd.

[15] In 1969 the Supreme Court held that the House cannot exclude any member-elect who satisfies the qualifications set out in Article I, Section 2, Clause 2; see page 292.

2. Each House may determine the rules of its proceedings, punish its members for disorderly behavior, and, with the concurrence of two-thirds, expel a member.

3. Each House shall keep a journal of its proceedings, and, from time to time, publish the same, excepting such parts as may, in their judgment, require secrecy; and the yeas and nays of the members of either House, on any question, shall, at the desire of one-fifth of those present, be entered on the journal.

4. Neither House, during the session of Congress, shall, without the consent of the other, adjourn for more than three days, nor to any other place than that in which the two Houses shall be sitting.

SECTION 6. *Compensation, Immunities, and Disabilities of Members*

1. The Senators and Representatives shall receive a compensation for their services, to be ascertained by law, and paid out of the treasury of the United States. They shall, in all cases, except treason, felony, and breach of the peace,[16] be privileged from arrest during their attendance at the session of their respective Houses, and in going to, and returning from, the same; and for any speech or debate in either House, they shall not be questioned in any other place.[17]

2. No Senator or Representative shall, during the time for which he was elected, be appointed to any civil office under the authority of the United States, which shall have been created, or the emoluments whereof shall have been increased during such time;[18] and no person, holding any office under the United States, shall be a member of either House during his continuance in office.

SECTION 7. *Revenue Bills, President's Veto*

1. All bills for raising revenue shall originate in the House of Representatives; but the Senate may propose or concur with amendments as on other bills.

2. Every bill which shall have passed the House of Representatives and the Senate, shall, before it become a law, be presented to the President of the United States; if he approve, he shall sign it, but if not, he shall return it, with his objections, to that House in which it shall have originated, who shall enter the objections at large on their journal, and proceed to reconsider it.[19] If, after such reconsideration, two-thirds of that House shall agree to pass the bill, it shall be sent, together with the objections, to the other House, by which it shall likewise be reconsidered, and, if approved by two-thirds of that House, it shall become a law. But in all such cases the votes of both Houses shall be determined by yeas and nays, and the names of the persons voting for and against the bill shall be entered on the journal of each House respectively. If any bill shall not be returned by the President within ten days (Sunday excepted) after it shall have been presented to him, the same shall be a law, in like manner as if he had signed it, unless the Congress, by their adjournment, prevent its return, in which case it shall not be a law.

3. Every order, resolution,[20] or vote, to which the concurrence of the Senate and House of Representatives may be necessary (except on a question of adjournment), shall be presented to the President of the United States; and before the same shall take effect, shall be approved by him, or, being disapproved by him, shall be repassed by two-thirds of the Senate and House of Representatives, according to the rules and limitations prescribed in the case of a bill.

SECTION 8. *Powers of Congress*

The Congress shall have power:

1. To lay and collect taxes, duties, imposts, and excises, to pay the debts, and provide for the common defence and general welfare of the United States; but all duties, imposts, and excises, shall be uniform throughout the United States;

2. To borrow money on the credit of the United States;

3. To regulate commerce with foreign nations, and among the several States, and with the Indian tribes;

---

16 *Treason* is strictly defined in Article III, Section 3. A *felony* is any serious crime. A *breach of the peace* is any indictable offense less than treason or a felony; hence this exemption from arrest is of little real importance today.

17 This "cloak of legislative immunity" extends to committee rooms and official publications of Congress, such as the *Congressional Record* and committee reports—but it does not extend to outside speech or publication.

18 In 1909 President Taft appointed Philander C. Knox as Secretary of State. His eligibility for the post was challenged because Congress had raised Cabinet officers' salaries while Knox was in the Senate. Congress resolved the problem by reducing the pay of the Secretary of State to its former figure. This same procedure has been followed twice since: in 1973, when President Nixon appointed Senator William B. Saxbe Attorney General; and in 1980, when President Carter appointed Senator Edmund Muskie Secretary of State.

19 The President must accept or reject a bill in its entirety; the President does not possess an *item veto*; see pages 410, 716.

20 *Concurrent resolutions* (which usually relate to the internal management of Congress—for example, creating a joint committee) do not have the force of law and so are not submitted to the President; nor are joint resolutions which propose amendments to the Constitution.

4. To establish a uniform rule of naturalization, and uniform laws on the subject of bankruptcies, throughout the United States;

5. To coin money, regulate the value thereof, and of foreign coin, and fix the standard of weights and measures;

6. To provide for the punishment of counterfeiting the securities and current coin of the United States;

7. To establish post offices and post roads;[21]

8. To promote the progress of science and useful arts, by securing, for limited times, to authors and inventors, the exclusive right to their respective writings and discoveries;

9. To constitute tribunals inferior to the Supreme Court;

10. To define and punish piracies and felonies, committed on the high seas, and offences against the law of nations;

11. To declare war, grant letters of marque and reprisal,[22] and make rules concerning captures on land and water;

12. To raise and support armies; but no appropriation of money to that use shall be for a longer term than two years;

13. To provide and maintain a navy;

14. To make rules for the government and regulation of the land and naval forces;

15. To provide for calling forth the militia to execute the laws of the Union, suppress insurrections, and repel invasions;

16. To provide for organizing, arming, and disciplining the militia, and for governing such part of them as may be employed in the service of the United States, reserving to the States respectively the appointment of the officers, and the authority of training the militia, according to the discipline prescribed by Congress;

17. To exercise exclusive legislation in all cases whatsoever, over such district (not exceeding ten miles square) as may, by cession of particular States, and the acceptance of Congress, become the seat of the Government of the United States, and to exercise like authority over all places, purchased by the consent of the legislature of the State in which the same shall be, for the erection of forts, magazines, arsenals, dockyards, and other needful buildings;—And

18. To make all laws which shall be necessary and proper for carrying into execution the foregoing powers, and all other powers vested by this Constitution in the Government of the United States, or in any department or officer thereof.[23]

SECTION 9. *Powers Denied to Congress*

[1. The migration or importation of such persons as any of the States now existing shall think proper to admit, shall not be prohibited by the Congress prior to the year one thousand eight hundred and eight; but a tax or duty may be imposed on such importation, not exceeding ten dollars for each person.][24]

2. The privilege of the writ of *habeas corpus*[25] shall not be suspended, unless when, in cases of rebellion or invasion, the public safety may require it.

3. No bill of attainder or *ex post facto* law shall be passed.[26]

4. No capitation, or other direct tax, shall be laid, unless in proportion to the census or enumeration hereinbefore directed to be taken.[27]

5. No tax or duty shall be laid on articles exported from any State.

---

[21] "Post" comes from the French *poste* meaning mail; "post roads" are those routes such as turnpikes, canals, rivers, streets, paths, and airways over which the mail is carried.

This power, "to establish post offices," which was granted to Congress, continued the precedent that had been established under the Articles of Confederation.

[22] *Marque* is the French for "boundary"; the word "reprisal" comes from the French *représaille*, meaning retaliation. Hence, originally "letters of marque and reprisal" were licenses to cross the boundary into an enemy country to capture or destroy. As used here it means a commission authorizing private citizens to fit out vessels (privateers) to capture or destroy in time of war. They are forbidden in international law by the Declaration of Paris, 1856, to the principles of which the United States subscribes.

[23] This is the Necessary and Proper Clause—or, as it is also known, the Elastic Clause. *Necessary* here does not mean absolutely or indispensably necessary, but rather *appropriate*. The Clause has made it possible for Congress and the courts to extend the meanings of other provisions in the Constitution. The constitutional basis for the existence of the *implied powers*, those which are not specifically stated in the Constitution but which may be reasonably implied from the expressed powers, is found in this Clause.

[24] Temporary provision; the phrase "such persons" was a euphemism (an agreeable substitute) for "slaves."

[25] A *writ of habeas corpus*, the "great writ of liberty," is a court order directing a sheriff, warden, or other public officer, or a private person, who is detaining another person to "produce the body" of the one being held in order that the legality of the detention may be determined by the court; see page 160.

[26] A *bill of attainder* is a legislative act which inflicts punishment without a judicial trial. See Article I, Section 10, and Article III, Section 3, Clause 2. An *ex post facto* law is any criminal law which operates retroactively to the disadvantage of the accused. See Article I, Section 10. See also page 161.

[27] See note 3, page 788, and the 16th Amendment (1913) which permits the levying of an income tax without regard to this prohibition.

6. No preference shall be given by any regulation of commerce or revenue to the ports of one State over those of another; nor shall vessels bound to, or from, one State, be obliged to enter, clear, or pay duties, in another.

7. No money shall be drawn from the treasury, but in consequence of appropriations made by law; and a regular statement and account of the receipts and expenditures of all public money shall be published from time to time.

8. No title of nobility shall be granted by the United States; and no person holding any office of profit or trust under them shall, without the consent of the Congress, accept of any present, emolument, office, or title, of any kind whatever, from any king, prince, or foreign state.

SECTION 10. *Powers Denied to the States*

1. No State shall enter into any treaty, alliance, or confederation; grant letters of marque and reprisal; coin money; emit bills of credit;[28] make anything but gold and silver coin a tender in payment of debts; pass any bill of attainder, *ex post facto* law, or law impairing the obligations of contracts, or grant any title of nobility.

2. No State shall, without the consent of the Congress, lay any imposts or duties on imports or exports, except what may be absolutely necessary for executing its inspection laws; and the net produce of all duties and imposts, laid by any State on imports or exports, shall be for the use of the treasury of the United States; and all such laws shall be subject to the revision and control of the Congress.

3. No State shall, without the consent of Congress, lay any duty of tonnage,[29] keep troops, or ships of war, in time of peace, enter into any agreement or compact with another State, or with a foreign power, or engage in war, unless actually invaded, or in such imminent danger as will not admit of delay.

Article II

EXECUTIVE DEPARTMENT

SECTION 1. *Term, Election, Qualifications, Salary, Oath of Office*

1. The executive power shall be vested in a President of the United States of America. He shall hold his office during the term of four years,[30] and together with the Vice President, chosen for the same term, be elected as follows:

2. Each State shall appoint, in such manner as the legislature thereof may direct, a number of Electors, equal to the whole number of Senators and Representatives, to which the State may be entitled in the Congress; but no Senator or Representative, or person holding an office of trust or profit, under the United States, shall be appointed an Elector.

[3. The Electors shall meet in their respective States, and vote by ballot for two persons, of whom one, at least, shall not be an inhabitant of the same State with themselves. And they shall make a list of all the persons voted for, and of the number of votes for each; which list they shall sign and certify, and transmit, sealed, to the seat of the Government of the United States, directed to the President of the Senate. The President of the Senate shall, in the presence of the Senate and House of Representatives, open all the certificates, and the votes shall then be counted. The person having the greatest number of votes shall be the President, if such number be a majority of the whole number of Electors appointed; and if there be more than one, who have such majority, and have an equal number of votes, then, the House of Representatives shall immediately choose, by ballot, one of them for President; and if no person have a majority, then, from the five highest on the list, the said House shall, in like manner, choose the President. But in choosing the President, the votes shall be taken by States, the representation from each State having one vote; a quorum for this purpose shall consist of a member or members from two-thirds of the States, and a majority of all the States shall be necessary to a choice. In every case, after the choice of the President, the person having the greatest number of votes of the Electors shall be the Vice President. But if there should remain two or more who have equal votes, the Senate shall choose from them, by ballot, the Vice President.][31]

4. The Congress may determine the time of choosing the Electors, and the day on which they shall give their votes; which day shall be the same throughout the United States.[32]

---

[28] The phrase "bills of credit" means paper money; "tender" means *legal tender*—any kind of money that must by law be accepted in payment of a monetary debt.

[29] *Tonnage* is a vessel's internal cubical capacity in tons of one hundred cubic feet each. Tonnage duties are duties upon vessels in proportion to their capacity. These duties are paid as a ship enters a port.

[30] The Constitution did not originally set a limit to the number of times a person may be elected President. The 22nd Amendment (1951) now limits a President to two terms or not more than 10 years in office.

[31] Superseded by the 12th Amendment (1804).

[32] Congress has set the date for the choosing of electors as the Tuesday after the first Monday in November every fourth year and for the casting of electoral votes as the Monday after the second Wednesday in December of that year.

5. No person, except a natural-born citizen, or a citizen of the United States at the time of the adoption of this Constitution, shall be eligible to the office of President; neither shall any person be eligible to that office, who shall not have attained to the age of thirty-five years, and been fourteen years a resident within the United States.

6. In case of the removal of the President from office, or of his death, resignation, or inability to discharge the powers and duties of the said office, the same shall devolve on the Vice President, and the Congress may by law provide for the case of removal, death, resignation or inability, both of the President and Vice President, declaring what officer shall then act as President, and such officer shall act accordingly, until the disability be removed, or a President shall be elected.[33]

7. The President shall, at stated times, receive for his services a compensation, which shall neither be increased nor diminished during the period for which he shall have been elected, and he shall not receive, within that period, any other emolument from the United States, or any of them.

8. Before he enter on the execution of his office, he shall take the following oath or affirmation:

"I do solemnly swear (or affirm), that I will faithfully execute the office of President of the United States, and will, to the best of my ability, preserve, protect, and defend the Constitution of the United States."

SECTION 2. *President's Powers and Duties*

1. The President shall be Commander in Chief of the army and navy of the United States, and of the militia of the several States, when called into the actual service of the United States; he may require the opinion, in writing, of the principal officer in each of the executive departments upon any subject relating to the duties of their respective offices,[34] and he shall have power to grant reprieves and pardons[35] for offences against the United States, except in cases of impeachment.

2. He shall have power, by and with the advice and consent of the Senate, to make treaties, provided two-thirds of the Senators present concur; and he shall, nominate, and, by and with the advice and

consent of the Senate, shall appoint ambassadors, other public ministers, and consuls, judges of the Supreme Court, and all other officers of the United States whose appointments are not herein otherwise provided for, and which shall be established by law; but the Congress may by law vest the appointment of such inferior officers, as they think proper, in the President alone, in the courts of law, or in the heads of departments.

3. The President shall have power to fill up all vacancies that may happen during the recess of the Senate, by granting commissions which shall expire at the end of their next session.

SECTION 3. *President's Powers and Duties*

He shall, from time to time, give to the Congress information of the state of the Union, and recommend to their consideration such measures as he shall judge necessary and expedient; he may, on extraordinary occasions, convene both Houses, or either of them, and in case of disagreement between them, with respect to the time of adjournment, he may adjourn them to such time as he shall think proper; he shall receive ambassadors and other public ministers; he shall take care that the laws be faithfully executed, and shall commission all the officers of the United States.

SECTION 4. *Impeachment*

The President, Vice President, and all civil officers[36] of the United States, shall be removed from office on impeachment for, and conviction of, treason, bribery, or other high crimes and misdemeanors.

Article III

JUDICIAL DEPARTMENT

SECTION 1. *Courts, Terms of Office*

The judicial power of the United States shall be vested in one Supreme Court, and in such inferior courts as the Congress may from time to time ordain and establish. The judges, both of the Supreme and inferior courts, shall hold their offices during good behavior, and shall, at stated times, receive for their services a compensation which shall not be diminished during their continuance in office.

SECTION 2. *Jurisdiction*

1. The judicial power shall extend to all cases, in law and equity, arising under this Constitution, the

---

[33] Modified by the 25th Amendment (1967), which provides expressly for the succession of the Vice President, for the filling of a vacancy in the Vice Presidency, and for the determination of presidential inability.

[34] The only authority in the Constitution for the President's Cabinet. There is no act of Congress which defines the membership of the Cabinet; rather, the matter is subject to the President's discretion.

[35] A *reprieve* is the postponing of the execution of a sentence; a *pardon* is legal (but not moral) forgiveness for an offense. The President may grant reprieves or pardons only in federal cases.

[36] *Civil officers* subject to impeachment include all officers of the United States who hold their appointments from the National Government, high or low, and whose duties are executive or judicial. Officers in the armed services are not civil officers; neither are Senators and Representatives so considered. Instead of the impeachment process, either house of Congress may expel one of its own members by a two-thirds vote (Article I, Section 5, Clause 2).

laws of the United States, and treaties made, or which shall be made, under their authority; to all cases affecting ambassadors, other public ministers, and consuls; to all cases of admiralty and maritime jurisdiction; to controversies to which the United States shall be a party; to controversies between two or more States, between a State and citizens of another State, between citizens of different States, between citizens of the same State claiming lands under grants of different States, and between a State, or the citizens thereof, and foreign states, citizens, or subjects.[37]

2. In all cases affecting ambassadors, other public ministers and consuls, and those in which a State shall be a party, the Supreme Court shall have original jurisdiction. In all the other cases before mentioned, the Supreme Court shall have appellate jurisdiction, both as to law and fact, with such exceptions and under such regulations as the Congress shall make.

3. The trial of all crimes, except in cases of impeachment, shall be by jury; and such trial shall be held in the State where the said crimes shall have been committed; but when not committed within any State the trial shall be at such place or places as the Congress may by law have directed.[38]

Section 3. *Treason*

1. Treason against the United States shall consist only in levying war against them, or in adhering to their enemies, giving them aid and comfort. No person shall be convicted of treason unless on the testimony of two witnesses to the same overt act, or on confession in open court.

2. The Congress shall have power to declare the punishment of treason, but no attainder of treason shall work corruption of blood, or forfeiture except during the life of the person attained.[39]

---

[37] Restricted by the 11th Amendment (1795).

[38] Trial by jury is here guaranteed in federal courts only. The right to trial by jury in *serious* criminal cases in the *State* courts is guaranteed by the 6th and 14th Amendments (see note 49, page 796). Crimes committed on the high seas or in the air are tried in the United States District Court for the judicial district in which the offender is landed or in which the offender is first apprehended.

[39] These very specific provisions are intended to prevent indiscriminate use of the charge of treason. The law of treason covers all American citizens, at home or abroad, and all permanent resident aliens. The maximum penalty is death, but no person convicted of the crime has ever been executed by the United States. Note that treason may be committed only in wartime; but Congress has also made it a crime for any person (in either peace or wartime) to commit espionage or sabotage, to attempt to overthrow the government by force, or to conspire to do any of these things.

Article IV

RELATIONS OF STATES

Section 1. *Full Faith and Credit*

Full faith and credit shall be given in each State to the public acts, records, and judicial proceedings of every other State. And the Congress may, by general laws, prescribe the manner in which such acts, records, and proceedings shall be proved, and the effect thereof.

Section 2. *Privileges and Immunities of Citizens*

1. The citizens of each State shall be entitled to all privileges and immunities of citizens in the several States.[40]

2. A person charged in any State with treason, felony, or other crime, who shall flee from justice, and be found in another State, shall, on demand of the executive authority of the State from which he fled, be delivered up, to be removed to the State having jurisdiction of the crime.[41]

3. No person held to service or labor in one State, under the laws thereof, escaping into another, shall, in consequence of any law or regulation therein, be discharged from such service or labor, but shall be delivered up on claim of the party to whom such service or labor may be due.[42]

Section 3. *New States; Territories*

1. New States may be admitted by the Congress into this Union; but no new State shall be formed or erected within the jurisdiction of any other State, nor any State be formed by the junction of two or more States, or parts of States, without the consent of the legislatures of the States concerned as well as of the Congress.

2. The Congress shall have power to dispose of and make all needful rules and regulations respecting the territory or other property belonging to the United States; and nothing in this Constitution shall be so construed as to prejudice any claims of the United States, or of any particular State.

Section 4. *Protection Afforded to States by the Nation*

The United States shall guarantee to every State in this Union a republican form of government, and

---

[40] The meaning is made more explicit by the 14th Amendment (1868).

[41] This section provides for what is known as *interstate rendition* or *extradition*. Although the Constitution here says the fugitive "shall . . . be delivered up" custom and court decisions have changed it to read "*may* . . . be delivered up." Governors sometimes refuse to return a fugitive.

[42] The phrase "person held to service" referred to slaves. Since the ratification of the 13th Amendment in 1865, the Fugitive Slave Clause has been of historical interest only.

shall protect each of them against invasion; and on application of the legislature, or of the executive (when the legislature cannot be convened), against domestic violence.

Article V

PROVISIONS FOR AMENDMENT

The Congress, whenever two-thirds of both Houses shall deem it necessary, shall propose amendments to this Constitution, or, on the application of the legislatures of two-thirds of the several States, shall call a convention for proposing amendments, which, in either case, shall be valid, to all intents and purposes, as part of this Constitution, when ratified by the legislatures of three-fourths of the several States, or by conventions in three-fourths thereof, as the one or the other mode of ratification may be proposed by the Congress; provided [that no amendment which may be made prior to the year one thousand eight hundred and eight shall in any manner affect the first and fourth clauses in the ninth section of the first Article;][43] and that no State, without its consent, shall be deprived of its equal suffrage in the Senate.

Article VI

NATIONAL DEBTS, SUPREMACY OF NATIONAL LAW, OATH

SECTION 1. *Validity of Debts*

All debts contracted and engagements entered into, before the adoption of this Constitution, shall be as valid against the United States under this Constitution, as under the Confederation.

SECTION 2. *Supremacy of National Law*

This Constitution, and the laws of the United States which shall be made in pursuance thereof, and all treaties made, or which shall be made, under the authority of the United States, shall be the supreme law of the land; and the judges in every State shall be bound thereby, anything in the constitution or laws of any State to the contrary notwithstanding.

SECTION 3. *Oaths of Office*

The Senators and Representatives before mentioned, and the members of the several State legislatures, and all executive and judicial officers, both of the United States and of the several States, shall be bound, by oath or affirmation, to support this Constitution; but no religious test shall ever be required as a qualification to any office or public trust under the United States.

Article VII

RATIFICATION OF CONSTITUTION

The ratification of the conventions of nine States shall be sufficient for the establishment of this Constitution between the States so ratifying the same.[44]

Done in Convention, by the unanimous consent of the States present, the seventeenth day of September, in the year of our Lord one thousand seven hundred and eighty-seven, and of the Independence of the United States of America the twelfth. *In Witness* whereof, we have hereunto subscribed our names.

Attest: *William Jackson,* SECRETARY
　　　George Washington
　　　PRESIDENT AND DEPUTY FROM VIRGINIA

NEW HAMPSHIRE	NEW JERSEY	DELAWARE	NORTH CAROLINA
John Langdon	*William Livingston*	*George Read*	*William Blount*
Nicholas Gilman	*David Brearley*	*Gunning Bedford, Jr.*	*Richard Dobbs Spaight*
	William Paterson	*John Dickinson*	*Hugh Williamson*
MASSACHUSETTS	*Jonathan Dayton*	*Richard Bassett*	
Nathaniel Gorham		*Jacob Broom*	SOUTH CAROLINA
Rufus King	PENNSYLVANIA		*John Rutledge*
	Benjamin Franklin	MARYLAND	*Charles Cotesworth Pinckney*
CONNECTICUT	*Thomas Mifflin*	*James McHenry*	*Charles Pinckney*
William Samuel Johnson	*Robert Morris*	*Dan of St. Thomas Jennifer*	*Pierce Butler*
Roger Sherman	*George Clymer*	*Daniel Carroll*	
	Thomas Fitzsimons		GEORGIA
NEW YORK	*Jared Ingersoll*	VIRGINIA	*William Few*
Alexander Hamilton	*James Wilson*	*John Blair*	*Abraham Baldwin*
	Gouverneur Morris	*James Madison, Jr.*	

---

[43] Temporary provision, relating particularly to the slave trade.

[44] Ratified by the ninth State on June 21, 1788, but not immediately effective; see page 58.

AMENDMENTS

1ST AMENDMENT. *Freedom of Religion, Speech, Press, Assembly, and Petition*[45]

Congress shall make no law respecting an establishment of religion, or prohibiting the free exercise thereof; or abridging the freedom of speech, or of the press; or the right of the people peaceably to assemble, and to petition the government for a redress of grievances.

2ND AMENDMENT. *Bearing Arms*

A well-regulated militia being necessary to the security of a free state, the right of the people to keep and bear arms shall not be infringed.

3RD AMENDMENT. *Quartering of Troops*

No soldier shall, in time of peace, be quartered in any house, without the consent of the owner; nor, in time of war, but in a manner to be prescribed by law.

4TH AMENDMENT. *Searches and Seizures*

The right of the people to be secure in their persons, houses, papers, and effects, against unreasonable searches and seizures, shall not be violated; and no warrants shall issue, but upon probable cause, supported by oath or affirmation, and particularly describing the place to be searched and the persons or things to be seized.[46]

5TH AMENDMENT. *Criminal Proceedings; Due Process; Eminent Domain*

No person shall be held to answer for a capital, or otherwise infamous, crime, unless on a presentment or indictment of a grand jury, except in cases arising in the land or naval forces, or in the militia, when in actual service, in time of war, or public danger; nor shall any person be subject, for the same offence, to be twice put in jeopardy of life or limb; nor shall be compelled, in any criminal case, to be a witness against himself;[47] nor be deprived of life, liberty, or property, without due process of law; nor shall private property be taken for public use, without just compensation.[48]

6TH AMENDMENT. *Criminal Proceedings*

In all criminal prosecutions, the accused shall enjoy the right to a speedy and public trial, by an impartial jury of the state and district wherein the crime shall have been committed, which district shall have been previously ascertained by law; and to be informed of the nature and cause of the accusation; to be confronted with the witnesses against him; to have compulsory process for obtaining witnesses in his favor; and to have the assistance of counsel for his defence.[49]

7TH AMENDMENT. *Civil Trials*

In suits at common law, where the value in controversy shall exceed twenty dollars, the right of trial by jury shall be preserved; and no fact, tried by a jury, shall be otherwise re-examined in any court of the United States than according to the rules of the common law.

8TH AMENDMENT. *Punishment for Crimes*

Excessive bail shall not be required, nor excessive fines imposed, nor cruel and unusual punishment inflicted.[50]

9TH AMENDMENT. *Unenumerated Rights*

The enumeration in the Constitution of certain rights shall not be construed to deny or disparage others retained by the people.

10TH AMENDMENT. *Powers Reserved to the States*

The powers not delegated to the United States by the Constitution, nor prohibited by it to the States, are reserved to the States respectively, or to the people.

11TH AMENDMENT. *Suits against States*[51]

The judicial power of the United States shall not be construed to extend to any suit in law or equity, commenced or prosecuted against one of the United States by citizens of another State or by citizens or subjects of any foreign state.

---

[45] The first 10 amendments, the Bill of Rights, were each proposed by Congress on September 25, 1789 and ratified by the necessary three-fourths of the States on December 15, 1791. They restrict only the National Government—*not* the States. But beginning in 1925 the Supreme Court has held most of their provisions applicable to the States through the Due Process Clause of the 14th Amendment; see pages 123–126, 151.

[46] The guarantees of the 4th Amendment (including the Weeks Doctrine—the "exclusionary rule") apply against the States through the Due Process Clause of the 14th Amendment.

[47] The prohibition of double jeopardy and the guarantee against self-incrimination each apply against the States through the Due Process Clause of the 14th Amendment.

[48] Acting under its inherent power of *eminent domain*, the Government may take (condemn) private property for public use. This provision restricts the exercise of that power by requiring a fair payment to the owner of any property so taken.

[49] The rights to counsel, to speedy and public trial, to trial by jury (in *serious* criminal cases), of confrontation, and to compel witnesses apply against the States through the Due Process Clause of the 14th Amendment.

[50] The protection against cruel and unusual punishment applies against the States through the Due Process Clause of the 14th Amendment.

[51] Proposed by Congress March 4, 1794; ratified February 7, 1795 (but official announcement of the ratification was not made until January 8, 1798).

12TH AMENDMENT. *Election of President and Vice President*[52]

The Electors shall meet in their respective States,[53] and vote by ballot for President and Vice President, one of whom, at least, shall not be an inhabitant of the same State with themselves; they shall name in their ballots the person voted for as President, and in distinct ballots the person voted for as Vice President; and they shall make distinct lists of all persons voted for as President, and of all persons voted for as Vice President, and of the number of votes for each, which lists they shall sign, and certify, and transmit, sealed, to the seat of the Government of the United States, directed to the President of the Senate; the President of the Senate shall, in the presence of the Senate and the House of Representatives, open all the certificates, and the votes shall then be counted; the person having the greatest number of votes for President shall be the President, if such number be a majority of the whole number of Electors appointed; and if no person have such a majority, then, from the persons having the highest numbers, not exceeding three, on the list of those voted for as President, the House of Representatives shall choose immediately, by ballot, the President.[54] But in choosing the President, the votes shall be taken by States, the representation from each State having one vote; a quorum for this purpose shall consist of a member or members from two-thirds of the States, and a majority of all the States shall be necessary to a choice. And if the House of Representatives shall not choose a President, whenever the right of choice shall devolve upon them, [before the fourth day of March next following,][55] then the Vice President shall act as President, as in case of death, or other constitutional disability, of the President. The person having the greatest number of votes as Vice President, shall be the Vice President, if such number be a majority of the whole number of Electors appointed; and if no person have a majority, then, from the two highest numbers on the list, the Senate shall choose the Vice President; a quorum for the purpose shall consist of two-thirds of the whole number of Senators; a majority of the whole number shall be necessary to a choice. But no person constitutionally ineligible to the office of President shall be eligible to that of Vice President of the United States.

13TH AMENDMENT. *Slavery and Involuntary Servitude*[56]

SECTION 1. Neither slavery nor involuntary servitude, except as a punishment for crime, whereof the party shall have been duly convicted, shall exist within the United States, or any place subject to their jurisdiction.

SECTION 2. Congress shall have power to enforce this article by appropriate legislation.

14TH AMENDMENT. *Rights of Citizens*[57]

SECTION 1. All persons born or naturalized in the United States, and subject to the jurisdiction thereof, are citizens of the United States and of the State wherein they reside.[58] No State shall make or enforce any law which shall abridge the privileges or immunities of citizens of the United States; nor shall any State deprive any person of life, liberty, or property, without due process of law, nor deny to any person within its jurisdiction the equal protection of the laws.

SECTION 2. Representatives shall be apportioned among the several States according to their respective numbers, counting the whole number of persons in each State, excluding Indians not taxed. But when the right to vote at any election for the choice of electors for President and Vice President of the United States, Representatives in Congress, the executive and judicial officers of a State, or the members of the legislature thereof, is denied to any of the male inhabitants of such State, being twenty-one years of age, and citizens of the United States, or in any way abridged, except for participation in rebellion or other crime, the basis of representation therein shall be reduced in the proportion which the number of such male citizens shall bear to the whole number of male citizens twenty-one years of age in such State.[59]

---

[52] Proposed by Congress December 9, 1803; ratified June 15, 1804.

[53] Modified by 23rd Amendment (1961), which provides presidential electors for the District of Columbia; see also the text of the proposed amendment relating to the representation of the District of Columbia, page 800.

[54] Only two Presidents, Thomas Jefferson in 1801 and John Quincy Adams in 1825, have been chosen by the House of Representatives.

[55] Changed by the 20th Amendment (1933), which sets the presidential inauguration date as January 20th.

[56] Proposed by Congress January 31, 1865; ratified December 6, 1865.

[57] Proposed by Congress June 13, 1866; ratified July 9, 1868.

[58] This clause was primarily intended to make Negroes citizens, but it has much wider application. "And subject to the jurisdiction thereof" excludes children born to foreign diplomats in the United States or to alien enemies in hostile occupation.

[59] The provisions of the second sentence here have never been enforced. Some authorities argue that they were nullified by the 15th Amendment (1870). The sentence is at least obsolete from disuse; also, it is not in accord with the 19th and 26th Amendments (1920, 1971).

SECTION 3. No person shall be a Senator or Representative in Congress, or elector of President and Vice President, or hold any office, civil or military, under the United States, or under any State, who, having previously taken an oath, as a member of Congress, or as an officer of the United States, or as a member of any State legislature, or as an executive or judicial officer of any State, to support the Constitution of the United States, shall have engaged in insurrection or rebellion against the same, or given aid or comfort to the enemies thereof. But Congress may, by a vote of two-thirds of each House, remove such disability.

SECTION 4. The validity of the public debt of the United States, authorized by law, including debts incurred for payment of pensions and bounties for services in suppressing insurrection or rebellion, shall not be questioned. But neither the United States nor any State shall assume or pay any debt or obligation incurred in aid of insurrection or rebellion against the United States, or any claim for the loss or emancipation of any slave; but all such debts, obligations, and claims shall be held illegal and void.

SECTION 5. The Congress shall have power to enforce, by appropriate legislation, the provisions of this article.

15TH AMENDMENT. *Right to Vote—Race, Color, Servitude*[60]

SECTION 1. The right of citizens of the United States to vote shall not be denied or abridged by the United States or by any State on account of race, color, or previous condition of servitude.

SECTION 2. The Congress shall have power to enforce this article by appropriate legislation.

16TH AMENDMENT. *Income Tax*[61]

The Congress shall have power to lay and collect taxes on incomes, from whatever source derived, without apportionment among the several States, and without regard to any census or enumeration.

17TH AMENDMENT. *Popular Election of Senators*[62]

The Senate of the United States shall be composed of two Senators from each State, elected by the people thereof, for six years; and each Senator shall have one vote. The electors in each State shall have the qualifications requisite for electors of the most numerous branch of the State legislatures.

When vacancies happen in the representation of any State in the Senate, the executive authority of such State shall issue writs of election to fill such vacancies: Provided, That the legislature of any State may empower the executive thereof to make temporary appointment until the people fill the vacancies by election as the legislature may direct.

This amendment shall not be so construed as to affect the election or term of any Senator chosen before it becomes valid as part of the Constitution.

18TH AMENDMENT. *Prohibition of Intoxicating Liquors*[63]

SECTION 1. After one year from the ratification of this article the manufacture, sale or transportation of intoxicating liquors within, the importation thereof into, or the exportation thereof from the United States and all territory subject to the jurisdiction thereof for beverage purposes is hereby prohibited.

SECTION 2. The Congress and the several States shall have concurrent power to enforce this article by appropriate legislation.

SECTION 3. This article shall be inoperative unless it shall have been ratified as an amendment to the Constitution by the legislatures of the several States, as provided in the Constitution, within seven years of the date of the submission hereof to the States by Congress.[64]

19TH AMENDMENT. *Equal Suffrage—Sex*[65]

The right of citizens of the United States to vote shall not be denied or abridged by the United States or by any State on account of sex.

Congress shall have power to enforce this article by appropriate legislation.

20TH AMENDMENT. *Commencement of Terms; Sessions of Congress; Death or Disqualification of President-Elect*[66]

SECTION 1. The terms of the President and Vice President shall end at noon on the 20th day of January, and the terms of Senators and Representatives at noon on the 3d day of January, of the years in which such terms would have ended if this article had not been ratified; and the terms of their successors shall then begin.

---

[60] Proposed by Congress February 26, 1869; ratified February 3, 1870. The amendment was intended to guarantee suffrage to newly-freed Negro slaves but is of much broader application today.

[61] Proposed by Congress July 12, 1909; ratified February 3, 1913. The amendment modifies the restrictions on the power to levy direct taxes, set out in Article I. (Section 2, Clause 3 and Section 9, Clause 4).

[62] Proposed by Congress May 13, 1912; ratified April 8, 1913. The amendment repealed those portions of Article I, Section 3, Clauses 1 and 2 relating to the election of Senators by the respective State legislatures.

[63] Proposed by Congress December 18, 1917; ratified January 16, 1919.

[64] The 18th Amendment was repealed in its entirety by the 21st Amendment (1933).

[65] Proposed by Congress June 4, 1919; ratified August 18, 1920.

[66] Proposed by Congress March 2, 1932; ratified January 23, 1933. The provisions of Sections 1 and 2 relating to Congress modified Article I, Section 4, Clause 2, and those relating to the President, the 12th Amendment.

SECTION 2. The Congress shall assemble at least once in every year, and such meeting shall begin at noon on the 3d day of January, unless they shall by law appoint a different day.

SECTION 3. If, at the time fixed for the beginning of the term of the President, the President-elect shall have died, the Vice President-elect shall become President. If a President shall not have been chosen before the time fixed for the beginning of his term, or if the President-elect shall have failed to qualify, then the Vice President-elect shall act as President until a President shall have qualified; and the Congress may by law provide for the case wherein neither a President-elect nor a Vice President-elect shall have qualified, declaring who shall then act as President, or the manner in which one who is to act shall be selected, and such person shall act accordingly until a President or Vice President shall have qualified.

SECTION 4. The Congress may by law provide for the case of the death of any of the persons from whom the House of Representatives may choose a President whenever the right of choice shall have devolved upon them, and for the case of the death of any of the persons from whom the Senate may choose a Vice President whenever the right of choice shall have devolved upon them.

SECTION 5. Sections 1 and 2 shall take effect on the 15th day of October following the ratification of this article.

SECTION 6. This article shall be inoperative unless it shall have been ratified as an amendment to the Constitution by the legislatures of three-fourths of the several States within seven years from the date of its submission.

21ST AMENDMENT. *Repeal of 18th Amendment*[67]

SECTION 1. The eighteenth article of amendment to the Constitution of the United States is hereby repealed.

SECTION 2. The transportation or importation into any State, Territory, or possession of the United States for delivery or use therein of intoxicating liquors, in violation of the laws thereof, is hereby prohibited.

SECTION 3. This article shall be inoperative unless it shall have been ratified as an amendment to the Constitution by conventions in the several States, as provided in the Constitution, within seven years from the date of the submission hereof to the States by the Congress.

22ND AMENDMENT. *Presidential Tenure*[68]

SECTION 1. No person shall be elected to the office of the President more than twice, and no person who has held the office of President, or acted as President, for more than two years of a term to which some other person was elected President shall be elected to the office of the President more than once. But this Article shall not apply to any person holding the office of President when this Article was proposed by the Congress, and shall not prevent any person who may be holding the office of President, or acting as President, during the term within which this Article becomes operative from holding the office of President or acting as President during the remainder of such term.

SECTION 2. This article shall be inoperative unless it shall have been ratified as an amendment to the Constitution by the legislatures of three-fourths of the several States within seven years from the date of its submission to the States by the Congress.

23RD AMENDMENT. *Presidential Electors for the District of Columbia*[69]

SECTION 1. The District constituting the seat of Government of the United States shall appoint in such manner as the Congress may direct:

A number of electors of President and Vice President equal to the whole number of Senators and Representatives in Congress to which the District would be entitled if it were a State, but in no event more than the least populous State; they shall be in addition to those appointed by the States, but they shall be considered, for the purposes of the election of President and Vice President, to be electors appointed by a State; and they shall meet in the District and perform such duties as provided by the twelfth article of amendment.

SECTION 2. The Congress shall have power to enforce this article by appropriate legislation.

24TH AMENDMENT. *Right to Vote in Federal Elections—Tax Payment*[70]

SECTION 1. The right of citizens of the United States to vote in any primary or other election for President or Vice President, for electors for President or Vice President, or for Senator or Representative in Congress, shall not be denied or abridged by the United

---

[67] Proposed by Congress February 20, 1933; ratified December 5, 1933. This amendment is the only one which has thus far been submitted to the States for ratification by conventions rather than by the State legislatures. See Article V. It is also the only amendment that specifically repealed a previous amendment. It also modified the scope of the commerce power, Article I, Section 8, Clause 3.

[68] Proposed by Congress March 24, 1947; ratified February 27, 1951. The amendment modified Article II, Section 1, Clause 1.

[69] Proposed by Congress June 16, 1960; ratified March 29, 1961. The amendment modified Article II, Section 1, Clause 2 and the 12th Amendment.

[70] Proposed by Congress September 14, 1962; ratified January 23, 1964.

States or any State by reason of failure to pay any poll tax or other tax.

SECTION 2.   The Congress shall have power to enforce this article by appropriate legislation.

25TH AMENDMENT. *Presidential Succession, Vice Presidential Vacancy, Presidential Inability*[71]

SECTION 1.   In case of the removal of the President from office or of his death or resignation, the Vice President shall become President.

SECTION 2.   Whenever there is a vacancy in the office of the Vice President, the President shall nominate a Vice President who shall take office upon confirmation by a majority vote of both Houses of Congress.

SECTION 3.   Whenever the President transmits to the President *pro tempore* of the Senate and the Speaker of the House of Representatives has written declaration that he is unable to discharge the powers and duties of his office, and until he transmits to them a written declaration to the contrary, such powers and duties shall be discharged by the Vice President as Acting President.

SECTION 4.   Whenever the Vice President and a majority of either the principal officers of the executive departments or of such other body as Congress may by law provide, transmit to the President *pro tempore* of the Senate and the Speaker of the House of Representatives their written declaration that the President is unable to discharge the powers and duties of his office, the Vice President shall immediately as-

sume the powers and duties of the office as Acting President.

Thereafter, when the President transmits to the President *pro tempore* of the Senate and the Speaker of the House of Representatives his written declaration that no inability exists, he shall resume the powers and duties of his office unless the Vice President and a majority of either the principal officers of the executive department or of such other body as Congress may by law provide, transmit within four days to the President *pro tempore* of the Senate and the Speaker of the House of Representatives their written declaration that the President is unable to discharge the powers and duties of his office. Thereupon Congress shall decide the issue, assembling within forty-eight hours for that purpose if not in session. If the Congress, within twenty-one days after receipt of the latter written declaration, or, if Congress is not in session, within twenty-one days after Congress is required to assemble, determines by two-thirds vote of both Houses that the President is unable to discharge the powers and duties of his office, the Vice President shall continue to discharge the same as Acting President; otherwise, the President shall resume the powers and duties of his office.

26TH AMENDMENT. *Right to Vote—Age*[72]

SECTION 1.   The right of citizens of the United States, who are eighteen years of age or older, to vote shall not be denied or abridged by the United States or by any State on account of age.

SECTION 2.   The Congress shall have the power to enforce this article by appropriate legislation.

---

[71] Proposed by Congress July 6, 1965; ratified February 10, 1967. This amendment contains the only typographical error in the Constitution. In the second paragraph of Section 4, the word "department" should properly read "departments."

[72] Proposed by Congress March 23, 1971; ratified July 1, 1971.

Two proposed amendments are now before the State legislatures. In 1972 Congress submitted the Equal Rights Amendment to the States:

SECTION 1.   Equality of rights under the law shall not be denied or abridged by the United States or by any State on account of sex.

SECTION 2.   The Congress shall have the power to enforce, by appropriate legislation, the provisions of this article.

SECTION 3.   This amendment shall take effect two years after the date of ratification.

And in 1978 it submitted another, to grant representation in Congress to the District of Columbia:

SECTION 1.   For purposes of representation in the Congress, election of the President and Vice President, and

Article V of this Constitution, the District constituting the seat of government of the United States shall be treated as though it were a State.

SECTION 2.   The exercise of the rights and powers conferred under this article shall be by the people of the District constituting the seat of government, and as shall be provided by the Congress.

SECTION 3.   The twenty-third article of amendment to the Constitution of the United States is hereby repealed.

In both instances, Congress fixed a seven-year time limit on the ratification process. The deadline for ratification of the Equal Rights Amendment was extended in 1978, however; it is now June 30, 1982. The deadline for approval of the District Representation Amendment is August 22, 1985.

To 1981, the Equal Rights Amendment had been ratified by 35 State legislatures, and the District of Columbia Representation Amendment by nine.

Note: Entries with a page number followed by an "n", as 365n, denote reference to a footnote on that page.

Klopfer v. *North Carolina:* 125, 163
Knights of Labor: 587-588
Knox, Henry: 393, 456
Korea: 408, 467-468, 480, 486
Korean Pact: 475
Korematsu v. *United States:* 123n

Labor: 580-593; discrimination outlawed, 77; pressure groups, 270; relations with management, 587-593. *See also* Labor Department; Labor unions
Labor Department: 544, 581-587, 587, 635; Secretary, 393-394, 581, 593
Labor Management Services Administration: 586-587
Labor Statistics Bureau (BLS): 582
Labor unions: 139, 141-142, 161, 188, 202, 538; collective bargaining, 589-592; development of, 587-588; government regulations of relations with management, 589-593; independent, 589; membership today, 588-589
LaFollette, Robert M.: 194, 381n
Laissez-faire theory: 28
Land and Natural Resources Division, Justice Department: 668
Land and Water Conservation Fund Act: 600-601
Land-grant colleges: 639-640
Land Management Bureau: 598-600
Land policy, federal: 598-599
Landon, Alfred: 265
Landrum-Griffin (Labor Management Reporting and Disclosure) Act: 161, 586, 590, 592-593
Latin America: 462-464, 474
Law: bill becoming, federal, 315-326, bill becoming, State, 701-704; Common, 736-737; equal justice under, 148-177; equity, 737; fundamental and statutory, 686; kinds applied by State courts, 735-738; na-

tional, 85-87; and order, 126. *See also* Constitution, U.S.
Law Enforcement Assistance Administration (LEAA): 671-672
Laxalt, Paul: 183
League of Nations: 405, 465, 480
League of Women Voters: 272, 274, 567
Lebanon: 408
Lee, Richard Henry: 43-44, 46, 51, 57-78
Lee v. *Washington:* 175
Legal Counsel, Office of: 667
Legal tender: 515
Legal Tender Cases: 337
Legation, right of: 444
Legislative branch: 20-21. *See also* Congress.
Legislative Reorganization Act: 310
Legislatures, State: 680; amendment proposal, 682-685; bicameralism, 691-692; direct legislation, 705-706; improving, 704-705; judge selection, 730; legislative process, 701-704; organization of, 700-701; overriding veto, 717; powers, 697-700; qualifications, elections, terms, and compensation, 694-697, sessions, 697, 716; size and apportionment, 692-694
Lemon v. *Kurtzman:* 131
Lend-Lease Act: 465
L'Enfant, Pierre-Charles: 762
Lenin, Vladimir Ilyich: 31-33
Levitt v. *CPERL:* 132
Lewis, John L.: 588
Libel: 134
Liberal-constructionists: 331-332, 343-345, 516, 681
Libertarian Party: 186
Library of Congress: 339, 547
Lie, Trygve: 483
Limited government: 19, 39-40, 46, 53, 63, 120-121, 330, 680
Limited Test Ban Treaty: 484
Lincoln, Abraham: 23, 29, 72, 160n, 190, 362n, 379n, 396, 398, 407-408, 556
Line agencies: 418, 611n
Literacy, voting and: 217, 220
Literary Digest: 265-266
Litigant: 648

Livingstone, William: 50
Lobbying: regulation of, 277-278; in States, 702; tactics, 274-277; value of, 278-279
Local government: cities, 752-764; counties, 743-749; expenditures, 778; financing, 769-778; legal status of, 741-743; metropolitan areas, 765-766; revenues, 769-776; special districts, 751-752; suburbanitis, 764-765; towns and townships, 749-751
Locke, John: 18, 55
London Company: 40
Long, Huey: 324
Louisiana: law, consitutionality of, 128, 172; open primary, 240
Louisiana Purchase: 462, 487
Louisiana v. *Resweber:* 168, 169
Loving v. *Virginia:* 175
"Lulu payments": 91
Luther v. *Borden:* 87

McAdoo, William G.: 504
McCarran (Internal Security) Act: 139-141, 668
McCarran-Walter (Immigration and Nationality) Act: 106-107, 115
McCarthy, Eugene: 236
McCollum v. *Board of Education:* 129
McCulloch v. *Maryland:* 86, 343-345, 496, 517, 770
McDaniel v. *Paty:* 133
McGovern, George: 193, 244-245, 374
McGowan v. *Maryland:* 132
McKinley, William: 192, 362n, 373n, 382, 507
Madison, James: 49-52, 56-59, 64, 126, 129-130, 190, 352, 397, 416, 444, 652, 709
Magistrates, U.S.: 661
Magna Carta: 39
Maine, U.S.S.: 463
Malfeasance: 405
Malloy v. *Hogan:* 125, 166
Management and Budget, Office of (OMB): 390-392; Director, 393, 396
Mann Act: 535
Mao Tse-tung: 31
Mapp v. *Ohio:* 125, 158